ISBN 978-0-266-11873-2
PIBN 10939280

1 MONTH OF
FREE
READING

at

www.ForgottenBooks.com

---◆---

By purchasing this book you are eligible for one month membership to ForgottenBooks.com, giving you unlimited access to our entire collection of over 700,000 titles via our web site and mobile apps.

To claim your free month visit:

www.forgottenbooks.com/free939280

English
Français
Deutsche
Italiano
Español
Português

www.forgottenbooks.com

Mythology Photography **Fiction**
Fishing Christianity **Art** Cooking
Essays Buddhism Freemasonry
Medicine **Biology** Music **Ancient**
Egypt Evolution Carpentry Physics
Dance Geology **Mathematics** Fitness
Shakespeare **Folklore** Yoga Marketing
Confidence Immortality Biographies
Poetry **Psychology** Witchcraft
Electronics Chemistry History **Law**
Accounting **Philosophy** Anthropology
Alchemy Drama Quantum Mechanics
Atheism Sexual Health **Ancient History**
Entrepreneurship Languages Sport
Paleontology Needlework Islam
Metaphysics Investment Archaeology
Parenting Statistics Criminology
Motivational

FIFTH ANNUAL REPORT

OF THE

STATE BOARD OF HEALTH

OF THE

STATE OF CONNECTICUT,

FOR THE

Fiscal Year ending November 30, 1882.

Printed by Order of the Legislature.

HARTFORD, CONN.:

PRESS OF THE CASE, LOCKWOOD & BRAINARD COMPANY.

1883.

State of Connecticut.

Office of the State Board of Health,
State House, Hartford, Dec., 1882.

To His Excellency, T. M. Waller,
Governor of the State of Connecticut.

Sir: In compliance with the laws of this State, I have the honor to present to you the Report of the State Board of Health for the year ending November 30, 1882.

Very respectfully,

C. W. CHAMBERLAIN, M.D.,
Secretary of the Connecticut State Board of Health.

MEMBERS OF THE BOARD.

CONTENTS.

INDEX.

GENERAL REPORT.

Before entering directly upon the usual review of the more prominent features in the sanitary history of the preceding year, it may be profitable to take a comprehensive glance at the general development and progress of public hygiene for the same period. The results of such a general survey can be fairly stated as very favorable, showing conclusively, substantial gains and important advances in different departments. As a matter of course there are serious obstacles and hindrances yet to be overcome, and much to be learned relating to the laws of disease, before we can fully control the needless loss of health and life by adaptation of cause and effect, and prevent the development and spread of disease by the removal of the essential factors, without which it cannot exist. One of the greatest needs now is experimental research into the ultimate cause and essential conditions of many of the zymotic diseases, and the atmospheric, telluric, and other influences that affect their prevalence.

One of the prominent proofs of advance in public hygiene is the constantly increasing interest in regard to all matters relating to health and sanitary science. This is shown in a multitude of ways, but plainest of all in the manner such subjects are treated by the press. The newspapers are quick reflectors of public sentiment, and in glancing over the columns of almost any of them, some reference to preventable diseases that were allowed to do their fatal work through negligence or ignorance of sanitary laws, brief, crisp articles on pure air, healthful, well-cooked food, sensible methods of clothing the body to avoid hampering development and growth, and many other like topics, are constantly encountered. The staider weekly papers often devote a column or more to topics relating to health, and present regularly to their readers well-written articles from good authorities, while the popular magazines abound in scientific essays on the more com-

2

plicated sanitary problems, that are more eagerly read, oftentimes, than the liveliest stories. A few years ago scientific health journals were almost unknown—the *Sanitarian* fought the battle against odds, nearly single handed; now this journal is forced to a weekly issue to meet the demands upon it, while the *Sanitary Engineer* has a large circulation and has given to its youngest rival, the *Hydraulic and Sanitary Plumber*, a portion of its original title. Many scientific journals have a sanitary department, or discuss some sanitary subject more or less in each issue. The period of indifference among the thinking and reading classes has pretty well passed by, and many of the principles of sanitary science have become quite extensively popularized. In this connection it may be allowable to refer to the demand for our own publications. The increase in the number of Reports enabled us to supply the physicians of the state generally, and to send a few to other professional men, but the supply is not half equal to the demand. Indeed it would appear that the clergy, as leaders of thought in many departments, have nearly equal claims to be supplied as the physicians.

The demand for the sanitary tracts issued by the Board has also steadily increased during the year, and in one or two instances new editions have been required to meet this demand. This increased interest in sanitary literature is a very encouraging indication, for all that is needed to secure most of the sanitary reforms that we wish is for the people to thoroughly understand their nature and value, when their accomplishment will be placed beyond doubt. This tendency is unfortunately mainly restricted to the cities and larger towns, where the evils resulting from unsanitary surroundings have forced themselves upon the attention of the people. Those that live in the country, where the praises of pure air have been sung from time immemorial, cannot yet fully realize that a man may so infect his own originally healthy surroundings by carelessness; that the water he drinks and the air he breathes, may be polluted by the products of the putrefactive decay of the waste substances incident to his occupancy; nor does he realize that if the natural movement of the ground-water is impeded by the intervention of impervious strata or from other cause, that the site he selects for a dwelling, even if on elevated ground, may be permanently damp and unhealthy; and thus his health and vigor may be slowly undermined.

The attitude of the plumbers towards sanitarians also indicates substantial progress, and that too in the right direction. Even when not compelled by law the plumbers are voluntarily investigating the relations of traps and drains to sewer gases, and the proper ventilation of house drains, and are mastering some of the laws of health relating to their special work; so that while a few years ago it was impossible to obtain a plumber that could properly trap and ventilate the fixtures and drains of a house without the constant superintendence of an expert, or a sanitary engineer, and even when supplied with proper instructions would return to old methods and declare the impossibility of any other; now it is not difficult to find one that is well qualified to plan and carry out the whole work, and that has a fair idea of the evils to be overcome and the best method of accomplishing the desired results. Nor are they so ready to pronounce old, faulty work as properly trapped. In fact, one or two clever little pamphlets have been issued by plumbers in this State upon the proper methods of house-drainage, mainly for advertising purposes, but quite generally correct in the advice offered. Nearly all have been forced by popular sentiment to pay some attention to the subject, which indicates that the public mind is becoming informed upon the relation of sewer-polluted air to the health of those compelled to breathe it. There should be some legal standard for tenement-houses in this State, and none allowed to be occupied that fall below that standard. Perhaps this can better be accomplished by city ordinances, as a sanitary inspector would be required.

The organization of voluntary sanitary associations, like the American Public Health Association, composed of sanitarians of all professions, physicians, educators, clergymen, business men, in fact of all interested in sanitary science and its development and progress, affords another illustration of the hold these subjects have upon the minds of both thinking and working men—men that are prominent in the work and progress of the day in all departments of human enterprise.

When the Association was first formed its speedy dissolution was predicted, but it survived, was the pioneer of all important movements in public and State hygiene, and is now one of the largest and most prosperous of the voluntary societies of the country; so large has it become that it has been obliged to classify its members into the active members, those actually engaged in sanitary work, or writers and investigators in some special branch of sanitary science, and associate members, those interested in public hygiene, and willing to aid in its progress. The Social Science Association has a section devoted to public health, which is constantly increasing in vigor and importance. The same can be said of the section on state medicine in the American Medical Association, now, usually, one of the most interesting of any, formerly scarcely noticed. The latest organization for sanitary improvement is the National Society for Sanitary and Rural Improvement, inaugurated at Greenwood Lake last summer, which has the promise of great usefulness. There are other scientific associations that are either forming special departments for the discussion of sanitary subjects, or else considering them much more extensively than formerly. The Sanitary Conventions, organized by the Michigan State Board of Health, and held in different parts of the State, where papers are read and discussions held, open to all to increase public interest in sanitary subjects, and also to popularize its principles, afford another illustration.

The International Sanitary Congress, which from small beginning has become a large and important body, whose sessions excite increasing interest each year, and whose contributions to sanitary literature and knowledge are of inestimable value, is a striking illustration in the same line. The importance, also, of the section on Public Health, in the Medical Congress held last year at London, and the ability of the essays and nature of the discussions, indicate the talent devoted to this department and the nature of the work there accomplished. But enough has been written to indicate the strength of this movement, and the earnestness of the workers in this field also to prove the brightness of the future outlook.

The establishment of the Museum of Hygiene at Washington, under the auspices of the Navy Department, with a library already of over four thousand volumes, and an experimental laboratory at the commencement fairly well stocked with apparatus, for the experimental study of disease, is one of the most important advances made during the year. Indeed, progress in our knowledge of the causes and control of disease can only come by the aid of carefully conducted experiment, and as the result of the experimental method. This is, in fact, one of the most imperative requirements of our own State Board of Health—an experimental laboratory where investigations can be made on adulterations in food, the pollution of water, the relation of climatology to disease, infected meat and milk, the relations of the soil, its structure, geological formation, humidity, and pollution to disease, researches into the ultimate causes of certain zymotic diseases, and a host of kindred topics that readily suggest themselves, without further enumeration. The value of such an accessory would increase from year to year as its records accumulate. We are indebted to the Agricultural Experiment Station for considerable aid in this direction, but there is enough specific work to warrant the addition to our means of usefulness.

The voluntary associations in cities and towns like the Sanitary Associations of Newport and Lynn were alluded to last year, but their example is so worthy of imitation that the reference will bear repetition; besides it is but another movement in the same direction with those under discussion just now. The formation of sanitary and rural improvement societies can scarcely be too highly commended. The good results that they have already secured where established is a criterion for the accomplishments to be secured in the future. It is intended to issue a circular with constitution, rules for action, and a description of the province and scope, more especially with regard to the sanitary work they can accomplish, of such organizations, during the ensuing year. Several applications for information on the subject have already been received. A similar society to the Public Health Association is to be organized in Canada, and the voluntary associations are increasing in number very fast. Several have been started in Connecticut the last year.

As before stated, the increase in the number and continued interest manifested in these voluntary associations as well as the practical work done by them, is an indication of progress, and shows the influence exerted upon the public by sanitary principles and ideas. Their continuance, increasing vigor and effectiveness is perhaps a stronger proof in this respect than the mere increase in numbers.

A striking proof of the practical results directly secured by sanitary science is given in the report of the registrar-general of England, showing that the death rate in twenty-three and a half

years had been decreased 12.2 per cent. in city populations, and
8.5 per cent. in rural populations. The enormous saving of life
and health involved in this statement can be faintly imagined
when the large populations involved are considered, and this large
aggregate must be multiplied by five at least to get at a numerical
estimate of the reduction in sickness involved. If thought desirable, the money value of each healthy life saved to the nation could
be figured out by the curious. This period is too long for the
result to be in any manner attributed to periodical movements in
disease or the rise and fall of epidemics. It is a solid achievement and stands unchallenged. Similar results can be shown on
a smaller scale in this country, but as there has been no general
or national system of vital statistics, no comparisons can be made on
a large scale. This result also means the prolongation of healthy,
vigorous lives, and the lengthening of the average duration of the
productive period, when men are a portion of the state's wealth.
It is a mistaken idea that has been advanced that prolonged duration of life involves continual bother and effort to preserve it, so that
the result is hardly worth the trouble, which might be in a measure
true were such the case, although much good work in literature,
science, and art has been done by valetudinarians, so to speak, i. e.,
men that were obliged to watch carefully over their lives, knowing
that any indiscretion on their part would soon result in a forfeit of
the life held by so frail a tenure. But sanitary science implies the
reverse of all this, namely, placing the man in a healthy environment
and amidst such surroundings that the exercise of the most ordinary
care would be all that would be required of him; in other words,
it is one of the aims of sanitation to prevent a man from ever
knowing by experience that he has a stomach or liver; to preserve
the purity of the air he breathes, and the food that he eats and
drinks, so that if the sanitary regulations of the community in
which he dwells are faithfully executed, he has only to regard the
plain and simple requirements of personal hygiene to secure long
life without vexatious annoyance and perpetual worry.

That is but a poor caricature of sanitary science that pictures
a multitude of anxieties upon this or that, taking up the minutiae
of daily life, and putting each detail through a sanitary catechism,
terminating with the query, Is life worth prolonging by such constant and close attention? That in very many respects there must
be a very great change in the present method or rather want of

method, in dealing with subjects relating to life, and health, and the maintainance of healthy lives is obvious, and that during the transition period, there must be considerable discussion and a clear treatment of many disagreable subjects is also very true ; but that anything like the representations alluded to will be the order of things under the reign of sanitary law is out of the question. In fact if we could but have perfectly physiological specimens of the human race, free from all inherited tendency to disease, and from the vices and depravities of constitution that are the resultant of the sins of a long train of ancestors, the problem would be very much simplified. But in the ideal city of health, but little friction if any will result from the execution and maintenance in perfection of sanitary laws and requirements. It is because we have departed so far from an ideal standard of perfection in sanitary matters that the change appears at all burdensome.

The saving of human life from destructive disease has been no less marked than the increase in the duration of life; as stated by Dr. Kedzie in his address to the Public Health Association this year at Indianapolis: "The saving of life by vaccination every year is equal to one-tenth of the standing armies of Europe. In Mexico, three and a half millions perished by one visitation of this fell disease. If one hundredth part of this number should now die in any nation by a single epidemic, the world would stand aghast in horror." He also states that the mortality from small-pox has been reduced from ninety-six per thousand in England and sixty-six and one-half in Germany to less than one in a thousand. The results in other forms of zymotic disease which, if unopposed, attack the strong as well as the weak are also as important. The results of this saving of life are shown ultimately in an increase in the average duration of life.

But it must be borne in mind that when the statement is made that by certain measures so many lives are saved each year, that this means men and women in the prime of life and the possession of vigorous health, allowed to round out the full term of life, that otherwise would fill untimely graves, or be wrecked in health and fortune by wasting disease. That it means the young allowed to reach maturity and complete honorable lives, that would otherwise be cut off, just as life was opening before them with its rewards, and prizes lost. That it means the bread winner spared to care for his loved ones and provide for them against want, or the wife,

the centre of the home, spared to train her children to lives of
usefulness, and the child to complete the span of life allotted to
him.   The idea that by the saving of life is meant the nursing of
pale, sickly specimens of the race, is an entirely erroneous idea of
sanitary science; as much so as the idea of the means by which it
can be secured, as exciting a constant worry and anxiety over trifling
details.

The amount of study and investigation in all departments of
sanitary science, and upon allied topics and collateral subjects,
illustrates the strength of this movement, and the recognition of its
claims by those best qualified to judge their value.   The vast army
of practical workers is backed by one of scientific investigators,
including in its ranks the brightest intellects of the world, and
many of the best workers and thinkers in the special departments.
In fact no subjects have taken a more prominent place or excited
a deeper interest in the world of thought, than those relating to
the development and preservation of life, and the nature of the
agencies which threaten its continuance.   If the deductions and
theories are disproved, the facts remain a permanent contribution
to knowledge.

The discovery of the mitigation of disease in animals by inoculation is a decided advance which promises fair for future usefulness.   Certainly if it stands the test of time, the fact that the virus
of disease can be rendered comparatively harmless by the successive cultivation of certain forms of bacteriae, whether these be the
cause or the carriers of the disease is immaterial, a great step in
advance has been taken, and a new and powerful weapon given us
against the ravages of disease; as this would give us a weapon
against contagion, which we have heretofore had in scarcely any
disease except small-pox.   Against direct contagion, almost the only
present resource in most instances except quarantine, is a condition
of health which gives the best chance for resistance, and purity of
the surroundings to give as little aid to the maleficent agent as
possible.

Much practical work has been done in relation to the influence
of electrical conditions, ozone, climatic and meteorological agencies
upon disease, in relation to the adulteration of foods and drugs,
the analysis of water and soils, and in a multitude of other directions which are interesting and valuable in their several aspects.
The investigations in regard to the diseases of animals more or

less communicable to man, especially bovine tuberculosis, should not be left out of account in this condensed summary.

The organization of local boards of health, the attention paid to the causes of disease that come within human control, and the willingness to act upon well settled principles of sanitary science is also an evidence of progress. The question of cause and effect has only to have a rational demonstration to secure in most instances appropriate action. The changes in the law in regard to local health boards, rendering their organization easier and less complicated, has already proved very beneficial and enabled prompt action to be taken upon the appearance of contagious diseases, preventing their spread.

There are so many States that now have efficient State Boards of Health, that it is easier to enumerate those that have none, and the number of these is steadily decreasing. None of the twenty-seven States that have established State Boards of Health have ever abolished them, while many have increased their powers and field of action. The publications of many of them have been of practical value, and will be standards for reference for all who are at work in the same field. Several of the publications of our own Board of Health have been ranked by others in this category, and have been largely copied and reprinted. The essay on Vaccination by Prof. Lindsley has been largely quoted—and is reprinted in full by one State Board. The essay of Prof. Brewer on the relation of health boards to material prosperity is another illustration. The attention called to the methods of ventilation and other sanitary regulations of the Bridgeport High School, was instrumental in their adoption in the construction of the new Normal School building. The edition of our report was soon exhausted, and a condensed reprint was made in the *Sanitary Engineer*. It was also reprinted in the report of the Board of Education, and is quoted often as a reference for those interested in the ventilation of school-houses, and as this is written, an application comes to hand from an Educational Journal for permission to reprint this article. Many others might be mentioned that have been repeatedly republished, but these are upon topics of such general interest, that it did not seem out of place to make the allusion to the fact. The sanitary reports each month, although of a more transient character, have had a wide circulation through the medical and sanitary journals in many instances.

3

Several of the State Boards of Health have been reorganized, and new powers and privileges granted. The State Board of Health of West Virginia, like that of Illinois, has the regulation of medical practice under control, and like that Board it has done a work of inestimable value in driving quackery in all of its forms out of the State, and protecting the lives of the people from the dangers they would be exposed from uneducated and unqualified practitioners. A diploma is not always evidence of proper qualifications, nor can it be as long as Medical Colleges are dependent entirely on the fees of students. Some feeble and weak institutions will sell diplomas after a few months study, or the mockery of it—without regard to the attainments of the purchaser, or rather in disregard of his utter lack of any. And under pressure of various kinds in some schools, where one would expect better things, students are graduated that have the merest smattering of a knowledge of their profession. The reports of the Boards of Health of Illinois and West Virginia on this subject, show the magnitude of the evil there. Fortunately it is not so great here, but it is bad enough.

From what has been accomplished by the application of sanitary principles already, it is safe to say that one-third of all the deaths from zymotic diseases can be prevented. Much larger claims are made, but at the estimate given, the saving of human life would be of greater value to the State than the cost of all the sanitary improvements, a thousand fold. This estimate takes into consideration only what would result from measures of State hygiene, and the sanitary regulations of cities and towns. If the whole field be included, it is by no means a large estimate to state that fully one-third of the deaths which occur from all causes could be prevented, were the principles of sanitary science fully understood, and its laws obeyed. This, of course, involves to a considerable extent domestic hygiene, and also individual obedience to sanitary regulations to a certain extent; not that to secure this all vice must be abandoned, but that men should be placed in a sanitary environment as a rule, instead of exceptionally, which as all experience shows of itself, tends to check vice and crime. As all evil associations are linked together, so vice, and crime, and unsanitary surroundings are usually associated.

Without entering further into detail, the evidence of progress is manifest in almost every direction. Such elements of discouragement as exist are transient, and to be expected, as sanitary progress and development cannot expect to escape all checks and temporary discouragements. .

PREVALENT DISEASES.

At the commencement of the year small-pox was attracting the greatest attention not only in this State but throughout the country generally. Constant reports of its prevalence extensively in different regions of the country, and the carelessness of the emigrant service, by which the disease was largely spread and the restrictions upon the National Board of Health, intensified the alarm. In most instances in this State, wherever it appeared, the greatest care was taken to prevent its spread. Places that had no pest-house were in several instances badly caught, but generally a quick way out of the difficulty was found. Several illustrations of the need of a law to repress the careless spread of the disease were afforded by the conduct of nurses in pest-houses, and in one or two instances patients with the disease well marked were found strolling about at large. The fact that no cases have been reported as resulting from such exposures, that is, from persons recently broken out with small-pox, is another illustration of the statement made on the experience of the old New York Hospital, when its patients were largely sailors, that infection from small-pox usually did not occur until the fifth day after the appearance of the eruption, that is, when the pustules commenced to maturate. Too much confidence, however, should not be placed in this, because under some conditions all rules fail apparently in such diseases as small-pox. An epidemic influence might intensify the infection.

There has not been during the year any extensive epidemic. In two places there were quite a large number of cases, and in one or more there were several sets of cases and quite a number of deaths; still there was no general or even partial epidemic anywhere. ' There was some unnecessary exposure from friction in the execution of the laws which were not fully understood, as there had been so little necessity for their execution. In general, after the first onset, the disease was well managed. As a general rule, as far as I can learn, there was the greatest spread in places where vaccination had been neglected. Where special attention had been paid to vaccination, in but few instances was there more than one case. In several instances the disease was introduced by servants brought up from New York, and usually emigrants that had been in this country but a little while. In one or two instances the contagion was charged to the rags used for paper stock, but there were not many cases at one time any where in the State. The disease appeared in a large number of places, and reappeared in some of the cities for the third time even, but as has been before stated so general has been the practice of vaccination that there has been but little spread of the disease. There may be something too in the material used in vaccinating. The greatest care has been exercised in securing pure virus, and as a rule, the bovine virus has been used, and if any other, that one remove only from the bovine. The usual plan in the central part of the State, and as far as I can learn pretty generally, has been to use the animal virus. In very obstinate cases, the humanized has been tried, that one remove having been found quite certain in its action, and at times almost too energetic. There were a few cases reported of spurious vaccine sores, both of the raspberry growths and a peculiar form of induration that is not described by any authors, which lasted several months, without any of the characteristics of a true vaccine sore.

From time to time during the year, there has been a case of small-pox here and there in different parts of the State, the last fatal cases reported from Manchester in the Autumn, but there was no diffusion of the disease. The law passed at the last session of the legislature gave the school visitors, or board of education, the power to order compulsory vaccination of school children. It is a good measure in some respects, although not likely to be of much service. In some respects it is objectionable, as it is better to have all such matters under one control, and the boards of health are the proper bodies for such powers to be vested in if they are to be granted to any. The results of the recent epidemic of small-pox in Hayti would appear enough to prove the value of vaccination were all other evidence wanting. It will be discussed more fully later in the report.

TYPHOID AND MALARIAL FEVERS.

The most interesting feature in the sanitary history of the State is the movement of typhoid fever towards its former rank, as one of the principal causes of disease among those of the zymotic order, which has been shared by malarial fevers, until from a comparatively small beginning they had usurped nearly the whole of the place occupied by typhoid, except in those parts of the State that had not been invaded by malaria, and even there there had been a very great decrease in the frequency of the occurrence of typhoid fever. From causing four or five hundred deaths in a year it had so decreased in importance that three years ago it was credited with only one hundred and fifty-nine deaths; an unprecedently low number. Since then, however, there has been a steady increase, although so far as the returns have been received no decrease in the number of deaths from malarial fevers save that sixty-three per cent. of the deaths in 1881 from malarial fevers were from typho-malarial fever, which most closely resembles typhoid fever of any of the types. There has been since 1881 a steady increase in the frequency of typhoid fever. It appeared earlier than usual ; was unusually frequent, almost epidemic in some places, and especially frequent in several of the cities where before it had been of very infrequent occurrence. In the regions where malarial fevers had longest been prevalent, cases of acute intermittent have been reported as exceptional, while the obscure forms, and those more like the type of continued fever, and typho-malarial fevers have been common. Meanwhile the existence of typhoid fever again and again at the same time that various forms of malarial fever were prevalent, has been seen so often that the idea of any necessary incompatibility between the two forms is no longer tenable. The idea has been advanced that there was an antagonism between the types so that they could not exist together. This was used to explain the decrease of typhoid on the appearance of malaria, and its almost total disappearance in the malarial belt. It appears probable now that this decrease was but part of a great periodic movement of rise and fall in typhoid fever. As the movement in malarial fevers, which has finally extended over the greater part of Connecticut has extended largely into Massachusetts, and reached Rhode Island, commenced in the southwestern part of Connecticut, it is a question whether this movement in malarial fever did not set in motion the movement in typhoid which afterwards became so general. In other words, was the invasion of Connecticut by the malarial type of disease the inception of the movement in typhoid fever, the disturbing element which interfered with the usual routine occurrence of typhoid fever each autumn, and thus set in motion the long train of causes whose results are now beginning to be fully apparent ? The question is easier asked than answered, and can safely be left for further consideration.

As the epidemic of malaria was followed by a decrease, and in places almost if not quite a total disappearance of typhoid, this return of typhoid fever to its former importance and relative frequency may be an intimation of the decrease and disappearance of malaria. The tendency towards typhoid fever commenced several years ago, and has steadily grown stronger each year, as shown by the increased prevalence, tendency to unusual frequency and severity, and the increase each year of deaths from this cause. As the decrease in the frequency of typhoid was an intimation of the extension of the malarial influence, so its increase may precede the entire disappearance of malaria, and gives us some ground for hope that such a disappearance will take place. The disappearance of epidemics of malarial fever, on a large scale, has often been followed by an unusual prevalence of typhoid fever or an extensive epidemic. The epidemics of malarial fever of 1807 and 1824, which are stated to have extended over all Europe, were followed by typhoid fever. Of course it is as yet but an inference that the present malarial influence which has extended continuously over the greater part of this State into Massachusetts and Rhode Island is subsiding and leaving its first points of invasion. But there is much to encourage such an idea. It is quite a prevalent impression that there has commenced a steady decrease in the general frequency of malaria in the west and southwestern parts of the State. However that may be the return of typhoid fever, the tendency towards a continued type shown by malarial fevers, the large percentage of typho-malarial fever, forming sixty-three per cent. of the mortality from malarial diseases last year, or two hundred and twenty-two out of three hundred and fifty-two deaths, are obvious facts. Whether or not malaria will become endemic in any part of the State is a question of interest that time only can determine. The idea has been advanced that the southwestern part of the State is a border land where the epidemic influence from the southwestern regions (especially Westchester county, where malaria is endemic), finds a resting place whence, if reinforced repeatedly, or strong enough originally, it invades other parts of the State. The prevalent tendency to greater severity in regions where malaria has existed for some time is a marked feature, while few cases comparatively of acute intermittent occur. Thus congestive chills are oftener reported, and usually fatal. A singular fact often illustrated is the tendency to acute intermittent shown by new comers into regions where malaria has prevailed several years, even if they came from a malarious region, and had had ague previously. Thus what at first looked like a fresh recurrence of acute intermittent in the vicinity of Hartford, was found on investigation to be almost wholly confined to the new families that had recently moved from New Jersey.

Finally taking into consideration the whole movement that commencing about 1876 there was a general decrease in the frequency of typhoid fever throughout this State, Massachusetts, and part of New England, certainly, as well as elsewhere, and that during the last three years, the present included, the increase has been about as marked as the decrease, until at the present time there would seem to be a pandemic wave, the prevalence is so extensive we have before us one of the most interesting and important problems of sanitary science, to wit: What are the ultimate causes of these periodic movements in disease, what is their starting-point, and what are the laws of their development and progress?

Why should a disease, like typhoid fever, which has been of regular occurrence in certain regions, in other words, endemic so long that it was supposed that everything concerning its nature was known, leave its usual limits, and appear in epidemic form in places where its occurrence, if at all, was exceptional, certainly more than exceptional as an epidemic; yet this autumn there have been extensive epidemics of typhoid fever in Paris and other places, and a quite extended prevalence. Enough is now known to show that this is no sudden precipitate result, but that the agencies that induced it have been long at work.

The return, however, appears to be partly, at least, due to a general influence, so widespread is the increase of typhoid as compared with its infrequency of late together with the epidemics in places where there has been very little prevalence of typhoid heretofore. This brings it in the category of extensive epidemics, and, as stated by Hertz, we have no insight into the conditions that govern the periodical rise of epidemics. That malaria should leave its "endemic haunts" and extend over large areas has become a familiar idea by the manifestations in New England recently, and that local epidemics of typhoid fever occur not unfrequently, due to easily ascertainable local causes as a rule,

is also well known; but that typhoid fever should become so
generally epidemic is not a familiar idea, although extensive epidemics are on record; but I have not yet found any account of
such a decisive rise and fall as has occurred from 1876 to 1882,
inclusive. Were this movement confined to the region invaded
by malaria and the adjacent territory, the explanation could be
found readily; but such is not the case, and especially is this true
of the recent increase, as the epidemic in Paris and prevalence in
other places testifies. Hertz* states that malarial epidemics and
pandemics stand in some, thus far, inexplicable relation to epidemics of other diseases which have either preceded or immediately followed the march of malaria. Typhoid fever has more
often followed malarial epidemics than any other form of disease;
the other forms mentioned are the cholera, the plague, and influenza. That we are threatened next season (1883) by a visitation
of cholera, is a significant fact in this connection. Epidemics of
typhus fever and malaria have existed side by side, and of dysentery. Hertz* asserts that the same is not true of typhoid, not that
there is a law of complete mutual exclusion, but that where
malarial fevers are indigenous typhoid is of the rarest occurrence;
in proof of which he cites Amsterdam, where malaria is endemic
and typhoid unknown almost, and the malarial regions of the
Rhine, and cites a case where typhoid increased as malaria, previously endemic, decreased. This idea of the antagonism of the
two types of disease had apparently strong confirmation in the
extensive decrease in typhoid fever in Connecticut, Massachusetts,
and Rhode Island, as malaria appeared, and its decrease in other
portions of these states not invaded by malaria was not conspicuous,
or was attributed to the extension of the malarial influence—one
of the changes that preceded the appearance of malaria. But the
return of typhoid to the regions where malaria is still existing, and
even where the malarial influence is the strongest, as shown by
the prevalence of acute intermittents and the typical varieties of
malarial fevers, is evidence that there is no complete law of exclusion between the two types of disease. The epidemics in cities
apparently contravene the statement that typhoid fever is a disease
of the country, and has been almost banished from the cities. But
the exception only proves the rule—the epidemic influence past;

---

* Zimssen's Cyclopædia, Vol. 2, pp. 555 et seq.

things resume their ordinary routine. The behavior of epidemics differs very much from that of indigenous diseases, and they are to be controlled by different agencies. The manifestations of epidemics that are localized, that is confined to one city or town, are better understood, yet why they should occur at one time rather than another, is not always explained readily. Epidemics are apparently due to the introduction of a virus from without; that is, epidemics on a large scale, and the epidemic influence is maintained by a *vis a tergo*, so to speak; that is, by a more or less constant reinforcement of the external force. When we know how the epidemic is spread, we exclude the agency that produces it, as by quarantine against cholera and yellow fever, and limit the spread of small-pox by vaccination. The science of epidemiology is not as yet very far advanced. We know many very important facts relating to certain forms of disease, and have learned that contagion must be counteracted by isolation of the centre from which it spreads; which is, in many instances, the individual that manufactures the poison, which is multiplied many thousand fold in his system during the development of the disease, and by destroying the developed virus, by disinfectants and otherwise, as thoroughly and efficiently as possible. The important point is to obtain control of the centre of infection at once. There are conditions favorable to the spread of certain diseases that we can control and remove, as impure water supply aids in the spread and malignancy of cholera and typhoid fever, while filth, polluting air, water, or soil, is favorable to almost all types of diseases. Yet when the whole field of epidemic disease is surveyed our facts appear too few even to theorize very confidently upon. But what we do know already about certain types of disease is of the utmost practical value, as witnessed by the control exercised over yellow fever, small-pox, and cholera, although repeatedly brought to our shores. This subject is one of the most interesting in the whole range of sanitary science, and had we access to a complete series of vital statistics of all nations for a few centuries, many of the vexed questions could be satisfactorily settled and the basis for a definite science laid. Unfortunately such statistics are out of the question, as even in the enlightened nations the statistics do not extend much farther than fifty years into the past—not far enough, even if they were sufficiently numerous, to derive any laws of periodicity where

3

the intervals of recurrence are long. Our own statistics give intimation of periodicity in many diseases, but none could be proven by one series of observations. The indications, however, are valuable. The tables in the registration report relating to these diseases are important in this connection, the table showing the rate of mortality from typhoid fever in each county, from 1854 to 1881, supplements the one showing the mortality by towns on pages seventy-seven to eighty-two of the Registration Report. Although they each show fluctuations, there is no such definite movement in typhoid fever as the rise and fall during the last six or eight years.

We have perhaps more knowledge about cholera than most of the epidemics, but this movement in relation to typhoid fever suggests

A LAW OF PERIODICITY

in other diseases of the same order, that when thoroughly under-stood will greatly aid in controlling their tendencies to become epidemic. A knowledge of the nature of the virus or contagion that produces a particular form of disease also gives great aid in its control. As the periodic rise and fall of typhoid fever has been by no means confined to regions affected by malaria, as shown by the same movement in typhoid fever in portions of this State, Massachusetts, Rhode Island, and elsewhere, where there was no malaria, and by the present strong tendency towards epidemics of typhoid fever, not only in the malarial belt of New England, where the two types exist side by side, but also at the forward edge of the malarial wave, as in Providence, where, judging from analogy, the malarial influence would exclude typhoid, but per contra an epidemic exists of typhoid fever, it may be that the movement in typhoid-fever is entirely independent of malaria. The future developments will be watched for with great interest, as they promise to be very instructive. Many of the points now so involved will then become clear.

This epidemic tendency apparently intensifies local causes that otherwise would not be so efficient. Thus, in the case of Paris, if the account of the sewerage and drainage of the houses is correct, as given in the *Lancet*, it is a wonder that typhoid has not occurred before. Although the general sanitary supervision of the city is excellent, the writer states in this article that the houses are seldom provided with traps, nor are the house drains ventilated. In the change from the cess-pools and vaults, to the sewers, with their rapid removal of filth, trapping and ventilation were not thought of, as their necessity did not then appear so urgent in the desire to escape the annoyances from the cesspools. This neglect is quite general, if the article is to be relied upon, which is in all probability the case. Thus, in untrapped sewers, the virus of any disease, if it be introduced, finds a ready channel of access wherever the sewers extend. This has been reported repeatedly in the case of scarlet fever, which has been traced along the course of the sewers through untrapped drains into houses and schools, and the cause demonstrated, the center of infection found, and further spread checked.*

Thus, in diseases like typhoid fever, scarlet fever, and diphtheria, local unsanitary influences intensify the activity of the disease germs or virus, and increase the tendency towards severity and malignancy, and towards a local epidemic. The epidemic wave that is seen, in different diseases, extending over wide areas, also intensifies local unsanitary conditions, and under that influence they are followed by results that at other times do not occur. Some diseases have an annual wave curve apparently, and if, like diarrheal diseases, they are influenced by the season, its height may be determined by that. The trough of the wave is often as well marked as the crest. These movements in disease, and their periodicity, furnish very interesting subjects for study. A great many of the apparent irregularities in the local appearances of disease, and the reason why local unsanitary conditions are at certain times apparently so inert, and at others so energetic in the production of disease and death, will be, in part, at least, made clear. That there are periodic movements best described by the comparison to a wave, that rises and falls with a regular curve, in many diseases, becomes more and more probable as we trace their history and manifestations over large periods and over large areas of territory. The contributions to our available means of counteracting and preventing the rise and spread of these destructive diseases, that have already resulted from what we have learned concerning epidemiology, is an earnest of what is in store for the patient investigations of future workers in this field.

* See Carpenter on Preventive Medicine and Public Health, etc.

LUNG FEVER.

From January to April inclusive, lung fever and acute lung diseases were the prevalent type, and were more frequent in occurrence than usual. The cases were many of them severe, and the mortality was somewhat in excess of the usual ratio, judging from the reports without exact statistics. Double pneumonia also was frequently reported, and many cases of typhoid-pneumonia. An insidious variety with rapid filling up of the lungs, or an extensive exudation suddenly succeeding bronchitis, was also very common. Indeed, what at first appeared like an ordinary case of bronchitis, requiring but little attention, often suddenly assumed alarming symptoms, and was rapidly fatal, so that upon close examination cases of apparent bronchitis were found to have diffused pneumonic exudation here and there in small patches. Such cases were almost invariably very severe, often fatal. In many, exposure brought on extensive trouble before they considered themselves at all seriously sick. The severity continued far into spring, as has been stated; even in April they continued to be the prevalent forms of disease, and still later were unusually frequent, although there was a great decrease after April, which was continuous and quite rapid as spring advanced.

DIPHTHERIA.

Although there have been no extensive epidemics of diphtheria, it has been quite prevalent during the year, and has contributed its full share to the mortality list. In January and March it was reported from a large number of places, and occasionally throughout the year. In the latter part of the summer, and early in the autumn, there was another increase; it was very frequent in some parts of Hartford, and very malignant and fatal. It was followed by

SCARLET FEVER,

Which has been more prevalent than usual this year, especially during the early winter. If it follows a rule that the mortality for several years would suggest that there is an increased prevalence and fatality about every third year—a decided increase in the mortality from this disease may be expected during the coming year. The period of prevalence is at times prolonged over several years, but the curve of depression is apparently more often two years. A similar tendency is observable in diphtheria. This much appears quite probable in many of the contagious diseases: that the period of great prevalence is followed by as proportionate a decrease. As the individual element must be also taken into account, it may be that the decrease in the number susceptible to the disease is a factor in causing the decline. Apart from this, however, there is apparently a regular increase in the strength of the infection at a point when it reaches its height, and a steady but not uniform decline. If the infection be a germ, one would thus outline its life history. Scarlet fever, although eminently a contagious disease, may depend upon filth for its continuance. Dr. Carpenter, of England, who has made special investigations in this field, reports many instances of this nature. An illustrative case may be not uninteresting in this connection. Scarlet fever continued to reappear, in an epidemic form, in a school at Croydon, notwithstanding every precaution that sanitary science apparently could suggest. At length, upon systematic investigation of the sewage, connections were found with an unused cesspool that had been discarded when sewers were introduced, but into which the washings from a slaughter-house near by had found way. These were bloody, and both hot and cold water was used. The virus of the disease was apparently kept alive by these conditions, as upon their discontinuance there has been no epidemic of scarlet fever for eight years, nor any cases originating in the school, as was the case repeatedly before while the conditions described lasted. The cesspool did not create the disease, but, after the infection was once introduced, increased its severity and perpetuated it for several years. The conclusion he draws from a series of such instances is that scarlet fever may as often arise from sewage emanations and sewage contaminated with the scarlatina germs as from personal contact.* An inference is drawn from this: that hot water and waste steam serve to perpetuate and spread the germs of disease, and especially when in connection with decomposing animal matter. The apparent influence of the putrefying waste from slaughter-houses on scarlet fever has been noted in several instances. The general testimony is in favor of the unfavorable influence of filth in increasing the mortality of scarlet fever, while the propagation of the poison of the disease outside

*Sanitary Record, March 15, 1882, page 362.

the human body is not considered as proven. The circular of the Michigan State Board of Health (1881) concerning the restriction and prevention of scarlet fever admits the possibility of such propagation, and states that filth, uncleanliness,* and imperfect ventilation may increase the danger of spreading the disease. That of Massachusetts (1878)† states that filth may be considered to promote scarlet fever, or -to increase its mortality, as anything which deteriorates the health and renders the system liable to disease. The general statement is made by many circulars for the prevention of scarlet fever that filth increases the danger of spreading the disease.

That it is one of the most contagious diseases, is well known; also, that it is infectious and may be conveyed by infected articles long distances, and more readily than almost any other form of disease. There is good evidence as to the spread of scarlet fever by milk that had stood in the room occupied by a patient in the desquamative stage. The danger of the spread of the disease by mild cases, and those that are convalescent mingling too soon with their fellows, is very apt to be overlooked, except in a severe epidemic, when the fears of the people are aroused. While contagion is the principal factor in spreading the disease, the unsanitary conditions that act as contributory must not be overlooked. The subject will be discussed more in detail in connection with the circular on restriction and prevention. As the disease has made its appearance in a malignant type, it deserves a fuller discussion. The evidence of its spread from the bodies of those who have died from it is unequivocal, and the fact is well established.

THE PROGRESS OF MALARIAL DISEASES.

Reference has already been made to one phase of these diseases; that is, their relation to the prevalence of typhoid fever, which, with the reappearance of typhoid, presents some new phases. There is no subject of more interest and importance to this section of the country, if not quite generally, than the etiology of malaria; and any investigations that present any new features in the manifestations of the disease, or show facts in a clear or plain light, are of great value. The essay and illustrative map prepared by Dr. G. H. Wilson, of this board, present the movement of malarial

---

* Transactions, 1881, page 217.
† Ninth Report, p. xxxii, et seq.

diseases over New England, and especially Connecticut, in a very clear and striking manner. The isochronal lines appeal to the eye directly, and impress the facts strongly and unmistakably. The law of progress is outlined here, and the relative importance of many phenomena placed in their true relations. The subject presents so many interesting phases that each demand attention in order to comprehend the complicated whole, that at times one phase assumes more than its relative importance. The work presents in itself the evidences of careful and painstaking endeavor, and will be a valuable contribution to the permanent literature of the subject. From the very nature of the case, malaria and its manifestations must occupy a prominent place in the sanitary literature of this state, and the subject will be brought up in various connections in different parts of the report.

The theories of origin are in fully as unsettled a condition as when the last report was issued. The germ theory has not been proven; that is, the bacillus malariæ has not been demonstrated to be the cause. The restriction of the field of operations of the National Board of Health caused the abandonment of the investigations inaugurated by them with the co-operation of several State Boards of Health. It is to be hoped that the present Congress will pursue a more enlightened policy, and enlarge, rather than restrict, the field of study at least of the National Board of Health.

NERVOUS DISEASES.

The increase of diseases of the nervous system, the occurrence of paralysis, and other forms in the young comparatively, and the prevalence of insanity, present topics of interest and importance, and worthy of the most careful study. What are the guilty agencies in modern life, and especially in America, that are increasing the number of nervous invalids—prematurely wrecking the lives of many earnest workers for fame and honor, as well as for the more material prizes of life? What are the causes that are increasing the number of the insane out of proportion to the growth of the population, and filling our asylums with incurable life pensioners upon the state? These are questions of the utmost interest and importance, and involve practical issues that must, more especially in relation to insanity, be sooner or later met.

In this connection, the discussion on the

by Dr. Page, of Hartford, who has for some years been one of the physicians of the Retreat for the Insane, is a very timely paper, and presents the subject in a clear light. The tendencies in modern life that are at work in the production of insanity are discussed in a broad and philosophical manner, while specific details are given whenever required for the elucidation of any statement. The paper will well repay a careful study, and is exceedingly suggestive. There are many points in regard to mental diseases that the public should better understand, and one of these is the danger to be apprehended from apparently mild cases of insanity, and how unsafe it is to endeavor to treat and care for such at home unless the constant care and attendance of a skilled attendant is provided, and *never omitted*, until reason regains its throne. Especial attention is directed to the discussion of that part of the subject by Dr. Page, emphasized as it has been by the recent painful illustration in a neighboring state. The frequent desire of friends to conceal mental aberrations, and their reluctance to separate an insane relative from familiar surroundings and associations, has led to many acts of violence. When the irresistible insane impulse seizes the mildest and, as one would suppose, gentlest and most harmless person, no act is so atrocious or so shocking as to cause repulsion or prevent its execution. It is fortunate that these tendencies often take a suicidal turn, as in such cases less harm is done than results from the slaughter of some innocent victim in the full possession of all his mental faculties.

LAWS RELATING TO INSANITY.

Although no glaring instances of false incarceration of sane persons on a charge of lunacy for various nefarious purposes has been brought to light in this state, yet their frequency in other states suggests such a possibility. The principal point in the laws relating to the insane that might render such a false commitment possible is that the signature of but one reputable physician is required on a certificate of lunacy; and as the requirements by law upon any person that may wish to practice medicine are not very stringent, the possibility of such an occurrence is obvious. That any respectable, educated physician would be thus guilty is, of course, out of the question; but when the other class referred to are considered, the case is not so clear. The law in most states requires the signature of two physicians, which is none too stringent a regulation. The subject, although not of pressing importance, is still worthy of attention.

DANGEROUS TOYS AND AMUSEMENTS.

The nefarious toy pistols (a cheaply-made implement of destruction) have produced their quota of accidents and lock-jaw in this State, and it seems about time that their manufacture and sale should be prohibited by law, or least their sale, which would produce about the same result. They are of no service to any one; do not aid in any way in producing good marksmanship, as the thing aimed at is seldom the one that is hit. Their capacities for evil would seem to be sufficiently well demonstrated to result in their suppression. The recent shooting of an actress upon the stage, in a foolhardy imitation of Tell's feat, with the substitution of a rifle for the strong-bow, shows that, with an unerring marksman and the perfection of rifles, accidents that result in death will occur. Such amusements should be prohibited by law. Their fascination lies in the element of danger. Such exhibitions are demoralizing, as well as dangerous, and the sooner they are ended the better for all concerned.

CROSSINGS AT GRADE.

Whether anything further can be done by general legislation to prevent the crossing of streets and roads at grade, by railroads, is a subject worthy of consideration. The lives that are lost each year at such crossings, especially in populous places, and at those death-traps where a sharp curve brings the unwary traveler without warning directly upon the track, render any action desirable upon the subject that is possible for the protection of life. Where, as in several cities, horse-railroad tracks also cross, and especially, as in Hartford, at the bottom of a steep hill, the possibilities of accident are much increased. Leaving out of account the interference to travel and the inconvenience caused, the danger to life requires the application of any possible remedy.

THE CORONER SYSTEM.

The evils of this antiquated system have long been recognized in other states than our own. But of late we have had several

conspicuous instances of the failure to secure the requisite evidence
to convict the guilty, by the defects in the coroner's quest law,
which, when analyzed, appears to be rather a bundle of traditions
than a system of law. If, in each case where a sudden and untimely death occurs with suspicion of foul play, a physician skilled
in pathology and having special knowledge of medical jurispru-
dence were summoned, the evidence necessary to convict the guilty
party would be made available to the commonwealth, and there
would be no chance for any disputed points as to the cause of
death, if there were any evidence to show such cause. There are,
in all such cases, two questions involved. The first is: What is
the cause of death? the second: If from violence, who was the
guilty person that committed this crime? The first question is
purely a medical question, and no one but a physician can properly
investigate it. If he be unskilled, and seldom, if ever, have occasion to make a *post-mortem* examination, the chances are that it
will be imperfectly done and plenty of loopholes left for a skilled
lawyer to plan the escape of his client through. Evidence may be
destroyed as well as overlooked, and, from the neglect of proper
precautions, the identification of the results with the body of the
deceased may be rendered impossible. We have been almost
tempted to issue plain and explicit directions for the conduct of
an autopsy, when the questions of cause of death and the detection
of crime are points at issue, although the subject does not come
entirely within our jurisdiction; that is, its use would not be compulsory. In Germany, it has been stated, such compulsory instructions are given. The second question is purely a legal one, and
here the physician usually fails, as he knows little of the rules of
evidence and the proper way of conducting a judicial inquiry.
Still, taking into consideration all the points involved, a physician
succeeds better as coroner than a lawyer. The Massachusetts law
recognizes the dual nature of the case and provides a medical
examiner, who is first called, and if the death is due to natural
causes that is the end. If there be suspicion of foul play, he calls
the legal associate, and together they pursue the investigation,
and, without any machinery of jury and a farce of trial before a
coroner, the case is prepared for police court or whatever tribunal
it is to be tried, and each point is clearly and systematically established. The law has worked, as far as can be learned, very successfully in Massachusetts for six years, has been under discussion

some time in New York before the Medico-Legal Society, and will probably be presented to the Legislature this winter. A movement for reform has also been started in Pennsylvania. The draft of a law like that of Massachusetts was printed in our last report, and, with some modifications, will be presented to the Legislature. Some change appears to be needed, and at present this method seems to have the most advantages and to offer the best chances for future success. It appears to be founded on a right idea of the principles involved in the inquiries that come before such an organization.

THE ADULTERATION OF FOOD.

A draft for a law on this subject, that has been very carefully prepared and passed by New York, Massachusetts, and one or more other states, was also printed in the report last year. If it is desirable to pass any general law on this subject just at present, there could be no better law framed than this.. Any law of this kind, to be efficiently executed, implies several expert examiners to detect the adulterations. Much of the work could be done by this Board if we had an experimental laboratory. Indeed, a series of examinations, where the microscope is the chief agent in detecting adulterations, is already planned and partly under way. But in addition to this local examiners would be needed in many places. The laws at present on the statute book are inoperative, and several of them were evidently passed without much consideration. Some local regulations will be referred to in another connection. But there is one topic allied to this that requires attention, and that is the

EXACTNESS AND PURITY OF DRUGS AND MEDICINES.

The adulteration of drugs would come under the provisions of a general law, but there are other points involved that are important. The regulation compelling all proprietary and patent medicines to have their formulæ printed upon the labels, and providing a severe penalty for those that do not, upon assay, come up to a certain standard, would prevent much mischief. But there is a more insidious danger, because coming from a source comparatively unexpected, and that is the temptation to short weight in expensive drugs after a reputation and sale has been secured. The recent analyses of two-grain quinine pills, published in the

Medical News, reveals a condition of affairs which, if general, requires some legal interference.

In five out of the seven leading manufacturing houses whose
products were examined, the pills sold as containing two grains of
quinine in reality contained much less. The best had 1.91 grains,
the worst 1.61; nor were scarcely any two analyses alike. Two
manufacturers out of the seven sold their products as represented;
that is, analysis showed that there was the quantity claimed in
each pill. The price at which they were sold was no criterion, as
the one having the least amount of quinine was sold at the highest
rate. If all such products were compelled to have a certain
standard and to be occasionally tested by assay, with severe penalties for any below a fixed standard, the physician and patient
would both be benefited, especially the latter. There is no place
where adulteration is productive of greater harm, even if, as in the
present case, a harmless substance is used to make up the weight.

DANGEROUS DYES.

It is a question whether the use of arsenical preparations should
not be prohibited by law, and where the preparation is soluble, as
in many brilliant colors, especially those used in the cheaper
grades of goods, in wall papers, especially those that have a
flocculent surface, portions of which are more or less readily de-
tachable, and generally in fabrics for use or ornament, where any
considerable amount of surface is to be exposed. There are already several firms that advertise wall-papers without the use of
arsenic in their manufacture, but analysis does not always bear out
the assertions of the sellers of non-arsenical paper-hangings, however it may be with the supply of such goods in the market. The
fact that so many light and popular shades, especially of green,
can readily be made by the use of arsenic, and the difficulty of
obtaining a brilliant green otherwise, has been a powerful influence
for its retention. Its use, however, is not confined to the bright
shades, nor to the green tints exclusively. Several of the creamy
tints and light shades contain arsenic in large amounts. During
the year several instances of severe skin eruptions, resulting from
arsenical coloring matters, have been investigated. Generally the
dye was quite readily soluble in water, and caused some staining of
the skin temporarily at least, but in one case the irritation apparently was caused by an excess of arsenic in the substance, which

was dissolved by the profuse perspiration, and then absorbed. High fever with the eruption, and great prostration, with congestion of the kidneys were the usual symptoms of severe cases. The cases of poisoning of operatives in a manufactory of artificial flowers, in New York, and the symptoms produced, show how dangerous the compounds are that are used to produce the brilliant greens and different tints and shades in artificial flower work. A case of persistent eruption on one side of the face and neck, extending behind the ear, and involving nearly all of one ear, after recurring for the third time was traced to a leafy branch of artificial flowers; the under sides of the leaves were thick and downy, and owing to some defect in manufacture yielded considerable pulverulent material, which, on testing, was found to be largely arsenic.

These fabrics, however, usually contain arsenic in very insoluble combinations, so that the operatives are the chief if not only sufferers. The number of materials into which arsenical coloring matters enter is very great, and the sole reason that greater harm does not result is that very many of them are insoluble. Were not this the case the evil would be insupportable. As the question is frequently asked, whether the use of Paris Green, a compound of arsenic, will not increase the proportions of arsenic in the soil to a dangerous extent, and especially contaminate wells and springs and even rivers, the investigations of the Michigan State Board of Health are again referred to in reply. It was very conclusively shown there that there is always iron enough in the soil to unite with all the arsenic that can ever be added in the applications to plants, and a hundred fold as much. Also, that there is a chemical reaction between this compound and the iron which invariably takes place, resulting in an arseniate of iron, one of the most inert and insoluble compounds known, so that no danger can possibly arise from this source. Other forms of domestic poisons will be considered later.

HATTING AS AFFECTING HEALTH.

This is the second article we have published relating to health of operatives. The first was on the manufacture of rubber as affecting health, by Dr. Bartlett of New Haven. The present essay is by Dr. Dennis of Newark, New Jersey, and was originally prepared for the Board of Health of that State. As the occupation is one extensively followed in parts of this State the essay is especially appropriate. Moreover, many of the facts were derived from the manufacture as carried on here. It is republished by the courtesy of the New Jersey State Board of Health and the kind permission of the author. Our special acknowledgment for the favor is here duly made to both parties.

SPECIAL INVESTIGATIONS.

These have been more frequent than ever during the past year, which has been one of the busiest since the Board was organized. In fact it is beginning to be very difficult to get along without regular clerical assistance, which is out of the question under present regulations. The subjects included cover a wide range, and extend into nearly every branch of sanitary science. The pollution of wells, lead poisoning by conveying spring water long distances in lead pipes, extensive prevalence of zymotic diseases in families and neighborhoods, unsanitary surroundings of manufacturing establishments, nuisances caused by slaughter-houses, privies, cesspools, neglected filth, and other causes, errors in the disposal of excrementitious and other waste products that by putrefactive decay were polluting the soil or water, are subjects that have been brought to our attention among others. The consultations with

LOCAL BOARDS OF HEALTH

have been very numerous—as in the case of special investigations more frequent than during any previous year.. In the first part of the year they related more especially to small-pox, and the powers and duties of boards of health with regard to its restriction and prevention. The manner of organizing and calling together boards of health was frequently a subject of inquiry, especially after the modifications in the law, which have proved of very great service, in several instances enabling prompt and efficient action to be taken in preventing the spread of contagion. The consultations have covered a wide range, relating mainly to the best manner of dealing with nuisances and local unsanitary conditions, and concerning their powers and duties in general. The work done by various local health organizations is well worthy of commendation, and is in striking contrast with the previous apathy. The effect is seen in the low death-rate that follows their efficient work. This is nowhere more strikingly shown than in New Haven. Under the efficient supervision of its energetic Health Officer, Dr. Lindsley, the introduction and spread of pestilential diseases are controlled, and an efficient sanitary policing of the city maintained. Meriden has some of the beneficial features of this system, in that a sanitary survey is sometimes made, and thus many nuisances brought to light that otherwise would have been fruitful in the production of disease and death before they were noticed. This in one of the most important parts of sanitary science, the prevention of the commencement of disease ; in other words, anticipating it by removing the agencies that would produce it before their baleful work is begun. The comparatively low death-rate of New Haven, the absence of epidemics, although it is a seaport town, and peculiarly exposed to danger from the introduction of disease from without, as it is also on one of the main lines of through travel, and the centering point for other lesser lines, is a plain proof of the power of sanitation, and has continued too long to be, as the subsidence of certain forms of disease is sometimes, the result of periodic movements in other words, the lower part of a curve that will have as high a crest hereafter. The higher death-rates of other places that have a less efficient sanitary service, although more favorably situated for health, is also an evidence of the truth of the conclusion. The delay until nuisances are complained of before action is taken, when the natural disinclination of people to complain of their neighbors is considered, is one of the greatest evils in the sanitary service of most of our larger towns and cities.

VITAL STATISTICS.

It is one of the duties of the Board to supervise the collection of vital statistics and prepare them to be of use to the people of the State. These reports have received increased attention each year, as their importance warrants. Last year was the first since the inauguration of the service, in 1854, that the physicians generally were supplied with a copy of the registration report. It is hoped that the defects in the returns will be largely obviated when the results of negligence are thus made evident to those whose duty it is to make the returns from which these reports are derived. The State has one of the best systems for the collection of vital statistics, and their completeness depends upon the fidelity of the individual physicians and others who make the returns. The tables show the most important features in regard to the preva-

lence of disease throughout the State, and each one can trace the
history of his own town in this respect if he desire. Several new
features have been introduced of especial value at the present
time, and a fuller discussion of several topics of more especial
interest is presented. The registration laws are in somewhat of a
chaotic condition, due to frequent changes. A codification is submitted which will obviate all confusion, if the fragmentary
sections are repealed.

REGISTRATION.

The registration of vital statistics should be under the control
of the boards of health, at least in the cities. We cannot expect
to have, for some time to come, if ever, a registration of diseases,
and the facts to be learned by the returns of vital statistics are of
inestimable value to the work of a local board of health. It is
true that they receive the results periodically, but this does not
answer the purpose fully. If it were their duty, as it should be
and is generally in the larger cities throughout the country, to
receive and record these returns, collate and tabulate them, the
lessons they convey would be more forcibly presented, and they
would have a truer guide for their sanitary work. The gain to
the service would be inestimable. The registrar should be a
physician, a member of the board, and subject to removal by them
for unsatisfactory performance of his duties. There could be no
better results secured than have followed this method, and it is so
evidently a part of the legitimate work of health boards that its
adoption should require little effort. The use that could be made
of these statistics of benefit to all, and especially to the physicians
of the city, is obvious on reflection. At present the desirability
of any sanitary measure can only be estimated on general principles and the impressions of the physicians as to the comparative
healthfulness or unhealthfulness of any special locality, while, if
the statistics were carefully tabulated and arranged, as they are
when under the direction of boards of health, all such facts could
be learned definitely. In all cases the registrar should be a
physician. Not to allude to the curious work made with medical
terms by laymen that are registrars, no one else can so well perform the duties of the office. Many returns are made that require
to be classified by the registrar, and the same disease is returned
under several names, now one is used, now the other; and no

one but a physician can correctly straighten out the puzzling details and classify and arrange the different types and varieties. There are few offices in the gift of the State, using the word in the general sense, that are peculiarly adapted to the physician. This, however, is one, and one that no other can fill as satisfactorily in all details. It is not intended by this to depreciate the good work done by many registrars, but the fact remains that so far as the records of births and deaths are concerned the best results would follow the methods suggested. Although, as before stated, it is not probable that we shall very soon secure a registration of diseases, yet Prof. Lindsley has hit upon an excellent method for ascertaining the health of a city in the

SICKNESS AMONG SCHOOL CHILDREN AS AN INDEX OF HEALTH.

By an arrangement with the superintendent of schools, the teachers report each week the number absent from any illness of more than two or three days' duration, and the nature of the sickness. The plan has been but lately inaugurated, but the results thus far have been very satisfactory. The benefit to the teachers and principal of a school derived from this knowledge may be worth much more than the trouble of ascertaining and recording the facts. Indeed, with the present knowledge in regard to schools as means of spreading infectious diseases, such knowledge seems almost a necessity, and that an obligation rests on the teachers to secure it for their own benefit, if for no other purpose. It is a valuable contribution to the resources of a board of health.

PUBLICATIONS OF THE BOARD.

One of the methods of usefulness to the people is by the diffusion of practical sanitary literature—brief, concise articles concerning the causes and prevention of diseases, the agencies by which they are produced, the means by which they are communicated, and how to avoid them. It is also intended to cover all points where the "people perish through lack of knowledge," and to give plain directions concerning the preservation of health and maintenance of sanitary surroundings. The importance of pure air, soil, and water, and nutritious, unadulterated food being generally conceded, it is a part of our duty to show how the soil, air, and water can be polluted by negligence, and give plain directions for the prevention of such pollution. The dangers that threaten health and life are to be pointed out, and instructions given for their avoidance. Imaginary dangers are to be shown in their true colors, and panics and unreasonable alarm prevented as far as possible. The publications are, in addition to the yearly reports and bulletins each month which have already been referred to, comprised principally in the following list :

1. On the General Nature and Scope of Public Hygiene; three editions.

2. On Treatment of the Drowned;* two editions.

3. On the Claims and Results of Public Hygiene, by Dr. J. S. Butler.

4. On the Prevention of Diphtheria; three editions.

5. On Rural Hygiene; two editions.

6. On Disinfection.*

7. Restriction and Prevention of Typhoid Fever.

8. Relation of Modern Health Boards to Prosperity and Wealth, by Prof. Brewer.

9. Restriction and Prevention of Small-Pox; two editions.

10. The Disposal of Sewage, by Prof. Lindsley.

11. Restriction and Prevention of Scarlet Fever.

Those that are starred are out of print. A new edition of the one relating to the treatment of the drowned is planned for the next year.

In addition to these, articles on sanitary subjects have been contributed to different papers in the State, and topics of especial local interest have been discussed. The usual number of lectures have been given, and several before farmers' clubs, which is a new feature. With sufficient notice in advance, the Secretary is always ready to render such services without any expense to those that wish them, as this is one means of extending and popularizing sanitary science. In this connection the

SYLLABUS OF SANITARY LECTURES,

By Prof. Brewer, prepared for use in Sheffield Scientific School, is worthy of especial attention. Information is often sought for the best method of taking up these subjects. The plans here authorized give just the information on these points that is desired, and may be of especial benefit to the various scientific associations in the State, the village improvement societies, and similar organizations. If our high schools and colleges would present such a course of instruction, it would displace some of the subjects which have no other excuse for attention than to discipline the mind.

USE OF NOSTRUMS.

The timely article of Prof. Lindsley recently published on the abuse of medicine by the constant use of different remedies, each highly vaunted and put forth as a cure for several diseases, calls attention to a growing evil. The deleterious effects of constant drugging, whether from patent medicines or proprietary articles, cannot be too strongly emphasized. The article in this report by Prof. Lindsley presents forcibly some of the phases of this evil, and also some features in the manufacture of medicines, that deserve thoughtful attention and may require legal action.

CONVEYANCE OF DISEASE BY MILK.

The agency of milk in the transmission of disease has been pretty thoroughly established. A brief account of the subject is given, and some of the methods by which milk is contaminated set forth. The attention of producers is called to the care they should exercise, whenever a case of transmissible disease occurs where it is liable to contaminate the milk supply in any of the methods mentioned. In England the subject has excited so much attention, that regular inspections of dairies by health officers is under discussion.

SANITARY IMPROVEMENTS.

The year has been marked by a general improvement along the whole line, as has been shown. Some special features will be taken up later. One subject that deserves special mention is the care now almost universally exercised in securing a pure ice supply, so that even if you see an ice-house in suggestive proximity to a sewer-polluted stream or pond, the inference is not to be drawn that the ice stored is gathered from thence. This, which was formerly quite generally the case, is so no longer. The companies have been forced by public opinion to discard all such sources of supply, as such ice, if the source were known, would be unsalable, and rightly. The fact has been slowly accepted, but is now pretty generally credited, that sewage-polluted water is not safe to use for drinking purposes, and that neither boiling nor freezing renders it innocuous.

The attention directed to the high-pressure system of education is also bearing fruit. In the discussions among intelligent men they no longer set aside these ideas as unworthy of· consideration. Education must, however, be placed upon a physiological basis, and the true place of the physician recognized as an adviser in such matters before the desired results will be obtained. The highest products of the present system are, as results in after life show, often failures, and are outstripped tenfold by their school and college inferiors. This indicates the radical defect in the whole system. When pushed it results in brain exhaustion and bodily weakness, with high-strung nervous irritability that has quickness but no depth. The powers are "led out" with a vengeance (e-duco) and little remains. With the physiological system a creative brain results, with a healthful, energetic body to execute its commands. The attention paid to the sanitary construction of school houses, especially in cities, manifested of late, and the recognition of one source of evil in the abolition of the tall-tower style of architecture in the new High School building at Hartford, are also important indications of progress.

There are many other topics that might be discussed in this connection relating to sewerage, the increased attention to securing a pure water supply, and kindred topics with illustrative examples, but space forbids. Several of these will be considered later in another connection. The year has been characterized by the work accomplished as decidedly one of great progress. The voluntary association of the plumbers in New Haven for mutual improvement and the discussion of sanitary matters, however, deserves mention in this connection as an indication of progress. The attention paid by plumbers to sanitary science has been already mentioned. Since that was written the notice of .this society was printed in one of the sanitary journals. Since the account of the Sanitary Convention in Michigan was written, full accounts of a very successful sanitary convention in Minnesota were received, which was very largely attended and elicited great interest.

The sanitary protection society in Stamford, which has recently been inaugurated, also should be mentioned here. But if each improvement were to be detailed, much space would be consumed. The final success of the people of Wallingford in securing a full supply of pure water, and thus avoiding local contamination of water by cesspools, vaults, and sink-drains, must not be forgotten. Any successful effort to obviate local sources of disease is certainly worthy of commemoration.

THE LIBRARY.

The accessions have been very valuable in many directions. We are especially indebted to the Census Bureau and to the Smithsonian Institute for important publications; and to our members of Congress, especially Hon. Joseph R. Hawley, who has repeatedly remembered our needs. The statistical reports of the Italian government relating to education and vital statistics are especially valuable. Our exchanges with other Health Boards are an important addition; and it is intended to secure all important works on sanitary science, as far as our means allow. The importance of this auxiliary to our work cannot well be exaggerated, and each year adds to its value. It has also been consulted quite frequently by others than members of the Board, and we extend every facility in our power for such consultations. As a matter of necessity it is mainly a reference library, and exceptions can but rarely be made. If any one is coming from a distance, a previous notification to the Secretary of the intention will secure the desired result, and the consultation will be arranged.

NOTIFICATION OF INFECTIOUS AND CONTAGIOUS DISEASES.

There is on the statute books a general law requiring the health authorities to be notified upon the appearance of any contagious or pestilential disease, but its provisions are so vague that it is of little use, except in case of small-pox, for which it was especially framed. There should be a statute requiring physicians and householders to give immediate information to the health authorities upon the appearance of a case of small-pox, cholera, diphtheria, or scarlet fever. By diphtheria, is not meant every slight affection of the throat, even with exudation in patches, but genuine contagious diphtheria. There should also be a clause in the statute forbidding any children attending school from families where there are cases of the diseases mentioned until a certificate that they may safely do so is given by the attendant physician. In this way the greatest danger of spreading an epidemic by schools would be obviated. In fact, with such surveillance it is doubtful

if occasion to close the schools would ever arise; certainly if the
law was enforced there would be little or no necessity, except in
the general prevalence of an epidemic. The children in many
cases might be less exposed in the school-room than they would
be on the streets or playing about infected houses, and even
perhaps with the children from such houses, for while such children can be kept from school, they can hardly, except in severe
cases, be shut up in the house all the time ; hence the chances of
contagion. Some of these points can be met by a city ordinance,
but a general, explicit statute would be generally useful. In scattered communities where the school is the only means of calling
the children together, closing the school is the safer course.

The question whether public funerals in case of death from contagious diseases should not be forbidden by law, has been referred
to us by the health authorities of several cities, by one with special
reference to an ordinance upon the whole subject discussed in
this connection. Many cities have such a law, and its usefulness
is unquestionable. As before stated, it should be explicit and
plain in details, so that no confusion can arise. It seems desirable
beyond question that if public funerals are not generally prohibited,
health boards in the towns and cities should have power to prohibit them in times of special danger from contagion. Meanwhile, before such laws are secured and enforced, public sentiment
can bring a force to bear that will cause such funerals to be rarely
celebrated. No one thinks of such a thing in case of small-pox, and
when the dangers in regard to the other diseases are as well understood there will be little if any opposition. The notice of death, and
of the funeral, should state the cause of death, if from contagious
disease, and then people can exercise their own discretion in the
matter. Especially is this the case with reference to scarlet fever
and diphtheria, as for lack of it, in several instances, children have
been taken to funerals of those that died from scarlet fever or
diphtheria, when their parents would have never allowed such
reckless exposure had the facts been known.

HATTING,

AS AFFECTING THE HEALTH OF OPERATIVES.

By L. DENNIS, M.D.

Republished from the Third Report of the New Jersey State Board of Health by the
courtesy of the Board and kind permission of the Author.

HATTING,

AS AFFECTING THE HEALTH OF OPERATIVES.*

BY L. DENNIS, M.D.

At the request of the State Board of Health, of New Jersey, I have, for some months past, been investigating the sanitary relations of the business of hatting.

Inquiry reveals the fact that in the U. S. Medical Library, at Washington, there is no entire volume in English on this subject. Neither in the Astor Library, in New York, nor in the Mercantile Library, in the same city, could anything be found on the healthfulness of trades in general. Which facts would seem to indicate the need of an awakening of our individual physicians as well as boards of health to a more thorough examination of all the hygienic conditions of factory life.

A paper by Dr. J. Addison Freeman, of Orange, on the "Mercurial Diseases Among Hatters," appeared in the published transactions for 1860, of the New Jersey State Medical Society, in which it was stated that more than one hundred cases of this disease had occurred in Orange alone. The symptoms were: "Swelling and ulceration of the gums, loosening of the teeth, fetor of the breath, abnormal flow of saliva, tremors of the upper extremities, or a shaking palsy and frequently some febrile action." These cases recovered under the usual remedies for mercurial salivation, especially iodide of potassium, or without any treatment if the work was abandoned for a time. This disease occurred exclusively among the hat finishers, and, the presence of mercury having been established by chemical tests in the hat bodies before going through the process of finishing, it seemed clear that the hot iron volatilized the mercury, and the close, ill-ventilated rooms

---

* Republished from the Third Report of the New Jersey State Board of Health, by courtesy of the Board and kind permission of the author.

favored the absorption of it in the system, and so the workmen were poisoned. The greater prevalence than usual of the disease, at that time, was found to be due to the use of a larger amount of mercury in order to render poor materials fit to work up into hats. The author suggested, therefore, that better material be used in the manufacture in order to admit of the diminution of the amount of mercury, and that the finishing room be large and well ventilated.

Some time after, a committee, of which Dr. S. Wickes, of Orange, was chairman, reported to the Essex County Medical Society substantially the same facts as those mentioned in Dr. Freeman's paper, and, after adding that most of the stock is imported, close their report as follows:

"The committee deem this a proper subject to, bring to the notice of the State Society. In the eastern section of the State there is a very large number of this class of operatives, and they have a claim upon us as conservators of the public health, to do what we can in their behalf. The facts in the case should be brought to the knowledge of our representatives in Congress, that such prohibitory laws may be enacted as shall secure the importation of proper and healthy materials. It may be proper to add that the importers have been appealed to by those interested in the hat manufacture, who declare that they cannot control or remedy the evil."

These two reports constitute all the available literature on the subject at our command. The dangers to workmen which they suggest as liable at any time to occur, and the fact that individual cases of the disease above mentioned come to the notice of the profession more or less frequently, prompted a more detailed examination into the whole business. To this end the wholesale dealers in furs, Messrs. White, 63 Broadway, and Hitchcock, Dermody & Co., 91 Mercer street, New York, were visited; also the factory of the latter firm on Park avenue, between Walworth and Sanford streets, Brooklyn, N. Y., in which are employed about two hundred hands, then in full operation.

The factory of Messrs. White is situated in Danbury, Conn., and employs about seventy-five hands.

The following hatting establishments in Newark and vicinity were also visited and inspected carefully:

NAME.	LOCATION.	NUMBER HANDS.
V. Hermann	42 Hunterdon street	42
Fairchild & McGowan	Market and Congress	125
R. & A. Fulcher	New and Hoyt	85
G. Graah	227 N. J. R. R. avenue	23
E. Sealy, Jr.	119 N. J. R. R. avenue	29
J. Schumann	457 Court	39
C. F. Seitz	31 Ward	127
C. Crossley	10 Front	134
Brown & Hyde	Kinney & McWhorter	53
Tichenor & Klein	N. J. R. R. avenue and Green	56
W. Carrolton	61 Lock	63
Hoefler & Hoepner	25 Exchange alley	27
T. R. Austin	157 Summitt	28
Roth & Rummell	McWhorter	73
J. Mercy & Co.	Market & Union	87
Mason	First street	26
E. K. Carley	144 Canal	59
Nichols & Mason	233 Central avenue	53
Yates, Wharton & Co.	142 Commerce	260
C. B. Alston & Co.	39 Liberty	40
E. A. Dodd	Jersey street	32
Stern & Co.	1 Commercial wharf	11
Wheaton's	N. J. R. R. avenue and Market	17
Messrs. Gill	Orange, N. J.	85
M. Mercy	22 Scott	65

1589

In this work I have to acknowledge with thanks the very kind assistance rendered in making up the lists of the workmen, in some cases by the proprietors, and in others by the book-keepers, at the establishments of Messrs. Graah, Sealy, Tichenor & Klein, Carrolton, Mason, Yates & Wharton, Dodd, and Stern. The lists of the remaining factories were made mainly by Mr. E. P. Roberts, of Elizabeth, N. J., a graduate of the Stevens' Institute, Hoboken. The latter gentleman also prepared, at my suggestion, the appended summary:

In order to make clearer the nature of the dangers to which the operatives are exposed in this business a brief description is herewith subjoined of each process in the manufacture from the crude fur to the finished hat. Ordinary felt hats are the only ones studied.

"The furs most largely used for the manufacture of hats are

those of the hare, coney, and rabbit, all of them rodent quadrupeds belonging to the genus *lepus*, and differing mainly in size and the quality of their fur. The hare is the largest of the family and its fur is the finest. Great quantities of the skins of these animals are brought from England and France, where the breeding of them for market is a regularly established business of considerable magnitude. The English rabbit has been domesticated in Australia, and for a few years past the importations from that country have been large and increasing. Many hare skins come from Russia, the fur being a longer staple than the English, but not as fine. Wild rabbits are found in large numbers in our Middle and Southern States, and their fur is extensively used, though hardly equal in quality to the best from Europe.

"For the finer grades of felt hats, and more especially for fur caps, nutria and beaver furnish the choicest material. They are both amphibious rodents, closely resembling each other in general appearance, the principal difference being that the former has a round tail and the latter a broad, flat one. The nutria is a native of South America, and is very prolific along the rivers of the Argentine Republic. The beaver is at home in colder climates, and flourishes in our Northern and Western States."

The preparation of the fur for hatting is termed "carroting," and the chemicals are called "carrot" from the fact that their action on the hair colors it yellow like the vegetable of the same name. A mixture is made consisting of one pound of quicksilver, three pounds of nitric acid, and thirteen pounds of water; this is stirred with heat until the quicksilver is entirely dissolved, thus forming a strong solution of nitrate of mercury. This, with the aid of a short wisp brush, the hands of the workmen being protected by rubber gloves, is thoroughly rubbed into the hair, the skin being held firmly on an inclined plane and the hair brushed both with the grain and against it, so that each hair, for about two-thirds of its length, is thoroughly wet with the solution.

These skins, when dried in a well-ventilated and heated room, upon racks prepared for the purpose, are then sent to the brushing room, where each one is held upon a large rapidly revolving horizontal cylindrical brush, until the fur, matted down by the "carrot," is perfectly smoothed, freed from dust, loose hair, and the adhesive particles of dried nitrate of mercury. They are then sent to the cutting room. "The machines which shave the fur from the skins are fitted with sharp, swiftly revolving knives, which remove the fur in an entire sheet, the skin being reduced to shreds. Then follows sorting of the fur into several grades, and packing in five-pound bundles." The small fragments of the skins which are torn off in the process of scouring, together with clippings purchased from furriers, are carefully sorted; the larger pieces, and those having longer and more valuable fur, are laid aside to be cut by hand.

"The remainder of the furriers' scraps, and all the clippings from the skins used in the factory, are put into a cylindrical machine, and indiscriminately mixed by means of revolving skeleton wheels. They are then spread upon endless aprons, and are thus carried into the mouths of the cutting machines. These machines have teeth something like the ordinary threshing machines. The skins are cut into small square bits, and the fur is removed after the manner of grain from the stalks. This hodgepodge of hide and fur is then screened. After passing from one machine to another the fur is entirely removed from the particles of the skins, is thoroughly cleansed by the process, and is ready for the packers. This is called short fur, and looks like thistle down."

It is sold to the hatters at a lower price, to be used with the more expensive stock as "filling in" material.

This process of "carroting" the fur is evidently the one in which there is greatest liability to mercurial poisoning, by reason of the concentration of that mineral in the wash employed. To guard against this, and also against the corrosive action of the solution, the hands of the workmen are protected, as stated above, by rubber gloves. In the establishment of Messrs. Hitchcock, Dermody & Co., the workman longest at this branch of the business had only been employed about six years. He stated that he had never had the tremors, but had suffered some from sore mouth and gums, and thought his teeth were beginning to be affected.

One of the Messrs. White stated that they have a number of old men in their factory, some of whom have at various times had the "shakes" and sore mouth, but that of late years there has been no complaint of these troubles since giving the workmen an abundant supply of fresh air.

He also stated that the demand for an increase of "carrot" in the stock has arisen within the past few years. The competition

is so close and the margin of profit so small in the hat manufacture that employers are calling for a stock that will felt rapidly,
and thus materially reduce the time and expense of production.
He stated that the process of "carroting" with mercury is a
French discovery and was called "*le secret*," all knowledge of its
use being for a time kept from other nations, and it being given
out that only acids were employed for that purpose. Hence for
years in the shops of Great Britain "carroting" was done with a
mixture of one pint of nitric acid and four parts of vinegar, and
the felting was aided by mixing with fur a certain proportion of
Saxony and Spanish lambs' wool. Consequently the workmen
were entirely free from mercurial diseases.

A microscopic examination of various specimens of fur which,
by the kindness of Prof. C. F. Eickhom, of Newark, were made
with his instrument, magnifying about eight hundred and fifty
diameters, revealed the fact that the action of the nitrate of mercury on the hair was to roughen its edges and deepen the natural
depressions which exist on its surface, evidently thus favoring the
adhesion and entanglements of the parts composing the felted
mass. It will be readily understood from this why a fur of short
fibre, or inferior quality, should need a greater amount of the
"carrot" to cause it to work up satisfactorily, and why workmen
are thereby more quickly poisoned. In some instances all the
hand in a shop have, in a few days, been either rendered unfit for
work or their health seriously impaired by handling stock so
treated, compelling the employers to return it to the dealers as
unfit for use. Just what, in a chemical way, is wrought by the
"carrot," could not be satisfactorily determined in the time at my
disposal. Some suppose the whole effect of the drug to consist in
its dissolving from the fur the oily and other animal matters which
coat its surface, and so prevent the felting. It is a matter of such
importance, however, that he who should discover the exact nature
of the change produced in the fibre of the fur, and be able to
suggest some agent less harmful than nitrate of mercury for the
accomplishment of the same work, would certainly be saving
hundreds of workmen from much suffering, and very many from
the premature wasting of their powers, and possibly early death.
We heartily commend the subject to the consideration of sanitarians, chemists, and microscopists throughout the country.

The fur, prepared as above described, is now mixed by weight and shaken together by hand in various proportions, according to the quality of the hat to be made, from one-half to one-eighth part being a coarse, poor material called "shoddy," composed of short and inferior furs, trimmings of hat brims, etc., which is worked in with the finer qualities to save expense. This material is then passed through a machine called a mixer, in which the fur is passed between a pair of rolls and immediately seized by a cylinder, studded with wires, called a "picker," making eighteen hundred revolutions a minute, by which it is whirled to the top of an enclosing box. It then falls upon an apron and is passed through another set of rolls and over another "picker," by which the several kinds of fur are uniformly and properly mixed.

The same work is done in other factories by an instrument called a "devil," consisting of a cone set with spikes and revolving very rapidly in a case also set with spikes. A set of projecting flanges at the base of the cone produce a strong draught over its surface, and the fur fed in an opening of the case near the top of the cone is by this current drawn between the whirling spikes and sent flying in a cloud in a close room which acts as a receiver. Here, as in the other machine, all grades are perfectly blended. After mixing, the fur is placed in a machine called a "blower," somewhat similar in construction to the mixer, but having sets of four to six pickers. Just underneath each one and leading from it to an endless apron is a grating, so inclined as to catch bits of matted fur and pieces of skin with fur attached, called "dags," also all the heavy, long, and coarse hairs as by their weight they fall down from the revolving picker, which throws the fur to the top of a grated box, whence it falls upon an apron and is carried forward to another picker, and so on through the set, emerging from the last a delicate, fleecy mass, winnowed entirely free from dust, dirt, hair, and "dags." The "dags" are collected upon an apron and sent back to be again put through the machine, and at last are collected to be cut and torn for poorer material. The hair and other impurities are collected in a box underneath the machine and thrown away. In this department the air is constantly charged with dust, so dense and heavy that everything is viewed through a cloud; and a stay of but a few minutes in the room produces in one unaccustomed to it a sense of dryness and unpleasant tingling in the nasal passages, with discharge of mucus which lasts for several hours after leaving the building.

Even the next day, sixteen hours after spending about forty-five minutes in the room, the mucus discharged from the nose was discolored with the same dust as on the previous day on just leaving the factory, showing that it had penetrated very deeply between the folds of the nasal mucous membrane. Some of the hands wear a thin cloth over the nose and mouth while at work feeding the machines and receiving the fur from them; others use no precautions. Boys are mainly employed in this work, but some men were found who had been so engaged for ten to twenty years. Some complain of catarrh, bronchitis, chronic coughs, spitting of blood, and loss of flesh. Of thirty-nine hands, five are more or less affected. The dust is also loaded more or less with finely-divided particles of nitrate of mercury from the "carroted" stocks; hence some have suffered from sore mouth and tremors. Of the thirty-nine workmen, eight cases of these diseases were found.

This dust seems less injurious to the bronchial surfaces than that from metals and minerals, perhaps partly from the fact that it is chiefly of an animal nature, and thus more readily softened by contact with the secretions of the mucous surfaces, and so loses part of its irritating properties, and, being lighter than the mucus floats on the surface, and so is easily expectorated.

Another reason for this difference is suggested by an English writer thus:—"Dust of every kind irritates, but not in an equal degree. Much, I conceive, depends on the size and figure of the particles which enter the air tube. The dust from the roads produces no apparent mischief, while the mason's chippings from the stone occasions serious and often fatal injury to his lungs. The dust from old iron, which is thrown off so copiously as to deposit a thick brown layer on the dress of the dealers in this article, produces no inconvenience; while the less apparent detachment of particles by the file is decidedly baneful to the workers in iron. It is then the form rather than the material, the spicular, the angular, or pointed figure of the particles detached, which we conceive the chief cause of injury. The bronchial membrane is mechanically irritated or wounded, and from daily repetitions of this injury the lungs at length become seriously diseased, and a vast majority die consumptive." In very few of the shops visited is any effort made to get rid of this dust. In some establishments ventilators have been put in the ceilings of the blowing rooms, and one manufacturer stated that he had heard much less complaint of sore mouth since that change.

Without doubt, at a trifling expense, with the aid of a fan connected with the main shaft, a gentle current of air could be introduced at various points into these rooms, in warm weather from without, and in cold weather heated by a steam coil so as to make it comfortable for the workmen, and this being allowed to pass out at the upper part of the room would not only perfectly ventilate it, but carry off the greater part of the fine dust which now fills the room. , If, in addition to this, the workmen were protected by close-fitting respirators of cotton wool, such as are recommended by Professor Faraday, the greater part of the evil would be remedied.

The fur is next weighed out into parcels of from two and a half to five ounces, according to the size and quality of the hats to be made. Each is then spread separately upon the apron of a feeding machine supplied with a revolving cylinder similar to a "picker," by which it is thrown forward upon another large roller also studded with wire, which projects it forward and upward toward a large inverted cone, in the gill machine, open at the top, into which it is drawn by the action of a fan from the bottom. In the lower part of this open cone, upon a revolving pedestal is placed a perforated copper cone upright, between two and three feet in height, from whose interior the air is exhausted by the fan above mentioned. This latter cone being moistened and set in its place, and the door of the outer enveloping, inverted cone being closed, the fan draws all the enclosed air immediately toward the copper cone, and with it the fine spray of fur admitted to the top from the feeding machine. This fur, by the revolution of the copper cone, is then deposited in a uniform delicate, thin film upon its surface. When the required amount previously weighed out has been laid on the cone it is covered with a conical cloth, sides and top, over which a metallic cover is placed, and the whole removed to be immersed for a few seconds in a hot-water bath to contract and compact the material. The covers being removed, the cone is inverted and the felt gently loosened, stripped off, and laid aside for further manipulation. In the Burr machine the copper cone is fed through an open funnel, the fur being blown by a fan and suction made on the inside of the cone, as in the Gill machine.

The hat now consists of an immense open bag, which, when

7

flattened out, measures from eighteen inches in breadth at the
bottom by twenty-four in length, for the smaller sizes, to thirty by
forty for the larger.   It is first subjected to a process called "hardening," which consists of gently rolling and pressing it in a cloth
from side to side and end to end, so as to interlace the fibres of
the fur more compactly.   At the same time it is examined closely
within and without, and if there are any thin spots they are
patched with bits of fur with the aid of a brush, so as to make
the body of uniform thickness.   The hands in this department are
called "weighers," "feeders," "coners," "wetters," and "hardeners."   The first two are handling only the dry stock; the last
three the wet stock.   The "coners" and "wetters" have their
hands moistened constantly with water in which there must be
considerable nitrate of mercury in solution.   Hence fourteen out
of seventy-four workmen, about 25 per cent., have had some form
of mercurial diseases.   The "hardeners" hold the damp hats on
the arms bared to the elbow, in order the more closely to inspect
them by letting the light shine through, and so have a larger
absorbent surface exposed to the action of the nitrate.   Consequently out of thirty-nine men examined, 25, or over 60 per cent.,
are found to have had some form of mercurial disease.

Among these men inquiry revealed another class of ailments,
evidently due to the same cause, namely, a wasting or diminution
in size, not very marked but still noticeable, of the muscles, particularly of the arms from the elbows to the wrists; and this, notwithstanding these muscles were in constant exercise and so ought
to be expected to increase in size and strength.   In one case,
besides the general shrinkage, there was a distinct depression
between the muscles of the left forearm, so deep that an ordinary
lead pencil would lie in the furrow.   This man had been working
thirteen years at hardening.   He complained of impaired memory,
lack of power of concentration of his thoughts, had tremors, and
general muscular weakness; had not used stimulants for the last
eight or nine years.   Two others, working thirteen and fourteen
years respectively, have the same mental symptoms, also increasing
physical weakness and diminished size of muscles, though not so
marked as in the first instance.   Of the nine "hardeners" examined with reference to this in three shops, six were more or less
affected, and one of those exempt had only worked in that department sixteen months.   In view of this condition and the special

dangers in this department our manufacturers should be cautioned against attempting to work up poor materials at the risk of the health of their workmen. The mischief is evidently at the present time not due to imported stock, but to the effort on the part of our manufacturers to supply the market cheaply.

The conical bag above mentioned is now put into the hands of the "sizer" or "maker," who reduces its dimensions to that of an ordinary hat, by rolling it in a cloth and rubbing it back and forth with others on an inclined plank. Four to eight men work about one kettle of water, kept boiling by means of a steam jet. This water is acidulated with sulphuric acid, the action of this being to make the material felt more rapidly. Frequently the fingers are made sore at the edges of the nails, and occasionally, when the acid is used in too large quantity, the nails are eaten badly by it, and the fingers rendered very sore. These men are in a steam bath constantly, and in the winter time this is so dense that it is impossible to see more than a few feet in any direction in the room. The frequent dipping of the hats in the kettle, and the splashing and slapping of them on the planks, spatters the water over the bodies of the men, so that they are most of the time wet. Hence in some cases rheumatic diseases are found among them. About three per cent. of the workmen examined report this disease contracted in this room. Only two cases, however, of mercurial disease of the whole number examined who had ever been "makers," probably amounting to four hundred and fifty, ascribe its origin to this department. The comparative exemption of this class from disease is probably due to several causes. The rooms are, as a rule, better ventilated than any others in the factories. For while there is a very small average air space to each man, as shown upon the appended table, yet the lattice work in the upper part of the rooms, with which nearly all are supplied, is kept constantly open, and so furnishes an abundance of fresh air. The work is vigorous, and of itself would tend to develop strong, active bodies. It is possible, even probable, that the addition of the sulphuric acid and the supply of an abundance of water effect decompositions and recompositions of the salts of mercury, producing several less readily soluble than the nitrate, and thus less deleterious to the workmen. Time did not permit a more critical and chemical examination of this matter.

As a result of these combined causes there is a much larger proportion of old men here than in most other departments of the business, the average ages being only exceeded by those of the "hardeners," "clippers," "dyers," and "blockers," none of whom have as hard work as the "makers," and would, therefore, natu-rally draw the older men to join them. Then, too, in past times it was customary for apprentices to learn several branches of the business, and as the finishers became incapacitated by age and dis-ease from doing that work they took position in the making room. In examining the men at work, one would infer in this room the existence of a better state of health than in most others, from the exuberance of spirits manifested. In many cases there was sing-ing and laughing—in nearly all, loud, good-natured, hilarious talk-ing, which was in marked contrast with the quiet of some of the other rooms.

After being sized properly the hats are sent to a drying room, heated to a temperature of 160° to 170° Fahrenheit, whence they go through the hands of a workman who dips them in a solution of shellac, either the brim alone or the whole hat, according to the final finish desired, whether a stiff brim and soft crown or an entirely stiff hat. They are then passed between a pair of rollers to press out any superfluous shellac, when they are ready for a second "sizing." This consists in passing them between a pair of rollers, on the surface of which are prominent raised disks, inclined at such an angle to the surface of the roller as to give, when in revolution, a wavy back-and-forth motion. A number of the hats are rolled in a cloth so as to form a long bundle, which is then thrown in the midst of a set of four rollers of the above pattern, which turn it rapidly about, the disks giving a wavy motion to the surface of the rolls, and thus the size of the hats is still further diminished. They are now taken to the blockers to receive the first stretching into a shape resembling a hat. Here one machine rounds out the crown somewhat, another pulls it over a cylindrical-shaped block, and at the same time seizes the brim, turns it up, and stretches it into shape. It is now ready for the dyer.

Ordinary black hats are produced by successive baths composed of logwood, copperas, and verdigris. In the production of brown, blue, etc., the aniline dyes, bicromate of potash, many varieties of woods, and various other substances are used by different manu-facturers, some of which are irritating to the hands of the workmen if they have sores upon them. Inquiry failed to discern any specially deleterious effect from these processes, though many workmen, and some employers, were found who believe the "shakes" and sore mouth are due chiefly to impurities in the dyes. After dyeing and drying, the hat is again blocked more thoroughly, when, after another drying, it is ready for "pouncing." After leaving the "makers," the processes of drying, stiffening, clipping, dyeing, and blocking seem to be comparatively free from disease. Only two cases of mercurial disease in the whole number of workmen examined refer their origin to either of these processes.

"Pouncing" consists in rubbing off, with the aid of a block of wood covered with a piece of emery paper, all the coarse, rough hairs, which in the process of felting the hat have gradually worked outward and are bristling from all parts of the surface. Formerly this was done by hand entirely, and the air of the rooms in which the men worked was filled with dust; the floor, walls, and ceiling were loaded with it. This dust was composed of particles of hair and fur, the "carrot" in the stock, and all the chemicals used in the process of dyeing. A few cases of disease of the respiratory organs and also of mercurial disease are referred therefore to this department. Of late years in most of the shops this work is done in good part by machinery. Rapidly-revolving conical rollers, covered with emery paper, clean the brim, and another instrument sweeps over the crown, set on a revolving block. Over each machine is placed an open funnel connected with a pipe leading to a larger pipe, the air from which is exhausted by a rapidly-revolving fan, so that a strong draft is thus made. The dust and hair are rubbed off and swept out of the room at once, to the great comfort and benefit of the workmen. In the manufacture of white hats in the pouncing room, preparations of French chalk or soapstone are rubbed into the body of the hat. No diseases seem to result exclusively from the use of these substances.

Next in order of sequence, but first in importance in a sanitary point of view, is the process of finishing. This consists, in the case of black hats, in ironing off smoothly with the aid of a little water the whole hat, crown and brim, with a very hot iron and shaping it to a particular pattern, if it be a stiff hat, upon a block or mold of the required dimensions. The workman is bending

over the iron with his face but a few inches from his work, and
this for the greater part of the working day.

Here there are conditions favorable to the absorption of mercurial vapors, viz., the highest temperature to which the hat has
been exposed in the whole process of manufacture, thus permitting the volatilization of the contained salts of mercury, and the
position of the workmen favoring the inhalation of the fumes as
they rise. Hence of the one hundred and sixty-eight cases of
mercurial disease whose origin is traceable one hundred and seven
or 63 per cent. are found to have arisen in the finishing department. Of the four hundred and thirty-eight men at present
employed in this work eighty-nine either now have or have had in
the past some form of mercurial disease. Of that number only
four admit that they now have the disease. This is accounted for
in several ways. Several furriers who are said to have used large
quantities of mercury, in "carroting" the stock, have gone out of
the business. At the time these examinations were made, during
the months of September, October, and November, all the windows and doors of the rooms were open, thus giving perfect ventilation and preventing the breathing in of the mercurial vapors.
Again, the style of finishing black hats has changed materially
within a few years, less of what is called "glazed" surface being
produced by the iron. The hatter now uses more moisture, and
develops a soft, smooth finish without the gloss. The latter
requires more persistent dry ironing, and would be likely, therefore, to volatilize more freely the mercury in the fur. It should
be remarked in this connection also that for one reason or another
many of the workmen examined seemed unaware that they had
any disease, whereas a critical questioning would frequently reveal
evidences of it. Many doubtless supposed they were answering
honestly, having failed to notice slight indications of disorder, and
so reported themselves well. For example, one of the hardeners,
above referred to, suffering from muscular weakness and wasting,
reported that he had no "shakes." Yet, on being requested to
stretch out his hand, there was a distinct tremor observable.
Some were disposed to make light of the matter, and gave frivolous and evasive answers. Some no doubt had a false pride in
regard to a confession of ill health. Very few indeed would
admit that the disease was contracted in their present places of
work, and were rather disposed to charge it upon some other shop.

These facts being considered, it will be readily inferred that the figures in the table appended will understate the numbers of those more or less affected by this class of diseases. In white hat finishing the dangers are much less, because the iron is used but little.

The subsequent operations, viz.: trimming, flanging, and packing, were nearly exempt from all these forms of disease.

The trimmers attach the band, braid, and lining to the hat. These are usually young girls. They work crowded in rooms often sadly ill-ventilated, as very little provision seems to be made for this in any of the factories. The average time in the business is short, for obvious reasons, many leaving it to enter upon married life. Hence, no conclusions are readily deducible as to the healthfulness of their work. Like all persons of sedentary occupations, they are rather disposed to look pale, thin, and worn.

The flange, or curl, in the brim of the hat is set on the mold by putting on it a bag of hot sand, thus dispensing with the iron. In this work, therefore, no complaint of disease is made. The packing consists simply in putting the hats in boxes for the market, and of course involves no greater dangers than the subsequent handling and sale of them in the stores.

Attention should be called briefly to some significant facts exhibited in the appended table, and others which were developed in conversation with the employers as well as their men, and not here tabulated.

Each individual in the factories above mentioned was visited, and personal inquiry made as to all the facts in his history relating to the three classes of diseases specified. The dimensions of the rooms were taken, and the number of the hands in each. It should be stated that the time at which these inquiries were made was near the end of the busy season; consequently fewer men were found at work than are often engaged. About fifteen hundred were employed, while the capacity of these shops is two thousand to twenty-five hundred hands. The figures representing the number of cubic feet of air space to one person would, therefore, be materially changed if the factories were full. The averages, also, are much raised by several instances of a few men being at work in very large rooms, e. g., the packing rooms. In addition to what has been said in reference to ventilation in the blowing and pouncing rooms, particular attention should be called

to the finishing rooms.   Here the air is necessarily charged with
poisonous vapors, and should be renovated by artificial means.
The most that is done in this direction in any shop is the furnishing of a skylight or open funnel with lattice work to permit the
free passage outward of the heated air.

No provision is made for forcing into the rooms a current of
pure air from without, thus insuring their rapid and perfect ventilation.   It will be observed from the table that in this, the most
dangerous work, the lowest minimum of air space of all is found,
and the average is too low for health.   Dr. Parkes estimates that
fifteen hundred cubic feet of air per hour are necessary for each
individual for healthy respiration.   Of course a larger volume
still is needful if it be vitiated by poisonous chemical fumes in
addition to the carbonic-acid gas exhaled in the breath.   It will
be seen that with an average air space of nine hundred and ninety-six cubic feet to a man, as in these rooms, in order to support
healthy respiration alone the entire volume of the air of the rooms
should be renewed every forty minutes.   That this rate should be
much increased when mercurial vapors load the air must be evident.   All the manufacturers who have observed the health of
their workmen agree in stating that mercurial diseases prevail·
much more extensively in winter, when the rooms are closed, than
at any other time.   The inference is clear, therefore, that wherever disease breaks out ventilation is insufficient.   Undoubtedly if
an arrangement were employed for drawing off the air from the
finisher's bench, such as is in successful operation in the pouncing
room for carrying away the dust and hair, there would be very
little complaint of disease from mercurial fumes.   For so successfully does this little appliance act that the smoke from the pipe of
a workman standing before it is drawn gently downwards and
swept out of the room.   Much more would the fumes from the
heated iron just in the mouth of the funnel be safely disposed of.

All degrees of severity of mercurial diseases reported are
included in the two classes, from a trifling soreness of the gums
and tongue to entire loss of the teeth, and from a slight tremor
of the hands and arms to such violent spasmodic jerking of the
muscles as to render the patient incapable of feeding himself or
carrying a cup of fluid to the mouth without spilling the whole or
the greater part of it, the latter being accompanied by great loss
of strength and manifest impoverishment of blood.

CLASS.	Number.	Average Age.	Average Time Hatting.	RESPIRATORY ORGANS. Past.	Present.	"SHAKES." Past.	Present.	SORE MOUTH. Past.	Present.	RHEUMATISM. Past.	Present.	WHERE CONTRACTED. Mercurial.	Rheumatic.	Respiratory.	Number Using Stimulants.	Number Using Tobacco.	VENTILATION. NUMBER CUBIC FEET OF AIR SPACE TO EACH MAN. Maximum.	Minimum.	Average.	Number of Fathers Hatters.
1 Mixers and Blowers...	39	31	7	..	5	2	2	1	7	...	...	14	..	5	18	30	8983	2580	3846	2
2 Weighers and Feeders	44	21	4	..					3	...	...	3	..				4000	1208	2415	4
3 Coners and Wetters...	74	36	10	1	..	1	2	11	...	...	...	15	..	1	45	61	4000	1203	2361	4
4 Hardeners	39	38	17	..		14	8	8	9	1	..	23	1	..	9	15	4000	1203	2389	4
5 Makers	379	37	20	1	3	16	2	..	1	12	1	2	15	..	337	316	2215	294	869	86
6 Dryers...............	4	21	1	..								2	..		9	4	9000	3300	6150	...
7 Stiffeners	11	27	16	..		1									9	10	7200	895	3313	2
8 Clippers	2	56	30	..											2	1	572	572	572	...
9 Dyers................	45	38	10	..		1						2	..		28	36	8250	866	2654	2
10 Blockers............	16	40	21	..		1				1	..				9	14	2700	925	2050	4
11 Pouncers	118	30	10	2	2	4	..	1				1	..	4	98	100	8400	213	1417	13
12 Finishers, white ...	48	28	10	..		5	1	1				1	..		28	42	1400	514	939	9
13 Finishers, black....	438	30	14	3	..	54	4	31		4	..	107	4	2	310	877	3686	200	996	87
14 Trimmers.	252	23	5	..													1639	261	729	38
15 Flangers............,	19	37	11	..		2	..			1					13	15	5280	924	3369	5
16 Packers.............	18	22	11	..		2	..	3							11	14	26400	533	6886	5
Total..................	1546	32	12	7	10	102	14	56	20	19	1	168	20	12	919	1035	6108	944	2559	265

The column marked "where contracted" represents, as far as
could be ascertained, in what particular room each class of disease
was first developed, taking the whole factory through, and is not
confined to the number of workmen at the present in that room.
Thus one hundred and seven report having contracted the mercurial diseases in black hat finishing, but a number of those are not
now engaged in that work, having gone to other departments,
since but eighty-nine now report the disease in that room.

Hence, two sets of figures were necessary, one to represent the
present condition of the men, and the other to indicate where,
including both past and present, the greatest amount of disease
had been developed. A glance at the table shows that rooms 1,
3, 4, and 13 have developed most · mercurial diseases; 5; most
rheumatism, and 1 and 11 most respiratory diseases. The reasons
for these results are evident from the description of the processes
carried on in the respective rooms. Assuming that the numbers
employed in the past are about the same as at present, in rooms 1,
3, 4, and 13, we have one hundred and fifty-nine cases of mercurial disease to five hundred and ninety workmen, an average of
about 27 per cent.

In order to maké some estimate of hereditary influences the occupation of the father was ascertained in each case.   In the table is
given only the number of those whose fathers were hatters.   Of
this number, twenty-six report having had mercurial disease.
About 13 per cent. of those whose parents were not hatters had
the disease, whereas only 11 per cent. of those whose parents were
hatters developed it.   These figures are insufficient, however, as a
basis for any general conclusions.

In conversation with the employers as to the diseases to which
their men were subject, in fully three-fourths of the cases the
statement was made that the chief cause of ill-health among them
was intemperance.   Since all writers on the articles used as medicines represent muscular tremors as one of the most common
effects of the excessive and long-continued use of alcoholic stimulants, it seemed necessary to inquire what proportion of the men
were addicted to them, in order to judge, if possible, what influence this might have on the disease.   The figures attached to each
class represent a condition of things sufficiently deplorable to fully
justify the statements of the manufacturers.   Again, Dr. Phillips,
of England, a careful writer on materia medica and therapeutics,
says of the chronic effects of tobacco: "General nervous depression has frequently been produced, showing itself in restlessness,
insomnia, and a tremulous condition of the limbs, not very
unlike the phenomena of chronic alcoholism."   Dr. H. C. Wood,
of Philadelphia, says of nicotia in poisonous doses: "In one or
two instances violent muscular tremblings have come on shortly
after the ingestion of the poison and ended in general clonic convulsions."· It is worth considering, therefore, how far the constant
and excessive use of this drug may have assisted in the production
of this class of diseases.

The data here likewise are insufficient, since the element of time
is not taken into the account.   Independent of that, however,
taking only the classes of work in which the men have had the
"shakes," out of twelve hundred and twenty-eight hands there
are found—

800 using stimulants and tobacco, with 80 cases of shakes,   10 per cent.
106   "   "   but not tobacco, with 8 cases of shakes,   7   "   "
216   "   tobacco, but not stimulants, with 20 cases of shakes, 9   "   "
 75   "   neither, with 8 cases of shakes,   ·   10   "   '

Of the whole number of persons examined, leaving out the weighers, feeders, and trimmers, who are girls, and do not, as a rule, use either stimulants or tobacco, there are left twelve hundred and fifty. Of these nine hundred and nineteen, or seventy-three per cent., use stimulants, and one thousand and thirty-five, or eighty-two per cent., use tobacco. Of course very many of them use both to excess, thus wasting hard-earned wages, undermining health, destroying the peace and prosperity of families, and in some cases preparing the way for entrance into our prisons and poor houses. He who shall succeed in so vividly and truly painting the dangers attending the use of these two articles as to deter healthy men from taking them, will confer a priceless blessing on humanity. Perhaps more is to be looked for from early training than any other agency, and it is incumbent on every sanitarian to urge the necessity of teaching thoroughly in all our public schools and institutions of learning the laws of sound health and right living. It may safely be assumed that one of these fundamental laws would teach that, to the human body in a state of health, both stimulants and tobacco are not only worthless, but positively detrimental.

American Public Health Association.

TENTH ANNUAL SESSION.

AMERICAN PUBLIC HEALTH ASSOCIATION.

TENTH ANNUAL SESSION.

The following account is mainly derived from various published reports of the transactions in local and other journals. The session was held in Indianapolis, October 17th to 19th, and although a day shorter than usual, as much important business was transacted, and the papers and discussions were fully as interesting as usual. There was less distraction from outside sources to divert the attention of the members from business, and as a natural consequence a closer attention was paid to the direct work of the Association. The attendance was smaller than usual; the failure to secure the transportation facilities that have been so freely and generously granted by the Southern railroads, and the time required to be spent in traveling, were perhaps factors in producing this, but there were enough present for all practical purposes, and the different sections of the country were well represented.

The meetings were held in the Park Theater, and commenced at ten o'clock Tuesday morning, the President, Prof. R. C. Kedzie of Michigan, presiding. After the usual opening exercises, Dr. A. L. Gihon reported the plan of the National Museum of Hygiene, established in Washington under the direction of the Navy. The favorable action upon the subject by the Association last year, and of the American Medical Association, was also stated. The report indorsing the plan was received and adopted. The Museum is intended to be a working-place for experimenters. Four thousand volumes are already accumulated in the library, and an experimental physiological laboratory with valuable apparatus has already been opened.

An amendment to the constitution which had been upon the printed circulars sent to each member was, after a lively discussion, adopted by a large majority. Several amendments to this were proposed, some quite radical in their nature, but they were rejected

in turn. This amendment divides the members into active and
associate, the former constituting the permanent body of the
Association, and entitled to vote. All old members are made
active members, and the· status of each new member is to .be
determined ·by the executive committee. All active workers in.
sanitary science, investigators, writers, and teachers of its principles are entitled to active membership. Associate members are
elected for one year, but may be reëlected; they have no vote;
anyone ·interested in sanitary science is eligible. The plan of
choosing an Advisory Committee by nominations from the delegates of each State was rejected, as were several other propositions
for amendments.

The first paper was by Dr. Horatio R. Storer of Newport, R. I.,
on the Newport ˙System of Sanitary Protection, 'which gave an
account of the origin of the plan of " sanitary protection " based
upon the principle of mutual life insurance as promulgated by
Prof. Fleming Jenkin of Edinburgh, in 1878. The Newport
association was formed in the autumn of that year, and proving a
success, has been copied in Lynn, Mass., Trenton, N. J., Brooklyn,
Savannah, Montreal, and other cities and towns. As had been˙
anticipated, very great . aid could be given by such protective
associations to local Boards of Health, to State Boards, and even
the National Board of Health. The association had ˙labored
earnestly for an independent board of health for Newport, but
without success as yet, but local public sentiment had been so
enlightened that not only was the special change desired close
at hand, but there had arisen a demand for other far-reaching
municipal progress. The traditional conservative feeling was
peculiarly strong, and great opposition was at first aroused at the
clear statements concerning˙ the unsanitary conditions found and
the reforms needed. A vigilance committee was even suggested,
but at a recent meeting of citizens it was determined to overthrow
the present system. Due acknowledgment was given to Dr. John
C. Peters of New York, a summer visitor, who had preached a
volunteer crusade in the New York newspapers in behalf of the
Sanitary Protection Association. The account in detail was then
given of measures employed for insuring complete inspection of
the houses occupied by permanent residents and transient visitors,
and a digest of the public and private work done during the year.

The paper was followed by " A History of Health Work in

Indiana," to date, which recounted the success of the efforts to secure a State Board of Health, and the organization of the State Board of Health of Indiana.

At the evening session the address of welcome was given by the Mayor of Indianapolis in a very appropriate speech, recognizing fully the nature of the work undertaken by the Association.

Gov. Porter then addressed the Association, welcoming them to the State on behalf of its citizens, stating his hope that the result of the session would be "to add much to a knowledge of the means by which sickness may be prevented, physical suffering diminished, and human life prolonged." There were some passages in his address that are of general interest, as the following extracts will illustrate:

"It is said that the prevention of disease is to be attained by avoiding or removing causes of disease, and by making the body less susceptible to these causes. To avoid or remove these causes the interposition of State or municipal regulations is often indispensable. The spread of contagions or epidemics cannot ordinarily be arrested by merely private agency. Municipal or State authority must be exerted to secure efficiency. Quarantine regulations, sewerage, drainage, disinfection, isolation, the construction of buildings in populous districts with reference to ventilation and an exclusion of noxious gases, and other measures of like nature must be adopted and enforced.

The extent to which the rise and spread of diseases have been prevented by the application of a knowledge of sanitary science furnishes a high incentive to continue efforts so successfully begun. Intelligent work in this almost limitless field is of very recent origin. Before an efficient beginning was possible, the superstition that diseases are of supernatural origin had first to be confuted and to be replaced by the theory, supported by the best observation, that nature is a friend to all those who obey her laws, or who, having violated them, strive to return to obedience. This fact has begun to be so well recognized that it has been justly said that the enlightened physician, before the administration of drugs, will usually look for the presence of any deleterious agencies or unremoved causes of disease. Little has been attained toward the prevention of diseases compared with the infinite amount yet to be attained, but the efforts made have been crowned with the saving of a countless number of human lives and a great amount of human suffering. In the work which has been accomplished, the efficient aid rendered by the American Public Health Association has been recognized by the most authoritative writers. The Association has been specially efficient in impressing upon the people the necessity

9

of public efforts toward prevention, and therefore in a great majority of
States State Boards of Health have been established by the Legisla-
tures. It gives me pleasure to say that Indiana is one of those States,
and that the law creating the board is sufficiently complete in its provisions to enable the board to do much good. The law has, however,
so recently come into force that time enough has not yet elapsed to give
it full efficiency.

It gives me pleasure, also, to say that the practice of underdraining
the soil has, in this State, been found so greatly to increase its productiveness that, in proportion to the area of the State, it is said we
have more underdrained soil than any of the States. Underdrainage
has everywhere been followed by a great lessening of sickness, and
intermittent fever, once so common, has become so rare that it is a good
deal less prevalent than in some of the oldest of the States. Our laws
relating to drainage have been recently much improved, and a disposition to relieve the soil in every portion of the State of all excess of
moisture tending to lessen its productiveness and to bring on sickness
is everywhere evident.

Although in the beginning of these remarks I have referred especially
to the disinterested earnestness of the physicians here met, in studying
how best to prevent disease, I am not unaware that some of the most
efficient members of your Association are not members of the medical
profession. It is also true, I know, as admitted by the best writers, that
some of the most valuable suggestions with respect to sanitary measures
have been furnished by persons not connected with the profession.
There are in every profession certain limitations which always render
non-professional coöperation in all efforts toward progress and reform
of real service."

The annual address was then given by the president, Prof.
R. C. Kedzie of Michigan. After a just tribute to the memory of
Dr. C. B. White, recently president of the Association, Medical
Director of the Auxiliary Sanitary Association of New Orleans,
and President of the Louisiana State Board of Health, who had
died since our last meeting, and allusion to others whose lives had
ended during the year, he proceeded to discuss the objects of
sanitary science, which, he stated, included everything that can
prevent disease and thus promote the public health. He quoted
Dr. Stokes' definition:

"The subject of public sanitation, which implies preventive medicine
in its widest sense, as distinguished from curative medicine, touches
every hearth and home in the country; every man, woman, or child,
from the highest to the lowest, every institution in the State, its power,

its defenses, its manufactures, every trade, every occupation, domestic purity, domestic happiness, national prosperity, national health, longevity, and morals, the duties of property, the exercise of charity, and the blossoming and the fruit of our common Christianity. Its end is to improve and to preserve man's body in the best condition, and through it his immortal part. The body of man, says Dr. Ackland, is not only the casket which contains the soul. It is more—it is a casket which, under certain conditions, moulds and modifies the soul. There is a class of persons, I am happy to say rapidly diminishing in number, who seem to be of the opinion that we who are engaged in sanitary work are somewhat fanatical, and that because it is connected with our material frame it is, therefore, a second-rate subject, fit only for inferior men. If I can read anything in the history of the globe, it is this: that the great qualities of a people depend in large measure (except in rare instances) upon the physique of the nation. I appeal to all who have studied the philosophy of history whether it is not the fact that some of the highest of human qualities have been shown in a most eminent degree in days when there was no systematic education, according to the modern notion of book learning. So far as the comparative national health is concerned, I say there is no possibility of exaggerating the importance, not to our own country alone, but to the world, of fostering and caring for the body of man."—*Journal of the Royal Dublin Society*, 1875.

He then discussed some of the unpleasant features of the work, and objections made, the imputation of sordid motives, the association with those that do not fully appreciate the greatness of the work, and the cavillers at the good to be secured by sanitary science. In reply to the charge that the result secured is not worth the constant watchfulness and anxiety required to secure it, expressed by the French proverb, "The health that is secured by constant watchfulness is itself a kind of disease," he very tersely says, after pronouncing this a travesty upon preventive medicine, "The man who prevents disease is not to be mistaken for the valetudinarian who spends life in dodging death." A prudent man will exercise the same care in protecting life and health as in the acquisition of property or in securing any other good. The man who builds his house so as to avoid all danger from defective flues is not to be classed with the man who, mousing around at untimely hours, awakens you with the exasperating inquiry, "Don't you smell fire?" Sanitary science strikes at causes rather than effects.

The results secured in reduction of the death-rate and prolonging the average duration of life were then discussed, and the con-

trol exercised over various forms of zymotic disease clearly stated.
He deprecated the semi-science that regarded these preventable
deaths as weeding and pruning processes by which to make the
race better and stronger, and showed its fallacy, as the strong were
as liable to be smitten as the weak. "Preventable sickness is a
crime against society, preventable death a crime against God." The
degree of development and length of life reached by the domestic
animals under the fostering care of man, the rate of speed attained
by the race-horse, were compared with their original condition
before cultivation. In the vegetable world the various luscious
fruits were compared with the originals, the crab-apple, choke-
berries, and the like. "Beyond the pale of man's intelligent aid,"
says Dr. Jarvis, "life is apparently stationary." If man would give
as much attention to the improvement of his own race by attention
to the laws of heredity and a wise care of its environment, might
not as striking results be secured in human development as already
have been secured in stock breeding?

The outlook for the future was declared to be encouraging, and
among the causes for hopefulness he named the following:

1st. Extension of the knowledge of the causes of contagious
diseases.

2d. The prevention of such diseases as charbon by inoculation.

3d. The discovery of the bacillus which is the cause of consumption, by Dr. Koch of Berlin. If science shall finally reach
forth the hand of healing and guard mankind as effectually from
consumption as she has saved us from small-pox, or the lower
animals from splenic fever, what a shadow will be lifted from the
face of our common humanity.

4th. Another element of hopefulness is the world-wide interest now taken in questions of public health.

5th. In our own land the sky is bright with promise in the
organization of so many State Boards of Health, and we greet
with hearty welcome Indiana, who has so lately joined this sister-
hood of the order of mercy. Foremost among the voluntary
organizations he placed the Sanitary Council of the Mississippi
Valley. Without funds or patronage, without authority to command a single individual, with no power save the high purpose
and courage to do good, and the confidence which such qualities
inspire, the Council put down shot-gun quarantine, and for the

past two years has kept the Valley of the Mississippi open to commerce and travel, but closed to pestilence.

The discouragements were then mentioned, or rather some of them. 1. There is so much to do, and so few workers. 2. A few who profess to be reapers are wasters. 3. The hostile indifference of Congress and the Executive to the National Board of Health. But for the timely action of the National Board of Health, and the efficient aid of a few State Boards of Health, the Northwest would have been one widespread hospital for small-pox, and the commerce of this vast region closed for a time. Yellow fever has lately started up into an epidemic, destroying life and wasting large communities with sickness, and crippling the commerce of our Gulf coast, inflicting a money loss exceeding tenfold the entire cost of the National Board of Health, to say nothing of the suffering and death thus entailed. Cholera is now laying waste the islands of the Indian Ocean, and will soon start on its sweep westward. Thus light and shadow alternate, but the light grows stronger, and the shadows grow less sombre. With wider knowledge and more general enforcement of sanitary law, this diminution of infant mortality and expansion of human life will go forward with ever-increasing momentum till life will attain its normal limits. "Not only will life be extended, but the long life will be full of joyful activities, and man shall fill his days. For this we toil and hope, God speed the day!"

At the executive session the second day, one hundred and fifty new members were received in the two classes of active and associate, as proposed by the Executive Committee, and a Standing Committee of five appointed on the National Museum of Hygeine. A paper on the relative size of the liver and spleen, and the normal temperature of Texas cattle, was read by Dr. Rauch in the absence of its author, Dr. J. R. Smith, U. S. A. The conclusion was, that no danger to northern cattle could result from the transportation of Texas cattle, which were apparently healthy when shipped North. It appeared from the discussion that such cattle were peculiarly subject to northern climatic influences—diseases being developed to which they were never subject in Texas. On motion of Dr. Harris, a resolution was passed requesting the Committee on Diseases of Cattle to consider the pathological and etiological relations of Texas cattle-disease. Drs. J. R. Smith and E. Harris were added to the Committee.

The evils incident to the present methods of stock transportation were then presented in a paper by Dr. E. E. Holman, of Chicago. These were deprivation of food and water for long intervals, and the cruelty of crowding sheep or hogs into cars with cattle to fill up the spaces between the legs of the latter. The account of cruelties was almost incredible. The use of the flesh of animals bruised and maimed by transportation was almost as bad as that of those that had died. Dr. Verdi, of Washington, gave an interesting account of an abbattoir at Turin, where a veterinary surgeon was employed to examine stock before and after killing.

The next paper was by Dr. T. P. Wilson, of Ann Arbor, Mich., on "Life on Wheels." The lack of fresh air was stated as one of the greatest evils in railroad traveling; the oxygen of the air is soon exhausted—sleeping-cars are a little worse, and the lower berths the worst of all. The drinking-water in the tanks was condemned. In the discussion of the paper Dr . Bell thought that upholstered furniture was liable to catch and retain the infection of contagious diseases, and he confirmed the statement as to the filthy and impure water used in the tanks.

One of the most important papers read was .by Dr. S. W. Abbott, of Wakefield, Mass., on the Uses and Abuses of Animal Vaccination.

After an interesting history of the gradual substitution. of animal. virus for humanized, and an account of the old methods, he states that nine-tenths of all the virus now used is of animal origin. The practice is reasonable and preferable to any other mode. Reasons for its use are, 1. The impossibility of securing a supply of virus from humanized sources large enough and with sufficient promptness to use in an epidemic. Large numbers often have to be vaccinated at once, while from a single susceptible animal 1,000 to 2,500 points may be charged; others state 4,000 or 5,000 or even higher. 2. The certainty of avoiding inoculation of human diseases; the opponents of vaccination are disarmed of the most potent argument thus far urged by them. As there have been within the United States alone, within the last ten years, three or four millions at least vaccinated with bovine virus, if there were any cases of transmission of bovine disease, the fact would be noted; but a careful search through anti-vaccine litera- ture shows no such case.

Without making any claims of superior protective power, its

efficiency was declared equal to the humanized.   Care is necessary in the selection of animals; they should be well fed, and housed, and kept clean.   After experiments upon all ages, he has found that cows from three to six years old are better than calves. , The thinness of the hide is the practical point, as virus takes equally well at all ages and in both sexes.

The immense demand during the last two epidemics has given rise to adulterations, dilutions, and other frauds.   Points and quills armed with lymph have been largely used.   The substances used for dilution have been blood serum, egg albumen, mucilage. The first is the most difficult to detect; in fact its inertness is almost the only sure test; the others are more readily detected. Crusts contain epithelium, and lymph corpuscles; there may be pus corpuscles, fat globules, hairs, connective tissue, starch granules, dirt, and the dust from the stables.   The paper was followed by a lively discussion, in which the necessity for Government supervision was suggested .

Dr. A. N. Bell read a paper on Sanitary Inspection, which he stated depended upon a knowledge, (1) of physics and chemistry, especially with relation to methods of analysis in searching for impurities in air, water, food, and soil; (2) pneumatics and hydrostatics with reference to the principles of ventilation, the laws of heat, and the distribution of water; (3) of habitation, use and tenantry, comprehending structure, building material, lighting, care, food and water supply, physical geography, and meteorology; (4) contagious and infectious diseases; (5) preventive measures. Dr. Coggeshall, of Michigan, advocated the contagiousness of consumption, and also its parasitic nature as taught by Koch.   He claimed that the milk of tuberculous cows was pre-eminently contagious and reproduces the disease if drank.

Dr. Compton, of Indiana, sent a paper on Combined Sewers dangerous to health, which was read by Dr. E. M. Hunt.   The system of separate sewers was endorsed, and the construction of sewers to receive rain water and sewage condemned, and their use declared dangerous to health.   In the discussion of the paper that followed, it was generally agreed that no one system was generally applicable, and that, if properly trapped and ventilated, there were no dangers to be apprehended from large sewers.   In reply to a question, it was stated that no association of Engineers had declared in favor of any system; but all asserted that the necessities of each place should determine the size of the sewers. There were some that thought that large sewers furnished better facilities for the growth of the lower forms of life, the bacteria and the like, and that when flushed by storms the foul gases they contained were forced back into houses. The engineers present claimed that the only advantage of the separate system was in the less cost, and that it did not invariably possess this advantage. If properly ventilated, no evils that had been mentioned could result from large sewers.

An interesting paper on the work of the National Board of Health was read by its President, Dr. Cabell, and after an expression of opinions from individual members, the National Board of Health and its results were endorsed in a series of resolutions that reviewed the whole subject at issue, and in the most emphatic terms commended the methods, plans, and investigations of the National Board of Health, and affirmed the urgent need of such an organization in strong terms. The Board was urged to continue its work in the hope of a just recognition by the next Congress.

At the business session the following officers were elected for the ensuing year:

President—Dr. E. M. Hunt, New Jersey.
First Vice-President—Dr. A. L. Gihon, U. S. N.
Second Vice-President—Dr. J. E. Reeves, Wheeling, W. Va.
Treasurer—Dr. J. B. Linsley, Nashville, Tenn.
Executive Committee—Dr. T. L. Neal, Ohio; Dr. F. J. Turner, U. S. N.; Dr. S. P. Conn, New Hampshire; Dr. J. S. Billings, U. S. A.; Dr. J. H. Speed, Louisville, Ky.; Dr. H. S. Fraser, Charleston, S. C.

The next session is to be held at Detroit. Papers were read on Vital Statistics; on Requiring Infectious Diseases to be reported; on Sanitary Government, and the Relations of Health Associations to the Practice of Medicine, and briefly discussed. An important paper by Dr. Thornton, on the Negro Mortality of Memphis, was read by the author. Its discusses the subject in a very exhaustive manner, but must be read in full to be appreciated. Cholera and small-pox are the principal epidemic diseases that have proven most fatal among the negroes. They are superstitious, and under the idea that they have been "tricked," are affected by symptoms much resembling nostalgia, or home sickness in whites. They are very slightly susceptible to the malarial fevers of the South, and especially the severer forms. The per cent. of increase for the last ten years was 29.20 for the white population, 34.67 for the colored. But the colored race is not reinforced by immigration as is the white, and in the cities at least the birth-rate is less than the death-rate. There will not therefore be any great preponderance of the negro race very soon.

Several papers on Small-pox and Vaccination were read, leading to a renewed discussion of the subject. These were followed by papers of more or less interest, which fully occupied the time to adjournment that was not required for business. After the usual votes of thanks to the local committees, and all that had shown courtesies to the Association and to the officers of the session, the President-elect was introduced, and in a brief speech returned thanks for his election. He stated that twenty-eight States had been represented at the meetings, and commended the papers and discussions highly. The Association then adjourned. There should be many more members from this State—the yearly fee is but five dollars, which entitles one to the volume of Transactions, which alone is worth more than the expense of membership. The Secretary of the State Board of Health will forward any names sent to him before the next meeting of the Association at Detroit, which will be assigned to their appropriate section as active or associate members.

SANITARY ARRANGEMENTS

OF THE

NEW HOSPITAL BUILDING,

AT MIDDLETOWN.

———•◆•———

By A. M. SHEW, M.D.

SANITARY ARRANGEMENTS OF THE NEW HOSPITAL BUILDING AT MIDDLETOWN.

BY A. M. SHEW, M. D.

With the introduction into dwelling-houses of water by gravity improvements and conveniences in closets and bathing appliances necessarily followed. The cold out-house or privy gave way to the warm modern water-closet. Stationary wash-bowls superseded the pump and tin basin. It was soon found, however, that while these improvements added much to the daily comfort of individuals, it exposed them to a new, insidious, and dangerous foe in the form of poisonous sewer-gas. To overcome this serious difficulty water-traps of the simple S form were attached to waste-pipes. But it soon became evident that these traps were easily emptied of water by the simple law of syphonage, thus affording only partial protection. Inventive genius came to the rescue with various forms of improved traps, such as the " Round," " Adee," " Cudell," and the " Bowers," each possessing some peculiar feature to meet an ascertained defect in the other. While all of these traps are useful, repeated tests carefully made at this institution, have convinced me that the " Bowers " rubber ball trap is the safest protection for ordinary use.

In the sanitary studies of this subject, it was found by actual experiment, that syphonage of traps was measurably lessened by having larger sized soil pipes carried up through the house with a free opening high above the roof. This insures a continuous circulation of air through the sewer and soil pipe, and effectually prevents putrefaction and accumulation of poisonous gases.

In buildings for the accommodation of the insane, it seems necessary to have the water-closets, lavatories, and bath-rooms accessible to, or connected with the wards. This being the case, unusual care should be exercised in planning and perfecting the arrangements. Any expense, however large it may seem, should be made to secure the best material and workmanship.

Insane persons cannot be depended upon to use judgment or care in operating closet-appliances. In fact, it is necessary to have automatic supplies of water and air. For this purpose many ingenious appliances have been designed; as for instance, a spring-valve in the water-pipe which permits a flow of water whenever the closet seats are occupied; also a chain attachment to the valve and door, by which a flow of water is secured whenever the door is opened or closed.

While these means are measurably successful, they are both open to the objection of being easily disarranged or broken, thus requiring frequent repairs.

In the McFarland Automatic Flushing Tank, attached to the short English iron hopper, we have the nearest approach to a perfect closet for the wards of a hospital. Having used these for three years in the main hospital, they were adopted and placed in all the water-closets in the new building. The subjoined diagram shows a sectional plan of the arrangement of closet and bath-rooms, together with traps and flushing tanks.

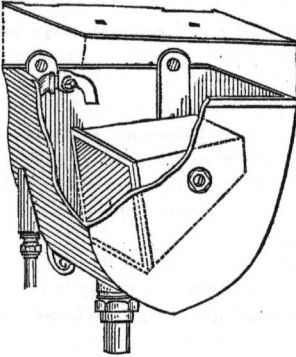

Section and Perspective of Tank D

The new hospital consists of three separate buildings: a central structure and two pavilions separated from the center by an open space of eight feet. All of these are constructed of brick, with brown stone window-caps and sills, water-tables and foundation walls, surmounted by a steep slate roof, which is relieved by large dormer windows, gables, and a central tower. The style of architecture is simple, yet pleasing. Each pavilion may be described as a flattened or broad letter H, with a bay projection on the front face. The linear front of each pavilion is 151 feet, the depth of end projection 64 feet, and of the immediate section 36 feet. The projecting bay is 27 feet in width, by 38 feet in length. This bay, on all of the stories, is used as the sitting-room or day-room for each ward, and is well lighted by eight large windows. A corridor 10 feet in width and 154 feet in length, extends through the entire pavilion. The accommodations for patients in each ward are as follows: There are four dormitories each in size 24 by 24 feet, at the four extreme corners of the projections. Each dormitory has ample space for eight beds. There are nine single rooms on the corridor; also a room for the attendants, a front and rear stairway, a bath-room and clothes-room, water-closet, drying-room, and broom-closets. The large day-room or bay, already described, opens in its full size from the corridor. As thus planned, with so many large windows opening into the dormitories, the sitting-rooms and the ends of the corridor, the pavilion is light, cheerful, and well ventilated. It is three stories in height, with an attic which is used as a trunk room and for storage purposes. The rooms and corridors are heated by twenty stacks of "Gold" radiators placed in the basement of the corridors, with flues leading independently to the different stories. Pure air is supplied to each stack by flue-boxes leading directly out of doors. In addition to this indirect radiation, there is placed in each dormitory, in the day room, and the extremities of the corridors, a direct radiator which can be used in extremely cold weather. Ventilating flues for the removal of vitiated air, extend from near the floor in every room and out on the roof, each as a separate chimney flue. There are also two large, open fire-places in each of the day-rooms, and similar ventilating flues in each of the dormitories. This arrangement for the rapid change of air has been found to work satisfactorily without the aid of a fan.

This general description of the north pavilion, which is occupied by males, applies to the three stories of the south, which is occupied by females. Owing to a slope in the land at the extreme south end of the pavilion, a cellar was constructed under the basement story, and the latter floor-level, which is three feet above ground, was made into a strong ward with nine rooms and the necessary closets, bath and day-rooms for the accommodation of a class of destructive female patients. Each of the ward bath-rooms contain a "Mott" improved cast-iron hospital bath-tub, hot and cold water supply, with the McFarland waste and overflow. A steam fire-proof drying closet opens from each bath-room, in which towels, mops, brooms, or soiled bedding can be properly

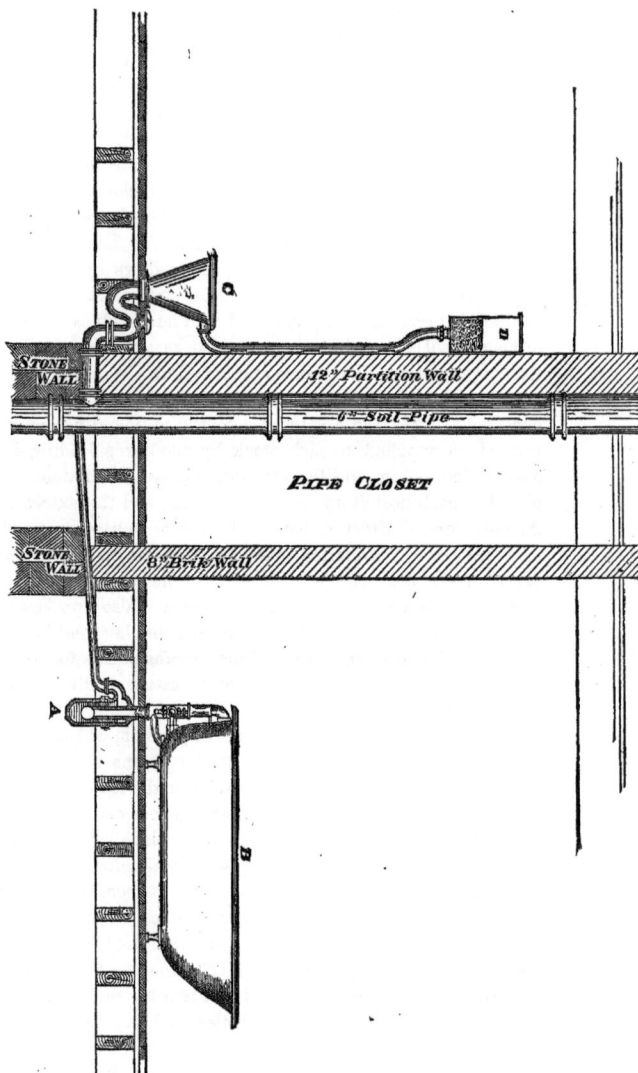

dried. Each water-closet is furnished with two cast-iron stationary hoppers which are flushed automatically, at regular intervals with a gallon of water from, a McFarland Automatic Flushing Tank, placed high up on the wall, immediately above the hopper.

These cisterns can be adjusted to discharge as frequently as desired. They consist of an iron bucket hung in a cistern, working in brass journals. The filling of this tilting bucket is adjusted by a valve inside of the cistern, and when full tips over, emptying the entire contents at once, thereby charging the pipes and giving a thorough wash to the closets and urinals. It has been our custom to so arrange them that the discharge will occur every two minutes. This quantity of water, precipitated into the hopper through a large pipe, is found to be much more effectual in removing waste than a running stream.

A conveniently large slop-hopper and urinal with the same automatic supply has been placed in each of the closets.

Two galvanized iron wash basins, on permanent frames, furnish the necessary facilities for personal cleanliness. All of the waste-pipes from bath-tubs and wash sinks are effectually closed by "Bower's" traps. In further explanation of the system of sewerage, I would mention that all of the main soil pipes are of heavy cast-iron, six inches in diameter, extending from the main sewer outside of the buildings, up through the closets and out above the roof, thus affording a continuous and complete circulation of air through the main sewer and soil-pipes. From this description it will be seen that all of the soil-pipes are of heavy cast iron with leaded joints, thus effectually preventing any escape into the air of the buildings.

The center building is 104 feet in length, 36 in width, three stories in height, surmounted by a slate roof.

A one-story projection in the rear of the center contains the kitchen, scullery, and store-room. A clock tower 17 feet square is carried up in front and above the main building. The first story of the center is divided into two large dining-rooms with a covered passage way leading from each to the corresponding pavilion. Each dining-room is furnished with tables and seats for 150 persons.

The dish-closets and wash-sinks are in the rear, between the dining-rooms and the kitchen. The kitchen proper is 40 feet in length by 20 feet in width. It is furnished with a range 16 feet in length, a steak-broiler and a meat-roaster; also two large soup-

11

kettles, four vegetable kettles, an improved coffee-kettle and a similar tea-kettle, all supplied with steam-pipes and hot and cold water.   Heavy iron wash-sinks stand in convenient places, both in the kitchen and scullery.   This apparatus was manufactured by Mr. E. Whitely, of Boston, and has thus far worked to our entire satisfaction.   There are two windows and one door on the north, and the same on the south side of this kitchen, and a large sky-light opens from above, and two doors open into the scullery in the rear, thus at all times affording perfect ventilation and an abund-ance of light in this most important department.   Two store-rooms for supplies, each 12 by 14 feet, adjoin the scullery at the rear.   A connecting passage way, 9 feet in length, separates this building from the boiler-house, which is 27 feet wide by 40 in length, one story in height.   In this are placed two tubular boilers, 16 feet in length by 5 feet in diameter.   Each boiler contains 58 flues.   In these is generated the steam used in heating the entire building, the water for washing and bathing purposes, and to supply the kitchen apparatus.   The boilers were manufactured by Peter Amerman, of Hartford, and the entire heating apparatus supplied and put in place by the Walworth Manufacturing Co., of Boston. A chimney stack with an inner flue of 2 feet 4 inches by 2 feet 4 inches is carried up 76 feet.   A 12-inch opening is made from the main sewer into this chimney flue, through which there is a continuous current.

The second story of this center building is divided into rooms for the assistant physician, the house-keeper, and the farmer and his family.   The third story is divided into four rooms for the servants on the north side, and two large sewing-rooms on the south side.   For convenience of going to and from the wards to the sewing-rooms, a small passage way has been recently com-pleted.

The cursory description of the new Hospital would be incom-plete without reference being made to a comparatively new feature in its construction.   All of the external walls consist of an 8-inch outer wall, a 4-inch air space, and an 8-inch inner wall.   These two walls are bound together by galvanized iron clamps.   All of the partition walls between the halls, dormitories, and rooms are brick.   For the purpose of economy it was decided to omit plas-tering wherever it could be done, and in carrying out this idea all of the passage ways, bath-rooms, store-rooms, closets, dormitories, kitchen, and scullery are finished in four coats of paints, laid directly on brick walls; and the long corridors in the pavilion to a height of 5 feet are finished in the same manner. By this arrangement it is believed that there was not only economy in the original construction, but that also the subsequent repairs will be less than where ordinary plaster is used in finishing. The floors throughout the entire building are of selected hard maple, planed, tongued, and grooved. The wood-work of doors and window-casings is of white pine, oiled and varnished. The entire cost of these buildings, including furniture and fixtures, was $130,000.

Situated on a dry, elevated plateau, sloping gradually on all sides, with carefully planned architectural arrangements for ventilation, and the most approved system of piping and plumbing—this building seems to offer a thoroughly hygienic hospital for the sick, as well as a home for those wards of the State whose mental defect or disease renders their stay among friends or relatives impracticable.

SYLLABUS

OF A

COURSE OF LECTURES

ON

SANITARY SCIENCE.

BY

WILLIAM H. BREWER.

SYLLABUS

OF A COURSE OF LECTURES ON SANITARY SCIENCE.

BY WILLIAM H. BREWER.

(In lecturing to classes in the Sheffield Scientific School of Yale College, it has been my habit to prepare a synopsis of topics in the order of their treatment, for the use of the students attending. The following scheme has been wrought into its present shape in the experience of several years' courses on elementary Sanitary Science. The headings indicate chief divisions of the subject rather than the apportionment into the several lectures.)

I.—Sanitary Science.

Objects and aims of Sanitary Science.
Its relation to other physical sciences:
How it differs from personal hygiene.
Methods of investigation in Sanitary Science.
Classification of causes of death.
Death-rates and the argument of averages.
What is meant by preventable diseases.
Some of the special dangers incident to modern civilization.
Some of the results already achieved.

II.—Epidemics, Plagues, and Pestilences.

What they are, how they travel and spread.
The part they have played in history.
Their relations to the social, moral, and religious life of a
    community.
Their relations to material prosperity and commerce.
    "   "   " the history and growth of Sanitary Science

III.—**The Germ Theory of Disease.**

Fermentation, general features, and phenomena.
> The chemical changes involved.
> The physical conditions required.
> The nature of living ferments.

Putrefaction and its relations to fermentation.
Zymotic diseases, general character.
> Infections and contagions.
> Bacteria and Microbia.

Vegetable parasites of man and animals.
Parasitic diseases of plants.
>   "   "   in general.

Disinfectants, Antiseptics, and Deodorizers.
Present status of the "Germ Theory."
Differences between scientific demonstration, working theory,
> hypothesis, and mere suggestion.

IV.—**Water.**

Chemical and physical properties.
The kinds, sources, and characters of natural waters.
The requirements of potable waters.
Organic matter in water, and its relations to health.
>   "   "   "   "   oxydation by air or in the
> soil.

Quantities of water required in city and country.
The pollution of streams.
Health aspects of sewage pollution.
City wells, and sources of contamination.
Artificial purification of water.
Ice contamination.
Lead poisoning, and other special impurities.

V.—**Decay and its Relations to Health.**

The gases of decay.
Oxydation in air, water, and soil.
Alleged influences of decaying organic matter on health,—
>   a. As carriers of specific infection.
>   b. By breeding disease germs.
>   c. By increasing the malignancy of zymotic diseases.

d. By increasing infant mortality.

e. By producing or favoring malaria.

VI.—Disposal of Filth.

Kinds of filth incident to civilized life,—

  a. Human excrement.

  b. Household slops and kitchen garbage.

  c. Animal excrement and stable manure.

  d. Slaughter refuse.

  e. Manufacturers' waste.

  f. Street dirt.

  g. The dead.

Systems of sewering.

Other methods of disposal of excreta and slops.

Garbage and its disposal.

Street dirt and its disposal.

VII.—Topography and Climate.

Relations of health to dampness of soil.

Ground water and its removal.

Agricultural drainage and public health.

Other relations to topographical features.

Relations to geological features.

  " " dryness of air.

To light, shade, and exposure.

VIII.—Vocations and Industries.

General relation of longevity to vocation.

Workmen are affected by,—

  a. Bad air.

  b. By dust.

  c. Gases and vapors.

  d. Exposure.

  e. Excessive temperatures.

  f. Chemicals.

  g. Infected goods.

Poisonous trades.

Offensive industries,—

    a. By noise.

    b. By smoke.

    c. Odors.

    d. Poisonous gases.

    e. Dust.

Effluvium nuisances.

IX.—Food.

Sanitary relations, as to kinds and abundance.

Unwholesome kinds of foods.

Food adulterations,—

    a. Merely fraudulent.

    b. Unwholesome and fraudulent.

    c. Accidental.

    d. Incidental to methods of preparation or preservation.

Special dangers incident to the household preparation of food.

    "   "   "   " manufactured food preparations.

Diseases of domestic animals affecting their flesh for food.

Milk supply of cities,—

    a. Sources and character.

    b. Adulterations.

    c. Relation to the health, feed, and treatment of the animals.

    d. Infections carried by it.

Cookery in its sanitary aspects.

X.—Social Customs and Education.

Sanitary aspects of certain social facts.

    Of fashions in dress.

    Of materials used about our persons and houses.

Of alcohol and narcotics.

Of divers other social customs and facts.

Disposal of the dead.

School hygiene.

XI.—Healthy Houses.

Situation and external conditions.

Internal dangers to be avoided.

Plumbing and disposition of waste.
Buildings for industrial and commercial uses.
Public buildings.

XII.—Sanitary Administration.

Official sanitation,—Boards of health, their kinds and
functions.
Quarantine,—Epidemics and their treatment.
Social statistics and their local use.
Sanitary laws,—Scope and function.
In criminal law the accused must have the benefit of the
doubt; in public sanitation, the public must have that
benefit.
The rights and duties of neighbors.
Unofficial sanitary societies and organizations.
Sanitary engineering, its field and function.
Professional sanitarians.
Sanitation of armies in peace and war.
Sanitation of ships and vessels.

XIII.—Conclusion.

Present status of sanitary science.
Effect on the average expectation of life.
Relations to public wealth and material prosperity.
The history and growth of sanitary literature.
War, pestilence, and famine,—the modern methods of deal-
ing with the three great scourges contrasted with the
ancient methods.

THE UNCERTAINTIES AND RISKS

ATTENDING THE USE OF

Proprietary and other Ready-made Medicines.

By Prof. C. A. LINDSLEY, M.D.,

Medical Department of Yale College.

THE UNCERTAINTIES AND RISKS ATTENDING

THE USE OF

PROPRIETARY AND OTHER READY-MADE MEDICINES.

The field over which the State Board of Health has cognizance is not limited to the study of the *causes* of disease, but includes also, to some extent, the means of curing diseases and of restoring health. It will not therefore be transgressing the legitimate boundaries of its functions to make inquiry about the quality of certain medicines which have of late years been coming more and more into use in the treatment of the sick. Such inquiry is the more justifiable because non-professional men, solely for mercenary reasons, and uninfluenced by the circumstances and personal relations which excite the philanthropy of the true physician, have of late assumed a very conspicuous and important part in providing these medicines.

Time was within the memory of many practitioners yet active, when the remedies advised for a sick person were prepared for administration, either by the physician who advised them, or by the apothecary. The symptoms which the patient presented and the indications for treatment formed the guide to the doctor for the composition of his prescription. Then he combined his medicines in such proportions as his judgment dictated, and relied upon his own or the pharmaceutical skill of his druggist to compound them. These duties of the pharmacist necessarily compelled some acquaintance with, and practical knowledge of drugs; so that with men of integrity of character and judgment, the patient was afforded reasonable security that he would be cared for not only with skill, but that the skill should not fail of its deserved success through misplaced confidence in the purity and quality of the medicine used.

In these later days this is greatly changed. Enterprise in business has developed a new industry. Manufacturing chemists' have appeared, and are growing in numbers with alarming rapidity. Not content with supplying the non-perishable officinal preparation for which there is possibly a legitimate demand, they have presumptously encroached upon the domain of the therapeutist and boldly propose new compounds, and recommend them to physicians with instructions as to the mode of use, and the maladies to which they are adapted. Then with all the art of skillful advertising they *make*, literally *make*, a market for their pretended discoveries in the art of curing disease.

Every firm of manufacturing chemists seems to think it is a privilege, if not a duty, to publish a new formula of combined medicines, invent some meaningless name for it ending in *ine*, and then by the aid of printer's ink and paper promulgate far and wide the assumed, though untried, merits of the preparation. The great variety and the constantly increasing numbers of these medicinal novelties have become a source of embarrassment, not only to practitioners, but especially to apothecaries. No one apothecary shop in the State has the requisite space capacity for a stock of all the different varieties in the market. For the most part their brief existence has not afforded sufficient experience with them to establish any decided preference for one preparation over others of like kind, or even to justify their existence at all in place of the extemporaneous prescriptions of judicious practitioners when prepared by competent pharmacists.

But the unnumbered and confusing multitude of these medicinal compounds is not the only evil attached to their general use. Many of these factory-made medicines are perishable, and lose or change their qualities by time and exposure.

The traffic in them is carried on solely for pecuniary profit, and not at all in the interest of science or philanthropy. The druggist is a man of business, and does not replenish his stock until the old supply is exhausted. Accordingly if he gets a prescription for Mixem, Quackem & Co.'s Compound Elixir of ———, the order is filled without reference to the present condition of the medicine. Whether it be spoiled or not, he probably does not know, or whether it may be an agent of cure or of injury to the patient. He can supply the article written for in the doctor's prescription, and the patient must take his chances of its being in good condition.

It is no exaggeration of the facts to say that large quantities of ready-made medicinal compounds are sold which by age and exposure have been deprived of whatever virtues they may have at first had, and have become either inert or absolutely hurtful to the sick to whom they may be given.

Again, an evil of no small magnitude threatens from the temptation to fraud on the part of the manufacturers of factory-made medicines. Several of the most prominent manufacturing chemists publish the formulas of their preparations, professing to give all the ingredients and their relative proportions in the medicinal preparations they make.

It has been often objected that the medical profession and their patients have no means of assurance that the manufacturers of these compounds are of unimpeachable integrity, and that the medicines are the exact representatives of the formulas they give—that there is a strong temptation (which has rarely been for long successfully resisted in other business enterprises under like opportunities) to cheat in the manufacture of their products, by reducing the proportions of expensive ingredients, or substituting cheaper constituents than the published formulas require.

In answer to this objection it is always urged that it would not be for the interest of the manufacturers to commit any fraud in their production—that the risk of detection is great, and the consequences to their reputation and trade would far over-balance any profits resulting from the frauds. That because of this high value which they put upon their reputation for fair dealing, their customers have the most perfect security against any deception in their manufactured preparations.

This argument is the manufacturers' strongest defence, is always offered in behalf of the integrity of their productions, and is boldly urged, as if it ought to be satisfactory and convincing, notwithstanding it is in the face of insinuations or positive statements made by themselves in most of the advertisements that the article specially advertised is to be preferred because of the unreliability of other producers, and the deceptions which it is intimated are practiced by other makers of the same class of medicines. So that even while these manufacturers indirectly accuse each other of cheating, they expect their customers to believe that their productions are reliable because it is not for their interest to cheat.

The argument resolves itself then into a question of business

13

interests; and who can tell how often in the careful estimation of probabilities the manufacturer may not reach the conclusion that it will pay to practice a fraud in this, that, or the other thing, where it will not be easily detected?

The argument based on the pecuniary interests of the manufacturers is a very weak one when it is carefully analyzed. It is only this: whenever detection of fraud is easy, it is better to be honest, and make the most of it for a reputation; but whenever a fraud is difficult of detection and not very likely to be discovered, and at the same time profitable, it is for the interest of the manufacturer to cheat, and he probably will.

There have been a good many illustrations of this latter way of the working of the argument of self-interest, but the most recent exposure of it has been made in a late number of the *Medical News*, in which it is stated that an analysis of the two-grain quinine pills placed in market by seven of the most prominent manufacturing chemists in the country, revealed the fact that there was no sort of uniformity in the amount of quinine in the pills of different makers, and that five of the seven made their pills deficient in weight to a degree that ought, according to the argument they urge in their own behalf, to sadly damage their reputation and their business.

It is to be seriously hoped that throughout the long list of drugs on sale in a finished state, ready for administration, there is not a like defect in the honesty of their preparation.

It is not intended to make the sweeping assertion that every manufacturing chemist is dishonest. But the daily investigations in almost every kind of manufactured merchandize reveals so much adulteration and fraud, of which manufactured medicines show their full share, as published in the current literature of the day, that it is not unreasonable to suspect the crime, wherever there is a profitable opportunity for it.

There is no official and authoritative supervision of the production of the many medicinal compounds with which the market is so largely supplied. The detection of fraudulent practices is not easy by those who use these medicines, and the profit may be very large. Hence the opportunity is abundant, the inducement great, and human nature is frail.

The attention of the medical profession cannot be too urgently called to the consideration of the questions involved in this subject. Indeed, it is worthy of reflection whether the readiness with which physicians trust to and employ ready-made doses, and endorse certificates to the virtues of unproved compounds, has not given a dangerous impetus to this sort of merchandise, and developed a traffic prejudicial to the welfare of their patients, and even detrimental to the best interest and progress of medical science. The impossibility of any ordinary druggist keeping a full stock of fresh preparations of even one manufacturer is further shown by the advertisement of one of the large manufacturing concerns, which advertises that their list comprises about *four hundred varieties of Formulæ.*

The enterprise of the *Medical News* in undertaking investigations of this character is to be highly commended. It suggests the need of legislative action to protect the people against the dangers to which they are liable from this source at times when they are most helpless themselves, when prostrated with sickness and disease.

We have an experimental station in behalf of the agricultural interest, to protect our farmers from deception and fraud in fertilizers. It surely is as important to protect ourselves and our families when sick, from the dangers of fictitious and fraudulent medicines.

SECRETARY'S REPORT.

The year has been one of unusual activity, although there have been no extensive epidemics. The recurrence of small-pox in different parts of the State, and the increase in the frequency of typhoid fever, which has shown a marked tendency to become epidemic, have given occasion for constant watchfulness, and frequent consultations with the local health authorities in many of the towns and cities of the State. The appearance of scarlet fever in several places, and its severity as shown more particularly in the autumn months, has attracted especial attention to that form of disease and the methods of its spread. It shows a disposition to take on an epidemic form and has been quite malignant. The tendency to greater frequency after several years of decided decrease in prevalence and severity, as shown to some degree by the mortality tables in this State, the increase often occurring the third year, while there has been but little mortality from scarlet fever for several years, make the chances for its prevalence in the coming year seem good. That there are recurrent elevations and depressions in the death-rate from scarlet fever is shown by the mortality tables. Generally the periods are not definitely known, nor are they exactly uniform, although if we knew all the factors in the case the regularity, or rather obedience to law, would perhaps be more evident. The depressing effect of unsanitary surroundings, and their influence in spreading the disease, have been shown repeatedly. Public funerals in case of persons dying from scarlet fever and diphtheria should be avoided, and, if not altogether prohibited by law, it should be in the discretion of the local Boards of Health to forbid them whenever the danger of spreading an epidemic demands such action.

In addition to the work in connection with the different varieties of zymotic diseases and investigating cases of unusual frequency and severity, and in consultations with local health authorities concerning emergencies and the best way to meet them, consultations have been held concerning almost every variety of local nuisances, slaughter-houses and their management, so as to be made inoffensive to health and comfort; the proper location of pig-pens, privies, and cesspools, and the best practicable location of the latter with refer- ence to the safety of the well-water from contamination; the drainage of a house site,—of cellars, and of the grounds in the immediate vicinity of dwelling houses; the location and ventilation of school-houses; the best methods of water supply, and other subjects, the most important of which will be taken up in detail, or rather some of those more important and generally interesting, as to fully discuss them all would take much more than the available space.

The water supply of the cities has taken also an important place among the subjects that have been under especial study, and some interesting facts will be found in this connection. The ice supply has also received some attention, although we were not fully prepared to undertake the work microscopically until late in the year. As we are now well armed and equipped for microscopical investigation, work of this kind will be pushed to a much greater extent during the coming year. A series of weekly examinations of the water supply of several places has been planned, and it is hoped to make it complete by chemical analyses also. This work is not to be confined to the cities, nor to those towns that have a public water supply, but as far as obtainable specimens of well-water will be analyzed and examined especially with reference to prevalent diseases. Considerable work has been done the present year in regard to the healthfulness or the reverse of well and spring water; also of the water from small reservoirs used in common by several families, and of cistern water. We are prepared to examine water from such sources, and any specimens of potable water, qualitatively and microscopically, free of charge, and hope to be able to obtain the necessary appa- ratus to make quantitative examinations of such substances as are deleterious in a sanitary sense. An exact detail of every mineral is not always of value. The following schedule, as followed by the National Board of Health in the work they had commenced with regard to water supply and its relation to disease, is complete enough for all sanitary purposes, especially if supplemented by a microscopical examination of the sediment and of any floating organic particles. There often appears in water that is kept for examination, if not seen when first obtained, small bright specks, which become readily visible after awhile. These can be removed by aid of a pipette and placed under the glass, when they are found to be usually confervoid growths, in various stages of development. The bright, refractive specks usually are spores. The following is the schedule mentioned:

Color, odor, total solids, loss on ignition, characteristics on ignition, fumes, peaty odor, growing dark, etc.; chlorine, nitrous acid, nitric acid, free ammonia, albuminoids, oxygen required to reduce organic matters. This is quite complete. The amount of lime, iron, and other mineral constituents give us very little aid in determining sanitary questions concerning water. In some connections they are desirable, as it is well to know the general characters of a particular water supply, but once ascertained the other elements are those that reveal the most in a sanitary sense.

There are many impurities offensive to the senses that are not deleterious to health. Thus many of the lower forms of plant and animal life that are visible to the eye, or by the aid of low powers of the microscope, are not dangerous to health if drank even in quite large quantities. These are the specimens caught by filters and shown in a glass of water by the vendors of the same. There is no evidence that they have ever done any harm; and as in many other cases agents that look much less offensive, or are altogether invisible, produce infinitely more mischief. The bad odors and tastes in ponded waters are at times very offensive, but the only harm they do is to disgust one with the water that thus offends; no ill-health or sickness has ever been caused by water otherwise ordinarily pure that smells badly. The causes of these odors will be alluded to in another connection.

The use of lead pipes to carry spring water any distance, especially if the water is from any cause long in contact with the lead, as the ends of the pipe in the cistern at the house, for instance, has, in several instances, produced enough contamination of the water to cause lead poisoning. Several such instances have occurred during the year. It is well known that the purer the water the greater the danger of its dissolving lead, and also water that contains nitrates and other products resulting from vegetable decay dissolves more. Iron pipes are much more preferable; the outside can be coated with some of the preparations in common use to prevent rust. So far as our experience reaches, tin lined lead pipes are worse than lead pipes; there is apt to be some break in the coating, and then chemical action between the two metals intensifies the process of solution, and greater contamination results. Several instances have been noted of contamination of water by lead, usually spring or rain water.

There is one precaution that is observed in many places to preserve the purity of cistern water, and that is, to allow the first rain that falls to wash the air, and roof, and gutter pipes along the roof, but not to allow it to run into the cistern. When water is scarce this is often collected in a separate cistern or tank, and used for other purposes than for drinking. If the cistern water be filtered, of course the impurities will for the most part be removed, but those held in solution will remain.

The liability of wells, as generally constructed, to contamination from surface water, has been forcibly brought to notice repeatedly during the past year. In many cases the facts have been verified by personal inspection of the premises; in others, the description of the well and its surroundings left no chance for doubt that the well received the washings from a large area which was to a great extent used as a receptacle for the deposit of the kitchen waste, the laundry filth, and other excrete and waste products, as vault and cesspool were included in the area of drainage that the well drew from. Every moderately heavy rain would dissolve more or less of the filth that there was no vegetation to utilize, and as the water trickled down the sides of the well, these substances were carried in solution. It is unfortunately the case that the soluble products of putrefaction do not have a bad taste nor odor, so that water containing a large percentage of the chemical products of the putrefactive decay of fœcal matters, would taste clear and appear bright and sparkling. If compared with a specimen of distilled water, one would be very apt to select the contaminated specimen. The well at a certain college was the most popular, and the other nearer several rods to half the rooms passed by to reach it, whose water was found on analysis after an unusual prevalence of diarrheal and dysenteric troubles among those that had used it freely, to be grossly polluted from the vault that was used by three hundred or more people, which was but a few rods distant. The use of this water was discontinued and the well filled up, to the great improvement in health of the inmates of the college buildings. Several instances of contamination of well

water from surface water collected from an area that from its near-
ness to the house and stables as a matter of course receives more
filth than can be disposed of except by decay have been noticed.
The analysis of the water before and after a smart shower showed a
gain in organic matter after the rain of over a third, and in one
instance after a long drought of more than half; a marked increase can usually be detected unless the water is always badly
contaminated, when there would not be as much difference.

The care that should be taken in obtaining specimens of well
water, that they should represent the top, middle, and bottom of
the level of water in the well, was illustrated last year by the different results from analysis of the water from the same well where
water at different levels was sent each time. The sugar test is so
easily applied and in general is so reliable that it will bear frequent
repetition. If the water in the well or from any source is suspected
to contain too much organic matter, to be contaminated by surface
drainage, or from the vault or sink drain or cesspool, it can readily
be determined by this test. Take a four or six-ounce bottle of
white glass; wash clean and rinse several times with the water to
be examined; then fill it two-thirds full, and add a few grains of
white sugar, loaf sugar preferably, as the most pure; cork it tightly
and place it in a moderately warm room in the light. It should
remain clear and free from floating specks for two weeks. If it
become at all milky or turbid, the water is polluted by organic
matter. The extent of the turbidity and the rapidity with which
it occurs are indications of the amount of pollution. Bright floating specks are usually the spores of compound plants that develop
after a while into quite a colony of these organisms, entangled by
their mycelial threads. The remedy for surface pollution of wells
is to cement thoroughly the inside of the well, and better yet, lay
the upper third of the wall with cement and coat the inside also.
A curious case, illustrating the necessity of a knowledge of the
geological formation before expressing an opinion as to the sanitary perfection of the surroundings of a house, came to notice
during the year, and another just as this report was in press. The
surface drainage was excluded from the well, and apparently every
precaution had been taken that was practicable. But sickness
occurred, and upon investigation it was found that the upper layer
of ground for a foot was loam. Then came several feet of hard
clay, and then coarse gravel; below this sand. The privy vault and

cesspool were dug down to the coarse gravel. As the vault received a large amount of liquid waste, neither vault nor cesspool
were cleaned. The well water finally received its full share, as of
course the well was deeper than the other openings, which were not
more than thirty feet distant. When a rain fell, the soil below the
clay was washed to an extent varying with the rain fall, and part of
the filth, washed out of the soil around vault and cesspool, as it
passed along readily through the gravel, as a matter of course
reached the well. So after all sub-soil pollution, if it is hidden and
out of sight, is just as undesirable. In the second instance the
lower level (the third layer) was quicksand, and similar results, to
a less degree, followed. The safer construction of vault or cesspool, if anywhere near a well, is to thoroughly cement the bottom
and sides, and clean often. If one has a small lawn, subirrigation
is the best method of disposal of kitchen and laundry fluids. A
series of small tile drains, laid under the surface eight or ten
inches, will dispose effectually of all such waste, so that no danger
to health can ever arise. A small plot would suffice for an ordinary household. Almost every house in the country has a grass
plot sufficiently large for the purpose. If one of the pipes is
clogged, a brighter green of the grass or its lodging will indicate
it, or else a wet spot. That tile can be dug up without disturbing
the others, cleaned, and replaced. There is no subject of greater
relative importance than the obtaining of a plentiful supply
of pure water for domestic purposes, and the preservation of its
purity against the chances and dangers that threaten in different
directions and from diverse sources.

SPECIAL INVESTIGATIONS.

These have been very numerous during the past year, and upon
many different subjects. In addition to those upon well-water, and
the systematic examination by Dr. Lewis of the water supplied to
several cities of the State, a series of examinations have been made
upon the ice supplied to several cities, the results of which will be
found in detail farther along in the report. It is evident that
much greater care has been taken of late in regard to securing
pure ice, as the results were much more favorable than had been anticipated. The first special examination since those reported last
year, and in some respects partly made then, although not regularly
acted upon, was in reference to the

14

EXPOSURE OF THE BED OF A NATURAL POND

In Union. There is a small village in this town clustered closely
about a pond that was formerly used for local manufacturing purposes. This was connected with a larger pond some distance above,
which was the reservoir. These formed part of a series or chain of
ponds connected by small streams, which extended into Massachusetts. Since the discontinuance of its use by local parties the water
power has passed into the hands of an outside company. During
the extreme dry weather for several summers, the second pond has
been, as was stated, drawn down entirely, leaving only a very narrow
stream running through the centre, and so maintained during the
summer and autumn until the heavy fall rains. In order to draw
down the water in the first and largest pond, which was a natural
pond fed mainly by springs, although having quite an extensive
water-shed, the second pond had to be emptied and the natural
channel of communication cut lower. This state of affairs had
continued for several years, it was stated. When the pond was
first drawn down, and while the decaying materials at the bottom
of the pond, which probably extended over thirty or forty acres
at least, were drying, offensive odors were complained of, and
it was stated that they caused nausea and vomiting. Diarrheal
and dysenteric troubles were stated to be then unusually frequent.
No cases of malaria were reported as having originated in any
part of the town, nor have there been any cases reported as yet.
Several large ponds were noted, in driving from Palmer, Mass.,
to Union, that were completely drawn down and their beds exposed, but upon inquiry no cases of malaria were reported as
originating in that region. The remedy asked for was to leave the
lower pond covered with a few inches of water. There appears to
be a causal relation between the exposure of the pond
and its loss of moisture and the sickness complained of, and the
request a reasonable one, that the bed of the pond should be
covered at all seasons of the year or else uncovered. Such a report was made to the parties at interest, and no new features in
the case have since been reported to the Board. An equally good
result would eventually follow the discontinuance of the middle
pond altogether, if that were possible, although it would take some
time for the grass to cover the bed of the pond. The pond is not
drawn down so much with reference to the comparatively small

supply of water that its capacity enables it to store, but to enable the large pond to be drawn, if need be, very low. The natural outlet provided only for an overflow, but this has been deepened, so that a large volume of water is rendered accessible. The region is thinly settled, and there are few houses around the other ponds mentioned, and none very near the large pond. A small village had grown up around the smaller pond when the manufacturing firm commenced operations, but its growth ceased when that removed to another place. The case is interesting in many features, as quite a large area is exposed to the sun, and a large amount of vegetable matter exposed every summer.

THE CAUSE OF MALARIA.

A communication was received from the National Board of Health with reference to the plan proposed in our last report, of a conjoint study of the etiology of malaria, with especial reference to the germ theory as a working basis, and incidental investigations, as facts warranted. The theory of Laveran was also to be considered, and it was confidently expected that if the primal origin of malaria were not discovered, that facts of permanent value might be collated and observed that would form a valuable addition to our knowledge on the subject. The State Boards of Health of New York, Massachusetts, and Rhode Island were interested in the work, and were to assist in all possible ways, as was the case with our own State Board of Health. A preliminary meeting was held in Boston, where delegates from each organization interested met, and the rough outline of the work was determined upon. Considerable enthusiasm was excited, and much was expected from the plan adopted, which involved geologic, atmospheric, and biological studies, as well as microscopical investigations ; in fact, every agency known or supposed to have any relation to the subject. The microscopical part was under the especial charge of the National Board of Health, who had selected one of the most expert workers in that department in this country, with one of the best equipped laboratories to work in to be found. The action of Congress in temporarily restricting the field of action of the National Board of Health, checked all concerted action at once, and all the possibilities of achievement remain as before. A brief account of some work done in relation to this subject accompanies other detailed statements in this report. The following is a pre-liminary circular prepared by Dr. Wallcot, of the Massachusetts State Board of Health, under direction of the convention held at Boston.

MAY 15, 1882.

DEAR SIR:—The National Board of Health has decided to undertake certain investigations upon the nature of the malarial poison, and more especially to attempt to determine the correctness of the observations published in Europe within the last two years with regard to the exist-ence of a definite germ or parasite connected with the disease.

It is proposed to repeat the experiments of Klebs and Tommasi-Crudelli, as well as those of Sternberg, as to the effects upon animals of materials collected from or near malarial localities, and to compare these with similar material collected from localities as yet free from malarial diseases.

It is also desired to investigate blood, with a view to prove or disprove the results announced by Eklund and Laveran.

The National Board proposes to undertake the laboratory work of the investigation, including culture experiments and experiments upon animals. This work will, for the present at least, be carried on at Boston in the laboratory of Dr. W. S. Bigelow, by W. F. Whitney, M.D., Curator of the Warren Anatomical Museum.

The State Boards of Health of Connecticut, Massachusetts, and New York have agreed to furnish the materials for this research, and to collect information in their respective States as to the conditions appear-ing to influence local outbreaks of the disease.

It is especially desired that early notice of the appearance of malarial fever in districts where it was previously unknown may be at once given to this Board.

Will you kindly aid in the investigation by furnishing answers to the subjoined questions?

1. Has malarial fever in any of its forms prevailed in your town or vicinity during the past year, or does it now prevail?

2. If so, please state:

a. The number of cases of which you are cognizant.

b. At what season of the year the disease has prevailed.

c. Whether the persons so affected reside near any pond, reservoir, or stream, and if so, how near and in what direction.

d. How many of the persons included in answers to questions a, b, and c have had malarial fever in previous years, and how many have been exposed to malaria in other places.

e. Can the disease in any case be traced to the use of drinking water from malarial districts.

3. Has malarial fever been known in your vicinity in previous years?

4. Did it exist, the year previous to its appearance in your town, in any town nearly adjacent? If so, please state where and how far away.

5. If malarial fevers have ceased to prevail during this or any previous year, state any causes which may appear to you sufficient to explain this relief.

6. What other diseases have been endemic or epidemic in the town at any time during the year?

It is also desired that the information sought in this circular should be furnished at any subsequent time if the present condition with regard to the existence or non-appearance of malarial fever should change.

It is not intended by either the National Board or State Boards to publish at present the localities where malarial fever exists.

NATIONAL BOARD OF HEALTH.

The following resolutions passed at a regular session of the Connecticut State Board of Health may perhaps as well be placed in this connection as elsewhere:

1st. *Resolved*, That in our judgment a National Board of Health is necessary for the adequate protection of the health and lives of the people of this country against many dangers that threaten from sources that are beyond the control and jurisdiction of local and State Boards of Health, but which could be averted by such an organization. It is also an important agency for investigation into the origin, causes, and methods of prevention of disease that are common to large areas and cannot be fully comprehended by any limited local organization.

2d. *Resolved*, That we especially regret the restriction of the field of action of the National Board of Health at the very inception of an extensive and critical investigation upon the subject of malaria, the essential conditions upon which it depends, and its causes and manner of diffusion, undertaken with the coöperation of the State Boards of Health of New York, Massachusetts, and Connecticut. The reappearance of malarial diseases in New England and their extension over the southwestern portion renders this proposed study one of peculiar interest and value.

3d. *Resolved*, That the work done by the National Board of Health in the way of scientific and practical investigations upon the origin and prevention of infectious diseases and upon other subjects in different departments of sanitary science has been of inestimable value.

4th. *Resolved*, That in our judgment the field of action of such a Board should be enlarged rather than restricted, and that every possible

facility should be afforded it for the diffusion among the people of the
information it secures.

5th. *Resolved*, That the National Board of Health, in its system of
inspection of emigrants and in the execution of its plans for the prevention of the spread of disease and infection by the internal transportation system of the country through railroads and steamboats, had
inaugurated a service that cannot be so adequately nor so fully executed
by any other agency.

6th. *Resolved*, That we unhesitatingly state that the good results
already accomplished by the National Board of Health in these and
other directions which have not been particularized warrant the continuance of such an organization and the enlargement of its sphere of
action, while its possibilities for the future present still greater and more
imperative claims. In our opinion such an organization should be an
independent department of the government.

By order State Board of Health of Connecticut.

C. W. CHAMBERLAIN,

Secretary.

It is certainly to be hoped that the investigations in regard to
malaria alluded to in this connection will be resumed, and
under better auspices carried to completion. No very definite results could be expected immediately; a study so complicated would
of necessity extend over a long period, but incidentally many facts
of value would be ascertained. The diseases that occur regularly
and do not depend upon some epidemic influence, but each year
contribute to the mortality lists, cause a hundred fold more deaths
than epidemics that by their sudden action terrify the people and
frighten them into sensible treatment of some sanitary subjects.
Yet the unsanitary surroundings of houses, the poor ventilation
of schools, and many a form of disease that no effort is made to
check or to save the lives its ravages needlessly waste, each
and all slay more victims than many a virulent epidemic. The
whole field of sanitary science should be open for the investigations of a National Health Board and all causes that needlessly
destroy health and life come by right under its jurisdiction.

INFANT MORTALITY.

The largely increased mortality among infants during the pro-tracted heated term for the last year or two, extending in one or two instances until late in September, has drawn special attention to the causes and means of prevention. One of the most fruitful sources next to unsanitary surroundings perhaps is poor food. This applies especially to the bottle-fed babies, who of course depend upon the nutritious quality of the milk for health, development, and life. The evils of adulterated milk and its influence in pro-ducing infantile diarrhea and infantile debility, even if no delete-rious substances are added to the milk, were discussed last year. In some places the local governing powers have taken action, and a bill fair enough in its provisions if executed, was passed at the last session of the legislature. These will be found printed in full with some general remarks on the subject, in their proper con-nection. The influence on infantile life of removing a large per-centage of the nutritious elements of the food, can be readily im-agined. The sight of the wasted, puny bodies of the victims of this practice would not delight the dreams of the most indifferent milk vendor. The following conclusions of a convention of German physicians and scientists are very forcibly stated:

1. That the mother's milk (woman's milk) is the only true material that is suited to the development of the child.

2. That cow's milk is the only substitute.

3. That the various artificial preparations are to be entirely and completely rejected during the first year of the child's life.

The plan of Dr. Gill of Illinois has been successful in some cases where an easily digestible, nutritious food was required. It is as follows: add ten grains of pepsin to a pint of milk; beat it in well, then set the milk on a warm stove and allow it to stand until curdled; sometimes it requires a half hour. When solid beat up the curd with a spoon and strain; add half as much water as there is whey; sweeten to the taste of mother's milk. If found to digest well some of the soft curd may be worked through into the whey, or a little cream may be added, a teaspoonful for each feed-ing. The following instructions as to the care of infants, by Dr. C. A. Lindsley, Health Officer of New Haven, are especially valuable.

"Infantile diarrhea always prevails most when the weather is the hottest. But the influence of heat as it directly affects the infant is not the chief factor in producing the disease, because it rarely happens that infants in a pure and wholesome atmosphere, who are well fed from nature's fountains, suffer from the disorder. The influence of heat is *indirectly*, however, a very potent cause of intestinal disorder. Potent, through its agency in promoting rapid decomposition and putrefaction of organic matter, with the result of charging the air with poisonous gases emanating from the decomposing filth. Infants are far more susceptible to the effects of such poisoned air than adults. Daily experience demonstrates that infantile diarrhea prevails most and is most fatal wherever filth is most abundant, and the sources of air pollution most prolific. The dwellings connected with cesspools, with privy vaults, with stinking garbage heaps, with foul and unventilated cellars, the houses with such defective plumbing that sewage and sewer gases are admitted or retained within the walls. These are the sure and certain causes where if there are babies living in them, they will be sick and many will die. And their chance of living is greatly lessened if they are also of the unfortunate class who are bottle-fed. Almost all the victims of this disease who die are fed with artificial diet. Their mothers do not nurse them. Hence attention to the diet of infants during the hot weather is of supremest importance.

"The welfare of the babies then requires that two things shall be most carefully provided for them, viz.: PURE AIR and GOOD FOOD. If they could have these two necessities constantly furnished them, there would be little difference in infantile mortality in July and January.

"Parents who are anxious to preserve their babies' lives should, therefore, clean up their houses and all about them. Let nothing remain within their reach that can make a smell or defile the air or the water. Let them wash the children twice a day in cold water, and oftener if it is very hot. Keep the doors and windows wide open, and as much as practicable keep the children out of doors wherever the air seems most wholesome.

"Overfeeding disorders the bowels, and is a fruitful cause of trouble. A nursing baby one or two months old should be allowed the breast only once in two or three hours. A six-months baby not more than five times in twenty-four hours. If the baby seems thirsty between times, give it a little water, *without sugar*. Avoid, however, a habit of giving it a sugar or some sweetened catnip tea at every whine it makes; that is the invention of some modern she-Herod, yclepeda nurse, and cannot be too strenuously resisted. Be regular and systematic; nurse it by the clock; and it will soon learn to keep time with as much accuracy.

"No hard and fast rules will apply to all these babies alike. Individual cases must be studied, and the special form of diet adapted to their needs.

"The ordinary substitute for mother's milk is cow's milk. It is to be had in two forms, viz.: Fresh from the cow, and preserved as 'condensed milk.'

"Really *fresh* milk is not attainable, especially by the poor.

"That served by milkmen at our doors was fresh the day before. In very hot weather it changes rapidly, and should be tested with blue litmus paper to determine if it is soured at all. Litmus paper can be had at any drug store, and when wet with milk will turn red if the milk is in the least acid.

"Cow's milk should be diluted for young infants.

"It may be diluted with pure water, with barley water, or with oatmeal water. If with the latter, the barley or oatmeal should be well cooked and strained. These different diluents are suited to different cases.

"As soon as the milk is received prepare a sufficient quantity for the child until the next supply. Add a pint of boiling water to an equal amount of milk; put in a small pinch of table salt, and slightly sweeten with pure loaf sugar and strain. Set it in refrigerator in a closely-covered vessel.

"Take from it only so much as the child will need at each feeding and warm it, adding a teaspoonful of lime water.

"Too much attention cannot be given to secure absolute purity and cleanliness of the nursing bottle. A filthy nursing bottle will poison any baby.

"After the baby is two months old a gradual increase in the proportion of milk should be made, as the digestion grows better and the baby stronger. If instead of water, barley or oatmeal water is used, a less proportion of milk will be required. For costive children oatmeal is preferred. After the child is fed always lay it upon its *right* side or back, and let it be quiet and sleep. Never place it upon the left side when the stomach is full.

"Condensed milk is sometimes more digestible than the fresh cow's milk, especially as the latter is supplied in cities. The Eagle

15

brand (Borden's Condensed Milk) is generally preferred to the imported. It is too often insufficiently diluted with water. A small teaspoonful to four ounces of 'bottle' is usually enough for a young infant. It requires no sweetening. It should be kept in a cool place, and the directions accompanying the package should be carefully observed.

"There are other forms of artificial food, some of them much employed, but they should only be used under the direction of an experienced physician, in cases where the more common forms of diet have not agreed. I conclude by reasserting that the essential requirements for healthy infants are *pure air* and *good food.*"

<h2 style="text-align:center">SCARLET FEVER.</h2>

There have been local epidemics of scarlet fever for the last few years in different parts of the State, but the whole number of deaths has not indicated any general diffusion. It has several times preceded diphtheria or croup, the former more especially when there was apparently a general contamination of the atmosphere of the place. There are those, and their number is not small, especially in England, that believe that zymotic diseases can be produced directly from filth, without the contagion of a preceding case. They find to support their view many cases like the following: A family in the northern part of Michigan were remote from any other people and from any line of travel. Their winter supplies had long ago been laid in in bulk, and to complete the isolation they had been snowed in for nearly two weeks, even if the cold weather had allowed any intercourse with the distant trading station. Yet one night the oldest child, a boy about six years old, was seized with vomiting, and the next morning had clearly developed the rash of scarlet fever. Many physicians that practice in the rural districts are firmly convinced of the direct origin of scarlet fever from unsanitary surroundings. There are, however, more that believe the spontaneous origin of other zymotic diseases, but exclude scarlet fever, tracing that invariably to contagion; still some of these believe that the contagion of the disease can be propagated outside the human body by putrefactive filth, as by cesspools, sewers, and decaying organic matter. Dr. A. Carpenter, of London, an eminent authority, holds this view, and has collected a series of cases, one of which is quoted in the first part of this report. The circular of the Michigan State Board of Health admits the possibility of the propagation of the virus or germ of the disease outside the human body, but states it as not yet proven. The conveyance of the disease by filth, as through sewers, is more generally admitted. The instructions for prevention of scarlet fever of State and City Boards of Health generally recognize filth and unsanitary conditions as agencies favoring the spread and severity of scarlet fever, invariably so far as I have had access to them, from Massachusetts, the oldest, to Iowa, one of the youngest State Boards of Health.

The disease is one that is especially dangerous to children, and most of the cases are among them. It is one of the most contagious and infectious of diseases, as repeatedly demonstrated and generally believed. The personal element that enters into every case, and affects every variety of disease as well as scarlet fever, has so impressed some people, however, that they deny the contagiousness of the disease. There are several elements to be considered in the production of any sickness. The first is the virus or poison of the disease; second, the *nidus*, so to speak (that is, there are certain essential conditions for the multiplication or spread of disease); and third, a condition of receptivity. Each is of importance, which varies with the type of the disease. The existence of every condition that is given by the best authorities as essential for the production of disease, or rather a certain form of disease, may exist for an indefinite time, and yet no such disease occur, when by chance a case is brought from without, and if the conditions existed on a grand scale an epidemic follows at once. This explains why unsanitary conditions are not uninterruptedly producing disease and epidemics in places where they certainly exist. If the personal conditions that are favorable for the development of the disease are wholly confined to certain individuals, they alone will be liable to have that disease. In a large population some would always be found in a condition to receive infection. But if there be no persons that are in proper form to receive the virus or contagion, no cases will result. Were it not for these kindly provisions of an all-wise Creator, the first epidemic pestilence would nearly exterminate the race. In the contagious diseases the second link is of least consequence of the three. Nature is marvelously systematic, and, as in the vegetable kingdom, not every blossom produces fruit, but out of an apparently prodigal waste of blossoms some perfect fruit is evolved. So man walks secure among a myriad threatening dangers. Bullets kill, yet did every one in ten "find its billet " in some human frame, the world would stand aghast in horror at the bloody war. Even if disease does originate *de novo* from filth, there is some process that must be worked out and a union of complex agencies that must take place to evolve the malignant agency. Were the personal receptivity of no account, where would be the limit to the spread of contagion? or if, as appears almost if not quite certain, when by accumulation of cases the atmosphere becomes infected so that isolation would no longer protect, where would be the limit of a pestilence as long as any food for it to feed upon remained ? So that if an unprotected person sleeps in the same bed with a patient sick with confluent small-pox, and escapes the disease, no one should infer that small-pox was not contagious.

A few illustrations of the contagiousness and infectiousness of scarlet fever may be interesting in this connection.

In a school at Blackheath scarlet fever appeared in 1868, when the fact of its importation was established almost with certainty; this was in October; it reappeared in July, 1871, March, 1874, and again in October, 1874. In the last instance four boys were attacked within twenty-four hours of each other, which indicated a common cause. The introduction of infection from without was carefully examined and no trace found. Upon close examination it was discovered that these four boys sat where they were exposed to a more or less direct current from a water-closet whenever a volume of water passed through the latrines. The only link now lacking was the presence of the virus of scarlet fever in the sewer. This fact was not known when this theory of origin was given, but inquiry showed that scarlet fever was very prevalent in houses connected with the sewer, into which the water-closet discharged. When the soil-pipe of the water-closet and the room itself was ventilated, and also the latrines, and the school-room so arranged as to cut off all such cross currents from the water-closet and latrines, the disease disappeared and has not returned. The general health of the scholars and teachers also improved, and sick-headaches, before common, became rare, as stated by the principal three years after.* The case the author states is

*Carpenter, Preventive Medicine and Public Health, page 812.

selected out of a series, and he gives four similar cases in an article already quoted from. It is now quite generally admitted that scarlet fever can be conveyed by milk, although the instances on record are not as numerous as in case of diphtheria, nor anything like the frequency of such transmission in case of typhoid fever. To avoid repetition, detailed cases of such conveyance will be given under the head of milk as a medium for the transmission of infection.

The virus of scarlet fever retains its vitality for an indefinite period. . An illustration of this was published in an earlier report, where every new comer that was placed in a certain dormitory had scarlet fever, and this had continued several years. A rigidly thorough sulphur fumigation prevented the recurrence, as not a case followed. The cases where unused bedding has retained infection for years, which, when the bedding was used, produced the disease, are so numerous that any specific case loses interest. An instance where infected clothing sent to relatives of the deceased party produced scarlet fever was published in our last report. These cases, where articles worn or much handled by persons sick or dead from scarlet fever, are fully as numerous as the class just mentioned. Dr. Talham, of Salford, describes an epidemic caused to a great extent by articles from a pawnbroker. The poor people would pawn any article not needed for immediate use early in the week, and redeem them Saturday night. Many of these were stored in a room occupied by a son of the pawnbroker that was nearly well, but in the *peeling* stage. The removal of the patient and the disinfection of the room and its contents, and other objects that had become infected, was followed by an immediate cessation of the spread of the disease.

Dr. MacCabe, of Dublin, relates a case where a lad at school at Rugby conveyed the disease to his aunt, with whom he resided. He was sent home, as the school was closed on account of an epidemic of scarlet fever; and, although he himself escaped, he apparently conveyed it to his aunt, as there was no other source of contagion that the most careful search could discover. The lady recovered, and the doctor, upon his visits during convalescence, found her handling a ball dress, which she stated was for a friend in a not-distant city. The young lady received the dress, and scarlet fever with it, of which she died.*

---

* London Sanitary Record, 1880, page 59.

There was a case reported to us where a family were driving through a village where scarlet fever was prevalent. The child, about three or four years old, was thirsty, and they stopped at a house by the side of the road to get a glass of water. There were two cases of scarlet fever in the house—one convalescent, if not both. The man from the house took the child in his arms for some reason or other, although he was not carried into the house. In a week after the child had well-marked scarlet fever. There are several cases on record where scarlet fever has been conveyed by a letter. Two such are reported from Michigan. The families had been in both cases isolated for a longer period than the incubation period of scarlet fever, and were well in the backwoods at best. There were no neighbors to convey infection, and the cases followed the receipt of the letter at the proper period. So generally is it believed that the disease can be conveyed, especially to children, by the bodies of the dead, that in many places public funerals are forbidden by law. In many other cases the good sense of the people induces them to dispense with a public funeral, and to disinfect the body and bury it soon after death. The change in this respect is a strong proof of the advance in public hygiene, and the diffusion of sanitary principles among the people. The idea at first is not a popular one, but after the results are seen when a malignant type of the disease prevails there is little need to urge the discontinuance of public funerals. There are all varieties of this disease—from the simplest, where no medical attendance is summoned, to the most malignant type. A volume could be filled with illustrations of its contagious and infectious nature, but a few recent cases have been selected. The following circular has been prepared for general distribution, as in case of the one on diphtheria:

SCARLET FEVER.

Scarlet fever is stated to be a highly contagious disease. It is oftenest seen in children under ten years of age. Adults are less liable to the disease, and oftener have it in a milder form than that prevalent among children at the same time. They can, however, communicate a malignant variety from a mild case. The same is also true of children, and often explains the spread of the disease, which may have been unnoticed in the first case. It usually

appears about a week after exposure to contagion, but the period
may be longer or shorter.

Scarlet fever, scarlatina, and canker rash are all names for one
and the same disease.

Scarlet fever is very infectious. The small bran-like scales from
the outer skin that are shed so freely may lodge in any article
in use about the patient, and become a source of contagion.
The contagion is mainly in the matters from the skin, head, and
nose. All the excretions of the patient are more or less contagious.
Some of these products retain their vitality for years, and under
favorable circumstances reproduce the disease.

Scarlet fever is believed to be due to a specific poison or contagion,
which is conveyed by personal contact or by any infected article.
Mild cases can induce malignant and fatal results in others, and
the subjects of mild attacks themselves are liable to the severe
complications that follow malignant attacks. The disease is often
communicated from a mild case, the patient convalescent, apparently
nearly well, having mingled with his fellows while the process of
shedding these infective particles still continues. Thus the isolation of the mild cases, and all where desquamation is still going
on, is as important as in the more acute cases.

Filth, unsanitary surroundings, and imperfect ventilation increase the severity of the disease and the danger of its spreading
and becoming epidemic, also overcrowding, together with all
agencies that depress vitality and strength.

RULES FOR PREVENTION.

When a person is attacked with scarlet fever, place him in a
room by himself, and remove all unnecessary articles from the
room. Carpets, woolen curtains, and upholstered goods are
especially liable to become infected.

If possible, let only one attendant enter the room and nurse the
sick person. Children especially should not be allowed to enter
the room.

The contagion is contained in all the excretions of the patient,
and in the bran-like scales of the outer skin that are shed so freely
in convalescence. The matters that come from the head, throat,
nose, and skin are especially contagious.

The excreta should be received in vessels containing a strong
solution of some disinfectant. The solution of copperas, a pound

and a half to a gallon of water, is the best, but solutions of zinc or other disinfectants may be used. All linen and cotton articles used about the patient should be at once placed in a solution of four ounces of sulphate of zinc, two ounces common salt, to a gallon of water. Under no circumstances should the sheets or underclothing be carried from the room dry, and care should be taken not to shake off the branny scales to infect other articles.

Dust and dirt must be removed by damp cloths, as sweeping and dusting are objectionable. These cloths should be at once thrown into the zinc and salt solution.

Books, toys, and articles used to amuse the patient when couvalescent are best disposed of by burning them in the room. Under no circumstances should toys *be borrowed to return,* nor used for the well.

No children should be allowed to go to school from the house, nor allowed to play with others that have not had the disease. As a rule the slightest cases, where the child is not confined to the bed, oftenest spread infection, as little care is exercised for prevention.

When fully convalescent, the patient should receive a warm bath in carbolized water, or carbolic soap may be used. When no roughness of skin remains there is little if any danger to be apprehended of conveying the disease. It is difficult to fix any definite period when there is no longer any danger of conveying the disease, as the types and varieties are so numerous, and of all grades of severity. From a wide experience in treating the disease, the average period of six weeks after convalescence is fairly established has been stated; the more cautious give eight weeks as the proper period before a child should attend school and mingle freely with others. The best guide is given by the condition of the skin; if that be perfectly smooth the danger is slight, if any. As the sequels of scarlet fever are so severe, this period is not oppressive, and in fact is demanded by the best interests of the child.

Inunction during the "peeling process" is useful in preventing infection. The body, head, and limbs should be thoroughly anointed with vaseline, camphorated oil, or similar substance, as the attending physician may direct, should he think it proper to use them.

The dishes used in the sick-room should be washed separately, and after use washed in the zinc and salt solution, then in hot water. For many purposes linen or cotton rags are useful instead of handkerchiefs, etc., especially when the throat symptoms are severe. After use they should be at once burned together with all fragments and refuse.

Perfect cleanliness should be enjoined, especially if the attendant is obliged to mingle with other people. As the hands are very liable to be infected from the necessary care of the patient, a disinfecting solution, chlorinated soda, or the solution of zinc and salt, already mentioned, should be used. To avoid all confusion, this zinc and salt solution if desired can be used exclusively for all purposes. After the use of the disinfecting solution the hands should be washed with plain soap and water. The disinfectant solution should be also provided for the physician's use on leaving the room, should he desire.

The more malignant the type the greater need is there of these precautions, and isolation is as necessary in the milder forms to prevent the spread of the disease. If the disease partakes at all of the nature of an epidemic, the utility of these precautions will be all the more apparent.

In case of death from scarlet fever the body should be wrapped in a sheet wet with a zinc solution double the strength of that advised for general use, *and be buried with as little delay as possible.* It is advised that if a newspaper notice of the death be given the cause of death be stated. The body should not be exposed to view, and the burial should in all cases be private.

After the patient is removed from the room it should be thoroughly disinfected by burning sulphur, and afterwards, if possible, exposed to free currents of fresh air for several days. The articles used in care of the patient should be spread out so as to expose the greatest amount of surface. Heavy articles, blankets, and other woolen articles that cannot be washed in the zinc solution, should be fumigated with sulphur. The amount of sulphur to be used should be at least two pounds for every thousand cubic feet of air space. The number of cubic feet of air space in a room may be ascertained by multiplying together the length, width, and height of the room. All openings should be tightly closed, and the room kept closed for twenty-four hours. Care should be taken to secure the burning of all the sulphur. An iron pan placed upon a pan of hot coals will best secure this. A tub half filled

16

with water may be placed in the center of the room, and bricks piled up above the level of the water. The pan of live coals may be placed on this, and the iron pot with the sulphur upon the coals. Ignite the sulphur with a few coals or by a little alcohol set on fire by a match. Be careful not to breathe the fumes.

After the disinfection the room should be washed with the zinc solution and the walls brushed over with the same. The ceiling should be freshly white-washed or kalsomined. Carpets are best disinfected on the floor, but should afterwards be thoroughly beaten and aired, as should all woolen articles, and clothing exposed to infection. The whole house should be as thoroughly aired as possible, and whenever practicable where there have been several malignant cases the whole house should be fumigated with sulphur. Fresh air should be plentifully supplied throughout the sickness, care being taken to avoid draughts, especially upon convalescents.

The disinfection of the excretions has been advised, but in addition a strong solution of copperas should be poured down water-closets, and the house-drains, which otherwise may become infected.

The best preventive is to avoid the special contagion of the disease. Adults can do with impunity that which would result in the production of the disease in children. As it is possible that scarlet fever can be propagated by filth,-care should be taken to prevent all unsanitary conditions. Decaying organic substances that pollute the air or water, contribute to the severity of scarlet fever, and intensify the virus, if they do not directly produce it. "Of the unsanitary conditions external to the body liable to spread scarlet fever perhaps the most common are infected air, infected water, and contact with infected substances or persons." Clothing worn by persons during sickness or convalescence from scarlet fever may convey the disease for many months. Milk may convey scarlet fever if infected.

It must be remembered that every person that has scarlet fever, whether in a mild or severe degree, creates around himself an atmosphere in which others that have not had the disease are liable to become infected, and that when death ensues the body, while unburied, continues to be a centre of infection.* The infectious particles thrown off retain their vitality for a long period, undetermined as yet, but for several years at least from authentic accounts.

---

* Circular of Kentucky State Board of Health on Scarlet Fever.

In case of an epidemic especial care should be taken in removing all decomposing animal and vegetable matter. "All sources which contaminate the air with foul gases should be removed, and in times of an epidemic be declared a nuisance."[*] Physicians should co-operate with local health authorities in preventing the spread of the disease.

A hospital for contagious diseases would save many lives, as in crowded tenement houses isolation is out of the question. The idea at first is not a popular one, but once established its powers for good would soon dispel all objections.

As can easily be seen, schools form a ready medium for the spread of scarlet fever. The teachers are vigilant and alert as a rule, and when the fact is known that scarlet fever or like contagious diseases exist in a house, do not allow other children from such a house to attend school. Physicians could do good service here by notifying teachers of the existence of such diseases, and supplying certificates showing that the child can no longer be considered as a source of infection when convalesence is established. Public sentiment can secure the abolishment of public funerals and exposure of the body, but a legal enactment is desirable for many reasons. The removal of bodies from the town in which the persons died to another is prohibited by law, if the death is due to a contagious disease, unless the body is placed in an air-tight coffin, or properly disinfected.

DISINFECTANTS.

1· For cotton and linen goods, for washing the hands, and almost all uses, sulphate of zinc four ounces, common salt two ounces, water a gallon. Double the strength should be used about the bodies of those dying from scarlet fever.

2. Copperas, a pound and a half to a gallon of water, for sewers, drains, and execreta.

This circular is published with a view to lessen the prevalence of scarlet fever and prevent unnecessary deaths in this State, from this cause. The State Board of Health in issuing it invite the co-operation of all physicians in securing its circulation where needed. Any communication on the subject may be addressed to the State Board of Health, State House, Hartford, Conn. Copies will be furnished for free distribution.

Please read carefully and preserve for future use.

---

[*] Official memoranda Local Government Board Great Britain, 6th report, page 308.

SCHOOLS IN RELATION TO INFECTIOUS DISEASES.

The readiness with which the school may become a center for the spread of contagious diseases has been so many times illustrated, that, as stated with reference to scarlet fever, the teachers often exercise great care in preventing attendance from houses where there are any sick. But this does not fully meet the emergency in a threatened epidemic, especially as the teachers are not always informed in time to prevent mischief, and disease has already been conveyed. If, as suggested, the physicians would coöperate with the teachers and inform them of the occurrence of disease in their districts, much better results could be secured. If the disease becomes fairly epidemic, however, the risks are too great in assembling the children from such diverse relations, and the preservation of life becomes the paramount question. The practical difficulty is to steer clear between a fussy interference when there is no need, and the danger of infection on a large scale. In cities where there is a health inspector a constant surveillance can be maintained over infected localities, and prompt notice given of danger from any locality, and the convalescents can be watched, lest they too soon mingle with the uninfected. It is not easy to mention any definite time when there is no danger of conveying diphtheria—the condition of the throat is a better guide: as long as the deep, dusky redness and infiltrated condition of the membrane continue, the disease is not over. In many instances this has been shown, and some relapses of a diphtheroid nature have shown the same fact. Dr. Page in the *Practitioner* for Nov., 1882, states that a month has been the usual period that was useful for the schools to be closed in case of scarlet fever—this of course would be modified by the state of the epidemic. There are, as he states, instances where the children run greater risks in playing about the streets than they would in school, especially if there be an efficient supervision of infected families. In the country where the children are brought together from scattered houses, many of them living at a considerable distance, the closing of the school promptly is advisable. The children here are brought together only during school hours, and if the school is closed there will be no general assemblage. Here the action should be prompt, as soon as the disease shows an epidemic disposition.

If there be any suspicion that the school-room has been infected, it should be thoroughly fumigated with sulphur, and afterwards ventilated for several days. The relation of the health of school children to that of the community generally is an interesting question. In New Haven, Prof. Lindsley is receiving regular reports of the absences from any form of sickness that causes an absence of more than two days, and comparing with the mortality returns, as an index of the health of the city. The first report is here given:

HEALTH OF SCHOOL CHILDREN AS AN INDEX OF PUBLIC HEALTH.

"By favor of the superintendent of public schools and the various teachers employed, I am furnished with a statement of the number of pupils absent from each school more than two consecutive days on account of sickness during the month of October. This report shows that the sick among all the children in the public schools was nearly 10 per cent. of the average number registered, the actual rate being 9.91. In a few of the schools there were no absences from sickness, and among the others the number varied in all degrees up to 27.24 per cent. I have visited several of the schools in which the sick rate was above the average, and do not find that any epidemic is prevailing except at the Woodward school in Fair Haven East, where whooping cough has kept a large number of children at home during the last month. This monthly report of sickness among the children of the public schools affords a means of getting information respecting the health of the town better and more directly than any other way available. The health of children is the most sensitive meter of unsanitary conditions known; and it may be considered a safe rule that ill-health will prevail in a community very much in proportion to illness among children. The reports from the various schools will also serve to distinguish before long the unhealthy sections of the town, to detect the beginning of epidemics, and afford a sure and reliable guide for sanitary work."

SMALL-POX AND VACCINATION.

The law passed at the last session of the legislature gave power to School Visitors and Boards of Education to order compulsory vaccination of school children whenever in their judgment it was necessary for the public safety. This measure caused considerable discussion, and brought out the anti-vaccination arguments in full force. If there were ever any strength to the objections against vaccination, the substitution of animal for humanized virus removes it. The danger of communicating disease was infinitesimal and could be entirely obviated by care. There is no evidence that I have been able to find to show that the vaccine lymph itself, even if the source be impure, transmits disease; if such ever results it must be from the blood or lymph. The instances on record compared with the number of successful vaccinations is so small as to reduce the chances to such an infinitely small ratio as to be hardly worth consideration; but this is unnecessary and out of the question with the use of animal virus. Without entering into an extended statement of the results secured by vaccination, a statement of some of the benefits thus derived seems to be called for. It would not be needful to go outside our own State to find convincing proof of the protective power of vaccination. The repeated recurrence of the disease from importation mainly, afforded every opportunity for the development of an epidemic repeatedly, yet none has occurred, as the people are so well protected by vaccination. Where this practice has been most completely followed, the exemption has been most complete. But even in cases where vaccination had been neglected, a prompt attention to the duty, and vaccination of all exposed and unprotected persons has again and again been found effectual. The prevalence of the disease in the northwestern States, and the arrest of its progress by a cordon of vaccinated persons just in advance of its spread, was a striking illustration of the power of vaccination. An insurmountable barrier was thus formed against its further progress.

In Tennessee, Dr. Clark reports that small-pox appeared at forty different places, yet but in one single instance did a second family contract the disease after its discovery; and further, that where vaccination could be promptly applied, there were but a few instances of the second case in the same family.

The experience of New York is also in the same line, as reported by the Superintendent of the Health Board for the month of January, 1882. During the month there were 166 cases; the ratio of deaths to admissions without regard to the number in the hospital at the beginning or end of the month was 28.92 per cent. Of the 166 patients, 85 had been vaccinated, 78 had not, and of three there was no history. Of the 48 that died, only one had been vaccinated, 44 had never been vaccinated, and of three there was no history. Of the 85 in vaccinated persons, 77 were of a mild type, and none of the confluent, hemorrhagic variety. Of the 78 un-vaccinated, 20 were discrete, 29 semi-confluent, and 19 were of some variety of hemorrhagic type. The history of St. Louis, where vaccination had been thorough, shows no deaths from small-pox during five years. The manifestations in Sydney, New South Wales, as reported by Dr. Hill,* are very conclusive for several reasons. There was a large amount of unvaccinated material for the disease to attack. There was very few cases among the vaccinated, and those of a mild type. No nurses contracted small-pox. *In every instance* where vaccination was refused, severe and fatal cases were the rule without exception. In households part of whom were vaccinated, the unvaccinated contracted small-pox.

Small-pox appeared in Hayti in the latter part of 1881, and spread rapidly over the entire island; the number of deaths reached 50,000, as no active means were taken to check the disease until early in the year 1882. Dr. Terres states that although attending two or three hundred severe cases of small-pox every day during the height of the epidemic, neither himself nor any of his family or servants took the disease (thirteen persons in all) their only protection was in successful vaccination. In forty families numbering about three hundred persons that he vaccinated successfully, only six had small-pox, and they all recovered. All these persons were exposed daily, as they insisted on visiting their sick friends. The scholars and teachers of three schools, five hundred in all, were successfully vaccinated, and only one case occurred. Dr. Terres states that not a single death occurred among vaccinated persons. These two latter statements from Sydney and Hayti are very conclusive, and furnish incontrovertible evidence of the protective power of vaccination.

· Dr. Guy, President of the Statistical Society, in a review of two hundred and fifty years of small-pox in London, shows very conclusively that as compared with other epidemic maladies, the mortality from small-pox stands alone in the reduction it has undergone during the present century, the reduction in other diseases being from a 44th to an 11th of that from small-pox. Taking ten per cent. of the deaths from all causes in a year as the measure of an epidemic, the entire absence of an epidemic of small-pox during the

---

*British Medical Journal, October 7, 1882.

present century is a certain presumption in favor of vaccination as a preventive of small-pox, strengthened by the fact that small-pox, up to the very close of the 18th century, had undergone no considerable abatement, and the longest interval between epidemics, as well as the lowest returns of deaths by small-pox, are found in the 19th century. While the epidemics of measles, scarlet fever, diphtheria, whooping-cough, fever, and diarrhea all undergo a decrease in the last forty years, the highest figure of decrease does not amount to a tenth part of the decrease in small-pox.

This disposes of the argument that the decrease in small-pox is due to sanitary improvements and reforms, so far as London is concerned, for there is no reason why the decrease in the mortality from small-pox should be so much greater than that of the other diseases mentioned, except vaccination.

The history of vaccination in India as given in the official reports furnishes a strong confirmation of the protective power of vaccination. The number of deaths caused by small-pox where vaccination was unknown would excite a panic in this country did any such occur, but its prevalence afforded a clear field to test the protective power of vaccination, and the results have been invariably satisfactory. A singular instance of the effects of prejudice was shown by one of the interior tribes. As they valued the female children at a very low estimate, they consented after considerable pressure to allow them to be vaccinated, but when small-pox next appeared these female children were exempt, while almost all the others had it, and many died. They now demanded that the boys should be vaccinated, and also that the doctor would vaccinate them also. They appeared quite indifferent to the fate of the female children.

The results in India show the protective power of vaccination on a large scale, as the population is dense, and until the Vaccination Department commenced operations there had been little if any systematic vaccination. In the Province of the Punjab they commenced in 1864, but in 1880 in ten of the thirty-five districts operations had not been commenced. In the sixteen years since 1865, when deaths from small-pox were first recorded, there were 443,283 fatal cases, 270,509 of which occurred in the first eight years, and 172,774 in the second eight, or nearly one hundred thousand less. The heavy mortality in 1879, when there were in round numbers 50,000 deaths, shows that vaccination has not been

complete enough to prevent the recurrence of excessive epidemics.*
The results in other provinces are as decisive.

Small-pox has been brought into this State repeatedly by domestic servants, as was the case last year, usually by emigrants
recently arrived. The Emigrant Inspection Service inaugurated
by the National Board of Health proved the imperfection of
former methods, and was an efficient measure to provide a complete vaccination of all unprotected emigrants, and thus prevent.
the diffusion and spread of small-pox all over the country. The
supervision of railroads and steamboats conveying emigrants to
the Western States and Territories completed the protection and
reduced the dangers to the lowest possible degree. It is to be
hoped that the present Congress will enable the National Board of.
Health to continue this beneficial service, the value of which has
been so often made evident. The speeches of Senator Harris of
New York and others, in reply to attacks made upon the National
Board of Health, were striking evidences of the progress of sanitary science in this country. Such a clear and logical presentation.
of the claims of preventive medicine upon the country, and of the
benefits already secured, strengthened by so strong an array of
facts, would have been out of the question a few years ago, nor
would they have been listened to with such close attention, if, indeed,
much if any notice would have been taken. The testimony of so
many of the officials of the various land and water transportation
companies, more especially of the West and Northwest, and of the
South and East also, but not so generally perhaps, as to the importance and value of the internal quarantine system of the National
Board of Health, seemed strong enough to convince any un-
prejudiced mind.

In addition to the introduction of small-pox, as usual, rags used
for paper manufacture receive the blame for producing several
cases. The importance of all workers in paper. mills being fully
protected by vaccination has been repeatedly shown, by cases of
small-pox due to infected rags. As instances of small-pox charged
to rags used in paper stock have been reported nearly every year
since small-pox has reappeared, it appeared useful to investigate
the probability of the

* Sanitary Measures in India, Vol. xiv, page 23.

17

INFECTIOUSNESS OF RAGS.

A commission appointed under the Local Government Board of England a few years ago made a very careful and thorough study of this whole subject. They found that small-pox was the principal disease communicated by infected rags, and upon inspecting all the large paper manufacturing establishments found that such transmission was not very uncommon. Those most exposed are the wrokers in dusting, assorting, and cutting the rags. As the rags come in compressed bales, there does not appear to be any easy method of disinfection. Certainly they cannot be disinfected in bulk. This question was brought up when the plague was rife in regions whence rags are largely collected, and fears had been expressed that the infected rags might convey the disease to other countries. The prompt action of the dealers in calling in their agents from the neighbourhood of infected districts, and receiving no more supplies from such quarters, obviated the danger, so the question received no practical solution. There is a law in this State that throws the expense of caring for the victims of small-pox in part upon the manufacturers if they employ unvaccinated persons. There have not been many instances where more than one or two cases at a time have been thus caused, so it is very probable that the employees are generally vaccinated. That this is the case has been the general statement of all employees that I have asked on this point:

Dr. C. O. Baylis of West Kent, England, relates an outbreak of small-pox in three sets—the first of twenty-five cases, from April 9th to 23d; the second of eleven cases, from May 2d to 7th, and the third of four cases May 16th. Three cases occurred in an adjoining workhouse from infection from these cases. As the cases developed, it was noticed that they were all women, except those in the workhouse, and rag-cutters in the same paper-mill, and upon inquiry it was learned that some of the rags were of a more dirty and offensive character than usual. Dr. Baylis is of the opinion that the dust in the rags contained the infective material. A disinfecting solution was used with a sprinkler as the rest of the rags of the same lot that apparently produced the small-pox passed through the duster, and no more cases of small-pox occurred.

There is no doubt of the possibility of the introduction of small-pox by infected rags; of course the principal reliance for protection is the vaccination of the employees, and revaccination when required. If a bale of rags has caused small-pox, or a part of any lot of bales from similar sources, the method adopted upon the recommendation of Dr. Baylis is apparently a protection against any further danger,—that is, sprinkling the rags with a disinfecting solution as they pass through the dusting machine. He advised a dilute solution of carbolic acid, but the solution of sulphate of zinc four ounces, common salt two ounces, water a gallon, is inodorous, does not stain, and is more effectual in destroying infection than the carbolic acid.

From a series of observations carefully made it appears that the dust produced in sorting the rags, in addition to the possibility of acting as a medium for conveying small-pox directly, favors chronic diseases of the lungs and the air passages. There is in general too little attention paid to preserving health from this danger, as the methods of ventilation in use are usually very imperfect. The intervention of glass between the workers and the rags, so that they can see their work, with openings for the hands and arms, has been used in some places, so arranged that the glass can be raised or lowered as occasion may require. The rags are also placed over a grating connected with a downward shaft, which has a strong draft downward, so the dust does not fall by gravity alone. The glass partition separates the room into two divisions horizontally, an upper one filled with pure air and a lower one filled with dust. If no arrangements are provided that remove the dust completely, the use of respirators over the mouth and nose is very useful in excluding the dust, and completely prevents its inhalation. A diluted gargle of carbolic acid and water, to rinse the mouth after the close of the day's work, is also advised. The outside garments should be of densely-woven stuff, impervious to dust, of linen or wash-linen, and made so that they can be drawn tightly around the wrists and neck. This dust is not as rapidly fatal as that from stone-cutting or metal-grinding, as the particles are not as irritating. A pigmentary staining of the lungs has occasionally been found before any decided inflammatory changes have commenced. The dust from buffing leather and some manufactures producing similar dust gives rise to about the same effects as that from rags. The constant inhalation of air largely charged with dust of any kind should be avoided.

SANITARY PROVISIONS OF FACTORIES AND WORKSHOPS.

The following investigation and report were made by special request, and serve to illustrate conditions that exist elsewhere, but are not noticed until the occurrence of disease compels attention. The complete discussion of the subject is not attempted, but some inferences and suggestions from this and other instances to which special attention has been called will be presented. The first inspection was with reference to an unusual prevalence of typhoid fever, and also typho-malarial, confined mainly to the operatives in a large factory. There were three hundred or more operatives under essentially the same conditions. The privy was found in a very foul condition. A trough was provided that emptied into the stream supplying the mill, and if there was a sufficient rain-fall this was flushed and kept clean. It was, however, usually offensive in the summer, and there had been several times an extensive prevalence of diarrheal troubles, especially among those that worked on the side of the building nearest to this vile-smelling vault, if such it could be called. The well used as a source of water supply was but a few rods distant, and examination showed plain evidence of contamination. It was not until a case of typhoid fever had been introduced, and thus the special contagion provided, that there was any other sickness than the diarrheal diseases before mentioned. The general health of the operatives, however, improved so generally after a well-cemented and ventilated vault was provided, that there is little doubt but that this state of affairs had had a depressing effect upon the general health. Subsequent examination of the well-water showed no excess of organic matter.

The second was a more complicated case. Here, in addition to a foul privy similar in very many respects to the one before described, as I find the form a very common one in connection with factories of all kinds, a long, comparatively shallow trough, discharging into a stream, and flushed by the rain water from the roof; sometimes the waste water of the factory is used, and then the condition is a little improved. Sometimes the privy is built over a small stream which only in spring and autumn is large enough to remove the deposits it receives, as a consequence it becomes an open, elongated vault, as the stream is polluted a long distance, and does not remove its pollution rapidly enough to prevent putrefaction.

But, to return to the case in hand, a well in the cellar of one of the factories, largely used as a supply for drinking water, was found to be polluted by infiltration from an obstructed drain; but as this drain conveyed no fœcal matters, but a considerable amount of organic matter in an alkaline, soapy state, the water doubtless was simply deleterious to the general health of those that used it. At first these were supposed to be sufficient causes, but when there were a large number of cases in a very short time, including many that had no connection with this factory, it was evident that some other agencies were at work. These were not difficult to find. There was quite a stream which ran through the town, and in its course had been repeatedly dammed for water power. These ponds were polluted with the waste of the factories—grease more or less saponified by alkalies, and wool washings, garbage of various kinds, and sewage from various sources; so that when it reached the last pond in a very dry season the water was very thick, and could almost be called semi-solid. This pond gave off bubbles of very offensive gases, polluting the air. Radical changes in relation to all the contributory causes were made, and as radical an improvement in health followed. A curious illustration of the mingling of the types typhoid and malarial was here given. The onset was variable; they were taken with vomiting often, and a copious eruption of watery vesicles was characteristic. There was an unusual prevalence of malarial fever more remote from the center described, although all the cases there were not typho-malarial. The death-rate was large, and all deaths were reported as from typho-malarial fever.

In another instance the following condition of affairs was found: Two quite extensive establishments were situated very near each other; but one employed, from the nature of the work, a very large number of operatives of both sexes. The question involved in the inspection was the proper disposal of the privy waste of the larger establishment, so that it might not be injurious to health. The method in use at the time was exceedingly faulty, and was, in our opinion, clearly a nuisance. The privy for the female operatives was near the middle of the building, and was very offensive. Its proximity could be readily detected long before it was reached; but the other that provided for the men was, with its connections, also exceedingly objectionable. In the first place, it was situated so that there was a constant and direct

current from it through a corner of the next establishment, stronger
at certain states of the wind. This corner was known in that shop as
the "unhealthy corner," as there had been more absences from
ill-health and cases of acute sickness from that corner than from
all the rest of the shop put together.

The privy had a shallow trough about two feet deep and nearly
as wide, and was used by about two hundred men and boys. The
floor of the urinal was saturated and gave off a very strong am-
moniacal odor, which, however, could not disguise the fœcal odor.
This trough was flushed by rain water, and whenever there was
any waste water it was sent through; but in summer, and especially
in such a dry season as that of last year, there was little or no
rain to flush the trough. This trough was connected by a tile
drain with two larger cesspools a few rods from the other
establishment. These had an overflow for fluids mostly by a
shallow ditch along a peaty soil and emptying alongside the railroad ditch, causing an unmitigated nuisance.

At first it was supposed that an ample water supply could be had
for water-closets and subirrigation of a piece of land that lay convenient for such purpose was advised. When the wind was in the
right direction the odor from these cesspools was strongly complained
of by the operatives exposed by their work on that side of the
shop. When it was found that the subirrigation plan was not
feasible for want of water, it was advised that a large vault be
dug, stoned and cemented at the bottom and sides, and cleaned
at least twice a year, to be thoroughly limed after it was emptied.
The discontinuance of the privy for female operatives was also
advised, and a double building to be constructed over this vault,
the side for female operatives to be entered from a corridor, as at
present, but cross-ventilation provided to protect the air of the
work-rooms. The vaults should be ventilated, and a tall chimney
adjacent was mentioned for this purpose, as it did not communicate
with the interior of the buildings and the draft upwards was very
powerful. The flooring on the men's side was to be slate flagging;
the artificial stone laid at an angle, with a gutter leading to the
vault, so that all liquids would readily flow off and not remain to'
pollute the air, as in the present instance. If separate ventilation
was desirable, it could be readily provided for by running an iron
pipe along the outside of the chimney. The effect of the
general influence towards typhoid—the pandemic wave, as it is

sometimes expressed—was seen here in the production of cases of typhoid fever. The same causes, without the effect of the special poison of typhoid fever, produced various forms of ill-health, diar-rheal, and dysenteric troubles; but the epidemic influence apparently intensified the local unsanitary conditions. The neglect of proper provisions to effectually dispose of the fœcal matter that accumu-lated in such quantities, and while retained in the immediate vicinity are a source of offense and a constant menace to health, beside the constant risk that is incurred of taking again into the system these waste matters before they have been reconverted into their original elements by the chemistry of plant life, is but too common, not only in connection with large and small manufactur-ing companies, but on a smaller scale around our dwelling-houses. The sanitary directions of Moses have never been excelled, and, whenever possible, the best method of disposing of all these waste products is to place them where the rootlets of plants can convert them into new forms of life, utility, or beauty.

It would seem a dictate of common sense to effectually dispose of such matters, instead of storing them up to saturate the sub-soil, where nature's chemistry has slight chance for action, or to allow them to contaminate the air, and become dissolved and pol-lute the water they are dissolved in, which is directly taken into the system to satisfy thirst. Argument seems hardly needed to impress upon the mind the urgent need of preserving the purity of one's surroundings rather than allowing them to become a source of offence and danger. The soil, a thin covering over long, deep-stored corruption; the air, which extends deep down into the soil and thence is drawn, especially in winter, into the cellar from this polluted subsoil, and from that permeates the whole house; the water from a shallow well, a solution of sur-face and subsoil filth, furnishes a picture not pleasant to contem-plate. Still it is to a certain extent true. If a man never cleans his vault but when full, and the surrounding soil no longer leaches it away, covers this over with the soil dug out for a new vault, and so on indefinitely, and pursues the same course with his cess-pool, in the course of time the full extent of the picture drawn would be realized, and evil results proportionately recur. The ills that result from a partial transgression are severe enough. In some portions of our country that have been overrun by pestilence the picture above drawn would be no exaggeration; and where there have been repeated deaths from typhoid fever and cerebro-spinal meningitis I have found essentially similar conditions. If it were not for the fact that there is a personal element in every case, and that a person must be in a certain condition to succumb to *any* contagion, although his strength and vitality may be in-sidiously overcome by unsanitary influences, the race would have been decimated by neglect of the effectual disposal of filth.

Another illustration of neglect in a little different direction, is as follows, although cases of insufficient provisions for the removal of filth where there are no sewers could be multiplied, the conditions are so very similar. A large number of employees,' shallow vaults, sometimes entirely upon the surface, and thus polluting the air on a large scale, and long-continued neglect to remove the accumu-lated materials, are the usual features. Where practicable the bucket system is the best, and if once started it will usually main-tain itself,—that is, some one can almost always be found that will cart the buckets to and fro, empty, clean, and replace them, for the value of the fertilizer obtained; but the buckets must be provided. The expense after, except for repairs and worn-out materials, will be slight, if any. Nature's method is to return all such waste to the vegetable kingdom, and the rootlets of plants will transmute the vile, dead putrefaction into living forms of beauty. The sub-irrigation plan, when water carriage can be secured, and the pail, bucket, or tub, as the size needed may dictate when there is no water supply, are the most effectual methods of disposing of such filth, so that it will not convey disease, nor death, nor ever again enter the system, as filth or filth product, through the medium of air, water, or milk. Where there is no sewerage, and for small towns or villages, as well as dwelling-houses, and institutions, these plans are the most effectual. The pail system, however, has not been very largely adopted in this country, except by scavengers in cleaning vaults. It is successfully used in the Tennessee Prison, at Nashville.

The third instance which will be given in this connection was of annoyance and illness caused by sewer gases in a large institution. The odors came from a large number of water-closets. The soil pipes were well ventilated, and the room itself, yet these odors persisted, and on some days were very sickening. The cause was very puzzling. At length, from experience in a similar case, a large trap, eight feet square, which received the rain-water pipe, and was the junction of several large drain pipes with the main drain leading to the sewer,—that is, they all discharged here, and the running trap discharged into the main sewer. It was found that this large trap was unventilated, and had a deposit two feet deep of horribly smelling putrescent matter. One of the drains emptied nearly a foot below the surface of this, and, as was shown while the examination was taking place, when two of the drains emptied, this whole mass was stirred up, and the trap, which was ten feet deep, was half filled before it could discharge the sudden rush. Of course, when closely shut, as it was before the top was removed, there was no other escape for the gases or foul air, with which it was filled, except through the traps of the water-closets, which were forced every time. The top was replaced firmly as before, and the drains allowed to discharge as usual, when the air could be heard boiling through the traps like a cauldron over a fierce fire, and the odors were distinctly recognized as the same that had been so annoying before., When this large trap was thoroughly ventilated there was no more trouble, and the general health was very much improved. There have been many unsanitary conditions found in connection with similar inspections of manufactories, schools, and houses, and in various connections, some of which will be taken up as the subjects they especially illustrate are discussed. Enough has been stated on this part of the subject to illustrate the work of the year in this direction. Although other instances might be related, they each simply accumulate the evidence, now very voluminous, that the laws of health cannot be neglected with impunity, and that the excretions and organic refuse contaminate and poison, unless properly and effectually disposed of, which does not mean simply placed out of sight.

TYPHOID FEVER.

The return of typhoid fever, until it has nearly reached its former prominence, has been already discussed. Besides the well-marked form of typho-malarial fever there have been very many modifications in the symptoms of typhoid fever, one of the most singular being the breaking up of the fever by a distinct chill after the usual run of typhoid fever. The period of defevervescence was thus ushered in by a chill. The following cases, reported by Dr. Brownson of New Canaan, are so characteristic of some features of typhoid fever, and give such positive evidence of

18

the contagion by the dejections, that they are given entire. They were all in one family, which makes the evidence the more con- clusive.

CASE FIRST.—George, aged 22, hatter, had been living in New Jersey six months, started for home February 8th, stopping over night in Nor- walk, with relatives, when he first complained of feeling unwell. He reached home the 9th, with the usual premonitory symptoms of typhoid fever fully developed. The case was very severe; March 1st and 2d he had severe hemorrhage from the bowels; this was checked, but recurred more profuse than before, March 9th, when death ensued the afternoon of the same day.

CASE SECOND.—Frank, aged 25, taken about March 1st. Similar train of symptoms, except coming down more rapidly for first ten days. Temperature ranging from 102° to 104°, pulse 100 to 130, more stupor and delirium, profuse eruption, considerable perspiration, very offensive and sickening odor from all the cases. Moderate hemorrhage from the bowels, in the third week, followed by gradual improvement till pulse was down to 84 for a week, and bowels in very satisfactory condition. Owing to scarcity of help in nursing, he was left alone a short time, left his bed, went to the pantry, ate heartily, had a relapse, followed by invol- untary discharges, tympanitis, a low grade of pneumonia with severe cough, characteristic sputa, rales, etc., several slight hemorrhages, with gradual convalescence. Though yet obliged to keep his bed, with some delirium remaining, and evident effusion in the brain, the prospects at this writing seem very favorable for complete recovery.

CASE THIRD.—About March 10th, Vanila (sister, maiden), aged 27, had epistaxis, chilliness, headache, malaise, took to her bed in about three or four days. Bowels moderately loose, some tympanitis, but much less than in the other cases, one light hemorrhage in third week, symptoms gen- erally less severe, no pneumonia, recovered, now able to do a little work.

CASE FOURTH.—Jerry, aged 20, youngest, farmer, taken March 19th, prostrated at once, obliged to keep his bed entirely after first day. Great pain and restlessness, high pulse and temperature, very frequent and profuse evacuations, with extreme tympanitis, pneumonia and intestinal hemorrhage in second week, profuse, rusty sputa, and distressing cough throughout the disease. Hemorrhage of the bowels again in third week, checking with slight improvement till April 18th and 19th, when he had large quantities of clotted blood pass the bowels, resulting in exhaustion and death on the morning of April 22d. In this case, but little delirium till the last few days.

CASE FIFTH.—Mrs. Olive, the mother of above cases, aged 48, taken about March 29th, had been for nearly fifty days in service day and night, anxiously nursing the four children. Gave up soon, no epistaxis, much nausea and vomiting, cephalalgia, restlessness, but few evacuations, excessive tympanitis, no hemorrhage. After first few days, she was passive and indifferent, seeming to suffer but little. Pneumonia in second week. Respiration, 50. Expectorating bloody mucus, great aversion to food or medicine, pulse 140, gradual decline, death on morning of April 20th. The husband and father, the only remaining member of the family at home, has thus far escaped.

"Such is an imperfect description of one of the most remarkable family afflictions I have known.

I have not time, nor did I think it necessary to give you the daily details of respiration, pulse, temperature, etc., in each case, with the course of treatment pursued.

The usual impression that there must be some cess-pool, defective drain, impure water, or something in the line of local causation to account for all this, we have endeavored to verify, without satisfactory results. Great attention has been given to ventilation, and disinfectants have been freely used. The dejections have been immediately taken a long distance from well or house, and burned or covered with ashes or earth.

These cases have all occurred upon a street running north and south, about one mile from the southern to the northern case. The ground is high, the extreme elevation being at the residence of T. S.,* sloping a little in each direction. None of the cases seemed to originate there, except, possibly, the case of the child, T. S.

The family of Mr. R. were all remarkably strong and healthy. The mother belonged to a family, six of whom, with their partners (twelve in all), weighed on the scales a little more than 2,400 lbs. Mrs. R. was very fleshy, weighing perhaps from 225 to 250 lbs. Frank, when taken sick, weighed 215 lbs. The sister and younger brothers were some lighter, but all large and strong.

So far as we have been able to determine, there were no local causes to account for this outbreak. The first case was evidently imported. Another noticeable fact is that cases following the first one in the R. family seemed to contract the disease in the direct order of the amount of exposure to the bodies and dejections of the sick, except in the case of the mother. Frank was most of the time with his brother, often sleeping in the same room with him, when not on duty. Vanila was with him less, and was taken a week or so later. Jerry was on duty nights a part of the time;

---

* Several cases in the town preceding these were mentioned.

during the day, working with his father in the woods. His case came on still later, while the mother, exposed most of all from the first, was the last one taken and the shortest time sick. Whether from the dejections, the breath, the sickening odor of the perspiration, etc., or from all these combined, the impression with me is strong, and I think is shared by my professional brethren, that direct, personal contagion, rather than any local causation, accounts for the propagation and continuance of the disease."

The cases are very instructive. The contagion from the first case was very strong evidently. An analysis of the water of the well, after the first case, would have been of value to determine whether the same care was used in the disposal of the dejections as was manifested later. The exclusion of other causes leaves little if any doubt but that the cases were caused by infection from the first case.

TYPHOID FEVER IN PORTLAND.

Portland is a town of a little over four thousand inhabitants, situated on the Connecticut river opposite Middletown. The village is situated mainly upon a hill, which rises rapidly from the river. At the northern part of the town are the brown-stone or sandstone quarries, so well known from the brown-stone fronts of Fifth Avenue, New York, and extensively used in that city and elsewhere. The stone contains fine specimens of bird or reptile tracks, illustrations of which have been preserved at the bottom of several of the quarries. The stone extends back from the river to a considerable distance, and enormous quantities have been quarried. The business gives occupation to a large number of foreigners, who live in a village near the river and back of the quarries. As can readily be imagined, this village is often in anything but a hygienic condition.

The general sanitary condition of the town has been much improved of late by a wide-awake and active village improvement association that have, it is true, but recently commenced work in this department, but give promise of excellent work in the future. This collection of quarrymen and their families, or "Quarryville," as it is called, is fortunately situated mainly on a steep hill slope, so that the rains wash the ground clean so far as the surface is concerned, and vegetable garbage is pretty well disposed of by various domestic animals. There is unfortunately no public water supply, and no sewerage nor systematic drainage. As before stated, the steep hillside gives good natural facilities for drainage, so the ground is not so much saturated as it might otherwise be in that part of the town. The tableland at the top of the hill, however, is not thus naturally drained, and here were the instances of well-pollution, and here is the greatest liability to danger from contamination of the soil from vaults, cesspools, and sink drains. The street through the centre is wide, and in the village above Quarryville the houses are well situated and separated by quite extensive grounds generally. The Air Line Railroad passes through the town, and there are extensive manufacturing interests. Epidemics in the lower village are not uncommon, as the people are variable—now one nationality predominating, now another— the mixed races producing at times fierce quarrels, as the workers in the quarries are of necessity strong, powerful men for the most part. The town is well but not densely shaded by elms for the most part, which, from their more open habit, are the best shade trees. For much of the data concerning the prevalence of typhoid fever I am indebted to the kindness of Dr. C. E. Ham mond, to whom I am also under many obligations for opportunities for personally inspecting many of the unsanitary conditions.

The fever commenced about the middle of August in a tenement house in the centre of the village. There were three families in the house, each of which took men that worked in the quarries to board. In other words, it was a large boarding-house for workers in the quarries, but kept by three families, each having its set of boarders. There were about twenty-five men, women, and children in the house. All used a privy at the corner of the house, which was joined to the building. There was no vault, and never had been any. The excrementitious matters spread out over the ground for several feet, forming a reeking, offensive mass, that had doubtless been instrumental in producing much ill-health, especially among the women and children that were more directly and for a longer period exposed to its influence. The introduction of the typhoid infection illustrated its influence; for, as has been previously stated, unsanitary conditions may exist a long time without apparently directly producing disease, but their predisposing influence is seen when infection is introduced. There was a well where these people obtained their drinking water, about twenty-five feet distant from the privy, but as the deposit was spread out upon the ground six or eight feet the excrementitious matters were only seventeen to nineteen feet distant, and could not fail to drain into the well; that is, a solution from them after every rain. There were ten cases of typhoid fever in this tenement house, and two deaths. If it were not for the personal element involved, one would expect here that every person would have been attacked, and an enormous fatality. The fact, however, that the men were absent the greater part of the time doubtless exercised some protective influence. Indeed it has been asserted that the periodical appearance of zymotic disease depends upon the persons present (that is, living in the locality) that are liable to the disease.*

The influence of unsanitary conditions in inducing disease, if this view be correct or partially true, is thus emphasized, as by them the system is predisposed to disease, if they do not actually cause the disease. If the occurrence of an epidemic depends on those ready to take the peculiar form partly or wholly a causative relation between unsanitary conditions and disease is established.

From this tenement house the disease spread rapidly, but was mainly confined to a radius of a half mile. New cases continued to appear until about Nov. 1st. There were upwards of sixty cases and eleven deaths, a mortality of about one in five. Nearly all the deaths were among Swedes, lately arrived in this country; many were poor, and badly nursed. The majority of the cases were among the Swedish population. The duration of the febrile stage was seldom less than twenty-one days, frequently twenty-seven days or more. Nearly every case commenced with a bad diarrhea, and in most of the cases that terminated fatally the diarrhea kept up until the end of the case. Diarrheal diseases were also more than usually prevalent. In the cases that were near the tenement house, where the disease commenced, the surroundings were in a very unsanitary condition. Around this square there were a large number of cases.

Some of the isolated cases gave strong presumptive evidence of direct origin from unsanitary surroundings. In one instance a water-closet had been introduced, supplied from a cistern in the garret, which depended upon the rain-fall for water. It was in a bath-room directly adjacent to his bed-room. Owing to the dry weather the cistern became empty, and the use of the closet was

---

* J. W. Tripe, Sanitary Record, Dec. 15, 1882, page 253.

continued by the aid of pails of water supplied when used. This, however, proved very unsatisfactory, but before attention was fully drawn to the matter the sides of the soil-pipe and trap were coated with more than the usual deposit, so that even when water was poured in it failed to entirely remove it. The quantity of water used was evidently not enough in all cases to entirely change the contents of the trap, or at least the filth that passed into the trap did not all pass out until fermentative changes had commenced. Again, from the experiments of Bowditch and Philbrick, water suddenly poured into fixtures is very liable to syphon the traps, so that this probably happened more or less often. From these contingencies—direct exposure to very unsanitary conditions—a constant pollution of the air resulted. The fever in this case resembled very closely the form that has been often called "centennial fever," so many cases resulted from the conditions on the grounds of the exhibition; at least they were charged with its causation. Quite a number of the isolated cases were of this type, and closely resembled it.

In one instance where there were several cases in one house, which was a tenement house, there was a veranda at the first and second floors, and in the corner at the end of the house a privy on both verandas. There was no vault and the deposit was seldom removed, scarcely ever regularly, except when used as a fertilizer of the ground in the spring. The well was in very close proximity. The persons that slept in the corner rooms near to the privy were earliest taken sick, and the cases were more severe.

The same conditions are to be found in connection with the greater number of the cases that exist in every village that is more or less thickly settled. There is a small yard, and if the houses are on a square several such small lots join each other. In every yard there is a well, a privy, and either a cesspool or a spot of land saturated with filth from the sink-drain. Children especially sicken and die in such places, health is undermined, and prosperity prevented by the negligence in the proper removal of filth. The excrementitious waste is the most dangerous; yet it is stored up in the sub-soil or upon the surface of the soil, away from the roots of plants that can render it harmless.

There had been the usual decrease of typhoid fever in Portland during the prevalence of malaria, and yet there have been cases of malarial fever during the prevalence of typhoid.

. The worst of the unsanitary conditions described in relation to the commencement of the disease have been remedied; substantial vaults have been constructed, and privies, disconnected with the house, placed over them, at as great a distance from the wells as the lots will allow, the mass of filth described removed, and the soil thoroughly disinfected. In several other places nearly as bad, similar improvements have been made. The work of sanitation has been vigorously pushed, and the results are very satisfactory.

TYPHOID FEVER—WATER AND AIR POLLUTION.

The following cases are not all of them clearly typhoid, but that is the governing type. They were reported by Dr. Griswold of Guilford, through whose kindness the opportunity of investigating the cases was afforded. The investigations were made with Prof. Lindsley, with the assistance of Dr. Griswold, who gave the local data and the following conclusions were formed as to the cause of the unusual prevalence. The history of the cases is essentially as given by Dr. Griswold, condensed in some places. No other changes are made:

" In a family of seven, six have been sick, or are now sick, with typhoid fever, or a mixture of malaria and typhoid. They were not all taken at once, but one after another at intervals of about a week. Two of the nurses of these patients have been sick in the same way, but no other families in the neighborhood. The cellar, drainage, and well appear to be all right." The symptoms as detailed appeared to be decidedly typhoid, somewhat modified by malarial influence, but not enough to be typho-malarial, except that in some constipation was more marked throughout than any tendency to diarrhea. The general appearance of the premises appeared excellent. More than usual attention had been paid to cleanliness, and the removal of all decaying matters. There had formerly been a cesspool that never required cleaning, as it leached into the sand which was the soil at the bottom. There was now in place of the cesspool a long wooden trough, which was tightly covered, although thinly, by a board and a layer of earth, frozen at the time of inspection. This trough emptied upon the open ground, and there was quite a pool of water, or rather quite a patch of ice, indicating the amount discharged. It was stated that this drain at times became obstructed, and had to be cleaned out. At the house end there was a large

tin pipe which fitted over the end of the lead sink-drain pipe, and
reached down to the bottom of the drain. Here was the source of
the pollution of the air; the kitchen was of course warmer than
the outer air, and an upward draft was created through the trough
up the pipe into the house. Several instances of this kind have
been observed where a current of air followed a drain-pipe a long
distance. The trough was of wood, and, as a matter of course,
various substances adhered to the rough surfaces and there slowly
decayed. It was learned that the covering had to be removed
every little while and the obstructions cleaned out. Grease
especially, upon cooling, would probably adhere and rapidly become
offensive. A long space was thus given for the production of putrefactive gases, aided by the warm water that often was poured
through the sink.

The well was apparently all right, but upon close inquiry
a source of contamination was discovered which in all probability has produced some effect, as the specimen taken for
examination contained a larger amount of organic matter than it
should; although not to a very great degree, still more than enough
to cause suspicion. The upper portion was stated to be cemented to
exclude surface-water, but the well reaches the quicksand, which
boils up into the well after heavy rains. As vault and cesspool
drain into the quicksand, the sources of organic impurity are not
far to seek. Whether the degree of organic contamination would
be sufficient alone to produce disease is an open question; that it
was a contributing cause is quite likely; also that the quantity of
organic matter at one time would probably be very much in
excess of that at another. The pollution of the air as described is
more probably the principal cause, as the amount of organic matter
is not enough alone to wholly condemn the water, and much is drank
that contains very much larger proportions without any disease
resulting. But as quality has some influence also, that must not be
overlooked; if the contagion of typhoid from the first case reached
the well, the importance of the pollution is to be measured rather
by its qualities than the exact amount, be that greater or less, and
as there is enough to create a suspicion without the presence of
the typhoid contagion, with the possibility of its presence, the
pollution becomes all the more serious.

After the nature of the disease was known, great care was exercised in the disposal of the dejections. The probability is that

19

these unsanitary conditions had predisposed to the disease if they had not caused it directly, hence its spread.

PROTECTION AGAINST QUACKERY.

The work of the State Boards of Health of West Virginia and Illinois in the execution of the medical practice act brings to light some queer characters. The protection afforded the people from the harpies that feed upon them is one of the most beneficent works accomplished. Allusion is especially made here because of the danger of the attempt to establish a mill for selling diplomas to anyone that will pay the price, regardless of qualifications or study, near here in Boston or vicinity. In fact there have been pretenders claiming to have credentials from the Bellevue Medical Institute of Boston, which has never had an existence, who have been exposed by these Boards. The gross ignorance of some of these pretenders in the west and southwest is astonishing and amusing, were it not for the dangers to life and health involved. A very interesting account of quackery in Missouri was given at the last session of the State Medical Society by one of the physicians that had made a special study of the subject. He mentioned an old impostor in the northern corner of that State that informed his patients that he used only three vegetable remedies, all from a certain root. *Highbobalorum* was obtained by peeling the root *upwards* and was a certain emetic. *Lobobahirum* was obtained by peeling the same root *downwards* and was a sure cathartic, and *Hilobustem* by peeling the root around, was a rank poison and would carry everything before it, and was only used when the others had failed. Among the varieties of quacks *Spankers* and Faith doctors are mentioned. The law concerning medical tramps has proved very beneficial in many parts of this State, but there is one clause that furnishes a loophole of escape, and that should be repealed. That is the phrase " not an inhabitant of this State." Several impostors by pretending to become permanent residents or claiming residence in some distant part of the State have managed to elude the provisions of the law. There has scarcely any recent law that has been passed which has been productive of more good results than this. If the mischief these unscrupulous pretenders cause were well understood there would be no difficulty in securing the most stringent laws.

LOCAL BOARDS OF HEALTH.

As has been stated, our relations with local boards of health have never been more satisfactory than during the past year, nor have the consultations upon various subjects been more frequent during any previous year. The publication of the sanitary laws, and the attention thus called to the fact that every town had, in name at least, a Board of Health, had some influence in leading to a better organization, or, in many cases, to the first regular action upon the subject. The appearance of small-pox in so many parts of the State also caused the towns adjacent to that in which it appeared to take action to protect themselves. The increased facilities for organization given by the changes made in the law by which the methods were clearly stated for calling meetings, and organizing for active work, had also a beneficial influence. The results that have been accomplished by the New Haven Board of Health in the control of contagious diseases and the reduction of the death rate, although a seaport city, and on one of the central lines of travel, and thus constantly exposed to imported disease, furnish a constant illustration of the effect of a well-planned organization, faithful inspection, and prompt · action in sanitary matters. No other city in the State has a board of health so well planned for effectual action. Meriden has one of its good features in the sanitary inspector, but in most of the cities the health boards are appointed by political influences that have little or no reference to efficiency. It is only by accident that any good results can follow such a method. The only plan that can be acted upon to any extent under such circumstances is to wait until complaints are made, but never to anticipate any danger, or remove nuisances until unbearable. The work of the New Haven Board of Health has been alluded to in several connections in this report. As full reports of their proceedings are published each year, the details are accessible to those interested. The following analysis of the causes of the deaths from infantile diarrhea in July is in point, as it has a general interest in relation to the etiology of that scourge of infant life :

"There were forty-three deaths in New Haven from infantile diarrhea in July. The health of a delicate infant is the most sensitive metre of local salubrity known. It follows that the most insalubrious localities in New Haven are where infantile mortality is greatest. The forty-three deaths occurred in thirty-two different streets, and in thirty-eight different houses. But the most remarkable fact is, that thirty-four of the forty-three victims were living upon streets in which there is no public sewer, and in houses about which are still tolerated those beastly abominations called cesspools and privy vaults. In most of the nine cases where the houses had sewer connections they were only for kitchen and laundry purposes, and the stinking privy still maintained its position in the back yard. Observe this fact, also : a considerable majority of the population of New Haven reside upon the sewered streets, and yet only nine out of forty-three deaths from a disease that is chiefly caused by foul air occurs among the majority, while thirty-four of the forty-three are among the minority who reside in dwellings surrounded by the time-honored filth-pits. Any one can draw intelligent and reasonable inferences from the above plain facts."

Among the evidences of sanitary progress, or rather among the illustrations, should be mentioned the increased attention paid to the purity of the milk supply. The subject has been discussed repeatedly in our reports, and last year specific illustrations were given of adulterations, and of the influence of adulterated milk upon infantile life, especially in the cities, where the use of cows' milk for infant food is so extensive. The dangers resulting from diseases in the cows, temporary derangements, from changes in their food, over-driving, and the like, are enough to run without the addition of adulteration of the milk, even if water alone is used, as by this means it is robbed of its nutrient qualities, as the purchaser of course supposes it to be pure milk, and dilutes it accordingly. The law passed at the last session of the Legislature upon the adulteration of milk will be found among the sanitary laws. In addition to this some cities have passed ordinances of their own for further protection. The only one that has been reported to us completely is that passed by the Common Council of Hartford, which has been the means of a great improvement in the quality of the milk supply. The following is the text of the ordinance :

SECTION 1. It shall hereafter be the duty of the Sealer of Weights and Measures of the City of Hartford in addition to the duties now devolving upon him under the ordinances of the city to inquire into and investigate the quality of milk which may be sold or kept, offered or exposed for sale within said city, and to make such examinations and inspections thereof as may be necessary to ascertain whether adulterated or impure milk is sold or kept, offered or exposed for sale within said city, contrary to statutes of the State of Connecticut, and to report all violations of said statutes relating to the sale and adulteration of milk to the city prosecuting attorney for prosecution forthwith.

SEC. 2. Said Sealer of Weights and Measures shall, for the purposes of this ordinance, have the power to enter any store, house, building, or yard, and upon any premises within said city where milk is sold or kept, offered or exposed for sale, or where it is believed to be sold or kept, offered or exposed for sale, at any reasonable time, to make an examination and inspection as provided in the preceding section, and it shall be lawful for him for the purposes of inspection and examination to stop and detain any team, wagon, or vehicle within said city which is used in the sale of milk or for the transportation of milk which is to be sold or kept, offered, or exposed for sale, or to be delivered on sale, and to stop and detain any person carrying milk which is to be sold or kept, offered or exposed for sale, or to be delivered on sale.

SEC. 3. It shall be the duty of every policeman to assist the Sealer of Weights and Measures in the performance of his duties aforesaid, when required, and to report to said Sealer of Weights and Measures any violation of the statutes of the State in relation to the sale of milk, which may come to his knowledge.

SEC. 4. Said Sealer of Weights and Measures shall receive for his compensation for the performance of the foregoing duties in addition to the compensation now allowed to him by ordinance for the performance of his other duties, the sum of $200 annually.

The intelligent action taken upon questions relating to health and life was mentioned as an indication of progress in public hygiene, and the brief mention of the work of several local health boards here made furnishes illustrations in point. A complete statement of the year's work by each would show this progress still plainer. Any question that clearly relates to sanitary improvements or the protection of health and life is sure of a candid consideration and treatment upon its merits, whether the desired action be taken or not. The following discussion of a subject that is prominent just now in sanitary literature, in this region at least, is of such general interest that it is republished entire, except certain local references that relate to other subjects. It is from the last report of the Board of Health of New Britain, which under the able direction of Dr. Comings has done much good work:

No general epidemic has prevailed during the year; tertian malaria, or chills and fever, has materially diminished during the year, whether from the removal of local causes which have heretofore existed, or from gradual changing of the forms of disease, is not easy to determine.   Our citizens have suffered much more during the last year from the secondary forms of malaria than from chills and fever.   For the last four or five years typhoid fever has been almost unknown, malarial fever having taken its place.   Last autumn the typhoid type seemed to return, modified by malarial influence.   During the war the term typho-malarial was applied to this form of fever, and is now generally recognized by the medical profession.   We are not able to report the exact number of cases which occurred, but nine deaths were reported to the town registrar prior to January 1, 1882.

The causes of malarial and other miasmatic diseases are not identical, though similar, and not unfrequently prevail in a given locality at the same time.   Such was the case on Whiting street late last autumn, where diphtheria and typho-malarial fever appeared simultaneously. The hygienic measures which are required to prevent the miasmatic or the whole class of zymotic diseases are the same.   They all thrive where filth and decomposing vegetable matter abound.

The conditions which favor the development of malaria, for instance, are well known, but the exact cause is not known, and perhaps never will be.   Neither do we know why or how the same locality furnishes the conditions for the development of diseases apparently so unlike as diphtheria and malaria.   The virus of one is suspended by the cold, and the other prevails at all seasons of the year.

Three conditions are essential factors in the development of malaria:
1.   The presence of the malarial germ.
2.   A high temperature and dry atmosphere.
3.   Favorable conditions of soil.

The absence of either of these conditions will suspend or prevent its action.   We have no power over the first two conditions.   The third we may remove or so treat that it shall become inert.

Cold suspends the action of malaria, but does not destroy it.   After the first autumn frost the germ remains dormant till a return of dry atmosphere and high temperature.

A generous rain in the vicinity has, we think, invariably suspended its action.   And yet a previous condition of moisture is essential to its manifestation.   All deposits of vegetable matter, such as muck, sink-drainage, heaps of decaying vegetable matter, or even wet, spongy land furnish the essentials for its support—but it is requisite that the soil shall have been very wet, or covered with water some portions of the year. It is doubtful whether muck that is well drained and dry the whole year will cause malaria. The banks of streams and ponds, as well as marshy swamp lands, that are covered with water in the spring and are dry in the summer are specially favorable to malaria, and are sure to foster it if the germs are in the vicinity and frequently abound, year after year.

MEANS OF DESTROYING MALARIA.

A generous crop of grass, and perhaps other vegetable substance, are known to prevent malaria. Emigrants and travelers who camp at night on the open prairie are exempt, while the pioneer farmer who has turned open the turf and exposed the virgin soil suffers severely, and is constantly subject to chills and fever, but if he can live long enough to bring the new soil under cultivation a few years he, too, will escape the chills. In 1880 nearly all the families east and southeast of the school fund lot, corner of Commercial and Elm streets, had malaria; only four on Franklin street escaped. Late in the autumn of that year the Health Committee caused those lots, which are largely a deposit of muck, to be plowed, dragged, and sowed with grass seed. Last season there was a heavy crop of grass and weeds, with an almost entire exemption from chills and fever in the neighborhood. At one time nearly every person occupying the Ætna boarding house suffered from chills and fever. The next year, after the low places in the vicinity were filled in and the filthy deposits in the bed of the old stream covered, malaria disappeared.

It will be remembered that in 1876, from the 28th of June to the 26th of July was a very remarkably hot period, when the highest average daily temperature for 28 days was over 90°. Ten days from commencement of this temperature there were six cases of chills and fever in the vicinity of Cook's pond; in 20 days there were 56 cases in a population of 84. Some 30 acres of swampy land had been overflowed the previous winter by raising the mill-dam. In May the pond had been drawn so as to expose all this land, some of which was muck. During last summer (1881) this land was protected by vegetation, mostly by a fine water grass. There were no cases of chills and fever in that vicinity during the year.

The opinion has been expressed that the malarial influence is dying out from natural causes. In our opinion the natural causes are the changes in the condition of the soil. We have noticed that where the malaria has emanated from the banks of mill-ponds that are covered during the wet season and exposed during dry weather and not protected with vegetation the malarial influences have prevailed unabated.

Last summer a tract of land, which had probably never been under cultivation, was plowed, graded, and otherwise improved; later in the season several families living south and east from said land had chills and fever of a severe form, showing no abatement from former exhibitions in other localities.

From the first malaria has not prevailed in those portions of our city where vegetable deposits and filth are absent.

Quite late in the autumn we were threatened with a severe epidemic on Whiting street. Within a few days, in fact almost simultaneously, there were five cases of typho-malarial fever and two of diphtheria—all of a severe type. An attending physician reported the matter to the Board of Health. On the north of Whiting street, between South Main and Cherry streets, there are several acres of rich muck, a portion of which has been under cultivation several years, while the balance was down to grass; this tract of land has been drained for twenty years, more or less, by a large ditch running east and west in the rear of the lots which front on Whiting street. The sink water and sewerage of most of the residences on Whiting street have been conveyed back to the main ditch in open ditches. Previous to the appearance of this epidemic these ditches had become dry half their length, thus exposing a muck bottom saturated with sink discharges. Here we have a variation of local causes producing, apparently, two varieties of miasmatic diseases. The Board of Health ordered drain tile to be laid in all these ditches, which were to be filled. Before the order could be complied with an unusually severe rain storm rendered it impracticable to prosecute the work. The rain storm, however, caused the prevailing sickness to abate as suddenly as it had commenced.

It is with great pleasure that we assure you that the health of those streets in which sewers have been laid has been remarkably good. No cases of miasmatic diseases have occurred along the line of the sewers, except on Elm street, where the cause was of such a nature as not to be remedied by a sewer. All the sewers constructed last year were much needed, and have already contributed to the health of the city.

The work of local boards of health is also illustrated in connection with various inspections, and in other connections in relation to different subjects discussed in the report. Some features that did not find their appropriate place elsewhere are here given. As indicated, substantial gains have been made in sanitary ordinances, in the recognition of the efficiency and value of sanitary inspectors, and in the management of contagious diseases. The recognition of the dangers that may arise from schools in relation to infectious diseases, and the plan of sanitary superintendence by exclusion of the children from infected quarters, is a great step in advance.

INSPECTION OF DWELLING-HOUSES.

One of the greatest evils yet to be overcome relates to the tenement house, or in other .words, houses that are rented. There should be some reasonable standard adopted by city ordinance, if not by a general law, in regard to the sanitary provisions, absolutely required in order to render a house inhabitable, and no building that did not possess these provisions should be allowed to be rented for a dwelling-house. This would· place the duties of inspector upon some member of the health board, who should receive a reasonable compensation for his services. If no sanitary inspectors were employed by the city or town health board, a certain sum might be required for a certificate of compliance with the law. A better plan would be to have the office a salaried one, and permanently occupied by one person as long as the duties were satisfactorily performed. The most unsanitary conditions have been found in houses of the better class, occupied often by people that recognize the evils they suffer, but have no redress. Some of the conditions referred to will be discussed in another connection, but no harm will be done even if they are repeatedly mentioned, for the evil is a great one, and not easily overcome. The enormous tenement-house mortality in New York city, even now, since it has been so materially reduced by the efforts of the board of health, and the high death rate in such quarters everywhere, are conspicuous and crying evils, that show the vast amount of work yet to be done in this one phase of sanitary work. But apart from the overcrowded tenement houses, and entirely distinct, is the question that it was proposed to discuss.

The point raised for discussion was the necessity of some standard, fixed by law, for the sanitary provisions that should be required in order to allow a building to be rented for a dwelling-house. An inspection of the ingeniously contrived unsanitary appliances, and the neglect of the plainest and simplest precautions against the pollution of the air by sewer gases in such houses, for half a day, would convince almost any reasonable person of the need of such a law. The greatest evil in many houses that have been built some time, or without any regard to sanitation, is the scattering of water-closets, bath-tubs, and other appliances without any system, so that horizontal waste-pipes are carried in all directions, often of lead, that open at the top seams,

20

and allow the escape of vile odors, and when the pipe is full, of liquids also.   If the fixtures are grouped in order they can more readily be trapped and ventilated, and the house thoroughly protected from sewer-polluted air.   This lack of orderly arrangement leads to a concealment of pipes that run almost everywhere and can never be inspected.   The pipes should all be carried in a pipe-closet, as shown in the illustration of the Asylum at Middletown, and thus be easy of access, for not only must there be good plumbing, but it must be looked after occasionally.   Another great evil is placing water-closets in the middle of a double house, one above the other, so that the closet itself cannot be ventilated.   Too often these open directly out of bed-rooms, and in addition to the odors of necessity following its use, the soil pipe is unventilated, and the occupants of the lower floors have the benefit of the foul air in the soil-pipe above them whenever the closets are used, and by wholesale when the bath-tubs are emptied, syphoning the traps, and by the complete filling of the waste-pipe, forcing out the foul air along the whole length of the pipe above them, and even the liquid contents of the traps below.   By this action the traps below the floor upon which the bath-tub was emptied are either sucked out, or else have their contents driven out by the down-ward pressure, and are thus left unsealed for the unobstructed admission of sewer gases.   This condition has been again and again found connected with disease and ill-health, and is perhaps one of the most common evils encountered.   Another is the re-liance upon one large trap where the main drain leaves the house for the protection of the whole house from sewer gases.   The connection of the traps of water-closets with basins by carrying the waste-pipe of the basin into the trap, thus making it a ventila-tor for the trap, is also very common.   But the most common fault is the entire lack of ventilation.   If the soil pipes were only carried full size through the roofs and provided with a revolving cowl to prevent clogging by snow a great improvement would result.   I have yet to encounter the house kept for rent that has proper ventilation of the soil-pipes, unless there have been special influ-ences brought to bear to secure it.   This subject is so closely related to the health of the people, more especially of cities and towns, that it deserves a full and complete discussion, and constant agitation, until the desired reforms are secured.   The proper pro-visions for the disposal of waste in villages where there are no

sewers, and where, from the limited space allowed around each
house, the dangers of soil and water pollution are multiplied, are
no less important, and demand the attention of sanitary workers
no less than the evils from sewer gases.   The disposal of the waste
products around country houses also opens another important department of the subject, and each furnish problems of a more or
less complicated nature.   In the discussion of the causes of disease
the unsanitary conditions incident to each receive due attention.
As has been shown, from cess-pool and sink-drain similar if not
identical effects are produced that result from sewer gases; the
types of zymotic disease fostered may vary.   The object desired is
the same in all cases; that is the rapid and complete removal of
all refuse, and its disposal so that the products of its decay can
never pollute the air of the house, or the water supply.   The conditions vary in each case, but the ultimate object is the same.

THE SYPHONAGE OF TRAPS.

The experiments made under the auspices of the National Board
of Health, recently published in the *Sanitary Engineer*, present
some new features in relation to this subject that have not generally been understood.   That the momentum of a downward
current could remove the water-seal of traps below the level at
which the water entered the drain-pipe was well-known, but that
traps were so readily syphonized by water poured through the
fixtures to which they are attached, was not known.   The only
remedy that fully meets the evil is separate ventilation at the
the crown of each trap.   This is, of course, the most efficient
means of ventilation, but the protection afforded by open soil
pipes, even if the traps are syphoned, remains as before.   The
combination of the two methods, whenever practicable, is to be
advised in every case.   The round trap was the only one that retained its water-seal.   This trap is objectionable from its liability to
retain filth, owing to its depth.   Still, if it is unsealed, under any
ordinary conditions of open soil pipes, the small amount retained
may be less objectionable than the risk of unsealing.   The experiments, if verified in the practical working of traps and drains,
will cause a new estimate to be placed upon fixtures now confidently relied upon as not liable to be syphoned under any circumstances.   The liability of syphonage increases as the size of

the drain-pipe decreases; that is, the smaller the pipe from sink or wash-basin, in proportion to that of the soil-pipe into which it empties, the greater the influence exerted by changes of pressure of the atmosphere of the soil-pipe.

The danger of·polluting the air of houses· by forcing out the air from the drain-pipes through the fixtures in the lower rooms, when the waste-pipe is full in the 'stories above, and must displace the air below the water somewhere, in order that it may flow, has been acknowledged, although the knowledge is not always acted upon. If the waste-pipes on the lower floors are small in comparison to those above, or if there is considerable volume in the pipes, the water in ·the traps, as well as the air in the pipes, may be driven out before the advancing current of water from the upper stories. The only complete remedy for this syphoning is the ven· tilation of each trap, from its crown, by as large a pipe as can conveniently be used, directly into an independent ventilating shaft or into the soil-pipe if open at the top. If the soil-pipe is open at the top and ventilated near the bottom, the danger of syphoning is apparently lessened. The ventilation of the soil-pipe, independent of its relation to the syphonage of traps, is of sufficient importance and value as a sanitary measure to induce its use invariably.

SEWER GASES AND GROWTHS.

The exact nature of all the organic compounds that exist in the atmosphere of sewers, doubtless many of them of complicated construction, has never been fully determined. That there are subtle agencies that steal away our strength, sap constitutional vigor, and predispose to disease, appears evident, and also that the warm, moist atmosphere of sewers affords a congenial medium for the perpetuation of the virus of disease. There is little doubt that the conditions are here favorable for the growth of the confervoid vegetations, and, if the germ theory of disease be true, for the propagation of the germs of disease. That the virus of diph-. theria, scarlet fever, and typhoid fever, and like diseases, can be conveyed by sewers, appears to be true in either case. Dr. Thomas Field, of Birmingham, England, reports a case where a surveyor opened a sewer that was contaminated by diphtheritic products, and it produced in him a severe diphtheritic attack. An instance was reported to·us where two boys, playing around an untrapped,

sewer-opening near a house in which there were cases of diphtheria, were seized with the disease, and one of them died. So
intense was the sewer poison that one of them was overcome by
its influence, and unable to proceed to his home. When he
reached home he at once took to his bed, and in a day or two the
characteristic membrane appeared, and the case was rapidly fatal.

It is probable that the germs of disease are conveyed by sewers,
and if the spores of the bacteria are not the agents that cause
disease, they may be its carriers.

The neglect of measures whose utility has been repeatedly
tested for the protection of health and life, in the plumbing of
tenement houses, and even in the dwelling houses of the better
class, has been so repeatedly brought to our attention that the
need of a building inspector, and a standard for sanitary plumbing established by law, appears to be unquestionable. The law
passed by the New York Legislature for the cities of New
York and Brooklyn provides that all plumbing and draining shall
be executed according to a plan approved by the Board of Health,
and that the work must not be covered or concealed in any way
until after it has been examined by an inspector of the Board of
Health. The registration of plumbers is also required by the
same statute. The following rules adopted by the Board of
Health of New York are so plain and excellent in every way,
that we reproduce them in this connection:

PLAN OF DRAINAGE AND PLUMBING APPROVED BY THE BOARD OF HEALTH.

The following plan of construction has been approved by the Board
of Health. When the work is completed, and before it is covered from
view, the Board must be notified, that it may send an inspector.

1. All materials must be of good quality and free from defects; the
work must be executed in a thorough and workmanlike manner.

2. The arrangement of soil and waste-pipes must be as direct as possible.

The drain, soil, and waste-pipes, and the traps, should, if practicable,
be exposed to view for ready inspection at all times, and for convenience in repairing. When placed within walls or partitions, they should
be covered with woodwork fastened with screws, so as to be readily
removed. In no case should they be absolutely inaccessible.

It is recommended to place the soil and other vertical pipes in a special
shaft, between or adjacent to the water-closet and the bath-room, and

serving as a ventilating shaft for them. This shaft should be at least two and a half feet square. It should extend from the cellar through the roof, and should be covered by a louvered skylight. It should be accessible at every story, and should have a very open but strong grating at each floor to stand upon.

3. Every house or building must be separately and independently connected with the street-sewer by an iron pipe caulked with lead.

4. The house-drain must be of iron, with a fall of at least one-half an inch to the foot, if possible.

It should run along the cellar wall, unless this is impracticable, in which case it should be laid in a trench cut at a uniform grade, walled up on the sides and provided with movable covers, with a hydraulic concrete base of four inches in thickness, on which the pipe is to rest.

It should be laid in a straight line, if possible. All changes in direction must be made with curved pipes, and all connections with Y-branch pipes and one-eighth bends.

It must be provided with a running trap placed at an accessible point near the front of the house. The trap must be furnished with a hand-hole for convenience in cleaning, the cover of which must be properly fitted and the joints made tight with some proper cement.

There should be an inlet for fresh air entering the drain just inside the trap, of at least four inches in diameter, leading to the outside air and opening at any convenient place not too near a window.

No brick, sheet-metal, or earthenware flue shall be used as a sewer-ventilator, nor shall any chimney flue be used for this purpose.

5. Every soil-pipe and waste-pipe must be of iron and must extend at least two feet above the highest part of the roof or coping, of undiminished size, with a return bend or cowl. It must not open near a window nor an air-shaft ventilating living rooms.

Horizontal soil and waste-pipes are prohibited.

There should be no traps on vertical soil-pipes or vertical waste-pipes.

6. All iron pipes must be sound, free from holes, and of a uniform thickness of not less than one-eighth of an inch for a diameter of two, three, or four inches, or five-thirty-seconds of an inch for a diameter of five or six inches; and for large buildings the use of what is known as extra heavy soil-pipe is recommended, which weighs as follows:

2 inches,	$5\frac{1}{2}$	pounds per lineal foot.				
3 "	$9\frac{1}{2}$	"	"	"	"	
4 "	13	"	"	"	"	
5 "	17	"	"	"	"	
6 "	20	"	"	"	"	
7 "	27	"	"	"	"	
8 "	$33\frac{1}{2}$	"	"	"	"	
10 "	45	"	"	"	"	
12 "	54	"	"	"	"	

Before they are connected they must be thoroughly coated inside and outside with coal-tar pitch, applied hot, or some other equivalent substance.

Iron pipes, before being connected with fixtures, should have openings stopped, and be filled with water and allowed to stand twenty-four hours for inspection.

7. All joints in the drain-pipes, soil pipes, and waste-pipes, must be so caulked with oakum and lead, or with cement made of iron filings and sal-ammoniac, as to make them impermeable to gases.

All connections of lead with iron pipes should be made with a brass sleeve or ferrule, of the same size as the lead pipe, put in the hub of the branch of the iron pipe and caulked in with lead. The lead pipe should be attached to the ferrule by a wiped joint.

All connections of lead pipe should be by wiped joints.

8. Every water-closet, sink, basin, wash-tray, bath, and every tub or set of tubs, must be separately and effectively trapped. The traps must be placed as near the fixtures as practicable. All exit-pipes should be provided with strong metallic strainers.

9. Traps should be protected from syphonage by a special metallic air-pipe not less than one and one-half inch in diameter; if it supply air to a water-closet trap, not less than two inches in diameter, the size to increase with the number of water-closets.

These pipes must either extend two feet above the highest part of the roof or coping, the extension to be not less than four inches in diameter to avoid obstruction from frost, or they may be branched into a soil-pipe above the inlet from the highest fixture. They may be combined by branching together those which serve several traps. These air-pipes must always have a continuous slope, to avoid collecting water by condensation.

10. Every safe under a wash-basin, bath, urinal, water-closet, or other fixture, must be drained by a special pipe not directly connected with any soil-pipe, waste-pipe, drain or sewer, but discharging into an open sink, upon the cellar floor, or outside the house.

11. No waste-pipe from a refrigerator shall be directly connected with the soil or waste-pipe, or with the drain, or sewer, or discharge into the soil, but it should discharge into an open sink. Such waste-pipes should be so arranged as to admit of frequent flushing, and should be as short as possible, and disconnected from the refrigerator.

12. All water-closets inside the house must be supplied with water from a special tank or cistern, the water of which is not used for any other purpose. The closets must never be supplied directly from the Croton supply pipes. A group of closets may be supplied from one tank, if on the same floor and contiguous.

The overflow-pipes from tanks should discharge into an open sink or into the bowl of the closet itself, not into the soil or waste-pipe, nor into the drain or sewer. When the pressure of the Croton is not sufficient to supply these tanks, a pump must be provided.

13. Cisterns for drinking-water are objectionable; if indispensable, they must never be lined with lead, galvanized iron, or zinc. They should be constructed of iron or of wood, lined, with tinned and planished copper. The overflow should be trapped, and should discharge into an open sink, never into any soil or waste-pipe, or water-closet trap, nor into the drain or sewer.

14. Rain-water leaders must never be used as soil, waste, or vent-pipes; nor shall any soil, waste, or vent-pipe be used as a leader.

When connected with the house-drain, the leaders should be trapped beneath the ground, with a deep seal, to avoid evaporation, and if placed within the house, must be made of cast-iron, with leaded joints.

15. No steam exhaust will be allowed to connect with any soil or waste-pipe.

16. Cellar and foundation walls should be rendered impervious to dampness, by the use of asphaltum or coal-tar pitch in addition to hydraulic cement.

Subsoil drains should be provided whenever necessary.

17. Yards and areas should always be properly graded, cemented, flagged, or well paved, and drained by pipes discharging into the house-drain. These pipes should be effectively trapped.

18. No privy-vault, or cesspool for sewage, will be permitted in any part of the city when a sewer is accessible.

By order of the Board,
CHARLES F. CHANDLER, President.

EMMONS CLARK, Secretary.

This set of rules is worth careful study. The result when a house is drained in accordance cannot fail to be satisfactory. No unreasonable or fanciful measures are called for; it is a practical, sensible arrangement of fixtures. If convenience in the use and care of these conveniences and comforts of modern life alone were the object no better plan could be followed, and good materials, while they may be perhaps a little more expensive at first than the cheap, unreliable stuff that is too often used, are certainly the cheapest in the end.

There are those that assert that it is practically impossible to protect a house from the admission of sewer gases, if there are connections with the sewers and the usual fixtures, no matter what plans are followed for trapping and ventilation.

The remedy proposed by the most radical is the disuse of all wash-basins, bath-tubs, and the like modern conveniences, or else placing them in a sort of wing disconnected with the house by cross-ventilation. They advise in addition to traps and ventilation a constant supply of a disinfecting solution which shall all the time trickle slowly through the pipes. This would prevent the growth of bacteria as well. While an ideal perfection perhaps cannot be reached, the modern methods insure a degree of safety that more than repays their use. That fixtures may become defective, and that obstructions, from the coating of the interior of the pipes, or from deposits of grease may occur, and that time brings decay, must be acknowledged. The danger from such causes should be remembered and a constant care and watchfulness exercised. The remark of Professor Varona that house drains are "a small system of sewers within the dwelling," is an index of the care required. That negligence is too often shown must be admitted.

POLLUTION OF STREAMS.

A bill was introduced at the last legislature for a special commission to be appointed from the State Board of Agriculture, the Commissioners on Fisheries, and the State Board of Health, to investigate the pollution of rivers with reference to the effect such pollution produces upon the interests with which each organization is particularly concerned. Whether the waste material could not be employed to advantage for agricultural purposes, would be one of the phases of the question; another would be the effect exercised upon the food fishes in our rivers; and the effects upon the health of the people another. These indicate the divisions of the questions involved. So far as the question relates to health, it is one of the most important in sanitary science. The disposal of sewage, the influence of the flow of streams upon the sewage they receive, and the feasibility of the use of water that has been once polluted by sewage as a source of supply for cities and towns, are all involved in such an investigation.

That small streams are polluted to the point of saturation, and even beyond, so that they become elongated cesspools, polluting the air and rendering the spread of zymotic diseases possible and easy, if they do not directly induce such diseases, is but too frequently true. Such streams are often again and again obstructed by dams,

21

and areas of deposit for the putrescible materials they hold in suspension are thus formed usually in or near populous places, and when the germ or virus of disease is introduced, are associated with epidemics. If the statement is true that epidemics are due to the number of people in any locality that are in a condition to take that form of disease, the baleful influence of such conditions is placed in a stronger light. It is generally conceded that such unsanitary influences are depressing and debilitating, and if the history of the cholera is any guide the theory advanced is rendered probable, to say the least. When cholera was raging in London part of the city was supplied with pure water, and part with unfiltered, polluted water; the prevalence of the epidemic was governed by the impure water supply. This was repeated twice at least in different years. Since then cholera has been excluded by quarantine. In a general sense then these polluted streams are a menace to health by predisposing the system to disease.

Another sanitary evil is the use of such polluted streams for a supply of potable water for towns and cities. In our first report an instance was given where an epidemic of diarrhea was caused by sewage polluted-water. A large sewer emptied within a few feet of the grating of the pumping works, and a current in the river carried the sewage directly over the pipe. These had existed for years in nearly the same situations, and the deaths from dysentery and epidemics of that form of disease were somewhat more frequent than in other places, but low water and an obstruction in the river causing the current mentioned increased the evil. The sediment from the water examined at the time microscopically resembled ditch-water. It was loaded with diatoms, and infusoriae and confervae, and other impurities, nor were traces of sewage entirely wanting. The subject is too extensive to be discussed here. Enough has been stated to show the nature of the work in our department. One of the most interesting and important questions is in relation to the profitable disposal of water-carried sewage, and it practically interests many cities and towns in this State.

But a few years ago it was the common practice to cut ice from polluted water; even that which was quite extensively contaminated by sewage was used as a source of supply. In fact it was with extreme difficulty that the popular idea that water was purified by freezing, so that ice would be pure if the water were polluted was corrected, and the public mind disabused of the widespread prejudice. The publication of a series of cases of sickness clearly caused by impure ice was of great assistance in teaching correct views. Still many, especially ice-dealers, assert the contrary belief, and are only compelled by popular sentiment to supply pure ice, that is ice frozen from pure water. The fact is that instead of puri- fying the water by the process of freezing, the impure products it con- tains, especially those from sewage, are condensed and the quantity in a certain bulk may be increased. This point will be considered in another connection. Taking all the points involved in all their details, and it is readily seen that there would be plenty of work in the proposed plan for the member representing the Board of Health. Many of the questions involved will come up for a practical solu- tion before many years, and at present there are no reliable data for the disposal satisfactorily of the greater part of the points in- volved. Of the practical results that would follow such an inves- tigation, rightly managed, there can be no doubt. The subject is certainly worthy of very careful consideration, and if disposed of upon its merits would doubtless be carried into effect. So far as can be learned the other parties mentioned have expressed their approval of the measure and their willingness to co-operate. There seems to be no reason for doubting the usefulness of the plan.

SCHOOL HYGIENE.

Under this apparently innocent title are included a multitude of complicated questions that as yet have never received anything like a satisfactory solution, as well as many that have been theoret- ically settled but never carried into practical effect. The whole system and plan of education is involved, as well as the external surroundings of the scholar during the period of school life. Our work for the most part has been concerned with the school-house and its surroundings, the proper method of drainage, water supply, and ventilation. The questions that have been directly sub- mitted to us have related to such topics almost wholly. We have been called upon to inspect the plumbing and ventila- tion of several large buildings, and found the main opening to the ventilation shaft boarded up only once. One of the greatest evils in such buildings that we have encountered is in regard to the water-closets. In repeated instances these have been found placed in the basements, and whatever care has been exercised in ventilation, more or less odor can be traced often to the highest story.   Such large buildings act as chimneys, and the upward draught is excessive.   This is seen in case of a fire, especially if it gain access to the stairways.   In several instances such closets have been removed, to the great benefit of the air of the rooms.   In other instances the small water-closets provided for teachers' use have been found unventilated and in bad condition.   The sink drains are usually well trapped, but in one place where a room was complained of as offensive, a large sink in the basement underneath was found untrapped.   But one very marked instance of overcrowding was noticed; there were only three square feet of floor-space instead of twenty-five, which is the sanitary standard for each scholar, and fifty-eight cubic feet of air-space instead of three hundred.   In the school buildings recently built the sanitary arrangements are much better than in the older buildings, especially with reference to ventilation, plumbing, and lighting.

. Another evil often found is the use of doors and windows in order to secure anything like proper ventilation.   This, with the modern improvements in ventilation, is entirely unnecessary, and it is extremely doubtful whether the exposure to a direct draft is not worse than breathing the impure air.   This is especially true of the smaller buildings in the country, where any attempt at systematic ventilation is the exception rather than the rule.   In the majority of the school-houses in the cities, unless of recent construction, the windows have to be thus used more or less.   The use of windows to entirely change the air of the rooms, while the scholars are out of them, as at recess, is, of course, to be commended and urged, but the other practice cannot be too strongly condemned.

The absence of proper provision for the disposal of wet over-clothes in stormy weather is not confined to the smaller buildings. The ill effects upon the atmosphere of the rooms of a mass of wet, steaming coats and shawls is obvious; also the harm that would result from their use while still wet.   The remedy in buildings already constructed is not easy to suggest, except in the larger ones; but attention is especially directed to the subject, that in new buildings the matter may receive the attention its importance deserves.   The relation of schools to infectious diseases has already been discussed; also the health of school children as an index of the health of a town or city.   There are several other unsanitary conditions that have been brought to our attention during the year, which will be discussed fully when the results are more complete. The neglect of physical exercise during the formative period of school-life is, after all, one of the greatest evils encountered. There is nothing to take the place of the out-door games in the English public schools, neither does exercise, nor the culture of the physical system, have any adequate consideration in the educational plan.

The high-pressure system leaves no room nor energy for exercise. The mind is cultivated at the expense of the body, and with little or no attention paid to brain development. In addition, the pressure of exciting competition is used to excite the energies to the utmost; and, still further, an elaborate system of prizes, in one form or another, is often used, together with the other stimulants. The age at which systematic education begins is much too young, as in the mental task-work of the schools the abstract idea is often presented and required, while the perceptive faculties of the mind only are developed. The adoption of the Kindergarten methods in the primary rooms is the only mitigation of the evil, but in the ungraded schools no such plan can well be followed. The result is a parrot-like, unthinking repetition of words as the basis of the child's power of acquiring knowledge. Ideas entirely beyond the comprehension of his faculties are made a part of his task-work. No intelligence is awakened, no interest excited. The abstract idea of the shape of the world, zones, and segments, and the philosophy of language, are the topics presented, while the world of natural science is teeming with facts that would awaken intelligent interest, and render the child an eager votary, in the place of a conscientious plodder at a piece of task-work.

There is so much vague assertion concerning the subject that it was determined to make the effort to secure some definite knowledge, if possible, of the results of the unsanitary methods pursued. The investigation involves no hostility to the school system, nor antagonism with the teachers and managers. There are evils inherent in every system, and those that appear such are often magnified beyond their just proportions. The following circular and questions have been sent to the physicians generally, and materials enough have already been received for a valuable contribution upon the subject. But it is of too much importance to be treated without careful reflection and every endeavor to secure a complete knowledge of all the influences at work in the case.

It is not intended to publish names, nor publish individual cases reported, unless the cases are of very unusual interest; but it is desired to accumulate a solid foundation of facts before any inferences are drawn. Cases are also desired where the school-life has been a contributing influence in the production of the evils named, but these are to be carefully distinguished from the others where the results were direct and plain. The circular and questions, as will be seen, cover considerable range, but that is a matter of necessity in investigating so complex a subject. It is true that the young are subjected to a great many unsanitary influences apart from school-life. These will be excluded, as far as possible. It is almost a truism that the educational methods in vogue are not entirely based upon physiological principles, but are the logical results of the solution of the problem, how shall the greatest amount of knowledge be acquired within a specified time, rather than upon the physiological basis, what are the mental faculties successively developed, and what subjects best exercise these faculties. What is the relation between the development of the mind and that of the body, and how can the two be developed systematically to reach the highest standard of excellence in mental and physical culture? By physical culture is not meant training like that of the athlete, but the symmetrical development of the physical system, so that it shall be a perfect instrument to execute the commands of the mind. The result aimed at—a mind conscious of its powers, and able to use them to the best advantage, and a body quick to execute the designs of the intellect. As has been before stated, the high-pressure system results in quick, irritable brains, of little executive capacity or penetration. It is the nervous, excitable temperaments, ambitious to excel, that are goaded on beyond their strength by the stimulative plan, while the careless, phlegmatic student passes through unharmed. The following is the circular:

STATE HOUSE, HARTFORD,
STATE BOARD OF HEALTH, 1882.

DEAR DOCTOR:

There are many points in relation to the educational methods at present adopted that require the intervention of the physician, and many related topics that need thorough investigation and research before exact and satisfactory knowledge can be acquired concerning them. As a matter of course those that appeal the strongest to the physiologist and sanitarian relate to the healthy and natural development of the mind, and body. In brief, the question might be stated somewhat as follows: Do educational methods now in common use in any manner hinder the physical growth and natural development of the body to a vigorous and healthy maturity? In other words, does the school life of a boy or girl (with all that that implies as to the surroundings, incentives, motives, and discipline that control a child through the greater part of the formative period of life) result in a sound physical frame?

That our teachers and masters have contrived a system by which the largest array of facts on various subjects can be acquired within a certain time can perhaps be safely granted; whether what is accomplished is secured at the expense of physical health and vigor, or methods and subjects are used in advance of the natural development of the brain and before the child possesses the mental powers necessary to understand its task work is another question. It is not intended to make any attack upon systems and methods in use, but simply to arrive at some facts in regard to school hygiene that will be useful to parents and welcomed by none more heartily than those having in charge our schools and the methods to be pursued in them.

Contributions of facts are earnestly desired, individual instances of ill health resulting from school life are especially requested; as far as possible the social habits of the child should be also stated. The habit in regard to meals is another related topic of interest,—whether the nervous system is so strongly taxed by mental labor required that appetite for food is impaired, or whether school hours compel irregularity at meals. Disorders of the pelvic organs in girls, from too much stair climbing, diseases of the nervous system from unnecessary worry, and strife for rewards, and those resulting from too mechanical and rigid discipline are suggested, but space and time forbid an enumeration of the ill effects that are possible, perhaps inseparable from any system that must include all kinds, classes, and races, with their inherited, diseased tendencies. A few questions are appended as suggestions, but it is not desired to limit the range. Shortsightedness and other eye affections have been reserved for a separate and special study; more is known also in that direction, perhaps, than of any other subject connected with school hygiene.

It is requested that physicians will, as they visit their families, inquire as opportunity offers for cases of ill health, acute sickness, and the like resulting from school life, and report the results to the Secretary of the State Board of Health, with any suggestions resulting from their experience, and as full details as possible, also direct answers to the second set of questions.

By order of the Board,

C. W. CHAMBERLAIN, Sec'y.

QUESTIONS AND TOPICS.

1. Can you give instances where ill health has been caused by excessive study, too many studies pursued at one time, too many hours of study required, too severe tasks either in regard to length or difficulty of the subjects in hand ? In all cases give as full details as possible.

2. Has ill health resulted from methods of study, emulation, and incentives to over effort by rewards or punishments, or from a too rigid scheme of study and discipline during school hours?

3. Give instances where pelvic derangements have resulted in girls from too much stair climbing.

4. Has sickness or ill health resulted from unsanitary punishments, denying recess,—detaining after school so that proper attendance upon the wants of nature was impossible, or from any other form or method ?

5. Has sickness resulted from using windows for ventilation ?

6. Have spinal injuries resulted from prolonged constrained positions of pupils when seated, or from desks illy adapted to the height of the pupil ?

7. Have evils resulted from overcrowding, placing too many pupils together, especially nervous disorders?

The following can be answered more directly :

1. How many hours of study can safely be allowed, at different ages, e. g., from seven to ten ?   ; ten to fifteen ?

2. At what age should school life begin ?

3. Should children be forbidden to ask their parents to assist them in learning their lessons ?

4. Is one sex more susceptible to ill effects from school life than the other ?

Any additional facts in regard to sickness or ill health from school life will be welcome. The subject is one that will occupy our attention whenever opportunity occurs. As will be seen, but few phases of the subject are here considered.

The neglect of physiology and hygiene in the course of studies pursued is a mistake that will sooner or later be rectified. The lack of a good text-book on the latter subject is perhaps one obstacle. There are many studies pursued that might be set aside for these with profit to all parties. A knowledge of the methods of maintaining the highest standard of vitality, and of those by which the body is built up and kept in vigorous health should be cultivated. Strong, robust health is such an unequivocal good that it is worth every effort to secure. The real end of the educational plan should be to best prepare those that are trained under it for the active duties of life. It is of little importance whether a thousand and one facts are at one's tongue's end, if the mind is unable to exercise its powers upon new and unfamiliar tasks.

While the body grows rapidly in childhood, the growth of the brain is fully as rapid, especially up to the seventh year, when the brain is double its original weight. There are many physiological reasons for selecting the seventh year for the commencement of school life. The development of the brain has so far advanced that thenceforward its growth is steady and uniform, more nearly in proportion to that of the body, and not as rapid as it was previously. The aggregate loss of life in childhood is so great that that alone should teach us how impressionable is the whole organization of the child, and how readily it succumbs to hostile influences. One-half the children born never see their sixth year, and from that on through the period of school life the death-rate is large. School life is to a certain extent unnatural. Especially is it so for children from four to seven, when nature demands frequent muscular action, and sleep when demanded. School life demands quiescence and constant application. The restraint when in ill-adapted seats, for long hours, if it does not directly produce serious diseases, may strengthen any predispositions, and dwarf physical development. An improper and unnatural interference with the normal attention to the calls of nature may result in diseases of the bladder, and a condition that is a curse for life, called by surgeons irritable bladder. This may be due to improper punishments, which take the form of refusal of recess, and detention after school, which is sometimes added to refusal of recess. Cases have occurred, where the active interference of a physician, and days of sickness, have followed this course. Compelling attention to a long set of martinet rules may injure children, causing nervous irritability. But a full discussion on these topics will accompany the report on the answers to the questions.

There has been considerable progress in many of the city schools in regard to unnecessary restraints. In primary rooms the hours are shorter, and the discipline is considerably relaxed; object teaching and kindergarten methods are more and more used, and also light gymnastics; but in the ungraded schools many of the old evils remain. In the older pupils cases of diseases of the spine and general anaemia would be germane; also that general depression of vitality, to which the expressive name, neurasthenia, has lately been given. Nervous exhaustion results from overwork, unneces-

22

sary strain to attain some fanciful standard, and the diversion of the energy required for digestion and assimilation to brain stimulation.

This partial treatment of some points indicates the nature of the information we seek, although it is not limited by any rigid lines. Any instances of unsanitary punishments or forms of discipline, or requirements like marching all the pupils down three flights of stairs through a basement, cold in winter, damp in summer, before they are allowed to commence to ascend what is thus made four flights; the requirement of one fixed position to be retained to the last pitch of endurance, or any ordeal of the kind used unnecessarily in the school-room, also comes within the scope of our inquiries. When there are contributing causes, indulgences to excess, in novel-reading, or any faulty conditions in home-life, these should be mentioned. The evil effects of stair-climbing upon girls, inducing various pelvic derangements, has been mentioned, and discussed briefly in our reports several times, but as long as the conditions remain unchanged the subject must receive attention. The description and plans of the Hartford High School deserve especial attention, because all the evils of stair-climbing are obviated. The building for school purposes is two stories high only, and is well proportioned, and well arranged. The attention paid to sanitary matters in the construction of the Normal School and the High School buildings in Hartford and Bridgeport shows substantial progress since the days, alas, now too prevalent in many of the towns and villages, when it was thought that any building that would contain the pupils was proper for a school-house, and action taken accordingly.

An inspection of the school-houses and surroundings in the State is planned for the present year, in connection with the study indicated in the circular and questions. A complete investigation of the topics suggested by the questions may not be fully accomplished, but the replies already received show that the subjects have received thoughtful attention. Cases in point under every topic are especially desired. The names of the reporters will not be used in any way, and individual cases will be used to derive inferences and decide the points at issue, unless they are so clearly separated from contributory causes that they are typical illustrations. Instances under each topic, where the school-life has been a partial cause, are also valuable. The whole case should be given, however.

The desire of making the best show of work accomplished lies at the foundation of many of these evils, and to it pupils and teachers alike are sacrificed. Every teacher must have a certain percentage ground out for the grade above or else step down to a lower grade, hence the flagging energies are stimulated to renewed exertion. In proportion to their relative numbers more teachers break down than pupils, and in many cases it is only a question of time. Many of the evils of the present system arise from the unwillingness of the people to provide enough teachers, so that they can lead their scholars instead of driving them, and have some opportunity to study individual peculiarities. The whole question has been surrendered by the parents, who find how unchangeable and rigid the system is if they attempt any suggestions in regard to good or evil tendencies in their children's minds or physical constitutions.

Nor can it be much otherwise as long as the present idea of the importance of the teacher's vocation continues. If one person must teach all branches to as many as can conveniently be put under his charge, some of the subjects will of necessity be treated mechanically, if not all. If the different departments were each under the charge of specialists, that is of those that had perfected themselves in that line, and were themselves interested in the studies pursued under them, mere task work would be a thing of the past. The eagerness of the pupils to understand the mysteries of science, and comprehend the bearing of the ideas that were stimulating them to a healthier endeavor than any competitive spur ever induced, would show well the difference between real study and being taught. The powers of the brain being rationally exercised, new strength would be developed, and as physical culture would of necessity be a part of such a method, mind and body would be developed symmetrically. The marked increase in the prevalence of nervous diseases, and the premature breaking down of men comparatively young has forcibly turned attention towards the causes for such evils. The neglect of proper attention to physical culture, persistently ignoring the demands of the body as a machine that can transmute force but cannot create it, and the neglect of rest and recreation, are the pricipal features in inducing these results.

QUOTATIONS FROM REVIEWS OF THE REPORTS OF THE BOARD.

A few extracts from reviews of reports, illustrating what is thought of our work abroad and at home may not be out of place.

We are not pioneers in this respect, but follow good custom if any excuse were needed. Those that were conveniently at hand were taken without any attempt at completeness or method of selection.

The *Sanitary Record*, of London, England, the best English journal on sanitary subjects, made quite an extended review of the last report. The following is an extract:

This volume contains a large amount of very interesting matter. The extent of the ground covered in the report prevents us from making anything like an exhaustive analysis of its contents. We would, however, point out that among other interesting subjects discussed in the report of the board is the question of the part played by filth in the causation of disease. The author protests against the doctrine that the only requisite for the production of disease is filth, and says that the fight against filth is so bitter because experience has shown that it furnishes an essential element for the origin and development of the germs of disease, and the best medium for their dissemination, but that filth alone does not produce disease except through the intervention of a germ. That the former statement is correct few will doubt, but as regards the latter there is by no means a general consensus of medical opinion in this country. Malarial disease appears to have been very prevalent in Connecticut, and to have the same limit in the easterly part of the State as in colonial days, and for several years it has halted on the west bank of the Thames and, its tributaries, showing a great disinclination to cross rivers. The report on this subject is of great value, extends over more than 100 pages, and includes notices of its behavior in about 130 towns and other localities.

In the report of the sewerage of Stamford the question of the effects of soils is discussed, and especial reference is made to the circulation of air and sewage gases in gravelly soils. This is a very important matter as regards Stamford, as well as many localities in England, where the soil is gravelly and the sewage is discharged into the soil, and thus pollutes the ground air of the soil, and thus produces disease. As the interstices between the stones and sand in gravel amount from one-third to one-half the bulk of the soil, a consideration of the quality of the ground air is most important.

The article on trichinous infection is short, but sufficient for the purpose. A very large number of statistical tables on the births and the causes of deaths in the various counties are also contained in the report. —*Sanitary Record*, London, September 15, 1882, p. 127.

The following is taken from the notice of the Fourth Report by the *Sanitary Engineer:*

The "Fourth Annual Report of the Connecticut State Board of Health " forms a handsome volume of 300 pages, which is bound with the report on the vital statistics of the State for the year 1880. Professor C. A. Lindsley of Yale College contributes an instructive paper on vaccination, in which he concludes that in point of protective power bovine virus is superior to humanized virus. The Secretary has a special report on malaria in Connecticut, which is interesting in a historical point of view. Following this is a report on malaria in Western Connecticut by General E. S. Viele, in which a topographical survey of the State is urged. There is no doubt that such a survey would furnish sanitary data of great practical importance. * * * Taken as a whole the report is a valuable one, and reflects much credit upon those that have contributed to its preparation.—*Sanitary Engineer*, April 20, p. 435.

The *American Journal of Medical Sciences* is the standard medical quarterly, and is one of the best medical journals of this country. The following is from a long article reviewing the report. Previous issues have been even more kindly mentioned:

The report from Connecticut opens with a general summary of the progress made and work done in hygiene during the past year. In regard to the prevalence of diseases in Connecticut, it is stated that the deaths from typhoid fever and from diarrheal diseases generally have been more numerous, and that small-pox has been introduced into many of the cities and towns, but being for the most part carefully managed, according to the excellent " Instructions " (issued in pamphlet form by the State Board), in but few instances has there been any spread of the disease. Professor Lindsley contributes a valuable ·and timely article on " Vaccination." The last important essay is on the Natural History and Pathology of the Trichinous infection of Man and Animals, by Noah Cressey, M.D., V.S., of Hartford. The paper is well illustrated by several instructive and generally accurate figures and plates.—*American Journal of the Medical Sciences*, April, 1882, p. 527.

The following generous commendation is from the North Carolina *Medical Journal:*

We congratulate the State of Connecticut upon the work her Board of Health is doing. Through the arduous efforts of Dr. Chamberlain, the secretary, and his confreres, the present report is a credit to him and to them, and will undoubtedly give a new impetus to sanitary work and sanitary legislation.—March, 1882, p. 152.

The Connecticut Health Report opens with a concise yet comprehensive digest of the sanitary investigations it records, furnished by the able Secretary of the Board, Dr. C. W. Chamberlain, from which we gather the gratifying intelligence that an improved public sentiment in regard to sanitary matters is manifested throughout the State. A thoughtful and suggestive letter from Prof. W. H. Brewer upon Public Health *vs.* Public Wealth is worthy of a wide circulation among the legislators of other communities besides those of New Haven, to which it is addressed. Among the special reports that of Robert Briggs, the eminent civil engineer of Philadelphia, upon the plans for warming and ventilating the Bridgeport school-house, should be carefully studied by all sanitarians. Dr. Chamberlain's paper upon sewerage problems is of particular local interest, but it also contains much general information upon the subject of our means for the disposal of waste and polluted water. The question of the transmission of tuberculosis by the meat and milk of infected animals is discussed by Dr. Noah Cressey. The subject is of great interest and importance.—Extract from Review of Third Report, *American Journal of Medical Sciences,* 1881, page 526–7.

Your valuable report is received, for which please accept thanks. It is a good report, full of instructive matter. The vital statistics interest me. I am glad you discuss that matter of divorce.

LOWELL, Feb. 21, 1881.   NATHAN ALLEN.

Your very full and able Annual Report for 1881 is at hand. * * * Its general appearance and great labor expended on its contents is deserving of great commendation.   E. ADDICKS.

PHILADELPHIA, February 24, 1882.

Please accept my thanks for your kindness in forwarding me a copy of the Fourth Annual Report of the Board of Health of your State. Like the former it is able and highly practical, and is worthy of especial study and preservation.

D. P. WELFLY,
Cumberland, Md.

I was much interested in the Report of your State Board of Health which you sent me at the request of my friend, Professor Johnson. * * * Can you let have the three preceding ones which have been issued ? * * *

SHIPPEN WALLACE,
Chemist to the New Jersey State Board of Health.

Please accept my thanks for the Annual Report of your State Board. It is full of matter of great interest.

Dr. E. M. SNOW,
Providence, R. I.

I hope you will continue to favor me annually with these valuable documents, from which I gather every year important facts and conclusions to enrich my lectures on hygiene at the university.

JOSEPH G. RICHARDSON,
Professor of Hygiene at the University of Pennsylvania.

The following kind note is from the Secretary of the California State Board of Health:

' Please accept thanks for your very interesting report. I regard it 'as a valuable contribution to the subject of practical hygiene.

SACRAMENTO, March, 1881. F. W. HATCH.

Dr. H. B. Baker, Secretary of the Board of Health of Michigan, one of the ablest sanitarians in this country, who has by his talents and untiring energy placed the State Board of Michigan at the head of all similar organizations in this country, and whose reports are a model of excellence, writes thus of our third report:

Accept thanks for your last Annual Report, and my hearty congratulations upon its great value and interest. Treating as it does of several subjects not elsewhere entered upon so vigorously, and not yet touched by our State Board of Health, I have already had occasion and have taken the liberty to recommend persons in this State studying special subjects to apply to you for a copy of your last report. I sincerely hope that through the liberality of your State you may be able to spare a copy of your report to such persons as I have mentioned, and thus the excellent public health service in your State may promote the public health in other States, as it undoubtedly does so efficiently in Connecticut.

LANSING, Mich., March 4, 1881. HENRY B. BAKER.

The Third Annual Report of the State Board of Health of Connecticut for the fiscal year ending Nov. 30, 1880, has been received. It forms a handsome volume of 252 pages, with maps and plans . . . The report itself should be in the hands of all who are interested in sanitary matters . . . The report of the Secretary is a plain, practical, common-sense paper, relating mainly to the means of preventing the spread of smallpox and the adulteration of milk . . . Taken as a whole, the report is a valuable educational document, and should be widely distributed.— *Sanitary Engineer, page*.189.

The Second Annual Report of the State Board of Health of Connecticut fulfills the promise that the report of last year led us to await. The number of correspondents of the Board has steadily increased, and the zeal and interest in the work in like proportion. The monthly sanitary reports have grown more comprehensive. A large number of copies of circulars on diphtheria have been distributed.—*Boston Medical and Surgical Journal, May*, 1880.

✦ The depressing influence of epidemics, or excessive prevalence of prominent forms of disease, on the material circumstances of communities, and its relation to the purblind tolerance of filthy local conditions, is forcibly shown and illustrated by numerous cited examples, well calculated to interest and instruct the people. "The Functions of the Modern Boards of Health" is the subject of a special paper by Prof. W. H. Brewer, which admirably shows the importance of skilled workmen in this department of the public service.—*Sanitarian*, 1880, *page* 231.

Though this Board was only constituted at the beginning of last year, it has already settled down steadily and earnestly to work. In the absence of local authorities it has enlisted correspondents from every part of the State, and has secured the co-operation of the medical profession in its useful work, besides educating the public mind by the circulation of memoranda on hygiene. In addition to the President's address the book contains a paper on the "Pollution of Streams," another on the "Registration of Vital Statistics in the State," and a workmanlike account of the "Epidemics of the Year," by the Secretary.— *London Sanitary Record*, 1879, *page* 380.

We have received the Second Annual Report of the State Board of Health for the college library. I desire to obtain the first one which would enable me to start with a perfect file. So valuable reports are much to be desired in the library of an educational institution, and if you would have the kindness to send me the First Report you would confer a favor on the college.

B. A. RICH,
Middletown, Conn.

TOPOGRAPHICAL SURVEY OF THE STATE.

The subject has received the attention of the legislature at different sessions, and has been generally admitted as a necessity. It has also been recently recommended in the messages of one or more of the former governors of the State. The only plausible objection urged was that the boundary of the State was still unsettled. No such obstacle now remains, and the value of the measure seems unquestioned. In a sanitary sense it is of very great importance, as the local conditions that influence disease are, many of them, still undetermined, and cannot be until the data is supplied by such a survey and map. The work could not be properly accomplished much if any under seven years, and the expense any one year would not be large. The work of the coast survey has lessened the expense of the work very much, as the work done by them cannot be excelled and would not require to be repeated. There has never been any really satisfactory geological survey, and if it is too much to hope that any other studies could be added to the topographical survey proper, that is certainly a matter that should not be delayed when the time that must elapse before it can be completed is taken into consideration.

There is one topic that requires brief mention before closing the report, relating to

Under the pressure of the widespread epidemic influence that caused small-pox to appear in so many parts of the country, the dealers occasionally· may have yielded to the pressure put upon them for vaccine, and sent out quills or ivory points, as the case might be, that were not properly armed, although no dangerous or rather directly poisonous substances were used. · The abomination of cones was shown last year. They contain foreign substances of necessity. Fortunately we have not suffered so badly in this respect as others, yet if inefficiency and inertness is a test, we have had nearly our share. The worst of this is the discredit thrown upon vaccination and the lack of protection when perhaps most needed. It would be a legitimate duty of a State Board of Health to superintend a vaccine farm, and thus guarantee a supply that would be reliable and free from adulteration. The National Board of Health have undertaken such duties. We are gravely told that vaccination causes more deaths than small-pox, and that a large number of infantile deaths are due to the contamination of blood by some baneful poison introduced through vaccination. The use of animal or bovine virus renders all such assertions unworthy of argument, and the individual cases are usually found due to other causes than impure vaccine.

There was a charge made that septicaemia resulted from a vaccination, and that one death had been caused and another child lay at the point of death. In circulating from mouth to mouth the numbers soon began to increase rapidly, until the story began to assume large proportions. Investigation showed that one child had died and that another was dangerously sick, and also that inoculation of pus was the cause.

- The mother had obtained what she supposed was vaccine virus from a neighbor, whose child had been vaccinated by a physician four days before. That is, four days after a physician had vaccinated a child, what was thought to be vaccine matter was taken from that child's arm and placed between two pieces of glass. As the vaccine vesicle is not mature until the eighth day, it was

23

impossible to obtain it then from that child's arm. This matter, probably pus, like the matter of an abscess, was used by the father, and introduced under the skin of the arms of both children. The day after it was put in the arms were very sore, red, and swollen; no physician was called to see the child until it had been sick nine days, and the tenth day one of the children died; the other had the same symptoms, but in a milder form, and recovered. The physician who saw the matter between the two pieces of glass said that it looked like pus. The facts have been carefully investigated, and are as stated. No physician saw the boy that died until nine days after his inoculation. The case shows the danger of attempting to do that which one knows nothing about; everyone with ordinary intelligence could make some sort of an abrasion and rub on virus; but properly done, vaccination is quite another affair, and requires intelligence and skill. If anything, the operation does not receive the attention it deserves from physicians. The protection a successful vaccination affords is well worth some trouble and attention to secure.

THE HARTFORD HIGH SCHOOL.

Attention is especially called to the description of the sanitary arrangements of the Hartford High School. The heating is on the principle advocated by the late Robert Briggs of Philadelphia, with modifications by the architect, Mr. George Keller of Hartford. The attention now given by architects to sanitation is an encouraging sign of progress, this is especially true in school architecture. The article will well repay careful study. A beautiful well-proportioned building, adapted in every respect for school purposes is here provided without the usual flight after flight of stairs, which, while accommodating a large number of pupils, is in every way symmetrical and convenient.

HISTORY OF PROTECTIVE INOCULATION.

This subject is one of great interest in view of the recent studies of Pastern and others, and in its relations to the germ theory of disease. The paper of Dr. Cressey discusses the present aspects of the question, and is of value not only in regard to the new features in veterinary medicine, but is of interest to all students of the theory of medicine.

TREASURER'S REPORT.

Expenditures from Dec. 1, 1881, to Dec. 1, 1882,	$1,890.25
Salary of Secretary,	1,000.00
	$2,890.25
Cash on deposit,	312.88
Total,	$3,203.13

RECEIPTS.

Cash,	$3,000.00
Balance from old account,	203.13
	$3,203.13
Bills outstanding about,	480.00

C. W. CHAMBERLAIN, M.D.,

Treasurer.

Approved,

C. A. LINDSLEY, M.D.,

Auditor.

DETAILED STATEMENT.

Printing,

For Bureau of Vital Statistics,	$255.13	
Sanitary Department,	184.00	
		$439.13
Sanitary Engineers,		305.00
For Library,		194.60
Traveling Expenses,		220.50
Photo-Lithographic Company,		341.00
Postage, Express, and Telegrams,		185.50
Clerical Services and Copying,		140.25

Stationery and Sundries, ...   68.27
Incidental Expenses in Investigations,   .   .   76.00
                                                    ─────────
                                                    $1,890.25

C. W. CHAMBERLAIN, M. D.,
Treasurer.

I have examined the accounts of the Treasurer of the State Board of Health for the year ending Nov. 30, 1882, and have compared them with the accompanying vouchers, and find them correct.

C. A. LINDSLEY, M.D.,
Auditor for the Board.

The following is the report of the public auditors upon the accounts of the year:

HARTFORD, Conn., Jan. 25th, 1883.

This will certify that we have examined the foregoing statement of C. W. Chamberlain, Treasurer, for the year ending with Nov. 30, 1882, compared the vouchers therewith, and find the same correct, showing a balance due the State amounting to three hundred and twelve dollars and eighty-eight cents.

THOMAS I. RAYMOND, ⎫   *Auditors of*
JAMES S. PARSONS,   ⎬   *Public Accounts.*

HOW CAN WE ESCAPE
INSANITY?

By CHARLES W. PAGE, M.D.,

ssistant Physician, Retreat for Insane, Hartford, Conn.

HOW CAN WE ESCAPE INSANITY?

CHARLES W. PAGE, M.D.,

Assistant Physician, Retreat for Insane, Hartford, Ct.

The insane asylums in the United States accommodate in all about 40,000 * patients, while there remains a still larger number scattered throughout the country, for whom no special hospital accommodations have as yet been provided.

Such facts, coupled with the knowledge that new cases are not only rapidly swelling these numbers, but in an increasing ratio— out of proportion to the growth of the population, suggest a problem alarming in its import and difficult of solution.

The history of insane asylums is a record of the earnest en, deavors of large hearted men to understand this subject and to prevent or alleviate in some degree the immense total of human suffering involved.

The circle of interest gradually enlarged until the financial aspect of the question has become of sufficient importance to command the attention of the whole State.

When lunatic asylums were first provided, the insane were committed to them as a matter of convenience or necessity, rather than from sense of duty, which resulted in the collection of a large proportion of acute and curable cases.

With the advantages of hospital seclusion, discipline, etc., on such a class of patients, the early superintendents achieved a flattering success, and a high percentage of their admissions was restored to reason and to active offices in society.

In their efforts to influence the public to provide more asylums, specialists, and other interested parties, made use of such facts as the basis of their appeals, and from this the idea came to prevail that lunatic asylums, if large enough to accommodate them, would

---

* Journal Nervous and Mental Diseases, April, 1882, page 243.

cure nearly all who might become insane, and in some way largely prevent attacks of insanity in the future.

In neither respect have such hopes been realized.

It has been impossible for institutions to restore the large per cent. expected, and their power to prevent insanity can accomplish little until they have the intelligent sympathy and hearty coöperation of the medical profession and the general public.

If then the means for curing insanity are so unsatisfactory, cannot more be done in the way of prevention ?

It is the invariable conclusion of those who study the subject, that very many who ultimately become insane, might have avoided the painful attack by the application of intelligent means at the suitable moment, and when the records of asylums are examined this conclusion is abundantly confirmed.

The same exciting causes of insanity operate in all communities, in that degree at least to which various places correspond in social and political respects; if then for the sake of convenience and special application, the statistics of this State are examined, at the same time, the subject can be considered in its broadest sense and bearings.

The last annual report* of the Connecticut Hospital for Insane, tabulates the exciting causes which led to the admission of 2,333 patients, the whole number received up to that date. Condensing the table for convenience, it reads as follows, viz.:

Not insane, .	23
Causes unknown,	957
Old age, brain disease, fevers, etc., etc.,	263
Ill health,	331
Connected with religion, the affections, domestic trouble, .	198
Dissipation and vice,	116
Intemperance, tobacco, opium,	226
Over-work and over-study, .	72
Anxiety in business, fluctuation of fortunes, etc., .	147
Total,	2,333

Nine hundred and fifty-seven cases, or forty one per cent. of all, could not be referred to a special exciting cause; yet, while no point of departure from the normal state could be decided upon,

* Sixteenth Annual Report, Conn. Hospital for Insane, 1882.

no doubt the history of each case would reveal very many minor influences which had value in the sum total of causation, but so complex and evenly balanced the conditions that it would be un-just, as well as impossible with our present knowledge, to tabulate such cases under a single heading, or to decide how many were preventable. However, if to this class are added those not insane, and the 263 cases in which insanity followed natural, accidental, or unavoidable causes, as old age, injury to head, organic brain disease, fever, sunstroke, etc., the total is only 1,243, or little more than one-half the whole number. In the other half of the cases insanity was brought about by such agencies as poor health, disappointed affections, vice, intemperance, tobacco, over-study, over-work, anxiety from various causes, and loss of sleep—conditions largely under the control of man.

In most cases attributed to definite causes, there can be dis-covered many previous lapses from a healthy standard not suffi-cient in themselves to dethrone the mind, but all leading up to the final overthrow of reason.

And when insanity develops in individuals with an uneventful history, the same is usually true of them, but it is hard to allot responsibility to the several contributing causes, and the accom-panying physical debility is accepted as reliable enough to answer the requirements for ordinary statistics, and the cases stand on the books charged to ill health. In the table quoted 331 cases, or fourteen and eighteen one hundredths per cent., are so rated. In this connection, ill health is not a definite term, but signifi-cant. It conveys the idea that the final breaking down was the result of a long train of physical debility and suffering, com-mencing quite likely in a delicate constitution, feeble by inheritance, with subsequent over-work, anxiety, grief, want, neglect, or abuse, and insomnia almost invariably. Through such agencies, it is easy to trace the insidious advances of nervous invalidism to ultimate insanity, which on the whole is but the climax of a series of accumulating vicious influences attributable to natural heritage, and the enfeebling, disorganizing conditions to which from acci-dent or choice the individual is subjected. From the end, how easy to follow back along the lines of causation which in case after case are so direct and parallel that the unmistakable drift of such conditions ought to be better understood and more successfully antagonized.

24

That the various exciting causes charged with producing one-half of all insanities are in constant operation upon millions, while comparatively few break down under the strain, clearly shows that for the greater number the subjects of insanity were predisposed; that such persons had suffered a diminution of the power of resistance, and in this sense hereditary or acquired weakness is at the bottom of most cases of insanity, a conclusion which signifies that the percentage of insanity in a state is an index of the degree of physical and mental degeneracy in that community.

At this point then should commence the study of insanity and all practical efforts at suppression.

Heredity is a biological law. The most careless observers recognize the fact that insanity runs in certain families; yet not only is overt insanity liable to break out in a direct line of descendants; but acquired habits even which affect the constitution in one generation may become diseased conditions in the next.

Since no serious results follow immediately, individuals and whole communities are pursuing methods of both work and play quite at variance with nature's laws of perfect life and development. They are subjecting themselves to deteriorating forces which eventually drive to the wall the weaker members, continually involve fresh stock, and entail upon future generations that instability of the nervous system recognized as the insane diathesis.*

And yet those most interested are entirely apathetic, or give little heed to the necessity for avoiding all those undermining influences which induce or accelerate the invariable tendency towards disastrous results.

The question of hereditary bias is undoubtedly a very serious matter, although it has become too popular as an excuse for results, which through ignorance or design are often obscure. True, if the original defect was due to malign influences which continue to embarrass individuals in the same line of descent, a serious explosion can be safely predicted; but for the most part the

---

* It is noteworthy that the great increase of insanity is among those cases in which the symptoms are obscure.

"Out of the cases of insane murderers in Broadmoor, insanity had been recognized in twenty-nine before the act was committed, but the persons were regarded as harmless; in thirty-three they were not regarded as harmless, but insufficient precautions were taken, and in seventy-five no one had recognized insanity at all."—Tukes History of Insanity in British Isles, page 282.

so-called hereditary limitations are conditional, and need seldom evolve the worst or even bad results if only proper attention be given to antagonizing the inimical tendency; for the law of heredity, if unimpeded, is most marked in the effort to eliminate defects, and to bring back a species from accidental errors to the normal type.

Predisposition is by no means synonymous with predestination. A vastly more important element for individual good or ill is the subject of environment, the moulding influences of instruction, associations, example, and habit. The offspring of virtuous, healthy parents, if early subjected to vicious influences and corrupt training, are pretty certain to swell the ranks of the diseased and immoral classes; while on the other hand, by removal from disorderly homes, with timely and wholesome instruction, the children of the depraved are often bred to careers of usefulness and honor. Such results are so commonly illustrated, that all are obliged to acknowledge the supreme importance of pure associations, wise discipline, and judicious physical and mental education to develop the best side of human nature, to counteract inherited evil traits, and to hasten on the work of elevating mankind.

Every strong emotion, or train of thought, temporarily affects the nutrition of the nerve centers, and if such excitations are frequently repeated, there results an organic physical condition which becomes the basis of habit and character. This is especially true of the susceptible brains of children; which suggests reason enough why in the young every laudable thought and emotion should be fostered, and those which are corrupting or excessive be smothered or controlled. Nor should such precautions be neglected in later years, for what we are pleased to call the accidents of life are seldom the visitation of mere chance. Careful watch is incumbent upon the fortunate possessors of a constitution free from ancestral taint, and whose high duty it is to preserve and transmit the priceless boon; but doubly important is it for that other large class, whose advance in life is trammeled by the incubus of diseased progenitors, for it is possible, through prudent direction in early years and subsequent self-control, for such even to prevail over infirmities and to rise superior to the "tyranny of a bad organization."

The springs of action should rise from a code of strict morals—self-discipline is to be encouraged, and self-feeling repressed. An education should be planned on the broadest grounds—not the sort which is mere book learning, but that which cultivates the natural powers of observation, comparison, and judgment; engaging the attention and stimulating interest in many channels and a wide variety of subjects. Other things being equal, breadth of base always contributes stability, and as concentration of the faculties obtains, the possibility of fatigue and strain increases, and the more difficult it becomes to regulate the mental hygeine when there is impending insanity or actual aberration. When by undue self-examination subjective feelings are magnified into morbid states and false proportions, it becomes impossible for the individual to control the habit by direct force of will, whether it be attempted through personal fears or by professional advice.

The remedy in such cases is to completely occupy the attention in other directions—a course which if successful promises most, be the object to prevent or cure insanity. When other means have completely failed in such attempts, the moral treatment of the insane asylum frequently succeeds, and the whole secret consists in presenting marked contrasts to former surroundings. The fascination which comes from observing other patients, or perhaps the substitution of a genuine annoyance or subject of anxiety for trivial or imaginary trouble, is often the first step which leads to gratifying results in treating mental disease.

In the table which forms the basis of this paper, there are 198 cases, about five and a half per cent., placed under the moral causes, religion, the affections, and domestic trouble. That sentiments of unalloyed religion will derange a sound mind is very improbable. On the contrary, a well grounded religious faith is calculated to keep at a minimum the influence of many mind-destroying agents, and to safely tide its possessor over the natural or accidental emergencies of life. It serves the practical advantage of withdrawing the mind periodically from the tiresome circle of care and business, affording a necessary break in the exhausting concerns of life, and permitting not only true rest, but a renewal of duties, with a clearer mind and fresh vigor. As a means of conserving human energy, the benefits of the Sabbath-day rest are inestimable. Then too the wise Christian should of all men be a true philosopher, and hold the favors of this world in such estimation that their acquisition or loss would not seriously disturb his equanimity.

There are, however, extra emotional minds in every community, apt to take on irregular action through wrapt attention on any subject appealing to the emotions, and who are often crazed through the excitement incident to some forms of religious fervor. For this rather numerous class, the gospel of common sense would be a much safer doctrine than theories of personal infallibility, leading to less mental disease and more practical Christianity.

But it is minds of quite another order that are liable to serious injury through the affections. It is a law of nature that intensity is opposed to permanency. So when those very demonstrative, overmuch persons are disturbed or thwarted in their love plans, there may be an explosion quite out of magnitude with its cuticular shallowness, but the first sweet zephyr usually clears up their heaven, while the retiring, amiable, sweet-natured ones may be mentally wrecked for life, on account of dismay, regret, or the rude shock accompanying the disappointment of fond hopes and expectations. That pure, absorbing love often witnessed between members of a family or particular friends, is a sacred influence, inspiring and beautiful to behold, but it may promote unsymmetrical development, and become a source of emotional or mental strain. Especially is this true when such affection for a deceased relation or friend is unduly cherished and magnified as the months or years roll on; a morbid mental condition results, reacting upon the physical organization until a burden of sickness or lunacy is superadded to the original affliction. In the sad history of all those who become bankrupt in sound sense through unfortunate bestowal of the affections, a time can be pointed when a knowledge of the truth and discipline, self imposed or otherwise provided, might have averted deplorable results.

Likewise with the victims of domestic trouble; a mutual effort towards duty or forbearance, the kind office of a mediator, or the stern hand of law and justice, should necessarily be tested in their behalf, before classifying such cases as unavoidable.

One hundred and sixteen cases, about five per cent., are returned as due to dissipation and vice. That such cases are largely preventable in a moral community, ought not to be questioned.

The number credited to intemperance is 218—about ten per cent. of all cases. This is below the per cent. attributed to the same cause in the average returns of other institutions; while some good authorities claim that fifty per cent. of all cases of mental disease, result directly or indirectly from the excessive use of alcoholic liquors. The lack of uniformity in such reports may depend upon the predominant class of the population, and their habits respecting the use of stimulants, as they vary in the several localities of the different observers. Then perhaps the theoretical bias of some leads them to strain every point to sustain a favorite theory; but without question intemperance occupies the first place among the physical causes of insanity. Dr. Carpenter asserts that "twenty-five per cent. would be small enough an estimate for Great Britain."

In such returns and estimates, temporary madness and delirium tremens are not included, only cases of marked insanity, though many have a distinctive alcoholic character. The sensitive brain tissue which presides over mental manifestation is shocked and blunted by the presence of alcohol in the blood, and when its long-continued use has resulted in a profound disturbance of nutrition in the nervous system, the patient exhibits symptoms of partial paralysis in both mind and body—as judgment and will-power are impaired, an emotional, childish disposition becomes a prominent feature of the case. Hallucinations, delusions, or suspicions fill the otherwise vacant mind, and there results a permanent loss of the finer feelings and higher development of character. There are many others, however, which have not these special aspects of "rum cases," but classify under the common terms for the different phases of insanity. They represent a large class who by inherited, accidental, or acquired causes are predisposed to mental derangement, and in whom mental balance is overpowered before the nervous system becomes saturated to the destructive point with the irritating poisonous fluids. In official reports such cases may be assigned to other classes; still intemperance was no less the exciting cause, and to it is chargeable all the suffering, personal and family-wise, besides the financial burden thus imposed upon self, friends, or the State.

Even habits of moderate drinking, especially in the lower classes, produce a considerable crop of insanity. The money squandered for the worse than useless liquor, nine-tenths of which is not what it purports to be,* amounts to millions,† the most of

---

* Encyclopaedia Britannica—Adulteration.

† Careful estimates make the amount for whole country not less than $600,000,000, and for Connecticut not less than $15,000,000."—*Conn. Temperance Union.*

which comes from those who at their best can scarcely make suitable provision for themselves and those dependent upon them.

The theory that lager beer is a comparatively harmless bev-
erage, and could wisely be substituted for distilled liquors, is a
gratuitous fallacy, judging from the experience of the Connecticut Mutual Life Insurance Company.*

Because of this waste of funds whole families are deprived of
clothing, food, shelter, and medical care in sickness, to an extent
which is destructive of all principles of wholesome living; leading
to malnutrition, over-work, beggarly idleness, cankering care, or dull
despondency, which glide into insanity in many weak systems, and
involve in all some degree of physical or mental degeneracy—an
indebtedness to nature which must be liquidated sooner or later at
the expense of human well-being.

To a large extent the increased consumption of alcohol is symptomatic of the increased prevalence of neuropathic constitutions—
of a rapidly increasing class who feel an insatiable nervous craving
for some excitant or stimulant, and lack the will-power to triumph
over the weakness.   But alcohol, when adopted, is no remedy for
such diseased conditions; it only accelerates the same evil in a
vicious circle.   The abuse of alcohol as it affects the user is worthy
the most serious consideration, but the stupendous total of suffering and disease descending upon the innocent children of hard
drinkers would be appalling if generally recognized in its extent
and menacing import.   The heredity of dipsomania is insisted
upon by all authorities.   They are agreed that parents enslaved to
stimulants always bestow upon their posterity inherent defects, exceedingly liable to develop alcoholism, insanity, or idiocy; at times
skipping a generation to break out later as a distressing malady.

This wide-spread disease, the result of moral and physical vice,
is not self-limiting; by inheritance and example, fresh recruits are
daily augmenting this inglorious army, who for the sake of a
temporary "fool's paradise" thus hazard every honor in life, both
for themselves and their posterity.   Most certainly some measure

* "What beer may be, and what it may do in other countries and climates I do not know
from observation. That in this country and climate its use is an evil, only less than the
use of whiskey, if less on the whole—that its effect is only longer delayed, not so immediately and obviously bad, its incidents not so repulsive, but destructive in the end
I have seen abundant proof. It is peculiarly deceptive at first: it is thoroughly destructive at the last."—Colonel JACOB L. GREENE, President Conn. Mutual Life Ins. Co.—*Hartford Daily Courant*, Nov. 29, 1882.

should be projected to counteract this immense evil, and a large share of the responsibility would seem to rest on physicians. The effect of intemperance in its immediate and remote relations upon families, and a succession of families, should be traced and recorded. Already some institutions work on this scheme, but the general practitioner must do a large share of the work, for who else is trained, and has opportunity for such public service.

The State Board of Health, a modern institution of great power for good, is ready to give the widest publicity to all reports and statistics on subjects affecting the public interest as this does. Waiving personal sentiments respecting temperance, the physician ought to take a vital interest in this subject, for he is confronted daily with the pernicious influence of this king of diseases: moreover, cultivating broad views in any field of knowledge assists wonderfully in cheering and stimulating one's labors in individual routine. Then there is open to the profession a grand opportunity to shape public opinion on this subject, which at present is far· from settled, else settled very erroneously. Cold science must furnish the facts and argument for the work, but kind-hearted philanthropy must take a new, earnest departure on this subject. Instead of threatening tracts and glittering generalities, the unpleasant truth must be brought home to the unfortunate, the mistaken, and the vicious, in a spirit of kindness, thus disarming antagonism with friendly sympathy and assistance.

The use of tobacco is another method of satisfying the abnormal sensations of the nervous system, so destructive to physical well-being if not regularly fed, when once the appetite is recognized or has become a habit.

The injurious effects arising from excessive use are too masked or remote to admit of numerical expression, and the conclusions warranted by statistics, but it is the common belief of those who see much of nervous disease that tobacco as used by many is a serious detriment.

Of the 2,333 cases, only one is reported as due to the opium habit.

As a prolific source of insanity, and results injurious to health and constitution, next to alcoholic intemperance comes "intemperance of work;" that intense, unremitting application which leads to mental and physical strain, directly conducing to insanity or systemic defects which may reappear in succeeding generations. Every one admits that the ambitious, intense haste characteristic of the present day is too fierce for general good. Still the most marked exponents of this impolitic fashion push on, wrapped in the delusion of personal exemption from the universal reign of law.

The youngest members of the community are soon involved, for our school practice conforms to the general high pressure system. Encouraged by parents, enterprising teachers impose a multiplication of tasks; a complex course of study is blocked out, and all comers, regardless of capacity, or ultimate ends in life, are hastily crowded through the rigid machine. During the years of tender life, when the physical growth is of prime importance, the brain is overtaxed to memorize a mass of dry disconnected facts and generalities, for the most part to be early forgotten, and of little practical importance beyond the dress parade of the exciting, injurious examination day.

Such practice may be teaching, but it is not educating in the proper sense or healthy way.

Nearly all for whom public schools are designed will succeed in life only by personal application to some form of labor, and that which they can make use of alone constitutes the graduate's true knowledge. Running superficially through the whole field of science and history, and inculcating often ideas of talent, merit, and promise, which are mere conceits when the material limitations of the individual are considered, are among the errors often charged to our public schools, but of much graver mischief is the antagonism which over-study precipitates between brain-growth and body-growth.

When mental preoccupation absorbs the whole energy of the young scholar, the powers of nutrition are chiefly expended upon the nervous system, in response to the local brain stimulation, and in efforts to recuperate the perpetual nervous exhaustion which must follow. The result of such perverted physiological activity is unsymmetrical development. The nutrition and functions in one set of organs are excessive, while in others they are retarded, and this eventuates in refinement, delicacy, and intensity of the nervous system at the expense of stamina and reserve power. It produces subjects inclined to headache, backache, and the never-

25

ending variety of nervous disturbances which go to make up the modern disease, American Neurasthenia.*

When the ordinary school requirements have such a depressing tendency, what can possibly excuse the folly of grafting fashionable society excitements and frivolities upon our public school system, thus doubling, without prospective benefit, the risks of mental over-work and strain. At a season when the legitimate school tasks require for their mastery the fullest and calmest mental attention of the pupils, subjects stirring up scheming, pride, envy, and excitement are forced upon them in a manner so alluring that imprisonment of the mind must become a secondary consideration. At an age when the judgment is unformed, social privileges and equalities are so meted out that the heads of some are completely turned—erroneous ideas of rank and future possibilities are formed; the correct, modest beginning, requisite for final success in life, is slighted, and years, perhaps a life-time, may be wasted struggling along on a plane to which the individual is unfitted by circumstances of life and fortune. Of the many who, by genius and personal efforts, have raised their position from lower to higher stations in life, none have made the advance through such channels, nor in accordance with such artificial standards.

As a consequence of the mental and nervous strain from these causes, how many scholars, brilliant according to school test, disappoint all expectation by making no mark in after life. But the obscure character of the mischief is its worst feature. If exhaustion is noted, a rest is prescribed, with the expectation that a few days of idleness will obliterate all traces of harm; and since there are no certain means of comparing the subsequent life with what might have been, it is hard to demonstrate the importance of this factor in diminishing good health. Yet how many go through life crippled in energies, suffer as chronic nervous invalids, or become downright lunatics, through this fruitful source of degeneration.

In the conflict between mental tension and physical development, the female system suffers greatest injury through refinement of

---

* During the last school year twenty-five per cent. of the girls in the Cleveland High School withdrew, from one cause or another. Of these seventy-five per cent. left, wholly or in part on account of ill-health, and thirty-three per cent. of those who left were compelled to do so on account of physical trouble. The health of more than half the children drops below the level when attending school.—*The Medical Record, Nov.* 12, 1881.

organization and delicate harmony of physiological functions, upon the integrity of which depend both individual well-being and race progression, for "if any class of organs become predominant in their development, it conflicts with the great law of increase."* Such one-sided modifications as the excessive nervous temperament represents, become more and more difficult to rectify or sustain. Nature has appointed woman to bear the strain of perpetuating the species, and the quantity and quality of animal life in the mother largely determines the character of the offspring, for "the first requisite of a gentleman is that he be a good animal," a conclusion of the philosophical Emerson, so recently quoted and emphasized by Herbert Spencer.

"So commonly do I find ill health associated with brilliant scholarship," writes Dr. Goodell, "that one of the first questions I put to a young lady seeking my advice is, 'Did you stand high at school?'" That undue brain work will undermine the health of girls cannot be denied.† The popular out-cry against stair-climbing for school girls indicates public alarm over some grave evil; nevertheless it repeats an old error by mistaking the symptoms for the disease, and fails to recognize one of the original causes, and a grand remedy for the prevalent lassitude of young women.

Not that schools deserve all the blame in this matter; in truth, if the days of the young were well ordered in every other respect, school duties would make a less serious impression; but as part with, and akin to the mistakes of the school system, is the common home practice of forcing children ahead of their years—a most unfortunate American custom. No other device would so well serve to keep the mind and emotions in that constant exercise which alters character and depresses vitality. The various accomplishments are attempted; too much time may be devoted to music, painting, and dancing; and such excesses, with reading sensational novels, and participating in exhausting pleasures, certainly help the young to understand the ways of the world, but do not contribute abundant health, length of days, nor strong links in the chain of evolution.

---

* Dr. Nathan Allen, *Popular Science Monthly*, Nov., 1882.

† If woman's health must be sacrificed upon the altar of a higher education, the time may come when, to renew the worn-out stock of this republic, it may be necessary for our young men to take the hint thrown out by another, and make matrimonial incursions into lands where educational theories are unknown.—*The Danger and the Duty of the hour.* WM. GOODELL, A.M., M.D., 1881.

Two marked, local, cases of "over-study" are thus explained: "One of our girls who graduated in very delicate health read from the Institute Library one hundred and ten bound novels in six months, while she was attending school. Another young lady who came near breaking down the last half year of her high school course, saw company, either at home or elsewhere, every night during that winter. She said she never commenced to study her lessons until after eleven o'clock at night, and seldom went to her bed before one o'clock."*

Aside from the "society claim" cases, over-study is most liable to harm those who become anxious or worried about their success in reaching imposed standards, or their own ambitious aims, and the same rule holds good in professional or commercial life, for over-taxing the mind and strength, in the sense here used, covers the cares and anxieties of business. It is not so much that a man conducts business on a large scale, as the too frequent haste, anxiety, and worry about it—the strife and fret for greater success, or the conjuring into prominence of uncertainties, actual risks, or possible reverses, which lead to exhaustion or premature decay. When every thought is given to business, as to any other one object, by exclusion, capacity for interest and enjoyment is gradually narrowed, and when too late it is found that the whole attention gravitates in one channel, direct attempts to arrest its course in view of foreseen danger are as futile as planning to obliterate a stream by constructing a dam—the power behind accumulates until the barrier is thrust aside, having served the mischievous purpose of adding volume to the flood which follows.

There is much corporeal over-work, particularly in the agricultural districts. Severe and constant manual labor leaves little time for cultivating the cheerful and better sentiments, or that education which contributes power and stability to mind and character. Years of constant drudgery combined, as is quite commonly the case, with innutritious food, improperly selected or poorly cooked, are so destructive of vital economy that exciting causes, harmless under other circumstances, are sufficient in these to derange the mind. The frequency with which insanity breaks out in farmers' families best illustrates this. The lot of a farmer's wife in many instances is exceedingly hard. In addition to the demands upon

---

*Letter.—JOSEPH HALL, A.M., Principal Hartford Public High School.

her strength and system incident to rearing a family, she usually performs all her housework, including family sewing and managing a dairy. Her efforts to please her husband and children, and to do her part in paying off a mortgage or depositing a few dollars in the savings bank, become so absorbing that she labors on in earnest, unselfish devotion; in pure country air, to be sure, and with a plenty of wholesome food obtained from the farm, perhaps, but with no restful moments, only a short sleep when exhausted to interrupt the grinding, wearying toil; heeding no admonition, she accumulates burden after burden, undermining strength and health until the human machine collapses; if sooner or later depends upon the constitution inherited. "Only think of it," said a farmer's wife in the Retreat happily convalescing after an attack of insanity. " Dr. Butler is keeping me here and I have six children and fourteen cows to take care of at home." " Twenty excellent reasons for you remaining here until cured," was the timely answer.*

Injurious to mind and body as overwork is, idleness on the whole works greater havoc in deteriorating the race. Those who possess abundant physical vigor seldom adopt indolent habits, but the delicate and emotional, especially if in wealthy circumstances, often neglect all occupation which would require healthy attention or interest, and in luxurious ease read light literature, build air castles, and imagine the most fascinating personal romances. They selfishly dwell upon subjective feelings, developing more and more complete egoism ; they magnify sensations into symptoms, and symptoms into diseases, until nervous invalids result by the hundred.

With emotional or intellectual capacity cultivated at the expense of physical development ; with serious, sensible views of life repressed by the engrossing cares of an artificial society life ; with wills untrained through perpetual indulgence, and with theories of human nature imbibed from French novels, French plays, and French operas, what wonder the middle ground between positive health or disease, sanity or insanity, is occupied with so large a class.

Admitting such to be exceptional cases still, while well supplied tables, lager beer, and cod liver oil are successful in maintaining a

*First Annual Report Conn. State Board of Health, 1879.

good standard of physique, it is a growing conviction that " women in the New England Family, are being gradually modified in physical organization, instincts, and character."*

True, healthy living requires both labor and recreation, and is best obtained by a systematic variety in subjects examined or undertaken, and by diversifying the channels of thought and action to combine exercise, change, rest, and amusement, thus strengthening the mind and character and affording the best preparation for success in any department of life. The professional man should follow a course of investigation or labor that would, through interest, not self-discipline, break into sedentary habits with regularity and profit. The business man and the farmer should adopt some course of reading or study which might be found most agreeablè, or best educate the faculties for personal success, or the assistance that could be unselfishly rendered others.

With children the same scheme of recreation and amusements must be employed if the happiest results are desired. It is not enough to declare a holiday, but judicious plans and careful supervision should attach to the entertainment òf the young.. Impressions leading to habits are so easily fixed that silly and vicious associations should be discountenanced, and those encouraged which stimulate interest in all things purè and refining, while giving rise to physical development, innocent mirth, and buoyancy of spirits.

Our native population inherited from the sturdy settlers of New England a coldness and austerity of manner, and there is great necessity for more methods of infusing warmth and sweetness into the lives and homes of our honest, strong-willed people. Much, therefore, remains to be done in educating the public in practical ways for rational enjoyment. Whatever customs evoke extreme sentiment, insipid or tart, and lead to apathy or frenzy, should be avoided. Unrestrained indulgence in exciting, frivolous pastimes is dissipation, and fond parents who provide for their children a

*Nathan Allen, M.D., L.L.D.
The Law of Human Increase.—*Popular Science Monthly*, Nov., 1882.
The New England Family.—*The New Englander*, March, 1882.
The Danger and the Duty of the Hour.—WM. GOODELL, A.M., M.D.
Incompatibility of the Higher Education with the Duties of Motherhood.—HENRY K. PALMER, M.D.
The Transitional American Woman.—KATE GARNET WELLS. *Atlantic Monthly*, Dec., 1880.
Editorial.—*Scribner's Magazine*, Feb., 1881.

continuous round of intoxicating gaieties, all unconsciously, perhaps, are substituting a trifling, artificial life for one of true dignity and worth. It is little realized how the young are being unfitted by this process for the sober realities of life.

Again the wear and tear inseparable from some popular forms of amusement—the Fourth of July celebration, for instance—are greatly in excess of any possible benefit. Such play-spells supply recreation with a vengeance, and are "better honored in the breach than the observance" Holidays and festivals which lead to cheerful, healthy recreation should be multiplied and utilized by all classes. Families and local communities could well afford to spend more time in salutary fellowship. The plan of village improvement societies so successfully inaugurated by Secretary Northrop of the State Board of Education, was well conceived, and suggests the happiest possibilities in the way of variety and entertainment in localities where it is extremely difficult to vary the monotony of life. More should be done in providing opportunities for recreation and amusement for the large classes who, if unassisted, have neither means, time, nor inclination for securing their own best interests. The English plan of public coffee club-houses might well be adopted in all thickly settled communities. Such places when conducted with sense, made attractive by music and games, supplied with books and current literature, would promote social improvement, and might rival even the public schools in spreading practical education among those not likely to find at home sufficient cheer and variety to satisfy the natural taste, and who, if neglected, would gravitate into associations and habits certain to diminish the powers of both body and mind, and verge toward pauperism, crime, or insanity.

But more important than all else in building minds and character is the family influence. Here rest the foundations of society, and here, in gentle patience, are engaged daily more heroism and grander virtues than are celebrated in the annals of military warfare. The laws of complete life are grounded on principles which must be indelibly impressed on the very young, and in faith, through example and precept, the parents must sow the moral seed.

Truth, obedience, love, and industry should be thoroughly taught as cardinal points, and with such foundations, knowledge and wisdom such as books of themselves can never teach, will generate spontaneously with the growth of the person, enriching and perfecting individual character—the safeguard for future human progress. The nurture and admonition for such training need not be irksome. In those families when the actual motives in life correspond to such doctrines, principles do not require formulation. Instruction is possible without a schoolmaster. There can be discipline without drilling, and correction without antagonism. Who has not been admitted to family circles where such a system prevails without friction or discord; where correction with love, and firmness with sympathy is so mingled, that the bestower with each instance is rewarded by stronger ties of endearment on the part of the recipient. One is always charmed in contemplating such harmonious promising family groups, where unselfish love and devotion to each other is the ruling motive of all, and feels assured of the safety of the race, so long as our land is filled with such homes and such families—the most sacred institutions on earth.

The prominent causes of insanity have been discussed, but underlying and largely accounting for them, as well as detected in numerous other directions as responsible for much actual disease and race degeneration, is the common fierce desire for the acquisition of riches. . To give direction and tone to popular notions as to worthy objects in life, there is great opportunity and necessity in this country for a wealthy cultured class, for men willing to pursue scientific investigations free from all anxiety for maintenance or gain; for men who would undertake public duty for honor, secure above the temptations of bribes, and more men, in imitation of some noble examples, who would desire to earn renown through the practice of Christian philanthropy. But in accordance with the money-gauge of nobility, the better impulses are trampled down in the rush for financial gains, and when favored by fortune, the grand climax of a successful life is claimed, even when to accomplish this, comfort, character, or life may have been ruthlessly sacrificed.

Our interest in the agencies which cause insanity are broader than the field embraced by any single topic. From the same centers radiate the malignant influences which cast upon society and its progress these great burdens—poverty, crime, and insanity. It is probably true of all these evils, that fifty per cent. is a low estimate for the amount due to gross ignorance or selfish disregard of known laws, and which might be largely prevented if the leading causes were better understood and suitable provision for correcting faulty living were at the command of an intelligent and interested public. Interested the public should be, for the unity of human interest is such that whatever affects the individual affects society. We prate of our independence and respect the rights (?) of others even in suicidal courses, but can we escape all responsibility? "Am I my brother's keeper?" was the unavailing excuse of the man who invented murder. The diminution of marriages and the birth rate, and the frequency of divorces in the native New England population can be explained on this physiological theory* of the one-sided development resulting from wrong methods in society, in study, and in business, though it is impossible to draw a line of demarkation between moral and physical influence in such connection. The unfavorable showing from statistics on these subjects, with the prevalence of poverty, intemperance, crime, and disease, and the frequency of shocking social explosions in quiet old orthodox districts in New England, indicate a decided undercurrent, demoralizing and deteriorating in its tendency. The recognition of such a state of things does not argue pessimism—it is but the diagnosis requisite for scientific treatment—and fortunately such conditions are the exception, for without doubt there is in the main an enlargement and progress in human affairs, but it is no less our duty, while retaining what is good, to detect, control, and remove what in modern life and manner is evil. Crying temperance in all things, and preaching the ".gospel of relaxation" is not enough to stem the torrent of baneful influences. The moral law is always the law of progress, and public sentiment must be held to the highest standards. The results of noxious habits, errors, and vices must be undertood and taught, and correction suggested. That narrowness of attention and asymmetry of development, as exhibited in forms of amusement, systems of education and application to business, must be realized as likely to defeat the very hopes which prompt such courses by their direct tendency to physical impairment—a condition inviting disease either in the individual or descendants.

From the limits of New England have gone out a great multitude distinguished for pure faith, pure aims, and pure blood. It has been an acknowledged center for the best moral and religious sentiments, but its honorable prestige may give place to a fame

---

* *New Englander*, Mar., 1882, p. 149.—D. ALLEN.

quite undesirable, if the elements of decay and disintegration are not retarded in their onward march.* We are justly proud of our high state of civilization; but every civilization that has risen into prominence but to decline, has been sacrificed to internal processes of decay. When to appearances at the height of their glory the whole fabric of society was permeated with corrupting, disintegrating habits and forces.

Typical for all time of the false sense of security bred of human pride, was that warning vision revealed to the king of great Babylon. "Its brightness was excellent," for as presented in his dream this remarkable human image was crowned with a head "made of fine gold." But when the inspired prophet scanned the same apparition from head to foot, marking how successively materials of a retrograde quality entered into its composition, until an incoherent mass of iron and clay made up the fragile feet on which it rested; he proclaimed in dismay that "its form was terrible."

Man follows scientific laws in propagating and cultivating every species under his control, excepting only his own, and this indifference comes because the lines connecting cause and effect in the growth or decay of man are so attenuated—often through the years of several generations, that a single observer has personal knowledge of disconnected sections only; but if such vitally interesting panoramas could be focused within a single field of vision, to be known and read of all men, it is safe to assume that attempts to perfect man would be the first business of the State. No systematic attempts have as yet been made to prevent insanity, but with the clearer knowledge yearly accumulating, the enormous money considerations involved and the increasing general interest in the subject point to the inauguration at an early day of efforts in the right direction. Not that insanity can be stamped out except in an ideal State, but it can be largely obviated in a working, practical commonwealth.

* Let us see to it that the New England idea which is creeping towards the far West and lengthening out its slimy trail towards our own home, which is breaking up households and gnawing into the core of our national prosperity—let us, I say, see to it that this canker does not take root in our soil."—DR. GOODELL, at Balt., Md., 1881.

Epidemic Intermittent Fever;

ITS

ANNUAL PROGRESS

IN CONNECTICUT AND OTHER PARTS OF NEW ENGLAND.

BY

G. H. WILSON, M. D.,

MERIDEN,

MEMBER OF THE STATE BOARD OF HEALTH.

EPIDEMIC INTERMITTENT FEVERS.

I desire to present a study of the movement of the present malarial epidemic in Connecticut and other parts of New England, illustrated by a map with isochronal lines, showing the extent and direction of its annual progress during the past twenty-three years.

The data upon which this article is based have been obtained from personal observations, and reports of medical men and others in nearly every town in the three States of Connecticut, Massachusetts, and Rhode Island, and are believed to be reliable. Some little variation in the particular year when the first cases of ague appeared in the respective localities was to be expected, owing to the comparative suddenness or insidiousness with which it changed the type of disease, as well as the degree of familiarity of the observer, with the forms he had to deal with.

In some instances, manifest errors in the returns have been corrected; but in nearly all other cases, including some doubtful ones, the lines of annual progress have been drawn upon the map as near to the reported date as was compatible with clearness of representation.

In a few instances the reported dates so far failed to correspond with those from adjoining towns, that they were inclosed in circles by themselves to indicate their exception from the general classification.

This fidelity to the sources of information interferes here and there with the symmetry of the diagramatic representation, but the alternative would be liable to sacrifice the truth.

To avoid confusion, a few lines have been dropped, or lost, in that of the year preceding, where the movement for several years was not lateral, but forward only.

With these exceptions, each annual line is drawn to include the towns in which malarial affections, chills and fever, had at that time appeared.

Having no means of showing intensity, or comparative prevalence, it may be remembered that the mode of invasion has been
so uniform, in nearly all towns, and sections of towns, districts,
and hamlets reporting, that we may assume for all, that the cases
were few the first year, ten times as many the second year, and
only became general on the third or fourth year.

It will be seen that the course, as shown by the successive
waves, and later, by the concentric lines of its annual progress,
indicates an advance in one definite direction, independent of any
known or recognized influence, whether atmospheric, telluric,
magnetic, or climatic, and through the most diverse conditions of
surface, soil, humidity, and temperature, general and local.

We are unfortunately constrained by long usage to denominate
the class of diseases under consideration malarial, and so in a
sense endorse by word, what in the argument we must disown.
Our inability to say what the cause of ague is, does not debar us,
however, from proving what it is not. In fact, if the question can
be cleared of the halo of error, which has hitherto surrounded it,
the truth may more readily appear ; and the object of this paper
is to show, how little its conclusions agree with the favorite
opinions of laymen and physicians, from Lancisi down, regarding
the cause of ague, and its future in Connecticut.

In this epidemic we may be sure that ague is not produced by
"heat, moisture, and decay," arising from ponds, reservoirs,
swamps, or low grounds, overflowed by freshets, or exposed by
evaporation; for new cases arise at any and all seasons of the year,
and upon the highest land, as it has done in one-third of the towns
in the State; nor by uncovering lately submerged lands, for in
most towns no such lands exist. Not only does the disease not
appear under the conditions appropriate to the paludal theory,
but it does not confine itself to, or remain in, the alluvial tracts,
even when established upon them.

Not from "disturbance of earth," by grading, ditching, or railroad building in the country, or by laying down sewers, or gas or
water pipes in towns; for these operations have been going on for
ages, while no ague came because of them, and it did appear at
the same relative time in territory whose surface had or had not
been disturbed.

Not from the "transportation of clay, manures, or other decaying and fermenting substances, from New Jersey and New York,"

or of sawdust in the river beds, floated down from the mills of the north; for in several towns so affected none of these things have been introduced to this day, and in others, the disease failed to appear at the time called for by the theory.

Not from "stagnant, or even foul water," no matter how offensive to smell or taste; for water with these qualities has always existed in many towns free from ague, and, on the other hand, many tracts of dry and sandy soil have been its favorite haunts.

Not from *bacillus malariæ* in the water, which would be carried *with* the current; while ague moves up stream, and *against* the current of every principal river in Connecticut.

It cannot be from germs carried by winds; for the direction for the year, in the State, and in New England generally, is north of west, and is very rarely, and for a short time only, in the direction of the ague movement.

Probably no error is so common among the people of towns, as that it may be caused by imperfect drainage, by the filth of houses. Doubtless bad conditions lower the vitality and decrease the resisting power of the system. and promote the liability to suffer from exposure to specific influence, but no amount of filth or degree of debility will produce one case of ague *de novo*.

Ague is specific, and can only be produced by its own cause. That ague is found in all these conditions is fortunate for the handy hypothesis of local influence, and the daily use of talkative laymen and lazy physicians; but *post hoc* is not *propter hoc*.

These alleged causes of ague might have been left to the defence of their inventors, and not have burdened this paper, but for the benefit of the contrast which the lessons and conclusions of the map present to the unsettled condition of thought on that subject.

In its invasion of this State the ague crossed, diagonally but decidedly, every one of our main rivers. Starting on the coast, west of the Housatonic, it crossed its valley the next year, but did not ascend it, more than about fifteen miles, in as many years. It next crossed the Naugatuck, within five miles of its mouth. The Quinnipiac, it first reached and crossed, in South Meriden, sixteen miles from East Haven; the Connecticut at Middletown, twenty-five miles from the Sound; and the tributaries of the Thames in Coventry, forty miles from the sea.

I would mention that in Rhode Island, also, it entered at

Westerly, and passed through the State to the northeast, leaving the southeast and northwest portions unaffected.

CLASSIFICATION.

The following table shows the towns affected by malarial diseases, grouped according to the years when the present epidemic first appeared:

1860. Southport.

1861. Fairfield, Milford, Orange.

1862. Darien, Bridgeport, Hamden Plains.

1863. Mt. Carmel, Centerville.

1864. Hamden, New Haven.

1865. The western border of North Haven and Wallingford, southeast corner of Cheshire, South Meriden.

1866. Woodbridge and East Haven.

1867. South Norwalk, Cheshire.

1868. Norwalk, Derby, North Haven.

1869. Wallingford, Meriden.

1870. New Canaan, Wilton, Middletown, Portland, Cromwell, Wethersfield.

1871. Stamford, Westport, Huntington, Southington, Berlin, New Britain, Newington, Middlefield, South Glastonbury.

1872. Weston, Seymour, Oxford, Birmingham, Hartford, East Hartford, Haddam, Durham, Rocky Hill.

1873. Easton, Trumbull, Naugatuck, West Hartford, Old Saybrook, Essex.

1874. Ridgefield, Burlington, Watertown, South Manchester, East Haddam.

1875. Greenwich, Beacon Falls, Roxbury, Woodbury, Torrington, Avon, South Windsor, East Windsor, Chatham, Chester, Westbrook.

1876. Southbury, West Oxford, Canton, East Granby, Warehouse Point, Manchester Center, Lyme, Saybrook, Guilford, Madison, Clinton, East Lyme.

1877. Monroe, Newtown, Brookfield, Bridgewater, New Fairfield, New Milford, Kent, Salisbury, Sheffield, Mass., Suffield, Ellington, Coventry, Columbia, Old Lyme, Glastonbury.

. 1878. Greenwich Town, Canaan, North Canaan, Norfolk, and Lenox, Mass., Hartland, Granby, Simsbury, Somers, Willington,

Lebanon, Waterford, Killingworth, and Agawam and Springfield,
Mass.

1879. Cornwall, Bozrah, Montville, Great Barrington, Lanes-
boro, West Springfield, Chicopee, Northampton, Hadley, Hatfield,
Brimfield, Dudley, Mass.

1880. Litchfield, Warren, Goshen, Winchester, Stafford, Tolland, Mansfield, Windham, Sprague, New London. In Massachusetts, Lee, West Stockbridge, North Adams, Southwick, Long
Meadow. In Rhode Island, Westerly, South-East Providence,
Barrington.

1881. Norwich, Thompson. In Massachusetts, Williamstown.
In Rhode Island, fourteen towns.

The general direction taken by the main line of annual progress
in this malarial invasion, will be seen, by reference to the dates on
the map at the head of each successive wave, to be northeast by
north, slightly curving to the left; and this course was pursued
during fifteen years, or until 1875, when it had reached the town
of Windsor on the Connecticut. After that time, the radiation, or
lateral spread of the disease, became more decided, covering finally,
nearly every town in this State, passing the line of Massachusetts,
at Agawam, in 1878. In the next four years it had attacked all
the towns in Western Massachusetts and a few scattered over the
eastern part of that State, and, invaded Vermont and New Hampshire, as well as Rhode Island.

Or, to be more definite: The epidemic approached New England,
through this State from the south, and first touched the shore, in
two places, at about the same time, or within a year, the first being
in the southern part of Fairfield and the second in Darien, from
neither of which did it spread to any considerable extent, but
gradually increased in intensity, as it usually has done, in the different towns, since that time.

The third point was in Milford in 1861, whence it extended
over a great part of the State, reaching Orange the same year, and
Hamden Plains in 1863, Mount Carmel in 1864, and New Haven
later the same season.

In 1865 it passed the village of Quinnipiac, the eastern border
of Cheshire, and the western part of North Haven and Wallingford, to South Meriden, where it crossed the Quinnipiac river.
In 1866 it appeared at Morris Cove in East Haven, and at Wood-

bridge. During the next three years its advance was slow but steady, reaching Branford, the villages of North Haven, Walling-ford, and the southwestern quarter of the city and town of Meriden in 1869; in 1870, the northwestern part of Meriden, and crossed the mountains to Middletown, Cromwell, Portland, and Wethers-field. In 1871 it passed to Berlin, New Britain, Southington, Newington, South Glastonbury, and Middlefield; in 1872, north to Hartford, East Hartford, Rocky Hill, and south to Haddam. In 1873 it advanced to West Hartford, on the north, Easton and Trumbull, on the west, and made a skip to Old Saybrook and Essex on the east, the towns between Branford and Essex not being affected until 1876-8. In 1875 it reached Windsor and spread laterally, involving many towns north and west. 1876 added a few towns to round out the concentric lines—Guilford, Madison, Clinton, Saybrook, Lyme, East Lyme, Canton, East Gran-by, and Warehouse Point. 1877 was remarkable for the number of towns attacked, although the progress was not much greater than before, but, extending eastwardly along the whole line from the seaboard to Massachusetts, it took in Old Lyme, Hebron, Columbia, Coventry, Ellington, and Suffield.

On the west, a similar wave included every town in the Housa-tonic valley, from Monroe to Sheffield.

1878 completed the width of the State, and added Agawam and Springfield, as well as the noted town of Lenox, Mass., and a tier of eastern towns, between Somers and Waterford.

In 1879-80 it made the usual advance in all directions except the west, which was already under its influence, finished the Litch field region, and the journey to the State of Rhode Island, where three towns were first included in the reports. So also were all the towns in the four western counties of Massachusetts, and a few scattering ones farther east.

In 1881 it invaded anew the States of Vermont and New Hampshire, and more than half the towns in Rhode Island.

Among the important exceptions to the general movement, now described, was the outbreak in Danbury, Bethel, and part of New-town, in 1865, twelve years before the main line reached them, and Sherman the previous year, 1876.

This region adjoins Westchester County, New York, where ague is perennial, and may have received its impulse from that direction. In fact, it seems very natural to include the whole

Housátonic valley above Trumbull, in a southwesterly wave from the neighboring State. Our information regarding the movement from that direction, though meager, strengthens the idea of a north-easterly movement similar to that in central Connècticut. the same year, which reached from Old Lyme to Suffield.

There may be a question, also, whether the Litchfield region re-ceived its ague from the east or west. Colchester and Enfield may be included in the exceptions.

In reference to the source from which the ague reached us, it will be seen that its main line of progress, as has been said, is a slight curve northeast and southwest. Now by following it back-ward we naturally reach that part of Long Island where ague was rife from 1850–60, and continuing the course it carries us to New Jersey. The same rule would apply to the wave in western Con-necticut.

In conclusion, it appears that New England is now suffering from an epidemic of intermittent, which has moved from the first, and is still moving, northeasterly, with an irregular front, continuous in time, but sometimes interrupted in manner.

It is not too much to suppose, that it came over from Long Island and New Jersey, and possibly further south, as well as from the same region over Westchester County; that its front ex-tends from the Hudson on the west, to Buzzard's Bay on the east; that it has moved a hundred miles north and east, and still reaches out its favors to those belated northmen and down-easters, who have hitherto mocked us.

MICROSCOPICAL EXAMINATION

OF

POTABLE WATERS

IN THE

State of Connecticut.

BY

WILLIAM J. LEWIS, M.D.

MICROSCOPICAL EXAMINATION OF POTABLE WATERS IN THE STATE OF CONNECTICUT.

Of the many interesting subjects open to the professional sanitarian for original investigation, none assume a greater importance than the relations of potable water to health and disease. It has long been known that contaminated drinking water, when taken into the human system, is capable of producing serious and oftentimes fatal diseases. Those who believe in the germ theory consider the active principle of contagion to consist of minute organisms, or germs transmittible from one person to another, and capable of reproducing, under favorable circumstances, the specific disease from which it derived its being. For instance, the excreta from a person suffering from typhoid fever may be thrown where it percolates its way into a well or stream, and parties using this water for drinking purposes may come down with the same disease, though living miles away from the source of contamination, while others residing in the immediate vicinity, but depending upon another water supply, are unaffected. In such a case it is evident the disease germs have been transmitted through the medium of drinking water. Exactly what the germs are has not yet been satisfactorily demonstrated, and it is largely due to our want of knowledge on this subject that so much useless alarm has been caused to the general public through articles published in our newspapers and popular periodicals of the day. To illustrate this: A few years ago a case occurred in the upper part of New York city, where a woman was suffering from "snakes in the abdomen." She assigned the origin of her strange malady to a clear spring of water from which she had drunk freely while at a picnic. Some embryo scientist procured a specimen of this water, and after submitting it to examination under his compound microscope, announced to the public that there were worms of a peculiar kind in the water, some of which having been swallowed by the patient in question, undoubtedly had grown to an enormous size, and taken up their permanent abode in the woman's abdomen. From this time on daily reports of the case were published in the city papers, and the possible consequences of swallowing microscopic and visible animals were discussed by the newspaper writers. Many original and startling theories were advanced, experimented on; and proven to the satisfaction of the originators. As the snake-eater, as she was familiarly called, showed signs of early dis solution, or, as her doctor announced, "the snakes were getting the best of her,". the *denouement* was awaited with interest. At her death a post mortem examination was held, though strongly opposed by the family physician, and the result, as announced to the Board of Health, was death from general tuberculosis.

In the summer of 1881 a statement was published in one of our Hartford. papers that the cause of the bad taste and odor then existing in Hartford water was the decay of fresh water shrimp, with which the water, and consequently the city pipes, were filled. The precise object which was thus designated as the "shrimp" escaped my observation, although I was making a careful examination of the water at the time.

In the use of the microscope it may well be said a little knowledge is a dangerous thing. A tyro, viewing for the first time a *Cyclops quadricornus* enlarged a hundred diameters, sees a most formidable animal, and may rush into print, giving an alarming account of his discovery. Yet water containing them in large numbers may be drunk with perfect impunity, as the people of Bridgeport can testify.

There are, however, certain forms of animal life found in drinking water which may produce serious mischief, such as certain forms of minute leeches, which have been observed more commonly in the waters of tropical countries. Trichinosis has been transmitted to the human subject, in a number of instances, in consequence of drinking water from streams upon the banks of which were located slaughter-houses. Though these are rare cases, yet they are worthy of note, as showing the care which should be exercised in collecting and storing a large supply of water for drinking purposes.

The water supplies of most of our large New England towns and cities derive their sources from small streams and springs, combined with the surface drainage immediately surrounding the reservoirs or places of storage. The dangers from contamination in water collected in this way are two-fold. In the first place there is always danger of sewage from small streams, if running through inhabited districts, and the same difficulty arises with surface shed water. This is a real and never-failing source of danger. Where there are people there must of necessity be more or less sewage, and also, though independent of it, more or less disease ; and if a case of an infectious nature arises, and the excrement be thrown into, or it in any way enters the water used for drinking purposes, that water, as has been demonstrated time and again, is absolutely dangerous to life, though in appearance it be as clear as crystal and refreshing as a mountain spring. Even with our present knowledge it is fair to say that fully one-half the cases of typhoid fever are caused by drinking water contaminated with the germs of this disease. Dr. M. C. Furnell, Sanitary Commissioner for Madras, believes that water is the chief means by which cholera is spread in India. There is no country in the world subject to such frequent cholera epidemics as India ; nor is this to be wondered at when we know that the reservoirs or "tanks" are used for public bathing and clothes-washing, as well as to supply water for cooking and drinking purposes !

To illustrate how a small amount of diseased sewage may cause incalculable mischief, I will quote the famous Broad street case, as given by Dr. Furnell in a recent lecture delivered to the people of Madras, India.*

" Here, in 1854, the people of a well-to-do and otherwise healthy district suffered immensely from cholera. This led to a minute inquiry into the surrounding circumstances, and it was discovered that a child who had been ill with cholera, died at No. 40 Broad street, and that its excreta had been emptied into a cess-pool situated only three feet from the well of the public pump in Broad street, from which most of the surrounding people took their water. It was further discovered that the bricks of the cess-pool were loose and allowed its contents to drain into the pump well. In one day 140 to 150 people were attacked, and it was discovered, on investigation, that nearly all the persons who had the malady during the first few days of the outbreak drank the water from the pump. When the pump was closed to public use the epidemic subsided, but the most curious case connected with it is this:

---

* Water, and its connection with Public Health. A lecture delivered at Pacheappa's Hall on 1st April, 1882, by M. C. Furnell, M D., F. R. C. S., Madras, 1882.

28

There occurred at West End, Hampstead, many miles away from Broad street, a single case of cholera which proved fatal, in the person of a woman aged fifty-nine years. Now this woman had formerly lived in Broad street, but had not been there for many months. *But mark this*, a cart went from Broad street to West End every day, taking out, amongst other things, a large bottle of water filled from the pump in Broad street, because the lady in question liked this water; she had drunk it all her life, and preferred it to all others. A niece who was on a visit to this lady also drank this water. She returned to her residence in a high and healthy part of Islington, was attacked with cholera and died. There was no cholera at the time either at the West End or in the neighborhood."

The second source of contamination in ponded water is the growth of vegetable and animal life, mostly of the minuter forms, and which at times imparts to it a disagreeable odor and taste. It is with these minuter forms of life found existing in the potable waters of Connecticut, and their significance in the water and effect on public health, that we have principally to deal in this paper.

The methods employed in examining water are two—chemical and microscopical—each incomplete in itself. With the microscope we can determine the structure of the lower organisms, study their habits, methods of propagation, and full natural history from their origin to death, and through the stages of decay. We can, in many instances, determine the source from which a given sample of water was procured, whether from a well, mineral spring, river, brook, ditch, or bog, by microscopical examination of its sediment, and determine, with a fair degree of accuracy, whether or not it is fit for drinking purposes. But to ascertain the *action* of various substances on the water, the changes they produce in its composition, we must call chemistry to our aid. It is only by the aid of systematic microscopical and chemical research combined, and extending over a period of years, that we may expect to satisfactorily solve the many problems now exercising the minds of professional sanitarians in this connection. The present paper will be confined to the report of a systematic microscopical examination made during the summer and fall of 1882, for the purpose, chiefly, of ascertaining the cause or causes of certain obnoxious odors and tastes prevailing at irregular intervals in impounded waters throughout the State.

BRIDGEPORT.

The water supply of this city, we are informed, is derived from several small ponds in a swampy piece of woodland, with hilly ground near. The bottom of the ponds is a black peat, with bog-grass at the margin, in some instances. Nothing has been done to properly prepare the beds of the ponds, nor do we learn that any pains have been taken to remove the leafy deposits, or the sediment of drift materials, that exist in some localities to quite an extent. The water flows from one pond to another in its course. The ponds are very much alike in formation; some embanking and a little excavating has been done to form some of them, but natural configuration of the land was the main reliance. In its course from one pond to another, the water flows through "shoddy pipes," so called,—that is, sheet iron pipe, lined and covered with cement,—and is conveyed in the same manner to the distributing reservoir. The water usually flows in a steady stream, larger or smaller, as the case may be. Some portion of this pipe has been replaced by the cast-iron pipe commonly used for mains. The reservoir is divided into two parts, the first of which is intended for a settling-reservoir, while from the second the distribution is made. There is no attempt at filtration. As this supply is not adequate, water is pumped from a lake near by, having a swampy margin. In dry seasons the ponds in the woods are drawn very low, and then the main reliance is upon water pumped from the lake.

Many of the people of Bridgeport have complained of the water furnished by that city for domestic purposes, as being at times bad tasting, and turbid in appearance. In July last samples of this water were furnished me, some taken from reservoirs, mains, flushing hydrants, and some drawn from faucets in private houses. All these specimens contained a great excess of both animal and vegetable forms of microscopic life. The samples taken from houses showed a larger proportion of organic matter than those taken from reservoirs, and it may be said here that this is almost a universal rule. At the time this examination was made, July 21st, this water could hardly be considered fit for drinking purposes. Filled with the *Cyclops quadricornus, Canthocamptus minu-tus*, and other *Copepoda*, themselves visible in a strong light to the unaided eye; teeming with the *Anguillula fluviatilis*, visible as thread-like worms; containing specimens of the *Annelida, Vorticel-lina*, etc., to say nothing of the various forms of vegetable life, it resembled very dilute ditch water. None of these animals are directly injurious to health, and they are formidable only in name. Their significance lies in the fact that they are what might be called scavengers, and exist in large numbers only in impure water. The inorganic matter in this water was not in excess, and consisted mostly of silica and carbonate of lime. The forms of vegetable life most prevalent were the *Chaetophoraceae, Conferva-ceae, Zygnemaceae*, and *Diatomaceae*. Fortunately representatives of the *Nostochaceae*, though by no means wanting, were not numerous.

It is easy to see that it would be difficult to assign a bad taste or smell to any one special ingredient of this water. The sediment, in samples of water drawn from the pipes, contained a considerable deposit of decaying animal and vegetable matter, while in that taken from the reservoir these forms of life were in a comparatively healthy condition. So far as known there was at this date nothing in this water of a positively injurious nature, though if drunk to excess it would be prone to produce irritative diarrhea, because of the large amount of decaying matter it contained. The difficulty could be obviated in a measure by thoroughly boiling and filtering the water prior to use.

NEW LONDON.

Lake Konomoc, which is the retaining and distributing reservoir supplying the New London water works, is a natural pond, enlarged by a dam constructed about ten years ago, with a storage capacity of 600,000,000 gallons, and an area of about 230 acres. It has comparatively little shallow water, there being a general depth of some twelve feet or more, while in some places it is forty-five to fifty feet deep. The bottom of the lake is mainly a deposit of sand and gravel, and its water-shed appears favorable for the purpose, both in formation and configuration.

An examination of the water supplied by this city was made August 21st. Two samples were furnished in glass bottles containing 500 c.c. each. This water was clear, without odor, and contained a small deposit. Sample number one, taken from a main, contained beautiful specimens of *Rotifera*, mostly the *Rotifer vulgaris* in active motion; fragments of *Chaetophora elegans;* *Chydorus sphaericus;* spiculae of the *Spongilla fluviatilis* ; grass pollen, also pollen from water lily. A few scales from butterflies' wings were also present. The quantity of organic matter was minute, and not in excess of the inorganic.

Sample number two was taken from lake Konomoc at the surface, near the effluent pipes. This sample contained several types of the *Diatomaceae*, mostly *Astrionlèla formosa ; Vorticella nebulifera* (active), tops of *Chaetophora elegans*, and numerous cells of Protophytes and escaped endochrome.

This second sample does not give a fair estimate of the quality of water contained in the lake, as a comparison with sample one, taken from a main, will show. This water as a whole is good, and much better than the average supplied to the cities and villages in Connecticut.

NEW HAVEN.

A small stream called Mill river, taking its rise in the Cheshire hills, is the source of Whitney-lake, which constitutes one of the principal water supplies of this city. A description of the formation of this lake is furnished by Prof. Bronson in his historical account of intermittent fever in the New Haven region, from which we make the following extract : " In the spring of 1860 the New Haven Water Company began, and in December, 1861, completed their works for supplying New Haven with water from Mill river. They constructed a dam thirty feet high, with water-wheels, forcing-pumps, etc., at Whitneyville, two miles north-northeast of the public square, on a site which had long been improved, the new dam taking the place of an old one eight feet high. In this way a deep, narrow pond, two miles long, called Lake Whitney, was formed, the water flowing back and submerging two mill privileges higher up the stream. Owing to the general deep banks, not much new ground, or ground not covered by the three old ponds, was flooded. In all, however, there were several acres, mostly at the upper end of the lake and at the mouth of Pine-marsh creek, (a small stream, with low, marshy, and peaty margins, coming from the southwest and south, two miles long,) up which the water flowed many rods. The stumps, roots, grass, turf, and vegetable debris on the land thus newly-covered were not removed. · . . . . The summer of 1869 was drier than any known for many years, the usual rains having been withheld till late in autumn. The water in Lake Whitney fell four feet below the top of the dam, and many acres were laid bare near the upper end. In the course of this year the water company, desiring to increase the power of their pumps, raised their dam four feet and eight inches. The work was completed in September, 1869, the capacity of the lake increased 59,000,000 gallons, and its whole area augmented to one hundred and· thirty acres. This done, the water set back up the valley nearly two and a half miles, spreading out above and below Pine-marsh creek, covering deeply the places which were before shallow, and submerging a wide margin outside the previous shore line. In addition to this, the valley ·of the creek, including the broad tract called Pine-marsh swamp, abounding, as it did, in peat bogs, coarse grass, roots, decaying leaves, and standing bushes, was inundated, more or less completely; for more than a mile, and to the extent, probably, of fifty miles. As but little shed-water flows into the valley to increase the supply derived from springs, this level is not much affected by rains."

A second source of supply is from Wintergreen lake, which is a natural pond, enlarged by a dam constructed in 1864 by the New Haven Water Company, and is fed mainly by springs, but also has a small water-shed of uncultivated land. Some sixty acres of swamp, meadow and wood land, with the usual living and decaying vegetable growths thereon, were flowed in the formation of this lake.

The waters from Whitney and Wintergreen lakes mix in the mains, there being no separate supply from either source.

Of water from this city four specimens were furnished in bottles containing each 900 c.c., and an examination was made August 22d.

Sample number one, taken from Wintergreen lake, had a slightly offensive odor after being exposed in a warm laboratory some hours. It contained long filaments of decaying algae of various types, horny parts of water and land insects, and many of the *Nostochaceae* in a state of semi-decomposition, and was swarming with Bacteria. The inorganic was largely in excess of the organic matter. While the quality of this water could certainly be improved upon, it is not seriously objectionable for potable purposes.

Sample number two, taken from Whitney lake, contained a few specimens of the *Cyclops quadricornus*, a small amount of amorphous granular matter, while a large proportion of the solid ingredients consisted of inorganic matter. The inorganic matter consisted almost entirely of the silica deposits of plant life. Judging from these two samples the water in Whitney lake is much purer than that in Wintergreen lake, though the solid ingredients are about equal, by volume, in both, and much greater by weight in the latter.

Sample number three was labeled "from a well much used," and contained types of the *Diatomaceae* and *Desmidiaecae* in small numbers, cells of *Protoccocus*, and granular inorganic matter, consisting mostly of minute granules of carbonate of lime. The deposit in this water, though taken from 900 c.c., was scarcely visible to the unaided eye. If the chemical constituents of this water are what they should be, and there is nothing microscopically to show they are not, it is a first-class drinking water in every respect.

Sample number four, drawn from a faucet, contained much more deposit than those taken from Wintergreen and Whitney lakes. Deposit consisted of amorphous granular matter, disintegrating algae, and a considerable amount of silica of the same form as mentioned in sample number two. Byrotulate spiculae from *Spongilla fluv.* were numerous. A specimen of the *Arachnida* in the form of *Macrobiotus Hufelandii* was found. The *Rotifera* were well represented, mostly by the *Rotifer vulgaris* and *Brach ionus amphiceros.*

At the date of this examination, New Haven water in quality was well up to its average; by no means so bad as it has been or will in all probability be again.

Water from a Pump on New Haven Green.—A sample of this water examined October 9th, showed it to be the purest drinking water of any of the Connecticut waters examined by me during the present year. It was perfectly free from odor, taste or color, and the sediment from 900 c.c. invisible to the unaided eye. The sample furnished for examination contained of the *Entomostraca* a *Pleuroxus trigonellus,* a little amorphous inorganic granular matter,

Chydorus sphericus, and minute fragments of carbonate of lime. This is unusually pure well water.

NORWALK.

A clear and concise description of this water supply, furnished me by Mr. W. C. Burke, Jr., at the same time specimens of the water were provided for examination, I will introduce in his own words:

"The water supply for the Borough of Norwalk and the city of South Norwalk is derived from different sources, although in the same neighborhood, being only about two miles apart. That for the Borough of Norwalk is taken from the west branch of the Norwalk river, about six and one-tenth miles from the distributing reservoir located on the hill west of the town. This stream in dry seasons as now (August 15, 1882), becomes almost if not entirely dry. The storage reservoir is made by a dam about twenty (?) rods wide; the banks are of gravel, the water sets back about one mile and is of pretty uniform width; from here it is carried to the distributing reservoir through composition pipes, *i. e.*, sheet iron encased and lined by water lime, and also distributed through pipes of same. (Norwalk storage reservoir, twenty-six acres area.)

"South Norwalk derives her supply from a small brook on high ground east of Norwalk reservoir, dry or nearly so during the latter half of June, July, August, and September. The storage reservoir of seventeen acres, holding about 250,000 gallons of water, has a pretty uniform depth of twenty-nine feet when full. The banks are of rock except for a short distance, when they are of gravel. The banks are very precipitous. From here the water is drawn off in the old bed of the brook, the banks of which are alluvial and gravel about equally divided. Water runs through this bed to the distributing reservoir one and a half miles distant. This is small, about fifteen feet deep when full; banks are gravel principally, although there is considerable alluvial deposit around margins. This reservoir, in my opinion, is not what it should be. But it is now proposed to build a sand dam shutting off a small portion immediately around mouths of pipes to act as a filter. At present, all water is drawn directly into pipes through a charcoal and sponge filter, from thence to town about seven miles through iron pipes. The storage reservoir is certainly one of the finest in the State. The care of the pipes in the town is by no means what it should be. The flushing of them is done at irregu- ler periods, too long apart, and even then it is very doubtful if it is so done as to do much more than to stir up sediment. . . . "

The examination of Norwalk water was made August 23d, from five samples furnished in bottles, containing each 475 c.c.

Sample number one, taken from the storage reservoir, contained a granular epithelial cell, disintegrating algae of various types and in various stages of decomposition, a few of the *Cyclops quad- ricornus*, and the *Grammarus pulex*, in considerable numbers. The vegetable matter was largely in excess of what it should be to constitute good drinking water. The entire deposit was, in all respects, what is usually found in ponded water when the reservoir is made by damming a stream and forcing the water to flood its banks, these being pretty generally of loam.

Sample number two, taken from the distributing reservoir, did not differ essentially from that from the storage reservoir.

Sample number three was taken from flushing a fire hydrant on one of the largest mains, and of course could not be expected to furnish any idea of the quality of water in general use. It con- tained a very large amount of decaying organic matter, and indeed it was difficult to detect portions of plant life sufficiently preserved to determine their classification. It is unnecessary to say that this sample would be condemned at once for any potable or culi- nary purposes. •

Sample number four, taken from a faucet connected with large main, contained more solid ingredients than samples from either reservoir. They consisted mostly of a flocculent precipitate of decaying masses of the *Confervoideae*, swarming with bacteria.

Sample number five, washings from filter house hydrant, con- tained *Cyclops quadricornus*, *Rotifera* of various types, spiculae of *Spongilla fluv.*, grass pollen, and many forms of *Confervoideae*.

From this examination it will be seen there is room for great improvement in the quality of Norwalk water. The organic mat- ter contained therein is in excess of what might be called its normal standard. The presence of a human epithelial cell in sam- ple number one leads us to suspect that at times this water may become contaminated to a dangerous extent.

29

SOUTH NORWALK.*

Six samples of South Norwalk water were furnished in bottles, each containing 475 c.c. Nearly all animal matter, both Protozoa and the higher orders, was in a decaying condition. It may be accounted for by the fact that the samples were collected some two weeks before they were received for analysis. The examination was made August 26, 1882.

Sample number one, taken from the stream connecting the storage with the distributing reservoir, contained a moderate deposit consisting mainly of *Confervoideae,* many of which were of the *Nostochaceae.*

Sample number two, taken from distributing reservoir at a time when the water was very low. This contained a heavier deposit than found in sample number one, though not excessive, and consisted of *Desmidiaceae, Diatomaceae, Branchionus amphiceros* (several), claws and antennae of various microscopical water and land insects, in addition to the plants found in sample number one.

Sample number three, taken from the large storage reservoir, had less deposit than either of the preceding samples. It was composed of algae in partial decomposition, and a small earthy deposit of sand and carbonate of lime.

Sample number four, taken from the brook supply for South Norwalk, contained various forms of *Infusoria,* and minute plant life with very little inorganic matter.

Sample number five, taken from a faucet at a private residence, contained considerable deposit, consisting of cells of *Protophytes, Rotifera,* mostly *Branchionus amphiceros,* and decomposing algae mixed with sand. This sample contained too heavy a deposit of decaying organic matter to constitute even a tolerable drinking water.

Sample number six, taken from the flushing of a hydrant on a by-street, that had not been opened for several months, contained, besides a large amount of amorphous granular matter, a considerable number of *Spongilla fluv.* spiculae. The odor of this water was strong and offensive. Decomposition of the organic matter had taken place to such an extent as to render it impossible even to distinguish the animal from the vegetable organisms.

---

* For a description of South Norwalk water supply see preceding report on Norwalk water.

This water, if freed from the excessive amount of decaying organic matter, ought to be of good quality. This can be done only by some proper method of filtration. The filter at present used, containing sponges and charcoal, should be abolished at once. When sponges enter into the composition of filters, the very method used to purify the water tends to contaminate it by holding the plant and animal life caught in the meshes, which not only have no purifying properties, but instead promote decay and rapid disintegration.

NORWICH.

In an article upon the water supply of this city, Prof. Silliman furnishes the following description of its source: "The reservoir is a natural lake formed by a dam built across a ravine between two hills of chrystalline rocks of the granite family, situated about two-and-a-half miles northwest of your city, and draining both into the Yantic and Shetucket rivers. This situation fortunately permits the excess of water, in times of flood, to escape in the direction away from your distributing outlet, thus giving no occasion to provide for an overflow in the direction of your mains. The margin of the reservoir is quite clean, and free from any causes of impurity. The water-shed discharging into this reservoir is largely in grass or upland mowing ground, with some woods and orchards, with but few houses or farm buildings on the slopes (1873); consequently no sewage or water contaminated with animal matter finds its way into your reservoir. An excellent *dry wall* more than two miles in circuit encloses the reservoir and shuts off, to a great extent, the shallow margins. * * * * * This wall is pierced at intervals with frequent openings for the admission of the water collected during the rains and winter snows from the surrounding hills. The northern end of the reservoir alone shows shallow water to any noticeable extent. The bottom was prepared for flowage by removing twenty thousand stumps of trees, the entire bed of the land cleaned over, and all soil containing roots removed—three hundred thousand cart loads removed. Average depth, over sixteen feet; at lower end near well house, over thirty feet (stated). The maximum capacity said to be three hundred and sixty million (U. S. standard) gallons."

Examination of Norwich water, made August 25th, from two samples furnished in bottles, each containing 900 c.c.

Sample number one, drawn from a faucet, had a very light sediment. It contained silica spiculae of the *Spongilla fluviatilis*. Specimens of *Volvox globator*, *Diatomaceae*, and *Desmidiaceae*, were found. Carbonate of lime and small particles of sand were present.

Sample number two, taken from the reservoir, contained only bodies foreign to the water, namely, scales of insects, grass pollen, particles of bark, and small wood fibers. This deposit was invisible to the naked eye.

If the samples furnished for examination were fair specimens, the Norwich water is one of the best in the State.

NEW BRITAIN.

This city derives its supply from Shuttle Meadow Lake, from which the water is received into a distributing reservoir on a hill overlooking the city. No process of filtration is attempted.

There has been much complaint during the past summer of the condition of water furnished in New Britain. At the time this examination was made, November 4th, the water in Shuttle Meadow lake was of a dull bluish green color, and a distinct odor was observed on the leeward side of the lake. This odor is said to have been very strong during the hot weather of July and August, and water drawn from the pipes in the city was decidedly offensive to both taste and smell. A bottle of this water viewed by transmitted light, showed it to be filled with granular particles which gave to it its peculiar color. Water drawn from a faucet in the railway passenger depot had the same appearance. These granular particles must have been of about the same specific gravity as the water, for they neither rose nor sank in a jar of it which stood in a cool place for nearly a week, but remained equally diffused throughout its entire volume. From the immense amount of these minute particles, both in the lake and city water, it seemed as though they must be accountable, at least to some extent, for the bad odor and taste prevailing during the hot weather preceding.

A microscopical examination of this sediment, or rather ingredient, showed it to consist entirely of plant life belonging to the *Nostochaceae*. There were immense numbers of spores entangled with partly decayed portions of the growth, in a condition in which one would expect to find these algae at this season of the year. None of the *Spongilla fluv.* were observed on the shores of

Shuttle Meadow lake, and no traces of it seen on microscopical examination. In this instance the only thing found capable of imparting a bad odor and taste was this abundant growth of Nostocs.

The city of Hartford is supplied with impounded water collected chiefly from natural surface drainage, which is retained in three storage reservoirs. The largest supply is drawn from reservoir No. 2, or the "new reservoir," which was built by damming what is known as the Cadwell basin. This reservoir receives its water almost exclusively from Dead Swamp, and from the natural surface drainage of the surrounding high lands. Located on the north bank, within a few feet of the water, is a large barn and barnyard, the entire surface of which must be thoroughly washed into the reservoir by every heavy shower. The shores are shallow and marshy, except the northeast end, which is formed by the dam. Water from this reservoir is conducted to the West Hartford distributing reservoir, partly through a large pipe and partly through an open brook. Reservoirs No. 1 and No. 3 are formed by damming natural basins, and receive their water from surface drainage, brooks, and springs. The water from these is conducted through open brooks to the distributing reservoir. The supply of water in the three storage reservoirs on the 1st day of March, 1882, as stated in the report of the Board of Water Commissioners of that date, was 1,026,000,000 gallons, which, with the water in the distributing reservoir, gave a total supply of 1,111,000,000 gallons.

An examination of the water supplied to this city was made November 28th, the samples used having been taken from the distributing reservoir. Sample number one was the purest water obtainable for examination from the distributing reservoir, and in appearance was much clearer than that near the gate house. It contained more sediment than should be found in good drinking water. The sediment was composed of various foreign substances, such as grass pollen, and portions of land insects, together with considerable decaying vegetable matter. Numerous members of the *Rotifera* were present, the most common being the *Branchionus amphiceros*. The organic matter was far in excess of the inorganic.

Sample number two, was taken from the shores of the large storage reservoir, No. 2, and is a fair specimen of all its shore water with the exception of that by the dam. This sample differed in no material respect from any other stagnant bog water. Filled with the lower animal organisms, and all manner of vegetable growths capable of imparting an obnoxious odor and taste to the water, it only needed a hot July and August sun to render it absolutely injurious to health, if used for drinking. None of the bright green algae found in almost all pure drinking water were seen; indeed, they cannot long exist in stagnant, marshy places. This impure water, as already stated, is to be found only along the shore, where the water is very shallow. Fortunately, the reservoir is of great capacity, and its large body of water is of good quality, so that the swampy water of its shores becomes sufficiently diluted, before being used, to render it no longer disagreeable. At certain periods however, when the meteorological influences have been especially favorable to the rapid development of the organisms above mentioned, and a fair collection of them becomes stored away in the city's pipes, then there necessarily must be a recurrence of the odors and tastes which heretofore have rendered this water so very unpalatable.

Old Well in City Hall Grounds, corner of State and Main Streets.—An examination of this water made November 17th, showed it to be of good quality. It contained but little sediment, and this was composed mostly of inorganic matter, such as particles of silica, carbonate of lime, and a minute quantity of iron rust. The organic matter consisted mostly of single cells of unicellular plants. No animal life found in the specimens examined.

In a review of the preceding examinations, there are a few points worthy of special note. It will be observed that water drawn from faucets in the cities always contains a larger proportion of sediment than samples taken from reservoirs, and that this sediment, when composed largely of microscopic plants, is almost always in a more advanced stage of decomposition.

So much has been said and written upon the power of the fresh water sponge, or *Spongilla fluviatilis*, to contaminate drinking water, and render its taste and smell obnoxious, since its relation to the potable water supplied to the city of Boston was first pointed out by Prof. Ira Remson, in his report on the condition of Boston water in November, 1881, that it may be well to mention here that spiculae of this sponge not unfrequently occur in considerable numbers·in water free from smell and taste, and again are absent in⁻ potable waters most foul. In the case of Bridgeport water, although particles of the sponge are found, there was a sufficient amount of other organic matter, which, in an advanced stage of decomposition, would render it unfit for drinking. Fortunately the Bridgeport aquarium seems to be in a favorable condition to promote and sustain the animal life therein, so that the people of that city are enabled to swallow the inhabitants alive, in which state the stomach is not so quick to rebel. In New Britain, where the water has had a bad smell and taste all summer, no traces of sponge could be found, though. that does not preclude the ·possibility of its being present.⁻ The contamination here seems to have been caused entirely by an abundant growth of *Nostocs.* That the *Spongilla fluv.*, in a state of decay, does in some cases produce a decided odor in the water cannot be doubted, but from microscopical and chemical analyses made, from time to time, of impounded waters throughout the country, it is evident that no one cause for the disagreeable odors and tastes prevailing at irregular· intervals can be assigned, which will be applicable in all cases.

The question of a wholesome water supply is a most serious one, and cannot be overlooked without detriment to the general public health. At present we have much to learn before we can arrive at any satisfactory remedy for this evil of impure water. A great many observations are now being made in this connection, and theories advanced and plans devised for an alleviation of the trouble. Some good already has been accomplished, and we hope for more to follow. But much scientific investigation and energy is being thrown to waste for the want of a uniform system to work by. Probably no satisfactory means can be arrived at for the purification of all potable waters, applicable to all cases where a bad odor and taste exist, without a more complete knowledge of the effect upon the water of the different organisms found therein, and a fuller knowledge of their natural history and causes which promote their growth. I would strongly recommend that a systematic research be made into the condition of the waters of some half dozen cities in Connecticut, somewhat after the following plan: 1st. The examinations to extend over a period of *at least* five years, and to be conducted during this period, so far as practicable, by the same parties. 2d. The examinations to be made of impounded water taken from several cities or towns, and to consist of at least two samples taken, one from the main reservoir, and the other from some faucet in the city or town; two such samples taken from each of the chosen cities or towns to be provided for examination every month during April, May, June, July, August, and September; a careful local daily record of the temperature and state of the weather and condition of water, including rain-fall, to be kept. The examination of water to be as follows: the amount, by weight, of the solid ingredients of the water, and the relative proportion of organic to inorganic matter. A chemical examination for free and albuminoid ammonia might be deemed advisable. A thorough microscopical examination into the nature of the solid constituents to be made, and the results faithfully noted.

With some such uniform plan of carefully recorded observations to enable a comparison of the condition of various waters, one year with another, we may reasonably hope to have our efforts crowned with success.

MILK

AS A

MEDIUM FOR THE TRANSMISSION OF DISEASE.

By C. W. CHAMBERLAIN, M. D.,

SECRETARY OF THE BOARD.

30

ON MILK AS A MEDIUM FOR THE TRANSMISSION OF DISEASE.

The possibility of transmitting disease by different articles of food is so thoroughly proven by the results of carefully conducted investigations and well observed facts, that it is no longer doubted by physicians generally. This transmission may take place from infection of articles of food by the virus of disease, or from diseases of animals whose flesh is used for food that are communicable to mankind. The fact that diseases can be thus transmitted has not long been established, nor have we as yet so definite a knowledge concerning the second method, nor so clear proofs on all points as could be desired. Still, in proportion to the time that has elapsed since the enunciation of the belief of such transmission, as much progress in the way of demonstration has been made as could be expected. The subject to be discussed, however, comes under the first division—the transmission of diseases by infection of articles of food, and especially milk. It is not intended to discuss the adulterations of milk except incidentally, as the transmission of typhoid fever, for instance, by adding to the milk water that had been polluted by drainage, from the excretions of a typhoid fever patient, nor the diseases induced in infants by the impoverishment of the milk when water is added or the cream partially removed. The principal subject for discussion will be the transmission of infectious or contagious diseases, like typhoid fever, scarlet fever, or diphtheria, by infected milk. Several of the diseases communicable to man have already been discussed in our reports, as the transmission of trichniæ by pork, and tuberculosis by the meat and milk of tuberculous cattle. Others will be considered in turn as the time seems opportune. As Vacher states, considering its liability to be associated as served to the public with another familiar fluid, it becomes probable that there is no food so liable to transmit disease as milk. I am indebted to him for the following excellent summary of the various ways in which it is possible to transmit disease by milk, and also for many valuable facts and suggestions:

1st. The milk may be derived from a cow suffering from the cattle plague, pleuro-pneumonia, splenic fever, or foot and mouth disease. The danger is slight, as the milk is either entirely arrested at an early stage of the diseases, or so changed in its appearance as to preclude its sale. Anthrax may be communicated, and an eruption caused by the milk from animals with foot and mouth diseases, but this would occur only rarely.

2d. The milk may be derived from a tuberculous cow.

3d. Milk may be drawn from an inflamed udder. This when mingled with a large quantity of good milk is oftenest sold. It may, when thus mixed, cause indigestion and diarrhea. As it contains pus, blood, and broken-down tissues, it must be unwholesome. Unmixed, its appearance would preclude its sale.

4th. The milk may have undergone chemical or fermentative changes. This is liable to occur where sour milk and buttermilk are drank, and sold to be drank. The lower forms of life, bacteria and the like, may develop in such milk, and are stated to cause a not very severe form of pharyngitis, or sore throat. I have not seen any report of this as having occurred in this country. If it has the cause has been overlooked. No serious injury to health is stated, but the fact seems to be recognized in England, as it is not mentioned as anything strange or unfamiliar.

5th. The milk may have become infected with the contagium of an animal disease, as the glanders for instance, or the foot and mouth disease.

6th. The milk may have become infected by the contagium of a human disease, which is the particular topic for consideration. The others, with the exception of the transmission of diseases of animals communicable to mankind, such as tuberculosis, are seldom liable to occur, but their enumeration is essential to a complete presentation of the subject, that is, so far as milk may be the agent for conveying disease.

The knowledge on this subject is of recent acquisition, and while the fact is pretty generally known that certain diseases can be thus conveyed, the manner of such transmission is not so well known. Frequently in the medical journals are the notices to be met of the outbreak of typhoid fever from infected milk, but not as often as the occurrence of outbreaks from polluted water. In point of fact, these are due to polluted water secondarily, for it is almost invariably the case where typhoid fever has been conveyed by milk, that the milk has been infected by the addition of water, either innocently or otherwise, that has been polluted by the dejections of some typhoid patient. Where the water is added to adulterate the milk, a practice by far too common in spite of the lactometer, the way of infection is made clear. The innocent method alluded to was the use of such contaminated water to cleanse the utensils by which the milk is collected and distributed. It is proper perhaps to admit the latter method, but the suspicion will recur that in some way or other more of the water got into the milk than is accounted for by the cleaning and rinsing of the pails and pans. The frequency with which outbreaks of typhoid fever were traced to infected milk, led to the suspicion that other diseases might be thus transmitted, and it was not a great while before the spread of diphtheria, scarlet fever and possibly measles and smallpox, were traced to the use of infected milk. The indigestion and diarrheal diseases caused by the adulterated milk sold in cities, especially large cities, to the poor, is due rather to the character of the detestable fluid, or rather compound, itself. It seems a pity that an article so valuable as food, whose restorative powers are so needed by the poor and weak, and the victims of the wasting diseases that so afflict such people, should be so hard to obtain by those that most require the recuperative qualities pure milk possesses.

The milk may become infected by water which is contaminated by the contagium of typhoid fever or other form of disease, but the instances are chiefly from infection by the typhoid excretions; or it may become infected by the absorption of the contaminated atmosphere emanating from a patient sick with scarlet fever, diphtheria, and possibly measles in the family of the farmer or of his assistants, or even by the illness of some of the laborers themselves, though rarely. The chief danger, however, arises from the presence of a case of the disease which is transmitted in the family of the dealer, or of some of his assistants. The closeness which links unsanitary conditions with the spread of disease is here finely illustrated. Were efficient means used in the disposition of filth, and the typhoid dejections properly disinfected and *entirely* removed, so that neither our soil nor drinking water could be polluted by them, typhoid fever could not be transmitted by milk, and were all cases of diphtheria and scarlet fever properly isolated, no danger would remain of the transmission of those diseases by milk. In brief, then, the whole case may be briefly stated as due to ignorance and filth. Negligence, perhaps, should be included, as it is certainly one of the prime agents in the transmission of infectious diseases generally.

The absorptive qualities of milk are well known. Every housewife knows how readily milk, if shut up in a close cupboard with any substance that has a decided odor, will acquire that odor, and even acquire the taste of articles that have a strong and decided flavor under the same circumstances. That it should absorb an infected atmosphere, does not appear at all strange nor unreasonable; in fact it seems strange that such absorption was not earlier recognized and acted upon. The close proximity of wells to drains, privies, and cesspools, has repeatedly been declared to be a source of danger. The water in such wells can hardly be expected under such circumstances to be pure, or even safe for drinking purposes during many months of the year. A series of analyses of the water of such wells taken at random has once or twice been made, with the almost invariable result of finding the water badly polluted by organic matters, the nitrates, chlorides, and albuminoid ammonia were often found in such proportions as to render the water unsafe for use.

When this proximity of the places for the disposal of filth to the wells used to obtain a supply of drinking water, and water for all domestic purposes, is considered in connection with the fact that the dejections of typhoid fever patients contain the contagium of the disease, whatever other ways there may be of causing it, and the vitality of the contagium, the readiness with which such water might be infected is apparent. Now if the water is infected by the contagium of typhoid fever the readiness with which a pollution of milk might occur is as evident. Brooks and springs used for a water supply are generally safer, but there are several instances on record where small streams used as a supply of water have been contaminated with the contagium of typhoid fever from the proximity of garbage heaps upon which had been thrown the dejections from a case of typhoid fever. The length of time that this contagion of typhoid fever retains its vitality also contributes to the liability of contamination of such water. Instances are on record where the contagium of typhoid fever has been conveyed by polluted water for long distances by underground channels. As water is thus liable to become infected by the germs or virus of typhoid fever, which retain their vitality for an indefinite period, for several years at least, and as such water is extremely likely to gain access to the milk in some way, the greater frequency of the communication of typhoid by milk be comes clear. Moreover, the *contagium* of typhoid retains its vitality if stored undisturbed in a heap of filth or in some vault, and if then placed where it is dissolved, or rather carried in water, it is capable of reproducing the disease, so that in towns and villages where there is no sewer system the contagium of typhoid fever not unfrequently gains access to water used for domestic purposes either from some old case or from carelessness in the disposal of the excretions of a recent case and neglect in disinfecting them thoroughly. While it is probable that these cases occur in this country more or less, yet they have been investigated and recorded more clearly in England, where sanitary inspectors are more com- mon than they are in this country. A few instances where the connection has been traced will serve to illustrate the danger of such contamination and the way to prevent its occurrence. Dr. Parsons describes an outbreak of typhoid fever at Bridlington dur- ing the last week of September and first of October 1881. A large number of persons were attacked, especially those living in a certain district; the cases occurred simultaneously or in rapid suc- cession. It was observed that the great majority of the households in which the fever had broken out obtained their milk from a dairy- man residing about a hundred yards from the house in which the first case occurred. The house was in close proximity to the stables, which also had inhabited rooms on three sides of them and over them on the second story. The yard was unpaved, had no slope, nor provisions for drainage. At the time of inspection it was very foul. In this yard was a well eighteen feet deep, sunk in loose gravelly soil and covered only with boards and earth. During the hot weather deep cracks formed in the ground over the well, so that when the rains came foul matters could be the more readily washed into it than before. The well was but a few feet distant from a huge pile of manure from the stables, and two privies with covered shallow vaults were but thirteen feet distant from the well The water, raised by a pump, was used both for dairy purposes and for domestic use, but when it was analyzed it was pronounced to be very badly contaminated by sewage and unfit for use. Three cases of typhoid fever occurred in the early part of October in the house adjoining the dairyman's. It was stated that the water from the well was used to rinse the cans used for the milk only after it had been boiled. Of the eighty-three families supplied there were forty-eight cases of fever undoubted and severe, and only twenty-seven escaped out of the eighty-three houses. The suddenness of the outbreak, its confinement at first to the families supplied from the same source, and the absence apparently of any other satisfactory explanation, and the undoubted pollution of the water of the well, together with the probability of the addition of the specific contagium of typhoid fever, make out a pretty clear case of the conveyance of typhoid fever by infected milk.*

The cases of the conveyance of typhoid fever by infected water are quite frequently recorded in the medical literature of this country, and there would be no difficulty in adding a large number to them from our own experience, but there have not been, as before stated, as yet many cases of disease traced to infected milk in this country, so the proofs must come from the observations of others for the most part. Dr. Ernest Hart, in a paper read recently before the section on State Medicine of the International Medical Congress, gave in a tabular form the particulars of seventy-one recent epidemics due to infected milk, sixty-seven of which have been carefully investigated since 1873, when, with Dr. Murchison, he studied and reported the Marylebone epidemic of typhoid fever that was caused by contaminated milk. There were three diseases included in the table as communicated by infected milk—typhoid fever, scarlet fever, and diphtheria; fifty of the epidemics were of typhoid fever, fourteen of scarlet fever, and seven of diphtheria. The total number of cases that were caused by infected milk in these seventy-one epidemics was stated as 4,800, divided as follows: typhoid fever, 3,500; scarlet fever, 800; diphtheria, 500. As before intimated, the usual manner of infection in typhoid fever is the pollution of well water by soakage from the dejections of typhoid fever patients.

The well-water in the reports from the dairymen is reported as having been used to *wash the milk cans*, but, as Dr. Hart well says, this is too often, it is feared, " a convenient euphemism for the di-

---

* London Sanitary Record, Sept., 1881.

lution of the milk itself; " at least the infection of the milk from the addition of polluted water appears very much more probable.

An epidemic in houses widely separated and provided with superior sanitary appliances was reported at Clapham, England. A milk dealer that obtained his supply from two dairy farms, furnished his customers what he called nursery milk, and ordinary milk, and of course some took both. The typhoid fever was entirely limited to those that took ordinary milk alone. The ordinary milk was supplied from both farms, and both were accordingly inspected. Neither had proper sanitary provisions for a dairy farm. The water from the well of one was found on analysis to be largely contaminated by sewage, and unfit for domestic use for drinking or culinary purposes. About eight yards from the dairy and twelve from the well was a brook which, before it reached the farm, flowed through a large stone sewer. The previous winter there were six cases of typhoid fever in the village above, and the excreta of the last were thrown into a vault that was emptied into this stone sewer. Thus the specific *contagium* of typhoid fever was easily traceable to the milk, and, as in other instances where zymotic diseases are spread by infected milk, the selection of the houses and persons using such milk was very clear.

Thus when several houses on a street have a different milk supply, they escape entirely until the epidemic influence is so strong as to spread the disease independently of the first infection. In two families in the same house, the same has been shown repeatedly, and even, in a few instances, in families where there was a double milk supply, the same exemption is shown in the case of those using the non-infected supply. In the outbreak at the Leicester Infirmary, where there were twelve cases of typhoid fever, all the persons that used milk freely as food in an uncooked state were attacked. The well was found near a leaky cesspool, and analysis showed the water to be largely contaminated by sewage, which probably received the special *contagium* of typhoid, as upon the change of the milk supply the typhoid fever ceased, without any change in the drainage. The Marylebone epidemic has been mentioned, not to multiply instances, which vary only in the clearness with which the infection by the *contagium* of typhoid fever is traced, a brief account of that will close the enumeration of instances of the transmission of typhoid fever. Of the 244 cases of typhoid fever at Marylebone, nine-tenths were in households that consumed milk

31

from one dairy; that is, 218 out of 244 cases. In three weeks 148 cases of the 218 occurred. There were only ten cases in families not thus supplied, and with but one exception wherever the milk supply from this particular dairy stopped, then the fever stopped. The map of the distribution of the milk supply resembles very closely the area of the outbreak, and it only extended into regions thus supplied, and, as in Clapham, was confined to the houses of those in prosperous circumstances, where the sanitary appliances were good. As before stated to be the rule, the disease selected the streets supplied by this dairy, and also houses in streets where other houses that were supplied from elsewhere, escaped. As a matter of course, when the epidemic influence was fully established, the disease was spread by that means, as is usually the case, independent of the special means of infection that first caused it to originate and spread. Thus, of 132 infected houses, 14 only did not receive this milk supply, and eleven out of the 88 streets into which the fever extended. Still more direct was the evidence before alluded to, that in some instances those only that used the milk as it came from the dairy,—that is, un-cooked,—were taken, and also those that had used the milk very freely. Dr. Radcliffe, from whose report this account is derived,* mentions some such instances. The mistress and kitchen maid were the only ones that drank uncooked milk in one family. They both had typhoid fever. The two children that did not drink milk escaped. A physician drank every night half a pint of cold milk, uncooked, and was the only one in the household that did thus, also the only one that had the fever. A young lady, while on a visit to her aunt at Marylebone, drank much milk while there. On her return, or rather soon after, she had typhoid fever. A child, visiting one of these families, drank freely of milk, and shortly after had the same fever. He also mentions ten cases of persons that drank exceptionally large quantities of uncooked milk that had the fever. The first cases were among those using a special variety furnished by the dairy, called nursery milk, and at first it was thought that this only was infected, but afterwards cases frequently occurred in those using the ordinary milk, so called. Strangely enough, there was an independent group of cases in another district which were supplied from the same dairy. The cases were twelve in number; eleven had been supplied with

* Report of Medical Officer of the Privy Council and Local Government Board, New Series, No. 11, page 108 et seq.

milk from this same dairy. These were at St. Anne's, Soho, and, as at Marylebone and Paddington, were people not of the poorest class. Inspection of the farms showed that the infection came from one only, that from which the nursery milk was supplied— about $\frac{1}{32}$ of the whole quantity. It was sent to London in a different and separate can, or "churn," as it was called, and distributed in sealed cans. It was collected from a few selected cows, and sold to those that objected to the mingled milk from many animals for nursery or other use. There were objections urged against the explanation of the cause of the epidemic by infected milk, and one was that in 63 families living in Pimlico, supplied from the implicated dairy, there were no cases of fever. It was found, however, that these 63 families were supplied with ordinary milk only, nor was nursery milk supplied to the carriers, and thus their exemption was explained. The other objections were the entire exemption of several streets and the irregular distribution of cases within the area supplied, especially the marked predominance in some streets over others. This was explained by the manner of disposal of the nursery milk. As the regular customers left town in July, it was either set for cream, sent into the shop to be sold across the counter, or used to fill out the general supply, if it fell short. When set for cream, the skim-milk was sent to the Soho branch to be sold. If used to fill out a short supply, it was added to the cans of the carrier last served. Cases of infection occurred from milk drank over the counter, and the use to supplement the general supply explains both the exemption of several streets and the irregular distribution in others. This should occasion an increase two weeks after it was first used. The exodus of July 12 was very marked, and, as shown by the books from the dairy, the outbreak of typhoid among the families using ordinary milk occurred after the "nursery milk" was used as a partial supply. On the week ending July 26, after the proper incubative period ordinary to the disease, the attacks among households using milk increased from 5 per cent. to 86 per cent., or 17 times, while among those using "nursery milk" the virulence was a week earlier, when the increase was from 8 to 33 per cent.

The farm from which the infected milk was received was situated between two villages, about a mile distant from each. During the fourteen months ending Aug. 31st, there had been fourteen indigenous cases of typhoid fever in one of these villages, and two imported cases. During June and July there had been nine cases in five families in the other village. One of these persons was attacked while at work on the farm in question. On the 8th of June the occupier of the farm died from latent typhoid fever; profuse diarrhea and hemorrhages from the bowels, were early symptoms. The disregard of the directions not to allow the patient to raise himself to an erect posture resulted in his death. The dejections, by order of the medical attendant, were not cast in the common privy, but buried in an ash-heap, where all the slops incident to the sickness were cast; no disinfectants were used. On the 12th of August, a son of the above patient aged thirteen had a slight but well marked attack of typhoid fever. The buildings were old and incommodious, the water was obtained from a well in the yard adjoining the farm-house, which was mainly fed by another, through an underground conduit; this was at some distance, in a meadow. The privy was higher than the well, and fifty-six feet distant. The premises, dairy, and farm-house were drained by a surface and underground drain; the latter ran close to the dairy well. The surface drain was a simple ditch emptying into a distant ditch which also received the discharge from the underground drain. The water from the well was not used for dairy purposes, as it had become polluted; that is, its use was discontinued after the first part of August. Carefully made excavations showed that there had been no soakage from the privy nor the surface yard drain, neither from the underground drain. There had been an increasing offensiveness in the well water, which finally led to its disuse as a regular supply; it had gradually become unfit for dairy purposes, as the examination was made in September. A line of soakage was however clearly and distinctly made out along the foundations of the yard wall leading directly to the well. One side of the pig-sty was a wall whose foundations were continuous with those of the yard wall, thus a direct line of soakage from the well to the pig-sty was proven; some clay in a piece of made ground in the line was reduced to a thin paste. This accounted for the increasing bad taste in the water of the well which led to its final disuse. Along this same wall was the ash-heap that had received the typhoid dejections from the 1st to the 8th of June. By an unhappy chance, these excreta were placed on the only spot in the farm premises where they would certainly find their way into the water used for dairy purposes, while endeavoring to prevent mischief. From the literature of typhoid fever, it appears that there is no fact as to the causation of typhoid fever more clearly established than its propagation and spread by water polluted by the discharges of a typhoid patient. The outbreak of typhoid fever from the infected milk commenced on the week ending July 5th; as the ordinary period of inoculation is fourteen days, the cause must have been in operation June 21st; this allows two weeks for the soakage from the typhoid dejections to reach the well. The epidemic lasted six weeks from the onset, and then there were three weeks of decline before it entirely ceased. The only water at this time used on the farm for all dairy purposes was that obtained from this well contaminated as described. It was generally used cold for rinsing; the utensils were scalded in London when they were emptied. Of course it was impossible to prove at that date that water from the well had been directly added to the milk, however true this might have been. The infection had probably ceased before the discovery of the cause of the outbreak. As this case has been so carefully studied, it is quoted quite fully from the official report. The increasing degree of the offensiveness of the water of the well, which at last led to its disuse, shows without doubt the fact of pollution ; and the connection with excremental filth from a typhoid fever patient is also as conclusively shown. Most of the laborers came from the villages where typhoid fever had prevailed extensively. There were a great many ways in which the infection could have reached the milk, but taking the whole train of facts, one could scarcely desire a more clear and evident a demonstration of cause and effect.

The subsidence of the epidemic as the use of the milk was discontinued is also a significant fact.

The spread of typhoid fever by infected milk adds to the strength of the argument that the excretions from typhoid fever patients should be disinfected. The vitality of the germ that reproduces typhoid fever is indefinite; unless the putrescent process is superseded by the potent chemistry of plant life, the maleficent agent may be dormant for months and even years, and then be dissolved in drinking water, and if not drank with the water may find its way into milk and thus gain access to a human system. The germ of typhoid fever finds its appropriate conditions for life and growth in the body, if from some previous agency that has destroyed the vital resistance of the membrane it can insinuate itself within the tissue and appropriate the nutrition sent to repair the debilitated tissue for its own reproduction. Thus, if there are no abrasions of the mucous membrane of the mouth and digestive tract certain deadly animal poisons can, it is said, be swallowed with impunity,—such as the rattlesnake poison; but if any abrasions exist the poison is absorbed and death follows rapidly. There is some such protection against the germs of disease; there is an individual equation which complicates the problem very much. The germs of disease are used because the theory that they cause disease or are its carriers,—for repeated experiments show that the fluids in which they grow are as potent as the bacteria themselves in transmitting disease,—is the best theory to work on and to push forward investigations that has as yet been advanced. The facts already learned concerning this infinitesimal world, the domain of the microscope, and its multitudinous denizens are extremely valuable, whatever the upshot may be.   One most significant discovery is that by regulating their food the character of the germs may be changed ; for instance the bacillus found in infusions of hay, if transplanted to a fish gelatine solution, becomes the bacillus anthracis, it is stated, or the form that produces malignant pustule in man and charbon in animals, and malignancy is lost by free supply of. oxygen. For purposes of discussion and study, then, the germ theory is the most convenient and promises the best results. In fact, on the old lines there is not much to be expected in the way of progress.

Accepting, then, the germ theory as a convenience, without affirming or denying its truth, we can proceed more readily. The germ of typhoid rapidly multiplies in the body, and if its vitality be not destroyed has many chances of again finding access to the human system to reproduce the disease and also the germs for a multitude of other cases under favorable circumstances. As our country is not so compactly built up as are the long settled acres of foreign lands there is less chance for this to happen. Still the excreta from a typhoid patient may be placed where sooner or later they may be dissolved in water used for drinking, they may infect the milk supply, or. they may be thoroughly dessicated and taken up into the atmosphere and gain access to the blood through the lungs. Still further, they may find appropriate conditions for growth and development in sewer air, and thus gain access to the body. The methods are but two, it is true—by solution in water or suspension in the air. The attention of the people is directed to this danger by sanitarians generally, but never more forcibly than now. Pamphlets similar to that on typhoid fever issued by our own State Board of Health are becoming frequent, and the importance of disinfection as a powerful means of prevention is becoming appreciated, as it deserves.

The germ theory has, to all appearance, settled the question of spontaneous generation, so far as demonstration can show such a theory to be untrue. As has been stated, the character of the bacteria can be _changed from an innocent germ to one associated with the most malignant diseases, and on the other hand by proper cultivation malignancy is lost or greatly modified. Malignancy would appear to be an attribute that may, under certain conditions, be associated with any germ. If this be generally true there seems no logical reason for doubting that diseases can be produced without contagion from a prevailing case, if the proper conditions are supplied. The theory offers a tempting field for investigation, and if demonstrated would explain many anomalies. The search then would be for the essential conditions, which learned, the control of the disease would follow logically.

The temptation to stray into side questions in writing upon disease is very great, and hard to resist, but these theories illustrate the fact that unsanitary conditions predispose to disease, and render it more malignant if they do not directly induce it, that there is a personal element in disease, and that there is a third agent which acts like the spark to the magazine which is probably biological, in other words, a germ. There are three principal factors in the production of disease, whether they shall prove to be in accordance with the analysis just given or not. In brief they are the virus or contagium, the conditions upon which it depends, and the receptivity of persons exposed. It is the virus or contagium that is destroyed by disinfecting the typhoid excreta, and thus a more direct blow is struck than by attempting to remove the essential conditions. This subject has of late received much attention from sanitarians as the proof that typhoid fever can be thus spread amounts to a demonstration. This being so, if the contagium can be so readily destroyed, it becomes a duty to regard the general

interests of public hygiene and take the extra trouble of disinfection, even if one's immediate friends are not likely to be benefited.
The solution of copperas is useful and best; the zinc solution is also
a strong germicide.

One of the later instances of typhoid fever from infected milk
was in Glasgow, in the western district. Out of fifty-nine cases
fifty had milk from the source of infection. As before stated,
where an epidemic starts cases spread from the first sources of
infection, which under favorable circumstances also become centres
of infection. All the deaths, six in number, were free consumers of
the infected milk. In seven contiguous streets supplied from
other sources, after a house to house visitation, not a single case
of typhoid fever was found. The epidemic closed with the discontinuance of the use of the milk.*

The following account of scarlet fever from infected milk is
from the official reports of England for 1879. The epidemic was
at Fallowfield, England, reported by Dr. Airy. There were a few
cases among adults, resembling scarlet fever, the last week in July,
without the characteristic rash. July 31st, there was a decided case
in a child, not connected with the subsequent cases. Sunday,
Aug. 3d, two children in one family, and four of another, not
neighbors, were taken with scarlet fever, and during that night
and Monday, Aug. 4th, there were eighteen cases in eleven families
belonging to Fallowfield. Aug. 5th, there were two more cases
in two families. Aug. 6th, there was a slight case of sore throat
which would not have been noticed had not others in the same
family had the fever from contagion of this case a week or two
later. Including some cases partly undeveloped, there were thirty-
five persons in eighteen families attacked within a month, twenty-
four of them within thirty-six hours. Vomiting and profuse
diarrhea were very prominent symptoms, suggesting an irritant poison. The twenty-four cases in thirty-six hours pointed to a
common cause.

The milk was suspected, and upon investigation it was found
that all the families attacked received milk from one dairy, while
families adjacent, receiving their milk from another source, escaped.
It was also learned that one of the milkers had his lodgings in a
house where there was a patient in the peeling stage of scarlet

* Brit. Med. Journ., July, 1882.

fever. It was learned that the people, who were of the better class, had not assembled at any gathering within the limits of any possible incubation of scarlet fever, and that they lived in detached villas mostly. In fact, intercourse between any two of the families, with a few exceptions, had been exceedingly rare, if there had been any at all. There was no community in church attendance. Only two of the eighteen families employed the same laundry. There was no scarlet fever in the family of the postman or news-agent. There was no community of drainage. Water was supplied from the Manchester water-works. The conclusion is thus irresistible that the scarlet fever was supplied with the milk.

The milking was done by the daughter of the farmer's widow who kept the dairy, a young man who lodged at the farm-house, and an old man who lodged at the house of his married son, in a crowded block. The most was done by the two first named, but each milker took a cow as it happened until all were milked. The milk was passed into two delivery cans, the first half into one, the second into the other, through a straining cloth which was kept scrupulously clean. In the morning two carts were sent out, one to the north, the other to the south. One was driven by milker No. 2, the other by a nephew of the farmer's daughter, who himself had scarlet fever August 4. Soon after starting, a can from a small dairy was poured into one or the other of the morning cans, and the can was left to be returned in time for the evening. At night only one cart was sent out. The customers living near the dairy were supplied by milker No. 3 in person morning and night. Had the fever been spread by personal contagion from one of the milk servers one of the three groups should have had all the cases. Although all the groups were attacked they were not all attacked with the same severity. There were eleven families supplied daily by milker No. 3: in six there were children, three had only servants. Out of six families that had children, who are much more susceptible to scarlet fever than adults, in five there were cases. In the north group there were twenty-five families; ten were affected. Four of the fifteen had left servants only, who were generally supplied in the evening, and six had no children. Thus out of fourteen susceptible families, in ten there were cases of scarlet fever. Of the south group two out of thirty families were attacked. A child had stopped at the farm August 2d, and probably had drank very freely of milk; two days later she had

32

active characteristic symptoms of scarlet fever; she resided two miles from Fallowfield, and was on her way home from a town where there had been no cases of scarlet fever when she stopped at the farm. There were four or five cases of rapid onset of the fever after exposure.

As before stated, while there was no scarlet fever at the farm before August 4, there was a case in the family of milker No. 3, that of his grandchild, who was in the peeling stage at the time of greatest infection. The child lay on the ground floor in a back room, and the old man always went in and out the back door. "Considering the average amount of sanitary knowledge of the family, their confined lodgings, imperfect ventilation, lack of cleanliness, it is difficult to believe that the old man could leave the house without carrying the scarlatinal infection." The evidence is not as conclusive as in the previous case, but there is little doubt but that the contagion was thus derived, and on one special occasion the milk that went to the northern group was especially contaminated. The rapidity of the six cases traced as mentioned, where the period of incubation was forty-eight hours, indicates this to have been August 2d. The careful exclusion of all other causes, and the existence of a case of scarlet fever in connection with the dairy, complete a long chain of proof that leaves little room for doubt.

Dr. Lovett reported an instance of the transmission of scarlet fever by infected milk. As in the previous cases almost all the cases were in families supplied from the same dairy. There were found to be two cases of scarlet fever in the family of one of the milk carriers; one of them was in the peeling state. The two cases were removed, and proper precautions taken with regard to disinfection, and there were no more new cases. There was no scarlet fever on the farm itself. The case appears plainer when the milk is directly exposed by standing in a room near one occupied by a case of scarlet fever, or in the very room itself. This has been reported in cases where scarlet fever has been spread through neighborhoods and families where milk was supplied to but a few, and that from which the cream had been wholly or partially taken was also sold. Instances of the infection of milk thus directly have been reported, but it does not seem to be the case in widespread epidemics, as such an occurrence could hardly happen in a large dairy where the milk is kept in a separate building, if stored

at all. In one case where several families were supplied from one
source, the milk was kept in a room adjacent to the one where
there was a case of scarlet fever. The door was open much of the
time, and the mother of the sick child, who attended him closely
through his illness, received the milk as it was brought to the
house night and morning, and poured it into each customer's pail.
The milk was carried by a member of another family to each
customer. In each of the three families supplied there were cases,
and where there were several children in one family the cases all
commenced within a few hours of each other, which showed clearly
that there was a common source of infection. From this one
case ten others originated through the infected milk supply. The
fact that several cases received the scarlet fever by contagion
from one or two of these ten cases, and again themselves infected
others, at first confused the search for the original cause very
much, but the first ten cases occurred so nearly at the same time
and had no other connecting link except the milk supply. Singularly enough the house stood on the border line of three towns, so
the families supplied had each different associations in regard to
church, school, post-office, and social intercourse, so that there
could be no other method of access of the scarlet fever infection
except through the milk supply.

In one epidemic of scarlet fever in families supplied from one
dairy, the milkers were found to be convalescents from scarlet
fever. Epidemics of dipththeria have also been traced to the
milk supply, but not as clearly as in the case of scarlet fever or
typhoid. Not to occupy too much space in the repetition of details that closely resemble each other, it is sufficient to state that
in repeated instances where there have been epidemics in a limited
area, the facts of a common milk supply, the exclusion of other
causes, and the presence of the disease at the dairy farm, or in connection with the families of one or more of those that act as milkers or carriers also appear. The direct method by which the milk
became infected with the germs or virus of diphtheria has not, so
far as I can learn, been shown in any case, as has been done so
clearly in case of typhoid fever when spread by infected milk, and
quite distinctly in some of the instances of the spread of scarlet
fever. The circumstantial evidence, however, is as strong as possible, and as the case has been so clearly proven in relation to the

other diseases, one can add the argument of analogy if it is thought to be needed.

The milk from distillery fed cows, or swill milk, as it is appropriately called, is fortunately not much used in this State, if anywhere. Such milk is found to be strongly acid in reaction, while milk from grass or hay fed cows is slightly alkaline. Singularly enough Dr. Percy found that the milk of nursing women living in damp, dark cellars, with insufficient and inappropriate food, was also strongly acid, while in healthy women it is decidedly alkaline. Swill milk soon becomes putrid after it has become soured; as it is deficient in sugar it does not become sour quite as soon as milk generally. The use of swill milk unmixed with other milk causes diarrhea and vomiting, and emaciation in children, with extreme languor; the children soon become exceedingly fretful and irritable. A wasting, rapid usually, is produced, called consumption of the bowels; emaciation is extreme.

The acid reaction of such milk is stated by general standard authorities, as well as demonstrated by the experiments of Dr. Percy. The phosphoric organic compound found in pure milk is entirely absent in swill milk. Pure milk is the only food that nourishes the entire body; every tissue finds its appropriate food. In swill milk there is no food for the nervous system, hence the depression and irritability that results, and the arrest of growth and substitution of a wasting process. Swill milk is also deficient in butter and sugar, hence entirely unfit for infants' food. I have never seen but one stable where distillery swill was used, and that not a large one. Such milk should not be sold, and if its use is not prohibited by law, its sale should be prohibited under severe penalties.

The blue color of milk which is acquired after long standing, has lately been stated to be due to the influence of certain fungus, discovered by Fuerstenberg, by which the constituents of the milk are decomposed, giving rise to a compound standing in near relation to the aniline dyes. Before the color is fairly established vibriones bacteria and mycelial germs are shown by the microscope. No ill effects upon health have been ascribed to this fungus; its appearance may, it is stated, be prevented usually by extreme cleanliness and the use of disinfectants. The exact nature of the compound that colors the milk blue has not been proven. This does not refer to skim milk, as the fungus may be found on the surface of the cream also. When milk sours or decomposes we find it to contain various forms of fungus, as a matter of course, and also bacteria and other forms of microscopical life. These facts are interesting in regard to the germ theory of disease. If milk affords a medium for the growth and development of innocent germs it does not appear unreasonable that it should act in the same relation towards malignant germs. However that may be, the contagion of certain diseases is doubtless conveyed by milk.

The influence of substances eaten by cows upon the milk has been deleterious in some instances, and occasionally disordered conditions have produced digestive and diarrheal disturbances in the consumers of the milk. But the transmission of disease by infected milk is a much more serious matter. Examination has also shown that in cattle drinking impure and stagnant water the milk was loaded with the same microscopical organisms found in the water, and if mixed even in small quantities with pure milk would produce the same changes in the whole mass.

The subject is of increasing importance. As our population becomes more dense large dairy farms will become of necessity more numerous and many of them will be near populous places where cases of zymotic disease will be of frequent occurrence. If the fact is recognized that under certain conditions milk may become infected and the medium for the transmission of disease, greater care will be exercised to prevent the possibility of such an occurrence.

Perfect cleanliness is at the foundation of safety in securing a pure milk supply. Pure water is no less a requisite, and good sanitary surroundings, as well as due regard to the laws that control the diffusion of diseases that can be conveyed by infected milk. The proper care of the dairy stock is also a matter of the greatest importance, plenty of pure air, nutritious and proper food, and pure water for drinking purposes are essential. It is not strange that the question of governmental inspection over the milk supply should be seriously considered. While self-interest and the intrinsic value of blooded stock will induce proper care in the more intelligent, there are those that, bent only on gain, will run any risks if any outlay is required to improve the sanitation of their dairy farms. All dealers and venders of milk in cities should properly be licensed, and all sales by unlicensed parties forbidden.

But in that case an intelligent inspector is needed, who will carry his investigations back of the venders to the parties that produce the milk, and so determine whether the sellers had a supply of pure milk at the start or not.   As long as water is cheaper than milk the temptation to increase the quantity by dilution with water will be a strong one.   The inspector should also teach the use of proper instruments to test pure milk to the sellers and pro-. ducers.   Of course all milk from diseased animals should be excluded from sale.   We have a law to that effect now, yet I have been informed that milk from tuberculous cows in the last stages has been sold, mixed with that of the rest of the stock.

After what has been said of the powers of absorption of milk, it would appear unnecessary to state that milk should not be kept in rooms used for sleeping purposes, nor where it is directly exposed to contamination by the air from adjacent rooms, used for patients with contagious diseases.   It would also appear undesirable to allow one recently convalescent from scarlet fever to act as milker for a part or the whole of a dairy.

Absolute cleanliness from first to last appears to be the rule for dairy farmers, milk sellers, and inspectors.   This implies an intelligent understanding of what is meant by filth in a sanitary sense, and of the methods by which disease can be transmitted by milk. As constant vigilance is the price of safety, an inspector is desirable whose duties shall cover the whole field of the purity of the milk, both in regard to freedom from adulteration and from infection, and the proper management of the dairy, its buildings and water supply, both for the domestic use about the milk utensils and the water supply for the stock.   The milk should also be once in a while tested at the barns as well as at the carts of the venders.   The case is not fully met when a law is passed directing skim milk to be plainly labeled if offered for sale; unless there is some one to enforce the law it is liable to be neglected. Milk from which a part of the cream has been sold should also be distinguished by a plain label from whole milk, that is, milk from which none of the cream has been taken.   In some of the cities ordinances have been passed for inspection of the milk as sold in the streets of the city.   While such a course is productive of inestimable benefit to the citizens of the particular city, the whole case is not met, as it is not known whether the supply was unadulterated to start with, unless the producers vend the milk them-selves.

While it is possible to produce disease from the qualities of the milk itself, as has been shown, from the food or drink of the herd, or disorders in the animals, or unsanitary stables, yet the greatest danger of spreading epidemic diseases arises from infec-tion of the milk after it has been drawn. Of the numerous epi-demics, a summary of which was given, and in the recent cases reported, all were due to infection from polluted water, or direct infection of the milk by the virus of the disease. The dangers that menace health and life are closely correlated. The storage of ex-cremental filth, the neglect to destroy contagion by disinfection, and disregard of sanitary laws, are as potent here to produce dis-ease and death as in other relations.

SOME OF THE ORGANIC IMPURITIES

FOUND IN

DRINKING WATER,

BY

C. W. CHAMBERLAIN, M.D.,

SECRETARY OF THE BOARD OF HEALTH.

33

SOME OF THE ORGANIC IMPURITIES FOUND IN DRINKING WATER.

It is the intention in the following paper to give a brief account of some of the common forms of plant and animal life found in rivers, streams, and ponds that are used as sources of water supply by cities and towns. The paper is in some respects supplementary to the one of Dr. Lewis, and is intended to pave the way for a more systematic study of the water supplies in this State. Most of the organisms described are microscopical, and they all can be studied by amateur microscopists; in fact some of them require only a low magnifying power to be clearly and distinctly seen, and the minuter can be seen by the aid of the powers usually supplied in a good physician's microscope. There is too little use made of the microscope by physicians generally; even those that have them neglect their use. Much can also be learned of the myriad forms of life with which the water and air are teeming, and such studies once commenced would prove too interesting to be discontinued. In this field, too, there is much that the general practitioner, and especially those more isolated, could contribute in relation to these minute organisms and disease. The progress of medical science, at least for the immediate future, appears to be connected with these minute forms of life. Apparently in some as yet unexplained way they have a causal relation to zymotic diseases. Whether they cause disease directly, act as carriers, or induce and play an essential part in changes that evolve the virus of disease, is uncertain, or whether, in some way yet to be learned, innocent germs become malignant, and *vice versa* malignant germs become harmless. That this transformation can be effected in regard to certain forms of bacterial life has been asserted by several different experimenters, and repeated trials have shown that by changing the food malignancy has been acquired by germs before harmless. Whether this is a partial or general truth is however by no means determined. The skill required for microscopical researches is not so very great, unless one is to be a specialist; then, indeed, mechanical dexterity and skill in manipulating small objects becomes an essential attribute. But for general work any one with ordinary average abilities can without much difficulty become master of the microscope. While one learns for his own gratification the life history of the more common forms of microsopical life that are common to the water, the mossy bog, or even muddy pool,. he can perchance record some fact of value in regard to the variations of plant or animal life in the water supply upon the manifestations of diseases, The subject is almost wholly unexplored and has all the charm of novelty. Some observations have been commenced but never completed in relation to drinking water and malaria. As can be readily seen there is a wide field here for much work upon many problems relating to health and disease, and also in regard to water itself, and how it is influenced by these growths.

It is not intended here to attempt anything like completeness, but the common forms of plant and animal life should be more or less familiar to prevent unnecessary alarm when their presence is shown. Especially should there be some idea of those that are harmless, and those whose presence means that the water is, to say the least, to be looked upon with suspicion, As the germ theory of disease is likely to occupy a prominent place in literature for some time, if not permanently, it is well that something should be popularly known about the common types of the small organisms that are to be found in all water, more or less, that has access to the light and air. A few will be considered that can be seen by the unaided eye, but for the most part those will be described whose individual characteristics cannot be made out without the aid of a glass, while the massed growth is distinguishable.

The larger plants, eel-grass, pickerel-weed, and the like, are well known, but not the mass of water weeds of this region which belong to a few genera and are small, obscure plants.* They all start from roots at the bottom of the pond or stream, and as they are not very tough are often broken off and washed ashore in heaps. There is a plant that floats in immense masses closely covering wide areas, having no fixed roots nor stems or leaves. These are roundish

---

* Farlow on Vegetable Growth, 1st Report of State Board of Health, Lunacy and Charity, Mass., pp. 131, et seq.

grass-green disks about a quarter of an inch in diameter, with delicate roots on the under side.* They, as well as the other flowering
water plants, do no harm and impart no unhealthful elements to the
water.   Farlow mentions a water plant that was transported to
England by Professor Babington, which grew so luxuriantly as to
choke small water courses, and was called Babington's curse.   The
botanical name is *Anacharis Canadensis.* This grows so abundantly in
Fresh Pond, used as a water supply for Cambridge, Mass., that the
pond has to be dredged periodically. Some others seem to grow more
luxuriantly in artificial ponds, upon embankments and masonry,
which were rarely met before in any abundance.   As with larger
plants these also have plants that grow upon them, and animal parasites which are often more interesting than the plants themselves.

The question naturally arises whether the larger water plants, if
decaying in masses, would not pollute the water by the products
resulting.   I have never personally known of any such result; nor
found any statements from others to that effect, that is, from the
natural decay every autumn of what are usually termed pond weeds.
There are some plants that have an offensive odor, either in a fresh
state or while decaying, but the quantity of the ordinary water-
weeds is not large enough to affect a reservoir to any extent.   If
by any changes in the level of the pond or otherwise large amounts
of vegetable growths are suddenly destroyed, as has occurred several times, the case would be altogether different.   Still, in that
case no danger to health has been ascribed to water thus affected;
the odor may be offensive, but the products with which it is changed
are entirely harmless.

One of the common forms of water plants that has no roots, but
floats upon the surface in still pools in coves along rivers, and in
ponds, is the *Chara coronata.*   This belongs to the *Characeae*, plants
of a grass green color, that multiply by spores.   The spore cells can
be seen as black dots in the illustration.   These plants sometimes
form long, spray-like growths, over a foot long.   There are quite a
number of species, but the one figured is the most common.
After high water in rivers, that has cleaned out the coves in
autumn, I have found masses of this, nearly a foot deep, cast up
on the shore and entangled in fallen brushwood, and producing in
decay no marked odor; that is the species figured.   Some of
the species are of a more gelatinous nature, and have a very disa-

* These are the *Lemnae*, or duck meats, as they are called.

greeable odor. The latter varieties, however, are more often found in shallow water, and are not associated with the sources of water supply. Farlow states that, strong as the peculiar odor is, it is not readily communicated to water, even when the plants grow in a confined space. They were formerly classed among the *Algae*. They are filamentous in structure, with whorls of branches. The main stem is tubular, the branches are smaller tubes, and what appear like leaves are still smaller tubes. The species figured is often found in large quantities, nearly covering the surface of still water. It is rather beneficial than otherwise, as, in its growth, it feeds upon impurities that the water contains. Many of the such so-called impurities that are found in water are useful, as they feed upon and remove from the water substances that are deleterious, while in themselves harmless. This is also true of many of the minute forms of life, but their presence in large quantities indicates that there are many impurities to remove.

There are plants which grow along the margins of ponds and in shallow water, such as the pickerel-weed, that have an offensive odor which is communicable to the water, but these do not ordinarily grow in water used for drinking purposes in sufficient quantities to affect the whole supply; that is, the water-weeds belonging to flowering plants.

Among the *Algae*, which is a large family of flowerless plants, containing many genera of marine and fresh-water plants, there are both odorless and offensive forms. These are of infinite

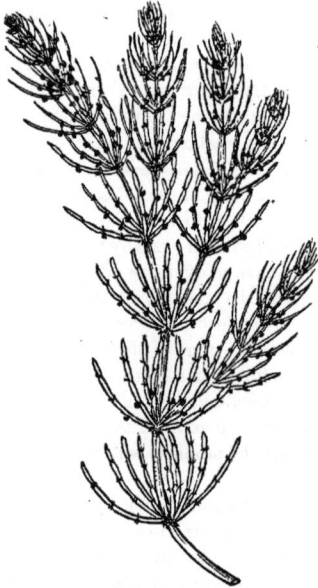

CHARA CORONATA.*

* Allen's Characæ of America, Part 1, plate 3.

variety, from one-celled plants that seem from the simplicity of their construction scarcely to possess life, invisible unless in masses, and then their structure unrevealed to the unaided eye, to plants of several inches in length, or even, though rarely, several feet. There is an almost infinite variety of shapes, colors, forms, and sizes. One variety of the unicellular *Algae* is shown in plate 1, the *Protococcus*, which consists of spherical cells, imbedded in a gelatinous mass of a bright green color. This is but one of an immense variety of one-celled plants with which fresh waters teem. Stagnant or quiet water contains large quantities of these plants, while ditch water swarms with them. Another genus, with almost endless species, is that of the *Diatoms*, some of which are figured in plate 2. When the water was reversed in the pipes, and a large amount sent through that had been standing all summer undisturbed in a reservoir in Hartford, I found, on allowing a pint to settle, in one specimen put under the microscope, fifteen different species of *Diatoms*, as well as representatives of the *infusorial* and other types of microscopic life. The water in the ditches in the North Meadows, when they received sewage, was especially rich in *Diatoms*. As indicated, these plants are found in polluted water in the greatest abundance, and, as well as some other varieties of *Algae*, are an indication of contamination when found in large quantities. But it must be remembered that all water exposed to light and air contains more or less life, and would soon become unfit for use were this not the case.

In 1859, Dr. Torrey* examined a bright green mass that had been driven by the wind to the outlet of Croton Lake, where it formed a considerable stratum in a quiet recess near the shore. This he found to consist of small, straight filaments, with occasional large, green spherical cells, filled with green spores, and others with a yellowish fluid, but no green spores. On distilling this in water, the odorous principle was obtained in a concentrated form, and found to be identical with the offensive odor that had been complained of in the water. No unwholesome qualities were attributed to it.

There are many varieties of filamentous *Algae* which are harmless in every respect. Upon examination the filaments in most genera are seen to consist of a series of cells, of different shape ·

---

* Waller, Report on Croton Water, pages 9-10.

in each species, joined at the ends and thus forming filaments varying in length, shape, and size.

In 1871 these Crotonic confervæ were reported by Dr. C. T. Jackson to exist in Hartford water. The undue quantity was reported as caused by the lack of animal life and stagnation of the water. In Cochituate lake the presence of minute crustacea, called *Cyclops*, in immense numbers, apparently checked the super-abundance of confervæ, as the water was purest when these were most abundant. This account is from the 18th report of the Hartford Water Commissioners.

As the Cyclops has been mentioned in this connection, perhaps some account might as well be given here of this species of impurity, although it belongs to the animal kingdom, and as has been stated, is one of the crustaceans. The species figured here is the *Cyclops quadricornis*. This is a lively little animal, which is often shown in a glass of water as one of the triumphs of some adjustable or self cleansing-filter. It shows up well under a low power of the microscope, but is harmless to life and health. Its presence indicates rather an undue amount of the filamentous *Algæ*, which form its principal food, and, while it offends the

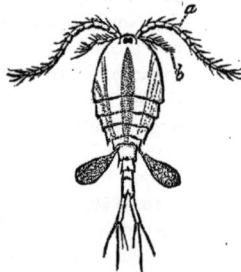

Male.   Female.

CYCLOPS QUADRICORNUS.

eye and induces all manner of unpleasant suggestions, is not so objectionable as the invisible forms that live upon sewage and whose presence indicates sewage contamination, especially if found in large quantities. Like the *Daphnia*, and other species, it belongs to the shrimp and lobster family, which contain many varieties largely used as food, and these minute forms are not injurious in any way when taken into the stomach. These are magnified, the male fifteen diameters, the female twenty-five. In the male, the letters *a b* indicate the superior antennae; in the female, *a* the superior, *b* the inferior antennae.

Farlow states that the bulk of the larger filamentous water-plants belong either to the *Zoösporae* or *Conjugateae*. They neither affect very deep water, but grow along the edges where they form large masses upon the surface; they are attached to sticks, stones, large plants, or any convenient object. The grass-green *Algae* have no injurious effect usually upon the water in which they grow, and will not themselves grow in impure water.

It is a common idea that every drop of water, if put under a microscope, would be found to be teeming with strange and repulsive forms of life. The animal life is much more familiar than the vegetable. While in a drop of stagnant ditch-water many varieties would always be found, both of plant and animal life, in case of water from rivers and ponds, this is far from being the case. In water badly polluted by sewage the proportion would be greater, but in ordinary reservoir water the sediment from quite a large quantity has to be collected. Thus a common method is to fill a large glass jar and allow it to stand carefully covered for a day, then, without disturbing the jar, siphon off all but the lower third or fourth, and then fill up the jar with more water from the source that is under examination. After a turbid sediment is obtained, the amount of water required varying with its purity, this is poured into a tall, conical jar and allowed to settle, the upper two-thirds siphoned off, and the rest kept for examination. Sometimes certain forms, large enough to be seen, can be removed by a pipette. There are various ways to condense the specimens of plant and animal life, which need not be mentioned here, but unless the water is very foul the sediment from a large amount must be collected. In cases where the wonders that a drop of water contains are exhibited, the drop represents a part of a carefully prepared specimen, and not water that is like the average water supplied for drinking. Often these organisms are cultivated for such purposes, and the stock is kept up by design. This is true where the exhibitor desires to show a battle royal on a screen, for some of these creatures fight viciously, and the victor consumes the vanquished. In that case, in one specimen for instance, the *Cyclops* would be cultivated, and in another the *Hydra*. By mixing the two on a slide, and throwing the magnified image on a screen, the results would not long remain undecided, for these fights are short and quick, as they are for life, defeat invariably means death. This is a favorite object in exhibitions with the

34

solar microscope. Thus it is seen that one does not consume so large a number of microscopic lobsters in the raw state, when drinking water, as has been supposed. The filter has allowed some gallons to run through before enough sediment is collected to exhibit well. Still, there are in all water exposed to light and air, many forms of vegetable and animal life, the former largely predominating, the purer the water the less the amount.

In the rivers and ponds, in the ditches and drains, in shallow pools, in boggy meadows, even in wet moss, forms of life are found. Their functions are not wholly known, but they play an important rôle in the economy of nature, in the transformation of dead matter to living forms, and preserving the changeless youth and freshness of nature. It is hard to draw the line between the animal and the vegetable, and now and then a variety is transferred from one to the other in the systems of classification. Thus many class the *Diatoms* as belonging to the animal kingdom. They have a silicious envelope, and greater powers of motion than most of the unicellular *Algae.* The confervoid plants form the lowest order of *Algae,* and are mostly microscopic.

The *Algae* that communicate offensive odors, either when growing or during decay, are generally of a bluish green color, at times becoming almost black, which is due to a characteristic coloring matter peculiar to the group, soluble in water but not in alcohol. Chlorophyl, the usual green coloring matter of plants and leaves is not soluble in water, but is in alcohol. The great number of the filamentous *Algae* that produce odors belong to the genus *Nostoc,* and to avoid the use of technical terms most of the other genera will be omitted. The paper of Professor Farlow presents this part of the subject in a very clear manner, and to it I am indebted for many of the facts relating to plant life. The valuable monograph of Professor Wood on the Fresh Water Algae of North America is the standard authority on the subject; to it I am indebted for the illustrations of many of the species shown. The last edition of the Micrographic Dictionary, and Professor Waller's exhaustive summary have also been freely used in the preparation of this article; also the reports of Prof. Nichols. But most of the forms mentioned I have verified by personal observation.

One of the most common forms that is repeatedly mentioned in the report of Dr. Lewis is the *Clathrocystis æruginosa,* which is found forming a scum or jelly-like mass upon the surface of the water, or diffused. The method of growth is quite complicated. The illustration in plate first shows a colony. Species of *Caelospherium* are also abundant in the water supplies examined; the cells of these are oblong while these of the former are spherical. When floating on the surface they are surrounded by a colorless film of mucus. If cut through, the interior would be found to be a jelly-like substance with bands of a firmer consistence. The colonies of the former are hollow at first spheroidal then tubulated. These two species of *Nostocs* which closest resemble each other are illustrated in plates one and two. Mature colonies are there shown. The color should be bluish green in both, although different in the plates, as there was not enough room on plate one. Other varieties of filamentous *Algae* are shown in the plate, each of which has its own peculiar odor. The bad odor of the Springfield water supply in 1875, or rather that from the Ludlow reservoir, was found to be due to the presence of *Clathrocystis æruginosa*, which was found to be very abundant in the water. This is also said to be a parasite on fishes, and to destroy them by cutting off the air supply, as the growth covers the gills. The following list is given by Professor Farlow of the plants which possess an offensive odor. Several of them are illustrated in the following plates:

Lynbyæ, suffocating odor.
Oscillariæ, " "
Beggiatoa, sulphurous odor.
Nodularia litorea.
Plectonema Wollei, pig-pen odor.
Anabæna, " " "

The last two give a marked odor while decaying, the others while still living. It has been stated that carbonic acid intensifies the odors from these plants, so that dealers in mineral waters have often been badly annoyed and put to considerable expense to obtain supplies of pure water.

As seen by the descriptions and illustrations the spores and plants have no resemblance to the bacteria that are associated with certain forms of disease. The spores and ciliæ are shown in the plates. These can be compared with the bacteria in the illustrations of a succeeding article. These odors, while objectionable, and the offensive tastes thus caused, while undesirable, have never rendered such water to be associated in any causative rela-

tion to disease, nor is there any reason for the idea that disease
could be produced by such water in any way. As just stated
the bacteria which are associated with disease have no characteristics in common with these; the germs are infinitely small and the
mature organisms are much smaller than any of the *Nostocs*.
Apart from theory, careful investigation has eliminated all possibilities of danger. The functions of these plants are twofold:
first, to purify the water by removing decaying impurities through
the chemistry of plant life, reconverting dead matter to the uses
of-life, and second, to serve as food for the water animalculae and
thus maintain a proper equilibrium between plant and animal life.

The filamentous variety of *Algae* found on submerged iron is
called *Lyngbya ochracea*, and is, like the others, harmless. A similar
species causes the scum-like iron-rust that is often seen at or near the
edges of ponds and in shallow water. It looks like a gelatinous mass
stained yellow, but under the microscope appears to be a filamentous plant which is yellowish-brown instead of green. This appears
under several names, the last one usually the same. The *Beggiatoa*
give off an odor like sulphuretted hydrogen (rotten eggs); they
grow by preference in house-drains and stagnant ditches that receive the waste from steam-pipes. The filaments oscillate rapidly.

The greater number of these *Algae* are only visible to the unaided eye when in masses, and then no individual structure can be
determined. The appearance like meal on the surface of ponds to
the windward is caused by such plants. The spores appear in the
water like bright shining dots, from their property of refracting
light. The *Zoösporae* are plants which multiply by zoöspores which
move rapidly for some time after set free, then become invested with
a membrane and attach themselves to some object, or they may form
colonies or masses varying in size. The *Zoösporae* are illustrated
by the *Cladophora glomerata* in plate 1, one of the commonest
forms. Sometimes this appears like a scum floating upon the
surface, at others like a web attached to some object and stretching
out into the water, at others floating masses varying in color, den-
sity, and size. The *Conjugatae* multiply in a different manner,
which is more complicated. They are illustrated by a form of
spirogyra in plate 1. The green scum commonly called frogs' spittle
is a common variety of filamentous *Algae*. Most of these plants
prefer shallow, quiet water. Some of them grow best in polluted
water. A few grow best in a current and stretch out long fila-.

ments in the direction of the flow. The desmids, especially a star-like species, the *Pediastria*, are found almost wholly in pure clear water that is exposed freely to sunlight; the *Diatoms* are found alike in all conditions; the *Infusoria* prefer stagnant, polluted water; the *Rotiferae* on the contrary are oftener found in clear water. Nor does the *Cyclops*, unless in profusion, indicate contamination, and then is associated with profuse plant life. Thus in several instances the profusion of *Algae* causing bad tastes and odors has been due to the absence of *Cyclops*. It appears to be the function of this animalcule to prevent the too luxuriant growth of certain varieties of water plants.

One of the commonest forms of the *Nostoc* family is the *Nostoc comminutum*, shown in plate two. Another species about as frequently met is the *Nostoc commune*. These are typical forms of many of the filamentous *Algae*. As seen in the illustration, the filaments are made up of a series of jointed cells varying in shape and size with the species. The spore cells are shown, and also some free zoöspores; those in the plate have two cilia on one end. Some varieties have cilia all around instead of only at one extremity, but those are not as common. The cells are sometimes enclosed in a glutinous envelope, and at others by a layer of cellulose alone. The interior green protoplasmic mass is called the endochrome. In the protococcus the spherical cells are sometimes imbedded in a mass of protoplasm, from which the unicellular spheres are formed, at other times a colony of spherical cells form a larger sphere, which is invested with a gelatinous layer.

The *Nostocs* have an offensive odor—in many of the species, at least this is the case—and are at times so abundant as to communicate a taste and odor to large ponds. What the particular species of *Nostoc* is that is so abundant in the water supply of New Britain I have not yet fully made out, as it was not brought under observation until late in the autumn. Both the above varieties of *Nostoc* illustrated were found in a specimen allowed to develop in a warm room, but the one that is so abundant is apparently another variety.

Some of these plants grow in winter as well as in summer, and ice is sometimes contaminated by them. When the ice is formed in shallow water at the windward side of ponds, plants are sometimes entangled in it to such an extent as to make the water from such ice offensive.

The microscopic life in water is most profuse in the warm months; both plants and animals decrease as winter approaches. One fact in the construction of the New Britain reservoir explains the presence of so much vegetation, and indicates a time in the future when it will be clear. That is, when the reservoir was constructed, the stumps of trees and brushwood were not grubbed out, but the water was allowed to cover them. There is therefore a large amount of material from vegetable decay for this plant-life to feed upon, which is really beneficial, as they feed upon the products of decay and become themselves in turn food for minute microscopical animals, which themselves become food for larger forms, and thus the cycle of nature is illustrated; constant change in form and shape, but no new particles of matter, nor the destruction of a single one of the old. The other varieties shown in the plate are typical forms that are found generally in this region, in ponded waters and in river coves more abundantly. Many of them have been mentioned in the preceding paper by Dr. Lewis, and are found in connection with other varieties. Our knowledge of many of them, and of the effects they produce is quite limited, and doubtless there are many species as yet undescribed.

There is also a periodicity in the appearance of different species of microscopical life in water, including both plant and animal life, while some are found all the year round. At certain times some species will be very plentiful, and in the same pond a short time after be almost entirely absent; this is especially true of some varieties of diatoms. The *Cyclops* is a constant inhabitant, found in both pond and river water. I have seen but one account of its presence in such quantities as to render the water offensive.* There is almost always a specimen of this water flea, as it is often called, in any collection of pond or river water. They belong to the crustaceans and to the order *Entomostraca*. Their enemies are the *Hydra*, a fresh water polyp whose tentacles seize them. The hydra is the animalcule that if cut up into many pieces, each piece will grow again to a perfect hydra.

One of the strangest plants, that from its power of motion is often classed as an animalcule, is the *Volvox globator*. This is a movable sphere crossed by a network of bars, and containing several smaller spheres. It appears as a pale green globe covered with dots, from each of which project two cilia, the motion of which causes it to

* Trenton, N. J., 1877. It has been accused of producing diarrhœa when very abundant.

revolve. In the interior there are from two to twenty globes, and these sometimes contain others still more minute.

It is found in clear still water free from much filth, and was not at first supposed to exist in this country, but it is now known to be quite common. I have found it in several of the reservoirs in this State, but not abundantly. In the autumn the internal globes sometimes become of an orange color.

There are also two other typical forms of *Nostocs* represented in the plates which have already been mentioned, *Caelospherium*, and *Clathrocystis aeruginosa*. These are found singly or forming scums on the surface of the water. In the latter case they form gelatinous masses in which the cells are imbedded. *Baccillus rods* are often found attached to the *Caelospherium*, forming a sort of fringe; the bacillae are attached to the layer of colorless mucus which surrounds them. The *Clathrocystis* develops into a hollow mass of spheroidal shape, and then puts forth buds, which drop off and sail away to form new colonies, which result in the appearance shown in the plate.

The *Oscillatoriaciae* are illustrated by the *Lyngbya muralis* in plate 1. This family, which contains many genera, differs from all other confervoids in a very marked manner. The filaments are not made up of a series of cells in a row, but of a cylindrical thread of protoplasm of different color, gray, green, brown, or purple. The ends of the filaments are narrower, and show no trace of striations. As they grow older, striations appear as a double row of dots. They ultimately break up into segments on the lines of the striations. In a few orders the filaments oscillate; in the *Lyngbyae* they are motionless.

The *Chaetophora elegans* is a variety of another family. This genus, illustrated in plate 1, forms little green protuberances on sticks and stones, and other objects in fresh water. The *Zoöspores* have four cilia. The filaments are branched and imbedded in a gelatinous mold. Its habitat is stagnant pools; hence its presence indicates a suspicion of the freshness and purity of the water, especially if found abundantly.

The *Cladophora Glomerata*, in plate 1, serves to introduce another genus of confervoid *Algae*. Like the former, the filaments are branched. They are composed of cylindrical cells, attached end to end. This genus is the true confervæ of the older writers.

The form illustrated is of a dark green color, and grows in long, drawn-out skeins in running water. Hence its presence is an indication of purity and freshness. The facts concerning the habitat of the various forms of animal and vegetable microscopic life are of great importance, as they enable us to judge somewhat of the character of the water from their presence.

The *Anabaenae* are chiefly interesting from the odors they produce. The filaments are moniliform and usually curved. They are of a dark bluish-green color. The cells are of three different kinds—the vegetative cells, which are oval and multiply by fission, that is, each cell dividing into two large nearly spherical cells, colorless or yellow, called heterocysts, and the spore cells. The vegetative cells increase the length of the filament by dividing transversely. The plant is reproduced by spores, and by the separation of the part between two heterocysts. As it grows in shallow water the spores sink into the mud, and thus preserve the plant in summer from drought and from cold in winter.

When large quantities of such *Nostocs* decay they produce that odor in water which is very suggestively described as the pig-pen odor. Farlow describes a case where this odor was caused by large quantities of *Anabaenae*, and also *Lyngbya Wollei*, an American variety. This was at Horn Pond in 1876, and again in 1879, when the *Clathrocystis* was more abundant. The decay was caused by the fall of the water, from exceedingly dry seasons, in 1879. As the water receded, the stones and pebbles along the shore were colored blue. From this one can imagine the quantity of such vegetation, as the color was derived from these plants. At South Framingham, in 1879, a similar odor was discovered. This was found to be caused by masses of *Caelospherium*, associated with *Anabaenae*. The sudden disappearance of these odors is a singular and often inexplicable phenomena. In one case the disappearance of a variety of *Anabaenae* was found due to the results of a unicellular vegetable parasite. The list of varieties that can produce odors has been given. The species of the Crotouic *Confervae* was not determined. It apparently was not any of these just named, as it was a bright grass green. It was a variety of *Nostoc*. This apparently caused the trouble in the Meriden reservoir in the winter of 1874–5, as the water was tinged a delicate green color. When this decayed in the pipes it formed a black deposit and evolved an offensive gas.

In 1877, the water in the reservoir at Plymouth, Mass.,* was affected by a taste and odor similar to those described. Prof. W. R. Nichols found this due to a variety of filamentous *Nostoc*, which, as it was of a bright green color, may have been identical with the Crotonic *Confervae*. A similar condition existed in the reservoir at Rahway, New Jersey, in January, 1877. In Poughkeepsie, New York, a similar disagreeable odor and taste was found due to a species of *Oscillatoria*, which belongs to the *Nostoc* class. Prof. Waller enumerates several other instances that are interesting, but similar to those quoted. In one case the development was prevented by placing a hood over the pond to exclude light.

At the time these papers were written the cucumber-like odor and taste was not explained, and Prof. Waller enumerates a number of instances where this odor and taste prevailed, and no unusual quantity of any form of vegetation was found to account for it. The conclusion was that there were other agencies also at work, and that while the pig-pen odor and some others could generally be explained by the presence of some form of confervoid vegetation, there were other cases where neither this nor any other cause could be discovered. One cause for this cucumber-like odor, if not the sole cause, was discovered by Prof. Ira Remsen, of Baltimore, in one of the reservoirs supplying Boston. Thus another important fact is added to our list, and by its aid perhaps the remaining mysteries will be solved.

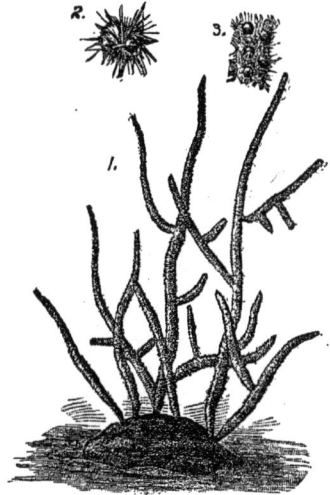

SPONGILLA FLUVIATILIS.

The cause of this cucumber-like odor was found to be a species of fresh water sponge, the *Spongilla fluviatilis*. The illustration

---

* Report of E. Waller on Croton Water,

was originally taken from Johnston's British Sponges. The cucumber-like odor is produced by this sponge. Several cities in our
own State have suffered from it, Hartford in 1871, New Haven
in 1864–65 and 1872, and Norwich for several years successively.
Other cities as well as Boston have suffered; Baltimore also in
1880–81. This sponge possesses the cucumber odor while living,
which is intensified by decay, and it easily decomposes. Prof.
Remson states, " These masses, growing upon the bottom, easily
become disintegrated and undergo decomposition, and both the
growing masses and the disintegrated parts must contribute to the
taste of the water, although naturally the principal effect is due
to decomposition. As this decomposition takes place the more
readily the nearer the masses approach the surface of the water,
the water near the surface has a stronger taste than that near the
bottom." The engraving is one-third natural size; when living the
sponge is green but becomes brown in decay; it multiplies with
great rapidity. No. 2 shows a bud surrounded by spicules; these
latter are silicious and the presence of the sponge can be detected
by them; if found in the water. No. 3 is a small fragment, highly magnified. The sponge grows attached to sticks and stones,
and is somewhat tough and leathery. If any doubt exists whether
a specimen is of this variety of sponge, a small fragment may
be burned on a piece of mica, and the ash moistened with a
little dilute muriatic acid, and the residue examined with a low
power of the microscope, when the silicious spicules will appear
if the specimen were sponge.

The *Cyclops quadricornis* has already been illustrated. This is one
of the commonest forms, found at all seasons of the year, and is
one of the trophies of the vendors of filters. The following is one
of the commonest form of water fleas, and resembles the Cyclops;
it is called *Daphnia pulex*, and is quite frequently encountered, or
similar species, in the water of ponds and rivers.* We have seen
how plentiful the microscopical plant life is, although we have
illustrated but a few types out of an almost endless variety. To
display all the forms and varieties of any one order would take a
large volume, but enough has been shown to show the principal
types. It is not of so much importance in a sanitary sense to identify each particular species, if one can assign the specimen to its
proper class and order, and perhaps genus. In fact there are
many as yet unnamed varieties in several orders, *Diatoms* for in-

stance. The chemical charges that are constantly occurring in water, the amount of decaying materials received every autumn, and the need of some agency to transform this dead matter to living forms again, indicates one function of plant life. The super-abundance of plant life is prevented by the almost endless forms of minute animal life, which in their turn furnish food for larger animals, and thus the endless cycle of nature is maintained. There is also a species somewhat similar to those already shown belonging to the order *Copepoda*, which is a fair type of the order; it is called *Canthocamptus minutus*, and as shown in the cut is en-larged about thirty diame-ters. In the paper on the microscopical examination of the water supplies of several of the cities, *Copepoda* are mentioned as having been frequently seen, and as this is one of the commoner forms it was selected for

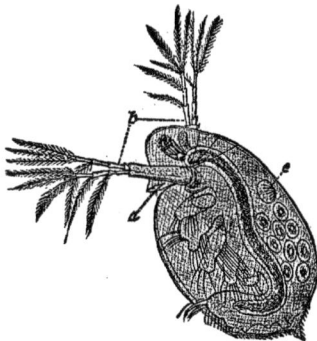

DAPHNIA PULEX.

illustration. It is usually of a pink color, and thus oftener attracts attention than the colorless varieties. The species can with difficulty be distinguished by the eye, although large enough to be seen under favorable circumstances, the pink color will also aid in distinguishing this variety. As before stated, this and the *Cyclops* selected as types of the *Copepoda* which are

CANTHOCAMPTUS.

often found in the rivers and ponds of this State.

There are very many other of the *Entomostraca*, and also of the crustaceans that might be used to illustrate the subject, but we close the list with one about as commonly met as any, the *Chydorus sphericus*. This is olive green in color, and is not quite as com-mon as the other varieties. There is scarcely a large pool of water in which specimens of *Cyclops* cannot be found. They also belong

to the order *Copepoda*, and vary in color and appearance, also with age. They are extremely active and dart about with great velocity. All the specimens of crustaceans illustrated are active and quick in their movements. This part of the subject has been illustrated so freely because these species are often shown to frighten people into the purchase of small filters; not but that such filters, if properly constructed and often cleaned, are most useful things, whose sale should be encouraged by all legitimate means. But these crustaceans are innocent objects enough, and as a rule offend the eye mainly. They act as scavengers to remove CHYDORUS SPHE- decaying materials and to check the superabund-
RICUS. ance of plant life. The great abundance of one variety of confervoid plants in one instance was in fact stated to be due to the absence of *Cyclops quadricornis*, as before stated in this article.

The next class of animals that have been mentioned as common in ponded water is the *Infusoria*. These are microscopical animals that have neither vessels nor nerves, but internal spherical cavities. Motion is effected by means of cilia. They are called infusoria because common in infusions which have been set aside for a time. They are almost invariably present in stagnant water which contains organic matters in solution. They have flexible bodies, sometimes covered with vibratile cilia, or these are collected around a mouth in rows. Some of these cilia move constantly, and others voluntarily. These cilia are the principal organs of locomotion and ingestion. The food is drawn towards the mouth by the currents established by them, and when it is received into the mouth they close to prevent its escape. The species are very numerous. One of the commonest forms is the *Vorticella nebulifera*, which is here shown. These are upon long stalks, which are either spiral or straight; one or two that have separated by fission are shown. These will float away VORTICELLA NEBULIFERA. and form other colonies. They increase in several ways, but the one shown is perhaps the common-

est. Some of the *Infusoria* are covered with cilia, as well as supplied with them around the mouth. The variety shown is sometimes a parasite upon other animals. To the eye it appears like a slimy mass attached to a stick or stone, or blades of grass, and floating out into the water. There are many species that' form colonies like the *Vorticella*, and more perhaps that remain distinct. Some of them are stationary, others float about. They are most abundant in stagnant water. If found in large quantities they are more significant of impurities than most of the others mentioned. But one illustration is given as the species are easily recognized.

The next order is somewhat higher in organization and structure, this is the *Rotiferae*. These have a nervous system, and some of them have eyes. At the anterior extremity is a retractile, often lobed disk, upon which are placed vibratile cilia which, when in motion, present the appearance of revolving wheels, hence the name. One of the commonest forms is here shown, the *Rotifer vulgaris*. There are four families, each with their genera and species. The illustration is typical, and almost any of the species can be easily identified. They are found in pure water, and are not associated with putrefactive decay.

The principal types of microscopical life, both plant and animal, found in the waters of this State, have been illustrated, and their functions, so far as known, pointed out. The low infusorial forms, if found in abundance, indicate pollution. In fact, water that contains an unusual amount of the lower forms of life is to be looked upon with suspicion. This is especially true if the spores of fungoid plants, bacteria and the like, occur in considerable quantities. The bacteria that accompany putrefactive decay, and the lower forms that derive their substance from organic decay, are undesirable constituents. As can plainly be seen from the description of the microscopic forms of plant life, they are entirely distinct and dissimilar from the spores, germs, and bacteria connected with disease, and the presence of the latter is connected with an entirely different set of conditions than pertains to the microscopic forms of plant life; nor are the bad odors and tastes that are produced by such plants as the *Algae* the cause of any noxious qualities in the water. Whether the odors

ROTIFER
VULGARIS.

and tastes are caused by the soluble constituents of the plants
themselves, or by the decay of *Algae*, or in whatever way produced in connection with microscopic plant or animal life, they
impart no dangerous qualities to the water. Such water may be
offensive to taste and smell, but is not deleterious to health. The
fungoid spores and bacteria point to dangerous compounds with
which they are associated. The bacteria and vibriones present as
minute objects as the microscopist is called upon to examine.
From one-thousandth to one ten-thousandth of an inch is the
range they take in diameter, or even less. The *Amoebae* are the
simplest forms of the *Protozoa*, and are little more than a mass
of protoplasm; yet they possess motion, the power of secretion,
and each one is a complete individual.

The lowest forms of animal life are jelly-like masses, which, as
stated, are difficult to distinguish from plants. The *Protozoa* are
simply masses of protoplasm, very like jelly. *Rhizopods*, or root-
footed animals, are represented by the *Amoeba Proteus*, and a few
other species. These are irregular shaped, jelly-like masses,
which throw out from any part projections of every conceivable
size and shape that is proportionate to the size of their bodies.
They open and enclose a *Diatom*, or *Desmid*, or a plant of some
other species of the *Algae*, and when it is digested, reject it from
whatever part of their periphery it may be nearest. Sometimes
they can be seen with a long plant, which is covered in the middle
and free at both ends. If the *Rhizopod* is watched, it will shortly
be seen to have entirely surrounded the plant, which may have
been several times as long as the *Rhizopod* was when the process
was commenced. It has the curious property of shooting out pro
jections from its surface, of all shapes and sizes. Thus, in the
case instanced, the greater part of the body may preserve nearly a
round shape, while that which took in the plant is a long, narrow
parallelogram, so that it appears like a globe resting on a narrow
base, which extends equal distances each side. These projections
are called *Pseudopodia*.

The *Infusoria* are next in order. Almost invariably found in
stagnant water, they have a mouth and rudimentary digestive
cavity, and move by means of cilia. The *Rotifera* have a complete alimentary canal, and a nervous system. They are not
usually associated with putrefaction. The *Crustaceans* come next,
of which the *Cyclops* and *Daphnia* are types. As a rule, they are

found only in good water. They are large enough to be seen when water is held up to the light. If water be steril- ized and exposed to the air, it will soon contain some va- riety of *Algae*, the germ of which came from the air. Al- most all are invisible to the unaided eye. The *Desmidiaceae* is one of the families of the *Algae*, the only illustration given is in figure 5, plate 2, the *Cosmarium* which is of this family. They are all unicellular, but most of them are nearly divided into two sections by a central suture, which divides them into two equal segments. Their color is a vivid green. *Diatoms* are found in both fresh and salt water, in stagnant water and swift currents. They exist in all climates, and under all condi- tions, even as parasites on other plants. Their envelopes are silicious, unlike all other plants which are made up of cellulose, and the silicious envelopes are preserved in fossil forms. They are usually of a yellowish-brown color. The interior green por- tion of these plans is called the endochrome, and around it is often a gelatinous envelope. The spores, or zoöspores, as they are oftener called, possess the power of motion. They are round, or oval, and have cilia at one end usually, as shown in the plate, or else all around. They move with great rapidity when first set free. but soon become coated with cellulose, and then develop rapidly. The *Desmids* are usually found in pure water, and free sunlight is needed for their development and growth. Their presence is beneficial in removing the excess of carbonic acid from the water and removing the products of vegetable decay. The same is true of the water plants generally. The only objectionable feature in regard to the *Diatoms* is in the liability of the decay of the gelatinous envelope, which is greater than in the other forms. There is little doubt but that the decay of the *Algae*, especially in the water pipes, may be one source of the bad odors and tastes, but when, why, or how this occurs, so as to affect large reservoirs, we are as yet ignorant. The ultimate conclusion is, that the plant and animal life is beneficial, rather than deleterious, and is in fact essential to the purity of the water. There are many other organic impurities, but this article has been restricted to the com- moner living forms, not including the bacteria nor vibriones, one variety of which is illustrated in another connection.

The pollen of grasses and other plants, fragments of the plant and animal forms that have been mentioned, and other fragments of land and water plants of nearly all kinds, vegetable fibres, woody tissue, scales of insects, the eggs of parasites, and also their young, and certain varieties of worm-like polyps and even insects, are among organic impurities that may be found in water. This account excludes almost entirely the characteristic forms in sewage-polluted water, although some reference has been made incidentally. While the general rule is true that the organic life in water is beneficial, it may, under certain conditions prove the reverse. This is the case, if there is an undue proportion of either class or of special forms, or if by drought large quantities are left to decay and pollute the water. There are also certain plants decidedly offensive, but scarcely any injurious unless they become so in some such manner as above described.

DESCRIPTION OF PLATES.

PLATE I.

Fig. 1, *Clathrocystis æruginosa*, *a* shows a mature colony, *b* an unformed mass surrounded by a gelatinous envelope.

Fig. 2, *Anabæna gigantea*, from Wood's 'Algae of North America. The fourth division is a hecterocyst; the second below this is the large spore-cell, the partly developed spores showing plainly; magnified 750 diameters.

Fig. 3, *Chætophora elegans* magnified 150 diameters, the branch and ciliated zoöspore, magnified 300 diameters, are shown at the side.

Fig. 4, *Spirogyra quinina*, showing conjugation magnified 200 diameters, the green spore-cells are formed from the contents of two cells.

Fig. 5, *Lyngbya muralis*, one of the plants which produces a pig-pen odor; magnified 300 diameters.

Fig. 6, *Cladophora glomerata*; *b* shows zoöspores forming, and the method of escape when fully formed at *b*, which is the club-shaped branch; magnified 600 diameters.

Fig. 7 Shows a variety of *Nostoc* surrounded by a gelatinous sheath; *b*, *Nostoc* showing spore cell.

Fig. 8, *Protococcus* at various stages.

Fig. 9, *Hyalotheca dissiliens*, a variety of *Desmid*.

PLATE II.

Fig. 1, *Nostoc sphæricum*, a single filament.

Fig. 2, *Nostoc comminutum* magnified 800 diameters.

Fig. 3, *Nostoc commune* magnified 850 diameters.

Fig. 4, *Cælosphærum* magnified 600 diameters; a mature colony.

Fig. 5, *Cosmarum Botrytis*. Two unicellular individuals have ruptured their contents and united to form the spore seen at center, which is not yet perfect.

Fig. 6, *Lyngbya*, a variety, magnified 200 diameters.

Fig. 7 to 11, Different species of *Diatoms* magnified from 200 to 450 diameters.

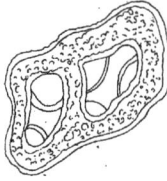

Fig. 2.

Fig. 1.

Fig. 4.

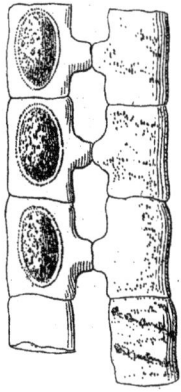

Fig. 3.

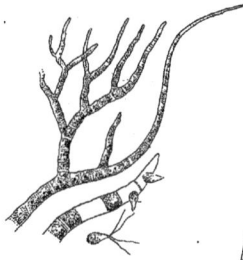

Fig. 5.

Fig. 6.

Fig. 7.

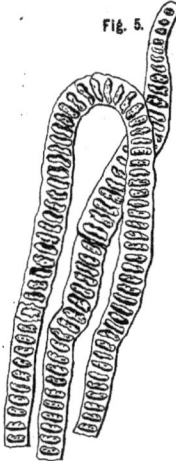

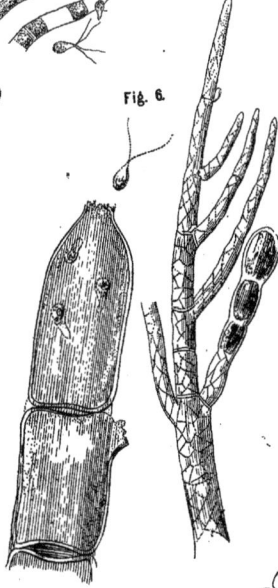

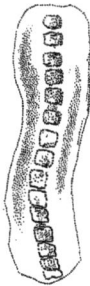

Fig. 9.

Fig. 8.

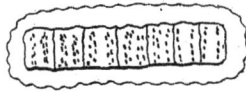

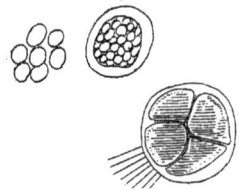

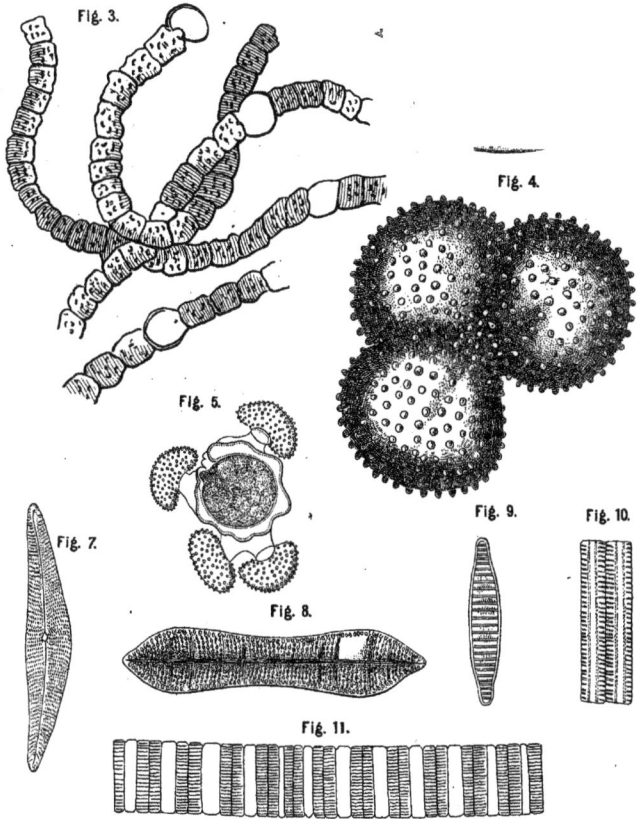

Fig. 2.

Fig. 3.

Fig. 4.

Fig. 5.

Fig. 7.

Fig. 9.

Fig. 10.

Fig. 8.

Fig. 11.

The Hartford Public High School.

A GENERAL DESCRIPTION OF THE WARM-ING AND VENTILATION.

GEORGE KELLER, ARCHITECT,

HARTFORD, CONN.

HARTFORD HIGH SCHOOL.

THE HARTFORD PUBLIC HIGH SCHOOL.

The Hartford Public High School was destroyed by fire January 24, 1882, and a town meeting was immediately called, at which James G. Batterson, James L. Howard, Rev. Edwin P. Parker, Rev. George L. Walker, and Edward S. White were appointed a Building Committee, and an appropriation of $200,000 was made to pay for erecting a new building—$30,000 additional was afterwards appropriated to pay for the furnishing of the school.

While the architect, Mr. George Keller of Hartford, has exercised the utmost freedom in preparing the design, he has successfully embodied the ideas of the Building Committee, to which in general, and its Chairman, James G. Batterson, in particular, many of the excellent features of the design are due. The suggestions and experience of the Principal, Mr. Joseph Hall, have been invaluable in the preparation of plans, the following description of which is taken from the Hartford *Daily Times* of June 9, 1882 :

TWO STORIES AND FIRE-PROOF.

Following the public opinion so emphatically expressed, both in and out of the town meeting, Mr. George Keller, the accomplished architect of this city, prepared plans with a view to a fire-proof building, of but *two stories* in height, exclusive of the attic. To secure school-room enough, it was necessary to enlarge the area of the building, as the burnt structure was of three stories. Mr. Keller laid out his work on an area of 22,000 square feet, and on looking at his plans it is found that he has occupied no more space than was necessary. His corridors are twelve feet wide, there are five exits, and a spacious hall 100 by 64 feet in width. He has arranged the stairways in the most convenient manner, as well as the reception, cloak, and recitation rooms, and the scientific

PLATE I.

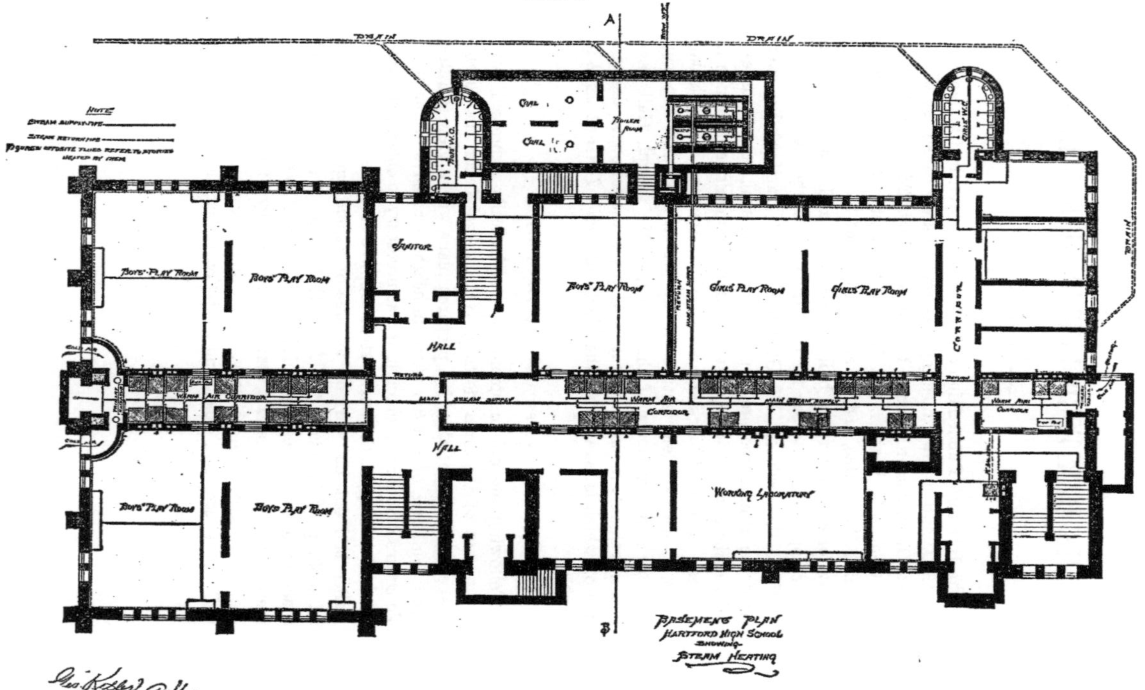

DRAIN
DRAIN
COAL
COAL
BOILER ROOM
BOYS' W.C.
GIRLS' W.C.
NOTE
JANITOR
BOYS' PLAY ROOM
BOYS' PLAY ROOM
BOYS' PLAY ROOM
BOYS' PLAY ROOM
BOYS' PLAY ROOM
GIRLS' PLAY ROOM
GIRLS' PLAY ROOM
CORRIDOR
HALL
HALL
WARM AIR CORRIDOR
MAIN STEAM SUPPLY
WARM AIR
CORRIDOR
WORKING LABORATORY
A
B
BASEMENT PLAN
HARTFORD HIGH SCHOOL
SHOWING
STEAM HEATING

PLATE II.

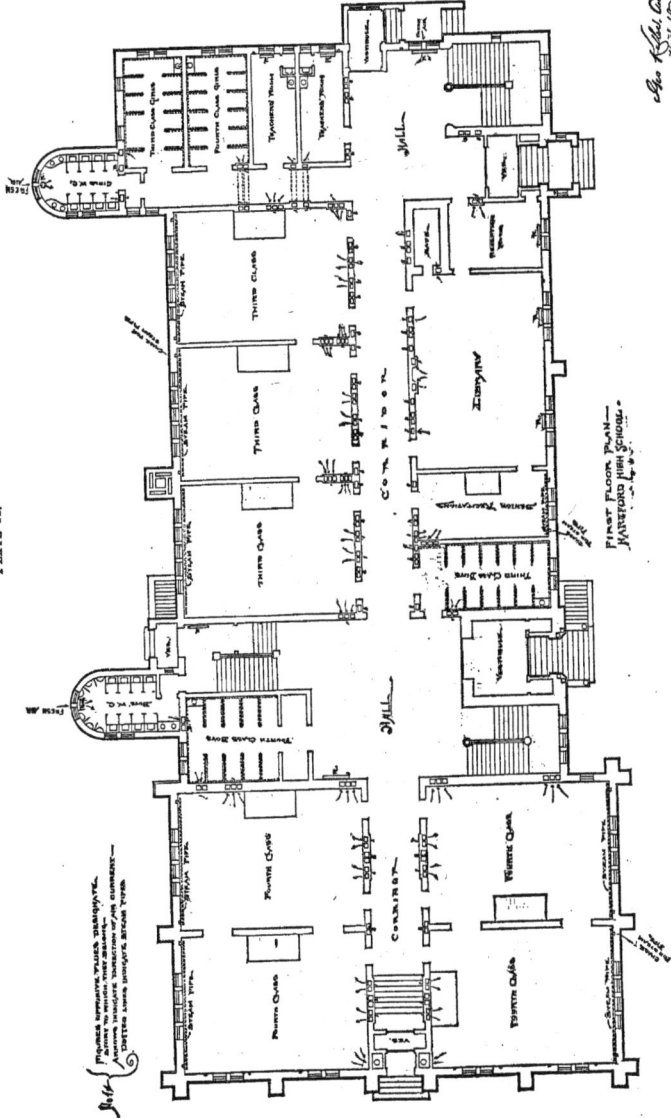

FIRST FLOOR PLAN
HARTFORD HIGH SCHOOL

PLATE III.

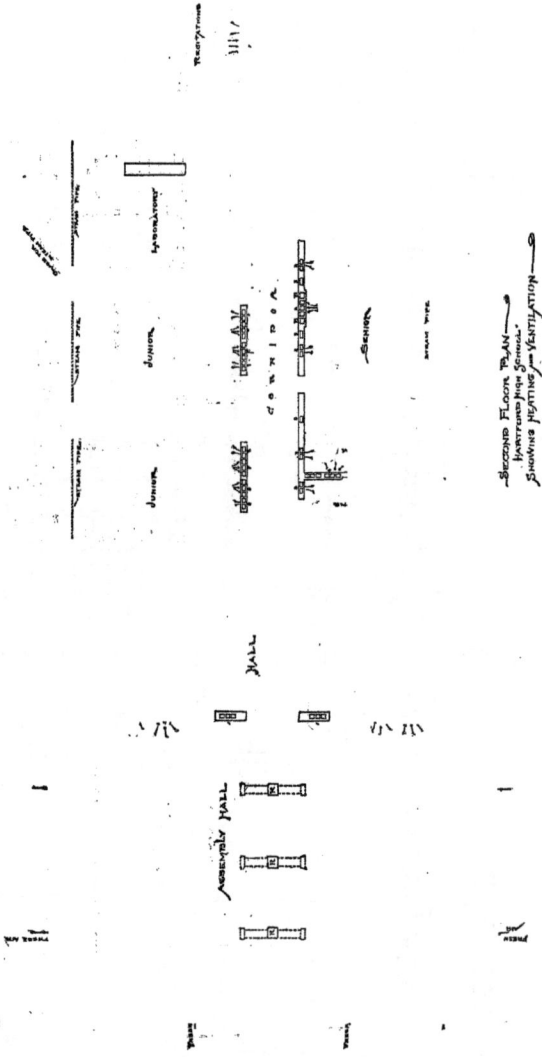

SECOND FLOOR PLAN
HARTFORD HIGH SCHOOL
SHOWING HEATING AND VENTILATION

apartments. Convenience, readiness of access, light, ventilation, have all been considered; and admirably well has Mr. Keller succeeded in accomplishing these desirable objects. There are fifteen rooms on the first floor and thirteen on the second, with a room for draughting purposes in the attic, where five or six more rooms may be utilized when found necessary.

A glance at the perspective elevation shows that Mr. Keller has succeeded in producing an imposing school-house; it tells its own story in characterizing itself as a school-house; and he has done this without wasteful expense in useless ornamentations, yet the building has a finished appearance, with all the exterior ornament that is necessary in a fine and substantial structure of this character. It is to be an enduring building. With brick arches for the floors and iron beams, there will be no decay, and 300 years hence the building will undoubtedly be as strong and useful as it will be the first year after it is completed. It will cost $25,000 or $30,000 extra to establish this object of durability and safety to the lives of the scholars; but it will be money well expended. The saving in insurance will be more than half enough to pay the interest on the extra cost.

A FULL DESCRIPTION.

The new high school building measures on the ground 236 feet in length and averages 95 feet in width, covering over 22,000 square feet, which is over double the area of the old buildings as they stood before the fire. It is planned for a two story building, having seven of the class-rooms on the first floor and but three on the second floor, so that practically two-thirds of the pupils will occupy the first floor and but one-third the second floor. The class rooms on the second floor are intended for the members of the junior and senior classes, which comprise the older scholars attending the school. A glance at the plans explains the arrangements.

FIRST FLOOR.

The ground floor shows a central corridor, twelve feet wide, running the whole length of the building from north to south. At the south end are placed four rooms for the fourth class scholars; two rooms on each side of the main corridor. The third class occupy three rooms adjoining each other on the west side of the building, and the reception, library, and senior recitation rooms occupy the principal part of the east front. The wardrobes for each class are arranged conveniently near each group of rooms, and the water-closets are planned *entirely outside the occupied part* of the building. Separate closets are provided level with each floor, so that the scholars are not obliged to descend or mount stairs to reach them. The boiler room is under ground, outside of the building.

There are five exits from the building, two on the east, and one each on the north, south, and west sides; and three ample stone staircases lead by easy ascent to the second story.   All the stair-cases are placed in the most convenient positions, yet so situated that the exercises in the different class-rooms are not disturbed by the noise of the scholars passing up and down the stairs. The clock tower, occupying the same position at the northeast angle as in the old building, contains one staircase.

SECOND FLOOR.

On the second floor, immediately over the four rooms of the fourth class, at the south end of the building, is placed the large assembly hall, 64 by 100 feet. It is reached by two staircases, placed a few feet on each side of the large doors to the hall.   Two junior class-rooms and the laboratory occupy the west side of the second floor, immediately over the third class-rooms below; and the senior class-room and recitation rooms are placed on the east side over the library and reception room of the first floor. The wardrobes, water-closets, etc., occupy corresponding positions to those on the first floor.

ATTIC.

But one room of the attic is intended to be finished off. It is to be used as a drawing room, and is placed at the north end of the building, behind the clock tower.

OBSERVATORY.

Advantage has been taken to arrange the senior wardrobe, so that its walls could be carried up and serve to support an observatory, instead of placing the observatory in the clock tower as was its position in the old building.

The building is designed in the Gothic style. The treatment of the exterior has been kept simple, the aim being to design a building which would proclaim its purpose at a glance, and one in which a proper use has been made of the materials to build a plain, substantial, and economical building. It is intended to build the walls up to the water-table of rock-faced brown stone, and above that of brick, faced with Philadelphia pressed brick, with brown stone caps and sills to the windows and other openings. The roofs are steep and are to be slated.

The height from floor to ceiling, in each story, is thirteen feet.

GENERAL DESCRIPTION OF THE WARMING AND VENTILATION.

The building is two stories high, with an attic and basement. On the first floor there are seven class-rooms, and on the second floor there are four class-rooms and a large assembly hall. Each class-room contains between fifty and sixty scholars, and it is proposed to ventilate each room with a supply of fresh air amounting to 30 cubic feet of air per minute for each scholar.

To accomplish this the arrangement for the introduction of air is to admit the fresh air after it has been adequately heated at an opening placed at the back or inner wall of each room, remote from the windows and cool outside walls, the effective cooling average surface of which—windows and walls—being as near equidistant from the point of admission of warm air as the form of the room will permit. This opening for the admission of warm air is placed about seven feet above the floor, so that the incoming current is not thrown upon any person standing near the opening. The direction of inflow will be made toward the windows, at the same time rising toward the ceiling. The warm air receives guidance from the outlet of the flue, and is also induced by the action of the windows and outside walls in demanding a greater or less supply of air for the downward currents against or near them.

The provision for the extraction of air is to withdraw the cooler and partially vitiated air from the surface of the floor through openings to flues placed as near the inner walls of the rooms as

37

practicable. The cold sheet of air traversing the panes of glass is intercepted before it falls or follows the wall to the floor by a broad and level window seat which throws the air inward to mingle with the warmer air of the room. Supplementary steam pipes are run under the windows the whole width of the room, to counteract the cooling effect of the glass.

Each room by itself and of itself, together with its inlet and outlet flues, is considered as one shaft or chimney. Such a shaft, starting as a flue at A, as shown in Diagram I, from an air chamber B, at the ground level, and having a small or limited sectional area, rises some height to an enlargement C, the room itself, the sectional area of the room being so out of proportion to that of the flue that the velocity of flow through it or the eddies occasioned by the flow may be imperceptible; and thence again to another flue D of limited section rising to and above the roof.

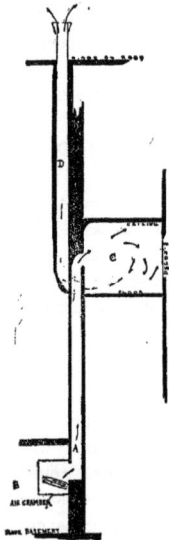

In order to make this "chimney" to draw, heat is supplied by radiators at the bottom, and during mild weather is further assisted by heat supplied to the outgoing flue above the room, either by gas jets or coils of steam pipe, as may be most suitable.

THE APPLICATION.

The High School is 236 feet long, running north and south, and averages 100 feet in width. It is divided almost in the middle by a twelve-foot wide corridor extending the whole length of the building from north to south. The different class-rooms, library, recitation-rooms, etc., open into this corridor on the right and left, so that the side walls of the corridors are also the inner walls to all the rooms. This arrangement admits of the introduction of the warm air to the different rooms of the building, at the end of the room farthest from the windows, by devoting the corridor in the basement for its whole length to an enclosed fresh-air duct, communicating by independent hot-air flues with each room. The fresh air is taken in at both ends, as shown on basement plan.

Diagram 1.

(Plate I.)' The fresh air passes through primary radiators placed at
the ends of corridor, which temper the air before it comes in contact
with the radiators placed at the mouth of each hot-air flue in the
basement. Each of these hot-air flues is provided with an independent radiator through which the fresh air in the corridor passes
and is warmed before it enters the flue to supply fresh warm air
to the room above.

The temperature of the air admitted to the rooms above is regulated without reducing the quantity of fresh-air supply, in the
following manner:

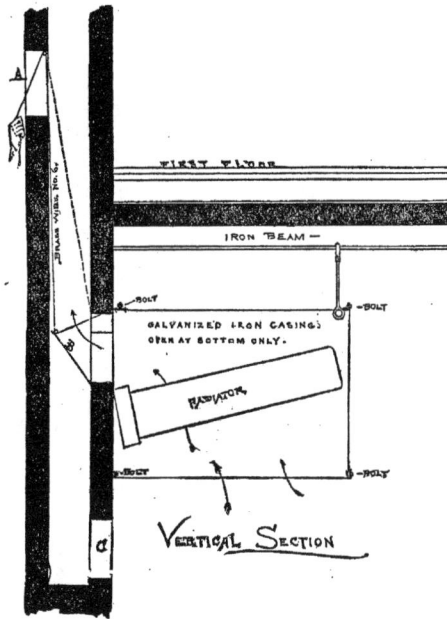

Diagram 2.

In an ordinary school room when the air becomes too warm the
teacher causes the registers to be closed, which shuts off the heat
and of course the ventilation at the same time. In the ar-

PLATE V.

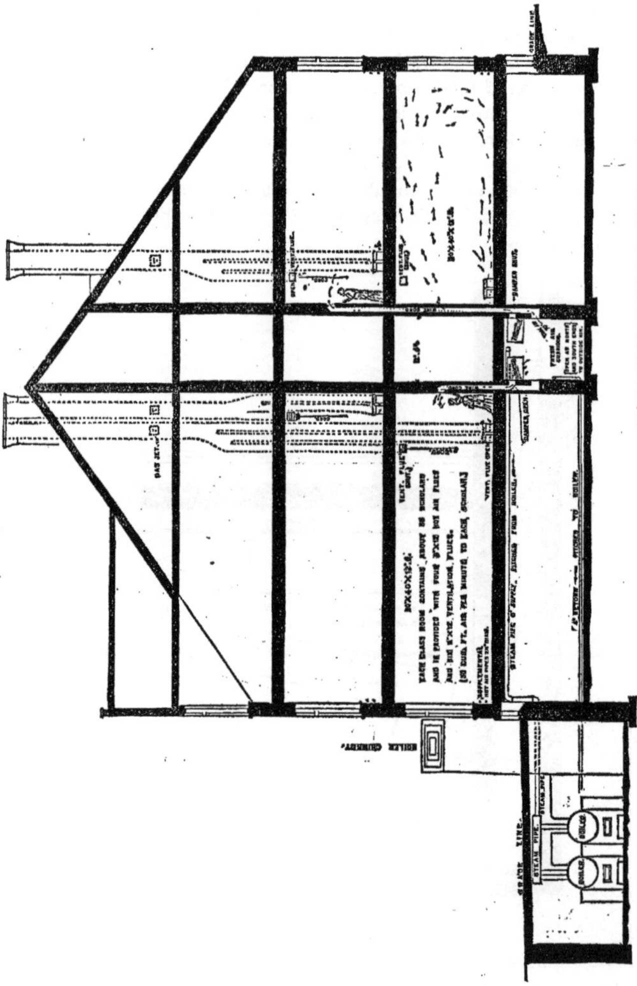

SECTION ON LINE A-B BASEMENT PLAN

rangement shown on Diagram 2, there is only a grating at A. The damper B is controlled from the school-room, and is so arranged that when it is open it admits the warm air to the flue, and when shut it admits cool air from the corridor through an opening into flue placed below radiators at C, and vice-versa.

The damper can also be placed at any intermediate position so that the temperature of the admitted air at A can be regulated to any degree from 140° to 70°, and adjusted to that which is necessary to keep the room at 68°, or, as some prefer, 70°. Each scholar is supplied with 30 cubic feet of air per minute, and the provision for supplying fresh air and withdrawing vitiated air changes the atmosphere every 11 minutes in ordinary weather. Each class-room is supplied with fresh air as above described through four 8″x12″ hot-air flues entering the class-rooms about seven feet above floor. Each class-room is also provided with six ventilation flues 8″x12″ (Plate V.) placed in the cross walls, and as near the inner wall of the room as practicable. The openings to four of these ventilation flues are placed at the level of the floor and are constantly open, and the openings to the remaining two flues are placed just below the level of the ceiling, and are closed, except when the air in the room becomes overheated, when these registers are opened, allowing the overheated air to escape. As indicated on the ground plans, a continuous line of steam-pipe is run along the partitions in cloak rooms, close to the floor, so as to dry the clothing in wet weather. Ample ventilation flues are provided in each cloak room, and the doors are provided with open transoms above and are three inches from the floor at the bottom, thus admitting a free circulation of air.

The main corridors on first and second floors, and the large assembly hall on the second floor are provided with direct radiators in addition to the warm air supplied to them by the indirect radiators in the basement. There are eight of these direct radiators in the assembly hall, and they are placed under the window stools of the east, west, and south

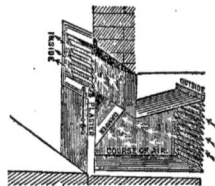

Eureka Ventilator.

outside walls. Each direct radiator is supplied with fresh air through what is known in Boston as the "Eureka Ventilator," built in the outside wall immediately behind each radiator. These ventilators are provided with dampers so as to control the admission of fresh outside air, as shown by the accompanying illustration.

In addition to the ventilation flues elsewhere described, the assembly hall, which will accommodate over 1,100 persons, is to be provided with three of "Boyle's Patent Air Pump Ventilators" for the extraction of overheated and vitiated air. These are automatic ventilators placed on the ridge of the roof, and communicating through galvanized iron ducts with a large ventilating register opening in the ceiling of the assembly hall. Rev. Newman Hall's Church, London, England, is ventilated by these patent ventilators, and wherever they have been adopted, they have given full satisfaction.

The system of warming and ventilation of the building is similar to that already carried out by Mr. Keller, in the new buildings designed by him for the State Hospital for the Insane at Middletown, Conn., which were completed about two years ago at a cost of $130,000. Mr. Charles B. Richards, C. E., of Philadelphia, one of the foremost investigators of this subject, was entrusted with the planning of the warming and ventilation of the new hospital in coöperation with the architect. The good results in the Middletown building led Mr. Keller to engage the services of Mr. Arthur C. Walworth, an accomplished engineer of Boston, Mass., to assist him in the planning of the warming and ventilation of the High School building. Much valuable advice and assistance was received from Mr. Charles B. Richards, and free use was made of the very able report of the late Robert Briggs, C. E., of Philadelphia, on the "Warming and Ventilation of the Bridgeport High School," published in the Third Annual Report of the Conn. State Board of Health, 1881. The system there advocated by Mr. Robert Briggs is practically the system adopted in the Hartford High School Building, and corresponds very closely to the system previously carried out in the Middletown State Hospital Additional Buildings for the Insane before referred to.

IMPURE ICE.

BY DR. C. W. CHAMBERLAIN,

SECRETARY STATE BOARD OF HEALTH.

IMPURE ICE.

The question of the purity of the ice supplied for domestic use is one of no inconsiderable importance when we take into consideration the amount of ice-water drank by the people of this country, and the free use that is made of ice to supply the deficiencies in the reservoir water, whenever, for any reason, that acquires an offensive taste or odor. Ice is used in so many ways that it has become one of the leading industries to supply the demand, and the ice crop is as important as many of the food products. It would be an interesting question to determine whether, as has been charged by the English, this free use is in any degree injurious to health; but that is a subject by itself, that would require considerable investigation and experiment before anything definite could result. The relation of many of the impurities that water contains to the ice frozen from it, has not as yet been fully determined, and the literature of the subject is very meagre.

In connection with the studies on the microscopical impurities in the water supplies of various cities, a systematic examination of the ice sold in the State has been commenced, and some studies made incidentally in regard to ice frozen from water contaminated by sewage. The old idea that water purifies itself by freezing is now pretty generally abandoned. The publication of the results of the use of impure ice at Rye Beach, and in our own State of a series of cases of dysentery caused by impure ice, were timely illustrations of its fallacy. Ice-houses now are seldom if ever filled with ice cut from ponds badly contaminated by sewage, nor from rivers that contain a very large percentage of such pollution. Public sentiment is so strong that such ice would be unsalable were its origin known. Indeed, most companies guarantee the purity of their sources of supply. Even ice used for markets and refrigerators, where it does not come into actual contact with objects to be preserved, is seldom cut from polluted water, and indeed pure ice should be used in all cases.

38

Pasteur has shown that while the fully-developed bacteria, bacillae, and similar organisms, can be destroyed by boiling or freezing, their germs or spores are not thus destroyed, but will retain their vitality even if exposed to a temperature very much below the freezing point; also, that many germs may remain dried for years and not lose their vitality, and if again placed under circumstances favorable to their development, will grow and multiply.

Prof. Pumpelly has found that most soils have but little capacity for retaining germs that are held in suspension in water that is passing through them, and that fine sand possesses such filtering properties least of all. This was tested for a layer one .hundred feet in thickness, and would doubtless be as true for thicker layers. As these germs are not readily oxidized or destroyed if they once gain access to water, it follows that water once polluted by sewage to any extent is wholly unfit ever after as a source of water supply. Freezing and boiling does not destroy the germs, filtering does not remove them. Unless their vitality is destroyed, they accompany the water to its ultimate outlet.

The utility of disinfectants, and the duty to use them wherever contagion or germs of disease can be reached, is thus forcibly shown. While their life remains, the power of the germs to reproduce themselves, and to cause disease, continues. Whether or no their infectiousness is lessened by freezing, is not known. That malignancy can be acquired and lost, seems to have been proven.

Freezing is a form of crystalization, and the general rules apply so far as inorganic pollution is in question. Ice frozen from water holding in solution mineral salts, will contain less of these than the water from which it was frozen, and by repeatedly dissolving in distilled water and refreezing, nearly all inorganic impurities can in time be removed from the ice. .But in case of *organic* pollution, the reverse is true. Often the process of freezing may, and does, concentrate such impurities so that the ice contains more in a given weight than the water from which it was frozen. This was shown by the experiments of the Committee of the National Board of Health. This appears different from what one would anticipate, although when water is mixed with substances that freeze at a different temperature, the latter may be concentrated by freezing the water, but may be separated from it, although the ice will retain a portion of such substance. Thus, in freezing a mixture of cider and water, for instance, the cider will be concentrated in the center of the ice and separated from the water, yet the whole bulk of the ice will be slightly sour.

The difference in specific gravity of ice and water probably is one reason for the excess of pollution in the ice. Such portions of the sewage as were lighter than the heavier water below the film of forming ice would naturally float to the surface and become entangled in the ice. From the results of some incomplete experiments of my own in this direction, it appears that the amount of dilution of the sewage, and the distance from the point of entrance, perhaps also the oxidation or partial destruction of the portions readily decomposed, are important factors in determining the relative amounts of pollution in ice and water. In specimens taken from a badly polluted stream near the outlet of a large trunk sewer, there were several grains more ($1\frac{1}{2}$) of organic residue from the ice than from the water of the river, while half a mile below the ice contained almost exactly the same amount of organic residue as the water. Similar results were obtained from ice cut from a pond four miles below the city, which sewers into the river of which the pond is a part. The pond results from a dam across the river.

The following experiment shows that the germs of bacteria are not destroyed by freezing or boiling or both. After the sewage-polluted ice was melted, while evaporating to secure the solid residue, a condenser was attached and the water received in a Florence flask which had been carefully washed in boiling water. The space between the tube of the condenser and the neck of the flask were filled with cotton wool to exclude the germs of the air as far as possible. When the flask was half full it was placed over a lamp and the water boiled, the neck sealed with cotton wool until the water boiled freely. The flask, after the water had been thoroughly boiled, was sealed and placed in a warm room. In two weeks bright spots appeared, and soon the whole became turbid. Microscopic examination then showed the presence of bacteria and bacillus rods. Ice cut from the centre of a block which was cut from a sewage polluted pond was placed in sterilized infusions by Prof. Pumpelly, and the flasks sealed. The development of bacteria showed that the vitality of their germs had not been destroyed by freezing.

There is another point to be considered in relation to the amount of contamination in ice from water polluted by sewage. As all chemical changes are less in winter under the influence of cold, the water from which the ice is formed would contain more sewage-pollution in a given bulk than in summer, because less would be removed by oxidization and still less by vegetation; so that the ice would probably contain a greater percentage of sewage-pollution than the water in summer. The microscopic life is also very considerably lessened in winter, so that source of puri-fication of the water would be removed. The cold would also have a tendency to prevent rapid changes in the sewage itself, so these products would accumulate. Thus it is readily seen that if such water is unfit to be used as a source of drinking water in summer, it is unfit for a source of ice supply in winter.

There has been but little work done in the way of exact analysis to determine the relative amounts of sewage in ice and the polluted water from which it is frozen. The following conclusions of Dr. Storer* in the investigations relative to the Newport ice supply, embody what is definitely known on the subject. They are derived from reports from different experts to which the subject was referred. They are in substance as follows:

While the *inorganic* impurities in water may be partly eliminated by freezing, the purification is at best but partial and imperfect. The more dangerous *organic* impurities resulting from human and other animal waste are retained in ice unchanged both as to quality and quantity, the latter indeed being likely to be increased. The germs of infectious diseases are retained in ice unaffected, and from their comparative lightness are so concentrated in ice that they exist in greater quantities than in the same amount of water at any other time of the year. The ordinary sewage or organic impurities, if there be no germs of infectious diseases, are likely to produce dangerous diseases in persons using the ice, as was the case at Rye Beach. In several instances the amount of albuminoid ammonia, one of the evidences of organic impurities, has been greater in the ice than in the same amount of the water of the pond from which it was obtained. Thus it appears that so far as organic pollution is concerned the quantity is rather increased and concentrated by freezing rather than diminished. This is the result of the experiments of Prof. Pumpelly, which were very complete and exact so far as the power of analysis can determine. The effect of freezing upon the infective power of germs has not been fully determined, although their

* Sanitarian, May 1882.

vitality remains. But even if infectious diseases cannot be conveyed by impure ice the diarrheal diseases induced are sufficient
to exclude the use of ice from such sources.

The following case has been analyzed very closely, and the connection is apparently clear: There occurred a fatal case of
typhoid fever in a gentleman who for some months had been living alone, his family being absent during the summer and
early autumn. As the sanitary arrangements were as perfect
as wealth and intelligence could make them, the cause of this
isolated case was for a long time a mystery. The fact that he
was inordinately fond of ice-water led to a suspicion that this
might be the cause, and an investigation followed. The ice used
was cut from a pond near the houses of laborers on his farm, and,
unknown to him, the drains from these houses had been connected
with this pond. During the summer there had been in these
houses three cases of typhoid fever, one fatal, and the dejections
had been thrown into the water-closets without any disinfection. The common practice of the neighborhood was for the
house-drains to empty upon the open ground whenever a lower
level could be reached, or else in some convenient ditch, but as
this pond was quite near the houses, the drains were led into it. As
the pond had been used for filling the ice-house for years, there
was no suspicion of any contamination until after the mischief had
been caused. The connection seems clear. There is no doubt
concerning the pollution of the water by the dejections from
typhoid fever patients as reported, nor the other facts as stated.
Had the ice been used by others to any extent, the proof would
have been clearer.

During the summer I examined thirty specimens of ice-water
from ice as supplied to customers from the carts in five different
cities. In none of those was there any evidence of sewage contamination, although one was suspicious, as the organic matters
were largely in excess in comparison with the others. The refusal
of several companies to sell to the person that was sending specimens, after they had learned by chance the purpose for which it
was wanted, led me to suspect that the source of supply was not
above suspicion.

The plan adopted was to have from twenty-five to fifty pounds
of the ice melted and the sediment with about a quart of water
sent. To secure uniformity, when the larger quantity had been

melted, half the quantity sent was used. In twelve of the specimens there was no sediment deposited. In six there was not
enough to cover the bottom of a quart bottle, and in the remaining
twelve the deposit varied from an eighth to nearly half an inch.
None developed offensive odors except in two instances, though
the bottles were kept corked in a warm room four months, some of
them. The bulk of the deposits was formed evidently of substances held in suspension in the water. The field and water
grasses broken in small fragments were most frequently encountered. Next to these an amorphous flocculent deposit of partly
decayed vegetable matter that had been held in suspension in the
water. The microscope revealed some diatoms and fragments of
microscopic plants and animals, such as are most common in fresh
water, and some few specimens nearly complete. In one there were
fragments of woody tissue, and several twigs and bits of bark;
sand and dirt were not uncommon. In one there was an unusual
quantity of specimens of various forms of microscopic plant and
animal life, in connection with fragments of water, weeds, and
grasses. There were but a few that developed any large amount
of microscopic plant and animal life; in fact, but two. In these
there were extensive colonies of filamentous *Algae* developed. In
but six was there any unusual amount of organic residue upon
evaporation and incineration, and that apparently was of vegetable
origin entirely. The water was not discolored in any instance.
The only indications that resulted from the work, as far as carried,
were, that there was considerable carelessness shown in cutting ice
from shallow water, and from the windward edge of ponds, and
storing ice that plainly showed that it held in suspension large
amounts of dirt, grit, sand, and vegetable matter, when clean, clear
ice might as well have been selected. Ice cut at some distance
from the margins of ponds or rivers, and from water several feet
deep, appears to be desirable. The specimens from which there
was no sediment showed what could be accomplished with care.
Turbid, dirty water, in a glass of ice water, or poured from an ice
pitcher is objectionable, if not deleterious to health, and as by the
exercise of a little more care this can be avoided, the remedy is in
the hands of the people, as it was in the case of sewage-polluted ice.
    One has only to compare these results with those in several
cases a few years ago, when I examined specimens of ice-water
from suspected sources. Upon uncorking the bottles that contained

the water a vile odor escaped that quickly made itself felt. One did not have to examine the specimens closely. The water was of a greenish hue, swarming with vibriones and bacteria, or became so in a short time. The sediment showed sewage contamination plainly when examined under the microscope, and the rapidity with which a solution of permanganate of potash was decolorized, left no room for doubt as to the qualitative nature of the water in question. The rapidity with which decomposition set in in such water, and the offensive odors were characteristics that were un-mistakable.

It is evident that there are but few venders of ice that would venture to store ice from polluted water. If the private ice-houses are filled with as intelligent a discrimination of the possible sources of pollution of ponds and rivers in populous districts, and when used as a final outlet for drains, one source of danger to health and life would be eliminated that is often insidious and obscure. The change in regard to public supplies, and the ice stored by companies in our cities and towns, is an encouraging sign of progress in sanitary science, or rather that its principles are becom-ing popularized and acted upon. Had the examination here de-tailed been made a few years ago, there would have been little difficulty in finding among so many different companies more than a half-dozen that had stored polluted ice, in the place of one or two suspicious cases where specimens were not readily obtained. While there is probably little danger in the undesirable practices mentioned, if there be any, as long as an improvement can be so easily made, it seems worthy the effort so that all the ice stored shall rival the artificial ice in clearness and purity.

A series of experiments have been commenced to determine more fully the relative amounts of organic pollution in ice cut from impure water, and the water itself; so far as any results have been reached, they indicate that when ice is cut from a sewage polluted stream after the water has had a short run, the ice usually contains more organic residue and albuminóid ammonia than the water, but may contain less mineral or inorganic compounds.

PROTECTIVE INOCULATION.

By NOAH CRESSY, M.D., V.S., Ph.D.

PROTECTIVE INOCULATION.

The sterling achievements in comparative pathology, which the last decade has wrought relative to the germ theory, have not only awakened new zeal among scientific men, both at home and abroad, but have necessitated the recognition of a biological factor in the study of the etiology of many forms of disease. The results of these researches have revolutionized in a great measure all previous conceptions of the intimate nature of contagion; and it has now been conclusively demonstrated by the concurrent testimony of competent observers, that the disease-bearing germs of anthrax and possibly certain other infectious maladies, are tiny parasitic organisms that belong to the marvelous world of microscopic plant life. The practical advantages already foreshadowed by these investigations have attracted the attention of biologists throughout the world. Everywhere earnest workers are searching for the evidence to establish or disprove the assertions; that each contagious disease is due to some specific germ, that bacteria can be metamorphosed at will, that their malignancy can be controlled by successive cultivations, and their very nature changed by modifications of temperature and food supply.

Even consumption, which has long been considered the very type of a disease due to hereditary tendencies, had hardly been shown to be only exceptionally thus induced, when from the laboratory of the daring young German experimenter, Dr. Koch, comes the confirmation of the contagiousness of the disease with the exhibition of the very bacillus that produces it, faithfully portrayed by nature's artist in the micro-photograph, which reproduces the wonderful revelations of the microscopic lens.

To such an extent has the zeal and enthusiasm of the microscopists been carried, that real progress has been retarded by their eagerness to identify themselves with the discovery of a species of bacteria, as the primal cause of some particular form of

disease, which has induced them to announce, as scientific veri-
ties, theories; based upon partially observed facts, and experiments that have not been repeated by independent observers, who
should have secured the same results, while unbiased by any desire to confirm the same.

That all contagious diseases have a continuous existence like
organized beings, and thus arise from special causes, no competent
pathologist will deny. As in the vegetable world, each seed produces its kind, and the acorn never contains the germ of any other
tree but the sturdy oak ; so each infectious disease has its own
specific virus, which can induce no other malady than the one from
which it was derived. Thus every disease germ must come
from pre-existing ones, and consequently the spontaneous origin
of any infectious malady is quite as untenable in the present state of science, as the equivocal generation of plants and
animals.

Long before the *contagium vivum* had been discovered, patholo-
gists believing that the morbific principle, affecting the system, in
a large group of epidemic and sporadic forms of disease, closely
resembled the action of a ferment, proposed the zymotic theory,
which though vague in its chemico-physiological significance, has
been almost universally accepted by modern authors. The analogy
seemed very striking in many respects, even when first enunciated,
but the discovery that the active agent of fermentation was a
minute vegetable organism, which grew and multiplied at the expense of the saccharine liquid, virtually paved the way for the
germ theory of disease.

DIFFUSION OF GERMS.

These tiny, floating particles are found in the atmosphere everywhere, and only await a congenial soil to spring into active life
and reproduce themselves with almost inconceivable rapidity, so
that if not retarded in any way the offspring of a single germ
would in a few hours be numbered by millions. Bacteria,
and their germs, exist in the water, as well as in the air, and permeate the moist earth everywhere, they are diffused by moisture and
are wafted into the atmosphere as the sun dries up the moisture
from the wetted surfaces upon which they were deposited; they
also reach the air from dried solid matters which, in the form of
dust or impalpable powders, are scattered broadcast by the winds.

There is a wide difference between bacteria and germs, although both terms are used indiscriminately. The bacteria are produced by germs, and are, it is supposed, the fully developed organisms; they also multiply by fission, that is a division into two equal parts, each of which becomes a complete living organism. The bacteria are exceedingly minute, some of them so small that they cannot be measured with certainty, the one which is the ferment of ordinary putrefaction is $\frac{1}{25000}$ of an inch in diameter; it is a little longer than it is broad. The *bacillus anthracis* is larger, from $\frac{1}{3000}$ to $\frac{1}{10000}$ of an inch long. The vibriones are about $\frac{1}{2000}$ of an inch long. The germs in the vacine lymph are $\frac{1}{25000}$ of an inch in diameter and are spherical. The corpuscles in the silk worm disease are $\frac{1}{8000}$ of an inch long. The cells of the yeast plant are $\frac{1}{3000}$ of an inch in diameter. The germs and flagellæ are at the extreme limit of microscopic vision, the former often appear as bright dots from their power of refracting light.

These micro-germs are exceedingly tenacious of life, freezing does not destroy them, neither do they lose their vitality at the boiling temperature of water, nor from dessication, for if moisture is again supplied the dried germ becomes as lively as ever. The period of time required to kill them has never been determined, and so far vitality has been preserved as long as they have been under observation, many years in repeated instances. This is not true of the mature bacteria which are very easily destroyed, in some varieties by a change of even a few degrees of temperature.

The bacteria and their germs revel in a damp, warm atmosphere, and are found in greater numbers in the summer air than in that of winter, and in larger proportions, in warm climates decreasing as the frigid zones are approached, where the air contains but few. So too after a warm rain, or if a long summer rain follows a continued drought, these organisms are found to be four times as numerous as before. This increase suggests a reason for the prevalence of malarial diseases under the conditions above mentioned, if they are caused by bacteria as has been so strongly asserted.

The bodies of animals always contain innocent germs so that they are found in the food we eat, as well as the water we drink. The human body also contains them, thus there are four different varieties of innocent bacteria in the mouth, as many in the intestinal tract, and others in different tissues of the body, although

Pasteur, Koch, and Ehrlich state that they have never found them in any animal except in disease.

There are four fundamental types of bacteria, each of which includes different species, some of them, a very large number. These are the spheroid, the rod-shaped, the thread-like, and the spiral. There has been a vast deal of discussion whether bacteria are properly plants or animals, but they are now generally classed among the fungi from the absence of green coloring matter. That they are of vegetable origin is shown by the presence of cellulose. They are distinguished from inorganic particles by the power of motion either in a straight or curved line, and by their arrangement into pairs, triplets, or chains. Molecular motion, that is motion without progress, may be possessed by inorganic matter. There are many chemical tests to differentiate fat cells and the like, but the best method of proving the nature of germs is by cultivation artificially.

As so many references are made to the different varieties of germs, a brief statement of the principal orders seems expedient. The word bacteria has been used as a general term for all germs, and also for one order causing considerable confusion; there are five orders, *Micrococcus, Bacterium, Bacillus, Vibrio, Spirillum.* The first are spherical granules, which occur either singly, in beaded chains, or irregular masses. The latter are called *Zooglea,* and are shown in the spores of bacillus in the plate, Fig. 3. Fig. 19 is a *zooglea* mass of bacilli, not as highly magnified as the other figures. The spores of bacillus are shaped like micrococci, and at Fig. 2 can be seen the fission or division into two spores which is one of the ways in which micrococci multiply. A species of the micrococcus is the germ supposed to cause diphtheria.

Bacteria, using the word in its limited sense, are oval and sometimes have flagellæ, that is minute filaments at the end, as shown in the bacillus, Fig. 6, and Fig. 20. The flagellæ are tests of microscopic vision, as their diameter is not more than the $\frac{1}{800000}$ of an inch. Bacteria seldom multiply in any other way than transverse fission.

The *bacillus* is the rod-shaped type; one species has been fully illustrated in the plate, the figures magnified in the upper part

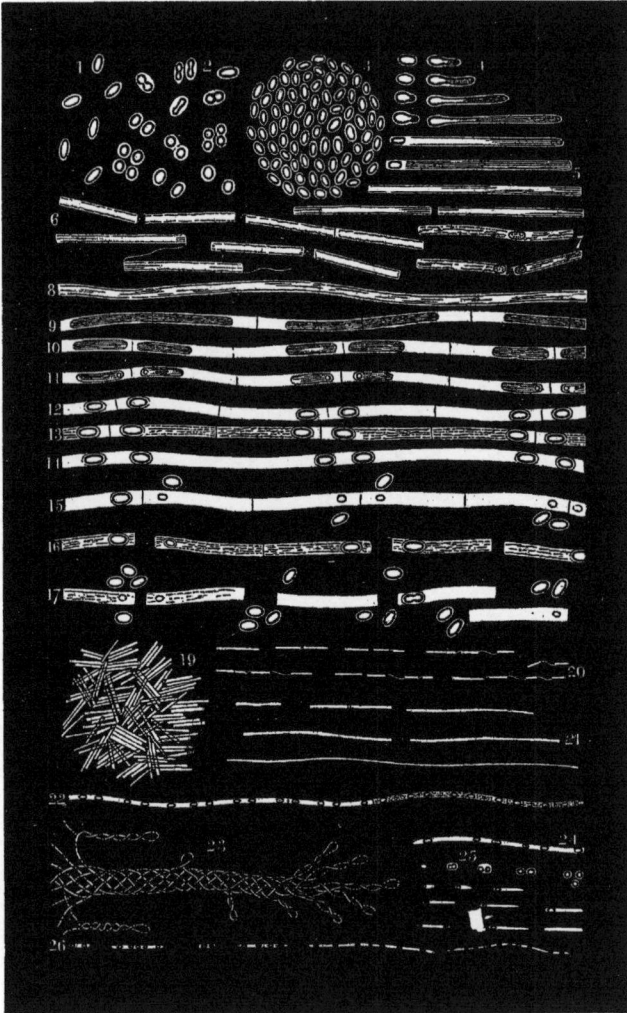

LIFE-HISTORY OF BACILLUS ANTHRACIS.

3,000 diameters, in the lower part less. The baeillus rods themselves vary from $\frac{1}{3000}$ to $\frac{1}{10000}$ of an inch in diameter.*

The *vibrio* resembles the *bacillus*, but is flexible, often curved, like
the letter S. *Vibriones* are the thread-like forms; they move by a
vibrating motion, hence the name. Any one familiar with microscopical examination of urine has often seen different species of them.

The *spirillum* is explained by its name, the spiral form. The
spores closely resemble the comma used in punctuation. A species
is associated with relapsing fever.

DESCRIPTION OF THE PLATE.

The plate, in a general way, illustrates the life history of all
microbes. The two principal methods of multiplication are shown
by the development of spores and transverse fission. Figs. 1 to 3
show the spores of *Bacillus anthracis*, Fig. 2 binary fission, and
Fig. 3 the *zooglea* form. The development of the spore into a
complete rod or *bacillus* is shown in Fig. 4, the resulting *bacillus* in
the next figure, which shows the commencement of transverse
fission complete in Fig. 6, which has lengthened into a filament at
Fig. 8. At the next figure (nine) the protoplasm of the interior
has commenced to contract, and the lines of fission where the filament is to break up into rods are shown. The contraction of the
protoplasm into spores is shown in Figs. 9 to 14, and the escape of
the spores by the breaking up of the filament into rods, i. e.,
bacilli, is shown in the next three figures. The second subdivision
is seen in Figs. 10 and 11, and the complete germs in Fig. 14 .

In Fig. 22 the modifying effects of cultivation at a fixed temperature are seen in the long filament which results. The spore-
bearing filaments are often smaller than the others, as seen in Fig.
26, also Figs. 20 and 21. A curious form is seen in Fig. 23, a
"double spiral rope work," instead of the usual *zooglea* mass shown
in Fig. 19, formed from the *bacilli* shown in Figs. 20 and 21. The
development of these cultivated spores is shown in Fig. 25.

The rope-work has been compared to a tangled skein of silk.
The silken threads, studded with brightly refractive spores, present a beautiful appearance under the microscope.

---

* "Carpenter on the Microscope," 6th edition, from which the plate is
taken.

METAMORPHOSIS OF GERMS.

It has been asserted that innocent bacteria may be developed into malignant forms by changing their food-supply, and in other ways. Thus one of the germs found in the mouth may be transformed into the one that kills by producing septicæmia, that is, blood poisoning. The bacillus from an infusion of hay may be converted into the one that produces anthrax by feeding it with egg albumum and the serum of the blood. By varying temperature, supply of oxygen, and by successive cultivations qualities may be changed almost at will. This has been done with a large number of bacteria, a few are alluded to above as illustrations. That malignancy and infectiousness have been placed under control, will be fully shown farther on.

In carefully studying the life-history of the *Bacillus anthracis*, microscopists have found that the rod, in living tissues, multiplies indefinitely by a process of transverse fission but it is not proved to lengthen out into filaments. If a moderate temperature, however, be kept up for several hours after death, and with other conditions favorable, it may assume the filamentous form. But in a short time, the protoplasm, of which the filament is largely composed, gradually contracts, segregation into globular masses occurs, and thus myriads of spores are formed. These in turn may either germinate and at once grow into rods again, or subdivide into four distinct sporules, which then germinate, and form rods, similar to the original type, thus completing a vegetative cycle of existence.

But when these bacilli are cultivated under artificial conditions, on the warm stage of the microscope, they have sometimes been observed to become mobile, but after being alternately in motion and at rest for some hours, the rod lengthens out into an exceedingly long filament, which has become much more "attenuate" than ever found under natural conditions, as shown in Fig. 22. In this state the protoplasm of the filament undergoes similar changes as before, but undoubtedly with altered properties.

MODE OF ACTION.

The production of disease by bacteria, or their germs, has been explained in several different ways, the following being the principal. First, that the germs are the carriers only of contagion or infection. Second, that the necrobiotic changes they induce in the tissues produce a chemical virus which causes the disease. Third, that the germs penetrate the tissues directly, enter the blood-vessels and permeate the corpuscles, and thus produce disease. Fourth, that the innocent germs in the body acquire malignancy, consequently increased powers of motion, penetration, and rapidity of growth, thus using the tissues and fluids of the body for their own nourishment. However this may be, it is true that innocent germs use the body as a pasture-ground, hence the probability that disease-germs may do the same. The fact that bacteria can be transferred from animal to animal while their life history is so obscure, at least that of the greater number, and can be so modified in their characteristics, strengthens the probability still further that these organisms play a causative role in the production of infective disease.

VARIOLOUS INOCULATION.

Early in the sixteenth century, when the ravages of small-pox were rife among the people and had attracted a wide-spread interest, the inoculation of the active virus was resorted to, with a view of diminishing the fatal effects of the malady. This method of producing the disease at will, in a milder form, which experience, gathered from the secrets of the past, had shown was equally efficacious as a protective measure, became a common practice in Persia, Hindostan, and other oriental nations, and received the endorsement of the most enlightened physicians of the age.

Variolous inoculation was introduced into England in 1722, by Mrs. Mary Wortley Montague, wife of the Embassador to Turkey, who, on her return home, had her daughter inoculated, according to the almost universal custom which they had observed in the East, of having the children submitted to this operation every autumn, and where their son, five years previously, had passed through this induced malady with favorable results. This made a deep impression on the minds of the English people, who were already very solicitous about the matter. Dr. Keith, with much confidence and anxiety, followed the example by the inoculation of his son, and this new practice therefore, under such sanction, soon became popular throughout the British isles.

Caroline, Princess of Wales, one of whose daughters, Princess Anne, had nearly died from small-pox, which very much disfigured

40

her, became anxious that the rest of her children should be protected by inoculation against such a misfortune. But as she had not acquired sufficient confidence, some further demonstrations became necessary, and George the First offered pardon to six condemned criminals, if they would consent to be inoculated for the good of the public. Five of them were favorably affected, the sixth not at all, and a seventh felon escaped the ordeal of the gallows by allowing a few small-pox scabs to be thrust up her nose as an experiment.

After variolation had been successfully practiced on several children at the parish of St. James, the Princesses Amelia and Caroline submitted to the operation, which resulted in a very satisfactory manner. As the practice, however, became more general, a fatal case now and then occurred, so that at the end of eight years, out of 845 inoculations, 17 had proved fatal. Thus showing that this induced affection, instead of being perfectly harmless, as it was at first supposed, had been attended with two per cent. of mortality, even under the most favorable circumstances. But to make this practice more availing in a sanitary point of view, a small-pox hospital was erected in 1746, for the benefit of the poor, who had already contracted the disease, and for the free inoculation of the children, as well as for adults who had hitherto escaped the disease. This charitable movement, however, greatly increased the mortality from small-pox, which for ten years, including four after the opening of the institution, had averaged 72½ in every 1,000; increased during the second decade, to 103, and in the next, to 111; from which we are forced to conclude, that the inoculation of the unmodified virus has a tendency to disseminate the germs of this loathsome and contagious malady.

The protective inoculation of small-pox was initiated in this country about the middle of the last century, and for a time was extensively practiced by a privileged class, who, in those days, united the office of priest and physician. During the winter of 1777 and '78, twelve hundred persons were inoculated at Middletown, Conn., and pock-houses were established in many towns in this and other states. But this method of protection, notwithstanding its many advocates on both sides of the Atlantic, was superseded in the progress of comparative pathology, by that very efficient, safe, and much more wholesome practice of Vaccination.

INOCULATION OF SHEEP-POX.

The horse, cow, and sheep are especially subject to an eruptive disease which is analogous to the small-pox in man, but modified by the peculiarities of the animal in each case. The virus of sheep-pox has been used successfully to inoculate flocks to prevent the spread of the disease. The protective power of the ovine virus has been also tested on the human subject, but with unsatisfactory results. Many other animals, and birds also, have a similar form of disease, which occurs independent of small-pox in man.

VACCINATION.

The beneficial results that have accrued to mankind from Jenner's discovery of vaccination are now so plainly evident that it would be more rational to deny the daily rotation of the earth upon its axis, or to doubt the truth of the law of gravitation, than to question their reality. Thus, instead of seeing in every other person a disfigured victim of this dreadful malady, a pitted face is seldom encountered in these days, and those decimating epidemics of small-pox which formerly numbered their victims by thousands are now unknown, except in the uncivilized regions where vaccination is not practiced. Well may our mother country boast of the honor of having given birth to that immortal philanthropist who in his zealous love for the truth, and with an ambition that was never daunted, has thus rescued the precious lives of millions, subdued the scourge whose malignancy had hitherto been ineffectually opposed, and raised a barrier against the unchecked progress of this pestilence.

DEVELOPMENT OF THE IDEA OF PROTECTIVE INOCULATION.

The chain of discoveries that led to the idea of protective inoculation is long and somewhat complicated. A complete history would take more time and space than can be here devoted to the subject. A few of the connecting links only can be considered, and these not always consecutively. One of the most important steps in the development of the germ theory of disease, and incidentally in the preparation for protective inoculation, was the discovery that the essential elements of the vaccine lymph of the small-pox matter, and of the virus of sheep-pox, were minute microscopic particles. This was demonstrated by filtering them through porcelain, when it was found that the liquid that had passed through would not produce any results when the germs or particles were thus removed. It may convey some idea of the minuteness of these particles when it is remembered that the virus of sheep-pox, for instance, may be diluted ten thousand times its bulk, and still produce the disease when inoculated. The discovery that fermentation was due to the development and growth of germs into confervoid organisms, the yeast plant, and the researches of Pasteur upon this subject were progressive steps in this direction. In fact, the development of the germ theory of disease, and all the subjects that relate to it, are also interwoven with the history of protective inoculation. One direct result, apparently, of the researches of Pasteur was the application of his conclusions to human surgery by Lister, who ascribed a similar fermentative action to the atmospheric germs absorbed by wounds, which, he asserted, led to suppuration, blood poisoning, and other great evils.

The studies of Pasteur in fermentation also led to his employment to solve the mystery which surrounded the disease of silkworms, which threatened to destroy one of the most profitable industries of France. It had already been noticed that there were tiny microscopic particles in the fluids of the diseased worms, but no one knew their nature, or whether they had any connection with the trouble in question. To these Pasteur directed his attention, and in them he found the cause of the disease of the silkworms; he discovered them to be germs, which in their development and growth into mature organisms used the silkworm as a food supply, destroying its vitality in the process. By studying their life history he was enabled to establish a method by which the disease could be stamped out, thus conferring an inestimable practical benefit upon the whole nation, in saving one of their most extensive industries from total extinction. Lessons in microscopy are given to the more intelligent employees. Women are the best manipulators. Small, inexpensive instruments are required, and the appearance of the parasite is noted at once, before it has extended its ravages. The prompt destruction of every infected silkworm stamps out the contagion, and prevents any interference with the usual progress of the industry.

With the promulgation of the theory that contagious diseases are produced by the agency of organic germs—microbes, as they are appropriately called—and the discovery of special forms in certain diseases, as the *bacillus anthracis* in splenic fever, a new impulse was given to the study of the natural history and habitat of the myriad forms and species of germs that swarm in the air, earth, and water, and also, as has been stated, find congenial homes in the various tissues and fluids of human and animal bodies. It is with the malignant microbes, however, that we are mostly concerned, and their action in the production of disease as well as the methods by which their malignancy can be tamed.

Davaine found in the blood of sheep and oxen that had died of anthrax, a malignant disease that has caused hitherto great devastation in the flocks and herds of Europe, a microbe that he termed *bacillus anthracis*. This discovery was verified by numerous independent experimenters, and it was furthermore found that these germs, if inoculated in sheep and cattle, would invariably produce anthrax. This is the most plainly demonstrated fact, in the germ-theory of disease, and is apparently unshaken by all attacks or endeavors to discredit it. Toussaint soon after identified the germ that produces chicken cholera, and since then numerous experimenters in different countries have announced the discovery of a microbe as the cause of certain forms of disease. One of the latest and most brilliant of these discoveries is that of the *bacillus tuberculosis*, by Koch, the microbe that produces consumption, which has been confirmed by many observers in different countries, and has a strong probability of truth in its favor, if not yet fully demonstrated. Time and space will not permit the enumeration of the germs that have been associated with different diseases,— some of which are quite probable, others mere conjecture. Long continued observations and experiments alone can determine the truth or falsity of these assertions.

An important step in the development of protective inoculation was the endeavor to control the qualities of germs, and modify them at will.

Though we have stated the different views held in relation to the connection of germs with disease, yet the experiments of

Koch, as verified by Klein and Toussaint, have apparently demonstrated that it is the germs themselves, and not the organic media in which they are found, which, when inoculated, produce anthrax, the swine plague, and chicken cholera. We are therefore led to infer that the same is true with all, for by removing these germs as far as possible from all sources of contamination, cultivating them in different media from those in which they were originally found, and invariably producing by their inoculation the very diseases from which they were taken, they proved that these tiny organisms were the cause of the maladies.

Thus, in 1876 Dr. Koch succeeded in isolating the *bacillus anthracis*, that little rod-like bacterium illustrated in the plate, selected not only because so much of its life history is known, but because it was the first disease germ that was cultivated outside of the animal body. Soon after this Klein isolated and cultivated the microbe associated with the swine plague, followed by Toussaint, who did the same with the bacterium of chicken cholera. Pasteur, dissatisfied with the culture-medium previously employed, found, after repeated experiments, that clear chicken soup was the best for the cultivation of this microbe. He introduced the germs into the soup by dipping the point of a needle into the infected blood, and then placed it in the soup,* which was maintained at a proper temperature with the germs of the air excluded as far as possible. Another quantity of soup was infected from the germs developed in the first, and so on indefinitely; but some degree of malignancy was lost at each successive cultivation. When the desired strength was acquired, it was used to inoculate fowls, inducing in them a mild form of disease, which afterward protected the chickens against a future attack of this very disastrous and contagious malady. But he found, by a very singular and interesting observation, that if the infected soup was freely exposed to oxygen, the same attenuation, or decrease of malignancy was produced.

Bacillus anthracis.—This microbe, which gives rise to anthrax in cattle and sheep, and to wool-sorter's disease in mankind, as well as malignant pustule, has been perhaps more thoroughly studied than any other form of bacteria. The invariable results that follow its inoculation in the hands of every skillful experimenter, the readiness with which it can be isolated and cultivated, render it a

---

*One source of error is apparent, that is the engrafting of other germs from the air or implements used.

typical illustration of a disease germ, and the real foundation on which the theory rests. Pasteur found the best medium for its cultivation also was the chicken-broth, although his efforts in this direction were at first defeated by its persistency in running to spores; but by maintaining a certain temperature this tendency was overcome, and it multiplied itself by fission, as shown at Fig. 7, in the plate. If the culture medium was kept at this temperature, he found that this microbe could be cultivated with essentially the same results as the germs of chicken cholera, but attenuation followed exposure to the atmosphere much more rapidly. He also found that any degree of malignancy could be produced, as was the case with the germs of chicken cholera, and that when sufficiently attenuated, if inoculated upon sheep and cattle, it produced only a slight disturbance of the system; yet it protected the animal as effectually against anthrax as was known to be the case in animals that had recovered from the disease. .

The tenacity of life of these germs is remarkable. Pasteur found the vitality undiminished of those taken from pits, where animals that had died from anthrax had been buried ten years. The agency of earth-worms in spreading this disease is also very curious. When such animals are buried, the worms bring the germs to the surface of the ground; these germs are taken into the stomachs of sheep and cattle as they crop the herbage, and thus give rise to epidemics of anthrax.

RESULTS OF PROTECTIVE INOCULATION.

As the annual loss to France from anthrax was nearly a million sterling, the commercial value of protective inoculation soon attracted general attention, and accordingly public tests on a large scale were demanded. Thus, at Melun, twenty-five out of fifty sheep were publicly inoculated with modified virus and marked. Two weeks afterwards the whole fifty were inoculated with anthrax. In the twenty-five marked sheep no results followed, and the others died within two days, of anthrax. The same results followed in other public tests, a few months later.

Within the last two years the benefits of protective inoculation have been extended far and wide, and the ravages of anthrax sensibly diminished.

In all those regions where anthrax prevails as an endemic disease, the inoculation of an attenuated virus is unquestionably very beneficial; but in other places, where the disease is unknown, the practice of such inoculation is uncalled for, and of very doubtful expediency, as Dr. Klein has so clearly shown it to be in England For the introduction of foreign germs into animals whose haoits and surroundings are essentially different may result in a recrudescence of malignancy, and thus propagate the disease in question.

We must not omit, however, to make mention of Willem's inoculation of pleuro-pneumonia, which was made in 1852, and which has now become a popular practice with veterinarians, though the germ has not been so thoroughly studied as the importance of the subject demands. The Russian cattle-plague and the foot-and-mouth disease have also been inoculated, with a view of prevention, but with questionable results.

"Thus," says Dr. Fleming, "though inoculation for the artificial production of certain contagious diseases of man and beast has been practiced for more than a century, yet the recent advances in histology and experimental pathology have placed the subject in an entirely new light, and demonstrated that with two or three, if not with all these maladies, protection may be afforded against them by inducing them, in an extremely modified form, through inoculation with their cultivated virus. This has been done with such fatal diseases as anthrax, symptomatic anthrax, fowl cholera, and to a certain extent with rabies; and it is in the range of possibility that all the other scourges which owe their development and extension to microscopic germs will soon be included in the list." *

SANITARY CONCLUSIONS.

The results of the power intimated by the control of germs, as described in modifying contagion, are plainly evident. The importance of disinfection and destruction of the virus of disease, whenever practicable, as in typhoid fever, for instance, is emphasized by what has been shown concerning the tenacity of life of disease germs. Every person affected by a contagious disease, soon surrounds himself by an infected atmosphere, which he maintains during its continuance, his body becoming, for the nonce, a laboratory for the manufacture of disease germs, and these infect other objects than the atmosphere, according to the nature of the malady.

---

* Veterinary Journal, London, Aug., 1882, page 119.

So long as the person is a hot-bed, swarming with tiny microscopic organisms, he is of little significance, except as an individual. But when the malignant germs are eliminated from the body by millions, each tenacious of life, and all his excretions are loaded with them, the danger threatened confers on him a new importance, yet convalescents are allowed to scatter disease germs by thousands wherever they go. The importance of exercising a supervision over those affected with contagious diseases, is shown plainly by this theory of disease. The relations of comparative pathology, and the transmission of diseases from animal to man, are also explained by the agency of disease germs. As it was to Jenner's observations of a peculiar eruption on the cow, that we owe the discovery of vaccination, so it is the investigations upon diseases of domestic animals, as Cameron observes, that has enabled the veterinary surgeons of France to make such important contributions to science, which clearly affect the vital interests, not only of animals merely, but of mankind, and show plainly the value of comparative medicine and pathology, whose function it should be to investigate the varied theories as to the diseased condition of every living thing and their relations to the diseases of man.

We have thus seen some methods of modifying the malignancy of germs, and the resulting control of contagion. There are probably other methods of varying the qualities of germs, which, if known, would produce equally important results. Whether the germ theory is universally true or not, it is the best one to work by, and promises the richest rewards for honest investigations.

41

ADDITIONS TO THE LIBRARY.

Adulteration of Foods, Bell.
Allen, Commercial Analysis, Vols 1, 2.

Bell, History of the Water Supply of the World.
Blythe, on Foods.
Browne, Water Supply.
Burdett, Pay Hospitals of the World.

Census Reports, Part I, Tenth Census.   Population.
    Bulletin on Machinery.
    Cotton Production.
    Forestry Bulletin.
    Indebtedness of Cities.
    Oyster Industry.
    Seal Islands of Alaska.
Cheyne on Croup.
Circulars of Bureau of Education.
Constantine, Practical Ventilation.

Darwin, Vegetable Mould.
Drake, Diseases of the Mississippi Valley.

Ekin, Potable Water.

Farlow, Marine Algæ of North America.
Fournier, Syphilis and Marriage.
Frankland, Water Analysis.

Gerber Analysis of Milk, Condensed Milk, and Infants Milk Foods.
Gerhardt, House Drainage.   Presented by the author.

Health Hints from the Bible.
Health Primers, 2 vols.
Hill & Cooper, Syphilis.
Hitchcock, Synopsis of Rhizopods.
Holbrook, Marriage and Parentage.
    "   Herald of Health, 1881, 1882.
Howard, Salt the Forbidden Food.
Huxley, Science and Culture.

Journal of the Statistical Society, 1882.

Leidy, Rhizopods of North America.
Leuckardt's Parasites.
Lubbock, Fifty Years of Science.
Luys, The Brain and its Functions.

Macdonald, Naval Hygiene.
Morselli, Suicide.

National Board of Health, 1st and 4th Annual Reports.
Navy, U. S., VI Report of Surgeon-General.
Normand and Noad, Chemical Analysis.
Norris, Pathology of the Blood.

Oakey, Building a Home.
Oswald, Physical Education.

Pasteur, Fermentation.
Paterson Health Statistics.
Proceedings Engineers' Club, Philadelphia.—from Col. Waring.
Proceedings, Alumni Association, Phil. Coll. Pharmacy.
Parry, on Water.
Public Acts, January Session 1882.

Rance, Water Supply of England.
Ray, Mental Hygiene.
Registration Report, Ontario, 1881.
Registration Report, Rhode Island, 1881.
     "   "   Massachusetts, "
     "   "   England,   ··
         "   Scotland,   "
         "   Philadelphia, "
         " '   Ontario,   "
         "   City of Albany, "
         "   " Providence.
         "   " London, Eng., Quarterly.
     "   Reports, Weekly, London, Edinburgh, Dublin, Rome,
Vienna, Paris.
Report Board of Health, City of Detroit.
     "   "   "   " Burlington.

Report Board of Health, City of Utica.
   " " " " Albany.
   " " " " Boston.
   " " " " Bridgewater.
   " " " " Concord.
   " " " " Dayton.
   " " " " Memphis.
   " " " " New Britain.
   " " " " New Haven.
   " " " " Reading.
   " " " " San Francisco.
   " " " " Somerville.
Report of Board of State Commissioners of Public Charities, Illinois; Tabular Statements.
Report, Board of Agriculture, Conn., and Conn. Experimental Station, 1882.
Report of Railroad Commissioners, 1882.
Report, On Education in Italy.
 " Alabama State Board of Health.
 " American Medical Association, 1881.
 " American Pharmaceutical Association.
 " Biennial, Maryland State Board of Health.
 " Board of Health, Boston, 1881.
 " Connecticut Hospital for Insane.
 " State Board of Education, Conn., 1882.
 " Hartford Retreat for Insane.
 " Health Officer, District of Columbia.
 " Homoepathic Medical Society, Penn., 1882.
 " Illinois State Board of Health, 3d.
 " Iowa State Board of Health, 1st.
 " Mass. State Board of Health, Lunacy, and Charities, 3d.
 " Michigan State Board of Health, 9th.
 " Minnesota State Board of Health, 8th.
 " New Hampshire State Board of Health, 1st.
 " New Jersey State Board of Health, 5th.
 " New York State Board of Health, 2d.
 " Rhode Island State Board of Health, 4th.
 " State Asylum for Insane Criminals, Auburn, N. Y.
 " State Homeopathic Asylum for Insane.
 " State Medical Society, New York, 1882.

Report South Carolina State Board of Health, 3d.
"   Tennessee State Board of Health.
"   Vital Statistics, Italy.
"   Wisconsin State Board of Health, 6th.
Reports, New York State Museum, 23-4, 31.
Ribot, Diseases of Memory.
Ridge, Principles of Organic Life.

Sanitarian, Vol. X, 1882.
Sanitary Record,   "
Sanitary Engineer,   "
Scientific American, Supplement.
Smithsonian Report, 1874-5, 1878—1881.
Spon's Cyclopedia of Industries, Vol. II.
Systems and Tables of Life Insurance.

Thwaite, Health of Factories and Workshops.
Thornton, On Foods.
Thudicum, Analysis of Medical Chemicals.
Thurber, Coffee; Plantation to the Cup.
Transactions, Institute of Surveyers, 8–10.
"   Social Science Association.
"   American Public Health Association, 7th.
Tidy, Legal Medicine, Vol. 1.
Truman, On Food.
Training Children.
Tuckerman's Lichens of North America.
Tucker, On Sugar Analysis.
Tyndall, Floating Matters in the Air.
Vaccination Enquirer, 1882.

Walford, Deaths from Accidents.
Wilson's Guide to Inspectors of Nuisances.
Woolsey, On Divorce. Presented by the author.

Yellow Fever in the Plymouth.
Yeo, Health Resorts.

ENGLISH PAMPHLETS.

Alkali Report.
"   "   Inspector's.

Animals Act, Report, 1881.
Army Medical Report.

China, Sanitary Regulations.
   "   Medical Report, 22.
Cholera Reports, 1855.
Contagious Diseases, Report, 2, Evidence.
      "   "   Memorials.
      "   "   of Animals Return.
              "   Act, Report.
                 " Report of Committee.

Dublin Hospital Report, 2d.
   "   "   "   3d.

Educational Theories.
Effluvium Nuisances, Report.
East India Sanitary Measures.

Habitual Drunkards, Report.
Hong Kong, Sanitary Condition.
   "   Papers, '79, '82.
Hospitals for Infectious Diseases, Report.

London Water Supply.
Lodging Houses, Queenstown, Report.
Lunacy Commission, Report.
   "   Scotland, Report.

Medical Officer's Report, 1880.
Metropolitan Board of Works, Report.
Model By-Laws.

Navy, Health Report of.

Prison Commissioners' Report, 4, 5.
Parliamentary Papers.

Rivers, Pollution, Report, Angus, Smith.
Rawlinson's Sanitary Papers.

Sanitary Condition, Birkenhead.

Searle, Nervous Diseases.
Sewer Gas, and Effects.
Supervision Report, 1881.
Simons's Report on Vaccination, 1857.

Vaccination Report and Evidence, 1871.
    "   " Scotland, 1881.
Vivisection.

White Lead Works, Employment in, Report.
Winslow, Influence of Light.

PAMPHLETS.

Bartlett, Adulteration of Food.
Baker, Systematic Study of Sickness, etc.

Circular, Resuscitation of the Drowned, California.
    "   Method for testing Inflammable Oils, Elliot.
    "   Prevention of Small-Pox, Mich.
    "   Work of Health Officers, "
    "   Contagious Diseases,   ".
    "   Scarlet Fever.
    "   "   Kentucky.
Conn. Ventilation.

Prevention of Diphtheria, New York State Board of Health.
Disinfection.   "   "   "   "
Procedures of Local Health Boards, "   "   "
Small-Pox Hospitals,   "   "   "   "
Contagious Disease Refuges,   "   "   "   "'
Prevention of Small-Pox,   "   "   "   "
Prevention of Contagious Diseases in Schools, "   "
Report on Methods of Sewerage,   "   "   "
Rules for Registration,   "   "   "   "
Immigrant Inspection Service in Michigan.
              "   "   " District of the Lakes.
Government Protection Needed, H. B. Baker, M.D.
Northerly Winds of California, Bonte.
Vaccination of School Children, Order for; Illinois State Board of
    Health.
Prevention of Small-Pox,   "   "   "

Personal Sanitary Responsibilities, J. R. Allen.
Registration of Plumbers, Health Department, New York.
Prevention of Small-Pox, Wisconsin.
Circular, Restriction of Scarlet Fever, Iowa.
    "   "   "   "   "   Kentucky.
    "   "   "   "   "   Michigan.
    "   "   "   "   "   Minnesota.
Infectious Diseases, Ordinance, Baltimore.
    "   "   "   New Britain.
Remsen, Report on Boston Water Supply.
Report Water Commissioners, New London.
    "   "   "   Hartford.
Resolutions International Medical Congress respecting Signalmen,
    etc.   Presented by Dr. Jeffries.

Suburban School Houses.

Thomson, Storage of Electricity.

Waring, Death-Rate, Memphis.
    "   Report on Sewerage of Buffalo.
    "   "   "   Worcester.
    "   Separate System Sewerage.   Reply to Clarke.
Watson, Common Law Citations.

State Board of Health.

BUREAU OF VITAL STATISTICS,

STATE OF CONNECTICUT.

REGISTRATION REPORT

FOR THE

Year Ending December 31, 1881.

NEW SERIES.—No. 4.

Printed by Order of the Legislature.

HARTFORD, CONN.:

PRESS OF THE CASE, LOCKWOOD & BRAINARD COMPANY.

1882.

CONTENTS.

State of Connecticut.

Office of the
Bureau of Vital Statistics,
State House, Hartford, Dec. 31, 1882.

To his excellency, H. B. Bigelow,

      Governor of the State of Connecticut:

Sir: In accordance with the laws of this State, I have the honor to submit the Annual Registration Report relating to Births, Marriages, Deaths, and Divorces which occurred in the State of Connecticut during the year 1881.

      Your very obedient servant,

              C. W. CHAMBERLAIN, M.D.,

              Superintendent of Registration of Vital Statistics.

State Board of Health

BUREAU OF VITAL STATISTICS.

Dr. JOHN S. BUTLER, Hartford, President.

Prof. C. A. LINDSLEY, M.D., New Haven.

Prof. W. H. BREWER, New Haven.

Hon. A. E. BURR, Hartford,

Hon. A. C. LIPPIT, New London.

Dr. G. H. WILSON, Meriden.

Dr. C. W. CHAMBERLAIN, Hartford, Secretary,

AND Superintendent of Registration of Vital Statistics.

REGISTRATION REPORT.

1881.

The report of the vital statistics of the State for the year presents many interesting features, and in connection with those of the last few years reveals indications of periodic movements in disease which will well repay study. In point of fact our knowledge of epidemics is very limited, especially with reference to the inducing causes of such wide-spread effects and influences, and their laws of periodicity, so that with regard to epidemics the guilty agencies that originate them are as a rule not well understood. The indications are, however, quite strongly in favor of the idea that many of the diseases that commonly occur more or less each year, are marked by periodic influences at intervals of varying length, as well as the recognized epidemics and pandemics that appear only at intervals and sweep over vast areas.

A few typographical errors have occurred; in fact, in such complicated tables it is almost impossible to prevent one now and then. They are, however, comparatively unimportant this year but one instance of transposition which is the most annoying.

Some improvement in the returns of occupations followed from the publication of the table; as was anticipated. When no use was made of them, there was no inducement for painstaking; there is however still room for improvement, and the attention of physicians is invited to their duty in this regard. A table showing the aggregate for ten years is in course of preparation, but cannot be in readiness this year. As no tables have been made for any of these years, the whole ground must be canvassed. There are several other comparative tables that have been planned and only await time and opportunity to complete. As all this has to be done with little clerical assistance, except to verify results, the need of time is apparent.

The mortality shows an increase over that recorded last year of

499, the year ranking here, as elsewhere, as upon the whole not characterized by conditions favorable to health. The protracted heated term, long-continued dry weather, and unseasonable warm weather, intensified unsanitary conditions that otherwise might have remained quiescent. The returns are completer than they have been in preceding years, and as physicians generally are now supplied with these reports, and the glaring evils of incomplete and inaccurate returns are brought to their notice, a greater improvement may be hoped for, in the future. The greatest difficulty now is to secure proper returns for small towns near cities, and villages where the larger amount of the practice is in the hands of non-resident physicians. The tables show how very inaccurate such returns are. Thus, in West Hartford, a town of nearly two thousand inhabitants, but 8 deaths are returned, the death rate from the records 4.4 per thousand, while the average of the county is 18 9. Stratford a death-rate of 5.1; that of the county 17.1; other instances could be cited. As a rule these very low rates indicate imperfect returns from some such cause. These returns however are slowly lessening each year, so that they are now almost entirely restricted to the towns indicated where non-resident physicians make no returns.

There have been no extensive epidemics to increase the mortality, nor any great accidents or calamities. The increase is mainly confined to diarrheal and enteric diseases, and those favored by debilitating and depressing influences, especially among children; the deaths of those not over five years comprising 30 per cent. of the total mortality; this increase is one and a half per cent. less than last year however. Lung fever has been very prevalent for the last two years, and deaths from nervous diseases and insanity have increased largely.

There were recorded in 1881, 14,616 births, 4,850 marriages, 10,907 deaths; 787 *more* births than in 1880, 105 *more* marriages and 499 *more* deaths. There were 404 divorces recorded, 72 more than in 1880, which gives a ratio of one divorce to every 12 marriages. There is as yet no very good reason for not attributing the decrease to the repeal of the omnibus clause to some extent. Even with the increased number of divorces, the ratio of marriages to divorces is still favorable to a gain by the repeal of that provision. The last legislature indicated no disposition to restore it, and it is to be hoped that changes will be made in the direction of more stringency in the divorce laws, if any are to be made. It has been stated that a part at least of the increase is more apparent than real, and due to the clearing up of old cases that had been some time on the docket.

The excess of births over deaths is 3,709, which is 288 more than last year, an improvement also over the figures of 1880, which were very much less than the preceding year. The returns of births are not as complete however, as those of deaths. By the efforts of some of the registrars, considerable improvement has been made over previous years' returns, so that in several instances where the returns at first indicated an excess of deaths over births, in several places by a little effort in neglected quarters something like accuracy was secured. Probably in the cities and larger towns from 20 to 25 per cent. of the births are unrecorded.

The population as finally revised by the census bureau is 622,700, which gives

Births,	22.4	to each 1,000 population.
Marriages,	7.7	" " "
Deaths,	17.4	" " "
Excess of births over deaths,	5.9	" " "

The daily average of natural increase was——

Daily average of births, male 20.9, female 19.5, total 40.4	
Marriages,	13.5
Deaths,	29.8
Average daily natural increase,	10.1

There has been a steady increase in the death-rate for the last few years, due to the same influences that have been felt all around us, and manifested in a similar manner in adjoining States, but the increase this year is one per cent. less than last. In 1880 it was 1.7%, this year, 1881, it is but seven-tenths of one per cent. The increase in births and marriages is an indication of returning prosperity, as the decrease in marriages especially was marked during the period of depression in business.

The following table gives a summary of the vital statistics of the State, from 1848, the date of the first registration report, up to the present time. The birth and death-rates are calculated by adding the proportional increment to each years' population, as the census every ten years is the only resource, no State census having yet been taken.

Years.	Births.	Birth-rate per 1,000.	Marriages	Deaths.	Death-rate per 1,000.	Excess of Births over Deaths.	Divorces.	No. of Marriages to each Divorce.
1848	6,850	20	2,816	4,379	12.4	2,471	...	...
1849	7,238	20	2,920	5,049	14	2,189	...	...
1850	7,578	20.4	2,884	5,170	14	2,408	...	...
1851	8,362	22	2,995	4,767	13	3,595	...	...
1852	8,302	21.4	3,136	5,596	14.4	2,706	...	...
1853	8,439	21.3	3,202	5,646	14.2	2,793	...	...
1854	10,012	24	4,286	6,094	14.6	3,918	...	...
1856	11,139	25	4,089	6,324	14.9	4,805	...	...
1857	11,355	26	3,747	6,585	16	4,770	...	...
1858	11,299	25	3,737	6,618	15.6	4,681	...	...
1859	11,259	25	3,778	6,533	15	4,726	...	...
1860	11,873	26	4,036	7,602	16.3	4,271	310	13
1861	11,934	25	3,757	7,735	16.5	4,199	275	13.9
1862	10,803	23	3,701	8,541	18	1,262	257	14
1863	9,885	21	3,467	8,442	18	1,443	291	12
1864	9,734	20	4,107	9,109	19	625	426	9.6
1865	10,202	20.8	4,460	7,950	16	2,252	404	11
1866	11,623	23	4,978	7,520	15	4,103	488	10
1867	12,029	23.2	4,779	7,343	14.3	4,676	459	10.4
1868	12,469	23.4	4,734	7,549	15	4,947	478	9.9
1869	12,481	23.5	4,754	8,417	15.6	4,064	491	9.6
1870	13,136	24.2	4,871	8,895	15	4,241	408	11.9
1871	13,114	24	4,882	8,166	14.2	4,948	409	11.9
1872	13,805	25.3	5,023	9,970	18	3,935	464	10.8
1873	14,087	25.6	4,841	9,822	17.4	4,265	457	10.6
1874	14,450	26.2	4,694	8,939	17.2	5,511	492	9.5
1875	14,328	26	4,385	9,883	17	4,485	476	9.4
1876	13,800	25	4,320	10,187	17.5	3,613	396	10.9
1877	14,072	26	4,319	9,696	16	4,376	427	10.1
1878	13,499	24	4,315	9,352	15	4,147	401	10.7
1879	14,051	22.4	4,373	9,394	15	4,657	316	12.7
1880	13,829	22.2	4,745	10,408	16.7	3,421	332	14.2
1881	14,616	22,4	4,850	10,907	17.4	3,709	404	12

The highest birth-rate is in 1874, 26.2, the lowest 1864, 20. The highest death-rate 1864, 19, the lowest 1848, but the returns were not then very complete. The most favorable ratio of marriages to divorces is 1880, 14.2, the least 1875, when there was one divorce for every 9.4 marriages, nearly one in nine.

TABLE 1.

BIRTHS, MARRIAGES, AND DEATHS IN THE SEVERAL TOWNS, FOR THE YEAR ENDING DECEMBER 31, 1881.

HARTFORD COUNTY.

TOWNS.	BIRTHS.		MARRIAGES.	DEATHS.		Death-rate per 1,000.
	Sex.	Parentage.		Sex.	Nativity.	
Hartford,						23.7
Avon,						11.3
Berlin,						17.4
Bloomfield,						14.8
Bristol,						12.9
Burlington,						21.
Canton,						18.2
East Granby,						17.2
East Hartford,						23.7
East Windsor,						14.9
Enfield,						23.5
Farmington,						7.2
Glastonbury,						13.4
Granby,						14.1
Hartland,						14.
Manchester,						19.3
Marlborough,						28.1
New Britain,						17.1
Newington,						18.2
Plainville,						14.5
Rocky Hill,						10.8
Simsbury,						18.9
Southington,						16.4
South Windsor,						14.6
Suffield,						12.1
West Hartford,						4.4
Wethersfield,						16.6
						17.0

B

NEW HAVEN COUNTY.

TOWNS	Population in 1880	BIRTHS Male	Female	Not stated	Total	Birth-rate per 1,000	Both American	Both Foreign	Am. Mother, Por. Father	Am. Father, Por. Mother	Both For. of diff. Nations	Not stated	MARR. Both American	Both Foreign	Hus. American, Wife Foreign	Hus. Foreign, Wife American	Not stated	Total	Hus. non-resident	Both non-resident	DEATHS Male	Female	Not stated	Total	American	Foreign	Not stated	Death-rate per 1,000
New Haven	62,882	1050	940	2	1992	31.6	632	693	74	40	21	552	303	199	38	49	5	594	46	8	676	659	3	1338	926	366	46	21.2
Beacon Falls	379	13	8		21	55.4	7	8	4	1	1		1			1		2	1		8	7		15	13	2		39.6
Bethany	637	6	12		18	28.2	12	4				2	7	2	1			7			5	8		13	13			20.4
Branford	3,047	38	28		66	21.6	40	16	5	2		1	7	31	1			14	3	1	29	35	1	65	53	11	1	21.3
Cheshire	2,284	31	28		50	21.8	35	8	4			2	6	2	1	3		8	2		18	20		38	35	3		16.6
Derby	11,650	186	149		335	28.8	112	126	34	23	17	23	68	4	5	16	1	120	3	1	99	83	3	185	142	43	1	15.8
East Haven	3,057	19	21		40	13.	26	6	3			3	14		1			17			10	14		24	23			7.9
Guilford	2,782	22	24		46	16.5	35	7		1			18	2	1	1		23	1		11	15		26	24	2		9.3
Hamden	3,408	23	18		41	12.2	25	9	4	2	2		12	1	1		1	15	3		20	20		40	32	8		11.7
Madison	1,672	10	10		20	11.9	15	4				1	10		1			12	1		11	16		27	27			16.
Meriden	18,340	286	290	3	579	31.5	178	341	19	14	23	4	76	39	13	17	1	146	7	1	147	130	12	289	203	74	12	15.7
Middlebury	687	4			9	13.1							4					4			4	6		10	6	4		14.5
Milford	3,347	35	31		66	19.7	43	14	5	1	8	1	22	7	2	2		24	2		25	34	1	60	55	5		17.9
Naugatuck	4,274	76	59		135	31.5	52	57	6	12	3	5	28		5			44	4		29	26	3	58	35	15	8	13.5
North Stamford	1,025	7	4		11	10.7	11												4		16	18		34	18	13	3	20.4
North Haven	1,763	8	7	1	16	9.	10	5	2	1		4	10	1	1	4		11	2		11	5		18	12	6		10.2
Orange	3,341	23	36		59	14.6	30	17		3		2	23	1				27	4		27	21		48	44	4		14.3
Oxford	1,120	9	11		20	17.8	14					6	4			2		4			10	11		21	18			18.7
Prospect	492	4	4		8	16.2	8	8					4					12			2	2		4	4		3	9.6
Seymour	2,318	25	24		49	20.6	26	23	2		2		10	1	1	2		7	3	5	26	23		49	45	4		20.6
Southbury	1,740	14	9		23	13.2	16	6	8	11		6	21		8			29			12	14		26	26			15.
Wallingford	4,686	69	45		115	24.5	59	29	59	24	2	118	97	3	10	17	2	165	10		42	37		79	57	10	12	16.6
Waterbury	20,270	334	285	6	625	30.8	222	202	1				41								172	168	7	347	241	95	12	17.1
Wolcott	493	2	4		6	12.1	8														9	3		12	6		24	24.3
Woodbridge	829	4	6		10	12.	5	1	1	1			3		1	1		4	1		6	7		13	7	1		8.4
Total	156,523	2298	2049	13	4360	27.8	1628	1578	229	142	78	705	754	335	83	114		1293	90	16	1425	1365	30	2820	2058	656	106	18.

NEW LONDON COUNTY.

TOWNS.	Population in 1880.	BIRTHS — Male	BIRTHS — Female	BIRTHS — Not stated	BIRTHS — Total	Birth-rate per 1,000	PARENTAGE — Both Amer.	PARENTAGE — Both Foreign	PARENTAGE — Am. Mother For. Father	PARENTAGE — For. Father Am. Mother	PARENTAGE — For. Mother Am. Father	PARENTAGE — Both For. of diff. Nations	PARENTAGE — Not stated	MARR. — Both American	MARR. — Both Foreign	MARR. — Hus. American Wife Foreign	MARR. — Hus. Foreign Wife American	MARR. — Not stated	MARR. — Total	MARR. — Hus. non-resident	MARR. — Both non-resident	DEATHS — Male	DEATHS — Female	DEATHS — Not stated	DEATHS — Total	DEATHS — American	DEATHS — Foreign	DEATHS — Not stated	Death-rate per 1,000
New London,	10,537	117	121		238	22.4	134	66	18	15		5		68	16	4	13		101	10	5	95	121	1	217	180	37		20.5
Norwich,	21,143	286	263		549	25.9	233	207	60	33		16		118	39	12	21		190	15	2	203	194		397	300	97		18.7
Bozrah,	1,155	18	11		29	25.1	11		3	4	2	2		5	4							7	9		16	13	3		13.8
...ér,	2,974	31	31		62	20.8	35	21	4	1	1		2	15		2	4		25	1	1	27	20		47	39	5	3	15.7
East Lyme,	1,731	4	2	9	6	8.7	4						1	5					11			16	14	1	31	31		3	18.5
Franklin,	686	30	33	10	73	26.6	36	19	9				1	15					3	2		6	8		14	13	1		20.4
...ld,	2,745	50	35		85	16.6	70	6	5	1	1	8	1	16	13	1	3		41	6	1	28	53	25	53	44			19.3
Groton,	5,128	18	11	1	29	15.7	24	9				2		38	4	2	2	2	17	4	1	37	53	1	90	86	4		17.5
Lebanon,	1,845	17	16		33	24.	30	6	2	1	1			13		1			7	1	1	10	20		30			30	16.2
Ledyard,	1,373	4	9		13	20.6	6	5	1					7	1							12	14	1	26	25		1	18.9
Lisbon,	630	6	7	1	14	13.6	13	4	2					1					6	1		4	3		7			7	11.1
Lyme,	1,025	29	16	2	47	17.6	33	1	1	3	1			6	2				13	3		30	16	1	47	36	8	11	11.7
Montville,	2,664	14	18		32	18.	26		2		2		24	12	1				5			19	11		30	30		7	16.8
...th Stonington,	1,769	15	15	9	24	17.3		4	1	2	3		2	5					6	1		8	5	1	14	13	1	11	17.6
Old Lyme,	1,387	17	20	2	39	15.4	28		1	1				6	1		1		17	3	1	20	23	1	44	40	4	1	16.8
Preston,	2,523	3	4		7	12.2	6	4	1		2			3	1		2		5	2		4	10		14	12		2	10.1
Salem,	574	44	45		89	38.5	12	57	9	10				37	16	1	2		22	9		34	24		58	39	19		17.4
Sprague,	3,207	79	52	1	132	17.9	78	35	13	6	1		1	3	10	7	2		56	2	1	59	68	2	129	115	14		24.3
Stonington,	7,355	24	16		40	33.7	14													9	11	11	10		21	18	3		18.
...rn,	1,186	12	20		32	11.8	32				1			18					20			23	20		43	43			17.5
Waterford,	2,701																												17.7
Total	74,338	839	748	16	1603	21.5	847	482	131	79	36	36	28	402	106	31	50	2	591	54	22	657	675	8	1340	1077	206	57	18.

FAIRFIELD COUNTY.

TOWNS	Population in 1880	BIRTHS — Male	Female	Not stated	Total	Birth-rate per 1,000	Both Amer.	Both Foreign	Am. Mother For. Father	Am. Father For. Mother	Both For. of diff. Nations	Not stated	MARRIAGES — Both American	Both Foreign	Hus. Foreign Wife American	Hus. American Wife Foreign	Not stated	Total	Hus. non-resident	Both non-resident	DEATHS — Male	Female	Not stated	Total	American	Foreign	Not stated	Death-rate per 1,000
Danbury,	11,666	126	117	2	245	21.	137	64	25	15	4	..	67	19	10	8	..	104	8	..	95	108	15	218	167	33	..	18.6
Bridgeport,	29,148	539	398	9	946	32.4	404	324	122	63	33	..	192	45	22	36	..	295	24	4	324	268	8	600	464	134	2	20.5
Bethel,	2,727	28	28	..	56	20.5	44	10	2	..	..	..	14	1	1	..	..	16	..	..	28	23	..	51	46	5	..	18.7
Brookfield,	1,152	13	13	..	26	22.5	21	5	..	1	..	..	5	1	..	..	..	7	..	..	10	8	..	18	17	1	..	15.6
Darien,	1,949	8	17	..	25	12.8	17	10	2	..	1	..	6	1	..	..	..	7	..	..	11	8	..	19	17	2	..	9.7
Easton,	1,145	5	3	..	8	6.9	7	..	..	..	..	..	6	..	..	..	..	6	..	..	10	6	..	16	14	2	..	13.9
Fairfield,	3,748	32	29	..	61	16.2	40	9	3	9	1	..	15	7	..	1	..	16	3	..	25	24	1	49	42	6	1	13.
Greenwich,	7,892	48	59	..	107	13.5	66	22	12	6	5	..	26	11	1	..	..	30	8	3	46	53	..	99	82	17	..	12.5
Huntington,	2,499	23	34	..	57	22.8	32	13	3	4	1	..	7	1	..	..	..	8	1	2	24	20	..	44	40	4	..	17.6
Monroe,	1,157	4	8	..	12	10.3	8	..	3	1	..	..	8	..	..	..	..	8	..	..	6	8	..	14	14	..	..	12.1
New Canaan,	2,673	28	25	..	53	19.7	36	9	6	..	1	..	12	2	..	..	..	12	1	..	20	23	1	44	41	3	..	17.1
New Fairfield,	791	8	5	1	14	17.5	12	..	..	4	..	..	3	..	..	..	..	3	..	..	6	4	..	10	9	1	..	12.6
Newtown,	4,013	52	33	..	85	21.1	31	24	23	19	2	21	82	7	9	5	..	107	19	3	39	41	..	80	55	13	..	19.9
Norwalk,	13,956	147	135	..	282	20.2	180	50	..	4	10	..	82	11	..	..	..	11	16	1	127	119	1	247	210	34	3	17.8
Redding,	1,540	19	14	..	33	21.4	26	6	1	19	..	..	6	..	1	..	..	23	1	..	15	16	..	31	29	2	..	30.1
Ridgefield,	2,028	17	16	1	34	16.7	32	6	..	18	..	..	10	..	1	..	..	8	..	..	17	16	..	33	31	2	..	16.2
Sherman,	828	3	6	..	8	10.8	8	..	1	..	..	1	..	..	..	..	..	..	..	..	3	5	..	8	7	..	1	9.6
Stamford,	11,297	138	125	24	287	25.4	141	105	18	18	5	..	62	14	..	9	..	89	16	..	92	104	..	196	147	49	..	17.3
Stratford,	4,251	20	7	..	27	6.6	20	3	1	..	2	..	21	..	1	1	..	23	..	..	8	14	..	22	21	1	..	5.1
Trumbull,	1,323	11	5	..	16	12.1	14	13	5	..	..	..	7	..	1	..	..	8	6	..	10	11	..	21	19	2	..	15.8
Weston,	918	31	23	..	54	58.8	30	14	3	4	..	..	17	5	..	2	..	25	..	..	29	21	..	50	40	8	2	54.4
Westport,	3,477	9	11	..	20	3.2	14	2	..	..	..	..	11	..	1	..	..	11	..	..	12	11	..	20	19	1	..	5.7
Wilton,	1,864	14	6	..	20	10.7	14	2	3	1	..	1	11	..	1	..	..	11	1	..	17	13	..	30	29	1	..	16.
Total,	112,042	1323	1108	37	2468	22.	1329	672	231	149	63	24	587	107	55	62	..	811	93	13	974	921	25	1920	1559	322	39	17.1

WINDHAM COUNTY.

TOWNS.	Population in 1880.	BIRTHS — Male	Female	Not stated	Total	Birth-rate per 1,000	Parentage — Both American	Both Foreign	Am. Mother, For. Father	For. Mother, Am. Father	Both For. of diff. Nations	Not stated	MARRIAGES — Both American	Both Foreign	Hus. American, Wife Foreign	Hus. Foreign, Wife American	Not stated	Total	Hus. non-resident	Both non-resident	DEATHS — Male	Female	Not stated	Total	Nativity — American	Foreign	Not stated	Death-rate per 1,000
Brooklyn,	2,308	34	19	…	53	22.9	20	30	2	1	…	…	7	…	…	…	…	7	1	…	28	20	…	48	39	9	…	20.8
Ashford,	1,041	9	7	…	16	15.3	16	…	…	…	…	…	9	…	…	…	…	9	1	…	5	11	…	16	14	2	…	15.3
Canterbury,	1,272	14	5	…	19	14.9	11	5	…	3	…	…	14	…	…	…	…	14	2	…	10	8	…	18	…	…	18	14.1
Chaplin,	627	8	4	…	12	19.1	7	3	…	2	…	…	5	…	…	…	…	5	…	1	5	7	…	12	12	…	…	19.1
Eastford,	855	7	6	1	14	16.3	14	…	…	…	…	…	9	…	…	…	…	9	1	…	9	6	…	15	15	…	…	17.5
Hampton,	827	9	8	…	17	20.5	11	5	…	…	1	…	6	1	…	…	…	7	…	5	4	9	…	13	11	…	2	15.7
Killingly,	6,921	82	89	1	172	24.8	76	78	12	5	1	…	31	23	4	2	…	60	5	1	66	55	…	121	101	20	…	17.4
Plainfield,	4,021	44	36	…	80	19.8	27	35	12	5	1	…	9	10	4	1	…	24	3	4	28	21	…	49	38	11	…	12.1
Pomfret,	1,470	9	9	…	18	12.2	12	4	…	2	…	…	12	…	…	…	…	12	1	…	10	10	…	20	18	2	…	13.6
Putnam,	5,827	127	86	3	216	37.	64	113	18	17	2	2	33	16	6	9	…	64	8	8	58	56	…	114	90	24	…	19.6
Scotland,	590	4	6	…	10	16.9	9	1	…	…	…	…	4	…	…	…	…	4	…	…	3	3	…	6	6	…	…	10.1
Sterling,	957	4	12	…	16	16.7	12	4	…	…	…	…	4	1	…	…	…	5	3	2	3	6	…	9	9	…	…	9.4
Thompson,	5,051	87	76	1	164	32.4	13	145	3	3	…	…	14	47	…	2	…	63	5	3	35	48	1	84	54	25	5	16.6
Windham,	8,264	97	91	…	188	22.7	62	104	8	13	…	1	35	21	6	7	6	75	8	3	81	77	3	161	98	53	10	19.4
Woodstock,	2,639	11	14	…	25	9.4	14	4	2	1	1	3	16	…	…	…	…	16	7	1	8	7	…	15	12	3	…	5.7
Total,	42,670	546	468	6	1020	23.9	368	531	56	48	10	7	208	119	20	21	6	374	45	28	353	344	4	701	517	149	35	16.4

LITCHFIELD COUNTY.

TOWNS.	Population in 1880.	BIRTHS — Sex Male	Female	Not stated	Total	Birth-rate per 1,000.	BIRTHS — Parentage Both Amer.	Both Foreign	Am. Mother, For. Father.	For. Mother, Am. Father.	Both For. or diff. Nations.	Not stated.	MARRIAGES — Both American.	Both Foreign.	Hus. American, Wife Foreign.	Hus. Foreign, Wife American.	Not stated.	Total.	Hus. non-resident.	Both non-resident.	DEATHS — Sex Male.	Female.	Not stated.	Total.	DEATHS — Nativity American.	Foreign.	Not stated.	Death-rate per 1,000.
LITCHFIELD,	3,410	39	37		76	22.3	42	20	4	5	1	4	18	3	1	2		19		1	26	18		44	34	3	7	12.9
Barkhamstead,	1,297	7	9		16	12.3	14	2					9					9			5	4		9	9			6.9
Bethlehem,	655	4			8	12.2										2			1		7	4	1	12	12			18.3
Bridgewater,	708	5	10		15	21.1	14	1	1	1		8	4					6	1		4	4			8			11.3
Canaan,	1,157	7			10	8.5	7	1					3					3			4	1		5	5			4.3
Colebrook,	1,148	5	3		8	6.9	5	1		1			7		1			7	1		13	8		21	14	1	7	18.3
Cornwall,	1,583	15	13		28	17.6	16	3	2						1			10	1		10	10		20	19	1		12.6
Goshen,	1,093	10	14		24	21.9	18	6		2			10		1			7	1		9	6		15	14	1		13.7
Harwinton,	1,016	7			14	13.7	12						5					5	2		12	9		21	20	1		20.6
Kent,	1,622	19	19		38	23.4	32	3			1	8	5	1		2		6			10	9		19	11	2		11.7
Morris,	627	6			7	12.7	6						3			1		7			9	9		17	11			17.5
New Hartford,	3,302	69	89		78	23.6	36	28	8	1			15	9	1			27	1		27	26		53	40	9	4	15.9
New Milford,	3,907	33	24		57	14.5	44	5	5	2	2	1	21			2	2	24	2		31	31		62	37	4	21	14.5
Norfolk,	1,418	8	6	1	15	10.5	10		2					3		1		8			11			20	16	4		11.
North Canaan,	1,537	9	13		22	14.3	15	7	3		1		8	7		2	1	20	8	4	11	6		17	14	3		20.
Plymouth,	2,350	17	16		34	14.4	24	2		1			2					10		1	22	25		47	42	5	7	22.1
Roxbury,	950	11			11	25.3	12						7			1		16	3		11	11			20	20			12.8
Salisbury,	3,715	53	39	2	94	14.6	51	33	8	5		4	12	14				31	2		30	17		48	43	5		14.6
Sharon,	2,580	21	17		38	25.3	26	4	3	1	1	1	7	2		4		24			20	18		38	27	4	7	9.
Thomaston,	3,225	53	43		96	29.8	42	38	9		1		12			2	2	16	3		11	18		30	26	4		15.
Torrington,	3,327	36	56		92	27.6	41	41	8	5			11		1		1	13	1		26	18		50	38	12		14.4
Warren,	639	6			8	12.5	8						1					12			4	3		8	8		5	14.4
Washington,	1,590	19	13	2	34	21.3	23		1				5	5		2		12			6	16		23	21	2		14.4
Watertown,	1,897	12	26		38	20.	30	7	19		1		11		2		3	12	3		13	14		27	22	3	2	14.4
Winchester,	5,142	75	57	1	182	25.6	71	35	1		2	1	26	11	5	3		45	1		33	41		74	68	6	1	13.5
Woodbury,	2,149	28	10		38	17.6	32						12					16	4		17	12		29	23			14.
Total,	**52,044**	**544**	**485**	**6**	**1035**	**19.8**	**635**	**260**	**77**	**29**	**13**	**21**	**248**	**57**	**19**	**28**	**1**	**353**	**29**	**7**	**381**	**345**	**6**	**732**	**608**	**76**	**48**	**14.**

MIDDLESEX COUNTY.

BIRTHS

TOWNS	Population in 1880	Sex Male	Sex Female	Sex Not stated	Total	Birth-rate per 1,000	Both Amer.	Both Foreign	Am. Mother, For. Father	For. Mother, Am. Father	Both For. of diff. Nations	Not stated
Middletown,	11,732	128	133	1	262	22.3	119	78	27	18	12	8
Haddam,	2,419	27	18	1	46	19.	27	6	4			7
Chatham,	1,967	18	17		35	17.7	23	11		1		
Chester,	1,177	14	15		29	24.6	24	2	2			
Clinton,	1,402		12		26	18.5	23			2	2	1
Cromwell,	1,640	19	9		28	17.	12	9	5			
Durham,	990	8	4		12	12.1	7	3		1		
East Haddam,	3,032	22	19		41	13.5	35	2	3		1	2
Essex,	1,855	12	17		29	15.6	25	4		2		
Killingworth,	748	8	2		10	13.3	7	1		2		1
Middlefield,	928	7	7		14	15.	10	1	2	5		
Old Saybrook,	1,302	19	13		32	24.5	20	6	1	4	3	
Portland,	4,157	48	61		109	26.2	25	73	1	1		
Saybrook,	1,362	8			15	11.	14		4			
Westbrook,	878	4	11		15	17.	14					
Total,	**35,589**	**356**	**345**	**2**	**703**	**19.7**	**385**	**197**	**49**	**87**	**26**	**9**

MARRIAGES

TOWNS	Both American	Both Foreign	Hus. American, Wife Foreign	Hus. Foreign, Wife American	Not stated	Total	Hus. non-resident	Both non-resident
Middletown,	57	10	6	12		85	5	2
Haddam,	11		1			12	1	
Chatham,	12	1				13		
Chester,	8					8		1
Clinton,	11	1	1			11	1	
Cromwell,	4					8	2	
Durham,	5			2		5	2	
East Haddam,	16	1	1			17		
Essex,	14					14		
Killingworth,	7					7		
Middlefield,	8	1		1		6		
Old Saybrook,	13	31	3			9	9	
Portland,	7	7				47	3	
Saybrook,	11					11		
Westbrook,								
Total,	**189**	**44**	**12**	**15**		**260**	**14**	**3**

DEATHS

TOWNS	Sex Male	Sex Female	Sex Not stated	Total	Nativity American	Foreign	Not stated	Death-rate per 1,000
Middletown,	136	124		260	192	62	6	22.1
Haddam,	11	17		28	23	5		11.5
Chatham,	13	13		26	24	2		13.2
Chester,	11	11		22	21	1		18.6
Clinton,	15	12		27	16	1	10	19.2
Cromwell,	14	11		25	19	6		15.2
Durham,	14	9		23	20	3		23.3
East Haddam,	19	18		37	32	5		12.2
Essex,	18	14		32	31	1		16.7
Killingworth,	12	13		25	25			33.4
Middlefield,	5	14		19	17	2		20.4
Old Saybrook,	9	11		20	19			15.3
Portland,	49	45		94	72	22		22.6
Saybrook,	10	8		18	16	2		13.2
Westbrook,	8	9		17	17			19.3
Total,	**344**	**329**		**673**	**544**	**113**	**16**	**18.9**

TOLLAND COUNTY.

TOWNS.	Population in 1880.	BIRTHS. Male.	Female.	Not stated.	Total.	Birth-rate per 1,000.	Both Amer.	Both Foreign.	Am. Mother, For. Father.	For. Mother, Am. Father.	Both For. of diff. Nations.	Not stated.	MARRIAGES. Both American.	Both Foreign.	Hus. American, Wife Foreign.	Hus. Foreign, Wife American.	Not stated.	Total.	Hus. non-resident.	Both non-resident.	DEATHS. Male.	Female.	Not stated.	Total.	American.	Foreign.	Not stated.	Death-rate per 1,000.
Tolland,	1,169	13	14		27	23.1	21	4	1	1			2	1		1		3		1	8	3		11	9		2	9.4
Andover,	428	3	2	2	5	11.6	4	1					4					4	1		2	3		5	5			11.6
Bolton,	512	9	7		16	31.2	15						4					4			12	1		13	13			25.4
Columbia,	757	5	8		13	17.1	12						3					3			4	8		12	11	1		15.8
Coventry,	2,043	17	22		39	19.	26	9	2		2		8	1				11			10	14		24	18	6		11.7
Ellington,	1,569	13	11		24	15.1	14	9	1				5					6			5	6		11	10	1		7.
Hebron,	1,243	8	9	1	17	13.6	12	4	2	1			7	1				7	1		6	6		12	12			9.6
Mansfield,	2,154	12	19	1	32	14.8	27	2					14					14	1		14	12		26	25	1		12.
Somers,	1,242	12	10		22	17.7	19		10	6	3		4					4	3		8	8		16	15	1		12.8
Stafford,	4,455	46	54	3	103	23.1	58	26					26			3		34	5		34	31	1	66	53	7	6	14.8
Union,	539	2	5		7	12.9	7														6	3		9	8	1		16.7
Vernon,	6,915	107	89		196	28.3	61	83	24	17	11	1	30	16	3	10		58	5	4	65	56		121	90	29	1	17.8
Willington,	1,086	16	10		26	23.9	19	3	2	1	1		6	2				6			16	9		25	24	1	1	23.
Total,	24,122	263	260	4	527	21.8	295	146	43	26	17	1	113	21	6	14		154	16	5	190	160	1	351	293	48	10	14.1

RECAPITULATION BY COUNTIES.

COUNTIES	Population in 1880.	BIRTHS Male	Female	Not stated	Total	Birth-rate per 1,000.	Both Amer.	Both Foreign	Am. Mother, For. Father	For. Mother, Am. Father	Mixed Foreign.	Not stated.	MARRIAGES Both Amer'n.	Both Foreign.	Hus. Amer'n, Wife Foreign.	Hus. Foreign, Wife Amer'n.	Not stated.	Total.	Hus. non-resident.	Both non-resident.	DEATHS Male.	Female.	Not stated.	Total.	American.	Foreign.	Not stated.	Death-rate per 1,000.
Hartford,.....	125,382	1491	1394	15	2900	23.1	1247	1035	223	188	85	122	646	200	84	80	4	1014	72	25	1188	1170	12	2370	1827	532	11	18.9
New Haven,..	156,523	2298	2049	13	4360	27.8	1628	1578	229	142	78	705	754	335	83	114	7	1293	90	16	1425	1365	30	2820	2058	656	106	18.
New London,.	74,338	839	748	16	1603	21.5	847	482	131	79	36	28	402	106	31	50	2	591	54	22	657	675	8	1340	1079	206	57	18.
Fairfield,.....	112,012	1323	1108	37	2468	22.	1329	672	231	149	63	24	587	107	55	62	..	811	93	13	974	921	25	1920	1559	322	39	17.1
Windham,.....	42,670	546	468	6	1020	23.9	368	531	56	48	10	7	208	119	21	20	6	374	45	28	353	344	4	701	517	149	35	16.4
Litchfield,.....	52,044	544	485	6	1035	19.8	635	260	77	29	13	21	248	57	19	28	1	353	29	7	381	345	6	732	608	76	48	14.
Middlesex,...	35,589	356	345	2	703	19.7	385	197	49	37	26	9	189	44	12	15	..	260	14	3	344	329	...	673	544	113	16	18.9
Tolland,.......	24,112	263	260	4	527	21.8	295	146	43	26	17	...	113	21	6	14	..	154	16	5	190	160	1	351	293	48	10	14.1
Total,....	622,700	7660	6857	99	14616	22.4	6734	4901	1039	698	328	916	3147	989	311	388	20	4850	413	119	5512	5309	86	10907	8483	2102	322	17.4

TABLE 2.

EXHIBITING THE NUMBER OF BIRTHS IN THE SEVERAL COUNTIES
FOR EACH MONTH IN THE YEAR ENDING DECEMBER 31, 1881.

COUNTY.	SEX.	January.	February.	March.	April.	May.	June.	July.	August.	September.	October.	November.	December.	TOTAL.
Hartford,....	Males, ...	126	125	123	112	122	122	119	136	138	138	128	102	1,491
	Females,...	105	100	114	100	114	116	110	132	118	130	133	122	1,394
	Not stated,	2	1	2	....	2	1	4	....	....	....	2	1	15
New Haven,.	Males, ...	204	189	218	187	177	162	170	220	210	210	168	183	2,298
	Females,...	159	166	174	161	167	138	169	183	186	183	149	214	2,049
	Not stated,	2	3	....	....	....	....	1	2	1	-1	1	2	13
New London,	Males, ...	69	61	71	70	74	67	67	63	76	80	76	65	839
	Females,...	63	57	67	48	68	57	62	66	79	59	60	62	748
	Not stated,	1	....	3	2	1	1	1	...	3	3	....	1	16
Fairfield,....	Males, ...	106	100	116	98	118	100	132	122	106	100	128	97	1,323
	Females,...	112	86	93	84	73	97	93	100	95	79	100	96	1,108
	Not stated,	8	2	5	2	2	6	2	....	3	4	1	2	37
Windham,...	Males, ...	39	35	61	41	48	55	48	56	41	48	39	35	544
	Females,...	44	46	39	42	44	28	36	42	44	35	26	42	468
	Not stated,	....	1	....	1	....	1	....	....	1	....	....	2	6
Litchfield,...	Males, ...	46	44	40	51	46	48	42	43	42	42	47	53	544
	Females,...	33	38	42	40	44	42	38	44	49	39	39	37	485
	Not stated,	....	..	....	....	....	....	2	...	2	....	....	2	6
Middlesex, ..	Males, ...	39	29	24	24	40	27	33	28	30	35	19	28	356
	Females,...	30	26	30	25	26	24	35	30	40	24	32	23	345
	Not stated,	....	....	....	1	....	....	1	....	....	....	....	....	2
Tolland, ...	Males, ...	26	13	27	16	30	27	23	17	11	26	23	24	263
	Females,...	19	23	23	20	21	18	22	30	22	22	20	20	260
	Not stated,	....	....	....	1	....	....	2	....	....	....	1	....	4
Total,...	Males, ...	655	596	680	599	655	608	634	685	654	679	628	587	7,660
	Females,...	565	542	582	520	557	520	565	627	633	571	559	616	6,857
	Not stated,	13	7	10	7	5	9	13	2	10	8	5	10	99
Grand Total, ...		1233	1145	1272	1126	1217	1137	1212	1314	1297	1258	1192	1213	14,616·

TABLE 3.

EXHIBITING THE NUMBER OF DEATHS IN THE SEVERAL COUNTIES FOR EACH MONTH IN THE YEAR ENDING DECEMBER 31, 1881.

COUNTY.	SEX.	January.	February.	March.	April.	May.	June.	July.	August.	September.	October.	November.	December.	TOTAL.
Hartford,	Males, ...	93	86	89	104	94	74	128	128	116	114	91	71	1,188
	Females,...	117	94	93	100	80	64	99	122	98	113	94	96	1,170
	Not stated,	....	....	2	1	2	1	1	1	1	3	....	....	12
New Haven,	Males, ...	120	106	161	107	100	113	139	128	109	124	100	118	1,425
	Females,...	112	103	130	109	125	97	120	117	112	140	95	105	1,365
	Not stated,	3	2	1	3	2	3	2	4	2	1	2	5	30
New London,	Males, ...	66	50	53	63	57	55	58	56	56	51	46	46	657
	Females,...	51	52	73	58	55	50	44	74	68	42	53	55	675
	Not stated,	1	....	3	1	1	..	2	....	....	....	....	....	8
Fairfield,	Males, ...	93	70	76	84	78	57	96	105	90	89	79	57	974
	Females,...	88	57	74	70	80	66	74	90	80	80	76	86	921
	Not stated,	1	.1	2	....	....	1	6	5	1	2	3	3	25
Windham,	Males, ...	30	34	15	23	31	24	32	26	47	33	30	28	353
	Females,...	40	36	33	30	24	19	30	28	35	25	22	22	344
	Not stated,	1	....	1	....	....	....	....	....	....	1	1	....	4
Litchfield,	Males, ...	37	24	39	23	33	22	29	32	35	26	32	49	381
	Females,...	29	32	30	25	19	30	23	39	36	26	24	32	345
	Not stated,	....	....	....	....	....	1	....	....	2	1	1	1	6
Middlesex, ..	Males, ...	33	18	.20	19	27	18	29	41	36	34	38	31	344
	Females,...	33	33	31	28	23	18	22	38	26	22	26	29	329
	Not stated,	....	....	....	....	....	....	....	....	....	....	....	....	......
Tolland, ...	Males, ...	15	22	18	12	13	14	18	20	11	16	11	20	190
	Females,...	12	15	16	16	10	10	16	19	10	14	12	10	160
	Not stated,	....	....	....	....	....	....	....	....	....	....	1	....	1
Total,...	Males, ...	487	410	471	435	433	377	529	536	500	487	427	420	5,512
	Females,...	482	422	480	436	416	354	428	527	465	462	402	435	5,309
	Not stated,	6	3	9	5	5	6	11	10	6	8	8	9	86
Grand Total,....		975	835	960	876	854	737	968	1073	971	957	837	864	10,907

TABLE 4.

CAUSES OF DEATHS ARRANGED BY TOWNS AND COUNTIES.

ORDER I.—MIASMATIC.

TOWNS IN HARTFORD CO.	Carbuncle.	Diarrhœa.	Cholera Infantum.	Malarial Fever.	Intermittent Fever.	Congestive Fever.	Typho-Malarial Fever.	Rheumatism.	Cerebro-Spinal Meningitis.	Caries and Necrosis.	TOTAL. M. F.	Male.	Female.	Sex not stated.	TOTAL.
Hartford,			83	12			6				4	122	143		
Avon,															
Berlin,															
Bloomfield,															
Bristol,															
Burlington,															
Canton,															
East Granby,															
East Hartford,															
East Windsor,															
Enfield,															
Farmington,															
Glastonbury,															
Granby,															
Hartland,															
Manchester,															
Marlborough,															
New Britain,															
Newington,															
Plainville,															
Rocky Hill,															
Southington,															
South ...r,															
Suffield,															
West Hartford,															

TOWNS IN HARTFORD CO.	Senile Gangrene.	Hydrocephalus.	nal Disease.	uralgia.	TOTAL.	Pneumonia.
				3 SYSTEM.		
HARTFORD,		4				95
Avon,						1
Berlin,						5
Bloomfield,						2
Bristol,						2
Burlington,						1
Canton,						9
East Granby,						3
East Hartford,						5
East Windsor,						
Enfield,						
Farmington,						
Glastonbury,						
Granby,						
Hartland,						
Manchester,						
Marlborough,						
New Britain,						
Newington,						
...lle,						
R.xy Hill,						
Simsbury,						
Southington,						
South Windsor,						
Suffield,						
West Hartford,						
Wethersfield,						
W s.r,						
W s.r Locks,						

CLASS III.—LOCAL DISEASES—Continued.

Towns in Hartford Co.	Order 4.—Digestive Organs. Total	Order 5.—Urinary Organs. Total	Order 6.—Generative Organs. Total	Orders 7 and 8. Male	Orders 7 and 8. Female	Total for Class III. Males	Total for Class III. Females	Total for Class III. Sex not stated	Total for Class III. TOTAL
Hartford	26	32		8	11	184	193		377
Avon	1	1				2			2
Berlin	3					7	8		15
Bloomfield	5					5	4		9
Bristol			1			14	13		27
Burlington	2					4	4		8
Canton	5			3		3	6		9
East		1		2		3	4		7
East Hartford	11	3				15	12		27
East						8	8		17
Enfield	2	1	1		1	24	20		44
Farmington	1	3				8	3		11
Glastonbury		4				5	10		15
Granby	2					7	4		11
Hartland	1					2	3		5
Marlborough	2		1			17	18		35
New Britain	12	1	1			3	3		6
Newington		2				29	47		76
Plainville	2					1	4		5
Rocky Hill	5	2				5	4		9
Simsbury						5	3		6
Southington	2	3		1	1	5	7		12
South Windsor						12	5		17
Suffield						6	4		6
West Hartford	1	2				2	11		17
Windsor						2	2		4
Windsor Locks	5					15	8		10
						5	4		23
									9
Total,	89	53	1	13	12	402	417		819

CLASS IV.—DEVELOPMENTAL DISEASES.   CLASS [V.]   [VIO]LENT DEATHS.

TOWNS IN HARTFORD CO.	Premature Birth and Debility	Stillbirth	Old Age F.	Atrophy and Debility M.	Atrophy and Debility F.	Total for Class IV Male	Female	Not stated	Total	Order 1.—Accident Negligence: Fracture and Contusion	Wounds	Burns and Scalds	Poison	Drowning	Suffocation	Otherwise	Suicide M.	Orders 3,4,5: Classed	Cause not Reported	Total for Class V
HARTFORD,	4		31	2	2	77	82		159	12		3		3	2	9	2		6	6
Avon,			3			2	3		5										1	1
Berlin,			1		1	1	1		2	1					1					
Bloomfield,							1		3	1									4	4
Bristol,	2		2			1	2		4			1				1			1	1
Burlington,	6					4			9											
East Granby,			2		2	1	5		1	4			2				1		2	2
East Hartford,									4			1							1	1
East [Windsor],	3		7			4	4		6		1	1								
Enfield,			1		1	4	2		1			1							2	2
Farmington,			1			2	4		3	1									9	9
Glas[tonbury],			4	1	4	6	7		0	1						1			1	1
Granby,			1		1	2	1		3		1				1				2	2
Hartland,			1				4		5											
Manchester,						0	1		8			1				1				
Marlborough,							1													
New Britain,			7		7	6	5		8	1		2			1	2			4	4
Newington,			1		1		2		2											
Rocky Hill,			1		1	1	3		4			1							4	4
Simsbury,							2		2							1				
Southington,			1		1	7	1		6			2				2			1	1
South [Windsor],						8	8		0	1				2					1	1
Suffield,						2	1		2										1	1
West Hartford,												1				1			1	1
Win[dsor],														2						
Wi[nd]sor Locks,																				

CLASS I.—ZYMOTIC DISEASES.

Towns in New Haven Co.	Order I.—Miasmatic																							Order II.—Enthetic								Order III.—Dietic						Total for Class I.			
	Small-pox	Measles	Scarlet Fever	Diphtheria	Quinsy	Croup	Whooping Cough	Typhoid Fever	Erysipelas	Puerperal Fever	Carbuncle	Dysentery	Diarrhœa	Cholera Infantum	Malarial Fever	Intermittent Fever	Congestive Fever	Remittent Fever	Typho-Malarial Fever	Rheumatism	Cerebro-Spinal Meningitis	Total M.	Total F.	Syphilis	Septicæmia	Caries and Necrosis	Stomatitis	Stricture	Hydrophobia	Total M.	Total F.	Purpura and Scurvy	Privation and Neglect	Alcoholism	Total M.	Total F.	Male	Female	Sex not stated	Total
New Haven	2	1	9	35		16	6	6	1	1	1	8	11	57	10	5		8	20	12	8	129	144	7		1	1			8	7		1	6	8	7	137	151		288
Beacon Falls				2				2						4					1			3	3														3	3		6
Bethany			1			1		1											1	2			1															1		1
Branford			5	5		6	2	1		1		3	2	3		3			1	3	1	3	8											3	3	3	3	8		11
Cheshire			2	2				2			1			6					4	2	1	6	2	1			1										6	2		8
Derby				1		1		1		1								1	8	1		28	17	1						3	2			3	3		26	19		45
East Haven			1	1								1		1						1		4	2	1						1						4	3		7
Guilford				3				2								3						2	3								1			1	1		3	3		6
Hamden		5		1		2	2					1	7									2	5	1	1					1	1						2	6		8
[Madison]				3				14						23			1		11		3	44	26	1	1					1	1			1	1	1	45	26	2	73
Meriden								2									1			2		3	2							1	1			1	1		1	3		4
Middlebury				5		1		2						1	4				3			4	7														3	7		10
Milford								2					7									4	4														5	4		9
Naugatuck	2															5						6	2													2	2		2
North Branford															4				1		1	3	4							1				1	1	5	4		9
[Orange] Haven			1	2		1	2	2	1	1				1					1	1	2	7	9							1				1		6	6		12
Oxford																					1	2	1							1				1	1	3	2		5
Prospect			4	2				2						1	5							5	4																	
Seymour														3					2			2	1	1						1	1			1	1		7	9		16
Southbury				2		8	1	4		3		3	3	22				1	1	7	1	5	7	1						1	1			2	1	1	2	1		3
[Wallingford]	2			12				8														34	36							1	1		2	2	1	1	6	7		13
Waterbury			4					1												7																	35	37	2	74
Wolcott																							1																	1
Total	9	1	126	70		34	11	168	23	20	2	16	25	123	21	9	2	10	53	32	17	288	293	8	5	1	2			17	13		2	6	8	7	305	306	4	615

CLASS II.—CONSTITUTIONAL DISEASES.   CLASS III.

TOWNS IN NEW HAVEN CO.	Gout	Dropsy and Anæmia	Cancer	Senile Gangrene	Total M.	Total F.	Scrofula	Tabes Mesenterica	Phthisis	Hydrocephalus	Total M.	Total F.	Male	Female	Sex not stated	Total	Apoplexy	Paralysis	Insanity	Epilepsy	Tetanus	Convulsions	Chorea	Meningitis	Brain Disease	Spinal Disease	Total M.	Total F.	Embolism	Heart Disease	Aneurism	Pericarditis	Phlebitis	Capillary Bronchitis	Pleurisy	Lung Disease	Bronchitis	Pneumonia	Laryngitis	Asthma	Total M.	Total F.
New Haven	6		1		15	33	3	53	206	4	136	130	151	163		314	26	25	8	5	4	50		29	18	4	88	81		54		4	4	10	5	11	20	93	6	8	107
Beacon Falls						1			2	2	1	2	1	2		2		1				1		1	1	1	1	1		1						1	1			1
Bethany		1	1		3				2		4	2	6	2		14	1	1						2	1		1	2		1						1	4			5
Branford	1	4			1	1		1	7	2	4	5	6	8		14	5	2				2		1			2	3		2		1				1	4			3
Cheshire	1		5	1	1	7		4	20	5	12	9	13	23	1	37	2	2		1		12		1	2	2	18	14		6					1	1	1	4		1	9
Derby			1		2	2		1	3		2	1	2	2		3	2					2		1			4	2		3					1	1	7			3
East Haven									3		2	3	4	2		5	4					2			1		2	3		5							2			
Guilford			1		1			2	3		4	3	3	3		6	2	8				1					2	1		1							7			8
Hamden	9	6		1	2				46	2	28	21	32	32		64	4	1	1	1	1	19		5	7		21	24	1	9			2		3	3	16	3	3	21
Middlebury	1		2	1	2	1		1	11	1	2	6	2	8		8				1								1		1					1	1	2	1		1
Milford	1	1	3		2	3		1	7	7	5	3	5	6		13	5	8		1		3					2	3				1				1	2			3
Naugatuck		1			1				2		5	3	6	6		12	2	1						1			2	1		1						1	3			3
North Branford			2						4	1	3	1	4	1		6	4			1		1			1		4	1				1				1	2			4
North Haven			1		2	2			2	1	1	2	1	4		7		3									4	3								1	3			3
Orange		1							4		3	1	3	1		6	5	1		1							4	3		1		2			1	1	4			4
Oxford	2				1	1			11	1	4	8	5	8		13	2		1			1		1	1	1	7	4		1						2	2	1		5
Prospect					1	1			2		1		1	2		2		6						1			22	7		1						2	3			3
Seymour		1	1		1	1		1	13	1	8	6	8	7		15	4		2			2		1			1	27		1		2		3	5	2	3	19		2	25
Southbury		7	1		3			1	50	6	22	34	25	38		63	23	6				16		14	5	1	22	27	1	23			3			1	2	2		4	5
Wallingford									1		1		1	1		2	5	6						1			1	2		2			1			1					5
Waterbury	2		1	1	3	4		1	1		8		2	2		2	3	1		1		2		4		1	1	2	3	2		2			1	4	2		4	
Wolcott																																							
Woodbridge																																							
Total	21	74	10	32	73		4	67	404	20	248	246	279	320	1	600	70	60	11	9	6	108		168	37	7	186	191	4	114		9		19	5	23	36	189	10	16	218

D

Table: Towns in New Haven Co. — Orders 4–8

Towns in New Haven Co.	Order 4.—Digestive Organs.																	Order 5.—Urinary Organs.												Order 6.—Generative Organs.					Orders 7 and 8.										
	Gastritis.	Enteritis.	Peritonitis.	Ascites.	Ulceration of Intestines.	Intussusception.	Hernia.	Stricture Intestines.	Stomach Disease.	Colic.	Hepatitis.	Jaundice.	Liver Disease.	Fistula.	Male.	Female.	Total.	Disease of Spleen.	Bright's Disease.	Nephritis.	Diabetes.	Calculus.	Cystitis.	Kidney Disease.	Prostatitis.	Uræmia.	Male.	Female.	Total.	Ovarian Tumor.	Ovarian Dropsy.	Uterine Tumor.	Disease of Uterus.	Total.	Arthritis.	Phlegmon.	Tumor.	Joint Disease.	Disease of Skin.	Male.	Female.	Males.	Females.	Sex not stated.	Total.
New Haven	8	8	13	1		2	1		3	1	2	5	20		28	36	64		19	1	1	1	2	3	3	5	26	15	41	4			1	5	5	1				2	4	251	245		4
Beacon Falls																			1								1		1													2	2		
Bethany		1	1			1						1	1		1	2	2				1						1		2				1	1								2	2		
Branford	1	1	1		1	1	1				2	1	1		1	3	4		3								1		6				1	1	1			1			1	7	6		
Cheshire		1	2				1		1			1	1		4	4	8		1							1	6		6						1							6	11		
Derby	1	1									1				1	2	2		1								1		1	1							1					38	28	1	
East Haven	1				1								1		1	2	2																									5	6		
Guilford		2	1						1			1				2	2							1				2	4								1				1	6	8		
Hamden	1					1						1	1		1	2	2		1												1											4	12		
Madison	2		1						1							2	3		3								2	2	4						1		1					10	4		
Meriden		1	7		1	1			1	1		2	1		3	6	9		4		1	1	1				4	1	4		1						1			1		47	49		
Middlebury															2		2		1								2		2													1	1		
Milford			2								1	1	1		3	2	5		1				1		2		2	1	2		1				1							12	8		
Naugatuck		1	3		1	1	1						1		3	3	4		1	1	1				1		1	1	2													8	7		
North Branford			1												2		2		1		1						2	1	1		1				1							7	3		
North Haven		1				1					1				1	2	2		1								1		1											1		5	2		
Orange	1	1	2			1	1				1		1		2	2	3							2			2		2									1		1	1	11	8		
Oxford															1		1		1		1			1			2		1													6	6		
Prospect	1														1		1										1															1	7		
Seymour																																										3	2		
Southbury			2			1										2	2										2	2	4													7	4		
Wallingford			3						1		1		1			1	1				1	1		1			1	2	6						1	1						3	6		
Waterbury	2	4	8		1	1						3	2		10	11	21				1		1	1	2		2	2	4	1	1				1	1			1	1	2	14	16		
Wolcott																			3		1				6		6	2	6						1						1	64	74		
Woodbridge															1							1																				6	2		
Total	16	18	40	1	3	4	2		4	3	5	11	27		160	75	135		40	1	4	2	3	7	5	6	55	23	78	4	2		3	9	9	2	4			7	8	525	512	1	

CLASS IV.—DEVELOPMENTAL DISEASES. CLASS V.—VIOLENT DEATHS.

Towns in New Haven Co.	ORDER 1.—Of Children.								ORDERS 2, 3, and 4.					TOTAL FOR CLASS IV.				ORDER 1.—Accident and Negligence.										Homicide.	Suicide.	Violent not Classed Casualty.		Cause not Reported.		Hemorrhage.	ORDERS 3, 4, and 5. TOTAL FOR CLASS V.			
	Stillborn.	Premature Birth and Debility.	Cyanosis.	Spina Bifida.	Malformations.	Teething.	Total M.	Total F.	Childbirth.	Old Age M.	Old Age F.	Atrophy and Debility M.	Atrophy and Debility F.	Male.	Female.	Sex not stated.	Total.	Fracture and Contusion.	Wounds.	Burns and Scalds.	Poison.	Drowning.	Suffocation.	Otherwise.	Total M.	Total F.		F.	M. F.		M. F.		Hemorrhage.	Male.	Female.	Not stated.	Total.
New Haven,	65	37	11	1	.	2	76	39	.	26	35	4	10	104	84	3	191	6	9	5	6	5	1	6	22	10	1	1	.	.	3 21	19 24	16	33	16	.	49
Beacon Falls,	2	.	.	.	.	.	2	1	1	1	.	.	.	3	.	.	3	.	.	.	.	1	1	.	.	.	.	.	.	.	.	.	.	.	.	.	.
Bethany,	2	1	.	.	.	.	1	1	.	.	.	.	2	3	2	.	3	.	.	.	.	1	1	1	1	.	.	1	.	.	.	.	.	1	1	.	2
Branford,	1	1	1	1	1	.	2	2	.	2	5	.	2	6	8	.	14	.	.	.	.	1	.	.	2	1	.	.	.	.	5	.	.	7	5	1	13
Cheshire,	.	.	.	1	.	.	1	1	.	3	1	.	.	6	6	1	7	1	.	.	.	1	.	.	2	.	.	.	.	.	3	.	.	1	1	.	2
Derby,	15	1	.	1	1	.	3	5	1	3	1	.	2	14	6	1	21	2	.	.	.	.	.	2	2	1	.	.	1	.	3	5 3	1	8	7	.	16
East Haven,	.	1	1	.	.	.	1	1	1	3	1	.	.	4	3	.	3	.	.	.	1	.	.	.	.	.	.	.	1	.	1	1	.	1	1	.	1
Guilford,	.	1	.	.	.	.	1	1	1	1	1	.	.	2	2	.	3	.	.	.	.	.	.	.	.	1	.	.	.	.	.	.	.	.	1	.	2
Hamden,	.	.	.	.	.	.	1	.	.	1	.	.	2	2	.	.	3	.	.	.	.	.	.	.	.	.	.	1	.	.	1	.	.	.	1	.	.
Madison,	16	10	.	.	.	.	8	9	1	2	5	.	1	12	5	.	7	2	2	2	.	.	.	.	3	2	.	.	1	.	1 1	1	3	11	5	1	17
Meriden,	.	1	.	.	.	.	.	3	1	4	8	.	1	2	18	9	39	2	.	2	.	.	.	3	2	.	.	.	.	.	1	.	3	3	3	.	6
Middlebury,	3	1	1	.	.	.	.	1	.	4	6	.	1	2	8	.	.	.	.	.	.	.	.	.	2	.	.	.	.	.	1	.	2	3	1	.	4
Milford,	4	3	1	.	1	.	6	3	.	2	2	.	1	9	8	.	11	.	.	.	.	.	1	.	3	.	.	.	1	.	.	.	.	2	1	.	.
Naugatuck,	.	.	.	.	.	.	.	.	.	.	.	.	.	3	.	.	18	.	.	.	.	.	.	.	.	.	.	.	.	.	.	.	.	.	.	.	.
North Branford,	.	2	.	.	.	.	4	.	.	1	.	.	1	5	3	.	3	.	.	2	.	.	.	.	2	2	1	.	.	1	.	.	.	2	1	.	2
North Haven,	.	.	.	.	.	.	2	1	.	3	.	.	.	2	1	.	8	1	.	1	.	1	.	.	2	1	.	.	.	.	2 7	.	.	2	1	.	3
Orange,	2	5	1	.	.	.	2	1	.	1	2	.	.	5	2	.	.	.	.	2	1	.	1	1	3	2	.	1	1	.	1	3	3	5	3	.	8
Oxford,	.	1	.	.	.	.	.	1	1	3	2	.	.	.	3	.	1	.	.	.	.	.	.	.	.	.	.	1	.	1	.	.	.	12	2	.	16
Prospect,	.	.	.	.	.	.	2	1	.	1	.	1	.	2	.	.	6	.	.	.	.	.	.	1	2	1	.	1	.	1	.	.	.	9	3	.	9
Seymour,	18	2	.	.	.	2	28	14	3	2	5	1	8	39	19	5	63	1	1	2	1	1	1	3	3	1	4	1	2 7	1	1 3	3	8	12	4	1	2
Southbury,	.	1	.	.	.	.	.	1	.	.	.	.	.	1	.	.	1	.	1	.	.	.	.	.	5	.	1	.	1	.	.	.	1	9	1	.	.
Wallingford,	.	3	3	.	.	.	2	2	.	3	3	.	.	1	.	.	1	1	.	2	.	.	.	.	3	.	.	.	.	.	1 3	.	1	1	.	.	1
Waterbury,	.	21	.	.	.	.	.	.	.	.	.	.	.	1	.	.	.	.	.	.	.	.	.	.	.	.	4	1	.	.	.	.	2	.	.	.	.
Wolcott,	.	.	.	.	.	.	.	.	.	.	.	.	.	.	.	.	1	.	.	.	.	.	.	.	.	.	1	.	.	.	.	.	.	1	.	.	2
Woodbridge,	.	.	.	.	.	.	.	.	.	.	.	.	.	.	.	.	.	.	.	.	.	.	.	.	.	.	.	.	.	.	1	.	.	1	1	.	.
Total,	129	85	17	4	1	2	145	80	7	56	76	19	15	217	177	20	414	15	12	10	9	12	4	6	65	114	1	10	6	1	3 21	19 24	16	99	50	4	153

CLASS I.—ZYMOTIC DISEASES.

Towns in New London Co.	Small-pox	Measles	Scarlet Fever	Diphtheria	Quinsy	Croup	Whooping Cough	Typhoid Fever	Erysipelas	Puerperal Fever	Carbuncle	Dysentery	Diarrhœa	Cholera Infantum	Malarial Fever	Intermittent Fever	Congestive Fever	Remittent Fever	Typho-Malarial Fever	Rheumatism	Cerebro-Spinal Meningitis	Total M	Total F	Pyæmia	Syphilis	Hydrophobia	Stomatitis	Caries and Necrosis	Total M	Total F	Privation and Neglect	Purpura and Scurvy	Alcoholism	Total M	Total F	Male	Female	Total
																																				Order III—Dietic		
New London,			6	18		4	2	5	2	1		1	1	8	8	1			4		1	21	21		1					1			3	1		22	24	46
Norwich,				9		6	1	6	1	1		1	7	13	13	1	1		4	4	2	27	36													27	36	63
Bozrah,			1		1									4								2	3													2	3	5
East Lyme,				1				3				1	1	3		1						3	6													3	6	9
Franklin,														1								2	2													2	2	4
Griswold,			7	3		3				1		1	3		1		1					7	5													7	5	12
Groton,				3		2								1	7				3		1	12	15													12	15	27
Lebanon,						2		2						2	2				2			2	4													2	4	6
Ledyard,			4	1				1						1	1							4	6													4	6	10
Lisbon,														2								3	1													3	1	4
Lyme,			1	1				2	1	1		1	1	1								1	1		1											1	1	2
No. Stonington,				6		2								1	1		5			1		6	3				1		1							6	3	9
Old Lyme,				3		4				1		1	1	7	7				1	1		7	4													7	4	11
Preston,			2	1		1		1						5	5							1														1		1
Salem,														6	6	1						2	8													2	8	12
Sprague,				3		1								4	4				3			10	2													10	2	5
Stonington,			2					2		1		1										10	7		1											10	7	17
Voluntown,				6																		10	15													10	15	25
Waterford,		2	1	1		1		2	1	1		1	1	6	6	1			3			3	4													3	4	7
Total,	3		34 52		124		323		5	5		7 15		66	3	5	6		17	7	7	133	150		2					1			3	3	1	135	153	288

CLASS II.—CONSTITUTIONAL DISEASES.   **ORDER 1.—NERVOUS SYSTEM.**

Towns in New London Co.	Dropsy and Anæmia	Cancer	Senile Gangrene	Diathetic Total M.	Diathetic Total F.	Scrofula	Tabes Mesenterica	Phthisis	Hydrocephalus	Tubercular Total M.	Tubercular Total F.	Male	Female	Total for Class II	Apoplexy	Paralysis	Insanity	Epilepsy	Chorea	Tetanus	Convulsions	Meningitis	Brain Disease	Neuralgia	Dislocation of Cord	Nervous Total M.	Nervous Total F.	Embolism	Heart Diseases	Aneurism	Pericarditis	Phlebitis	Capillary Bronchitis	Pleurisy	Lung Disease	Bronchitis	Pneumonia	Laryngitis	Asthma
New London	7	6	.	5	9	1	1	30	.	8	24	13	33	46	4	9	.	.	.	1	2	.	4	.	.	11	9	.	10	.	.	.	2	.	3	2	11	.	.
Norwich	8	16	1	11	14	6	1	62	4	39	34	50	48	98	7	15	1	2	.	1	6	17	12	.	1	37	25	1	12	3	4	.	.	.	2	1	11	.	.
Bozrah	1	.	.	1	1	1	.	3	3	2	2	3	3	5	.	.	.	1	.	.	1	3	2	.	.	3	4	.	3	.	.	.	1	.	.	.	.	.	.
Colchester	1	.	.	3	.	1	.	10	6	4	2	7	3	10	2	1	.	1	.	.	1	3	.	.	.	4	4	.	3	.	.	.	1	.	.	.	2	.	.
East Lyme	1	3	1	1	1	.	.	6	.	4	2	7	6	13	2	1	.	.	.	.	2	1	.	.	.	4	1	.	1	.	.	.	.	.	.	.	1	.	.
Franklin	.	.	.	.	.	.	.	.	.	.	.	.	.	.	2	1	.	.	.	.	1	.	1	.	.	1	3	.	1	.	.	.	.	.	.	.	.	.	.
Griswold	.	1	.	.	2	2	.	14	1	10	6	10	8	18	3	1	.	.	.	.	.	.	1	.	.	1	5	.	2	.	.	.	1	.	.	.	7	.	.
Groton	.	1	.	1	1	.	1	10	.	4	6	6	10	14	.	1	.	.	.	.	.	1	1	1	.	1	1	.	3	.	.	.	1	.	.	.	2	.	.
Lebanon	1	1	.	1	2	.	.	6	1	3	3	4	4	8	4	1	.	1	.	.	.	.	1	.	.	2	1	.	2	.	.	.	1	.	.	.	1	.	.
Ledyard	1	1	.	1	1	.	.	3	.	1	2	3	2	7	.	.	.	.	.	.	.	.	1	.	.	.	3	.	2	.	.	.	.	.	.	.	1	.	.
Lisbon	3	1	♦	1	1	2	.	.	.	.	.	2	2	4	4	1	.	.	.	.	.	.	.	.	.	1	1	.	3	.	.	.	1	.	1	.	2	.	.
Lyme	.	1	.	.	1	.	.	.	.	.	1	.	2	.	.	1	.	.	.	.	.	1	1	.	.	2	1	.	1	.	.	.	.	.	.	.	.	.	.
Montville	1	1	1	.	1	.	.	2	.	1	1	2	2	4	2	1	.	1	.	.	.	.	1	1	1	.	.	.	3	.	.	.	1	.	.	.	1	.	.
No. Stonington	2	.	.	2	2	.	.	1	1	.	1	2	2	4	.	.	.	.	.	.	2	.	1	.	.	3	.	.	2	.	.	.	.	.	.	.	2	.	.
Old Lyme	.	1	.	2	2	.	.	2	.	.	1	2	2	4	2	1	.	1	.	.	.	1	1	.	.	3	1	.	2	.	.	.	1	.	.	.	1	.	.
Preston	2	.	.	2	2	.	1	2	.	4	.	4	2	6	.	1	.	.	.	.	.	.	1	.	.	2	.	.	4	.	.	.	.	.	1	.	2	.	.
Salem	1	.	.	.	.	.	.	.	.	.	.	.	.	.	.	.	.	.	.	.	.	.	.	.	.	.	1	.	.	.	.	.	.	.	.	.	3	.	.
Sprague	1	2	.	2	2	.	.	14	.	7	9	9	9	18	.	.	.	.	.	.	2	2	.	.	.	1	1	.	2	.	.	.	.	.	.	.	2	.	.
Stonington	1	3	.	1	1	.	.	24	2	9	13	10	16	26	3	3	.	.	.	.	5	2	7	.	.	11	8	.	4	.	.	.	1	.	.	.	3	.	.
Voluntown	.	.	.	1	1	.	.	4	1	3	1	4	1	5	.	1	.	.	.	.	.	.	.	.	.	1	1	.	2	.	.	.	.	.	.	.	2	.	.
Waterford	2	1	2	3	2	.	.	4	.	2	2	5	4	9	6	.	.	2	.	.	.	.	.	.	.	3	5	.	2	.	.	.	.	.	.	.	.	.	.
Total	**34**	**41**	**5**	**34**	**46**	**12**	**3**	**195**	**7**	**100**	**117**	**134**	**163**	**297**	**38**	**34**	**2**	**7**	.	**2**	**22**	**25**	**30**	**1**	**2**	**88**	**75**	**1**	**58**	.	**4**	.	**6**	.	**8**	**3**	**51**	.	.

CLASS III.—LOCAL DISEASES—Continued.

Towns in New London Co.	Order 4.—Digestive Organs.														Order 5.—Urinary Organs.												Order 6.—Generative Organs.					Orders 7 and 8.—							Total for Class III.				
	Gastritis.	Enteritis.	Peritonitis.	Ascites.	Ulceration of Intestines.	Intussusception.	Hernia.	Stricture Intestines.	Stomach Disease.	Colic.	Hepatitis.	Jaundice.	Liver Disease.	Fistula.	Male.	Female.	Total.	Disease of Spleen.	Bright's Disease.	Nephritis.	Diabetes.	Calculus.	Cystitis.	Kidney Disease.	Prostatitis.	Uræmia.	Male.	Female.	Total.	Ovarian Tumor.	Ovarian Dropsy.	Uterine Tumor.	Disease of Uterus.	Total.	Arthritis.	Abscess.	Tumor.	Joint Disease.	Disease of Skin.	Male.	Female.	Males.	Females.	Sex not stated.	Total.
New London,	4	4			2						2	1	1		4	4	14		3		1		1	1			2	4	6						1	1				1	1	33	37		70
Norwich,	7	12	1		1	2			1		1		3	1	18	10	28		13					1			7	7	14	1						1				1	1	80	60		140
Bozrah,	1	1													2	2	2							1	1		1	1	2						1					1		3	2		5
Hier,	1						2								3	1	4										1	1	2											1		13	8		21
East Lyme,									1				1		1	2	3							1				1														8	3		11
Franklin,						2									2	1	3																				1					2	5		7
ield,					1	1			1				1		2	1	1		1					1			1	1	2			2		2			1			1		4	9		13
Groton,		1											2		2	2	4			1				1				1														8	7		15
Lebanon,															1	1	3										1	1														3	9		12
Ledyard,						1									2	1	1												1														4	5		9
Lisbon,																	1																											1		1
Lyme,					1			2							5		5		1					2					2													2	3		5
Montville,															2	1	3										1	2									1				1	13	3		17
No. Stonington,		1													1	1	2		1								2	2	2													8	3		11
Old Lyme,			2												1	2	3									1		2	4													4	6		7
Preston,		1	1										1		1	2	2																				1			1		4	6		10
Salem,			3												1	3	1		2								2		2													7	4		7
Sprague,		1				1							1		1	2	4		2					2			4		4								1			1		19	16		11
Stonington,	1														1	3	1								1																	3	2		35
iern,								1																																		4	6		5
Waterford,																																														10
Total,	15	30			5	5	5	5	3		3	2	11		142	39	81	1	22	1			1	5	2	1	118	15	33	2				3	2	2	3			3	4	222	199		421

CLASS IV.—DEVELOPMENTAL DISEASES. — CLASS V.—VIOLENT DEATHS.

Towns in New London Co.	Stillborn	Premature Birth and Debility	Cyanosis	Spina Bifida	Other Malformat'ns	Teething	Order 1 Total M	Order 1 Total F	Childbirth	Old Age M	Old Age F	Atrophy and Debility M	Atrophy and Debility F	Class IV Male	Class IV Female	Class IV Not stated	Class IV Total	Fracture and Contusion	Wounds	Burns and Scalds	Poison	Drowning	Suffocation	Otherwise	Acc. Total M	Acc. Total F	Homicide F	Hemorrhage	Suicide M	Suicide F	Violent not Classed M	Violent not Classed F	Cause not Reported M	Cause not Reported F	Class V Male	Class V Female	Class V Not stated	Class V Total	Grand Total Males	Grand Total Females
New London	7	2	·	·	·	2	8	8	9	3	9	9	6	20	26	1	47	1	·	1	·	2	1	·	4	1	·	1	2	2	·	·	·	2	7	1	·	8	95	121
Norwich	39	5	·	·	·	·	18	26	3	10	13	7	5	35	47	·	82	3	·	2	·	3	·	1	9	·	·	1	2	·	·	·	2	1	11	3	·	14	203	194
Bozrah	1	·	·	·	·	1	1	1	·	2	·	·	·	3	·	·	3	·	·	·	·	·	·	·	1	·	·	·	·	·	·	·	·	1	1	·	·	1	7	9
Colchester	·	·	·	·	·	·	1	1	·	·	2	·	·	3	1	·	4	1	·	·	·	·	·	·	1	1	·	·	·	·	·	·	1	1	1	1	·	2	27	20
East Lyme	3	·	·	·	·	·	1	2	·	2	2	·	·	3	·	·	8	·	2	·	·	·	·	·	·	1	1	·	·	1	·	·	·	·	·	1	·	1	16	14
Franklin	·	·	·	·	·	·	3	3	1	2	1	·	·	5	3	·	3	1	·	·	·	1	·	·	·	1	·	·	·	·	·	·	·	·	·	·	·	·	6	8
Griswold	2	·	·	·	·	·	1	2	·	5	11	2	·	8	14	·	22	1	·	·	1	·	·	·	4	·	·	1	·	·	·	·	1	7	2	·	·	2	28	25
Groton	·	·	·	·	·	·	1	·	·	1	1	·	2	3	·	·	4	·	·	·	·	·	·	·	1	·	·	·	·	·	·	·	·	·	·	·	·	·	37	53
Lebanon	·	·	·	·	·	·	1	·	·	1	·	·	·	1	3	·	3	·	·	·	·	·	·	·	1	1	·	·	·	·	·	·	·	·	1	·	·	1	10	20
Ledyard	·	·	·	·	·	·	·	·	·	·	·	·	·	1	1	·	2	·	·	·	·	1	·	·	·	·	·	·	·	·	·	·	·	·	·	·	·	·	12	14
Lisbon	2	·	·	·	·	·	2	2	·	2	·	·	·	4	2	·	3	·	·	·	·	·	·	·	1	1	1	1	1	·	·	·	5	4	2	1	·	2	4	3
Lyme	·	·	·	·	·	·	2	·	·	·	4	·	1	4	4	·	6	·	·	·	·	·	·	·	1	·	·	·	·	·	·	·	4	3	1	1	·	2	4	7
Montville	·	1	·	·	·	1	·	·	1	2	1	1	·	1	·	·	1	·	·	·	·	·	·	·	1	·	·	·	·	·	·	·	2	2	3	·	·	3	30	16
No. Stonington	·	·	·	·	·	·	·	·	·	·	1	·	·	·	1	2	1	·	·	·	·	·	·	·	1	·	·	1	·	·	·	·	9	12	2	12	·	·	19	11
Old Lyme	·	·	·	·	·	·	·	2	·	·	6	·	·	·	2	·	7	·	1	·	·	1	1	·	·	·	·	·	·	·	·	·	·	·	·	·	·	·	8	5
Preston	2	·	·	·	·	·	·	·	·	4	1	·	·	·	9	2	·	1	1	·	·	·	·	·	2	·	·	·	·	·	·	·	·	1	2	2	·	9	20	23
Salem	·	·	·	·	·	·	·	·	·	·	·	·	·	·	·	·	·	·	·	·	·	·	·	·	·	·	·	·	·	·	·	·	·	·	·	·	·	·	4	10
Sprague	·	6	·	·	·	·	6	2	·	4	6	1	6	6	9	·	8	·	1	·	·	·	1	·	·	1	·	·	·	·	·	·	2	·	2	2	·	4	34	24
Stonington	2	4	·	·	2	·	9	3	·	·	1	·	·	8	9	2	19	·	·	1	·	·	·	·	2	·	·	·	·	·	·	·	9	12	12	12	·	24	59	68
Voluntown	·	3	·	·	·	·	3	2	·	2	1	·	·	1	3	·	9	·	·	·	·	·	·	·	·	·	·	·	·	·	·	·	·	·	·	·	·	·	11	10
Waterford	2	·	·	·	·	·	2	2	·	·	1	·	·	4	3	·	7	1	1	·	1	·	·	1	3	1	·	1	·	·	·	·	1	·	4	·	·	4	23	20
Total	60	33	·	·	2	4	48	43	15	35	50	21	14	105	121	8	234	8	5	4	2	6	4	2	25	6	1	6	6	6	1	1	23	31	60	40	·	100	657	675

CLASS I.—ZYMOTIC DISEASES.

Towns in Fairfield Co.	Total for Class I: Male	Female	Sex not stated	Total
Danbury,	23	23	.	46
Bridgeport,	91	67	1	159
Bethel,	8	4	.	12
Brookfield,	1	1	.	2
Darien,	2	1	.	3
Easton,	1	1	.	2
Fairfield,	5	5	.	10
Greenwich,	5	12	.	17
Huntington,	5	6	.	11
Monroe,	1	1	.	2
New Canaan,	7	6	.	13
New Fairfield,	1	3	.	4
Newtown,	5	6	.	11
Norwalk,	28	24	.	52
Redding,	5	2	.	7
Ridgefield,	3	2	.	5
Sherman,	1	.	.	1
Stamford,	27	27	.	54
Stratford,	1	3	.	4
Trumbull,	2	3	.	5
Weston,	4	3	.	7
Westport,	9	1	.	10
Wilton,	2	2	.	4
Total,	237	203	1	441

CLASS II.—CONSTITUTIONAL DISEASES.

Towns in Fairfield Co.	Order 1.—Diathetic. Dropsy and Anæmia.	Cancer.	Otes Sarcoma.	Senile Gangrene.	Total. M.	Total. F.	Order 2.—Tubercular. Scrofula.	Tabes Mesenterica.	Phthisis.	Hydrocephalus.	Total. M.	Total. F.	Total for Class II. Male.	Female.	Sex not stated.	Total.
Danbury,	1	5	..	1	4	3	..	..	22	..	17	5	21	8	..	29
Bridgeport,	6	8	..	1	7	8	2	15	63	6	43	43	50	51	1	102
Bethel,	....	2	..	..	2	..	..	1	7	..	2	6	4	6	..	10
Brookfield,	....	..	..	..	..	..	..	..	1	..	1	....	1	....	..	1
Darien,	....	1	..	1	1	1	..	1	2	..	3	....	4	1	..	5
Easton,	....	1	1	..	..	2	..	..	....	1	1	....	1	2	..	3
Fairfield,	....	1	..	..	..	1	..	..	4	..	3	1	3	2	..	5
Greenwich,	6	3	1	1	6	5	..	1	13	1	10	5	16	10	..	26
Huntington,	....	..	..	..	..	..	..	1	5	..	5	1	5	1	..	6
Monroe,	....	..	..	..	..	..	..	..	3	..	1	2	1	2	..	3
New Canaan,	1	..	..	..	..	1	..	1	7	1	4	5	4	6	..	10
New Fairfield,	....	..	..	..	..	..	..	..	....	..	....	....	...	...	..	....
Newtown,	2	1	..	1	2	2	..	..	7	..	4	3	6	5	..	11
Norwalk,	5	8	..	1	5	9	2	5	29	2	20	18	25	27	..	52
Redding,	2	1	..	..	2	1	..	..	1	..	1	....	3	1	..	4
Ridgefield,	1	3	..	..	..	4	..	..	4	..	1	3	1	7	..	8
Sherman,	....	..	..	..	..	..	..	..	2	..	....	2	...	2	..	2
Stamford,	7	..	..	..	4	3	2	..	32	..	13	21	17	24	..	41
Stratford,	....	..	..	..	..	..	..	..	1	..	....	1	...	1	..	1
Trumbull,	1	..	..	1	1	1	..	..	3	..	2	1	3	2	..	5
Weston,	1	1	..	..	1	1	..	..	1	..	....	1	1	2	..	3
Westport,	1	1	..	..	1	1	..	..	8	..	3	5	4	6	..	10
Wilton,	1	1	..	..	1	1	..	..	....	..	....	....	1	1	..	2
Total,	35	37	2	7	37	44	6	25	215	11	134	123	171	167	1	339

Towns in Fairfield Co.	Order 1.—Nervous System. Apoplexy.	Paralysis.	Insanity.	Epilepsy.	Chorea.	Tetanus.	Convulsions.	Meningitis.	Brain Disease.	Spinal Disease.	Neuralgia.	Total. M.	Total. F.	Embolism.	Heart Disease.	Aneurism.	Pericarditis.	Phlebitis.	Capillary Bronchitis.	Pleurisy.	Lung Disease.	Bronchitis.	Pneumonia.
Danbury,	5	7	2	..	..	..	2	..	1	..	..	8	9	..	5	..	..	..	....	..	1	5	1
Bridgeport,	13	10	..	1	..	1	16	15	14	3	..	43	30	3	17	1	2	..	4	..	15	4	2
Bethel,	5	..	..	..	..	..	..	..	2	1	..	5	3	..	1	..	..	..	....	..	..	..	
Brookfield,	1	3	..	..	1	..	..	..	..	..	..	3	2	..	3	..	..	..	....	..	..	..	...
Darien,	1	1	..	..	..	..	..	1	..	..	1	1	2	..	1	..	..	..	1	..	..	1	...
Easton,	1	1	..	1	..	..	..	..	..	..	..	4	....	..	3	..	..	..	....	..	..	..	...
Fairfield,	1	4	..	..	..	..	3	1	..	..	..	3	6	..	5	..	..	..	1	..	..	..	
Greenwich,	1	5	..	..	..	..	3	1	..	..	..	5	5	..	9	1	..	..	....	..	1	..	
Huntington,	1	..	..	..	1	..	3	1	..	..	..	3	3	..	5	..	..	..	....	..	..	..	
Monroe,	..	..	..	..	..	..	..	1	..	1	..	1	1	..	....	..	..	..	....	..	..	..	
New Canaan,	1	2	..	..	..	..	..	2	..	..	..	1	4	..	1	..	..	..	....	..	..	2	
New Fairfield,	..	..	..	..	..	..	..	..	..	..	..	....	....	..	1	..	..	..	....	..	..	..	
Newtown,	4	1	..	..	..	..	4	2	4	..	..	5	10	..	4	..	..	..	....	1	..	..	
Norwalk,	5	9	..	2	..	1	7	2	4	..	..	19	11	..	11	1	1	..	4	..	..	5	1
Redding,	5	..	..	..	..	..	..	..	..	..	..	2	3	..	....	..	..	..	....	..	..	..	
Ridgefield,	1	..	..	..	..	..	..	..	1	..	..	....	2	..	2	..	..	..	....	..	..	1	
Sherman,	1	..	..	..	..	..	..	..	..	..	..	1	....	..	....	..	..	..	....	..	..	..	...
Stamford,	6	2	..	..	..	..	3	..	2	..	..	6	7	..	9	..	..	..	....	..	1	..	1
Stratford,	1	1	..	..	..	..	1	..	..	..	..	1	2	..	1	..	..	..	....	..	..	..	...
Trumbull,	..	2	..	..	..	..	..	..	..	..	..	1	1	..	3	..	..	..	....	..	..	..	...
Weston,	1	1	..	..	..	..	..	..	..	..	..	2	....	1	2	..	..	..	....	..	..	..	...
Westport,	..	..	..	1	..	..	1	1	1	..	..	3	1	..	2	..	..	..	....	..	3	..	
Wilton,	3	1	..	1	..	..	..	..	4	..	..	5	4	..	1	..	..	..	....	..	..	..	
Total,	57	50	2	6	2	2	43	27	33	5	1	122	106	4	86	3	3	..	10	1	21	18	

CLASS III.—LOCAL DISEASES—Continued.

Towns in Fairfield Co.	Order 4.—Digestive Organs: Gastritis	Enteritis	Peritonitis	Ascites	Ulceration of Intestines	Intussusception	Hernia	Stricture Intestines	Stomach Disease	Colic	Hepatitis	Jaundice	Liver Disease	Fistula	Male	Female	Total	Order 5.—Urinary Organs: Disease of Spleen	Bright's Disease	Nephritis	Diabetes	Calculus	Cystitis	Kidney Disease	Prostatitis	Uræmia	Male	Female	Total	Order 6.—Generative Organs: Ovarian Tumor	Ovarian Dropsy	Disease of Uterus	Uterine Tumor	Total	Orders 7 and 8.—: Abscess	Tumor	Joint Disease	Disease of Skin	Arthritis	Male	Female	Total for Class III.: Male	Female	Sex not stated	Total
Danbury	.	.	2	1	.	1	.	1	.	.	1	.	.	.	2	.	2	.	1	.	1	.	.	.	.	.	2	.	2	.	.	1	.	1	1	.	.	.	1	2	2	22	25	.	47
Bridgeport	6	1	12	1	.	1	.	.	2	.	1	.	6	.	13	20	33	.	12	.	3	.	1	5	.	.	11	11	22	.	.	1	.	1	3	.	.	.	.	2	2	115	91	.	206
Bethel	.	.	.	.	.	.	.	1	.	1	.	.	.	.	.	1	1	.	.	.	.	1	1	.	.	.	.	.	.	.	.	.	.	.	1	1	.	.	.	1	.	10	6	.	16
Brookfield	.	.	.	.	.	.	.	.	.	.	1	.	.	.	.	.	.	.	.	.	.	.	.	.	.	.	1	.	1	.	.	.	.	.	.	.	.	.	.	.	1	6	5	.	11
Darien	.	.	.	.	.	.	.	.	.	.	.	.	.	.	1	.	1	.	.	.	.	1	1	.	.	.	1	1	1	.	.	.	.	.	.	.	.	.	.	.	.	4	3	.	7
Easton	.	.	.	1	.	1	.	.	.	.	.	.	.	.	1	.	1	.	.	.	.	.	.	.	.	.	.	.	.	.	.	.	.	.	.	.	.	.	.	.	.	7	.	.	8
Fairfield	.	.	2	.	.	.	.	.	3	.	1	.	2	.	3	3	6	.	.	.	.	.	.	.	.	.	.	2	.	.	.	1	.	1	.	.	.	.	.	.	.	11	14	.	25
Greenwich	.	.	.	.	.	.	.	.	.	.	.	.	.	.	1	3	6	.	1	.	.	.	.	.	.	.	1	.	1	.	.	.	.	.	1	1	.	.	.	.	.	14	23	.	37
Huntington	.	.	1	.	.	1	.	.	.	.	1	.	.	.	1	1	1	.	.	.	.	.	.	.	.	.	1	.	1	.	.	1	.	1	1	.	.	.	.	.	.	9	9	.	18
Monroe	.	3	.	.	.	.	.	.	.	.	.	.	.	.	.	.	1	.	.	.	.	.	.	.	.	.	.	.	.	.	.	.	.	.	.	.	.	.	.	.	.	1	2	.	3
New Canaan	.	.	1	.	.	.	.	.	.	.	.	.	.	.	1	.	1	.	.	.	.	.	.	.	.	.	.	.	.	.	.	.	.	.	.	.	.	.	.	.	.	7	.	.	13
New Fairfield	.	.	.	.	.	.	.	.	.	.	.	.	.	.	.	.	.	.	.	.	.	.	.	.	.	.	.	.	.	.	.	.	.	.	.	.	.	.	.	.	.	.	18	.	18
Newtown	.	3	1	.	.	.	.	.	.	.	5	.	.	.	6	5	8	.	1	.	.	1	.	.	.	1	1	1	3	.	.	1	.	1	2	.	.	.	.	.	.	18	41	.	36
Norwalk	3	.	3	.	.	2	.	.	1	.	1	.	5	.	6	10	16	.	1	.	.	.	.	1	.	.	1	4	15	.	.	1	.	1	.	.	.	.	.	.	.	59	.	.	100
Redding	2	.	.	.	.	.	.	.	.	.	.	.	.	.	.	3	3	.	.	.	.	.	.	.	.	.	.	.	1	.	.	.	.	.	.	.	.	.	.	.	.	4	10	.	14
Ridgefield	.	.	.	.	.	.	.	1	.	.	1	.	.	.	.	.	.	.	.	.	.	.	.	.	1	.	1	.	1	.	.	.	.	.	.	.	.	.	.	.	.	5	4	.	9
Sherman	.	.	.	.	.	.	.	.	.	.	.	.	.	.	.	.	.	.	.	.	.	.	.	.	.	.	.	.	.	.	.	.	.	.	.	.	.	.	.	.	.	.	.	.	1
Stamford	.	1	3	1	.	.	.	.	3	.	1	.	5	.	5	8	13	.	1	.	.	1	1	.	.	2	2	2	4	.	.	1	.	1	1	.	.	.	.	.	.	20	33	.	53
Stratford	.	.	2	.	.	.	.	.	.	.	.	.	2	.	.	2	2	.	.	.	.	.	.	.	.	.	2	.	2	.	.	.	.	.	1	.	.	.	.	.	.	4	5	.	9
Trumbull	.	.	.	.	.	.	.	.	.	.	.	.	.	.	.	.	.	.	1	.	.	1	.	.	.	.	1	1	.	.	.	1	.	1	.	.	.	.	.	.	.	5	3	.	8
Weston	1	.	2	.	.	2	.	.	1	.	.	.	.	.	3	.	2	.	1	.	.	.	.	.	.	.	2	.	2	.	.	.	.	.	.	.	.	.	.	.	.	6	2	.	8
Westport	.	1	.	.	.	.	.	.	.	.	.	.	1	.	.	1	1	.	1	.	.	.	1	.	.	.	1	1	.	.	.	1	.	.	1	.	.	.	.	.	.	9	11	.	20
Wilton	.	.	1	.	.	.	.	.	1	.	.	.	.	.	2	.	3	.	1	.	.	.	1	.	.	.	1	1	.	.	.	.	.	.	.	.	.	.	.	.	.	11	7	.	18
Total	14	6	28	3	.	4	3	1	11	1	5	1	22	1	142	58	100	2	30	2	6	3	4	6	1	5	39	20	59	.	1	3	.	4	6	6	.	.	1	7	.	351	324	.	675

CLASS IV.—DEVELOPMENTAL DISEASES. | CLASS V.—VIOLENT DEATHS.

Towns in Fairfield Co.	Stillborn	Premature Birth and Debility	Cyanosis	Other Malformations	Teething	Total M	Total F	Sex not stated	Childbirth	Old Age M	Old Age F	Atrophy and Debility M	Atrophy and Debility F	Class IV Male	Class IV Female	Class IV Not stated	Total for Class IV	Fracture and Contusion	Wounds	Burns and Scalds	Poison	Drowning	Suffocation	Otherwise	Order 1 Total M	Order 1 Total F	Homicide M	Homicide F	Hemorrhage	Suicide M	Suicide F	Violent not Classed M	Violent not Classed F	Cause not Reported M	Cause not Reported F	Class V Male	Class V Female	Class V Not stated	Total for Class V	Grand Total Male	Grand Total Female
Danbury,	13	2			1	9	7		2	3	11			12	20		32	1		2	1	1	1	3	3	5				1				13	27	17	32	15	64	95	108
Bridgeport,	26	25		1		27	22	3	7	5	9	11	7	43	45	3	91	2		2		3		6	10	2			2					14	10	24	14	1	39	324	268
Bethel,	6	6				2				2	2	1		3	6	3	9	1							1	1								2	1	3	3		4	28	23
Brookfield,	1													3	2		4																							10	8
Darien,						1				2	1			2	1		4	1			1				1	2		1							1	1	1		3	11	8
Easton,											2			1	1		2								1	1													1	10	6
Fairfield,	1	1							2	4	5		1	5	7		8	1				1			2	1				1				1		4	1		5	25	24
—		3				3	2			2				7	2		14			1		1			2	2			4					1	1	3			5	46	53
Huntington,	2					2					5	2		2	1		4	1							1								2			2			3	24	20
Monroe,		1						1	2			1		1	1		3																							6	8
New —																						1			1										1		1		1	20	23
New Fairfield,	2	1				2				2	3			3	9		16																	1						6	4
Newtown,	8	5				7	5	1		5	15	1	3	7	22	1	35	2		1	1	1		2	2	2								1	1	3	3		8	39	41
Norwalk,		2				2				1	2	1		2	3		5	1					1		2	2			1		1					2	2		4	127	119
Redding,		8				7			6	12	8	1		4	3		7								2											3	3		1	15	16
Ridgefield,	2	2			3	1			1	1	3	1	2	16	19		35	1		1					2	2				1	2			2	9	12	12		13	17	16
—man,				1						1		1		4	4		5									1											1		3	3	5
Stamford,	1	1		1			1			1		1	1	1	1		5			1				1	1	1					1			1	1	2	2		3	92	104
Stratford,								1			8	1			4		5					1											2			1	1	1	3	8	14
Trumbull,	1	1				3					3			2			5																						1	10	11
Weston,										2		1		2	3		4	3											1							2			1	12	8
Westport,		1				1				1	2	1	1	2	3		5			1		1			1	1				1	2	1				2	3		5	29	21
Wilton,												1	1	2	2		4	1						1	4				1					1	1	2	1		2	17	13
Total,	65	42	1	2	4	60	49	5	19	47	70	18	18	125	156	5	286	14	2	9	4	12	4	11	34	18		7	8	1	2	1	44	45	89	71	16	176	974	921

Towns in Windham Co.	Small-pox	Measles	Scarlet Fever	Diphtheria	Quinsy	Croup	Whooping Cough	Typhoid Fever	Erysipelas	Puerperal Fever	Carbuncle	Dysentery	Diarrhœa	Cholera Infantum	Malarial Fever	Intermittent Fever	Congestive Fever	Remittent Fever	Typho-Malarial Fever	Rheumatism	Cerebro Spinal Meningitis	Total M.	Total F.	Septicæmia	Syphilis	Caries and Necrosis	Stomatitis	Stricture	Hydrophobia	Total M.	Total F.	Purpura and Scurvy	Privation and Neglect	Alcoholism	Total M.	Total F.	Male	Female	Sex not stated	Total
Brooklyn,			1	3				4				1	1	5			1	1				11	6											1	1		12	6		1
Ashford,								2														1	1														1	1		
Canterbury,				1	1																		1															1		
Chaplin,														1					1				1															1		
Eastford,													1	1								3															3			3
Hampton,		1	3	7		1		7		1				10						1	3	16	18														16	18		3
Killingly,						1		7			1	2		3							2	12	3														12	3		
Plainfield,						1		2												1		1	3														1	3		
Pomfret,		1	1			1			1			2		13					4			8	15														9	15		2
Putnam,																															1			1	1					
Scotland,							2							1								2	2														2	2		1
Sterling,		1		3				7	1			2		5					4		1	6	10	1													6	10		2
Thompson,			1	1				1		1				6					1	1	2	8	10									1					8	12		
Windham,																						1	3								1						1	3		
Woodstock,																																								
Total,		3	5	15		5	2	30	2	2		9	3	44			1	1	10	3	8	69	74	1							1	1		2	2	1	71	76		147

CLASS II.—CONSTITUTIONAL DISEASES.

Towns in Windham Co.	Order 1.—Diathetic. Otes Sarcoma.	Dropsy and Anæmia.	Cancer.	Senile Gangrene.	Total. M	Total. F.	Order 2.—Tubercular. Scrofula.	Tabes Mesenterica.	Phthisis.	Hydrocephalus.	Total. M.	Total. F.	Total for Class II. Male.	Female.	Total.
BROOKLYN,	..	....	1	..	1	..	..	..	3	3	2	4	3	4	7
Ashford,	..	....	..	..	..	..	..	..	3	..	1	2	1	2	3
Canterbury,	..	....	..	..	..	..	..	..	3	..	....	3	....	3	3
Chaplin,	..	....	1	..	..	1	..	..	2	..	1	1	1	2	3
Eastford,	..	....	..	..	..	..	..	..	6	..	3	3	3	3	6
Hampton,	1	....	..	..	1	..	..	..	1	..	....	1	1	1	2
Killingly,	..	....	3	1	2	2	1	3	17	1	11	10	13	13	26
Plainfield,	..	....	3	..	1	2	..	1	2	..	3	....	4	2	6
Pomfret,	..	....	..	..	..	..	..	..	4	..	1	3	1	3	4
Putnam,	..	....	4	..	2	2	1	1	17	1	8	12	10	14	24
Scotland,	..	....	1	..	..	1	..	..	1	..	....	1	....	2	2
Sterling,	..	....	..	1	..	1	..	..	....	..	....	....	....	1	1
Thompson,	..	4	3	2	2	7	1	..	12	2	5	10	7	17	24
Windham,	..	....	2	1	1	2	1	..	32	..	15	18	16	20	36
Woodstock,	..	....	..	..	..	..	..	..	4	..	2	2	2	2	4
Total,	1	4	18	5	10	18	4	5	107	7	52	71	62	89	151

Towns in Windham Co.	Order 1.—Nervous System. Apoplexy.	Paralysis.	Insanity.	Epilepsy.	Chorea.	Tetanus.	Convulsions.	Meningitis.	Brain Disease.	Spinal Disease.	Neuralgia.	Total. M.	Total. F.	Embolism.	Heart Disease.	Aneurism.	Pericarditis.	Phlebitis.	Capillary Bronchitis.	Pleurisy.	Lung Disease.	Bronchitis.	Pneumonia.	Laryngitis.	Asthma.
BROOKLYN,	..	..	..	..	..	..	2	..	1	..	..	3	....	..	2	..	1	..	....	..	1	..	2	..	..
Ashford,	..	..	..	..	..	..	..	..	..	..	1	....	1	..	....	..	..	..	....	..	..	..	2	..	..
Canterbury,	..	..	..	1	..	..	..	..	..	..	..	1	....	..	....	..	..	..	....	..	..	..	3	..	..
Chaplin,	1	1	..	..	..	..	..	..	..	..	..	1	1	..	1	..	..	..	....	..	..	..	3	..	..
Eastford,	..	..	..	..	..	..	..	..	..	..	..	....	....	..	1	..	..	..	....	..	..	..	3	..	..
Hampton,	..	1	1	..	..	..	..	..	..	..	..	....	2	..	....	..	..	..	....	..	..	..	2	..	..
Killingly,	5	..	..	..	..	1	1	11	..	..	..	10	8	..	10	..	..	..	....	..	..	..	14	..	..
Plainfield,	1	..	..	..	..	..	..	2	2	..	..	1	4	..	8	..	..	..	....	..	1	..	4	..	..
Pomfret,	2	1	1	..	..	..	..	1	1	..	..	3	3	..	1	..	..	..	....	..	1	..	1	..	..
Putnam,	1	..	..	..	..	..	..	5	2	..	..	6	2	..	3	..	..	..	....	..	..	1	6	..	1
Scotland,	..	..	..	..	..	..	..	..	..	..	..	....	....	..	....	..	..	..	....	..	..	..	..	..	..
Sterling,	1	..	..	..	..	..	..	..	..	..	..	1	....	..	1	..	..	..	....	..	..	..	..	..	..
Thompson,	1	..	..	..	..	..	2	1	2	..	..	6	....	..	4	..	..	..	....	..	..	..	4	..	..
Windham,	2	3	..	..	..	..	2	..	1	..	..	5	3	..	1	..	..	..	....	..	..	..	7	..	..
Woodstock,	..	..	..	..	..	..	..	..	..	..	..	....	....	..	2	..	..	..	....	..	..	..	1	..	..
Total,	14	6	2	1	..	1	7	20	9	..	1	37	24	..	34	..	1	..	....	..	3	1	52	..	1

CLASS III.—LOCAL DISEASES—Continued.

Towns in Windham Co.	Order 4.—Digestive Organs.																	Order 5.—Urinary Organs.												Order 6.—Generative Organs.					Orders 7 and 8.—							Total for Class III.			
	Gastritis.	Enteritis.	Peritonitis.	Ascites.	Ulceration of Intestines.	Intussusception.	Hernia.	Stricture Intestines.	Stomach Disease.	Colic.	Hepatitis.	Jaundice.	Liver Disease.	Fistula.	Male.	Female.	Total.	Disease of Spleen.	Bright's Disease.	Nephritis.	Diabetes.	Calculus.	Cystitis.	Kidney Disease.	Prostatitis.	Uremia.	Male.	Female.	Total.	Ovarian Tumor.	Ovarian Dropsy.	Uterine Tumor.	Disease of Uterus.	Total.	Arthritis.	Abscess.	Tumor.	Joint Diseases.	Disease of Skin.	Male.	Female.	Males.	Females.	Sex not stated.	Total.
Brooklyn,			1												1	1	1							1			1		1													6	5		11
Ashford,																																										1	2		3
Canterbury,													1	1	1		1							1			1		1													5	1		6
Chaplin,																																										3	3		6
Eastford,																			1					1			1	1	2													3	1		4
Hampton,															1	1	1											1					1	1				1			1	3			7
Killingly,	2													4	4	2	2		1									1	2													24	20		44
Plainfield,			1							3						2	4																									8	13		21
Pomfret,																									1		1															6	3		9
Putnam,			1				1				1								1								1						1	1								15	10		25
Scotland,																																													
Sterling,			1											1	1	2	3				1											1		1								1	1		2
Thompson,		1	4				1				1		2	4	4	2	6		3								3		3											1		9	8		17
Windham,												1															1	2	3		1			1								17	9		26
Woodstock,																											1		1													3	1		4
Total,	2	1	8				1			3	1	1	3	11	8	19		5	1	1			2	1	1	8	2	10	1	1	1	1	2				1	1	1	103	82		185

	CLASS IV.—DEVELOPMENTAL DISEASES.																	CLASS V.—VIOLENT DEATHS.																				GRAND TOTAL FOR ALL CLASSES.	
	ORDER 1.—OF CHILDREN.								ORDERS 2, 3, AND 4.					TOTAL FOR CLASS IV.				ORDER 1.—ACCIDENT AND NEGLIGENCE.											ORDERS 3, 4, AND 5.						TOTAL FOR CLASS V.					
TOWNS IN WINDHAM CO.	Stillborn.	Premature Birth and Debility.	Cyanosis.	Spina Bifida.	Other Malformat'ns.	Teething.	TOTAL M.	TOTAL F.	Childbirth.	Old Age M.	Old Age F.	Atrophy and Debility M.	Atrophy and Debility F.	Male.	Female.	Not stated.	TOTAL.	Fracture and Contusion.	Wounds.	Burns and Scalds.	Poison.	Drowning.	Suffocation.	Otherwise.	TOTAL M.	TOTAL F.	Homicide.	Hemorrhage.	Suicide M.	Suicide F.	Violent, not Classed M.	Violent, not Classed F.	Cause not Reported M.	Cause not Reported F.	Male.	Female.	Not stated.	TOTAL.	Males.	Females.
Brooklyn,	3						2	2		1			1	3	3		6	1		2		2			2	2	2						1	1	4	4	2	6	28	20
Ashford,	1	1	1		1		1	2		2	2		1		5		5	1							1					1			1	1	2	1		3	5	11
Canterbury,	2	1					4		2		1			4	3		7	1							1								1		1			1	10	8
Chaplin,				2							1				1		1																1		1			1	5	7
Eastford,	1	1						1							1		1			1					1									1		1		1	9	6
Hampton,					1			1	1	1		1	2		1		2																	1		1		1	4	9
Killingly,	4						6	1	1	1	1	7		7	4		11	5	1			1			6	1	1			1			1	1	6	2		6	66	55
Plainfield,	2			1				3	1	1	1	2	2	2	2		4	1							1							2	1	4	2	1		3	28	21
Pomfret,		3							1					4			4		1						1			3		1						1		1	10	10
Putnam,	1						2	2		2	4	1	2	4	6		10	5	1						5	1			1		1		14	19	20	11		31	58	56
Scotland,							1	1		1	1	1		2	1		3	1	1						1	1							1		1	1			3	3
Sterling,			1					3			1				1		1	1							1											1		1	3	6
Thompson,	9						6	3	1	1	1	2	6	9	6	1	16	1	1						3	1		2			1		6	4	4	7		11	35	48
Windham,	2	5					5	2	3	3	3	6	5	14	15		29	1		3					3			2	3				21	21	26	21	3	50	81	77
Woodstock,	2						2			2	2			2	1		3	1							1														8	7
Total,	25	11	1	2	2		12	14	7	14	19	8	10	49	50	1	100	17	4	4		3			21	8		5	5		1	1	40	32	68	47	47	118	353	344

CLASS I.—ZYMOTIC DISEASES.

Towns in Litchfield Co.	Small-pox	Measles	Scarlet Fever	Diphtheria	Quinsy	Croup	Whooping Cough	Typhoid Fever	Erysipelas	Puerperal Fever	Carbuncle	Dysentery	Diarrhœa	Cholera Infantum	Malarial Fever	Intermittent Fever	Congestive Fever	Remittent Fever	Typho-Malarial Fever	Rheumatism	Cerebro-Spinal Meningitis	Total M.	Total F.	Syphilis	Caries and Necrosis	Septicæmia	Hydrophobia	Worms	Stricture Urethra	Total M.	Total F.	Privation and Neglect	Purpura and Scurvy	Alcoholism	Total M.	Total F.	Male	Female	Sex not stated	Total
Litchfield						1						5		3								6	3			1				1	1	1					6	4		10
Barkhamsted														1					1															1	1		1			
Bethlehem				1		1																	3															3		3
Bridgewater																																								
Cornwall								1	1					1								1	1														1	1		1
Goshen								1														1	1														1	1		1
Harwinton				2										2					2			2	2														2	2		3
Kent				1		6		2	1					2			1				1	1	6														4	6		4
Morris								3				1										3	4														4	2		1
New Hartford									1				1				1		1		2		2															2		12
New Milford				2	1		1					1		3	1				1			3	5														5	6		8
Norfolk										2												3	3														1	2		2
North Canaan								3				2	2	3							2	3	3									1		1	2		3	5		7
Plymouth														6			1		1		1	8	8														3	3		3
Roxbury																																								
Salisbury						1		3				1		1								2	6															8		16
Sharon						2				2		2		1					1		2	2	6														2	1		2
Thomaston								2				1		1					1		1	8	1														6	6		6
Torrington				1		3	1					1		4			1			1		1	7					1		1	1			2	2		3	3		15
Warren																																								
Washington	1			2				2	1			1		1								8	1											2				7		4
Wi...n																																								
Woodbury																						1	1															1		
Total	1		2	10	1	15	1	18	4	2		11	3	29	1		2		6	1	7	58	60			1		1		1	1	1		2	4	5	64	61		125

CLASS II.—CONSTITUTIONAL DISEASES.

TOWNS IN LITCHFIELD CO.	Gout	Dropsy and Anemia	Cancer	Senile Gangrene	ORDER 1.—DIATHETIC TOTAL M.	F.	Scrofula	Tabes Mesenterica	Phthisis	Hydrocephalus	ORDER 2.—TUBERCULAR TOTAL M.	F.	Male	Female	Sex not stated	TOTAL FOR CLASS II.	Apoplexy	Paralysis	Insanity	Epilepsy	Tetanus	Convulsions	Chorea	Meningitis	Brain Disease	Spinal Disease	ORDER 1.—NERVOUS SYSTEM TOTAL M.	F.	Embolism	Heart Disease	Anurism	Pericarditis	Phlebitis	Capillary Bronchitis	Pleurisy	Lung Disease	Bronchitis	Pneumonia	Laryngitis	Asthma
Litchfield						3			3		3		3			3	7	2	2					1			9	3		2								3		
Barkhamsted		1	1	1	1				1		1		2			2														1				1			1	1		
Bethlehem																		1												1										
Bridgewater		1	1	1	1				1	1				1		2	1	1									1	4										1		
Canaan					1				2	2		1	2			2	1	6	1	1							3	4		2							2	2		
Colebrook		2		1				1	2				2	1		3	1	4				1					3	2		1								1		
Cornwall		1							1		1		1			2		4						1			2	1		1							1			1
Goshen		2		1		1			2	1			2	1		3	2	4		1					4		5	2		2				2				6		
Harwinton		1	3	1	2			2	7	2		3	7	3		10	3	3				2					5	4		5						1		5	1	
Kent									1	3			1			4	3	2				1		1	2		1	2		1								5		1
Morris									1				1			1	1			4					4		4	1										9		
New Hartford		3	1	2	3				4	4		6	3	4		14	2	2	1	1							4	3		2			4		1		1	2		
New Milford		2	1		2	3		2	4	1		5	2	3		14	2	2	1			1			1		4	4		5					1	1		1	1	1
Norfolk		1	1						1	1				1		4	1			1		1					2	3		1								3		
North Canaan																4	1										1	2												
Plymouth		5		2	4									4		5	2										4			2								2		
Roxbury																	2	2		4				1	2		4	4		5			4		1	1		2		
Salisbury		3	1		3	6			8	7			5	3		15	3	3		1					4			3								1	1	3		
Sharon			1	2	2	3			4	1		1	1	2			2	2	2	1				2	1		4	2		2							1	3		
Thomaston		1		3									3			5	1	1				1		3			1	4		5						2				
Torrington		2	1	1	2	5			7	1		6	6	4		14	3	2	1	1		1			1		1	3		1						1		3		
Warren																	3	1		1		1					4	4		2										
Washington		2	1	1		5			10			8		6		9	1	2	1					2				4									1	3	1	
Watertown			1	1	1	10	1		6			3	10	16		19	3	2				1		3	1		3	4		2					2		1			1
Winchester		2	4	1		4	2	2	4			3	4	6		19	3	2				1		3	4		7	4		2			4	2				3		
...	1		1		1		1				3		3			9	2	1				1					2	1		2							1	2		1
Total	1	23	16	8	23	24	5	9	75	1	42	48	65	72	1	138	34	32	4	4		8		9	17		58	49	1	32				8	2	7	6	53	1	2

F

CLASS III.—L[ocal Diseases]

Towns in Litchfield Co.	Order 4.—Digestive Organs																	Order 5.—Urinary Organs												Order 6.—Generative Organs					Orders 7 and 8										
	Gastritis.	Enteritis.	Peritonitis.	Ascites.	Ulceration of Intestines.	Intussusception.	Hernia.	Stricture Intestines.	Stomach Disease.	Colic.	Hepatitis.	Jaundice.	Liver Disease.	Fistula.	Male.	Female.	TOTAL.	Disease of Spleen.	Bright's Disease.	Nephritis.	Diabetes.	Calculus.	Cystitis.	Kidney Disease.	Prostatitis.	Uræmia.	Male.	Female.	TOTAL.	Ovarian Tumor.	Ovarian Dropsy.	Uterine Tumor.	Disease of Uterus.	TOTAL.	Ulcer.	Abscess.	Tumor.	Joint Disease.	Disease of Skin.	Male.	Female.	Males.	Females.	Sex not stated.
Litchfield,											1				1		1							1			1	1	1							1	1				1	14	5	
Barkhamstead,																																										2	3	
Bethlehem B.,		1																																								2		
Bridgewater,													1		1		1												1													3	2	
?,																			2				1				1	1	2													3	2	
Colebrook,			1																1				1				1		2													3	4	
?,																			1								1														4	2	
Goshen,																							1		1		2		2													4	4	
Harwinton,			1			1							3		3	1	3						1				1		2			1		1								6	3	
Kent,						1		1					1		3	1	4		1				1				1		1													5		
Morris,																																										12	11	
New Hartford,			1								1				1	1	2																									10	4	
New Milford,																								1			1		1													7	6	
Norfolk,																												2	2													6	4	
North ?,																1	1		2								2		3			1		1								10	12	
Plymouth,		1									1					1	1							1			1	1	1													4	5	
Roxbury,																			1								1		1							1				1		8	5	
Salisbury,																																										4	8	
Sharon,			2																																							6	9	
Thomaston,																			2					1			2	1	3				1	1								10	5	
Torrington,											1		1		1	1	1		1					1			1		1							1	1			1		3	2	
Warren,																						1					1		1													2	3	
?,																																										5	6	
Watertown,			1		1					1			1		2	2	3		3								2	2	3	1			1	1		1					1	14	4	
?,																1	3										2		3													2	12	
?,																																											3	1
Total,	4	1	8		2			1			2		6		16	8	24		15			1	6	5	2		19	12	31	2			2	4		2	1			2	1	159	122	1

CLASS IV.—DEVELOPMENTAL DISEASES.   CLASS V.—VIOLENT DEATHS.

TOWNS IN LITCHFIELD CO.	Stillborn	Premature Birth and Debility	Cyanosis	Spina Bifida	Malformations	Teething	Total M	Total F	Sex not stated	Childbirth	Old Age M	Old Age F	Atrophy and Debility M	Atrophy and Debility F	Class IV Male	Class IV Female	Class IV Sex not stated	Class IV Total	Fracture and Contusion	Wounds	Burns and Scalds	Poison	Drowning	Suffocation	Otherwise	Accid. Total M	Accid. Total F	Homicide M	Homicide F	Suicide M	Suicide F	Violent not Classed M	Casualty F	Cause not Reported M	Cause not Reported F	Hæmorrhage	Class V Male	Class V Female	Class V Not stated	Class V Total
LITCHFIELD,		1						1			5	1	1		1	7		8											1				2	1		1	2	2		4
Barkhamsted,												2				3		6							1	1							1	1	1	1	2			2
B[loomfield],										1	2	1			1			1	1																		1			1
Bridgewater,																																								
Canaan,					1			2		1	4	4			4	2		6			2				2					1					3	1	3	3		6
Colebrook,								3			2	2			3	2		5																1	1	1	1	1		2
Cornwall,		4					1				1	4			3	2		6	1				2			2									1		3	1		4
Goshen,							1			1	1	3			2	1		4																		1	1			1
Harwinton,				1							1				1			1																						
Kent,		1					1	2			1	1			2	1		2		1			1		2	2					1			2			2	2		3
Morris,		1									1				2	1		3							2	2	1								3		5	2		7
New Hartford,	4										6	9			10	15		25			1		1	1	1	3				1				3	2	2	5	2	1	1
New Milford,		1		1						1	1				1		1	1			1																1			1
Norfolk,								5				5		1		7		7		1						3				1					1		4	1		1
North Canaan,		1					5	1	1		2	2			11	5		16			1					1							3	3		4	4		5
Plymouth,		1					1	1			1	1			2	2		4		1	1									1						1	4	1		1
Roxbury,			2																																					
Salisbury,	12		2					3			2	2	1		2	2		4		1						1										1		1		1
Sharon,							2				1	1			2	2		5																						
[Bri]ton,								3					1		1	2		1																2	2		3	3		6
Torrington,	1	1						1		1					1			4		1					3	3				1					3		3	3		6
Warren,		1					1	1			1	2			2	2		4																						
Washington,							1	1			1	1		1	1	2		1		1																1		1		
Watertown,		5	2					3							2	2		5			1									1				2	2	2	3	2		3
W[eth]er,	1	2					3	3	1		3	3		1	5	6	1	11	3		1					3	1							3	3		3	3		6
Woodbury,							3	4			1				4	1		5									1									2	3		2
Total	**18**	**21**	**3**	**1**	**1**	**1**	**22**	**20**	**3**	**6**	**33**	**38**	**4**	**3**	**59**	**67**	**3**	**129**	**7**	**3**	**2**		**3**	**1**	**2**	**16**	**2**		**1**	**4**	**2**			**13**	**13**	**8**	**34**	**23**	**1**	**58**

CLASS I.—ZYMOTIC DISEASES.

Towns in Middlesex Co.	Total for Class I. Total	Total for Class I. Female	Total for Class I. Male
MIDDLETOWN,	62	28	34
Haddam,	9	5	4
Chatham,	3	2	1
Clinton,	4	·	4
Durham,	6	2	4
East Haddam,	5	2	·
Essex,	15	9	6
Middlefield,	10	4	6
Old	3	1	2
Portland,	1	1	·
Saybrook,	4	2	2
	33	14	19
	3	2	·
	5	4	1
Total	**167**	**77**	**90**

CLASS II.—CONSTITUTIONAL DISEASES.

Table of disease statistics by towns in Middlesex Co. (rotated table). Principal divisions: ORDER 1.—DIATHETIC; ORDER 2.—TUBERCULAR; TOTAL FOR CLASS II; ORDER 1.—NERVOUS SYSTEM (with respiratory/circulatory columns).

Towns in Middlesex Co.	Dropsy and Anemia	Cancer	Senile Gangrene	Total M.	Total F.	Scrofula	Tabes Mesenterica	Phthisis	Hydrocephalus	Total M.	Total F.	Male	Female	Total for Class II	Apoplexy	Paralysis	Insanity	Epilepsy	Chorea	Tetanus	Convulsions	Meningitis	Brain Disease	Neuralgia	Dislocation of Cord	Total M.	Total F.	Embolism	Heart Disease	Aneurism	Pericarditis	Phlebitis	Capillary Bronchitis	Pleurisy	Lung Disease	Bronchitis	Pneumonia	Laryngitis	Asthma	Total M.
Middletown	5	4	1	3	7	3	4	43	2	25	27	28	34	62	3	11	17	.	.	.	.	1	4	.	1	22	15	1	7	.	.	.	.	3	4	2	12	.	2	18
Haddam	1	.	.	1	.	.	.	2	.	.	2	1	2	3	1	.	.	.	.	1	.	1	1	.	.	2	2	.	3	.	3	.	.	.	.	.	4	.	.	1
Chester	3	3	.	2	1	.	2	3	.	3	.	3	2	4	1	1	1	.	.	.	.	3	.	.	.	2	3	.	2	.	.	.	.	.	.	.	1	.	.	5
Clinton	.	.	.	.	.	.	.	.	.	.	.	3	2	4	2	1	1	.	.	.	1	.	1	.	.	1	3	.	1	.	.	.	.	.	.	1	1	.	.	.
All	.	.	.	.	.	.	.	5	.	.	4	3	4	7	1	1	1	.	.	1	.	3	.	.	.	3	1	.	2	.	.	.	.	1	.	.	2	.	.	2
Durham	.	2	2	.	3	.	.	.	.	.	.	2	2	4	.	.	.	.	.	.	.	.	1	.	.	3	2	.	1	.	.	.	1	.	.	.	4	.	.	6
East	.	2	1	.	1	.	.	2	.	1	1	3	4	1	.	1	.	.	.	1	1	.	2	.	.	3	3	.	4	.	.	.	.	1	2	1	1	1	.	5
Essex	1	.	.	1	.	.	.	1	.	1	.	1	1	1	.	.	.	.	.	.	1	.	.	.	.	1	1	.	3	.	.	.	1	.	.	.	.	.	.	2
	2	.	.	.	3	3	.	1	.	1	.	2	.	4	.	6	6	.	.	.	1	.	2	.	.	5	5	.	1	.	.	.	1	.	.	.	3	.	.	6
Md.	.	1	1	.	1	.	2	2	.	2	.	2	3	5	2	.	.	.	.	.	1	2	.	.	.	1	3	.	2	.	.	.	.	.	.	.	1	.	.	5
Old Saybrook	.	.	.	.	.	.	2	3	.	2	.	2	3	5	1	2	6	.	.	.	1	.	7	.	.	7	3	.	1	.	.	.	.	1	.	.	8	.	.	4
Portland	1	1	1	1	.	.	.	7	.	5	4	5	3	10	2	.	2	.	.	.	1	.	.	.	1	7	5	.	2	.	.	.	1	1	.	.	1	.	.	6
Saybrook	.	.	.	1	.	.	.	1	.	1	.	5	5	1	.	.	.	.	.	.	.	.	.	.	.	2	1	.	4	.	.	.	.	1	.	.	.	.	.	4
	.	.	.	.	.	.	.	.	.	.	.	.	.	.	.	.	.	.	.	.	.	.	.	.	.	.	1	.	.	.	.	.	1	1	.	.	1	.	.	1
Total	12 13	.	3	9 19	5	8	73	2	46	42	55	61	116	16 22 21	22 21	.	.	3	.	5 12 17	.	2	52	46	1	31	.	3	.	2	6	6 4	4	42	1	2	53

CLASS III.—LOCAL DISEASES—Continued.

Towns in Middlesex Co.	Gastritis	Enteritis	Peritonitis	Ascites	Ulceration of Intestines	Intussusception	Hernia	Stricture Intestine	Stomach Disease	Colic	Hepatitis	Jaundice	Liver Disease	Fistula	Male	Female	Total	Disease of Spleen	Bright's Disease	Nephritis	Diabetes	Calculus	Cystitis	Kidney Disease	Prostatitis	Uremia	Male	Female	Total	Ovarian Tumor	Ovarian Dropsy	Disease of Uterus	Abortion	Total	Ulcer	Abscess	Tumor	Joint Disease	Spinal Disease	Male	Female	Male	Female	Sex not stated	Total
					Order 4.—Digestive Organs.													**Order 5.—Urinary Organs.**												**Order 6.—Generative Organs.**					**Orders 7 and 8.**							**Total for Class III.**			
Middletown,	3	6	1		1							2	2		6	9	15		1					2			2	1	3	3						2		3		3	2	51	40		91
Adam,			1												1	1	1																			1					1	3	5		8
Har,		1											1		1	1			1										1													8	9		17
Chn,		1													1	1	2		1						1			1	2	2												2	5		7
nil,			1									1											1																	1		7	5		12
																																										5	3		8
Durham,		2														2	2										2		2	2												5	7		12
East Haddam,												1					2		1				1		1			1		1				1	1								11	5		16
Essex,																2																											5	4		9
Killingworth,			1												2	1	3		1						1			2	1	2				1	1								5	8		13
Middlefield,			1												2					1								1															3	6		9
Old ...k,																																										5	4		9
Portland,			1									2			2	1			1									1		1				1	1						2	2	14	12		26
Saybrook,			1														1		1											1													8	2		10
...k,																	1										1		1													1	2		3
Total	5	8	6	.	1	.	.	.	.	.	.	5	3	.	12	16	28	.	6	1	1	.	1	2 3	3	.	10	4	14	.	.	.	2	2	1	5	1	3	.	4	6	6 131	117	.	248

CLASS IV.—DEVELOPMENTAL DISEASES. — CLASS V.—VIOLENT DEATHS.

Towns in Middlesex Co.	Stillborn	Premature Birth and Debility	Cyanosis	Spina Bifida	Other Malformat'ns.	Teething	Total M.	Total F.	Childbirth	Old Age M.	Old Age F.	Atrophy and Debility M.	Atrophy and Debility F.	Class IV Male	Class IV Female	Class IV Not stated	Class IV Total	Fracture and Contusion	Wounds	Burns and Scalds	Poison	Drowning	Suffocation	Otherwise	Accident Total M.	Accident Total F.	Homicide	Hemorrhage	Suicide M.	Suicide F.	Violent not Classed M.	Violent not Classed F.	Cause not Reported M.	Cause not Reported F.	Class V Male	Class V Female	Class V Not stated	Class V Total	Grand Total Males	Grand Total Females
MIDDLETOWN	10	5			2		8	10		2	6	2	2	12	18		30	3	3			4		2	8	1			2		1	1	1	3	11	4		15	136	124
Haddam	2						1	1						1	1		2								2	1					1			3	2	4		6	11	17
...m	1	1							1	1	3			1	3		2			1		1			1						1	1		1	1			2	13	13
Clinton											1			2	1		5								1									1					11	11
...ll	1	1			1					2				3			4	2							2				2				3	1	4	3		7	15	12
Durham																	2																	1					14	11
East ...m	1							2		1	2			1	5		1					1						2											19	9
Essex		2		1				1		4	2		1	5	5		2								1								3	1	2			1	18	18
...	1	4			1		3				3			3	4		10	2				1		2	2						1				2				12	14
Middlefield	1			1			1	2					1				7						1										3	1				1	14	13
Old Saybrook								1		2	8			1	12		4								2	3		1					3	1	6	3		3	9	14
Portland	4	3					3	4			1			5	1		2	2				1			3	1										3		7	49	11
Saybrook					1	1	1			2							17								1										1			3	10	45
Westbrook										3		1	1	5			5	2						2	1								1	1	3			4	8	10
Total	19	15		1	3	2	20	21	1	17	27	3	5	40	54		94	10		1		2	7	4	20	6		3	4		1	1	3	9	28	20		48	344	329

CLASS I.—ZYMOTIC DISEASES.

Towns in Tolland Co.	Order I.—Miasmatic.																							Order II.—Enthetic.								Order III.—Dietic.						Total for Class I.			
	Small-pox	Measles	Scarlet Fever	Diphtheria	Quinsy	Croup	Whooping Cough	Typhoid Fever	Erysipelas	Puerperal Fever	Carbuncle	Dysentery	Diarrhœa	Cholera Infantum	Malarial Fever	Intermittent Fever	Congestive Fever	Remittent Fever	Typho-Malarial Fever	Rheumatism	Cerebro Spinal Meningitis	Total M.	Total F.	Syphilis	Septicæmia	Caries and Necrosis	Stomatitis	Stricture	Hydrophobia	Total M.	Total F.	Purpura and Scurvy	Privation and Neglect	Alcoholism	Total M.	Total F.	Male	Female	Sex not stated	Total
Tolland,	·	·	·	·	·	·	·	1	·	·	·	·	·	·	1	·	·	·	·	1	1	2	1	·	·	·	·	·	·	·	·	·	·	·	·	·	1	1	·	2
Andover,	·	·	·	·	·	·	·	1	·	·	·	2	·	·	·	·	·	·	1	·	1	3	1	·	·	·	·	·	·	·	·	·	·	·	·	·	2	1	·	3
Bolton,	·	·	·	·	·	·	·	·	1	·	·	·	·	1	·	·	·	·	1	1	·	3	1	·	·	·	·	·	·	·	·	·	·	·	·	·	3	1	·	4
Columbia,	·	·	·	·	·	·	·	1	·	·	·	·	·	1	·	·	·	·	·	1	·	2	3	·	·	·	·	·	·	·	·	·	·	·	·	·	2	3	·	5
Coventry,	·	·	·	1	·	·	·	2	·	·	·	·	·	·	·	·	·	·	·	·	·	1	1	·	·	·	·	·	·	·	·	·	·	·	·	·	1	1	·	2
Ellington,	·	·	·	·	·	2	·	1	·	·	·	·	·	1	·	·	·	·	·	·	·	1	1	·	·	·	·	·	·	·	·	·	·	·	·	·	1	1	·	2
Hebron,	·	·	1	7	·	1	·	·	·	·	·	·	·	·	·	·	·	·	·	·	·	·	·	·	·	·	·	·	1	·	1	·	·	·	·	·	·	1	·	1
Mansfield,	·	·	·	·	·	·	·	3	·	·	·	·	·	1	·	·	·	·	·	·	1	4	·	·	1	·	·	·	·	·	·	·	·	·	·	·	4	·	·	4
Somers,	·	·	·	·	·	·	·	·	·	1	·	·	·	·	·	·	·	·	·	·	1	·	2	·	·	·	·	·	·	·	·	·	·	·	·	·	·	2	·	2
Stafford,	·	·	·	4	·	5	6	5	·	1	·	1	1	7	·	·	·	·	·	1	1	7	9	·	·	·	·	·	·	·	·	·	·	·	·	·	7	9	·	16
Union,	·	·	·	·	·	·	·	·	·	·	·	·	·	·	·	·	·	·	·	·	·	2	1	·	·	·	·	·	·	·	·	·	·	·	·	·	2	1	·	3
Vernon,	·	1	·	·	·	·	·	·	·	·	·	·	2	·	·	·	·	·	3	·	24	12	·	·	·	·	·	·	·	·	·	·	·	·	·	24	12	·	36
Willington,	·	·	·	·	·	·	·	·	·	·	·	·	·	·	·	·	·	·	·	·	·	·	·	·	·	·	·	·	·	·	·	·	·	·	·	·	·	·	·	·
Total,	·	1	1	13	·	8	6	15	1	2	·	2	5	12	1	·	·	·	8	4	47	32	·	1	·	·	·	·	1	·	·	·	·	·	·	·	47	33	·	80

CLASS II.—CONSTITUTIONAL DISEASES.

Co.	Order 1.—Diathetic. Dropsy and Anæmia.	Cancer.	Otes Sarcoma.	Senile Gangrene.	Total. M.	Total. F.	Order 2.—Tubercular. Scrofula.	Tabes Mesenterica.	Phthisis.	Hydrocephalus.	Total. M.	Total. F.	Total for Class II. Male.	Female.	Sex not stated.	Total.
.....	....	..	..	..	..	..	..	1	1	..	1	1	1	1	..	2
.....	....	..	..	..	..	..	..	..	....	..	....	....	...	...	..	....
.....	....	..	..	..	..	..	..	..	....	..	....	....	...	...	..	....
.....	....	2	..	..	..	2	..	..	1	..	....	1	...	3	..	3
.....	....	1	..	..	..	1	..	..	5	..	2	3	2	4	..	6
.....	....	..	..	..	..	..	..	..	....	..	....	....	...	...	..	....
.....	1	1	..	..	1	1	..	..	....	..	....	....	1	1	..	2
.....	1	2	..	..	2	1	..	..	7	..	2	5	4	6	..	10
.....	2	1	..	..	2	1	..	..	....	..	....	....	2	1	..	3
.....	1	1	..	..	1	1	..	1	7	3	6	5	7	6	..	13
.....	....	..	..	..	..	..	..	..	....	..	....	....	...	...	..	....
.....	4	5	..	..	3	6	..	1	13	..	3	11	6	17	..	23
.....	1	..	..	..	1	..	..	..	5	..	3	2	4	2	..	6
.....	10	13	..	..	10	13	..	3	39	3	17	28	27	41	..	68

CLASS III.—LOCAL DISEASES.

Co.	Order 1.—Nervous System. Apoplexy.	Paralysis.	Insanity.	Epilepsy.	Chorea.	Tetanus.	Convulsions.	Meningitis.	Brain Disease.	Spinal Disease.	Neuralgia.	Total. M.	Total. F.
.....	..	1	..	..	..	..	..	..	..	..	..	....	1
.....	..	..	..	..	..	..	..	..	..	..	..	....	....
.....	..	..	..	1	..	..	..	..	..	..	..	1	....
.....	..	..	..	..	..	..	..	..	..	1	..	....	1
.....	2	..	..	..	..	..	..	..	1	..	..	2	1
.....	..	..	..	..	..	..	..	..	1	..	..	....	1
.....	1	..	..	..	..	..	..	..	..	..	..	....	1
.....	1	.	1	..	..	..	..	..	..	..	..	1	1
.....	..	1	1	..	..	..	..	..	..	..	..	1	1
.....	2	..	..	..	..	..	1	2	4	..	..	4	5
.....	..	..	..	..	..	..	..	..	..	..	..	....	....
.....	2	..	..	3	..	..	6	4	2	..	..	8	9
.....	3	2	..	..	..	..	..	..	..	..	..	5	....
.....	11	4	2	4	..	..	7	6	8	1	..	22	21

Co.	Orders 2 and 3. Embolism.	Heart Disease.	Aneurism.	Pericarditis.	Phlebitis.	Capillary Bronchitis.	Pleurisy.	Lung Disease.	Bronchitis.	Pneumonia.	Laryngitis.	Asthma.	Total. M.	Total. F.
.....	..	1	..	..	..	....	..	..	..	1	..	..	2	....
.....	..	1	..	..	..	....	..	..	..	....	..	..	....	1
.....	..	1	..	..	..	1	..	..	..	....	..	..	2	....
.....	..	....	..	..	..	1	..	..	..	2	..	..	2	1
.....	..	4	..	..	..	....	..	..	1	....	1	..	3	3
.....	..	....	..	..	..	....	..	..	..	3	..	..	2	1
.....	..	....	..	..	..	....	..	..	..	2	..	..	1	1
.....	1	1	..	..	..	1	..	..	..	1	..	..	3	1
.....	..	....	1	..	..	....	..	..	..	3	..	..	3	1
.....	..	3	..	..	..	1	1	..	..	7	..	..	8	4
.....	..	....	..	..	..	....	..	..	..	2	..	..	2	....
.....	..	4	..	1	..	....	..	..	..	3	..	..	3	5
.....	..	1	..	..	..	....	..	..	..	3	..	..	1	3
.....	1	16	1	1	..	4	1	..	1	27	1	..	32	21

CLASS III.—LOCAL DISEASES—Continued.

Towns in Tolland Co.	Gastritis	Enteritis	Peritonitis	Ascites	Ulceration of Intestines	Intussusception	Hernia	Stricture Intestines	Stomach Disease	Colic	Hepatitis	Jaundice	Liver Disease	Fistula	Male	Female	Total	Disease of Spleen	Bright's Disease	Nephritis	Diabetes	Calculus	Cystitis	Kidney Disease	Prostatitis	Uræmia	Male	Female	Total	Ovarian Tumor	Ovarian Dropsy	Uterine Tumor	Disease of Uterus	Total	Ulcer	Abscess	Tumor	Joint Disease	Spinal Disease	Male	Female	Males	Females	Sex not stated	Total
Tolland,																																										2			3
Andover,			1	1														2											2												1	1			1
Bolton,															2		2												2																5
Columbia,	1														1	1		2	1										2																4
Coventry,		1			1					1		1	1		1	1		2	1								1		1					1		1						5	6	2	12
Ellington,	1																																									2	3		6
Hebron,			1										1		1	1		3	1				1							1				1								3			4
Mansfield,		1	1												1	1		2									1	1						2								6	3		9
Somers,			2												2	1		2					1					1								1					1	5	3		8
Stafford,															1	1													2	2				2								15	10		25
Union,								1							1	1																										2			2
Vernon,															1	1		1	1								1	1		1				1		1					1	13	14		27
Willington,															1	1		1	1								1			2				2						1	1	8	5		13
Total,	2	1	5	1	2		1	1				1	2		11	4	15		4				2				4	2	6					6		2				2	2	69	50		119

CLASS IV.—DEVELOPMENTAL DISEASES.　CLASS V.—VIOLENT DEATHS.

TOWNS IN ——LLAND CO.	Stillborn.	Premature Birth and Debility.	Cyanosis.	Other Malformat'ns.	Teething.	TOTAL M.	TOTAL F.	Sex not stated.	Childbirth.	Old Age M.	Old Age F.	Atrophy and Debility M.	Atrophy and Debility F.	Male.	Female.	Not stated.	Total for Class IV.	Fracture and Contusion.	Wounds.	Burns and Scalds.	Poison.	Drowning.	Suffocation.	Otherwise.	Total M.	Total F.	Homicide M.	Hemorrhage.	Suicide.	Violent, not Classed M./F.	Cause not Reported M./F.	Male.	Female.	Not stated.	Total for Class V.	Male.	Female.	Not stated.	Total.
——nd,		1								2				3			3						1		1							1			1	8	3		11
——er,	1										1				1		1	1							1										1	2	3		5
——bia,				2		2										3	3																			12	1		13
——ntry,										1					2										1				1	1	1		1		1	4	8		12
——gton,							2				2			1	2		3	1						1	1	1							1		1	10	14		24
——on,						2	1			1	1			1	1		2													1		1	1		1	5	6		11
——field,							2			2	2			2	2		4	1							1								1		1	6	6		12
——rs,			1				4				1				4		8	1					1		2							2			4	14	12		26
——rd,		3			1	2			1			1		3			8											1			2		2		3	8	8		16
——a,		9	5	2	3	3	6	2		2			1	15	9	1	24	5		3		1		1	5				1	2	2	7	4		11	34	31	1	66
——on,										1																										6	3		9
——ngton,		9	1	2		2		1	2	2	2	1		15	9	1	24	1				1		1	5			1		1	2	2	4		11	65	56		121
——,		1					1			1	1			2			4													2		2			2	16	9		25
Total,.....	14	8	1	2	5	19	10	3	3	11	10	1	1	31	24	1	56	8		3		1	1	2	10	5	1	1	1	2	2	16	12		28	190	160	1	351

Recapitulation of Table 4.

CAUSE OF DEATH.	Hartford Co.	New Haven Co.	New London Co.	Fairfield Co.	Windham Co.	Litchfield Co.	Middlesex Co.	Tolland Co.	TOTAL	PER CENT. TO TOTAL MORTALITY.				
										1881.*	1880.*	1879.	1878.	1877.
ZYMOTIC DISEASES.														
ler 1, Miasmatic,	591	581	283	426	143	118	161	79	2,383	22.67	23.56	18.59	21.51	25.49
2, Enthetic,	7	16	2	6	1	2	3	1	37	.36	.26	.11	.22	.19
3, Dietic,	19	18	3	9	3	5	3	...	60	.57	.45	.41	.37	.46
4, Parasitic,	...	...	...	...	...	...	...	...	...	...	.06	...	...	...
Total, Class I,	617	615	288	441	147	125	167	80	2,480	23.60	23.35	19.13	23.10	26.14
CONSTITUTIONAL DISEASES.														
ler 1, Diathetic,	83	105	80	82	28	48	28	23	477	4.54	3.98	4.11	4.49	4.34
2, Tubercular,	338	495	217	257	123	90	88	45	1,653	15.73	15.14	15.16	15.90	17.03
Total, Class II,	421	600	297	339	151	138	116	68	2,130	20.27	19.12	19.49	20.39	21.37
LOCAL DISEASES.														
ler 1, Nervous System,	266	377	163	228	61	108	98	43	1,344	12.79	13.69	13.29	13.09	12.75
2, Organs of Circulation,	125	127	66	96	35	33	35	19	536	5.09	5.41	5.16	4.87	4.92
3, Organs of Respiration,	257	297	68	175	57	79	63	34	1,030	9.81	10.51	10.31	7.34	8.78
4, Organs of Digestion,	89	135	81	100	19	24	28	15	491	4.66	4.57	5.14	3.67	4.24
5, Urinary Organs,	53	78	33	59	10	31	12	6	282	2.68	2.63	2.50	2.28	2.05
6, Generative Organs,	4	9	3	4	2	4	2	...	28	.27	.49	.41	.22	.39
7, Organs of Locomotion,	6	...	2	1	1	...	3	...	13	.11	.02	.20	.12	.32
8, Integumentary System,	19	15	5	12	1	3	7	2	64	.61	.47	.26	.24	.54
Total, Class III,	819	1038	421	675	186	282	248	119	3,788	36.03	37.85	37.34	31.83	33.98
DEVELOPMENTAL DISEASES.														
ler 1, Children,	172	240	99	114	42	45	41	30	783	*3.69	*3.27	6.40	5.77	6.07
2, Women,	13	7	15	19	7	6	1	3	71	.68	.36	.68	.64	.81
3, Old People,	123	133	85	117	33	71	44	21	627	5.96	5.27	5.56	5.78	3.23
4, Nutrition,	14	34	35	36	18	7	8	2	154	1.46	1.46	1.54	1.36	2.41
Total, Class IV,	322	414	234	286	100	129	94	56	1,635	11.79	10.40	14.15	13.55	14.52
VIOLENT DEATHS.														
ler 1, Accident,	62	68	31	52	29	18	26	15	301	2.86	3.45	3.26	3.76	3.10
2, Homicide,	...	1	1	...	...	...	...	...	2	.02	.02	.07	.13	.11
3, Suicide,	18	16	7	9	6	6	5	2	69	.65	.47	.70	.61	.57
4, Execution,	...	...	...	...	...	...	...	...	...	.01	.01	...	...	...
Iden, Cause unascertained,	23	28	8	10	8	8	5	3	93	.88	.72	.35	.37	.21
ase not stated,	88	40	53	108	74	26	12	8	409	3.89	4.85	5.43	6.27	...
Total, Class V,	191	158	100	179	117	58	48	28	874	8.31	9.04	9.83	11.13	8.99
and Cause not stated,	...	...	...	...	...	...	...	...	...	...	.24	.06	...	...
Grand Total,	2370	2820	1340	1920	701	732	673	351	10,907	100.00	100.00	100.00	100.00	100.00

*Stillborn not included.

TABLE 5.

DEATHS IN TOWNS. ALPHABETICAL ARRANGEMENT, DISTINGUISHED BY AGE, NATIONALITY, AND SEASON.

NAME OF TOWN.	Under 1.	1 to 5.	5 to 10.	10 to 20.	20 to 30.	30 to 40.	40 to 50.	50 to 60.	60 to 70.	70 to 80.	80 to 90.	90 to 100.	Over 100.	Unknown.	Birthplace, Conn.	All other States.	Birthplace, Ireland.	Birthplace, Germany.	Birthplace, England.	Birthplace, Sweden.	Birthplace, Canada.	All other Foreign Countries.	Unknown.	Deaths in Spring.	Deaths in Summer.	Deaths in Autumn.	Deaths in Winter.	Total.
Andover,	2									2		1			5									2	2		1	5
Ashford,	3														13	3								3	6	3	4	16
Avon,	1														10	1	1							3	2	3	4	12
Barkhamsted,	8														8		1								2	3	4	9
Beacon Falls,	7	2			5										13	2									5	8	2	15
Berlin,	2	2												4	33	3	5	1						17	10	10	5	42
Bethany,		1													12		1							3	6	2	2	13
Bethel,	14	2													35	9	5	1	1					10	14	16	11	51
Bethlehem,	2														11									3	2	3	4	12
Bloomfield,	3	2													13		7							3	5	8	4	20
Bolton,	1	1													12								1	1	6	3	3	13
Bozrah,		4													13	3								3	5	5	3	16
Branford,	11	3													49	2	9		2		2		1	17	14	16	18	65
Bridgeport,	125	101	51	24	75	46	42	42	34	38	17	5			388	76	70	31	27	4			4	144	153	139	164	600
Bridgewater,		2	1												8									1	2	3	2	8
Bristol,	9	9													51	5	8		3			1	1	12	17	18	22	69
Total,	**193**	**128**	**63**	**45**	**110**	**73**	**60**	**75**	**68**	**88**	**48**	**11**		**4**	**674**	**105**	**108**	**33**	**33**	**4**	**2**	**1**	**6**	**222**	**251**	**240**	**253**	**966**

TABLE 5.—Continued.

NAME OF TOWN.	Under 1.	1 to 5.	5 to 10.	10 to 20.	20 to 30.	30 to 40.	40 to 50.	50 to 60.	60 to 70.	70 to 80.	80 to 90.	90 to 100.	Over 100.	Unknown.	Birthplace, Conn.	All other States.	Birthplace, Ireland.	Birthplace, Germany.	Birthplace, England.	Birthplace, Sweden.	Birthplace, Canada.	All other Foreign Countries.	Unknown.	Deaths in Spring.	Deaths in Summer.	Deaths in Autumn.	Deaths in Winter.	Total.
Brookfield,															16									6	2	6	4	18
Brooklyn,	12														34									8	13	18	9	48
Burlington,	4														18									7	6	9	4	26
Canaan,															5									1	2	1	1	5
[illegible],	2																							4	3	3	8	18
Chaplin,	13														33									9	7	14	12	42
Chatham,															12									2	3	4	3	12
Cheshire,	4														24									1	10	6	9	26
[illegible],	9														31									7	7	15	9	38
Clinton,	3														18									6	6	4	6	22
Colchester,	1														16									4	5	9	9	27
[illegible],	6														38									10	14	9	14	47
[illegible],															12									7	6	3	5	21
Cornwall,	1														9									2	4	2	4	12
Coventry,	4														18									4	8	6	2	20
Cromwell,	2														13									6	6	5	7	24
[illegible],	3														17									8	8	4	5	25
Danbury,	44														148									42	65	70	41	218
Total,	108	58	32	35	59	51	38	46	64	72	64	22			462	50								134	175	188	152	649

																								Total
Darien,	2								2									1	1	3	3	6	7	19
Derby,	39	27	5	20	15	16		2	1	2	6	16	14	13	16	128	32	45	2	47	46	47	45	185
Durham,	2	1	5	2	5	16		1	2		1					19		6	2	1	6	4	8	23
Eastford,	2	1			4	1		2	2		4					11		4	1	1	4	3	4	15
Easton,	1			1				1	3		1	2	2			12		4			6	5	3	16
East Granby,		1	1	5	1	1	1		4		3	2	2			10		3	3		2	4	1	13
East Haddam,	6	4	3	8	3	3	1	3	6	2	2	3	3	1		31		4	1		9	13	7	37
East Hartford,	13	7	2	4	2	2	1	1	2		5	5	5			62		5			20	18	25	83
East Haven,	4	2	1	3	8	9	3	5	5		10	12	15			20		3		2	5	4	6	24
East Lyme,	5	8	3	2	2	2	5	3	3		2	4	1			31		5	1	4	7	9	4	31
East [illegible],	11	6	3	1	3		12	6	6		4	10	10		3	32	5	3	2	1	15	11	11	45
[illegible]ington,		1						10	5		10	5	5			10			4		8	8	26	11
Enfield,	24	14	8		22	16	23			5	13	13	9	3		125	5	42	6	5	42	39	26	159
Essex,	3	1		2	2		3	2	7		1	2	2	2		28		8	1	1	8	4	8	32
Fairfield,	6	5		1	2	1	1	5	5		3	14	14	1	1	35		12	1		12	13	12	49
Farmington,	1	1			3	6		1	2		5	3	3			16		4		1	4	12	3	22
Franklin,					1	1		1	4		4	6	4	1		12	2	7		2	8	7	2	14
Glastonbury,	4	2		4				8		1	10	2	9	7		41	1	1			3	3	16	48
[illegible],	6				3			3		2	2	5	8		2	14					13	3	4	15
Granby,	3	1	7	2	2	1		2	6		6	10	10	2	1	14		3	1		6	3	3	19
Greenwich,	19	4	5	9	2			6	10	4	16	10	10	16	3	15	1	25	2	5	23	29	24	99
[illegible],	12	6	2	4	5	2		10	10	2	2	5	9			57		4		7	11	14	13	53
Groton,	7	10			2			13	5	1	14	10	9			40		7		2	38	11	22	90
Guilford,	2				9	9		3	10		3	3	2			79		1		1		6	10	26
Haddam,	8	2	2	4	4			2	9	2	6	1	1	1		23	3		2		8	10	6	28
Hamden,				4	4			5	2		6	5	2	4	4	23		3	2		3	3	13	40
Hampton,	4	2		3	1	1	4	1			2	2	1	7	7	29				2	4	7	2	13
Hartford,	245	125	63	103	89	91	91	59	72	90	120	640	170	22	4	9				7	290	247	227	1012
Hartland,	1		1	1	2	1		4	7		2	7	2	2	7	7				2	1	1	1	9
Harwinton,		1	1		1		1	5				20		1		20			1	2	5		5	21
Hebron,	11	6			1	1		6	7			7				11		2	1	1	2	2	3	12
Huntington,		1	1	1	4	6	6	3	5	2	2	38	3		1	38	1	9			11	13	11	44
Kent,	1				3			3	3	5	3	14				14		7			3	3	6	19
Total,	445	233	75	114	206	196	162	192	231	241	186	31	311	1655	234	268	47	7	35	22	575	622	584	545	2326

NAME OF TOWN	Under 1	1 to 5	5 to 10	10 to 20	20 to 30	30 to 40	40 to 50	50 to 60	60 to 70	70 to 80	80 to 90	90 to 100	Over 100	Unknown	Birthplace, Conn.	All other States	Birthplace, Ireland	Birthplace, Germany	Birthplace, England	Birthplace, Sweden	Birthplace, Canada	All other For. Countries	Unknown	Deaths in Spring	Deaths in Summer	Deaths in Autumn	Deaths in Winter	Total
Killingly,	31	17	4	12	17	3	4	4	8	14	7				82	19	1	1	4		14			30	21	35	35	121
Killingworth,							1	1	4	9	4				24	1								6	6	2	11	25
Lebanon,	6	2	1	1	3	1	5	3	4	4	3	1			23	2						1		13	4	7	6	30
Ledyard,	3	4	3		3	1	2	2	4	3	1								2				30	6	7	8	5	26
Lisbon,	1	1		1	1				1	2	1	1		7		3		1					7	2	2			7
Litchfield,	4				2	1	2	5	9	15	2	1			31		1		2	1				8	12	13	11	44
Lyme,	2			1	4	1			2	2	2	3			12	3								5	3	2	2	12
Madison,	1	14	1		13	6	7	2	7	9	7				23	4	6		2					6	3	7	11	27
Manchester,	24	2	12	14	2	1	2	7	10	13	6	2		19	83	5	29				6	2		27	26	40	33	126
Mansfield,	1			2	4			1	3	8	2				21	4				1				6	5	4	11	26
Marlborough,						1	2		5	2	1				9									3	3	1	3	11
Meriden,	67	26	12	21	39	16	19	22	19	21	7	2	2	19	178	25	30	30	18		6	2		79	85	66	59	289
Middlebury,						2	2		1	1		5	5		6		1		3					4	1	1	4	6
Middlefield,	1			2		3		1	2	4	3	1	2		16		2	1	1					3	4	1	8	19
Middletown,	45	15	7	12	21	29	19	34	33	29	14	1	5		166	26	42	9	13	1		2		59	63	63	75	260
Milford,	5	6	3	5	6	3	11	3	5	5	3	2	2		50	5	4	1	1	1				15	15	13	17	60
Monroe,	2	2			2	1	1	1	1	1	1	1	1		13	2								3	2	4	5	14
Montville,	10		3	5	8	1	3	2	3	8				4	35	1	5				3			14	17	8	8	47
Total,	209	92	42	75	125	70	78	89	121	145	64	21		23	772	98	116	35	43	2	24	3	61	289	279	282	304	1154

Town																						Total
Morris,	2	4	2	3				7	2	9	2		3	4		1		1			2	2
Naugatuck,	9	11	23	15	7	2	4	7	17	35		1	3	5	4	2	7	2	3	7	3	9	14
New Berlin,	67	62	57	54	3	4	14	44	13	147			3	21	21	20	32	10	16	32	5	25	71
New Canaan,	4	8	13	19			14	1	1	28		1	7	6	6	3	4	1	2	4	2	7	7
New Fairfield,	3	9					2			9			2					2		1			
New Hartford,	18	5	15	6	4	3	1	5	5	33	3	1	7	4	6			2	9	7	9	8	10
New Hn.	314	317	353	354	46	6	48	254	150	776	1	9	62	77	108	122	117	127	137	55	58	122	340
Newington,	3	7	5	2			3	1		15		1		2	4		2		2	1		2	1
New London,	42	50	54	71	18	1	2	26	22	158		4	13	20	16	17	15	26	16	14	12	31	33
New Milford,	14	16	12	20	12			3	3	37		1	16	8	9	3	2	5	2	5			13
Newtown,	18	17	21	24			1	12	3	52		1	10	10	10	6	15	5	5	3	4	4	13
Norfolk,	3	9	5	3				1	1	15			2	4	3	3							
North Branford,	6	2	7	5				3	2	17				5	3	1	1			1			1
North Canaan,	10	4	1	4	3	1	1	3	2	12			3	3	4		3	1		1	8	4	3
North Haven,	3	4	6	7	3	3	1	1	1	11	1		3	1	4	3		1	6	2			4
North Stonington,	7	4	53	11			1		2	23		5	15	5	18	8	3		16	10	2	2	51
Norwalk,	58	66	53	70	3	9	3	27	51	159	5	3	21	25	33	2	21	22	32	26	9	27	107
Norwich,	111	101	99	86		6	1	64	35	265	3			42	3	3	29	31		3	8	28	
Old Lyme,	4	4	2	4			1	1	1	13			2	1	2	3	2	2	2	2	13	1	5
Old Saybrook,	5	15	9	4		2			3	16		1	3	4	2	1	1	1	1	4		5	11
Orange,	9	5	8	16	2		4		1	37	1		3	5	7	8	3	2	3	2			2
Oxford,	3	15	5	8			3		3	18			3	2	3		2		5	4		4	10
Plainville,	17	15	7	10			1		5	33		5	5	5	6	4		1	4	6	8	3	6
Plymouth,	8	9	6	17		2	1	4	2	25			6	6	7	3		2	1	2		2	4
Pomfret,	11	5	4	5			4	1	4	40		2	5	2	5	3	3	4	4	4	6	13	20
Portland,	16	4	3	18		3	1	17	1	14			11	7	7	2	4	9	6	9	4	8	6
Preston,	11	32	28	10		16			3	71			3	5	5	4	5	4	3	5			1
Prospect,		12	11		3		2		7	37					1	2	1			1		9	40
Putnam,	24	38	26	26	3	16		3	7	4	2	2	8	12	7	7	4	11	7	5	4	2	5
Redding,	7	9	8	7			2		1	83			3	6	3		2	2	1	3		1	3
Ridgefield,	7	12	8	6		16			7	29	3		3	4	6	3	2	4	2	2	1	1	1
Rocky Hill,	4	4	8	2			4	1	2	24	1	1	3	2		1	2		2				
										10													
Total,	826,345 9	874	865	894	46 94	751 46 94	76 81	485 76 81	364	2255	6 7	44	218	302	314	290	265	292	303	175	131	321	791

H

TABLE 5—CONTINUED.

NAME OF TOWN.	Under 1.	1 to 5.	5 to 10.	10 to 20.	20 to 30.	30 to 40.	40 to 50.	50 to 60.	60 to 70.	70 to 80.	80 to 90.	90 to 100.	Over 100.	Unknown.	Birthplace, Conn.	All other States.	Birthplace, Ireland.	Birthplace, Germany.	Birthplace, England.	Birthplace, Sweden.	Birthplace, Canada.	All other Foreign Countries.	Unknown.	Spring.	Summer.	Autumn.	Winter.	Total.
Roxbury,	3			3	2	1		2	3	2	4	1			19	1	1							3	6	2	10	21
Salem,	1			1			2	2	1	6	1				12								2	7	1	3	3	14
Salisbury,	16	6			5	2		2	5	4	3	3			33	10	5	1		1				13	8	14	13	48
Saybrook,	4		1		1		1	3	3	3	3				14	2		1	1					3	5	6	4	18
Scotland,					1		4		1	1					5	1								1	1	3	1	6
Seymour,	5	4	3	2	3		6	5	12	6	3	1			42	3	2		2				7	15	1	11	12	49
Sharon,	4	4		4	3	2	1	1	1	5	1	3		2	25	2	3	1	1					13	6	12	7	38
	1				1						2			1	7									1	1	5	1	8
	5				3	2	3	4	5	13	6	1			26	3	2	2	1					13	6	7	9	35
Somers,					1	1	1	1		2	2			1	14	1		3	1					4	4	4	4	16
Southbury,	6	11		2	3		3	4	9	9	6	2			23	3	12	3	4		1	1	6	8	9	8	6	26
Southington,	24	8	5	9	3	1	7	1	5	8	3	1	1		58	5	5	3	1		13	1		16	23	29	21	89
South Windsor,		7	7	2	5	5	2	3	5	8	4				22	2					2	2	6	6	4	9	7	28
Sprague,	22	9	5	6	2	3	2			5					35	4	5		1				6	23	16	9	10	58
Stafford,	17	25	7	5	6	3	16	5	6	24					40	13	46	1	3					14	14	17	48	66
Stamford,	30		7	11	21	24	16	13	17	4	13		5		105	42	38		8		2	2	6	46	59	43	48	196
Sterling,	2									4	2				6	3	1	1						2	4	1	2	9
Stonington,	21	12	8	11	16	3	10	5	14	15	9	5			88	27	10		3					35	24	37	33	129
Total,	170	79	32	42	78	49	59	53	91	114	66	17	1	3	574	123	84	9	23		16	8	21	220	202	220	212	854

Town	Total
Stratford,	
Suffield,	
...	
Tolland,	
Torrington,	
...	
Union,	
Vernon,	
...	
Wallingford,	
Warren,	
Washington,	
Waterbury,	
Waterford,	
Watertown,	
...	
West Hartford,	
Weston,	
Westport,	
Wethersfield,	
Willington,	
Wilton,	
Winchester,	
Windham,	
Windsor,	
Windsor Locks,	
Wolcott,	
Woodbridge,	
Woodbury,	
Woodstock,	
To tal,	

Recapitulation of Table 5.

	Total. 1881.	Total. 1880.	Total. 1879.	PER CENT. TO TOTAL MORTALITY.		
				1881.	1880.	1879.
AGES.						
Deaths under 1 year,............................	2,229	2,159	1,761	20.4	20.5	18.7
" from 1 to 5,............................	1,040	1,150	919	9.6	11.0	9.6
Total, First Period, Infantile,..............	3,269	3,309	2,680	30.0	31.5	28.3
Deaths from 5 to 10,.........................	425	357	401	3.9	3.4	4.2
" " 10 to 20,.........................	579	582	482	5.3	5.4	5.2
Total, Second Period, Youth,..............	1,004	939	883	9.2	8.8	9.4
Deaths from 20 to 30,........................	1,033	857	782	9.5	8.2	8.5
" " 30 to 40,........................	848	724	667	7.7	6.9	7.5
" " 40 to 50,........................	751	742	612	6.9	7.1	7.2
" " 50 to 60,........................	851	796	731	7.8	7.4	8.0
Total, Third Period, the Productive Age,...	3,483	3,119	2,792	31.9	29.6	31.2
Deaths from 60 to 70,........................	1,029	923	904	9.4	8.8	9.0
" " 70 to 80,........................	1,130	1,122	1,048	10.3	10.7	9.7
" " 80 to 90,........................	741	725	661	6.8	6.9	8.3
" " 90 to 100,........................	164	151	145	1.5	1.4	1.6
" over 100,........................	11	9	13	.1	.8	.1
Total, Fourth Period, Old Age,............	3,075	2,930	2,771	28.1	28.6	28.7
Age not stated,........................	76	111	268	.8	1.5	2.0
Total,........................	10,907	10,408	9,394	100.00	100.00	100.00
NATIONALITIES.						
Deaths of those born in Connecticut,............	7,404	7,036	6,524	67.9	67.6	69.8
" " " all other States,..........	1,105	1,105	958	10.1	10.5	9.9
Total for United States,..................	8,509	8,141	7,482	78.0	78.1	79.7
Deaths of those born in Ireland,..............	1,251	1,216	1,006	11.5	11.3	9.9
" " " Germany,..............	273	178	175	2.5	1.5	3.2
" " " England,..............	269	249	171	2.4	2.0	3.1
" " " Sweden,..............	23	20	7	.2	1.6	.1
" " " Canada,..............	162			1.4		
" " " all other Foreign Countries,	106	604	553	1.0	5.5	4.0
Total Foreign Births,..................	2,084	2,267	1,912	19.1	21.9	20.3
Total Unknown Births,..................	314			2.9		
Total,........................	10,907	10,408	9,394	100.00	100.00	100.00
SEASON.						
Deaths in Spring,........................	2,673	2,659	2,208	24.5	25.5	23.5
" Summer,........................	2,764	2,879	2,301	25.3	27.6	24.0
" Autumn,........................	2,784	2,417	2,095	25.5	23.2	20.0
" Winter,........................	2,686	2,453	2,790	24.7	23.5	32.5
Total,........................	10,907	10,408	9,394	100.00	100.00	100.00
BIRTHS.						
Births in Spring,........................	3,591	3,391	3,396	24.5	24.5	24.2
" Summer,........................	3,615	3,422	3,500	24.7	24.6	24.8
" Autumn,........................	3,663	3,540	3,558	25.1	25.5	25.4
" Winter,........................	3,747	3,476	3,597	25.7	25.2	25.6
Total,........................	14,616	13,829	14,051	100.00	100.00	100.00

TABLE 6.

NOSOLOGICAL ARRANGEMENT BY COUNTIES, WITH COMPARATIVE MORTALITY FOR SIX YEARS.

DISEASES.	Hartford Co.	New Haven Co.	New London Co.	Fairfield Co.	Windham Co.	Litchfield Co.	Middlesex Co.	Tolland Co.	Total 1881.	Per cent. to Total Mortality.*	1880.	1879.	1878.	1877.	1876.	Aggregate for 6 years.	Average for 6 years.
I. 1. MIASMATIC,																	
Small pox,	7	9	3	7	...	1	4	...	31	22.67	9	4	4	...	23	67	11.1
Varicella,	3	1	...	...	...	...	...	...	...	.29	...	1	...	4	...	5	.9
Measles,	7	26	34	4	3	2	2	1	14	.13	59	14	20	25	56	188	31.3
Scarlet Fever,	93	70	52	42	15	10	4	13	121	1.15	92	164	215	216	171	979	163.1
Diphtheria,	1	...	1	71	...	1	9	8	333	3.27	332	256	464	589	564	2548	424.6
...y,	...	34	...	5	5	...	...	6	8	.07	3	...	...	2	1	14	2.3
Croup,	43	11	24	...	2	15	5	15	178	1.69	181	149	178	178	221	1085	180.8
Whooping Cough,	29	68	3	3	30	4	1	1	59	.57	104	...	68	76	39	346	57.6
..d Fever,	52	23	23	32	2	18	19	6	257	2.45	242	59	260	321	361	1600	266.6
Erysipelas,	16	20	5	5	2	4	6	1	62	.59	55	49	56	49	61	332	55.3
Puerperal Fever,	9	2	...	6	2	2	...	2	46	.43	53	40	42	47	43	271	45.1
Carbuncle,	2	...	...	...	...	1	...	...	5	.04	1	5	6	3	...	20	3.3
Influenza,	...	...	7	20	9	11	10	2	...	.96	...	...	...	8	25	33	5.5
Dysentery,	26	16	7	20	9	11	10	2	101	.96	69	75	86	83	106	520	86.6
Diarrhea,	32	25	15	12	3	3	14	5	109	1.04	108	86	60	84	98	555	92.5

* Still births not included.

TABLE 6.—CONTINUED.

DISEASES.	Hartford Co.	New Haven Co.	New London Co.	Fairfield Co.	Windham Co.	Litchfield Co.	Middlesex Co.	Tolland Co.	Total, 1881.	Per cent. to Total Mortality.*	1880.	1879.	1878.	1877.	1876.	Aggregate for 6 years.	Average for 6 years.
Cholera Infantum,	144	123	66	83	44	29	25	12	526	5.01	570	351	422	447	605	2921	486.8
Intermittent Fever,	1	9	5	11			11		37	.35	32	35	54	37	11	206	34.3
Remittent Fever,	8	10			1		2		25	.24	7	25	11	8	11	87	14.5
Typho-Malarial Fever,	70	53	17	42	4	6	24		222	2.12	153	117	78	28		598	99.6
Congestive Fever,	3	2	6	6	10	2	10	1	30	.29	33					84	14.
Malarial Fever,	15	21	3	1	1	1	1	8	43	.40	40	21	43	51	47	83	13.8
Rheumatism,	21	32	7	11	3	7	7	4	90	.86	60		43	51		591	98.5
Cerebro Spinal Meningitis,	9	17	7	16	8	7	7		75	.72	65	59	47	39	47	285	47.5
I. 2. ENTHETIC,																	
Syphilis,	5	8	2	1		1			16	.36	10		8	8	8	50	8.3
Stricture of Urethra,				1					1	.15				2		3	.5
Hydrophobia,									1	.01	1	2	7	8	4	23	4.
Malignant Pustule,					1					.01						1	.1
Pyaemia and Septicaemia,	1	5		2		1		1	12	.12	18	11	3		7	8	1.3
Caries and Necrosis,		1			3	1	7	1	1	.01		4	3	8	1	44	7.4
Stomatitis,	2	2		1		1	2		5	.05						17	2.8
																5	.8
I. 3. DIETIC,										.60							
Privation,	5	2		1	1	1	1	1	10	.09	6		5	3	1	25	4.1

Disease	Per cent.	Total	Rate
Purpura,	.02	18	3.
Alcoholism,	.49	201	33.3
I. 4. PARASITIC,			
Thrush,	.04	18	3.
Worms,	.03	4	.7
II. 1. DIATHETIC,	4.54		
Lupus,	.01	1	
Gout,	.01	7	1.1
Dropsy and Anaemia,	1.53	930	155.
Anaemia,	2.54	1340	223.3
Osteo Sarcoma,	.02	3	.5
Mortification,	.42	59	9.8
Senile Gangrene,	.01	91	15.1
Leucocythaemia,		3	.5
Exophthalmic Goitre,		1	.7
Addison's Disease,	.01	4	.7
II. 2. TUBERCULAR,	15.73		
Scrofula,	.41	239	39.8
Tabes Mesenterica,	1.39	547	91.1
Tubercular Consumption,	13.36	7961	1326.6
Hydrocephalus,	.57	385	64.1
III. 1. NERVOUS SYSTEM,	12.79		
Encephalitis,		105	17.5
Apoplexy,	2.94	1614	269.
Paralysis,	2.40	1551	258.3
Insanity,	.55	241	40.1
Chorea,	.02	14	2.3
Epilepsy,	.36	168	28.
Convulsions,	.16	110	18.3
Convulsions,	2.44	1498	249.7
Brain Disease,	1.84	1261	210.1

TABLE 6.—Continued.

DISEASES.	Hartford Co.	New Haven Co.	New London Co.	Fairfield Co.	Windham Co.	Litchfield Co.	Middlesex Co.	Tolland Co.	Total, 1881.	Per cent. to Total Mortality.*	1880.	1879.	1878.	1877.	1876.	Aggregate for 6 years.	Average for 6 years.
Meningitis,	23	68	25	27	20	9	12	6	190	1.82	164	134	143	140	159	930	155.
Neuralgia,	2		1	1	1				5	.04	9	3	2			17	2.8
Spinal Disease,	6	7	2	5				1	23	.22	26	8		5		64	10.6
III. 2. ORGANS OF CIRCULATION,										5.75							
Pericarditis,	4	9	4	3	1		3	1	25	.23	27	28	18	32	52	182	30.3
Aneurism,	1		3	3					8	.07	11	13	13	3	18	65	10.8
Heart Disease,	121	114	58	86	34	32	31	16	492	4.70	499	440	424	399	285	2559	426.5
Embolism,		4	1	4		1	1	1	12	.11	5	5	5			27	4.5
Phlebitis,				1					1		2	2				5	.8
Angina Pectoris,										.01	5		3	5		18	3.
Hemorrhage,	13	24	6	7	5	8	3	1	67	.64	28	22	30	5	39	186	31.
III. 3. RESPIRATORY ORGANS,										9.81							
Epistaxis,	1					1	1		20	.19	14	16	15	26	18	109	18.1
Laryngitis,	27	10	3	6	1	6	4	1	96	.92	173	136	83	86	80	654	108.6
Bronchitis,	23	36	6	18		8	2	4	72	.69						72	12.
Capillary Bronchitis,	1	19		10		2	6			.14		17				92	15.3
Pleurisy,		5		1					16		22		11	9	17		
Pneumonia,	183	189	51	116	52	53	42	27	713	6.78	712	626	458	478	776	3763	627.1

Asthma,	7	16		8	16	3	1	2	2	31	.30	38	21	10	28	12	140	23.3
Lung Disease,	14	23	8		23	21	3	6	2	82	.78	100	155	111	155	110	713	118.8
III. 4. DIGESTIVE ORGANS,																		
Gastritis,	12	16	15	14	2	4	2		5	70	.64	74	73	46	49	71	383	63.8
Enteritis,	2	18		6	1	1	1		8	37	.35	63	60	45	56	50	311	51.8
Peritonitis,	36	40	30	28	8	8	6	3	6	161	1.55	113	106	58	78	56	572	95.3
Ascites,		1			1		1	1		5	.04	8	6	10	6	12	41	6.8
Ulceration of Intestines,	3	2	5	3	2	2		1	2	15	.14	12	25	11	11	10	84	14.
Hernia,	1	2	5	4	4	1	1			13	.12	11	22	30	10	21	107	17.8
Intu-su-ception,		4	5	5						14	.13	4	2	5	8	6	39	6.5
Stricture of Intestines,				1	1	1				2	.01	11	9	11			34	5.6
Fistula,		1	1	1						3	.02	2	2		3	3	13	2.1
Stomach Diseases,	7	4	3	11	2	6	2	5	2	25	.24	36	40	48	58	32	239	39.6
Stricture Oesophagus,					3									1	1		3	.5
Colic,	1	3		1	3	2	1			9	.08	11	8	1	14	14	58	9.6
Hepatitis,		5	3	5	1	2		1	5	17	.16	25	21	16	17	28	123	20.5
Jaundice,		11	2	2	6			2	3	21	.19	14	18	15	16	11	9	15.1
Liver Disease,		27	11	22		6	6	3		98	.94	78	82	66	80	50	457	76.1
Spleen Disease,	24			2						2	.01	2	4	2	1		11	1.8
III. 5. URINARY ORGANS,																		
Nephritis,	4	11		2		1		1	1	19	.18	21	12	6	13	6	77	12.8
Bright's Disease,	27	40	22	30	2		15	5	6	149	1.42	138	103	110	80	88	668	111.3
Diabetes,	8	4	1	6	1	30		1	4	21	.19	27	29	24	27	32	160	26.6
Calculus,		2		3		6				6	.05	6	8	3	6	4	33	5.5
Cystitis,	6	3	5	4	3	3	6	5	2	23	.22	22	23	18	11	33	130	21.6
Kidney Disease,	5	7	1	6	4	2	5	2		32	.31	39	44	35	40	40	230	38.3
Uraemia,	1	7		5	2	1	1			17	.16	14	18	12	2	4	67	11.1
Prostatitis,	2	5	3	1	1		2	3		16	.15	3	3	5	10		37	6.1
III. 6. GENERATIVE ORGANS,																		
Ovarian Dropsy,	1	2	2	1						7	.27	5	6	6	6		30	5.
Ovarian Tumor,	2	4	1				2			9	.07	18	10	7	6		50	8.3
Disease of Uterus,	1	3	3	3	3		2	1		10	.10	23	14	8	17	11	83	13.8

TABLE 6.—CONTINUED.

DISEASES.	Hartford Co.	New Haven Co.	New London Co.	Fairfield Co.	Windham Co.	Litchfield Co.	Middlesex Co.	Tolland Co.	Total, 1881.	Per cent. to Total Mortality.*	1880.	1879.	1878.	1877.	1876.	Aggregate for 6 years.	Average for 6 years.
Uterine Tumor,											4	9		10	8	31	5.1
III. 7. ORGANS OF LOCOMOTION,																	
Arthritis,	1		2						4	.11	1	1	3	1	2	12	2.
Joint Diseases,	5	9		1	1	2	3		9	.03	2	13	5	22	14	65	10.8
III. 8. INTEGUMENTARY,																	
Abscess,	9			6			5		33	.08						33	5.5
Phlegmon,										.61	19	10	5	15	32	81	13.5
Ulcer,									5	.32	10	9	6	6	3	39	6.6
Skin Disease,	2	2	2				1		2	.05	4	4	2	3	5	17	2.8
fin,	8	4	3	6	1	1	1		24	.23	16		14	28	19	101	16.8
IV. DEVELOPMENTAL 1. Of Children,																	
Stillborn,	65	129	60	65	25	18	19	14	395	*3.69	343	286	300	337	413	2074	345.6
Premature Birth and Infantile Debility,	82	85	33	42	11	21	15	8	297	*** 2.83	245	242	290	141	139	1354	225.6
Atalectasis and Cyanosis,	10	17		1	1	3	1	1	34	.33	30	16	9	9		95	15.8
Spina Bifida,	2				2	1	1		10	.09	6	11	4			35	5.8
Other Malformations,	7	4	2	2	1	1	3	2	20	.18	18	24	19	21	23	125	20.8
Teething,	6	4	4	4			2	5	27	.26	38	37	15	43	26	186	31.

* Stillbirths not included.

Cause									Rate						Total	Per cent
IV. 2. OF WOMAN,																
Childbirth,	13	7	15	19	6	7		3	71	.68	37	64	24	71	53	320	53.3
Abortion,									2							2	.6
IV. 3. OF OLD PEOPLE,																	
Old Age,	123	132	85	117	71	33	71	21	626	5.96	531	522	606	476	574	3335	555.8
IV. 4. OF NUTRITION,																	
Atrophy and Debility,	14	34	35	36	18	7	8	2	154	1.46	147	111	127	220	207	966	161.
V. 1. ACCIDENT OR NEGLIGENCE,																	
Railroad,	5	5	3	10	9	3	2	2	39	2.86	16	15	37	23		130	21.6
Fractures and Contusions,	17	10	5	4	8	4	8	6	62	.37	102	83	60	89	96	492	82.
Wounds,	1	12	5	2	4	3	1		28	.58	35	22	26	16	17	144	24.
Sunstroke, Heat,	1			1	1	1	1		3	.02	2	2	5	9	9	21	4.
Burns and Scalds,	10	10	4	9	4	2	2	3	43	.40	42	28	43	25	58	239	39.8
Freezing,	2			4	1	1	2		5	.04	2	2	3		2	14	2.2
Poison,	3	9	2		3	2	2	2	21	.19	11	15	18	26	22	303	50.5
Lightning,			6	12	7	3						3	3		1	7	1.2
Drowning,	7	12			1		1	1	51	.48	74	55	50	51	71	352	58.6
Tornado,											11	11	30			30	5.
Suffocation,	4	4	4	1	1	1	1	1	16	.15	11	68	13	24	20	71	11.8
Otherwise,	15	6	2	11	2	2	4	2	42	.39	62		65		28	289	48.1
V. 3. HOMICIDE,																	
Homicide,			1						2	.02	2	7	12	10	3	36	6.
V. 4. SUICIDE,																	
Suicide,	18	16	7	9	6	6	5	2	69	.65	48	58	55	52	49	331	55.1
V. 5. EXECUTION,																	
Execution,											2	1				3	.5
V. 6. NOT CLASSED,																	
Violent Deaths,			1	2	3	3	2	2	10	.09	10	6				26	.4
Sudden,	10		1	1			12	8	19	.18	73	21	36	19	33	201	34.
Cause not stated,	88	40	53	108	26	74			409	3.89	442	419	282	592	635	2809	468.1

REPORT OF THE STATE BOARD OF HEALTH.

TABLE 7.

CAUSES OF DEATHS BY MONTHS, AGE, AND SEX.

DISEASE	Under 1	1 to 5	5 to 10	10 to 20	20 to 30	30 to 40	40 to 50	50 to 60	60 to 70	70 to 80	80 to 90	90 to 100	Over 100	Age not stated	Male	Female	Sex not stated	Total	Month not stated	December	November	October	September	August	July	June	May	April
Abscess,	1	1	2	4	8	2	7	4	3	1	2				20	15		35	5		4	3	3	2	2	2	1	2
A........ nt, not stated,	3	1	1	6	9	3	6	7	3	3	3				30	12		42	2	5	5	6	3	4		8		2
A i cltr, Total all causes,	13	30	20	30	33	31	30	29	21	14	9				197	64		261	34	34	23	25	23	33	21	25	10	17
Addison's Disease,						1										1		1										
Alcoholism,			1		4	20	11	5	6	3					39	10		49	4	4	4	4	4	4	7	4	5	5
Aneurism,									1	2	2				4	4		8		1	1	1	1	2	2			
Angina Pectoris,							1								1			1				1				1	1	1
Apoplexy,	4	1	2	2	14	7	23	50	68	78	51	14			169	139		308	27	27	30	22	30	22	22	19	27	31
Arthritis,					1	2	1	1			1					3		4			1			1	1	1	1	1
Ascites,									1	3	1				3	2		5							2		1	5
Asthma,	4		2		3	3	4	2	7	8	3				13	17	1	31	3	8	2	5	2	1	3	1	1	1
Ataxia Progressive,									1	1	1				1	1		1			1							
Abortion,							4	2							1	3		3	3	3	2	5	2	1	3	1	1	5
Brain Diseases,	26	28	10	17	11	14	13	19	22	24	8	1			111	81	1	193	1	1	8	24	21	19	12	15	11	17
Bright's Disease,	1	5	2	7	17	19	15	23	36	20	7				88	61		149	9	9	12	9	19	11	12	13	9	15
Bronchitis,	16	14	5	4	7	4	8	10	11	8	6				45	51		96	16	5	5	5	9	4	5	4	10	13
Bronchitis, Capillary,	51	9	3	8	7		2	2		2	3				43	29		72	7	7	7	4	9		2	1	5	2
Burns and Scalds,	5	18	3			3	2	3	2	2	1				21	22		43		2	5	4	5	3	1	1		5
Caries and Necrosis,				1	1	1		1								1		1									1	1
Calculus and Gravel,							2	1	1		1																	
Cancer,				2	4	21	48	57	55	57	19	3			5	1		6									1	
Carbuncle,	13	19	6	12	6	9	1	4	1						90	176		266	21	21	22	20	24	25	17	22	21	23
....								1	3						3	2		5			1	1	1	1				1
Cerebro-Spinal Meningitis,	13		6	12	6	9	3	4	3						37	37	1	75	2	2	3	5	8	7	5	4	3	11

Childbirth, Puerp...
Cholera...
Chorea...
Colic...
Consumption...
Convulsions...
Croup...
— Case not stated...
Cyanosis...
Cystitis...
Debility and Atrophy...
Diabetes...
Diarrhea...
Diphtheria...
Dropsy and Anæmia...
Do...
Drowning...
Embolism...
Enteritis...
Epilepsy...
Episraxis...
Erysipelas...
Fever, Congestive...
Fever, Intermittent...
Fever, Remittent...
Fever, Typhoid...
Fever, Typho Malarial...
Fever, Malarial...
Fistula...
Freezing...
Fractures and Contusions...
Gastritis...
Gout...
Hemorrhoids...
Heart Diseases...

TABLE 7.—CONTINUED.

DISEASE	Total	Sex not stated	Female	Male	Age not stated	Over 100	90 to 100	80 to 90	70 to 80	60 to 70	50 to 60	40 to 50	30 to 40	20 to 30	10 to 20	5 to 10	1 to 5	Under 1	Month not stated	December	November	October	September	August	July	June	May	April	March
Hemorrhage	57	1	33	23			1	2	5	8	10	9	7	1		1	1	12	4	4	6	7	4	3	3		6	5	2
Hemoptysis	6			4									1	4	2					1	4	1			1				2
Hematemesis	3		1	2					2		5	2	1	1	1				2	2	2	1	3		2	2	1	2	
Hepatitis	17		10	7			1	1	3	3	1	2	1	1				1	2	2	1	1	3	1	2	1	1	3	
Hernia	13		7	6				2	1	3				1	4	7	17		2	1	2	4	3	12	12	7	8	4	
Homicide	2			2									1	1			1	28											4
Hydrocephalus	60	1	27	32														28	1										
Hydrophobia	1			1																		1							
Influenza	1			1																								1	1
Insanity	58	1	32	26				2	8	12	8	12	9	5	2				6	3	1	6	6	7	3	3	5	5	6
Intussusception	14		7	7					1	6	4			3		1	4	3			2	1	2		2	3	1	3	
Jaundice	21		12	8					1		1	2	2	3	2	1		3	2		1	1		2	2	1	2	3	3
Joint Disease	9		3	6				3		9	6	4	2	1	2				2	4	1	1	1	1	3	3	4	1	
Kidney Disease	32	1	10	23				8	6	9	6	2	1	3		3	4	5	2	4	1	2	2	1	3	3	4	2	4
Laryngitis	20		3	9					10	1	24	12	7	1	1		1	2	5	3	7	7	8	8	10	8	7	6	8
Liver Diseases	98	1	47	51			2	3	11	27					2	3	12	14	2	4	2	12						12
Leucocythemia	1														10	15	2	20											
Lung Diseases	82	1	41	41				3	11	7	6	4	9	4			2	7	6	8	12	24	4	1	3	8	8	8	7
Malformations	20	1	9	11													3	49				5	3	23	3	2	1	1	4
Measles	14		7	7				3			5	3	10	18	2	3	3	67		1	1		23	23	2		1	18	14
Meningitis	190	1	93	97		2	1	3	3	2	5		2	2	10	15			10	10	24	1	1	9	2	22	2	2
Nephritis	19	1	9	16						7	3				23			7		1	5	5	1	1	9	16	2		
Neuralgia, Sciatic	4		7	2				3	3	2		3	1	2				2					1		1	3	3	2	2
Neurasthenia	2	1	3	2				2	1	7		2	1				1				1		2			1		1	
Old Age	626	361	265		3	9	121	324	136	33			1							60	52	56	53	63	38	39	44	45	56

Ovarian Tumor,
Ovarian Dropsy,
Neo Sarcoma,
Paralysis,
Pemphigus,
Pericarditis,
Peritonitis,
Pleurisy,
Pneumonia,
Premat'e Birth & Debility,
Privation and Neglect,
Prostatitis,
Puerp'ral Fever,
Puerperal Convulsions,
Purpura and Scurvy,
Poison by Accident,
Quinsy,
Rachitis,
Rheumatism,
Railroad Accidents,
Scarlet Fever,
Scrofula,
Senile Gangrene,
Sep' æmia,
Skin,
Small-pox,
Spina fila,
Spinal Disease,
Spleen Disease,
St mah Disease,
Stomatitis,
Stricture of Intestines,
St ure of Urethra,
Stillborn,
Sudden.

TABLE 7.—Continued.

DISEASE	Under 1	1 to 5	5 to 10	10 to 20	20 to 30	30 to 40	40 to 50	50 to 60	60 to 70	70 to 80	80 to 90	90 to 100	Over 100	Age not stated	Male	Female	January	February	March	April	May	June	July	August	September	October	November	December	Month not stated
Suffocation,	5			1	4	1	1	2	2	1					7	9	1	2			1	1	3	2	2	2	2		
Sunstroke,				2	2	16	18	14	7	8	2				53	16	7	3	8	8	5	7	9	6	4	8	3	6	
Suicide, Total,			1	1		5	8	4	1	2	1				15		1	2	1	2	3	2		1		1		2	
Suicide by Wounds,					2	3	4	2	3	2	1				10	6			3	2				3	2	1	1		
Suicide by Poison,			1			4	2	6	3	2	1				11	7	2	1	2	2	2	5	2	3	2	1	1	2	
Suicide by Drowning,					2	4	4	1	2	1					4	1							5			1	1		
Suicide by Hanging,					5			3	1	1	1				13	2		1	2	2	2		2		2		1	2	
Suicide Otherwise,							3	5	6						4	2			2	3	2		2		2		1	2	
Syphilis,	9	2			9		2	2		3	2	2			71	74	9	7	17	9	12	13	13	13	14	24	10	24	
Tabes Mesenterica,	86	22	3	2								1			17	10	4	2				2	1	2		2	3	4	
Teething,	18	9		1								1			10	8	3		1	3	2	2		1	3	3	3	2	
Tetanus,	6		2		3	3	3	5	6	3	2	2			11	13	8	7	4	1	4	2	2	1		3	3	1	
Tumor,			1		4			2							2	6	1	2		1	2		1	2			2	2	
Ulcer,					3	2	4	2							9	7	1			1	4	2	4		3	2	4	1	
Ulceration of Intestines,					4	1	4	4	4	4	1				10	10	3	2	3	1			3	2	3	3	2	1	
Uraemia,					1	1	3	3	3						7	3	1		1	1	2			2	1	3	1	2	
Uterus, Diseases of,		1			1	1	2			1						10	1	1	1						1	2	2	1	
Violent Deaths,	1				1		1								10	7	3		1	1				2	5	6		1	
Vomiting of Pregnancy,					1	4										3	1		1					1	1				
Whooping Cough,	2824		4	2	1	1									31	28	10	9		2	5	3	7	6	5	6			
Worms,	1	1			1	1				1	1				1	1			1					1					
Wounds,	1	3		2	6	4	4	3	2	1	2	2			25	3			3	4	1	4	1	6	3	3	3		

TABLE 8.

OCCUPATIONS AND AGES.

OCCUPATIONS.	15 to 20.	20 to 30.	30 to 40.	40 to 50.	50 to 60.	60 to 70.	70 to 80.	80 to 90.	90 to 100.	Over 100.	Total, 1881.	Total, 1880.
Agents,		2	2	2	1	2	1				10	3
Artists,			1	1	1	1					4	1
Actor,					1						1	1
Actress,		1									1	1
Army Officer,				1							1	...
Authoress,					1						1	...
Bakers,		1	2	1							4	5
Bankers,				2			2				4	1
Bartenders,		2	1								3	3
Barbers,			1		1		1				3	1
Baggage-master,						1					1	...
Basket-makers,					1			1			2	...
Blacksmiths,	1	5	5	7	6	6	4	2	1		37	35
Book-binders,				2	1		1				4	1
Book-keepers,		3	1	3	2	2					11	6
Brass-founder,		1									1	1
Bridge-builder,				1							1	1
Brickmakers,		1		3	1						5	1
Brakemen,	1	7	1								9	3
Brewers,			1			1					2	2
Brokers,					1		1				2	4
Burnishers,			1								1	4
Butchers,	1	2	2	3	2	3					13	9
Calkers,			1	1					1		3	1
Carmen,	1										1	1
Cashier,							1				1	1
Carpenters,		4	3	10	16	13	11	3			60	65
Carvers,		1	1								2	1
Carriage-painters,				1	1						2	4
Carriage-makers,		1	1	1	2	1	5	2			13	1
Cabinet-makers,					3		1	1			5	1
Coopers,					1	1					2	5
Cutlers,	1	2			1	2					6	...
Colliers,			1								1	2
Cooks,	1	1	2	1	1		2				8	1
Clerks,	9	21	14	8	7	4	2	1			66	34
Commercial Travelers,			1	1	3						5	1
Clergymen,			2	4	5	6	4	1	1		23	21
Cigar-makers,		1	1	1					1		4	5
Contractors,			2		1						3	3
Conductors,		1			1						2	1
Carpet-weavers,				2							2	1

TABLE 8.—Continued.

OCCUPATIONS.	15 to 20.	20 to 30.	30 to 40.	40 to 50.	50 to 60.	60 to 70.	70 to 80.	80 to 90.	90 to 100.	Over 100.	Total, 1881.	Total, 1880.
Coachmen,	..	1	1	....	....	....	....	....	....	..	2	1
Cloth finishers,	..	....	1	....	....	....	....	....	....	..	1	2
Clock-makers,	..	2	...	....	1	1	1	....	1	..	6	....
Corset-makers,	1	1	1	1	1	....	....	....	....	..	5	....
Coal-dealers,	..	....	....	1	1	....	....	....	....	..	2	....
Confectioner,	..	1	....	....	....	....	....	....	....	..	1	....
Dentists,	..	....	....	....	1	2	1	....	....	..	4	2
Druggists,	..	1	2	1	....	....	....	....	....	..	4	3
Dress-makers,	1	6	3	5	2	....	....	....	....	..	17	10
Domestics,	7	14	6	5	6	11	6	5	1	..	61	68
Deputy Sheriff,	..	....	1	....	....	....	....	....	....	..	1	....
Depot-master,	..	....	....	....	1	....	....	....	....	..	1	1
Dyers,	..	....	....	....	2	....	....	....	....	..	2	3
Draughtsman,	..	1	....	....	....	....	....	....	....	..	1	....
Die-sinkers,	..	....	1	....	1	....	....	....	....	..	2	....
Editors,	..	1	1	....	....	....	....	....	....	..	2	....
Engineers,	..	4	3	3	4	1	....	....	1	..	16	7
Engravers,	..	1	1	....	....	....	....	....	....	..	2	1
Expressmen,	1	1	1	3	2	....	....	....	....	..	8	6
Farmers,	14	45	44	54	78	138	238	153	24	1	789	678
File-cutters,	..	1	1	....	....	....	....	....	....	..	2	....
Fur-dresser,	..	....	1	....	....	....	....	....	....	..	1	1
Fishermen,	..	1	2	2	1	1	1	....	....	..	8	3
Firemen,	..	1	....	1	....	....	....	....	....	..	2	....
Foremen,	..	....	....	1	1	1	....	....	....	..	3	1
Gardeners,	..	....	....	....	1	....	2	1	....	..	4	3
Gas makers,	..	1	....	..	....	1	....	....	....	..	2	....
Grocers,	..	....	....	1	1	....	1	....	....	..	3	2
Grinders,	..	....	3	1	....	....	....	....	....	..	4	2
Gun-smiths,	..	....	....	..	....	....	1	....	1	.	2	....
Gold platers,	..	....	1	....	1	....	....	....	....	..	2	....
Glass-cutters,	1	1	1	....	....	....	....	....	....	..	3	....
Glass-blowers,	..	....	....	....	1	1	....	....	....	..	2	....
Hatters,	1	13	8	5	8	7	7	1	....	..	50	45
Hackmen,	..	....	1	1	....	....	....	....	....	..	2	1
Harness-makers,	..	1	....	2	1	2	1	....	....	..	7	2
Hose-makers,	..	....	....	1	....	1	2	....	....	..	4	....
Hostlers,	..	1	3	....	....	....	....	....	....	..	4	....
Housewives,	17	156	182	181	187	223	245	266	40	1	1498	1256
Housekeepers,	3	16	24	40	39	45	32	11	9	.	219	459
Hotel keepers,	..	2	1	3	4	3	....	1	1	..	15	8
Ice Dealers,	..	1	....	1	....	....	....	....	....	..	2	1
Insurance Agents,	..	2	2	1	....	....	....	....	....	..	5	....
Inspectors,	..	1	1	1	....	....	....	....	1	..	4	....
Jewelers,	..	....	1	1	....	1	....	....	....	..	3	2
Joiners,	..	2	1	2	1	4	1	....	....	..	11	4
Journeymen,	..	2	1	1	1	4	2	....	....	..	11	2
Laborers,	27	88	69	80	80	95	43	25	3	1	511	396
Lawyers,	..	....	1	1	1	4	3	....	....	..	10	12
Landlords,	..	....	....	....	....	1	2	....	....	..	3	....

TABLE 8.—Continued.

OCCUPATIONS.	15 to 20	20 to 30	30 to 40	40 to 50	50 to 60	60 to 70	70 to 80	80 to 90	90 to 100	Over 100	Total 1881.	Total 1880.
Lightermen,												1
Liverymen,			1	1		3					5	3
Liquor Dealers,			1	1	1	1					4	2
Locksmiths,		1	1	2	2	1	1				8	1
Manufacturers,	3	2	1	3	5	8	7	4	1		34	35
Masons,		1	3	2	5	4	3	2	2		22	13
Mail Carrier,					1						1	
Mariners,		1	2	7	4	5	4	1			24	38
Machinists,	4	6	4	7	7	2	1				31	9
Merchants,	1	12	22	14	34	26	26	11	1		147	83
Millers,				1	1	1	3				6	5
Milliners,		1	1	1		1	2				6	2
Mechanics,	9	75	52	47	53	34	42	10	3		325	152
Musicians,		1	2	1	1						5	8
Miners,		1	1								2	
Moulders,		6	3	8	2	3	2				24	6
Nurserymen,		1	1	1							3	1
Nurses,			2	3	3	2	1	2	2		15	2
Overseers,			1		1						2	
Oystermen,			1			1	1				3	1
Operatives,	42	35	19	12	12	14	9				143	102
Organ Grinders,			1	1							2	
Paupers,					1	2	3				6	6
Paper Makers,		1		1		2	1		1		6	1
Paper Hanger,				1							1	
Pattern Makers,			1	1							2	
Painters,	3	4	7	6	7	9	1	1	1		39	21
Peddlers,			1	1			1				3	3
Prisoners,												4
Printers,	2	3	2	1		1			1		10	4
Physicians,		1	5	4	4	5	5	1			25	24
Pilots,				2							2	
Publisher,						1					1	1
Polishers,		2	2	3	4						11	2
Post-masters,												2
Policemen,		1	1		1						3	1
Plumber,		1	1			1					3	1
Photographer,			1								1	
Quarrymen,			2	2			1	1			6	10
Railroad Hands,		2	1	1	2	1	1				8	10
Railroad Builders,					1						1	1
Retired Merchants,						2	1	2	1		6	1
Restaurant Keeper,					1						1	1
Rope-makers,					1			1			2	
Saloon Keepers,		3	4	8	3	1					19	5
Salesmen,		1	1	1							3	4
Students,	14	6									20	13
Shoemakers,	1	6	3	10	8	8	14	7	1		58	27
Sailmakers,			1		1	2					4	
Seamstress,		2	2	1	1	1	1				8	7

TABLE 8.—CONTINUED.

OCCUPATIONS.	15 to 20.	20 to 30.	30 to 40.	40 to 50.	50 to 60.	60 to 70.	70 to 80.	80 to 90.	90 to 100.	Over 100.	Total 1881.	Total 1880.
Saddlers,	..	1	1	...	...	...	1	1	...	...	4	....
Seamen,	2	2	1	2	2	3	3	1	...	...	16	7
Sextons,	..	...	...	1	...	...	...	...	...		1	1
Sea Captains,	..	...	...	...	1	1	...	...	...	..	2	5
Servants,	7	20	18	16	9	8	3	2	1	..	84	21
Stage Drivers,	..	...	...	...	1	1	...	...			2	1
Station Agent,	..	...	...	...	1	...	...	...			1	1
Shears Makers,	.	...	1	1	...	...	...	...			2	1
Scythe Makers,	..	...	...	1	...	...	...				1	1
Switchmen,	..	...	...	1	...	1	...	...			2	1
Spinners,	..	...	1	2	1	...	...	...			4	1
Superintendents,	..	...	...	1	1	...	...	...			2	3
Stone Cutters,	..	1	1	2	6	3	2	...	...		15	3
Ship Builders,	..	...	...	...	1	1	...	...			2	3
Speculators,	..	...	...	1	...	1	1	...	...		3	1
Sister of Charity,	..	...	...	1	...	...	...	...			1	1
Saw-makers,	..	1	1	...	...	...	...				2	....
Solders,		...	...	...	..	...	...				...	2
Surveyor,	..	...	...	...	1	...		..			1	....
Silk Finisher,	..	...	...	1	...	...		..			1	....
Tailors,	..	1	1	2	1	7	2	1	1	..	16	8
Tanners,	..	1	...	...	1	1	1	...			4	2
Tailoress,	..	1	1	1	...	1	1	...			5	5
Tinkers,	..	1	...	1	...	...	...				2	1
Teachers,	3	10	4	3	2	2	2	1	1	..	28	26
Tinners,	1	2	1	2	1	1	2	1	...		11	10
Tool-makers,	..	...	1	1	...	...	...				2	....
Telegraph Operator,	..	1	...	...	...	...					1	1
Teamsters,	1	6	3	1	5	3	2	1	...		22	3
Turners,	..	2	1	2	...	...	...				5	4
Tramps,	..	1	1	...	...		1	...			3	....
Undertakers,	..	...	...	1	1	1	...				3	2
Upholsterer,	..	...	1	...	...	...					1	1
Wheelwright,	..	...	...	...		1	1	...			2	....
Watchmen,	..	1	...	1	1	1	2	1	...		6	2
Waiters,	2	1	1	1	1	...	...				6	....
Washerwomen,	..	3	2	3	1	...	...				9	1
Weavers,	5	6	5	2	1	4	1	...			24	3
Wire-workers,	..	1	1	1	...	...	..	..			3	....
Woolcarders,	..	...	...	1	...	...	1				2	1
Whaler,	..	...	1	...	...	...	...				1	1

TABLE 9.

DEATHS FROM MALARIAL FEVERS IN EACH TOWN, BY COUNTIES, FOR FIVE YEARS, CONTRASTED WITH THOSE FROM TYPHOID FEVER FOR TEN YEARS. MALARIAL IS USED FOR ALL THE VARIETIES, INTERMITTENT, CONGESTIVE, ETC., EXCEPT TYPHO-MALARIAL FEVER.

TOWNS.	Population in 1880.	1881 Malarial	1881 Typho-Malarial	1881 Typhoid	1880 Malarial	1880 Typho-Malarial	1880 Typhoid	1879 Malarial	1879 Typho-Malarial	1879 Typhoid	1878 Malarial	1878 Typho-Malarial	1878 Typhoid	1877 Malarial	1877 Typho-Malarial	1877 Typhoid	TYPHOID FEVER 1876	1875	1874	1873	1872
HARTFORD.																					
Avon,	42,553	12	6	27	24	2	13	3	12	11	2	3	22			22	26	35	14	29	33
Berlin,	1,058		3		1	1	1	1		1	1	1	1			1		1	3	1	5
Bloomfield,	2,385	1						1		1								2		1	4
Bristol,	1,346	1		7	2		4		3	1			4			4	2	1	3	3	8
Burlington,	5,347					5			5	8	1		2			2	15	4	9	6	1
Canton,	1,224									3							2			3	2
East Granby,	2,299	2	1		5	1	1	2	2	3			1		4	1		1	2	1	
East Hartford,	754	2	11	1		3	4		2		4	4	1			1	3		1	2	2
East	3,500		2			1	1		5		2		2			1		2	2	4	1
Enfield,	3,019	2	19	1	5	3	4	2	2			1					5	5	3	3	5
Farmington,	6,754		3		1		1		5	1	1		1	1		2	3	4	4	12	1
Glastonbury,	3,014	1	1		1			1				2				1	3	2	3	2	3
Granby,	3,580			2		12	5		5					4			2		1		2
Hartland,	1,340				4	6	2		4										6		5
Manchester,	643	1	5	6	1	3	1	1		1			1	1		1	2	1	3	3	1
Marlborough,	6,462					1												16	1		18
New Britain,	391	2	9	4	4	6		6	5	1	2		7		1	7	8		6	7	
Newington,	13,978		2		1	3		1	4	1	1	1								1	
	934				1												1				1
Rocky Hill,	1,930			1	1		3			1	1	1	2			2	1	3	1	2	5
	1,109				1			2	2	1	1	1				1	2	12	1	1	2
Southington,	1,830	2	2	1	1	4	3	2	6	1	1	1	1			1	3		1	3	8
	5,411																				

TABLE 9.—CONTINUED.

TOWNS.	Population in 1880.	TYPHOID FEVER. 1872	1873	1874	1875	1876	1877 Malarial	1877 Typho-Malarial	1877 Typhoid	1878 Malarial	1878 Typho-Malarial	1878 Typhoid	1879 Malarial	1879 Typho-Malarial	1879 Typhoid	1880 Malarial	1880 Typho-Malarial	1880 Typhoid	1881 Malarial	1881 Typho-Malarial	1881 Typhoid
South Windsor,	1,902	1			3	1	1		5									2			1
Suffield,	3,225	5	6	2	3		1		1		1			1		3		2		4	
West Hartford,	1,838		2	1	2	2				1	3				1			1			1
Wethersfield,	2,173		4	1		1						1	1					1		1	2
Windsor,	3,036	6	3	1	1	5			3			1			1			1		1	
Windsor Locks,	2,33?	1	1	1	1	23	1		3	3									1		2
NEW HAVEN.	62,882	53	55	47	37		1	17	15	5	6	13	6	20	12	13	27	18	30	14	28
Beacon Falls,	379	1	2	2	1				2			1		1				4		1	
Bethany,	637	2	1	1	5	3	1		1	1	4	1	2	1		1			1	1	1
Branford,	3,047	3	2	3	4	2			2		1	1		3			1		3	4	2
Cheshire,	2,284	7	1	4	1	3			2		9	3			1				1	3	
Derby,	11,649	9	2	1		2	1		1	1	1	1	2		1	1	1	1	1		1
East Haven,	3,067	2	3	3		1	3	2		1	12	8			1		3			1	2
Guilford,	2,782	1					2				2				5	2	7	2		1	14
Hamden,	3,408	1			21	5			9	4	1	4	2	4	5	5	1	5	1	1	2
Madison,	1,669			4		2			1				1		1	2	3	2	4	1	2
Meriden,	18,340	6	3	5	4	3	1	1	7	2	3					1	3	1	2	1	
Middlebury,	687	1	1	4	4		1		1		2									1	
Milford,	3,347				2	2	1			2	2		2			2			4		
Naugatuck,	4,272	2	1	1			1	2	1			4	1	2				2	2	1	2
North Branford,	1,025			1		2				3	3										
North Haven,	1,763	3	1		2	2	1				2	4	1		3		1		4	1	
Orange,	3,341																		2		
Oxford,	1,120																				
Prospect,	492					2	2	2	1												2
Seymour,	2,318	3	1	1	2	2	1			1	3	4	1		3	2	1	3	5		
Southbury,	1,740	2	1			3	1		1	1	1		1		1	2					2

Town	Population
Wallingford,	4,686
Waterbury,	20,269
Wolcott,	493
Woodbridge,	829
NEW LONDON.	10,529
Norwich,	21,141
Bozrah,	1,155
Colchester,	2,974
East Lyme,	1,731
Franklin,	686
Griswold,	2,745
Groton,	5,127
Lebanon,	1,845
Ledyard,	1,373
Lisbon,	630
Lyme,	1,025
Montville,	2,666
North Stonington,	1,769
Old Lyme,	1,387
Preston,	2,519
Salem,	574
Sprague,	3,207
Stonington,	7,353
Voluntown,	1,186
Waterford,	2,701
FAIRFIELD.	11 69
Danbury,	29,148
Bridgeport,	2,726
Bethel,	1,152
Brookfield,	1,948
Darien,	1,145
Easton,	3,748
Fairfield,	7,892
Greenwich,	2,499
Huntington,	

TABLE 9.—CONTINUED.

TOWNS.	Population in 1880.
Monroe,	1,157
New-Fairfield,	2,673
Newtown,	791
Norwalk,	4,013
Redding,	13,956
Ridgefield,	1,540
Sherman,	2,028
Stamford,	828
Stratford,	11,298
Trumbull,	4,251
Weston,	1,323
Westport,	918
Wilton, WINDHAM.	3,477
Brooklyn,	1,864
Ashford,	2,308
Canterbury,	1,041
Chaplin,	1,272
Eastford,	627
Hampton,	855
Killingly,	827
Plainfield,	6,921
Pomfret,	4,021
Putnam,	1,470
Scotland,	5,827
Sterling,	590
	957

	Population
(Windham),	5,051
Windham,	8,265
Woodstock,	2,639
LITCHFIELD.	
Barkhamsted,	3,410
Bethlehem,	655
Bridgewater,	708
Canaan,	1,157
Colebrook,	1,148
Cornwall,	1,583
(Goshen),	1,093
Harwinton,	1,016
Kent,	1,622
Morris,	627
New Hartford,	3,302
New Milford,	3,907
Norfolk,	1,418
North Canaan,	1,537
(Plymouth),	2,350
Roxbury,	950
Salisbury,	3,715
Sharon,	2,580
Thomaston,	3,225
Torrington,	3,327
Warren,	639
Washington,	1,589
Watertown,	1,897
Winchester,	5,142
(Woodbury),	2,148
MIDDLESEX.	
(Middletown),	11,731
Haddam,	2,419
Chatham,	1,967
(Chester),	1,177
Clinton,	1,402

TABLE 9.—CONTINUED.

TOWNS.	Population in 1880.	1872	1873	1874	1875	1876	1877 Typhoid	1877 Typho-Malarial	1877 Malarial	1878 Typhoid	1878 Typho-Malarial	1878 Malarial	1879 Typhoid	1879 Typho-Malarial	1879 Malarial	1880 Typhoid	1880 Typho-Malarial	1880 Malarial	1881 Typhoid	1881 Typho-Malarial	1881 Malarial
	1,640	2	1	1	2					3		1				1				1	1
Durham,	990	3	5	3	6		3			2		1			1	2	2		1	1	1
East Haddam,	3,032	2	1	2	2	1	2			3		1							1	5	1
Essex,	1,855			1						1		2									1
Killingworth,	748	2	3	1	1	2	2	2				2	1		1	1			1		3
Middlefield,	928	5	3	3	3	2	3			4					1	2	2			5	3
Old Saybrook,	1,302			5		2				1									3	1	
Portland,	4,156			1		1				2		1	1		1	1	2		1		
Saybrook,	1,362				1	1	1														
Westbrook,	878					1	1			1							2	2				
TOLLAND.	1,169					1				1			1								
Andover,	428			1			1														
Bolton,	512		1	6							1		1				2				
Columbia,	757	4	4	1	5	2	2			1			1			1	1				
Coventry,	2,043	3		2	2					1						3	3	2			
Ellington,	1,569	2	1			2				1		1	1	1		3	2	1			
Hebron,	1,243																				
Mansfield,	2,154			1	1	8	3			1			2						3		
Somers,	1,242	4	1	8	12	8	10			7			4			6			1		
Stafford,	4,455	3	11		1	1				2			1			2			5		
Union,	539	2																			
Vernon,	6,915	9		8		1				2		1	1	1	1	2		1	1		1
Willington,	1,086																				

VITAL STATISTICS OF THE COLORED POPULATION BY COUNTIES.

COUNTIES.	BIRTHS.										MARRIAGES.								DEATHS.										
	Males.	Females.	Total.	1880.	1879.	1878.	1877.	1876.	Aggregate for 6 years.	Average each year.	1881.	1880.	1879.	1878.	1877.	1876.	Aggregate for 6 years.	Average each year.	Males.	Females.	Sex not stated.	Total.	1880.	1879.	1878.	1877.	1876.	Aggregate for 6 years.	Average each year.
Hartford....	32	33	65	55	59	46	63	56	344	57.3	15	5	15	18	23	27	103	17.2	30	34	..	64	56	54	57	28	24	283	47.1
New Haven..	40	32	72	74	60	70	46	63	385	64.1	5	4	38	30	25	33	135	22.5	52	47	5	104	65	79	79	13	87	427	71.1
New London,	15	15	30	32	39	22	17	29	169	28.1	16	6	8	13	11	15	69	11.5	9	26	..	35	37	23	30	30	11	166	27.6
Fairfield...	17	22	39	60	41	42	49	46	277	46.1	15	3	8	3	23	19	71	11.8	19	32	1	52	53	23	42	42	20	232	38.6
Windham....	9	4	13	7	22	11	8	12	73	12.1	2	2	4	5	4	3	20	3.3	5	4	..	9	7	20	7	6	7	56	9.3
Litchfield...	11	12	23	17	16	16	28	11	111	18.5	4	4	5	5	5	5	28	4.6	8	9	..	17	18	9	11	15	23	93	15.5
Middlesex..	3	4	7	4	6	9	7	5	38	6.3	2	2	4	4	3	3	18	3.	5	1	..	6	8	8	10	5	20	57	9.5
Tolland.....	3	3	6	5	4	5	8	1	29	4.8	1	1	1	2	2	2	9	1.5	..	1	..	1	7	3	4	1	2	18	3.
Total.....	130	125	255	254	247	221	226	223	1,426	237.6	60	27	83	80	96	107	453	75.5	128	154	6	288	251	219	240	140	194	1,332	222.2

There are eight cases of mixed marriages included in this table. In two the groom was an Indian, the bride a negro; in the other cases the woman was white, the man black, with one exception, when the reverse was the case.

As shown by the table, the births for the last six years exceed the deaths by 94. The marked decrease in the marriages for 1880, only about a third of the average, would seem due to neglect in reporting the colored marriages separately.

BIRTHS.

The total number of births reported—14,616—exceeds the number in 1880 by 787, and the average for the last ten years previous to 1881, by 712. An increasing birth-rate in excess of the death-rate is an indication of prosperity, which is strengthened by an increasing marriage-rate. A high birth-rate also offsets in some degree a high death-rate, in striking the balance of the year in relation to gain or loss in population, an element of no inconsiderable importance in the health of the State. The natural increment of population this year is 3,709; that is, the excess of births over deaths,—a gain of ten a day in round numbers (10.13). This exceeds the gain in 1880 by 388,—a trifle over one a day,—but does not quite equal the average for the last ten years, 4,335, falling short 626—not quite two a day.

There were 7,660 male births to 6,857 female, an excess of male births of 803, about the usual average. The ratio is a little over 111 males to every 100 females, or 55.5 males to 44.5 females. The average for the last ten years is 110 males to 100 females, or 55 males to every 45 females. In Massachusetts the ratio is stated to be pretty uniform ; for the last three years it was 105.3 males to every 100 females. In England, the Registrar-General's report for 1880 shows 103.6 males to 100 females, which is stated to be the lowest, except in one year (1871), and never to have been equally low except on three other occasions (1868, 1877, and 1879). The proportion in England and Wales is smaller than in any other European country, and has been steadily decreasing for several years. No explanation is given of this curious fact. The following table shows the ratio in several countries for ten years, 1870–79, which is the highest in this State:

Connecticut,	110.0	Holland,	106.1
Italy,	107.1	Belgium,	105.9
Australia,	106.8	Scotland,	105.7
France,	106.4	Ireland,	105.6
Switzerland,	106.3	England and Wales,	103.9
German Empire,	106.2		

There were reported 395 still-births, the returns probably quite incomplete; 211 of these were males, 152 females, 32 sex not stated, which gives 138.8 males to every 100 females. In 1880 the ratio was 148 males to 100 females. This disproportion of males to females in still-births is quite general; the ratios given are about the same as in Massachusetts.* The greater fatality in males is ascribed to their greater size and weight, which exposes them to greater risks in child-birth. - What the excess of male births in the illegitimate class is caused by is not so obvious, unless the greater vitality of the father might be a cause, but this, if true, is not so universally, and until more is known of the influences which determine sex *in utero*, perhaps speculations might as well be omitted on these points. There was reported one still-birth to each 37 living births; the average was but slightly in excess of one for each day of the year. In 1880 there were 40 living births reported to each still-birth. As these details have an important relation to the whole system of statistics, it is hoped that physicians will exhibit greater care in making their returns complete.

The following table shows the number of twin and illegitimate births by counties for the last five years:

COUNTIES.	1881.		1880.		1879.		1878.		1877.		Total.		Average for 5 years.	
	Twin.	Illegitimate.	Twin.	Illegitimate.	Twin.	Illegitimate.	Twin.	Illegitimate.	Twin.	Illegitimate.	Twin.	Illegitimate.	Twin.	Illegitimate.
Hartford.........	35[1]	33	28[1]	34	32	44	33	36	20	38	148	185	26.6	37.0
New Haven......	40	41	27[2]	35	40	45	30	25	36	47	173	193	34.6	38.6
New London.....	16	18	22	23	10	16	8	17	16	10	72	84	14.4	16.8
Fairfield.........	18	30	28	23	24	28	28	23	25	24	123	128	24.6	25.6
Windham........	44	13	13	14	13	8	12	11	9	17	91	63	18.2	12.6
Litchfield........	12	6	9	8	17	7	14	10	12	15	64	46	12.8	9.2
Middlesex	16	3	3	3	9	6	7	4	3	3	38	19	7.6	3.8
Tolland..........	4	8	4	6	9	6	3	2	6	1	26	23	5.2	4.6
Totals	185	152	134	146	154	160	135	128	127	155	735	741	147.0	148.2

[1] Including one case of triplets, Southington.
[2] Including two cases of triplets.

The plurality births are much more frequent in the foreign born population, and those whose ancestors have not been for many generations in this country. There are but few, comparatively, reported out of the manufacturing towns where the foreign element is massed. The illegitimate births are mainly reported

*Registration Report, Mass., 1881, page 25.

from the centers of population; the element of nationality has not
been as definitely traced. The numbers in each class are somewhat in excess of the average for the last five years. A few instances of triple births are, for sake of convenience, included
among the twin births.

The following table shows the number of children born of
American and foreign-born parents, and the percentages to the
whole number of births for four years, as long as the data are
obtainable. This table will be of increasing value as its limits are
extended.

Years.	Parents American.	Per Cent.	Parents Foreign.	Per Cent.	American Foreign.	Per Cent.	Not Stated.	Per Cent.
1881,	6,734	46.	5,229	35.7	1.737	12.	916	6.3
1880,	6,585	47.	5,101	37.	1,656	12.5	487	8.5
1879,	6,672	47.	4,848	34.6	1,748	13.	733	5.4
1878,	6,150	45.	5,704	41.	1,289	9.	356	5.
Aggregate,	26,141	46.2	20,882	37.	6,430	11.6	2,542	5.

The greater part of those in the third class, rated as American,
are in all probability descended from foreign-born parents that
have been naturalized in this country. It is impossible to trace
nationalities after one generation, as all those born in this country
return their children, of course, as of American parentage, so that
the foreign element cannot be traced beyond a limited extent without great labor and detailed investigations. The greater part of
those where the nationality is not stated are probably of foreign
descent; that is, so recently can the parent stock be traced to other
lands that the descendants have not as yet become entirely assimilated, but retain enough of their characteristic qualities to enable
their race to be determined without any trouble. At best less than
fifty per cent. of the births are of American parents, and doubtless there is some foreign admixture here, that is, foreign one or two
generations ago. The proportionately higher birth-rate in our
manufacturing towns is also another indication of the larger birth-
rate in the foreign population and those of foreign descent.

The following table shows the birth-rates by counties for the last three years.

	1881.	1880.	1879.
Hartford,	23.1	22.2	23.5
New Haven,	27.8	24.6	25.8
New London,	21.5	21.1	20.1
Fairfield,	22.	20.8	19.1
Windham,	23.9	25.4	25.
Litchfield,	19.8	19.6	19.7
Middlesex,	19.7	18.8	20.2
Tolland,	21.8	19.7	21.4
Connecticut,	22.4	22.2	22.4

New Haven county shows the highest birth-rate, except 1880, when Windham county stands first, and occupies second place in the other two years. The influence of the foreign population, massed in the manufacturing centers, is shown strongly in this table, but still more so by a comparison of the birth-rates of the towns themselves.

The highest birth-rate for 1881 is that of Beacon Falls, which reports 21 births in a population of 379, giving a birth-rate of 55.4 for every one thousand of population. This, however, is an exceptional occurrence, but is from the record. The birth-rate of Weston is printed larger, but the lines belonging to that town and Westport were transposed, except the population, so that the birth and death-rates of these towns are not correct, and the rest of the line printed opposite Weston should be read for Westport, and vice versa. The next highest birth-rates were Sprague, 38.5, Putnam 37, Meriden and Naugatuck each 31.5, Waterbury 30.8, Derby 28.8, Manchester 28.4, New Britain 27.7, Canton 24.3. The lowest birth-rate is 6.9 in two towns. Several very low birth-rates are caused by the failure of the physicians to return the births—especially non-resident physicians. Thus the recorded rate of Stratford is 6.6, returning 27 births to a population of 4,251, not quite seven to a thousand; North Haven 9, North Stamford, 10.9 to each thousand, and so on. After thoroughly ventilating this subject, and calling the attention of the registrars and negligent physicians directly to it, unless decided improvement is shown in the returns, the only recourse would seem to be a legal procedure, as the law is explicit on the point requiring the physicians to make the returns, and the registrars to see that the returns are made. In some instances the registrars, by considerable effort, complete the returns themselves, as the registrar in East Hartford, whose records are a model of completeness and accuracy.

Although there is some compensation for these duties, still much must be done from public spirit and a sense of duty. Any intelligent man, upon reflection, can see the great value of the records of the vital statistics of a town, and also that accuracy and completeness are essential requisites in records that are oftentimes the last and conclusive evidence of contested rights, and are so closely linked with the most complicated relations of human life. Yet few towns are willing to pay for indexing these records, to enable references to be readily made, and to preserve, oftentimes, otherwise perishable matter that time has rendered nearly illegible, nor to recompense a registrar for extra work in completing the records by adding data that he can attest, but which will soon become unattainable. The law provides for such work during the registrar's term of office, but the work is even more valuable if he can supply the deficiencies of previous years by exact knowledge.

Owing to the high death-rate, the number of towns where the death-rate exceeds the birth-rate is much larger than usual, although the total excess of births over deaths is considerably larger than last year. In quite a number they vary but slightly, while in seven the birth and death-rate are exactly equal, showing neither gain nor loss by natural causes. These were Seymour, Montville, Ashford, Chaplin, Sharon, Warren, and Andover. This is an unusually large number, as it is seldom that these ratios exactly balance. The rule is for the birth-rate to be considerably the larger.

The following table shows the birth and death-rate in other places as well as Connecticut:

	1880.			1880.	
	Birth-rate.	Death-rate.		Birth-rate.	Death-rate.
Connecticut,	22.2	16.7	England,	34.2	20.5
Massachusetts,	24.8	19.8	Denmark,	31.8	20.4
Ontario, Canada,	27.4	18.	Austria,	37.3	29.6
Sweden,	29.4	18.1	Prussia,	37.9	25.5
Hungary,	42.9	38.6	Italy,	33.6	30.5
Belgium,	32.		Germany,	37.7	26.1

As shown by the table, the birth and death-rates each are less in Connecticut than in any of the countries cited. They are both slightly larger in 1881,—the birth-rate 22.4, and the death-rate 17.4. There is little doubt but that the birth-rate should be increased to 25 per cent. at least. The death-rate is probably still too small; in fact, it is nearly as certain as the same statement concerning the birth-rate, for many towns that are exceedingly faulty in giving too low rates lower the general average obviously, as well as a wide-spread omission of a few in each place.

RATE. OF BIRTHS TO POPULATION, 1881.

Connecticut,	one birth to every				42.6	Hartford,	one birth to every			37.3
Hartford Co.,	"	"	"	"	43.2	New Haven,	"	"	"	"	31.1
N. Haven	"	"	"	"	35.9	Bridgeport,	"	"	"	"	30.6
N. London	"	"	"	"	46.4	Norwich,	"	"	"	"	38.6
Fairfield	"	"	"	"	45.4	Waterbury,	"	"	"	"	32.4
Windham	"	"	"	"	42.6	Meriden,	"	"	"	"	31.5
Litchfield	"	"	"	"	40.2	New Britain,	"	"	"	"	36.5
Middlesex	"	"	"	"	53.4	Norwalk,	"	"	"	"	49.0
Tolland	"	"	"	"	46.0	New London,	"	"	"	"	36.2

As indicated by the rate per thousand, also, New Haven County makes the best showing,—one birth to every 35.9, Bridgeport, the best among the cities; the manufacturing cities and towns generally show the highest birth-rates in proportion to population. The returns of births from New Haven and Bridgeport are probably the most complete, although by special effort the registrar of Hartford has each year supplied many of the deficiencies in the returns by a careful canvass in certain parts of the city, where past experience has revealed the greatest negligence. The large number of births that are not attended by physician or midwife, and the neglect and ignorance of many midwives, account for a large percentage of the missing facts, and the forgetfulness of the doctors—to use a mild expression—completes the list of principal causes of the deficiencies in birth-returns. The registrars deserve in many instances great credit for their efforts to secure complete returns. The time is near at hand, we hope, when all the physicians can be honestly commended for their work. In discussing the subject among representatives from other states, much surprise was expressed that the fee paid did not prove sufficient inducement. In many of the states that have but recently established

general laws no fees are paid. While this is wrong, still the fact
that the work *is* adequately paid for should increase the sense
of obligation which every intelligent physician must feel in
regard to the proper performance of these duties. There is now
no excuse for incomplete returns of births, as we have at considerable trouble provided a record (that the physician may and should
keep himself) of all the births that he attends, and then, as he goes
his rounds, he can secure the names and records of births without
special effort. After the first returns are made the book can be
trimmed to the size of the stubs, and then readily carried for completing the record in after months, if the child has not been
named promptly; and when the names are secured the registrar
can complete the record from this and return to the owner, who
thus has a record of his obstetric practice that is exact, and from
which deductions can safely be drawn. Notes and even a short
history of the case can be written on the reverse of the stub.

This form of certificate is very popular, and it is hoped that
practical results will follow its extended use.

Births as Influenced by Seasons.

The greatest number of births in any month were in August;
September next; April has the least. There were the most births
in winter,—the least in spring. There is some caprice in this evidently, as last year October had the greatest number of births of
any month, and May the least; autumn and winter had the most,
and spring least, as this year. August has the greatest number of
male births, March next; September, which had the largest number of male births last year, has the greatest number of female
this. The record of 1879 is the same as 1881, in that there were
the most births in winter and the least in spring. The following
table shows the nationalities of the parents when these were born
in foreign countries.

COUNTIES.	Irish,	English.	German.	Canadian.	Scotch.	French.	Dane.	Italian.	Swiss.	Swedes.	American and Foreign.	Mixed Foreign.
Hartford,	628	82	163	85	5	3	3	..	2	25	471	83
New Haven,	1,146	94	240	80	9	5	1	3	3	9	371	78
New London,	226	28	26	187	11	..	2	..	..	2	210	36
Fairfield,	453	56	112	9	8	1	1	1	..	10	380	63
Windham,	122	8	3	288	1	..	..	..	..	3	104	10
Litchfield,	157	25	24	23	8	8	..	2	2	1	106	13
Middlesex,	124	13	22	2	1	..	..	4	2	29	86	26
Tolland,	45	10	63	33	1	..	..	1	3	..	60	17
Total,	2,901	316	853	707	44	17	5	13	12	79	1,737	328
Total, 1880,	2,682	303	600	794	41	9	13	24	4	55	1,678	434

There were several other nationalities represented by so few that they were not included in the table. Portuguese, nine (in New London County), Polanders, five; Russians, two; Hungarians, two; Dutch, one; and one native of New Brunswick; one from Wales. These figures, except those in the last two columns, represent the nationalities of both parents. In the next to the last, one parent is of American birth, the other of foreign birth; but, as before stated, the probability is that those of American' birth are descended from foreign-born parents. The Canadians and Germans appear to be increasing, and the Swedes to less extent. As a rule the Germans and Canadian French are much more prolific than the Americans, as are the Irish. The higher death-rate, due largely to the unsanitary conditions that surround life during infancy, is a check to the gain over the American-born that to a considerable extent counterbalances the larger birth rate.

The following table shows the comparative ages of American and foreign mothers at the birth of the first to the twentieth child. As before stated, many of these born in this country were from a parentage born in foreign countries, so that the comparison is not strictly between native and foreign. The totals for the last three years are added for comparison and the number unreported. Attention is directed to the large number still unreported, although there has been a marked improvement since the first table was

constructed. The value of complete certificates in making returns
of either births or deaths is partly illustrated by the deficiencies
they cause in the tables. A little care and thoughtfulness by each
physician in the discharge of this duty, would soon remedy these
imperfections in the returns. From the first to the third child
the American mothers have very decidedly the precedence, but
from this point they lose it, and in large families the foreign population largely excel, as the table very clearly indicates. The
youngest mother reported was but fourteen, and during the three
years three such cases have been given. The oldest mentioned during the same period was sixty-nine, and two other cases where the
mother was over fifty have been reported. In constructing this
table the large number of births in manufacturing towns was
quite noticeable; this was also indicated by the birth-rates in
these places, which range proportionally much higher than in any
other kind of a community. The influence of the foreign element
is manifest also here in the native birth-rate in the manner stated,
that is, from the Irish-Americans, German-Americans, and in some
parts of the state the Canadian-Americans. The numerical importance of the Canadian emigrants is increasing each year, and they
already figure very largely in the returns. The multiplicity of
influences at work in and among the people is indicated by the
rapidly increasing number of nationalities represented, and the
growth in number of each delegation. In the eastern part of the
state the Canadians have apparently increased by emigration more
rapidly than any other race. To what extent this complex foreign
element will assimilate itself to the spirit of our institutions, time
alone will show. In many instances they come imbued with
prejudices and socialistic habits that exist in their own countries.
The extensive strikes, and the terrorism exercised to gain success
indicate this. But experience shows that all such hatreds and
prejudices grew less and less in successive generations, and the
experience of the past teaches us that there is power enough in
our institutions and nationality to assimilate and reconstruct the
most diverse elements.

NUMBER OF MOTHERS AT BIRTH OF	AMERICAN MOTHERS 14	15 to 18	18 to 20	20 to 30	30 to 40	40 to 50	TOTALS 1881	1880	1879	FOREIGN MOTHERS 15 to 18	18 to 20	20 to 30	30 to 40	40 to 50	TOTALS 1881	1880	1879	AMERICAN AND FOREIGN TOTALS 1881	1880	1879
1st child	1	118	410	1,623	317	90	2,554	2,637	2,308	17	170	857	184	35	1,263	1,157	777	3,817	3,794	3,085
2d "		15	73	1,297	375	45	1,805	1,638	1,748		25	586	311	18	940	933	884	2,745	2,571	2,632
3d "			21	695	387	25	1,128	1,163	1,404		24	392	373	22	811	906	814	2,039	2,069	2,218
4th "			3	384	395	57	839	793	739		5	417	382	75	879	819	642	1,718	1,612	1,381
5th "			1	243	287	40	571	487	454			287	390	85	762	659	551	1,333	1,146	1,005
6th "				68	276	70	414	319	367			75	332	71	478	531	387	892	850	754
7th "				31	125	58	214	195	87			34	300	66	400	510	135	614	705	222
8th "				4	55	14	73	75	58			4	114	35	153	128	72	226	203	120
9th "					29	13	43	51	30				78	51	129	87	82	171	138	112
10th "					15	12	27	30	11				49	45	94	64	40	121	94	51
11th "					13	5	18	25	7				15	26	41	27	20	59	52	27
12th "					4	8	12	15	5				24	10	34	36	18	46	51	18
13th "					2	4	6	6	4				2	7	9	7	5	15	13	9
14th "					2		2		2				5	3	8	6		10	6	2
15th "								1					1	3	4			4	1	
16th "																3			3	
17th "						2	2						1	2	2			4		
18th "						1	1							2	3					
19th "																				
20th "						1	1						2	2	4			5		
Total	1	128	508	4,345	2,282	445	7,709	7,435	7,294	17	224	2,651	2,543	568	6,003	5,869	4,422	13,723	13,304	11,646
Not reported																		893	525	2,405

MARRIAGES.

For several years there was a steady decrease in the number of marriages reported in this State, which reached the highest number in 1872, when over five thousand were reported. This period of decrease can fairly be stated to have commenced in 1874, as in the year previous, although there were less marriages reported than in 1872, still the number was fully equal to that of previous years, except '72. This decrease was not great in any one year, but the number fell below the average and continued so until 1879, when the reaction commenced. This period corresponded to one of general business depression, and the increase also corresponded to an increase in business prosperity, and has increased as that has increased and continued. This period does not indicate any peculiar hardship and lack of prosperity in this State, as the same state of affairs existed over this country generally, and over England and Europe; so also did it exert the same influence on the marriage rate, although not everywhere synchronous. In England and Wales the decrease in marriages commenced in 1874; in France, Prussia, and in the German Empire, in 1873; in Switzerland and Italy, about 1875; and was general as far as statistics are available. The forty-third report of the Registrar-General of England, to which I am indebted for many facts, states that the decrease in the frequency of marriages in England and Wales commenced in the mining districts, from thence extended to the manufacturing, reaching the agricultural last; and the increase followed the same order. In this State, as nearly as can be learned, and that partly by inference, the decrease was first shown in manufacturing districts and the cities, reaching the agricultural districts last, with the least fluctuation in them, although the decrease was felt.

A similar depression in the birth-rate was felt to some extent, but not as uniformly. But there are other causes that influence the birth-rate than business depression, especially among American women. It is difficult to secure exact figures here, as the native Americans involved with the foreign element so extensively. Enough is indicated, however, to show that if the table could be constructed to contrast American and foreign mothers, including in the latter all those whose great-grandparents were emigrants, the comparatively small number of American born women that would figure in the column reporting the birth of the second or third child, to say nothing of larger families, would be very marked, especially in the cities. In the country, American women of physical stamina are much more frequently found.

It would require a larger space, a bolder pen, and a different handling of the theme than is here allowable, to fully analyze all the causes which are at work in decreasing the marriage and birth-rates among the native race, or, rather, the race that succeeded the indigenous race, as, strictly speaking, the wild Indians have the best claim to be considered as the native race in this State and country. It is at least apparently true that the natural tendency to increase and multiply is as strong in the American race as in any other, and that, unless interfered with in some way, the birth-rate would be as high, and large families as much the rule, as in the foreign people among us. Of course, as the country grows older, and the means of living harder to gain, marriage is delayed of necessity, and one check is felt. The same influences render large families undesirable, or any increase in the burden, now just endurable, and a similar check is given to the birth-rate. This influence is still more strongly felt in the cities and towns where the population is massed, and all the values of desirable and needed materials are enhanced. To this must be added the results of the high-pressure system of education, which unfits a person for hard plodding drudgery and renders one discontented with anything short of wealth; also one phase of the modern idea of culture, which scouts the sacredness of maternity, and denies its importance in the scheme of woman's life.

Of course, it is the evil tendencies that are involved that are under discussion. It is not by any means affirmed that the necessary outcome of education and culture are in the direction intimated. But it cannot be denied that our educational systems, and the whole tendency of modern life is calculated to induce unrest and discontent, and a feverish desire for success in reaching a higher plane than that upon which circumstances started one in life. One of the resultants of this is of necessity a decrease in the marriage and birth-rate, as all cannot gain wealth or renown.

Another element that is of no small importance is the physical incapacity of many American women for the burdens of maternity, which often seems to be in a direct ratio to the culture of the mind, and the acquirement of what are called accomplishments. Not that this, either, is a necessary result, but it occurs because the mind is cultivated at the expense of the body. Of course work is out of the question for girls these days, and exercise is neglected; the result, a nervous, broken-down invalid after the birth of one child, if, indeed, the burdens of motherhood are assumed at all.

The culture of the mind to the fullest extent does not of necessity imply physical or constitutional weakness, or deterioration of the power to resist disease and strain of any kind. Indeed, the reverse is true. That educational method that advances as the natural development of the brain and mental powers directs, and recognizes the requirements of the body, securing its physiological development by proper exercise and due regard to the requirements of digestion, assimilation, and the development of its various functions (all of which require nervous force for their accomplishment, which must not be unduly diverted) results in a directly opposite condition—a sound mind in a sound body.

But the training of the schools is but one of the factors involved, although the high-pressure system, with its essential evils of worry, and the nervous irritability induced by unnecessary refinements in exactitude, produces its full share of evil, but faulty methods of life are all contributory to the result outlined. The home and social life may be as unphysiological as the school life, and the same condition results from disregard of physiological requirements in both cases. As it seems exceedingly difficult to secure for physiology and hygiene their proper place as a basis of the educational scheme, an intelligent appreciation of its laws and penalties is a thing of the future. The physician sees and deplores the results of the high pressure system in school life, the lack of right training, especially of the body, at home, and the erroneous methods in social life upon American girls in a multiplication of the difficulties and dangers of childbirth, the large number that are permanently broken down by this strain on a system with little strength or reserve power, so that they are hopeless invalids ever after, and in a multitude of ways. The outcome is to increase the disinclination for marriage, in the educated class especially, and to induce a still greater disinclination for the cares and burdens of motherhood. That which is a temporary inconvenience only to the robust and physically well-developed foreign girl, is by total neglect of the requisite means for the healthy growth and development of the body a difficult or even dangerous ordeal to the imperfectly developed physical system of the other. This imperfect physical development of many American women is also shown in the inability to nurse their own offspring, which apparently is becoming more and more common instead of a rare exception. These tendencies of modern life, together with the mistaken methods pursued during the formative period of life are, however, constant factors, while the influence of prosperity or business depression upon the rate of marriages varies.

The tendency towards individual extravagance and luxury, and the disinclination to begin small, and by self sacrifice and economy gradually secure the prizes of life, must also be taken into account among the influences decreasing the marriage-rate. This is as great in one sex perhaps as in the other, although manifested in different methods. The tendency towards individualization and separate interests, as fostered by modern thought and various social movements, as well as by the laws fixing more clearly distinct property rights, proper enough, but showing the drift, and the laxity of the divorce laws, were considered in the last report. When the physician takes his proper place in relation to education, and the influences that surround the formative period of life are regulated by the laws of physiology and hygiene, the duration of life will be prolonged, and its enjoyment in health and vigor much oftener the rule. Early marriage at the period when the sexes are mutually attracted towards each other seems to be nature's law, and transgression, due to the refinements of modern social life, brings its sure punishment in a deterioration of the race and in vice and crime. The constant introduction of fresh blood and physical vigor from the country, and also the foreign intermarriages, assist to maintain the standard aided by the natural tendency of all species to return to the original type.

The age at which marriage takes place is another indication of prosperity, and of the conditions of existence in a country. Of course the possessors of inherited health will swell the marriage rate to some extent, but if the ratio of those who marry at or near the marriageable age is proportionately large, so are the conditions of life comparatively easy, and a general state of business prosperity exists; the reverse indicates business depression and an increased difficulty in securing the necessary means for existence.

M

It is needless to remark that the state of morals, and the ratio of vice and crime, are more favorable to good order in the first case than the second. If early marriages are the rule, the chances for the formation of evil habits and tendencies of all kinds are much lessened. In fact many of the temptations to evil are removed by marriage, and a wife and children are powerful restraining influences against excesses of all kinds, and stimulating to all good qualities one is endowed with. This theme is so extensive, and the points where the dry figures of the statistician touch interesting and important questions of social economy are so frequent, that an occasional digression is perhaps pardonable. The greatest trouble is to refrain, but as it is impossible to exhaust the topics that one is thus led to take up, an incomplete presentation must serve of necessity.

The total number of marriages reported was 4,850, which is 105 more than in 1880, and thus continues the increase that commenced in 1879. Of these, in 3,147 both parties were born in this country, but how many of these are Irish-Americans, German-Americans and the like, no one can tell precisely, nor at all beyond one generation. In 989 both parties were of foreign birth. In 311 the husband was American, the wife of foreign birth; in 383 the husband was of foreign birth, the wife American. In 20 the nationality was not stated—this is a gain in completeness over last year, when there were 48 not reported. The husband was not a resident of this State in 413 instances, and both parties were non-residents in 119 instances. There were four towns where there were no marriages celebrated, but this does not of *necessity* mean that none in these towns were married during the year, as marriages are recorded in the town where the marriage is celebrated, not that in which the parties live, unless they are married at home. The towns referrred to are Marlborough, Wolcott, Union, and Lisbon. Sherman and Warren report each one marriage. In five towns two marriages were reported in each, these were Newington, Beacon Falls, Middlebury, Prospect, and Westport. The marriage and birth-rates of Beacon Falls hardly correspond this year, as it had the highest birth rate of any place in the State. There were three marriages reported in each of the following towns, East Granby, Columbia, Franklin, New Fairfield, Bridgewater, and Tolland. In eight towns there were four marriages in each, and in the same number of towns five in each; in forty towns there were over five, and less than ten in each, so that in eighty-three towns there must have been more than ten marriages in each.

The following table shows the ages of the parties at marriage, and the number of second, third, and fourth marriages reported in 1881, and also the totals for the two preceding years for comparison:

BRIDES, NO. OF FROM	Under 15.	15 to 20.	20 to 30.	30 to 40.	40 to 50.	50 to 60.	60 to 70.	70 to 80.	80 to 90.	Total, 1881.	Total, 1880.	Total, 1879.
First Marriage,..........	..	701	2,832	611	57	14	3	1	..	4,219	4,145	3,817
Second "	..	4	124	154	94	41	20	2	..	439	462	411
Third "	..	...	3	9	5	7	3	1	..	28	16	6
Fourth "	..	...	....	...	..	..	..	1	..	1	2	....
Total,................	..	705	2,959	774	156	62	25	5	..	4,687	....	....
" 1880,...........	..	5	860	2,819	669	183	55	24	10	..	4,625	....
" 1879,...........	..	736	2,788	436	151	80	25	2	2	....	....	4,234
GROOMS. First Marriage,..........	..	89	3,049	669	106	22	7	....	..	3,944	3,915	3,630
Second "	..	...	116	243	168	88	50	20	3	688	683	580
Third "	..	...	....	9	23	10	7	1	1	51	24	22
Fourth "	..	...	....	...	2	...	1	...	1	4	3	2
Total, ...	..	89	3,165	921	299	122	65	21	5	4,687	....	....
" 1880, ...	..	207	3,134	898	214	116	43	18	5	....	4,625	....
" 1879, ...	..	114	2,988	634	281	127	82	7	1	....	....	4,234
Not reported,...........	..	...	....	...	..	..	..	...	..	163	120	139
										4,850	4,745	4,373

More than five times as many women as men marry under twenty, according to the average for three years as given in the table, while in the second period from twenty to thirty, more men are married than women between these ages; and from that on, the ratio of men exceeds that of women, until during the whole period from twenty to eighty, the excess is balanced which was so largely in favor of the females under twenty.   The total number of marriages is given for each year, so that the relative proportions can be calculated if desired.

The number of men that marry more than once is quite largely in excess of that of women.   There is one case of a woman marrying for the fourth time, and four of men, while the number of third marriages in men is nearly double that reported in the case of women, there are nearly a third more instances of widowers that have remarried the second time, than of widows. It would be an interesting fact if ascertainable, whether more widows die than widowers, as so many more of the latter remarry. There were no marriages reported at unusual ages; the youngest bride reported in the three years was twelve years of age, and there were four that were fourteen. Of those over fifty, as reported, more men than women marry, two to one, so that the majority must marry women considerably younger than themselves. Of the total number reported in the table, which is 146 less than the total number of marriages, eighty-five per cent. were bachelors, fifteen per cent. widowers; the number of the divorced that remarry is not stated, nor how many bachelors married widows.

In the English report for 1880 five per cent. of bachelors married widows, and forty per cent. of the widowers married widows. Of the total number of women reported in the table ninety per cent. were spinsters, ten per cent. widows. From the records of England and Wales for thirty-six years it appears that of every 100 bachelors that marry, on an average sixteen eventually marry a second time; while out of every 100 spinsters that marry, only ten in round numbers afterwards remarry. The number of living widows is always much greater than of widowers, as men marry later in life and live a shorter time, on an average.

How much of this would be true here, it is not easy to determine; but probably the proportions would not vary very much. The percentage of first marriages varies but slightly for the three years. It is identical for the last two, and less than one per cent. different from 1879, and the percentages of subsequent marriages are nearly as uniform.

A short time since, the attention of those that make these returns was called to the nationality of the parents of those that marry. The returns have hitherto been so imperfect that no attempt to tabulate them was made. This year, while incomplete, they are apparently correctly returned, and in the most of the state fairly complete. The nationality of the parents of the brides and grooms, as reported, are as follows:

	Brides.	Grooms.
American, ...	1,794	1,778
Foreign, ...	1,435	1,397
American and Foreign, . .	13	29
Total, ...	3,242	3,204

In several instances the nationality of the parents of the bride was given and that of the groom omitted, probably the same as that stated, but, as not stated, the totals vary slightly. More than half the parentage is reported as American, fifty-five per cent. in each instance. The foreign parentage is mainly from the manufacturing towns. In the country, among the agricultural population, the foreign born element is quite small. It does not figure largely in the returns, as the increase by immigration is so small that the first comers are assimilated and begin to make returns as native to the soil, before the fresh arrivals contribute much of anything towards vital statistics. This is quite generally true in all the departments, as well as the one specially under consideration.

The third division, American and foreign, includes those where one parent (and usually the mother) is American, the other foreign; as, out of the forty-two reported, in twenty-seven the mother was American. The returns next year, it is expected, will be complete in many respects, as the blanks now in use are generally uniform, and the value of completeness is more apparent. Even in this department of vital statistics, the returns are not always promptly and correctly made. The claims of morality and good order of society would seem to be enough to induce prompt returns by those whose duty it is to solemnize marriages, even if the parties are themselves careless; but there is room for improvement here.

DIVORCES.

Many of the causes that prevent marriage have a tendency also to render divorces more frequent. This is especially true of the tendency in modern life towards individualism, making the individual the central idea rather than the home. The modern idea of woman's rights, and the higher education and culture of woman, has a strong bearing in this direction. In fact, so plainly has this been made apparent in some directions that the ground has been taken that the higher education of woman unfits her for the routine of home life, and especially for the duties and burdens of maternity. That a disinclination towards marriage and the desire to avoid maternity is a legitimate result of the modern idea of culture, in some at least of its phases, is obvious. Still farther, the ground has been taken that such education and training unfits woman for the burdens of motherhood.

The lack of physical exercise involved in so protracted an educational course; the diversion of nervous energy required for the proper development of the physical framework, and especially such diversion at the age when it is demanded for the development of new functions and for the establishment of the nerve centres requisite for the proper maintenance and healthful future exercise of these functions, tends to produce the results charged. It is not sufficient answer to state that such neglect of exercise is not necessary, and that the education, if pursued with due regard to the physical constitution, need have no such results, as long as such rational plans are not pursued. The tone of thought, and the aims and objects in life that are often tactily if not openly held up as worthy of effort to secure, are not such as the quiet happiness of home life, with its uneventful routine, will satisfy. These and similar tendencies in modern life which exalt the individual, his or her hopes, aims, and aspirations, at the expense of the home, with its blending of interests, hopes, and aims, for the common welfare of the family, have an influence in the increase of the number of divorces. The central idea of individualism is disorganizing. It may be stated thus: Every individual has certain inalienable rights and privileges that every one else is bound, under every and all circumstances, to respect, although this does not include all its modifications. With this idea the dominant one, it is easy to see how slight incompatibilities in disposition are at once magnified; fancied neglect causes the deadly plunge into licentiousness, in the mad search for the ideal bliss that marriage failed to realize.

The relation of licentiousness to divorce has been recently pretty freely discussed by the Divorce Reform Association; and grave charges are made against New England, and Connecticut especially. The decrease in the marriage rate and the increasing difficulties in maintaining a home are, it seems, more closely related to licentiousness than the mere number of divorces, especially if the decrease in marriages is caused chiefly by the difficulty in securing a maintenance and supporting a family. The cry against the small families among Americans is proper enough, but is it safe to rely upon philosophy to support ten children, when a sudden illness, or any unexpected tax upon one's resources is liable to throw one upon public aid for bread to put into the mouth of four, and one's rate of earning is permanently fixed ? That this evil is more prevalent where the question of ways and means of support has no bearing upon the matter, must be granted. Yet it is equally true that the question as stated is one that is intensely practical in very many instances. While there are no statistics available to prove the statement, it does not appear probable that the relative increase or decrease of the divorce rate has any relation to the relative amount of licentiousness, in this State at least, nor that laxity in the divorce laws produces any such results, unless in so far as the increase in divorces is considered as an evidence of licentiousness. The tendencies in modern life that have been alluded to, a logical if extreme outcome of which would be that one may seek his own comfort and present gratification at all hazards so far as others are concerned, and with as little regard to their comfort as he may, and escape retributive sufferings, have a greater effect in the production of licentiousness than laxity in the divorce laws, or frequency of divorce.

The number of divorces reported this year is 404; an increase over last year of 72. This increase, however, may be more apparent than real, as many of the cases, it has been stated, were on the docket, and the clearing the list caused the larger returns.

The ratio of divorces to marriages, while less favorable than it has been for the past two years, is still much more so than it was before the repeal of the omnibus clause ; so that unless the present year shall show an increase very decidedly over this, the proof will be pretty strongly in favor of the decrease having been partly due to this repeal. It has been intimated that the first results were more decided, because a greater stringency in the divorce laws was supposed to result from this repeal than was really the case. This at best, however, can be only a surmise.

The fact that divorce laws are intended to remedy evils, and do not produce them, as stated by Prof. Robinson, in an able article on the "Diagnostics of Divorce," and that the evils they remedy would still exist were the laws repealed, has been to a great extent overlooked by over-zealous reformers. People cannot be made holy and righteous by order of the legislature. Neither can peaceful homes be made by legislative enactment. If there are manifest evils in the laws on any subject of course a revision should be secured, but beyond a certain point very little can be secured by law in preventing the frequency of divorces. The convictions expressed by divorce legislation are very concisely stated by the author just mentioned, viz.: 1st, "That a permanent estrangement between man and wife ought to result in their permanent separation. 2d, That if permanently separated from each other neither ought to be condemned to a life of solitude, but should be allowed to form new ties of marital relationship." These commend themselves to the judgment of nearly all that have legislated upon the subject, at least in this country, and the only argument that can be urged against them is that adultery is the only cause sanctioned by the Christian religion. The attack upon divorce laws can produce no radical good while the causes that rendered the laws necessary are allowed to produce their results unopposed. The author also states that divorces are increasing, are usually in those that have been married less than ten years, and are more frequent among the middle classes, where the burdens of life and the strife for advancement embitter life and undermine affection.

The increase is favored by the increased difficulties in securing a competence, and the results in such instances follow that of necessity, end in divorce. The want of training for the duties of life by which a woman would be enabled to aid in securing the comforts of a home, and the disinclination of American women for what they term domestic drudgery, the legitimate result of education above their rank in life, or faulty home discipline, or none, have been before discussed. They are, however, fruitful agencies in producing divorce.

It is, however, easier to point out evils than to suggest remedies. That there is a wide field for effort here for a long time to come is plainly to be seen. But that any real improvement can result from narrowing the causes for which divorces can be granted to one while the present social tendencies exist, and the present agencies are at work, appears more than problematical.

The following tables show the number of divorces and the alleged causes. As several causes are often assigned, the numbers in the two tables do not balance :

NUMBER OF DIVORCES BY COUNTIES FOR THE LAST TEN YEARS.

COUNTY.	Husband's Petition.	Wife's Petition.	TOTAL IN—									
			1881.	1880.	1879.	1878.	1877.	1876.	1875.	1874.	1873.	1872.
Hartford, ...	35	45	80	49	51	74	72	91	73	86	70	75
New Haven,......	33	88	121	96	84	111	97	103	52	131	107	119
New London,.....	16	22	38	32	35	52	44	54	51	63	67	61
Fairfield,.........	29	49	78	63	63	74	92	58	73	76	71	84
Windham,........	11	25	36	33	27	28	35	17	36	46	51	28
Litchfield, ...	13	22	35	32	23	23	36	25	45	39	40	31
Middlesex, ...	1	5	6	11	14	18	23	21	25	18	25	25
Tolland,..........	5	5	10	16	19	21	28	27	21	33	26	41
Total,..........	143	261	404	332	316	401	427	396	476	492	457	464

The number of divorces to marriages in 1881 for Hartford County is 1 to 12.6, an increase in the ratio of the past two years, which was about 1 divorce to every 20 marriages, a much better showing. In New Haven the ratio was 1 to 10.6, an increase in the number of divorces, but not so great as in Hartford County. The ratio last year was 1 to 12.8, and in 1879 it was 1 to 13.5. In New London County it was 1 to 15.5, in 1880, 1 to 20. In Fairfield County the ratio was 1 to 10.4, a slight increase over that of the pre. ceding year, 1 to 11. In Windham and Litchfield Counties it was 1 to 10, against 1 to 11 in 1880. In Middlesex County there is the most favorable showing, 1 divorce to every 43 marriages ; last year, 1 to 24. Tolland County stands second, with a ratio of 1 to 15 ; last year, 1 to 13. The usual proportion is shown between the number of instances in which the wife was petitioner, to those where the husband was petitioner ; it appears by the table about twice as many women apply as men.

N

CAUSES.

	Hartford County.	New Haven County.	New London County.	Fairfield County.	Windham County.	Litchfield County.	Middlesex County.	Tolland County.	Total.
Adultery, ...	17	32	9	17	8	5	2	4	94
Intemperance, ...	24	35	3	21	5	12	1	..	101
Infamous Crime, ...	..	1	7	..	..	..	..	..	1
Cruelty, ...	15	20	16	11	8	6	1	6	74
Desertion, ...	34	52	..	40	15	17	2	10	176
Fraudulent Contract	..	..	..	1	..	..	..	..	1
Misconduct, ...	2	1	..	..	..	..	..	..	3
Life Imprisonment,	..	..	..	..	..	..	..	..	
Imbecile, ...	1	..	1	..	..	..	..	..	2

Desertion stands first as a cause for divorce, but it must be remembered that in many cases two and even three causes are alleged. This is apparently its usual rank here. Among the causes commonly assigned, intemperance, as usual, stands second. In the frequency with which this is alleged, is indicated its agency in causing domestic unhappiness and misery. When it is considered how long and persistently women endure the abuse of an intemperate husband before applying for a divorce, the magnitude of this curse becomes more apparent. That a woman should be doomed to life-long misery, and chained to a brutal sot, without hope of relief, does not appear conducive to social order, nor does her release appear to be a contribution to the increase of licentiousness. Adultery ranks third among the causes, and cruelty fourth. There are but a few cases where any other cause is assigned. The law for registration of divorces, if passed, will enable us to analyze the agencies that produce divorces more closely.

CAUSES OF DEATH.

The most interesting questions relating to prevalent diseases are those connected with the relations between malaria and typhoid fever, and to the special manifestations of each disease. That there is a well marked form of fever distinct in symptoms and course, in its clinical history in a word, which is rightly named typho-malarial, whether it is of a mixed character, or an independent type, would seem to be established. This variety of fever becomes of especial interest at this time, as it is credited with sixty-three per cent. of the deaths reported as due to malarial diseases in 1881, and the proportion of cases reported has increased steadily. Moreover it is, judging from analogy of the form most likely to persist after the other varieties have nearly if not entirely disappeared. Typho-malarial fever also, as stated before, is the variety apparently the most influenced by unsanitary conditions, although there is no evidence to show that it is conveyed by the excretions, as is the case with typhoid fever.

There has also apparently been developed a peculiar variety that is perhaps only a transitional form, called for convenience malarial fever, which is apparently a simple continued fever with malarial complications, the resultant of chronic malarial poisoning; in some instances, its period of convalescence is tedious and relapses are common; clearly marked cases of remittent fever are infrequent. Where malarial diseases have but recently appeared, on the forward edge of the wave, as it may be stated, acute intermittents and the like acute types are the ones most frequently occurring.

The relative movements in typhoid fever and malaria present many interesting and complicated questions. The relations of malaria to different diseases have been discussed repeatedly. In this state it has been claimed that the existence of malaria conferred an immunity from tubercular consumption, and in certain places the number of deaths has decreased, and for several years there have been no deaths reported from tuberculosis; on the contrary, others claim that the influence of malaria has increased the tendency to consumption and its fatality. Hertz,* after quoting the conflicting views, states that if intermittent fever is grafted on to the pulmonary affection, the progress of the latter seems to be

---

* Zeimssen's Cyclopædia, pp. 555 et seq.

accelerated, and that the existence or non-existence of phthisis or
tuberculosis in malarious regions is not to be accounted for by the
presence of intermittent fever. As the relative mortality from
consumption throughout the state has not decreased perceptibly,
there can hardly have been any marked influence upon it from
intermittent fever.

The idea that malaria displaces typhoid and the reverse has
been quite strongly advocated, but that one necessarily excludes
the other does not appear from the developments of the last few
years. Indeed the developments in both diseases, of late, render
it necessary to revise some opinions that have been regarded as
well settled. One would suppose as typhoid fever had been so
long prevalent in New England, that everything was learned that
was possible relating to its regular manifestations and peculiarities. But the extensive movement of the last six or eight years
has presented new complications and given us topics for extended
study. That there should be so marked a decrease, amounting in
many localities nearly if not quite to a total disappearance, extending over so wide an area with such diversified conditions, and not
to be accounted for by any atmospheric or telluric changes, or
other like influences that have been noted if they exist, appears at
present inexplicable from its previous record. The return to its
former frequency along the whole line where the disease had
extended, also with no known atmospheric or telluric influences
adequate to explain it; including the states of Massachusetts,
Rhode Island, and Connecticut, from which there are definite
reports, and in localities presenting the most diverse local
conditions, is also nearly as strange.

Thus, from producing on an average nearly five per cent. of the
total mortality from known causes, and in exceptional years six
per cent., as in 1854, 1867, or even seven and three-quarters per
cent., as in 1865, it decreased and increased as follows:

1875.	1876.	1877.	1878.	1879.	1880.	1881.
5.11	3.58	3.32	2.70	1.77	2.51	2.45

There is every indication that the mortality in 1882 will be very
much increased. The increase in the percentage of diarrheal
diseases, malarial fevers, and in pneumonia and other diseases,
influenced by climatic changes, causes the relative percentage of
increase of typhoid fever to appear less in 1881 than it is in
reality, as the total number of deaths from typhoid is in excess of
1880, but not very markedly—fifteen more deaths.

Thus a change of opinion in regard to the extent of the antagonism between malaria and typhoid fever has been compelled by
the recent increase of typhoid fever and its reappearance in
malarial regions. Whether the decrease in typhoid was induced
by the malarial miasm, and whether the return of typhoid is an
indication of the subsidence of malaria, are questions of the deep-
est interest, which will bear repetition until more is known. The
tendency toward the typhoid type is shown very strongly in the
regions where malaria has existed for the longest period. There
the increased frequency of typho-malarial fever is shown by the
table of deaths in each town on pages seventy-seven to eighty-two.
The comparative infrequency of acute intermittent, the mongrel
malarial fever, more and more approaching the continued type,
chronic malaria with obscure symptoms, and remittent fever, the
typho-malarial being the most common type, show the subsidence
of the malarial influence. At the forward edge of the malarial
wave the reverse is true, and acute intermittent is the more
common form. The fact, as shown by the table, that the decrease
in typhoid fever in 1879, at least in mortality, was as great in
those counties where malarial fevers have not even yet reached,
and its increase proportionately as great; and the fact that the
same decrease in the frequency of typhoid fever extended pretty
generally over the whole of Massachusetts, as shown by the last
registration report, and that the increase has been almost as rapid
as the decrease, although but a small part of the state has been
invaded by malaria, and still less had been when the decrease commenced, indicates that the movement in typhoid fever was due to
some law of periodicity in that disease, rather than to any direct
influence exerted by malaria.

The deaths in New Haven County from typhoid fever do not indicate very strongly any antagonism between the two types of disease.
From 1854 to 1861 the average number of deaths from typhoid fever
in the county was sixty-eight. Malarial fevers appeared about
1861, and had become very prevalent in the southern part of the
county, and have remained prevalent, more or less, ever since.
Yet the average increased from 1861 to 1866 to seventy-nine, and
from 1867 to 1876 to 118. Then the decrease began. Nor was
there any essential difference between the southern towns, where
malaria prevailed, and the northern, where it did not appear before
1876. It may be true that the extent of territory invaded by

malaria in 1875 inaugurated the decrease in typhoid fever, but the more closely the relative mortality is situated the clearer does it appear that there was no causative relation between the decrease in typhoid and the spread of malaria, and their existence side by side now is further proof. This, however, does not preclude the idea that the return of typhoid indicates the disappearance of malaria, nor that the onset of malaria might have, so to speak, disturbed the equilibrium and so inaugurated the movement in typhoid, without there existing any necessary antagonism between the two. Whether or no malaria will disappear, is a question for time to decide. The table shows the deaths by counties from 1854.

DEATHS FROM TYPHOID FEVER BY COUNTIES.

1854–1881.

	Hartford Co.	New Haven Co.	New London Co.	Fairfield Co.	Windham Co.	Litchfield Co.	Middlesex Co.	Tolland Co.	Total.	Per cent. known causes.
1854	83	74	13	26	23	40	17	8	284	6.20
1855	58	62	38	15	25	28	27	20	273	5.50
1856	47	62	31	16	29	36	20	15	256	4.62
1857	61	58	28	15	27	35	29	14	267	4.55
1858	58	68	25	35	25	34	16	24	285	4.89
1859	78	55	25	48	26	36	17	22	307	5.30
1860	59	91	24	28	35	40	20	17	314	4.60
1861	92	74	32	34	42	32	23	31	360	5.25
1862	99	83	45	46	24	36	24	24	381	5.10
1863	112	96	61	39	19	45	28	27	427	5.71
1864	97	117	52	43	18	54	29	32	442	5.44
1865	129	97	80	56	60	57	42	27	548	7.79
1866	77	79	49	37	36	20	15	19	332	4.95
1867	117	105	38	37	25	46	19	28	415	6.39
1868	81	104	32	33	31	30	30	25	366	5.54
1869	84	130	34	59	38	48	38	30	458	5.63
1870	77	124	31	54	37	44	35	25	427	5.49
1871	64	111	25	53	31	34	29	5	352	4.93
1872	134	134	37	67	39	39	32	24	506	5.76
1873	114	117	37	43	33	41	24	21	430	5.00
1874	69	109	48	31	32	32	28	21	370	4.68
1875	103	119	38	45	40	44	32	28	449	3.11
1876	76	78	42	42	25	32	12	20	327	3.58
1877	80	80	33	40	25	26	17	28	321	3.32
1878	39	55	30	28	27	27	25	15	260	2.70
1879	30	24	34	26	14	15	5	11	159	1.77
1880	40	47	32	31	34	21	19	18	242	4.51
1881	52	68	23	32	30	18	19	15	257	2.45

As seen by the table, there have been, previously, fluctuations in the frequency of typhoid, especially in the different counties, but no such general and extensive movement as that which commenced in 1876. There are years when the mortality was very largely in excess of the average, but no uniform period intervenes between them. Many of the town records in the table, on page seventy-seven, are exceedingly interesting, and the table, as a whole, will well repay study. The developments of the next few years will be watched with great interest.

CEREBRO—SPINAL MENINGITIS.

The evidence of a close association between this type of disease and malaria continues to accumulate. It remains frequent in the towns where malaria prevails, and often, as was the case when malaria first appeared in Hartford, takes on an epidemic type. In the earlier history of the state it is seldom noted, if ever, except as an epidemic, occasionally of great severity, and causing great mortality. It now appears to have taken on more of the characteristics of an endemic disease. The number of deaths is seventy-five, ten greater than last year. It is not confined to any age, although it is more frequent among those under twenty years of age, and among children, as was the case in epidemics in former years.

PNEUMONIA AND ACUTE LUNG DISEASES.

The prevalent type of disease for the last two years, from January to April, has been lung fever and other acute inflammatory affections of the respiratory system. The greatest mortality has been from lung fever, and is about the same as last year—713—which exceeds the average for the last six years by eighty-six, and forms six and seventy-eight one-hundredths per cent. of the total number of deaths from all causes, the percentage of the whole order being nine and eighty-one one-hundredths, the average for the past five years being nine and thirty-six one-hundredths per cent.

The prevalence of pneumonia does not seem to become fully established until January, at least the highest ratio of deaths. There are more deaths in January than in both November and December. Strangely enough, there are as many deaths in May from lung fever as in December, and no very great excess in November over the mortality in June. This extension into the summer

months has apparently been more marked of late than in former
years. This may be partly due to a closer diagnosis, as in these
spring months the type of broncho-pneumonia is more common;
that is, a general bronchitis, with diffused pneumonic patches, so
to speak, or solidification of the lung succeeding a general bronchitis. It is more than probable that many of these were formerly
reported as influenza, which does not figure to any extent in the
mortality reports of late. There are more deaths, from pneumonia,
of males than of females—392 males to 321 females, an excess of
seventy-one—about the same as in 1880, or ten per cent. more
males than females. In Canada, Province of Ontario, the excess
of males in 1880 was twenty-seven per cent.; the greatest mortality
was in March and April. Here the greatest mortality was in
January, February, and March, nearly half the total number, 334;
the number for each of these months nearly the same. The greatest
immunity is from five to twenty, and the greatest fatality from one
to five and from forty to eighty. From twenty to forty the disease is a little more frequent than from five to twenty, and very
much less than in the other periods named.

THE TEN HIGHEST CAUSES OF DEATH.

Consumption holds the first place, and has, without a near rival,
from the first. Even when epidemics prevail extensively, there is
no approach to the number of deaths caused by consumption in
the State. Pneumonia ranks second, but quite a long way behind
consumption. Old age comes next, cholera infantum fourth. The
following table shows the number from the ten highest causes of
death in 1881:

Consumption,	1,404	Diphtheria,	333
Pneumonia,	713	Apoplexy,	308
Old Age,	626	Infantile Debility,	297
Cholera Infantum,	526	Cancer,	266
Heart Disease,	492	Convulsions,	258

These represent, for the most part, the ten leading causes for
the last ten years, except that typhoid fever has usually been included, and the order has varied a little. Still, on the whole, the
table represents fairly the leading causes for the period named,
with no very radical changes. The displacement of typhoid fever
from its usual rank is the most marked change.

ZYMOTIC DISEASES.*

Small-pox, the first in the list, leads off with a larger mortality than for six years, and shows a rapid increase. There was complete exemption in 1877–8; then four deaths were reported, the next year nine, and in 1881, thirty-one, all counties being then represented except Windham and Tolland. These are more remote from the central lines of travel, which is a very significant fact with reference to the introduction of the contagion. This has been largely due to foreign emigrants, often brought into the State as domestic servants; as usual, a case or so was imputed to rags used for paper stock. The protective power of vaccination has been repeatedly shown by the exemption from the disease when repeatedly introduced in towns where vaccination has been most thorough, and its spread where this has been neglected. Measles show a marked decline, which one would expect after the epidemic of 1880. Scarlet fever is in the third year of its depressed period; the next year should show a decided increase, which should continue or be still more marked the following year, if there is any inference to be drawn from the manifestations for several such periods. Diphtheria presents a similar relation, but the changes have not been so uniform. When it reaches a high point it stays several years; that is, it has done so several times. It is time for an increase to begin. Croup presents the same average as for the last six years, and does not appear to fluctuate very much. By mistake, the mortality from whooping-cough for 1879 dropped out in the table, so the average is less than it should be. It is printed fifty-seven, and should be seventy, which makes the mortality less than the average for six years. Erysipelas shows an increase, although not very large. Diarrheal diseases show a very marked increase, especially infantile. The other principal diseases in this class have already been discussed.

AGES AND NATIONALITIES.

The greatest increase in deaths is in the productive period from twenty to sixty, when each death needlessly is a loss to the state of $1,300, as usually estimated. The increase is a little over two per cent. over 1880, in numbers 364; the data are given for estimating the value of the increase, and if one-third, the usual average estima-

* See table 6, page 61.

ted, were needless or preventable deaths, the waste in dollars would be $157,300. The incidental loss can be better imagined than described. The proportions of the nationalities have been essentially the same for the last three years—about sixty-seven per cent. born in Connecticut, ten in other states; and, among those of foreign birth, the Irish exceeding all others nearly tenfold. The deaths are pretty evenly divided among the seasons. The percentages are, at the most, but one in excess of the smallest; thus—twenty-four per cent. die in spring, and twenty-five per cent. die in autumn—a. difference, as stated, of one per cent. The deaths in summer come next to those in autumn, with two-tenths of one per cent. difference, in numbers twenty. No very important deductions can be made here.

Nor is there any very marked difference in the mortality each month; with one or two exceptions, they average very nearly alike. The highest mortality was in August, 1,073; the lowest in June, 737. With the others, a variation of about a hundred was the ordinary limit. Last year July stood highest, and in 1879 January. One of the summer months is perhaps more often reported with the greatest mortality; that is, either July or August, and more commonly July.

There was one death reported from Vernon of a man stated to have been 112 years old. The statement was declared to be probably true; but no registration of the birth, of course, could be obtained, as the only record at the time of his reputed birth was that kept of baptisms by churches. The number reported to be more than one hundred was eleven—about as usual for the last few years. The number of deaths of old people is considerably larger than last year; the greatest increase is between the ages of sixty and seventy, although each period shows a slight advance. As the total number of deaths is larger than last year, the proportion to the total number is about the same. The following is rather remarkable:

On the 25th of January, 1880, Ann C., wife of Thomas R., of Hampton, gave birth to a child which died in four days on account of malformation. The mother was quite sick at the time and for two or three weeks after. On the 28th of December, 1880, said Ann C. gave birth to a child, with an interval of but eleven months between the two.

REGISTRATION LAWS.

The following are the various acts as successively passed. Many of the provisions are repealed. A digest follows, and a proposed act uniting all the parts of acts now in force.

MARRIAGE.

Sec. 1. No man shall marry his mother, grand-mother, daughter, grand-daughter, sister, aunt, niece, step-mother, or step-daughter; no woman shall marry her father, grand-father, son, grand-son, brother, uncle, nephew, step-father or step-son; and if any man or woman shall marry within the degrees aforesaid, such marriage shall be void.

Sec. 2. No persons shall be married until one of them shall inform the registrar of the town in which the marriage is to be celebrated, or in case of his inability, the town clerk, of the name, age, color, occupation, birth-place, residence, and condition (whether single, widowed, or divorced) of each. Such registrar or town clerk shall thereupon issue his certificate that the parties therein named have complied with the provisions of this section, which certifies shall be a license for any person, authorized to celebrate marriage, to join in marriage, within said town only, the parties therein named; but no such certificate shall be issued if either of the parties is a minor, under the control of a parent or guardian, until such parent or guardian shall give to the registrar or town clerk his written consent; and any registrar or town clerk who shall knowingly issue such certificate, without such consent, shall forfeit to the State one hundred dollars; and any person who shall join any persons in marriage, without having received such certificate, shall forfeit one hundred dollars.

Sec. 3. Every person who shall join any persons in marriage, shall certify, upon the license certificate, the fact, time, and place of such marriage, and return it to the registrar of the town where it was issued, before or during the first week of the month next succeeding such marriage, and upon failure thereof shall forfeit ten dollars. The penalties for joining persons in marriage in violation of this and the preceding section, shall be paid to the town where the offense is committed, and the registrar shall sue therefor.

SEC. 4. The certificates, required by the preceding sections of this Chapter, shall be *prima facie* evidence of the facts therein stated.

SEC. 5. All judges, justices of the peace, and ordained or licensed clergymen belonging to this State, or any other State, so long as they continue in the work of the ministry, may join persons in marriage; and all marriages attempted to be celebrated by any other person shall be void; but all marriages, which shall be solemnized according to the forms and usages of any religious denomination of this State, shall be valid.

Registrars of births, marriages, and deaths shall receive for ascertaining and recording each birth, marriage, or death, ten cents; for issuing a certificate of license for marriage fifty cents; for making an abstract for the State Librarian two dollars; for each name on such abstract, over two hundred, two cents.

REGISTRAR OF BIRTHS, MARRIAGES, AND DEATHS.

SECTION 1. Every registrar of births, marriages, and deaths shall hold office for one year from the first Monday in January next succeeding his appointment, and until his successor is appointed and qualified.

SEC. 2. The registrar shall ascertain, as accurately as he can, all the births, marriages, and deaths occuring in his town, and record the same in a book or books kept by him for that purpose, in such form and with such particulars as shall be prescribed by law. He shall give licenses to marry, according to the provisions of law, and shall make and perfect all records of the birth of any child born in his town, upon the affidavit of the father or mother, stating the date of birth, the name and sex, the names, ages, color, and residence of the parents, and the occupation of the father; and his record of births shall state, in separate columns, the date of each birth, the child's name, (if any,) its sex, the names, ages, color, and residence of its parents, and the occupation of its father.

His record of marriages shall state, in separate columns, the date of each marriage solemnized in his town, the name, age, color, occupation, and birth-place of each of the parties, the residence of each prior to and at the time of marriage, the condition of each, (whether single or widowed,) immediately prior to the marriage, and the name and residence of the minister or magistrate by whom the parties were joined in marriage ; and his record of deaths shall state, in separate columns, the date of each death, the disease, or other cause producing such death, the name, age, color, sex, birth-place, last occupation, residence, and condition, (whether single or widowed,) immediately prior to the marriage, and the name and residence of the minister or magistrate by whom the parties were joined in marriage ; and his record of deaths shall state, in separate columns, the date of each death, the disease, or other cause, producing such death, the name, age, color, sex, birth-place, last occupation, residence, and condition, (whether single, married, or widowed,) of the deceased ; and he shall amend his records, as he may discover omissions or mistakes therein ; and annually, on or before the twenty-fifth day of January, shall send the State Librarian an attested abstract of said records for the year next preceding the first day of said January, which shall be made in such form as shall be prescribed by said Librarian, and shall deposit a true copy thereof with the town-clerk.

Sec. 3. Every physician or midwife, who shall have professional charge of the mother at the birth of any child, and every attendant, who may act as midwife at such a time, where no physician or midwife is employed, shall, during the first week of the month next succeeding such birth, furnish the registrar of the town wherein such birth may have taken place, a certificate, signed by such physician, midwife, or attendant, stating from the best information which the signer of said certificate can obtain, the date of such birth, the child's name, (if any,) and sex, the names, ages, color, and residence of its parents, and the occupation of its father; and every sexton or person having charge of any public or private burial place, shall, during the first week of each month, deliver to the registrar of the town in which such burial place is situated, a list of the names and dates of burial of the persons buried therein, during the month next preceding; and the physician who shall attend any deceased person shall, during the first week of the month next succeeding such decease, leave with the registrar a certificate signed by him, containing all the particulars relating to said deceased required by the preceding section to be recorded; and in case no physician attended such deceased person, the nearest of kin shall procure such certificate from some other physician or substantial inhabitant of the town, and shall leave it with the registrar within fifteen days thereafter.

SEC. 4. Each person, who shall perform the duties required by the preceding section, shall receive for each certificate so given, twenty-five cents, to be paid by the town in which such birth or death may occur.

SEC. 5. Every certificate of death shall be in the following form:

I certify from the best information which I can obtain, that   died at   on the   day of   A. D. 18 , aged   years,   months, and   days. Sex, ; condition,   ; born in   ; residence at the time of death,   ; disease, or cause of death,   ; occupation,   ; color,   .

Dated at   this   day of   , A. D. 18 .

————————————— Attending physician,

(or—Inhabitant of said town,

as the case may be.)

And the registrar of each town shall distribute to all persons therein, who in his judgment are likely to need them, blank forms for the certificates and returns required by law.

SEC. 6. No person shall take the body of a deceased person out of the town, wherein he died, without having first left with its registrar a certificate, similar in all particulars to the one prescribed in the preceding section; and the registrar shall give a permit for the removal of such body, upon receipt of said certificate.

SEC. 7. The State Librarian shall annually prepare and furnish to the registrars of the several towns, blank books for their records, and a sufficient number of blank forms for all the certificates and returns of births, marriages, and deaths, required by law; accompany the same with such instructions and explanations as he may think necessary; receive said returns, and prepare, or cause to be prepared therefrom, such tabular statements as will render them of practical utility and exhibit their results in convenient form; make report thereof annually to the General Assembly; and do whatever may be necessary to carry the provisions of this Part into effect.

Sec. 8. When any birth or death shall happen, concerning which no certificate shall be returned to the registrar, he shall obtain the information required by law respecting such birth or death, for which he shall be entitled to the compensation provided in the fourth section.

Public Acts, Revision of 1875.

AN ACT IN RELATION TO THE REGISTRATION OF BIRTHS, MARRIAGES, AND DEATHS.

Every person who shall violate any of the provisions relating to the registration of births, marriages, and deaths, shall pay for every such offence, a fine of ten dollars, to the use of the town wherein such offence is committed.

Public Acts, 1875, p. 41.

CHAPTER LXXXIII.

AN ACT IN ADDITION TO AND ALTERATION OF AN ACT CONCERNING THE REGISTRATION OF BIRTHS, MARRIAGES, AND DEATHS.

SECTION 1. Certificates of births shall state the name of each child (if it have any); the place and date of its birth; its sex; the name of its father, and the maiden name of its mother; the ages, color, residence, and nativity of its parents; the occupation of its father; the number of the child, with the name and address of the medical attendant.

SEC. 2. Certificates of death shall state the full name of the deceased; the date and place of death; the age, sex, color, and condition (single, married, or widowed—if a wife or widow, of whom); the occupation; birth-place and residence (if in a tenement house, with how many families); the name of the father; the cause or causes of death, and the duration of the decease, with the name and address of the medical attendant.

SEC. 3. No person shall open any grave for the interment or disinterment of the body of any deceased person; or deposit such dead body in any grave, vault, or tomb, in any public or private cemetery, or burial place; or disinter or remove such dead body from the town in which the death took place, without having procured from the registrar a permit therefor.

SEC. 4.   On the receipt by the registrar, of a certificate of death, properly made in the form hereafter to be furnished by the state librarian, and containing the specific facts required by section two of this act, the registrar shall issue a permit for the interment, disinterment, or removal (as the case may be,) of the body of any deceased person, stating therein the locality of the interment, disinterment, or removal.   No permit for the disinterment of the body of any deceased person during the months of June, July, August, or September, shall be issued, except when required for the purposes of a legal investigation.

SEC. 5.   Every sexton, or other person having charge of a cemetery, or other place of burial, shall, during the first week of every month, return to the registrar a list of all the interments, disinterments, or removals made by him during the month next preceding, with the dates thereof.

SEC. 6.   All laws or parts of laws that are inconsistent with this act, are hereby repealed.

SEC. 7.   This act shall take effect on the first day of January, 1877.

Public Acts, 1876, p. 129.

AN ACT IN AMENDMENT OF AN ACT ENTITLED AN ACT IN ADDITION TO AND ALTERATION OF AN ACT CONCERNING THE REGISTRATION OF BIRTHS, MARRIAGES, AND DEATHS.

SECTION 1.   That section three, chapter eighty-three, of the public acts of 1876, be, and hereby is, repealed, and the following substituted therefor: No person shall open any grave for the disinterment of the body of any deceased person, in any public or private cemetery or burial-place; or disinter or remove such dead body from the town in which the death took place, without having procured from the registrar a permit therefor.

SEC. 2.   That section four, chapter eighty-three, of the public acts of 1876, be, and hereby is, repealed, and the following substituted therefor: On the receipt by the registrar of a certificate of death, properly made in the form hereafter to be furnished by the state librarian, and containing the specific facts required by section two of the acts to which this is an amendment, the registrar shall issue a permit for the disinterment or removal of the body of any deceased person, stating therein the locality of the interment, disinterment, or removal. No permit for the disinterment of the body of any deceased person during the months of June, July, August, or September, shall be issued, except when required for the purpose of a legal investigation.

SEC. 3. Every registrar of births, marriages, and deaths, shall receive for issuing each permit as herein provided, the sum of twenty-five cents.

SEC. 4. Any registrar of births, marriages, and deaths, or any sexton neglecting or refusing to comply with the provisions of this act, shall be punished by a fine not exceeding twenty-five dollars.

SEC. 5. All acts and parts of acts inconsistent herewith are hereby repealed.

SEC. 6. This act shall take effect from its passage.

Public Acts, 1877, p. 160.

AN ACT RELATING TO RETURNS OF DIVORCES.

SECTION 1. The returns of divorces required of clerks of the superior court to the state librarian, by section three, part sixteen, chapter one, title three, of the general statutes, shall hereafter be made to the secretary of the state board of health, which returns shall be tabulated and published in the annual report of said board.

SEC. 2. This act shall take effect from its passage.

Public Acts, 1879, p. 427.

AN ACT CONCERNING THE REGISTRATION OF BIRTHS, MARRIAGES, AND DEATHS.

SECTION 1. The registrar for completing each record of birth by inserting the full name of the child, shall receive from the town ten cents, and for ascertaining, recording, and indexing each birth of which no certificate has been furnished, fifty cents.

SEC. 2. Every physician residing without the town wherein a birth or death occurred under his charge shall make return thereof to the registrar of such town, and he shall receive therefor from the registrar an order on the treasurer of such town for the fee prescribed by law.

SEC. 3. No deceased person shall be buried in any town having an incorporated city within its limits, until a burial permit, stating the place of burial and that the certificate of death required by law has been returned and recorded, has been given by the registrar, who upon receipt of such certificate shall issue such permit; and upon application, when permits are required, the attending physician of the deceased, and the coroner in case of an inquest, shall give such certificate; or if there be no attending physician, or his certificate cannot be obtained early enough, or where immediate burial is required, any member of the local board of health, or any physician employed to have charge of the poor of said town or city, shall give such certificate to the best of his knowledge and belief, and the registrar shall record the place of any burial other than in a public cemetery, and for each permit shall receive twenty-five cents from the town.

SEC. 4. In all towns the secretary or committee of each cemetery association shall report to the registrar of the town in which such cemetery is situate, the name of the sexton at present in charge of such cemetery, and of any change hereafter.

SEC. 5. Every person having charge of any burial place shall during the first week of every month return a list, for which he shall receive fifty cents, of all the interments, disinterments, and removals made by him during the next preceding month, with the dates thereof to the registrar of the town, who shall record the same in a book to be furnished by the bureau of vital statistics.

SEC. 6. Every person violating any of the provisions of this act shall be punished by a fine not exceeding twenty-five dollars.

SEC. 7. All acts and parts of acts inconsistent herewith are hereby repealed.

Public Acts, 1879, p. 454.

AN ACT ESTABLISHING A STATE BOARD OF HEALTH.

SEC. 8. That it shall be the duty of the State Board of Health to have the general supervision of the State system of registration of births, marriages, and deaths. Said board shall prepare the necessary methods and forms for obtaining and preserving such records, and to insure the faithful registration of the same in the several counties, and in the central bureau of vital statistics at the capital of the State. The said board of health shall recommend such forms and amendments of law as shall be deemed to be necessary for the thorough organization and efficiency of the registration of vital statistics throughout the State. The secretary of said board of health shall be the superintendent of registration of vital statistics. As supervised by the said board, the clerical duties and safe keeping of the bureau of vital statistics thus created shall be provided for by the Comptroller of the State, who shall also provide and furnish such apartments and stationery as said board shall require in the discharge of its duties.

TOWN OR CITY BY-LAWS.

Any town or city may enact by-laws, not contrary to law, more effectually to obtain a perfect registration of births, marriages, and deaths; and the registrar of the town in which such by-laws may be enacted shall execute their provisions under the same oath and penalty as if they were the statute laws of the State.

AN ACT CONCERNING THE BODIES OF DECEASED PERSONS.

The custody and control of the remains of deceased residents of this state is hereby granted, and shall hereafter pertain, to the husband or wife of the deceased, but if the surviving husband or wife had abandoned, and at the date of death was living apart from the deceased, or if there be no husband or wife surviving, then such custody and control is granted and shall pertain to the next of kin; but the court of probate for the district of the domicil of the deceased may at any time, upon the petition of any of the kin, award such custody and control to that relation who may seem to said court most fit for the time being to have the same.

Approved, March 1, 1882.

AN ACT CONCERNING THE RECORDS OF BIRTHS, MARRIAGES, AND DEATHS.

It shall be the duty of the registrars of births, marriages, and deaths, in the several towns, where no fire-proof safes are provided for their use, to keep the records of their office in the vaults provided for the land records in said towns.

Approved, March 9, 1882.

AN ACT IN ADDITION TO AN ACT RELATING TO CORONERS' INQUESTS.

Section one, chapter two, part one, title sixteen (page 205) of the general statutes, is hereby amended by adding at the end of

said section the following : "and it shall be the duty of said justice of the peace forthwith to leave with the registrar of births,
marriages, and deaths, a certificate signed by him, containing all
the particulars relating to said deceased, so far as can be ascertained by him, required by section two, part five, chapter three,
title three (page 28) of the general statutes, for which service he
shall receive twenty-five cents, to be taxed in his bill of costs."

Approved, March 22, 1882.

The following is the code of registration laws submitted to the
legislature. With a few exceptions in securing uniformity, it is
what is now in force in the unrepealed parts of acts, brought together in one chapter.

AN ACT IN RELATION TO THE REGISTRATION OF BIRTHS, MARRIAGES, AND DEATHS.

*Be it enacted by the Senate and House of Representatives in General
Assembly convened :*

SECTION 1. Every registrar of births, marriages, and deaths
shall be sworn to the faithful performance of his duties, and shall
hold his office for one year from the first Monday in January next
succeeding his appointment, and until his successor is appointed
and qualified.

SEC. 2. It shall be the duty of the state board of health to have
the general supervision of the registration of births, marriages, and
deaths, and the secretary of said board shall be the superintendent
of registration of vital statistics. Said board shall prescribe such
methods, and prepare such forms, as may seem to it to be necessary to obtain and preserve the faithful registration of all births,
marriages, and deaths.

SEC. 3. Every registrar shall ascertain as accurately as he can
all the births, marriages, and deaths occurring in his town, and
record the same in a book or books kept by him for that purpose,
in such form and with such particulars as shall be prescribed by
said board of health. He shall give licenses to marry, according
to the provisions of law; shall make and perfect all records of the

birth and death of the persons born or deceased in his town; and
when any birth or death shall happen of which no certificate shall
be returned to him, he shall obtain the information required by
law respecting such birth or death. He shall distribute to all
persons in his town, who in his judgment are likely to need them,
blank forms for the certificates and returns required by law to be
made to him; shall execute the provisions of all by-laws, not contrary to law, that may be enacted by any town or city to more
effectually insure therein a perfect registration of births, marriages, and deaths; shall record in the books furnished by the
bureau of vital statistics such facts concerning the births, marriages, and deaths in his town as may be therein required; shall
amend his records as he may discover mistakes or omissions therein; shall keep the records of his office, when a fire-proof safe is
not provided for his use, in the vaults provided for the land
records of his town; shall annually, on or before the 25th day of
January, send to the superintendent of vital statistics an attested
abstract, made in such form as may be prescribed by him, of said
records for the year next preceding the first day of said January,
and shall deposit a true copy thereof with the town clerk.

SEC. 4. Every physician, or midwife, who shall have professional charge of the mother at the birth of any child, and every
attendant who may act as midwife at such a time, where no physician or midwife is employed, shall, during the first week of the
month next succeeding such birth, furnish the registrar of the
town wherein such birth may have taken place a certificate, signed
by such physician, midwife, or attendant, and stating, from the
best information which can be obtained, the name, if it have any,
of such child; the place and date of its birth; its sex; the name
of its father, and the maiden name of its mother; the ages, color,
residence, and nationality of its parents; the occupation of its
father; the number of the child, and the name and address of the
medical attendant.

SEC. 5. Every physician who shall have attended any person in
his last sickness shall, unless the same shall have been done before,
during the first week of the month next succeeding such decease,
leave with the registrar a certificate signed by him, and stating,
from the best information that can be obtained, the full name of
the deceased; the place and date of death; the age, sex, color,
and condition (single, married, divorced, or widowed, and if a

wife or widow, of whom); the occupation, birth-place, and residence (if in a tenement house, with how many families); the name of the father; the cause or causes of death; the duration of the disease, and the name and address of the medical attendant. And in case no physician attended such deceased person, the nearest of kin shall procure such certificate from some other physician, or substantial inhabitant of the town, and leave it with the registrar within fifteen days after such death.

SEC. 6. The physician who may have attended any person during his last sickness, and the coroner, in case of an inquest, shall, upon application, when burial permits are required, give such certificate of death as may be required under the preceding section, and in case a physician were not in attendance, any member of the board of health of the town in which such person died, or any physician employed to take charge of the poor of said town or city, shall upon application give such certificate according to the best of his knowledge and belief.

SEC. 7. No deceased person shall be buried in any town having an incorporated city within its limits until a burial permit, stating the place of burial and that the certificate of death required by law has been returned and recorded, has been given by the registrar, who shall issue such permit whenever said certificate of death has been received by him, and the registrar shall record the place of any burial other than in a public cemetery.

SEC. 8. No person shall open any grave for the disinterment of the body of any deceased person in any public or private cemetery or burial place, or disinter or remove such dead body from the town in which the death took place, without having procured from the registrar a permit therefor.

SEC. 9. On receipt by the registrar of a certificate of death properly made, and containing the facts required by section six of this act, the registrar shall issue a permit for the disinterment or removal of the body of any deceased person, stating therein the locality of the interment, disinterment, or removal, but no permit for the disinterment of the body of any deceased person during the months of June, July, August, or September shall be issued, except when required for the purpose of a legal investigation.

SEC. 10. In all towns the secretary or committee of each cemetery association shall report to the registrar of the town in which such cemetery is situated the name of the sexton at present in charge thereof, and of any change hereafter.

SEC. 11. Every person having charge of any burial place shall, during the first week of every month, return a list of all the interments, disinterments, and removals made by him during the next preceding month, with the dates thereof, to the registrar of the town, who shall record the same in a book to be furnished by the bureau of vital statistics.

SEC. 12. Any person violating any of the provisions of the preceding sections of this act shall be punished by a fine not ex ceeding twenty-five dollars nor less than ten dollars.

SEC. 13. No person shall remove the body of any deceased person from or into the limits of any town in this State otherwise than for immediate burial in a cemetery adjacent to the town in which such person died, unless there shall be attached to the coffin or case containing such body a written or printed permit, signed by the registrar of deaths in said town, certifying the cause of death or disease of which said person died; and further certifying, in case said disease or cause of death appears by said permit to have been cholera, yellow fever, diphtheria, scarlet fever, small-pox, or other pestilential disease, that said body is enclosed in an air-tight coffin or case, hermetically sealed, or has been disinfected, or both; and any person who shall violate any provision of this section, or who shall knowingly sign any false permit, or knowingly cause or allow any false permit to be used in lieu of a permit required by this section, shall be fined not more than five hundred dollars, or imprisoned not more than six months, or both.

SEC. 14. The registrars of births, marriages, and deaths are hereby authorized and empowered to administer oaths in all cases coming before them.

SEC. 15. To the person performing the duties required by this act the following fees shall be allowed, to be paid, except in cases of license to marry and removal permits, by the town wherein the same are done: To the registrar, for completing each record of birth by procuring and inserting the full name of the child, or for recording each marriage or death, ten cents; for ascertaining, recording, and indexing each birth or death, of which no certificate has been returned to him, or for issuing a certificate of license to marry, fifty cents; for issuing each burial or removal permit, twenty-five cents; for making an abstract for the superintendent of vital statistics and the town clerk, three dollars, and when such abstract is of a record that in the aggregate contains more than two hundred names, two cents additional for each name over said two hundred. To the person furnishing the certificate required by the fourth, fifth, and sixth sections of this act, twenty-five cents for each certificate; and to the sexton or other person making the return required by the eleventh section of this act, fifty cents for each monthly return.

SEC. 16. All provisions of the several statutes and public acts hereinafter named as are now in force are hereby expressly repealed, viz.: Part five, chapter three, title three of the revised statutes; chapter twenty, title thirteen of the revised statutes; chapter seventy of the public acts of 1875; chapter eighty-three of the public acts of 1876; chapter twenty-eight of the public acts of 1877; chapter one hundred and five of the public acts of 1879; chapter fifty-nine of the public acts of 1880, and chapters five and one hundred and fourteen of the public acts of 1882.

ERRATA.

Page 10. North Branford is printed North Stamford.

Page 12. The lines, after population, for Weston and Westport are transposed.

Page 23. In class 4, there are eight, sex not stated, required to account for the total. These were omitted in the table.

Page 24. In the table septicæmia was transposed to the second order, but the total was not subtracted from the total of order one, nor added to order two; so the errors balance each other in the general total.

Page 25. "Malarial fever, 10," should be, intermittent fever, 10, in New Haven.

Page 28. "Arthritis, 9," should be, abscess, 9, in New Haven.

Page 43. "Drowned, 1," should be, Suffocation, 1, in New Hartford.

In the tables for New London and Middlesex Counties, Diseases of the Cord is printed, "Dislocation of the Cord."

Page 77. Newington is a new town, hence no deaths from typhoid fever in the columns. Beacon Falls also is a new town.

Page 77. In 1875 there were 15 deaths reported from *fever* in East Hartford, probably malarial; in 1876 there were six such cases.

Page 97. Near the bottom, for inherited health, read inherited wealth.

REPORT

BANK COMMISSIONERS

OF THE

STATE OF CONNECTICUT,

TO THE

GENERAL ASSEMBLY,

January Session, 1883.

Printed by Order of the Legislature.

HARTFORD, CONN.:
The Case, Lockwood & Brainard Co., Printers.
1883.

BANK COMMISSIONERS.

SAMUEL Q. PORTER, Unionville.

JAMES W. HYATT, Norwalk.

INDEX.

4   INDEX.

REPORTS OF SAVINGS BANKS (*Continued*):

State of Connecticut.

BANK COMMISSIONERS' REPORT.

OFFICE OF THE BANK COMMISSIONERS,
HARTFORD, January 3, 1883.

To the General Assembly of the State of Connecticut.

The Bank Commissioners, as required by law, have the honor to submit their annual report relative to the institutions coming under their supervision. Detailed reports from all the Savings Banks, State Banks, and Trust Companies are appended, and will amply repay a careful examination at the hands of the General Assembly.

SAVINGS BANKS.

The Operatives', at New Haven, having declined further business, there are now but eighty-four Savings Banks in the State, and two of these—the Dime of Middletown and the Eastford Savings Bank—are not receiving deposits, but are, as stated in the last report, closing up their affairs under direction of their officers. Some progress has been made during the year, but the final settlement with depositors cannot be made until a few pieces of real estate can be disposed of, and several mortgages closed up. Better results, it is believed, will be reached by further delay. The following is a

SUMMARY OF THE REPORTS.

RESOURCES.	October 1, 1882.	Increase since Oct. 1, 1881.	Decr'ase since Oct. 1, 1881.
Loans on Real Estate,	$38,381,167.11	....	$1,427,789.41
Loans on Stocks and Bonds,	6,310,603.84	$2,265,469.00	....
Loans on Endorsed Notes,	4,404,361.26	1,360,193.58	....
Invested in Bank Stock,	5,366,521.13	511,474.26	....
Invested in Railroad Stocks and Bonds,	7,041,311.35	2,447,791.56	....
Invested in United States Bonds,	5,649,570.58	....	1,073,908.99
Invested in State, Town, City, & Corporation Bonds	12,692,441.61	1,227,249.45	....
Real estate owned, including banking houses,	5,366,521.13	....	809,301.30
Miscellaneous Assets,	382,085.24	32,102.10	....
Cash in Bank and on hand,	3,189,094.71	542,737.75	....
Total Resources,	$88,915,870.50	$8,387,017.70	$2,810,999.70

LIABILITIES.	October 1, 1882.	Increase since Oct. 1, 1881.	Decr'ase since Oct. 1, 1881.
Deposits, - - - - - - - - -	$84,942,410.55	$4,420,109.68	....
Interest and Surplus, - - - - - -	3,894,085.77	458,700.17	....
Other Liabilities, - - - - - - -	79,374.18	....	$205,074.81
Total Liabilities, - - - - - -	$88,915,870.50	$4,878,809.85	$205,074.81

MISCELLANEOUS ITEMS.

Number of depositors having $500 or less, - -	187,471	10,508	....
Amount of such deposits, - , - - - -	$23,481,558.11	$1,775,598.92	....
Depositors having over $500 and less than $1,000, -	26,039	1,124	....
Amount of such deposits, - - - -	$18,973.110.78	$1,786,170.68	....
Depositors having $1,000 and not over $2,000, - -	18,329	587	....
Amount of such deposits, - - - - - -	$24,595,635.93	$53,991.45	....
Depositors having over $2,000, - - - - -	6.154	458	....
Amount of such deposits, - - - - -	$17,892 105.73	$854,353.68	....
Total number of depositors, - - - - -	237,993	12,627	....
Total amount of deposits, - - - -	$84,942,410.55	$4,420,109.68	....
Largest amount due a single depositor, - -	$34,833.57	$1,737.08	....
Number of accounts opened during the year, - -	40,767	3,787	....
Number of accounts closed during the year, - -	28,140	2,613	....
Income received during the year, - - -	$4,684,845.75	$226,549.26	....
Dividends declared during the year, - - -	$3,327,342.10	$156,749.32	....
Office expenses including salaries, - - -	$228,936.07	$8,874.55	....
United States and State taxes, - - - -	$188,815.70	$12,626.39	....
Deposits including interest credited, - - -	$20,440,615.26	$1,823,423.79	....
Withdrawn during the year, - - - -	$16.115,711.70	$1,507,311.15	....
Net amount from real estate owned, - - -	$122,207.97	$20,471.67	....
Amount of assets yielding no income for the year, -	$809,001.78	....	$428,010.79
Largest amount loaned to one individual, society, or corporation, - - - - - -	$400,000.00	....	....

STATE BANKS.

In January last the Union Bank of New London ceased to be a national bank and resumed its powers as a State Bank. Notice was immediately given the Bank Commissioners, as required by statute, and upon examination we found that all legal requirements had been complied with. The United States Trust Company, as authorized by the last General Assembly, has assumed the name of United States Bank, so that there are now six State Banks—three in Hartford, two in New Haven, and one in New London. The following is a summary of their condition:

ASSETS.		LIABILITIES.	
Loans and Discounts,	$3,896,340.57	Capital Stock,	$1,849,880.00
Due from Banks and		Due Depositors,	2,880,940.17
Bankers,	933,425.68	Due to Banks and Bankers,	463,847.08
Stocks and Bonds,	285,387.08	Surplus Earnings, Profit and	
Specie, Demand Notes, and		Loss, Unpaid Dividends,	329,496.06
Cash Items,	277,305.44	Circulation,	19,375.00
Real Estate,	151,079.54		
Total Asse s,	$5,543,538.31	Total Liabilities,	$5,543,538.31

TRUST COMPANIES.

The number of Trust Companies is one less than last year—there are six doing a banking business, and three dealing wholly in real estate securities.   The following is a summary of the condition of those doing a banking business:

ASSETS.		LIABILITIES.	
Notes Discounted,	$2,434,359.10	Capital Stock,	$926,600.00
Mortgage Loans,	276,769.77	Deposits,	2,611,191.03
Due from Banks and		Due Banks and Bankers,	172,006.23
Bankers,	430,073.16	Surplus, Earnings, and	
Stocks and Bonds,	268,713.14	Profit and Loss,	153,228.95
Cash and Cash Items, and		Dividends unpaid, and all	
Over-Drafts,	124,749.42	other liabilities,	3,680.29
Real Estate,	309,261.35		
Expense, Interest, Taxes,			
etc.,	22,780.56		
Total Assets,	$3,866,706.50	Total Liabilities,	$3,866,706.50

A summary of the business of the Trust Companies dealing in real estate securities shows their condition to be as follows:

ASSETS.		LIABILITIES.	
Real Estate,	$2,740,108.18	Capital Stock,	$1,675,000.00
Mortgage Notes and		Outstanding Bonds, Cer-	
Loans,	3,481,993.77	tificates, and Coupons,	4,725,434.00
Due from Banks, Cash		Interest and Sundry	
and Cash Items,	224,416.37	Credits,	168,222.86
Interest due, and other		Surplus, Earnings, and	
assets,	221,802.62	Unpaid Dividends,	159,308.62
Corporation Bonds,	30,895.00		
Expense, Insurance, Taxes,			
Safe, and Fixtures,	28,749.54		
Total Assets,	$6,727,965.48	Total Liabilities,	$6,727,965.48

DEPOSITS.

The increase in deposits during the year reaches the large sum of $4,420,109.68, a larger amount than in any year since 1872.

The total deposits aggregate $84,942,410.55, an amount never before reached.   The number of depositors, too, is greater than ever before reported, being 237,993, an increase during the year of 12,627.   Of this number 10,508 deposited $500 or less, making the total number of depositors in this class 187,471.   The number of depositors having less than $1,000 on deposit is 213,510, with an aggregate of deposits amounting to $42,454,668.89.

These facts are highly gratifying, and show that the class in whose interests savings banks were organized are largely bringing to them their savings to be cared for.

INVESTMENTS.

During the year there has been a very noticeable increase in investments in railroad bonds, amounting to $2,447,791.56 over the previous year.

Your commissioners have carefully watched these investments, and when, owing to imperfect information, unauthorized bonds have occasionally been purchased, have promptly notified the banks, and the necessary changes have been cheerfully made. The law as it now stands is a good one, and has worked to the advantage of the banks.

Another noticeable increase in investments has been in bonds of towns, cities, and other corporations, the aggregate increase amounting to $1,227,249.45. Still another large increase has been in loans upon stocks and bonds, the aggregate of such loans amounting to $6,810,603.84, an increase during the year of $2,-265,469.

The increase in bank. stock investments during the year amounts to $511,474.26, swelling the total of such investments to $5,366,521.13. There has been a decrease of $1,073,908.99 in United States bonds, largely if not wholly occasioned by the redemption calls of the government.

The cash on hand upon the 1st of October amounted to $3,189,094.71, and was generally on deposit in banks and drawing interest at about two or three per cent.

LOANS UPON REAL ESTATE.

The loans upon real estate have decreased during the year $1,427,789.41. In our report of last year, we alluded to one of the causes which tended to reduce the volume of real estate loans. The same reason still exists, viz. :—the taking of desirable loans by other moneyed institutions, which can loan a greater amount than one-half the appraised value, and at lower rates than savings banks feel warranted in doing. In 1876, with assets aggregating $81,336,631, the loans upon real estate

amounted to $55,403,988. In 1882, with assets amounting to
$88,915,870, the loans upon real estate amount to but $38,381,-
167, a decrease of $17,022,821. Deduct from this amount an
increase of $4,599,303 in real estate owned, or taken by fore-
closure, and we have a net decrease in real estate loans since
1876 of $12,423,518, with an increase in assets during the same
time of $7,579,239.

LOANS ON ENDORSED NOTES.

The aggregate of loans upon endorsed notes is $4,404,361.26,
an increase during the year of $1,360,193.58. Some portion of
these loans are of a permanent character and are legitimate, but
we regret to feel called upon to report that some of the savings
banks are in the market as purchasers of commercial paper,
which we do not consider a wise or legitimate investment of
their funds. National and State banks, and Trust companies,
are owned by stockholders who place their money at the risks of
the business, and know that the discounting of commercial paper
is often attended with very great hazards, a risk to which savings
bank depositors should not be subjected. Attention has been
called to this matter in former reports of the Bank Commissioners,
but no action has been taken by the General Assembly. The
evil has now risen to such magnitude as to justify us in again
calling attention to the matter and urging legislative action.

INCOME AND DIVIDENDS.

The earnings of the Savings Banks, the past year, aggregate
$4,634,345.75, an increase over the previous year of $226,549.26.
The dividends paid during the year amount to $3,327,342.10, an
increase of $156,749.32.

Estimating the average assets for the year at eighty-four
millions dollars, the earnings have been a fraction over five and
one-half per cent.—a slight increase over the rate of the previous
year. The earnings have exceeded the dividends $1,307,003.65,
of which amount $458,700.17 appears in the surplus account,
and the balance has materially strengthened the banks in other
ways—by charging off premiums on investments and in writing
down the book value of foreclosed real estate. Estimating the
average amount of deposits at eighty-two million five hundred
thousand dollars, the rate of interest paid is a fraction over four
and one-fourth per cent.

The following comparative table shows the rates paid by
different savings banks in 1881 and 1882, with the amount of
deposits in each class:

Per cent. of Dividends.	Number of Banks, 1882.	Amount of Deposits Oct., 1882.	Number of Banks, 1881.	Amount of Deposits Oct., 1881.
6	2	$352,693.68	2	$333,324.29
5¼	0	....	1	423,985.70
5	18	12,499,383.58	19	11,745,020.47
4¾	0	....	2	586,560.96
4½	17	11,802,549.47	10	9,757,698.35
4¼	1	92,977.39	2	432,082.06
4	42	59,926,453.96	44	56,753,337.45
3½	2	214,847.59	1	103,381.77
3	0	....	1	226,840.77
2	1	13,451.09	1	118,323.60
None.	1	40,053.79	2	41,795.45
	84	$84,942,410.55	85	$80,522,300.87

REAL ESTATE.

One of the most gratifying features of the report of the
savings banks is the reduction in the amount of real estate
owned. Each successive report since 1877 has shown an increase in the aggregate value of this asset. This year we are
enabled to report a diminution of $309,301.30. It is hoped, now
that the tide has turned, that the banks may rapidly be relieved
of the care of this species of property.

It will be noticed, also, that the assets yielding no income—
largely real estate owned—have been reduced $428,010.79.

REPORTS OF RECEIVERS.

The receivers of the Townsend Savings Bank, New Haven,
report but very little change in the condition of affairs during
the year. The nominal value of the assets on hand is $848,136.19,
estimated value, $288,045.60. The cash on hand is $57,824.70;
no dividends have been declared during the year, and the expenditures have been but $30.

The receivers of the Willimantic Trust Company have, during
the year, paid a dividend of twelve and one-half per cent. to
creditors, making 62½ per cent. thus far paid. The suit for
about $32,600, brought against the officers of the Trust Company
and others, to secure the refunding of money paid by the com-

pany for a portion of its capital stock, still lingers in the courts.
If the decision is in favor of the receivers, creditors will probably be paid in full, otherwise there will be a loss of twenty-five
per cent., or thereabouts. The receivers report assets on hand
of a nominal value of $51,850.78; estimated value, $11,929.90.
Expenses for the year, $201.

The receiver of the Thompsonville Savings Bank has closed
up its business and made his final report to the court.

CONCLUSION.

The exibit herein made of the Savings Banks shows them to
be in an exceedingly satisfactory condition, more so than at any
time since the financial disturbance of 1873. The increase in
the volume of deposits might have been much greater had the
banks taken all the funds offered, instead of wisely limiting
their receipts from individuals to a sum much less than the
maximum amount authorized by statute.

Securities in which Savings Banks are authorized to invest
yield but about four per cent. upon their market value, and are
daily becoming more difficult to obtain. The fact that the banks
are authorized to invest in certain specified securities increases
their commercial value and correspondingly reduces their net
interest return.

The time is not far distant when it will be wise in view of
these facts, and the further fact that the government has established an interest rate of three per cent. upon its bonds, for
savings banks to readjust their dividend rates. So long as they
continue to pay higher rates than the government, so long will
they be pressed to receive deposits from parties abundantly able
to care for their own property. The New Haven Savings Bank,
with deposits amounting to nearly five million dollars, has already adopted a graduated scale of interest rates, paying four
per cent. upon deposits of two thousand dollars and less, and
three per cent. upon all sums in excess of that amount. The
best banks in New York and other places make a similar discrimination in favor of small depositors, and the general adoption by
our Savings Banks of a graduated scale for the payment of
interest, is a point worthy of serious consideration. It would
relieve them of much of the pressure to receive deposits from
persons having large sums to invest and who are quite content

with four per cent. free of taxes, and would enable the banks to invest in the most solid securities, even if they did not yield as large an income as others coming within the law.

The officers of the Savings Banks are fully alive to the responsibilities of the important trust in their hands, and we take pleasure in bearing testimony to the care and fidelity with which their duties are discharged. There is no important interest in our State, we are confident, which is managed more intelligently and with greater economy.

SAMUEL Q. PORTER, } *Bank*
JAMES W. HYATT, } *Commissioners.*

REPORTS OF SAVINGS BANKS,

October 1, 1882.

2

BERLIN SAVINGS BANK, KENSINGTON.

ROYAL R. UPSON, Treasurer.   INCORPORATED, 1873.

STATEMENT, OCTOBER 1, 1882.

LIABILITIES.		ASSETS.	
Whole Amount of Deposits,	$101,922.78	Loans on Real Estate, .	$59,784.00
Surplus Account, }		Loans on Stocks and Bonds,	12,100.00
Interest Account, } . . 4,455.20		Loans on Endorsed Notes, .	985.00
		United States Bonds, . .	1,021.25
		Town Orders, . . .	7,000.00
		Bank Stocks in Connecticut,	13,062.00
		Bank Stocks in other States,	4,773.75
		Cash in Bank, . . .	6,330.88
		Cash on hand, . . .	1,321.10
Total Liabilities, . . $106,377.98		Total Assets, . . $106,377.98	

INVESTMENTS.

DESCRIPTION.	PAR VALUE.	COST.	MARKET VALUE.
UNITED STATES BONDS.			
4s of 1907, coupon, ... $	1,000.00	1,021.25	1,180.00
TOWN ORDERS.			
Town of Berlin, ...	7,000.00	7,000.00	7,000.00
BANK STOCKS.			
33 shares Conn. River Banking Co., Hartford,	1,650.00	1,485.00	1,683.00
12 " Farmers & Mechanics Nat. Bank, Hfd.,	1,200.00	1,368.00	1,620.00
10 " First National Bank, Hartford, .	1,000.00	1,012.50	1,220.00
7 " National Exchange Bank, Hartford,	350.00	476.00	539.00
44 " City National Bank, Hartford, .	4,400.00	4,555.50	3,960.00
13 " Middletown National Bank, . .	975.00	1,354.00	
1 " American " " Hartford,	50.00	68.50	70.00
14 " Conn. Trust & Safe Dep. Co., "	1,400.00	1,886.00	1,575.00
10 " Hartford Trust Co., . . .	1,000.00	1,002.50	1,010.00
3 " Middlesex County National Bank,	300.00	354.00	
20 " Merchants' Ex. Nat. Bank, N. Y. City,	1,000.00	1,000.00	980.00
10 " American " " " "	1,000.00	1,251.25	1,310.00
20 " Fourth National " " "	2,000.00	2,522.50	2,460.00

MISCELLANEOUS ITEMS.

1. . Number of depositors having $500 or less,   311; total amount, $26,854.41
2. Number of depositors having over $500 and
   · less than $1,000; . . . . 44; total amount,   29,362.69
3. Number of depositors having $1,000 and not
   over $2,000, ... 29; total amount,   35,047.05
4. Number of depositors having over $2,000,   5; total amount,   10,658.63

5. Total number of depositors, ... 389; total deposits, $101,922.78

BERLIN SAVINGS BANK.—Continued.

MISCELLANEOUS ITEMS.—Continued.

6. Largest amount due a single depositor, $2,223.14.
7. Number of accounts opened during the year, 72; number closed, 20.
8. Amount of income received during the year, $5,127.43.
9. Amount of dividends declared during the year, $4,301.23.
10. Amount deposited, including interest credited, the past year, $34,630.49.
11. Amount withdrawn during the year, $16,526.64.
12. Increase of deposits the past year, $18,103.85.
13. Amount carried to surplus or profit and loss during the year, $612.54.
14. Rate of dividend the last year, 5 per cent.; paid, January 1st and July 1st.
15. State tax during the past year, $91.16; U. S. tax, none.
16. Total office expenses the past year, including salaries, $100.00.
17. Net amount of income during the year from real estate owned, none.
18. Amount of assets yielding no income during the year, $1,710.00.
19. Are all loans upon real estate secured by first mortgage? Yes.
20. Largest amount loaned to one individual, company, society, or corporation, $10,000.00.
21. Date of annual meeting for choice of officers, third Wednesday July.

OFFICERS.—President, Alfred North; Treasurer, Royal R. Upson; Directors or Trustees, Alfred North, Henry N. Galpin, J. T. Hart, William H. Risley, Edward E. Stevens, William Bulkley, John Norton.

BRIDGEPORT SAVINGS BANK.

ALEX. HAWLEY, Treasurer.   INCORPORATED, 1842.

STATEMENT, OCTOBER 1, 1882.

LIABILITIES.		ASSETS.	
Whole Amt. of Deposits,	$3,009,320.39	Loans on Real Estate,	$1,466,621.00
Surplus Account,	153,313.98	Loans on Stocks and Bonds,	365,600.00
Interest Account,	52,748.01	United States Bonds,	586,200.00
Rent Account,	590.91	Town, City, and Corp. B'ds,	557,300.00
		School District Note,	6,000.00
		Railroad Bonds,	5,000.00
		Bank Stocks in Connecticut,	17,500.00
		Bank Stocks in other States,	29,988.00
		Real Estate by Foreclosure,	99,477.40
		Banking House,	50,000.00
		Profit and Loss,	21.99
		Expense Account,	2,871.88
		Land in Madison, Wis.,	3,800.00
		Cash in Bank,	24,394.68
		Cash on hand,	1,198.34
Total Liabilities,	$3,215,973.29	Total Assets,	$3,215,973.29

INVESTMENTS.

DESCRIPTION.	PAR VALUE.	COST.	MARKET VALUE.
UNITED STATES BONDS.			
Fives of 1881, Registered (Extended 3½s),	$ 200,000.00	200,000.00	201,500.00
Fours of 1907, Registered,	305,000.00	305,000.00	364,856.25
Fours of 1907, Coupon,	1,200.00	1,200.00	1,435.50
Three per cents,	80,000.00	80,000.00	80,000.00
TOWN, CITY, AND CORPORATION BONDS.			
Bridgeport Town Bonds, 4½s,	39,000.00	39,000.00	40,950.00
" " " 6s,	7,500.00	7,500.00	8,025.00
Middletown " " 6s,	1,000.00	1,000.00	1,140.00
Fairfield " " 6s,	37,000.00	37,000.00	41,500.00
Danbury " " 5s,	20,000.00	20,000.00	21,000.00
Hartford " " 4½s,	60,000.00	60,000.00	63,000.00
Bennington, Vt., Town Bonds, 4s,	60,000.00	60,000.00	61,800.00
Bridgeport City Bonds, 5s,	60,000.00	60,000.00	70,200.00
New Haven " " 7s,	10,000.00	10,000.00	12,600.00
Danbury Water Bonds, 4½s,	77,000.00	77,000.00	80,850.00
Fair Haven, Vt., " 5s,	31,800.00	31,800.00	34,344.00
N. H. Quinnipiac Bridge Bonds, 4s,	100,000.00	100,000.00	104,000.00
Cleveland City Bonds, 4s,	54,000.00	54,000.00	55,620.00
SCHOOL DISTRICT NOTE.			
Newfield School District,	6,000.00	6,000.00	6,000.00
RAILROAD BONDS.			
Milwaukee & St. Paul Railroad Co.,	5,000.00	5,000.00	6,500.00

BRIDGEPORT SAVINGS BANK.—Continued.

INVESTMENTS.—Continued.

DESCRIPTION.	PAR VALUE.	COST.	MARKET VALUE.
BANK STOCKS.			
15 shares Metropolitan National, New York, $	1,500.00	1,500.00	2,625.00
20 " Park " "	2,000.00	2,000.00	3,140.00
20 " Hanover " "	2,000.00	2,000.00	2,700.00
26 " Gallatin " "	1,800.00	1,800.00	1,755.00
40 " American Exchange Nat., "	4,000.00	4,000.00	5,200.00
50 " Commerce National, "	5,000.00	5,000.00	7,500.00
8 " Bank of State " "	800.00	800.00	1,040.00
140 " Chatham "	3,500.00	3,500.00	4,375.00
51 " Phœnix " "	1,020.00	1,020.00	1,040.40
52 " Manuf. & Merchants Nat., "	468.00	468.00	In Liq.
15 " Continental National, "	1,500.00	1,500.00	1,800.00
66 " Merchants " "	3,300.00	3,300.00	4,290.00
30 " Importers and Traders, "	3,000.00	3,000.00	7,500.00
6 " Shoe & Leather, National, "	600.00	600.00	750.00
30 " Ætna " Hartford,	3,000.00	3,000.00	4,000.00
70 " Connecticut " Bridgeport,	7,000.00	7,000.00	9,450.00
10 " City " "	1,000.00	1,000.00	1,300.00
45 " First " "	4,500.00	4,500.00	7,425.00
20 " Pequonnock " "	2,000.00	2,000.00	2,500.00

MISCELLANEOUS ITEMS.

1. Number of depositors having $500 or less, 6,737; total amount, $885,935.39
2. Number of depositors having over $500 and less than $1,000,. 938; total amount, 659,385.00
3. Number of depositors having $1,000 and not over $2,000, 762; total amount, 1,109,629.00
4. Number of depositors having over $2,000, 121; total amount, 354,371.00

5. Total number of depositors, . . . 8,558; total deposits, $3,009,320.39
6. Largest amount due a single depositor, $7,017.
7. Number of accounts opened during the year, 1,244; number closed, 1,062.
8. Amount of income received during the year, $167,743.06.
9. Amount of dividends declared during the year, $130,941.85.
10. Amount deposited, including interest credited, the past year, $448,030.06.
11. Amount withdrawn during the year, $495,168.97.
12. Decrease of deposits the past year, $47,138.91.
13. Amount carried to surplus or profit and loss during the year, $17,898.41.
14. Rate of dividend the last year, 4¼ per cent.; when paid, Jan. 1882, 2¼ per cent., and July, 1882, 2 per cent.
15. State tax during the past year, $7,028.48; U. S. tax, none.
16. Total office expenses the past year, including salaries, 7,852.57.
17. Net amount of income during the year from real estate owned, $2,858.85.
18. Amount of assets yielding no income during the year, $10,866.40.
19. Are all loans upon real estate secured by first mortgage? Yes.
20. Largest amount loaned to one individual, company, society, or corporation, $100,000.00.
21. Date of annual meeting for choice of officers, June.

Officers.—President, E. S. Hawley; Treasurer, Alexander Hawley; Vice-Presidents, S. C. Trubee, L. W. Clark; Directors or Trustees, Andrew E. Joy, Ezekiel Birdsey, W. R. Higby, Edward Sterling, Curtis Thompson, Philip Conrad, T. B. DeForest, F. B. Hawley, W. H. Perry, F. N. Benham.

BRISTOL SAVINGS BANK.

MILES L. PECK, Treasurer.   INCORPORATED, 1870.

STATEMENT, OCTOBER 1, 1882.

LIABILITIES.		ASSETS.	
Whole Amount of Deposits,	$643,959.62	Loans on Real Estate, .	$436,526.00
Surplus Account, }		Loans on Stocks and Bonds,	32,856.00
Interest Account, } . .	26,090.63	Loans on Endorsed Notes,.	3,774.25
		United States Bonds, . .	11,000.00
		Town, City, and Corp'n Bonds,	70,500.00
		School District Orders, .	8,200.00
		Railroad Bonds, . . .	6,000.00
		Bank Stocks in Connecticut,	81,250.00
		Bank Stocks in other States,	2,000.00
		Real Estate by Foreclosure,	2,000.00
		Banking House, . . .	8,000.00
		Cash in Bank, . . .	4,737.00
		Cash on hand, . . .	3,207.00
Total Liabilities, . .	$670,050.25	Total Assets, . .	$670,050.25

INVESTMENTS.

DESCRIPTION.	PAR VALUE.	COST.	MARKET VALUE.
UNITED STATES BONDS.			
4s of 1907, Registered, ... $	10,000.00	10,000.00	11,800.00
TOWN, CITY, AND CORPORATION BONDS.			
Hartford, Town Bonds, ...	11,000.00	11,412.50	11,385.00
Brooklyn, N. Y., City Bonds, . . .	21,000.00	23,650.00	23,650.00
Rochester, N. Y., Bonds, . . .	5,000.00	5,800.00	5,800.00
Cincinnati, O., Bonds, ...	15,000.00	18,365.00	18,365.00
Chicago, Ill., Bonds, ...	6,000.00	6,840.00	6,840.00
Bath, Maine., Bonds, ...	7,500.00	8,012.50	8,000.00
SCHOOL DISTRICT ORDERS.			
Bristol First School District, ...	3,000.00	3,000.00	3,000.00
Bristol Third " "	4,000.00	4,000.00	4,000.00
Bristol Second " "	1,000.00	1,000.00	1,000.00
Bristol Eighth " "	45.00	45.00	45.00
Burlington Fifth School District, . .	155.00	155.00	155.00
RAILROAD BONDS.			
New York Central & Hudson River, . .	5,000.00	6,687.50	6,600.00
BANK STOCKS.			
44 shares Hartford National Bank, Hartford,	4,400.00	6,600.00	7,700.00
60 " Exchange " " " .	3,000.00	4,000.00	4,500.00
289 " American " " " .	14,450.00	18,174.00	20,280.00
11 " Charter Oak " . " " .	1,100.00	1,375.00	1,540.00
8 " Ætna " " " .	800.00	960.00	1,040.00
7 : City " " " .	700.00	714.00	630.00
20 " Mercantile " " " .	2,000.00	2,440.00	2,600.00
28 " First " " " .	2,800.00	3,780.00	3,360.00

BRISTOL SAVINGS BANK.—Continued.

INVESTMENTS.—Continued.

DESCRIPTION.	PAR VALUE.	COST.	MARKET VALUE.
BANK STOCKS.—CONTINUED.			
61 shares Yale National Bank, New Haven, $	6,100.00	7,200.00	7,320.00
6 " Merchants " " "	300.00	325.00	345.00
15 " Tradesmen " " "	1,500.00	2,250.00	2,250.00
13 " Home " " Meriden, .	1,300.00	1,530.00	1,560.00
10 " First " " .	1,000.00	1,100.00	1,120.00
12 " Central " " Middletown,	900.00	1,272.00	1,272.00
10 " First " " "	1,000.00	1,140.00	1,150.00
50 " First " " Norwich, .	5,000.00	5,600.00	5,750.00
100 " Merchants " " "	4,000.00	4,000.00	4,080.00
5 " First " " Portland, .	500.00	565.00	565.00
9 " Rockville " " Rockville,	900.00	990.00	990.00
30 " Pahquioque " " Danbury, .	3,000.00	3,630.00	3,690.00
15 " Deep River " " Deep River,	1,500.00	2,100.00	2,100.00
60 " Bristol " " Bristol, .	6,000.00	6,000.00	7,200.00
25 " New Britain " " New Britain,	2,500.00	3,250.00	3,750.00
10 " First " " Wallingford,	1,000.00	1,000.00	1,000.00
25 " Conn. Trust Co., Hartford, . .	2,500.00	2,325.00	2,800.00
20 " Fourth National Bank, New York,	2,000.00	2,240.00	2,500.00

MISCELLANEOUS ITEMS.

1. Number of depositors having $500 or less, . 2,060; total amount, $221,225.23
2. Number of depositors having over $500 and less than $1,000, ... 234; total amount, 162,323.78
3. Number of depositors having $1,000 and not over $2,000, ... 135; total amount, 190,381.37
4. Number of depositors having over $2,000, . 29; total amount, 70,029.24

5. Total number of depositors, . . . 2,458; total deposits, $643,959.62
6. Largest amount due a single depositor, $3,923.97.
7. Number of accounts opened during the year, 539; number closed, 369.
8. Amount of income received during the year, $37,251.13.
9. Amount of dividends declared during the year, $27,815.36.
10. Amount deposited, including interest credited, the past year, $224,493.40.
11. Amount withdrawn during the year, $139,429.99.
12. Increase of deposits the past year, $85,063.41.
13. Amount carried to surplus or profit and loss during the year, $3,976.87.
14. Rate of dividend the last year, 5 per cent.; when paid, January and July.
15. State tax during the past year, $1,274.62; U. S. tax, 190.00.
16. Total office expenses the past year, including salaries, $1,824.88.
17. Net amount of income during the year from real estate owned, $150.35.
18. Amount of assets yielding no income during the year, none.
19. Are all loans upon real estate secured by first mortgage? Yes.
20. Largest amount loaned to one individual, company, society, or corporation, $16,000.00.
21. Date of annual meeting for choice of officers, third Wednesday in July.

OFFICERS.—President, Henry A. Seymour; Treasurer, Miles L. Peck; Directors or Trustees, William W. Carter, Nathan L. Birge, Julius R. Mitchell, Edward N. Pierce, Henry Beckwith, John H. Sessions, Samuel P. Newell, N. Taylor Baldwin, Laporte Hubbell, Gad Norton.

BROOKLYN SAVINGS BANK.

CLARENCE A. POTTER, Treasurer.   INCORPORATED, 1872.

STATEMENT, OCTOBER 1, 1882.

LIABILITIES.		ASSETS.	
Whole Amount of Deposits,	$444,735.57	Loans on Real Estate,	$184,245.00
Surplus Account,	8,000.00	Loans on Stocks and Bonds,	54,075.00
Interest Account,	2,256.76	United States Bonds,	12,345.00
Rent Account,	89.30	State Bonds,	1,500.00
		Town, City, and Corp'n Bonds,	65,834.08
		Town, City, and B'gh Orders,	3,000.00
		Railroad Bonds,	55,605.61
		Bank Stocks in Connecticut,	14,545.50
		Real Estate by Foreclosure,	42,842.69
		Insurance Account,	7.25
		Expense Account,	169.85
		Expense on R. Est. and Taxes,	3,327.89
		Cash in Bank,	15,639.01
		Cash on Hand,	1,944.75
Total Liabilities,	$455,081.63	Total Assets,	$455,081.63

INVESTMENTS.

DESCRIPTION.	PAR VALUE.	COST.	MARKET VALUE.
UNITED STATES BONDS.			
4½s of 1891, Registered, ... $	12,000.00	12,345.00	14,280.00
STATE BONDS.			
State of Connecticut 6s of 1885, . . .	1,500.00	1,500.00	1,575.00
TOWN, CITY, AND CORPORATION BONDS.			
Newton, Mass., 6s, Water Loan, 1905,	10,000.00	10,525.00	13,150.00
Providence, R. I., 4½s, High St. School, 1884,	3,500.00	3,548.75	3,525.00
Meriden, Conn., 6s, Improvement, 1893,	10,000.00	10,350.00	12,500.00
Hartford, " 6s, Capitol, 1897,	7,000.00	7,000.00	9,100.00
Lawrence, Mass., 6s, Water Loan, 1890,	3,000.00	3,315.00	3,600.00
Lynn, " 6s, General " 1891,	2,000.00	2,210.00	2,300.00
Boston, " 5s, City " 1885,	6,000.00	6,285.00	6,420.00
Cleveland, Ohio, 6s, Street Imp't Loan, 1883,	3,000.00	3,120.00	3,060.00
Essex (Town), Ct., 4½s, General Loan, 1900,	5,000.00	5,200.00	5,300.00
Cincinnati, Ohio, 7₁₀⁶s, " 1902,	5,000.00	6,550.00	6,550.00
" " 7s, " 1908,	6,000.00	7,735.33	7,735.33
TOWN, CITY, AND BOROUGH ORDERS.			
Town of Brooklyn, Conn., ...	3,000.00	3,000.00	3,000.00
RAILROAD BONDS.			
Norwich & Worcester Railroad, 1st 7s, . .	10,000.00	11,600.00	12,000.00
Chicago & Alton " 1st 7s, . .	20,000.00	24,300.00	25,000.00
New York & Harlem " 1st 7s, . .	15,000.00	19,705.61	20,250.00
BANK STOCKS.			
95 shares Windham County National, Brooklyn,	9,500.00	11,145.50	11,400.00
10 " First National, Killingly, . .	1,000.00	1,200.00	1,200.00
55 " Merchants National, . . .	2,200.00	2,200.00	2,255.00

BROOKLYN SAVINGS BANK—Continued.

MISCELLANEOUS ITEMS.

1. Number of depositors having $500 or less,   818; total amount, $111,999.67
2. Number of depositors having over $500 and
       less than $1,000, ...   174; total amount,   120,948.77
3. Number of depositors having $1,000 and not
       over $2,000, ...   :   113; total amount,   149,938.77
4. Number of depositors having over $2,000,   .   23; total amount,   61,848.36

Total number of depositors,   .   .   .   1,123; total deposits, $444,735.57
Largest amount due a single depositor, $4,702.71.
Number of accounts opened during the year, 181; number closed, 116.
Amount of income received during the year, $25,517.04.
Amount of dividends declared during the year, $16,771.77.
10. Amount deposited, including interest credited, the past year, $98,969.26.
11. Amount withdrawn during the year, 73,550.12.
12. Increase of deposits the past year, $25,419.14.
13. Amount carried to surplus or profit and loss during the year, $6,059.92.
14. Rate of dividend the last year, 4 per cent., paid March and September.
15. State tax during the past year, $776.60; U. States tax, $8.22.
16. Total office expenses the past year, including salaries, $1,360.55.
17. Net amount of income during the year from real estate owned, $2,112.66.
18. Amount of assets yielding no income during the year, $17,172.85.
19. Are all loans upon real estate secured by first mortgage? Yes.
20. Largest amount loaned to one individual, company, society or corporation,
       $16,250.
21. Date of annual meeting for choice of officers, third Wednesday in July.

OFFICERS.—President, William Woodbridge; Vice-President, Frank E. Baker; Treasurer, Clarence A. Potter; Directors or Trustees, Enos L. Preston, William N. Putnam, Lewis Searls, John P. Wood, Alfred Pray, Thomas R. Baxter, Preston B. Sibley.

CITY SAVINGS BANK, MERIDEN.

C. L. ROCKWELL, Treasurer.   INCORPORATED, 1874.

STATEMENT, OCTOBER 1, 1882.

LIABILITIES.		ASSETS.	
Whole Amount of Deposits,	$476,800.69	Loans on Real Estate, . .	$341,325.00
Surplus Account, . .	10,000.00	Bank Stocks in Connecticut,	111,400.00
Interest Account, . .	6,763.05	Bank Stocks in other States,	18,620.00
		Tax Account, . . .	532.34
		Expense Account, . .	32.20
		Cash in Bank, . . .	21,654.20
Total Liabilities, . .	$493,563.74	Total Assets, . .	$493,563.74

INVESTMENTS.

DESCRIPTION.	PAR VALUE.	COST.	MARKET VALUE.
BANK STOCKS.			
405 shares First National Bank, Meriden, . $	40,500.00	42,500.00	47,790.00
400 " Home " " . .	40,000.00	42,000.00	50,000.00
27 " Meriden, " " . .	2,700.00	2,700.00	3,375.00
100 " Nat. Bank of Norwalk, . . .	10,000.00	10,000.00	11,000.00
30 " Fairfield Co., " . . .	3,000.00	3,000.00	3,600.00
50 " First National, So. Norwalk,	5,000.00	5,000.00	5,500.00
3 " First National, Middletown, . .	300.00	300.00	360.00
15 " New Britain, New Britain, . .	1,500.00	1,500.00	2,100.00
110 " Merchants, Norwich, . . .	4,400.00	4,400.00	4,400.00
66 " Bank of No. America, New York City,	4,620.00	4,620.00	4,620.00
100 " Bowery National, New York City,	10,000.00	14,000.00	15,000.00

MISCELLANEOUS.

1. Number of depositors having $500 or less,   1,088; total amount, $138,785.42
2. Number of depositors having over $500 and less than $1,000, . . .   140; total amount,   94,601.20
3. Number of depositors having $1,000 and not over $2,000, ...   137; total amount,   162,161.79
4. Number of depositors having over $2,000,   31; total amount,   81,252.28

   Total number of depositors, . . .   1,396; total deposits, $476.800.69
   Largest amount due a single depositor, $6,257.10.
   Number of accounts opened during the year, 345; number closed, 182.
   Amount of income received during the year, $28,291.66.
   Amount of dividends declared during the year, $21,575.69.
10. Amount deposited, including interest credited, the past year, $142,991.78.
11. Amount withdrawn during the year, $90,176.79.
12. Increase of deposits the past year, $52,814.99.

28 BANK COMMISSIONERS' REPORT.

CITY SAVINGS BANK, MERIDEN.—Continued.

MISCELLANEOUS ITEMS.—Continued.

13. Amount carried to surplus or profit and loss during the year, $4,417.
14. Rate of dividend the last year, 5 per cent.; when paid, January and July.
15. State tax during the past year, $1,097.69; United States tax, $90.
16. Total office expenses the past year, including salaries, $1,111.28.
17. Net amount of income during the year from real estate owned, do not own any.
18. Amount of assets yielding no income during the year, none.
19. Are all loans upon real estate secures by first mortgage? Yes.
20. Largest amount loaned to one individual, company, society, or corporation, $35,000.
21. Date of annual meeting for choice of officers, second Monday in July.

OFFICERS.—President, John D. Billard; Treasurer, Chas. L. Rockwell; Directors or Trustees, W. W. Lyman, John C. Byxbee, Ratcliffe Hicks; N. L. Bradley, Wm. Lewis, Chas. L. Upham, Geo. W. Smith, Dexter W. Parker, Erwin D. Hall, H. L. Schleiter, W. H. Miller, John Tait, Seth J. Hall, Randolph Linsley.

CANAAN SAVINGS BANK.

JOSEPH W. PEET, Treasurer.   INCORPORATED, 1872.

STATEMENT, OCTOBER 1, 1882.

LIABILITIES.		ASSETS.	
Whole Amount of Deposits,	$92,593.45	Loans on Real Estate, .	$26,103.68
Surplus Account, . .	3,523.20	Loans on Stocks and Bonds,	2,080.00
Interest Account, . .	1,865.74	Loans on Endorsed Notes, .	4,580.04
		United States Bonds, . .	11,901.89
		State Bonds, . . .	5,491.05
		Town, City, and Corp'n Bonds,	4,579.10
		Town, City, and Boro' Orders,	1,000.00
		Railroad Bonds, . .	25,777.50
		Bank Stocks in Connecticut,	1,277.50
		Bank Stocks in other States,	6,160.12
		Cash in Bank, . . .	5,970.75
		Cash on hand, . . .	3,110.76
Total Liabilities, . .	$97,982.39	Total Assets, . .	97,982.39

INVESTMENTS.

DESCRIPTION.	PAR VALUE.	COST.	MARKET VALUE.
UNITED STATES BONDS.			
4s of 1907, registered, ... $	7,300.00	} 11,901.89	12,120.00
4s of 1907, coupon, ...	2,800.00		
STATE BONDS.			
State of Missouri, 6 per cent., . . .	5,000.00	5,491.05	5,500.00
TOWN, CITY, AND CORPORATION BONDS.			
City of St. Louis, 6 per cent., . . .	3,000.00	3,220.00	3,300.00
City of Cincinnati, 7-30, ...	1,000.00	1,359.10	1,359.10
TOWN, CITY, AND BOROUGH ORDERS.			
Town of No. Canaan, 5 per cent., . . .	1,000.00	1,000.00	1,000.00
RAILROAD BONDS.			
Chicago, Rock Island & Pacific, 6s, . .	11,000.00	13,795.00	14,300.00
New York Central & Hudson, 7s, . .	9,000.00	11,982.50	12,100.00
BANK STOCKS.			
10 shares National Iron Bank, . .	1,000.00	1,277.50	1,277.50
10 " Fourth National New York, . .	1,000.00	1,072.50	1,280.00
5 " Metropolitan "	500.00	586.25	880.00
31 " American Exchange " . .	3,100.00	3,503.87	4,216.00
10 " Central National " . .	1,000.00	997.50	1,280.00

CANAAN SAVINGS BANK.—Continued.

MISCELLANEOUS ITEMS.

1. Number of depositors having $500 or less, 327; total amount, $36,819.80
2. Number of depositors having over $500 and less than $1,000, ... 44; total amount, 29,557.06
3. Number of depositors having $1,000 and not over $2,000, ... 17; total amount, 22,224.34
4. Number of depositors having over $2,000, 1; total amount, 3,992.25

5. Total number of depositors, . . . 389; total deposits, $92,593.45
6. Largest amount due a single depositor, $3,992.25.
7. Number of accounts opened during the year, $104; number closed, 66.
8. Amount of income received during the year, $4,116.43.
9. Amount of dividends declared during the year, $2,949.47.
10. Amount deposited, including interest credited, the past year, $62,676.05.
11. Amount withdrawn during the year, $44,252.66.
12. Increase of deposits the past year, $19,423.39.
13. Amount carried to surplus or profit and loss during the year, $975.70.
14. Rate of dividend the last year, 4 per cent.; when paid, April and October.
15. State tax during the past year, $77.46; United States tax, $13.14.
16. Total office expenses the past year, including salaries, $416.10.
17. Net amount of income during the year from real estate owned, none.
18. Amount of assets yielding no income during the year, $8,842.00.
19. Are all loans upon real estate secured by first mortgage? Yes.
20. Largest amount loaned to one individual, company, society, or corporation, $2,600.00.
21. Date of annual meeting for choice of officers, second Tuesday in July.

Officers.—President, Frederick Watson; Treasurer, J. W. Peet; Directors or Trustees, Jay A. Underwood, N. C. Ward, Geo. W. Cowdry, J. B. Reed, Geo. S. Fuller.

CHELSEA SAVINGS BANK.

GEORGE D. COIT, Treasurer.   INCORPORATED, 1858.

STATEMENT, OCTOBER 1, 1882.

LIABILITIES.		ASSETS.	
Whole Am't of Deposits,	$3,378,025.01	Loans on Real Estate, .	$949,176.00
Surplus Account, . .	32,600.00	Loans on Stocks and Bonds,	793,450.00
Interest Account, . .	10,219.68	Loans on Endorsed Notes,	56,700.00
Rent Account, . .	1,210.82	United States Bonds, .	535,000.00
Profit and Loss Account,	97,533.10	Town, City, and District B'ds,	280,000.00
		Town Orders, . . .	63,000.00
		Railroad Bonds, . .	395,000.00
		Bank Stocks in other States,	66,800.00
		Real Estate by Foreclosure,	254,422.48
		Banking House, . .	23,450.00
		Insurance and Tax Account,	2,588.38
		Expense Account, . .	494.00
		Premium Account, . .	32,691.50
		Loans on Call, . . .	50,000.00
		Cash in Bank, . . .	14,967.82
		Cash on hand, . . .	1,848.43
Total Liabilities, .	$3,519,588.61	Total Assets, .	$3,519,588.61

INVESTMENTS.

DESCRIPTION.	PAR VALUE.	COST.	MARKET VALUE.
UNITED STATES BONDS.			
4½s of 1891, Registered, ... $	60,000.00	60,000.00	67,650.00
4s of 1907, Registered, ...	475,000.00	475,000.00	562,875.00
TOWN, CITY, AND DISTRICT BONDS.			
20 Town of New Haven, 6s, 1889, .	20,000.00	20,000.00	22,000.00
24 " Old Saybrook, 5s, 1894, .	24,000.00	24,000.00	25,200.00
25 " Vernon, 6s, 1883 to 1887,	25,000.00	25,000.00	25,750.00
10 City of Norwich S'k'g F'd, 5s, 1907, .	10,000.00	10,000.00	11,200.00
69 " Cincinnati, gold, 6s, 1906, .	69,000.00	69,000.00	82,800.00
27 " " cur., 6s, 1909, .	27,000.00	27,000.00	32,400.00
2 " " 7s, 1902, .	2,000.00	2,000.00	2,500.00
12 " " 7s, 1904, .	12,000.00	12,000.00	15,000.00
3 " " 7s, 1908, .	3,000.00	3,000.00	3,750.00
4 " " 7-30s, 1902, .	4,000.00	4,000.00	5,200.00
15 " " 7-30s, 1906, .	15,000.00	15,000.00	19,500.00
5 " Cleveland, 6s, 1896, .	5,000.00	5,000.00	5,750.00
1 " Chicago, 7s, 1892, . .	1,000.00	1,000.00	1,200.00
6 " " 7s, 1894, .	6,000.00	6,000.00	7,380.00
20 " Syracuse, 7s, 1900, .	10,000.00	10,000.00	13,000.00
12 " " 7s, 1900, .	12,000.00	12,000.00	15,600.00
10 " Buffalo, 7s, 1917, .	10,000.00	10,000.00	14,000.00
25 Dist. of Columbia, Funded, 5s, . 1899, .	25,000.00	25,000.00	28,500.00

CHELSEA SAVINGS BANK.—Continued.

INVESTMENTS.—Continued.

DESCRIPTION.	PAR VALUE.	COST..	MARKET VALUE.
TOWN ORDERS.			
Town of Norwich, ... $	63,000.00	63,000.00	63,000.00
RAILROAD BONDS.			
100 Louisiana and Missouri River First Mortgage, 7s, 1900, ...	100,000.00	100,000.00	118,000.00
150 St. Louis, Jacksonville, and Chicago First Mortgage, 7s, 1894, ...	150,000.00	150,000.00	177,000.00
5 Cincinnati, Hamilton, and Dayton Consolidated, 6s, 1905, ...	5,000.00	5,000.00	5,500.00
79 Norwich and Worcester, First Mortgage,	79,000.00	79,000.00	93,220.00
15 New York Central and Hudson River, First Mortgage, 7s, 1903, . . .	15,000.00	15,000.00	19,950.00
4 Columbus and Xenia, First Mortgage, 7s, 1890, ...	4,000.00	4,000.00	4,400.00
14 Morris and Essex, First Mortgage, 7s, 1914,	14,000.00	14,000.00	18,900.00
13 Chicago and Alton, " " 7s, 1893,	13,000.00	13,000.00	15,600.00
15 Jeffersonville, Madison, and Indianapolis, 7s, 1906, ...	15,000.00	15,000.00	17,700.00
BANK STOCK.			
120 Shares Fourth National, New York City,	12,000.00	12,000.00	15,360.00
37 " Ninth " "	3,700.00	3,700.00	4,514.00
66 " Central " "	6,600.00	6,600.00	8,250.00
30 " Imp'rs and Traders, Nat., "	3,000.00	3,000.00	7,650.00
50 " Nassau, "	2,500.00	2,500.00	3,150.00
10 " Corn Exchange, "	1,000.00	1,000.00	1,670.00
100 " American Exc., Nat., "	10,000.00	10,000.00	13,200.00
80 " Merchants, " "	4,000.00	4,000.00	3,800.00
275 " Phenix, " "	5,500.00	5,500.00	5,775.00
60 " Hanover, " "	6,000.00	6,000.00	8,100.00
25 " National Shoe and Leather, "	2,500.00	2,500.00	3,250.00
100 " Continental, National; "	10,000.00	10,000.00	12,000.00

MISCELLANEOUS ITEMS.

1. Number of depositors having $500 or less, 3,191; total amount, $487,748.50
2. Number of depositors having over $500 and less than $1,000,. . . . . 874; total amount, 618,045.09
3. Number of depositors having $1,000 and not over $2,000, . . . 756; total amount, 1,039,532.91
4. Number of depositors having over $2,000, 348; total amount, 1,232,698.51

5. Total number of depositors, . . . 5,169; total deposits, $3,378,025.01
6. Largest amount due a single depositor, $30,852.96.
7. Number of accounts opened during the year, 711; number closed, 526.
8. Amount of income received during the year, $187,963.11.
9. Amount of dividends declared during the year, $129,615.10.
10. Amount deposited, including interest credited, the past year, $686,662.71.
11. Amount withdrawn during the year, $609,973.78.
12. Increase of deposits the past year, $76,688.93.
13. Amount carried to surplus or profit and loss during the year, $8,400 to surplus; $27,119.32 to profit and loss.

CHELSEA SAVINGS BANK.—Continued.

MISCELLANEOUS ITEMS.—Continued.

14. Rate of dividend the last year, 4 per cent., paid March and September 1882.
15. State tax during the past year, $7,244.30; U. S. tax, none.
16. Total office expenses the past year, including salaries, $6,392.32.
17. Net amount of income during the year from real estate owned, $8,309.81.
18. Amount of assets yielding no income during the year, $8,873.70.
19. Are all loans upon real estate secured by first mortgage? Yes.
20. Largest amount loaned to one individual, company, society, or corporation, $125,000.
21. Date of annual meeting for choice of officers, third Wednesday in September.

OFFICERS.—President, Lorenzo Blackstone; Vice-Presidents, Henry Bill, John F. Slater, John T. Wait; Directors, James A. Hovey, John P. Barstow, O. J. Lamb, Oliver P. Avery, Edward Harland, George D. Coit, Henry H. Gallup, David A. Billings, Charles L. Richards; Counsel, Jeremiah Halsey; Attorney, John M. Thayer; Secretary and Treasurer, George D. Coit; Assistant Treasurer, Charles B. Chapman.

CHESTER SAVINGS BANK.

E. C. HUNGERFORD, Treasurer.   INCORPORATED, 1871.

STATEMENT, OCTOBER 1, 1882.

LIABILITIES.		ASSETS.	
Whole Amount of Deposits,	$92,977.39	Loans on Real Estate, .	$46,090.93
Surplus Account, . .	1,600.00	Loans on Endorsed Notes,	5,950.00
Interest Account, . .	655.13	Town, City, and Corp'n Bonds,	19,020.00
		Bank Stocks in Connecticut,	15,545.00
		Bank Stocks in other States,	6,206.25
		Safe, etc., ...	220.00
		Expense Account, . .	3.75
		Cash in Bank, . . .	1,176.16
		Cash on hand, . . .	1,020.43
Total Liabilities, . .	$95,232.52	Total Assets, . .	$95,232.52

INVESTMENTS.

DESCRIPTION.	PAR VALUE.	COST.	MARKET VALUE.
TOWN, CITY, AND CORPORATION BONDS.			
Cincinnati, Ohio, 6s currency, due, 1909, . $	3,000.00	3,217.50	3,450.00
Cincinnati, Ohio, 6s gold, due, 1906, .	3,000.00	3,300.00	3,450.00
St. Louis, Mo., 6s gold, due, 1890, .	3,000.00	3,405.00	3,500.00
St. Louis, Mo., 6s gold, due, 1891, .	3,000.00	3,375.00	3,600.00
Cleveland, Ohio, 4s currency, due, 1888, .	3,000.00	3,000.00	3,150.00
Columbus, Ohio, 4s currency, due, 1912, .	3,000.00	3,120.00	3,150.00
BANK STOCKS.			
59 shares Deep River National, Deep River, .	5,900.00	7,670.00	7,670.00
25 " First National Bank, Middletown, .	2,500.00	2,500.00	2,750.00
20 " Nat. Bk. of New England, E. Haddam,	2,000.00	2,405.00	2,500.00
30 " City National Bank, Hartford, .	3,000.00	2,970.00	2,700.00
10 " National Park Bank, New York City,	1,000.00	1,013.75	1,500.00
20 " Central National, " "	2,000.00	2,081.25	2,400.00
11 " Fourth National, " "	1,100.00	1,126.25	1,300.00
40 " Merchants Exc. Nat., " ".	2,000.00	1,985.00	2,000.00

MISCELLANEOUS ITEMS.

1. Number of depositors having $500 or less,   332; total amount, $26,622.89
2. Number of depositors having $500 and less
   than $1,000, ...   39; total amount, 26,502.84
3. Number of depositors having $1,000 and not
   over $2,000, ...   24; total amount, 29,648.08
4. Number of depositors having over $2,000,   4; total amount, 10,203.58

5. Total number of depositors, . . .   399; total deposits, $92,977.39
6. Largest amount due a single depositor, $3,286.77.
7. Number of accounts opened during the year, 81; number closed, 22.
8. Amount of income received during the year, $4,954.45.

CHESTER SAVINGS BANK.—Continued.

MISCELLANEOUS ITEMS.—Continued.

9. Amount of dividends declared during the year, $3,366.42.
10. Amount deposited, including interest credited, the past year, $27,277.91.
11. Amount withdrawn during the year, $9,511.01,
12. Increase of deposits the past year, $17,766.90.
13. Amount carried to surplus or profit and loss during the year, $506.81.
14. Rate of dividend the last year, 4¼ per cent.; when paid, 2¼ per cent. February 1st, and 2 per cent. August 1st.
15. State tax during the past year, $75.68; U. S. tax, $8.13.
16. Total office expenses the past year, including salaries, $417.50.
17. Net amount of income during the year from real estate owned, none.
18. Amount of assets yielding no income during the year, none.
19. Are all loans upon real estate secured by first mortgage? Yes.
20. Largest amount loaned to one individual, company, society, or corporation, $2,000.00.
21. Date of annual meeting for choice of officers, second Monday in July.

OFFICERS.—President, Charles L. Griswold; Treasurer, Edward C. Hungerford; Directors, George W. Smith, Ambrose Pratt, Fisk Shailer, S. W. Turner, George Jones, Hiram H. Clark, John W. Marvin, N. C. Perry, C. G. Ladd.

CITIZENS SAVINGS BANK, STAMFORD.

W. C. HOYT, Treasurer.   INCORPORATED, 1869.

STATEMENT, OCTOBER 1, 1882.

LIABILITIES.		ASSETS.	
Whole Amount of Deposits,	$855,160.21	Loans on Real Estate, .	$284,435.00
Surplus Account, . .	11,000.00	Loans on Stocks and Bonds,	259,575.00
Interest Account, . .	4,215.92	United States Bonds, .	100,000.00
		State Bonds, . . .	20,000.00
		Town, City, and Corp'n Bonds,	63,500.00
		Town, City, and Bor'gh Orders,	7,723.56
		Railroad Bonds, . .	81,800.00
		Bank Stocks in Connecticut,	20,900.00
		Bank Stocks in other States,	16,850.00
		Real Estate by Foreclosure,	6,000.00
		Cash in Bank, . . .	9,592.57
Total Liabilities, .	$870,376.13	Total Assets, . .	$870,376.12

INVESTMENTS.

DESCRIPTION.	PAR VALUE.	COST.	MARKET VALUE.
UNITED STATES BONDS.			
Fours of 1907, Registered, ... $	60,000.00	60,000.00	72,000.00
Three per cents, ...	40,000.00	40,000.00	40,800.00
STATE BONDS.			
Missouri, ...	20,000.00	20,000.00	21,400.00
TOWN, CITY, AND CORPORATION BONDS.			
Greenwich, Conn., ...	2,000.00	2,000.00	2,400.00
Stamford, "	31,500.00	31,500.00	37,700.00
Middletown, "	10,000.00	10,000.00	12,000.00
New York City, ...	10,000.00	10,000.00	12,000.00
Brooklyn "	10,000.00	10,000.00	12,000.00
TOWN, CITY, AND BOROUGH ORDERS.			
Darien, Conn., ...	7,723.56	7,723.56	7,723.56
RAILROAD BONDS.			
Union Pacific, ...	15,000.00	17,000.00	17,400.00
Rock Island, ...	10,000.00	12,000.00	12,800.00
New York Central, ...	30,000.00	39,600.00	40,200.00
New York & Harlem, ...	10,000.00	13,200.00	13,400.00
BANK STOCKS.			
140 shares First National, Stamford, . .	14,000.00	19,900.00	24,500.00
10 " City National, So. Norwalk, . .	1,000.00	1,000.00	1,000.00
6 " Metropolital National, New York,	600.00	750.00	1,050.00
100 " Fourth National, New York, .	10,000.00	11,900.00	12,500.00
35 " National Park Bank, New York, .	3,500.00	4,200.00	5,950.00

CITIZENS SAVINGS BANK.—Continued.

MISCELLANEOUS ITEMS.

1. Number of depositors having $500 or less,   1,426; total amount, $224,522.05
2. Number of depositors having over $500 and less than $1,000, ...   321; total amount,   224,897.09
3. Number of depositors having $1,000 and not over $2,000, ...   200; total amount,   262,934.06
4. Number of depositors having over $2,000,   50; total amount,   142,807.01

5. Total number of depositors, . . . 1,997; total deposits, $855,160.21
6. Largest amount due a single depositor, $11,597.97.
7. Number of accounts opened during the year, 461; number closed, 303.
8. Amount of income received during the year, $45,231.38.
9. Amount of dividends declared during the year, $31,002.51.
10. Amount deposited, including interest credited, the past year, $272,459.50.
11. Amount withdrawn during the year, $210,718.18.
12. Increase of deposits the past year, $61,741.32.
13. Amount carried to surplus or profit and loss during the year, $3,000.
14. Rate of dividend the last year, 4 per cent.; when paid, January and July.
15. State tax during the past year, $1,905.38; U. S. tax, $3.52.
16. Total office expenses the past year, including salaries, $2,502.87.
17. Net amount of income during the year from real estate owned, $150.
18. Amount of assets yielding no income during the year, $3,500.
19. Are all loans upon real estate secured by first mortgage? Yes.
20. Largest amount loaned to one individual, company, society, or corporation, $100,000. ·
21. Date of annual meeting for choice of officers, first Thursday in July.

OFFICERS.—President, Wells R. Ritch; Treasurer, W. C. Hoyt; Directors or Trustees, C. W. Brown, W. R. Ritch, T. H. H. Messinger, Charles Gaylor, Wm. Hoyt, Seth S. Cook.

CITY SAVINGS BANK, BRIDGEPORT.

S. M. MIDDLEBROOK, Treasurer.   INCORPORATED, 1859.

STATEMENT, OCTOBER 1, 1882.

LIABILITIES.		ASSETS.	
Whole Amt. of Deposits,	$1,982,228.75	Loans on Real Estate, .	$729,807.62
Surplus Account, . .	40,000.00	Loans on Stocks and Bonds,	29,700.00
Interest Account, . .	23,665.05	Town, City, and Corp'n Bds.,	817,976.19
		Railroad Bonds, . . .	110,489.01
		Bank Stocks in Connecticut,	5,000.00
		Real Estate by Foreclosure,	312,210.94
		Sundry Temporary Account,	813.74
		Cash in Bank, } . .	39,946.30
		Cash on hand, }	
Total Liabilities, .	$2,045,893.80	Total Assets, . .	$2,045,893.80

INVESTMENTS.

DESCRIPTION.	PAR VALUE.	COST.	MARKET VALUE.
TOWN, CITY, AND CORPORATION BONDS.			
Bridgeport City, 7 per cent., ...	$ 175,000.00	178,291.00	217,000.00
Cincinnati " 6 " "	125,000.00	135,190.80	146,250.00
Rochester " 7 " "	100,000.00	104,653.00	125,000.00
New York " 7 " "	100,000.00	103,510.00	125,000.00
Brooklyn " 7 " "	100,000.00	103,510.00	140,000.00
Cincinnati " 5 " "	50,000.00	53,000.00	57,500.00
" " 7$\frac{3}{10}$ " "	25,000.00	32,875.00	33,000.00
" " 7 " "	10,000.00	13,195.00	13,500.00
St. Louis, Gold, 6 " "	50,000.00	58,701.44	60,000.00
New York, 7 " "	25,000.00	25,000.00	31,250.00
RAILROAD BONDS.			
Chicago & Rock Island, 6 per cent., . .	50,000.00	63,558.24	63,558.24
New York Central & H. R.R., 7 per cent., .	35,000.00	46,880.77	46,880.77

MISCELLANEOUS ITEMS.

1. Number of depositors having $500 or less, 5,305; total amount, $955,283.39
2. Number of depositors having over $500 and
   less than $1,000, ... 466; total amount, 339,893.74
3. Number of depositors having $1,000 and not
   over $2,000, ... 336; total amount, 456,021.23
4. Number of depositors having over $2,000,   86; total amount, 231,030.39

5. Total number of depositors, . . . 6,193; total deposits, $1,982,228.75
6. Largest amount due a single depositor, $7,336.18.
7. Number of accounts opened during the year, $1,483; number closed, 781.
8. Amount of income received during the year, $113,606.57.
9. Amount of dividends declared during the year, $88,947.44.
10. Amount deposited, including interest credited, the past year, $547,591.46.

CITY SAVINGS BANK.—Continued.

MISCELLANEOUS ITEMS.—Continued.

11. Amount withdrawn during the year, $418,354.09.
12. Increase of deposits the past year, $129,237.37.
13. Amount carried to surplus or profit and loss during the year, $15,000.00.
14. Rate of dividend the last year, 4½ per cent.; when paid, January and July.
15. State tax during the past year, $3,793.24; United States tax, $306.46.
16. Total office expenses the past year, including salaries, $5,935.48.
17. Net amount of income during the year from real estate owned, $9,038.85.
18. Amount of assets yielding no income during the year, none.
19. Are all loans upon real estate secured by first mortgage? Yes.
20. Largest amount loaned to one individual, company, society, or corporation, $150,000.00.
21. Date of annual meeting for choice of officers, July.

OFFICERS.—President, Ira Gregory; Treasurer, S. M. Middlebrook; Directors or Trustees, D. F. Hollister, Horace Nichols, Horace F. Hatch, Lewis W. Booth, C. K. Averill, George P. Stockwell, Nathan Buckingham, David M. Read, Edward A. Lewis, S. M. Middlebrook, Courtland Kelsey, Henry S. Peck, F. W. Parrott, Josiah Bayliss, Burr Curtis, Lewis B. Booth, George K. Birdsey, Edwin Banks, John M. Wheeler, Wm. N. Middlebrook.

COLCHESTER SAVINGS BANK.

J. N. ADAMS, Treasurer.   INCORPORATED, 1874.

STATEMENT, OCTOBER 1, 1882.

LIABILITIES.		ASSETS.	
Whole Amount of Deposits,	$192,601.81	Loans on Real Estate, .	$80,332.71
Surplus Account, . .	3,610.18	Loans on Endorsed Notes,	12,743.24
Interest Account, . .	813.88	United States Bonds, .	11,500.00
		Town and Corporation Bonds,	41,225.98
		City Bond, . . .	1,000.00
		Railroad Bonds, . .	1,000.00
		Bank Stocks in Connecticut,	34,760.09
		Savings Bank Deposits, .	6,263.68
		Safe and Furniture, . .	1,200.00
		Ecclesiastical Order, .	200.00
		Cash in Bank, . . .	6,063.42
		Cash on hand, . . .	736.84
Total Liabilities, .	$197,025.87	Total Assets, . .	$197,025.87

INVESTMENTS.

DESCRIPTION.	PAR VALUE.	COST.	MARKET VALUE.
UNITED STATES BONDS.			
4½s of 1891, Registered, ... $	6,500.00	6,755.00	7,328.00
4s of 1907, Registered, ...	5,000.00	5,150.00	5,920.00
TOWN, CITY, AND CORPORATION BONDS.			
Norwich City Bond, 5s, ...	1,000.00	1,025.00	1,075.00
Hartford Town Bonds, 4½s, ...	3,000.00	3,120.00	3,120.00
TOWN, CITY, AND BOROUGH ORDERS.			
Town of Colchester Orders, ...	38,225.98	38,225.98	38,225.98
ECCLESIASTICAL ORDERS.			
Baptist Church, ...	200.00	200.00	200.00
BANK STOCKS.			
24 shares Rockville National Bank, . .	2,400.00	2,700.00	2,701.00
25 " Middlesex County Bank, Middletown,	2,500.00	3,081.00	3,081.00
120 " First National Bank, Norwich, .	12,000.00	13,200.00	13,200.00
134 " Merchants " " .	5,360.00	5,578.00	5,578.00
5 " Willimantic " " .	500.00	612.50	612.50
22 " Thames :: " .	2,200.00	3,362.00	3,362.00
44 " Norwich " " .	4,900.00	5,685.00	5,685.00
78 " Uncas " " .	3,900.00	4,600.00	4,600.00
2 " City Bank, New London, . .	200.00	200.00	200.00
8 " Union " " . .	800.00	800.00	800.00

COLCHESTER SAVINGS BANK.—Continued.

MISCELLANEOUS ITEMS.

1. Number of depositors having $500 or less,   674; total amount, $57,564.38
2. Number of depositors having over $500 and
      less than $1,000, ...   77; total amount,   52,692 81
3. Number of depositors having $1,000 and not
      over $2,000, ...   33; total amount,   41,724.81
4. Number of depositors having over $2,000,   12; total amount,   40,619.81

5. Total number of depositors,   796; total deposits, $192,601.81
6. Largest amount due a single depositor, $8,633.91.
7. Number of accounts opened during the year, 164; number closed, 110.
8. Amount of income received during the year, $9,230.83.
9. Amount of dividends declared during the year, $6,729.67.
10. Amount deposited, including interest credited, the past year, $84,069.42.
11. Amount withdrawn during the year, $54,891.47.
12. Increase of deposits the past year, $29,177.95.
13. Amount carried to surplus or profit and loss during the year, $1,044.41.
14. Rate of dividend the last year, 4 per cent., paid April and October.
15. State tax during the past year, $282.61; U. S. tax, none.
16. Total office expenses the past year, including salaries, express, appraisals,
      telegraphy, etc., $712.65.
17. Net amount of income during the year from real estate owned, nothing.
18. Amount of assets yielding no income during the year, nothing.
19. Are all loans upon real estate secured by first mortgage? Yes.
20. Largest amount loaned to one individual, company, society, or corporation,
      $10,000.
21. Date of annual meeting for choice of officers, last week day in August.

OFFICERS.—President, S. C. Gillette; Vice-President, Wm. H. Hayward;
Treasurer, J. N. Adams; Directors or Trustees, S. C. Gillette, J. N. Adams,
E. Ransom, Russel Way, P. A. Dawly, Wm. S. Curtis, Wm. H. Hayward, J. N.
Pelton, A. A. Baker, H. P. Buell.

COLLINSVILLE SAVINGS BANK.

SAMUEL N. CODDING, Treasurer.   INCORPORATED, 1853.

STATEMENT, OCTOBER 1, 1882.

LIABILITIES.		ASSETS.	
Whole Amount of Deposits,	$285,147.11	Loans on Real Estate, .	$196,564.00
Surplus Account, ⎫		Loans on Endorsed Notes,	33,240.00
Interest Account, ⎭ . .	9,201.03	United States Bonds, .	11,000.00
		Town, City, and Corp'n Bonds,	17,650.00
		Town, City, and Bor'gh Orders,	10,750.00
		School District Orders, .	2,650.00
		Railroad Bonds, . .	1,800.00
		Real Estate by Foreclosure,	11,331.39
		Expense Account, . .	271.35
		Interest Account, . .	164.56
		Western Real Estate Bond,	1,000.00
		Premium Account, . .	1,138.37
		Cash in Bank, . . .	2,021.87
		Cash on hand, ...	4,766.60
Total Liabilities, .	$294,348.14	Total Assets, . .	$294,348.14

INVESTMENTS.

DESCRIPTION.	PAR VALUE.	COST.	MARKET VALUE.
UNITED STATES BONDS.			
4½s of 1891, Registered, ... $	5,000.00	5,000.00	5,650.00
4½s of 1891, Coupon, ...	6,000.00	6,000.00	6,780.00
TOWN, CITY, AND CORPORATION BONDS.			
Hartford, ...	4,000.00	4,174.00	4,160.00
New Haven, ...	2,000.00	2,082.24	2,080.00
Providence, ...	2,000.00	2,020.00	2,020.00
Boston, ...	2,000.00	2,148.61	2,020.00
Rochester, ...	5,000.00	5,590.00	5,500.00
St. Joseph, ...	2,650.00	2,650.00	2,650.00
RAILROAD BONDS.			
Connecticut Western, ...	2,000.00	1,800.00	

MISCELLANEOUS ITEMS.

1. Number of depositors having $500 or less, .   745; total amount, $95,084.31
2. Number of depositors having over $500 and
     less than $1,000, ...   92; total amount,   61,825.32
3. Number of depositors having $1,000 and not
     not over $2,000, ...   61; total amount,   87,791.48
4. Number of depositors having over $2,000, .   14; total amount,   40,446.00

5. Total number of depositors, ...   912; total deposits, $285,147.11

COLLINSVILLE SAVINGS BANK.—Continued.

MISCELLANEOUS ITEMS.—Continued.

6. Largest amount due a single depositor, $5,351.53.
7. Number of accounts opened during the year, 185; number closed, 76.
8. Amount of income received during the year, $14,557.74.
9. Amount of dividends declared during the year, $11,789.70.
10. Amount deposited, including interest credited, the past year, $63,015.82.
11. Amount withdrawn during the year, $46,748.50.
12. Increase of deposits the past year, $16,267.32.
13. Amount carried to surplus or profit and loss during the year, $1,437.01.
14. Rate of dividend the last year, 4½ per cent.; when paid, July and January.
15. State tax during the past year, $502.30; U. S. tax, none.
16. Total office expenses the past year, including salaries, $800.
17. Net amount of income during the year from real estate owned, $600.
18. Amount of assets yielding no income during the year, $1,800.
19. Are all loans upon real estate secured by first mortgage? Yes.
20. Largest amount loaned to one individual, company, society, or corporation, $7,500.
21. Date of annual meeting for choice of officers, July 17, 1882.

Officers.—President, Charles H. Blair; Treasurer, Samuel N. Codding; Directors or Trustees, J. B. Bodwell, Ebenezer Sexton, Samuel N. Codding, John D. Andrews, Sherman Fancher, C. H. Thayer, Romeo Elton, Charles H. Blair, H N. Goodwin.

CONNECTICUT SAVINGS BANK, NEW HAVEN.

ELLIOTT H. MORSE, President.   INCORPORATED, 1857.

STATEMENT, OCTOBER 1, 1882.

LIABILITIES.		ASSETS.	
Whole Amt. of Deposits,	$3,038,352.69	Loans on Real Estate,	$1,477,925.00
Surplus Account,	66,825.41	Loans on Stocks and Bonds,	232,000.00
Interest Account,	29,773.82	Loans on Endorsed Notes,	232,901.10
		United States Bonds,	300,000.00
		State Bonds,	7,000.00
		Town, City, and Corp'n B'ds,	201,000.00
		Town, City, and Bor'gh Orders,	62,000.00
		School District Orders,	4,000.00
		Railroad Bonds,	387,750.00
		Bank Stocks in Connecticut,	74,000.00
		Bank Stocks in other States,	48,150.00
		Real Estate by Foreclosure,	50,982.25
		Banking House,	25,000.00
		Expense Account,	1,292.67
		Profit and Loss Account,	69.62
		Cash in Bank,	27,636.04
		Cash on hand,	3,245.24
Total Liabilities,	$3,134,951.92	Total Assets,	$3,134,951.92

INVESTMENTS.

DESCRIPTION.	PAR VALUE.	COST.	MARKET VALUE.
UNITED STATES BONDS.			
4½s of 1891, Registered,	$ 100,000 00	100,000.00	113,000.00
4s of 1907, Registered,	200,000.00	200,000.00	239,000.00
STATE BONDS.			
State of Missouri,	7,000.00	7,000.00	7,630.00
TOWN, CITY, AND CORPORATION BONDS.			
District of Columbia, 7s,	5,000.00	5,000.00	6,750.00
St. Louis, Mo., 6s,	50,000.00	50,000.00	57,000.00
Cincinnati, Ohio, 5s,	50,000.00	50,000.00	56,000.00
" " 6s,	10,000.00	10,000.00	12,000.00
" " 7³⁄₁₀s,	10,000.00	10,000.00	13,000.00
Cleveland, " 6s,	16,000.00	16,000.00	18 000.00
Columbus, " 6s,	5,000.00	5,000.00	5,600.00
Milwaukee, Wis., 7s,	5,000.00	5,000.00	6,500.00
Albany, N. Y., 6s,	4,000.00	4,000.00	4,200.00
Brooklyn, " 7s,	1,000.00	1,000.00	1,030.00
New York, N. Y., 7s,	5,000.00	5,000.00	5,250.00
Newark, N. J., 7s,	10,000.00	10,000.00	12,000.00
Providence, R. I., 5s,	10,000.00	10,000.00	11,400.00
New Haven City, 7s,	6,000.00	6,000.00	7,800.00
New Haven Water Co., 7s,	14,000.00	14,000.00	16,800.00

CONNECTICUT SAVINGS BANK.—CONTINUED.

INVESTMENTS.—CONTINUED.

DESCRIPTION.	PAR VALUE.	COST.	MARKET VALUE.
TOWN, CITY, AND BOROUGH ORDERS.			
Town of Derby, ... $	30,000.00	30,000.00	30,000.00
Town of Naugatuck, ...	32,000.00	32,000.00	32,000.00
SCHOOL DISTRICT ORDERS.			
Central School District, Wallingford, . .	4,000.00	4,000.00	4,000.00
RAILROAD BONDS.			
N. Y. Central & Hudson R. R., 1st 7s, .	136,000.00	170,000.00	180,880.00
New York & Harlem, 1st 7s, .	38,000.00	47,500.00	50,160.00
Chicago, Burlington & Quincy, 1st 7s, .	50,000.00	50,000.00	63,500.00
Morris & Essex, 1st 7s, .	25,000.00	31,250.00	34,500.00
Chicago & Milwaukee, 1st 7s, .	20,000.00	20,000.00	24,400.00
Lake Shore & Michigan Southern, 1st 7s, .	50,000.00	50,000.00	62,500.00
Cleveland & Toledo, 1st 7s, .	18,000.00	18,800.00	18,900.00
Columbus & Xenia, 1st 7s, .	1,000.00	1,000.00	1,100.00
BANK STOCKS.			
250 shares Second National Bank, New Haven,	25,000.00	25,000.00	40,000.00
250 " Yale " " "	25,000.00	25,000.00	29,250.00
40 " Tradesmens National B'k "	4,000.00	4,000.00	6,600.00
600 " New Haven County Nat. B'k, N. H'n,	6,000.00	6,000.00	8,400.00
40 " Merchants Nat. Bank, New Haven,	2,000.00	2,000.00	2,480.00
100 " First National Bank, W. Meriden,	10,000.00	10,000.00	11,700.00
20 " Home " " "	2,000.00	2,000.00	2,500.00
75 " Nat. Bank of Commerce, New York,	7,500.00	7,500.00	11,250.00
120 " " " Republic, "	12,000.00	12,000.00	15,600.00
150 " American Exc. Nat. B'k, "	15,000.00	15,000.00	19,800.00
300 " Phenix National Bank, "	6,000.00	6,000.00	6,600.00
39 " Seventh Ward Nat. Bank, "	3,900.00	3,900.00	3,900.00
50 " German American Nat. B'k, "	3,750.00	3,750.00	3,750.00

MISCELLANEOUS ITEMS.

1. Number of depositors having $500 or less, 6,395; total amount, $999,038.99
2. Number of depositors having over $500 and less than $1,000. . . . .   992; total amount,   748,052.49
3. Number of depositors having $1,000 and not over $2,000, ...   564; total amount,   768,344.40
4. Number of depositors having over $2,000,   183; total amount,   522,916.81

5. Total number of depositors, . . . 8,134; total deposits, $3,038,352.69
6. Largest amount due a single depositor, $10,243.42.
7. Number of accounts opened during the year, 1,994; number closed, 1,072.
8. Amount of income received during the year, $169,762.26.
9. Amount of dividends declared during the year, $107,990.16.
10. Amount deposited, including interest credited, the past year, $1,100,439.48.
11. Amount withdrawn during the year, $838,634.01.
12. Increase of deposits the past year, $261,805.47.
13. Amount carried to surplus or profit and loss during the year, 7,023.41.
14. Rate of dividend the last year, 4 per cent.; when paid, Jan. 16th, July 17th.
15. State tax during the past year, $6,751.51; U. S. tax, none.
16. Total office expenses the past year, including salaries, $7,350.00.

CONNECTICUT SAVINGS BANK.—CONTINUED.

MISCELLANEOUS ITEMS.—CONTINUED.

17. Net amount of income during the year from real estate owned, $2,735.32.
18. Amount of assets yielding no income during the year, $12,077.64.
19. Are all loans upon real estate secured by first mortgage? Yes.
20. Largest amount loaned to one individual, company, society, or corporation, $115,000.
21. Date of annual meeting for choice of officers, July.

OFFICERS.—President, James E. English; Treasurer, Elliott H. Morse: Directors or Trustees, Charles R. Ingersoll, Daniel Trowbridge, Charles Peterson, Amos F. Barnes, Henry H. Bunnell, Luzon B. Morris, Lucius R. Finch, Horace J. Morton, Philo Chatfield, Benjamin R. English, Thomas Attwater Barnes.

CROMWELL DIME SAVINGS BANK.

S. P. POLLEY, Treasurer.   INCORPORATED, 1881.

STATEMENT, OCTOBER 1, 1882.

LIABILITIES.		ASSETS,	
Whole Amount of Deposits,	$99,538,78	Loans on Real Estate, .	$62,599.00
Surplus Account,)		Loans on Endorsed Notes,	7,561.56
Interest Account, } . .	2,732.80	United States Bonds, .	14,100.00
Rent, ...	12.00	Town, City, and Corp'n B'ds,	5,000.00
		Bank Stocks in Connecticut,	400.00
		Real Estate by Foreclosure,	5,200.00
		Banking House Furniture,	623.82
		Tax Account, . .	948.69
		Insurance Account, . .	70.50
		Expense Account, . .	689.99
		Premium Account, . .	2,481.43
		Cash in Bank, . .	1,245.70
		Cash on hand, . . .	1,363.40
Total liabilities, . .	$102,283.59	Total Assets, . .	$102,283.59

INVESTMENTS.

DESCRIPTION.	PAR VALUE.	COST.	MARKET VALUE.
UNITED STATES BONDS.			
4s of 1907, Coupon, ... $	14,100.00	15,925.50	16,920.00
TOWN, CITY, AND CORPORATION BONDS.			
Town of Chatham, ...	5,000.00	5,500.00	5,750.00
BANK STOCKS.			
4 shares Middlesex County Bank Stock, .	400.00	480.00	480.00

MISCELLANEOUS ITEMS.

1. Number of depositors having $500 or less,   390; total amount, $22,886.56
2. Number of depositors having over $500 and
    less than $1,000, ...   20; total amount,   12,502.74
3. Number of depositors having $1,000 and not
    over $2,000. . . . . . .   22; total amount,   31,777.71
4. Number of depositors having over $2,000,   12; total amount,   32,371.78
5. Total number of depositors, ... 444; total deposits, $99,538.79
6. Largest amount due a single depositor, $4,210.00.
7. Number of accounts opened during the year, 46; number closed, 25.
8. Amount of income received during the year, $4,850.48.
9. Amount of dividends declared during the year, $3,719.12.
10. Amount deposited, including interest credited, the past year, $45,520.77.
11. Amount withdrawn during the year, $42,112.66.
12. Increase of deposits the past year, $3,408.11.
13. Amount carried to surplus or profit and loss during the year, none.

CROMWELL DIME SAVINGS BANK.—Continued.

MISCELLANEOUS ITEMS.—Continued.

14. Rate of dividend the last year, 4 per cent.; paid, July and January.
15. State tax during the past year, $94.20; U. S. tax, $54.87.
16. Total office expenses the past year, including salaries, $387.50.
17. Net amount of income during the year from real estate owned, $236.00.
18. Amount of assets yielding no income during the year, $1,870.93.
19. Are all loans upon real estate secured by first mortgage? Yes.
20. Largest amount loaned to one individual, company, society, or corporation, $3,929.00.
21. Date of annual meeting for choice of officers, October 9, 1882.

OFFICERS.—President, John Stevens; Treasurer, S. P. Polley; Directors or Trustees, John Stevens, Bulkley Edwards, L. S. Smith, Elisha Stevens, Charles P. Sage, Richard Gay, J. K. Sage, H. W. Stocking, Russel Frisbie, D. C. Tryon, M. R. Warner, E. S. Coe, Wm. Hurlbert.

DEEP RIVER SAVINGS BANK.

HENRY R. WOOSTER, Treasurer.   INCORPORATED, 1851.

STATEMENT, OCTOBER 1, 1882.

LIABILITIES.		ASSETS.	
Whole Amount of Deposits,	$595,330.07	Loans on Real Estate, .	$232,010.00
Surplus Account, . .	6,174.69	Loans on Stocks and Bonds,	54,970.00
Interest Account, . .	16,303.67	United States Bonds, . .	26,170.00
		Town, City, and Corp'n B'ds,	123,500.00
		Railroad Bonds, . . .	87,000.00
		Bank Stocks in Connecticut,	19,447.00
		Bank Stocks in other States,	35,235.06
		Real Estate by Foreclosure,	333.45
		Banking House, . . .	3,500.00
		Tax Account, . . .	685.93
		Expense Account, . .	1,022.29
		Premium Account, . .	24,081.29
		Cash in Bank, . . .	6,481.95
		Cash on hand, . . .	3,371.46
Total Liabilities, . .	$617,808.43	Total Assets, . .	$617,808.43

INVESTMENTS.

DESCRIPTION.		PAR VALUE.	COST.	MARKET VALUE.
UNITED STATES BONDS.				
4s of 1907, Registered, ...	. $	16,000.00	16,170.00	18,880.00
Currency 6s, ...	.	10,000.00	11,000.00	13,100.00
TOWN, CITY, AND CORPORATION BONDS.				
District of Columbia, 6s, . . .	.	10,000.00	11,339.29	11,413.00
City of Bridgeport, 7s, . . .	.	10,000.00	10,000.00	12,000.00
" New London, 7s, . . .	.	10,000.00	10,000.00	12,000.00
" New York, 6s, . . .	.	5,000.00	5,588.54	6,000.00
" Boston, 6s, . . .	.	5,000.00	5,738.46	5,950.00
" Providence, 5s, . . .	.	5,000.00	5,360.00	5,900.00
" Fall River, 5s, . . .	.	5,000.00	5,186.20	5,300.00
" St. Louis, 6s, . . .	.	9,000.00	9,478.42	9,540.00
" " 6s, . . .	.	1,000.00	1,053.72	1,060.00
" " 6s, . . .	.	5,000.00	5,807.69	5,800.00
" Chicago, 6s, . . .	.	5,000.00	5,960.94	6,050.00
" " 7s, . . .	.	10,000.00	11,919.65	12,400.00
" Cincinnati, 7$\frac{3}{10}$s, .	.	7,000.00	7,797.50	7,870.00
" " 6s, 1884, . .	.	5,000.00	5,100.00	5,100.00
" " 6s, 1909, . .	.	5,000.00	5,326.00	6,000.00
" Detroit, 7s, . . .	.	2,000.00	2,047.50	2,070.00
" Cleveland, 7s, . . .	.	3,000.00	3,446.00	3,500.00
" Dayton, 8s, . . .	.	5,000.00	5,825.00	5,825.00
" Columbus, 6s, . . .	.	5,000.00	5,442.00	5,600.00
Town of Chester, 6s, . . .	.	10,000.00	10,000.00	10,700.00
" Beloit, 6s, . . .	.	1,500.00	1,500.00	1,500.00

4

DEEP RIVER SAVINGS BANK.—Continued.

INVESTMENTS.—Continued.

DESCRIPTION.		PAR VALUE.	COST.	MARKET VALUE.
RAILROAD BONDS.				
Chicago Burlington & Quincy,	7s, $	10,000.00	11,000.00	11,875.00
United New Jersey Railroad & Canal Co.,	6s,	10,000.00	11,266.66	11,900.00
Kalamazoo, Allegan, & Grand Rapids,	8s,	10,000.00	11,320.34	11,550.00
Little Miami,	6s,	19,000.00	19,000.00	19,000.00
Rensselaer & Saratoga,	7s,	5,000.00	6,248.49	6,500.00
Norwich & Worcester,	6s,	5,000.00	5,797.80	5,850.00
Buffalo, New York & Erie,	7s,	5,000.00	6,612.50	6,612.50
Shamokin Valley & Pottsville,	7s,	5,000.00	6,325.00	6,325.00
Cincinnati & Baltimore,	7s,	5,000.00	6,175.00	6,175.00
St. Louis, Jacksonville & Chicago,	7s,	5,000.00	5,912.50	5,912.50
Joliet & Northern Indiana,	7s,	3,000.00	3,847.50	3,847.50
Oswego & Rome,	7s,	3,000.00	3,847.50	3,847.50
Columbus & Xenia,	7s,	2,000.00	2,283.33	2,300.00
BANK STOCKS.				
90 shares Deep River National Bank, . .		9,000.00	9,000.00	12,330.00
25 " Middletown " . .		1,875.00	2,347.00	2,600.00
20 " Meriden " . .		2,000.00	2,360.00	2,400.00
32 " Home " Meriden,		3,200.00	3,360.00	3,840.00
20 " First " Hartford,		2,000.00	2,380.00	2,400.00
38 " Nat. Bank of Commerce, New York,		3,800.00	4,427.50	5,700.00
10 " Nat. Shoe and Leather Bk., "		1,000.00	1,000.00	1,300.00
38 " Continental National Bank, "		3,800.00	3,800.00	4,560.00
28 " Central " " "		2,800.00	2,800.00	3,500.00
15 " Ninth " " "		1,500.00	1,500.00	1,830.00
50 " American Exc. " " "		5,000.00	5,235.42	6,600.00
15 " St. Nicholas, " " "		1,500.00	1,500.00	1,875.00
168 " Mechanics, " " "		4,200.00	5,633.50	6,468.00
54 " Merchants, " " "		2,700.00	3,207.39	3,564.00
25 " Metropolitan, " " "		2,500.00	2,928.13	4,400.00
25 " Bank of America, "		2,500.00	3,203.12	4,025.00

MISCELLANEOUS ITEMS.

1. Number of depositors having $500 or less, 1,126; total amount, $138,978.21
2. Number of depositors having over $500 and less than $1,000, ... 192; total amount, 127,915.94
3. Number of depositors having $1,000 and not over $2,000, ... 129; total amount, 185,401.96
4. Number of depositors having over $2,000, 44; total amount, 43,033.96

5. Total number of depositors, . . . 1,491; total deposits, $595,330.07
6. Largest amount due a single depositor, $15,000.
7. Number of accounts opened during the year, 213; number closed, 92.
8. Amount of income received during the year, $33,188.38.
9. Amount of dividends declared during the year, $23,725.32.
10. Amount deposited, including interest credited, the past year, $132,292.41.
11. Amount withdrawn during the year, $68,663.19.
12. Increase of deposits the past year, $63,629.22.
13. Amount carried to surplus or profit and loss during the year, $1,387.88.
14. Rate of dividend the last year, 4½ per cent.; paid, 2½ per cent. in November, and 2 per cent. in May.

DEEP RIVER SAVINGS BANK.—Continued.

MISCELLANEOUS ITEMS.—Continued.

15. State tax during the past year, $1,219.79; U. S. tax, $153.41.
16. Total office expenses the past year, including salaries, $2,181.98.
17. Net amount of income during the year from real estate owned, $67.00.
18. Amount of assets yielding no income during the year, $4,200.00.
19. Are all loans upon real estate secured by first mortgage? Yes.
20. Largest amount loaned to one individual, company, society, or corporation, $20,000.
21. Date of annual meeting for choice of officers, first Monday in July.

OFFICERS.—President, Asa R. Shailer; Vice-President, Milon Pratt; Treasurer, Henry R. Wooster; Director or Trustees, Richard P. Spencer, W. F. Willcox, Henry L. Shaler, Joseph E. Silliman, Horace P. Denison.

DERBY SAVINGS BANK.

Thos. S. Birdsey, Treasurer.   INCORPORATED, 1846.

STATEMENT, OCTOBER 1, 1882.

LIABILITIES.		ASSETS.	
Whole Am't of Deposits,	$1,077,867.64	Loans on Real Estate, .	$653,643.47
Surplus Account, }		Loans on Stocks and Bonds,	7,800.00
Interest Account, } · .	77,421.90	Loans on Endorsed Notes,	224,858.05
		United States Bonds,.	40,000.00
		Town, City, and Corp'n B'ds,	3,000.00
		Town, City, and Bor'gh Orders,	21,674.20
		School District Bonds, .	14,000.00
		Bank Stocks in Connecticut,	101,825.00
		Bank Stocks in other States,	57,100.00
		Real Estate by Foreclosure,	2,793.58
		Expense Account, . .	2,464.28
		Birmingham Water Co. Bonds,	8,000.00
		Derby Gas Co. Bonds, .	2,500.00
		Cash in Bank, . , . .	8,345.30
		Cash on hand, . .	12,285.71
Total Liabilities, .	$1,155,289.54	Total Assets, . .	$1,155,289.54

INVESTMENTS.

DESCRIPTION.	PAR VALUE.	COST.	MARKET VALUE.
UNITED STATES BONDS.			
4s of 1907, Registered, ... $	40,000.00	40,000.00	48,000.00
TOWN, CITY, AND CORPORATION BONDS.			
Birmingham Water Co.'s, ...	8,000.00	8,000.00	8,000.00
Derby Gas Co.'s, ...	2,500.00	2,500.00	2,500.00
TOWN, CITY, AND BOROUGH ORDERS.			
Town of Derby, ...	3,000.00	3,000.00	3,000.00
Borough of Birmingham, ...	21,674.20	21,674.20	21,674.20
SCHOOL DISTRICT ORDERS.			
Sixth School District of Town of Derby, Bonds,	14,000.00	14,000.00	14,000.00
BANK STOCKS.			
300 shares New Haven County Nat. B'k, N. H'n,	3,000.00	3,000.00	3,450.00
110 " Yale National Bank, New Haven,	11,000.00	11,000.00	12,650.00
59 " The Second Nat. Bank, New Haven,	5,900.00	5,900.00	9,145.00
154 " Merchants " "	7,700.00	7,700.00	8,470.00
5 " National Tradesmens B'k, "	500.00	500.00	700.00
23 " National New Haven " "	2,300.00	2,300.00	3,450.00
21 " First National Bank of Bridgeport,	2,100.00	2,100.00	3,150.00
63 " Bridgeport National, "	3,150.00	3,150.00	4,725.00
62 " City " "	6,200.00	6,200.00	7,812.00
27 " Connecticut " "	2,700.00	2,700.00	3,780.00
40 " Pequonnock " "			

DERBY SAVINGS BANK.—Continued.

INVESTMENTS.—Continued.

DESCRIPTION.	PAR VALUE.	COST.	MARKET VALUE.
BANK STOCKS.—CONTINUED.			
41 shares Middletown Nat. of Middletown, $	3,075.00	3,075.00	4,100.00
40 " Central " "	3,000.00	3,000.00	4,000.00
‚ 86 " First " of Norwich,	8,600.00	8,600.00	9,460.00
366 " Birmingham " of Birmingham,	34,600.00	34,600.00	43,250.00
40 " Citizens " of Waterbury,	4,000.00	4,000.00	5,000.00
88 " Metropolitan " of N. Y. City,	8,800.00	8,800.00	13,200.00
48 " Union " "	2,400.00	2,400.00	3,360.00
80 " Fourth " "	8,000.00	8,000.00	9,600.00
50 " Hanover " "	5,000.00	5,000.00	6,250.00
100 " American Exc. Nat., "	10,000.00	10,000.00	12,000.00
225 " Nat. Bank of Commerce, "	22,500.00	22,500.00	31,500.00
4 " Bank of New York, "	400.00	400.00	560.00

MISCELLANEOUS ITEMS.

1. Number of depositors having $500 or less,   3,089; total amount, $339,867.04
2. Number of depositors having over $500 and less than $1,000, ... 238; total amount,   234,400.33
3. Number of depositors having one thousand and not over $2,000, ... 128; total amount,   322,237.04
4. Number of depositors having over $2,000, 61; total amount,   181,363.23

5. Total number of depositors, . . . 3,516; total deposits, $1,077,867.64
6. Largest amount due a single depositor, $12,415.78.
7. Number of accounts opened during the year, 757; number closed, 385.
8. Amount of income received during the year, $72,651.66.
9. Amount of dividends declared during the year, $48,861.92.
10. Amount deposited, including interest credited, the past year, $250,694.39.
11. Amount withdrawn during the year, $160,572.63.
12. Increase of deposits the past year, $50,964.39.
13. Amount carried to surplus or profit and loss during the year, $10,229.08.
14. Rate of dividend the last year, 5 per cent.; when paid, January and July.
15. State tax during the past year, $2,412.44; U. S. tax, $200.56.
16. Total office expenses the past year, including salaries, $3,576.25.
17. Net amount of income during the year from real estate owned, $106.14.
18. Amount of assets yielding no income during the year, none.
19. Are all loans upon real estate secured by first mortgage? Yes.
20. Largest amount loaned to one individual, company, society, or corporation, $50,000.
21. Date of annual meeting for choice of officers, June 30th.

OFFICERS.—President, Jos. Arnold; Vice-President, Sidney A. Downs; Treasurer, Thos. S. Birdsey; Directors or Trustees, S. N. Summers, Wm. E. Downes, David Torrance, Henry A. Nettleton, Clark N. Rogers, A. B. Ruggles, Truman Piper.

DIME SAVINGS BANK, HARTFORD.

J. W. WELCH, Treasurer.   INCORPORATED, 1870.

STATEMENT, OCTOBER 1, 1882.

LIABILITIES.		ASSETS.	
Whole Amount of Deposits,	$185,159.05	Loans on Real Estate,	$84,925.00
Surplus Account,	7,741.35	Loans on Stocks and Bonds,	31,150.00
Interest Account,	5,184.83	Loans on Endorsed Notes,	7,950.00
		United States Bonds,	4,500.00
		Bank Stocks in Connecticut,	12,825.00
		Real Estate by Foreclosure,	46,000.00
		Cash in Bank,	9,145.27
		Cash on hand,	1,589.96
Total Liabilities,	$198,085.23	Total Assets,	$198,085.23

INVESTMENTS.

DESCRIPTION.	PAR VALUE.	COST.	MARKET VALUE.
UNITED STATES BONDS.			
4s of 1907 Registered, ... $	4,500.00	5,025.00	5,355.00
BANK STOCKS.			
40 shares Mercantile National, Hartford,	4,000.00	5,137.25	5,280.00
12 " Farmers and Mechanics Nat., Hartford,	1,200.00	1,563.00	1,680.00
16 " Ætna National, "	1,600.00	2,160.00	2,160.00
34 " Middlesex County Nat., Middletown,	3,400.00	4,075.00	4,080.00
21 " Middletown " "	1,575.00	2,331.00	2,352.00
14 " American " Hartford,	700.00	1,050.00	1,092.00

MISCELLANEOUS ITEMS.

1. Number of depositors having $500 or less,   5,176; total amount, $129,043.63
2. Number of depositors having over $500 and less than 1,000, ... 59; total amount,   39,597.78
3. Number of depositors having $1,000 and not over $2,000, ... 12; total amount,   14,449.85
4. Number of depositors having over $2,000,   1; total amount,   2,067.79

5. Total number of depositors, . . . 5,248; total deposits, $185,159.05
6. Largest amount due a single depositor, $2,067.79.
7. Number of accounts opened during the year, 360; number closed, 1,350.
8. Amount of income received during the year, $14,270.43.
9. Amount of dividends declared during the year, $10,081.33.
10. Amount deposited, including interest credited, the past year, $55,890.34.
11. Amount withdrawn during the year, $97,572.06.
12. Increase of deposits the past year, nothing.
13. Amount carried to surplus or profit and loss during the year, $7,741.35.
14. Rate of dividend the last year, 5 per cent., paid Oct. 1, 1881, and April 1, 1882.
15. State tax during the past year, $317.21; U. S. tax, nothing.
16. Total office expenses the past year, including salaries, $3,334.75.

DIME SAVINGS BANK.—Continued.

MISCELLANEOUS ITEMS.—Continued.

17. Net amount of income during the year from real estate owned, $2,028.45.
18. Amount of assets yielding no income during the year, $1,000.
19. Are all loans upon real estate secured by first mortgage? Yes.
20. Largest amount loaned to one individual, company, society, or corporation, $6,700.
21. Date of annual meeting for choice of officers, third Wednesday in July.

Officers.—President, A. E. Burr; Treasurer, J. W. Welch; Directors or Trustees, A. E. Burr, H. Sidney Hayden, J. W. Welch, W. A. Healy, James Bolter, Silas Goodell, Horace Lord, C. C. Kimball, John R. Redfield, Thomas Sisson, Chas. R. Chapman, Elisha Johnson, D. A. Rood, C. S. Davidson, W. H. Goodrich, J. C. Britton, Peter Chute, Owen McCabe, Rush P. Chapman, John Fairman.

DIME SAVINGS BANK, MIDDLETOWN.

ABEL C. ALLISON, Treasurer.   INCORPORATED, 1870.

STATEMENT, OCTOBER 1, 1882.

LIABILITIES.		ASSETS.	
Whole Amount of Deposits,	$40,304.80	Loans on Real Estate, .	$12,525.00
Interest Account, . .	1,845.76	Bank Stocks in Connecticut.	4,251.00
		Real Estate by Foreclosure,	17,860.82
		Furniture, ...	145.00
		Cash in Bank, . . .	7,368.74
Total Liabilities, . .	$42,150.56	Total Assets, . .	$42,150.56

INVESTMENTS.

DESCRIPTION.	PAR VALUE.	COST.	MARKET VALUE.
BANK STOCKS.			
8 shares Middlesex Co., Middletown, . . $	800.00	937.00	960.00
31 " Central National, " . .	2,325.00	2,880.00	3,410.00
4 " First " " . .	500.00	484.00	484.00

MISCELLANEOUS ITEMS.

1. Number of depositors having $500 or less, 603; total amount, $17,149.49
2. Number of depositors having over $500 and less than $1,000, ... 2; total amount, 1,312.30
3. Number of depositors having $1,000 and not over $2,000, ... 11; total amount, 15,418.78
4. Number of depositors having over $2,000, 3; total amount, 6,424.23

5. Total number of depositors, . . . 619; total deposits, $40,304.80
6. Largest amount due a single depositor, $2,276.37.
7. Number of accounts opened during the year, ; number closed, 37.
8. Amount of income received during the year, $2,846.04.
9. Amount of dividends declared during the year, none.
10. Amount deposited, including interest credited, the past year, none.
11. Amount withdrawn during the year, $1,724.88.
12. Decrease of deposits the past year, $1,724.85.
13. Amount carried to surplus or profit and loss during the year, none.
14. Rate of dividend the last year, per cent.; when paid, none.
15. State tax during the past year, $3.00; U. S. tax, none.
16. Total office expenses the past year, including salaries, $200.00.
17. Net amount of income during the year from real estate owned, $219.07.
18. Amount of assets yielding no income during the year, $1,550.00.
19. Are all loans upon real estate secured by first mortgage? yes.
20. Largest amount loaned to one individual, company, society, or corporation, $2,500.00.
21. Date of annual meeting for choice of officers, second Tuesday in July.

OFFICERS.—President, Curtis Bacon; Treasurer, Abel C. Allison; Directors or Trustees, Curtis Bacon, S. S. Allison, Abel C. Allison, Chas. A. Pelton, C. R. Fagan, J. S. Bailey, A. M. Colegrove, F. J. Chaffee, J. S. Fairchild, F. L. Gleason,. R. S. Hayes, S. T. Hull, C. A. Newell, Thos. Walsh, E. J. Paddock.

DIME SAVINGS BANK, NORWICH.

J. HUNT SMITH, Treasurer.   INCORPORATED, 1869.

STATEMENT, OCTOBER 1, 1882.

LIABILITIES.		ASSETS.	
Whole Amt. of Deposits,	$1,206,202.55	Loans on Real Estate, .	$518,234.00
Surplus Account, . .	10,000.00	Loans on Stocks and Bonds,	123,300.00
Interest Account, . .	23,340.97	Loans on Endorsed Notes,	5,700.00
Profit and Loss, . .	3,719.09	United States Bonds, .	35,350.00
Rent, ...	3,835.81	Town, City, and Corp'n Bonds,	24,955.00
		Town, City, and Bor'gh Orders,	55,000.00
		Railroad Bonds, . .	56,630.00
		Bank Stocks in Connecticut,	1,700.00
		Real Estate by Foreclosure,	167,805.91
		Banking House, . .	12,800.00
		Tax Account, . . .	1,266.46
		Expense Account, . .	1,296.64
		Real Estate Advances, .	444.12
		Business Paper, . .	200,000.00
		Cash in Bank, . .	5,126.23
		Cash on hand, . .	37,490.06
Total Liabilities, .	$1,247,098.42	Total Assets, . .	$1,247,098.42

INVESTMENTS.

DESCRIPTION.	PAR VALUE.	COST.	MARKET VALUE.
UNITED STATES BONDS.			
4s of 1907, Registered, ... $	30,000.00	30,300.00	35,512.50
4s of 1907, Coupon, ...	5,000.00	5,050.00	5,981.25
TOWN, CITY, AND CORPORATION BONDS.			
City of Cincinnati, 6s of 1909, . . .	22,000.00	23,870.00	26,620.00
" " 6s of 1906, Gold, . .	1,000.00	1,085.00	1,210.00
TOWN, CITY, AND BOROUGH ORDERS.			
City of Norwich, ...	55,000.00	55,000.00	55,000.00
RAILROAD BONDS.			
St. Louis, Jacksonville, and Chicago, 7 per cent.,	32,000.00	32,000.00	36,800.00
Louisiana and Missouri River, 7 per cent., .	20,000.00	20,000.00	22,800.00
Joliet and Northern Indiana, 7 per cent., .	4,000.00	4,630.00	4,800.00
BANK STOCK.			
6 shares Shetucket Nat. Bank, Norwich, .	600.00	600.00	750.00
10 " Norwich " " " .	1,100.00	1,100.00	1,100.00

DIME SAVINGS BANK.—Continued.

MISCELLANEOUS ITEMS.

1. Number of depositors having $500 or less,   4,735; total amount, $349,187.83
2. Number of depositors having over $500 and
   less than $1,000, ... 352; total amount,   247,842.24
3. Number of depositors having $1,000 and not
   over $2,000, ... 275; total amount,   382,099.43
4. Number of depositors having over $2,000,   . 84; total amount,   227,073.05

5. Total number of depositors,   .   .   . 5,446; total deposits, $1,206,202.55
6. Largest amount due a single depositor, $6,970.68.
7. Number of accounts opened during the year, 690; number closed, 600.
8. Amount of income received during the year, $67,638.01.
9. Amount of dividends declared during the year, $44,612.25.
10. Amount deposited, including interest credited, the past year, $345,457.34.
11. Amount withdrawn during the year, $294,301.64.
12. Increase of deposits the past year, $51,155.70.
13. Amount carried to surplus or profit and loss during the year, $7,382.90.
14. Rate of dividend the last year, 4 per cent.; when paid, May and November.
15. State tax during the past year, $2,401.82; U. S. tax, $52.38.
16. Total office expenses the past year, including salaries, $3,242.09.
17. Net amount of income during the year from real estate owned, $4,263.68.
18. Amount of assets yielding no income during the year, $1,000.00.
19. Are all loans upon real estate secured by first mortgage? Yes.
20. Largest amount loaned to one individual, company, society, or corporation,
    $200,000.00.
21. Date of annual meeting for choice of officers, second Wednesday in May.

OFFICERS.—President, E. R. Thompson; Vice-Presidents, H. H. Osgood, Horace Whitaker, W. R. Austin; Secretary and Treasurer, J. Hunt Smith; Assistant Treasurer, Frank L. Woodard; Directors or Trustees, Jas. Burnet, W. C. Osgood, F. J. Leavens, W. R. Burnham, Chas. D. Browning, Wm. G. Abbot, J. Hunt Smith, E. G. Bidwell, Gardiner Greene, Jr.

DIME SAVINGS BANK, THOMPSON.

HIRAM ARNOLD, Treasurer.   INCORPORATED, 1871.

STATEMENT, OCTOBER 1, 1882.

LIABILITIES.		ASSETS.	
Whole Amount of Deposits,	$421,517.72	Loans on Real Estate, .	$208,825.00
Surplus Account, . .	12,719.04	Loans on Endorsed Notes, .	200,747.54
Interest Account, . .	2,333.49	Bank Stocks in Connecticut,	11,358.00
Rents, etc., from		Real Estate by Foreclosure,	12,691.24
Real Estate Foreclosures, }	651.86	Expense Account, . .	68.87
		Cash in Bank, . . .	3,531.46
Total Liabilities, . .	$437,222.11	Total Assets, . .	$437,222.11

INVESTMENTS.

DESCRIPTION.	PAR VALUE.	COST.	MARKET VALUE.
BANK STOCKS.			
80 shares Thompson National Bank, . . $	8,000.00	8,928.00	9,120.00
12 " Home " " Meriden,	1,200.00	1,380.00	1,440.00
10 " First " " "	1,000.00	1,050.00	1,200.00

MISCELLANEOUS ITEMS.

1. Number of depositors having $500 or less,   673; total amount, $82,354.58
2. Number of depositors having over $500 and less than $1,000, . . .   167; total amount,   130,864.62
3. Number of depositors having $1,000 and not over $2,000, ...   95; total amount,   125,293.26
4. Number of depositors having over $2,000,   28; total amount,   83,005.26

5. Total number of depositors, . . . 963; total deposits, $421,517.72
6. Largest amount due a single depositor, $5,892.23.
7. Number of accounts opened during the year, 199; number closed, 52.
8. Amount of income received during the year, $22,205.58.
9. Amount of dividends declared during the year, $16,849.68.
10. Amount deposited, including interest credited, the past year, $114,915.26.
11. Amount withdrawn during the year, $70,154.05.
12. Increase of deposits the past year, $44,761.21.
13. Amount carried to surplus or profit and loss during the year, $1,732.90.
14. Rate of dividend the last year, 4½ per cent., paid February and August.
15. State tax during the past year, $811.96; U. States tax, $110.87.
16. Total office expenses the past year, including salaries, $1,576.85.
17. Net amount of income during the year from real estate owned, $526.88.
18. Amount of assets yielding no income during the year, $6,870.00.
19. Are all loans upon real estate secured by first mortgage? They are.
20. Largest amount loaned to one individual, company, society or corporation, $25,000.
21. Date of annual meeting for choice of officers, last Tuesday in July.

OFFICERS.—President, Lucius Briggs; Treasurer, Hiram Arnold; Directors or Trustees, Thomas D. Sayles, Jeremiah Olney, James N. Kingsley, James M. Munyan, Jerome F. Crosby, Henry G. Rawson, Marcus F. Towne, David Chase, George H. Nichols, John D. Converse.

DIME SAVINGS BANK, WALLINGFORD.

JOHN ATWATER, Treasurer.   INCORPORATED, 1871.

STATEMENT, OCTOBER 1, 1882.

LIABILITIES.		ASSETS.	
Whole Amount of Deposits,	$100,628.41	Loans on Real Estate, .	$64,211.66
Surplus Account, }		Loans on Endorsed Notes, .	25,674.00
Interest Account, } . .	2,592.63	Town, City, and Corp'n Bonds,	7,780.00
		Bank Stocks in Connecticut,	5,000.00
		Cash in Bank, ...	200.75
		Cash on hand, . . .	345.63
Total Liabilities, . .	$103,221.04	Total Assets, . .	$103,221.04

INVESTMENTS.

DESCRIPTION.	PAR VALUE.	COST.	MARKET VALUE.
TOWN, CITY, AND CORPORATION BONDS.			
Tax relief 1890 of City of New York, 7 per cent.,	$ 3,000.00	3,780.00	3,690.00
Central School District of Wallingford, 5 per ct.,	4,000.00	4,000.00	4,000.00
BANK STOCKS.			
50 shares First National Bank of Wallingford,	5,000.00	5,000.00	5,250.00

MISCELLANEOUS ITEMS.

1. Number of depositors having $500 or less,   661; total amount, $54,786.96
2. Number of depositors having over $500 and less than $1,000, ...   34; total amount,   22,367.32
3. Number of depositors having $1,000 and not over $2,000, ...   17; total amount,   23,474.13
4. Number of depositors having over $2,000,   0; total amount,
5. Total number of depositors, ...   712; total deposits, $100,628.41
6. Largest amount due a single depositor, $2,000.
7. Number of accounts opened during the year, $170; number closed, 123.
8. Amount of income received during the year, $4,852.66.
9. Amount of dividends declared during the year, $3,954.06.
10. Amount deposited, including interest credited, the past year, $40,197.04.
11. Amount withdrawn during the year, $28,957.12.
12. Increase of deposits the past year, $11,239.92.
13. Amount carried to surplus or profit and loss during the year, none.
14. Rate of dividend the last year, 4¼ per cent.; when paid, 2¼ per cent. Jan., and 2 per cent. July.
15. State tax during the past year, $107.67; United States tax, none.
16. Total office expenses the past year, including salaries, $293.23.
17. Net amount of income during the year from real estate owned, none.

DIME SAVINGS BANK.--CONTINUED.

MISCELLANEOUS ITEMS.—CONTINUED.

18. Amount of assets yielding no income during the year, $10,000.00.
19. Are all loans upon real estate secured by first mortgage? Yes.
20. Largest amount loaned to one individual, company, society, or corporation, $8,119.00.
21. Date of annual meeting for choice of officers, July.

OFFICERS.—President, Samuel Simpson; Treasurer and Secretary, John Atwater; Directors or Trustees, Phineas T. Ives, Charles N. Jones, Hezekiah Hall, Hugh Mallon, J. A. F. Northrop, Walter J. Leavenworth, John Munson; Secretary, Thomas Pickford.

DIME SAVINGS BANK, WATERBURY.

G. S. PARSONS, Treasurer.

INCORPORATED, 1870.

STATEMENT, OCTOBER 1, 1882.

LIABILITIES.		ASSETS.	
Whole Amount of Deposits,	$844,689.59	Loans on Real Estate, .	$513,600.00
Surplus Account, . .	35,000.00	Loans on Stocks and Bonds,	58,250.00
Interest Account, . .	17,529.04	Loans on Endorsed Notes, .	188,985.85
		State Bonds, . .	10,000.00
		Town, City, and Corp'n Bonds,	54,795.00
		Town, City, and Boro' Orders,	500.00
		Railroad Bonds, . . .	5,000.00
		Bank Stocks in Connecticut,	21,061.00
		Bank Stocks in other States,	1,500.00
		Real Estate by Foreclosure,	8,168.00
		Real Estate, ...	6,118.72
		Tax Account, . . .	246.80
		Insurance Account, . .	99.45
		Safe Account, . . .	1,000.00
		Cash in Bank, . . .	13,633.12
		Cash on hand, . . .	29,260.69
Total Liabilities, . .	$897,218.63	Total Assets, . .	$897,218.63

INVESTMENTS.

DESCRIPTION.	PAR VALUE.	COST.	MARKET VALUE.
STATE BONDS.			
State of Connecticut 6s, ... $	10,000.00	10,000.00	10,500.00
TOWN, CITY, AND CORPORATION BONDS.			
City of Waturbury 7s, 1897, . . .	5,000.00	5,650.00	6,500.00
" " 4½s, 1904-5, . .	10,000.00	10,645.00	10,645.00
" Cincinnati, 7$\frac{3}{10}$s, . . .	20,000.00	26,000.00	26,000.00
" Chicago, water, 7s, . . .	10,000.00	12,500.00	12,500.00
TOWN, CITY, AND BOROUGH ORDERS.			
Town of Middlebury, Conn., . . .	500.00	500.00	500.00
RAILROAD BONDS.			
Chicago, Burlington & Quincy 8s, . . .	5,000.00	5,000.00	5,000.00
BANK STOCKS.			
100 shares Waterbury National Bank, . .	5,000.00	7,600.00	9,000.00
50 " Citizens " " . .	5,000.00	6,265.00	6,750.00
24 " Bridgeport " " . .	1,200.00	1,596.00	1,596.00
30 " Hurlbut " " . .	4,000.00	5,600.00	6,000.00
12 " Shoe and Leather National, N. Y.,	1,200.00	1,500.00	1,500.00

DIME SAVINGS BANK.—Continued.

MISCELLANEOUS ITEMS.

1. Number of depositors having $500 or less,   4.215; total amount, $347,950.05
2. Number of depositors having over $500
   and less than $1,000, ...   278; total amount,   185,565.70
3. Number of depositors having $1,000 and
   not over $2,000, ...   169; total amount,   202,097.70
4. Number of depositors having over $2,000,   86; total amount,   109,076.14

5. Total number of depositors, . . .   4,698; total deposits, $844,689.59
6. Largest amount due a single depositor, $12,414.44.
7. Number of accounts opened during the year, $1,288; number closed, 765.
8. Amount of income received during the year, $43,915.54.
9. Amount of dividends declared during the year, $26,479.70.
10. Amount deposited, including interest credited, the past year, $436,947.88.
11. Amount withdrawn during the year, $286,354.39.
12. Increase of deposits the past year, $150,593.49.
13. Amount carried to surplus or profit and loss during the year, $10,000.
14. Rate of dividend the last year, 4 per cent.; when paid, April and October.
15. State tax during the past year, $1,685.34; United States tax, $161.98.
16. Total office expenses the past year, including salaries, $2,732.13.
17. Net amount of income during the year from real estate owned, none.
18. Amount of assets yielding no income during the year, $10,500.
19. Are all loans upon real estate secured by first mortgage? Yes.
20. Largest amount loaned to one individual, company, society, or corporation,
    $30,000.
21. Date of annual meeting for choice of officers.

Officers.—President, E. Leavenworth; Treasurer, Guernsey S. Parsons; Directors or Trustees, Henry C. Griggs, Theodore I. Driggs, Henry Merriman, E. N. Lathrop, Charles W. Gillette, Henry H. Peck, F. A. Spencer, E. C. Lewis.

DIME SAVINGS BANK.—WILLIMANTIC.

JOHN L. WALDEN, Treasurer.   INCORPORATED, 1872.

STATEMENT, OCTOBER 1, 1882.

LIABILITIES.		ASSETS.	
Whole Amount of Deposits,	$568,559.47	Loans on Real Estate, .	$228,524.00
Surplus Account, }		Loans on Stocks and Bonds,	102,512.00
Interest Account, } . .	6,702.57	Loans on Endorsed Notes,.	103,189.50
Profit and Loss, . .	7,679.28	Town, City, and Corp'n Bonds,	25,569.80
		Town, City, and B'gh Orders,	28,250.00
		School District Orders, .	4,500.00
		Bank Stocks in Connecticut,	44,651.00
		Insurance Account, . .	3.00
		Certificate of Deposit, .	8,000.00
		Furniture and Fixtures, .	1,050.00
		Cash in Bank, . . .	28,082.47
		Cash on hand, . . .	8,659.55
Total Liabilities, . . .	$582,941.32	Total Assets, . . .	$582,941.32

INVESTMENTS.

DESCRIPTION.	PAR VALUE.	COST.	MARKET VALUE.
TOWN, CITY, AND CORPORATION BONDS.			
Norwich City Sinking Fund, 5 per cent., 1908, $	10,000.00	10,300.00	10,500.00
City of Cincinnati, Gold, 6 " " .	11,000.00	12,741.80	14,520.00
City of Minneapolis, 8 " " .	2,000.00	2,528.00	2,568.00
TOWN, CITY, AND BOROUGH ORDERS.			
Borough of Willimantic, ...	26,000.00	26,000.00	26,000.00
Town of Coventry, ...	1,500.00	1,500.00	1,500.00
" " "	500.00	500.00	500.00
" " "	250.00	250.00	250.00
SCHOOL DISTRICT ORDERS.			
Second School District of Willimantic, . .	4,500.00	4,500.00	4,500.00
BANK STOCKS.			
85 shares Mer. Loan and Trust Co., Willimantic,	8,500.00	9,043.00	9,435.00
69 " First National Bank, Hartford, .	6,900.00	7,416.00	8,280.00
28 " " " " Willimantic,	2,800.00	2,800.00	3,800.00
9 " National Exchange Bank, Hartford,	450.00	594.00	666.00
15 " Rockville National " Rockville,	1,500.00	1,540.00	1,875.00
12 " Stafford " " Stafford,	1,200.00	1,278.00	1,278.00
120 " Second " " Norwich,	12,000.00	13,800.00	14,400.00
30 " Thames " " "	3,000.00	4,050.00	4,800.00
35 " Shetucket " " "	3,500.00	4,130.00	4,375.00

DIME SAVINGS BANK.—CONTINUED.

MISCELLANEOUS ITEMS.

1. Number of depositors having $500 or less, .   2,213; total amount, $145,773.55
2. Number of depositors having over $500 and less than $1,000, ...   171; total amount,   119,247.47
3. Number of depositors having $1,000 and not over $2,000, ...131; total amount,   171,888.80
4. Number of depositors having over $2,000, .   14; total amount,   31,649.65

5. Total number of depositors,   .   .   . 2,529; total deposits, $568,559.47
6. Largest amount due a single depositor, $3,000.00.
7. Number of accounts opened during the year, 525; number closed, 392.
8. Amount of income received during the year, $31,229.52.
9. Amount of dividends declared during the year, $22,541.55.
10. Amount deposited, including interest credited, the past year, $204,450.37.
11. Amount withdrawn during the year, $147,241.37.
12. Increase of deposits the past year, $57,209.00.
13. Amount carried to surplus or profit and loss during the year, $6,338.99.
14. Rate of dividend the last year, 4½ per cent.; when paid, April and October.
15. State tax during the past year, $1,148.64; U. S. tax, $8.09.
16. Total office expenses the past year, including salaries, $2,041.64.
17. Net amount of income during the year from real estate owned, none.
18. Amount of assets yielding no income during the year, none.
19. Are all loans upon real estate secured by first mortgage? Yes.
20. Largest amount loaned to one individual, company, society, or corporation, $50,000.00.
21. Date of annual meeting for choice of officers, third Wednesday in July.

OFFICERS.—President, James Walden; Treasurer, John L. Walden; Executive Committee, James Walden, Ansel Arnold, James E. Murray, Fred. Rogers, William C. Jillson, E. G. Sumner, A. T. Fowler, J. L. Walden.

EASTFORD SAVINGS BANK.

H. B. BURNHAM, Treasurer.   INCORPORATED, 1871.

STATEMENT, OCTOBER 1, 1882.

LIABILITIES		ASSETS.	
Whole Amount of Deposits,	$13,451.09	Loans on Real Estate, .	$5,260.00
Interest Account, . .	362.58	Loans on Endorsed Notes, .	2,364.66
Other Liabilities, . .	116.71	Real Estate by Foreclosure,	5,759.71
		Expense Account, . .	32.34
		Other Assets, . . .	373.32
		Cash in Bank, . . .	28.73
		Cash on hand, . . .	111.62
Total Liabilities, . .	$13,930.38	Total Assets, . .	$13,930.38

MISCELLANEOUS ITEMS.

1. Number of depositors having $500 or less,. 144; total amount, $6,991.33
2. Number of depositors having over $500
    and less than $1,000, . .   5; total amount,   3,658.07
3. Number of depositors having $1,000
    and not over $2,000, . . .   2; total amount,   2,801.69
4. Number of depositors having over $2,000, none; total amount,   none.

5. Total number of depositors, . .   151; total deposits, $13,451.09
6. Largest amount due a single depositor, $1,630.07.
7. Number of accounts opened during the year, 1; number closed, 21.
8. Amount of income received during the year, $542.52.
9. Amount of dividends declared during the year, $315.18.
10. Amount deposited, including interest credited, the past year, $436.30.
11. Amount withdrawn during the year, $2,522.98.
12. Increase of deposits the past year, none.
13. Amount carried to surplus or profit and loss during the year, none.
14. Rate of dividend the last year, 2 per cent.; when paid, January.
15. State tax during the past year, none; U. S. tax, none.
16. Total office expenses the past year, $32.34. ǀ
17. Net amount of income during the year from real estate owned, none.
18. Amount of assets yielding no income during the year, $5,759.71.
19. Are all loans upon real estate secured by first mortgage? Yes.
20. Largest amount loaned to one individual, company, society, or corporation,
    $4,000.00.
21. Date of annual meeting for choice of officers, July 30th.

OFFICERS.—President, J. D. Barrows; Vice-President, S. G. Bowen; Treasurer, H. B. Burnham; Directors or Trustees, George Bugbee, Isaac Warner, S. O. Bowen, Amasa Keyes, H. B. Burnham, J. M. Keith, J. D. Barrows, Albert Kenyon, E. W. Warren, John Holman, H. H. Burnham, C. E. Barrows.

ESSEX SAVINGS BANK.

E. W. REDFIELD, Treasurer.   INCORPORATED, 1851.

STATEMENT, OCTOBER 1, 1882.

LIABILITIES.		ASSETS.	
Whole Amount of Deposits,	$610,338.52	Loans on Real Estate, .	$393,448.00
Surplus Account, . .	14,605.96	Loans on Stocks and Bonds,	14,580.00
Interest Account, . .	8,462.63	Loans on Endorsed Notes,	10,578.10
Rents, ...	802.76	Town, City, and Corp'n Bonds,	94,500.00
Sundry Accounts, . .	146.51	Railroad Bonds, . .	11,000.00
		Bank Stocks in Connecticut,	10,959.00
		Bank Stocks in other States,	19,761.24
		Real Estate by Foreclosure,	28,437.75
		Banking House, . .	3,651.69
		Expense Account, . .	624.21
		Office Furniture, Safe, etc.,	759.70
		Sundry Accounts, . .	185.27
		Premium Account, . .	19,240.83
		Cash in Bank, . . .	24,224.29
		Cash on hand, . . .	2,406.30
Total Liabilities, .	$634,356.38	Total Assets, . .	$634,356.38

INVESTMENTS.

DESCRIPTION.	PAR VALUE.	COST.	MARKET VALUE.
TOWN, CITY, AND CORPORATION BONDS.			
Middletown, 6 per cent., . . . $	1,000.00	1,000.00	1,050.00
Borough of Danbury, 7 " . . .	1,000.00	1,000.00	1,100.00
Town of Lyme, 5 " . . .	500.00	500.00	500.00
Town of Essex, 4½ " . . .	20,000.00	20,000.00	20,800.00
City of Brooklyn, 7 " . . .	1,000.00	1,000.00	1,300.00
" Cincinnati, 7 " . . .	8,000.00	8,000.00	9,520.00
" " 7 3/10 " . . .	24,000.00	24,000.00	31,200.00
" " 6 " . . .	10,000.00	10,000.00	12,000.00
" Chicago, 7 " . . .	19,000.00	19,000.00	22,420.00
" St. Louis, 6 " . . .	10,000.00	10,000.00	11,200.00
RAILROAD BONDS.			
Central Pacific, 6 per cent., ...	1,000.00	1,000.00	1,140.00
New York Central & Hudson R., 7 per cent.,	10,000.00	10,000.00	13,000.00
BANK STOCK.			
20 shares Phœnix National, Hartford, . .	2,000.00	1,979.00	3,400.00
15 " Hartford Trust Co., " . .	1,500.00	1,500.00	1,515.00
20 " Second National, New Haven, .	2,000.00	2,160.00	3,200.00
6 " Yale " " .	600.00	690.00	690.09
10 " Middletown National, Middletown,	750.00	1,000.00	1,000.00
2 " Saybrook " Essex, .	200.00	270.00	250.00
50 " Merchants " Norwich,	2,000.00	2,100.00	2,100.00
20 " Uncas " " .	1,000.00	1,260.00	1,260.00

ESSEX SAVINGS BANK.—Continued.

INVESTMENTS.—Continued.

DESCRIPTION.		PAR VALUE.	COST.	MARKET VALUE.
BANK STOCKS.—CONTINUED.				
28 shares Bank of Commerce, New York,	$	2,800.00	2,800.00	4,200.00
20 " Marine National, "		1,000.00	1,000.00	690.00
30 " American Exchange, "		3,000.00	3,257.50	3,900.00
11 " Continental, "		1,100.00	1,563.75	1,320.00
10 " Bank of America, "		1,000.00	992.50	1,610.00
20 " Park, "		2,000.00	2,062.50	3,140.00
30 " Chatham, "		750.00	635.62	900.00
24 " Union, "		1,200.00	1,051.87	1,800.00
18 " Ninth National, ::		1,800.00	1,900.00	2,196.00
8 " Shoe and Leather, "		800.00	1,100.00	1,040.00
10 " Bank of New York, "		1,000.00	1,005.00	1,400.00
24 " Delaware & Hudson Canal Co., N.Y.,		2,400.00	2,392.50	2,736.00

MISCELLANEOUS ITEMS.

1. Number of depositors having $500 or less,   1,506; total amount, $169,682.65
2. Number of depositors having over $500 and less than $1,000,. . . . .   192; total amount,   134,301.43
3. Number of depositors having $1,000 and not over $2,000, . . . 121; total amount,   171,490.29
4. Number of depositors having over $2,000,   43; total amount,   134,864.15

5. Total number of depositors, . . . 1,862; total deposits, $610,338.52
6. Largest amount due a single depositor, $9,925.27.
7. Number of accounts opened during the year, 202; number closed, 123.
8. Amount of income received during the year, $33,650.58.
9. Amount of dividends declared during the year, $25,566.25.
10. Amount deposited, including interest credited, the past year, $93,739.87.
11. Amount withdrawn during the year, $64,355.40.
12. Increase of deposits the past year, $29,384.47.
13. Amount carried to surplus or profit and loss during the year, $1,475.
14. Rate of dividend the last year, 4½ per cent., paid 2¼ in January, 2 in July.
15. State tax during the past year, $1,189.78; U. S. tax, $191.98.
16. Total office expenses the past year, including salaries, $2,282.35.
17. Net amount of income during the year from real estate owned, $821.09.
18. Amount of assets yielding no income during the year, none.
19. Are all loans upon real estate secured by first mortgage? They are.
20. Largest amount loaned to one individual, company, society, or corporation, $7,500.
21. Date of annual meeting for choice of officers, fourth Monday in July.

OFFICERS.—President, James Phelps; Treasurer, E. W. Redfield; Directors or Trustees, James Phelps, Henry G. Smith, J. H. Tucker, Benjamin Post, N. H. Williams.

FAIRFIELD COUNTY SAVINGS BANK, NORWALK.

LESTER S. COLE, Treasurer.   INCORPORATED, 1874.

STATEMENT, OCTOBER 1, 1882.

LIABILITIES.		ASSETS.	
Whole Amount of Deposits,	$392,307.48	Loans on Real Estate, .	$151,975.00
Surplus Account, . .	5,000.00	Loans on Stocks and Bonds,	89,900.00
Interest Account, . .	2,862.36	Loans on Endorsed Notes,	1,050.00
		United States Bonds, . .	15,575.00
		Town, City, and Corp. B'ds,	52,983.50
		School District Orders, .	13,600.00
		Bank Stocks in Connecticut,	14,509.00
		Bank Stocks in other States,	32,274.88
		Real Estate by Foreclosure,	12,866.33
		Insurance Account, . .	50.73
		Cash in Bank, . . .	15,385.40
Total Liabilities, . .	$400,169.84	Total Assets, . .	$400,169.84

INVESTMENTS.

DESCRIPTION.	PAR VALUE.	COST.	MARKET VALUE.
UNITED STATES BONDS.			
5s of 1881, Registered (extended 3¼ per cent.), $	5,000.00	15,575.00	15,000.00
TOWN, CITY, AND CORPORATION BONDS.			
Brooklyn, N. Y., City, ...	14,000.00	15,557.50	15,557.50
Bethel Borough, ...	12,000.00	12,456.00	13,800.00
New York City, ...	20,000.00	24,450.00	24,450.00
Norwalk War, ...	500.00	520.00	500.00
SCHOOL DISTRICT ORDERS.			
Over River School District, ...	10,000.00	10,000.00	10,000.00
Center " " . . .	3,600.00	3,600.00	3,600.00
BANK STOCKS.			
40 shares Continental, New York, . .	4,000.00	4,000.00	4,760.00
55 " Phenix, "	1,100.00	1,100.00	1,144.00
50 " Fourth National, "	5,000.00	4,790.63	6,400.00
30 " Norwalk " . . .	3,000.00	3,810.00	3,810.00
26 " Fairfield County, . .	2,600.00	3,114.00	3,250.00
30 " Park, New York, . .	3,000.00	3,180.00	4,710.00
50 " Republic, " . .	5,000.00	5,050.00	5,000.00
30 " Mercantile, " . .	3,000.00	2,850.00	3,600.00
30 " Central, " . .	3,000.00	3,098.00	3,000.00
35 " St. Nicholas, " . .	3,500.00	3,500.00	3,500.00
100 " Merchants Ex., " . .	5,000.00	4,706.25	4,650.00
20 " First, Westport, Ct., . .	2,000.00	2,020.00	2,020.00
10 " " Norwich, " . .	1,000.00	1,065.00	1,100.00

FAIRFIELD COUNTY SAVINGS BANK.—Continued.

MISCELLANEOUS ITEMS.

1. Number of depositors having $500 or less,   712; total amount, $138,763.49
2. Number of depositors having over $500 and less than $1,000, ...   179; total amount,   94,514.59
8. Number of depositors having $1,000 and not over $2,000, ...   90; total amount,   124,715.74
4. Number of depositors having over $2,000,   17; total amount,   34,313.66

5. Total number of depositors, . . .   998; total deposits, $392,307.48
6. Largest amount due a single depositor, $2,936.99.
7. Number of accounts opened during the year, 245; number closed, 162.
8. Amount of income received during the year, $21,160.64.
9. Amount of dividends declared during the year, $13,726.80.
10. Amount deposited, including interest credited, the past year, $107,250.70.
11. Amount withdrawn during the year, $43,504.02.
12. Increase of deposits the past year, $63,746.68.
13. Amount carried to surplus or profit and loss during the year, $4,481.95.
14. Rate of dividend the last year, 4 per cent.; when paid, April and October.
15. State tax during the past year, $760.97; U. S. tax, none.
16. Total office expenses the past year, including salaries, $875.41.
17. Net amount of income during the year from real estate owned, none.
18. Amount of assets yielding no income during the year, $12,866.33.
19. Are all loans upon real estate secured by first mortgage? Yes.
20. Largest amount loaned to one individual, company, society, or corporation, $10,000.
21. Date of annual meeting for choice of officers, fourth Wednesday in January.

OFFICERS.—President, Winfield S. Moody; Treasurer, Lester S. Cole; Directors or Trustees, Winfield S. Moody, Edward H. Nash, Edward Merrill, Alfred H. Camp, Martin S. Craw, Elbert Curtis, Sherman Morehouse, Charles E. St. John, Asa B. Woodward.

FALLS VILLAGE SAVINGS BANK.

U. H. MINER, Treasurer.   INCORPORATED, 1854,

STATEMENT, OCTOBER 1, 1882.

LIABILITIES.		ASSETS.	
Whole Amount of Deposits,	$409,236.89	Loans on Real Estate,	$156,082.74
Surplus Account,	6,500.00	Loans on Stocks and Bonds,	24,900.00
Interest Account,	2,356.20	Loans on Endorsed Notes,	73,174.74
		United States Bonds,	25,298.25
		State Bonds,	7,630.00
		Town, City, and Corp'n Bonds,	40,000.00
		Town, City, and Boro' Orders,	345.80
		Bank Stocks in Connecticut,	13,915.00
		Bank Stocks in other States,	11,200.00
		Real Estate by Foreclosure,	32,979.76
		Banking House,.	12,230.28
		Insurance Account,	26.15
		Expense Account,	329.10
		Other Assets,	2,000.00
		Cash in Bank,	13,492.59
		Cash on hand,	4,488.68
Total Liabilities,	$418,093.09	Total Assets,	$418,093.09

INVESTMENTS.

DESCRIPTION.	PAR VALUE.	COST.	MARKET VALUE.
UNITED STATES BONDS.			
4s of 1907, Coupon, $	25,100.00	25,298.25	29,743.50
STATE BONDS.			
Missouri, 6 per cent., 1889,	6,000.00	6,630.00	6,630.00
Minnesota, 4½ per cent., 1891,	1,000.00	1,000.00	1,000.00
TOWN, CITY, AND CORPORATION BONDS.			
Cincinnati, Ohio, 6 per cent., 1909,	10,000.00	10,700.00	12,000.00
Cleveland, Ohio, 6 per cent., 1898,	20,000.00	23,400.00	23,400.00
Rochester, N. Y., 7 per cent., 1893,	5,000.00	5,900.00	6,250.00
TOWN, CITY, AND BOROUGH ORDERS.			
Canaan,	345.80	345.80	345.80
BANK STOCKS.			
131¼ shares National Iron, Falls Village,	13,125.00	13,915.00	15,750.00
112 " Continental National, N. Y.,	11,200.00	11,200.00	13,440.00

FALLS VILLAGE SAVINGS BANK.—Continued.

MISCELLANEOUS ITEMS.

1. Number of depositors having $500 or less,   857; total amount, $128,190.25
2. Number of depositors having over $500 and
    less than $1,000, ... 136; total amount,   73,780.59
3. Number of depositors having $1,000 and not
    over $2,000, ... 88; total amount,   118,890.38
4. Number of depositors having over $2,000,   27; total amount,   88,375.67

5. Total number of depositors, .   .   .   1,108; total deposits, $409,236.89
6. Largest amount due a single depositor, $6,916.14.
7. Number of accounts opened during the year, 184; number closed, 128.
8. Amount of income received during the year, $19,641.66.
9. Amount of dividends declared during the year, $15,076.84.
10. Amount deposited, including interest credited, the past year, $111,019.51.
11. Amount withdrawn during the year, $79,309.75.
12. Increase of deposits the past year, $31,709.76.
13. Amount carried to surplus or profit and loss during the year, $1,000.
14. Rate of dividend the last year, 4 per cent., paid January and July.
15. State tax during the past year, $727.06; U. S. tax, $35.30.
16. Total office expenses the past year, including salaries, $1,876.61.
17. Net amount of income during the year from real estate owned, $520.14.
18. Amount of assets yielding no income during the year, $1,000.
19. Are all loans upon real estate secured by first mortgage? Yes.
20. Largest amount loaned to one individual, company, society, or corporation,
    $13,000.
21. Date of annual meeting for choice of officers, September.

Officers.—President, Daniel Brewster; Treasurer, U. H. Miner; Directors or
Trustees, Uriel H. Miner, Daniel Brewster, James H. Barnum, O. M. Brinton,
C. Brown, P. C. Storm, H. E. Wetherell.

FARMERS & MECHANICS SAVINGS BANK, MIDDLETOWN.

GEO. N. WARD, Treasurer.   INCORPORATED, 1858.

STATEMENT, OCTOBER 1, 1882.

LIABILITIES.		ASSETS.	
Whole Amt. of Deposits,	$1,305,550.51	Loans on Real Estate, .	$601,508.00
Surplus Account, .	39,000.00	Loans on Stocks and Bonds,	16,422.00
Interest Account, . .	12,192.16	Loans on Personal Security,	9,250.00
Profit and Loss Account, .	8,386.11	United States Bonds, .	34,800.00
Premium Account, . .	45.00	Town, City, and Corp'n B'ds,	321,377.50
Miscellaneous Account, .	11.58	Bank Stocks in Connecticut,	149,812.50
		Real Estate by Foreclosure,	157,535.56
		Bank Block, . . .	34,906.01
		Tax Account, . . .	1,170.84
		Expense Account, . .	1,609.57
		Fixture Account, . .	5,000.00
		Steam Heating Account, .	3,460.22
		Cash in Bank, . . .	26,850.64
		Cash on hand, . . .	1,482.52
Total Liabilities,	$1,365,185.36	Total Assets, . .	$1,365,185.36

INVESTMENTS.

DESCRIPTION.	PAR VALUE.	COST.	PAR VALUE.
UNITED STATES BONDS.			
4s of 1907, registered, ... $	30,000.00	34,800.00	35,512.50
TOWN, CITY, AND CORPORATION BONDS.			
Town of Middletown, Ct., 6s, . . .	132,000.00	132,000.00	147,840.00
" " " " 7s, . . .	55,500.00	58,500.00	65,490.00
" " Portland, " 7s, . . .	17,600.00	17,600.00	20,768.00
" " Middlefield, " 7s, . . .	8,900.00	8,900.00	10,502.00
" " Chatham, " 5s, . . .	7,200.00	7,200.00	7,560.00
City of Rockland, Me., 6s, . . .	5,000.00	5,210.00	5,210.00
" " St. Louis, Gold, 6s, . . .	6,000.00	6,900.00	6,900.00
" " " Park, 6s, . . .	5,000.00	6,025.00	6,050.00
" " Cleveland, 6s, . . .	4,000.00	4,630.00	4,630.00
" " Columbus, 6s, . . .	5,000.00	5,512.50	5,600.00
" " Cincinnati, 6s, . . .	10,000.00	10,700.00	12,000.00
" " " $7\frac{3}{10}$s, . . .	10,000.00	13,000.00	13,100.00
" " Milwaukee, 7s, . . .	7,000.00	8,925.00	8,960.00
" " Detroit, 7s, . . .	5,000.00	6,725.00	6,725.00
" " Rochester, 7s, . . .	25,000.00	29,500.00	30,000.00
BANK STOCKS.			
255 shares Middlesex Co. Nat., Bank, Middleto'n,	25,500.00	28,505.00	30,600.00
142 " Central " " "	10,650.00	14,762.00	15,975.00
141 " Middletown " " "	10,575.00	15,581.00	15,721.50
260 " First " " "	26,000.00	27,815.00	31,200.00

FARMERS & MECHANICS SAVINGS BANK.—Continued.

INVESTMENTS.—Continued.

DESCRIPTION.	PAR VALUE.	COST.	MARKET VALUE.
BANK STOCKS.—CONTINUED.			
91 shares First National Bank, Meriden, $	9,100.00	10,081.50	10,738.00
14 " Meriden, . " " "	1,400.00	1,698.00	1,820.00
78 " Home " " "	7,800.00	10,446.00	10,446.00
111 " Thames, " " Norwich,	11,100.00	16,785.50	16,785.50
150 " First " " "	15,000.00	16,205.00	17,325.00
71 " First " " Portland,	7,100.00	7,843.00	8,520.00
5 " Nat. Bank of Commerce, N. London,	500.00	590.00	600.00

MISCELLANEOUS ITEMS.

1. Number of depositors having $500 or less, 2,000; total amount, $266,554.20
2. Number of depositors having over $500 and less than $1,000, ... 390; total amount, 275,203.12
3. Number of depositors having $1,000 and not over $2,000, ... 373; total amount, 544,501.13
4. Number of depositors having over $2,000, 71; total amount, 219,292.06

5. Total number of depositors, . . . 2,834; total deposits, $1,305,550.51
6. Largest amount due a single depositor, $19,890.29.
7. Number of accounts opened during the year, 451; number closed, 292.
8. Amount of income received during the year, $74,182.15.
9. Amount of dividends declared during the year, $40,728.58.
10. Amount deposited, including interest credited, the past year, $269,182.75.
11. Amount withdrawn during the year, $204,339.69.
12. Increase of deposits the past year, $64,843.06.
13. Amount carried to surplus or profit and loss during the year, $14,454.76.
14. Rate of dividend the last year, 4 per cent.; when paid, after August 10th and February 10th.
1 State tax during the past year, $2,044.66; U. S. tax, $297.28.
1 Total office expenses the past year, including salaries, $5,905.47.
1 Net amount of income during the year from real estate owned, $5,016.71.
1 Amount of assets yielding no income during the year, $3,606.84.
1 Are all loans upon real estate secured by first mortgage? Yes.
20 Largest amount loaned to one individual, company, society, or corporation, $23,000.00.
21. Date of annual meeting for choice of officers, second Wednesday in July.

OFFICERS.—President, Benjamin Douglas; Treasurer, Geo. N. Ward; Directors or Trustees, Benj. Douglas, Wm. R. Galpin, Jno. M. Douglas, O. Vincent Coffin, A. G. Pease, Hiram Veazey, L. Boardman, Jos. W. Douglas, Edwin Scovill, D. B. Coe, Hezekiah Scovill, Dr. L. Bailey, H. D. Hall, J. G. Baldwin, S. T. Camp, Dr. D. H. Chase, A. Cornwell, E. W. N. Starr, Wm. W. Wilcox, A. B. Calef, Cornelius Brainerd, E. B. Chaffee, Oscar Leach, A. H. Conklin, S. Stearnes, Jr.

FARMINGTON SAVINGS BANK.

JULIUS GAY, President.   INCORPORATED, 1851.

STATEMENT, OCTOBER 1, 1882.

LIABILITIES.		ASSETS.	
Whole Amt. of Deposits,	$1,806,582.03	Loans on Real Estate, .	$1,131,635.00
Surplus Account, . .	40,000.00	Loans on Stocks and Bonds,	17,400.00
Interest Account, . .	30,787.74	Loans on Endorsed Notes,	4,400.10
		United States Bonds, .	150,000.00
		Town, City, and Corp'n B'ds,	70,000.00
		Railroad Bonds, . .	240,000.00
		Bank Stocks in Connecticut,	155,900.00
		Bank Stocks in other States,	20,300.00
		Real Estate by Foreclosure,	34,350.00
		Banking House, . .	4,000.00
		Cash in Bank, . . .	39,849.09
		Cash on hand, . . .	9,535.68
Total Liabilities, .	$1,877,369.77	Total Assets, . .	$1,877,369.77

INVESTMENTS.

DESCRIPTION.	PAR VALUE.	COST.	MARKET VALUE.
UNITED STATES BONDS.			
4½s of 1891, Registered, ... $	70,000.00	71,733.75	78,837.50
4s of 1907, Registered, ...	80,000.00	79,867.50	94,900.00
. TOWN, CITY, AND CORPORATION BONDS.			
Hartford 4½ per cent., Town, ...	60,000.00	62,495.00	62,400.00
Bridgeport " "	10,000.00	10,305.00	10,400.00
RAILROAD BONDS.			
Chicago, Rock Island & Pacific, . . .	40,000.00	48,212.50	50,400.00
Morris & Essex, ...	10,000.00	13,035.00	13,900.00
Buffalo, New York & Erie, . . .	30,000.00	37,450.00	39,000.00
Pittsburgh, Fort Wayne & Chicago, . .	10,000.00	12,853.34	13,500.00
Chicago & Alton, ...	40,000.00	48,788.75	48,400.00
Chicago, Burlington & Quincy, . .	40,000.00	50,555.50	49,900.00
New York Central & Hudson River, . .	20,000.00	26,575.00	26,600.00
New York, Providence & Boston, . . .	5,000.00	6,631.25	6,700.00
Albany & Susquehanna, ...	45,000.00	53,057.66	52,000.00
BANK STOCKS.			
88 shares Charter Oak National, Hartford, .	8,800.00	10,469.50	12,320.00
150 " Farmers & Mechanics, " .	15,000.00	22,078.75	20,250.00
138 " National Exchange, " .	6,900.00	8,493.25	10,764.00
10 " Hartford National, " .	1,000.00	1,481.50	1,750.00
100 " City " .	10,000.00	10,978.25	9,000.00
40 " State .	4,000.00	4,731.00	4,440.00
60 " Phœnix National, .. .	6,000.00	8,332.00	10,500.00
17 " Mercantile " :: .	1,700.00	2,007.75	2,210.00
45 " Ætna " .. .	4,500.00	5,290.25	5,850.00
200 " First " " .	20,000.00	26,865.25	24,400.00
70 " American " .. .	3,500.00	5,285.00	5,040.00

FARMINGTON SAVINGS BANK.—Continued.

INVESTMENTS.—Continued.

DESCRIPTION.		PAR VALUE.	COST.	MARKET VALUE.
BANK STOCKS.—Continued.				
100 shares National New Haven, New Haven,	$	10,000.00	13,350.95	17,500.00
60 " Merchants National, "	.	3,000.00	3,470.00	3,600.00
50 " Meriden " Meriden,	.	5,000.00	5,475.00	6,250.00
207 " Home " .	.	20,700.00	22,223.00	25,875.00
200 " First " "	.	20,000.00	22,455.68	23,000.00
8 " Middlesex " Middletown,		800.00	800.00	920.00
50 " New Britain " New Britain,		5,000.00	5,660.00	7,000.00
106 " Merchants " New York,		5,300.00	6,890.78	6,890.00
50 " Nat. Bank of Commerce, "		5,000.00	7,360.51	7,500.00
100 " American Exc. Nat. B'k, "		10,000.00	11,304.41	13,000.00
100 " Nat. Bank of Norwalk, Norwalk,		10,000.00	10,858.50	11,000.00

MISCELLANEOUS ITEMS.

1. Number of depositors having $500 or less, 2,366; total amount, $303,283.03
2. Number of depositors having over $500 and less than $1,000, ...   481; total amount,   332,818.09
3. Number of depositors having $1,000 and not over $2,000, ...   446; total amount,   637,737.00
4. Number of depositors having over $2,000,   170; total amount,   532,744.00

5. Total number of depositors, . . . 3,463; total deposits, $1,806,582.03
6. Largest amount due a single depositor, $14,156.41.
7. Number of accounts opened during the year, 299; number closed, 266.
8. Amount of income received during the year, $106,753.79.
9. Amount of dividends declared during the year, $78,476.56.
10. Amount deposited, including interest credited, the past year, $302,675.09.
11. Amount withdrawn during the year, $254,959.07.
12. Increase of deposits the past year, $47,716.02.
13. Amount carried to surplus or profit and loss during the year, $11,597.41.
14. Rate of dividend the last year, 4½ per cent.; when paid, 2¼ per cent. January. 1st, 2 per cent. July 1st.
15. State tax during the past year, $4,068.48; U. S. tax, $148.61.
16. Total office expenses the past year, including salaries, $5,177.64.
17. Net amount of income during the year from real estate owned, $900.52.
18. Amount of assets yielding no income during the year, none.
19. Are all loans upon real estate secured by first mortgage? Yes.
20. Largest amount loaned to one individual, company, society, or corporation, $20,000.
21. Date of annual meeting for choice of officers, 3d Monday in January.

Officers.—President, William Gay; Treasurer, Julius Gay; Directors or Trustees, Augustus Ward, W. M. Wadsworth, John S. Rice, Charles L. Whitman, Franklin Wheeler, Edward Norton, Chauncey Deming, Henry W. Barbour.

FREESTONE SAVINGS BANK, PORTLAND.

JNO. H. SAGE, Treasurer.   INCORPORATED, 1865.

STATEMENT, OCTOBER 1, 1882.

LIABILITIES.		ASSETS.	
Whole Amount of Deposits,	$216,261.60	Loans on Real Estate, .	$133,988.00
Surplus Account, . .	5,300.00	Loans on Stocks and Bonds,	14,475.00
Interest Account, . .	2,226.90	Loans on Endorsed Notes,	12,033.03
		United States Bonds, .	5,000.00
		Town, City, and Corp'n Bonds,	15,800.00
		Bank Stocks in Connecticut,	14,350.00
		Bank Stocks in other States,	3,300.00
		Real Estate by Foreclosure,	22,000.00
		Insurance Account, . .	8.20
		Furniture and Fixtures, .	250.00
		Cash in Bank, . . .	2,584.27
Total Liabilities, .	$223,788.50	Total Assets, . .	$223,788.50

INVESTMENTS.

DESCRIPTION.	PAR VALUE.	COST.	MARKET VALUE.
UNITED STATES BONDS.			
4s of 1907, Registered, ... $	5,000.00	5,000.00	5,900.00
TOWN, CITY, AND CORPORATION BONDS.			
Town of Chatham, 7s, ...	3,000.00	3,000.00	3,390.24
" " Middletown, 7s, ...	2,000.00	2,000.00	2,260.00
" " Portland, 7s, ...	8,300.00	8,300.00	9,379.00
" " Middlefield, 6s, ...	500.00	500.00	540.00
" " Portland, 6s, ...	2,000.00	2,000.00	2,200.00
BANK STOCKS.			
74 shares First National Bank, Portland, .	7,400.00	7,400.00	8,584.00
40 " " " " Middletown, .	4,000.00	4,000.00	4,800.00
2 " Middletown National, "	150.00	150.00	220.00
15 " Middlesex Co. " "	1,500.00	1,800.00	1,800.00
5 " Thames National, Norwich, .	500.00	500.00	750.00
5 " First National, " .	500.00	500.00	590.00
33 " National Shoe and Leather, New York,	3,300.00	3,300.00	4,290.00

MISCELLANEOUS ITEMS.

1. Number of depositors having $500 or less, . 539; total amount, $59,287.92
2. Number of depositors having over $500 and less than $1,000, ... 58; total amount, 41,901.33
3. Number of depositors having $1,000 and not not over $2,000, ... 54; total amount, 80,837.1
4. Number of depositors having over $2,000, . 10; total amount, 34,235.21

5. Total number of depositors, ... 661; total deposits, $216,261.60

FREESTONE SAVINGS BANK.—Continued.

MISCELLANEOUS ITEMS.—Continued.

6. Largest amount due a single depositor, $7,238.71.
7. Number of accounts opened during the year, 61; number closed, 77.
8. Amount of income received during the year, $15,073.27.
9. Amount of dividends declared during the year, $12,016.31.
10. Amount deposited, including interest credited, the past year, $48,758.15.
11. Amount withdrawn during the year, $40,267.23.
12. Increase of deposits the past year, $8,490.92.
13. Amount carried to surplus or profit and loss during the year, $800.00.
14. Rate of dividend the last year, 6 per cent.; when paid, Feb. 1st and Aug. 1st.
15. State tax during the past year, $282.20; U. S. tax, $69.96.
16. Total office expenses the past year, including salaries, $718.97.
17. Net amount of income during the year from real estate owned, $1,012.56.
18. Amount of assets yielding no income during the year, $4,800.
19. Are all loans upon real estate secured by first mortgage? Yes.
20. Largest amount loaned to one individual, company, society, or corporation, $14,000.
21. Date of annual meeting for choice of officers, first Monday in July.

OFFICERS.—President, E. White; Vice-President, W. W. Coe; Treasurer, Jno. H. Sage; Directors or Trustees, Edwin Bell, Geo. W. Pettis, F. Gildersleeve, Hobart Davis, Nelson Shepard, E. Brainerd, H. S. Cooper.

GREENWICH SAVINGS BANK.

MARK BANKS, Treasurer.   INCORPORATED, 1870.

STATEMENT, OCTOBER 1, 1882.

LIABILITIES.		ASSETS.	
Whole Amt. of Deposits,	$119,499.05	Loans on Real Estate,	$90,242.50
Surplus Account,	1,114.84	Loans on Bonds,	1,225.00
Interest Account,	2,446.25	Loans on Endorsed Notes,	1,930.59
		Town Bonds,	5,250.00
		Real Estate by Foreclosure,	2,847.31
		Tax Account,	79.49
		Expense Account,	118.99
		Cash in Bank,	19,970.70
		Cash on hand,	1,400.59
Total Liabilities,	$123,060.14	Total Assets,	$123,060.14

INVESTMENTS.

DESCRIPTION.	PAR VALUE.	COST.	MARKET VALUE.
TOWN, CITY, AND CORPORATION BONDS.			
Town of Greenwich, $	5,000.00	5,250.00	5,250.00

MISCELLANEOUS ITEMS.

1. Number of depositors having $500 or less,   424; total amount, $42,724.90
2. Number of depositors having over $500 and less than $1,000,   44; total amount,   29,917.41
3. Number of depositors having $1,000 and not over $2,000,   27; total amount,   35,259.08
4. Number of depositors having over $2,000,   2; total amount,   11,597.66
5. Total number of depositors,   497; total deposits, $119,499.05
6. Largest amount due a single depositor, $9,187.08.
7. Number of accounts opened during the year, 139; number closed, 76.
8. Amount of income received during the year, $5,636.82.
9. Amount of dividends declared during the year, $3,575.60.
10. Amount deposited, including interest credited, the past year, $85,672.36.
11. Amount withdrawn during the year, $69,555.08.
12. Increase of deposits the past year, $16,117.28.
13. Amount carried to surplus, $4,392.00.
14. Rate of dividend the last year, 3 and 4 per cent.; when paid, January 1st and July 1st.
15. State tax during the past year, $114.09; United States tax, $34.48.
16. Total office expenses the past year, including salaries, $958.51.
17. Net amount of income during the year from real estate owned, $40.00.

GREENWICH SAVINGS BANK.—CONTINUED.

MISCELLANEOUS ITEMS.—CONTINUED.

18. Amount of assets yielding no income during the year, $1,930.59.
19. Are all loans upon real estate secured by first mortgage? Yes.
20. Largest amount loaned to one individual, company, society, or corporation, $9,000.00.
21. Date of annual meeting for choice of officers, first Thursday in July.

OFFICERS.—President, Robert M. Bruce; Treasurer, Mark Banks; Directors or Trustees, Solomon Mead, Lyman Mead, John G. Reynolds, Frank Shepard, Thomas Ritch, Benjamin Wright, Thomas A. Mead, Denham Palmer, Willis H. Wilcox, Odle C. Knapp, James H. Brush, William H. Briggs, H. W. R. Hoyt.

GROTON SAVINGS BANK.

A. H. SIMMONS, Treasurer.   INCORPORATED, 1854.

STATEMENT, OCTOBER 1, 1882.

LIABILITIES.		ASSETS.	
Whole Amount of Deposits,	$602,510.31	Loans on Real Estate, .	$413,850.93
Surplus Account, ⎰		Loans on Stocks and Bonds, .	9,000.00
Interest Account, ⎱ · ·	29,996.42	Town, City, and Corp'n Bonds,	42,000.00
		Town, City, and Bor'gh Orders,	2,000.00
		Bank Stocks in Connecticut,	27,225.60
		Bank Stocks in other States,	54,760.00
		Real Estate by Foreclosure,	74,023.98
		Cash in Bank, . . .	9,646.22
Total Liabilities, . .	$632,506.73	Total Assets, . .	$632,506.73

INVESTMENTS.

DESCRIPTION.	PAR VALUE.	COST.	MARKET VALUE.
TOWN, CITY, AND CORPORATION BONDS.			
Town of Greenwich, 6s, . . . $	10,000.00	10,500.00	10,500.00
City of Rochester, N. Y., 7s, . . .	5,000.00	5,642.33	6,475.00
" " Buffalo, N. Y., 7s, . . .	2,000.00	2,260.00	2,320.00
" " Burlington, Vt., 5s, . . .	10,000.00	10,500.00	10,500.00
" " Cincinnati, O., 6s, . . .	5,000.00	5,350.00	5,500.00
" " St. Louis, Mo., 6s, . . .	10,000.00	11,300.00	11,300.00
TOWN, CITY, AND BOROUGH ORDERS.			
Town of Groton, 6s, ...	2,000.00	2,000.00	2,000.00
BANK STOCKS.			
30 shares Nat'l B'k of Commerce, New London,	3,000.00	3,225.00	3,450.00
40 " Union Bank, New London, . .	4,000.00	4,071.75	4,200.00
116 " Mystic River National, Mystic River,	5,800.00	6,325.60	7,772.00
60 " Mystic National, Mystic, . .	3,000.00	3,377.00	3,480.00
20 " Pawcatuck National, Pawcatuck, .	1,000.00	1,000.00	1,100.00
60 " Uncas National, Norwich, . .	3,000.00	3,641.00	3,641.00
40 " Norwich National, " .	4,000.00	4,600.00	4,600.00
32 " Union National, N. Y.,	1,600.00	1,600.00	2,560.00
20 " Corn Exchange, " .	2,000.00	1,947.50	3,200.00
30 " Importers and Traders Nat'l, " .	3,000.00	3,000.00	7,200.00
50 " Nassau, " .	5,000.00	5,144.00	5,500.00
50 " Hanover, " .-	5,000.00	5,234.25	6,750.00
40 " Fourth National, " .	4,000.00	4,027.68	4,920.00
38 " Continental " / " .	3,800.00	5,079.00	4,560.00
40 " Marine " " .	9,000.00	15,000.00	12,600.00
50 " Pacific, " .	2,500.00	2,690.00	3,750.00
33 " Central National, " .	3,300.00	5,466.88	4,125.00
80 " Merchants Exchange Nat'l, " .	4,000.00	4,940.76	3,680.00
8 " Exchange, St. Louis, . . .	800.00	400.00	40.00
14 " Mechanics, " . . .	1,400.00	1,300.00	1,463.00

6

GROTON SAVINGS BANK.—Continued.

MISCELLANEOUS ITEMS.

1. Number of depositors having $500 or less, . 1,248; total amount, $146,310.84
2. Number of depositors having $500 and less than $1,000, ... · 209; total amount, 145,978.61
3. Number of depositors having $1,000 and not over $2,000, · . . . . . 105; total amount, 140,447.03
4. Number of depositors having over $2,000, 54; total amount, 169,773.83

5. Total number of depositors, . . . 1,616; total deposits, $602,510.31
6. Largest amount due a single depositor, $8,567.49.
7. Number of accounts opened during the year, 179; number closed, 87.
8. Amount of income received during the year, $34,438.44.
9. Amount of dividends declared during the year, $22,584.22.
10. Amount deposited, including interest credited, the past year, $95,684.64.
11. Amount withdrawn during the year, $65,069.26.
12. Increase of deposits the past year, $30,615.38.
13. Amount carried to surplus or profit and loss during the year, $8,087.65.
14. Rate of dividend the last year, 4 per cent.; when paid, April 1st and Oct. 1st.
15. State tax during the past year, $1,212.09; U. S. tax, $273.73.
16. Total office expenses the past year, including salaries, $1,690.75.
17. Net amount of income during the year from real estate owned, $870.69.
18. Amount of assets yielding no income during the year, $368.40.
19. Are all loans upon real estate secured by first mortgage? Yes.
20. Largest amount loaned to one individual, company, society, or corporation, $25,000.00.
21. Date of annual meeting for choice of officers, in July.

OFFICERS.—President, Henry B. Noyes; Treasurer, Abel H. Simmons; Directors or Trustees, Thomas S. Greenman, William H. Potter, Lemuel Clift, William Clift, John O. Fish, Abel H. Simmons.

GUILFORD SAVINGS BANK.

CHARLES GRISWOLD, Treasurer.   INCORPORATED, 1875.

STATEMENT, OCTOBER 1, 1882.

LIABILITIES.		ASSETS.	
Whole Amount of Deposits,	$132,945.57	Loans on Real Estate, .	$62,199.14
Surplus Account, . .	4,530.03	Loans on Endorsed Notes,	10,841.50
Interest Account, . .	2,105.83	Railroad Bonds, . .	3,990.00
		Bank Stocks in Connecticut,	55,233.50
		Expense Account, . .	229.11
		Safe Account, . . .	702.20
		Cash in Bank, . . .	1,487.33
		Cash on hand, . . .	4,948.65
Total Liabilities, .	$139,581.43	Total Assets, . .	$139,581.43

INVESTMENTS.

DESCRIPTION.	PAR VALUE.	COST.	MARKET VALUE.
RAILROAD BONDS.			
New York Central & Hudson R., 7 per cent., $	3,000.00	3,990.00	3,990.00
BANK STOCKS.			
117 shares Yale National, New Haven, . .	11,700.00	13,475.00	14,040.00
36 " Second " " . .	3,600.00	5,583.00	5,760.00
332 " New Haven Co. Nat., New Haven,	3,320.00	4,562.50	4,648.00
30 " Merchants National, "	1,500.00	1,825.00	1,860.00
6 " Mechanics " "	360.00	396.00	396.00
48 " First " West Meriden,	4,800.00	5,319.00	5,760.00
8 " Meriden " Meriden, .	800.00	1,040.00	1,040.00
14 " Middlesex Co. " Middletown,	1,400.00	1,732.00	1,732.00
10 " New Britain " New Britain,	1,000.00	1,520.00	1,520.00
12 " Nat. Bk. of New Engl'd, E. Haddam,	1,200.00	1,596.00	1,596.00
50 " First National, Norwich, . .	5,000.00	5,600.00	5,800.00
100 " Merchants National, Norwich, .	4,000.00	4,100.00	4,100.00
50 " Uncas " " .	2,500.00	3,125.00	3,200.00
2 " Shetucket. " " .	200.00	250.00	260.00
28 " Thames " " .	2,800.00	4,182.00	4,228.00
8 " Norwich " . " .	800.00	928.00	928.00

MISCELLANEOUS ITEMS.

1. Number of depositors having $500 or less, . 510; total amount, $52,206.06
2. Number of depositors having over $500 and less than $1,000, ... 49; total amount, 32,929.55
3. Number of depositors having $1,000 and not over $2,000, ... 34; total amount, 47,809.96
4. Number of depositors having over $2,000, . 0; total amount, 0.00
5. Total number of depositors, ... 593; total deposits, $132,945.57
6. Largest amount due a single depositor, $2,000.

GUILFORD SAVINGS BANK.—Continued.

MISCELLANEOUS ITEMS.—Continued.

7. Number of accounts opened during the year, 147; number closed, 78.
8. Amount of income received during the year, $7,264.57.
9. Amount of dividends declared during the year, $4,428.01.
10. Amount deposited, including interest credited, the past year, $51,482.07.
11. Amount withdrawn during the year, $35,695.11.
12. Increase of deposits the past year, $15,786.96.
13. Amount carried to surplus or profit and loss during the year, $1,545.58.
14. Rate of dividend the last year, 4 per cent.; when paid, January and July.
15. State tax during the past year, $177.08; U. S. tax, none.
16. Total office expenses the past year, including salaries, $559.16.
17. Net amount of income during the year from real estate owned, none.
18. Amount of assets yielding no income during the year, $702.20.
19. Are all loans upon real estate secured by first mortgage? Yes.
20. Largest amount loaned to one individual, company, or corporation, $4,000.
21. Date of annual meeting for choice of officers, first Tuesday in October.

OFFICERS.—President, Edward R. Landon; Treasurer, Charles Griswold; Directors or Trustees, Frederick Spencer, John N. Chittenden, John Bishop, Martin C. Bishop, Cyrus O. Bartlett, Henry E. Norton, Lewis R. Elliot, Edward Griswold, Alvan Talcott, John B. Wright, Samuel R. Crampton, E. F. Jones, Heman C. Stone, Nathan Evarts, Beverly Monroe, Christopher Spencer, H. Lynde Harrison, George E. Elliot, David Beach, George Rose, Edwin W. Bartlett, Samuel Chidsey, E. R. Landon, Rufus N. Leete, Charles Griswold.

HIGGANUM SAVINGS BANK.

E. D. GILBERT, Treasurer.   INCORPORATED, 1874.

STATEMENT, OCTOBER 1, 1882.

LIABILITIES.		ASSETS.	
Whole Amount of Deposits,	$25,357.56	Loans on Real Estate, .	$10,840.00
Surplus Account, . .	400.00	Loans on Endorsed Notes,.	10,415.00
Interest Account, . .	402.20	Bank Stocks in Connecticut,	2,000.00
		Expense Account, . , .	200.00
		Town of Haddam Note, .	2,000.00
		Safe and Fixtures, . .	645.77
		Cash on hand, . . .	306.99
Total Liabilities, . .	$26,209.76	Total Assets, . .	$26,209.76

INVESTMENTS.

DESCRIPTION.	PAR VALUE.	COST.	MARKET VALUE.
BANK STOCKS.			
5 shares Conn. Trust Co., ... $	2,000.00	2,000.00	2,240.00

MISCELLANEOUS ITEMS.

1. Number of depositors having $500 or less,   145; total amount, $9,254.93
2. Number of depositors having over $500 and less than $1,000, ...   8; total amount,   5,381.17
3. Number of depositors having $1,000 and not over $2,000, ...   7: total amount,   8,495.06
4. Number of depositors having over $2,000,   1; total amount,   2,226.40
5. Total number of depositors, . . .   161; total deposits, $25,357.56
6. Largest amount due a single depositor, $2,226.40.
7. Number of accounts opened during the year, 36; number closed, 7.
8. Amount of income received during the year, $1,471.50.
9. Amount of dividends declared during the year, $818.24.
10. Amount deposited, including interest credited, the past year, $13,625.59.
11. Amount withdrawn during the year, $3,488.26.
12. Increase of deposits the past year, $10,137.33.
13. Amount carried to surplus or profit and loss during the year, $400.00.
14. Rate of dividend the last year, 4½ per cent.; when paid, January and July.
15. State tax during the year, none; U. S. tax, none.
16. Total office expenses the past year, including salaries, $1,100.00.
17. Net amount of income during the year from real estate owned, none.
18. Amount of assets yielding no income during the year, $700.00.
19. Are all loans upon real estate secured by first mortgage? Yes.
20. Largest amount loaned to one individual, company, society, or corporation, $8,515.00.
21. Date of annual meeting for choice of officers, second Monday in August.

OFFICERS.—President, Geo. M. Clark; Treasurer, Edward D. Gilbert; Directors or Trustees, Geo. M. Clark, Thos. J. Clark, William J. Smith, Giles Thayer, E. D. Gilbert.

JEWETT CITY SAVINGS BANK.

HENRY T. CROSBY, Treasurer.   INCORPORATED, 1874.

STATEMENT, OCTOBER 1, 1882.

LIABILITIES.		ASSETS.	
Whole Amount of Deposits,	$409,531.31	Loans on Real Estate, . .	$82,960.00
Surplus Account, . .	6,150.00	Loans on Stocks and Bonds,	5,885.10
Interest Account, . .	7,185.27	Loans on Endorsed Notes, .	12,525.00
Rent Received, . . .	22.16	United States Bonds, . .	10,939.50
Other Liabilities, . . .	246.28	Town, City, and Corp'n Bonds,	62,125.00
		Railroad Bonds, ...	87,049.00
		Bank Stocks in Connecticut,	88,334.75
		Bank Stocks in other States,	42,105.25
		Real Estate by Foreclosure,	2,000.00
		Tax Account, . . .	396.61
		Expense Account, . .	362.05
		Deposit in Cranston Sav. Bk.,	458.52
		Furniture for Bank Room, .	70.98
		Bills due for Insurance, .	110.75
		Other Assets, . .	6,175.00
		Cash in Bank, . . .	12,342.82
		Cash on hand, . . .	4,294.69
Total Liabilities, . . $423,135.02		Total Assets, . . $423,135.02	

INVESTMENTS.

DESCRIPTION.	PAR VALUE.	COST.	MARKET VALUE.
UNITED STATES BONDS.			
4s of 1907, Coupon, ... $	10,000.00	10,939.50	11,950.00
TOWN, CITY, AND CORPORATION BONDS.			
City of Norwich, Conn., 5s of 1908, . .	15,000.00	15,375.00	15,900.00
" Cincinnati, Ohio, 6s of 1906, .	26,000.00	29,940.00	31,265.00
" " " 7$\frac{3}{10}$s of 1902-06, .	13,000.00	16,810.00	17,095.00
RAILROAD BONDS.			
New London Northern, 5s of 1910, . .	5,000.00	5,300.00	5,400.00
Norwich & Worcester, 6s of 1897, . . .	1,000.00	1,142.00	1,170.00
Morris & Essex, 7s of 1914, ...	20,000.00	26,900.00	27,200.00
St. Louis, Jacksonville & Chicago, 7s of 1894,	12,000.00	14,207.00	14,070.00
New York Central & Hudson Riv., 7s of 1903,	20,000.00	26,700.00	26,800.00
Shamokin Valley & Pottsville, 7s of 1901, .	10,000.00	12,800.00	12,800.00
BANK STOCKS.			
299 shares Thames National, Norwich, . .	29,900.00	40,684.00	44,850.00
149 " Second " " . .	14,900.00	17,046.00	17,880.00
72 " Norwich " " . .	7,200.00	7,816.00	7,920.00
26 " Uncas " " .	1,300.00	1,548.75	1,560.00
10 " First " Killingly, . .	1,000.00	1,180.00	1,200.00
129 " Nat. Bk. of Commerce, N. London,	12,900.00	13,803.00	15,996.00
10 " Ætna National, Hartford, . .	1,000.00	1,262.00	1,300.00
80 " Mechanics National, New York, .	2,000.00	2,505.00	3,000.00
122 " Fourth " "	12,200.00	14,821.00	15,372.00
137 " Central " "	13,700.00	16,293.00	17,947.00
50 " Corn Exchange, New York, . .	5,000.00	8,486.25	8,500.00

JEWETT CITY SAVINGS BANK.—Continued.

MISCELLANEOUS ITEMS.

1. Number of depositors having $500 or less, .   752; total amount, $99,687.50
2. Number of depositors having over $500 and less than $1,000, ...—.   107; total amount,   76,887.96
3. Number of depositors having $1,000 and not over $2,000, ...   88; total amount,   120,472.13
4. Number of depositors having over $2,000, .   33; total amount,   112,483.72

5. Total number of depositors,   . . .   980; total deposits, $409,531.31
6. Largest amount due a single depositor, $11,855.68.
7. Number of accounts opened during the year, 228; number closed, 55.
8. Amount of income received during the year, $20,524.45.
9. Amount of dividends declared during the year, $18,010.50.
10. Amount deposited, including interest credited, the past year, $129,189.36.
11. Amount withdrawn during the year, $45,452.25.
12. Increase of deposits the past year, $83,737.11.
13. Amount carried to surplus or profit and loss during the year, $1,215.
14. Rate of dividend the last year, 5 per cent.; when paid, October 15, 1881, and April 15, 1882.
15. State tax during the year, $725.62; U. S. tax, $141.84.
16. Total office expenses the past year, including salaries, $762.35.
17. Net amount of income during the year from real estate owned, $144.00.
18. Amount of assets yielding no income during the year, $6,633.52.
19. Are all loans upon real estate secured by first mortgage? Yes.
20. Largest amount loaned to one individual, company, society, or corporation, $10,000.
21. Date of annual meeting for choice of officers, second Wednesday in July.

OFFICERS.—President, Hezekiah L. Reade; Vice-Presidents, James O. Sweet, Alfred A. Young; Treasurer, Henry T. Crosby; Directors or Trustees, Cornelius Murphy, John R. Tracy, Francis S. Young, Albert G. Brewster, Henry L. Johnson, Joseph E. Leonard, Israel Mathewson, Charles H. Fanning, Daniel M. Brown, Stephen Tiffany, Allen B. Burleson, Louis K. Potter.

LITCHFIELD SAVINGS SOCIETY.

HENRY R. COIT, Treasurer.   INCORPORATED, 1850.

STATEMENT, OCTOBER 1, 1882.

LIABILITIES.		ASSETS.	
Whole Amount of Deposits,	$770,272.01	Loans on Real Estate, .	$287,796.07
Surplus Account, . .	21,500.00	Loans on Stocks and Bonds,	45,300.00
Interest Account, . .	18,862.17	Loans on Endorsed Notes,	31,300.00
		United States Bonds, . .	52,462.49
		Town, City, and Corp'n Bds.,	270,310.50
		Railroad Bonds, . .	2,000.00
		Bank Stocks in Connecticut,	73,333.25
		Bank Stocks in other States,	23,651.23
		Real Estate by Foreclosure,	8,688.63
		Tax Account, . . .	185.15
		Expense Account, . .	521.20
		Cash in Bank, . . .	15,135.66
Total Liabilities, . .	$810,634.18	Total Assets, . . .	$810,634.18

INVESTMENTS.

DESCRIPTION.	PAR VALUE.	COST.	MARKET VALUE.
UNITED STATES BONDS.			
4s of 1907, Registered, ... $	41,500.00	47,462.49	49,177.50
4s of 1907, Coupon, ...	5,000.00	5,000.00	5,925.00
TOWN, CITY, AND CORPORATION BONDS.			
City of Cincinnati, O., Municipal Gold, 6s, 1906,	20,000.00	24,650.00	25,000.00
" Hartford, Conn., 6s, 1899, . . .	4,000.00	4,740.00	4,800.00
" Brooklyn, N. Y., Soldiers' Aid, 7 per ct.,	1,000.00	1,203.75	1,200.00
" " " Bridge and Water,	9,000.00	10,933.75	10,500.00
" Buffalo, " Water, . . .	1,000.00	1,240.00	1,200.00
" Providence, R. I., 5 per cent., . .	9,000.00	9,720.00	9,500.00
" St. Louis, Mo., ...	18,000.00	20,530.00	20,500.00
" " "	7,000.00	7,700.00	7,500.00
" New York, N. Y., ...	10,000.00	11,800.00	12,000.00
County of " "	10,000.00	11,800.00	12,000.00
Town of Hebron, ...	5,000.00	5,150.00	5,500.00
" Greenwich, ...	30,000.00	32,400.00	33,000.00
" Litchfield, ...	82,000.00	82,000.00	88,000.00
" Washington, ...	6,000.00	6,000.00	6,250.00
" Roxbury, ...	8,100.00	8,100.00	8,500.00
" Morris, ...	16,600.00	16,600.00	17,500.00
Borough of Danbury, ...	15,000.00	15,743.00	16,000.00
RAILROAD BONDS.			
New York & Harlem, 1st mortgage, . .	2,000.00	2,000.00	2,700.00
BANK STOCKS.			
110 shares Waterbury National, Waterbury,	5,500.00	5,850.00	8,800.00
120 " Citizens' " "	12,000.00	12,070.00	15,000.00
10 " Birmingham " Birmingham,	1,000.00	1,000.00	1,200.00

LITCHFIELD SAVINGS SOCIETY.—Continued.

INVESTMENTS.—Continued.

DESCRIPTION.	PAR VALUE.	COST.	MARKET VALUE.
BANK STOCKS.—CONTINUED.			
25 shares Mercantile National, Hartford, $	2,500.00	2,500.00	3,175.00
112 " Phœnix " "	11,200.00	12,659.50	19,040.00
100 " Hartford " "	10,000.00	15,100.25	17,000.00
35 " Farmers & Mech's " "	3,500.00	4,025.00	4,520.00
21 " State, "	2,100.00	2,394.00	2,250.00
25 " National Exchange, "	1,250.00	1,918.00	1,950.00
50 " First National, "	5,000.00	5,660.00	6,000.00
10 " American " "	500.00	690.00	725.00
15 " Yale " New Haven,	1,500.00	1,530.00	1,600.00
15 " National Tradesmens, "	1,500.40	2,190.00	2,200.00
203 " New Haven County Nat., "	2,030.00	2,334.50	2,400.00
31 " City, "	3,100.00	3,472.00	3,500.00
30 " National Park, New York,	3,000.00	3,222.50	4,500.00
20 " American Exchange Nat., "	2,000.00	2,132.50	2,500.00
10 " St. Nicholas " "	1,000.00	1,000.00	1,100.00
20 " Importers & Traders " "	2,000.00	2,127.50	5,000.00
60 " Mechanics " "	1,500.00	1,591.23	2,150.00
25 " Continental " "	2,500.00	2,505.00	3,000.00
16 " Fourth " "	1,600.00	1,685.25	1,950.00
19 " Metropolitan " "	1,900.00	1,993.50	3,000.00
22 " Nat. Bank of the Republic, "	2,200.00	2,200.00	3,000.00
10 " " " Commerce, "	1,000.00	1,022.50	1,500.00
20 " Union National, "	2,000.00	2,026.25	2,150.00
15 " Bank of America, "	1,500.00	2,145.00	2,145.00

MISCELLANEOUS ITEMS.

1. Number of depositors having $500 or less,   1,788; total amount, $189,365.47
2. Number of depositors having over $500 and less than $1,000, ...   279; total amount,   212,898.62
3. Number of depositors having $1,000 and not over $2,000, ...   151; total amount,   172,323.93
4. Number of depositors having over $2,000, .   62; total amount,   195,683.99

Total number of depositors, .   .   . 2,280; total deposits, $770,272.01
Largest amount due a single depositor, $13,072.37.
Number of accounts opened during the year, 277; number closed, 181.
Amount of income received during the year, $44,923.89.
Amount of dividends declared during the year, $37,018.69.
10. Amount deposited, including interest credited, the past year, $102,249.30.
11. Amount withdrawn during the year, $76,125.94.
12. Increase of deposits the past year, $26,123.36.
13. Amount carried to surplus or profit and loss during the year, none.
14. Rate of dividend the last year, 5 per cent.; when paid, 2½ January 1st, and 2½ July 1st.
15. State tax during the past year, $1,383.60; U. S. tax, none.
16. Total office expenses the past year, including salaries, $2,505.43.
17. Net amount of income during the year from real estate owned, none.
18. Amount of assets yielding no income during the year, $12,598.86.
19. Are all loans upon real estate secured by first mortgage? Yes.
20. Largest amount loaned to one individual, company, society, or corporation, $30,000.
21. Date of annual meeting for choice of officers, last Saturday in June.

OFFICERS.—President, George C. Woodruff; Treasurer, Henry R. Coit; Directors or Trustees, George C. Woodruff, Frederick D. McNeil, Jesse L. Judd, George M. Woodruff, William H. Braman.

MARINERS SAVINGS BANK, NEW LONDON.

JOHN E. DARROW, Treasurer.   INCORPORATED, 1867.

STATEMENT, OCTOBER 1, 1882.

LIABILITIES.		ASSETS.	
Whole Amt. of Deposits,	$1,327,406.87	Loans on Real Estate, .	$432,450.00
Surplus Account, . .	35,823.25	Loans on Stocks and Bonds,	89,500.00
Interest Account, . .	6,331.76	Loans on Endorsed Notes,	15,600.00
Rent Account, . . .	24,590.86	United States Bonds, . .	93,350.00
		State Bonds, . .	3,180.00
		Town, City, and Corp'n B'ds,	189,767.00
		Railroad Bonds, . .	130,950.00
		Railroad Stocks, .	10,000.00
		Bank Stocks in Connecticut,	121,817.50
		Bank Stocks in other States,	69,260.00
		Real Estate by Foreclosure, .	208,604.48
		Expense Account, .	329.08
		Maintenance Account, .	15,909.51
		Sundry Charges, .	113.35
		Cash in Bank, . . .	7,500.00
		Cash on hand, . . .	5,821.82
Total Liabilities, .	$1,394,152.74	Total Assets, .	$1,394,152.74

INVESTMENTS.

DESCRIPTION.	PAR VALUE.	COST.	MARKET VALUE.
UNITED STATES BONDS.,			
5s of 1881, registered (extended 3½ per cent.), $	50,000.00	51,531.25	50,375.00
Currency 6s, 1895, ...	35,000.00	43,850.00	45,850.00
STATE BONDS.			
Connecticut 6s, 1884, ...	3,000.00	3,180.00	3,180.00
TOWN, CITY, AND CORPORATION BONDS.			
City of New London, 7s, various issues, .	79,000.00	79,705.00	94,800.00
" Cincinnati, 6s, 1909, ...	20,000.00	12,150.00	23,000.00
" " 7$\frac{3}{10}$s, 1906, ...	15,000.00	19,050.00	20,000.00
" Cleveland, 6s, 1896, . . .	5,000.00	5,800.00	5,800.00
" " 6s, 1898, . . .	25,000.00	29,250.00	30,000.00
District of Columbia, 6s, 1891, . . .	10,000.00	11,200.00	12,000.00
Town of Norfolk, 6s, 1890, . . .	6,000.00	6,000.00	6,900.00
" Greenwich, 6s, 1902, . . .	7,000.00	7,262.00	8,050.00
Equitable Trust Co., 5s, 1887, . . .	10,000.00	10,000.00	10,000.00
RAILROAD BONDS.			
N. Y. Central & Hudson River reg. 7s, 1903,	30,000.00	40,125.00	40,125.00
Chicago, Rock Island & Pacific reg. 6s, 1917,	10,000.00	12,575.00	12,800.00
Chicago & Alton coup. 7s, 1893, . .	20,000.00	24,700.00	24,750.00
Albany & Susquehanna coup. 7s, 1906, . .	10,000.00	12,800.00	12,800.00
Union Pacific coup. 6s, 1896-98, . . .	25,000.00	28,750.00	29,000.00
United N. Jersey R. R. & Canal Co. coup. 6s, 1901,	10,000.00	12,000.00	24,400.00

MARINERS SAVINGS BANK.—Continued.

INVESTMENTS.—Continued.

DESCRIPTION.	PAR VALUE.	COST.	MARKET VALUE.
RAILROAD STOCKS.			
New London Northern, ... $	10,000.00	10,000.00	11,400.00
BANK STOCKS.			
50 shares Marine National, New York, ,	5,000.00	7,000.00	7,250.00
100 " Metropolitan " "	10,000.00	15,200.00	17,600.00
100 " Continental " "	10,000.00	10,375.00	12,100.00
100 " American Exc. " "	10,000.00	11,610.00	13,400.00
100 " National Park, (·	10,000.00	12,200.00	16,000.00
50 " Nat. Bank of Commerce, "	5,000.00	6,700.00	7,550.00
50 " Nat. Bank of the State of New York,	5,000.00	6,175.00	6,600.00
100 " First National, Norwich, .	10,000.00	10,500.00	11,500.00
100 " Second " " .	10,000.00	11,300.00	11,800.00
200 " Thames· " " .	20,000.00	28,400.00	30,000.00
60 " Norwich " " .	6,000.00	6,705.00	6,600.00
100 " Uncas " . " .	5,000.00	5,075.00	6,250.00
125 " Merchants " " .	5,000.00	5,450.00	5,250.00
200 " Nat. Bk. of Comm'e, New London,	20,000.00	21,450.00	23,000.00
400 " National Whaling, "	10,000.00	12,000.00	14,000.00
200 " Union Bank, "	20,000.00	20,937.50	22,000.00

MISCELLANEOUS ITEMS.

1. Number of depositors having $500 or less, 1,796; total amount, $241,612.52
2. Number of depositors having over $500 and less than $1,000, ... 318; total amount, 226,317.69
3. Number of depositors having $1,000 and not over $2,000, ... 261; total amount, 350,609.55
4. Number of depositors having over $2,000, 147; total amount, 508,867.11

5. Total number of depositors, . . . 2,522; total deposits, $1,327,406.87
6. Largest amount due a single depositor, $20,279.41.
7. Number of accounts opened during the year, 369; number closed, 284.
8. Amount of income received during the year, $61,771.15.
9. Amount of dividends declared during the year, $49,367.34.
10. Amount deposited, including interest credited, the past year, $285,882.56.
11. Amount withdrawn during the year, $219,204.56.
12. Increase of deposits the past year, $66,678.
13. Amount carried to surplus or profit and loss during the year, $4,175.18.
14. Rate of dividend the last year, 4 per cent.; when paid, March and September.
15. State tax during the past year, $2,401.98; U. S. tax, $363.38.
16. Total office expenses the past year, including salaries, $3,399.95.
17. Net amount of income during the year from real estate owned, $11,657.03.
18. Amount of assets yielding no income during the year, $22,351.15.
19. Are all loans upon real estate secured by first mortgage? Yes.
20. Largest amount loaned to one individual, company, society, or corporation, $50,000.
21. Date of annual meeting for choice of officers, last Wednesday in July.

Officers.—President, William H. Barns; Treasurer, John E. Darrow; Directors or Trustees, Julius T. Shepard, William H. Allen, James Griswold, C. C. Comstock, Erasmus D. Avery, Samuel Green, William L. Peckham, Robert A. Morgan, Eldridge P. Beckwith, Daniel D. Latham, Henry L. Dudley, Daniel B. Hempstead, Frederick S. Newcomb.

MECHANICS SAVINGS BANK, HARTFORD.

WARD W. JACOBS, Treasurer.   INCORPORATED, 1861.

STATEMENT, OCTOBER 1, 1882.

LIABILITIES.		ASSETS.	
Whole Amt. of Deposits,	$1,342,844.24	Loans on Real Estate, .	$666,722.00
Surplus Account, . .	27,541.92	Loans on Stocks and Bonds,	179,825.00
Interest Account, . .	21,336.36	Loans on Endorsed Notes,	5,000.00
Profit and Loss, . .	2,201.92	United States Bonds, .	1,050.00
		State Bonds, . . .	35,892.50
		Town, City, County, and	
		Corporation Bonds, .	107,615.00
		Bank Stocks in Connecticut,	114,935.00
		Bank Stocks in other States,	12,500.00
		Real Estate by Foreclosure,	200,914.67
		Tax Account, . . .	1,797.21
		Expense Account, . .	2,742.60
		Loans to School District,	600.00
		Cash in Bank, . . .	61,122.68
		Cash on hand, . . .	3,207.78
Total Liabilities, .	$1,393,924.44	Total Assets, . . .	$1,393,924.44

INVESTMENTS.

DESCRIPTION.	PAR VALUE.	COST.	MARKET VALUE.
UNITED STATES BONDS.			
4s of 1907, Coupon, ... $	1,050.00	1,050.00	1,244.25
STATE BONDS.			
Missouri 6s, due in 1886, ...	16,000.00	17,320.00	17,120.00
" 6s, " 1887, ...	17,000.00	18,572.50	18,275.00
TOWN, CITY, AND CORPORATION BONDS.			
City of Chicago, Ill., 7s, due in 1890, .	15,000.00	17,965.00	17,250.00
" " " 7s, " 1894, .	10,000.00	12,725.00	12,000.00
" " " 7s, " 1896, .	5,000.00	5,000.00	6,150.00
" Cincinnati, Ohio, 6s, " 1885, .	1,000.00	1,000.00	1,030.00
" " " 6s, " 1890, . .	1,000.00	1,000.00	1,080.00
Cuyahoga Co., " 7s, " 1883, .	5,000.00	5,000.00	5,000.00
City of Dayton, " 8s, " 1888, .	5,000.00	5,925.00	5,800.00
" St. Louis, Mo., 6s, " 1883, .	1,000.00	1,000.00	1,000.00
" " " 6s, " 1887, .	5,000.00	5,000.00	5,250.00
" " " 6s, " 1888, .	6,000.00	6,000.00	6,360.00
St. Louis Co., " 6s, " 1883, . .	2,000.00	2,000.00	2,000.00
Vernon Town, Ct., 6s, ...	45,000.00	45,000.00	45,000.00
BANK STOCKS.			
150 shares Ætna Nat., Hartford,	15,000.00	15,000.00	19,950.00
400 " American " "	20,000.00	20,000.00	30,000.00
150 " City " "	15,000.00	15,000.00	18,500.00
50 " Charter Oak, " "	5,000.00	5,000.00	7,100.00

MECHANICS SAVINGS BANK.—Continued.

INVESTMENTS.—Continued.

DESCRIPTION.	PAR VALUE.	COST.	MARKET VALUE.
BANK STOCKS.—CONTINUED.			
10 shares Farmers & Mech's Nat., Hartford, $	1,000.00	1,000.00	1,360.00
300 " First " "	30,000.00	30,000.00	37,200.00
100 " Mercantile " "	10,000.00	10,000.00	13,000.00
100 " First " Norwich,	10,000.00	11,575.00	11,575.00
50 " " " Suffield, . .	5,000.00	5,000.00	5,000.00
75 " Metropolitan " New York,	7,500.00	7,500.00	13,200.00
50 " Nassau "	2,500.00	2,500.00	3,150.00
30 " Second National, New Haven,	3,000.00	4,860.00	4,860.00

MISCELLANEOUS ITEMS.

1. Number of depositors having $500 or less, 2,919; total amount, $394,014.50
2. Number of depositors having over $500 and less than $1,000, ... 472; total amount, 322,630.14
3. Number of depositors having one thousand and not over $2,000, ... 357; total amount, 498,714.48
4. Number of depositors having over $2,000, 48; total amount, 127,485.12

5. Total number of depositors, . . . 3,796; total deposits, $1,342,844.24
6. Largest amount due a single depositor, $9,675.78.
7. Number of accounts opened during the year, 712; number closed, 485.
8. Amount of income received during the year, $73,020.45.
9. Amount of dividends declared during the year, $48,653.70.
10. Amount deposited, including interest credited, the past year, $436,520.58.
11. Amount withdrawn during the year, $339,321.12.
12. Increase of deposits the past year, $97,199.46.
13. Amount carried to surplus or profit and loss during the year, none.
14. Rate of dividend the last year, 4 per cent.; when paid, Jan. 1st and July 1st.
15. State tax during the past year, $2,412.30; U. S. tax, $81.30.
16. Total office expenses the past year, including salaries, $6,267.63.
17. Net amount of income during the year from real estate owned, $3,454.41.
18. Amount of assets yielding no income during the year, $27,406.
19. Are all loans upon real estate secured by first mortgage? Yes.
20. Largest amount loaned to one individual, company, society, or corporation, $50,000.
21. Date of annual meeting for choice of officers, in July.

Officers.—President, George W. Moore; Treasurer, Ward W. Jacobs; Directors or Trustees, George W. Moore, Daniel Phillips, Edward W. Parsons, Henry Pease, Ward W. Jacobs, Hugh Harbison, Charles L. Lincoln, George A. Fairfield, Edwin D. Tiffany, John G. Root, John S. Welles, Edson Fessenden, Jeremiah M. Allen, John M. Holcombe, Henry C. Dwight, Frederick R. Foster, Jonathan B. Bunce.

MECHANICS & FARMERS SAVINGS BANK, BRIDGEPORT.

L. S. CATLIN, Treasurer.   INCORPORATED, 1871.

STATEMENT, OCTOBER 1, 1882.

LIABILITIES.		ASSETS.	
Whole Amount of Deposits,	$320,627.99	Loans on Real Estate, .	$184,900.00
Surplus Account, . .	1,304.87	Loans on Stocks and Bonds,	30,250.00
Interest Account, . .	7,301.22	Loans on Endorsed Notes, .	10,712.10
		Town, City, and Corp'n Bonds,	84,325.00
		Town, City, and Boro' Orders,	6,200.00
		Bank Stocks in Connecticut,	1,740.00
		Real Estate by Foreclosure,	2,253.72
		Safe and Furniture, . .	675.00
		Cash in Bank, . . .	7,245.23
		Cash on hand, . . .	933.03
Total Liabilities, . .	$329,234.08	Total Assets, . .	$329,234.08

INVESTMENTS.

DESCRIPTION.	PAR VALUE.	COST.	MARKET VALUE.
TOWN, CITY, AND CORPORATION BONDS.			
Bridgeport City, 5 per cent., ... $	4,000.00	4,120.00	4,480.00
Cincinnati " 6 " . . .	26,000.00	29,542.50	31,460.00
" " 7⅜ " . . .	7,000.00	8,607.50	9,240.00
" " 5 " . . .	24,000.00	27,240.00	27,240.00
Brooklyn " 7 " . . .	9,000.00	11,910.00	13,500.00
West Farms, guaranteed by New York City,	1,500.00	1,795.00	2,100.00
Cleveland City, 6 per cent., . . .	1,000.00	1,110.00	1,110.00
TOWN, CITY, AND BOROUGH ORDERS.			
Borough of West Stratford, ...	1,200.00	1,200.00	1,200.00
City of Bridgeport, ...	5,000.00	5,000.00	5,000.00
BANK STOCKS.			
12 shares Connecticut, ...	1,200.00	1,740.00	1,740.00

MISCELLANEOUS ITEMS.

. Number of depositors having $500 or less, 1,019; total amount, $133,858.95
. Number of depositors having over $500 and less than $1,000, . . . 135; total amount, 87,280.00
3. Number of depositors having $1,000 and not over $2,000, ... 75; total amount, 99,489.04.
4. Number of depositors having over $2,000, 0; total amount, 0.00

5. Total number of depositors, . . 1,229; total deposits, $320,627.99
6. Largest amount due a single depositor, $2,000.
7. Number of accounts opened during the year, 422; number closed, 190.
8. Amount of income received during the year, $15,062.59.
9. Amount of dividends declared during the year, $10,540.81.

MECHANICS & FARMERS SAVINGS BANK.—CONTINUED.

MISCELLANEOUS ITEMS.—CONTINUED.

10. Amount deposited, including interest credited, the past year, $182,058.13.
11. Amount withdrawn during the year, $93,761.43.
12. Increase of deposits the past year, $88,296.70.
13. Amount carried to surplus or profit and loss during the year, $675.47.
14. Rate of dividend the last year, 4½ per cent.; when paid, January and July.
15. State tax during the past year, $489.16; United States tax, none.
16. Total office expenses the past year, including salaries, $1,213.42.
17. Net amount of income during the year from real estate owned, $37.
18. Amount of assets yielding no income during the year, none.
19. Are all loans upon real estate secured by first mortgage? Yes.
20. Largest amount loaned to one individual, company, society, or corporation, $20,000.
21. Date of annual meeting for choice of officers, month of July.

OFFICERS. — President, William G. Lineburgh; Vice-Presidents, Andrew Burke, R. B. Lacey; Treasurer, Lyman S. Catlin; Directors or Trustees, David Wooster, S. C. Kingman, Isaac W. Smith, George W. Peck, Carlos Curtis, D. N. Morgan, H. C. Coggswell, H. R. Parrott, Fred. A. Mason, L. S. Catlin, Chauncey Morton, D. B. Lockwood, George W. Hayes, L. F. Curtis, George Keeler, M. E. Morris, I. B. Prindle, F. B. Hall.

MERIDEN SAVINGS BANK.

S. H. W. YALE, Treasurer.   INCORPORATED, 1851.

STATEMENT, OCTOBER 1, 1882.

LIABILITIES.		ASSETS.	
Whole Am't of Deposits,	$1,451,603.76	Loans on Real Estate, .	$939,635.83
Surplus Account, . .	14,468.87	Loans on Stocks and Bonds,	1,200.00
Interest Account, . .	80,751.50	Loans on Endorsed Notes,	139,722.43
		United States Bonds, .	180,718.75
		State Bonds, . .	100.00
		Town, City, and Corp'n B'ds,	40,370.37
		Railroad Bonds, . .	48,245.84
		Bank Stocks in Connecticut,	113,784.50
		Real Estate by Foreclosure,	5,844.89
		Banking House and Real Est.,	20,896.88
		Tax Account, . . .	1,550.58
		Cash in Bank, . . .	37,693.54
		Cash on hand, . . .	17,061.02
Total Liabilities, .	$1,546,824.13	Total Assets, . .	$1,546,824.13

INVESTMENTS.

DESCRIPTION.	PAR VALUE.	COST.	MARKET VALUE.
UNITED STATES BONDS.			
4½s of 1891, Registered, ... $	5,000.00	5,618.75	5,675.00
4s of 1907, Registered, ...	35,000.00	35,000.00	41,825.00
4s of 1907, Coupon, ...	100.00	100.00	119.50
Three per cents., ...	140,000.00	140,000.00	142,800.00
STATE BONDS.			
State of Connecticut, 6s, ...	100.00	100.00	106.00
TOWN, CITY, AND CORPORATION BONDS.			
Cincinnati, Ohio, 7s, ...	14,000.00	18,186.89	18,186.89
" " 7 3/10 s, ...	16,000.00	21,021.30	21,021.30
St. Louis, Mo., ...	500.00	583.60	583.60
Johnstown, N. Y., ...	500.00	578.58	578.58
RAILROAD BONDS.			
Chicago, Burlington & Quincy, 7s,	5,000.00	6,206.25	6,206.25
Albany & Susquehanna, 7s,	5,000.00	6,259.59	6,259.59
New York Central & Harlem River, 7s,	25,000.00	32,675.00	32,675.00
Morris & Essex, 7s,	2,800.00	3,105.00	3,175.00
BANK STOCKS.			
204 shares Meriden National, . . .	20,400.00	21,676.00	25,500.00
261 " Home " Meriden, . .	26,100.00	27,126.50	32,625.00
420 " First " " . .	42,000.00	42,720.00	49,560.00
99 " New Britain National, . .	9,900.00	10,404.00	14,850.00
14 " Middlesex Co., Middletown, .	1,400.00	1,400.00	1,680.00
30 " Winsted National, . . .	3,000.00	3,150.00	3,150.00
50 " Yale " New Haven, .	5,000.00	6,000.00	6,000.00
12 " Central " Middletown, .	900.00	1,308.00	1,308.00

MERIDEN SAVINGS BANK.—CONTINUED.

MISCELLANEOUS ITEMS.

1. Number of depositors having $500 or less, 4,077; total amount, $504,995.62
2. Number of depositors having over $500 and less than $1,000, ... 391; total amount, 257,626.05
3. Number of depositors having $1,000 and not over $2,000, ... 330; total amount, 435,259.08
4. Number of depositors having over $2,000, . 92; total amount, 253,723.01

5. Total number of depositors, . . . 4,890; total deposits,$1,451,603.76
6. Largest amount due a single depositor, $6,360.93.
7. Number of accounts opened during the year, 820; number closed, 515.
8. Amount of income received during the year, $83,089.69.
9. Amount of dividends declared during the year, $66,324.44.
10. Amount deposited, including interest credited, the past year, $318,472.79.
11. Amount withdrawn during the year, $210,848.23.
12. Increase of deposits the past year, $107,624.56.
13. Amount carried to surplus or profit and loss during the year, none.
14. Rate of dividend the last year, 5 per cent.; when paid, January and July 21st.
15. State tax during the past year, $3,575.79; U. S. tax, none.
16. Total office expenses the past year, including salaries, $3,284.58.
17. Net amount of income during the year from real estate owned, $1,129.64.
18. Amount of assets yielding no income during the year, about $8,000.
19. Are all loans upon real estate secured by first mortgage? Yes.
20. Largest amount loaned to one individual, company, society, or corporation, $50,000.
21. Date of annual meeting for choice of officers, first Monday after the 19th of July.

OFFICERS.—President, Levi E. Coe; Treasurer, S. H. W. Yale; Directors or Trustees, O. H. Platt, O. B. Arnold, Chas. Parker, Geo. W. Lyon, H. A. Yale, John P. Morse, Geo. R. Wilmot, John L. Billard, Isaac C. Lewis, J. W. Russell, A. C. Markham, A. Chamberlain, S. H. W. Yale.

MECHANICS SAVINGS BANK, WINSTED.

ELIAS E. GILMAN, Treasurer.   INCORPORATED, 1875.

STATEMENT, OCTOBER 1, 1882.

LIABILITIES.		ASSETS.	
Whole Amount of Deposits,	$366,818.96	Loans on Real Estate,	$184,878.84
Surplus Account,		Loans on Endorsed Notes, .	40,945.00
Interest Account, } . .	13,662.77	United States Bonds, . .	46,147.00
Other Liabilities, . .	319.50	Town, City, and Boro' Orders,	2,500.00
		School District Orders, .	4,850.00
		Bank Stocks in Connecticut,	82,397
		Tax Account, }	738.97
		Insurance Account, } .	
		Expense Account, . .	1,328.57
		Society Orders, . . .	946.25
		Cash in Bank, . . .	15,537.85
		Cash on hand, . . .	531.75
Total Liabilities, . .	$380,801.23	Total Assets, . .	$380,801.23

INVESTMENTS.

DESCRIPTION.	PAR VALUE.	COST.	MARKET VALUE.
UNITED STATES BONDS.			
4s of 1907, Registered, ... $	21,000.00	21,000.00	24,885.00
4s of 1907, Coupon, ...	50.00	50.00	59.00
Currency 6s, ...	20,000.00	25,097.00	26,800.00
TOWN, CITY, AND BOROUGH ORDERS.			
Town of Hartland, ...	1,000.00	1,000.00	1,000.00
Borough of Winsted, ...	1,500.00	1,500.00	1,500.00
SCHOOL DISTRICT ORDERS.			
Winchester, No. 1, ...	4,850.00	4,850.00	4,850.00
Ecclesiastical Society Orders, . .	946.25	946.25	946.25
BANK STOCKS.			
30 shares Pahquioque National, Danbury, .	3,000.00	3,825.00	3,825.00
35 " Birmingham " . .	3,500.00	5,525.00	5,525.00
20 " Tradesmens " New Haven,	2,000.00	3,200.00	3,200.00
74 " Second " "	7,400.00	11,796.00	11,796.00
22 " City " Bridgeport, .	2,200.00	2,933.00	2,933.00
84 " First " "	8,400.00	14,318.00	14,318.00
20 " Waterbury " . .	1,000.00	1,750.00	1,750.00
15 " Central " Middletown,	1,125.00	1,710.00	1,710.00
15 " New Britain " . .	1,500.00	2,310.00	2,310.00
29 " Home " Meriden, .	2,900.00	3,688.00	3,688.00
25 " Hartford " Hartford, .	2,500.00	4,125.00	4,125.00
22 " Phœnix " "	2,200.00	3,606.00	3,606.00
50 " Mercantile " "	5,000.00	6,750.00	6,750.00
14 " American " "	700.00	966.00	966.00
64 " First " Winsted, .	6,400.00	6,500.00	6,500.00
58 " Hurlbut " "	5,800.00	9,355.00	9,355.00

MECHANICS SAVINGS BANK.—Continued.

MISCELLANEOUS ITEMS.

1. Number of depositors having $500 or less,   857; total amount, $107,614.67
2. Number of depositors having over $500 and
   less than $1,000, ... 120; total amount,   82,121.54
3. Number of depositors having $1,000 and not
   over $2,000, ... 101; total amount, 138,109.37
4. Number of depositors having over $2,000, .   16; total amount,   38,973.38

5. Total number of depositors, ... 1,094; total deposits, $366,818.96
6. Largest amount due a single depositor, $3,177.58.
7. Number of accounts opened during the year, 302; number closed, 113.
8. Amount of income received during the year, $18,189.24.
9. Amount of dividends declared during the year, $12,375.12.
10. Amount deposited, including interest credited, the past year, $141,537.04.
11. Amount withdrawn during the year, $78,757.95.
12. Increase of deposits the past year, $62,779.09.
13. Amount carried to surplus or profit and loss during the year, none.
14. Rate of dividend the last year, 4 per cent.; when paid, January and July.
15. State tax during the past year, $685; United States tax, none.
16. Total office expenses the past year, including salaries, $1,328.57.
17. Net amount of income during the year from real estate owned, none.
18. Amount of assets yielding no income during the year, none.
19. Are all loans upon real estate secured by first mortgage? Yes.
20. Largest amount loaned to one individual, company, society, or corporation,
    $25,000.
21. Date of annual meeting for choice of officers, second Wednesday in July.

Officers.—President, Normand Adams; Treasurer, Elias E. Gilman; Directors
or Trustees, Normand Adams, Harvey B. Steele, M.D., L. R. Norton, Charles B.
Hallett, Joseph H. Norton, Harvey L. Roberts, Theodore Baird.

MIDDLETOWN SAVINGS BANK.

F. L. GLEASON, Treasurer.   INCORPORATED, 1825.

STATEMENT, OCTOBER 1, 1882.

LIABILITIES.		ASSETS.	
Whole Am't of Deposits, .	$5,290,844.35	Loans on Real Estate, .	$2,816,670.00
Surplus Account, . .	150,000.00	Loans on Stocks and Bonds,	201,000.00
Interest Account, . .	91,286.54	Loans on Endorsed Notes,	12,366.00
Profit and Loss Account, .	55,399.22	United States Bonds, .	734,550.00
Balance Sundry Accounts,	15,394.24	Town, City, and Corp. B'ds,	1,089,816.54
		Railroad Bonds, . .	12,500.00
		Railroad Stocks, . .	17,275.00
		Bank Stocks in Connecticut,	166,142.00
		Bank Stocks in other States,	55,000.00
		Real Estate by Foreclosure,	494,181.20
		Banking House, . .	31,000.00
		Insurance Account, . .	26.25
		Expense Account, . .	3,853.34
		Cash in Bank, . . .	507,273.52
		Cash on hand, . .	11,270.50
Total Liabilities, .	$5,602,924.35	Total Assets, . .	$5,602,924.35

INVESTMENTS.

DESCRIPTION.		PAR VALUE.	COST.	MARKET VALUE.
UNITED STATES BONDS.				
5s of 1881, Registered (extended 3¼ per cent.),	$	300,000.00	300,000.00	300,000.00
4s of 1907, Registered, ...		400,000.00	434,550.00	474,500.00
TOWN, CITY, AND CORPORATION BONDS.				
Town of Wallingford,	6s, . .	1,300.00	1,300.00	1,300.00
Central School District,	5s, . .	20,000.00	20,000.00	20,000.00
City of New Britain,	7s, . .	41,000.00	41,000.00	48,380.00
" Middletown,	6s, . .	3,000.00	3,000.00	3,360.00
" "	7s, . .	30,000.00	30,000.00	35,400.00
Town of "	6s, . .	40,000.00	40,000.00	44,800.00
" "	4½s, . .	115,000.00	119,510.45	119,510.45
" "	7s, . .	53,100.00	53,100.00	62,658.00
" " Registered,	6s, . .	1,000.00	1,000.00	1,120.00
" Middlefield,	7s, . .	13,000.00	13,000.00	15,340.00
" "	6s, . .	5,000.00	5,000.00	5,600.00
" Portland,	7s, . .	13,600.00	13,600.00	16,048.00
" "	6s, . . .	51,000.00	51,000.00	57,120.00
" Chatham,	7s, . .	16,000.00	16,000.00	18,880.00
" New Canaan,	4s, . .	40,000.00	40,000.00	40,000.00
City of Dubuque, Iowa,	6s, . .	11,500.00	11,500.00	11,500.00
" New York,	6s, . .	83,000.00	87,771.01	87,771.01
" "	7s, . .	71,000.00	80,425.00	80,425.00
" Brooklyn, N. Y.,	7s, . .	110,000.00	135,666.56	135,666.56
" Jersey City, N. J.,	7s, . .	100,000.00	100,000.00	106,000.00
" St. Louis, Mo.,	6s, . .	51,000.00	57,136.14	58,140.00
" Chicago, Ill., Water,	7s, . .	14,000.00	17,505.38	17,505.88
" Cleveland, Ohio,	4s, . .	86,000.00	86,000.00	87,290.00
" Dayton, "	6s, . .	15,200.00	16,302.00	16,302.00

MIDDLETOWN SAVINGS BANK.—CONTINUED.

INVESTMENTS.—CONTINUED.

DESCRIPTION.	PAR VALUE.	COST.	MARKET VALUE.
RAILROAD BONDS.			
Pittsburgh, Fort Wayne & Chicago, . . $	6,500.00	6,500.00	8,775.00
Sandusky, Mansfield & Newark, . . .	7,000.00	6,000.00	7,000.00
RAILROAD STOCKS.			
30 shares Housatonic, preferred, . . .	3,000.00	3,000.00	3,900.00
63 " New York, New Haven & Hartford,	6,300.00	7,800.00	11,380.00
79 " Cleve., Col., Cin. & Indianapolis, .	7,900.00	6,475.00	5,420.00
BANK STOCKS.			
40 shares Bank of the State of New York, .	4,000.00	4,000.00	5,200.00
100 " Nassau National, " .	5,000.00	5,000.00	6,300.00
50 " St. Nicholas " " .	5,000.00	5,000.00	6,450.00
100 " National Park, " .	10,000.00	10,000.00	15,700.00
50 " " Shoe & Leath., " .	5,000.00	5,000.00	6,500.00
260 " American Ex. Nat., " .	26,000.00	26,000.00	33,800.00
377 " First " Middletown, .	37,700.00	37,700.00	45,240.00
548 " Middletown " " .	41,100.00	41,351.00	61,102.00
122 " Middlesex Co. " " .	12,200.00	12,978.00	14,640.00
110 " Central " " .	8,250.00	8,698.00	12,375.00
133 " Thames " Norwich, .	13,300.00	19,550.00	19,950.00
51 " Yale " New Haven, .	5,100.00	5,100.00	6,050.00
50 " Meriden " Meriden, .	5,000.00	5,750.00	6,500.00
100 " First " " .	10,000.00	11,450.00	11,800.00
65 " Home " " .	6,500.00	8,465.00	8,710.00
100 " City " Hartford, .	15,100.00	15,100.00	13,590.00

MISCELLANEOUS ITEMS.

1. Number of depositors having $500 or less,   6,900; total amount, $925,494.73
2. Number of depositors having over $500 and less than 1,000, ... 1,168; total amount,   834,687.86
3. Number of depositors having $1,000 and not over $2,000, ... 1,204; total amount, 1,751,329.00
4. Number of depositors having over $2,000,   538; total amount, 1,779,332.76
5. Total number of depositors, . . . 9,810; total deposits, $5,290,844.35
6. Largest amount due a single depositor, $30,092.
7. Number of accounts opened during the year, 1,102; number closed, 1,020.
8. Amount of income received during the year, $258,451.57.
9. Amount of dividends declared during the year, $206,008.25.
10. Amount deposited, including interest credited, the past year, $974,660.96.
11. Amount withdrawn during the year, $907,314.63.
12. Increase of deposits the past year, $67,346.33.
13. Amount carried to surplus or profit and loss during the year, $35,820.19.
14. Rate of dividend the last year, 4 per cent.; when paid, November 25th and May 25th.
15. State tax during the past year, $11,099.36; U. S. tax, $220.32.
16. Total office expenses the past year, including salaries, $11,468.23.
17. Net amount of income during the year from real estate owned, $5,595.52.
18. Amount of assets yielding no income during the year, $15,380.
19. Are all loans upon real estate secured by first mortgage? Yes.

MIDDLETOWN SAVINGS BANK.—Continued.

MISCELLANEOUS ITEMS.—Continued.

20. Largest amount loaned to one individual, company, society, or corporation,
      $77,500.
21. Date of annual meeting for choice of officers, first Monday in June.

OFFICERS. — President, Elijah Ackley; Treasurer, Frederic L. Gleason; Directors or Trustees, William Southmayd, Henry G. Hubbard, John P. Bacon, Samuel Babcock, Chas. A. Boardman, Elijah H. Hubbard, George S. Hubbard, M. B. Copeland, John N. Camp, George W. Harris, George W. Burr, Henry Ward, Elisha B. Nye, L. M. Leach, Elijah Ackley, John H. Watkinson, Moses Culver, John S. Bailey, Samuel Rapell, William Wilcox, Henry Woodward, Edward Payne, George W. Atkins, James H. Bunce.

MILFORD SAVINGS BANK.

PHINEAS S. BRISTOL, Treasurer.   INCORPORATED, 1872.

STATEMENT, OCTOBER 1, 1882.

LIABILITIES.		ASSETS.	
Whole Amount of Deposits,	$104,758.07	Loans on Real Estate,	$61,574.00
Surplus Account,	2,133.96	Loans on Endorsed Notes,	3,091.64
Interest Account,	785.30	United States Bonds,	12,802.00
		Town, City, and Corp'n Bonds,	2,060.00
		Bank Stocks in Connecticut,	21,317.13
		Expense Account,	92.40
		Iron Safe,	222.00
		Cash in Bank,	6,003.07
		Cash on hand,	515.09
Total Liabilities,	$107,677.33	Total Assets,	$107,677.33

INVESTMENTS.

DESCRIPTION.	PAR VALUE.	COST.	MARKET VALUE.
UNITED STATES BONDS.			
4s of 1907, Coupon,	12,000.00	12,802.00	12,802.00
TOWN, CITY, AND CORPORATION BONDS.			
Town of Milford, 5 per cent.,	2,000.00	2,060.00	2,060.00
BANK STOCKS.			
84 shares Merchants National, New Haven,	4,200.00	5,013.00	5,013.00
10 " Yale " "	1,000.00	1,020.00	1,020.00
22 " New Haven " "	2,200.00	3,550.00	3,550.00
32 " Second " "	3,200.00	5,249.75	5,249.75
14 " Middlesex Co. National, Middletown,	1,400.00	1,711.50	1,711.50
21 " Meriden National, Meriden,	2,100.00	2,531.25	2,531.25
6 " Connecticut National, Bridgeport,	600.00	841.63	841.63
10 " Agawam Nat'l, Springfield, Mass.,	1,000.00	1,500.00	1,400.00

MISCELLANEOUS ITEMS.

1. Number of depositors having $500 or less, . 376; total amount, $48,281.76
2. Number of depositors having over $500 and less than $1,000, . 34; total amount, 23,243.49
3. Number of depositors having $1,000 and not over $2,000, . 19; total amount, 25,871.77
4. Number of depositors having over $2,000, . 3; total amount, 7,361.05
5. Total number of depositors, . 432; total deposits, $104,758.07
6. Largest amount due a single depositor, $2,795.09.
7. Number of accounts opened during the year, 107; number closed, 56.
8. Amount of income received during the year, $4,950.00.
9. Amount of dividends declared during the year, $4,141.64.

MILFORD SAVINGS BANK.—Continued.

MISCELLANEOUS ITEMS.—Continued.

10. Amount deposited, including interest credited, the past year, $54,953.42.
11. Amount withdrawn during the year, $32,528.62.
12. Increase of deposits the past year, $22,424.80.
13. Amount carried to surplus or profit and loss during the year, $509.11.
14. Rate of dividend the last year, 5 per cent.; when paid, January and July.
15. State tax during the past year, $91.98; U. S. tax, $2.17.
16. Total office expenses the past year, including salaries, $354.40.
17. Net amount of income during the year from real estate owned, none.
18. Amount of assets yielding no income during the year, none.
19. Are all loans upon real estate secured by first mortgage? Yes.
20. Largest amount loaned to one individual, company, society, or corporation, $7,000.00.
21. Date of annual meeting for choice of officers, July.

OFFICERS. —President, Isaac T. Rogers; Treasurer, Phineas S. Bristol; Directors or Trustees, Anon Clark, William G. Mitchell, John W. Fowler, James T. Higley, Phineas S. Bristol, Theodore Platt, George M. Gunn, William G. Cornwall, Charles W. Beardsley, H. B. Beardsley, Samuel B. Gunn, Marcus Merwin, Nathan E. Smith, Charles Lake, Miles B. Plumb, James McCarthy, Joseph W. Nettleton, David L. Clark, William Glumey, Treat C. Botsford.

MOODUS SAVINGS BANK.

EUGENE W. CHAFFEE, Treasurer.   INCORPORATED, 1870.

STATEMENT, OCTOBER 1, 1882.

LIABILITIES.		ASSETS.	
Whole Amount of Deposits,	$149,107.22	Loans on Real Estate, .	$74,685.00
Surplus Account, . .	4,053.46	Loans on Stocks and Bonds,	1,200.00
Interest Account, . .	1,267.15	Loans on Endorsed Notes, .	1,920.00
		United States Bonds, . .	11,000.00
		Town, City, and Corp'n B'ds,	26,800.00
		Town, City, and Boro' Orders,	6,500.00
		School District Orders, .	120.00
		Railroad Bonds, . . .	10,000.00
		Bank Stocks in Connecticut,	9,200.00
		Bank Stocks in other States,	500.00
		Real Estate by Foreclosure,	2,875.00
		Insurance Account, . .	7.18
		Expense Account, . .	6.20
		1st Ecc. Soc., E. Haddam, order,	150.00
		Premium Account, . .	6,684.00
		Cash in Bank, . . .	2,345.31
		Cash on hand, . . .	435.19
Total Liabilities, . .	$154,427.83	Total Assets, . .	$154,427.83

INVESTMENTS.

DESCRIPTION.	PAR VALUE.	COST.	MARKET VALUE.
UNITED STATES BONDS.			
4½s of 1891, registered, ... $	1,000.00	1,000.00	1,120.00
4s of 1907, registered, ...	5,000.00	5,000.00	5,900.00
Three per cents, ...	5,000.00	5,000.00	5,000.00
TOWN, CITY, AND CORPORATION BONDS.			
Hartford 4½ per cent., coupon, 1889-1904,	4,000.00	4,000.00	4,160.00
Saybrook 5 " " 1889-1899,	4,000.00	4,000.00	4,200.00
Essex 4½ " " 1890-1900,	2,000.00	2,000.00	2,060.00
Chatham 5 " " 1884-1904,	1,000.00	1,000.00	1,010.00
New York City 7 " registered, 1896,	1,000.00	1,000.00	1,800.00
" 7 " " 1900,	1,000.00	1,000.00	1,370.00
" 6 " " gold, 1901,	3,000.00	3,000.00	3,840.00
" 6 " " 1901,	800.00	800.00	1,000.00
" 6 " .. 1887,	1,000.00	1,000.00	1,090.00
Brooklyn, N.Y. 6 " " 1899,	1,000.00	1,000.00	1,200.00
" " 7 " " 1920,	2,000.00	2,000.00	2,800.00
Rochester, " 7 " " 1903,	3,000.00	3,000.00	4,110.00
Buffalo, " 6 " coupon, 1896,	2,000.00	2,000.00	2,360.00
Detroit, Mich., 7 " " 1893,	1,000.00	1,000.00	1,180.00
TOWN, CITY, AND BOROUGH ORDERS.			
East Haddam, ...	6,500.00	6,500.00	6,500.00

MOODUS SAVINGS BANK.—Continued.

INVESTMENTS.—Continued.

DESCRIPTION.	PAR VALUE.	COST.	MARKET VALUE.
SCHOOL DISTRICT ORDERS.			
Ninth School District of East Haddam, $	120.00	120.00	120.00
RAILROAD BONDS.			
N. Y. Central & Hudson Riv. 1st m. 7s of 1903,	5,000.00	5,000.00	6,600.00
New York & Harlem " " " 1900,	5,000.00	5,000.00	6,600.00
BANK STOCKS.			
64 shares Nat. Bk. of New England, E. Haddam,	6,400.00	6,400.00	8,000.00
10 " First National Bank of Portland, .	1,000.00	1,000.00	1,160.00
25 " Merchants " " Norwich, .	1,000.00	1,000.00	1,000.00
5 " Home " " Meriden, .	500.00	500.00	650.00
5 " Ninth " " New York,	500.00	500.00	600.00

MISCELLANEOUS ITEMS.

1. Number of depositors having $500 or less, . 596; total amount, $56,423.98
2. Number of depositors having over $500 and less than $1,000, ... 48; total amount,   34,591.28
3. Number of depositors having $1,000 and not over $2,000, ... 24; total amount,   32,041.19
4. Number of depositors having over $2,000, . 11; total amount,   25,062.83

5. Total number of depositors, .   .   . 679; total deposits, $149,107.28
6. Largest amount due a single depositor, $3,025.59.
7. Number of accounts opened during the year, 97; number closed, 54.
8. Amount of income received during the year, $7,755.96.
9. Amount of dividends declared during the year, $6,153.79.
10. Amount deposited, including interest credited, the past year, $35,326.21.
11. Amount withdrawn during the year, $24,360.02.
12. Increase of deposits the past year, $10,966.19.
13. Amount carried to surplus or profit and loss during the year, $781.35.
14. Rate of dividend the last year, 4½ per cent.; when paid, January and July.
15. State tax during the past year, $209.50; U. S. tax, none.
16. Total office expenses the past year, including salaries, $414.67.
17. Net amount of income during the year from real estate owned, $32.25.
18. Amount of assets yielding no income during the year, none.
19. Are all loans upon real estate secured by first mortgage? Yes.
20. Largest amount loaned to one individual, company, society, or corporation, $7,000.00.
21. Date of annual meeting for choice of officers, third Thursday in July.

OFFICERS.—President, Charles E. Brownell; Vice-President, Amasa Day; Treasurer, Eugene W. Chaffee; Directors or Trustees, William E. Cone, Theodore Fuller, David S. Purple, William L. Fowler, Jr., Albert E. Purple.

NATIONAL SAVINGS BANK, NEW HAVEN.

HOADLEY B. IVES, Treasurer.   INCORPORATED, 1866.

STATEMENT, OCTOBER 1, 1882.

LIABILITIES.		ASSETS.	
Whole Amt. of Deposits,	$633,056.75	Loans on Real Estate, .	$433,801.58
Surplus Account, . .	33,913.98	Loans on Stocks and Bonds,	31,050.00
Interest Account, ·. .	9,050.92	Loans on Endorsed Notes,	39,200.00
		United States Bonds, .	49,005.72
		Town, City, and Corp'n B'ds,	33,390.26
		Bank Stocks in Connecticut,	58,308.50
		Real Estate by Foreclosure,	12,931.13
		Expense Account, . .	1,037.42
		Cash in Bank, . . .	14,851.10
		Cash on hand, . . .	2,445.94
Total Liabilities, .	$676,021.65	Total Assets, . .	$676,021.65

INVESTMENTS.

DESCRIPTION.	PAR VALUE.	COST.	MARKET VALUE.
UNITED STATES BONDS.			
5s of 1881, Registered (extended 3½ per cent.), $	19,000.00	19,805.00	19,285.00
4½s of 1891, Coupon, ...	15,000.00	16,181.25	16,987.50
4s of 1907, Coupon, . . ، . .	18,000.00	18,019.47	15,502.50
TOWN, CITY, AND CORPORATION BONDS.			
City of New Haven, 7s, . . .	4,000.00	3,900.00	5,200.00
" " 1885, 6s, . . .	5,000.00	4,550.00	5,400.00
. " Chicago, 1888, 7s, . . .	18,000.00	15,156.26	15,600.00
Town of East Haven, 1907, 6s, . . .	3,000.00	3,332.00	3,360.00
City of Cincinnati, 1908, 7s, . . .	5,000.00	6,452.00	6,500.00
BANK STOCKS.			
179 shares Yale National, New Haven,	17,900.00	21,391.75	21,480.00
273 " Merchants " "	13,650.00	16,470.50	17,199.00
25 " Second " "	2,500.00	3,650.00	4,050.00
13 " Mechanics " "	780.00	1,066.25	910.00
55 " Middlesex Co., " Middletown,	5,500.00	6,725.00	6,765.00
65 " First " Meriden, .	6,500.00	7,715.00	7,865.00
10 " Home " " .	1,000.00	1,290.00	1,300.00

MISCELLANEOUS ITEMS.

1. Number of depositors having $500 or less, 1,331; total amount, $178,886.22
2. Number of depositors having over $500 and less than $1,000, ... 284; total amount, 167,440.80
3. Number of depositors having $1,000 and not over $2,000, ... 173; total amount, 201,249.48
4. Number of depositors having over $2,000, 21; total amount, 85,480.25

5. Total number of depositors, . . . 1,809; total deposits, $633,056.75

NATIONAL SAVINGS BANK.—Continued.

MISCELLANEOUS ITEMS.—Continued.

6. Largest amount due a single depositor, $10,719.03.
7. Number of accounts opened during the year, 370; number closed, 254.
8. Amount of income received during the year, $34,822.47.
9. Amount of dividends declared during the year, $23,901.11.
10. Amount deposited, including interest credited, the past year, $201,244.03.
11. Amount withdrawn during the year, $152,587.77.
12. Increase of deposits the past year, $48,656.26.
13. Amount carried to surplus or profit and loss during the year, $6,969.54.
14. Rate of dividend the last year, 4 per cent.: when paid, January and July.
15. State tax during the past year, $1,325.20; U. S. tax, none.
16. Total office expenses the past year, including salaries, $2,364.56.
17. Net amount of income during the year from real estate owned, $280.26.
18. Amount of assets yielding no income during the year, $3,006.38.
19. Are all loans upon real estate secured by first mortgage? Yes.
20. Largest amount loaned to one individual, company, society, or corporation, $25,000.
21. Date of annual meeting for choice of officers, first Wednesday in July.

OFFICERS.—President, Maier Zunder; Vice-President, George H. Watrous; Treasurer, Hoadley B. Ives: Directors or Trustees, Maier Zunder, George H. Watrous, H. B. Ives, Bernard Reilly, Abner L. Train, John E. Earle, Samuel Johnson, Julius Twiss, Cornelius Pierpont, Louis Feldman, Charles Atwater, Francis Donnelly.

NAUGATUCK SAVINGS BANK.

L. S. PLATT, Treasurer.   INCORPORATED, 1870

STATEMENT, OCTOBER 1, 1882.

LIABILITIES.		ASSETS.	
Whole Amount of Deposits,	$142,216.01	Loans on Real Estate, .	$122,289.58
Surplus Account, . .	4,559.88	Loans on Endorsed Notes, .	19,222.00
Interest Account, . .	1,879.98	Cash in Bank, . . .	5,432.06
		Cash on hand, . . .	1,662.23
Total Liabilities, . .	$148,605.87	Total Assets, . .	$148,605.87

MISCELLANEOUS ITEMS.

1. Number of depositors having $500 or less, . 568; total amount, $71,289.22
2. Number of depositors having over $500 and less than $1,000, ... 61; total amount, 41,430.11
3. Number of depositors having $1,000 and not over $2,000, ... 16; total amount, 18,742.06
4. Number of depositors having over $2,000, . 5; total amount, 10,704.62

5. Total number of depositors, ... 650; total deposits, $142,166.01
6. Largest amount due a single depositor, $2,615.59.
7. Number of accounts opened during the year, 219; number closed, 88.
8. Amount of income received during the year, $7,530.34.
9. Amount of dividends declared during the year, $5,690.69.
10. Amount deposited, including interest credited, the past year, $33,277.05.
11. Amount withdrawn during the year, $19,735.51.
12. Increase of deposits the past year, $13,541.54.
13. Amount carried to surplus or profit and loss during the year, $1,158.89.
14. Rate of dividend the last year, 5 per cent.; when paid, January 1st and July 1st.
15. State tax during the past year, $183.12; U. S. tax, $3.01.
16. Total office expenses the past year, including salaries, $528.
17. Net amount of income during the year from real estate owned, none.
18. Amount of assets yielding no income during the year, none.
19. Are all loans upon real estate secured by first mortgage? Yes.
20. Largest amount loaned to one individual, company, society, or corporation, $5,500.00.
21. Date of annual meeting for choice of officers.

OFFICERS.—President, Homer Twitchell; Treasurer, L. S. Platt; Directors or Trustees, L. S. Platt, J. H. Whittemore, B. B. Tuttle, E. B. Mallette, L. D. Warner.

NEW CANAAN SAVINGS BANK.

RUSSELL L. HALL, Treasurer.   INCORPORATED, 1859.

STATEMENT, OCTOBER 1, 1882.

LIABILITIES.		ASSETS.	
Whole Amt. of Deposits, .	$169,671.42	Loans on Real Estate, .	$90,735.98
Surplus Account, . .	450.00	Loans on Stocks and Bonds,	2,500.00
Interest Account, . .	1,223.34	Loans on Endorsed Notes, .	29,378.79
Bills Payable, . . .	8,195.53	Bank Stocks in Connecticut,	19,500.00
		Real Estate by Foreclosure, ·	34,070.84
		Expense Account, . .	385.69
		Other Assets, . . .	2,763.15
		Cash on hand, . . .	205.84
Total Liabilities, . .	$179,540.29	· Total Assets, . .	$179,540.29

INVESTMENTS.

DESCRIPTION.	PAR VALUE.	COST.	MARKET VALUE.
BANK STOCKS.			
195 shares First National, New Canaan, . .	$ 19,500.00	19,500.00	19,500.00

MISCELLANEOUS ITEMS.

1. Number of depositors having $500 or less, . ` 605; total amount, $64,665.34
2. Number of depositors having over $500 and less than $1,000, ... 41; total amount, 27,085.57
3. Number of depositors having $1,000 and not over $2,000, ... '49; total amount, 68,556.81
4. Number of depositors having over $2,000, . . 4; total amount, 9,413.70
5. Total number of depositors, ... 699; total deposits, $169,671.42
   Largest amount due a single depositor, $2,634.40.
   Number of accounts opened during the year, 59; number closed, 85.
   Amount of income received during the year, $8,746.85.
   Amount of dividends declared during the year, $6,895.13,
   Amount deposited, including interest credited, the past year, $25,857.34.
10. Amount withdrawn during the year, $37,284.92.
12. Decrease of deposits the past year, $11,427.57.
13. Amount carried to surplus or profit and loss during the year, $450.
14. Rate of dividend the last year, 4 per cent.; when paid, Jan. 10th and July 10th.
15. State tax during the past year, $237.00; United States tax, $16.08.
16. Total office expenses the past year, including salaries, $1,047.22.
17. Net amount of income during the year from real estate owned, $938.01.
18. Amount of assets yielding no income during the year, $5,000.
19. Are all loans upon real estate secured by first mortgage?
20. Largest amount loaned to one individual, company, society, or corporation, $16,551.79.
21. Date of annual meeting for choice of officers, June.

OFFICERS.—President, Henry B. Rogers; Treasurer, Russell L. Hall; Directors or Trustees, Henry B. Rogers, Joseph F. Silliman, Edwin Hoyt, John E. Whitney, P. A. Thatcher, E. J. Richards, Russell L. Hall.

NEW MILFORD SAVINGS BANK.

CHARLES RANDALL, Treasurer.   INCORPORATED, 1858.

STATEMENT, OCTOBER 1, 1882.

LIABILITIES.		ASSETS.	
Whole Amount of Deposits,	$626,170.46	Loans on Real Estate, .	$242,050.85
Surplus Account, . .	25,700.00	Loans on Stocks and B'ds, ⎱	16,152.82
Interest Account, . .	20,469.16	Loans on Endorsed Notes, ⎰	
Sinking Fund, . . .	8,152.95	United States Bonds, .	21,858.00
Loss and Gain, . . .	2,853.68	Town, City, and Corporation Bonds and Notes, .	320,651.15
		Bank Stocks in Connecticut,	43,009.00
		Real Estate by Foreclosure,	6,698.69
		Banking House, . .	11,885.82
		Expense Account, . .	1,753.63
		Furniture, Safe, and two Time Locks, . . .	1,971.40
		Cash in Bank, . . .	15,770.43
		Cash on hand, . . .	2,544.46
Total Liabilities, .	$683,346.25	Total Assets, . .	$683,346.25

INVESTMENTS.

DESCRIPTION.		PAR VALUE.	COST.	MARKET VALUE.
UNITED STATES BONDS.				
6s of 1881 (extended 3½ per cent.), . . $		6,500.00	6,500.00	6,500.00
4½s of 1891, Coupon, ...		4,000.00	4,356.00	4,520.00
4s of 1907, Coupon, ...		10,200.00	10,550.00	12,138.00
TOWN, CITY, AND CORPORATION BONDS.				
New Milford,	5s and 7s, .	32,200.00	33,012.92	33,012.92
New Haven, Town,	6s, .	4,200.00	4,220.00	4,780.00
Hartford, "	4½s, .	6,000.00	6,232.50	6,232.50
" City,	6s, .	1,000.00	1,160.00	1,160.00
Danbury Borough,	4½s, .	18,000.00	18,747.50	18,747.50
City of Rochester, N. Y.,	7s, .	7,000.00	8,895.00	9,730.00
Town of Portland,	6s, .	3,000.00	3,150.00	3,300.00
City of Middletown,	6s, .	4,400.00	4,664.00	4,708.00
" New York, Registered,	7s, .	21,500.00	24,990.50	95,388.00
" " Coupon,	6s and 7s, .	63,300.00	70,372.13	
" Cleveland, Ohio,	7s, .	11,000.00	13,282.50	13,282.50
" Chicago, Ill.,	7s, .	34,000.00	41,775.00	41,775.00
" Brooklyn, N. Y.,	7s, .	18,000.00	15,795.00	15,795.00
" Cincinnati, Ohio,	6s, .	4,000.00	4,225.00 ⎫	53,612.50
" " "	7s, .	23,000.00	26,692.50 ⎬	
" " "	7 3⁄10s, .	17,000.00	20,695.00 ⎭	
" St. Louis, Mo.,	6s, . .	16,000.00	17,950.00	18,700.00
" Buffalo, N. Y.,	7s, .	5,000.00	5,750.00 ⎫	7,300.00
" " "	6s, .	1,000.00	1,100.00 ⎭	
" Columbus, Ohio,	8s, .	1,000.00	1,181.60	1,181.60
" Detroit, Mich.,	7s, .	1,000.00	1,235.00	1,235.00
" Bridgeport,	6s, .	500.00	525.00	525.00

NEW MILFORD SAVINGS BANK.—Continued.

INVESTMENTS.—Continued.

DESCRIPTION.				PAR VALUE.	COST.	MARKET VALUE.
BANK STOCK.						
72 shares	First	National,	New Milford,	$ 7,200.00	8,180.00	10,224.00
10 "	Connecticut	"	Bridgeport, .	1,000.00	1,400.00	1,450.00
90 "	Poquonnock	"	" .	9,000.00	9,870.00	10,800.00
60 "	City	"	" .	6,000.00	6,970.00	7,800.00
80 "	Bridgeport	"	" .	4,000.00	5,678.00	6,000.00
15 "	National Iron Bank,		Falls Village, .	1,500.00	1,875.00	1,875.00
10 "	First National,		Middletown, .	1,000.00	1,140.00	1,140.00
15 "	Middlesex County,		" .	1,500.00	1,710.00	1,710.00
33 "	First National,		West Meriden,	3,300.00	3,696.00	3,696.00
60 "	Merchants,		Norwich, .	2,400.00	2,490.00	2,490.00

MISCELLANEOUS ITEMS.

1. Number of depositors having $500 or less, 1,981; total amount, $242,865.05
2. Number of depositors having over $500 and less than $1,000, ... 216; total amount, 151,486.73
3. Number of depositors having $1,000 and not over $2,000, ... 122; total amount, 170,577.79
4. Number of depositors having over $2,000, 18; total amount, 61,240.89
5. Total number of depositors, ... 2,337; total deposits, $626,170.46
6. Largest amount due a single depositor, $12,581.67.
7. Number of accounts opened during the year, 456; number closed, 338.
8. Amount of income received during the year, $36,031.28.
9. Amount of dividends declared during the year, $23,918.91.
10. Amount deposited, including interest credited, the past year, $146,738.39.
11. Amount withdrawn during the year, $139,775.91.
12. Increase of deposits the past year, $6,962.48.
13. Amount carried to surplus or profit and loss during the year, $6,200.
14. Rate of dividend the last year, 4 per cent.; when paid, April and October.
15. State tax during the past year, $1,395.52; U. S. tax, $14.30.
16. Total office expenses the past year, including salaries, $2,100.
17. Net amount of income during the year from real estate owned, $185.
18. Amount of assets yielding no income during the year, $7,000.
19. Are all loans upon real estate secured by first mortgage? Yes.
20. Largest amount loaned to one individual, company, society, or corporation, $13,000.
21. Date of annual meeting for choice of officers, July.

Officers. — President, R. E. Canfield; Vice-President, Isaac B. Bristol; Treasurer, Charles Randall; Directors or Trustees, Turney Soule, Chas. H. Booth, John S. Turrill, Geo. W. Anthony, V. R. Giddings.

NEW HAVEN SAVINGS BANK.

JOHN P. TUTTLE, Treasurer.   INCORPORATED, 1838.

STATEMENT, OCTOBER 1, 1882.

LIABILITIES.		ASSETS.	
Whole Amt. of Deposits,	$5,055,673.52	Loans on Real Estate,	$2,145,069.99
Surplus Account, . .	210,000.00	Loans on Stocks and Bonds,	357,800.00
Interest Account, . .	44,534.88	Loans on Endorsed Notes, .	91,000.00
Rents Collected, . . .	2,129.43	United States Bonds, . .	157,500.00
Profit and Loss Account, .	1,838.17	State Bonds, . . .	5,000.00
		Town, City, and Corp'n B'ds,	1,058,400.00
		Railroad Bonds, . . .	1,003,228.75
		Bank Stocks in Connecticut,	142,250.00
		Real Estate by Foreclosure,	232,160.63
		Banking House, . . .	11,000.00
		Tax Account, . . .	8,443.75
		Insurance Account, . .	232.40
		Expense Account, . .	2,899.00
		Taxes on mort. property, .	2,969.31
		Cash in Bank, . . .	5,518.32
		Cash on hand, . . .	90,703.35
Total Liabilities, .	$5,314,175.50	Total Assets, .	$5,314,175.50

INVESTMENTS.

DESCRIPTION.		PAR VALUE.	COST.	MARKET VALUE.
UNITED STATES BONDS.				
4½s of 1891, Registered, ... $		80,000.00	80,000.00	90,000.00
4½s of 1891, Coupon,		20,000.00	20,000.00	22,500.00
4s of 1907, Registered, ...		50,000.00	50,750.00	59,500.00
STATE BONDS.				
Missouri, 6 per cent., ...		5,000.00	5,000.00	5,318.75
TOWN, CITY, AND CORPORATION BONDS.				
City of Cincinnati,	$7\frac{3}{10}$ per cent., . .	160,000.00	192,000.00	209,600.00
" "	6 " . .	31,000.00	31,000.00	36,890.00
" "	5 " . .	50,000.00	50,000.00	56,500.00
" "	7 " . .	4,000.00	4,000.00	5,280.00
" Chicago,	7	63,000.00	63,000.00	80,640.00
" "	6	40,000.00	46,000.00	47,200.00
" Burlington, Vt.,	5 " . .	60,000.00	60,000.00	63,000.00
" New Haven,	7 " . .	63,000.00	63,000.00	81,900.00
" Rochester, N. Y.,	7 " . .	5,000.00	5,000.00	6,200.00
" New York,	6 " . .	26,000.00	26,000.00	29,380.00
" "	7 " . .	20,000.00	20,000.00	24,000.00
" Brooklyn,	5 " . .	100,000.00	100,000.00	120,000.00
" "	7 :: . .	5,000.00	5,000.00	7,500.00
" St. Louis,	6 " . .	53,000.00	53,000.00	59,360.00
" Milwaukee,	7 " . .	3,000.00	3,000.00	3,750.00

8

NEW HAVEN SAVINGS BANK.—CONTINUED.

INVESTMENTS.—CONTINUED.

DESCRIPTION.	PAR VALUE.	COST.	MARKET VALUE.
TOWN, CITY, AND CORPORATION BONDS.—CON.			
Town of New Haven, 6 per cent., . . $	102,000.00	102,000.00	112,200.00
" East Haven, 6 " . .	4,000.00	4,000.00	4,120.00
" Branford, 5 " . .	13,400.00	13,400.00	13,400.00
" Hartford, 4½ " . .:	125,000.00	125,000.00	128,750.00
" Saybrook, 5 " . .	18,000.00	18,000.00	18,720.00
Borough of Wallingford, 4 " water,	75,000.00	75,000.00	76,500.00
RAILROAD BONDS.			
N. York Central & Hudson River, 7 per cent.,	300,000.00	369,000.00	393,000.00
United N. J. R. R. & Canal Co., 6 "	80,000.00	89,600.00	95,200.00
Morris & Essex, 7 "	46,500.00	56,275.00	65,100.00
Chicago, Burlington & Quincy, 7 "	100,000.00	123,403.75	127,000.00
Shore Line, 4½ "	200,000.00	200,000.00	216,000.00
Chicago, Rock Island & Pacific, 6 "	102,000.00	122,400.00	181,580.00
New York & Harlem, 7 "	18,000.00	22,000.00	22,376.00
Pittsburgh, Ft. Wayne & Chicago, 7 "	15,000.00	20,550.00	20,550.00
BANK STOCKS.			
600 shares Merchants National, New Haven,	30,000.00	30,000.00	37,200.00
113 " National Tradesmens, "	11,300.00	11,300.00	18,419.00
81 " Mechanics National, "	4,860.00	4,860.00	5,751.00
20 " Waterbury " Waterbury,	1,000.00	1,000.00	1,600.00
1394 " N. Haven Co.," New Haven,	13,940.00	13,940.00	19,516.00
200 " Yale " "	20,000.00	20,000.00	23,800.00
85 " City "	8,500.00	8,500.00	10,370.00
125 " Second National, . "	12,500.00	12,500.00	20,000.00
10 " New Haven " "	1,000.00	1,000.00	1,660.00
10 " First " Westport, .	1,000.00	1,000.00	1,120.00
112 " Home " Meriden, .	11,200.00	11,200.00	14,560.00
121 " First " . "	12,100.00	12,100.00	14,520.00
85 " Thames " Norwich, . .	8,500.00	8,500.00	12,750.00
21 " Uncas " "	1,050.00	1,050.00	1,260.00
53 " First " " . /	5,300.00	5,300.00	5,936.00

MISCELLANEOUS ITEMS.

1. Number of depositors having $500 or less, 12,778; total amount, $1,795,671.52
2. Number of depositors having over $500 and less than $1,000, . . . 1,842; total amount, 1,284,575.00
3. Number of depositors having $1,000 and not over $2,000, ... 941; total amount, 1,272,095.00
4. Number of depositors having over $2,000, 157; total amount, 703,332.00

5. Total number of depositors, . . . 15,718; total deposits, $5,055,673.52
6. Largest amount due a single depositor, $9,585.
7. Number of accounts opened during the year, 3,078; number closed, 2,323.
8. Amount of income received during the year, $269,415.73.
9. Amount of dividends declared during the year, $179,365.15.
10. Amount deposited, including interest credited, the past year, $1,371,561.57.
11. Amount withdrawn during the year, $1,007,678.04.
12. Increase of deposits the past year, $363,883.53.
13. Amount carried to surplus or profit and loss during the year, none.

NEW HAVEN SAVINGS BANK.—Continued.

MISCELLANEOUS ITEMS.—Continued.

14. *Rate of dividend the last year, 4 per cent., when paid, January 1st and July 1st.
15. State tax during the past year; $10,590.96; U. S. tax, $518.76.
16. Total office expenses the past year, including salaries, $11,953.92.
17. Net amount of income during the year from real estate owned, $8,031.20.
18. Amount of assets yielding no income during the year.
19. Are all loans upon real estate secured by first mortgage? Yes.
20. Largest amount loaned to one individual, company, society, or corporation, $100;000.
21. Date of annual meeting for choice of officers, fourth Wednesday in May.

OFFICERS.—President, Andrew L. Kidston; Vice-Presidents, Matthew G. Elliott, Gardner Morse, Dr. E. H. Bishop, Dr. William B. DeForest; Treasurer, John P. Tuttle; Directors or Trustees, George J. Brush, Stephen B. Butler, Henry D. White, George W. Curtis, John P. Tuttle, N. H. Sanford, David T. Hotchkiss, Wallace B. Fenn, John H. Leeds, Samuel E. Merwin.

---

* Four per cent. on $2,000 and less; three per cent. on excess of $2,000.

NEWTOWN SAVINGS BANK.

HENRY T. NICHOLS, Treasurer.   INCORPORATED, 1855.

STATEMENT, OCTOBER 1, 1882.

LIABILITIES.		ASSETS.	
Whole Amount of Deposits,	$405,732.58	Loans on Real Estate, .	$211,067.93
Surplus Account, }		Loans on Stocks and Bonds,	18,322.23
Interest Account, }	12,000.00	Loans on Endorsed Notes,	70,016.34
Profit and Loss, . .	1,327.92	United States Bonds, . .	2,200.10
Collections, . . .	2,916.56	State Bonds, . . .	10,000.00
Rent Account, . . .	314.36	Town, City, and Corp. B'ds,	24,700.00
		Railroad Bonds, . . .	1,500.00
		Bank Stocks in Connecticut,	23,500.00
		Real Estate by Foreclosure,	15,500.00
		Insurance Account, .	170.09
		Reserve Account, ' . .	223.40
		Safe, ...	500.00
		Premium, ...	3,042.50
		Cash in Bank, . . .	32,242.09
		Cash on hand, . . .	9,306.74
Total Liabilities, . .	$422,291.42	Total Assets, . .	$422,291.42

INVESTMENTS.

DESCRIPTION.	PAR VALUE.	COST.	MARKET VALUE.
UNITED STATES BONDS.			
6s of 1881 (extended 3½ per cent.), . . . $	1,000.00	1,000.00	1,000.00
4s of 1907, Coupon, ...	1,200.00	1,200.10	1,434.00
STATE BONDS.			
Connecticut, 5 per cent., ...	10,000.00	10,000.00	10,600.00
TOWN, CITY, AND CORPORATION BONDS.			
Town of Middletown, 6 per cent., .	10,000.00	10,000.00	10,600.00
" New Haven, 6 " .	200.00	200.00	230.00
City of Bridgeport, 5 " .	5,500.00	5,500.00	5,830.00
" Brooklyn, N. Y., 6 " .	1,000.00	1,000.00	1,180.00
" Cleveland, Ohio, 6 & 7 " .	5,000.00	5,000.00	6,050.00
" Cincinnati, " 7 3/10 " .	1,000.00	1,000.00	1,200.00
" St. Louis, Mo., 6 " .	2,000.00	2,000.00	2,250.00
RAILROAD BONDS.			
Milwaukee & St. Paul, La Crosse Div., 7 per ct.,	1,000.00	1,000.00	1,120.00
Housatonic, 6 per cent., ...	500.00	500.00	525.00
BANK STOCKS.			
92 shares Bridgeport National, Bridgeport,	4,600.00	4,600.00	6,440.00
46 " Pequonnock " "	4,600.00	4,600.00	5,520.00
59 " City " "	5,900.00	5,900.00	7,817.50
10 " Uncas " Norwich, .	500.00	500.00	640.00
57 " First . " " .	5,700.00	5,700.00	6,555.00
4 " Norwich " "	400.00	400.00	460.00
20 " Merchants " " .	800.00	800.00	820.00
8 " Commerce, New London,	800.00	800.00	960.00
2 " New London City Nat., "	200.00	200.00	220.00

NEWTOWN SAVINGS BANK.—CONTINUED.

MISCELLANEOUS ITEMS.

1. Number of depositors having $500 or less,   808; total amount, $113,551.83
2. Number of depositors having over $500 and less than $1,000, .   .   . 166; total amount,   117,635.48
3. Number of depositors having $1,000 and not over $2,000, ... 92; total amount,   129,093.05
4. Number of depositors having over $2,000,   26; total amount,   45,452.22

5. Total number of depositors, .   .   . 1,092; total deposits, $405,732.58
6. Largest amount due a single depositor, $5,583.73.
7. Number of accounts opened during the year, 182; number closed, 180.
8. Amount of income received during the year, $18,620.14.
9. Amount of dividends declared during the year, $14,971.88.
10. Amount deposited, including interest credited, the past year, $113,615.53.
11. Amount withdrawn during the year, $94,974.28·
12. Increase of deposits the past year, $18,641.25.
13. Amount carried to surplus or profit and loss during the year, $1,183.81.
14. Rate of dividend the last year, 4 per cent.; when paid, April 1st and Oct. 1st.
15. State tax during the past year, $781.04; U. S. tax, $0.59.
16. Total office expenses the past year, including salaries, $958.39.
17. Net amount of income during the year from real estate owned, $160.59.
18. Amount of assets yielding no income during the year, $20,000.
19. Are all loans upon real estate secured by first mortgage? Yes.
20. Largest amount loaned to one individual, company, society, or corporation, $20,000.
21. Date of annual meeting for choice of officers, October.

OFFICERS.—President, Simeon B. Peck; Treasurer, Henry T. Nichols; Directors or Trustees, Charles C. Warner, Simeon B. Peck, Philo Clarke, Henry Sanford, William L. Terrill, Aaron Sanford, Monroe Judson, Jerome Judson, Wm. N. Northrop, Abel Stilson, Elliott M. Peck, Cyrus B. Sherman, Hosea B. Northrop, Daniel G. Beers, William Botsford, Henry G. Curtis.

NORWALK SAVINGS SOCIETY.

GEORGE E. MILLER, Treasurer.   INCORPORATED, 1849.

STATEMENT, OCTOBER 1, 1882.

LIABILITIES.		ASSETS.	
Whole Am't of Deposits, .	$1,672,328.84	Loans on Real Estate, .	$800,135.32
Surplus Account, . .	30,000.00	Loans on Stocks and Bonds,	417,200.00
Interest Account, . .	7,609.41	Loans on Endorsed Notes	
Profit and Loss, . .	16,324.14	and Personal Security, .	62,395.07
Rent Account, . . .	530.62	Town, City, and Corp'n B'ds,	154,861.25
		Town, City, and Boro' Orders,	10,000.00
		School District Orders and	
		Notes, ...	18,857.72
		Bank Stocks in Connecticut,	42,164.00
		Bank Stocks in other States,	28,630.47
		Real Estate by Foreclosure,	149,691.08
		Banking House and Lot, .	22,633.30
		Tax Account, . . .	1,957.47
		Expense Account, . .	1,484.24
		Furniture and Fixtures, .	2,000.00
		Revenue Stamps, . .	75.00
		Suspense Account, . .	2,455.36
		Cash in Bank, . . .	1,366.66
		Cash on hand, . . .	10,886.07
Total Liabilities, .	$1,726,793.01	Total Assets, . .	$1,726,793.01

INVESTMENTS.

DESCRIPTION.	PAR VALUE.	COST.	MARKET VALUE.
TOWN, CITY, AND CORPORATION BONDS.			
Town of Norwalk, War Bonds, 6s, $	14,500.00	15,330.00	15,225.00
Borough of " Water Fund, 7s,	77,500.00	77,500.00	85,250.00
City of Cincinnati, 1902–1906, 7 4/10 s,	50,000.00	62,031.25	66,000.00
TOWN, CITY, AND BOROUGH ORDERS.			
Town of Norwalk, ...	10,000.00	10,000.00	10,000.00
SCHOOL DISTRICT ORDERS.			
Down Town, Norwalk, ...	1,500.00	1,500.00	1,500.00
Center, "	12,600.00	12,600.00	12,600.00
Northwest, "	3,897.88	3,897.88	3,897.88
Over River, "	746.75	746.75	746.75
Broad River, "	113.09	113.09	113.09
BANK STOCKS.			
86 shares Fairfield Co. National, Norwalk, .	8,600.00	9,649.50	10,320.00
120 " National Bank of Norwalk, . .	12,000.00	12,901.50	13,200.00
15 " Central National, " .	1,500.00	1,500.00	1,725.00
55 " Danbury " . .	5,500.00	5,880.00	7,975.00
5 " First " Westport, . .	500.00	550.00	525.00
10 " " " South Norwalk,	1,000.00	1,120.00	1,120.00
25 " City " "	2,500.00	2,500.00	2,500.00

NORWALK SAVINGS SOCIETY.—Continued.

INVESTMENTS.—Continued.

DESCRIPTION.	PAR VALUE.	COST.	MARKET VALUE.
BANK STOCKS.—CONTINUED.			
50 shares Stamford National, . . . $	1,500.00	2,250.00	2,250.00
41 " Connecticut National, Bridgeport,	4,100.00	5,863.00	5,863.00
80 " Fourth " New York,	8,000.00	7,973.25	10,000.00
30 " Metropolitan " "	3,000.00	2,900.00	5,250.00
50 " National Park, "	5,000.00	6,256.25	8,000.00
66 " Merchants National, -- "	3,300.00	4,198.59	4,290.00
22 " Market " "	2,200.00	2,363.00	2,860.00
10 " National Shoe & Leather, "	1,000.00	1,080.00	1,300.00
50 " German American, "	3,750.00	3,859.38	3,562.50

MISCELLANEOUS ITEMS.

1. Number of depositors having $500 or less, . 3,684; total amount, $452,823.16
2. Number of depositors having over $500 and
   less than $1,000, ... 549; total amount, 389,867.66
3. Number of depositors having $1,000 and not
   not over $2,000, ... 389; total amount, 539,380.94
4. Number of depositors having over $2,000, . 94; total amount, 290,257.08

5. Total number of depositors, . . . 4,715; total deposits,$1,672,328.84.
6. Largest amount due a single depositor, $13,056.21.
7. Number of accounts opened during the year, 602; number closed, 485.
8. Amount of income received during the year, $90,443.89.
9. Amount of dividends declared during the year, $65,355.13.
10. Amount deposited, including interest credited, the past year, $355,958.97.
11. Amount withdrawn during the year, $370,559.75.
12. Decrease of deposits the past year, $14,600.78.
13. Amount carried to surplus or profit and loss during the year, $14,078.43.
14. Rate of dividend the last year, 4 per cent.; when paid, Jan. 10th and July 10th.
15. State tax during the past year, $3,818.44; U. S. tax, $208.38.
16. Total office expenses the past year, including salaries, $5,980.20.
17. Net amount of income during the year from real estate owned, $2,212.89.
18. Amount of assets yielding no income during the year, $80,570.12.
19. Are all loans upon real estate secured by first mortgage? Yes.
20. Largest amount loaned to one individual, company, society, or corporation, $200,000.
21. Date of annual meeting for choice of officers, fourth Wednesday in July.

OFFICERS.—President, William B. E. Lockwood; Treasurer, George E. Miller; Directors or Trustees, William B. E. Lockwood, Samuel E. Olmstead, George M. Holmes, Robert B. Craufurd, F. St. John Lockwood, Edward K. Lockwood, Asa Smith, William C. Street, George E. Miller.

NORFOLK SAVINGS BANK.

JOSEPH N. COWLES, Treasurer.   ,   INCORPORATED, 1856.

STATEMENT, OCTOBER 1, 1882.

LIABILITIES.		ASSETS.	
Whole Amount of Deposits,	$144,965.93	Loans on Real Estate, .	$66,482.04
Surplus Account, . .	3,369.66	Loans on Stocks and Bonds,	1,500.00
Interest Account, . .	1,260.10	Loans on Endorsed Notes, .	8,466.00
		Town Bonds, . . .	15,000.00
		City Bonds, . . .	11,497.64
		Railroad Bonds, . . .	5,723.75
		Bank Stocks in Connecticut.	17,448.75
		Bank Stocks in other States,	350.00
		Banking House, . . .	3,775.00
		Tax Account, . . .	233.91
		Expense Account, . .	215.49
		Cash in Bank, . . .	5,000.00
		Cash on hand, . .	13,903.11
Total Liabilities, . .	$149,595.69	Total Assets, . .	$149,595.69

INVESTMENTS.

DESCRIPTION.	PAR VALUE.	COST.	MARKET VALUE.
TOWN, CITY, AND CORPORATION BONDS.			
Winchester, ... $	10,000.00	10,000.00	10,600.00
Canaan, ...	5,000.00	5,000.00	5,300.00
TOWN, CITY, AND BOROUGH ORDERS.			
Cincinnati, ...	10,000.00	11,497.64	11,497.64
RAILROAD BONDS.			
Chicago & Alton, ...	1,000.00	1,171.25	1,171.25
Illinois Central, ...	4,000.00	4,552.50	4,552.50
BANK STOCKS.			
45 shares First National, Norwich, . .	4,500.00	4,918.00	4,918.00
25 " Thames, " . .	2,500.00	3,575.00	3,575.00
25 " Merchants, " . .	1,000.00	1,025.00	1,025.00
10 " Mercantile, Hartford, . .	1,000.00	1,350.00	1,350.00
20 " Middlesex Co., . .	2,000.00	2,480.00	2,480.00
10 " Birmingham, . . .	1,000.00	1,560.00	1,560.00
20 " Pahquioque, . . .	2,000.00	2,540.75	2,540.75
7 " Merchants, N. Y., . . .	350.00	350.00	350.00

MISCELLANEOUS ITEMS.

1. Number of depositors having $500 or less, . 527; total amount, $49,292.50
2. Number of depositors having over $500 and less than $1,000, . . . 60; total amount, 45,434.83
3. Number of depositors having $1,000 and not over $2,000, ... 23; total amount, 30,500.60
4. Number of depositors having over $2,000, . 8; total amount, 19,738.00

5. Total number of depositors, ... 618; total deposits, $144,965.93

NORFOLK SAVINGS BANK.—CONTINUED.

MISCELLANEOUS ITEMS.—CONTINUED.

6. Largest amount due a single depositor, $2,831.
7. Number of accounts opened during the year, 106; number closed, 46.
8. Amount of income received during the year, $6,625.46.
9. Amount of dividends declared during the year, $5,291.64.
10. Amount deposited, including interest credited, the past year, $53,651.29.
11. Amount withdrawn during the year, $35,635.25.
12. Increase of deposits the past year, $18,016.04.
13. Amount carried to surplus or profit and loss during the year, none.
14. Rate of dividend the last year, 4½ per cent.; when paid, January and July.
15. State tax during the past year, $146.58; U. S. tax, $17.40.
16. Total office expenses the past year, including salaries, $564.67.
17. Net amount of income during the year from real estate owned, $120.
18. Amount of assets yielding no income during the year, $405.
19. Are all loans upon real estate secured by first mortgage? Yes.
20. Largest amount loaned to one individual, company, society, or corporation, $4,766.
21. Date of annual meeting for choice of officers, second Monday in July.

OFFICERS.—President, Robbins Battell; Vice-President, William W. Welch; Treasurer, Joseph N. Cowles; Directors or Trustees, A. A. Spaulding, Plumb Brown, Erastus Burr, F. E. Porter, H. H. Riggs, Lyman Dunning, J. K. Shepard, Abel Camp, H. J. Holt.

NORWICH SAVINGS SOCIETY.

COSTELLO LIPPITT, Treasurer.   INCORPORATED, 1824.

STATEMENT, OCTOBER 1, 1882.

LIABILITIES.		ASSETS.	
Whole Amt. of Deposits, .	$7,647,215.24	Loans on Real Estate,	$2,592,318.58
Surplus Account, . .	100,000.00	Loans on Stocks and Bonds,	294,000.00
Interest Account, . .	131,848.37	Loans on Endorsed Notes,	·90,800.00
Profit and Loss, . .	218,289.12	United States Bonds, .	200,000.00
		State Bonds, . . .	481,500.00
	·	Town, City, & Corp'n Bds.,	1,246,361.25
		Railroad Bonds, . .	2,481,805.89
		Bank Stocks in Connecticut,	117,600.00
		Bank Stocks in other States,	36,000.00
		Real Estate by Foreclosure,	260,162.72
		Banking House, . .	28,610.77
		Insurance Account, . .	54.82
		Expense Account, . .	4,360.08
		Foreclosure Account, ˉ .	5,730.22
		Cash in Bank, . · .	238,299.54
		Cash on hand, . .	· 19,748.86
Total Liabilities, .	$8,097,352.73	Total Assets, . .	$8,097,352.73

INVESTMENTS.

DESCRIPTION.	PAR VALUE.	COST.	MARKET VALUE.
UNITED STATES BONDS.			
4s of 1907, Registered, ... $	200,000.00	200,000.00	236,000.00
STATE BONDS.			
Connecticut, 6s, Coupon, . . .	405,000.00	405,500.00	423,235.00
" 7s, Registered, ...	76,000.00	76,000.00	79,420.00
TOWN, CITY, AND CORPORATION BONDS.			
Town of Norwich, town debt, . . .	60,000.00	60,000.00	64,800.00
" " war "	40,000.00	40,000.00	43,200.00
Borough of New Britain, water fund, . .	30,000.00	30,000.00	31,200.00
Town of Hartford, ...	200,000.00	200,000.00	210,000.00
" Portland, ...	30,000.00	30,000.00	31,200.00
" Chatham, ...	25,000.00	25,000.00	25,000.00
" Preston, . . .	43,500.00	43,500.00	45,675.00
" Windham, funded debt, . . .	30,000.00	30,000.00	30,600.00
City of Norwich, 6 per cent., water bonds, .	101,000.00	101,000.00	111,100.00
" " 7 " . . .	1,000.00	1,000.00	1,120.00
" New London, water, ; . .	25,000.00	25,000.00	27,500.00
" Middletown, " . .	8,000.00	8,000.00	8,320.00
" Hartford, . . ; . .	25,000.00	25,000.00	27,000.00
" Wheeling, W. Va., . . .	12,000.00	10,200.00	10,200.00
" Vergennes, Vt., gold, . . .	26,000.00	26,000.00	26,000.00
" Cleveland, Ohio, . . .	250,000.00	250,000.00	271,250.00
" " " viaduct, . .	50,000.00	57,650.00	58,500.00
" Cincinnati, " sundry issues, .	246,000.00	284,011.05	304,710.00

NORWICH SAVINGS SOCIETY.—CONTINUED.

INVESTMENTS.—CONTINUED.

DESCRIPTION.	PAR VALUE.	COST.	MARKET VALUE.
TOWN, CITY, AND BOROUGH ORDERS.			
Norwich, ... $	30,000.00	30,000.00	30,000.00
RAILROAD BONDS.			
Cleveland, P. & A., ...	10,000.00	10,000.00	11,500.00
Little Miami, ...	57,000.00	57,000.00	58,500.00
St. Louis, Jacksonville & Chicago, - . .	150,000.00	150,000.00	195,000.00
New London Northern, ...	650,000.00	650,000.00	715,000.00
Chicago, Milwaukee & St. Paul, . . .	187,000.00	187,000.00	200,090.00
Columbus & Xenia, ...	36,000.00	36,000.00	38,500.00
Columbus & Hocking Valley, . . .	14,000.00	16,281.50	16,281.00
Chicago & Alton, ...	22,000.00	25,890.25	26,850.00
Joliet & Northern Indiana, ...	8,000.00	9,853.50	9,410.00
Warren, ...	29,000.00	35,224.00	36,002.00
New York Central & Hudson River, registered,	240,000.00	286,286.25	328,200.00
" " " " coupon,	85,000.00	136,122.25	116,240.00
Cincinnati & Baltimore, ...	99,000.00	120,161.25	122,760.00
The United Companies, ...	84,000.00	98,364.00	103,320.00
Chicago, Rock Island & Pacific, . . .	43,000.00	53,243.89	54,810.00
Burlington & Quincy, ...	9,000.00	9,000.00	9,270.00
Kalamazoo, Allegan & Grand Rapids, . .	29,000.00	32,696.75	33,785.00
Eastern Pennsylvania, ...	5,000.00	5,000.00	5,550.00
Shamokin Valley & Pottsville, . . .	117,000.00	145,606.50	149,175.00
New London Northern, ...	1,000.00	1,000.00	1,000.00
Jefferson, Madison & Indiana, . . .	91,000.00	108,064.00	110,110.00
Morris & Essex, ...	80,000.00	89,753.25	109,600.00
" "	2,000.00	2,652.50	2,740.00
South West, Penn., ...	2,000.00	2,540.00	2,600.00
New York & Harlem, registered, . . .	59,000.00	76,743.50	78,175.00
" " coupon, . . .	66,000.00	83,409.50	87,450.00
Burlington & Missouri, ...	4,000.00	4,603.00	4,670.00
Buffalo, New York & Erie, . . .	24,000.00	31,074.00	31,860.00
Elmira & Williamsport, ...	16,000.00	18,736.00	19,040.00
BANK STOCKS.			
500 shares Thames National, Norwich, .	50,000.00	50,000.00	75,000.00
172 " Norwich " " .	17,200.00	17,200.00	19,780.00
635 " Merchants " "	25,400.00	25,400.00	26,035.00
180 " First :: " .	18,000.00	18,000.00	20,880.00
70 : " " "	7,000.00	7,000.00	7,820.00
266 " Merchants " New York,	13,300.00	13,300.00	17,290.00
50 " Hanover . " "	5,000.00	5,000.00	6,750.00
200 " Broadway " "	5,000.00	5,000.00	11.950.00
75 " Metropolitan " .	7,500.00	7,500.00	13.200.00
32 " National Bank of Commerce, .	3,200.00	3,200.00	4,800.00
20 " " " State of New York,	2,000.00	2,000.00	2,600.00

NORWICH SAVINGS SOCIETY.—Continued.

MISCELLANEOUS ITEMS.

1. Number of depositors having $500 or less,   6,807; total amount, $960,116.24
2. Number of depositors having over $500 and
     less than $1,000,'   .   .   .   .1,766; total amount,   1,265,320.00
3. Number of depositors having $1,000 and not
     over $2,000, ...1,476; total amount,   2,032,062.00
4. Number of depositors having over $2,000, .   846; total amount,   3,389,717.00

5. Total number of depositors,   ' .   .   10,895; total deposits,$7,647,215.24
6. Largest amount due a single depositor, $34,761.69.
7. Number of accounts opened during the year, 1,273; number closed, 1,285.
8. Amount of income received during the year, $427,296.30.
9. Amount of dividends declared during the year, $300,331.98.
10. Amount deposited, including interest credited, the past year, $1,340,235.58.
11. Amount withdrawn during the year, $1,215,133.25.
12. Increase of deposits the past year, $125,102.33.
13. Amount carried to surplus or profit and loss during the year, $114,443.26.
14. Rate of dividend the last year, 4 per cent.; when paid, January and July.
15. State tax during the past year, $16,707.35; U. S. tax, 2,683.58.
16. Total office expenses the past year, including salaries, $12,521.06.
17. Net amount of income during the year from real estate owned, $1,984.62.
18. Amount of assets yielding no income during the year, $6,410.52 real estate.
19. Are all loans upon real estate secured by first mortgage? Yes.
20. Largest amount loaned to one individual, company, society, or corporation,
     $400,000.
21. Date of annual meeting for choice of officers, June.

OFFICERS.—President, Franklin Nichols; Treasurer, Costello Lippitt; Directors, Lucius W. Carroll, Amos W. Prentice, David Gallup, John A. Morgan, John Brewster, John Mitchell, Chas. Webb, Hezekiah F. Rudd, Henry Larrabee, Lucius Brown, Bela P. Learned, Frank Johnson, George R. Hyde.

PEOPLE'S SAVINGS BANK, ROCKVILLE.

E. S. HENRY, Treasurer.   INCORPORATED, 1870.

STATEMENT, OCTOBER 1, 1882.

LIABILITIES.		ASSETS.	
Whole Amt. of Deposits,	$235,344.60	Loans on Real Estate, .	$124,531.00
Surplus Account, . .	4,250.00	Loans on Endorsed Notes,	58,757.57
Interest Account, . .	4,964.18	Bank Stocks in Connecticut,	56,555.50
		Tax Account, . . .	218.54
		Expense Account, . .	161.87
		Safe and Fixtures, . .	1,175.00
		Cash in Bank, ...	2,301.62
		Cash on hand, . . .	862.63
Total Liabilities, .	$244,558.73	Total Assets, . .	$244,558.73

INVESTMENTS.

DESCRIPTION.	PAR VALUE.	COST.	MARKET VALUE.
BANK STOCKS.			
164 shares First National, Rockville, . $	16,400.00	20,140.00	22,140.00
78 " Rockville " "	7,800.00	8,580.00	9,360.00
40 " Stafford " Stafford, .	4,000.00	4,240.00	4,400.00
100 " Tolland Co. " Tolland, .	10,000.00	10,000.00	10,000.00
40 " First " Willimantic,	4,000.00	4,000.00	4,400.00
40 " " " Hartford, .	4,000.00	5,651.50	5,000.00
9 City " .	900.00	944.00	810.00
20 " Ætna " " .	2,000.00	2,500.00	2,600.00
5 " Hartford Trust Co., " .	500.00	500.00	500.00

MISCELLANEOUS ITEMS.

1. Number of depositors having $500 or less, 605; total amount, $79,904.60
2. Number of depositors having over $500 and less than $1,000, ... 75; total amount, 60,140.00
3. Number of depositors having $1,000 and not over $2,000, ... 75; total amount, 95,300.00
4. Number of depositors having over $2,000, ; total amount,
5. Total number of depositors, . . . 755; total deposits, $235,344.60
6. Largest amount due a single depositor, $2,000.
7. Number of accounts opened during the year, 178; number closed, 137.
8. Amount of income received during the year, $12,600.
9. Amount of dividends declared during the year, $10,055.16.
10. Amount deposited, including interest credited, the past year, $93,178.62.
11. Amount withdrawn during the year, $61,230.28.
12. Increase of deposits the past year, $31,948.34.
13. Amount carried to surplus or profit and loss during the year, $550.
14. Rate of dividend the last year, 5 per cent.; when paid, January and July
15. State tax during the past year, $346.31; U. S. tax, none.
16. Total office expenses the past year, including salaries, $877.53.

PEOPLE'S SAVINGS BANK.—Continued.

MISCELLANEOUS ITEMS.—Continued.

17. Net amount of income during the year from real estate owned, none.
18. Amount of assets yielding no income during the year, none.
19. Are all loans upon real estate secured by first mortgage?   Yes.
20. Largest amount loaned to one individual, company, society, or corporation, $18,000.
21. Date of annual meeting for choice of officers, July.

Officers.—President, George M. Paulk; Treasurer, E. S. Henry; Directors or Trustees, George M. Paulk, Cyrus Winchell, Francis Keeney, E. S. Henry, Dwight Marcy, R. G. Holt, Frederick Walker, Asaph McKinney, E. C. Chapman, A. N. Belding, C. Fitton, Robert Patton, Samuel Fitch.

PEOPLE'S SAVINGS BANK, BRIDGEPORT.

F. W. MARSH, Treasurer.   INCORPORATED, 1860.

STATEMENT, OCTOBER 1, 1882.

LIABILITIES.		ASSETS.	
Whole Amt. of Deposits,	$1,413,044.74	Loans on Real Estate, .	$607,635.00
Surplus Account, . .	39,637.54	Loans on Stocks and Bonds,	299,582.00
Interest Account, . .	30,130.18	Town, City, and Corp'n B'ds,	472,500.00
		Bank Stocks in Connecticut,	28,300.00
		Real Estate by Foreclosure,	10,025.55
		Banking House, . .	40,000.00
		Insurance Account, . .	30.00
		Municipal Notes, . .	7,000.00
		Cash in Bank, . .	17,194.34
		Cash on hand, . . .	545.57
Total Liabilities, .	$1,482,812.46	Total Assets, .	$1,482,812.46

INVESTMENTS.

DESCRIPTION.	PAR VALUE.	COST.	MARKET VALUE.
TOWN, CITY, AND CORPORATION BONDS.			
Bridgeport City, 6 per cent., $	500.00	500.00	515.00
" " 7 "	100,000.00	100,000.00	115,000.00
" " "Bridge," 7 "	28,500.00	28,500.00	30,210.00
" " 5 "	52,000.00	52,000.00	57,200.00
Danbury Water, 7 "	15,500.00	15,500.00	16,430.00
" Town, 5 "	20,000.00	20,000.00	21,000.00
Norwalk, 7 "	50,000.00	50,000.00	53,000.00
Middletown City School District, 5 "	74,000.00	74,000.00	77,700.00
Norwich City, 5 "	50,000.00	50,000.00	52,500.00
Hartford Town, 4½ "	50,000.00	50,000.00	52,500.00
Cincinnati City, 6 "	12,000.00	12,000.00	13,800.00
" " 7 "	10,000.00	10,000.00	12,500.00
" " 7$\frac{8}{10}$ "	10,000.00	10,000.00	12,900.00
MUNICIPAL NOTES.			
Town of Bridgeport, ...	7,000.00	7,000.00	7,000.00
BANK STOCKS.			
10 shares Poquonnock National, Bridgeport,	1,000.00	1,000.00	1,200.00
100 " Connecticut " "	10,000.00	10,000.00	14,000.00
166 " Bridgeport " "	8,300.00	8,300.00	12,450.00
90 " First " "	9,000.00	9,000.00	14,400.00

MISCELLANEOUS ITEMS.

1. Number of depositors having $500 or less, 3,228; total amount, $520,382.90
2. Number of depositors having over $500 and
    less than $1,000, ... 470; total amount, 327,194.60
3. Number of depositors having $1,000 and not
    over $2,000, ... 361; total amount, 535,925.97
4. Number of depositors having over $2,000, 12; total amount, 29,541.27

Total number of depositors, . . . 4,071; total deposits, $1,413,044.74

PEOPLE'S SAVINGS BANK.—Continued.

MISCELLANEOUS ITEMS.—Continued.

6. Largest amount due a single depositor, $4,212.27.
7. Number of accounts opened during the year, 931; number closed, 493.
8. Amount of income received during the year, $84,358.67.
9. Amount of dividends declared during the year, $65,758.64.
10. Amount deposited, including interest credited, the past year, $466,616.72.
11. Amount withdrawn during the year, $383,502.82.
12. Increase of deposits the past year, $83,113.90.
13. Amount carried to surplus or profit and loss during the year, $100.56.
14. Rate of dividend the last year, 5 per cent.; when paid, January and July.
15. State tax during the past year, $2,920.21; U. S. tax, $7.53.
16. Total office expenses the past year, including salaries, $3,959.44.
17. Net amount of income during the year from real estate owned, $3,189.06.
18. Amount of assets yielding no income during the year, none.
19. Are all loans upon real estate secured by first mortgage? Yes.
20. Largest amount loaned to one individual, company, society, or corporation, $150,000.
21. Date of annual meeting for choice of officers, second Monday in July.

OFFICERS.—President, George B. Waller; Treasurer, F. W. Marsh; Directors or Trustees, William E. Geeley, 1st Vice-President, Russell Tomlinson, 2d Vice-President, Samuel W. Baldwin, Edward W. Marsh, D. W. Kissam, Elbert E. Hubbell, C. B. Hotchkiss, Egbert Marsh, Eli C. Smith, John E. Pond, William B. Hincks.

PUTNAM SAVINGS BANK.

JEROME TOURTELLOTTE, Treasurer.   INCORPORATED, 1862.

STATEMENT, OCTOBER 1, 1882.

LIABILITIES.		ASSETS.	
Whole Am't of Deposits,	. $771,013.16	Loans on Real Estate, . .	$418,821.87
Surplus Account,	. 10,000.00	Loans on Stocks and Bonds,	45,029.25
Interest Account,	. . 17,672.78	Loans on Endorsed Notes, .	14,380.62
Profit and Loss, . . .	2,283.12	Town, City, and Corp'n B'ds,	60,895.86
		Fire District Orders, . .	11,000.00
		Railroad Bonds, . . .	12,525.00
		Bank Stocks in Connecticut,	79,200.00
		Bank Stocks in other States,	37,300.00
		Real Estate by Foreclosure, .	57,502.50
		Furniture and Fixtures, .	2,500.00
		Insurance Account, . .	13.69
		Cash in Bank, . . .	60,885.52
		Cash on hand, . . .	1,414.75
Total Liabilities, .	. $800,969.06	Total Assets, .	. $800,969.06

INVESTMENTS.

DESCRIPTION.	PAR VALUE.	COST.	MARKET VALUE.
TOWN, CITY, AND CORPORATION BONDS.			
Town of Portland, 6 per cent., untaxable, . $	30,000.00	30,000.00	31,800.00
City of Cincinnati, 7$\frac{3}{10}$ per cent., . . .	25,000.00	30,895.86	33,000.00
DISTRICT ORDERS.			
Putnam Fire District Notes, ...	11,000.00	11,000.00	11,000.00
RAILROAD BONDS.			
Chicago, Burlington & Quincy, 7s, 1903, .	10,000.00	12,525.00	12,700.00
BANK STOCKS.			
5 shares City National, Hartford, . .	500.00	500.00	450.00
23 " Thompson " Thompson, .	2,300.00	2,300.00	2,760.00
50 " Tolland " Tolland, . .	5,000.00	5,000.00	5,000.00
70 " Stafford " Stafford Springs,	7,000.00	7,000.00	7,560.00
50 " First Norwich National, Norwich,	5,000.00	5,000.00	5,900.00
154 " Uncas " "	7,700.00	7,700.00	9,240.00
100 " Thames " "	10,000.00	10,000.00	15,000.00
106 " Norwich "	10,600.00	10,600.00	11,485.00
300 " Merchants " "	12,000.00	12,000.00	12,600.00
191 " First Putnam " Putnam, .	19,100.00	19,100.00	23,875.00
100 " Hanover " New York,	10,000.00	10,000.00	12,800.00
104 " Am. Exchange " "	10,400.00	10,400.00	13,000.00
80 " Fourth " "	8,000.00	8,000.00	9,600.00
67 " Central " "	6,700.00	6,700.00	8,040.00
22 " Ninth " "	2,200.00	2,200.00	2,750.00

9

PUTNAM SAVINGS BANK.—Continued.

MISCELLANEOUS ITEMS.

1. Number of depositors having $500 or less, . 2,201; total amount, $313,226.34
2. Number of depositors having over $500 and less than $1,000, ... 332; total amount,   213,140.58
3. Number of depositors having $1,000 and not over $2,000, ... 136; total amount,   195,622.40
4. Number of depositors having over $2,000, .   15; total amount,   49,023.84

5. Total number of depositors, . . . 2,684; total deposits, $771,013.16
6. Largest amount due a single depositor, $6,551.67.
7. Number of accounts opened during the year, 482; number closed, 332.
8. Amount of income received during the year, $40,956.76.
9. Amount of dividends declared during the year, $28,108.75.
10. Amount deposited, including interest credited, the past year, $200,901.07.
11. Amount withdrawn during the year, $158,152.18.
12. Increase of deposits the past year, $42,748.89.
13. Amount carried to surplus or profit and loss during the year, $4,000.
14. Rate of dividend the last year, 4 per cent.; when paid, April and October.
15. State tax during the past year, $1,501.92; U. S. tax, $96.77.
16. Total office expenses the past year, including salaries, $1,800.64.
17. Net amount of income during the year from real estate owned, $2,439.55.
18. Amount of assets yielding no income during the year, none.
19. Are all loans upon real estate secured by first mortgage? Yes.
20. Largest amount loaned to one individual, company, society, or corporation, $47,500.
21. Date of annual meeting for choice of officers, third Monday in July.

OFFICERS. — President, J. H. Gardner; Treasurer, Jerome Tourtellotte; Directors or Trustees, J. H. Gardner, R. S. Mathewson, J. A. Carpenter, G. W. Phillips, Geo. W. Holt, Jr., Z. A. Ballard, C. M. Fenner, O. H. Perry, A. Houghton.

RIDGEFIELD SAVINGS BANK.

D. SMITH GAGE, Treasurer.   INCORPORATED, 1871.

STATEMENT, OCTOBER 1, 1882.

LIABILITIES.		ASSETS.	
Whole Amount of Deposits,	$65,903.35	Loans on Real Estate, .	$37,295.00
Surplus Account, . .	2,550.00	Loans on Endorsed Notes, .	10,944.06
Interest Account, . .	1,312.52	Bank Stocks in Connecticut,	5,850.00
		Real Estate by Foreclosure,	6,487.06
		Expense Account, . .	33.14
		Cash in Bank, . . .	5,996.18
		Cash on hand, . . .	3,160.43
Total Liabilities, . .	$69,765.87	Total Assets, . .	$69,765.87

INVESTMENTS.

DESCRIPTION.	PAR VALUE.	COST.	MARKET VALUE.
BANK STOCKS.			
50 shares National Bank of Meriden, . . $	5,000.00	5,850.00	5,850.00

MISCELLANEOUS ITEMS.

1. Number of depositors having $500 or less, 310; total amount, $38,510.25
2. Number of depositors having over $500 and less than $1,000, ... 20; total amount, 21,193.05
3. Number of depositors having $1,000 and not over $2,000, ... 5; total amount, 6,200.05
4. Number of depositors having over $2,000, 0; total amount, 0.00

5. Total number of depositors, . . . 335; total deposits, $65,903.35
6. Largest amount due a single depositor, $1,266.10.
7. Number of accounts opened during the year, 43; number closed, 18.
8. Amount of income received during the year, $3,320.77.
9. Amount of dividends declared during the year, $2,704.96.
10. Amount deposited, including interest credited, the past year, $29,594.27.
11. Amount withdrawn during the year, $28,703.63.
12. Increase of deposits the past year, $890.95.
13. Amount carried to surplus or profit and loss during the year, none.
14. Rate of dividend the last year, 4½ per cent.; when paid,
15. State tax during the year, $39.98; U. S. tax, none.
16. Total office expenses the past year, including salaries, $283.16.
17. Net amount of income during the year from real estate owned, none.
18. Amount of assets yielding no income during the year, $5,850.
19. Are all loans upon real estate secured by first mortgage? Yes.
20. Largest amount loaned to one individual, company, society, or corporation, $12,000.
21. Date of annual meeting for choice of officers, last Saturday in July.

OFFICERS.—President, L. H. Bailey; Treasurer, D. Smith Gage; Directors or Trustees, D. L. Adams, M.D., E. H. Smith, E. J. Couch, B. K. Northrop, Samuel M. Northrop, L. H. Bailey, Harvey K. Smith, Wm. H. Beers, Wm. A. Benedict, E. G. Northrop, D. S. Sholes, D. Smith Gage.

SALISBURY SAVINGS SOCIETY, LAKEVILLE.

THOS. L. NORTON, Treasurer.   INCORPORATED, 1848.

STATEMENT, OCTOBER 1, 1882.

LIABILITIES.		ASSETS.	
Whole Amount of Deposits,	$493,863.27	Loans on Real Estate, .	$178,607.52
Surplus Account, }		Loans on Stocks and B'ds, }	78,774.34
Interest Account, }	17,082.95	Loans on Endorsed Notes, }	
		United States Bonds, .	8,055.00
		Town, City, and Corp. Bonds,	121,815.00
		Town, City, and Bor'gh Orders,	5,182.68
		Railroad Stocks, . .	290.00
		Bank Stocks in Connecticut,	32,860.00
		Real Estate by Foreclosure,	30,791.29
		Banking House, . .	6,000.00
		Dist. of Col. 3-65 Bonds, .	4,993.75
		Premium Account, . .	1,955.37
		Furniture Account, . .	3,085.11
		Cash in Bank, . . .	20,609.53
		Cash on hand, . · .	17,926.63
Total Liabilities, . · ·$510,946.22		Total Assets, . . · $510,946.22	

INVESTMENTS.

DESCRIPTION.	PAR VALUE.	COST.	MARKET VALUE.
UNITED STATES BONDS.			
4s of 1907, Coupon, ... $	8,000.00	· 8,055.00	9,520.00
TOWN, CITY, AND CORPORATION· BONDS.·			
Town of Salisbury, 4½ per cent.; ··. . .	45,000.00	45,000.00	45,000.00
City of New York, 6 " . . .	10,000.00	11,725.00	12,700.00
" Boston, 4 " . . .	10,000.00	10,100.00	10,700.00
" Cincinnati, 7³⁄₁₀ " . . .	8,000.00	10,160.00	10,400.00
" " 6 " . . .	11,000.00	12,760.00	·13,090.00
" " 5 " . . .	5,000.00	5,675.00	·5,450.00·
" Cleveland, ·6 " . . .	·7,000.00	8,120.00	8,120.00
" Chicago, 7 " . . .	10,000.00	12,500.00	12,300.00·
" St. Louis, 6 " . . .	5,000.00	5,775.00	5,700.00
TOWN, CITY, AND BOROUGH ORDERS.			
Town of Sharon, ...	5,182.68	5,182.68	5,182.68
· . RAILROAD STOCKS.			
3 shares, Berkshire, . · . . .	300.00	290.00	330.00
· · · BANK STOCKS.			
80 shares National Iron, Falls Village,	8,000.00	8,210.00	9,600.00 ·
·9 " Phœnix · National, Hartford, ·	900.00	1,050.00	1,485.00
100 " First " Norwich, ·	10,000.00	11,500.00	11,600.00
50 " Uncas " "	2,500.00	3,000.00	3,200.00
220 " Merchants " "	8,800.00	9,100.00	9,020.00

SALISBURY SAVINGS SOCIETY.—Continued.

MISCELLANEOUS ITEMS.

1. Number of depositors having $500 or less, . 1,214; total amount, $152,824.25
2. Number of depositors having $500 and less than $1,000, ...—. 126; total amount, 96,250.40
3. Number of depositors having $1,000 and not over $2,000, · . . . . 83; total amount, 100,766.10
4. Number of depositors having over $2,000, 37; total amount, 144,522.52

5. Total number of depositors, . . . 1,460; total deposits, $493,863.27
6. Largest amount due a single depositor, $11,147.48.
7. Number of accounts opened during the year, 267; number closed, 183.
8. Amount of income received during the year, $24,046.86.
9. Amount of dividends declared during the year, $18,543.11.
10. Amount deposited, including interest credited, the past year, $123,871.10.
11. Amount withdrawn during the year, $94,887.42.
12. Increase of deposits the past year, $28,983.68.
13. Amount carried to surplus or profit and loss during the year, $2,309.80.
14. Rate of dividend the last year, 4 per cent.; when paid, April and October.
15. State tax during the past year, $837.38; U. S. tax, $335.50.
16. Total office expenses the past year, including salaries, $1,505.76.
17. Net amount of income during the year from real estate owned, $1,148.04.
18. Amount of assets yielding no income during the year, $6,900.
19. Are all loans upon real estate secured by first mortgage? With one exception.
20. Largest amount loaned to one individual, company, society, or corporation, $28,000.
21. Date of annual meeting for choice of officers, July.

OFFICERS.—President, Geo. B. Burrall; Treasurer, Thos. L. Norton; Directors or Trustees, Geo. B. Burrall, L. Tupper, S. S. Robbins, M. Reed, D. Allyn.

SAVINGS BANK OF ANSONIA.

EGBERT BARTLETT, Treasurer.   INCORPORATED, 1862.

STATEMENT, OCTOBER 1, 1882.

LIABILITIES.		ASSETS.	
Whole Amount of Deposits,	$495,771.78	Loans on Real Estate, . .	$299,117.00
Surplus Account, . .	8,723.79	Loans on Endorsed Notes, .	88,912.31
Interest Account, . .	8,212.41	Town, City, and Corp'n B'ds,	16,500.00
		Town, City, and Boro' Orders,	4,366.67
		School District Orders, .	6,800.00
		Bank Stocks in Connecticut,	41,159.50
		Bank Stocks in other States,	45,263.00
		Real Estate by Foreclosure,	3,850.00
		Tax Account, . . .	490.09
		Expense Account, . .	335.91
		Cash in Bank, . .	5,052.88
		Cash on hand, . . .	860.67
Total Liabilities, . .	$512,707.98	Total Assets, . .	$512,707.98

INVESTMENTS.

DESCRIPTION.	PAR VALUE.	COST.	MARKET VALUE.
TOWN, CITY, AND CORPORATION BONDS.			
Ansonia Water Co., ... $	11,500.00	11,500.00	11,500.00
Derby Gas Co., ...	5,000.00	5,000.00	5,000.00
TOWN, CITY, AND BOROUGH ORDERS.			
Borough of Ansonia, ...	1,200.00	1,200.00	1,200.00
Town of Derby, ...	2,000.00	2,000.00	2,000.00
" Naugatuck, ...	1,166.67	1,166.67	1,166.67
SCHOOL DISTRICT ORDERS.			
Fourth, Derby, ...	4,800.00	4,800.00	4,800.00
Fifth, "	2,000.00	2,000.00	2,000.00
BANK STOCKS.			
225 shares Ansonia National, ...	11,250.00	11,800.00	12,930.50
36 " Birmingham "	3,600.00	4,495.00	5,760.00
100 " Merchants " New Haven, .	5,000.00	5,950.50	5,750.00
100 " " " Norwich, .	4,000.00	4,100.00	4,100.00
100 " First " "	10,000.00	10,614.00	11,000.00
50 " Yale " New Haven, .	5,000.00	5,060.00	5,750.00
50 " American Exchange, New York, .	5,000.00	5,450.00	6,600.00
50 " Central, "	5,000.00	5,000.00	6,500.00
50 " Commerce, "	5,000.00	6,050.00	7,600.00
50 " Fourth, "	5,000.00	4,794.00	6,350.00
50 " Hanover, "	5,000.00	4,832.00	6,750.00
100 " Merchants Exchange, " .	5,000.00	4,987.00	5,000.00
70 " Shoe and Leather, "	7,000.00	8,650.00	9,100.00
125 " Tradesmens, "	5,000.00	5,500.00	5,750.00

SAVINGS BANK OF ANSONIA.—CONTINUED.

MISCELLANEOUS ITEMS.

1. Number of depositors having $500 or less, . 1,899; total amount, $205,658.15
2. Number of depositors having over $500 and
   less than $1,000, ... 166; total amount, 115,781.34
3. Number of depositors having $1,000 and not
   over $2,000, ... 127; total amount, 174,332.29
4. Number of depositors having over $2,000, . 0; total amount, 0.00

5. Total number of depositors, . . . 2,192; total deposits, $495,771.78
6. Largest amount due a single depositor, $2,000.
7. Number of accounts opened during the year, 691; number closed, 346.
8. Amount of income received during the year, $27,172.95.
9. Amount of dividends declared during the year, $20,543.55.
10. Amount deposited, including interest credited, the past year, $206,733.87.
11. Amount withdrawn during the year, $127,037.04.
12. Increase of deposits the past year, $79,696.83.
13. Amount carried to surplus or profit and loss during the year, $4,594.74.
14. Rate of dividend the last year, 5 per cent.; when paid, January and July.
15. State tax during the year, $956.18; U. S. tax, none.
16. Total office expenses the past year, including salaries, $1,412.76.
17. Net amount of income during the year from real estate owned, $125.
18. Amount of assets yielding no income during the year, none.
19. Are all loans upon real estate secured by first mortgage? Yes.
20. Largest amount loaned to one individual, company, society, or corporation, $20,000.
21. Date of annual meeting for choice of officers, first Monday in July.

OFFICERS.—President, William B. Bristol; Vice-President, Thomas Wallace; Treasurer, Egbert Bartlett; Directors or Trustees, Abraham Hubbell, Charles L. Hill, Egbert Bartlett, Henry J. Smith, John Lindley, Jonah C. Platt, Dana Bartholomew, Hobart Sperry, James Swan.

SAVINGS BANK OF DANBURY.

HENRY C. RYDER, Treasurer.   INCORPORATED, 1849.

STATEMENT, OCTOBER 1, 1882.

LIABILITIES.		ASSETS.	
Whole Am't of Deposits, .	$1,840,101.86	Loans on Real Estate, .	$1,007,282.50
Surplus Account, . .	74,064.88	Loans on Stocks and Bonds,	70,000.00
Interest Account, . .	5,064.74	Loans on Endorsed Notes,	303,668.88
		United States Bonds, .	66,212.50
		Town, City, and Corp. B'ds,	185,048.75
		Railroad Bonds, . .	13,950.00
		Bank Stocks in Connecticut,	21,756.50
		Bank Stocks in other States,	23,838.63
		Real Estate by Foreclosure,	167,831.67
		Banking House, . .	16,000.00
		Cash in Bank, . . .	31,239.40
		Cash on hand, . . .	12,402.65
Total Liabilities, .	$1,919,231.48	Total Assets, . .	$1,919,231.48

INVESTMENTS.

DESCRIPTION.	PAR VALUE.	COST.	MARKET VALUE.
UNITED STATES BONDS.			
4½s of 1891, Registered, ... $	35,000.00	36,287.50	39,375.00
4s of 1907, Registered, ...	30,000.00	29,925.00	35,400.00
TOWN, CITY, AND BOROUGH ORDERS.			
Bridgeport, 6 per cent., . .	1,500.00	1,410.00	1,530.00
Portland, 6 " . .	25,000.00	23,344.00	27,250.00
Washington, 6 " . .	29,000.00	27,840.00	30,450.00
Borough of Danbury, 7 " . .	3,000.00	3,000.00	3,200.00
" " Norwalk, 7 " . .	30,000.00	30,000.00	33,000.00
Cincinnati, Ohio, 7 " . .	14,000.00	16,410.00	16,410.00
" " 7 8/10 " . .	24,000.00	31,035.00	31,035.00
Cleveland, " 7 " . .	3,000.00	3,550.00	3,550.00
Chicago, Ill., 7 " . .	40,000.00	48,459.74	48,459.75
RAILROAD BONDS.			
Sandusky, Dayton & Cincinnati, 6 per cent.,	1,000.00	650.00	1,000.00
New York Central & Harlem River, . .	10,000.00	13,300.00	13,250.00
BANK STOCKS.			
162 shares Danbury National, Danbury, .	16,200.00	18,116.50	24,300.00
20 " National Pahquioque, " .	2,000.00	2,040.00	2,700.00
16 " National Bank of Norwalk, . .	1,600.00	1,600.00	1,760.00
75 " Ninth National, New York,	7,500.00	6,750.00	9,375.00
68 " Central " "	6,800.00	6,528.00	8,500.00
100 " North America "	7,000.00	6,300.00	
188 " Phenix, "	3,760.00	3,063.63	4,136.00
30 " Nassau, "	1,500.00	1,200.00	1,800.00

DANBURY SAVINGS BANK.—Continued.

MISCELLANEOUS ITEMS.

1. Number of depositors having $500 or less, 4,124; total amount, $566,619.70
2. Number of depositors having over $500 and
   less than $1,000, ...—.   562; total amount,   410,975.22
3. Number of depositors having $1,000 and not
   over $2,000, ...   429; total amount,   614,115.89
4. Number of depositors having over $2,000,   .   107; total amount,   248,391.05

5. Total number of depositors, ... 5,222; total deposits,$1,840,101.86
6. Largest amount due a single depositor, $6,015.25.
7. Number of accounts opened during the year, 886; number closed, 592.
8. Amount of income received during the year, $106,356.46.
9. Amount of dividends declared during the year, $69,586.64.
10. Amount deposited, including interest credited, the past year, $512,476.85.
11. Amount withdrawn during the year, $462,589.66.
12. Increase of deposits the past year, $49,887.19.
13. Amount carried to surplus or profit and loss during the year, $16,997.34.
14. Rate of dividend the last year, 4 per cent.; when paid, April 1st and Oct. 1st.
15. State tax during the past year, $3,725.94; United States tax, none.
16. Total office expenses the past year, including salaries, $3,800.
17. Net amount of income during the year from real estate owned, $4,751.10.
18. Amount of assets yielding no income during the year, $58,482.79.
19. Are all loans upon real estate secured by first mortgage? Yes.
20. Largest amount loaned to one individual, company, society, or corporation, $50,000.
21. Date of annual meeting for choice of officers, June.

OFFICERS.—President, Frederick S. Wildman; Treasurer, Henry C. Ryder; Directors or Trustees, Edgar S. Tweedy, Roger Averill, Lyman D. Brewster, George Raymond, Henry C. Ryder, William R. White, John W. Bacon, William Jabine, George Starr.

SAVINGS BANK OF NEW BRITAIN.

WILLIAM F. WALKER, Treasurer.   INCORPORATED, 1862.

STATEMENT, OCTOBER 1, 1882.

LIABILITIES.		ASSETS.	
Whole Am't of Deposits, .	$1,174,703.57	Loans on Real Estate, .	$612,166.00
Surplus Account, . .	35,000.00	Loans on Stocks and Bonds,	34,838.00
Interest Account, . .	19,356.48	Loans on Endorsed Notes,	15,275.00
Rent Account, . . .	194.20	United States Bonds, .	36,200.00
Suspense Account, . .	30.00	State Bonds, . . .	5,000.00
Profit and Loss Account, .	3,434.77	Town, City, and Corp. B'ds,	191,400.00
		Loans to Town N. Britain,	10,500.00
		Loans to City New Britain,	21,541.90
		Railroad Bonds, . .	33,500.00
		Bank Stocks in Connecticut,	175,915.00
		Bank Stocks in other States,	39,250.00
		Real Estate by Foreclosure,	18,771.47
		Banking House, . .	20,000.00
		Tax Account, . . .	1,347.75
		Insurance Account, . .	41.59
		Expense Account, . .	1,153.60
		Cash in Bank, . .	7,765.33
		Cash on hand, . . .	8,053.20
Total Liabilities, .	$1,232,719.02	Total Assets, . .	$1,232,719.02

INVESTMENTS.

DESCRIPTION.	PAR VALUE.	COST.	MARKET VALUE.
UNITED STATES BONDS.			
5s of 1881, Registered (extended 3½ per cent.), $	6,000.00	6,000.00	6,045.00
4⅛s of 1891, Coupon, ...	10,000.00	10,000.00	11,275.00
4s of 1907, Coupon, ...	20,200.00	20,200.00	24,038.00
STATE BONDS.			
Connecticut, 6 per cent., 1884, ...	2,000.00	2,000.00	2,080.00
" 5 " 1897, . . .	3,000.00	3,000.00	3,240.00
TOWN, CITY, AND CORPORATION BONDS.			
Town of New Britain (Park), 7 per cent., 1894,	34,000.00	34,000.00	42,500.00
City of " (Water),7 " 1892–8,	26,000.00	26,000.00	32,500.00
Town of Hartford, 4½ " 1905,	7,000.00	7,000.00	7,490.00
City of New York, 5 " 1884,	30,000.00	30,000.00	30,600.00
" Boston, 4 " 1910, .	20,000.00	20,000.00	21,000.00
" Cincinnati, 6 " 1909,	16,000.00	16,000.00	19,200.00
" " 6 " 1906,	14,000.00	14,000.00	16,800.00
' Chicago, 7 " 1890–9,	25,000.00	25,000.00	30,000.00
" St. Louis, 6 " 1905,	19,000.00	19,400.00	22,800.00
RAILROAD BONDS.			
N.Y. Central & Hudson Riv., 7 per cent., 1903,	20,000.00	23,500.00	26,000.00
N. Y., Providence & Boston, 4 " 1901,	10,000.00	10,000.00	10,400.00

SAVINGS BANK OF NEW BRITAIN.—Continued.

INVESTMENTS.—Continued.

DESCRIPTION.			PAR VALUE.	COST.	MARKET VALUE.
BANK STOCKS.					
330 shares New Britain National,	New Britain,	$	33,000.00	38,610.00	47,850.00
170 " Hartford	" Hartford, . .		17,000.00	25,500.00	28,900.00
111 " Phœnix	" " .		11,100.00	16,420.00	18,648.00
50 " Farm. & Mech.	" " .		5,000.00	5,450.00	6,500.00
75 " Mercantile	" " .		7,500.00	8,175.00	9,375.00
100 " First	" " .		10,000.00	10,500.00	12,000.00
19 " Ætna	" " . .		1,900.00	2,100.00	2,400.00
80 " City	" " .		8,000.00	7,560.00	7,600.00
250 " New Haven Co.	" New Haven,		2,500.00	2,800.00	3,300.00
4 " Tradesmens	" " .		400.00	600.00	650.00
100 " Second	" — " .		10,000.00	14,000.00	16,000.00
32 " Middletown	" Middletown,		2,400.00	3,000.00	3,500.00
60 " Central	" " ..		4,500.00	5,800.00	6,750.00
10 " Connecticut	" Bridgeport,		1,000.00	1,100.00	1,400.00
25 " First	" " .		2,500.00	3,300.00	4,100.00
100 " Bridgeport	" " .		5,000.00	6,500.00	7,500.00
100 " Thames	" Norwich, .		10,000.00	13,300.00	14,800.00
50 " Pahquioque	" Danbury, .		5,000.00	5,600.00	6,400.00
50 " Commerce	" New London,		5,000.00	5,600.00	6,000.00
75 " Am. Exchange	" New York,		7,500.00	8,250.00	9,750.00
100 " Commerce	" " .		10,000.00	14,000.00	15,000.00
50 " Hanover	" " .		5,000.00	5,500.00	6,500.00
100 " Mercantile	" " .		10,000.00	11,500.00	12,000.00

MISCELLANEOUS ITEMS.

1. Number of depositors having $500 or less, 3,210; total amount, $355,245.83
2. Number of depositors having over $500 and less than 1,000, ... 398; total amount, 270,986.94
3. Number of depositors having $1,000 and not over $2,000, ... 280; total amount, 364,539.01
4. Number of depositors having over $2,000, 74; total amount, 183,931.79

5. Total number of depositors, ... 3,962; total deposits,$1,174,703.57
6. Largest amount due a single depositor, $4,966.91.
7. Number of accounts opened during the year, 837; number closed, 543.
8. Amount of income received during the year, $69,634.09.
9. Amount of dividends declared during the year, $41,761.83.
10. Amount deposited, including interest credited, the past year, $451,926.63.
11. Amount withdrawn during the year, $336,248.13.
12. Increase of deposits the past year, $115,678.50.
13. Amount carried to surplus or profit and loss during the year, $2,000.
14. Rate of dividend the last year, 4 per cent.; when paid, January and July.
15. State tax during the past year, $2,528.00; U. S. tax, $46.19.
16. Total office expenses the past year, including salaries, $4,180.49.
17. Net amount of income during the year from real estate owned, $1,412.61.
18. Amount of assets yielding no income during the year, none.
19. Are all loans upon real estate secured by first mortgage? Yes.
20. Largest amount loaned to one individual, company, society, or corporation, $35,875.
21. Date of annual meeting for choice of officers, third Wednesday in July.

OFFICERS.—President, Levi S. Wells; Treasurer, Wm. F. Walker; Directors or Trustees, Levi S. Wells, Horace Eddy, C. B. Erwin, T. W. Stanley, Philip Corbin, J. A. Pickett, J. B. Talcott, George P. Rockwell, William F. Walker.

SAVINGS BANK OF NEW LONDON.

JOSHUA C. LEARNED, Treasurer.   INCORPORATED, 1827.

STATEMENT, OCTOBER 1, 1882.

LIABILITIES.		ASSETS.	
Whole Am't of Deposits,	$3,193,072.62	Loans on Real Estate, .	$936,374.26
Surplus Account, . .	65,601.47	Loans on Stocks and Bonds,	136,000.00
Interest Account, . .	53,267.96	Loans on Endorsed Notes,.	42,000.00
Real Estate Rents, . .	59.16	United States Bonds, . .	375,000.00
		State Bonds, . . .	6,000.00
		Town, City, and Corp'n B'ds,	925,500.00
		Railroad Bonds, . . .	251,000.00
		Railroad Stocks, . . .	43,300.00
		Bank Stocks in Connecticut,	106,000.00
		Bank Stocks in other States,	184,540.00
		Real Estate by Foreclosure,	244,292.79
		Banking House, . . .	8,944.06
		Expense Account, . .	1,268.47
		Profit and Loss Account, .	3,062.90
		Cash in Bank, . . .	37,469.14
		Cash on hand, . . .	11,249.59
Total Liabilities, .	$3,312,001.21	Total Assets, .	$3,312,001.21

INVESTMENTS.

DESCRIPTION.	PAR VALUE.	COST.	MARKET VALUE.
UNITED STATES BONDS.			
5s of 1881, registered (extended 3½ per cent.), $	60,000.00	60,555.00	60,600.00
4½s of 1891, registered, ...	90,000.00	104,225.00	101,523.00
4s of 1907, registered, ...	125,000.00	127,000.00	149,175.00
Currency 6s, ...	100,000.00	104,000.00	132,000.00
STATE BONDS.			
Michigan, ...	6,000.00	6,000.00	6,120.00
TOWN, CITY, AND CORPORATION BONDS.			
City of Cincinnati, ...	38,000.00	43,100.00	46,360.00
" New London, ...	90,000.00	90,000.00	106,200.00
" Brooklyn, ...	14,000.00	14,000.00	19,600.00
" " South St. Improvement, .	25,000.00	25,000.00	29,500.00
" " Park Loan, . . .	10,000.00	10,000.00	14,200.00
" " Bridge, . . .	50,000.00	50,000.00	70,000.00
" New York, Dock, . . .	71,000.00	71,000.00	92,300.00
" " Improvement, . .	40,000.00	40,000.00	46,000.00
" New London, Water, . . .	75,000.00	76,125.00	97,500.00
" Middletown, ...	23,000.00	20,123.00	27,600.00
" Buffalo, N. Y., ...	43,500.00	47,850.00	54,375.00
" Rochester, "	20,000.00	21,000.00	24,000.00
" St. Louis, Mo., ...	48,000.00	48,700.00	49,880.00
" Chicago, Ill., ...	58,000.00	65,366.00	70,760.00
" Cleveland, Ohio, ...	8,000.00	9,766.00	9,200.00
District of Columbia, ...	33,000.00	38,295.00	38,940.00

SAVINGS BANK OF NEW LONDON.—Continued.

INVESTMENTS.—Continued.

DESCRIPTION.	PAR VALUE.	COST.	MARKET VALUE.
TOWN, CITY, AND BOROUGH ORDERS.			
Town of New London, ... $	39,000.00	39,000.00	46,020.00
" Stamford, ...	70,000.00	70,000.00	81,200.00
" Wallingford, ...	20,000.00	20,000.00	24,000.00
" New Haven, ...	50,000.00	50,000.00	57,500.00
" Middletown, ...	25,000.00	25,000.00	28,750.00
" West Hartford, ...	20,000.00	18,600.00	23,200.00
" Montville, ...	30,000.00	30,471.00	36,000.00
" Greenwich, ...	30,000.00	31,600.00	34,200.00
RAILROAD BONDS.			
Hudson River, ...	10,000.00	9,800.00	10,800.00
Morris & Essex, ...	15,000.00	15,000.00	20,850.00
New York Central, ...	25,000.00	23,500.00	27,000.00
Chicago, Rock Island & Pacific, . . .	55,000.00	66,700.00	70,400.00
New London Northern, . . , . .	19,000.00	19,000.00	20,140.00
Central Pacific, ...	20,000.00	20,000.00	23,000.00
Albany & Susquehanna, ...	7,000.00	8,050.00	8,050.00
New York, Providence & Boston, . .	20,000.00	20,000.00	21,200.00
Chicago & Alton, ...	4,000.00	4,930.00	4,880.00
Union Pacific, ...	76,000.00	89,680.00	89,120.00
RAILROAD STOCKS.			
New York & New Haven, ...	12,600.00	12,600.00	22,932.00
New York Central, ...	14,500.00	14,500.00	19,430.00
Boston & Lowell, ...	· 4,000.00	4,000.00	4,120.00
Michigan Central, ...	7,200.00	7,200.00	7,200.00
Boston & Albany, ...	5,000.00	5,000.00	8,750.00
BANK STOCKS.			
145 shares North America, New York,	10,150.00	11,000.00	10,880.00
165 " Metropolitan, "	16,500.00	17,555.00	28,875.00
173 " Fulton, "	5,190.00	6,137.00	6,847.00
30 " Seventh Ward,	3,000.00	3,000.00	3,090.00
300 " Phenix, "	6,000.00	6,000.00	· 6,600.00
556 " Mechanics, "	13,900.00	14,750.00	20,155.00
15 " Leather Manufacturers, "	1,500.00	1,763.00	2,475.00
40 " State of New York, "	4,000.00	4,000.00	5,200.00
72 " Merchants Exchange, "	3,600.00	3,600.00	3,528.00
152 " Union, "	7,600.00	7,600.00	12,160.00
140 " Commerce, "	14,000.00	14,000.00	21,000.00
150 " America, "	15,000.00	15,000.00	24,000.00
134 " Merchants,	6,700.00	6,900.00	8,710.00
40 " Corn Exchange, "	4,000.00	4,160.00	6,680.00
174 " Continental, "	17,400.00	17,400.00	20,880.00
50 " City, · "	5,000.00	6,000.00	13,250.00
201 " American Exchange, "	20,100.00	21,000.00	.26,782.00
40 " North River, "	1,200.00	1,200.00	1,868.00
50 " Nassau, "	5,000.00	5,000.00	6,300.00
100 " United States Trust Co., "	10,000.00	10,700.00	42,500.00
80 " Fourth National, "	8,000.00	8,000.00	10,000.00
18 " Middletown, ... '	1,350.00	1,350.00	1,825.00
· 99 " New London City, . . .	9,900.00	9,954.00	10,395.00
330 " Union, New London, . . .	33,000.00	33,000.00	34,650.00

SAVINGS BANK OF NEW LONDON.—Continued.

INVESTMENTS.—Continued.

DESCRIPTION.		PAR VALUE.	COST.	MARKET VALUE.
BANK STOCKS.—CONTINUED.				
127 shares Bank of Commerce, New London,	$	12,700.00	12,700.00	13,970.00
68 " Whaling, "		1,700.00	1,700.00	2,155.00
400 " Thames, Norwich,		40,000.00	40,000.00	62,000.00
67 " Uncas, "		3,350.00	3,350.00	3,752.00
40 " Stafford, "		4,000.00	4,000.00	4,400.00
42 " Albany City, Albany, N. Y.,		4,200.00	4,200.00	4,704.00
25 " Union, " "		2,500.00	2,500.00	2,875.00

MISCELLANEOUS ITEMS.

1. Number of depositors having $500 or less, 3,910; total amount, $648,205.27
2. Number of depositors having over $500 and less than $1,000, . . . 740; total amount, 484,232.50
3. Number of depositors having $1,000 and not over $2,000, ... 653; total amount, 771,157.85
4. Number of depositors having over $2,000, . 335; total amount, 1,289,497.50

5. Total number of depositors, . . . 5,638; total deposits,$3,193,072.62
6. Largest amount due a single depositor, $34,833.67.
7. Number of accounts opened during the year, 743; number closed, 686.
8. Amount of income received during the year, $175,133.12.
9. Amount of dividends declared during the year, $124,065.27.
10. Amount deposited, including interest credited, the past year, $345,497.64.
11. Amount withdrawn during the year, $318,719.49.
12. Increase of deposits the past year, $26,778.15.
13. Amount carried to surplus or profit and loss during the year, $37,450.52.
14. Rate of dividend paid the last year, 4 per cent.; when paid, Jan. 1st and July 1st.
15. State tax during the past year, $6,848.20; U. S. tax, $866.36.
16. Total office expenses the past year, including salaries, $5,008.23.
17. Net amount of income during the year from real estate owned, $2,776.83.
18. Amount of assets yielding no income during the year, none.
19. Are all loans upon real estate secured by first mortgage? Yes.
20. Largest amount loaned to one individual, company, society, or corporation, $117,000.
21. Date of annual meeting for choice of officers, first Tuesday in June.

OFFICERS.—President, W. H. Chapman; Treasurer, Joshua C. Learned; Directors or Trustees, William C. Crump, Joseph B. Congdon, Charles Prentis, Charles Barns, Joshua C. Learned, Robert Coit, Horace Coit, Charles A. Williams.

SAVINGS BANK OF ROCKVILLE.

LEBBEUS BISSELL, Treasurer.   INCORPORATED, 1858.

STATEMENT, OCTOBER 1, 1882.

. LIABILITIES. .		ASSETS.	
Whole Amount of Deposits,	$758,053.97	Loans on Real Estate, .	$255,271.00
Surplus Account, . .	15,000.00	Loans on Stocks and Bonds,	85,400.00
Interest Account, . .	23,726.08	Loans on Endorsed Notes,	291,475.64
		Town, City, and Corp. B'ds,	2,500.00
		Railroad Bonds, . .	2,000.00
		Bank Stocks in Connecticut,	147,101.00
		Bank Stocks in other States,	24,050.00
		Real Estate by Foreclosure,	18,686.95
		Bank Fixtures, . . .	1,000.00
		Cash in Bank, . . .	19,295.46
Total Liabilities, .	$796,780.05	Total Assets, . .	$796,780.05

INVESTMENTS.

DESCRIPTION.	PAR VALUE.	COST.	MARKET VALUE.
TOWN, CITY, AND CORPORATION BONDS.			
Springfield, City, Ill., ... $	2,500.00	2,500.00	2,500.00
RAILROAD BONDS.			
Norwich & Worcester, 1st mortgage, . .	2,000.00	2,000.00	2,400.00
BANK STOCKS.			
400 shares First National, Rockville, .	40,000.00	42,890.00	50,000.00
30 " Rockville " "	3,000.00	3,000.00	3,600.00
50 " Tolland Co. " Tolland, .	5,000.00	5,000.00	5,000.00
85 " Stafford " Stafford Springs,	8,500.00	8,910.00	9,350.00
141 " Mercantile " Hartford, .	14,100.00	17,185.00	18,330.00
50 " City " "	5,000.00	5,000.00	5,000.00
58 " Ætna " " .	5,800.00	7,170.00	7,540.00
406 " American " " .	20,300.00	27,184.00	28,420.00
50 " Nat'l Ex. " . .	2,500.00	3,175.00	3,500.00
50 " Hartford " ..	5,000.00	7,970.00	8,000.00
7 " Farm.&Mech." .	700.00	700.00	900.00
9 " Phœnix " " .	900.00	1,350.00	1,440.00
142 " First " " .	14,000.00	16,042.00	17,000.00
25 " Nat. Bk. Commerce, New York, .	2,500.00	3,400.00	3,500.00
134 " Merchants National, " .	6,700.00	8,650.00	8,650.00
100 " Continental " " .	10,000.00	12,000.00	12,000.00
8 " First " Meriden, .	800.00	900.00	900.00
5 " Home " " .	500.00	625.00	625.00

SAVINGS BANK OF ROCKVILLE.—CONTINUED.

MISCELLANEOUS ITEMS.

1. Number of depositors having $500 or less, 2,114; total amount, $287,948.40
2. Number of depositors having over $500 and less than $1,000, ... 236; total amount, 165,002.04
3. Number of depositors having $1,000 and not over $2,000, ... 173; total amount, 244,552.09
4. Number of depositors having over $2,000, . 24; total amount, 60,661.44

5. Total number of depositors, . . . 2,547; total deposits, $758,053.97
6. Largest amount due a single depositor, $4,448.84.
7. Number of accounts opened during the year, 596; number closed, 379.
8. Amount of income received during the year, $47,212 04. .
9. Amount of dividends declared during the year, $32,557.27.
10. Amount deposited, including interest credited, the past year, $251,974.08.
11. Amount withdrawn during the year, $176,548.35.
12. Increase of deposits the past year, $75,425.73. .
13. Amount carried to surplus or profit and loss during the year, $5,000.
14. Rate of dividend the last year, 5 per cent.; when paid, April and October.
15. State tax during the past year, $1,554.86; U. S. tax, $42.84. .
16. Total office expenses the past year, including salaries, $2,759.47.
17. Net amount of income during the year from real estate owned, $400.
18. Amount of assets yielding no income during the year, $11,000.
19. Are all loans upon real estate secured by first mortgage? Yes. .
20. Largest amount loaned to one individual, company, society, or corporation, $21,000.
21. Date of annual meeting for choice of officers, third Tuesday in July.

OFFICERS.—President, B. H. Bill; Treasurer, Lebbeus Bissell; Directors or Trustees, George Talcott, William Butler, J. S. Dobson, E. I. Smith, B. H. Bill, Lebbeus Bissell, G. W. West, H. L. James, A. R. Goodrich, T. M. Durfee.

SAVINGS BANK OF STAFFORD SPRINGS.

ALVARADO HOWARD, Treasurer.   INCORPORATED, 1858.

STATEMENT, OCTOBER 1, 1882.

LIABILITIES.		ASSETS.	
Whole Amount of Deposits,	$306,844.01	Loans on Real Estate, . .	$96,954.00
Surplus Account, ⎫		Loans on Stocks and Bonds,	5,976.00
Interest Account, ⎭ . .	8,855.90	Loans on Endorsed Notes, .	35,407.49
		United States Bonds, . .	200.00
		Town, City, and Corp'n B'ds,	1,000.00
		Railroad Bonds, ...	59,000.00
		Bank Stocks in Connecticut,	51,500.00
		Bank Stocks in other States,	17,300.00
		Real Estate by Foreclosure,	8,580.00
		Prem. pd. on Stocks and B'ds,	22,610.00
		Safe and Fixtures, . .	1,000.00
		Cash in Bank, . . .	13,900.58
		Cash on hand, . . .	2,271.84
Total Liabilities, . .	$315,699.91	Total Assets, . .	$315,699.91

INVESTMENTS.

DESCRIPTION.	PAR VALUE.	COST.	MARKET VALUE.
UNITED STATES BONDS.			
4s of 1907, Coupon, ... $	200.00	200.00	200.00
TOWN, CITY, AND CORPORATION BONDS.			
City of Norwich, Conn., ...	1,000.00	1,000.00	1,000.00
RAILROAD BONDS.			
Louisiana & Missouri River, . . .	10,000.00	10,000.00	10,000.00
Chicago, Burlington & Quincy, . .	20,000.00	20,000.00	20,000.00
St. Louis, Jacksonville & Chicago, . .	5,000.00	5,000.00	5,000.00
New York & Harlem, ...	5,000.00	5,000.00	5,000.00
New York Central, ...	5,000.00	5,000.00	5,000.00
Rensselaer & Saratoga, ...	4,000.00	4,000.00	4,000.00
Morris & Essex, ...	10,000.00	10,000.00	10,000.00
BANK STOCKS.			
180 shares Stafford National, . . .	18,000.00	18,000.00	18,000.00
50 " Thames " Norwich, .	5,000.00	5,000.00	5,000.00
50 " Second " " .	5,000.00	5,000.00	5,000.00
25 " Thames Loan & Tr. Co., Norwich,	2,500.00	2,500.00	2,500.00
100 " City National, Hartford, .	10,000.00	10,000.00	9,500.00
35 " First " "	3,500.00	3,500.00	3,500.00
50 " American " " .	2,500.00	2,500.00	2,500.00
50 " Mercantile " "	5,000.00	5,000.00	5,000.00
100 " Amer. Exchange Nat'l, New York,	10,000.00	10,000.00	10,000.00
33 " Metropolitan National, " .	3,300.00	3,300.00	3,300.00
40 " Nat'l Bank of Commerce, " .	4,000.00	4,000.00	4,000.00

SAVINGS BANK OF STAFFORD SPRINGS.—Continued.

MISCELLANEOUS ITEMS.

1. Number of depositors having $500 or less, 989; total amount, $117,220.23
2. Number of depositors having over $500 and less than $1,000, ... 125; total amount, 84,531.33
3. Number of depositors having $1,000 and not over $2,000, ... 75; total amount, 100,932.78
4. Number of depositors having over $2,000, 2; total amount, 4,159.67

5. Total number of depositors, . . . 1,191; total deposits, $306,844.01
6. Largest amount due a single depositor, $2,089.54.
7. Number of accounts opened during the year, 192; number closed, 164.
8. Amount of income received during the year, $15,687.57.
9. Amount of dividends declared during the year, $11,269.65.
10. Amount deposited, including interest credited, the past year, $107,202.13.
11. Amount withdrawn during the year, $94,249.15.
12. Increase of deposits the past year, $12,952.15.
13. Amount carried to surplus or profit and loss during the year, none.
14. Rate of dividend the last year, 4 per cent.; when paid, April and October.
15. State tax during the past year, $606.25; United States tax, $1.77.
16. Total office expenses the past year, including salaries, $1,338.04.
17. Net amount of income during the year from real estate owned, none.
18. Amount of assets yielding no income during the year, $8,375.00.
19. Are all loans upon real estate secured by first mortgage? Yes.
20. Largest amount loaned to one individual, company, society, or corporation, $13,687.
21. Date of annual meeting for choice of officers, second Wednesday in July.

OFFICERS.—President, Chas. Warren; Treasurer, Alvarado Howard; Directors or Trustees, Robbins Patten, Orrin Converse, Seneca N. Page, M. P. J. Walker, Andrew Whiton, Smith W. Page, Lucian Holt, M. H. Kinney, Luman Orcutt, Lucius Blodgett.

SAVINGS BANK OF TOLLAND.

ARTHUR J. MORTON, Treasurer.   INCORPORATED, 1841.

STATEMENT, OCTOBER 1, 1882.

LIABILITIES.		ASSETS.	
Whole Amount of Deposits,	$94,948.54	Loans on Real Estate, .	$52,200.95
Surplus Account, . .	546.44	Loans on Endorsed Notes, .	8,000.00
Interest Account, . .	2,074.09	Bank Stocks in Connecticut,	30,100.00
Real Estate Rents, . .	80.94	Real Estate by Foreclosure,	3,117.92
		Tax Account, . . .	80.86
		Expense Account, . .	148.54
		Cash in Bank, . . .	3,896.51
		Cash on hand, . . .	105.23
Total Liabilities, . .	$97,650.01	Total Assets, . .	$97,650.01

INVESTMENTS.

DESCRIPTION.	PAR VALUE.	COST.	MARKET VALUE.
BANK STOCKS.			
218 shares Tolland County National, . . $	21,800.00	21,800.00	21,800.00
70 " Rockville " . .	7,000.00	7,000.00	7,700.00
13 " Stafford " . .	1,300.00	1,300.00	1,300.00

MISCELLANEOUS ITEMS.

1. Number of depositors having $500 or less, . 337; total amount, $33,705.67
2. Number of depositors having over $500 and less than $1,000, ... 88; total amount, 27,738.45
3. Number of depositors having $1,000 and not over $2,000, ... 21; total amount, 26,186.45
4. Number of depositors having over $2,000, . 2; total amount, 6,317.97
5. Total number of depositors, ... 398; total deposits, $94,948.54
6. Largest amount due a single depositor, $3,166.77.
7. Number of accounts opened during the year, 33; number closed, 81.
8. Amount of income received during the year, $4,876.99.
9. Amount of dividends declared during the year, $3,759.74.
10. Amount deposited, including interest credited, the past year, $10,502.59.
11. Amount withdrawn during the year, $33,877.65.
12. Decrease of deposits the past year, $23,375.06.
13. Amount carried to surplus or profit and loss during the year, $391.30.
14. Rate of dividend the last year, 3¼ per cent.; when paid, 1¼ per cent. January 1st, and 2 per cent. July 1st.
15. State tax during the past year, $161.72; U. S. tax, $7.42.
16. Total office expenses the past year, including salaries, $854.45.
17. Net amount of income during the year from real estate owned, $80.94.
18. Amount of assets yielding no income during the year, none.
19. Are all loans upon real estate secured by first mortgage? Yes.
20. Largest amount loaned to one individual, company, society, or corporation, $10,848.95.
21. Date of annual meeting for choice of officers, fourth Monday in June.

OFFICERS.—President, Charles Underwood; Treasurer, Arthur J. Morton; Directors or Trustees, Charles Underwood, Nathan Pierson, Edmund Joslyn, John B. Fuller, William Holman.

SOCIETY FOR SAVINGS, HARTFORD.

Z. A. STORRS, Treasurer.   INCORPORATED, 1819.

STATEMENT, OCTOBER 1, 1882.

LIABILITIES.		ASSETS.	
Whole Am't of Deposits,	$9,074,011.91	Loans on Real Estate,	$4,285,110.00
Surplus Account,	278,216.10	Loans on Stocks and B'ds,	554,225.00
Interest Account,	80,863.46	Loans on Endorsed Notes,	93,275.00
		United States Bonds,	1,099,875.00
		State Bonds,	1,500.00
		Town, City, and Corp. B'ds,	945,230.00
		Railroad Bonds,	1,065,525.00
		Railroad Stocks,	27,800.00
		Bank Stocks in Connecticut,	181,060.00
		Bank Stocks in other States,	82,480.00
		Real Estate by Foreclosure,	376,950.00
		Banking House,	15,000.00
		Expense Account,	4,634.00
		Profit and Loss Account,	1,860.37
		Cash in Bank,	727,032.42
		Cash on hand,	22,034.68
Total Liabilities,	$9,433,091.47	Total Assets,	$9,433,091.47

INVESTMENTS.

DESCRIPTION.	PAR VALUE.	COST.	MARKET VALUE.
UNITED STATES BONDS.			
4½s of 1891, registered,	$ 350,000.00	351,125.00	392,000.00
4s of 1907, registered,	25,000.00	26,332.80	29,750.00
4s of 1907, coupon,	50,000.00	49,875.00	59,500.00
Currency 6s,	200,000.00	200,000.00	260,000.00
Three per cents,	475,000.00	475,000.00	475,000.00
STATE BONDS.			
Connecticut, registered,	1,500.00	1,620.00	1,545.00
TOWN, CITY, AND CORPORATION BONDS.			
Meriden Town, 4¼ per cent.,	80,000.00	80,000.00	80,000.00
Haddam " 4¼ " due 1890,	20,000.00	20,000.00	20,000.00
Hartford " 4¼ " " 1905,	150,000.00	154,250.00	155,250.00
" " 4¼ " " 1904,	100,000.00	104,000.00	103,500.00
" City, 6 " " 1899,	28,000.00	27,230.00	30,240.00
" " 6 " " 1891,	70,000.00	70,000.00	74,900.00
" " 6 " " 1893,	2,000.00	2,000.00	2,160.00
Buffalo " 7 " " 1903,	50,000.00	50,000.00	70,000.00
Rochester " 7 " " 1905,	45,000.00	45,000.00	63,000.00
" " 7 " " 1893,	5,000.00	5,000.00	6,250.00
Springfield " 7 " " 1893,	20,000.00	20,000.00	24,000.00
Boston " 5 " " 1905,	40,000.00	40,000.00	47,600.00
" " 5 " " 1906,	25,000.00	25,000.00	29,750.00

SOCIETY FOR SAVINGS.—Continued.

INVESTMENTS.—Continued.

DESCRIPTION.	PAR VALUE.	COST.	MARKET VALUE.
TOWN, CITY, AND CORPORATION BONDS.—CON.			
Providence City, 5 per cent., due 1906, $	25,000.00	25,000.00	29,250.00
New Haven " 7 " " 1901,	75,000.00	101,250.00	102,750.00
Chicago " 7 " . .	59,000.00	74,062.50	73,750.00
Detroit " 6 " . due 1906,	7,000.00	8,890.00	8,890.00
St. Louis " 6 " " 1894,	10,000.00	11,700.00	11,500.00
Cleveland " 6 "	50,000.00	58,500.00	58,500.00
District of Columbia, 3.65 " due 1924,	35,000.00	35,000.00	37,800.00
Atlantic Dock Co., 5 " " 1901,	50,000.00	50,000.00	50,000.00
RAILROAD BONDS.			
Cleveland & Toledo, 7 per ct., due 1885,	32,000.00	32,000.00	33,920.00
Pitts. Ft. W. & Chicago, 7 " " 1912,	20,000.00	20,000.00	27,000.00
" " " 7 " " 1912,	22,000.00	28,840.83	30,360.00
Indianapolis & Cincinnati, 7 " " 1888,	20,000.00	17,525.00	21,400.00
N. Y. Cent. & Hudson R., 7 " " 1903,	25,000.00	31,931.25	33,250.00
" " reg., 7 " " 1903,	275,000.00	369,793.75	365,750.00
Chicago, R. I. & Pacific, 6 " " 1917,	50,000.00	59,173.75	63,000.00
" " reg., 6 " " 1917,	215,000.00	271,206.25	270,900.00
New York & Harlem, 7 " " 1900,	31,000.00	40,266.25	40,920.00
" reg., 7 " " 1900,	40,000.00	53,106.25	52,800.00
Cleveland & Pittsburgh, 6 " " 1892,	82,000.00	90,952.49	88,560.00
Norwich & Worcester, 6 " " 1897,	35,000.00	40,950.00	41,300.00
Rensselaer & Saratoga, 7 " " 1921,	26,000.00	35,482.50	35,360.00
Albany & Susquehanna, 7 " " 1888,	35,000.00	39,946.25	39,550.00
Morris & Essex, 7 " " 1914,	25,000.00	33,676.25	34,500.00
N. Y., Prov. & Boston, 4 " " 1901,	50,000.00	50,000.00	50,000.00
Chicago & Alton, 7 " " 1893,	32,000.00	39,380.00	38,400.00
Chicago & Milwaukee, 7 " " 1898,	53,000.00	65,301.25	64,660.00
RAILROAD STOCKS.			
273 shares New York, New Haven & Hartford,	27,300.00	27,300.00	49,686.00
BANK STOCKS.			
150 shares Hartford National, Hartford,	15,000.00	15,000.00	26,250.00
225 " Phœnix " "	22,500.00	22,500.00	39,375.00
294 " City " "	29,400.00	29,400.00	26,460.00
140 " Farmers & Mech. " "	14,000.00	14,000.00	18,900.00
300 " Ætna " "	30,000.00	30,000.00	39,000.00
239 " Charter Oak " "	23,900.00	23,900.00	33,460.00
120 " American " "	6,000.00	6,510.00	8,400.00
125 " First " Massillon, O.,	12,500.00	12,500.00	15,000.00
50 " Central " New York,	5,000.00	5,186.25	6,250.00
50 " American Exchange, " "	5,000.00	5,631.25	6,550.00
35 " Continental, " "	3,500.00	3,504.38	4,200.00
240 " Phenix " "	4,800.00	4,480.00	5,136.00
20 " Metropolitan " "	2,000.00	2,623.07	3,440.00
314 " Merchants " Norwich,	12,560.00	12,872.50	12,872.50
100 " First " "	10,000.00	11,700.00	11,700.00
150 " First " Litchfield,	15,000.00	19,200.00	19,200.00
27 " Hartford Trust Co., . . .	2,700.00	2,707.00	2,707.00

SOCIETY FOR SAVINGS.—Continued.

MISCELLANEOUS ITEMS.

1. Number of depositors having $500 or less, 21,874; total amount, $2,437,612.82
2. Number of depositors having over $500 and less than $1,000, ... 2,729; total amount, 1,917,835.71
3. Number of depositors having $1,000 and not over $2,000, ... 1,673; total amount, 2,293,566.37
4. Number of depositors having over $2,000, 753; total amount, 2,424,997,01

5. Total number of depositors, . . . 27,029; total deposits, $9,074,011.91
6. Largest amount due a single depositor, $10,200.
7. Number of accounts opened during the year, 3,792; number closed, 2,603.
8. Amount of income received during the year, $480,633.34.
9. Amount of dividends declared during the year, $334,670.11.
10. Amount deposited, including interest credited, the past year, $1,770,304.31.
11. Amount withdrawn during the year, $1,237,124.51.
12. Increase of deposits the past year, $533,179.80.
13. Amount carried to surplus or profit and loss during the year, none.
14. Rate of dividend the last year, 4 per cent.; when paid, June 1st and Dec. 1st.
15. State tax during the past year, $20,032.05; U. S. tax, none.
16. Total office expenses the past year, including salaries, $17,421.68.
17. Net amount of income during the year from real estate owned, none.
18. Amount of assets yielding no income during the year, $84,000.
19. Are all loans upon real estate secured by first mortgage? Yes.
20. Largest amount loaned to one individual, company, society, or corporation, $100,000.
21. Date of annual meeting for choice of officers, July.

OFFICERS.—President, Roland Mather; Treasurer, Zalmon A. Storrs; Directors or Trustees, Joseph Langdon, Charles Seymour, Drayton Hillyer, Chas. T. Hillyer, Rowland Swift, J. F. Morris, H. K. Morgan, John C. Parsons, A. R. Hillyer, G. W. Russell, Z. A. Storrs, Calvin Day, Francis B. Cooley, Lucius J. Hendee, Caleb M. Talcott, Wm. H. Post, J. Goodnow, Walter Keney, Geo. L. Chase, Theodore Lyman, William R. Cone, Charles Boswell, P. M. Hastings, John B. Corning, T. O. Enders, Wm. M. Stanley, Henry Keney, J. M. Allen, Chauncey Howard, Rodney Dennis, Nathaniel Shipman, Atwood Collins, Daniel R. Howe.

SOUTHINGTON SAVINGS BANK.

F. D. WHITTLESEY, Treasurer. INCORPORATED, 1860.

STATEMENT, OCTOBER 1, 1882.

LIABILITIES.		ASSETS.	
Whole Amount of Deposits,	$386,238.34	Loans on Real Estate,	$194,312.15
Surplus Account,	15,406.27	Loans on Stocks and Bonds,	5,475.00
Interest Account,	3,812.42	Loans on Endorsed Notes,	23,045.00
		United States Bonds,	12,000.00
		Town, City, and Corp. B'ds,	10,345.00
		Railroad Bonds,	13,150.00
		Bank Stocks in Connecticut,	121,456.08
		Bank Stocks in other States,	14,619.00
		Real Estate by Foreclosure,	6,081.60
		Banking House Safe,	500.00
		Cash in Bank,	520.70
		Cash on hand,	3,952.50
Total Liabilities,	$405,457.03	Total Assets,	$405,457.03

INVESTMENTS.

DESCRIPTION.	PAR VALUE.	COST.	MARKET VALUE.
UNITED STATES BONDS.			
4s of 1907, Registered, $	12,000.00	12,000.00	14,160.00
TOWN, CITY, AND CORPORATION BONDS.			
Town of West Hartford, 4 per cent.,	10,000.00	10,345.00	10,350.00
RAILROAD BONDS.			
New York Central & Harlem, 7s, 1903,	10,000.00	13,150.00	13,150.00
BANK STOCKS.			
20 shares National Exchange, Hartford,	1,000.00	960.00	1,560.00
22 " Ætna National, "	2,200.00	2,448.00	2,860.00
31 " Charter Oak " "	3,100.00	3,306.00	4,840.00
64 " First "	6,400.00	6,738.75	7,744.00
154 " American " "	7,700.00	9,635.00	11,242.00
9 " Farm. & Mech. " "	900.00	1,042.00	1,215.00
16 " Phœnix " "	1,600.00	2,400.00	2,800.00
40 " City " "	4,000.00	3,600.00	3,600.00
216 " Yale " New Haven,	21,600.00	22,399.00	25,920.00
158 " Merchants " "	7,900.00	8,042.00	9,480.00
35 " Tradesmens " "	3,500.00	5,678.75	5,740.00
152 " New Haven Co. " "	1,520.00	2,044.00	2,090.00
9 " Middletown " Middletown,	540.00	976.50	976.50
56 " Middlesex Co. " "	5,600.00	6,703.00	6,832.00
30 " First "	3,000.00	3,395.00	3,480.00
65 " First " Norwich,	6,500.00	7,116.00	7,475.00
50 " Thames " "	5,000.00	7,275.00	7,500.00
109 " First " Meriden,	10,900.00	11,598.83	13,080.00
97 " Home " "	9,700.00	11,508.25	12,901.00
30 " Birmingham " Birmingham,	3,000.00	4,590.00	4,680.00
72 " Nat. Bk. of Commerce, New York,	7,200.00	9,504.00	10,800.00
45 " Nat. Amer. Exchange, "	4,500.00	5,115.00	5,940.00

SOUTHINGTON SAVINGS BANK.—Continued.

MISCELLANEOUS ITEMS.

1. Number of depositors having $500 or less, 1,062; total amount, $118,470.50
2. Number of depositors having over $500 and less than $1,000, ... 117; total amount, 83,106.43
3. Number of depositors having $1,000 and not over $2,000, ... 71; total amount, 98,872.56
4. Number of depositors having over $2,000, 24; total amount, 85,788.85

5. Total number of depositors, . . . 1,274; total deposits, $386,238.34
6. Largest amount due a single depositor, $11,878.22.
7. Number of accounts opened during the year, 221; number closed, 169.
8. Amount of income received during the year, $22,768.99.
9. Amount of dividends declared during the year, $15,949.09.
10. Amount deposited, including interest credited, the past year, $115,077.63.
11. Amount withdrawn during the year, $96,103.32.
12. Increase of deposits the past year, $18,974.31.
13. Amount carried to surplus or profit and loss during the year, $4,539.36.
14. Rate of dividend the last year, 4½ per cent.; when paid, 2 per cent. in January and 2½ per cent. in July.
15. State tax during the past year, $774.04; U. S. tax, $96.14.
16. Total office expenses the past year, including salaries, $1,273.79.
17. Net amount of income during the year from real estate owned, $349.26.
18. Amount of assets yielding no income during the year, none.
19. Are all loans upon real estate secured by first mortgage? Yes.
20. Largest amount loaned to one individual, company, society, or corporation, $8,000.
21. Date of annual meeting for choice of officers, fourth Wednesday in June.

OFFICERS. — President, Wheaton L. Plumb; Vice-President, Marcus H. Holcomb; Treasurer, Francis D. Whittlesey; Directors or Trustees, Amon Bradley, Roswell A. Neale, George B. Finch, Charles D. Barnes, Merit N. Woodruff, James H. Pratt, James H. Osborne.

SOUTH NORWALK SAVINGS BANK.

JOHN H. KNAPP, Treasurer.   INCORPORATED, 1860.

STATEMENT, OCTOBER 1, 1882.

LIABILITIES.		ASSETS.	
Whole Amount of Deposits,	$246,657.77	Loans on Real Estate, .	$109,268.06
Surplus Account, . .	7,500.00	Loans on Stocks and Bonds,	106,859.50
Interest Account, . .	5,480.50	Loans on Endorsed Notes,	15,624.00
Profit and Loss Account, .	936.26	Town, City, and Corp. B'ds,	100.00
Rents Received, . . .	213.44	School District Notes, .	13,325.00
		Bank Stocks in Connecticut,	5,000.00
		Real Estate by Foreclosure,	9,000.00
		Tax Account, . . .	209.53
		Expense Account, . .	336.19
		Office Furniture, . .	87.52
		Cash in Bank, . . .	978.17
Total Liabilities, . .	$260,787.97	Total Assets, . .	$260,787.97

INVESTMENTS.

DESCRIPTION.	PAR VALUE.	COST.	MARKET VALUE.
TOWN, CITY, AND CORPORATION BONDS.			
Borough of Norwalk, Water, 7 per cent., . $	. 100.00	100.00	110.00
SCHOOL DISTRICT NOTES.			
South Norwalk Union, ...	. . .	. . .	. . .
South Five Mile River, ...	. . .	. . .	. . .
BANK STOCKS.			
5 shares First National, New Canaan, . .	500.00	500.00	500.00
15 " " " South Norwalk, .	1,500.00	1,500.00	1,620.00
30 " City " " .	3,000.00	3,000.00	3,000.00

MISCELLANEOUS ITEMS.

1. Number of depositors having $500 or less, 1,084; total amount, $101,032.47
2. Number of depositors having over $500 and less than $1,000, ... 106; total amount, 71,210.40
3. Number of depositors having $1,000 and not over $2,000, ... 39; total amount, 54,306.26
4. Number of depositors having over $2,000, 9; total amount, 20,108.64

Total number of depositors, ... 1,238; total deposits, $246,657.77
Largest amount due a single depositor, $2,676.94.
Number of accounts opened during the year, 432; number closed, 225.
Amount of income received during the year, $14,651.37.
Amount of dividends declared during the year, $7,975.12.
10. Amount deposited, including interest credited, the past year, $147,237.76.
11. Amount withdrawn during the year, $99,882.66.
12. Decrease of deposits the past year, $47,405.10.

SOUTH NORWALK SAVINGS BANK.—CONTINUED.

MISCELLANEOUS ITEMS.—CONTINUED.

13. Amount carried to surplus or profit and loss during the year, $2,936.26.
14. Rate of dividend the last year, 4 per cent.; when paid, January and July.
15. State tax during the past year, $416.77; United States tax, $4.19.
16. Total office expenses the past year, including salaries, $1,055.80.
17. Net amount of income during the year from real estate owned, $814.52.
18. Amount of assets yielding no income during the year, none.
19. Are all loans upon real estate secured by first mortgage? Yes.
20. Largest amount loaned to one individual, company, society, or corporation, $50,000.
21. Date of annual meeting for choice of officers, July.

OFFICERS.—President, Dudley P. Ely; Vice-President, Alden Solmans; Treasurer, John H. Knapp; Directors or Trustees, Dudley P. Ely, F. H. Nash, O. W. Weed, Alden Solmans, Edwin Adams, John H. Ferris, John H. Knapp, Henry I. Smith, Edwin Beard.

SOUTHPORT SAVINGS BANK.

CHAS. C. PERRY, Treasurer.   INCORPORATED, 1854.

STATEMENT, OCTOBER 1, 1882.

LIABILITIES.		ASSETS.	
Whole Amount of Deposits,	$504,150.19	Loans on Real Estate,	$179,600.00
Surplus Account,	9,900.00	Loans on Stocks and Bonds,	11,800.00
Interest Account,	15,161.20	Loans on Endorsed Notes,	10,000.00
		United States Bonds,	42,000.00
		Town, City, and Corp. Bonds,	196,000.00
		Railroad Bonds,	16,000.00
		Railroad Stocks,	4,800.00
		Bank Stocks in Connecticut,	3,600.00
		Bank Stocks in other States,	25,700.00
		Real Estate by Foreclosure,	22,000.00
		Banking House,	5,000.00
		Expense Account,	1,268.80
		Cash in Bank,	5,782.31
		Cash on hand,	660.28
Total Liabilities,	$529,211.39	Total Assets,	$529,211.39

INVESTMENTS.

DESCRIPTION.	PAR VALUE.	COST.	MARKET VALUE.
UNITED STATES BONDS.			
4s of 1907, Registered, $	42,000.00	42,000.00	49,770.00
TOWN, CITY, AND CORPORATION BONDS.			
New York City Acc. Debt, 1884, 7 per cent.,	12,000.00	12,000.00	12,360.00
" " " 1885, 7 "	50,000.00	50,000.00	52,000.00
" " " 1888, 7 "	30,000.00	30,000.00	33,000.00
" County " 1884, 7 "	10,000.00	10,000.00	10,300.00
Brooklyn City, Park, 1915, 7 "	30,000.00	30,000.00	42,000.00
" " Boulevard, 1883, 7 "	2,000.00	2,000.00	2,000.00
Bridgeport " 1900, 7 "	25,000.00	25,000.00	31,000.00
Cincinnati " 1904, 7 "	3,000.00	3,000.00	3,840.00
St. Louis " 1891, 6 "	16,000.00	16,000.00	17,760.00
" " 1894, 6 "	4,000.00	4,000.00	4,560.00
Town of Fairfield, 1883, 6 "	1,000.00	1,000.00	1,000.00
" " 1884, 6 "	3,000.00	3,000.00	3,030.00
Borough of Danbury, 1900, 4½ "	10,000.00	10,000.00	10,400.00
RAILROAD BONDS.			
Chicago, Bur. & Quincy, 1883, 8 per cent.,	10,000.00	10,000.00	10,000.00
Midland, New Jersey, 1910, 5 "	6,000.00	6,000.00	5,220.00
RAILROAD STOCKS.			
New York, Susquehanna & Western,	4,800.00	4,800.00	960.00

SOUTHPORT SAVINGS BANK.—Continued.

INVESTMENTS.—Continued.

DESCRIPTION.	PAR VALUE.	COST.	MARKET VALUE.
BANK STOCKS.			
16 shares National, Norwalk, . . . $	1,600.00	1,600.00	1,600.00
20 " First National, Norwich, .	2,000.00	2,000.00	2,300.00
10 " Hanover " New York,	1,000.00	1,000.00	1,850.00
180 " Phœnix " "	3,600.00	3,600.00	3,744.00
22 " Continental " "	2,200.00	2,200.00	2,640.00
40 " Fourth " "	4,000.00	4,000.00	5,200.00
50 " Third " "	5,000.00	5,000.00	5,750.00
14 " Central " "	1,400.00	1,400.00	1,750.00
5 " St. Nicholas " "	500.00	500.00	640.00
10 " American Ex. " "	1,000.00	1,000.00	1,300.00
50 " Nat. Bank of N. America, "	3,500.00	3,500.00	3,605.00
15 " " " Commerce, "	1,500.00	1,500.00	2,250.00
20 " " " State of "	2,000.00	2,000.00	2,600.00

MISCELLANEOUS ITEMS.

Number of depositors having $500 or less, . 855; total amount, $104,970.86
Number of depositors having over $500 and less than $1,000, ... 126; total amount, 89,868.75
Number of depositors having $1,000 and not over $2,000, ... 143; total amount, 198,055.36
Number of depositors having over $2,000, . 41; total amount, 111,255.22

5. Total number of depositors, . . 1,165; total deposits, $504,150.19
6. Largest amount due a single depositor, $5,947.12.
7. Number of accounts opened during the year, 152; number closed, 114.
8. Amount of income received during the year, $23,986.16.
9. Amount of dividends declared during the year, $20,241.57.
10. Amount deposited, including interest credited, the past year, $87,353.39.
11. Amount withdrawn during the year, $98,904.48.
12. Decrease of deposits the past year, $11,551.59.
13. Amount carried to surplus or profit and loss during the year, $2,600.
14. Rate of dividend the last year, 4 per cent.; when paid, January 1st and July 1st.
15. State tax during the past year, $1,101.11; U. S. tax, $5.60.
16. Total office expenses the past year, including salaries, $2,880.28.
17. Net amount of income during the year from real estate owned, $112.05.
18. Amount of assets yielding no income during the year, $12,800.
19. Are all loans upon real estate secured by first mortgage? Yes.
20. Largest amount loaned to one individual, company, society, or corporation, $10,000.
21. Date of annual meeting for choice of officers, July 1st.

OFFICERS.—President, ——; Vice-Presidents, Edwin Sherwood, Augustus Jennings; Treasurer, Chas. C. Perry; Directors or Trustees, F. D. Perry, Ebenezer Monroe, W. B. Meeker, O. B. Jennings, Oliver Bulkley, C. M. Taintor, George Bulkley, Francis Jelliff, Franklin Bulkley, Benjamin A. Bulkley, Simon C. Sherwood, Royal G. Skiff, John H. Wood, Edward Henshaw, John H. Perry, Chas. C. Perry.

STAFFORD SAVINGS BANK.

R. S. HICKS, Treasurer.   INCORPORATED, 1872.

STATEMENT, OCTOBER 1, 1882.

LIABILITIES.		ASSETS.	
Whole Amount of Deposits,	$424,952.84	Loans on Real Estate, .	$271,248.49
Surplus Account, . .	3,000.00	Loans on Stocks and Bonds,	53,100.00
Interest Account, . .	3,226.30	Loans on Endorsed Notes, .	9,000.00
		Railroad Bonds, . . .	4,240.00
		Bank Stocks in Connecticut.	76,217.00
		Bank Stocks in other States,	5,000.00
		Cash in Bank, . . .	10,485.87
		Cash on hand, . . .	1,887.78
Total Liabilities, . .	$431,179.14	Total Assets, . .	$431,179.14

INVESTMENTS.

DESCRIPTION.	PAR VALUE.	COST.	MARKET VALUE.
RAILROAD BONDS.			
New London Northern, 1st mort., 5 per cent., $	4,000.00	4,240.00	4,300.00
BANK STOCKS.			
379 shares Stafford National, . .	37,900.00	39,291.00	41,690.00
100 " Second " Norwich, .	10,000.00	11,400.00	12,000.00
100 " Uncas " " .	5,000.00	5,500.00	6,000.00
100 " American " Hartford, .	5,000.00	6,826.00	7,250.00
110 " Tolland Co. " Tolland, .	11,000.00	10,500.00	11,000.00
5 " First " Wallingford,	500.00	500.00	525.00
2 " Rockville " Rockville, .	200.00	200.00	220.00
20 " Winsted " Winsted, .	2,000.00	2,000.00	2,100.00
40 " Continental " New York, .	4,000.00	4,000.00	4,800.00

MISCELLANEOUS ITEMS.

1. Number of depositors having $500 or less, 1,135; total amount, $162,696.19
2. Number of depositors having over $500 and less than $1,000, ... 150; total amount, 106,395.68
3. Number of depositors having $1,000 and not over $2,000, ... 105; total amount, 149,721.26
4. Number of depositors having over $2,000, . 3; total amount, 6,139.71
5. Total number of depositors, . . . 1,393; total deposits, $424,952.84
6. Largest amount due a single depositor, $2,105.28.
7. Number of accounts opened during the year, 305; number closed, —.
8. Amount of income received during the year, $23,562.82.
9. Amount of dividends declared during the year, $19,618.64.
10. Amount deposited, including interest credited, the past year, $94,455.52.
11. Amount withdrawn during the year, $65,502.09.
12. Increase of deposits the past year, $28,953.43.
13. Amount carried to surplus or profit and loss during the year, $500.00.

STAFFORD SAVINGS BANK.—Continued.

MISCELLANEOUS ITEMS.—Continued.

14. Rate of dividend the last year, 5 per cent.; when paid, January and July.
15. State tax during the past year, $877.46; U. S. tax, $30.52.
16. Total office expenses the past year, including salaries, $1,662.82.
17. Net amount of income during the year from real estate owned, none.
18. Amount of assets yielding no income during the year, $3,780.
19. Are all loans upon real estate secured by first mortgage? Yes.
20. Largest amount loaned to one individual, company, society, or corporation, $35,000.
21. Date of annual meeting for choice of officers, third Wednesday in July.

OFFICERS.—President, L. W. Crane; Vice-Presidents, G. H. Preston, Wm. M. Corbin; Secretary and Treasurer, R. S. Hicks; Directors or Trustees, Chas. Holt, Davis A. Baker, D. E. Whiton, J. J. Ellis, G. Hall, Jr., D. F. Fairman, Geo. C. Parkess, S. C. Eaton.

STAMFORD SAVINGS BANK.

A. A. HOLLY, Treasurer.   INCORPORATED, 1851.

STATEMENT, OCTOBER 1, 1882.

LIABILITIES.		ASSETS.	
Whole Amt. of Deposits,	$1,487,158.52	Loans on Real Estate, .	$763,017.00
Surplus Account, . .	45,000.00	Loans on Stocks and Bonds,	318,610.00
Interest Account, . .	38,339.61	Loans on Endorsed Notes,	23,815.00
		United States Bonds, . .	150,000.00
		State Bonds, . . .	6,483.50
		Town, City, and Corp. B'ds,	160,187.50
		Railroad Bonds, . . .	61,070.00
		Bank Stocks in Connecticut,	6,937.00
		Real Estate by Foreclosure,	15,075.12
		Cash on hand, . . .	65,303.01
Total Liabilities, .	$1,570,498.13	Total Assets, .	$1,570,498.13

INVESTMENTS.

DESCRIPTION.	PAR VALUE.	COST.	MARKET VALUE.
UNITED STATES BONDS.			
4½s of 1891, registered, ... $	120,000.00	120,000.00	135,000.00
4s of 1907, registered, ...	30,000.00	30,000.00	35,700.00
STATE BONDS.			
Connecticut, 5 per cent., ...	2,000.00	2,120.00	2,120.00
Missouri, 6 per cent., 1886, ...	4,000.00	4,363.56	4,320.00
TOWN, CITY, AND CORPORATION BONDS.			
Town of Greenwich, ...	20,000.00	20,000.00	21,200.00
New York City Improvement, . .	50,000.00	50,000.00	55,000.00
" " Consolidated, . .	20,000.00	20,000.00	24,400.00
" " Accumulated, . .	20,000.00	20,000.00	22,000.00
Brooklyn Park, ...	5,000.00	5,000.00	7,250.00
" City, ...	10,000.00	11,462.50	13,000.00
Rochester City Water Loan, . . .	5,000.00	5,000.00	5,900.00
Cincinnati Public Wharf, . . .	1,000.00	1,000.00	1,100.00
" " Water, . . .	1,000.00	1,000.00	1,100.00
St. Louis City, ...	5,000.00	5,725.00	6,000.00
District of Columbia, ...	20,000.00	21,000.00	22,400.00
RAILROAD BONDS.			
Jefferson, Madison & Indianapolis, . .	9,000.00	10,000.00	10,620.00
Morris & Essex, ...	15,000.00	16,050.00	18,750.00
Columbus & Xenia, ...	5,000.00	5,000.00	5,600.00
Terre Haute & Indianapolis, . . .	26,000.00	29,020.00	29,900.00
New York Central, ...	1,000.00	1,000.00	1,020.00
BANK STOCKS.			
209 shares Stamford National, . . .	6,270.00	6,937.00	9,405.00

STAMFORD SAVINGS BANK.—CONTINUED.

MISCELLANEOUS ITEMS.

1. Number of depositors having $500 or less, 3,185; total amount, $515,040.45
2. Number of depositors having over $500
   and less than $1,000, ...   441; total amount,   305,784.28
3. Number of depositors having $1,000 and
   not over $2,000, ...   221; total amount,   302,036.42
4. Number of depositors having over $2,000,   104; total amount,   364,297.37

5. Total number of depositors,   .   .   .   3,951; total deposits, $1,487,158.52
6. Largest amount due a single depositor, $15,995.
7. Number of accounts opened during the year, 706; number closed, 565.
8. Amount of income received during the year, $82,130.92.
9. Amount of dividends declared during the year, $68,385.45.
10. Amount deposited, including interest credited, the past year, $306,325.27.
11. Amount withdrawn during the year, $219,263.32.
12. Increase of deposits the past year, $87,061.95.
13. Amount carried to surplus or profit and loss during the year, none.
14. Rate of dividend the last year, 5 per cent.; when paid, April and October.
15. State tax during the past year, $34.56; U. S. tax, none.
16. Total office expenses the past year, including salaries, $4,986.86.
17. Net amount of income during the year from real estate owned, none.
18. Amount of assets yielding no income during the year, $35,000.
19. Are all loans upon real estate secured by first mortgage? Yes.
20. Largest amount loaned to one individual, company, society, or corporation, $44,000.
21. Date of annual meeting for choice of officers, July.

OFFICERS.—President, George H. Hoyt; Vice-President, Charles A. Hawley; Treasurer, A. A. Holly; Directors or Trustees, Geo. Elder, F. Miller, C. M. Holly, Theodore Leeds, T. J. Daskam, R. Hoyt, W. H. Judd, J. B. Reed, W. W. Skiddy.

STATE SAVINGS BANK, HARTFORD.

J. W. STEDMAN, Treasurer.   INCORPORATED, 1858.

STATEMENT, OCTOBER 1, 1882.

LIABILITIES.		ASSETS.	
Whole Am't of Deposits, .	$1,977,550.86	Loans on Real Estate, .	$790,363.22
Surplus Account, . .	70,289.70	Loans on Stocks and Bonds,	85,470.00
Interest Account, . .	9,883.93	Loans on Endorsed Notes,	8,000.00
Rent Account, . . .	3,292.27	Judgment Account ., .	15,700.00
Suspense Account, . .	203.50	United States Bonds, .	8,045.63
		Town, City, and Corp'n B'ds,	219,040.00
		Railroad Bonds, . .	26,550.00
		Bank Stocks in Connecticut,	258,250.19
		Real Estate by Foreclosure,	578,978.80
		Banking House, . ₳ .	34,000.00
		Expense Account, . . .	6,771.88
		Cash in Bank, . . .	13,062.25
		Cash on hand, . . .	6,988.29
Total Liabilities, .	$2,061,220.26	Total Assets, . . .	$2,061,220.26

INVESTMENTS.

DESCRIPTION.	PAR VALUE.	COST.	MARKET VALUE.
UNITED STATES BONDS.			
4s of 1907, Registered, ... $	6,000.00	6,704.63	7,080.00
4s of 1907, Coupon, ...	1,200.00	1,341.00	1,416.00
TOWN, CITY, AND CORPORATION BONDS.			
City of Cincinnati, Municipal, 7$\frac{3}{10}$ per cent.,	160,000.00	209,600.00	212,800.00
" Rochester, 7 "	8,000.00	9,440.00	9,440.00
RAILROAD BONDS.			
New York Central & Hudson River, . .	20,000.00	26,550.00	26,600.00
BANK STOCKS.			
278 shares American National, Hartford,	13,900.00	18,765.00	20,850.00
32 " Ætna " "	3,200.00	3,266.00	4,320.00
144 " City " "	14,400.00	14,231.00	13,392.00
16 " Farm. & Mech. " "	1,600.00	1,900.00	2,240.00
253 " First " "	25,300.00	26,565.00	31,625.00
145 " Conn. Trust & Dep. Co., "	14,500.00	14,450.00	16,675.00
250 " Security Co., "	25,000.00	26,250.00	31,250.00
3 " Phœnix National, "	300.00	508.50	525.00
600 " Mercantile " "	60,000.00	72,000.00	79,200.00
15 " Conn. River Banking Co., "	750.00	900.00	795.00
10 " Hartford National, "	1,000.00	1,710.00	1,750.00
16 " Charter Oak " "	1,600.00	2,400.00	2,320.00
223 " New Haven Co. " New Haven,	2,230.00	3,122.00	3,122.00
46 " Central " Middletown,	4,875.00	7,495.00	7,495.00
250 " Thames " Norwich,	25,000.00	37,377.00	38,000.00
400 " Uncas " "	20,000.00	22,541.66	25,000.00
80 " Home " Meriden,	8,500.00	11,176.53	11,220.00
30 " First " "	3,000.00	3,592.50	3,600.00

11

STATE SAVINGS BANK.—Continued.

MISCELLANEOUS ITEMS.

1. Number of depositors having $500 or less, . 3,982; total amount, $501,119.42
2. Number of depositors having over $500 and
   less than $1,000, ... 696; total amount, 486,431.14
3. Number of depositors having $1,000 and not
   not over $2,000, ... 500; total amount, 682,052.89
4. Number of depositors having over $2,000, . 118; total amount, 307,947.41

5. Total number of depositors, . . . 5,296; total deposits,$1,997,550.86
6. Largest amount due a single depositor, $6,572.35.
7. Number of accounts opened during the year, 754; number closed, 511.
8. Amount of income received during the year, $116,334.66.
9. Amount of dividends declared during the year, $71,325.44.
10. Amount deposited, including interest credited, the past year, $510,753.42.
11. Amount withdrawn during the year, $323,107.60.
12. Increase of deposits the past year, $187,645.82.
13. Amount carried to surplus or profit and loss during the year, $1,350.30.
14. Rate of dividend the last year, 4 per cent.; when paid, August and February.
15. State tax during the past year, $3,066.29; U. S. tax, $263.40.
16. Total office expenses the past year, including salaries, $6,771.88.
17. Net amount of income during the year from real estate owned, $16,025.95.
18. Amount of assets yielding no income during the year, $52,527.25.
19. Are all loans upon real estate secured by first mortgage? Yes.
20. Largest amount loaned to one individual, company, society, or corporation,
    $46,000.
21. Date of annual meeting for choice of officers, third Wednesday in July.

OFFICERS.—President, Gustavus F. Davis; Vice-President, G. M. Bartholomew; Treasurer, John W. Stedman; Directors or Trustees, A. Spalding Porter, Henry Kellogg, Miles W. Graves, William Hamersley, Leverett Brainard, R. W. Farmer, D. W. C. Skilton.

STONINGTON SAVINGS BANK.

D. B. SPAULDING, Treasurer. INCORPORATED, 1850.

STATEMENT, OCTOBER 1, 1882.

LIABILITIES.		ASSETS.	
Whole Amount of Deposits,	$685,817.94	Loans on Real Estate, .	$312,780.02
Surplus Account, . .	26,102.55	Loans on Stocks and Bonds,	8,464.16
Interest Account, . .	9,942.55	Loans on Endorsed Notes, .	43,826.90
		United States Bonds, . .	35,437.50
		Town, City, & Boro' Orders,	163.26
		Railroad Bonds, . . .	51,036.00
		Bank Stocks in Connecticut,	73,470.50
		Bank Stocks in other States,	15,600.00
		Real Estate by Foreclosure,	164,372.77
		Tax Account, . . .	3,052.86
		Insurance Account, . .	98.84
		Expense Account, . .	6,120.27
		Cash in Bank, . . .	7,439.96
Total Liabilities, . .	$721,863.04	Total Assets, . .	$721,863.04

INVESTMENTS.

DESCRIPTION.	PAR VALUE.	COST.	MARKET VALUE.
UNITED STATES BONDS.			
4s of 1907, Coupon, ... $	35,000.00	35,437.50	41,518.75
TOWN, CITY, AND BOROUGH ORDERS.			
Stonington Borough Orders, 6 per cent., .	163.26	163.26	163.26
RAILROAD BONDS.			
New York Central, 6 per cent., .	4,000.00	3,720.00	4,110.00
Michigan Central, 8 "	1,000.00	1,000.00	1,000.00
Joilet & Northern Indiana, 7 " .	8,000.00	7,700.00	8,800.00
Chicago, Burlington & Quincy, 8 " .	16,000.00	15,324.75	16,320.00
New York & Harlem, 7 " .	5,000.00	4,750.00	6,550.00
Chicago, Rock Island & Pacific, 6 " .	15,000.00	18,541.25	19,050.00
BANK STOCKS.			
40 shares Fourth National, New York, .	4,000.00	4,000.00	5,120.00
50 " Am. Exch. " "	5,000.00	5,000.00	6,550.00
66 " Central " " .	6,600.00	6,600.00	8,250.00
200 " First " Stonington, .	20,000.00	20,000.00	28,000.00
40 " City " Hartford, .	4,000.00	4,000.00	4,000.00
161 " Uncas " Norwich, .	8,050.00	10,065.00	10,065.00
35 " Norwich " " .	3,500.00	4,060.00	4,060.00
173 " First " " .	17,300.00	19,044.00	20,068.00
291 " Merchants " " .	11,640.00	11,801.50	11,981.00
30 " Thames " " .	3,000.00	4,500.00	4,560.00

STONINGTON SAVINGS BANK.—CONTINUED.

MISCELLANEOUS ITEMS.

1. Number of depositors having $500 or less,   816; total amount, $106,444.95
2. Number of depositors having over $500 and
   less than $1,000, ...   156; total amount,   120,546.62
3. Number of depositors having $1,000 and not
   over $2,000, ...   121; total amount,   147,093.32
4. Number of depositors having over $2,000,   76; total amount,   311,733.05

5. Total number of depositors,   .   .   . 1,169; total deposits, $685,817.94
6. Largest amount due a single depositor, $13,963.02.
7. Number of accounts opened during the year, 138; number closed, 95.
8. Amount of income received during the year, $38,861.54.
9. Amount of dividends declared during the year, $26,096.08.
10. Amount deposited, including interest credited, the past year, $83,613.33.
11. Amount withdrawn during the year, $60,655.26.
12. Increase of deposits the past year, $22,958.57.
13. Amount carried to surplus or profit and loss during the year, $1,822.84.
14. Rate of dividend the last year, 4 per cent.; when paid, June 15th and Dec. 15th.
15. State tax during the past year, $1,067.90; U. S. tax, $598.40.
16. Total office expenses the past year, including salaries, $2,263.40.
17. Net amount of income during the year from real estate owned, $1,359.58.
18. Amount of assets yielding no income during the year, $48,233.93.
19. Are all loans upon real estate secured by first mortgage? Yes.
20. Largest amount loaned to one individual, company, society, or corporation,
    $27,000.
21. Date of annual meeting for choice of officers, June 26, 1882.

OFFICERS. — President, O. B. Grant; Vice-President, Moses Pendleton; Treasurer, D. B. Spalding; Directors or Trustees, Oliver B. Grant, Richard A. Wheeler, Joseph E. Smith, Alanson Brown, Moses Pendleton, Lodowick N. Latham, Thomas Burtch, Oliver D. Chesebro, Daniel B. Spalding; Auditors, Moses A. Pendleton, Horace N. Trumbull,

SUFFIELD SAVINGS BANK.

Samuel White, Treasurer.   Incorporated, 1869.

STATEMENT, OCTOBER 1, 1882.

LIABILITIES.		ASSETS.	
Whole Amt. of Deposits,	$134,552.08	Loans on Real Estate, .	$75,975.00
Surplus Account, . .	7,320.10	Loans on Stocks and Bonds,	2,700.00
Interest Account, . .	1,176.01	Loans on Endorsed Notes,	2,825.00
		United States Bonds, .	4,000.00
		Railroad Bonds, . .	14,105.00
		Bank Stocks in Connecticut,	36,960.00
		Bank Stocks in other States,	5,000.00
		Real Estate by Foreclosure,	1,025.00
		Expense Account, . .	75.00
		Cash in Bank, . . .	383.19
Total Liabilities, .	$143,048.19	Total Assets, . .	$143,048.19

INVESTMENTS.

DESCRIPTION.	PAR VALUE.	COST.	MARKET VALUE.
UNITED STATES BONDS.			
4s of 1907, Coupon, ... $	4,000.00	4,080.00	4,600.00
RAILROAD BONDS.			
5 Bonds Connecticut Western, . . .	5,000 00	1,500.00	1,500.00
8 " New York Central, ...	8,000.00	8,160.00	8,160.00
4 " " Elevated, . . .	4,000.00	4,605.00	4,605.00
BANK STOCKS.			
241 shares First National Suffield, .	24,100.00	24,100.00	24,100.00
60 " City " Hartford, .	6,000.00	5,900.00	5,100.00
28 " First " "	2,800.00	2,800.00	3,220.00
40 " Conn. River Bank. Co., " .	2,000.00	2,160.00	2,000.00
50 " Merchants National, Norwich, .	2,000.00	2,000.00	2,000.00
50 " Marine " New York,	5,000.00	5,000.00	7,000.00

MISCELLANEOUS ITEMS.

1. Number of depositors having $500 or less, 466; total amount, $49,894.39
2. Number of depositors having over $500 and less than $1,000, ... 40; total amount, 27,393.41
3. Number of depositors having $1,000 and not over $2,000, ... 37; total amount, 50,782.12
4. Number of depositors having over $2,000, 3; total amount, 6,482.16
5. Total number of depositors, . . . 546; total deposits, $134,552.08
6. Largest amount due a single depositor, $2,364.95.
7. Number of accounts opened during the year, 95; number closed, 60.
8. Amount of income received during the year, $3,069.37.
9. Amount of dividends declared during the year, $7,403.93.

SUFFIELD SAVINGS BANK.—Continued.

MISCELLANEOUS ITEMS.—Continued.

10. Amount deposited, including interest credited, the past year, $28,554.77.
11. Amount withdrawn during the year, $19,556.30.
12. Increase of deposits the past year, $8,998.47.
13. Amount carried to surplus or profit and loss during the year, none.
14. Rate of dividend the last year, 6 per cent.; when paid, Feb. 1st and Aug. 1st.
15. State tax during the past year, $170.03; U. S. tax, $1.21.
16. Total office expenses the past year, including salaries, $492.52.
17. Net amount of income during the year from real estate owned, $100.
18. Amount of assets yielding no income during the year, $5,000.
19. Are all loans upon real estate secured by first mortgage? Yes.
20. Largest amount loaned to one individual, company, society, or corporation, $5,500.
21. Date of annual meeting for choice of officers, first Wednesday in July.

OFFICERS.—President, William H. Fuller; Treasurer, Samuel White; Directors or Trustees, William H. Fuller, Albert Austin, Alfred Spencer, Horatio K. Nelson, Martin J. Sheldon, Mathew T. Newton, M. D., Samuel White, Samuel McAuley, Albert J. Miller, Benjamin F. Hastings, Clinton Phelps, Ralph P. Mather.

·THOMASTON SAVINGS BANK.

GEORGE H. STOUGHTON, Treasurer.   INCORPORATED, 1874.

STATEMENT, OCTOBER 1, 1882.

LIABILITIES.		ASSETS.	
Whole Amount of Deposits,	$264,152.65	Loans on Real Estate, .	$158,800.00
Surplus Account, . .	7,415.86	Loans on Stocks and Bonds,	18,500.00
Interest Account, . .	3,472.78	Loans on Endorsed Notes, .	43,509.00
Premium Account, . .	615.00	Town, City, and Corp. B'ds,	5,300.00
		Bank Stocks in Connecticut,	45,578.50
		Expense Account; . .	553.20
		Cash in Bank, . . .	1,259.79
		Cash on hand, . . .	2,155.80
Total Liabilities, . .	$275,656.29	Total Assets, . .	$275,656.29

INVESTMENTS.

DESCRIPTION.	PAR VALUE.	COST.	MARKET VALUE.
TOWN, CITY, AND CORPORATION BONDS.			
Town of Middletown, ... $	5,000.00	5,300.00	5,500.00
BANK STOCKS.			
10 shares Middlesex County, Middletown, .	1,000.00	1,240.00	1,240.00
15 " Birmingham, Birmingham, . .	1,500.00	2,415.00	2,415.00
50 " Manufactures, Waterbury, . .	5,000.00	5,000.00	5,200.00
105 " Waterbury, Waterbury, . .	5,250.00	8,620.00	8,620.00
40 " National Pahquioque, Danbury, .	4,000.00	5,160.00	5,160.00
50 " Winsted, Winsted, . . .	5,000.00	5,400.00	5,400.00
14 " First National, West Meriden, .	1,400.00	1,596.00	1,596.00
25 " Home " " .	2,500.00	3,025.00	3,025.00
5 " Yale " New Haven, .	500.00	490.00	600.00
23 " Second " " .	2,300.00	3,662.50	3,680.00
65 " Merchants, Norwich, . . .	2,600.00	2,705.00	2,705.00
5 " National Exchange, Hartford, .	250.00	315.00	390.00
11 " New Britain, New Britain, . .	1,100.00	1,650.00	1,650.00
40 " Bristol, Bristol, ...	4,000.00	4,300.00	5,000.00

MISCELLANEOUS ITEMS.

1. Number of depositors having $500 or less, 1,022; total amount, $112,927.21
2. Number of depositors having over $500 and less than $1,000, ... 101; total amount, 69,821.58
3. Number of depositors having $1,000 and not over $2,000, ... 61; total amount, 81,403.86
4. Number of depositors having over $2,000, 0; total amount, 0.00
5. Total number of depositors, . . . 1,184; total deposits, $264,152.65
6. Largest amount due a single depositor, $1,950.28.
7. Number of accounts opened during the year, 816; number closed, 160.
8. Amount of income received during the year, $16,787.52.

THOMASTON SAVINGS BANK.—Continued.

MISCELLANEOUS ITEMS.—Continued.

9. Amount of dividends declared during the year, $11,651.51.
10. Amount deposited, including interest credited, the past year, $102,971.53.
11. Amount withdrawn during the year, $82,479.68.
12. Increase of deposits the past year, $20,491.85.
13. Amount carried to surplus or profit and loss during the year, $153.
14. Rate of dividend the last year, 5 per cent., when paid, January and July.
15. State tax during the past year, $491; U. S. tax, none.
16. Total office expenses the past year, including salaries, $1,110.82.
17. Net amount of income during the year from real estate owned, none.
18. Amount of assets yielding no income during the year, none.
19. Are all loans upon real estate secured by first mortgage? Yes.
20. Largest amount loaned to one individual, company, society, or corporation, $150,000.
21. Date of annual meeting for choice of officers, last Wednesday in June.

OFFICERS.—President, Miles Morse; Treasurer, Geo. H. Stoughton; Directors or Trustees, Miles Morse, Aaron Thomas, Edwin P. Parker, G. A. Stoughton, Michael Ryan, Geo. H. Stoughton, I. B. Woodward, G. B. Pierpont, F. M. Foster.

TORRINGTON SAVINGS BANK.

ISAAC W. BROOKS, Treasurer.   INCORPORATED, 1868.

STATEMENT, OCTOBER 1, 1882.

LIABILITIES.		ASSETS.	
Whole Amt. of Deposits, .	$265,212.63	Loans on Real Estate, . . .	$109,215.00
Surplus Account, . .	2,344.20	Loans on Stocks and Bonds,	12,150.00
Interest Account, . .	3,103.29	Loans on Endorsed Notes, .	44,677.63
		United States Bonds, . .	51,000.00
		Town, City, & Corp'n Bds.,	18,600.00
		Town, City, & Boro' Orders,	11,000.00
		Bank Stocks in Connecticut,	10,700.00
		Cash on hand, . . .	13,317.49
Total Liabilities, . . .	$270,660.12	Total Assets, . . .	$270,660.12

INVESTMENTS.

DESCRIPTION.	PAR VALUE.	COST.	MARKET VALUE.
UNITED STATES BONDS.			
4½s of 1891, Registered, ... $	20,000.00	21,000.00	22,550.00
4s of 1907, Registered, ...	20,000.00	20,000.00	23,725.00
Three per cents., ...	10,000.00	10,000.00	10,000.00
TOWN, CITY, AND CORPORATION BONDS.			
Town of Saybrook, 5 per cent., . .	10,000.00	10,000.00	10,500.00
City of Boston, 1890, 4 " . .	2,000.00	2,000.00	2,070.00
" Providence, 1900, 5 " . .	3,000.00	3,300.00	3,510.00
" " 1906, 5 " . .	3,000.00	3,300.00	3,525.00
TOWN, CITY, AND BOROUGH ORDERS.			
Town of Torrington, ...	6,000.00	6,000.00	6,000.00
" Thomaston, ...	5,000.00	5,000.00	5,000.00
BANK STOCKS.			
55 shares First National, Litchfield, . .	5,500.00	6,050.00	6,875.00
31 · " Hurlbut " Winsted, . .	3,100.00	4,650.00	4,650.00

MISCELLANEOUS ITEMS.

1. Number of depositors having $500 or less,   966; total amount, $100,498.21
2. Number of depositors having over $500 and
     less than $1,000,   108; total amount,   73,772.63
3. Number of depositors having $1,000 and not
     over $2,000, ...   58; total amount,   74,159.54
4. Number of depositors having over $2,000, .   7; total amount,   16,782.25

5. Total number of depositors, . .   1,139; total deposits, $265,212.63
6. Largest amount due a single depositor, $2,641.72.
7. Number of accounts opened during the year, 266; number closed, 195.
8. Amount of income received during the year, $12,608.92.

TORRINGTON SAVINGS BANK.—Continued.

9. Amount of dividends declared during the year, $9,149.28.
10. Amount deposited, including interest credited, the past year, $108,369.55.
11. Amount withdrawn during the year, $80,230.69.
12. Increase of deposits the past year, $28,138.86.
13. Amount carried to surplus or profit and loss during the year, $624.54.
14. Rate of dividend the last year, 4 per cent.; when paid, January and July.
15. State tax during the past year, $469.56; U. S. tax, none.
16. Total office expenses the past year, including salaries, $842.54.
17. Net amount of income during the year from real estate owned, none.
18. Amount of assets yielding no income during the year, none.
19. Are all loans upon real estate secured by first mortgage? Yes.
20. Largest amount loaned to one individual, company, society, or corporation, $13,000.
21. Date of annual meeting for choice of officers, second Monday in July.

Officers.—President, Joseph F. Calhoun; Treasurer, Isaac W. Brooks; Directors or Trustees, Joseph F. Calhoun, Ransom Holley, Bradley R. Agard, Lyman W. Coe, Nelson Allyn, Elisha Turner, Isaac W. Brooks.

UNION SAVINGS BANK.

L. P. TREADWELL, Treasurer.   INCORPORATED, 1866.

STATEMENT, OCTOBER 1, 1882.

LIABILITIES.		ASSETS.	
Whole Amount of Deposits,	$600,599.29	Loans on Real Estate, .	$297,561.00
Surplus Account, . .	4,000.00	Loans on Stocks and Bonds,	6,150.00
Interest Account, . .	21,582.18	Loans on Endorsed Notes, .	212,782.08
		Town, City, & Boro' Orders,	18,500.00
		School District Orders, .	18,878.95
		Bank Stocks in Connecticut,	17,875.00
		Real Estate by Foreclosure,	30,000.00
		Banking House, . . .	8,800.00
		Tax Account, } Insurance Account, } .	284.49
		Cash in Bank, . . .	11,905.37
		Cash on hand, . . .	3,444.58
Total Liabilities, . .	$626,181.47	Total Assets, . .	$626,181.47

INVESTMENTS.

DESCRIPTION.	PAR VALUE.	COST.	MARKET VALUE.
TOWN, CITY, AND BOROUGH ORDERS.			
Notes, ... $	18,500.00	18,500.00	18,500.00
SCHOOL DISTRICT ORDERS.			
Notes, ...	18,875.00	18,875.00	18,875.00
BANK STOCKS.			
17 shares Danbury National, ...	1,700.00	2,550.00	2,550.00
95 " National Pahquioque, . . .	9,500.00	10,325.00	12,825.00
50 " City National, South Norwalk, .	5,000.00	5,000.00	5,000.00

MISCELLANEOUS ITEMS.

1. Number of depositors having $500 or less, 1,979; total amount, $269,769.29
2. Number of depositors having over $500 and less than $1,000, ... 189; total amount, 133,685.00
3. Number of depositors having $1,000 and not over $2,000, ... 114; total amount, 155,885.00
4. Number of depositors having over $2,000, 18; total amount, 41,260.00

Total number of depositors, . . . 2,300; total deposits, $600,599.29
Largest amount due a single depositor, $3,000.
Number of accounts opened during the year, 700; number closed, 400.
Amount of income received during the year, $32,097.89.
Amount of dividends declared during the year, $20,577.04.
10. Amount deposited, including interest credited, the past year, $400,582.54.
11. Amount withdrawn during the year, $330,215.36.
12. Increase of deposits the past year, $70,367.18.

UNION SAVINGS BANK.—Continued.

MISCELLANEOUS ITEMS.—Continued.

13. Amount carried to surplus or profit and loss during the year, $1,500.
14. Rate of dividend the last year, 4 per cent.; when paid, April 1st and October 1st.
15. State tax during the past year, $1,194.34; U. S. tax, $27.87.
16. Total office expenses the past year, including salaries, $1,900.
17. Net amount of income during the year from real estate owned, $1,650.
18. Amount of assets yielding no income during the year, $3,500.
19. Are all loans upon real estate secured by first mortgage? Yes.
20. Largest amount loaned to one individual, company, society, or corporation, $60,000.
21. Date of annual meeting for choice of officers, second Thursday in July.

Officers.—President, S. C. Holley; Treasurer, L. P. Treadwell; Directors or Trustees, Almon Judd, F. H. Austin, Martin H. Griffing, Jr., William J. Rider, Norman Hodge, David G. Penfield, James B. Wildman.

WATERBURY SAVINGS BANK.

F. J. KINGSBURY, Treasurer. INCORPORATED, 1850.

STATEMENT, OCTOBER 1, 1882.

LIABILITIES.		ASSETS.	
Whole Amt. of Deposits,	$1,958,853.54	Loans on Real Estate, . .	$974,522.80
Surplus Account, . .	100,000.00	Loans on Stocks and Bonds,	284,200.00
Interest Account, . .	22,803.60	Loans on Endorsed Notes, .	263,764.20
Over and Short, . .	201.13	United States Bonds, . .	201,100.00
		State Bonds, . . .	200.00
		Town, City, and Corp. B'ds,	53,000.00
		School District Orders, .	20,000.00
		Railroad Bonds, . . .	50,000.00
		Bank Stocks in Connecticut,	72,750.00
		Real Estate by Foreclosure,	26,742.38
		Cash in Bank, . . .	135,578.89
Total Liabilities, .	$2,081,858.27	Total Assets, .	$2,081,858.27

INVESTMENTS.

DESCRIPTION.	PAR VALUE.	COST.	MARKET VALUE.
UNITED STATES BONDS.			
5s of 1881, Registered (extended 3½ per cent.),	$ 200,000.00	200,000.00	200,500.00
4s of 1907, Coupon, ...	100.00	110.00	118.00
Currency 6s, ...	1,000.00	1,250.00	1,310.00
STATE BONDS.			
Connecticut, ...	200.00	212.00	212.00
TOWN, CITY, AND CORPORATION BONDS.			
Waterbury City, 7s, . . .	41,000.00	41,000.00	45,920.00
Cincinnati, Ohio, " 6s, ...	12,000.00	13,682.71	13,682.71
SCHOOL DISTRICT ORDERS.			
Waterbury, Center District, ...	20,000.00	20,000.00	20,000.00
RAILROAD BONDS.			
New York, Providence & Boston, 4s, . .	50,000.00	50,000.00	50,000.00
BANK STOCKS.			
400 shares Citizens National, Waterbury,	40,000.00	41,010.00	50,000.00
155 " Waterbury " "	7,750.00	8,800.00	11,625.00
40 " First " Portland, .	4,000.00	4,326.00	4,320.00
50 " Pahquioque " Danbury, .	5,000.00	6,150.00	6,150.00
100 " First " Litchfield, .	10,000.00	12,675.00	12,675.00
20 ' " " Meriden, .	2,000.00	2,340.00	2,340.00
40 " " " "	4,000.00	4,680.00	4,680.00

WATERBURY SAVINGS BANK.—Continued.

MISCELLANEOUS ITEMS.

1. Number of depositors having $500 or less, . 3,775; total amount, $771,253.54
2. Number of depositors having over $500 and
    less than $1,000, ... 547; total amount, 350,800.00
3. Number of depositors having $1,000 and not
    over $2,000, ... 328; total amount, 409,000.00
4. Number of depositors having over $2,000, . 150; total amount, 427,800.00

5. Total number of depositors, . . . 4,800; total deposits, $1,958,853.54
6. Largest amount due a single depositor, $10,069.80.
7. Number of accounts opened during the year, 875; number closed, —.
8. Amount of income received during the year, $109,466.87.
9. Amount of dividends declared during the year, $91,099.37.
10. Amount deposited, including interest credited, the past year, $416,031.77.
11. Amount withdrawn during the year, $339,976.06.
12. Increase of deposits the past year, $76,055.71.
13. Amount carried to surplus or profit and loss during the year, $6,861.79.
14. Rate of dividend the last year, 5 per cent.; when paid, Feb. 1st and Aug. 1st.
15. State tax during the year, $4,462; U. S. tax, none.
16. Total office expenses the past year, including salaries, $5,000.
17. Net amount of income during the year from real estate owned, $1,186.08.
18. Amount of assets yielding no income during the year, none.
19. Are all loans upon real estate secured by first mortgage? Yes.
20. Largest amount loaned to one individual, company, society, or corporation, $60,000.
21. Date of annual meeting for choice of officers, second Wednesday in June.

OFFICERS.—President, Willard Spencer; Treasurer, F. J. Kingsbury; Directors or Trustees, Willard Spencer, Nathan Dikeman, J. M. Burrall, C. B. Merriman, J. W. Smith, E. L. Frisbie, A. S. Chase, F. L. Curtiss, F. J. Kingsbury.

WESTPORT SAVINGS BANK.

B. L. WOODWORTH, Treasurer.   INCORPORATED, 1860.

STATEMENT, OCTOBER 1, 1882.

LIABILITIES.		ASSETS.	
Whole Amount of Deposits,	$81,904.22	Loans on Real Estate, . .	$71,975.00
Surplus Account, . .	5,141.33	Town Orders, . . .	5,000.00
Interest Account, . .	1,843.00	Bank Stocks in other States,	9,200.00
		Real Estate by Foreclosure,	2,079.94
		Expense Account, . .	68.50
		Cash in Bank, . . .	565.11
Total Liabilities, .	$88,888.55	Total Assets, . .	$88,888.55

INVESTMENTS.

DESCRIPTION.	PAR VALUE.	COST.	MARKET VALUE.
TOWN ORDERS.			
Westport, Town, ... $	5,000.00	5,000.00	5,000.00
BANK STOCKS.			
10 shares National Park, New York, . .	1,000.00	1,000.00	1,580.00
17 " Continental " . .	1,700.00	1,700.00	1,955.00
50 " Fourth National, " . .	5,000.00	5,000.00	6,150.00
15 " Amer. Exchange, " . .	1,500.00	1,500.00	1,987.50

MISCELLANEOUS ITEMS.

1. Number of depositors having $500 or less, 381; total amount, $40,272.19
2. Number of depositors having over $500 and less than $1,000, ... 25; total amount, 16,272.14
3. Number of depositors having $1,000 and not over $2,000, ... 13; total amount, 18,855.07
4. Number of depositors having over $2,000, . 2; total amount, 6,504.82

5. Total number of depositors, . . . 421; total deposits, $81,904.22
6. Largest amount due a single depositor, $4,018.78.
7. Number of accounts opened during the year, 33; number closed, 44.
8. Amount of income received during the year, $5,150.95.
9. Amount of dividends declared during the year, $3,758.31.
10. Amount deposited, including interest credited, the past year, $9,226.94.
11. Amount withdrawn during the year, $14,663.33.
12. Increase of deposits the past year, none.
13. Amount carried to surplus or profit and loss during the year, $736.14.
14. Rate of dividend the last year, 4¼ per cent.; when paid, 2 per cent. January and 2¼ per cent. July, 1882.
15. State tax during the past year, $86.02; U. S. tax, $12.98.
16. Total office expenses the past year, including salaries, $317.94.
17. Net amount of income during the year from real estate owned, $48.
18. Amount of assets yielding no income during the year, $500.

WESTPORT SAVINGS BANK.—Continued.

MISCELLANEOUS ITEMS.—Continued.

19. Are all loans upon real estate secured by first mortgage?   Yes.
20. Largest amount loaned to one individual, company, society, or corporation,
     $7,000.
21. Date of annual meeting for choice of officers, July 14, 1882.

OFFICERS.—President, E. W. Taylor; Vice-Presidents, E. S. Downes, George
S. Adams, W. E. Dikeman; Treasurer, B. L. Woodworth; Directors or Trustees,
E. A. Williams, Wm. H. Marvin, O. I. Jones, H. Staples, H. A. Ogden, Edward
Wheeler.

WILLIMANTIC SAVINGS INSTITUTE.

HENRY F. ROYCE, Treasurer.   INCORPORATED, 1842.

STATEMENT, OCTOBER 1, 1882.

LIABILITIES.		ASSETS.	
Whole Amount of Deposits,	$674,827.46	Loans on Real Estate, . .	$251,875.00
Surplus Account, . .	9,043.34	Loans on Stocks, B'ds, etc.,	51,422.60
Interest Account, . .	17,494.44	Loans on Endorsed Notes, .	202,133.75
Rent Account, . . .	1,537.50	School District Orders, .	2,000.00
		Bank Stocks in Connecticut,	44,190.00
		Bank Stocks in other States,	3,000.00
		Real Estate by Foreclosure,	47,975.00
		Banking House, . . .	24,960.00
		Tax Account, . . .	1,293.37
		Expense Account, . .	1,656.03
		Cash in Bank, . . .	65,116.60
		Cash on hand, . . .	7,280.39
Total Liabilities, . .	$702,902.74	Total Assets, . .	$702,902.74

INVESTMENTS.

DESCRIPTION.	PAR VALUE.	COST.	MARKET VALUE.
SCHOOL DISTRICT ORDERS.			
First, Windham, ... $	2,000.00	2,000.00	2,000.00
BANK STOCKS.			
30 shares Bank of America, New York, .	3,000.00	3,000.00	4,800.00
20 " Ætna National, Hartford, .	2,000.00	2,000.00	2,600.00
50 " First " Norwich, .	5,000.00	5,750.00	5,750.00
100 " Second " " .	10,000.00	11,500.00	12,000.00
83 " Uncas " " .	4,150.00	6,250.00	4,980.00
41 " Merchants " " .	1,640.00	1,640.00	1,640.00
60 " Nat. Bk. of Commerce, N. London,	6,000.00	6,000.00	7,500.00
64 " Windham National, Willimantic, .	6,400.00	6,400.00	7,680.00
40 " Winsted " Winsted, .	4,000.00	4,200.00	4,200.00
50 " Tolland Co. " Tolland, .	5,000.00	5,000.00	5,000.00

MISCELLANEOUS ITEMS.

1. Number of depositors having $500 or less, 1,974; total amount, $255,887.93
2. Number of depositors having $500 and less
   than $1,000, ... 254; total amount, 180,289.07
3. Number of depositors having $1,000 and
   not over $2,000, ... 130; total amount, 178,328.36
4. Number of depositors having over $2,000, 26; total amount, 60,322.10
5. Total number of depositors, . . . 2,884; total deposits, $674,827.46
6. Largest amount due a single depositor, $4,312.67.
7. Number of accounts opened during the year, 410; number closed, 288.
8. Amount of income received during the year, $36,002.35.

12

WILLIMANTIC SAVINGS INSTITUTE.—Continued.

MISCELLANEOUS ITEMS.—Continued.

9. Amount of dividends declared during the year, $23,422.04.
10. Amount deposited, including interest credited, the past year, $219,767.28.
11. Amount withdrawn during the year, $165,534.10.
12. Increase of deposits the past year, $54,233.18.
13. Amount carried to surplus or profit and loss during the year, $6,820.01.
14. Rate of dividend the last year, 4 per cent.; when paid, April 1st and October 1st.
15. State tax during the past year, $1,237.59; U. S. tax, $27.67.
16. Total office expenses the past year, including salaries, $2,146.59.
17. Net amount of income during the year from real estate owned, $2,610.21.
18. Amount of assets yielding no income during the year, $8,250.
19. Are all loans upon real estate secured by first mortgage? Yes.
20. Largest amount loaned to one individual, company, society, or corporation, $32,000.
21. Date of annual meeting for choice of officers, third Monday in June.

OFFICERS.—President, Whiting Hayden; Treasurer, Henry F. Royce; Directors, Mason Lincoln, Eugene S. Boss, George C. Martin, Charles E. Carpenter, Charles A. Capen.

WINDHAM COUNTY SAVINGS BANK, DANIELSONVILLE.

ANTHONY AMES, Treasurer.   INCORPORATED, 1864.

STATEMENT, OCTOBER, 1, 1882.

LIABILITIES.		ASSETS.	
Whole Am't of Deposits, .	$855,809.87	Loans on Real Estate, . .	$377,325.00
Surplus Account, . .	7,455.37	Loans on Stocks and Bonds,	132,000.00
Interest Account, . .	11,857.01	Loans on Endorsed Notes, .	65,528.34
		United States Bonds, . .	2,600.00
		Town, City, and Corp. B'ds,	26,990.00
		Town, City, and Boro' Orders,	22,986.85
		Bank Stocks in Connecticut,	54,300.00
		Bank Stocks in other States,	7,500.00
		Real Estate by Foreclosure,	120,560.57
		Banking House, . . .	16,350.00
		Tax Account, . . .	2,296.84
		Expense Account, . .	1,170.25
		Premium Account, . .	13,459.01
		Cash in Bank, . . .	26,677.69
		Cash on hand, . . .	5,378.20
Total Liabilities, .	$875,122.25	Total Assets, . .	$875,122.25

INVESTMENTS.

DESCRIPTION.	PAR VALUE.	COST.	MARKET VALUE.
UNITED STATES BONDS.			
6s of 1881 (extended 3½ per cent.), . . . $	2,500.00	2,500.00	2,500.00
4s of 1907, coupon, ...	100.00	100.00	118.00
TOWN, CITY, AND CORPORATION BONDS.			
Cincinnati, 7$\frac{3}{10}$ per cent., 1902, . . .	20,000.00	26,990.00	26,990.00
TOWN, CITY, AND BOROUGH ORDERS.			
Town of Killingly, ...	18,720.34	18,720.34	18,720.34
Borough of Danielsonville, ...	4,400.00	4,400.00	4,400.00
BANK STOCKS.			
138 shares First National, Killingly,	13,800.00	13,800.00	16,560.00
55 " Windham Co. " Brooklyn,	5,500.00	5,500.00	6,600.00
75 " Ninth " New York,	7,500.00	7,500.00	9,000.00
100 " Norwich " . . .	10,000.00	10,000.00	12,000.00
50 " First " Norwich,	5,000.00	5,000.00	6,000.00
100 " Second " "	10,000.00	10,000.00	12,500.00
100 " Thames " "	10,000.00	10,000.00	15,000.00

WINDHAM COUNTY SAVINGS BANK.---Continued.

MISCELLANEOUS ITEMS.

1. Number of depositors having $500 or less, 2,119; total amount, $282,899.05
2. Number of depositors having over $500 and
   less than $1,000, ... 332; total amount, 226,015.70
3. Number of depositors having $1,000 and not
   over $2,000, ... 224; total amount, 302,382.76
4. Number of depositors having over $2,000, . 19; total amount, 44,512.36

5. Total number of depositors, ... 2,694; total deposits, $855,809.87
6. Largest amount due a single depositor, $4,435.67.
7. Number of accounts opened during the year, 395; number closed, 313.
8. Amount of income received during the year, $32,987.28.
9. Amount of dividends declared during the year, $31,616.02.
10. Amount deposited, including interest credited, the past year, $187,797.96.
11. Amount withdrawn during the year, $146,412.50.
12. Increase of deposits the past year, $40,385.46.
13. Amount carried to surplus or profit and loss during the year, $2,067.63.
14. Rate of dividend the last year, 4 per cent.; when paid, April and October.
15. State tax during the past year, $1,598.94; United States tax, none.
16. Total office expenses the past year, including salaries, $2,613.98.
17. Net amount of income during the year from real estate owned, $3,000.
18. Amount of assets yielding no income during the year, $90,000.
19. Are all loans upon real estate secured by first mortgage? Yes.
20. Largest amount loaned to one individual, company, society, or corporation,
    $50,000.
21. Date of annual meeting for choice of officers, July.

Officers. — President, J. D. Bigelow; Vice-President, Wm. H. Chollar;
Treasurer, Anthony Ames; Directors or Trustees, Lysander Warren, E. L. Cundall,
J. A. Williams, Simon S. Waldo, Samuel Hutchins, E. H. Jacobs, Almond M.
Paine, Rowland R. James.

WINDSOR LOCKS SAVINGS BANK.

A. W. CONVERSE, Treasurer. INCORPORATED, 1871.

STATEMENT, OCTOBER 1, 1882.

LIABILITIES.		ASSETS.	
Whole Amount of Deposits,	$60,376.52	Loans on Real Estate,	$35,941.36
Surplus Account, }Interest Account, }	1,040.23	Loans on Endorsed Notes,	5,560.00
		Bank Stocks in Connecticut,	13,643.50
		Safe, etc.,	510.25
		Cash in Bank,	4,798.01
		Cash on hand,	963.63
Total Liabilities,	$61,416.75	Total Assets,	$61,416.75

INVESTMENTS.

DESCRIPTION.	PAR VALUE.	COST.	MARKET VALUE.
BANK STOCKS.			
50 shares First National, Suffield,	5,000.00	5,250.00	6,000.00
42 " " " Hartford,	4,200.00	4,196.50	5,324.00
40 " City " "	4,000.00	3,897.00	3,680.00
4 " American " "	200.00	300.00	300.00

MISCELLANEOUS ITEMS.

1. Number of depositors having $500 or less, 415; total amount, $28,384.32
2. Number of depositors having over $500 and less than $1,000, 28; total amount, 17,862.29
3. Number of depositors having $1,000 and not over $2,000, 5; total amount, 6,779.30
4. Number of depositors having over $2,000, 3; total amount, 7,350.61
5. Total number of depositors, 451; total deposits, $60,376.52
6. Largest amount due a single depositor, $2,699.81.
7. Number of accounts opened during the year, 102; number closed, 79.
8. Amount of income received during the year, $2,948.57.
9. Amount of dividends declared during the year, $2,314.21.
10. Amount deposited, including interest credited, the past year, $27,555.71.
11. Amount withdrawn during the year, $24,633.73.
12. Increase of deposits the past year, $2,921.98.
13. Amount carried to surplus or profit and loss during the year, none.
14. Rate of dividend the last year, 4 per cent.; when paid, April and October.
15. State tax during the past year, $17.63; U. S. tax, $3.62.
16. Total office expenses the past year, including salaries, $370.25.
17. Net amount of income during the year from real estate owned, none.

WINDSOR LOCKS SAVINGS BANK.—Continued.

MISCELLANEOUS ITEMS.—Continued.

18. Amount of assets yielding no income during the year, none.
19. Are all loans upon real estate secured by first mortgage? Yes.
20. Largest amount loaned to one individual, company, society, or corporation, $5,000.
21. Date of annual meeting for choice of officers, second Thursday in July.

OFFICERS.—President, Jabez H. Hayden; Treasurer, Alfred W. Converse; Directors or Trustees, J. H. Hayden, J. R. Montgomery, Allen Pease, T. B. Persse, James Colton, Charles E. Chaffee, J. W. Johnson, E. D. Dexter, S. R. Burnap, James T. Coogan, George P. Clark, J. H. Adams, William Mather.

WINSTED SAVINGS BANK.

GEORGE S. ROWE, Treasurer.   INCORPORATED, 1860.

STATEMENT, OCTOBER 1, 1882.

LIABILITIES.		ASSETS.	
Whole Am't of Deposits,	$848,685.19	Loans on Real Estate, .	$407,432.80
Surplus Account,	60,000.00	Loans on Stocks and Bonds,	13,850.00
Interest Account,	14,840.37	Loans on Endorsed Notes, .	181,196.22
Prepaid Interest,	421.92	United States Bonds, .	54,000.00
Profit and Loss, .	2,413.62	Town, City, and Corp. B'ds,	192,500.00
		Town, City, and Boro' Orders,	500.00
		School District Orders,	5,780.00
		Railroad Bonds, .	5,000.00
		Railroad Stocks, .	2,900.00
		Bank Stocks in Connecticut,	9,800.00
		Bank Stocks in other States,	39,225.00
		Real Estate by Foreclosure,	5,163.66
		Banking House, .	6,000.00
		Expense Account,	536.76
		Western Real Estate Bonds,	19,499.12
		Cash in Bank,	29,369.90
		Cash on hand,	3,607.64
Total Liabilities, .	$926,361.10	Total Assets,	$926,361.10

INVESTMENTS.

DESCRIPTION.	PAR VALUE.	COST.	MARKET VALUE.
UNITED STATES BONDS.			
6s of 1881 (extended 3½ per cent.),	34,000.00	34,840.00	34,000.00
4s of 1907, registered,	10,000.00	10,000.00	11,950.00
4s of 1907, coupon, .	10,000.00	10,000.00	11,950.00
TOWN, CITY, AND CORPORATION BONDS.			
Cook County, Illinois,	4,000.00	4,000.00	4,800.00
Town of Hartford, Conn.,	30,000.00	30,000.00	31,200.00
" Winchester, "	133,500.00	133,500.00	140,175.00
Borough of Winsted, "	25,000.00	25,000.00	26,150.00
TOWN, CITY, AND BOROUGH ORDERS.			
Borough of Winsted,	500.00	500.00	500.00
SCHOOL DISTRICT ORDERS.			
Fourth of Winchester,	5,650.00	5,650.00	5,650.00
Ninth of Barkhamsted,	130.00	130.00	130.00
RAILROAD BONDS.			
Burlington & Missouri River, Land Mortgage,	5,000.00	5,900.00	5,900.00
RAILROAD STOCKS.			
Hartford & Connecticut Western,	6,000.00	8,800.00	3,120.00

WINSTED SAVINGS BANK.—Continued.

INVESTMENTS.—Continued.

DESCRIPTION.	PAR VALUE.	COST.	MARKET VALUE.
BANK STOCKS.			
98 shares Hurlbut National, Winsted, . . $	9,800.00	12,298.00	14,700.00
50 " Nat'l Bank of Commerce, New York,	5,000.00	5,000.00	7,450.00
60 " American Ex. National, "	6,000.00	6,000.00	7,740.00
53 " Import. & Trad., " "	5,300.00	5,300.00	13,515.00
37 " National Bank of Republic, "	3,700.00	3,700.00	4,810.00
40 " Fouth National, "	4,000.00	4,000.00	4,920.00
100 " Nat'l Mechanics Bank. Asso., "	5,000.00	5,000.00	5,000.00
25 " German American, "	1,875.00	2,500.00	1,743.75
50 " Hanover National, "	5,000.00	5,000.00	6,750.00
67 " Merchants " "	3,350.00	3,350.00	4,455.50

MISCELLANEOUS ITEMS.

1. Number of depositors having $500 or less, 2,674; total amount, $245,700.99
2. Number of depositors having over $500 and less than 1,000, ... 347; total amount, 240,061.54
3. Number of depositors having $1,000 and not over $2,000, ... 202; total amount, 268,925.83
4. Number of depositors having over $2,000, 39; total amount, 93,996.83
5. Total number of depositors, . . . 3,262; total deposits, $848,685.19
6. Largest amount due a single depositor, $6,205.35.
7. Number of accounts opened during the year, 525; number closed, 387.
8. Amount of income received during the year, $42,826.83.
9. Amount of dividends declared during the year, $36,705.96.
10. Amount deposited, including interest credited, the past year, $182,370.22.
11. Amount withdrawn during the year, $178,889.48.
12. Increase of deposits the past year, $3,480.74.
13. Amount carried to surplus or profit and loss during the year, none.
14. Rate of dividend the last year, 4¼ per cent.; when paid, 2 per cent. January, and 2¼ July.
15. State tax during the past year, $1,901.11; U. S. tax, none.
16. Total office expenses the past year, including salaries, $2,154.42.
17. Net amount of income during the year from real estate owned, $82.
18. Amount of assets yielding no income during the year, $25,374.12.
19. Are all loans upon real estate secured by first mortgage? Yes.
20. Largest amount loaned to one individual, company, society, or corporation, $25,000.
21. Date of annual meeting for choice of officers, third Wednesday in July.

OFFICERS.—President, John Hinsdale; Treasurer, George S. Rowe; Directors or Trustees, John Hinsdale, Henry G. Colt, Henry Gay, John G. Wetmore, Rufus E. Holmes, James R. Alvord, Caleb J. Camp.

WOODBURY SAVINGS BANK.

DAVID S. BULL, Treasurer.   INCORPORATED, 1872.

STATEMENT, OCTOBER 1, 1882.

LIABILITIES.		ASSETS.	
Whole Amount of Deposits,	$169,527.28	Loans on Real Estate, .	$143,303.64
Surplus Account, . .	6,071.62	Loans on Endorsed Notes, .	8,622.05
Interest Account, . .	3,551.18	Town, City, & Boro' Orders,	525.00
		Bank Stocks in Connecticut,	9,150.00
		Banking House, . . .	10,637.55
		Cash in Bank, . . .	378.46
		Cash on hand, . . .	6,533.38
Total Liabilities, . .	$179,150.08	Total Assets, . .	$179,150.08

INVESTMENTS.

DESCRIPTION.	PAR VALUE.	COST.	MARKET VALUE.
TOWN, CITY, AND BOROUGH ORDERS.			
Town of Woodbury, ... $	525.00	525.00	525.00
BANK STOCKS.			
100 shares Waterbury National, . . .	5,000.00	9,000.00	9,000.00
2 " " " . . .	100.00	150.00	150.00

MISCELLANEOUS ITEMS.

1. Number of depositors having $500 or less, 802; total amount, $84,115.65
2. Number of depositors having over $500 and less than $1,000, ... 68; total amount, 45,218.97
3. Number of depositors having $1,000 and not over $2,000, ... 23; total amount, 33,200.97
4. Number of depositors having over $2,000, . 3; total amount, 6,991.69
5. Total number of depositors, ... 896; total deposits, $169,527.28
6. Largest amount due a single depositor, $2,497.11.
7. Number of accounts opened during the year, 134; number closed, 135.
8. Amount of income received during the year, $8,019.34.
9. Amount of dividends declared during the year, $6,468.57.
10. Amount deposited, including interest credited, the past year, $39,600.52.
11. Amount withdrawn during the year, $37,185.95.
12. Increase of deposits the past year, $2,414.57.
13. Amount carried to surplus or profit and loss during the year, none.
14. Rate of dividend the last year, 4 per cent.; when paid, Jan. 15th and July 15th.
15. State tax during the year, $268.52; U. S. tax, $1.28.
16. Total office expenses the past year, including salaries, $403.75.
17. Net amount of income during the year from real estate owned, none.

WOODBURY SAVINGS BANK.—Continued.

MISCELLANEOUS ITEMS.—Continued.

18. Amount of assets yielding no income during the year, $5,800.
19. Are all loans upon real estate secured by first mortgage? Yes.
20. Largest amount loaned to one individual, company, society, or corporation, $8,500.
21. Date of annual meeting for choice of officers, Monday next after June 17th.

OFFICERS.—President, George B. Lewis; Treasurer, David S. Bull; Directors or Trustees, George B. Lewis, Edward Cowles, Horace D. Curtiss, George P. Allen, Michael F. Skelly, Scovill Nettleton, David C. Porter, Benjamin S. Russell, George C. Bradley.

TOWNSEND SAVINGS BANK, NEW HAVEN.

Report of the Receivers, on the 10th day of July, 1882, with a statement of the assets of the Bank, and an estimate of their values, together with a detailed report of their expenses from July 10, 1881, to July 10, 1882.

ASSETS.

DESCRIPTION.	PAR VALUE.	ESTIMATED VALUE.
Loans on Real Estate, unpaid and in process of foreclosure,	$14,898.00	$5,758.00
Loans on Stocks, Bonds, and Personal security,	336,322.00	300.00
J. T. Clark loan,	142,162.13	5,000.00
STOCKS AND BONDS OWNED BY THE BANK.		
139 First Mortgage Bonds, Little Rock, Pine Bluff & N. O. R. R.,	27,800.00	41,700.00
227 First Mortgage Bonds, Miss., Ohio & Red River R. R.,	45,400.00	68,100.00
97 First Mortgage Land Bonds,	19,400.00	No value.
70 Louisiana State Bonds,	14,000.00	No value.
725 Credit Mobilier Stock,	18,125.00	18,125.00
Adirondack Mortgage,	40,000.00	No value.
Office Fixtures,	13,000.00	1,000.00
Cash Items,	32,618.86	5,000.00
Arkansas Bond Account,	76,860.00	76,860.00
Arkansas Land Bond Account,	6,141.50	6,141.50
Credit Mobilier Stock Account,	711.40	711.40
Covington R. R. Bond Account,	25.00	25.00
Real Estate owned by Bank,	2,848.10	1,500.00
Continental Bank Account,	1,193.16	1,193.16
Deposit in National New Haven Bank,	16,211.80	16,211.80
" Tradesmans Bank,	16,822.89	16,822.89
" Yale National Bank,	66.32	66.32
" Saybrook National Bank,	21,308.08	21,308.08
Cash and Cash Items,	2,222.45	2,222.45
Totals,	$848,136.19	$288,045.60

Expenses paid from July 10, 1881, to July 10, 1882.

Insurance, ... $30.00

T. E. DOOLITTLE, } Receivers of the
J. E. REDFIELD, } Townsend Savings Bank.

Personally appeared T. E. Doolittle and J. E. Redfield, Receivers of the Townsend Savings Bank, and made oath that the foregoing statement is true according to their best knowledge and belief, before me,

HERBERT C. WARNER, Notary Public.

WILLIMANTIC TRUST COMPANY.

Report of the Receivers on the 1st day of July, 1882, with a statement of the assets of the Company, and estimate of their value, together with a detailed statement of expenses.

ASSETS, JULY 1, 1882.

DESCRIPTION.	PAR VALUE.	ESTIMATED VALUE.
Notes of Individuals;	$19,423.45	$1,000.00
65-959 U. S. Watch Co., N. Y.,	5,200.00	1,500.00
277 shares Victor Sewing Machine Co.,	6,925.00	1,400.00
Overdraft not collectible,	272.43	
Deposit First National Bank, Willimantic,	708.27	708.27
Deposit Norwich Savings Society,	3,844.58	3,844.58
Cash Items,	477.05	477.05
246 shares Preferred, and 354 Common Stock St. Johnsbury & Lake Champlain R. R. Co.,	15,000.00	3,000.00
Totals,	$551,850.78	$11,929.90

Detailed statement of expenses of Receivers of Willimantic Trust Company from July 10, 1881, to July 1, 1882.

Rent,	$60.00
Stationery and Stamps,	14.80
Traveling and Sundries,	126.20
	$201.00

We have paid by order of the Superior Court of Windham County, a dividend of 12¼ per cent. to all creditors to the amount of $11,996.24.

BELA P. LEARNED, } Receivers.
W. H. OSBORN,

STATE OF CONNECTICUT, WINDHAM Co., ss.: July 10, 1882.

Personally appeared Bela P. Learned and W. H. Osborn, signers of the foregoing statement, and made oath of the truth of the same before me.

, A. J. BOWER, Justice of the Peace.

REPORTS OF STATE BANKS,

October 2, 1882.

CITY BANK, NEW HAVEN.

STATEMENT, OCTOBER 2, 1882.

LIABILITIES.

Capital Stock,	$500,000.00
Deposits,	419,701.68
Due Banks, Bankers, or Trust Companies in this State,	16,361.15
Due Banks, Bankers, or Trust Companies out of this State,	108,135.65
Dividends unpaid,	1,352.00
Surplus,	70,000.00
Profit and Loss,	16,147.30
Bills in Circulation,	9,800.00
Total Liabilities,	$1,141,497.78

ASSETS.

Banking House,	$20,000.00
Other Real Estate,	5,000.00
Due from Banks, Bankers, and Trust Companies in this State,	13,670.09
Due from Banks, Bankers, and Trust Companies out of this State,	222,407.13
Discounted for Directors,	84,247.50
Discounted for other parties in this State,	613,688.27
Discounted for parties out of this State,	92,181.20
Railroad Bonds,	16,000.00
Bank Stocks,	3,000.00
Manufacturing Stocks,	162.82
Specie, Currency, Checks, and Cash items,	67,783.51
Expense Account,	3,357.26
Total Assets,	$1,141,497.78

Past due paper, $7,395.51.
Liability of any one Director, $25,900.
Liability of any one firm, corporation, or person other than a Director, $74,040.60.
Par value of Stock, $100; market value, $122.
Rate per cent. of last Dividend, and when paid, 3 per cent., July 1, 1882.

GEORGE W. CURTIS, President.   SAMUEL LLOYD, Cashier.

DIRECTORS.—George W. Curtis, George H. Watrous, Wooster A. Ensign, Frederic Ives, David T. Hotchkiss, Charles B. Wooster, James D. Dewell, Henry C. Shelton, Elliott H. Morse.

CONNECTICUT RIVER BANKING COMPANY, HARTFORD.

STATEMENT, OCTOBER 2, 1882.

LIABILITIES.

Capital Stock,	$249,880.00
Deposits.	412,991.81
Due Banks, Bankers, or Trust Companies in this State,	-5,776.86
Due Banks, Bankers, or Trust Companies out of this State,	86,374.91
Dividends unpaid,	255.60
Profit and Loss,	33,612.34
Total Liabilities,	$788,891.02

ASSETS.

Banking House,	$20,000.00
Other Real Estate,	1,800.00
Due from Banks, Bankers, and Trust Companies in this State,	44,860.15
Due from Banks, Bankers, and Trust Companies out of this State,	81,488.15
Discounted for Directors,	7,000.00
Discounted for other parties in this State,	430,796.34
Discounted for parties out of this State,	159,854.51
Town, City, and Corporation Bonds,	10,500.00
Stocks,	19,000.00
Specie, Currency, Checks, and Cash items,	12,979.29
Overdrafts,	612.58
Total Assets,	$788,891.02

Past due paper, $8,822.
Liability of any one Director, $7,000.
Liability of any one firm, corporation, or person other than a Director, $37,500.
Par value of Stock, $50; market value, $55.
Rate per cent. of last Dividend, and when paid, 4 per cent., July 1, 1882.

SAMUEL E. ELMORE, President.   MILES W. GRAVES, Cashier.

DIRECTORS.—Richard W. H. Jarvis, Herbert R. Coffin, George M. Welch, John C. Parsons, Samuel T. Wolcott, Elizur S. Goodrich, Samuel N. Kellogg, Jeremiah M. Allen.

MECHANICS BANK, NEW HAVEN.

STATEMENT, OCTOBER 1, 1882.

LIABILITIES.

Capital Stock,	$300,000.00
Deposits,	306,900.11
Due Banks, Bankers, or Trust Companies in this State, " " " " out of this State,	85,637.77
Dividends unpaid,	499.20
Surplus,	25,000.00
Profit and Loss,	11,607.74
Total Liabilities,	$729,644.82

ASSETS.

Banking House,	$14,000.00
Other Real Estate,	20,000.00
Due from Banks, Bankers, and Trust Companies in this State, " " " " out of this State,	124,574.87
Discounted for Directors,	39,925.00
Discounted for other parties in this State,	386,275.28
Discounted for parties out of this State,	54,695.00
Railroad Bonds and Stocks,	25,000.00
Specie, Currency, Checks, and Cash items,	63,258.49
Overdrafts,	3.69
Expense Account,	1,912.50
Total Assets,	$729,644.82

Past due paper, none.
Daily average of Specie and Specie Funds for preceding three months, $654.
Liability of any one Director, $15,000.
Liability of any one firm, corporation, or person other than a Director, $43,176.
Par value of Stock, $60; market value, $72.
Rate per cent. of last Dividend, and when paid, 2 per cent., July 1, 1882.

CHAS. S. LEETE, President.   CHAS. H. TROWBRIDGE, Cashier.
JOHN P. TUTTLE, Vice-President.

DIRECTORS. — Thomas R. Trowbridge, Charles S. Leete, John P. Tuttle, Ruel P. Cowles, Edwin F. Mersick, Maier Zunder, Joel A. Sperry, Oliver S. White, George Alling.

13

STATE BANK, HARTFORD.

STATEMENT, OCTOBER 1, 1882.

LIABILITIES.

Capital Stock,	$400,000.00
Deposits,	647,446.09
Due Banks, Bankers, or Trust Companies in this State,	4,121.13
Due Banks, Bankers, or Trust Companies out of this State,	130,606.77
Dividends unpaid,	883.50
Profit and Loss,	79,094.43
Circulation,	9,575.00
Total Liabilities,	$1,271,726.92

ASSETS.

Banking House,	$50,000.00
Other Real Estate,	4,699.90
Due from Banks, Bankers, and Trust Companies in this State,	113,582.38
Due from Banks, Bankers, and Trust Companies out of this State,	197,462.68
Discounted for parties in this State,	657,090.95
Discounted for parties out of this State,	99,915.57
Railroad Bonds and Stocks,	105,962.50
Specie, Currency, Checks, and Cash items,	41,889.43
Overdrafts,	1,528.50
Non-resident Tax,	8.30
Internal Revenue Stamps,	91.71
Total Assets,	$1,271,726.92

Past due paper, $1,701.50.
Daily average of Specie and Specie Funds for preceding three months, $235,184.21.
Liability of any one Director, $13,737.82.
Liability of any one firm, corporation, or person other than a Director, $70,000.
Par value of Stock, $100; market value, $112.
Rate per cent. of last Dividend, and when paid, 3½ per cent., July, 1882.

C. H. BRAINARD, President.   GEORGE F. HILLS, Cashier.

DIRECTORS.—Asa S. Porter, William Gay, Joseph Toy, A. C. Hotchkiss, Nelson Hollister, James J. Goodwin, Charles H. Brainard.

UNION BANK, NEW LONDON.

STATEMENT, OCTOBER 1, 1882.

LIABILITIES.

Capital Stock,	$300,000.00
Deposits,	249,826.31
Due Banks, Bankers, or Trust Companies in this State,	26,357.53
Due Banks, Bankers, or Trust Companies out of this State,	475.31
Dividends unpaid,	924.50
Surplus,	43,000.00
Profit and Loss,	13,672.88
Total Liabilities,	$634,256.53

ASSETS.

Banking House,	$10,000.00
Due from Banks, Bankers, and Trust Companies in this State,	6,950.16
Due from Banks, Bankers, and Trust Companies out of this State,	26,781.18
Discounted for Directors,	19,800.00
Discounted for other parties in this State,	370,872.31
Discounted for parties out of this State,	131,673.41
Railroad Bonds and Stocks,	22,319.76
Specie, Currency, Checks, and Cash items,	40,920.28
Overdrafts,	4,642.86
Expense Account,	201.57
U. S. Treasurer,	95.00
Total Assets,	$634,256.53

Past due paper, $20,261.
Daily average of Specie and Specie Funds for preceding three months, $30,000.
Liability of any one Director, $11,000.
Liability of any one firm, corporation, or person other than a Director, $17,500.00.
Par value of Stock, $100; market value, $100.
Rate per cent. of last Dividend, and when paid, 3½ per cent., July.

W. H. CHAPMAN, President.   L. C. LEARNED, Cashier.
                                  J. L. CREW, Assistant Cashier.

DIRECTORS.—W. H. Chapman, Robert Coit, Charles Burtis, Nathan Belcher, J. N. Eggleston, George F. Fincker, E. Clark Smith, Israel Matson, Horace Coit, L. C. Learned, Arnold Rudd, Peleg Williams, John W. Luce.

UNITED STATES BANK, HARTFORD.

STATEMENT, OCTOBER 1, 1882.

LIABILITIES.

Capital Stock,	$100,000.00
Deposits,	844,074.67
Profit and Loss,	33,446 57
Total Liabilities,	$977,521.24

ASSETS.

Other Real Estate,	$5,579.64
Due from Banks, Bankers, and Trust Companies in this State,	11,139.83
Due from Banks, Bankers, and Trust Companies out of this State,	90,509.07
Discounted for Directors,	20,150.00
Discounted for other parties in this State,	403,890.51
Discounted for parties out of this State,	16,969.39
Bonds and Mortgage,	82,840.00
Town, City, and Corporation Bonds,	407.00
Stocks,	195.00
Specie, Currency, Checks, and Cash items,	36,873.51
Overdrafts,	22.56
Expense Account,	1,629.40
Loaned on Collateral,	307,315.33
Total Assets,	$977,521.24

Past due paper, none.
Liability of any one Director, $20,000.
Liability of any one firm, corporation, or person other than a Director, $34,000.
Par value of Stock, $100; market value, $120.
Rate per cent. of last Dividend, and when paid, 8 per cent., November 1, 1876.

THOMAS O. ENDERS, President.   HENRY L. BUNCE, Cashier.

DIRECTORS. — Thomas O. Enders, Morgan G. Bulkeley, James Campbell, Edgar T. Welles, William H. Bulkeley, Samuel G. Dunham, John B. Windsor, Charles J. Cole, Atwood Collins, John R. Hills, John W. Welch.

REPORTS OF TRUST COMPANIES,

October 1, 1882.

CONNECTICUT TRUST AND SAFE DEPOSIT COMPANY, HARTFORD.

STATEMENT, OCTOBER 1, 1882.

LIABILITIES.

Capital Stock,	$300,000.00
Deposits,	1,044,978.04
Due Banks, Bankers, or Trust Companies in this State,	35,138.41
Due Banks, Bankers, or Trust Companies out of this State,	97,013.34
Surplus,	50,000.00
Profit and Loss,	10,172.78
Total Liabilities,	**$1,537,302.57**

ASSETS.

Other Real Estate,	$6,996.86
Due from Banks, Bankers, or Trust Companies in this State,	101,561.52
Due from Banks, Bankers, or Trust Companies out of this State,	104,616.22
Discounted for Directors,	54,693.67
Discounted for other parties in this State,	761,050.75
Discounted for parties out of this State,	473,386.24
Specie, Currency, Checks, and Cash items,	32,446.32
Overdrafts,	2,551.49
Total Assets,	**$1,537,302.57**

Past due paper, none.
Liability of any one Director, $16,133.67.
Liability of any one firm, corporation, or person other than a Director, $40,000.
Par value of Stock, $100; market value, $110.
Rate per cent. of last Dividend, and when paid, 3½ per cent., July 1, 1882.

E. B. WATKINSON, President.　　　　　M. H. WHAPLES, Treasurer.
JNO. B. CORNING, Vice-President.

DIRECTORS.—Charles H. Brainard, George S. Gilman, Edward B. Watkinson, Henry C. Robinson, Henry Keney, George L. Chase, Gustavus F. Davis, Charles H. Smith, Charles Boswell, J. B. Corning, Asa S. Porter, Henry Corning, John J. Goodwin, Jacob L. Greene.

EQUITABLE TRUST COMPANY, NEW LONDON.

STATEMENT, OCTOBER 1, 1882.

LIABILITIES.

Capital Stock,	$1,500,000.00
Due Banks, Bankers, or Trust Companies out of this State,	72,091.68
Debentures due 1887 to 1891,	4,697,000.00
Coupons not presented,	3,734.00
Sundry creditors,	44,777.79
Excess of Assets over Liabilities,	90,604.18
Interest,	17,038.57
Total Liabilities,	$6,425,246.22

ASSETS.

Real Estate,	$2,725,485.12
Due from Banks, Bankers, and Trust Companies out of this State, and cash,	204,619.97
Expense Account,	2,188.76
Mortgage Loans and Contracts,	3,276,608.39
Interest due on Loans,	195,267.14
Insurance and Taxes advanced,	10,172.00
Sundry Debtors,	10,904.84
Total Assets,	$6,425,246.22

Mortgage Bonds outstanding, with guarantee of Company, $597,000.
Liability of any one Director, none.
Liability of any one firm, corporation, or person other than a Director; all Loans secured by mortgage.
Par value of Stock, $100; market value, $70.
Rate per cent. of last dividend, and when paid, 3½ per cent., March 1, 1878.

F. B. ELLIOTT, President.
H. R. BOND, Sec. and Treas.   EDWIN I. MARSTON, Asst. Sec. and Man.
HENRY R. PAYSON, Western Manager.

TRUSTEES.—John Jacob Astor, Charles Barns, William H. Barns, Henry R. Bond, Augustus Brandegee, Willett Bronson, Charles Butler, George C. Clark, Robert Coit, Jonathan Edwards, J. N. Harris, Adrian Iselin, Adrian Iselin, Jr., Eugene Kelly, Robert Lennox Kennedy, J. D. Leffingwell, George DeForest Lord, A. A. Low, Francis V. Parker, Joseph Patterson, Henry E. Pierrepont, William Remsen, George A. Robbins, James A. Roosevelt, Alfred Roosevelt, J. Gregory Smith, Gustav Stellwag, C. A. Williams, Samuel Willetts, Charles Stewart Wurts.

HARTFORD TRUST COMPANY.

STATEMENT, OCTOBER 1, 1882.

LIABILITIES.

Capital Stock,	$250,000.00
Deposits,	740,616.30
Due Banks, Bankers, or Trust Companies in this State, } out of this State, }	2,062.91
Dividends unpaid,	1,050.00
Profit and Loss,	29,606.23
Total Liabilities,	$1,023,335.44

ASSETS.

Banking House, Trust Co. Block,	$250,000.00
Other Real Estate,	7,978.12
Due from Banks, Bankers, and Trust Companies in this State, } out of this State, }	43,413.12
Discounted for Directors, } Discounted for other parties in this State, } Discounted for parties out of this State, }	666,330.56
Town, City, and Corporation Bonds,	10,100.00
Specie, Currency, Checks, and Cash items,	39,427.26
Overdrafts,	1,055.54
Expense Account,	2,525.37
Real Estate and Safe Deposit Departments,	2,505.47
Total Assets,	$1,023,335.44

Past due paper, $8,603.26.
Liability of any one Director, $3,000.
Liability of any one firm, corporation, or person other than a Director, $50,000, Collateral.
Par value of Stock, $100; market value, $105.
Rate per cent. of last dividend, and when paid, 3 per cent., July 1, 1882.

WM. FAXON, President.   CHAS. M. JOSLYN, Vice-President.
R. W. CUTLER, Sec. and Treas.

TRUSTEES.—Charles M. Pond, J. C. Webster, Henry Kellogg, Rodney Dennis, Joseph Bishop, Charles M. Joslyn, Theodore Lyman, David Gallup, C. B. Erwin, R. W. Farmer, Z. A. Storrs, R. D. Hawley, William Faxon, Alvan P. Hyde.

MERCHANTS' LOAN & TRUST COMPANY, WILLIMANTIC.

STATEMENT, OCTOBER 1, 1882.

LIABILITIES.

Capital Stock, ...	$51,600.00
Deposits, ...	8,025.00
Due Banks, Bankers, or Trust Companies in this State, . . .	11,768.37
Surplus, ...	1,500.00
Profit and Loss, ...	21.02
Total Liabilities, ...	$72,914.39

ASSETS.

Bank Stocks, Bonds, and Mortgages, ...	$72,914.39

Past due paper, none.
Liability of any one Director, none.
Liability of any one firm, corporation, or person other than a Director, none.
Par value of Stock, $100; market value, $100.
Rate per cent. of last Dividend, and when paid, 4 per cent., July 21, 1882.

Wm. C. Jillson, President.   Ansel Arnold, Vice-President.
              O. H. K. Risley, Secretary and Treasurer.

    Directors.—Wm. C. Jillson, Ansel Arnold, O. H. K. Risley, Hyde Kingsley,
E. S. Henry, S. G. Risley, J. N. Stickney, A. T. Fowler.

MIDDLESEX BANKING COMPANY, MIDDLETOWN.

STATEMENT, OCTOBER 1, 1882.

LIABILITIES.

Capital Stock, ...	$75,000.00
Dividends unpaid, ⎫	
Surplus, ⎬	24,502.38
Profit and Loss, ⎭	
Debentures outstanding, ...	24,700.00
Sundry Creditors, ...	2,273.68
Total Liabilities, ...	$126,476.06

ASSETS.

Other Real Estate, ...	$7,923.06
Due from Banks, Bankers, and Trust Companies in this State, .	3,980.12
Due from Banks, Bankers, and Trust Companies out of this State,	9,469.44
Specie, Currency, Checks, and Cash items, ...	222.51
Taxes, ...	1,223.78
Expense Account, ...	2,534.16
Safe Deposits and Furniture, ...	5,277.19
Interest accrued and due, ...	2,563.82
Sundry Debtors, ...	6,505.71
Real Estate Mortgage securities, ...	86,776.27
Total Assets, ...	$126,476.06

Past due paper, none.
Liability of any one Director, none.
Liability of any one firm, corporation, or person other than a Director, none
  unsecured by Real Estate.
Par value of Stock, $100; market value, no recent public sales.
Rate per cent. of last dividend, and when paid, 3 per cent., July 15, 1882.

ROBERT N. JACKSON, President.   MERRICK E. VINTON, 1st Vice-President.
D. T. HAINES, Secretary.   CHARLES E. JACKSON, 2d Vice-President.

TRUSTEES.—Robert N. Jackson, Merrick E. Vinton, Charles E. Jackson,
Russell Frisbie, Benjamin Douglas, John M. Douglas, Thomas G. Carson, Lindley
Vinton, William F. Graves, Emory H. Nash.

SECURITY COMPANY, HARTFORD.

STATEMENT, OCTOBER 1, 1882.

LIABILITIES.

Capital Stock,	$200,000.00
Deposits,	387,575.75
Due Banks, Bankers, or Trust Companies out of this State,	18,880.17
Surplus,	27,000.00
Profit and Loss,	12,126.90
Treasurer's Checks issued,	1,138.15
Total Liabilities,	$641,720.97

ASSETS.

Due from Banks, Bankers, and Trust Companies in this State, on deposit,	$51,123.11
Due from Banks, Bankers, and Trust Companies out of this State, on deposit,	29,738.81
Discounted for Directors, all on collateral security,	13,500.00
Discounted for other parties in this State, all on collateral security,	103,057.50
Discounted for parties out of this State, all on collateral security,	30,000.00
Town, City, and Corporation Bonds,	64,350.00
Railroad Bonds and Stocks,	42,057.25
Specie, Currency, Checks, and Cash items,	11,869.34
Expense Account,	2,700.77
Interest Accrued,	17,054.42
Loaned on Mortgage Security,	276,269.77
Total Assets,	$641,720.97

Past due paper, none.
Liability of any one Director, $13,500.
Liability of any one firm, corporation, or person other than a Director, $28,800.
Par value of Stock, $100; market value, $119 bid.
Rate per cent. of last Dividend, and when paid, 3¼ per cent., July 1, 1882.

ROBERT E. DAY, President.   WILLIAM L. MATSON, Treasurer.
JOHN C. ABBOTT, Secretary.

TRUSTEES.—John C. Abbott, Leverett Brainard, Newton Case, William R. Cone, Robert E. Day, Thomas O. Enders, C. C. Kimball, William L. Matson, John C. Parsons, Asa S. Porter, Cassius Welles.

THAMES LOAN AND TRUST COMPANY, NORWICH.

STATEMENT, OCTOBER 1, 1882.

LIABILITIES.

Capital Stock,	$100,000.00
Due Banks, Bankers, or Trust Companies in this State,	2,500.00
Surplus,	33,779.56
Profit and Loss,	9,229.87
Earnings,	1,192.63
Collections,	29,541.14
Total Liabilities,	$176,243.20

ASSETS.

Banking Furniture,	$200.00
Other Real Estate,	6,500.00
Due from Banks, Bankers, and Trust Companies in this State,	4,301.87
Discounted for Directors,	8,175.00
Town, City, and Corporation Bonds,	19,180.00
Railroad Bonds and Stocks,	11,043.00
Bank Stocks,	672.00
Specie, Currency, Checks, and Cash items,	3,647.46
Expense Account,	1,354.81
Suspense Account,	2,559.95
Real Estate Mortgage Bonds,	67,250.36
Mortgage Securities and Tax Certificates,	51,358.75
Total Assets,	$176,243.20

Past due paper, none.
Liability of any one Director, $4,087.50.
Liability of any one firm, corporation, or person other than a Director, none.
Par value of Stock, $100; market value, $——.
Rate per cent. of last dividend, and when paid, 2 per cent., April 1, 1879.

CHARLES BARD, President.   J. HUNT SMITH, Sec. and Treas.

TRUSTEES. — Franklin Nichols, James L. Hubbard, Lorenzo Blackstone, Charles Bard, Gardiner Greene, Hugh H. Osgood, John Mitchell, Edward N. Gibbs, James O. Sweet, J. Hunt Smith.

THOMPSONVILLE TRUST COMPANY.

STATEMENT, OCTOBER 1, 1882.

LIABILITIES.

Capital Stock,	$25,000.00
Deposits,	85,835.50
Due Banks, Bankers, or Trust Companies in this State,	7,394.36
Dividends unpaid,	1,021.12
Profit and Loss,	3,273.04
Total Liabilities,	$122,524.02

ASSETS.

Banking House,	$7,000.00
Due from Banks, Bankers, and Trust Companies in this State,	5,095.95
Due from Banks, Bankers, and Trust Companies out of this State,	29,889.86
Discounted for Directors,	3,786.96
Discounted for other parties in this State,	44,765.29
Railroad Bonds and Stocks,	3,000.00
Specie, Currency, Checks, and Cash items,	6,362.96
Safe,	500.00
Mortgage Bond,	500.00
Fire Insurance Stocks,	21,623.00
Total Assets,	$122,524.02

Past due paper, $263.25.
Liability of any one Director, $1,927.83.
Liability of any one firm, corporation, or person other than a Director, $5,000.
Par value of Stock, $25; market value, $25.
Rate per cent. of last Dividend, and when paid, 3½ per cent., April 1, 1882.

R. B. MORRISON, President.   LYMAN A. UPSON, Vice-President.
WILLIS GOWDY, Secretary and Treasurer.

DIRECTORS.—R. B. Morrison, J. L. Houston, G. A. Douglass, L. H. Pease, G. H. Barber, J. N. Allen, Lyman A. Upson, A. H. Mathewson, Willis Gowdy.

UNION TRUST COMPANY, NEW HAVEN.

STATEMENT, OCTOBER 1, 1882.

LIABILITIES.

Capital Stock, ...	$100,000.00
Deposits, ...	344,160.44
Due Banks, Bankers, or Trust Companies in this State, . . .	4,748.67
Surplus, } Profit and Loss, }	20,000.00
Total Liabilities, ...	$468,909.11

ASSETS.

Banking House, } Other Real Estate, }	$34,781.40
Due from Banks, Bankers, and Trust Companies in this State, } " " " " " out of this State, }	64,634.57
Discounted for Directors, } Discounted for other parties in this State, } Discounted for parties out of this State, }	283,788.13
Town, City, and Corporation Bonds, ...	5,162.50
Railroad Bonds and Stocks, ...	49,506.00
Specie, Currency, Checks, and Cash items, ...	31,036.51
Total Assets, ...	$468,909.11

Past due paper, none.
Liability of any one Director, $15,000.
Liability of any one firm, corporation, or person other than a Director, $10,000.
Par value of Stock, $100; market value, Stock not on the market.
Rate per cent. of last dividend, and when paid, 3 per cent., July 11, 1882.

HENRY L. HOTCHKISS, President.   WM. T. BARTLETT, Sec. and Treas.

TRUSTEES.—Henry L. Hotchkiss, Louis H. Bristol, Eugene S. Bristol, William T. Bartlett.

CONDENSED STATEMENTS.

1	Berlin Savings Bank, Kensington	$59,784.00	$12,100.00				$1,091.25
2	Bridgeport Savings Bank,	1,466,621.00	365,600.00				586,200.00
3	Bristol Savings Bank,	436,526.00	32 856.00				11,000.00
4	Brooklyn Savings Bank,	184,245.00	54,075.00				12,345.00
5	City Savings Bank, Meriden,	341,825.00					
6	Canaan Savings Bank,	26,103.68	2,080.00				11,901.89
7	Chelsea Savings Bank, Norwich,	949,176.00	793,450.00				535,000.00
8	Chester Savings Bank,	46,090.93					
9	Citizens' Savings Bank, Stamford	284,435.00	259,575.00				100,000.00
10	City Savings Bank, Bridgeport,	729,607.62	29,700.00				
11	Colchester Savings Bank,	80,332.71					11,500.00
12	Collinsville Savings Bank,	196,564.00					11,000.00
13	Conn. Savings Bank, New Haven,	1,477,925.00	232,000.00				300,000.00
14	Cromwell Dime Savings Bank,	62,599.00					14,100.00
15	Deep River Savings Bank,	232,010 00	54,970.00				26,170.00
16	Derby Savings Bank,	653,643.47	7,800.00				40,000.00
17	Dime Savings Bank, Hartford,	84,925.00	31,150.00				4,500.00
18	Dime Savings Bank, Middletown,	12,525.00					
19	Dime Savings Bank, Norwich,	518,234.00	123,300.00				35,350.00
20	Dime Savings Bank, Thompson,	208,825.00					
21	Dime Savings Bank, Wallingford,	64,211.66					
22	Dime Savings Bank, Waterbury,	513,600.00	48,250.00				
23	Dime Savings Bank, Willimantic,	228,524.00	102,512.00				
24	Eastford Savings Bank,	5,260.00					
25	Essex Savings Bank,	398,448.00	14,580.00				
26	Fairfield Co. Sav. Bank, Norwalk,	151,975.00	89,900.00				15,575.00
27	Falls Village Savings Bank,	156,082.74	24,900.00				25,298.25
28	Farmers and Mechanics, Middt'n,	601,508.00	16,422.00				34,800.00
29	Farmington Savings Bank,	1,131,635.00	17,400.00				150,000.00
30	Freestone Savings Bank,	133,988 00	14,475.00				5,000.00
31	Greenwich Savings Bank,	90,242.50	1,225.00				
32	Groton Savings Bank,	413,850.93	9,000.00				
33	Guilford Savings Bank,	62,199.14					
34	Higganum Savings Bank,	30,840.00					
35	Jewett City Savings Bank,	82,960.00	5,885.10				10,939.50
36	Litchfield Savings Society,	297,796.07	45,300.00				62,462.49
37	Mariners' Savings B'k, N. London,	432,450.00	89,500.00				93,350.00
38	Mechanics' Savings B'k, Hartford,	666,722.00	179,825 00				1,050.00
39	Mechanics & Farmers, Bridgep't,	184,900.00	30,250.00				
40	Meriden Savings Bank,	931,635.33	1,300.00				180,718.72
41	Mechanics' Savings B'k, Winsted,	184,878.84					46,147.00
42	Middletown Savings Bank,	2,316,670.00	201,000.00				734,550.00
43	Milford Savings Bank,	61,574.00					12,802.00
44	Moodus Savings Bank,	74,685.00	1,200.00				11,000.00
45	National Sav. B'k, New Haven,	433,801.58	31,050.00				49,005.75
46	Naugatuck Savings Bank,	122,289.58					
47	New Canaan Savings Bank,	90,735.98	2,500.00				
48	New Milford Savings Bank,	242,050.85					21,358.00
49	New Haven Savings Bank,	2,145,069.99	357,800.00				157,500 00
50	Newtown Savings Bank,	211,007.93	18,322.23				2,200.10
51	Norwalk Savings Society,	800,185.32	417,200.00				
52	Norfolk Savings Bank,	66,482.04	1,500.00	17,798.75	5,723 75		
53	Norwich Savings Society,	2,592,318.58	294,000.00	153,600.00	2,481,805.89		
54	Peoples' Savings B'k, Rockville,	124,581.00		56,555.50			
55	Peoples' Sav. Bank, Bridgeport,	607,635.00	299,582.00	28,800.00			
56	Putnam Savings Bank,	418,821.87	45,029.25	116,500 00	12,025.00		
57	Ridgefield Savings Bank,	37,295.00		5,850 00			
58	Salisbury Sav. Soc'y, Lakeville,	178,607.52		32,860 00	290.00		8,055.00
59	Savings Bank, Ansonia,	299,117.00		86,422.50			
60	Savings Bank, Danbury,	1,007,282.50	70,000.00	45,595.13	13,950 00		66,212.50
61	Savings Bank, New Britain,	612,186.00	34,838.00	215,165 00	33,500.00		36,200.00
62	Savings Bank, New London,	936,374.26	136,000.00	290,540 00	294,200 00		
63	Savings Bank, Rockville,	255,271.00	35,400.00	171,151 00	2,000.00		
64	Savings Bank, Stafford Springs,	96,954.00	5,976.00	68,800.00	59,000.00		
65	Savings Bank, Tolland,	52,200 95		30,100.00			
66	Society for Savings, Hartford,	4,985,110.00	554,225.00	213,540.00	1,092,825.00		
67	Southington Savings Bank,	194,312.15	5,475 00	136,075.08	13,150.00		
68	South Norwalk Savings Bank,	109,268.06	106,859.50	5,000.00			
69	Southport Savings Bank,	179,600.00	16,800.00	29,300.00	20,800.00		
70	Stafford Savings Bank,	271,248.49	53,100.00	81,217.00	4,240.00		
71	Stamford Savings Bank,	763,017.00	318,810.00	6,937.00	61,070.00		
72	State Savings Bank, Hartford,	790,863 22	83,470.00	268,250.19	26,550.00		8,045.6
73	Stonington Savings Bank,	312,780.02	8,464.16	89,070.50	51,036 00		35,437.5
74	Suffield Savings Bank,	75,975.00	2,700.00	41,960 00	14,105 00		4,000.0
75	Thomaston Savings Bank,	158,800.00	18,500.00	45,578 50			
76	Torrington Savings Bank,	109,215.00	12,150.00	10,700.00			51,000.0
77	Union Savings Bank, Danbury,	297,561.00	6,150.00	17,875.00			
78	Waterbury Savings Bank,	974,522 80	284,200.00	72,750.00	50,000.00		201,100.0
79	Westport Savings Bank,	71,975.00		9,200.00			
80	Willimantic Savings Institute,	251,875.00	51,422.60	47,190 00			
81	Windham Co , Danielsonville,	397,325.00	132,000.00	61,800 00			2,600.00
82	Windsor Locks Savings Bank,	35,941.36		13,543.50			
83	Woodbury Savings Bank,	148,303.64		9,150.00			
	Winsted Savings Bank,	407,432 80	13,850.00	49,025.00	7,900.00		54,000.0
		33,381,167.11	6,810,603 84	5,306,521.13	7,041,311.35	5,649,570.5	

						Liabilities.		
							$4,455.20	$106,377.98
		20,593.02	$6,693 87				206,061.99	3,215,973.29
		7,944 00					26,090.63	670,050.25
		17,588.76	3,504.99				10,256.76	455,081.63
		21,654.20	564.54				16,763.05	493,563.74
		9,081.51					5,388.94	97,982 39
11,070 15		16,816.25	35,773.88				140,352.78	3,519,588.61
343,000 00		2,196.59	223.75		92,977.39		2,255.13	95,282.52
19,020.00		9,592.57			855,160.21		15,215.92	870,376.13
91,223.56		39,946.80	818.74		1,982 228.75		63,665.05	2,045,893.80
817,976.19		6,800.36	7,668.68		192,601.81		4,424.06	197,025.87
42,225.98		6,788.47	2,574 28		285,147.11		9,301.03	294,348.14
31,050.00		30,881.28	1,862.29		3,038,352.69		96,599.23	3,134,951.92
274,000.00	5,000.00	2,609.10	4,190.61		99,538.79		2,783 80	102,283.59
70,952.20	123,500.00	9,853.41	25,789 51		595,330.07		22,478.36	617,308.43
5,848.82	49,174.20	15,631.01	2,464.23	1,155,489.54	1,077,887 64		77,421 90	1,155,289 54
3,833.45	79,955 00	10,735.23	145.00	198,085 23	185,159 05		12,926.18	198,085.23
2,798.58	7,780.00	7,368.74		42,150.56	40,304 80		1,845.76	42,150.56
46,000.00	65,295.00	5,126.28	8,007 22	1,247,098.42	1,206,202.55		37,060.06	1,247,098.42
17,860.82	58,319.80	3,581.46	68.87	437,222.11	421,517.72		15,052.53	437,222.11
180,605.91	94,500.00	555.38		103,221.04	100,628 41		2,592.63	103,221.04
12,691.24	66,583.50	42,893.81	1,346.25	897,218.63	844,689 59		52,529.04	897,218.63
14,286.72	47,975.80	44,692.02	1,053.00	582,941.82	568,559.47		14,381.85	582,941.82
5,759.71	321,377.50	140.35	405.66	18,930.38	13,451.09		362.58	18,930.38
32,089.44	70,000.00	26,630.59	20,810.01	634,356.38	610,338.52	949 27	23,068 59	634,356.38
12,866.33	15,800.00	15,385.40	50.73	400,169 84	892,307.48		7,862 36	400,169 84
45,210.04	5,250.00	17,981.27	2,355.25	418,093.09	409,236.89		8,856 20	418,093.09
192,441.57	44,000.00	28,333.16	11,240.63	1,365,185.36	1,305,550.51		51,192.16	1,365,185.36
83,350.00	2,000.00	49,384.77		1,877,869.77	1,806,582.03	8,442.69	70,787.74	1,877,869.77
22,000.00	62,125.00	2,584.27	258.20	223,788.50	216,261.60		7,526.90	223,788.50
2,847.31	270,810.50	21,371.29	193.45	123,060.14	119,499 05		3,561.09	123,060.14
74,023.98	192,947.00	9,646.22	931.31	632,506.73	602,510.81		29 996 42	632,506.73
2,000.00	444,107.50	6,885.98	547.77	139,581.43	132,945.57		6,635.86	139,581.43
8,688.68	90,525.00	806.99		26,209.76	25,357 56		852.20	26,209.76
208,604.48	40,470.37	27,090.03	7,115.39	423,135.02	409,777.59	22.16	18,335.27	423,135.02
200,914.67	7,350.00	15,135.66	656.85	810,634.18	770,272.01		40,362.17	810,634.18
2,253.72	1,039,816.54	13,331.82	16,351.94	1,394,152.74	1,327,406.87	24,590.86	42,155.01	1,394,152.74
26,741.77	2,060.00	64,330.46	4,539.81	1,393,924.44	342,844.24		51,080.39	1,393,924.44
525,181.20	33,420 00	8,176.26	675.00	829,234.08	320,627.99		8,606.09	829,234.08
2,875.00	33,390.26	54,754.56	1,550.58	1,546,824.13	451,603.76		95,220.37	1,546,824.13
12,931.18	320,651.15	16,069.60	3,013.79	380,801.28	366,818.96	819.50	13,662 77	380,801.28
34,070.84	1,063,400.00	518,544.02	3,879.59	5,602,924.35	5,290,844.35	15,394.24	296,685 76	5,602,924 35
18,084.51	34,700.00	6,518.16	814.40	107,677.33	104,758.07		2,919.36	107,677.33
243,160.63	183,718 97	2,780.50	6,847.33	154,427.83	149,107.22		5,320.61	154,427.83
15,500.00	26,497 64	17,297.04	1,037.42	676,021.65	633,056.75		42,964.90	676,021.65
172,324.38	1,727,861.25	7,094.29		148,605.87	142,166.01		6,439.86	148,605.87
3,775.00	479,500.00	205.84	8,148.84	179,540.29	169,671.42	8,195.53	1,673.34	179,540.29
288,773.49	71,895.86	18,314.89	3,725.03	683,346.25	626,170.46	2,129.48	57,175.79	683,346.25
50,025.55	131,991.43	96,221.67	14,544.46	5,314,175.50	5,055,673.52		256,372.55	5,314,175 50
57,502.50	27,066 67	41,548.83	8,935.99	422,291.42	405,732.58	3,230.92	13,327.92	412,291.42
6,487.06	185,048.75	18,903.11	7,972.07	1,726,793.01	1,672,828 84	530.62	53,933.55	1,726,793.01
36,791.29	228,441.90	258,048.40	449.40	149,595.69	144,965 98		4,629.76	149,595.69
3,850.00	931,500.00	3,164.25	10,145.12	8,097,352.73	7,647,215.24		450,137.49	8,097,352.73
183,831.67	2,500.00	17,739.91	1,550.41	244,558.73	235,344.60		9,214 13	244 558.73
33,771.47	1,000.00	61,800.27	30.00	1,482,812.46	1,418,044.74		69,767.72	1,482,812.46
253,236.85	946,730.00	9,155.61	2,513.69	800,969.06	771,013.16		29,955.90	800,969.06
18,686.95	10,345.00	38,586.16	33.14	69,765.87	65,903.35		3,862.52	69,765.87
8,580.00	18,425.00	5,913.50	5,040.48	510,946.22	493,863.27		17,082.95	510,946.22
3,117.92	196,000.00	43,642.05	826.00	512,707.98	495,771.78		16,936 20	512,707.98
391,950.00	166,671.00	15,818.53		1,919,231.48	1,840,101.86		79,129.62	1,919,231.48
6,081.60	219,040.00	48,718.73	2,542.94	1,232,719.02	1,174,708.57	224.20	57,791.35	1,232,719.02
9,000.00	163.26	19,295 46	4,331.37	3,813,001.21	3,168,072.62	59.16	118,869.48	3,812,001.21
27,000.00	5,800.00	16,172.42	1,000.00	796,780.05	758,053.87		38,726.08	796,780.05
15,075.12	37,378.95	4,001.74	28,610.00	315,699.91	306,844 01		8,855.90	315,699.91
612,978.80	73,200.00	749,067.10	229.40	97,650 01	94,948.54	80.94	2 620.53	97,650 01
164,372.77	5,000.00	4,473.20	6,494.37	9,433,091.47	9,074,011 91		359,079 58	9,433,091.47
1,025.00	44,000.00	978.17	500.00	405,457.03	386,238.84		19,218.69	405,457 03
38,800.00	49,976.85	6,442.59	633 24	260,787.97	246,657.77	213.44	13,916.76	260,787.97
26,742.38	525.00	12,873 65	1,268 80	529,211.39	554,150.19		25,061 20	529,211.39
2,079 94	198,780.00	65,308.01		431,179.14	424,952 84		6,226 30	431,179.14
72,935.00		20,050.54	6,771 88	1,570,498.13	1,487,158.52		83,389 61	1,570,498.13
136,910.57		7,489 96	9,271.97	2,061,220.26	1,977,550.86	3,495.77	80,173 63	2,061,220.26
10,637.55		333.19	75 00	721,863.04	685,817.94		36,045.10	721,863.04
11,163.66		3,415.59	553.20	143,048.19	184,552.08		8,496 11	143,048.19
		13,317 49		275,656.29	264,153.65	615.00	10,888.64	275,656.29
		15,349 95	284.49	270,660.12	265 212 63		5,447.49	270,660.12
		135,578.89		626,181.47	600,599 29		25,582.18	626,181.47
		565.11	68.50	2,081,858 27	1,958,853.54		123,004.73	2,081,858 27
		72,396.99	2,949 40	88,888 55	81,904.22		6,984.33	88,888 55
		32,055.89	16,925.60	702,902.74	674,827.46	1,537.50	26,537.78	702,902.74
		5,761.61	510.25	875,122 25	855,809.87		19,312.38	875,122 25
		6,911.84		61,416.75	60,876.52		1,040.23	61,416.75
		32,977.54	20,035.88	179,150 08	169,527.28	2,835 54	9,622 80	179,150 08
				926,361.10	848,685.19		74,840.37	926,361.10
5,548,713.67	12,692,441.61	3,189,094 71	332,085.24	88,915,870.50	84,942,410.55	79,374.18	3,894,085.77	88,915,870.50

STATE BANKS.

SUMMARY OF THEIR ASSETS AND LIABILITIES, OCTOBER 1st, 1882.

NAME OF BANKS.	ASSETS.						LIABILITIES.					
	Loans and Discounts.	Due from Banks and Bankers.	Other Bonds and Stocks.	Specie, Demand Notes, Overdrafts, Checks, and Cash Items.	Real Estate.	Total Assets.	Capital Stock.	Deposits.	Due Banks and Bankers.	Surplus, Earnings, Profit and Loss, unpaid Dividends, Suspense Account.	Circulation.	Total Liabilities.
City Bank, N. Haven,	$790,116.97	236,077.29	19,163.63	71,140.77	25,000.00	1,141,497.78	500,000.00	419,701.68	124,496.30	87,499.30	9,800.00	1,141,497.78
6th. River Banking Co., Hartford,	597,650.85	126,348.30	29,500.00	13,591.87	21,800.00	788,891.02	249,880.00	412,991.31	92,151.77	33,867.94		788,891.02
M's Bank, New Haven,	490,895.28	121,574.96	25,000.00	65,174.68	34,000.00	729,644.68	300,000.00	306,900.11	85,637.77	37,106.94		729,644.68
Ste Bnd,	757,006.52	311,045.06	105,963.50	43,013.94	54,659.90	1,271,726.92	400,000.00	647,446.09	134,727.90	79,977.93	9,575.00	1,271,726.92
Ufon Bank, New London,	532,345.72	33,731.34	23,319.76	45,859.71	10,000.00	634,256.53	300,000.00	249,826.31	26,832.94	57,597.38		634,256.53
Uted States Bank, Hartford,	746,325.23	101,648.00	83,449.00	38,526.47	5,579.64	977,531.94	100,000.00	844,074.67		33,446.67		977,531.94
Totals, $	3,896,840.57	933,425.08	285,387.08	277,305.44	151,079.54	5,543,538.31	1,849,880.00	2,880,940.17	463,847.08	329,496.06	19,375.00	5,543,538.31

TRUST COMPANIES DOING A BANKING BUSINESS.

SUMMARY OF THEIR ASSETS AND LIABILITIES, OCTOBER 1, 1882.

COMPANIES.	ASSETS								LIABILITIES					
	Notes Discounted.	Mortgage Loans.	Due from Banks and Bankers.	Stocks and Bonds.	Cash Items and Over-drafts.	Real Estate.	Expense, Interest, Sus-pense, Fixtures, Taxes, etc.	Total Assets.	Capital Stock.	Deposits.	Due to Banks and Bankers.	Surplus Earnings, Profit and Loss, etc.	Divi-dends unpaid, and all other Liabili-ties.	Total Liabilities.
nd Safe Deposit artford,	$1,289,130.66		206,177.74		34,997.81	6,996.86		1,537,302.57	300,000	1,044,978.04	132,151.75	60,172.78		1,537,302.57
t ny,	666,380.56		43,413.12	10,100.00	40,482.80	260,483.59	2,595.37	1,023,335.44	250,000	740,616.30	2,062.91	30,656.23		1,023,335.44
oan and Trust blic,			72,914.39	72,914.39				72,914.39	51,600	8,025.00	11,768.37		1,521.02	72,914.39
pany, Hartford,	146,567.50	276,269.77	80,861.92	106,407.26	11,869.34		19,755.19	641,720.97	200,000	387,575.75	18,880.17	39,196.90	1,188.15	641,720.97
e Trust Company,	43,553.25	500.00	34,985.81	24,625.00	6,362.96	7,000.00	500.00	122,534.02	25,000	85,895.50	7,391.36	3,273.04	1,021.12	122,534.02
Company, New	288,788.13		64,634.57	54,668.50	31,036.51	24,781.40		468,909.11	100,000	344,160.44	4,748.67	20,000.00		468,909.11
	2,434,369.10	276,769.77	430,073.16	268,718.14	124,749.42	309,261.35	22,780.56	3,866,706.50	926,600	2,611,191.03	172,006.23	153,228.95	3,680.29	3,866,706.50

TRUST COMPANIES DEALING IN REAL ESTATE SECURITIES.

SUMMARY OF THEIR ASSETS AND LIABILITIES, OCTOBER 1st, 1882.

OF COMPANIES.	Real Estate.	Mortgage Loans and Notes.	Due from Banks, Bankers, Cash, and Cash Items.	Interest Due, and other Assets.	Corporation Bonds.	Expense, Insurance, Taxes, Safe, and Fixtures.	Total Assets.	Capital Stock.	Deposits, etc.	Outstanding Bonds, Certificates, and Coupons.	Interest, Sundry Creditors, etc.	Surplus, Earnings, Dividends Unpaid.	Total Liabilities.
Trust Company, ...don.	$2,725,485.12	3,276,608.89	204,619.97	207,455.90		21,076.84	6,435,246.22	1,500,000.00		4,700,734.00	133,908.04	90,604.18	6,435,246.22
Banking Company, ...idletown.	7,998.06	86,776.27	13,672.07	14,846.72		3,757.94	126,476.06	75,000.00		24,700.00	2,273.68	24,502.38	126,476.06
...an and Trust, Norwich.	6,700.00	118,609.11	16,124.38		30,895.00	3,914.76	176,243.20	100,000.00			32,041.14	44,202.06	176,243.20
	2,740,108.18	3,481,993.77	234,419.37	221,802.69	30,895.00	28,749.54	6,727,965.48	1,675,000.00		4,725,434.00	168,222.86	159,308.62	6,727,965.48

ABSTRACT OF REPORTS OF SAVINGS BANKS,

From 1853 to 1882, inclusive.

	Number of Banks.	Number of Depositors.	Deposits.	Other Liabilities.	Loans on Real Estate.	Loans on Stocks, Bonds, and Personal Security.	Invested in U. S. Bonds.	Invested in other Bonds and in Stocks.	Real Estate, including Bank'g Houses	Other Assets, including Cash on hand.	Total Assets.	Excess of Assets over Liabilities.
53	23	50,850	$8,764,645	$994	$4,656,849	$2,502,226		$1,481,732	$29,248	$317,763	$8,987,819	$222,179
54	26	54,589	9,655,746	4,340	5,379,869	2,439,047		1,880,776	28,866	124,764	9,853,322	198,236
55	27	57,708	10,844,933	4,780	6,014,226	2,429,212		2,440,063	28,827	137,530	11,049,857	9,944
56	29	61,186	12,162,136	6,809	6,871,305	2,932,728		2,445,126	45,181	371,172	12,533,308	364,363
57	29	63,039	12,563,594	3,448	7,408,773	2,541,780		2,107,715	22,000	797,714	12,878,053	312,011
58	35	66,709	14,053,181	8,458	8,788,566	2,217,977		2,228,984	22,000	1,218,550	14,467,270	407,361
59	37	75,792	16,565,283	10,080	10,409,542	2,770,519		2,290,404	28,900	1,443,959	16,838,386	253,023
60	44	84,614	19,337,670	13,057	12,463,710	3,740,293		2,274,463	49,137	1,328,426	19,852,897	24,670
61	45	88,373	19,983,959	9,256	13,065,901	2,554,439		2,348,699	188,914	2,117,293	20,539,758	546,543
62	49	103,727	23,146,936	19,048	13,580,291	2,478,550	$2,507,919	2,386,462	178,970	2,220,483	23,648,492	482,508
63	48	116,681	26,954,802	45,431	12,850,258	3,250,683	6,481,550	2,466,729	204,892	2,311,618	27,565,731	565,498
64	49	121,683	29,142,288	61,554	12,831,399	3,141,593	7,109,648	2,734,865	220,901	5,048,739	31,087,145	1,883,603
65	50	107,572	27,319,013	80,191	11,491,197	2,752,242	8,194,280	2,836,493	194,239	3,433,061	28,891,454	1,492,250
66	53	126,823	31,180,390	78,380	13,268,487	3,230,046	9,180,943	3,302,732	210,492	3,958,165	33,150,865	1,892,184
67	54	138,846	36,283,660	88,280	16,787,715	4,119,581	10,191,713	3,590,895	234,841	3,719,142	38,643,891	2,272,150
68	55	149,919	41,803,681	43,775	21,031,619	4,570,204	10,585,029	3,678,073	307,578	4,376,963	44,549,466	2,702,008
69	64	165,692	47,904,834	120,463	26,081,163	5,601,305	9,188,484	3,968,855	385,111	6,027,148	51,202,065	3,177,768
70	73	177,887	55,297,705	69,585	32,144,663	7,332,226	7,183,436	9,877,706	412,139	1,699,608	58,619,779	3,252,488
71	78	195,937	62,717,814	81,705	38,265,514	8,476,413	5,336,154	10,601,242	429,154	1,838,989	65,307,460	2,507,949
72	79	201,742	68,523,397	161,046	43,174,015	9,495,818	4,771,970	11,651,691	423,342	1,754,557	71,271,395	2,586,950
73	87	204,741	70,769,407	151,407	47,236,893	8,596,818	4,039,564	11,695,325	519,840	1,599,140	73,677,589	2,756,767
74	86	206,274	73,783,802	99,028	51,552,293	7,042,492	4,141,645	11,196,366	581,946	2,360,304	76,875,049	2,992,219
75	86	208,030	76,489,310	655,847	55,363,219	5,060,709	4,974,423	10,554,859	574,743	3,009,702	79,537,656	2,392,499
76	86	203,514	78,524,172	233,434	55,403,988	4,715,266	,656	12,180,119	767,218	2,302,380	81,336,631	2,579,024
77	86	204,575	77,214,372	409,864	52,387,212	4,514,246	7,192,260	11,762,279	2,208,474	2,322,464	80,273,938	2,649,701
78	86	199,795	72,515,468	657,017	48,142,697	3,601,176	6,780,564	11,532,293	3,707,133	2,260,700	76,024,606	2,852,120
79	85	202,385	72,842,443	536,185	45,108,803	3,388,065	8,163,695	11,691,003	4,959,119	2,931,131	76,241,816	2,863,188
80	85	213,913	76,518,570	170,522	42,791,160	4,300,209	7,245,223	16,681,918	5,397,281	3,537,867	79,943,659	3,254,566
81	85	225,386	80,532,300	285,448	39,808,956	7,089,801	6,723,479	20,913,758	5,675,822	4,031,815	84,243,131	3,435,382
82	84	237,993	84,942,410	79,874	38,381,167	10,714,964	5,649,570	25,100,273	5,366,521	3,521,179	88,915,870	3,894,085

LAWS

RELATING TO

BANKS, TRUST COMPANIES,

AND

SAVINGS BANKS.

LAWS.-

[The changes rendered necessary by subsequent legislation in the General Statutes—Revision 1875—have been made in this compilation.]

TITLE XVII.

PRIVATE CORPORATIONS.

PART II.

BANKS AND TRUST COMPANIES.

ARTICLE I.

GENERAL PROVISIONS.

SECTION 1. All banks organized under the Act of 1852, entitled " An Act to authorize the business of banking," shall retain and enjoy all the rights and privileges conferred, and be subject to all the restrictions imposed by said Act, and the several acts in addition thereto; and all said acts shall remain in force as Private Acts for the government of said institutions only, and shall be subject to alteration, amendment, or repeal at all times by the General Assembly.

1855.
Banks organized under Act of 1852.

1872.
Reserve fund of
cash or bonds.

SEC. 2. Every bank and trust company shall always keep in its banking office gold and silver coin, bullion, bonds, legal tender notes of the United States, or national bank currency, to an amount not less than one-tenth of all its liabilities, except its capital stock; but the bonds of the United States so included in said reserve fund shall never exceed one-twentieth of said liabilities.

1837.
1842. 1872.
Dividends.

SEC. 3. No trust company or banking corporation shall declare any dividend except from its net earnings after deducting all losses, overdrafts, and obligations, suspended or over due; nor make any loan or discount on a pledge of its

Loans on its
stock.
Agencies.

own stock;* nor establish any branch office, or agency thereof, or employ any agent or person to make loans or discounts at any other place than the banking house.

1855. 1862.
Loans to one
party limited.

SEC. 4. No bank or trust company shall give credit to any party, who shall thereby become liable to it for more than fifteen *per cent.* of its capital stock actually paid in. The provisions of such bank charters, as limit the amount to be loaned to any one party to a sum less than fifteen *per cent.* of the capital actually paid in, are repealed; and every bank or trust company, which shall violate the provisions of this section, shall pay to the State not less than one thousand dollars.

1837.
Paper of cash-
iers and clerks.

SEC. 5. No bank shall discount any paper made, accepted, or indorsed by its cashier or any of its clerks, or by any partnership of which either is a member.

1859.
Loans out of
the State.

SEC. 6. When the loans and discounts of any bank to parties in this State shall in the aggregate amount to its capital stock, it may loan to parties out of this State any excess or surplus over the amount of its capital stock, and not otherwise.

1863.
Officers of
banks required
to mark all
counterfeit
bills, etc.

SEC. 7. The cashier or teller of any bank to which shall be presented a counterfeit or altered bank bill, or a paper purporting to be the bill of a bank which never existed, shall write or stamp upon all such counterfeit bills the word "counterfeit," and upon all such altered bills the word "altered," adding thereto the name of the bank and his initials.

Bills erroneous-
ly stamped.

SEC. 8. Any bank, an officer of which by mistake so writes upon or stamps a good bill, shall pay to the holder

---

* Such loan may be good between the parties. 26 Conn., 144.

its value on demand, and every bank shall include the amount of all counterfeit or altered bills, so stamped by its officers, in its returns to the Bank Commissioners. Amount re-
turned to Com-
missioners.

SEC. 9. When any false and counterfeit coin, made in imitation of any current gold or silver coin, shall be offered to the cashier of a bank, he shall seize it and deliver it to some justice of the peace, with the name of the person from whom it is taken; and if any officer shall fail to comply with the provisions of this section he shall forfeit one hundred dollars to this State. Counterfeit coin
to be seized.

SEC. 10. The State, and every college, ecclesiastical society, school corporation, and charitable corporation in this State, may subscribe at par to the stock of any bank in addition to its authorized capital stock, to the extent, in the aggregate, of ten *per cent.* of such capital actually paid in; but no such corporation (other than the State) shall subscribe to the stock of any one bank to a greater amount than five thousand dollars; and all stock so subscribed shall be not transferable, and may be withdrawn at any time on giving twelve months' notice to the bank; but such subscription, if withdrawn, shall not entitle such subscriber to any portion of the surplus in excess of the capital of such bank existing at the time of such subscription.* 1855.   1857.
Charitable
subscriptions.

SEC. 11. The Commissioner of the School Fund may at any time examine the books and accounts of any bank, in which there is stock belonging to the School Fund; and the Treasurer shall have the same right, in case of stock in any bank owned by the State, and purchased from its general funds. 1836.
Commissioner
of School Fund
and Treasurer
may examine
banks in which
School Fund or
State has stock.

SEC. 12. The stockholders of any bank, at the annual meeting, or at any special meeting, which any five stock-holders, owning no less in all than one hundred shares of stock, are authorized to call for that purpose, may examine the books, accounts, securities, and expenditures of the bank. 1842.
Stockholders
may examine
condition of
bank.

SEC. 13. No stock in any bank shall be voted on at any meeting of the stockholders, which is not transferable, or which has been transferred, hypothecated, or pledged to any bank, or to any person in trust for any bank; and when 1840.   1842.
What stock may
not be voted on.

---

*Act of 1855 applies only to banks organized under the Act of 1852. 26 Conn., 60. Non-transferable stock entitled to an equal dividend. 26 Conn., 269.

the number of shares to be held by any party is limited, no
stock held in trust for such party shall be voted on, beyond
what, with that standing in his name, shall equal the
amount so limited; and any person who shall vote upon
any shares of stock in any bank in violation of this section,
shall be disqualified from holding any office in such bank
for one year thereafter.

Proxy voting.   SEC. 14. No person shall vote at any meeting of the
stockholders of any bank as the attorney of another, without
the power of attorney; and when at any meeting the right
of any person to vote on any stock is denied, he shall not be
permitted to vote until he has lodged with the presiding
officer of said meeting his affidavit, stating his interest in
said stock, and also the character and amount of the interest,
if any, owned by any other person therein.

1850.
When stock-
holder shall file
his affidavit.

1839.
When president
or cashier not to
vote on proxies.

SEC. 15. No president or cashier of any bank shall vote
in the election of directors upon any other stock than his
own, nor request any stockholder to make to any person a
power of attorney to vote upon his stock, and no person shall
vote by virtue of a power so obtained.

1837.
When Commis-
sioner of School
Fund and Treas-
urer may vote.

SEC. 16. The Commissioner of the School Fund may vote
upon the transferable stock in any bank, which is appropriated for the use and benefit of the School Fund; and
the Treasurer of the State may vote upon the transferable
stock which belongs to the general or civil list funds of the
State.

ARTICLE II.

DIRECTORS AND CASHIERS.

1837. 1840.
Who may not
be directors.

SECTION 1. No person not a resident of this State shall
act as a director of any bank in this State, and no director
of any bank in this State shall act as a director in any other
bank.

SEC. 2.   No director in any bank shall be obligated to such bank to an amount exceeding five *per cent.* of its capital actually paid in; and no bank shall permit its directors to become obligated to it, to an amount at any one time exceeding in the whole the sum of twenty *per cent.* on its capital stock actually paid in.   Any bank which shall violate the provisions of this section shall forfeit to this State not less than five hundred nor more than one thousand dollars.

1858.
To what amount directors may be indebted.

SEC. 3.   If any director of any bank shall receive any compensation for indorsing any paper discounted by such bank, he shall forfeit to the State the full amount of such paper.

1887.
Penalty for indorsing notes for a premium.

SEC. 4.   The directors of any bank or trust company, in making any dividend, shall take the question thereon by yeas and nays, which shall be recorded on its records; and no such bank or company shall declare any dividend, except from its earnings, remaining after deducting all losses, all sums due for expenses, all overdue and unsecured debts, and an allowance for depreciation of securities and investments; and the directors voting for any dividend, not in conformity with the provisions of this section, shall be fined five hundred dollars, for which they shall be jointly and severally liable.

1842.
Dividends to be declared by yeas and nays.

SEC. 5.   The directors of any bank, by vote of its stockholders, may, at any time when the General Assembly is not in session, reduce its capital stock to such sum and such number of shares as the Bank Commissioners may determine; who shall make return of such proceedings to the next General Assembly for approval, and if approved such reduction shall thereupon be valid.

1842.
Reduction of capital.

SEC. 6.   When the State shall own stock to the amount of five thousand dollars in any bank, it shall be entitled to one director therein; and when the stock so held by the State in any bank shall amount to twenty thousand dollars, it shall be entitled to two directors therein, who shall be annually appointed by the General Assembly.

1839.
State directors.

SEC. 7.   The Governor may accept the resignation of any bank director appointed on the part of the State; and in case of the resignation or inability of any State director to attend to his duties, may appoint some other person to supply his place until the next General Assembly.

1853.
Resignation of State director.

Cashiers to give bond.

SEC. 8. If any cashier shall neglect to give the bond required by law, for thirty days after his appointment, his office shall become vacant.

1887.
Unclaimed dividends.

SEC. 9. The cashier of every bank shall annually prepare a written statement, containing the names of all its stockholders to whom, on the last Saturday of March, any dividend has remained due and unclaimed for one year and the amount due to each, and shall publish the same three weeks immediately succeeding said date in some newspaper published in the county where such bank is located.

1855. 1858.
Quarterly statements to Bank Commissioners.

SEC. 10. The cashiers of all banks and the treasurers of all trust companies shall, on the first Mondays of January, April, July, and October in each year, or within ten days thereafter, sign and deliver to the Bank Commissioners a particular statement of the condition of their respective institutions, exhibiting their resources and liabilities, and the daily average of specie and of specie funds during the three months last preceding, which statement shall be verified by oath and published in a newspaper in the county where such bank or trust company is located.

1871.
1872. 1873.
Annual statement to Bank Commissioners.

SEC. 11. The cashiers of banks and the treasurers of trust companies chartered by this State on or before the first day of April in each year, and oftener if required by the Bank Commissioners, shall transmit to them a sworn statement of the condition of their respective institutions, making a balance sheet, showing, among other things, the amount invested in real estate, the locality thereof, and its cash value; the amount invested in stocks or bonds, with the number of shares of said stock and the par value thereof, the actual cost of the institution, the actual market value at the time of said return, the number and amount of such bonds, and their description, and all other investments in personal property, specifying the value thereof and the original cost; also the amount of moneys held in trust and on deposit on the day of the return, the average amount of loans for the year, and the actual amount of loans on the day of the return, and the security held therefor.

ARTICLE III.

BANK COMMISSIONERS.

SECTION 1. The Bank Commissioners shall visit and examine every bank, savings bank, and trust company, semi-annually, or oftener, and may examine its books and papers in the presence of one or more of its officers, to ascertain whether it has been managed according to law; examine any persons under oath, in relation to its affairs, which oath such Commissioners may administer; may compel the attendance of witnesses, and the production of books and papers by suitable process; and in case any person, on request of the Commissioners, shall refuse to comply with any of the provisions of this section, may apply to a judge of the Superior Court, who shall cause such person to come before him and inquire into the facts set forth in such application, and may thereupon commit such person to jail until he shall comply with said provisions; but the Bank Commissioners shall not impart any information obtained by them in the course of such examination, except so far as may become necessary in the performance of their duties.

1844.   1872. Duties and powers.

May compel testimony.

SEC. 2. The Commissioners shall annually report to the General Assembly the condition of all such institutions examined by them, with such recommendations as they may deem proper: and shall also report to the General Assembly and to the State's Attorney in the county where any such institution is located any violation of law by it or any of its officers.

1867. Report to the General Assembly.

SEC. 3. The Comptroller shall apportion the salaries of the Bank Commissioners among the several banks, savings banks, and trust companies, in proportion to the aggregate amount of the capital and deposits of each, according to their average as nearly as can be ascertained, for the year preceding, and notify each by mail of the amount apportioned to it, and it shall pay the same to the State within twenty days from the time of mailing such notice; and any institution

1872. Fund for their salary, whence derived.

15

Penalty on
banks, etc.,
neglecting or
refusing to pay.

which shall not pay the same within said time shall forfeit two hundred dollars, together with the amount so apportioned, to the State.

[From Title III, Chapter I, Part VIII, as amended by the Act of March 22, 1877.]

1837,   1874.
1877.
Appointment,
term of office,
and disquali-
fications.

SECTION 1. Two Bank Commissioners, whose powers and duties shall be those specified in Chapter II of Title XVII, shall be appointed by the Governor, one annually, to hold office for two years, and until their successors are appointed and qualified; and he shall also fill any vacancy for any unexpired term. No officer of any bank, savings bank, or trust company, shall be eligible to said office; and if any Bank Commissioner at any time shall become indebted or obligated to any bank, savings bank, or trust company, or shall engage or be interested in the sale of securities as a busi-ness, or in the negotiation of loans for others, his office shall

Bank officers to
give notice of
indebtedness.

become vacant. The cashier of every bank and the treasurer of every savings bank or trust company to which a Bank Commissioner shall become indebted or obligated, shall forth-with give notice thereof to the Governor.

ARTICLE IV.

CLOSING BUSINESS OF BANKS.

1837.
Complaint for
forfeiture of
charter.

SECTION 1. When, in the opinion of the Bank Commis-sioners, the charter of any bank shall be forfeited, or the public are in danger of being defrauded by any bank, said Commissioners, or the State's Attorney in the county in which it is situated, shall prefer a complaint to the Supe-rior Court for such county, as a court of equity, if in ses-sion, or if not to a judge of the Supreme Court of Errors, praying that such bank may be enjoined from any further proceedings in its business, and that its charter may be revoked, and its property disposed of; whereupon said court or judge shall forthwith issue a citation to said bank, to be served upon the president, a majority of the directors, and the cashier, by leaving a true and attested copy with each, or at his last usual place of abode, if within this State, commanding it to appear before said court or judge, on a day and at a place named in such citation, to answer to said complaint. And if, upon the hearing, said court or judge shall be of opinion that the charter of such bank is forfeited, or that the public are in danger of being defrauded thereby, said court or judge shall issue an injunction to the agents of such bank, enjoining them from proceeding in transacting its business, and appoint not exceeding three disinterested persons to be receivers of such bank; and said court, at any term subsequent to the issuing Receivers. of said injunction, may, upon a hearing of all the parties, declare the charter of such bank to be null and void.

SEC. 2. Receivers of any bank whose capital is impaired 1867. Receivers on may be appointed by the Superior Court for the county in petition of stockholders. which such bank is located, on the petition of the holders of a majority of its capital stock, if the court finds that the interests of the stockholders require that the affairs of such bank should be closed.

SEC. 3. Receivers appointed under the provisions of this 1858. Notes and part may apply to a judge of the Superior Court for an order plates of bank to be destroyed in relation to the disposition to be made of the circulating on application of receiver. notes, and the note plates of such bank, who may, and in case of a perpetual injunction against the further transaction of business by the bank, or the repeal of its charter, shall order said plates and notes to be destroyed.

SEC. 4. The avails of the property of the bank shall be Avails of the property of appropriated ratably to the payment, first, of the charges and bank, how appropriated. expenses of settling its concerns; secondly, of the circulating notes; thirdly, of all deposits; fourthly, to the repayment of all sums which have been subscribed and paid in for its stock by the State, or School Fund; fifthly, to the payment of all other liabilities; and the surplus shall be paid and distributed among the stockholders.

SEC. 5. All payments and conveyances made by any such What payments and conveyan- bank in contemplation of insolvency, to or for the use of any ces are void. or all its creditors, with the fraudulent intent to prevent the distribution and appropriation of its effects in manner as here-inbefore prescribed, shall be utterly void.

Refusal to sur-render assets. SEC. 6. Any person who shall willfully neglect or refuse to deliver to the receivers, on demand, books, papers, or any evidences of title or debt, or property belonging to said bank, in his possession or under his control shall be fined not more than ten thousand dollars, or imprisoned not more than three years, or both.

ARTICLE V.

BANKS ORGANIZING UNDER UNITED STATES LAWS.

863, Corporate rights not terminated, but suspended. SECTION 1. When two-thirds of the stockholders of any bank shall vote or agree to become a national banking association, and such change shall be duly consummated, the corporate rights and existence of said bank shall not be deemed to be thereby terminated or altered; but the same shall be deemed suspended during the existence of said association, excepting that for three years next following such change, and until the termination of all suits by or against it, said bank may continue to exercise its corporate powers for **1868. Actions.** the sole purpose of closing up its concerns, and prosecuting and defending said suits; and may, at any time after the expiration of said three years, convey its real estate to such association, if the same was included as a part of its assets at the time of the conversion of said bank.

1865. Stockholders not dissenting, to be stockholders in the national bank. SEC. 2. When any bank has been, or shall be, converted into a national banking association, every stockholder who does not signify to such bank, in writing, his dissent thereto, within thirty days after notice in writing given him of such conversion, shall become a shareholder in said association to the amount of his stock in such bank; and said notice may be given by leaving the same with him, or at his usual place of abode, or depositing it, properly addressed to him, postage paid, in the post-office at the place where said bank is located.

SEC. 3. Executors, administrators, guardians, conserva-tors, and trustees may represent the stock in their control, in all matters touching the conversion of said bank into a national banking association, and subscribe to its capital stock. *Stock of deceased persons, and others, how represented.*

SEC. 4. Any stockholder in a bank so converted into a national banking association, who shall not become a share-holder in said association, shall be entitled to receive from said bank the value of his stock, to be ascertained by an appraisal, made as the directors may prescribe; and if the value so fixed shall not be satisfactory to any stockholder, he may appeal to the Bank Commissioners, who shall make a re-appraisal which shall be final; and if said re-appraisal shall exceed the value fixed by the directors, the bank shall pay the expenses of said re-appraisal, otherwise the appellant shall pay them ; and the value so ascertained shall be deemed to be a debt due to said stockholder from said association. *Persons not becoming stockholders to be paid for their stock.*

SEC. 5. Every bank which shall have been converted into a national banking association, in which, at the time of its conversion, this State or any charitable corporation held stock, which shall have refused to allow such stockholder to become a stockholder in said association, shall pay to it its ratable share of so much of the surplus of said bank as was accumulated during its ownership of said stock, the amount to be determined according to the provisions of the preceding section. *1865. Surplus, rights of holders of non-transferable stock in.*

SEC. 6. The officers of any national banking association, converted from a State bank, who shall be in office when such association shall cease to exist, shall continue in office after it shall have resumed its powers as a State bank, until others shall be appointed in their stead. *Officers to continue.*

SEC. 7. Every bank which shall resume its powers as a bank of this State, after having ceased to be a national banking association, shall forthwith deliver to the Bank Commissioners, and duly publish in a newspaper of the county in which such bank is located, such a particular and detailed statement, under oath, of its condition, as is required in the eleventh section of Article II of this Part. *Duty on resuming chartered powers.t*

Non-transfera-ble stock, when to become transferable. SEC. 8. Notice of the intention of any bank to become a national banking association shall be given to all holders of non-transferable stock, by sending a written notice to the Treasurer or institution holding the same, within ten days after such bank shall have made its said determination; and any such holder may, within thirty days after the receipt of said notice, elect in writing to continue to hold such stock as transferable stock, and to hold the same after the proposed change shall have been effected, as stock of said proposed national banking association; and thereupon such stock shall **Owner declin-ing to become a stockholder, may withdraw the same.** be deemed regular capital stock of said bank. If such holder does not make such election, it, at the expiration of said thirty days, shall be entitled to receive from said bank the par value of said stock, with interest from the date of the last dividend **The amount, how recover-ab e.** declared by said bank; and said amount shall be a debt due and payable to said owner or owners from said national banking association.

Notice to Comp-troller. SEC. 9. Any bank, which may organize as a national banking association, shall, within sixty days thereafter, notify the Comptroller thereof in writing; and any such bank failing to give such notice, or to comply with any of the provisions of this Article applicable to such bank, shall be deemed to have surrendered its charter, and the same shall be thenceforth considered as revoked, except so far as the same shall remain in force by virtue of the first section of this Article.

PART III.

SAVINGS BANKS.

SECTION 1. No more than three officers of any one sav- _{1874.} ings bank shall be officers of any one bank of discount or circulation, or trust company; and no cashier of a bank of discount or circulation shall be treasurer of any savings bank having over five hundred thousand dollars deposits.

Officers of banks of discount, when not to be officers of savings banks.

[Section 2 repealed by act of March 18, 1880.]

SEC. 3. No savings bank shall buy, or lend any money _{1873.} upon any obligation on which only one person or firm shall be holden, without taking additional security for the same equivalent to the guaranty or endorsement of some other responsible party.

One name paper.

SEC. 4. When any loan or investment is made by any _{1874.} savings bank, the names of the directors or trustees con- senting thereto shall be entered upon the records of said bank, and said record shall be at all times open to the inspection of the corporators and auditors of said bank and the Bank Commissioners, and be *primâ facie* evidence of the truth of the statements therein contained.

Record of consent of directors to loan or investment.

SEC. 5. Savings banks may receive on deposit from any _{1850. 1872.} one individual, in his own name or in the name of another, in any one year, a sum not exceeding one thousand dollars.

Deposits of individuals limited.

[Section 6 repealed by act of March 7, 1877.]

SEC. 7. Savings banks whose deposits shall exceed five _{1868. 1873.} hundred thousand dollars, may pay their presidents such compensation as the directors, managers, or trustees deem reasonable, not exceeding three hundred dollars a year.

Compensation of presidents

SEC. 8. The directors, managers, or trustees of any _{1867.} savings bank, assenting to a violation of any provision of law relating to savings banks, shall be jointly and severally liable to said savings bank for any loss which may result therefrom.

Officers, when liable.

[Section 9 repealed by act of March 13, 1877.]

[Section 10 repealed by act of March 23, 1877.]

SEC. 11. No officer of a savings bank shall be a bor- _{1874.} rower, or surety for a borrower, of any of its funds; nor receive any money or valuable thing for negotiating, pro- curing, or recommending any such loan from such bank, or for selling or aiding in the sale of any stocks or securities to such savings bank. And any such officer who shall violate any provision of this section, shall forfeit to the State one thousand dollars.

Officer not to be a borrower, etc.

SEC. 12. The treasurer of each savings bank shall, at least ten days before each meeting of the corporators, mail or deliver to each a written or printed notice of the day and hour of holding such meeting; and if he shall neglect to give such notice, he shall pay one hundred dollars to the town where such bank is located.

1870. Notices of meetings.

SEC. 13. The treasurer of each savings bank shall give bonds with surety, to the acceptance of the directors or trustees, in not less than ten thousand dollars, payable to said bank, and kept by the president thereof; and no president, director, or trustee of any such savings bank shall be surety in the bond of such treasurer.

1860. Treasurers to give bonds.

1874. President nor director to be surety.

[Section 14 repealed by act of March 7, 1878.]

SEC. 15. When a corporator of any savings bank shall neglect to attend its meetings for three successive years, or be convicted of any crime, he may be removed by a unanimous vote of said corporators at any annual meeting.

1871. Corporator, how removed.

SEC. 16. The directors, managers, or trustees of savings banks may fill any vacancy in any office and the person chosen to fill the same shall hold said office until another is chosen in his stead; and when any officer cannot perform the duties of his office they may appoint an assistant to him during their pleasure, until the next annual meeting of said corporation, who shall have the same powers and duties as such officer.

Vacancies in offices, how filled.

SEC. 17. The Bank Commissioners shall visit and examine every savings bank whose treasurer is cashier of any national banking association, at the same time the United States Examiner shall visit it.

1871. Commissioners to visit with United States Examiner.

SEC. 18. The provisions of Article IV of Part II of this Chapter, in regard to closing the business of banks, and the distribution of their assets, shall, so far as possible, be applied to savings banks.

1878. Proceedings in insolvency.

SEC. 19. Every person who shall violate any provision of law in relation to banks, savings banks, or trust companies, for which no other penalty is provided or provision made, shall be fined not less than one hundred dollars, nor more than five hundred dollars.

General penalty.

TITLE XXII.—Provisions for Defining and Establishing the
General Statutes.

SECTION 8. As used in these General Statutes . . . the *Defining the terms "banks"*
term "banks" shall include all incorporated banks; the term *and "savings banks."*
"savings banks" shall include savings banks, societies for
savings, and savings societies.

[An Act relating to Savings Banks.]

Be it enacted by the Senate and House of Representatives in
General Assembly convened:

SECTION 1. No savings bank or savings society in this *1875. Rate of interest*
State shall demand or receive on any loan, now or hereafter *which savings banks may take.*
to be made, by said savings bank or society, either as bonus,
commission, or tax, or in any other way, directly or indirectly,
more than the value of six dollars for the forbearance of one
hundred dollars a year, and at that rate for a greater or less
sum, or for a longer or shorter period; but the taking of
interest in advance for a period not to exceed six months, and
the reimbursement of any money paid by said bank or society
for insurance on property mortgaged to them, shall not be
deemed a violation of this act.

[The foregoing section is given as amended by the act of
March 12, 1877.]

[Section 2 repealed by act of March 27, 1878.]

SEC. 3. All special acts granting special privileges to any *1875. Repeal of special privileges.*
savings bank or savings society, heretofore passed, are hereby
repealed.

SEC. 4. All loans made by any savings bank or savings *Certain loans confirmed.*
society, on or before the first day of January, 1875, upon
which interest has been taken in advance for a period of six
months, or for a shorter period, at any one time, are hereby
ratified, confirmed, and declared to be legal and valid.

SEC. 5. This act shall take effect from its passage.

SEC. 6. All acts or parts of acts inconsistent herewith are
hereby repealed.

Approved, May 26, 1875.

[An Act relating to Savings Banks.]

Be it enacted by the Senate and House of Representatives in General Assembly convened:

[Sections 1 and 2 repealed by act of March 23, 1877.]

Returns by receivers of savings banks. SECTION 3. The receivers of any savings bank heretofore appointed, or which hereafter may be appointed by judicial authority, shall, on or before the tenth day of July next after such appointment, and annually thereafter so long as said receivers remain in charge and administration of the assets of such bank, render to the Bank Commissioners a sworn statement of all the assets of said bank, containing, so far as possible, a detailed enumeration thereof, with their cash values.

Penalty. SEC. 4. Any receiver or receivers who shall fail to make the return required by the preceding section, shall forfeit to the State a penalty of five hundred dollars.

When this act takes effect. SEC. 5. This act shall take effect from its passage, and the reports made by the savings banks of the amount of their deposits on the first day of July, 1875, and the taxes assessed on the same, shall be made and assessed under the provisions of this act.

Approved, July 8, 1875.

[An Act relating to Savings Banks.]

Be it enacted by the Senate and House of Representatives in General Assembly convened:

Loans by savings banks on real estate to be appraised. SECTION 1. That when any loan is made by any savings bank or savings society, upon real estate security, the property mortgaged to secure such loan shall be appraised by two or more suitable persons, who shall be well known in the community where such loan is made; and such appraisal, together with a certificate of title, shall be lodged and kept with the institution making such loan; and such appraisal shall express upon its face the amount at which said property is appraised.

Loans on personal security. SEC. 2. That no savings bank or savings society having more than twenty-five thousand dollars deposits shall loan on personal security to any one person, company, or interest more than three per cent. of its deposits at the time of making such loan.

Approved, July 23, 1875.

[An Act in Addition to an Act relating to Receivers.]

Be it enacted by the Senate and House of Representatives in General Assembly convened :

SECTION 1. Upon the appointment of receivers for any incorporated bank, savings bank, or trust company, the court making such appointment shall, in the absence of any statutory provision therefor, limit the time within which all claims against such corporation shall be presented to said receivers, and said court may, upon proper cause shown, extend such time, and shall cause such public notice of such limitation or extension of time to be given as it shall deem reasonable and just. And all claims not presented to said receivers within the period limited therefor shall be forever barred. *Limitation of time for presenting claims to receivers of banks, etc. Gen. Stat., p. 288.*

SEC. 2. Said receivers shall receive proof of, and allow or disallow, as justice and equity may require, the several claims which may be presented to them as aforesaid, and shall make report thereof to said court, specifying particularly those allowed and disallowed, and shall give such notice as said court may prescribe, to any party whose claim or any part thereof is disallowed. Any person aggrieved by the doings of said receivers, in the allowance or disallowance of any claims or any part thereof, may after said report shall have been returned to said court, and within such time as said court shall limit for that purpose, and not afterwards, make his complaint in writing to said court, setting forth with reasonable certainty the grievance whereof he complains, and said complaint being first served on said receivers, and upon any other party in interest who may be entitled to notice, in such manner as said court shall prescribe or deem reasonable, said court shall, by a committee or otherwise, inquire into the grievances complained of, and grant such relief in the premises as to law and equity may appertain. *Reception of claims by said receivers. Appeals.*

Inventory of
assets.

SEC. 3. Said receivers shall, as soon after their appointment as may be, make and return to said court an inventory and appraisal of the assets of such corporation, verified by oath according to their best knowledge, information, and belief, and shall from time to time thereafter make and return such additional or supplementary inventories and valuations, and render such reports of their doings and statements of accounts as shall be necessary for the information of said court, or as shall be required by the order of said court. They shall hold all the assets which shall come into their hands, as such receivers, subject to the order of said court, shall convert the same into money, with all reasonable dispatch, and for that purpose may sell and dispose of said assets, and make all proper conveyances thereof, and may compromise all doubtful claims for or against such corporation : *provided, however,* that no claim in favor of such corporation against any director, trustee, or other officer thereof, for breach or neglect of official duty, shall be compromised without the special authority and approval of said court. In cases of doubt or difficulty they may, upon written application, ask the advice of said court as to the manner in which they shall execute their trust. Said court may from time to time, of its own motion, or on complaint of any party interested, make all necessary and proper orders as to the proceedings of said receivers, their compensation and other expenses, and may make and render any and all proper judgments and decrees, as the exigencies of the case may require, for the right administration and final settlement of such estate according to law.

Claim against
an officer for
breach of trust
not to be com-
promised.

Claims in favor
of the corpora-
tion not barred
when..

SEC. 4. No claim in favor of such corporation not barred by the statute of limitation at the time of serving the citation on said corporation for the appointment of receivers shall be barred against said receivers in any suit for the recovery thereof, brought by them either in their own name or in the name of said corporation.

Dissolution of
attachment,
etc., on such
corporation.
Gen. Statutes,
p. 288.

SEC. 5. All attachments of the estate of any such corporation, made within sixty days of the filing of any complaint as prescribed in section one, article four, part two, chapter two, title seventeen of the general statutes, and all levies of execution upon the estate of said corporation

not completed within the period aforesaid, except such
levies as are made in pursuance of attachments which are
not herein invalidated, shall, upon the granting of the
prayer of said complaint and the appointment of receivers
of said corporation, be and become dissolved.

SEC. 6. Any judge of the supreme court of errors may exercise all the powers of the superior court included in the preceding sections, whenever the superior court of the proper county is not in session at a civil term, and the orders and doings of said judge in the premises shall be recorded with the records of said superior court. *Judge of supreme court may act, when*

Approved, July 23, 1875.

[An act in addition to and in Amendment of an Act relating to Savings
Banks.]

*Be it enacted by the Senate and House of Representatives in
General Assembly convened :*

SECTION 1. All loans and investments by savings banks, in United States bonds, bonds of this State, and the bonds of any of the counties, towns, cities, boroughs, and school districts of this State, shall be classed in the returns of the treasurers of said savings banks as real estate for the purposes of loans. *Treasurers of savings banks in their returns to class certain investments as real estate.*

SEC. 2. Power is hereby given to the directors of savings banks, in declaring dividends, to discriminate between deposits of two thousand dollars and less and those over that sum; such discrimination shall not exceed one per cent. per annum, and if at any time a discrimination becomes necessary such discrimination shall always be made in favor of those deposits the amount of which are less than two thousand dollars. *Savings banks may discriminate in declaring dividends.*

SEC. 3. All acts and parts of acts inconsistent herewith are hereby repealed. *Repeal.*

SEC. 4. This act shall take effect from its passage. *When takes effect.*

Approved, June 28, 1876.

[An act to Provide for the Election of Directors of Corporations.]

Be it enacted by the Senate and House of Representatives in General Assembly convened:

Who eligible as a bank director.   Any one of the directors or executive officers of any corporation incorporated by the laws of this State, owning stock in any of the banks or other corporations of this State, shall be eligible to be elected as a director of such banks or other corporations, at any meeting of the stockholders of such banks or other corporations, legally convened for the election of directors, and upon such election may act as director of such bank or other corporation, *provided, however,* that not more than one single person of such directors or executive officers shall be eligible to serve as such director at the same time.

Approved, June 28, 1876.

[An Act to amend the General Statutes in relation to the Reports of Savings Banks.]

Be it enacted by the Senate and House of Representatives in General Assembly convened:

Auditors of savings banks.   SECTION 1. The directors, managers, or trustees of savings banks shall annually appoint not less than two auditors, who shall not be directors, managers, or trustees thereof, who shall examine the books, accounts, and securities belonging to such bank, and make a sworn statement showing the true condition thereof on the first day of October in each year, which shall be kept on file in the office of said bank, and an attested copy forwarded to the Bank Commissioners on or before the first day of November in each year.

[Section 2 repealed by act of March 28, 1878.]

[Section 3 repeals acts omitted in this compilation.]

Approved, March 7, 1877.

[An Act in relation to Savings Banks.]

Be it enacted by the Senate and House of Representatives in General Assembly convened:

Savings bank dividends regulated.   SECTION 1. The net income of any savings bank in excess of a sum equal to one-eighth* of one per cent. of

---

*As amended by act of March 11, 1880.

its deposits, actually earned during the six months last preceding, and no more, may be semi-annually divided among its depositors.

SEC. 2. No savings bank shall make any dividend, ex-cept as provided in section one of this act, until its surplus shall have accumulated to an amount equal to three per cent. of its deposits. Such surplus shall be kept as a contingent fund; but no savings bank shall carry to its contingent fund a sum larger than an amount equal to ten per cent. of its deposits; but any surplus beyond that amount shall be divided among the depositors entitled to such dividends, in sums of not less than one per cent. of its deposits. *Savings banks required to keep a surplus fund.*

[Section 3 repeals a section of a law omitted in this compilation.]

Approved, March 13, 1877.

[An Act concerning Savings Banks.]

Be it enacted by the Senate and House of Representatives in General Assembly convened:

SECTION 1. The treasurer of every savings bank shall, on or before the tenth day of July annually, deliver to the comptroller a sworn statement containing the name and amount standing to his credit of every depositor who shall not have made a deposit therein or withdrawn therefrom any part of his deposit, or any part of the interest thereon, for a period of more than twenty years next preceding: *provided, however,* this act shall not apply to the deposit made by any person known to said bank to be living. *Annual returns to be made of those who have not increased or diminished their deposits for twenty years.*

SEC. 2. The comptroller shall communicate the statements hereinbefore provided, which have been delivered to him, to the succeeding session of the General Assembly thereafter, and on or before the third day thereof. *Comptroller to report to general assembly.*

Approved, March 13, 1878.

[An Act relating to Savings Banks.]

Be it enacted by the Senate and House of Representatives in General Assembly convened:

SECTION 1. The treasurer of each savings bank or savings society in this State shall, on or before the tenth day of *Returns by and tax on savings banks.*

January, A. D. 1879, and annually thereafter, on or before said day, deliver to the comptroller of this State a sworn statement of the amount of all its deposits, exclusive of surplus, on the first day of said month; and every such savings bank or savings society shall pay to the State an annual tax on its corporate franchise equal to one-fourth of one per centum on the amount of its deposits, exclusive of surplus, deducting, however, from said deposits the sum of fifty thousand dollars, and also the amount invested in any bonds issued by this State or by any town or city in this State in aid of the construction of any railroad, and which by the statutes of this State are exempt from taxation, and also the amount invested in real estate liable to taxation in this State, one-half of said tax to be paid on or before the twentieth day of January, and one-half on or before the twentieth day of July in each year, beginning with the month of January, 1879; and said tax shall be in lieu of all other taxes upon said savings banks or savings societies, their deposits and surplus, except upon the real estate owned by them, beyond what is required and used by them for the transaction of their appropriate business.

Powers of board of equalization. SEC. 2. The board of equalization shall have the same powers in regard to the returns required by section 27 as are conferred upon them by section 11 of chapter v, title xii, of the general statutes of 1875, in regard to the returns therein named.

United States taxes may be charged to depositors. SEC. 3. All taxes paid by the savings banks or savings societies of this State to the United States may be proportionately charged by said savings banks or savings societies to those depositors upon whose deposits said taxes are paid.

Penalty for violation of law relating to savings banks. SEC. 4. Any officer, director, or trustee of any savings bank or savings society who shall intentionally violate any provisions of the statute law of this State relating to savings banks shall be punished by a fine of not less than one hundred nor more than one thousand dollars, at the discretion of the court before whom the offense is tried, and it shall be the duty of the State's Attorney for the county where such bank or society is located to prosecute such violation on complaint thereof by the Bank Commissioners.

[Section 5 repeals certain acts and parts of acts which are omitted in this compilation.]

Approved, March 27, 1878.

———

[An Act relating to Receivers of Savings Banks.]

Be it enacted by the Senate and House of Representatives in General Assembly convened :

That it shall be the duty of all receivers of savings banks heretofore appointed, or which may hereafter be appointed, to include in the reports required by law to be made by them to · the Bank Commissioners a statement in detail of the expenses incurred by them in the administration of the affairs of such bank, including an estimate of the amount which they will ask the superior court to allow for their own services during the time covered by such report, and the first statement hereafter made by such receivers shall include in detail as aforesaid such expenses and estimated charges for the whole period of time elapsed since their appointment.

Reports made by receivers of savings banks.

Approved, March 27, 1878.

———

[An Act relating to Returns of Savings Banks.]

Be it enacted by the Senate and House of Representatives in General Assembly convened :

SECTION 1. The treasurer of each savings bank, on or before the first day of October in each year, and oftener if required by the Bank Commissioners, shall transmit to them a sworn statement of its condition, giving the par value, cost, and market value of its assets and answers to all particulars required in the annual statements of banks and trust companies to said commissioners.

Statement of condition of savings banks to be made annually.

[Section 2 repeals part of a public act which is omitted in this compilation.]

Approved, March 27, 1878.

16

[An Act in addition to an Act concerning Private Corporations.]

*Be it enacted by the Senate and House of Representatives in
General Assembly convened:*

Closing busi-
ness of trust
companies.
Gen. Stat.,
p. 288.

SECTION 1.   All the provisions of title seventeen, article
four of the general statutes relative to closing the business of banks are hereby extended to trust companies.

Acts of receiv-
ers confirmed.

SEC. 2.   All appointments of receivers for any trust
company, heretofore made by the superior court, are hereby validated and confirmed, and all the acts and doings of
the said receivers so appointed, done, and performed in
pursuance of the duties of their said appointment are
hereby ratified and declared to be legal and binding upon
all parties.

Duty of receiv-
ers.   Acts 1878,
p. 883.

SEC. 3.   It shall be the duty of all receivers for trust
companies, now in office or hereafter appointed, to make
the same reports to the Bank Commissioners relative to their
administration of the affairs of said trust companies and the
expense thereof as receivers of savings banks are now
required to make to said Bank Commissioners, by the
provisions of chapter one hundred and thirteen of the
public acts of 1878.

SEC. 4.   This act shall take effect from its passage.

Approved, March 4, 1879.

[An Act concerning Savings Banks.]

*Be it enacted by the Senate and House of Representatives in
General Assembly convened:*

Loans by sav-
ings banks to
manufacturing
or ecclesiastical
corporations.

SECTION 1.   That no loan shall hereafter be made by any
savings bank to a manufacturing corporation or ecclesiastical
society, secured by mortgage upon their property, unless the
same shall be accompanied by the individual guarantee of
some responsible party or parties, or by other collateral
security of equal value to the amount of the sum loaned, and
the directors or trustees of any such bank consenting to any
loan contrary to the provisions of this act shall be held indi-
vidually responsible to the full extent of such loan.

Savings bank
buildings.

SEC. 2.   No savings bank shall expend in the purchase or
construction of any building, for the purpose, in whole or in
part, of accommodating the business of said bank, a greater

sum than may be taken from the surplus of said bank, after allowing for the depreciation of assets and the reserve required by law, and subject in all cases to the approval of the Bank Commissioners.

Approved, March 19, 1879.

[An Act fixing the Fees of Receivers of Banks, Savings Banks, and Trust Companies.]

Be it enacted by the Senate and House of Representatives in General Assembly convened :

SECTION 1.   That the fees of receivers of banks, savings banks, and trust companies shall be one per cent. of the amount of dividends paid to depositors and other creditors, and may be drawn by said receiver or receivers at the time dividends are paid, and shall be in full for their personal and clerical services ; all other expenses to be taxed and allowed by the court: *provided,* that if in the settlement of such trusts it shall appear that the aggregate amount of dividends paid is less than two hundred and fifty thousand dollars, the court may allow such further sum as may be equitable and just. *(Fees of receivers of banks, savings banks, and trust companies.)*

SEC. 2.   That the act entitled "An Act fixing the Fees of Receivers of Banks, Savings Banks, and Trust Companies," approved March 27, 1879, be, and the same is hereby, repealed. *(Repealing act of 1879.)*

SEC. 3.   This act shall take effect from its passage.

Approved, March 12, 1880.

[An Act concerning Savings Banks, Banks, and Trust Companies.]

Be it enacted by the Senate and House of Representatives in General Assembly convened :

SECTION 1.   That the cashiers of banks and the treasurers of trust companies shall severally give bonds in the penal sum of not less than ten thousand dollars, with sufficient sureties for the faithful performance of the duties of their office, and the bonds of such cashiers and treasurers, and the bonds of treasurers of savings banks now required by law to be given, shall forthwith be recorded at length in the books of said banks, savings banks, and trust companies respectively, *(Bonds of treasurers to be recorded.)*

and shall at all times be subject to the inspection of the bank commissioners.

Bonds to be kept by president.

SEC. 2. It shall be the duty of the president of every bank, savings bank, or trust company to safely keep the original bond or bonds so given as aforesaid.

Approved, March 12, 1880.

[An Act concerning Savings Banks.]

Be it enacted by the Senate and House of Representatives in General Assembly convened :

SECTION 1. Savings banks may employ not exceeding half of their deposits in making loans on personal security, and in the purchase of the public stock or bonds of the United States, of any of the New England States, of the states of New York, New Jersey, Pennsylvania, Ohio, Kentucky, Michigan, Indiana, Illinois, Wisconsin, Iowa, Missouri, Kansas, or Nebraska, or of the District of Columbia, in the authorized bonds of any incorporated city in the New England states, of the cities of New York, Brooklyn, Albany, Syracuse, Utica, Troy, Rochester, and Buffalo in the state of New York, Philadelphia in the state of Pennsylvania, Detroit in the state of Michigan, Cleveland, Columbus, Dayton, and Cincinnati in the state of Ohio, Chicago in the state of Illinois, Milwaukee in the state of Wisconsin, and St. Louis in the state of Missouri ; also in the first mortgage bonds of any railroad company, located in any of the states aforesaid, which has paid dividends of not less than five per centum per annum regularly, on their entire capital stock, for a period of not less than five years next previous to the purchase of such bonds, or in the consolidated mortgage bonds of any railroad company chartered by this state, authorized to be issued to retire the entire bonded debt of said company, *provided* said company has paid dividends as aforesaid, or of any town or borough of, this state, or in the stock of any bank in this state, New York city, or Boston, or in the stock of any trust company in the cities of Hartford or New Haven, and all other loans shall be secured by mortgage of unincumbered real estate, in this state, worth double the amount of the loan secured thereon ; *provided* that the Stafford savings bank of

Deposits how to be invested.

Mortgages to be on lands in this state.

the town of Stafford, and the Stonington savings bank of the Stafford and Stonington
town of Stonington, may loan, the former on land located in banks may loan out of state.
the county of Hampden, in the state of Massachusetts, the
latter on land in the county of Washington, in the state of
Rhode Island.

SEC. 2. That investments in United States bonds, in bonds Bonds which may be classed
of this state, in bonds of towns, cities, boroughs, and school with loans on
districts in this state may be classed with loans upon real real estate.
estate, for the purpose of determining the proportion of loans
required upon such estate.

SEC. 3. That section two, part three of chapter two, title Repealing acts named.
seventeen of the general statutes, and chapter seventy-eight,
entitled, "An act in amendment of an act relating to savings
banks," approved July 23, 1875, be, and the same are hereby,
repealed.

SEC. 4. This act shall take effect from its passage.

Approved, March 18, 1880.

UNITED STATES LAW.

An Act to Amend the Laws relating to Internal Revenue.

Be it enacted, etc. * * * *

Insolvent bank not to pay tax. SECTION 22. That whenever and after any bank has ceased to do business by reason of insolvency or bankruptcy, no tax shall be assessed or collected, or paid into the Treasury of the United States on account of such bank, which shall diminish the assets thereof necessary for the full payment of all its depositors; and such tax shall be abated from such national banks as are found by the Comptroller of the Currency to be insolvent; and the Commissioner of Internal Revenue, when the facts shall so appear to him, is authorized to remit so much of said tax against insolvent State and savings banks as shall be found to affect the claims of their depositors.

Relating to tax on savings banks having no capital stock. That in making further collections of internal revenue taxes on bank deposits, no savings bank, recognized as such by the laws of its State, and having no capital stock, shall on account of mercantile or business deposits heretofore received, upon which no interest has been allowed to the parties making such deposits, be denied the exemptions allowed to savings banks having no capital stock and doing no other business than receiving deposits to be loaned or invested for the sole benefit of the parties making such deposits, without profit or compensation to the banks, if such bank has paid the lawful tax upon the entire average amount of such business or mercantile deposits; but nothing in this section shall be construed to extend said exemptions to deposits hereafter made, or in any way to affect the liability of such deposits to taxation.

That section thirty-four hundred and eight of the Revised Statutes be amended by striking out all after the thirtieth line, and inserting the following:

"Associations or companies known as provident insti- tutions, savings banks, savings funds, or savings institutions doing no other business than receiving and loaning or investing savings deposits shall be exempt from tax on so much of such deposits as they have invested in securities of the United States, and on two thousand dollars of savings deposits and nothing in excess thereof, made in the name of and belonging to any one person."

That all laws and parts of laws inconsistent with the provisions of this section be, and the same are hereby, repealed. * * *

Approved, March 1, 1879.

SYNOPSIS OF DECISIONS

OF THE

SUPREME COURT OF ERRORS OF CONNECTICUT,

RELATING TO SAVINGS BANKS.

DEPOSITS IN TRUST.

A widow with a considerable estate and no children deposited in a savings bank $250 in her own name as trustee for a boy thirteen years of age, whose parents were near neighbors and friends, and who was accustomed to do errands for her. Shortly after making the deposit she told the boy's parents that she had deposited that amount in the savings bank for their son, and again alluding to it remarked that it would be needed for his education. She kept the bank book herself, and two years thereafter drew out a part of the money, and a year later the balance with accrued interest, signing receipts in her own name, and appropriating the money to her own use. She died four years later, leaving a will in which no allusion was made to the deposit, and nothing was given to the boy. It was found by the court below that at the time she made the deposit she intended to make a gift, to take effect either then or at some future time. Held that she made a complete gift at the time of the deposit, and could not afterwards revoke it. Held also, that the trust was to be regarded upon the facts as only for the boy's minority, and that upon his becoming of age the legal title would vest in him without any further act to end the trust.—
Minor vs. *Rogers*, 40 Conn. Reports, p. 512.

DEPOSITS TO THE CREDIT OF ANOTHER.

A woman deposited $460 in a savings bank for E. K., her niece, the deposit being placed to the credit on the books of the bank of "E. K.—M. K. guardian;" she at the same time informing the guardian of her niece that she had made such a deposit. A bank book was delivered to her by the bank with the deposit so entered, but she retained possession of it, and afterward had the money transferred back to her by the guardian. The court below found that at the time the deposit was made she intended it as a gift to her niece. Held to be a complete gift, and beyond the power of revocation.—*Kerrigan* vs. *Rantigan.* 43 Conn. Reports, p. 17.

PAYMENT OF DEPOSITS ON FORGED ORDER.

A savings bank paid money on an order to a person who brought with it the depositor's bank book. It proved that the order was forged and that the bank book had been stolen. The savings bank had a standing rule, on account of the difficulty of identifying its depositors, that any person bringing the bank book of a depositor should, in the absence of suspicious circumstances, be taken to be the depositor, or to have an order from him; and the book contained in conspicuous letters on the cover the following notice: "Caution to depositors. This book should be preserved with great care. If it should be lost, give immediate information at this office." The by-laws of the bank were also printed on the cover of the book, one of which was as follows: "Payment on deposits shall be made only to the depositor or his order, or to his legal representatives, on the presentation of the depositor's book." The depositor had no actual notice of the rule of the bank except what would be conveyed by this by-law and caution. Held, in an action brought against the bank by the depositor to recover the amount paid out on the forged order, that the bank could not avail itself of that payment in defense, and that the plaintiff is entitled to recover. Had the book contained this further notice, that the presentation of the book shall be taken to be full authority for paying the money, and this rule been brought distinctly to the knowledge of the depositor, and assented to by him, the bank would have been justified in the payment on the forged order.—*Eaves* vs. *People's Savings Bank,* 27 Conn., p. 229.

SCALING DEPOSITS.

A savings bank in the course of its business met with a loss equal to 24 per cent. of its deposits, which sum was by vote of the directors apportioned *pro rata* among the depositors, and this action of the directors was afterwards validated and confirmed by resolve of the General Assembly. In an action by a depositor to recover his *pro rata* share of such loss, it was held that the defendant was merely the agent of the plaintiff to receive and hold his money, that the loss was occasioned by the plaintiff's own act through the instrumentality of his agent, and that independently of the resolve of the General Assembly he was not entitled to recover.— *Bunnell* vs. *Collinsville Sav. Soc.*, 39 Conn. Reports, p. 203.

SET-OFF.

A depositor in a savings bank, who is also a debtor to the bank as a borrower of its funds, cannot . . . . set off the amount of his deposits against his indebtedness. When, however, a man indebted to a savings bank as borrower deposited an amount less than the debt, intending to use the money so deposited for a payment upon the debt, it was held that the amount deposited could be set off against the debt. A savings bank is an agent for the depositors, receiving and loaning their money, and its losses are their losses, and are to be borne by them equally to their interest.— *Osborn* vs. *Byrne*, 43 Conn. Reports, p. 155.

TREASURER'S BOND.

The treasurer of a savings association appointed in 1851 was annually re-appointed until 1858. Upon his first appointment he gave bond with sureties for the faithful discharge of the duties of his office, and no new bond was afterward given. He committed no default until after his re-appointment in 1856. By the constitution of the corporation the directors were to be appointed annually, and they were to appoint the treasurer and other officers—all the officers of the corporation to continue in office until the next annual meeting, and until others should be elected in their stead. Held, that the office was an annual one, and that the obligation of the bond did not extend beyond the year for which the treasurer was first appointed. An official bond may be so drawn, in the case of an officer who is to be annually appointed, as to guarantee his fidelity while he remains in office under the first or successive appointments, but the language must be clear and definite, or the common law rule will control, and courts will treat it as an annual bond.— *Welch* vs. *Seymour*, 28 Conn. Reports, p. 387.

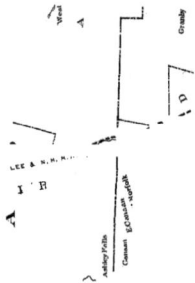

1883.

THIRTIETH ANNUAL REPORT

OF THE

RAILROAD COMMISSIONERS

OF THE

STATE OF CONNECTICUT,

TO WHICH ARE ADDED

STATISTICAL TABLES

COMPILED FROM THE

ANNUAL RETURNS FOR 1882 OF THE RAILROAD COMPANIES OF THIS STATE.

Printed by Order of the Legislature.

HARTFORD, CONN.:
PRESS OF THE CASE, LOCKWOOD & BRAINARD COMPANY.
1883.

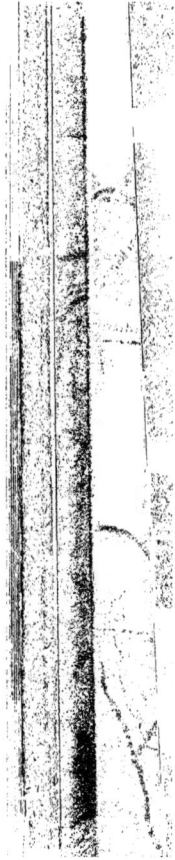

State of Connecticut.

To the Honorable General Assembly of the State of Connecticut, January Session, A.D., 1883.

ON the 1st of July next, thirty years will have elapsed since the passage of the act authorizing a State Board of Railroad Commissioners, and we herewith submit the thirtieth annual report, being for the year ending December 31, 1882.

It is alike interesting, and significant of the fact that our growth in population and business has been at established centers, rather than in sections before unsettled which would call for additional roads, to note that of the 962 miles of railroad in our State, 530, or an average of more than thirty-five miles a year, were opened during the fifteen years beginning with 1837, while during the last thirty years there have been opened only 432 miles, or an average of less than fourteen miles a year. If, however, we compare the business of the roads as appears in the first report, with that now reported, we find an equally significant indication of the general growth in population, wealth, and industries. The gross earnings then reported were $3,283,354.00; now, $15,353,656.04. The number of passengers then carried 3,202,490; now, 15,406,786. The tons of freight carried then 670,741; now, 6,646,838. The taxes paid the State then $29,622.69; now, $484,732.42.

In this same first report, we find the Commissioners recommending as a new thing a requirement "that a lantern shall be lighted and furnished with a reflector of not less than ten inches in diameter, and placed in front of the engine on all trains running in the night season." Now the head-light has come to be regarded so essential to safety, that the failure to make use of one for a short run after dark on a certain road a year or two ago, called out a most vigorous protest from the

patrons of the line. Another recommendation contained in
this report gives a hint of the comparatively comfortable
duties of train men in those days. After alluding to the fact
that all the companies except the "Stonington" required
their engineers and conductors to furnish their own watches,
and saying that it could hardly be expected that men with
such moderate compensation should keep their watches in reliable order, they add: "A safer practice would be for the
corporation to furnish at least each conductor daily with a
watch from the office, known to be right and in order; this
he should return to the office for comparison and adjustment,
after the duties of the day are performed." Such a picture
of home living as this recommendation suggests, it would be
difficult for many train men in our day even to imagine.

DRAW-BRIDGE STOPS.

A good deal of grumbling has been heard in the past few
years of the delay to travel caused by the stopping of trains
before crossing the draw-bridges, and the Commissioners are
authorized to dispense with the stop "when, in their opinion,
in can be done consistently with public safety." No such permission has been granted since the first year after the passage
of the law (except in the case of the Park River Draw on the
Connecticut Valley, at Hartford, and the disused one on the
New York & New England, at Hartford). The Commissioners then reported that there were seventeen draw-bridges
in the State, and that permission had been given to pass
twelve of them without stopping; the other five were, we suppose, all on the New York & New Haven. There has since
been added, the Connecticut River bridges on the Shore Line
and the Air Line, and the Mystic River bridge on the New
York, Providence & Boston, at all of which stops are made.
We hope some invention may be found which, when applied,
will justify us in permitting some or all of them to be passed
without stopping, but believe that public sentiment will uphold
us in refusing such permission until trains can run over draw-
bridges with as much apparent safety as they can run over
any other bridge.

Thirty years ago the Hartford, Providence & Fishkill Railroad Company operated only thirty-one miles of road, that between Hartford and Willimantic. Now the New York & New England, its outgrowth and successor, operates 452 miles; then the New York & New Haven operated 61 miles ; now the New York, New Haven & Hartford operates or controls 448 miles. In fact, all but one or two of our railroads may be said to belong to, or to be closely allied with one or the other of these two systems. The New London Northern particularly should be regarded as an exception, as it, through its lessor, the Central Vermont, and the Grand Trunk, forms a recognized link in the "long route " via Montreal between New York and the West, this route being authorized by the combined trunk lines to make freight rates from New York at about one-sixth less than the four trunk lines.

So far as through business for their main lines is concerned, both the systems above spoken of are claimants for some of the same patronage, but their chief objective points are directly opposite. That of the New York, New Haven & Hartford and its connecting roads being New York, and that of the New York & New England, and most of its connections, being Boston and the East. Hence it comes about that at almost all crossing points the local travel is subjected to serious delays, there being apparently no attempt to make close connection at any point in western Connecticut. The cure for this evil we are told lies in a law like the recent Vermont law to compel companies to make connections according " to the convenience of the traveling public."

In this law Vermont is only following about twenty-five years after Connecticut. If statutes would remove the trouble we have statutes enough. Our law provides that

" Every railroad company shall run it trains each way for passengers at such times and in such manner as to afford reasonable facilities for receiving passengers from, and delivering them to, the other railroads in this State, connected therewith; and when the business connections of the railroad of any company with the railroad of any other company are not convenient and reasonable for the accommodation of passengers over said road, said company shall make such connections as the public travel and business may require."

And gives to any person who shall be aggrieved by the neglect of any company to make such connections the right to bring his petition to a judge of the Superior Court, who, if the allegations in the petition are found to be true, shall order the company to make such connections on penalty of forfeiting *to the petitioner* not less than fifty dollars for each day that it shall fail to comply with the order.

The practical difficulty in this case, as under the kindred statute authorizing the Commissioners to make regulations for such business connections between railroads as shall be convenient and reasonable for the people living on the lines of them, is in the application of the law, the trouble being how to make an order which shall not be impossible or unreasonable in its requirements, and at the same time one that can not be easily evaded, or in other words the solving of the yet unsolved problem of how to run a railroad by statute laws. It is better for the traveling public that there should be no pretense of the connection of trains, rather than the time table should show connections which in the actual running are rarely made.

We took occasion last year to express our views upon the obligations of railroad companies to make their schedule time. If there was any call for such remarks at that time it has been much louder since. The failures in this respect have not been confined to any particular road.

When occurring on local roads, the fact that they have to wait for the trunk lines has caused the delays to be accepted as inevitable ; but in regard to the trunk lines the demands of the public are more exacting, nothing short of inevitable accident being accepted as sufficient excuse, and even then the requirement is that the obstructions should be removed in the quickest possible time. As to the New York, New Haven & Hartford, the few complaints which have come to us have been of failure to comply with this last requirement. Whether these particular complaints were just or not, it is both reasonable and proper that this corporation, with its ample means, should be held to the most stringent requirements both as to the condition of its road-bed, the comfort and sufficiency of its equipments, and its punctuality in the transportation of its passengers and the delivery of its freight.

That there has been a great want of punctuality both in the movement of passenger trains and the delivery of freight on the New York & New England road is a notorious fact, and is admitted by the officers of the company, than whom none more fully realize the disastrous consequence of such delays, and the importance of avoiding their continuance.

We ought to appreciate better than the general public the difficulties and embarrassments under which this company has been and still is laboring, and the efforts of the management to overcome these difficulties and remove these embarrassments. The business of most roads is of slow growth, but with the opening of its western extension there came upon this road a volume of traffic which their existing facilities were wholly inadequate to properly accommodate; so that, as the management has stated, about one-half of the time of their freight trains had to be spent on side tracks. An idea of the increase, so far as figures can give it, may be gained by a comparison of their report for this year with that for last year, a partial statement of which will be given elsewhere.

If now we recall the fact that before the Hudson river extension was opened the capacity of the road at and east of Hartford was severely taxed, we shall see that the problem with which the managers have had to struggle was one of no easy solution. We therefore forbore for a long time to take any formal action on the almost constant complaints made to us, but it finally seeming to us that the convenience, business prosperity, and rights of our citizens, and even public safety, demanded that we should call attention to certain indisputable evils and suggest such remedies as occurred to us, we did, after our fall inspection of that road, embrace in our report such of these suggestions as we deemed best. Some of these suggestions have been already adopted, and we believe the officers are exercising their best ability so to manage the affairs of the company that their road may deserve and receive a return of the popular favor which it has in some degree lost. The system of paying train men for the trips run instead of by the month is still continued on this road. If ever desirable, it is not in our judgment adapted to a road situated as is the New York & New England. Our views on this subject have been very fully given heretofore, and as it is not a matter calling for legislative action there is no necessity for repeating them here.

RAILROAD CONSTRUCTION.

pursuant to the authority granted by the last General Assembly, the Danbury & Norwalk Railroad Company has extended its track from the depot of the New York, New Haven & Hartford road at South Norwalk, to the Sound at Wilson's Point, two and three quarters miles; our hearing upon the approval of its location having been held on the 10th of February, and our certificate authorizing it to be opened for travel issued on the 11th day of August. All else in the way of construction during the year has been in the line of additional facilities on existing roads. One and two-tenths miles of second track has been laid on the New York & New England in this State, and fourteen and forty-five one-hundredths miles of siding on that and the other roads.

Nothing further has been heard from the New York & Connecticut Air Line Railway Company, since its articles of association were filed, October 22, 1881, but under the amended general railroad law it has ten months more in which to commence construction and expend thereon ten per cent. of its subscribed capital.

The proposed extension of the Valley road to Springfield has of course been abandoned, since the control of that road has passed to the New York, New Haven & Hartford Company.

MERIDEN & CROMWELL RAILROAD.

The articles of association of the Meriden & Cromwell Railroad Company were filed in the office of the Secretary of State on the 10th day of July, 1882, and hearings were had upon the approval of its location on the 20th and 29th days of September. The only question of much importance, involved in its location, was the crossing of the Hartford & Connecticut Valley Railroad at Cromwell, which was asked for at grade. This was opposed by those interested in that road, but after the approval given by the Legislature to the grade crossing of the New York & New England road at Hartford, by the proposed extension of the Valley road we did not feel authorized to refuse such a crossing at a point where it would be far less dangerous and perhaps equally expensive. No work has as yet been commenced on this road, and we understand some changes in location are contemplated.

HOUSATONIC VALLEY RAILROAD.

Articles of association of the Housatonic Valley Railroad Company were filed in the office of the Secretary of State on the 21st day of October, 1882, but no application has as yet been made for the approval of its location. This railroad is intended to connect the New York & New England at Sandy Hook in the town of Newtown, with Shelton and Birmingham, and undoubtedly also connect New Haven with the west by means of the New Haven & Derby, and the New York & New England roads.

The only changes in management or control of any of our railroads, has been the purchase of a controlling interest in the Hartford & Connecticut Valley Railroad Company by the New York, New Haven & Hartford Railroad Company, and by the lease by that company of the Boston & New York Air Line Railroad, as a substitute for the existing pooling arrangement, a copy of which lease will be found in the Appendix.

GROSS EARNINGS.

The total gross earnings of the companies reporting to us amounted to $15,353,656.04, an increase of $1,550,241.08, or a little more than eleven per cent. over those of the previous year; the passenger earnings having been $6,706,-

2

304.61, and the freight $7,376,878.75. Of this increase, the
New York & New England, with its additional miles of road,
earned about 40 per cent., the New York, New Haven &
Hartford 21 per cent., the New Haven & Northampton 9 per
cent., the New York, Providence & Boston, the Naugatuck,
and Norwich & Worcester, each about 7 per cent. Of all the
companies, the New York & New England shows the greatest
increase in gross earnings, both actual and proportional, the
increase having been as elsewhere stated, 22.6 per cent, with
an increase of 16.75 per cent. in the number of miles of road
from which the earnings were derived. The greatest proportionate increase with the same number of miles of road as
last year was by the Naugatuck road, amounting to 16 per
cent., of which nearly three-quarters was from freight earnings. Of the total gross earnings, 48 per cent. came from
freight, and 44 per cent. from passenger earnings.

OPERATING EXPENSES.

The total expenditures reported for operating expenses,
amount to $10,338,802.21, which is 68 per cent. of the gross
earnings. The operating expenses show an increase of
$1,763,514.63, being $213,273.55 more than the increase in
gross expenses. This increase in expenses is chiefly made
up of increased charges to the following items; repairs of
road-bed and track, $415,216.99; repairs of buildings, $198,-
951.71; repairs of locomotives, $81,914.51; repairs of cars,
$90,991.67; fuel, $145,415.18; salaries and labor other than
for repairs, $503,616.51; the total number of men employed
having increased 1,326, amounting to 10,959. It is true that
certain companies have charged the cost of new equipment
and of permanent improvements to the repairs of operating.

But after making all deductions which any one can possibly
claim ought to be made, on account of charges to operating
expenses of items which might be charged elsewhere, we still
have the undeniable fact that these expenses are, and for
some time have been increasing, out of proportion with the
increase in receipts. Admitting that the increased cost of

labor and supplies, on the one hand, and the reduction in rates on the other is the cause, it does not relieve the manager from his perplexity, since both processes are likely to continue in the future. The easiest means for immediate reduction of expenses is to " reduce the force " or " cut down the wages," an expedient necessarily temporary in its nature, and requiring no ability to adopt. The next step is to increase the hauling capacity of the engines, and the carrying capacity of the cars. This has been done till many think the limit nearly reached, and that what is gained in this direction is in part counterbalanced by increased wear of rails and expenditures needed to meet the additional strain upon, and vibration of, the bridges.

It is a matter of daily occurrence to hear railroad men complaining of the increasing inferiority of rails in wearing qualities, a complaint, no doubt, justly made· in part, but often made in apparent forgetfulness of the tremendous increase of the grinding and pounding to which they are subjected. Careful experiments on the London & Northwestern Railroad are said to have shown that the steel rails are subjected to a loss of one-third of a pound of steel for every mile run, so that fifteen hundred weight of steel is ground off the tracks of that road every hour of the day. It will readily be seen then how short-sighted is the too common practice of buying rails and wheels without reference to each other, and how much can be saved by having the one made to accommodate the pattern of the other. Again, it is said that an engine which will move a given load on a level track, can move but one-half that load on a grade of twenty-one feet to the mile, one-third the load on a grade of forty-two feet, one-fourth the load on a grade of sixty-three feet, and one-fifth of the load on a grade of eighty-four feet. A large saving can therefore be made in the expenses for motive power and train-men by reduction of grades. Considerable has already been done in this direction on our roads, and we do not know that there are any places in the State where the maximum grade can be reduced twenty-one feet, except at enormous expense ; but there are places where grades may be materially reduced at a cost which the increased capacity of the road thereby gained would justify.

NET EARNINGS.

Owing to the increase in operating expenses, the net earnings, after deducting $9,363.41, deficiency reported by the Hartford & Connecticut Western R. R. Company, are less by $213,273.55, or about 4 per cent., than last year, amounting, after making such deduction, to $5,014,853.83.

DIVIDENDS.

The same ten companies as last year paid dividends this year, amounting in all to $2,635,071.17, varying from 3 to 10 per cent., with an average of 8.23 per cent. on their total capital stock.

EARNINGS AND EXPENSES PER MILE OPERATED.

The gross earnings per mile of road operated show an increase of $772.42 over last year, the average being $10,-475.84; the Naugatuck, the New Haven & Derby, the New York, New Haven & Hartford, the New York, Providence & Boston, and the Norwich & Worcester being above the average, and the others below; the New Canaan road earning the smallest amount per mile, to wit, $1,820.31.

The gross expenses per mile operated averaged $7,054.19, an increase of $1,026 per mile. The net earnings per mile operated amounted this year to $3,421.64, the greater proportionate increase of expenses over gross earnings causing, of course, a falling off in net earnings.

EARNINGS AND EXPENSES PER MILE RUN.

The New Haven & Derby, and the Naugatuck, continue to lead in the amount of gross earnings per train mile, the former showing $3.03, and the latter $1.97; the average for all being $1.43.

The gross operating expenses per train mile were also highest on these two roads, amounting to $1.60 on the New Haven & Derby, and to $1.28 on the Naugatuck, the general average being $0.96.

The average net earnings per mile run show a falling off of eight cents per mile, having been $0.47.

MILEAGE AND FUEL.

The total train mileage for the year was 10,760,104, being an increase of 1,308,635 miles, of which the miles run by passenger trains increased 451,285, or 9 per cent., and the miles run by freight trains 487,267, or 13 per cent.; the total miles run by passenger trains was 5,481,783, and by freight, 4,123,846.

The cost of fuel for the 10,760,104 miles was $1,280,530.39, an average of ten cents and ninety-six one hundredths per mile; being one cent per mile less than last year.

The cost of fuel was lowest, or six and eight-tenths cents per train mile on the New Canaan road, where the cost of coal was $4.55 per ton, and highest, or fifteen and eight-tenths cents per train mile on the New Haven & Derby, where the cost of coal was $4.48 per ton. The average cost of fuel per train mile was eleven and nine-tenths cents. The average cost of coal was $4.95 per ton, or 34 cents less than last year.

MAINTENANCE OF ROAD.

The average cost of maintenance of road per mile operated was $1,399.75, being $267.94 per mile more than last year; the highest being of course the New York, New Haven & Hartford, with its double track, $2,833.96 per mile. The highest on a single track road was $1,768.79 on the New London Northern, on which a large amount of steel rails were laid, and the lowest $298.39 on the New Canaan.

STEEL RAILS.

There has been laid during the year in this State 102.36 additional miles of steel rails. The total number of miles so laid is now 844.39 or 65 per cent. of the whole number of miles of track, including sidings. At the present cost of steel rails, $40 per ton, we presume no renewals will be made with iron rails.

STOCK AND DEBT.

The total amount of stock issued and outstanding indebt-edness is reported at $83,710,289.60, an increase of $12,204,-243.65. The present amount of stock is $55,716,850.00, an increase of $9,368,500.00, of which increase $7,759,000.00 is. in the stock of the New York & New England, being amount. of "Berdell Bonds" converted into stock during the year; $1,586,000.00 is in the stock of the Hartford & Connecticut Western Railroad, $800,000.00 of which was the new stock authorized by the legislature last year, and issued in payment for the Rhinebeck & Connecticut Railroad, and $786,000.00 issued for $1,310,000.00 bonds converted into stock at 60 per cent.; and $229,500.00 is in the stock of the Boston & New York Air Line, issued for bonds converted into stock. On the other hand, the railroad of the New York, Housatonic & Northern Railroad Company having been bought by the Housatonic, the stock of the former, $261,200.00 as hereto-fore reported, is no longer included.

The outstanding indebtedness amounts to $27,993,439.60, an increase of $3,327,545.95, the funded debt of the New York & New England having increased $2,774,000.00, and their unfunded debt decreased $266,975.48; and the rest of the insured indebtedness being mostly made up of $276,265.67 in that of the Housatonic, $227,118.91 in that of the Hartford & Connecticut Western, and $147,000.00 in that of the Danbury & Norwalk.

LENGTH OF ROADS.

The total length of all the roads in the State is 962.45. miles; the length of double tracks 121.48, and the sidings 215.05, being a total of 1,298.98 miles of single track, an increase of 30.16 miles.

CONSTRUCTION AND EQUIPMENT ACCOUNTS.

The construction account shows an increase of $2,082,55 77, and amounts to $74,879,789.87. The increase is chiefly made up of an increase of $127,250.16 in the construction.

account of the Danbury & Norwalk, on account of the Wilson's Point extension; $736,000.00 in that of the Hartford & Connecticut Western; $165,747.05 in that of the New Haven & Northampton; $995,343.24 in that of the New England.

The equipment account amounts to $8,420,176.60, and shows an increase of $638,681.08, made up mostly of an increase of $115,904.00 in the account of the Hartford & Connecticut Western; $258,793.47 in that of the Housatonic; $105,361.15 in that of the New York & New England, and $95,868.65 in that of the New York, Providence & Boston.

PASSENGERS AND FREIGHT CARRIED.

The number of passengers carried during the year amounted to 15,406,786, an increase of 2,200,960 or 16 per cent., the passenger receipts averaging forty-three and one-half cents a passenger. The mileage was 322,526,920 miles, an increase of 39,340,725 miles.

The freight carried amounted to 6,646,838 tons, an increase of 807,480 tons, or very nearly 14 per cent.

ACCIDENTS.

It is a matter of congratulation that only one train accident resulting in injury to passengers occurred within the limits of our State during the year ending Sept. 30, 1882, and it indicates most thorough attention to the condition of road-bed, track, bridges, and equipment, and to the general management of trains on the part of the superior officers, and unceasing watchfulness and untiring faithfulness upon the part of engineers and the other employés. No passenger out of the 15,406,786 carried was killed through any fault of the companies or employés, and excepting the lady injured in the collision at Thompson, none injured but through their own want of care. Ten passengers in all, two less than last year, were injured. Of the three injured on the New York & New England, one fell between the cars of an excursion train and was killed, one jumped from a train in motion and dislocated his shoulder, and one was the lady bruised and wrist broken at Thompson. Of the seven injured on the New York, New Haven & Hartford, six either jumped or fell from trains in motion, and one had his arm, which was out of the car window, broken by a loose door on a passing freight train. The number of employés reported injured, however, shows a sad increase, the total having been 123, an increase of 54 per cent., while of that number those killed amounted to 79, more than two and a half times as many as last year.

The increase in the number employed, which is 14 per cent., can account for only a part of this increase in injuries. A still greater part is, we presume, attributable to the increasing business of the companies, calling for more work from the men in all departments, but especially in train men, yardmen, and switchmen, and rendering greater watchfulness on their part necessary when from fatigue they are less able to give it. The proportion of those injured in coupling or uncoupling cars is about the same as last year, being 32 per cent. of the whole number. The number of those injured in falling from the cars was 43, or 35 per cent. of all, instead of 25 per cent. as last year.

The collision at Pomfret on the New York & New England, in which one employé was fatally hurt, and five others more or less injured, did not occur till the 4th of November, and the number of injured are not therefore included in the statistics for the year. The circumstances attending this accident are being investigated by us, and the report thereon will be found in the Appendix.

The number of trespassers injured was 88, an increase of 18, but the proportion of those fatally hurt was less than last year, having been 54 per cent., instead of 60 per cent. Nineteen of the eighty-eight were injured at highway crossings, ten of them fatally, twice as many as last year.

CONDITION OF THE ROADS.

BOSTON & NEW YORK AIR LINE.

For the first time in several years we are not able to report any improvement in the track, road-bed, or superstructure of this road, but rather a deterioration. At our last examination no new rails, and but a limited number of new ties had been put into the track; the ditching had been neglected, and portions of the timber work of various bridges along the line needed renewal. As stated in another part of this report, this road has been recently leased by the New York, New Haven & Hartford Railroad Company for the term of ninety-nine years, at a guarantee of four per cent. on its preferred capital stock, and the lessees will, no doubt, on taking possession, make such repairs and renewals as are found necessary. The company has paid to its preferred stockholders dividends to the amount of three per cent. during the year.

DANBURY & NORWALK RAILROAD.

During the past year the relaying of the main line of this road with steel rails has been nearly completed, and its track and road-bed maintained in their usual excellent condition. Three of the most important bridges on the road are now being entirely rebuilt. One new locomotive and one first-class passenger car have been added to the equipment.

The main line of the road has been extended southerly from South Norwalk station for a distance of 2.65 miles to tide water at Wilson's Point, so called, on Long Island Sound, passing under the tracks of the New York, New Haven & Hartford Railroad just below said station. Ample docks, buildings, and other terminal facilities have been constructed at the new terminus. The docks which have been heretofore used by the company, are generally rendered inaccessible by ice during a great part of the winter, and being above two draw-bridges, and at the head of a long and crooked channel requiring skillful pilotage, have caused considerable incon-

3

venience and loss of freight to the company, all of which will be remedied by the new facilities afforded by the extension. The gross earnings of the road for the year, have been $200,-993.60, being an increase of $5,830.55 over those of the preceding year, and dividends at the rate of five per cent. per annum have been paid to the stockholders.

HARTFORD & CONNECTICUT VALLEY RAILROAD.

Nearly six miles of steel rails have been put into the track of this road during the past year, and fifteen short-span wooden stringer bridges have been replaced by iron girders. The filling of the Goodspeed's piling, and the pilings near Chester has been partially completed, over 90,000 cubic yards of material having been used for this purpose. The track and superstructure is in good condition, about ninety per cent. of the entire line being now laid with steel rails. The passenger trains of this company now arrive and depart at the Asylum street depot in Hartford, to the great convenience of the traveling public, and especially of those desiring to connect with trains of other roads.

The gross earnings of the road have been $195,873.61, nearly all of which, not used for running expenses, has been expended in prosecuting the work of track renewals, filling of pilings, and other permanent improvements above referred to.

HARTFORD & CONNECTICUT WESTERN RAILROAD.

The general condition of the track and road-bed of this line gives evidence of careful attention and continued improvement. A construction train has been continuously run on the road during the year, and the work of filling up its trestles and pilings, and rebuilding its bridges, is nearly completed. Nearly two miles of new side tracks have been put in. One hundred and twenty-six freight cars have been added to the equipment. New repair shops have nearly been built at Hartford, and equipped with proper machinery. Nearly one hundred thousand dollars has been expended in the purchase and improvement of real estate in Hartford heretofore leased by the company for terminal facilities.

The company has acquired by purchase the line of road between the New York State line and Rhinecliff on the Hudson, formerly called the Rhinebeck & Connecticut Railroad, thirty-six miles in length, and including its valuable docks, warehouses, and water front on the Hudson River, and furnishing a direct connection not only with the New York Central Railroad, but also with the canals terminating at Roudout, which connect directly with the Pennsylvania coal fields, enabling coal to be shipped from the mines to the docks of the company without breaking bulk. A large sum has been expended by the company upon this property since its acquisition, in building bridges, relaying track, and putting it in good order for business.

The total distance from Hartford to the Hudson by this line is 108.3 miles. The work of reconstruction of the road which has been so thoroughly and vigorously prosecuted during the past two or three years is now nearly completed, and it is hoped that when the necessity for these extraordinary expenditures has ceased, that the company may be able, with its increased business, to make a fair return to its stockholders.

HOUSATONIC RAILROAD.

The condition of this road has not materially changed during the year past. The track being of steel needs no renewals, and the bridges are few in number and in good condition. A new and convenient passenger station has been built at Danbury, and the freight house there considerably enlarged and improved. Two locomotives, two parlor cars, two smoking cars, and three hundred and fifty freight cars have been added to the equipment. The gross earnings have been about $8,000 less, and the operating expenses about $8,000 greater than for the preceding year. The usual dividend of eight per cent. per annum has been paid to the preferred stockholders.

NAUGATUCK RAILROAD.

A considerable amount has been expended on the line of
this road during the past year for permanent improvements.
The extensive yard grounds at Waterbury, acquired and graded
previous to our last report, are now occupied by a large number of switching and storage tracks, a commodious brick engine house partly completed, with turn-table, water tank, coal
sheds, and other necessary appliances. The new brick depot
at Thomaston, and the addition to the machine shop in Bridgeport have also been completed, and the depot at Beacon Falls
remodelled and improved. A new iron bridge of one hundred
and twenty-six feet span has been built over the Naugatuck
River, on the Watertown branch, and two small iron bridges
have been put in at Ansonia, and one near Burrville. Two
locomotives and fifty-three freight cars have been added to
the equipment. The track of the road being entirely of steel,
has required no renewals, and has been kept in good condition. We understand it is proposed soon to commence the
work of preparing the road-bed for a double track, from the
New York, New Haven & Hartford Railroad junction north
to Waterbury. The gross earnings show an increase of
$100,487.08, or over sixteen per cent., but owing to the cost
of the permanent improvements above named and increased
expense of operating, the charges made to running expenses
have increased $72,169.14, leaving the net earnings $28,317.94,
in excess of last year. Ten per cent. in dividends has been
paid to the stockholders.

NEW CANAAN RAILROAD.

This road continues to be operated by the trustees for the
first mortgage bond-holders. Its gross earnings have been
about the same as last year, and six per cent. interest has
been paid by the trustees to the holders of its bonds. The
track and road-bed are maintained in good condition for the
limited business of the road.

NEW HAVEN & DERBY RAILROAD.

We are glad to report for the first time a considerable progress in the permanent improvements of this road, by the filling up of much of its piling between Ansonia and Birmingham, and a partial filling of the Platte Valley trestle, so called, just east of Orange station. Substantial stone abutments are also being built at Wopawaug River preparatory to a new bridge in place of the old structure now there. About two miles of new steel rails have been put into the track, and the repair shops and machinery department have been considerably enlarged and improved. We are assured by the managers of the road, that its permanent improvement will be continued as rapidly as its earnings will permit, until our frequent recommendations as to the filling of its trestles and pilings have been fully carried out, and the track entirely relaid with steel.

The gross earnings of the road have increased $18,838.40, or about thirteen per cent., and the net earnings $11,836.14, or about seventeen and. one-half per cent. as compared with those of the preceding year. The road has now been in operation ten years, and its financial statement shows steady and gratifying yearly increase of earnings from $74,000 in 1873, to $166,000 in 1882.

NEW HAVEN & NORTHAMPTON RAILROAD.

This road has been maintained in its usual good condition during the past year, and no special permanent improvements have been made.

The gross earnings have increased $144,656.08, or over nineteen per cent., and the net earnings $33,315.61, or over twelve per cent. as compared with those of the preceding year.

NEW LONDON NORTHERN RAILROAD.

The relaying of this road with steel rails has been completed to the State line during the past year, about two thousand tons having been put in, thus replacing 23.38 miles of

iron that remained in the State. It has added to its equipment three mogul locomotives, one combination passenger
car, and twenty-six freight cars; has extended its sidings
at various places, and made additions to its repair-shops and
water facilities. Its track and road-bed have been maintained in good condition, and its numerous wooden bridges
and pilings have received careful attention.

We have several times recommended this road to publish
in Connecticut time when its trains leave Connecticut stations, but it has not yet done so. Six per cent. in dividends have been paid to the stockholders during the year.

NEW YORK & NEW ENGLAND RAILROAD.

The track, road-bed, and superstructure of this important
road have been maintained in excellent condition during the
past year. In the line of permanent improvements in this
State may be named the completion of double-track between
Hartford and Burnside, including the filling of the East
Hartford piling, a new freight-house at Hartford, a large increase of freight tracks and other yard facilities at East Hartford, six miles of additional side-tracks at various stations,
and the relaying of nearly twenty-four miles of main track
with steel. Twenty-two new locomotives have been recently
received, and twenty more are soon expected. Eight hundred twenty-ton freight cars have also been added to the
equipment.

At the date of our last report this road had just been
opened to the Hudson River, and the quantity of freight since
offered from this direction has exceeded the present facilities
possessed by the company for its transportation. It is therefore proposed to continue the construction of double track as
rapidly as possible, and this work is now in progress between
Burnside and Vernon, a distance of eight and two-tenths miles,
and between Hartford and Newington, five miles, and is about
to be commenced on the twenty-five miles between Putnam
and Willimantic. To further accommodate this business the

East Hartford freight yard is being considerably enlarged, and many new side-tracks are to be laid there.

We are glad to report that this road in its last public time-tables has adopted the standard time, as established by the Statute Law of 1881, as to all stations in this State, leaving only two roads that have not yet thus adopted it.

The gross earnings of the road show an increase of $610,-415.28, or nearly twenty-three per cent., and the net earnings $93,369.20, or over twelve per cent. The number of tons of freight carried one mile has increased from sixty four millions, as reported last year, to one hundred and three millions, or over sixty per cent.

NEW YORK, NEW HAVEN & HARTFORD RAILROAD.

The most noticeable improvement on the line of this road is the completion and opening of the elegant new passenger station at Meriden, and the enlargement and improvement of the freight yards and other freight facilities in the same city, so that there are now laid there nearly six miles in length of side-tracks, furnishing room for over one hundred and fifty freight cars to be unloaded at the same time by teams, without interference with each other. A new brick passenger station has been built at Fairfield in place of one destroyed by fire. The rock ballasting of the track near Wallingford has been continued, five and a quarter miles having been put in during the past year, making in all ten and one-half miles of double track thus treated, which was formerly the most dusty and unpleasant part of the road, but now among the cleanest. On the Shore Line Division stone arches and earth fillings are being substituted for some of the shorter pilings, this work having already been completed during the year at Westbrook and at Saltonstall Lake. A new passenger station has been built at Niantic. The piers of the Connecticut River bridge have been enclosed by cribs and stone-work, and thoroughly strengthened.

A desirable improvement is now in progress on the line of the road in the west part of the city of New Haven. The track is being lowered about eight feet to enable all the highways in that part of the city to be carried over the track, thus obviating the necessity of any grade crossings in that vicinity.

The relaying of the Middletown Branch with steel rails has been completed, over four hundred tons having been put in during the year, and five hundred tons of steel-capped rails in the main line has also been replaced by solid steel rails. The track, road-bed, and superstructure generally on all the various divisions and branches of the road have been maintained in their usual good condition.

The equipment of the road has been increased by the addition of five locomotives, twenty-seven elegant new passenger cars, and six freight cars.

The financial statement of the road includes this year the earnings and operating expenses of the Shore Line Division, and the gross receipts of both roads have increased $425,420.88. The operating expenses, however, having increased $777,130.53, the net earnings are $351,709.60 less than those of the preceding year.

The usual dividend of ten per cent. in all has been paid to the stockholders.

NEW YORK, PROVIDENCE & BOSTON RAILROAD.

The small part of this road in Connecticut has been maintained in its usual good condition, and several improvements made. Double track abutments and a new Howe truss bridge have been put in at Quambaug, the side tracks at Groton and Pequonnoc have been extended, new water facilities have been supplied at Groton and Stonington, and about a mile of new steel rails have been laid, in the track, and a double track is contemplated between Groton and Stonington. At Stonington a gas-house has been erected, with machinery for compressing gas into cylinders for use of the night trains and steamboats of the company.

We have recommended this company to adopt Connecticut standard time in its public time-tables and advertisements, as to stations in this State, but it has not yet done so.

The gross and net earnings each show an increase of eleven per cent. as compared with the preceding year, and eight per cent. in dividends have been paid to stockholders.

NORWICH & WORCESTER RAILROAD.

The general condition of this road is as last reported, no permanent improvements of importance having been made during the year.

It is still leased by the New York & New England Railroad Company, its superstructure is maintained in good condition, and about ten miles of its track has been relaid with steel rails since our last report.

The gross earnings of the road have increased $101.288.66, or nearly fourteen per cent., and the net earnings $89,640.46, or over thirty-two per cent., as compared with the preceding year.

Dividends to the amount of ten per cent. have been paid on the capital stock from rent received from the lessees.

SHEPAUG RAILROAD.

No special change in the general condition of this road has taken place during the past year. Its gross earnings do not vary materially from those of the two years last past. Its track and road-bed are reasonably well maintained, and we have advised that its future rail renewals be of steel instead of iron.

SOUTH MANCHESTER RAILROAD.

The condition of the track on this road continues in excellent condition. Many improvements in the depot grounds at South Manchester have been made, and substantial retaining walls constructed at the same place for the protection of the road-bed.

PETITIONS AND HEARINGS.

WILLIMANTIC DEPOT.

In their second annual report, made in 1855, the Railroad Commissioners said, "The depot at Willimantic, one of the most important east of Hartford, is poorly adapted to the wants of the public ; " a characteristic which, each year since, has become more and more striking until it has ceased to have any adaptibility " to the wants of the public."

In 1864 the Commissioners declared that its situation rendered it " one of the most inconvenient and unsafe stations in the State," and the General Assembly instructed them " to inquire into and examine the condition of the railroad station and grounds connected therewith at Willimantic," and to recommend such changes or alterations as they thought public safety and convenience required, reporting any neglect or failure to comply with such recommendations to the next General Assembly.

In their report for 1865, the Commissioners, after stating that they had given the subject their attention said, " while we are well satisfied that public convenience and safety require a radical change in the depot arrangements at this place, it seemed to us that as the Boston, Hartford & Erie Railroad Co. are about to construct a new station-house on this ground, it was advisable to wait for the maturity of their plans before giving any positive directions or recommendations." After waiting in vain seventeen years for the " maturity " of these plans, the citizens of Willimantic secured the passage of a resolution by the last legislature authorizing us, upon petition of the selectmen, to order such changes in the approaches or means of access to the depot as would make them safe and convenient for the public, or to change the location of the depot itself if we thought that the public could not otherwise be sufficiently protected. · Such a petition was brought on the 29th of September and heard on the 2d and 17th of November, and an order made, as will be found in full in the Appendix, providing for the changes regarded by us as necessary for public convenience and safety, involving the erection of a new depot to be completed by the 1st of July next.

DEPOT GROUNDS.

By an amendment to the general railroad law passed last winter, authority was given to all railroad companies, whether organized under that law or under special charters, after their

line of road has been located, approved, and established, to
take land for additional tracks, turn-outs, freight and passenger stations, and for supplying water. Six petitions have been
brought under this act.

AT MERIDEN.

The first, on the 9th of June, by the New York, New Haven
& Hartford Railroad Company, for land in Meriden adjoining
their new freight yard. This petition was heard on the 16th
and 23d days of June, and our approval given.

AT WALLINGFORD.

The second was by the same company on the 14th day of
August last, for a tract 35 feet wide by 1,550 long on the east
side of their tracks below the depot in Wallingford, for additional tracks and turn-outs. This was heard on the 7th and
22d days of September, and approval given without objection.

AT GREEN'S FARMS.

The third was by the same company, on the 6th of September, at request of certain citizens of Westport living near
Green's Farm station, for the location of a freight depot.
Hearings on this were had on the 19th of September and
the 3d of October. Objection was chiefly made to the location asked for as inconvenient and dangerous. As the petitioners did not seem inclined to abandon their application and
ask for land at another site, and we did not feel authorized to
refuse the accommodations asked for by the people of Green's
Farms, we granted the petition, though recommending a change
of location.

Another petition for leave to take land in Norwalk was
brought and hearings appointed, but the matter was adjusted
without a trial.

AT EAST HARTFORD.

The last petition was by the New York & New England
Railroad Company, for leave to take about five acres of land
in East Hartford as a part of their new freight yard at the

junction of their Eastern, Western, and Springfield Divisions.
One petition was brought on the 16th of October, upon
which a hearing was begun on the 24th of October and
adjourned to the 8th of November, at which time it was
withdrawn. Another petition covering the same subject
matter was brought on the 30th of October and heard upon
the 8th and 9th of November, and although considerable
opposition was made, chiefly on the ground that if the company were permitted to take the land asked for it would render
more dangerous and impracticable the use of certain " pent
roads " which had already been made inconvenient and dangerous by the laying of tracks across them on land then owned
by the company, yet the need of the land for the proper laying out of so important a freight yard seemed to us to out-
weigh the additional danger and inconvenience in the use of
the " pent roads," and permission was accordingly given to
take the land.

GATES AND FLAGMEN.

The increasing number of trains, and the consequent danger at grade crossings, has called out an unusually large number of petitions for gates, flagmen, or electric signals; particularly has this been the case on the line of the New York
& New England.

WILLIMANTIC CROSSINGS.

On the 17th of April the warden and burgesses of Willimantic petitioned for an order for gates at the Main, Union, and
Jackson street crossings of that road, and the Bridge street
crossing of that road, and of the New London Northern.
This petition was heard at Willimantic on the 27th of April,
and gates were ordered at said Main, Union, and Jackson
street crossings in place of a flagman, which had previously
been stationed there by our orders. At the Bridge street
crossing we were of opinion the flagman already stationed
there was all that public safety required.

PUTNAM CROSSINGS.

On the 12th of January the selectmen of Putnam brought their petition praying for gates at the crossings of the New York & New England road near Union Block and at May street. This petition was partially heard on the 26th of January, and the further hearing, by agreement of the parties, adjourned subject to the call of the Commissioners. On the 22d of June a further petition was brought, asking for gates at the crossings of both the New York & New England and of the Norwich & Worcester, at both said places; also for an order requiring the sides of the bridge over the tracks on the Rhodesville road to be covered. This was heard at Putnam on the 28th of July, and the order made as requested.

CROSSINGS IN HARTFORD.

On the 1st of August the selectmen of Hartford brought their petition for gates at the railroad crossings of Canton and Windsor, and Pleasant streets. We heard this petition on the 9th of August, and ordered the New York, New Haven & Hartford Co. to erect gates at the Canton street crossing, and the New York & New England to erect them at Windsor street. We did not think them required at Pleasant street.

WATERBURY CROSSINGS.

The mayor and common council of Waterbury brought their petition on the 15th of September, asking us to order gates, electric signals, or flagmen at the West Main and Bank street crossings of the Naugatuck Railroad, and the West Main street, Bank, and Riverside street crossings of the New York & New England Railroad. Hearings were held on this petition at Waterbury on the 9th and 10th of November, and gates ordered at the Bank street crossing of the Naugatuck Road, and at the Bank and West Main street crossings of the New York & New England, and an electric signal at the West Main street crossing of the Naugatuck. We did not think any further protection needed at the Riverside street crossing of the New York & New England.

CROSSINGS IN BRISTOL AND FORESTVILLE.

On the 30th of October the selectmen made their written request for gates or flagmen at the Main and Prospect street crossings of the New York & New England in Bristol, and a like request as to the Central street crossing at Forestville. These petitions were heard at Bristol and Forestville on the 16th of November, and gates ordered at the Main street crossing.

MANCHESTER CROSSINGS.

The last petition heard was that of the selectmen of Manchester, dated the 15th day of November, representing that public safety required gates to be established or flagmen stationed at the three highway crossings of the New York & New England Railroad next east of the Manchester depot, and asking that we order the railroad company to forthwith erect gates and station flagmen at the crossings, and also to order the company to move their freight depot, side-tracks, and switching yard so far west as to relieve the crossings from the frequent switching across them. At the hearing had upon this petition on the 23d of November, an agreement was made between the selectmen and the officers of the railroad company as to the subject matter of the petition, resulting in its withdrawal, a flagman to be stationed at the principal crossing until certain changes should be made.

PETITIONS FOR GRADE CROSSINGS.

Five petitions asking for six different grade crossings have been received and acted on.

SOUTHBURY.

The first was by the selectmen of Southbury, on the 1st of August, for a crossing of the tracks of the New York & New England road immediately west of the Southbury depot, as a means of access to it. The location was examined and the petition heard and granted on the 23d of August, as it was impracticable to carry the highway either over or under the track.

BREWERY STREET, NEW HAVEN.

The next was that of the City of New Haven on the 1st of October, for leave to extend Brewery street across the tracks of the New Haven & Northampton Company at grade. The right of the city to cross the tracks at all was denied, but it was conceded that the crossing, if made at all, must be at grade, and permission was given accordingly on the 13th of October.

PLAINFIELD.

On the 16th of September the selectmen of Plainfield filed their petition for two grade crossings, one of the New York & New England road near Almyville, and the other crossing both the Norwich & Worcester and the New York & New England tracks just above their junction at Plainfield. We examined these locations, and heard the parties on the 25th of October, when it appeared that the Almyville crossing was an old and established one, though the road had not before been made a public highway. This we allowed to remain at grade. The proposed crossing at Plainfield station would have been a most dangerous one if permitted to be at grade, and we accordingly ordered the highway to be carried over the tracks of both the railroads.

LIBERTY STREET, WATERBURY.

On the 15th of September, the mayor and common council of Waterbury asked leave to extend Burnham street across the New York & New England road at grade. This was heard on the 9th and 10th of November, and permission granted, it being agreed between the city and company that the Riverside street crossing should be discontinued, and no increase in the number of crossings made. On the 23d of October another petition was brought by them for authority to extend Liberty street across the Naugatuck Railroad at grade. This was heard on the 10th of November, the grade crossing disallowed, and it was ordered to the satisfaction of all parties in interest that the proposed extension be carried over the tracks by a bridge.

CHANGES IN HIGHWAY CROSSINGS AT CANTON.

On the 12th of June the selectmen of Canton brought their petition asking us to order the removal of certain obstructions to the sight at Case's crossing of the Hartford & Connecticut Western Railroad. An examination was made and a hearing had, and order made on the 22d of June for the removal by the town of the obstructions, at the equal joint expense of the town and the company.

FERRY PATH, NEW HAVEN.

On the 21st of June, the New York, New Haven & Hartford Railroad Company brought their petition, asking that the location of Ferry Path, a street in the city of New Haven be so changed, that instead of crossing the tracks of said company at grade, as it then did, it should be carried under the tracks in a line with the proposed extension of James' street. A hearing was ordered for the 13th of July, at which time an adjournment was by agreement made till the 12th of September, when, after a full hearing and careful examination, the change was ordered.

ROSE STREET, DANBURY.

Early in October the New York & New England Railroad Company asked for authority to so change the location of a portion of Rose street, in Danbury, then crossing their tracks at grade, that it should not cross at all. This was heard on the 23d of October, and the authority granted.

So far therefore as the action of the board is concerned, no addition has been made to the number of grade crossings during the year, except those on the Wilson's Point extension of the Danbury & Norwalk Railroad, and those that may be on the Meriden & Cromwell Railroad. The number of grade crossings differ very considerably on the different roads, there being sixty-six on the thirty-six miles of main road and branches of the Danbury & Norwalk, or nearly an average of one every half mile, while on the Norwich & Worcester they only average about one in a mile and a half.

SOUTHBURY.

On the 9th of January, the selectmen of Southbury brought their petition that the approaches of four crossings of the New York & New England Railroad might be improved. The attention of the railroad company was called to the matter, and the improvements made without any hearing being had.

HAMDEN.

The selectmen of Hamden, on the 3d of July, represented that the various highways crossed by the new location of the New Haven & Northampton Company had not been left in a proper condition for public travel. We made a special examination of all these crossings on the 8th of August, and ordered further work done at three of them, which has been attended to.

LOCOMOTIVE WHISTLING.

Only two applications have been received in regard to the matter of locomotive whistling. One was by the Common Council of Bridgeport on the 23d of June, asking that the whistle of westward bound engines might be sounded near South Avenue, as a signal to the gate-tenders at the Main and Water street crossings. The necessary order was issued at our request without any hearing.

SOUTH NORWALK.

The other was by the mayor and common council of South Norwalk on the 3d of August, complaining of the unnecessary whistling of the locomotives on both the New York, New Haven & Hartford, and the Danbury & Norwalk roads, of the obstruction of highways by switching of trains, and of the speed of certain trains in passing Washington and Main streets in that city. These complaints were fully heard on the 24th of August, and an order made requiring the flagman stationed at the Washington and Main street crossing to remain on duty till ten P. M. Recommendations were also made in regard to the other matters complained of, and over

5

which we had no absolute control. Much complaint, however, still continues to be made of the annoyance caused by what is thought to be unnecessary whistling.

PARKVILLE DEPOT.

On the 17th of January a petition was presented to us from citizens of Hartford, complaining that the New York & New England Railroad Company had closed their depot at Parkville, in said town, to the serious annoyance, expense, and danger of many patrons of the road, and therefore asking us to order said depot to be reopened. The 25th of January was assigned for the hearing upon the petition, and notice given, but before the day appointed the depot was reopened, and satisfactory arrangements made.

NEW HAVEN & DERBY RAILROAD STOP AT DERBY.

Permission was given by us on the 9th of June for all eastbound trains on the New Haven & Derby Railroad, which have come to a full stop at Birmingham Station, to cross the Naugatuck road at Derby without a second stop, whenever the signal is in proper position—the speed of such trains not to exceed six miles an hour till the crossing is passed.

FENCE PETITIONS.

Only two complaints were made to us in regard to railroad fences, both of which were attended to without formal hearings.

HOP BROOK DEPOT.

On the 10th of June, 1881, a petition was brought by a number of the electors of the town of Naugatuck, to Judge Carpenter, representing that the managers of the New York & New England Railroad ought to establish a station at some point in said town, on the west side of Hop Brook viaduct or arch, near to the road leading from Litchfield to New Haven, and that they had reason to fear that said managers did not intend so to do, and praying for the appointment of a practical engineer, skilled in the construction of railroads, who, with us, should hear said petition. Mr. Charles N. Yeamans, President of the New Haven & Northampton Company, was so appointed, and such hearing began on the 17th of February, 1882, and from time to time adjourned till the 23d of April, when, after a full hearing and on consideration, the engineer and the Commissioners concurred in the opinion that the company ought not to be required to establish a station on the location asked for, as they already had located and built one just east of the viaduct. The petition was therefore dismissed.

RAILROAD ACCOUNTS AND RETURNS.

The method of keeping the accounts of the railroad companies occupied the attention of the Legislature to some extent last year, and may again at the ensuing session. It may therefore be proper to recall the legislation on this subject, and give the existing state of our laws, for, although this subject was very fully discussed by us in our report six years ago, and again in 1878, yet few, if any, of your Honorable Body were members at that time, and few have given special attention to the subject.

All will agree that there may exist a form for making their returns which all the companies may strictly follow, while at the same time they may vary very much in their mode of keeping their books and accounts; that is, they may each report how much of their expenditures they have charged to repairs of track, and how much to construction account; how much they have charged to repairs of locomotives and cars, and how much to equipment account, while they differ as to how much of the cost of steel rails, or of the cost of filling an old trestle should be charged to repairs of track, and how much of the cost should be added to construction account; how much of the cost of new engines and cars should be charged to repair account as keeping the old equipment good, and how much of it should be added to equipment account; and generally whether good management dictates that the expense account should be kept down by charging all possible expenditures to construction, equipment, and property

account, or that these accounts, supposed to correspond in
some degree with capital account, should be kept down while
operating expenses are increased. We presume that it will
also be admitted that while as respects a particular company,
it is not of much consequence, either to the public, the stockholders, or the creditors, to which head expenditures are
charged, provided the facts appear, yet the value of the returns for comparison depends largely on a uniformity in the
classification of the accounts. Neither will it be denied but
that the State, if it can and does require returns to be made,
and to be made in a specified form, may also require the accounts upon which the returns are based to be kept in a prescribed manner.

Believing as we did not only in the right of the State to
require the accounts to be kept in accordance with certain
general and fixed principles, but also in the advisability of
making such a requirement, we in 1877 recommended the
adoption by our State of a form of accounts and returns with
the general instructions and rules relating thereto, which had
been recommended by the several Boards of Commissioners
for the New England States, and the State Engineer of New
York.

This recommendation, however, the General Assembly did
not see fit to adopt, but in lieu thereof a committee was appointed to prepare a new schedule for the form of annual
reports, which schedule is that now in use. We have not
changed our views as to the desirableness of having all the
railroad companies make their division of accounts upon the
same basis, but we have come to doubt whether such a requirement can be thoroughly carried out in practice. Our
chief reason for this doubt is that, as it seems to us, the attempt has not succeeded in that State where, if at all, it
might justly be expected to succeed. The Massachusetts
Board were authorized to, and did, prescribe a system upon
which the companies should keep their books and accounts in
a uniform manner; and the law requires the corporations to
keep their books and accounts in accordance therewith. It

is also made the duty of the board from time to time in each year to examine the books and accounts of all the corporations operating railroads to see that they are so kept, and " an accountant skilled in the methods of railroad accounting " is employed under the direction of the board to supervise the method in which the accounts are kept. Nothing would therefore seem to be wanting in the machinery for accomplishing the result desired.

Yet we find precisely the same practice prevailing there as with us; the old, well-established, and prosperous corporations, such as the Boston & Albany, the Old Colony, the Boston & Maine, the Boston & Providence, charging all or most of their expenditures for additional tracks, buildings, and equipment to the expense or operating account; while the new and struggling companies charge these and all other expenditures possible to construction, equipment, or property account. If we go a step farther we find that while all advocates of requirements for uniform railroad book-keeping agree to the general proposition that whatever expenditures add to the permanent value of a company's property, should be charged to either construction, equipment, or property account, and not to operating expenses, they also agree that in the past, construction account has been the place where most frauds and peculations have been covered up. We presume also that it will not be denied that even when honestly attempted the difficulty of determining to what accounts certain specific expenditures should be charged is much greater than it would seem to be on first thought. As, for illustration : Mr. Kirkman, the well-known authority, would charge to construction the cost of new side-tracks, less the cost of those taken up; the difference in value between permanent structures, as bridges of iron or stone, over the original cheaper ones; the value of steel rails over the iron ones for which they are substituted; while others, like Mr. Williams of Michigan, would charge these to the expense account, as being renewals just as much as they would have been had they been of a less permanent character which would themselves have to be the sooner renewed.

Again, if this division is to be made with that accuracy which alone can give it value, not only an inventory but also an appraisal of all the company's property must be annually made before it can be determined how much of the expenditures are to be charged to renewals and how much to permanent improvements. We do not think it possible for your Honorable Body, within any reasonable limits, to prescribe a system upon which the railroad companies shall keep their books and accounts, and direct to what account the vast multitude of items shall be charged. If done at all, it must be by delegating that authority to the Commissioners, with power to employ all necessary accountants. It is for you to say whether the interests of the public, the stockholders, or the creditors demand that it should be done.

COLOR BLINDNESS AND VISUAL POWER.

The subject of the visual power and defects of men controlling or directing the movement of vessels in the water, or locomotives on the land, has continued to command increasing attention, both in this country and abroad, and requirements for examinations are more general. The Massachusetts law, which only requires that the examination shall be by a "competent person," without defining in any way the qualifications necessary for competency in the examiner, continues, we believe, to give satisfaction to the Commissioners of that State, and to many, perhaps most of the railroad managers, but does not meet the approval of those who have most made the subject a study. Our own short-lived law was more correct, we think, in that particular. All arguments which apply in favor of having any physical examination conducted by an educated physician, instead of a layman, however intelligent, apply with tenfold force in the case of the examination of so delicate and complicated an organ as the eye. We are inclined however to think, in view of the fact that we were taking the initiative in legislation on this subject, that it was a mistake to forbid under penalty the employment of a person who did not possess a certificate of "freedom from color-blindness.' Had we required the examinations to be made just as was done, and a certificate given to the person examined, showing his condition, and a copy filed in our office for record, leaving to the companies the responsibility of employing men found incompetent by the examiners, no such alarm would have been given to the men, nor could such a law have furnished a plank for political platforms. We are satisfied that with such an examination and such a record, employment would have been found for any who were unfitted for the places occupied without any sudden change, while the public would have been amply protected.

One outgrowth of the interest in this subject every one will admit is of a most practical character. Those who have examined the green and red signal lights, have observed the entire want of a standard color, and also the need of a lens which would not diminish the quantity of light. This want the New England Glass Works undertook to supply, and with such success that the Secretary of the Navy authorized them to supply each of the thirty-six boards of local inspectors of steam vessels named in his order with one green and one red lantern, to be used as the standards of color. It is, therefore, in the power of our railroad managers to furnish their lines with switch lights and lanterns of a uniform color and best power for transmitting light.

CAR-COUPLERS.

The following act upon this subject was passed at the last session of the General Assembly, to wit:

SECTION 1. Every corporation, company, or association, operating any railroad located partially or wholly in this state, shall cause every freight car that shall be hereafter built or purchased for use on such railroad, to be provided with couplers so arranged as to render the presence of any person between the ends of the cars unnecessary for the purpose of coupling the same.

SEC. 2. No couplers shall hereafter be placed on any freight cars built or purchased as before stated, nor shall any new couplers be substituted for any that are now in use, until the same shall

have been approved by the Railroad Commissioners, and such couplers shall be hung at such height above the face of the railroad
track as shall be designated by such Commissioners.

SEC. 3. Every corporation, company, or association operating
any railroad, who shall permit a violation of this statute, shall forfeit for every such violation the sum of fifty dollars to the treasury of this state, the same to be recovered in a proper action
founded on this statute.

SEC. 4. This act shall take effect on the first day of July,
A. D. 1882.

Only five companies have made formal applications to us
for approval of couplers, four of which were granted and one
declined, as the coupler in question did not, in our judgment,
comply with the requirements of the law. The various companies report 1700 new freight cars added to their equipment,
a portion of which were, we presume, built or purchased since
the act took effect.

The act is it stands is chiefly valuable as indicative of the
sentiment of the State on the subject. Most of the managers
have evinced a desire to act in accordance with that sentiment, even though they questioned the practicability of the
law. As originally prepared, the bill made the companies
liable for an injury to an employé received from a car not
so equipped, without regard to the question of negligence of
himself or of a fellow employé. This was a variation from
the present rule in this country as to liability of employers
to employés, which would probably have prevented the passage of the act as originally drawn.

The rule of law on the subject of liability of employers for
injury to one employé arising from the neglect or wrongful
act of another, is different in this country, and to a certain
extent in England, from what it is on the continent of Europe.
There the doctrine that the employer is not liable for injuries
received under such circumstances, is not accepted. And
under the employer's "liability act" of Great Britain, passed
in 1880, an employé who receives an injury in consequence
of the neglect, or misconduct, or unskillfulness of another

employé; under whose orders he is acting, may recover from their common employer. A like rule has been laid down by the courts in two or three of the States of the Union, but the general rule here is the other way. It is not without interest to consider how diametrically opposite rules of law have come to be established in the old countries and in this. The European doctrine of liability is said to rest not only on the theory that the employer is supposed to order all that the servant does,—a theory which in practice is faulty, inasmuch as most accidents occur through a violation of orders, but upon the principle that the business is conducted by the employés for the employer's benefit and profit, and that therefore all damages occasioned in the carrying on of the business should be charged against the profits of the concern. On the other hand, it is said that the rule, as it prevails in this country, has its origin not so much in a disagreement as to the principles involved as in the necessities of the situation. Because it was thought to be necessary to the continued existence and growth of the new enterprises, whose means were limited, but whose success was essential to the prosperity of the country, that the liability of employers for the acts of employés should be confined to the narrowest limits consistent with justice. Hence has grown up the doctrine that the liability of an employé to accidents through the acts of his fellow servants engaged in the same business is a risk which can be, and is, taken into account in fixing the rate of wages, and that employés receive pay day by day, not only for the work performed, but also for the risk incurred. And that if an accident occurs, the damages sustained have already been adjusted, and included in the rate of wages.

It is undoubtedly true that the character of the work to be performed, its severity, unhealthfulness, and special liability to accident, is to some extent taken into consideration in fixing the rate of compensation, but so long as the number of men seeking employment is in excess of the demand for men, the risk incident to a particular employment will be an inconsiderable element in determining the rate of wages. But even

6.

were it true that railroad employés, for instance, were fully paid for the risks assumed, and that if his employment were made safer, his compensation would be made less, there still remains the question of humanity and public policy. It should be made for the pecuniary interests of employers to prevent accident to employés. As our railroad enterprises become more firmly established, thus removing the necessity which has led to the adoption of the American rule of restricted liability, we may reasonably expect to see the rule itself relaxed in favor of the employé.

The efficacy of the coupler act would undoubtedly have been greater had it retained something like its original provisions. It will be recollected that in recommending legislation on this subject, we acknowledged that the advisibility of compulsory legislation in so small a state as ours was by no means certain, but we thought it would be a step in the right direction. We have seen no occasion to change our minds. We however look for more efficient results to the action of the Master Car Builders' Association. With a membership made up as it will be under its revised constitution, and with the requirements in regard to recommendations of standards provided by its constitution, whatever recommendations it may make will be sure of almost universal adoption. Recommendation for standard height for draw bars (2 ft. 9 in.) and for dead blocks have already been made, and a committee appointed to investigate the subject of "Automatic Draw Bars," has reported that they " unanimously agree that an automatic coupler would be desirable, provided one can be found to meet the requirements." They also recommend certain ones for trial. Automatic car couplers seem to be particularly attractive objects for invention in these days. One hundred and sixty-one patents for such devices were issued for the six months ending June 30, 1882, and the *Official Gazette* gives twenty-two as issued in a single week in November.

STANDARD TIME.

The Legislature of 1881 enacted " that the standard time for the meridian of the City Hall in the city of New York

shall be and is hereby made the standard time for this State."
Provision was also made for furnishing this standard time
daily to all railroad companies in this State, and making it
the duty of such companies to keep at all their depots having
telegraph communication a clock regulated by said time. A
section requiring all companies to adopt this time was omitted
from the act on the assurance that, as soon as proper arrangements could be made, it would be voluntarily adopted by
several companies who opposed the insertion of this compulsory clause. Since the passage of the act we have urgently
recommended all companies not already doing so to advertise
the time of their trains, as to stations in this State, in Connecticut standard time, and all have complied with this recommendation except the New London Northern and the New
York, Providence & Boston companies.

As the neglect of these companies so to comply causes three
kinds of time to be now in use at New London by the railroads
centering there, and two kinds in like manner at Norwich and
Willimantic, it is hoped that in view of their connections at these
points these companies will find it for their interest as well as
for public convenience to make at an early day such changes
in their public posters and advertisements as will make them
conform to the uniform time established by law.

OBSTRUCTION OF HIGHWAY CROSSINGS BY TRAINS.

The present law in regard to the obstruction of highway
crossings by locomotives, cars, or trains standing upon or
across the same is wholly inadequate to prevent this great and
increasing inconvenience. The law gives to the person who
is prevented from crossing the right to recover the pecuniary
damage not exceeding fifty dollars. While this has the appearance of fairness we all know that the dislike to litigation,
and the delay and annoyance incident to it, would prevent
most persons from suing, even where the exact pecuniary
damages could be easily proved; while in most cases it would
be difficult to prove pecuniary damage, or to estimate in dollars and cents what ought to be paid for the delay, annoyance,

or exposure to the health arising from being compelled to wait in all kinds of weather, and at all hours of day or night, for the crossing to be opened to travel. Under the law as it existed from 1866 to 1878, it was made the duty of the person having charge of a freight train which was obliged to remain at any station in such a position as to obstruct the ordinary travel on any highway for more than five minutes, to cause the train to be so separated as to accommodate the public travel; and provided that any railroad company in whose employment any person should be who violated the above provision, should forfeit not more than ten dollars to any person who should sue therefor. It has been said that this was practically making the person in charge of the train pay the penalty, as the companies subjected to it would deduct it from the pay of the person in charge. And, also, that it gave to any maliciously disposed person the chance to annoy the company with really causeless suits. The evil has become so great that neither objection is longer regarded as valid by the suffering public. The Commissioners have frequently called the attention of offending companies to the matter, but are powerless to compel them to keep the highways open.

ANNUAL RETURNS.

The returns of the companies were sent in more promptly this year than last. Still the last were not received till November 30. We are satisfied that it is impracticable for the companies to make their returns, as now required, by the 1st of November, and we would recommend that the time be extended till November 15, with a like extension of the time when our own report must be presented to the General Assembly. All of which is respectfully submitted.

GEORGE M. WOODRUFF,
JOHN W. BACON,   *Railroad*
WILLIAM H. HAYWARD,   *Commissioners.*

HARTFORD, January, 1883.

APPENDIX.

The Boston and New York Air Line Railroad Company has let, and hereby demises and lets, for the term of ninety-nine years from and after the thirtieth day of September, 1882, unto The New York, New Haven and Hartford Railroad Company, all and singular the railroad of the party of the first part, from a point in the City and County of New Haven to a point in the village of Willimantic, in the County of Windham, in the State of Connecticut, and at present passing through the towns of New Haven, North Haven, and Wallingford, in the County of New Haven; Durham, Middlefield, Middletown, Portland, and Chatham, in the County of Middlesex; Marlborough, in the County of Hartford; Colchester and Lebanon, in the County of New London; Columbia and Hebron, in the County of Tolland, and Windham, in the County of Windham, as the said railroad is now and as it may hereafter be located and constructed, and all the lands that are or may hereafter be included in the location of said railroad, within the terminal points aforesaid; with all and singular the railways, rails, turn-outs, bridges, viaducts, fences, station-houses, freight-houses, depots, shops, buildings, structures of every kind, cars, engines, rolling stock, equipments, machinery, tools, ways, water-tanks, walls, fixtures; and all papers, documents, maps, and surveys, of every kind, showing the condition of the lessor's title to its land, hereby demised, and all its rights and obligations; and other appendages, privileges, contracts, rights, and leases thereto appertaining, and all property, right, and

interest of every description acquired and held by the lessor
for the maintenance and operation of its railroad; together
with all the tolls, income, issues, and profits to be derived
from the operation thereof by the lessee, and all rights to
demand, receive and recover the same, and to have and do
everything necessary for the use, improvement, and operation
of said railroad; the lessor covenanting with the lessee that
it has good right to lease said premises in manner as herein
set forth, and that it will suffer and permit the lessee (it
keeping all the covenants on its part as herein contained) to
occupy, possess and enjoy said premises during the term
aforesaid without hindrance or molestation; yielding and
paying as rent therefor in each year of said term one hundred
and twenty thousand dollars, which sum shall be paid in
equal semi-annual payments of sixty thousand dollars each,
the same to be distributed by the lessee on the first days of
April and October in each year during the continuance of this
lease, beginning April first, 1883, to such persons, and such
persons only, as shall be certified by the lessor to have the
right to receive the same by virtue of their respective hold-
ings in the preferred stock of the lessor, as such right may
appear on the stock-books of the lessor on the twentieth day
of the months of March and September next preceding said
days respectively, on the basis of two dollars on each share;
and if the whole of said rent is not required in accordance
with this provision, the balance shall, at the end of six
years from the time it becomes payable, be paid over to said
lessor.

And said lessee, in addition to the rent aforesaid, hereby
covenants and agrees to pay for the benefit of the lessor, to
the several holders thereof, the interest warrants or coupons
of the twenty-five thousand dollars of bonds of the Colchester Railway Company, the payment of which is guaranteed
by the lessor, and also the interest warrants or coupons of
the five hundred thousand dollars first mortgage bonds of the
lessor, upon presentation of the same at maturity; and the
interest warrants or coupons of any new bonds which may

be issued in lieu or extinction of the aforesaid bonds, shall in like manner be paid by the lessee during the term of this lease, to an amount not exceeding twenty-six thousand seven hundred and fifty dollars a year.

And the lessee further covenants with the lessor to pay, during each year of said term, all taxes, rates, charges, and assessments, ordinary and extraordinary, which may be lawfully imposed or assessed in any way upon the lessor, its capital stock, indebtedness, franchises, and revenues, the premises hereby let, or said rental or any part of the same; said payments to be made to the authority or treasurer entitled by law to receive the same, whether such law be that of the United States, the State of Connecticut, or any municipal corporation of or in said State, so that said lessor shall be saved harmless, during the said term of this lease, from any such tax, assessment, or charge, under laws or proceedings made or authorized by the United States or the State of Connecticut; and if any taxes or assessments shall be levied against the individual holders of the stock or bonds of the lessor in lieu of upon the lessor itself, its railroad and premises, the same shall be paid by the lessee.

And the lessee covenants with the lessor to make the several rental and other payments, hereinbefore stipulated, as the same become due and payable in each year of said lease; provided, nevertheless, that if any of said payments shall not be made within thirty days from the time when the same becomes payable, or if default be made for thirty days in the performance of any other of the covenants of the lessee in this indenture contained, and shall be thereafter continued for ten days after written notice of such default has been given to it by the lessor, then this lease shall expire and terminate at the option of the lessor, which may re-enter upon the demised premises, and the same have and possess as of its former estate, and without such re-entry may recover possession thereof by the statutory proceedings of summary process; it being understood that no demand for the rent, or any part thereof, and no re-entry for condition

broken as at common law, shall be necessary to enable the
lessor to recover such possession, but that all right to any
such demand or re-entry is hereby expressly waived by the
lessee ; saving to the lessor any right to damages for breach
of any of the provisions of this indenture.

And it is further provided that all the old rails, which were
formerly on the tracks of the lessor, but are or shall be before
the beginning of said term, renewed and replaced by new
rails, shall remain the absolute property of the lessor and
not pass as part of the demised premises.

And it is further provided that, whereas the lessor has
mortgaged said demised premises by its deed dated August
first, 1880, to secure its five per cent. bonds to the amount of
five hundred thousand dollars, and has further guaranteed
the bonds of the Colchester Railroad Company, secured by
mortgage of said Colchester Railroad, dated January first,
1878, to the amount of twenty-five thousand dollars, which
bonds will mature during the term of this indenture, the
lessor or the Colchester Railroad Company, or both, may
execute and deliver from time to time new mortgages to
secure new bonds, to be issued or guaranteed in renewal of,
or substitution for, said five hundred and twenty-five thousand
dollars of bonds now outstanding, or any part thereof, or in
renewal of or substitution for bonds issued in renewal of such
renewal bonds, and that all such mortgages shall be a lien on
the demised premises, so far as they may purport to cover the
same, paramount to this lease as fully as if executed and
delivered prior thereto, and the lessee covenants to pay the
necessary cost of preparing and issuing such new bonds and
mortgages, unless it elects to pay the old bonds as hereinafter
provided; but the total amount of bonds issued or guaranteed by the lessor, outstanding at any one time, shall never
exceed five hundred and twenty-five thousand dollars in par
value, or the rate of interest thereon exceed that now paid;
provided, however, that the lessee may, at its option, pay any
such bonds at maturity, and if it shall elect, so to do, the
lessor shall secure the lessee, by mortgage or other proper

instrument, for the repayment, within such period, not exceeding ten years (as the lessor may elect) from the expiration of this lease, of such sums of money as may be required in the payment of such bonds, with semi-annual interest thereon at the rates now paid, said interest to commence upon the termination of this lease.

And the lessee covenants with the lessor that it will maintain said demised premises and property during said term in as good order, repair and condition as when received at the beginning of said term, replacing and renewing whatever becomes defective or worn out, from time to time; all new property, improvements, and renewals to become part of the demised premises, and as such to be delivered up to the lessor at the expiration of this lease, whether occurring before or at the end of said term; provided, however, that an inventory and appraisal of all the personal property hereby demised shall be made within one hundred and twenty days from October first, 1882, by J. H. Franklin and E. M. Reed, or (if they do not agree) by them and a third person, to be agreed on by the lessor and lessee, and the action of a majority of said three persons shall be final and conclusive on both parties; and that at the expiration of this lease as aforesaid, the parties hereto shall cause a new inventory and appraisal of all the personal property then in use in connection with said leased railroads to be made by one person appointed by each, and if such two persons do not agree, then by them and a third person, to be agreed upon by the lessor and lessee, and the action of a majority of said three persons shall be final and conclusive on both parties; and that the lessor shall then have the option either to take all the personal property in said inventory described, or only so much thereof as equals in value at the appraisal the appraised value of said personal property hereby demised; and that in the first case the difference, if any, in favor of the lessee between the values of the property in the two inventories shall be paid by the lessor to the lessee, and in the second case the lessor shall have the right to select which of the articles in the inventory it will

7

take to the amount of the value of the articles in the original inventory.

And the lessee covenants with the lessor that it will save the lessor harmless from all suits, costs, damages, and expenses by reason of any act or omission of the lessee in the use of said demised premises, or otherwise, under this lease; and will, at its own expense, defend all suits brought against the lessor for any such cause, and pay the judgment, if any, therein recovered, when demanded on final process; and that it will make all returns, during said term, which could be—were there no lease—required by the laws of the State of Connecticut, or the United States, from or of the lessor, to any public officers or officer, or other legal authority or assembly; and that, should any such returns be required by law of the lessor, the lessee will furnish, on demand, so far as it has the means, all information necessary therefor.

And the lessee further covenants with the lessor, that it will keep and perform all and singular the contracts relative to the operation and maintenance of the demised premises, which are now in force and binding on the lessor, including all stipulations in deeds of real estate to the lessor or its predecessor in title, as on record, and in said lease of the Colchester Railroad, dated April third, 1878, and in the award of Chief Justice Park, as to the Middletown Railroad crossing, dated May second, 1881.

And the parties hereto mutually covenant each with the other that, in all other respects, the covenants herein contained shall enure to the benefit of, or be obligatory upon, the parties respectively and their respective successors and assigns.

And the lessor covenants with the lessee that it will maintain its corporate organization, and will, from time to time, if requested by the lessee, proceed to appropriate and condemn by appraisal such real estate as the convenient operation of the demised premises may render desirable; the lessee, however, advancing and paying all expenses thereby incurred, including legal expenses; and the lessor also agrees that the lessee may use its name in bringing or defending any suits so far as it is or may be necessary for the quiet enjoyment and protection of the demised premises, but at the sole expense of the lessee, saving the lessor harmless from all loss, costs or damages thereby accruing.

And the lessee further covenants with the lessor that it will furnish and keep all such books, forms and papers, and do and perform all such acts and things at its own cost and expense as may be required for the proper issue, record, and transfer of the stock of the lessor, and for the registration and transfer of any of the aforesaid bonds, and will provide a suitable person to act as the transfer agent of the lessor during the continuance of this lease ; provided, always, that all stock certificates and bonds shall be signed by the proper officers of the lessor.

It is understood that this lease, when approved by the parties hereto, by a stockholder's vote, as required by the laws of Connecticut (subject to which approval by both said lease is executed), shall be in lieu and discharge, from and after September thirtieth, 1882, of the existing contract between said parties, dated March twenty-first, 1879, saving to each party all rights under said contract accruing before October first, 1882.

In witness whereof, the said parties hereto, under the authority and direction of their respective Boards of Directors, have caused this instrument to be signed and sealed by their respective Presidents the thirty-first day of August, A. D. 1882.

THE BOSTON & NEW YORK AIR LINE RAILROAD COMPANY,

By H. B. Hammond, *President,*

T. L. Watson, *Secretary,*

BOSTON & NEW YORK AIR LINE R.R. CO.

Signed, sealed, and delivered in presence of

Frederick Sedgwick.

James B. Gregory.

THE NEW YORK, NEW HAVEN, &
HARTFORD
RAILROAD COMPANY,

By GEO. H. WATROUS, *President.*

Signed, sealed, and delivered in presence of
CHARLES P. CLARK.
WM. E. BARNETT.

STATE OF CONNECTICUT, ⎰ SS.
MIDDLESEX COUNTY.   ⎱

MIDDLETOWN, October 18, 1882.

Then and there personally appeared Henry B. Hammond, President, and Thomas L. Watson, Secretary of the Boston & New York Air Line Railroad Company, which company is a signer and sealer of the foregoing instrument, and they severally acknowledged the same to be the free act and deed of said company, and that the seal attached thereto was the corporate seal of said company, and that it was attached thereto by order of the board of directors of said company, before me.

Signed,   JOHN N. CAMP,
                         Notary Public.

STATE OF NEW YORK, ⎰ SS.
CITY AND COUNTY OF NEW YORK, ⎱

October 28, 1882.

Then and there personally appeared George H. Watrous, President of the New York, New Haven & Hartford Railroad Company, signer and sealer of the foregoing instrument, and acknowledged the same to be the free act and deed of said company, before me,

Signed,   WM. E. BARNETT,
                         Notary Public.

An Act of the Legislature Concerning Approaches to the Willimantic Railroad Depot.

Section 1. Whenever the majority of the selectmen of the town of Windham shall present a petition to the railroad commissioners alleging that the approaches or means of access to the present passenger depot located at Willimantic, in said town, are unsafe and dangerous for the public, it shall be the duty of said commissioners forthwith to give such notice to all the railroad companies interested in said petition, and to said selectmen, as they may judge reasonable, of the time and place when and where they will hear said petition; and if upon said hearing said commissioners shall find the allegations of said petition are true, they shall have power to order all railroad companies owning said depot to make such changes in the approaches or means of access to said depot upon the premises of said companies as they may determine will make said approaches or means of access safe and convenient for the public; and may make any other order or regulation that they may deem reasonable and proper in the premises, or in the management and operation of trains and cars crossing said approaches; and if they consider that the public cannot sufficiently be protected without the location of the depot being changed, they may order said depot to be located at such a point in said town as they may deem proper and suitable for the location of said depot. Said commissioners are empowered to apportion the expense arising from a compliance with their orders or regulations among the several companies affected by such orders or regulations, as they may deem reasonable and proper.

Sec. 2. No appeal shall be allowed from any order made by said commissioners under the provisions of the preceding section.

Sec. 3. If a change in the location of said depot shall be ordered by said commissioners, said railroad company or railroad companies shall have the right to take real estate for the location of the same in the same manner as is now provided by law for the taking of real estate for railroad purposes.

SEC. 4. Any railroad company who shall neglect to comply with any order made by said commissioners under the provisions of section one of this act, shall forfeit to the town in which the depot is located, concerning which said order is made, the sum of fifty dollars for each day of such neglect, to be recovered in an action brought by the town.

SEC. 5. This act shall take effect from its passage.

Approved, April 25, 1882.

ORDER OF THE RAILROAD COMMISSIONERS IN REFERENCE TO THE WILLIMANTIC DEPOT.

STATE OF CONNECTICUT,
OFFICE OF THE RAILROAD COMMISSIONERS,
HARTFORD, November 17, 1882.

Be it remembered, that on the 29th day of September the selectmen of Windham preferred their petition to us as follows, viz:

"*To the Hon. Board of Railroad Commissioners of the State of Connecticut :*

The undersigned, being a majority of the selectmen of the town of Windham, respectfully represent that the approaches and means of access to the present passenger depot located at Willimantic, in said town of Windham, and owned by the New York & New England R.R. Co. and by the New London Northern R.R. Co., are unsafe and dangerous for the public.

Wherefore, your petitioners request your Honorable Commission, in accordance with the provisions of the resolve of the last General Assembly, entitled a resolution "Concerning the Approaches to Willimantic Railroad Depot," to give due notice to all the railroad companies interested in this petition, and to your petitioners, of the time and place when and where you will hear this petition. And upon finding the allegations thereof true, that you will make such orders, regulations, and changes in and concerning said approaches and means of ac-

cess to said depot, as will make said approaches or means of
access to said depot safe and convenient for the public; or
that you will order the location of said depot to be changed,
or make such other orders and regulations in the premises
as your honorable Commission may deem reasonable and
proper.

And your petitioners, as in duty bound, will pray.

Dated at Windham, this 29th day of September, A.D. 1882.

M. EUGENE LINCOLN, } *Selectmen of the*
J. GRIFFIN MARTIN,   } *Town of Windham.*"

As by said petition on file will fully appear. Upon which
petition it was, on the 13th day of October, 1882, by us
Ordered, "That the same be heard at the office of said selectmen in Willimantic, on Thursday, the 2d day of November,
1882, at 9 o'clock in the forenoon, and that notice thereof be
given to said selectmen, and to the New York & New England R.R. Co., the New London Northern R.R. Co., the Central Vermont R.R. Co., and the Boston & New York Air Line
R.R. Co., by George T. Utley, by depositing in the post-office at
Hartford true and attested copies of said petition and of this
order; one addressed to the Selectmen, Willimantic, Conn.;
one to J. W. Perkins, Secretary N. Y. & N. E. R.R. Co.,
Boston, Mass.; one to J. A. Southard, Secretary N. L. N. R.
R. Co., New London, Conn.; one to Central Vermont R.R.
Co., St. Albans, Vt.; and one to T. L. Watson, Secretary B.
& N. Y. A. L. R.R. Co., Bridgeport, Conn., on or before the
14th day of October, 1882."

And on the said 2d of November, 1882, we met at the time
and place named in said order, which order we do find has
been duly complied with, when said petitioners appeared to
prosecute their said petition; and said New York & New
England R.R. Co. and said New London Northern R.R. Co.
also appeared, and by agreement an adjournment was had
till this day, when said parties again appeared and were fully
heard.

And upon such hearing we do find that the allegations of

said petition are true, and that certain changes in the approaches and means of access to said depot, and in the management and operation of trains and cars crossing said approaches are necessary to make said approaches and means
of access safe and convenient to the public.   And we further
consider that the public cannot sufficiently be protected without the location of said depot being slightly changed.

We do therefore order and direct said New York & New
England R.R. Co. and said New London Northern R.R. Co.,
before the first day of July, 1883, to locate a depot at said
Willimantic west of the west line of Railroad street were the
same extended south, and not more than three hundred feet
therefrom, and south of the north line of the land of said
New York & New England R.R. Co. in such place and manner that access may be had from Main street to said depot,
or to a suitable covered platform connected with the main
depot by a covered way without crossing any railroad tracks;
and in conformity with the agreement of said parties, we do
further order said companies to erect and on or before said
date complete to our satisfaction a new depot upon said location.

And we do further order that on or before said day said
New York & New England R.R. Co. shall cause to be removed
all of their railroad tracks, except their main track or tracks,
not exceeding two, between the east line of said Railroad
street and a point three hundred feet west of said street, and
shall thereafter cause to be discontinued the switching of
freight cars and the making up of trains between said points,
and the occupying of the main track or tracks with engines,
freight cars, or trains, except in cases of temporary necessity.

The expense arising from a compliance with these orders
to be by us hereafter apportioned between said New York &
New England R.R. Co. and said New London Northern R.R.
Co., in case of their failure to agree.

GEORGE M. WOODRUFF,
JOHN W. BACON,   } *Railroad*
WILLIAM H. HAYWARD, } *Commissioners.*

Collision at Pomfret.

This accident was a collision between east-bound passenger train No. 16 and west-bound freight train No. 47, second section, and occurred near the west switch at Pomfret Station, November 4, 1882, at 7.13 A. M., in a cut upon a curve, and neither train was in sight of the other till just before they struck. Myron Gladden, engineer of No. 16, jumped from his engine and was fatally injured; his fireman also jumped, and was badly hurt; one brakeman and the baggage-master on that train were also injured. Engineer Kendall and Fireman Wilson of the freight also jumped from their engine, and Kendall had his leg broken and was bruised about the head and otherwise. The passenger train should have left Pomfret for Putnam at 7.09 A. M., and so was about five minutes behind time, but this delay was not in any way the cause of the accident, nor were the passenger trainmen in any degree responsible therefor. The immediate cause of the accident was that Engineer Kendall ran his train past Pomfret Station in the face of and upon the time of the passenger train. The freight train left Boston at 11 o'clock on the night of the 3d, being two hours behind its regular leaving time. From Boston to Putnam it is said to have run without any special orders. At Putnam the following order was given for it: " Run to Willimantic as No. 47, second section. You will not leave Elliott's without special orders." This order was received at Putnam at 6.40 A. M., and receipted for by Conductor Bland for himself and Engineer Kendall. The "All right" was received at 6.42, and the train pulled out from Putnam at 6.45. It consisted of 27 cars, 19 loaded and 8 empty, and was drawn by a "consolidated" engine. The distance from Putnam to Pomfret is 4.8 miles, the larger part of it being up-grade, the schedule time for the run varying from 20 to 30 minutes, except for the Pier 50 express freight; the time for No. 47 was 30 minutes. As the schedule time for No. 16 to have left Pomfret was 7.09, there would have been only 24 minutes for the freight train to make the run, before it would have met No. 16, had it been on time ;

8

but, to prevent the possibility of collision, the rule would
have required the freight train to be on the side track at
Pomfret ten minutes before No. 16 was due, or at 6.59, leaving it only fourteen minutes in which to make the run. As a
matter of fact, at least twenty-seven minutes were consumed
in the run, and Pomfret Station was not passed till at least
three minutes after No. 16 should have left, going east. Evidently therefore the freight train was run, so far as its
engineer was concerned, without any expectation of meeting
No. 16 at Pomfret. Was this because he did not know of the
train, or because he forgot about it, or because he was misled
by the order under which he was running? There can be no
question but that he well knew of the train. It had run at
about the same hour for ten years, and Kendall had met it
frequently, once at least at Pomfret, and was familiar with its
time. He either therefore forgot it or was misled by his
order. We do not think it possible to decide absolutely which
was the case, since the testimony essential to the correct decision is wanting. Kendall claims that all the occurrences of
that night are a blank to him. Hence we cannot tell under
what theory he was running, and his present statements as to
how he should understand orders and rules are, of course, to
be received as those of a man anxious to avoid all possible
responsibility. We are, however, strongly inclined to the
opinion that he was misled by the order which he had received
at Putnam. He had run from Boston to Putnam without any
order, though from two to six hours behind time. At Putnam the order stated above was received. The first part of
the order, properly understood, simply made this train subject to all regulations which would have applied to No. 47.
The second part of the order required that it should not leave
Elliott's without special orders. Had no order been given, it
would have been its duty to continue on from Putnam under
the same rules and regulations as it had run to Putnam. Did
the direction not to leave Elliott's (which is only 4.1 miles
west of Pomfret) without special orders give the impression
to Kendall that he had a clear track to that point? We

think it may have done so. Kendall now says, should he receive such an order, he should consider he had a right to go
to Elliott's, but not beyond, without a special order, and that
as regarded regular trains, he should consider that the dispatcher had taken care to have the track clear for him.
There can be no question but that Kendall ran his train as
though he so understood the order. It will be remembered
that no order was necessary to enable him to run under the
rules. He receives an order to run to Willimantic only
nineteen minutes before he should be on the side track at
Pomfret, if he was to meet No. 16 there, and some part of
the nineteen minutes had to be used in getting off, and in
fact five minutes were so used. He runs into Pomfret some
three minutes after No. 16 should have been there, blows his
whistle for the station, the signal at the station is raised, sig-
nifying " Safety, go ahead ;" he opens the throttle, and goes
ahead till the collision occurs, though the speed has been
much checked by the application of the brakes by the conductor and brakemen. Under all the circumstances, we do
not think it very surprising that Kendall misunderstood his
duty under the order. On the other hand, we do not think
there was criminal negligence on the part of the dispatcher ;
but we do think that greater care should have been exercised
in sending out the train from Putnam so near the time of the
passenger train, and greater definiteness used in the form of
the order. The train ought not to have been allowed to leave
Putnam at the time it did without special orders, both to it
and to No. 16, to pass at Pomfret, or, if the responsibility of
the time for starting was properly left with the conductor and
engineer of the freight, we think the form of the order at one
time used on this road would have prevented the accident, by
recalling No. 16 to the memory of Kendall, viz.: " Run to
Willimantic as No. 47, second section, keeping out of the way
of all regular trains," etc. It is not sufficient answer to say
that is just what this *meant*, since it may have meant this to
Bland and something else to Kendall. The fact that Bland
sent back his acknowledgment of the receipt of the order,

and that he understood it, does not show *how* he or Kendall understood it. Rule 90 reads:

"ABBREVIATIONS. In addressing an order the abbreviations " C " and " E " may be used for conductor and engineman. The abbreviation " 12 " will be used at the end of an order immediately preceding the signature. "12 " signifies " *Do you acknowledge receipt of this order? How do you understand? Get my answer before leaving.*" Operatives and others will use the abbreviation " 13 " in repeating the order to despatcher. "13 " signifies " *We hereby acknowledge receipt of, and we understand and will fully execute the same.*"

But it will be observed that " 13 " does not say *how* the order was understood, either by the operator, or the conductor, or the engineer. In this case Bland understood it as it was meant, and tried to stop his train at Pomfret. He however apparently felt himself in some degree responsible for the collision, as he left immediately after its occurrence. Presumably he neglected both to inform himself as to the engineer's understanding of the order, and also to tell him to set off at Pomfret. Kendall might just as well have understood, so far as the *answer* indicated, that he had a clear track to Elliott's.

Rule 1 of the " Rules Governing the Use of Signals at Telegraph Offices on Single Track " in force at the time of the accident, read:

" The arm extended in a horizontal position by day or a red light by night will indicate danger ; stop. The arm lifted or lowered to a vertical position by day or a white light by night will indicate safety ; go ahead," etc., etc., etc.

It seemed to us that the wording of the rule was calculated to mislead, and might have confirmed Kendall in his impression that he had a clear track to Elliott's. The language was " the arm lifted or lowered to a vertical position " . . . . will indicate *safety* ; go ahead," while in fact it only meant there were no orders. We accordingly suggested to Superintendent Bent at the hearing on the 15th of November, that it would be less likely to mislead if the rule was made to *read* in that way. This suggestion was adopted and the rule now reads " will indicate no orders." This in our judgment is a much safer form of expression. The work of the train despatcher is the most important in the management of trains, and this department should be under the control of a thoroughly competent and practical railroad man, seconded by equally competent assistants, to whom every detail of the road to be managed should be familiar. These should have control of and be held responsible for the movement of the trains, and under no circumstances should this power be delegated to a mere telegraph operator, whose duties should be to execute, not originate orders. It is self-evident that all orders issued to trainmen should be so plain, explicit, and complete in themselves that if possible nothing should be left to be supplied from memory for their correct understanding.

GEORGE M. WOODRUFF, ⎫ *Railroad*
JOHN W. BACON,   ⎬ *Commissioners.*
WILLIAM H. HAYWARD, ⎭

January 2, 1883.

STATEMENT.

SHOWING THE SHORTEST DISTANCE BY RAILROAD FROM HARTFORD TO
THE VARIOUS STATIONS IN CONNECTICUT.

Abington,	49.	Colchester,	38.85	Grant's,	41.25
Allyn's Point,	54.2	Colebrook,	38.	Greeneville,	49.2
Andover, .	22.5	Collinsville,	24.	Green's Farms,	62.47
Ansonia,	48.9	Conn. River,	43.67	Greenwich,	81.46
Arnold's,	27.25	Cos Cob,	79.86	Grosvernordale,	60.2
Avon,	19.62	Cottage Grove,	4.	Groton,	61.75
Baltic,	41.9	Cook's,	11.7	Guilford,	52.47
Bartlett's,	56.	Crescent Beach,	53.17	Haddam,	26.5
Beacon Falls,	41.39	Cromwell,	12.75	Hampton,	43.3
Berlin,	10.625	Cornwall Bridge,	70.75	Hancock,	26.1
Bethel,	62.6	Danbury,	63.	Harrison's,	59.4
Birmingham,	47.16	Danielsonville,	64.	Hayden's,	9.
Blackhall,	45.75	Darien,	71.61	Hawleyville,	56.6
Bloomfield,	5.5	Dayville,	61.2	Hazardville,	19.6
Bolton,	16.6	Deep River,	34.5	Higganum,	24.
Botsford,	64.6	Derby,	46.62	HighRockGrove,	40.39
Branchville,	70.48	Eagleville,	38.5	Hitchcock's,	21.5
Branford,	44.61	East Canaan,	52.25	Hoadley's,	27.8
Bridgeport,	53.81	East Hampton,	24.25	Hop River,	26.3
Bristol,	17.9	East Hartford,	2.7	Hoskins',	13.5
Broad Brook,	14.6	East Haven,	41.51	Jewett City,	47.4
Brookfield,	62.6	East Lyme,	54.17	Kent,	79.75
Brookfield Junc.,	60.6	East River,	54.59	Lakeville,	64.
Brookside Park,	65.6	East Thompson,	64.6	Lanesville,	65.6
Buckland,	7.5	East Windsor,	8.8	Lebanon,	38.2
Burlington,	22.78	Ellithorpe,	52.8	Leete's Island,	49.62
Burnham's,	4.7	Ellington,	19.3	Liberty Hill,	36.3
Burnside,	4.1	Elliott,	49.2	Lime Rock,	62.75
Burrville,	39.5	Elmwood,	3.7	Litchfield,	47.7
Campville,	47.14	Enfield Bridge,	15.5	Long Hill,	61.81
Canaan,	54.75	Essex,	38.	Lyman Viaduct,	27.45
Cannon's	74.31	Fairfield,	58.88	Lyme,	44.11
Canterbury,	50.2	Fair Haven,	38.9	Madison,	54.15
Canton,	21.5	Fall Village,	60.75	Manchester,	8.7
Central Village,	57.6	Farmington,	16.99	Mansfield,	40.4
Centreville,	35.44	Fenwick,	45.	Maromas,	20.5
Chapinville,	59.5	Five Mile River,	70.3	Massapeag,	53.3
Charter Oak Park,	3.	Forestville,	15.5	Mechanicsville,	58.2
Cherry Brook,	25.	Franklin,	41.	Melrose,	16.3
Cheshire,	25.63	Georgetown,	71.72	Meriden,	18.
Chester,	33.5	Glen Brook,	74.8	Merrow,	42.
Clayton,	6.6	Goshen,	39.9	Merwinsville,	75.6
Clinton,	50.6	Goodspeed's,	29.75	Middlefield,	21.25
Cobalt,	20.95	Granby,	19.83	Middlef'd Centre,	20.25

Middletown,	15.25	Riverside,	79.47	Tolles,	24.9
Milford,	46.07	Rockfall,	18.65	Towantic,	40.6
Mill Plain,	67.6	Rocky Hill,	7.5	Torrington,	44.84
Mohegan,	51.4	Rockville,	16.7	Trumbull C'h,	58.81
Montowese,	35.25	Sadd's Mills,	18.	Turnerville,	35.25
Montville,	55.2	Salisbury,	62.25	Twin Lakes,	57.5
Moosup,	57.7	Sandy Hook,	51.4	Tyler City,	40.88
Mt. Carmel,	32.63	Sanford's,	68.08	Union City,	35.7
Mystic,	69.5	Saybrook Junc.,	42.25	Unionville,	19.86
New Britain,	9.1	Saybrook Point,	44.	Vernon,	12.3
New Hartford,	29.	Scotland, (H. & C. W.)	9.5	Versailles,	44.7
New Haven,	36.5	Scotl'd, (N.Y. & N.E.)	38.5	Yalesville,	20.5
Newington,	5.	Seymour,	48.49	Yantic,	44.2
New London,	61.	Shaker Station,	21.6	Wallingford,	24.
New Milford,	68.6	Simsbury,	15.	Walkley Hill,	25.25
Newtown,	60.6	Sound Beach,	78.25	Warehouse P't,	13.5
Noank,	67.	South Coventry,	36.8	Waterford, (S. L.)	57.92
Norfolk,	45.25	Southbury,	46.9	Watertown,	38.13
Noroton,	72.9	Southford,	43.9	Waterville,	29.9
North Cromwell,	11.5	Southington,	19.04	Waterbury,	32.4
Northford,	31.55	South Kent,	78.6	Wauregan,	59.
N. Grosvern'dale	61.7	South Lyme,	50.03	Weatogue,	16.86
North Haven,	29.625	S. Manchester,	10.95	Westbrook,	46.12
North Windham,	35.8	South Norwalk,	68.19	Westchester,	30.45
Norwalk,	69.69	Southport,	60.45	West Cornwall,	66.75
Norwich,	47.9	S. Wethersfield,	5.5	West Haven,	38.91
Norwich Town,	46.2	S. Willington,	44.25	West Mystic,	68.5
Oakville,	35.9	South Wilton,	76.36	West Norfolk,	48.
Oneco,	62.9	S. Windham,	34.9	Westport,	65.25
Orange,	42.69	South Windsor,	6.2	West Street,	15.5
Orcutt's,	54.1	Stafford,	51.9	West Thompson,	58.6
Ore Hill,	66.	Stamford,	76.25	West Winsted,	36.25

STATEMENT.

SHOWING THE SHORTEST DISTANCE BY RAILROAD FROM HARTFORD TO
THE VARIOUS STATIONS IN CONNECTICUT.

Abington,	49.	Colchester,	38.85	Grant's,	41.25
Allyn's Point,	54.2	Colebrook,	38.	Greeneville,	49.2
Andover,	22.5	Collinsville,	24.	Green's Farms,	62.47
Ansonia,	48.9	Conn. River,	43.67	Greenwich,	81.46
Arnold's,	27.25	Cos Cob,	79.86	Grosvernordale,	60.2
Avon,	19.62	Cottage Grove,	4.	Groton,	61.75
Baltic,	41.9	Cook's,	11.7	Guilford,	52.47
Bartlett's,	56.	Crescent Beach,	53.17	Haddam,	26.5
Beacon Falls,	41.39	Cromwell,	12.75	Hampton,	43.3
Berlin,	10.625	Cornwall Bridge,	70.75	Hancock,	26.1
Bethel,	62.6	Danbury,	63.	Harrison's,	59.4
Birmingham,	47.16	Danielsonville,	64.	Hayden's,	9.
Blackhall,	45.75	Darien,	71.61	Hawleyville,	56.6
Bloomfield,	5.5	Dayville,	61.2	Hazardville,	19.6
Bolton,	16.6	Deep River,	34.5	Higganum,	24.
Botsford,	64.6	Derby,	46.62	HighRockGrove,	40.39
Branchville,	70.48	Eagleville,	38.5	Hitchcock's,	21.5
Branford,	44.61	East Canaan,	52.25	Hoadley's,	27.8
Bridgeport,	53.81	East Hampton,	24.25	Hop River,	26.3
Bristol,	17.9	East Hartford,	2.7	Hoskins',	13.5
Broad Brook,	14.6	East Haven,	41.51	Jewett City,	47.4
Brookfield,	62.6	East Lyme,	54.17	Kent,	79.75
Brookfield Junc.,	60.6	East River,	54.59	Lakeville,	64.
Brookside Park,	65.6	East Thompson,	64.6	Lanesville,	65.6
Buckland,	7.5	East Windsor,	8.8	Lebanon,	38.2
Burlington,	22.78	Ellithorpe,	52.8	Leete's Island,	49.62
Burnham's,	4.7	Ellington,	19.3	Liberty Hill,	36.3
Burnside,	4.1	Elliott,	49.2	Lime Rock,	62.75

Bantam,	85.86	Naugatuck,	37.45	Springdale,	81.25
Beckleys,	13.125	New Canaan,	84.55	Steele's,	18.3
Chewink,	38.3	New Preston,	76.85	Talmadge Hill,	83.
East Berlin,	15.625	Romford,	80.54	Union C'y,(Naug)	36.54
Judd's Bridge,	71.35	Roxbury,	68.8	Washington,	75.67
Leonard's Br'ge,	87.95	Roxbury Falls,	65.07	Westfield,	17.625
Morris,	82.55	Shepaug,	61.44		

The distance to Collinsville should read,   -   -   -   -   -   **21.64**
"   "   " Pine Meadow "   " -   -   -   -   -   **27.04**
"   "   " New Hartford "   " -   -   -   -   -   **27.79**

Middletown,	15.25	Riverside,	79.47	Tolles,	24.9
Milford,	46.07	Rockfall,	18.65	Towantic,	40.6
Mill Plain,	67.6	Rocky Hill,	7.5	Torrington,	44.84
Mohegan,	51.4	Rockville,	16.7	Trumbull C'h,	58.81
Montowese,	35.25	Sadd's Mills,	18.	Turnerville,	35.25
Montville,	55.2	Salisbury,	62.25	Twin Lakes,	57.5
Moosup,	57.7	Sandy Hook,	51.4	Tyler City,	40.88
Mt. Carmel,	32.63	Sanford's,	68.08	Union City,	35.7
Mystic,	69.5	Saybrook Junc.,	42.25	Unionville,	19.86
New Britain,	9.1	Saybrook Point,	44.	Vernon,	12.3
New Hartford,	29.	Scotland,(H. & C. W.)	9.5	Versailles,	44.7
New Haven,	36.5	Scotl'd,(N.Y.& N.E.)	38.5	Yalesville,	20.5
Newington,	5.	Seymour,	48.49	Yantic,	44.2
New London,	61.	Shaker Station,	21.6	Wallingford,	24.
New Milford,	68.6	Simsbury,	15.	Walkley Hill,	25.25
Newtown,	60.6	Sound Beach,	78.25	Warehouse P't,	13.5
Noank,	67.	South Coventry,	36.8	Waterford,(S.L.)	57.92
Norfolk,	45.25	Southbury,	46.9	Watertown,	38.13
Noroton,	72.9	Southford,	43.9	Waterville,	29.9
North Cromwell,	11.5	Southington,	19.04	Waterbury,	32.4
Northford,	31.55	South Kent,	78.6	Wauregan,	59.
N. Grosvern'dale	61.7	South Lyme,	50.03	Weatogue,	16.86
North Haven,	29.625	S. Manchester,	10.95	Westbrook,	46.12
North Windham,	35.8	South Norwalk,	68.19	Westchester,	30.45
Norwalk,	69.69	Southport,	60.45	West Cornwall,	66.75
Norwich,	47.9	S. Wethersfield,	5.5	West Haven,	38.91
Norwich Town,	46.2	S. Willington,	44.25	West Mystic,	68.5
Oakville,	35.9	South Wilton,	76.86	West Norfolk,	48.
Oneco,	62.9	S. Windham,	34.9	Westport,	65.25
Orange,	42.69	South Windsor,	6.2	West Street,	15.5
Orcutt's,	54.1	Stafford,	51.9	West Thompson,	58.6
Ore Hill,	66.	Stamford,	76.25	West Winsted,	36.25
Osborn,	12.9	State Line,(N.L.N.)	50.1	Wethersfield,	3.75
Packerville,	52.5	Stepney,	63.81	Wheaton's,	27.1
Parkville,	1.6	Sterling,	61.1	Whiting River,	50.25
Pine Meadow,	28.	Stoney Creek,	48.11	Willimantic,	31.5
Plainfield,	54.5	Stonington,	73.	Wilson's, (H.& N.H.)	3.5
Plainville,	13.7	Stratford,	50.59	Wilson's (N. & W.)	63.8
Plantsville,	19.75	Stratton Brook,	17.5	Wilson's Point,	70.84
Pomfret,	51.3	Summit,	43.5	Wilton,	75.82
Pomperaug V'y,	46.9	Taftville,	51.	Windermere,	17.6
Portland,	16.25	Talcottville,	11.3	Windsor,	6.375
Poquonnock,	64.	Tariffville,	11.5	Windsor Locks,	12.
Pratt's,	7.4	Terryville,	22.2	Winnipauk,	71.37
Putnam,	56.1	Thamesville,	49.	Winsted,	35.5
Quinnipiack,	33.	Thomaston,	41.82	Woodland,	5.1
Quinnebaug,	71.1	Thompson,	60.2	Wolcottville,	44.84
Reading,	65.99	Thompsonville,	17.375	Woodmont,	42.46
Ridgefield,	74.48	Tolland,	46.		

STATISTICAL TABLES.

TABLE I.

Number	Names of Roads and Branches. [Branches in Italics.]	Chartered.	Opened for use.	Location of Road. From	Location of Road. To	Length of Main Line and Branches. Total.	Length of Main Line and Branches. In Conn.	Double Track. Total.	Double Track. In Conn.	Sidings. Total.	Sidings. In Conn.	Length of Single T Mile. Total.
1	Boston & New York Air Line,*	1875	1870-73	New Haven, Ct.	Willimantic, Ct.	50.	50.			5.05	5.05	55.05
2	Colchester,	1876	1877	Colchester, Ct.	Turnerville, Ct.	3.59	3.59			.50	.50	4.09
3	Connecticut Central, *Rockville,*	1871	1876	East Hartford, Ct. Rockville, Ct.	Mass. State Line. Melrose, Ct.	20.25 7.	20.25 7.			1.31	1.31	28.56
4.	Danbury & Norwalk,‡ *Ridgefield,* *Hawleyville,*	1850 1870 1872	1852 1870 1872	Danbury, Ct. Branchville, Ct. Bethel, Ct.	Wilson's Point, Ct. Ridgefield, Ct. Hawleyville, Ct.	26.50 4. 6.	26.50 4. 6.			5.30	5.30	41.80
5	Hartford & Connecticut Valley,†	1880	1871	Hartford, Ct.	Fenwick, Ct.	46.90	46.30			5.30	5.30	52.
6	Hartford & Connecticut Western, ‖	1881	1871	Hartford, Ct.	Rhinecliff, N. Y.	101.90	66.70			18.12	14.66	120.02
7	Housatonic, *Danbury,*	1886	1840	Bridgeport, Ct. Danbury, Ct.	Mass. State Line. Br'kfield Junc., Ct.	74. 5.50	74. 5.50			12.50	12.50	92.
8	Naugatuck,	1845	1849	Winsted, Ct.	{ Junction N. Y., N. H. & H. R.R. }	56.55	56.55			11.54	11.54	68.09
9	New Canaan,	1866	1868	New Canaan, Ct.	Stamford, Ct.	8.30	8.30			.47	.47	8.77
10	New Haven & Derby,	1864	1871	New Haven, Ct.	Ansonia, Ct.	13.	13.			1.96	1.96	14.96
11	New Haven & Northampton, *New Hartford,* *Tariffville,* *Williamsbury,* *Turner's Falls,*	1846	1848-81	New Haven, Ct. Farmington, Ct. Simsbury, Ct. Northampton, Mass. So. Deerfield, Mass.	Conway Junc., Mas. New Hartford, Ct. Tariffville, Ct. Williamsb'y, Mass. Turner's F'ls, Mass.	94.64 14.09 1.04 7.51 10.07	51.36 14.09 1.04			27.50	14.52	154.85
12	New London Northern,¹	1859	1849-67	New London, Ct.	Brattleboro, Vt.	121.	56.			23.48	18.15	144.48

No.	Name			From	To	A	B	C	D	E	F	
13	New York & New England,[2]	1873	1855–81	Boston, Mass.	Fishkill, N.Y.	216.77	134.18	30.88	2.70	88.16	39.56	4
	Woonsocket,			Willimantic, Ct.	Providence, R.I.	58.60	88.18					
	Dedham,			Brookline, Mass.	Woonsocket, R.I.	33.75	2.					
				Islington, Mass.	Dedham, Mass.	2.						
	Ridge Hill,			Dedham Junc., Mas.	" "	.91						
				Charles River, Mas.	Ridge Hill, Mass.	1.64						
				Dorrance St., Pr.R.I.		.83						
	Southbridge,			East Thompson, Ct.	Southridge, Mass.	17.50	5.					
	Freight,			Hartford, Ct		.50	.50					
14	New York, New Haven & Hartford,[3]	1871	1839–70	Harlem Junc., N.Y.	Spring'f'ld, Mass.	174.17	154.25	123.20	103.28	77.97	69.88	8
	Middletown,			New Haven, Ct.	New London, Ct.	10.	4.			11.		
	Suffield,			Berlin Junc., Ct.	Middletown, Ct.	4.	4.50				5.	
	New Britain,			Windsor Locks, Ct.	Suffield, Ct.	3.	3.	50.				
				Berlin Junc., Ct.	New Britain, Ct.							
15	New York, Providence & Boston,	1832	1837	Groton, Ct.	Providence, R.I.	62.50	17.	50.	5.50	11.	5.	1
	Warwick,			Auburn, R.I.	Buttonw. Bch., R.I.	9.875						
16	Norwich & Worcester,	1833	1840	Norwich, Ct.	Worcester, Mass.	59.75	41.25			14.87	9.97	
	Allyn's Point,			" "	Allyn's Point, Ct.	6.30	6.30					
	In Norwich,			" "		.43	.43					
17	Ridgefield & New York,[4]	1867		Ridgefield, Ct.	Port Chester, N.Y.							
18	Rockville,	1857	1863	Rockville, Ct.	Vernon, Ct.	4.50	4.50			.75	.75	
19	Shepaug,[5]	1873	1872	Litchfield, Ct.	Hawleyville, Ct.	38.98	38.98			1.52	1.52	
20	Shore Line,[6]	1864	1852	New Haven, Ct.	New London, Ct.	50.	50.	50.				
21	South Manchester,	1866	1869	S. Manchester, Ct.	Manchester, Ct.	2.25	2.25			1.36	1.36	
22	Watertown & Waterbury,	1869	1871	Watertown, Ct.	Waterbury, Ct.	4.60	4.60			.25	.25	
	Total,					1,377.915	962.45	204.08	121.48	809.41	215.05	

* Road commenced operations in 1870, under the charter granted to the New Haven, Middletown & Willimantic R. R. Company in 1867.
† Successor to the Connecticut Valley R. R. Company, chartered in 1868.
‡ Successor to the Connecticut Western R. R. Co., chartered in 1868.
§ Original charter granted to the Fairfield County R. R. Company in 1835, renewed in 1846, and name changed to D. & N. R. R. Company in 1850.
‖ The New London, Willimantic & Springfield R. R. Company was incorporated in 1847. In 1848, that Company and the New London, Willimantic & Palmer R
incorporated by the State of Massachusetts, were permitted, by the Legislature of Connecticut, to become one corporation, to be known as the N. L, W. & P. R. R.
mortgage of which having been foreclosed, the holders of the mortgage bonds were incorporated as the N. L. N. R. R. Company in 1859.
[2] Road commenced operations in 1867, under charter granted to the Boston, Hartford & Erie R. R. Company in 1863.
[3] Hartford & New Haven R. R. Company incorporated in 1833; Hartford & Springfield R. R. Company in 1835, and privileges of its charter conferred on H.
Company in 1842. N Y. & N. H. R. R. Company incorporated in 1844, and consolidated with H. & N. H. R. R. Company in 1872.
[4] Unfinished. Proposed line 23.29 miles, of which 15.94 are in Connecticut.
[5] Charter granted to Shepaug Valley R. R. Company in 1868.
[6] New Haven & New London R. R. Company incorporated in 1848; mortgage foreclosed and bondholders incorporated as Shore Line Railway Company in 1864.

TABLE II.—CAPITAL STOCK.

Number	RAILROADS.	14 Authorized by Charter.	15 Auth'rized by vote of Company.	16 Issued for Cash.	17 Issued for Bonds.	18 Issued for stock of other corporations.	19 Issued for undivided earnings.	20 Issued for increased valuation.
1	Boston & New York Air Line.	$4,000,000.00	$4,000,000.00		$3,800,800.00			
2	Colchester.	50,000.00	25,000.00	$25,000.00				
3	Connecticut Central,	800,000.00	800,000.00	361,600.00				
4	Danbury & Norwalk.	1,000,000.00	600,000.00	388,416.25			$101,583.75	$160,000.00
5	Hartford & ... Valley.	1,200,000.00	800,000.00		704,800.00			
6	Hartford & ... Western.	3,000,000.00	3,000,000.00		1,365,000.00			
7	Housatonic,	2,000,000.00	2,000,000.00	2,000,000.00				
8	Naugatuck,	2,000,000.00	2,000,000.00	397,696.00	273,000.00		142,700.00	448,825.00
9	New Canaan,	200,000.00	200,000.00	164,050.00				
10	New Haven & Derby.	700,000.00	457,000.00	447,100.00				
11	New Haven & ...mpton.	5,000,000.00	2,600,000.00	1,882,000.00	1,102,660.00		578,000.00	
12	New London Northern,	2,000,000.00	1,500,000.00	340,673.33		$56,666.67		
13	New York & New England.	20,000,000.00	20,000,000.00		16,502,000.00			
14	N. Y., N. H. & Hartford.	15,500,000.00	15,500,000.00	400,000.00		15,500,000.00		
15	N. Y., Providence & Boston,	4,000,000.00	4,000,000.00	3,000,000.00				
16	Norwich & ...er.	3,835,000.00	3,835,000.00					
17	Ridgefield & New York.	1,250,000.00	1,250,000.00	182,150.00				
18	Rockville,	120,000.00	100,000.00	108,750.00				
19	Shepaug,	700,000.00	800,000.00	89,750.00	210,000.00			
20	Shore Line,	1,000,000.00	1,000,000.00	62,845.20	678,125.00			259,029.80
21	South ...er...	40,000.00	40,000.00	40,000.00				
22	...wn & ...y,	-150,000.00	130,000.00	118,200.00				
	Total,	$68,585,000.00	$64,127,000.00	$12,162,580.78	$24,636,385.00	$15,556,666.67	$822,283.75	$867,854.80

TABLE III.—CAPITAL STOCK.

Number	RAILROADS.	21. Otherwise issued.	22. Total amount issued.	23. Total issue per last report.	24. Issued per mile of road.	25. Amount held in Connecticut.	26. Amount same per last report.
1	Boston & New York Air Line,	......	$3,800,800.00	$3,571,800.00	$76,000.00	$903,400.00	$ 7,300.00
2	Colchester,	......	25,000.00	25,000.00	6,963.79	25,000.00	25,000.00
3	Connecticut Central,	$86,900.00	48,500.00	448,500.00	16,495.41	25,000.00	25,000.00
4	Danbury & Norwalk,	......	600,000.00	600,000.00	16,438.35	273,000.00	220,000.00
5	Hartford & Conn. Valley,	......	704,800.00	652,000.00	15,255.41	88,800.00	88,800.00
6	Hartford & Conn.	800,000.00	2,65,000.00	579,000.00	21,246.31	1,084,200.00	490,400.00
7	Housatonic,	......	2,000,000.00	2,000,000.00	25,157.23	85,800.00	85,400.00
8	Naugatuck,	737,779.00	2,000,000.00	2,000,000.00	35,366.75	6,400.00	49,400.00
9	New	......	64,60.00	164,050.00	19,765.06	37,000.00	37,000.00
10	New Haven & Derby,	......	447,100.00	447,100.00	84,392.30	407,500.00	98,000.00
11	New Haven & Northampton,	......	60,000.00	90.00	11,464.46	970,600.00	69,700.00
12	New London	......	1,500,000.00	1,500,000.00	12,396.69	1,003,900.00	82,100.00
13	New York & New England,	......	16,502,000.00	8,743,000.00	49,656.95	62,500.00	26,300.00
14	N. Y., New Haven & Hartford,	......	15,500,000.00	15,500,000.00	110,163.38	6,950,700.00	88,700.00
15	N. Y., Providence & Boston,	......	3,000,000.00	3,000,000.00	41,436.96	65,500.00	65,500.00
16	Norwich & Worcester,	......	2,64,400.00	2,604,400.00	39,160.64	80,600.00	86,300.00
17	Ridgefield & New York,	46,400.00	28,50.00	228,550.00	9,813.22	71,500.00	71,500.00
18		......	108,50.00	08,750.00	22,625.25	108,50.00	108,750.00
19	Shepaug,	......	299,700.00	297,800.00	9,280.97	296,700.00	296,700.00
20	Shore Line,	......	1,000,000.00	1,000,000.00	20,000.00	63,600.00	62,600.00
21	South	......	40,000.00	40,000.00	17,777.77	40,000.00	40,000.00
22	Watertown &	......	118,200.00	118,200.00	25,595.65	118,200.00	118,200.00
	Total,	$1,671,079.00	$55,716,850.00	$46,348,350.00	$47,620.46	$16,458,650.00	$15,212,700.00

TABLE IV.—CAPITAL STOCK. DEBT.

Number.	RAILROADS.	27 Par value per share.	28 Number of stockholders in Conn.	29 Number of same per last report.	30 Rate of interest on funded debt.	31 Unpaid interest on same.	31 Total amount funded debt.	32 Amount of same per last report.
1	Boston & New York Air Line,	$100.00	335	257	5 per cent.	......	$00,000.00	$500,000.00
2	Colchester,	100.00	1	1	7 "	......	25,000.00	25,000.00
3	Connecticut Central,	100.00	139	180	7 "	$67,305.00	85,000.00	325,000.00
4	abry & Norwalk,	50.00	115	99	6 & 7	......	500,000.00	500,000.00
5	Hartford & ri. Tley,	100.00	16	59		......	95,200.00	
6	Hartford & nd. Wiern,	100.00	483	217	5, 6, & 7 "	......	140,000.00	
7	Housatonic,	100.00	417	385		......	1, 00,000.00	850,000.00
8	Naugatuck,	100.00	451	438		......		
9	New ren,	50.00	197	197	7 "	18,252.99	99,875.25	99,878.25
10	New Haven & Derby,	100.00	266	318	7 "	......	525,000.00	85,000.00
11	New Haven & Northampton,	100.00	193	204	5, 6, & 7 "	......	3,200,000.00	900.00
12	New London Northern,	100.00	224	222	5, 6, & 7 "	......	1,499,500.00	1,499,500.00
13	New York & New England.	100.00	14	10	6 & 7	......	11,742,000.00	8,968,000.00
14	N. Y., N. H. & Hartford,	100.00	1,938	1,827		......		
15	N. Y., ne & Boston,	100.00	18	18	6 & 7 "	......	1,300,000.00	1,360,000.00
16	Norwich & W.	100.00	30	29		......	400,000.00	400,000.00
17	Ridgefield & New York,	50.00	54	54		......		
18	Rockville,	100.00	47	47	6 "	......	6,000.00	6,000.00
19	Shepaug,	100.00	14	14	7 "	......	400,000.00	400,000.00
20	Shore Line, ster,	100.00	184	188	4½ "	154,000.00	200,000.00	200,000.00
21	South ster,	100.00	9	9		......		
22	Watertown & Waterbury,	50.00	56	56	7	11,880.00	19,000.00	19,000.00
	Total,	......	5,191	4,779	......	$251,497.99	$22,026,575.25	$19,316,378.25

TABLE V.—DEBT.

Number	RAILROADS.	34 Amount of bills payable.	35 Amt. of same per last report.	36 Accounts payable, etc.	37 Total.	38 Total per last report.	39 Proport'n per mile of road.	40 To al stock and dbt.
1	& New York Air Line,			$13,064.48	$513 04.48	$1, 9.46	$10,261.29	$4, 3,864.48
2					25,000.00	25, 0.00	6,963.79	50,000.00
3				12,914.16	405,219.16	82, 0.16	14,870.43	63,719.16
4	Danbury & Norwalk,	$147,000.00			647,000.00	60, 0.00	17,726.02	1, 27,000.00
5	Hartford & Conn. Valley,			268,284.06	363,184.06	29, 0.60	7,867.62	1, 08,284.06
6	Hartford & Conn.	25,000.00		76,711.98	241,711.98	14, 8.07	2,372.05	2, 06,711.98
7		188,008.37	$135,000.00	94,860.93	1,332,869.30	1, 65, 63.63	16,763.13	3,332,869.30
8				71,385.69	71, 8.69	71, 31.81	1,262.34	2, 01,385.69
9					18, 9.24	14, 31.00	14,232.31	282,178.24
10	New Haven & Derby,	9,806.00	16,678.99	78,212.35	63, 9.35	63, 45.71	47,155.25	1, 00,118.35
11	New Haven &	585,000.00	316,000.00	90,629.22	3, 35, 9.22	3,778, 76.17	30,432.89	6, 35,629.22
12		227,000.00	212,000.00	3,623.42	1, 30, 9.42	1, 74 42.33	14,298.54	3, 30,123.42
13	N.Y., Housatonic & Northern,	1,311,532.00	225,374.37			44.37		
14	New or & New	1,311,532.00	1,900,532.00	1,260,301.22	14,313,833.22	11,806,908.70	43,072.43	30,815, 83.22
15	N.Y., New Haven & Hartford	514,762.40	3,000.00	592,917.78	1,107,680.18	44,664.98	786.63	16, 07, 60.18
16	N.Y., Pe &				1,300,000.00	1,360,000.00	17,962.00	4 340, 00.00
17	Norwich & Worcester,	5,140.13	11,983.93	102,001.35	507,141.48	492,831.75	7,628.48	31, 51.48
18	& New York,							28, 50.00
19	Rockville,	12,549.75	15,549.75	849.35	19,399.10	22,276.01	4,041.47	28, 49.10
20	Shepaug,				4, 0.00	526,000.00	17,162.24	63,700.00
21	Shore Line,				200,000.00	200,000.00	4,000.00	1, 90, 00.00
22	So th			23,871.72	23 871.72	26,909.90	10,609.65	63, 81.72
23	&				0.00	29,550.00	6,718.04	49, 00.00
	Total,	$3,025,798.65	$2,836,119.04	$2,689,627.71	$27,993,439.60	$24,453,893.65	*$20,815.79	90

* Average.

TABLE VI.—CONSTRUCTION AND EQUIPMENT.

Number.	RAILROADS.	41 Construction.	42 Equipment.	43 Total and	43 c'ton m't.	44 Total per last report.	45 Per mile of road.
1	Boston & New York Air Line,	$4,431,984.45	$129,931.94	$4,561,916.39		$4,529, 96.54	$1, 88.32
2	Colchester,	50,000.00		50, 0.00		50, 00.00	13,927.57
3	Connecticut Central,	5		70,655.25		770, 65.25	28, 80.93
4	Danbury & Norwalk,	1,118,289.00	198,345.42	1,306,584.42		1,162, 82.46	35, 96.83
5	Hartford & 6th. Valley, 6m,			85,258.23		85, 82.05	19, 33.55
6	Hartford & 6th. 6th.	2, 62, 0.00	89,504.00	*2,771, 0.00		*1, 90, 00.00	27, 82.10
7	Housatonic,	2,207,279.81	80, 0.30	3,048,244.11		2, 62, 42.87	38, 494.95
8	Naugatuck,	1, 08,483.75	24,086.57	2,137,570.33		2,187,570.32	34,950.46
9	New 6th.	30,746.03	27,197.90	37,943.98		257, 93.93	31,077.58
10	New Haven & Derby,	970,816.77	45,141.53	1, 15, 43.29		1, 23, 20.57	85,804.48
11	New Haven & Northampton,	5, 60,894.06	61,457.03	6, 62,351.09		6, 90,467.77	50, 4.80
12	New London Northern,	2, 86,403.01	28,445.44	8, 5		3, 02, 40.27	25,659.90
13	New York & New England,	30, 39, 6.36	2,280,274.36	32,810,074.72		31,709,370.33	98, 30.36
14	New York & New Hartford,	13,578,547.38	2,154,454.71	15,733,002.09		15, 33, 02.09	111,819.49
15	N. Y., New Haven & Hartford,	2, 95,802.32	81	81		3, 82, 41.96	51,044.27
16	N. Y., Providence & Boston,	3,270, 8.36	87			3, 46,371.90	51,905.98
17	Norwich & Wr.,	96,450.00		3,450,710.08		96, 50.00	8,494.95
18	8rd & New York,	144,247.66	28,887.99	196,450.00		73, 65.65	96 043.67
19	Rockville,	8	11,064.20	173,105.65		73, 05.65	93.58
20	Shepaug,	1, 8		268,523.78		268,523.78	28,389.92
21	Shore Line,	1, 8		1, 60, 46.10		1,169,496.10	89
22	South 1h & 3y,	65 376.65	17,172.46	184,248.43		82,102.40	29,184.44
23		83				134,248.43	
	Total,	$74,879,789.87	$8,420,176.60	$84,195,224.50		$81,414,084.67	†$61,108.36

*See returns of H. & C. V. R. R. Co. and H. & C. W. R. R. Co.   † Average.

TABLE VII.—EARNINGS.

Number.	RAILROADS.	46 Passenger.	47 Freight.	48 Mails.	49 Express.	50 Rents.	[51 Other Sources.
1	(...n & ...w York Air Line,	$72,848.77	$73,492.72	$7,724.83	$3,600.00	.....	$147,445.02
2	Colchester,	.....	.....	.....	.....	.....	.....
3	Connecticut Central,	.....	.....	.....	.....	.....	.....
4	D...y & Norwalk,	93,564.73	98,546.39	2,897.57	3, 0.00	$2,384.91	.....
5	Hartford & ...n. Valley,	102,699.25	77,930.13	2,781.04	2,955.84	1,092.17	8,435.18
6	Hartford & ...n. Western,	110,110.30	184,078.24	5, 41.24	4, 43.34	2,883.67	.....
7	Housatonic,	230,282.98	46,956.13	12,356.57	15,000.00	.....	41, 2.08
8	...n.	253,884.88	45,409.41	6,276.14	10,500.00	1,512.50	7,315.08
9	New Canaan,	9, .872	4,477.16	689.75	200.00	100.00	3, 93.61
10	New Haven & ...y,	70,277.78	90,349.65	04.84	1,876.96	.....	18, 04.74
11	New Haven & ...n,	200,259.43	51,863.84	10,258.08	14,924.52	.....	2, 90.02
12	N...(...h	212,274.96	45,467.27	7,461.20	8,874.47	10,336.56	156, 91.96
13	N...w York & ...w England,..	1,171,623.02	1,837,880.35	48,898.38	87,475.77	.....	29, 82.25
14	N.Y., ...w Haven & ...rd,	3,393,513.86	2,065,855.52	144,256.48	234,867.93	69,481.60	16, 45.91
15	N.Y., Providence & Boston,	562,000.53	42,808.46	19,058.13	98	7,583.60	22, 21.89
16	Norwich & ...r..	203,798.35	56, 6.80	5, 2.96	17,112.12	2,522.51	.....
17	...l & ...w York,	.....	.....	.....	.....	.....	.....
18	...b,	.....	.....	.....	.....	.....	.....
19	Shepaug,	12,914.80	40,613.49	1,456.04	766.50	.....	7,056.00
20	Shore ...e,	.....	.....	.....	.....	125.00	.....
21	South ...er,	6,609.25	4,569.19	*50.04	.....	.....	.....
22	...n & Waterbury,	.....	.....	.....	.....	.....	.....
	Total,	$6,706,804.61	$7,376,878.75	$275,635.29	$434,451.18	$97,972.52	$462,413.74

*Includes amount received for express.

10

TABLE VIII.—EARNINGS.

Number.	RAILROADS.	52. Total.	53. Total per last report.	54. Per mile of road operated.	55. Total operating expenses.	56. Net earnings.	57. Same per last report.
1	Boston & New York Air Line,	$305,111.35	$282,582.67	$5,693.44	$113,262.86	$191,848.48	$146,116.14
2	Colchester,						
3	Danbury & Norwalk,						
4	Derby & New Haven,	90, 93.60	95,163.05	5,506.67	28, 02.67	72,990.93	88, 80.96
5	Hartford & Connecticut Valley,	195, 823.61	191,926.13	4,239.68	95, 63.88	789.79	23, 97.55
6	Hartford & Connecticut Western,	746.79	266,725.14	2, 97.21	36, 70.20	*9,363.41	10, 47.38
7	Housatonic,	746,327.76	30	5,899.83	57, 90.58	179,127.18	95, 48.53
8	Naugatuck,	714,898.01	43	11 688.97	63, 85.10	251,032.91	22, 74.97
9	New Haven & Northampton,	15,108.63	97	30,31	9, 88.56	5,840.07	7, 71.24
10	New Haven & Derby,	166,402.84	47, 4.44	12,800.22	87,929.36	78,473.48	67, 67.34
11	New Haven & Northampton,	94 20.61	51,614.53	6, 99.56	591,200.19	305,070.42	21, 6.81
12	New London Northern,	74.48	61,043.58	5 873.84	519,312.18	78,072.30	97, 1.34
13	New York & New England,	8,302,789.48	2, 62,874.20	86.66	2,445,068.45	-857,721.03	64,351.83
14	N. Y., New Haven & Hartford,	5,987,807.64	5, 65,766.05	29, 82.71	3,803, 678.97	2,184,128.67	2 22,857.04
15	N. Y., Providence & Boston,	1 65 60.31	97, 7.68	12 880.28	561,375.63	504,274.69	85,184.90
16	Norwich & New York,	70.63	26,481.97	21.84	473,423.66	364,346.97	274,706.51
17							
18	Rockville,						
19	Shepaug,	62,981.53	60,831.71	1,949.56	54,393.83	8,538.00	14,865.40
20	Shore Line,		416,620.71				212,981.28
21	South Manchester,	11,228.48	13,086.16	4,090.43	9,266.16	1,962.33	3,454.16
22	Watertown & Waterbury,						
	Total,	$15,353,656.04	$13,803,414.96	$10,475.84	$10,338,802.21	†$5,014,853.83	$5,228,127.38

*Deficiency.   † Deficiency reported by H. & C. W. R. R. Co. deducted.

TABLE IX.—OPERATING EXPENSES.

Number	RAILROADS.	58 Repairs of road-bed and track.	59 Repairs of bridges.	60 Repairs of fences.	61 Repairs of buildings and fixtures.	62 Repairs of locomotives.	63 Repairs of cars.	64 Repairs of machinery and tools.
1	Bo &c & New York Air Line,	$20,394.99	$11,440.83	$1,033.86	$1,623.93	$9,207.72	$10,419.68	$268.05
2	Colchester,							
3	Co ...							
4	Danbury & Norwalk,	33,026.93	3,957.17	770.90	8,070.34	8,670.59	9,714.81	999.58
5	Hartford & Conn. Valley,	24,852.1	8,084.67	2,925.21	2,661.77	7,131.11	12,824.07	748.81
6	Hartford & Conn.	188,067.93	29,815.96	2,277.42	10,235.79	9,150.96	8,811.40	485.31
7	Housatonic,	142,52.39	3,417.35	3,691.72	24,634.76	34,011.75	41,656.99	485. 9
8	Naugatuck,	95,0.90	10,921.03	242.15	49,311.40	37,885.34	43,038.61	4,835. 9
9	New Canaan,	2, 6.62		4.92	7.50	642.81	331.04	
10	New Haven & Derby,	13, 41.52	7,564.07	358.29	1,153.14	5,432.50	5,069.63	137.22
11	New Haven & Nor ...	25, 68.35	9,745.08	3,075.17	30,065.68	38,346.52	55,080.70	
12	New London N ...	68, 9.05	8,380.56	7,463.04	14,571.36	24,006.96	31,606.18	2,767.94
13	New York & New England,	34, 3.89	61,527.49	15,802.78	28,441.83	154,753.99	173,475.88	26,099.65
14	N.Y., New &c & Hartford,	539,502.01	47,135.44	12,879.48	229,528.18	144,107.34	392,228.50	32,350.21
15	N. Y., Providence & Boston,	115,896.09	14,146.52	2,937.31	11,561.95	13,615.36	32,226.94	3,319.29
16	Norwich & Worcester,	8.59	1,443.08	685.73	9,871.63	23,583.23	46,700.74	3,745.17
17	&c & New York,							
18								
19	S ...	18,628.39	1,153.16	509.27	293.20	5,428.34	1,903.80	78.28
20	Shore Line,							
21	S ... Mchester,	1,747.87			187.36	252.46	129.22	47.89
22	&c & Waterbury,							
	Total,	$1,841,777.18	$218,732.41	$54,657.25	$422,209.81	$516,176.98	$865,217.64	$81,683.39

TABLE X.—OPERATING EXPENSES—FUEL.

Number	RAILROADS.	LOCOMOTIVES AND CARS				STATIONS AND SHOPS				69 Total cost.
		65 COAL		66 WOOD		67 COAL		68 WOOD		
		Number of tons.	Cost.	Number of cords.	Cost.	Number of tons.	Cost.	No. of Cords.	Cost.	
1	Boston & New York Air Line,	2,628.	$13,796.91	75.	$235.00		$2,947.63			$16,969.54
2										
3	Connecticut Central,									
4	Danbury &	3,555.	16,774.87	50.	300.00	125.	750.00	25	$187.50	17,962.37
5	Hartford & Conn. Valley,	3,971.82	19,980.79	23.	105.48	275.59	1,444.93			21,531.20
6	& Conn. Western,	4,803.	30,354.96			248.	1,597.81			31,952.77
7	Housatonic,	12,871.	59,969.69			1,003.	4,846.69			4,816.88
8	Naug	8,203.11	40, 51.49	140.588	456.74	397.85	1,810.26			43, 18.49
9	Canaan,	273.	1, 22.15				60.60			1, 9.75
10	New Haven & Derby,	1,932.	8, 55.54		43.22		420.97			9,119.73
11	New Haven & mpton,	13,369.	65, 97.28			89.	8,894.40			69,851.68
12	New h Northern,	11,483.	55, 63.16	2,770.	10,036.17	598.	2,483.97			70, 0.30
13	New & New England,	88,257.5	28, 80.97			440.	29,288.06	450	1,611.00	37,629.03
14	N.Y. New Haven & Hartford,	75,267.	383,251.75	922.	5,091.61	2,103.	9,083.98			97, 2.34
15	N.Y., Providence & Boston,	14,950.	70,354.21			475.	2,171.49			72,525.61
16	& Worcester,	12,200.	59,781.40	60.	400.00	1,239.	6,689.03			66,870.43
17	& New York,									
18	Rockville,									
19	Shepaug,	1,356.5	7,274.38	8.	14.00	13.	90.10			7,378.48
20	Shore Li ster,									
21	South & Waterbury,	202.	1,284.30	5.5	24.90	11.	74.25			1,388.45
22										
	Total,	255,321.93	$1,263,883.85	4,053.088	$16,697.12	7,007.44	$67,654.08	475	$1,748.50	$1,349,933.55

TABLE XI.—OPERATING EXPENSES.

Number.	RAILROADS.	70 Salaries and labor not before stated.	71 Oil and waste.	72 Injuries to persons.	73 Damages to property.	74 Insurance.	75 Rent of other roads.	76 Other operating expenses.
1	Boston & New York Air Line,	$31,041.71	$1,677.61	$80.05	$1,291.68	$320.00	.....	$7,498.21
2	.....	.....	.....	.....	.....	.....	.....	.....
3	.....	.....	.....	.....	.....	.....	.....	.....
4	... & ... Valley,	40,939.12	995.37	.....	246.88	315.15	.....	4,328.96
5	... & ... Western,	69,568.88	1,709.82	137.85	5,072.25	533.73	.....	37,051.52
6	.....	25,698.03	3,537.23	.....	437.79	631.55	$6,040.00	49, 6
7	Housatonic,	150,981.80	6,312.26	68.25	1,029.78	2,440.50	74,075.92	11, 042
8	.....	151,059.11	5,914.30	525.00	1,611.07	2,679.60	.....	16,932.11
9	New ...	2,981.57	325.17	.....	.....	104.54	500.00	591.64
10	New Haven & Derby,	38,490.42	950.40	275.00	664.70	327.84	3,360.04	1,614.86
11	N... &	181,625.74	8,814.11	5,550.66	1,616.46	2,506.70	28,415.95	30,697.39
12	N...	43,127.08	7,103.24	334.06	491.72	2,472.00	.....	38,394.69
13	New York & New England,	873,892.41	21,186.27	18,588.64	29,381.34	10,486.53	74,965.90	164,042.88
14	N.Y., ... & ...,	1,088,023.65	52,976.63	20,263.72	9,001.79	2,777.75	100,000.00	845,576.93
15	N.Y., Providence & ...,	26, 639	7,742.49	.....	1,845.65	2,117.18	.....	67,224.84
16	Norwich & ...,	166,391.41	3,449.19	264.21	1,478.55	.....	37,210.00	35,501.67
17	... & New York,	.....	.....	.....	.....	.....	.....	.....
18	.....	.....	.....	.....	.....	.....	.....	.....
19	Shepaug,	16,104.85	585.18	.....	418.42	356.25	.....	1,561.21
20	Shore Line, ...,	.....	.....	.....	.....	.....	.....	.....
21	South ...	4,970.85	302.08	.....	.....	.....	.....	245.48
22	... & Waterbury,	.....	.....	.....	.....	.....	.....	.....
	Total,	$3,201,233.02	$123,531.35	$46,087.44	$54,583.06	$28,069.32	$824,567.81	$1,311,357.37

TABLE XII.

Number.	RAILROADS.	77 Total operating expenses.	78 Total per last report.	79 Per mile of road operated.	80 Paid for taxes.	81 Paid for interest.	82 Paid for dividends.	83 Dividends paid per last report.
1	Boston & New York Air Line,	$113,262.86	$136,416.53	$2,118.50	$19,694.10	$25,000.00	$90,000.00	......
2	Colchester,................	......	......	......	......	......	......	......
3	Connecticut Central,.......	......	......	......	......	......	......	......
4	...y & Norwalk..........	28, 02.67	06,892.09	3,506.92	9,836.69	33,632.50	32,491.17	$29,991.36
5	... & Con.	95,083.83	63,948.58	4,222.59	260.68	161.54	......	......
6	...d & Conn. Western,.....	36, 40.20	36,577.76	3,057.68	9,030.30	7,321.64	......	......
7	Housatonic,...............	567,200.58	59,364.57	4,483.80	12,447.71	69,351.97	94,400.00	94,400.00
8	...,......................	43, 85.10	91,695.96	7,594.45	27,247.99	......	200,000.00	200,000.00
9	New Canaan,..............	9,268.56	7,871.73	1,116.69	......	......	15,992.66	......
10	...w ...n & Derby,.......	87, 99.38	79,927.10	6,763.79	3,989.63	28,325.91	......	......
11	...w ...en & ....n,	91, 90.19	29,859.72	4,089.37	28,926.33	288, 97.21	......	......
12	...w ...on Northern,......	59, 33.18	...64	5,193.12	23,654.07	97,310.28	90,000.00	90,000.00
13	...w York & ...w England,.	2,44 68.45	92.37	6,349.34	117,816.81	91.68	......	......
14	N.Y., ...w ... ...H...d,	3,80 63.97	91	18,694.05	264,440.54	90.00	1, 050. 0	1,550,000.00
15	N. Y., ...ce & ...ton,..	93	62 532.22	6,785.22	28,943.96	83.18	240,000.00	0
16	... ... Worcester,..	95	96	7,121.29	44,046.23	8.55	50.00	50.00
17	Ridgefield & New York,....	......	......	......	......	......	......	......
18	...e,......................	......	......	......	555.27	1,236.05	2,400.00	2,400.00
19	Shepaug,..................	54,393.83	45,966.31	1,685.06	......	......	......	......
20	Shore Line,...............	......	203,639.43	......	13,973.10	9,118.46	50.00	78,500.00
21	South ... ...nester,.......	9,266.16	9,632.00	4,118.29	285.85	......	......	......
22	...n & Waterbury,.........	......	......	......	......	......	......	......
	Total,..............	$10,838,802.21	$8,575,287.58	*$7,054.19	$605,149.25	$1,569,357.87	$2,641,063.83	$2,575,071.36

* Average.   † Includes amount paid for insurance.   † Not paid on stock, but by trustees on account of interest due on bonds.

TABLE XIII.

PER MILE OF ROAD OPERATED. PERMANENT INVESTMENT DURING THE YEAR.

Number.	RAILROADS.	84 Maintenance of way.	85 Net earnings.	86 Construction.	87 Equipment.	88 Total.	89 Total per last report.
1	3ñ & New York Air Line,	$612.72	$3,579.93	$4,926.25	....	$4,926.25	$75,658.17
2	₲,	....	....	....	....	....	....
3	Connecticut Central,	1,013.26	1,999.75	127,250.16	$16,381.80	143,631.96	8,398.13
4	Danbury & ₲. ₶y,..	712.91	17.09	48,692.89	11,051.29	59,744.18	26,798.60
5	₶ & Conn.	1,622.06	....	736,000.00	115,904.00	851,904.00	....
6	₶,. ₶,	1, ₶3.91	1,416.02	27,307.77	258,793.47	286,101.24	100,104.46
7	Naugatuck,	1,750.36	4, ₶.52	....	....	....	....
8	New Cannaan,	298.39	₶3.62	....	....	....	....
9	₶ ₶ & Derby,..	1,613.50	6, ₶6.42	₶0	₶4.48	7,844.48	44,696.26
10	₶ ₶ & ₶on,	₶7.63	2, 10.37	₶5	₶7	₶2	₶9
11	New London Northern,	1,768.79	60.72	12,398.18	....	12,398.18	₶8.74
12	New York & ₶ ₶l.	1,029.29	2, 27.32	₶4	....	₶9	₶.64
13	N.Y., New ₶ ₶rd,	2,833.96	10, ₶3.66	....	105,361.15	1,100,704.89	2,682,
14	N.Y., ₶ce & 3₶,	1,571.79	6, ₶5.06	15,999.80	95,868.65	111,868.45	102,332.92
15	Norwich & ₶,	1,168.34	5, ₶0.84	₶1.93	....	1,181.93	....
16	₶ & ₶w ₶ork,	....	....	....	....	....	21,450.00
17	₶,	....	....	....	....	....	....
18	Shepaug,	612.81	264.50	....	....	....	....
19	Shore ₶e, ₶ster,.	....	....	....	....	....	....
20	South ₶n & ₶y.	776.61	872.13	446.71	....	446.71	345.67
21							
22							
	Total,	*$1,399.75	*$3,421.64	$2,136,293.98	$646,341.11	$2,782,635.09	$4,018,097.78

* Average.

TABLE XIV.—TRANSPORTATION.

Number.	RAILROADS.	PASSENGERS.			FREIGHT.		
		90 Whole number carried.	91 Whole no. carried per last report.	92 Number carried one mile.	93 Number of tons carried.	94 No. tons carried per last report.	95 No. tons carried one mile.
1	th & New York Air Line,	94,378	90,837	1,703,812	66,081	68,133	2,070,200
2	...,						
3	...dt Central,						
4	...y & Norwalk,	346,784	278,380	3,698,860	78,093	68,598	1,330,145
5	... & G. M,	330,984	299,077	4,883,750	63,846	81,578	1,800,142
6	... & Conn. Wn,	241,707	208,466	3,868,795	219,172	168,263	7,496,478
7	...c.	340,478	319,743	8,546,70	353,909	348, 14	17,510,670
8	Naugatuck,	415,391	404,403	8,971,196	61,571	268,965	9,363,634
9	...G,	41,369	41, 63	286,265	5,350	5,155	41,391
10	...n & Derby, Ph.,	197,749	57, 83	1,876,99	127,192	15,584	1,422,597
11	...n &	483,229	56, 76	8,726,851	498,631	540	24,800,865
12	...n W. M,	430,066	53, 85	7,207,61	458,281	400,372	20,421,443
13	...orR& New Ph,		3, 42, 60	55,853,672	1,522,374	1, 76,795	108,668,653
14	N.Y., w in & ford,	4,536,082	5 295, 93	185,261,407	1,908,323	1,665,513	117,459,231
15	N.Y., ...ole & 3d.,	6,897,385	92, 96	23,836,502	394,631	873,628	14,700,045
16	...n & Mr,	1,026,495	96, 94	7,273,405	605,553	548,763	84
17	...d & New York,	433,720					
18	Rockville,						
19	Shepaug,	16,524	15,828	320,164	29,787	23,873	635,651
20	Shore Line,		445,031			61,929	
21	South ...dr,	94,445	115,741	212,501	14,104	18,446	31,734
22	...n & g,						
	Total,	15,406,786	18,205,826	322,536,920	6,646,888	5,689,358	344,341,493

TABLE XV.—MILEAGE.

Number.	RAILROADS.	96 Passenger trains.	97 Freight trains.	98 Other trains.	99 Total.	100 Total per last report.	EMPLOYEES. 101 Employees, including officers.	EMPLOYEES. 102 Same per last report.
1	Boston & New York Air Line,	123,635	37,080	9,791	170,506	152,423	114	120
2	Colchester,							
3	Connecticut Central,							
4	Danbury & Norwalk,	74,745	33,877	15,110	123,732	110,635	132	18
5	Hartford & Conn. Val[l]ey,	111,523	63,955	52,546	228,024	221,518	190	95
6	Hartford & Conn. Western,	135,710	142,704	31,075	309,489	243,631	468	215
7	Housatonic,	222,188	292,676	24,606	539,470	544,810	525	32
8	Naugatuck,	154,650	152,340	55,756	362,746	531,116	325	311
9	New Canaan,	18,240			18,240	18,210	10	10
10	New Haven & Derby,	50,493		4,360	54,853	51,799	91	58
11	New Haven & [Northamp]ton,	372,185	231,638	27,910	683,322	484,774	539	378
12	New London Northern,	276,506	285,449	4,013	565,968	560,938	500	500
13	New York & New England,	1,297,888	926,074	564,981	2,788,893	2,272,509	3,845	[?]
14	N.Y., New Haven & Hartford,	2,017,635	1,559,388	120,208	3,697,211	2,883,626	3,014	[?]
15	N.Y., Providence & Boston,	431,731	148,951	60,671	641,353	677,276	700	579
16	Norwich & Worcester,	162,979	228,476	131,049	507,504	535,849	437	[49?]
17	[...] & New York,							
18	Rockville,	18,565	23,460	870	*52,845	152,617	60	59
19	Shepaug,							
20	Shore Line,					303,994		184
21	South [Manchester],	13,140	2,808		15,948	15,844	9	9
22	[...]n & Waterbury,							
	Total,	5,481,783	4,123,846	1,092,946	10,760,104	9,451,469	10,959	9,633

* Includes 9,980 miles run on Danbury & Norwalk road.

† Includes 9,887 miles run on Danbury & Norwalk road.

11

TABLE XVI.—ROLLING STOCK.

Number.	RAILROADS.	LOCOMOTIVES			106 Passenger cars.	107 Baggage and mail cars.	108 Merchandise and other cars.	109 Total.	110 Total per last report.	PASSENGER TRAIN CARS	
		103 Number.	104 With train brake.	105 Av. weight in tons.						111 With train brakes.	112 With patent platform, etc.
1	...n & New York Air Line,	7	3	54.	7	5	140	152	152	7	12
2	Colchester,										
3	...t Central,										
4	Danbury & Norwalk,	7	6	50.	10	3	90	108	102	13	13
5	Hartford & Conn. Valley,	9	8	32.	14	7	159	180	180	20	20
6	Hartford & ...h. Western,	13	6	52.—5	16	5	406	427	236	15	16
7	Housatonic,	24	16	48.5	26	12	885	928	570	37	37
8	Naugatuck,	13	9	50.	16	9	412	437	384	23	23
9	New Canaan,	2		26.	1		3	4	4		
10	New ...n & Derby,	4		51.	4	3	64	71	65	4	4
11	New Haven & Northampton,	25	16	53.	22	15	539	576	570	37	37
12	New London Northern,	23	13	45.	15	10	360	385	353	24	24
13	New York & New England,	101	50	62.	136	39	3,426	3,601	2,546	175	175
14	N.Y., New Haven & ...ll,	91	64	54.5	228	82	2,153	2,463	2,416	309	309
15	N. Y., Providence & Boston,	27	23	54.	35	13	346	394	373	53	53
16	Norwich & ...r,	17		40.	10	9	742	761	760	19	19
17	...d & New Y ...k,					1					
18	...le,	3			2	2	23	28	27	3	2
19	...u...,				3			3			
20	Shore ...ie,			50.							
21	S ...h ...ster,	1	1	28.	3			3	3	3	3
22	...n & Waterbury,										
	Total,	367	215	*46.2	548	215	9,748	10,511	8,741	716	747

* Average.

TABLE XVII.
CROSSINGS IN CONNECTICUT. BRIDGES IN CONNECTICUT.

Number.	RAILROADS.	113 Railroad at grade.	HIGHWAY. 114 Over the track.	115 Under the track.	116 At grade.	117 At grade with gates.	118 At grade with flagm'n.	WOOD. 119 Aggregate length in feet.	120 Spans over 25 feet each.	IRON. 121 Aggregate length in feet.	122 Spans over 25 feet each.	123 Stone arches. Aggregate length in feet.
1	Boston & New York Air Line,	1	12	6	51			8,355	5	5,230	18	
2	...				2							50.
3	Connecticut Central,	1			33			270	2			
4	Danbury & Norwalk,	1	2	2	66	2	2	1,270	21	167	1	
5	Hartford & G. Valley,	2	1	7	58		4	16,813	12	409	8	
6	Hartford & Conn. Western,	4	6	6	74	1	1	6,112	26	94	2	250.
7	...	4	1	3	118	1	2	975	4	163	1	105.
8	Naugatuck,	3	1	1	45		1	3,899	18			
9	New ...,	1	8	1	10			107	1			
10	New Haven & Derby,	1	17	8	19	2		5,560	7			
11	New Haven & ...,	3	3	9	86	2	2	663	5			
12	New ... Northern,	1	3	2	71		3	6,176	21	609	6	30.
13	New York & New England,	9	29	39	224	8	10	13,046	66	905	18	440.5
14	N. Y., New Haven & Hartford,	5	44	23	267	32	5	17,624	54	4,378	41	1,655.
15	N. Y., Providence & Bost. ...,		2	1	17	1	3	1,435	11			
16	Norwich & Worcester,	2	4	2	34		2	2,873	13	493	2	400.
17	... & New York,											
18	...,		2	1	6			66	1			
19	...,	2	1		37			2,244	8			59.
20	Shore Line,	2	6	6	67	1		12,402	35	280	1	
21	South ...,				5							
22	... & Waterbury,		1	3	8		2	1,531	5	125		
	Total,	41	140	121	1,226	49	35	98,518	280	12,573	97	2,989.5

TABLE XVIII.

Number	RAILROADS.	STATIONS. 124 On entire road.	125 In Conn.	126 On all roads operated by each company.	127 In Conn.	128 Av. number miles for each station in Conn.	STEEL RAILS. 129 Number of miles.	130 Number per last report.	131 New ties laid in Conn. past year.	OPERATED BY EACH CO. 132 Total miles.	133 In Conn.
1	Boston & New York Air Line,	15	15	16	16	3.33	41.	41.	17,500	53.59	53.59
2	Colchester,	2	2			1.80					
3	Connecticut,	10	10			2.72					
4	Danbury & Norwalk,	14	14	14	14	2.10	41.80	20.42	13,833	36.50	36.50
5	& Conn. Valley,	23	23	23	22	2.47	37.39	31.67	10,885	46.20	46.20
6	& Conn. Western,	38	27	40	27	3.53	39.28	23.28	28,951	103.50	66.70
7	&c.,	21	21	37	21	2.97	74.	74.	45,660	126.50	79.50
8	Naugatuck,	19	19	21	21	1.66	56.55	56.55	32,360	61.16	61.16
9	New	5	5	5	5	1.85			1,075	8.30	8.30
10	New Haven & Derby,	7	7	7	7	4.15	7.68	5.68	4,255	13.	B.
11	New & North,	29	16	30	16	2.43	106.	103.	31,789	144.57	66.39
12	New London Northern,	45	23	45	23	2.29	62.	33.62	33,110	121.	56.
13	New York & New,	144	75	168	86	2.63	236.99	198.54	72,399	385.09	203.71
14	N. Y., New & Hartford,	59	46	90	66	2.12	308.21	254.07	179,278	203.47	171.75
15	N. Y., & Boston,	36	8	49	8	3.06	95.75	90.	12,788	82.735	.17
16	Norwich &	25	16	25	16		18.50	8.80	2,873	66.48	47.98
17	Ridgefield & New York,										
18		4	4	12	12	1.30	.88	.38	17,928	32.28	32.28
19		12	12			2.69		49.78			
20	Shore Line,	21	21			2.88			300		
21	South Manchester,	2	2			1.13				2.35	
22	Watertown & Waterbury,	2	2	2	2	1.53	2.25	2.25	2,200		2.25
	Total,	532	367	583	362	*2.62	1,127.78	991.04	505,494	1,486.625	962.31

* Average.

TABLE XIX.—EXPENSE PER TRAIN MILE.

Number	RAILROADS.	184 Repairs of road-bed, track, and bridges.	185 Salaries, labor, etc.	186 Miscellaneous.	MAINTENANCE OF MOTIVE POWER AND CARS. 187 Repairs of locomotive.	188 Repairs of cars.	189 Fuel.	140 Oil and waste.
1	Boston & New York Air Line,	$0.187	$0.182	$0.295	$0.054	$0.061	$0.082	$0.009
2	Connecticut Central,							
3								
4	Danbury & Norwalk,	.299	.331	.405	.062	.078	.138	.008
5	Hartford & Conn. Valley,	.144	.305	.406	.031	.056	.088	.007
6	Hartford & Conn. Western,	.542	.083	.397	.029	.028	.098	.011
7	Housatonic,	.270	.278	.503	.063	.077	.111	.011
8	Naugatuck,	.295	.416	.571	.104	.118	.113	.016
9	New	.136	.163	.209	.035	.018	.068	.018
10	New Haven & Derby,	.353	.702	.519	.099	.092	.158	.017
11	New Haven & Northampton,	.198	.266	.401	.056	.081	.096	.013
12	New London Northern,	.312	.253	.352	.042	.055	.116	.012
13	New York & New England,	.142	.313	.421	.055	.062	.153	.007
14	N. Y., New Haven & Hartford,	.156	.294	.578	.039	.106	.105	.014
15	N. Y., Providence & Boston,	.203	.337	.335	.021	.050	.109	.012
16	Norwich & Worcester,	.153	.328	.452	.046	.092	.118	.006
17	Ridgefield & New York,							
18	Rockville,							
19	Shepaug,	.461	.305	.350	.102	.036	.137	.011
20	Shore Line,							
21	South Manchester,	.110	.312	.160	.015	.008	.082	.019
22	Watertown & Waterbury,							
	Average,	$0.191	$0.297	$0.472	$0.047	$0.080	$0.119	$0.011

TABLE XX.—PER TRAIN MILE.

Number.	RAILROADS.	Expenses					Earnings.			
		141 Maintenance of way.	142 Motive power and cars.	143 Miscellaneous.	144 Total.	145 Total per last report.	146 Gross.	147 Same per last report.	148 Net.	149 Same per last report.
1	Boston & New York Air Line,	$0.187	$0.207	$0.270	$0.664	$0.894	$1.789	$1.853	$1.125	$0.958
2	Colchester,									
3	Connecticut Central,									
4	Danbury & Norwalk,	.299	.286	.449	1.034	.965	1.624	1.764	.590	.798
5	Hartford & Conn. Valley,	.144	.183	.528	.855	.762	.859	.866	.003	.103
6	Hartford & nd. Western,	.542	.167	.313	1.022	1.053	.992	1.095		.041
7	Housatonic,	.270	.263	.518	1.051	1.026	1.388	1.385	.332	.358
8	Naugatuck,	.295	.353	.631	1.279	1.182	1.971	1.855	.692	.672
9	New Canaan,	.136	.139	.283	.508	.432	.828	.826	.320	.394
10	New Haven & Derby,	.383	.367	.853	1.603	1.543	3.033	2.848	1.430	1.305
11	New Haven & Northampton,	.198	.246	.421	.865	.989	1.311	1.550	.446	.560
12	New London Northern,	.312	.227	.378	.917	.786	1.087	1.089	.120	.352
13	New York & New England,	.142	.279	.456	.877	.848	1.184	1.185	.307	.336
14	N. Y., New Haven & Hartford,	.156	.264	.608	1.028	.978	1.606	1.767	.577	.788
15	N. Y., Providence & Boston,	.203	.193	.479	.875	.743	1.661	1.414	.786	.672
16	Norwich & Wor.,	.153	.263	.516	.932	.878	1.650	1.400	.718	.522
17	Ridgefield & New York,									
18	Rockville,									
19	Shepaug,	.461	.288	.367	1.029	.873	1.191	1.156	.161	.288
20	Shore Line,					.669	1.370	1.370		.700
21	South ater,	.110	.124	.346	.581	.607	.704	.825	.123	.218
22	Watertown & Waterbury,									
	Average,	$0.191	$0.450	$0.319	$0.961	$0.907	$1.427	$1.460	$0.466	$0.553

TABLE XXI.

Number.	RAILROADS.	RATES OF FREIGHT AND FARE PER MILE.				INCOME PER MILE CARRIED.			
		150 Average rate rec'd exclusive of commuters.	161 Average rate from commuters.	162 Average rate from all passengers.	158 Average rate of freight per ton.	154 From each passenger.	155 Same per last report.	156 From each ton of freight.	157 Same per last report.
1	Boston & New York Air Line, &c,	$0.0432	$0.0085	$0.0405	$0.0358	$0.0427	$0.0405	$0.0355	$0.0491
2									
3	Connecticut Central,								
4	Danbury & Norwalk,	.0350	.0099	.0256	.0750	.0253	.0237	.0740	.0826
5	Hartford & Conn. Valley,	.0223	.0093	.0214	.0433	.0210	.0212	.0433	.0345
6	Hartford & C nn Western,	.0297	.0088	.0285	.0246	.0285	.0285	.0246	.0357
7	Housatonic,	.0269		.0269	.0254	.0269	.0276	.0255	.0296
8	Naugatuck,	.0368	.0185	.0283	.0465	.0283	.0283	.0465	.0425
9	New Canaan,	.0463	.0221	.0410	.1447	.0337	.0848	.1081	.1041
10	New Haven & Derby,	.0303	.0072	.0371	.0630	.0374	.0395	.0630	.0538
11	New Haven & Northampton,	.0230		.0230	.0263	.0229	.0281	.0263	.0292
12	New London Northern,	.0300	.0072	.0290	.0160	.0294	.0310	.0169	.0178
13	New York & New England,	.0229	.0085	.0209	.0177	.0209	.0225	.0177	.0230
14	N. Y., New Haven & Hartford,	.0231	.0058	.0191	.0198	.0183	.0179	.0176	.0180
15	N. Y., Providence & Boston,	.0250	.0075	.0235	.0290	.0236	.0228	.0293	.0263
16	Norwich & Worcester,	.0300	.0090	.0280	.0270	.0280	.0280	.0271	.0271
17	Ridgefield & New York,								
18	Rockville,								
19	Shepaug,	.0403		.0403	.0650	.0403	.0403	.0649	.0718
20	Shore Line,						.0255		.0359
21	South Manchester,	.0451	.0171	.0311	.1432	.0311	.0290	.1440	.1253
22	Watertown & Waterbury,								
	Average,	$0.0319	$0.0087	$0.0290	$0.0501	$0.0208	$0.0215	$0.0214	$0.0235

TABLE XXII.—GENERAL PERCENTAGE.

Number.	RAILROADS.	158 Gross earnings to capital and debt.	159 Net earnings to capital and debt.	160 Net earnings to construction and equipment.	161 Net earnings to gross earnings.	162 Passenger receipts to gross earnings.	163 Freight receipts to gross earnings.	164 Operating expenses to gross earnings.
1	Boston & New York Air Line,	7.07	4.45	4.20	62.88	23.87	24.08	37.12
2	Colchester,							
3	Conn Central,							
4	Danbury & Norwalk,	16.12	5.85	5.58	36.31	46.55	49.03	63.69
5	Hartford & Conn Valley,	18.33			.40	52.43	39.78	99.60
6	Hartford & Conn. Western,	12.76	5.87	5.41	24.	35.85	59.97	76.
7	Housatonic,	22.41	12.11	11.74	35.11	30.85	59.88	64.89
8	Naugatuck,	34.51			38.65	35.39	60.76	61.35
9	New Canaan,	5.35	2.	2.24	47.50	63.81	29.63	62.5
10	New Haven & Derby,	15.69	7.40	7.03	34.03	42.23	54.29	65.97
11	New Haven & Northampton,	14.14	4.81	4.72	11.57	22.34	72.73	88.43
12	New London Northern,	18.18	2.11	2.19	25.97	36.14	58.81	74.03
13	New York & New England,	10.72	2.77	2.61	35.94	35.47	55.64	64.06
14	N.Y., New Haven & Hartford,	35.75	12.85	18.56	47.83	57.15	34.79	52.68
15	N.Y., Providence & Boston,	24.78	11.72	13.65	48.49	52.73	40.61	56.51
16	Norwich & Worcester,	26.89	11.71	10.55		24.32	70.01	
17	Ridgefield & New York,							
18	Rock ille,							
19	Shepaug,	7.37	1.	3.17	18.56	20.52	64.53	86.44
20	Shore Line,							
21	South Manchester,	17.58	3.07	2.37	17.47	58.86	40.69	82.53
22	Watertown & Waterbury,							
	Average,	18.34	5.99	5.95	33.66	43.68	48.04	67.34

TABLE XXIII.—ACCIDENTS IN CONNECTICUT RESULTING IN DEATH OR INJURY TO PERSONS.

No.	RAILROADS.	GENERAL STATEMENT								HIGHWAY CROSSINGS		EMPLOYES					PASSENGERS		TRESPASSERS	
		163 Passengers	164 Employes	165 Trespassers	166 Adults	167 Children	168 Total	169 Fatal	170 Not fatal	171 Fatal	172 Not fatal	173 Falling from car	174 Coupling or uncoupling cars	175 Other causes	176 Fatal	177 Not fatal	178 Fatal	179 Not fatal	180 Fatal	181 Not fatal
1	Boston & New York Air Line,			1	1		1	1											1	
2	Colchester,																			
3	Connecticut Central,																			
4	Danbury & Norwalk,		2		2		2	1	1				1	1	1	1				
5	Hartford & Conn. Valley,		1	2	2	1	3	1	2			1				1			1	1
6	Hartford & Conn. Western,		4	5	8	1	9	4	5	2		1	3			4			4	1
7	Housatonic,		10	4	13	1	14	6	8			5	4	1	2	8			4	
8	Naugatuck,																			
9	New Canaan,																			
10	New Haven & Derby,		2	1	3		3	1	2	1	1	2			1	1				1
11	New Haven & Northampton,		2	4	6		6	5	1			2			1	1			4	
12	New London Northern,		2	3	3	2	5	2	3			1		1	1	1			1	2
13	New York & New England,	3	40	23	66		66	19	47	4	1	14	12	14	9	31	1	2	9	14
14	N.Y., New Haven & Hartford,	7	55	43	98	7	105	36	69	2	7	16	16	23	12	43	1	6	23	20
15	N.Y., Providence & Boston,																			
16	Norwich & Wor.,		5	2	7		7	3	4	1		1	3	1	2	3			1	1
17	Ridgefield & New York,																			
18	Rockville,																			
19	Shepaug,																			
20	Shore Line,																			
21	South Manchester,																			
22	Watertown & Waterbury,																			
	Total,	10	123	88	209	12	221	79	142	10	9	43	39	41	29	94	3	8	48	40

TABLE XXIV.
ACCIDENTS IN CONNECTICUT FOR THE YEAR ENDING SEPTEMBER 30, 1882, RESULTING IN DEATH OR INJURY TO PERSONS.

No.	RAILROADS.	Oct.	Nov.	Dec.	Jan.	Feb.	Mar.	April.	May.	June.	July.	August.	Sept.	Total.
1	Boston & New York Air Line,							1						1
2														
3	Connecticut Central,													
4	Danbury & Norwalk,													
5	Hartford & Connecticut Valley,	1									1			2
6	Hartford & Connecticut Western,					1	1							2
7	Housatonic,		1	1	1			1	2	1	1	1		9
8	Naugatuck,		1	2	1	1		1	1		4	1	2	14
9	New Canaan,						1							1
10	New Haven & Derby,		1							1		1		3
11	New Haven & Northampton,	1	1					1	1		1		1	6
12	New London Northern,	1	1				1	1			1			5
13	New York & New England,	2	4	10	2	4	4	5	1	6	10	4	14	66
14	N. Y., New Haven & Hartford,	15	9	9	7	9	8	7	8	8	8	7	10	105
15	New York, Providence & Boston,													
16	Norwich & Worcester,	1				3		1	1		1			7
17	Ridgefield & New York,													
18	Rockville,													
19	Shepaug,													
20	Shore Line,													
21	South Manchester,													
22	Watertown & Waterbury.													
	Total,	21	18	22	11	18	15	18	14	16	27	14	27	221

COMPARATIVE STATEMENT FOR FIVE YEARS.

Number.	RAILROADS.	CAPITAL STOCK ISSUED.				
		1878.	1879.	1880.	1881.	1882.
1	Boston & New York Air Line,	$2,918,200.00	$...00.00	$3, ...00.00	$3,571,300.00	$3, ...00.00
2	Colchester,	25,000.00	25,000.00	25,000.00	25,000.00	25,000.00
3	Connecticut Central,	437,600.00	448,500.00	448,500.00	448,500.00	448,500.00
4	Hartford & Conn. Valley,	1,069,000.00	1, ...000.00	....	652,000.00	...00.00
5	Hartford & Conn. Western,	1,890,100.00	1,890,100.00	1,890,100.00	579,000.00	...00.00
6	Danbury & Norwalk,	600,000.00	...000.00	...00.00	600,000.00	...00.00
7	Hartford, Prov. & Fishkill,	2,087,939.98	....	....	....	....
8	Housatonic,	2,000,000.00	2,000,000.00	2,000,000.00	2,000,000.00	2,000,000.00
9	Naugatuck,	2,000,000.00	2,000,000.00	2,000,000.00	2,000,000.00	2,000,000.00
10	New ......,	164,050.00	164,050.00	164,050.00	164,050.00	164,050.00
11	New Haven & Derby,	445,600.00	447,100.00	447,100.00	447,100.00	447,100.00
12	New Haven & Northampton,	2,460,000.00	2,460,000.00	2,460,000.00	2,460,000.00	...00.00
13	New London Northern,	1,500,000.00	1,500,000.00	1,500,000.00	1,500,000.00	1,500,000.00
14	N.Y., Housatonic & Northern,	261,200.00	261,200.00	261,200.00	261,200.00	....
15	New York & New England,	5,817,000.00	6,186,000.00	7,146,000.00	8,743,000.00	5...2,000.00
16	N.Y., New Haven & Hartford,	15,500,000.00	15,500,000.00	15,500,000.00	15,500,000.00	5...000.00
17	N.Y., Providence & Boston,	300,000.00	300,000.00	300,000.00	3, ...000.00	3,000,000.00
18	N... & Worcester,	2,604,400.00	2,604,400.00	2,604,400.00	2,604,400.00	4...00.00
19	Ridgefield & New York,	207,100.00	207,...00	207,100.00	228,550.00	228,550.00
20	Rockville,	97,750.00	97,750.00	108,750.00	108,750.00	108,750.00
21	...,	297,000.00	297,000.00	297,000.00	297,300.00	299,700.00
22	Shore Line,	1,000,000.00	1,000,000.00	1,000,000.00	1, ...00.00	1,000,000.00
23	South Manchester,	40,000.00	40,000.00	40,000.00	4000.00	40,000.00
24	Watertown & Waterbury,	118,200.00	118,200.00	118,200.00	...00.00	118,200.00
	Total,	$46,490,139.98	$45,125,400.00	$45,388,700.00	$46,848,850.00	$55,716,850.00

† No report received since September 30, 1878.

COMPARATIVE STATEMENT FOR FIVE YEARS.

Number.	RAILROADS.	1878.	1879.	1880.	1881.	1882.
				FUNDED DEBT.		
1	oston B & New Ofk Air Line,	$500,000.00	$500,000.00	$00, 00.00	$500,000.00	$00, 00.00
2	Colchester	25, 00.00	25,000.00	25, 00.00	25,000.00	25, 00.00
3	...nt Central	312,500.00	325,000.00	325, 00.00	325,000.00	325, 00.00
4	...st Valley	2,250, 00.00	2,250,000.00	*1,000,000.00		95, 90.00
5	...ft ...Vın	2,945,500.00	2,945,500.00	3 90, 00.00		†140, 00.00
6	...ry & N ...onlk	500, 00.00	500,000.00	500, 00.00	500,000.00	500, 00.00
7	Hartford, Prov. & Fishkill	2,055,500.00				
8	...He	50, 00.00	550,000.00	850, 00.00	850,000.00	1, 400.00
9	Naugatuck					
10	New ...te	99,878.25	99,878.25	99,878.25	99, 88.25	99,875.25
11	New Hen & Derby	525, 00.00	525,000.00	525, 00.00	525, 00.00	525,000.00
12	New Hen & Northampton	2,181, 00.00	2,324,000.00	2, 89, 00.00	3,390, 00.00	3,200,000.00
13	New London N ...th	67,500.00	687,500.00	1,499,500.00	1,499,500.00	1,499,500.00
14	N.Y., t Hic & No Hirn,	249, 00.00	249, 00.00	249, 00.00	249, 00.00	
15	New York & New England,	400, 00.00	4,708,000.00	6,468, 00.00	8,968, 00.00	11,742, 0.00
16	N.Y., New Haven & Hartford					
17	N. Y., He & Boston	1,050,000.00	1,050,000.00	1, 00 000.00	1,360,000.00	1 300 0.00
18	N ...wh & Worcester	400, 00.00	400,000.00	400,000.00	400,000.00	400.00
19	Ridgefield & New He					
20	...Rie	6, 000.00	22,000.00	6, 000.00	6, 00 00	6 000.00
21	Shepaug	400, 00.00	400, 000.00	400,000.00	400 000.00	400.00
22	Shore Line	90, 00.00	200,000.00	200,000.00		200,000.00
23	South ...er					
24	Watertown & Waterbury	19,000. 0	19,000.00	19,000.00	19,000.00	19,000.00
	Total	$15,355,878.25	$17,779,878.25	$19,755,378.25	$19,316,878.25	$22,026,575.25

* Hartford & Connecticut Valley R. R. Co. † Hartford & Connecticut Valley R. R. Co. † Hartford & Connecticut Western R. R. Co.

COMPARATIVE STATEMENT FOR FIVE YEARS.

FLOATING DEBT.

Number.	RAILROADS.	1878.	1879.	1880.	1881.	1882.
1	Boston & New ... Air Line,	$40,976.15	$51,389.57	$13,647.07	$71,204.46	$13,064.48
2	Colchester,					
3	... ...al,	13,343.52	7,302.91	12,914.16	57,469.16	80,219.16
4	...ut Valley,	281,577.83	1,115,029.41	*36,419.39	299,200.60	268,284.06
5	... Wern,	37,839.04	196,107.41	59,124.36	14,593.07	101,711.98
6	Danbury & N ...rak,					147,000.00
7	Hartford, Prov. & Fishkill,	349,251.44				
8	Housatonic,		228,038.73	98,908.05	205,603.63	23,869.30
9	Naugatuck,		29,858.27		71,341.81	71,385.69
10	New ...n,		1,088.13	410.88	14,452.75	18,253.99
11	New Haven & Derby,	87,579.07	103,572.22		98,465.71	...35
12	New Haven & Northampton,	210,900.00	185,163.37	271,385.71	88,776.17	...2
13	New London Northern,	159,419.71	152,274.54		214,902.33	
14	N.Y., Housatonic & Northern,	225,374.87	225,374.37	225,374.37		
15	New York & New England,	720,977.24	459,291.76	2,791,863.60	2,838,908.70	2,571,833.22
16	N.Y., New Haven & Hartford,	3,000.00	428,978.48		4.68	1,107,680.18
17	N.Y., Providence & Boston,	200,000.00	47,622.00	235 106.35		
18	Norwich & Worcester,	31,928.61	394,588.24	...12	92,821.75	107,141.48
19	...d & New York,					
20	Rockville,	16,549.75	1,933.98		16,276.01	13,399.10
21	Shepaug,	33,950.00	24,000.00	6,000.00	126,000.00	154,000.00
22	Shore Line,					
23	South ...r,	27,000.00	46,327.25	31,071.00	26,909.90	23,871.72
24	Water town & Waterbury,				10,550.00	11,880.00
	Total,	$2,430,617.70	$3,697,920.64	$3,853,943.06	$5,137,515.40	$5,966,864.35

* Hartford & Connecticut Valley R. R. Co.

COMPARATIVE STATEMENT FOR FIVE YEARS.

Number.	RAILROADS.	TOTAL CONSTRUCTION AND EQUIPMENT.				
		1878.	1879.	1880.	1881.	1882.
1	...n & New York Air Line,...	$3,522,797.64	$4,358,317.20	$4,454,338.37	$4,529,996.54	$4,561,916.39
2	...r,...	50,000.00.	50,000.00·	50,000.00	50, 00.00	50,000.00
3	...d,...	754,195.60	770,655.25	770,655.25	70,655.25	70,655.25
4	Connecticut Valley,...				85,352.05	85,258.23
5	...t Western,...	3,090, 67.97	3,104,561.80	5,013,027.42	1,920,000.00	2,771, 0.00
6	...& Norwalk,...	5,012, 07.42	5,012,027.42	1,154,554.33	1,162,932.46	1,306,584.42
7	...nce & Fishkill,...	1,138, 60.08	1,138,680.08			
8	...c,...	5,200, 67.04				
9	Naugatuck,...	2,581, 06.38	2,605,920.76	2,663,088.41	2,763, 287	3,049,244.11
10	New ...n,...	2,162,981.77	2,187, 6.33	2,187,570.32	2,137,570.32	2 37,570.32
11	New ...n & Derby,...	257,448.93	97, 03	257,943.93	37,943.93	37, 93
12	New ...n & N ...pt,...	1,083 034.40	1,083, 8.40	1,084,724.31	1, 29, 8.57	1,115,458.29
13	New ...h Northern,...	...7.18	4,831, 73.55	5,389,757.58	6, 80, 4.77	6,462,351.09
14	N. Y., ...c & N	2,284 ...0.49	2, 95, 92.16	3,007, 91.53	3, 02, 8.27	3,104,848.45
15	New York & New ... ...d,...	...1.94	61, 81.94	61, 81.94		
16	N. Y., New ...n & ...d,...	21,419 500.06	25, 94, 02.73	29, 97, 05.69	81, 09, 20.33	32,810,074.72
17	New York, ...le & Boston,...	1 ...9.11	15, 33,002.09	15, 33,002.09	15, 33,002.09	15, 33,002.09
18	Norwich & Worcester,...	3,213, 50.06	3, 33, 07.81	3, 40, 29.04	3, 82, 41.96	3 694, 30.41
19	...d & New York,...	3,385, 36.07	3, 85, 90.31	3 456, 68.89	3, 86, 31.90	30, 70.08
20	Rockville,...	75,000.00	75,000.00	75,000.00	96, 40.00	96, 40.00
21	Shepaug,...	73, 05.65	73,105.65	73, 05.65	73, 05.65	73, 05.65
22	Shore ...e,...	88,524.28	88,523.78	88, 33.78	88, 33.78	88, 33.78
23	...chester,...	1, 69,496.10	1, 69,496.10	1,169, 66. 0	1, 69, 46.10	1, 69, 46.11
24	Watertown & Waterbury,...	67 000.00	67,000.00	67,000.00	83, 02.40	29.11
		...3	...3	134,248.23	134,248.43	134,248.43
	Total,...	$78,839,694.46	$77,959,280.71	$80,326,792.86	$81,414,084.67	$4 19?,224.80

* Hartford & Connecticut Valley R. R. Co.

COMPARATIVE STATEMENT FOR FIVE YEARS.

Number	RAILROADS	1878.	.	1880.	1881.	1882.
1	& New York Air Line,	$282,861.22	$259,497.23	$286,891.99	$282,533.67	$305,111.35
2	...er,					
3	...t ...l,			..., 74.86		
4	Connecticut Valley,	84,031.01	9? 848.36	?3	191,926.13	195,873.?1
5	...t ...e,	167,845.83	?4.15	?3	266,?.5?	307,106.79
6	Danbury & Norwalk,	227,?04.56	?4,236.30	?3	195,163.05	200,993.60
7	...e & Fishkill,	159,565.02				746,327.76
8	...c,	838,138.26	599,660.09	?0, ?.63	?4,513.10	?4,898.01
9	Naugatuck,	570,413.48	516,594.14	?2,151.54	?4, ?0.93	15,108.63
10	New Canaan,	193,4?0.05	13,372.70	14,163.56	15,042.97	166,402.84
11	New Haven & Derby,	13,004.36	?6,478.10	?2, ?6.39	147,564.44	896,270.61
12	New ... & N ...n,	102,112.56	588,280.50	?4,506.35	751, ?4.53	587,384.48
13	New Londan	548,199.73	500,491.86	?1,346.58	?1, ?3.58	
14	N. Y. ...c & Northern,	501,441.55	1, ?1, ?6.43	2,324,940.52	2 ?2,374.20	?8
15	New York & New England,	1,025,935.?4	3,997,892.96	?,360,182.85	5,095,766.05	?.64
16	N. Y., New ...n & ...,	3,924,365.89	?4 625.?9		957,717.62	?1
17	New York, ...e & Boston,	834,698.78	?1	854,072.96	736,481.97	837,770.63
18	N ... & ...r,	667,?82.12		?7,581.98		
19	...d & New ...k,					
20	...e,					
21	Shepaug,	47,646.25	54,174.76	61,304.45	60,831.71	62,931.83
22	Shore ...e, ...st ...r,	317,978.57	299,086.01	349,111.58	416,620.71	
23	...n ...i ...st ...,		*5,467.56	13,421.95	13,086.16	11,228.48
24	Watertown & ...y,					
	Total,	$10,806,494.18	$11,012,250.57	$12,390,878.51	$13,808,414.96	$15,853,656.04

TOTAL INCOME.

* For six months only.   † To June 1, 1880.   ‡ Hartford & Connecticut Valley R. R. Co.

COMPARATIVE STATEMENT FOR FIVE YEARS.

Number	RAILROADS.	TOTAL OPERATING EXPENSES.				
		1878.	1879.	1880.	1881.	1882.
1	...n & N ...w York Air Line,...	$208,007.46	$142,798.67	$127,440.80	$186,416.53	$113,262.86
2	...d,...					
3	Connecticut Central,........	69,841.37	74,325.33	†65, 2.60	...88	195,088.88
4	...tt Valley,........	45,248.19	150,697.74	†60,458.11	256,577.76	316,470.20
5	Connecticut Western,......	175,019.71	172,369.21	3, 26.51	106,822.09	128,002.67
6	...ly & Norwalk,......	11,443.77	128,918.80	124,327.40		
7	...ld, ...le & Fishkill,	62, 89.98	429,379.38	54,003.06	559, 8.57	567,200.58
8	...	49, 55.33	294,318.70	350,088.46	81, 65.96	43,865.10
9	N ...n ...,......	85, 00.15	11,843.04	7, 33.86	7, 81.73	9,268.56
10	New ...,......	11, 88.03	53,942.23	40.55	79, 97.10	87,929.36
11	New ...ven & Derby,....	60, 43.88	367,473.44	48, 28.85	49, 89.72	591,200.19
12	N ...y ...th,........	38, 0.13	30, 65.04	42, 35.70	43, 86.24	59,312.18
13	N ...y ...n & N	31, 6.34	11.97	1,600, 05.34	1, 98, 03.37	2,445,068.45
14	N ...y	80,347.49	2,085,212.65	2 36, 87.39	2 822, 09.01	3,803,678.97
15	N ...w York & N ...w England,...					
16	N. Y., N ...w ...ven & Hartford,...	2,013, 0.86	415,285.23	45,194.59	62, 82.72	561,375.62
17	Norwich & ...ch,......	97,189.33	392,372.29	46,191.50	41, 75.46	43,423.66
18	...d & ...w Y ...,......	397,104.87				—
19	Rockville,........					
20	Shepaug,........	37,609.14	35,570.23	41,456.16	45,966.31	54,393.83
21	Shore Line,........	216,439.14	155,915.18	194,625.13	203,639.43	9,266.16
22	South ...ter,........		*9,175.04	24,788.19	9,632.00	
23	...h & Waterbury,......					
	Total,........	$6,680,400.67	$6,719,005.67	$7,688,414.20	$8,575,287.58	$10,338,802.21

*For six months only.   †To June 1, 1880.   ‡Hartford & Connecticut Valley R. R. Co.

COMPARATIVE STATEMENT FOR FIVE YEARS.

Number	RAILROADS.	1878.	1879.	1880.	1881.	1882.
				INCOME FROM PASSENGERS.		
1	Boston & New York Air Line,	$102,517.11	?29	$158,720.01	$158,914.11	$72,848.77
2	...r,					
3	...ut Central,	29,822.11	30,053.26	† 18,144.79		
4	...ut Valley,	78,587.10	77,585.98	‡ 85,951.29	92,782.18	102,699.25
5	...ut Western,	85,732.53	82,808.58	?25	93,265.71	110,110.30
6	Danbury & Norwalk,	70,721.18	66,249.10	83,552.12	85,867.73	93,564.73
7	Hartford, Provi dence & Fishkill,	391,335.58				
8	Housatonic,	175,017.62	177,543.23	?67	217,215.96	230,282.98
9	Naugatuck,	178,711.88	178,920.56	206,521.54	226,944.96	253,884.88
10	New ...n,	7,742.93	7,650.04	9,678.35	9,974.13	9,641.72
11	New Haven & Derby,	46,501.15	48,373.02	52,223.60	58,981.56	70,277.78
12	New Haven & ...,	127,986.68	125,062.17	?5.90	158,110.61	200,259.43
13	New ...in Northern,	1640.99	162,016.99	?3.81	199,518.52	212,274.96
14	New York & New England,	932.88	788,216.95	893,516.51	1,029,585.75	1,171,623.02
15	N. Y., New Haven & Hartford,	8,222.29	2,142,252.12	2,337,506.77	2,741,021.97	3,393,513.86
16	New York, Providence & Boston,	74065.16	345,756.97	9?00.41	522,763.87	563,000.53
17	...h & Worcester,	182,419.12	178,442.64	181,486.15	186,771.35	2?6.35
18	...ild & New York,					
19	Rockville,					
20	Shepaug,	10,086.57	8,598.46	11,089.13	12,325.79	12,914.80
21	Shore Line,	235,433.37	206,526.18	241,033.99	308,827.07	
22	South ...ester,		* 3,078.38	6,564.35	7,569.23	6,609.25
23	...n & Waterbury,					
	Total,	$5,062,290.64	$4,651,279.92	$5,314,224.64	$6,110,390.50	$6,706,304.61

* For six months only.　　† To June 1, 1880.　　‡ Hartford & Connecticut Valley R. R. Co.

13

COMPARATIVE STATEMENT FOR FIVE YEARS.

Number.	RAILROADS.	INCOME FROM FREIGHT.				
		1878.	1879.	1880.	1881.	1882.
1	Boston & New York Air Line,..	$163,244.07	$555.22	$107,194.54	$105,107.05	$73,492.72
2	Colchester,....					
3	Connecticut Central,....	51,1063	60,192.45	441,557		
4	Connecticut Valley,....	80,015.20	80,583.90	197,582.01	90,664.60	77,930.13
5	Connecticut Western,....	133,238.33		140,492.28	160,742.30	184,0624
6	Danbury & Norwalk,....	81,204.98	90,350.20	94,007.13	101,548.96	93,546.39
7	Hartford, Providence & Fishkill,	383,412.39	397,681.41			
8	Housatonic,....	370,421.17	313,089.55	512,875.51	512,017.44	44,956.13
9	Naugatuck,....	291,684.94	313,089.55	360,820.90	363,509.66	485,409.41
10	New Canaan,....	4,286.61	4,355.18	3,431	4,150.94	4,477.16
11	New Haven & Derby,....	50,724.02	53,659.66	66,124.30	83,467.95	90,349.65
12	New Haven & Northampton,....	375,226.71	412,769.76	504,261.18	47,747.40	651,863.84
13	New London Northern,....	4,865.38	294,026.29	356,784.79	345,755.48	345,467.27
14	New York & New England,....	505,809.19	1,209.27	2,693	1,420,768.30	1,837,890.35
15	N. Y., New Haven & Hartford,..	1,778.08	1,492,261.88	1,651,168.70	1,923,460.54	2,065,855.52
16	... Providence & Boston,	249,663.10	310,775.73	318,775.20	366,671.65	432,808.46
17	... & Worcester,....	461,441.55	469,014.59	506,994.68	525,623.68	586,570.80
18	Ridgefield & New York,....					
19	Rockville,....					
20	Shepaug,....	27,044.70	36,663.97	41,148.01	39,309.50	40,613.49
21	Shore ..e,....	63,166.29	62,343.91	77,212.90	77,018.32	
22	South ... ..er,....		*2,389.18	4,358.60	5,201.63	4,569.19
23	..n & Waterbury,....					
	Total,....	$4,771,109.15	$5,291,791.24	$6,184,583.84	$6,672,145.40	$7,376,878.75

*For six months only.   †To June 1, 1880.   ‡Hartford & Connecticut Valley R. R. Co.

COMPARATIVE STATEMENT FOR FIVE YEARS.

Number.	RAILROADS.	NUMBER OF PASSENGERS CARRIED.				
		1878.	1879.	1880.	1881.	1882.
1	Boston & New York Air Line, ..	989	7,196	88,776	90,887	94,378
2	...er,			† 46,559		
3	...ticut Central,	6846	68,294	‡267,945	299,077	330,984
4	...ticut Valley,	193,848	962		966	984
5	...ticut Western,	161,307	167,303	179,047		207
6	...ry & N ...nk,	223,212	089	984	278,380	346,784
7	...d... ...e & Fishkill,	1,982				
8	...ic,	224	252,740	291,620	319,243	340,478
9	Naugatuck,	274,412	261,469	352,288	683	415,391
10	New ...n,	36,553	37,322	40,447	41,683	41,369
11	New ...n & ...,	212	118,437	123,445	157,783	197,749
12	New ...n & N ...th,	093	278,620	300,940	356,776	483,229
13	New ...n N ...n ...h,	281,889	250,560	349,046	353,815	420,066
14	New York & New ...B,	1,731,685	633,987	3,121,057	3,492,560	4,536,082
15	N. Y., New ...n & Hartford,	3,525,468	3,587,899	600,507	205,793	397,385
16	New York, ...e & ...ston,	657,742	692,608	859,843	982,936	026,495
17	Norwich & W ocester,	3600	380,226	400,181	396,974	423,720
18	...d & New York,					
19	...le,					
20	S ...bg,	13,636	10,956	14,569	15,828	16,524
21	Shore li...,	299,154	290,282	360,440	445,031	
22	S uth ...ster,		*23,181	46,869	115,741	94,445
23	Watertown & W erbury,					
	Total,	9,695,782	9,588,056	11,723,633	13,205,826	15,406,786

*For six months only.   † To June 1, 1880.   ‡ Hartford & Connecticut Valley R. R. Co.

COMPARATIVE STATEMENT FOR FIVE YEARS.

TONS OF FREIGHT CARRIED.

Number.	RAILROADS.	1878.	1879.	1880.	1881.	1882.
1	Bn & New York Air Line,...	170,814	107,569	54	68,132	66,081
2	Mr.,					
3	Gut Central,	53 35	56 67			
4	Gut My,	92	62		81,578	86
5	Gt Mn,	06,944	61	286,188	68 83	29,72
6	Danbury & Norwalk,	51,813	60,550	47 15	68 88	78,093
7	Hartford, de & Fishkill,	83 14		26		
8	Hc,	90, 67	25 67	81, 89	348,614	83, 09
9	Naugatuck,	78, 03	85	28, 96	88 65	61,571
10	New Canaan.	3, 30	42	4, 80	55	5, 30
11	New Hn & Derby,	51, 31	89	92, 87	64	27, 92
12	New Hn & Northampton,	23, 47	40	80, 34	45 50	88, 81
13	New Bn M,	94 80,	84	49, 60	62	48, 81
14	New York & New England,		871,187	06, 49	1,176,795	1, 82, 84
15	N. Y., New Hn & Hartford,	898,799	1, 09 80	1,348, 87	1, 513	1, 08, 82
16	New Yk, de & Bon,	279,345	85	83, 66	373,628	84, 81
17	Wn & Mr,	408,094	46	67, 92	93	65, 58
18	Md & New Y dk,					
19	Rockville,					
20	Shepaug,	14,885	20,538	26,238	23,873	29,787
21	Shore Ln,	43,405	43,265	58,310	61,929	
22	8th Mr,		*7,866	14,210	18,446	14,104
23	Wn & Wry,					
	Total,...	3,791,795	4,371,845	5,095,963	5,839,358	6,646,888

* For six months only.   † To June 1, 1880.   ‡ Hartford & Connecticut Valley R. R. Co.

COMPARATIVE STATEMENT FOR FIVE YEARS.

Number	RAILROADS.	AMOUNT PAID IN DIVIDENDS.				
		1878.	1879.	1880.	1881.	1882.
1	Boston & New York Air Line, ...				$30,000.00	$90,000.00
2	...r, ...					
3	...cticut Central, ...					
4	...cticut Valley, ...					
5	...cticut ...n, ...					
6	...ry & Norwalk, ...e & Fishkill,		$11,997.00	$14,905.70	29,991.36	32,491.17
7	Hartford, Provi...					
8	H...tc, ...	$94,400.00	94,400.00	94,400.00	94,400.00	94,400.00
9	Naugatuck, ...	200,000.00	200,000.00	200,000.00	200,000.00	200,000.00
10	New Canaan, ...					* 5,992.66
11	New ...n & Derby, ...					
12	New ...n & N ...,		3.00	1,245.00		
13	New ...in & N ...n, ...	90,000.00	90,000.00	90,000.00	90,000.00	
14	...w York & ...w England, ...					
15	N. Y., New Haven & Hartford, ...	1,550,000.00	1,550,000.00	1,550,000.00	1,550,000.00	1,550,000.00
16	New ...rk, ...e & ...lon,	300,000.00	255,000.00	240,000.00	240,000.00	240,000.00
17	Norwich & ...,	259,780.00		259,780.00	259,780.00	
18	...d & ...w York,		7, 0.00			
19	...e, ...			15,120.00	2,400.00	2,400.00
20	Shepaug, ...					
21	Shore Line, ...			75, 0.00	0	
22	South ...ster, ...	75,000.00	75,000.00			76,000.00
23	...n & Waterbury, ...					
	Total, ...	$2,569,180.00	$2,543,720.00	$2,540,540.70	$2,575,071.36	$2,641,063.83

* Not paid on stock, but by trustees on account of interest due on bonds.

COMPARATIVE STATEMENT FOR FIVE YEARS.

Number	RAILROADS.	AMOUNT PAID FOR INTEREST.				
		1878.	1879.	1880.	1881.	1882.
1	Boston & New York Air Line,	$ 86	$6,803.64	$35,000.00	$30,000.00	$25,000.00
2						
3	...t Central,	30, 49.71	14, 8. 9	8, 07.50		
4	...t Wy.,	1,636.67	1,829.34	*1,256.29	1,207.68	161.54
5	...t Western,	10,426.58	..3	8,978.42	5,795.45	7,321.64
6	Danbury & Norwalk,	34,771.25	..8	34,066.74	34,976.25	33,632.50
7	Hartford, Providence & Fishkill,	169, 44.80			785	69,351.97
8	Housatonic,	47,559.48	47,817.45	44,430.34		
9	N...k,		9.69		5,992.66	6, 92.66
10	New ...a & Derby,	175.00	24,566.95	24, 97.86	29, 32.51	23, 85.91
11	New Haven & N...	27, 44.84	62,555.77	65, 36.07	74, 30.00	88, 87.21
12	New Haven & N... ...on,	39, 87.51	45,125.00	51, 87.08	98, 61.98	97, 30.28
13	New ... ...ch,	45, 25.00	81,930.19	29, 21.62	05, 08.62	91, 21.68
14	New ...k & New England,	81, 55.90	30,000.00	130,000.00	43, 33.33	70, 00.00
15	N. Y., New ...n & Hartford,	30, 00.00	77,253.85	79,037.47	79,304.18	78, 42.18
16	New ...ok, ...le & Boston,	80, 87.35	24,029.42	45.00	25,198.07	24, 68.55
17	Norwich & ... or,	23, 88.74				
18	...d & ...w York,					
19	Rockvil d,	1,791.73	1,490.96	1,361.08	1,354.98	1,286.05
20	Shepaug,	2,718.55	2,250.74	92.40	78.50	
21	Shore Line, ...st d,	14,065.65	..7	14,081.87	9,044.67	9,118.46
22	South ...n & ...Wy.,					
23						
	Total,	$896,232.63	$889,238.17	$1,003,749.74	$1,395,774.73	$1,569,557.37

* Hartford & Connecticut Valley R. R. Co.

COMPARATIVE STATEMENT FOR FIVE YEARS.

| | | ACCIDENTS TO PASSENGERS IN CONNECTICUT. | | | | | | | | | |
Number.	RAILROADS.	1878.		1879.		1880.		1881.		1882.	
		Fatal.	Not Fatal.	Fatal.	Not Fatal.	Fatal.	Not Fatal.	Fatal.	Not Fatal.	Fatal.	Not Fatal.
1	Boston & New York Air Line,										
2	...r,										
3	...ut Central,			1							
4	...e Valley,										
5	...ut Western,	12			1			1	1	1	
6	Danbury & Norwalk,		70							1	
7	Hartford, Providence & Fishkill,	1									
8	Housatonic,										
9	...								1		
10	New ...an,										
11	New Haven & Derby,										
12	New Haven & Northampton,										
13	New London Northern,						8				
14	New Y...k & New Engl...nd,		1			2		1	2	1	2
15	N. Y., New Haven & Hartford,		6		4	1	3	1	5	1	6
16	New Y...k, Providence & Boston,		1								
17	...h & ...r,	1									
18	...d & New York,										
19	Rockville,										
20	S...g,										
21	Shore Line,										
22	S...uth ...st...e,										
23	S...th ...n & ...y,										
	Total,	14	78	1	5	3	11	3	9	2	8

SUMMARY OF THE FOREGOING TABLES.

	1881.	1882.	INCREASE.	DECREASE.
Capital stock issued,...............	$46,348,350.00	$55,716,850.00	$9,368,500.00	....
Capital stock held in Connecticut,..	15,212,700.00	16,458,650.00	1,245,950.00	....
Funded debt,.....................	19,316,378.25	22,026,575.25	2,710,197.00	....
Floating debt,...................	5,349,515.40	5,966,864.35	617,348.95	....
Total stock and debt,.......:.....	71,014,243.65	83,710,289.60	12,696,045.95	....
Construction and equipment,......	81,414,084.67	84,195,224.80	2,781,140.13	....
Expended for permanent invest- ment,....	4,018,097.78	2,782,635.09	....	$1,235,462.69
Gross earnings,..................	13,803,414.96	15,353,656.04	1,550,241.08	....
Operating expenses,..............	8,575,287.58	10,338,802.21	1,763,514.63	....
Net earnings, ...	5,228,127.38	5,014,853.83	....	213,373.55
Income from passengers,.........	6,110,390.50	6,706,304.61	595,914.11	....
Income from freight,..............	6,672,145.40	7,376,878.75	704,733.35	....
Paid for insurance,..,...........	36,722.66	28,069.32	....	8,653.84
Paid for taxes,..	479,818.02	605,149.25	125,331.23	....
Paid for interest,.................	1,386,730.06	1,569,357.37	182,627.31	....
Paid in dividends,.................	2,575,071.36	2,641,063.88	65,992.47	....
Paid for fuel,...!...............	1,204,017.79	1,349,933.55	145,915.76	....
Maintenance of way,..............	1,610,084.61	2,060,509.59	450,424.98	....
Maintenance of motive power and cars, ...:...................	2,449,186.41	1,854,859.52	....	595.326.89

	Miles.	Miles.	INCREASE.	DECREASE.
Total length of main line and branches, ...	1,312.195	1,377.915	65.72	....
Total of same in Connecticut,.....	958.940	962.450	3.51	....
Total length of sidings,..	279.830	309.410	29.58	....
Total of same in Connecticut,......	200.600	215.050	14.45	....
Total length of double track,......	193.700	204.080	10.88	....
Total of same in Connecticut,.	110.280	121.480	11.20	....
Track laid with steel rails,........	991.040	1,127.780	136.74	....
Run by passenger trains,..........	4,929,498	5,481,783	552,285	....
Run by freight trains,.............	3,625,579	4,123,846	498,267	....
Run by other trains,.............	876,635	1,092,946	216,311	....
Total run by all trains,............	9,451,469	10,760,104	1,308,635	....
Total passenger mileage,..........	283,176,195	322,526,920	39,350,725	....
Total freight mileage,.............	282,974,571	344,341,493	61,366,922	....

				DECREASE.
Number of passengers carried,.....	13,205,826	15,406,786	2,200,960	....
Number of tons of freight carried,..	5,839,358	6,646,888	807,480	....
Highway grade crossings in Conn.,.	1,196	1,226	30	....
Number of men employed,.........	9,633	10,959	1,326	....
Number of engines,.......	339	367	28	....
Number of cars, ...	8,741	10,511	1,770	1
Accidents to passengers—fatal,.....	3	2	....	1
Accidents to passengers—not fatal,.	9	8	....	1
Accidents to employees—fatal,.....	30	29	....	64
Accidents to employees—not fatal,.	50	94	20	2
Accidents to trespassers—fatal, ...	28	48	....	....
Accidents to trespassers—not fatal,.	42	40	....	....
Accidents at highway crossings— fatal,..................:....	5	10	5	....
Accidents at highway crossings— not fatal,.....................	5	9	4	....

Names of Railroad Commissioners, Commencement of Term, and Residence.

Name	Residence	Year	Notes
Zaccheus W. Bissell,	Sharon,	1853	
Moses B. Harvey,*	Stafford,	1853	
John Stewart,*	Chatham,	1853	resigned.
James N. Palmer,	New Haven,	1854	to fill vacancy.
John Gould,*	Fairfield,	1854	
John S. Jewett,			
Henry Hammond,	Killingly,	1856	
Patten Fitch,	Bolton,	1857	
John Gould,*	Fairfield,	1858	
George D. Wadhams,*	Torrington,	1859	
Henry Hammond,	Killingly,	1860	
Joseph W. Dudley,*	Madison,	1861	
John J. Jacques,	Waterbury,	1862	to fill vacancy.
Abel Scranton,*	Madison,	1862	
Samuel Fitch,	Stafford,	1863	
Abel Scranton,*	Madison,	1864	
William A. Cummings,*	Darien,	1865	
Samuel Fitch,	Stafford,	1866	
Albert Austin,	Suffield,	1867	
James Pike,	Sterling,	1868	
Charles H. Denison,	Stonington,	1869	resigned.
Simeon Gallup,	Groton,	1870	to fill vacancy
John I. Hutchinson,	Essex,	1870	
James Pike,	Sterling,	1871	resigned.
Simeon Gallup,	Groton,	1872	to fill vacancy.
Andrew Northrop,	Brookfield,	1872	
Charles W. Scott,*	Sprague,	1873	to fill vacancy.
George W. Arnold,*	Haddam,	1873	
George M. Woodruff,	Litchfield,	1874	
Minott A. Osborn,*	New Haven,	1875	
George W. Arnold,*	Haddam,	1876	
George M. Woodruff,	Litchfield,	1877	
John W. Bacon,	Danbury,	1877	to fill vacancy.
John W. Bacon,	Danbury,	1878	
Francis A. Walker,	New Haven,	1879	resigned, Nov.
W. H. Hayward,	Colchester,	1880	to fill vacancy.
George M. Woodruff,	Litchfield,	1880	
John W. Bacon,	Danbury,	1881	
W. H. Hayward,	Colchester,	1882	

Clerk,   -   -   GEORGE T. UTLEY,

HARTFORD, CONN.

OFFICE, Nos. 41 and 43 State Capitol, Hartford.

*Deceased.

14

CONTENTS OF TABLES.

---

67   Coal for stations and shops.
68   Wood "   "   "   "
69   Total cost of fuel.
70   Salaries and labor.
71   Oil and waste.
72   Injuries to persons.
73   Damages to property.
74   Insurance.
75   Rent of other roads.
76   Other operating expenses.
77   Total.
78   "   per last report.
79   "   per mile of road operated.

MISCELLANEOUS.

80   Paid for taxes.
81   "   "   interest.
82   "   "   dividends.
83   "   "   "   per last report.
84   Maintenance of way per mile of road operated.
85   Net earnings per mile of road operated.

PERMANENT INVESTMENT DURING THE YEAR.

86   For construction.
87   "   equipment.
88   Total.
89   "   per last report.

TRANSPORTATION.

90   Number of passengers carried.
91   "   "   "   "   per last report.
92   "   "   "   "   one mile.
93   Number of tons of freight carried.
94   "   "   "   "   "   "   per last report.
95   "   "   "   "   "   "   one mile.

MILEAGE.

96   By passenger trains.
97   " freight   "
98   " other   "
99   Total.
100   "   per last report.

MILES OPERATED BY EACH COMPANY.

132 Total number.
133   "   "   per last report.

EXPENSE PER TRAIN MILE.

134 Repairs of road-bed, track, and bridges.
135 Salaries, labor, etc.
136 Miscellaneous.
137 Repairs of locomotives.
138   "   ". cars.
139 Fuel.
140 Oil and waste.
141 Total maintenance of way.
142   "   "   " motive power and cars.
143   " miscellaneous.
144 Total.
145   " per last report.

EARNINGS PER TRAIN MILE.

146 Gross.
147   " per last report.
148 Net.
149   " per last report.

RATES OF FARES.

150 Average rate exclusive of commuters.
151   "   " from
152   "   "   " all passengers.
153   "   " of freight per ton.

INCOME PER MILE CARRIED.

154 From each passenger.
155   "   "   " per last report.
156   "   " ton of freight.
157   "   "   "   "   " per last report.

GENERAL PERCENTAGE.

158 Gross earnings to capital and debt.
159 Net   "   "   "   "   "
160   "   "   " cost of road and equipment.
161   "   "   " gross earnings.
162 Passenger receipts to gross earnings.
163 Freight   "   "   "   "
164 Operating expenses "   "   "

ACCIDENTS IN CONNECTICUT.

RAILROAD RETURNS.

BOSTON & NEW YORK AIR LINE RAILROAD.

Return of the Boston & New York Air Line Railroad Company for the year ending September 30, 1882.

EARNINGS AND EXPENSES.

STATEMENT OF GROSS EARNINGS.

From earnings under agreement with the N. Y., N. H. & H. R. R. Co., - - -	* $307,078.17
From rent of depots, depot grounds, etc., -	948.30
Total gross earnings, - - -	**$308,026.47**

* In the amount here given the September earnings are estimated, the correct figures for that month not having been ascertained at the time of making the return. The following statement shows the actual receipts:

From passenger transportation, - - - - - -	$71,934.47
From freight transportation, - - - - - -	73,492.72
From commutation, - - - - - - -	843 25
From express, - - - - - - -	3,600.00
From mails, - - - - - - -	7,724 83
From extra baggage, - - - - - -	71.05
From car service, - - - - - - -	2,203.94
Total earnings, - - - - - -	$159,870.26
From N. Y., N. H. & H. R. R. Co., over and above, - - -	145,241.08
	$305,111.34

RAILROAD COMMISSIONERS.

STATEMENT OF OPERATING EXPENSES.

For repairs of road-bed and track,	- -	$20,394.99
For repairs of bridges, - - -	-	11,440.83
For repairs of fences, - - -	-	1,033.86
For repairs of buildings and fixtures,	-	1,623.93
For repairs of locomotives,	- -	9,207.72
For repairs of cars, - - -	-	10,419.68
For repairs of machinery and tools,	-	268.05
For salaries and labor, not included above,	-	31,041.71

For fuel for locomotives and cars,—

2,628 tons of coal, $13,796.91		
75 cords wood, 225.00		14,021.91

For fuel for stations and shops,—coal and wood,	2,947.63
For oil and waste,	1,677.61

For damages, losses, and gratuities,—

to persons,	$80.05	
to property,	1,291.68	$1,371.73
For insurance, - - - -		320.00
For general office, etc., - - - -		7,493.21
Total operating expenses, - - -		$113,262.86
Net earnings, - - - -		$194,763.61

TOTAL RECEIPTS AND EXPENDITURES.

STATEMENT OF RECEIPTS FROM ALL SOURCES.

Cash on hand at date of last report, - -	$22,587.24
Bills and accounts receivable at date of last report,	64,441.73
From gross earnings, as stated, - - -	308,026.47
Materials on hand, as per last year's report, -	5,180.46
Total, - - - - -	$400,235.90

STATEMENT OF TOTAL EXPENDITURES.

For operating expenses, as stated, - -	$113,262.86
For taxes, - - - - -	19,694.10
For interest, - - - - -	25,000.00
For dividends (number, 3; rate per cent., 1% each),	90,000.00
Dates when paid,—Dec. 1, 1881, March 1, 1882, June 1, 1882.	
For construction account, less old rails sold, -	4,926.25
Decrease in current liabilities, viz.,—	
Current liabilities Sept. 30, 1881, $71,204.46	
" " 1882, 13,064.48	58,139.98
Transfers to profit and loss account, - -	26,526.66
Bills and accounts receivable this date, - -	37,141.08
Cash on hand to balance, - - - -	25,544.97
Total, - - - -	$400,235.90

GENERAL BALANCE-SHEET.

Assets.

Cost of property, representing the railroad formerly known as the "New Haven, Middletown & Willimantic Railroad," its road, equipment, rights and franchises acquired as an entirety by this company, - - - -	$3,928,104.06
New construction, expended by company, -	503,880.39
New equipment, - - - - -	129,931.94
Accounts receivable, - - - -	37,141.08
Cash and cash items on hand, - - -	25,544.97
Total, - - - - -	$4,624,602.44

Liabilities.

Bonds of the New Haven, Middletown & Willimantic Railroad Company outstanding and convertible into stock, - - -	$30,000.00
Capital stock, preferred, - - - -	2,970,000.00
" common, - - - -	830,800.00
" scrip, - - - -	27,720.88
First mortgage bonds, - - - -	500,000.00
Accounts payable, - - - -	13,064.48
Profit and loss, - - - - -	253,017.08
Total, - - - - -	$4,624,602.44

PRESENT OR CONTINGENT LIABILITIES NOT INCLUDED IN BALANCE

For damages, losses, and gratuities,—

to persons,	$80.05	
to property,	1,291.68	$1,371.73
For insurance,	- - - -	320.00
For general office, etc.,	- - - -	7,493.21
Total operating expenses,	- - -	$113,262.86
Net earnings,	- - - -	$194,763.61

TOTAL RECEIPTS AND EXPENDITURES.

STATEMENT OF RECEIPTS FROM ALL SOURCES.

Cash on hand at date of last report, - -	$22,587.24
Bills and accounts receivable at date of last report,	64,441.73
From gross earnings, as stated, - - -	308,026.47
Materials on hand, as per last year's report, -	5,180.46
Total, - - - - -	$400,235.90

STATEMENT OF TOTAL EXPENDITURES.

For operating expenses, as stated, - -	$113,262.86
For taxes, - - - - -	19,694.10
For interest, - - - - -	25,000.00
For dividends (number, 3; rate per cent., 1% each),	90,000.00

Dates when paid,—Dec. 1, 1881, March 1, 1882, June 1, 1882.

Capital stock issued should read as follows:

38,008 full shares of $100 each, - - -	$3,800,800.00
Stock issued for bonds, etc., - - - -	3,800,800.00

GENERAL BALANCE-SHEET.

Assets.

Cost of property, representing the railroad formerly known as the "New Haven, Middletown & Willimantic Railroad," its road, equipment, rights and franchises acquired as an entirety by this company,	$3,928,104.06
New construction, expended by company,	503,880.39
New equipment,	129,931.94
Accounts receivable,	37,141.08
Cash and cash items on hand,	25,544.97
Total,	$4,624,602.44

Liabilities.

Bonds of the New Haven, Middletown & Willimantic Railroad Company outstanding and convertible into stock,	$30,000.00
Capital stock, preferred,	2,970,000.00
" common,	830,800.00
" scrip,	27,720.88
First mortgage bonds,	500,000.00
Accounts payable,	13,064.48
Profit and loss,	253,017.08
Total,	$4,624,602.44

PRESENT OR CONTINGENT LIABILITIES, NOT INCLUDED IN BALANCE-SHEET.

Bonds guaranteed by this company, or a lien on its road, issued by the Colchester Railway Company,	$25,000.00

GENERAL INFORMATION.

CAPITAL STOCK.

Capital stock authorized by charter,	$4,000,000.00
Capital stock authorized by vote of company,	4,000,000.00
Capital stock issued, viz.:	
38,108 full shares of $100 each,	3,810,800.00

Stock issued for bonds of the New Haven, Middle-
town & Willimantic Railroad,   -   -   3,810,800.00
Amount of stock held in Connecticut,   -   -   903,400.00
Number of stockholders residing in Connecticut,   335
Whole number of stockholders,   -   -   -   549

BONDS OR UNFUNDED DEBT.

First mortgage, due August 1, 1905, rate of interest, 5 per cent.,   -   -   -   - $500,000.00
    Interest paid to August 1, 1882.
Guaranteed by this company,—
    First mortgage bonds of the Colchester Rail-
    way Company, 50 bonds of $500 each,   -   25,000.00
    Due July 1, 1907; rate of interest, 7 per cent.
    Interest paid to July 1, 1882.

DESCRIPTION OF ROAD.

Date when road, or different portions thereof, were
    opened for use, viz.:
        From New Haven to Middletown, Conn.,
        in August, 1870; from Middletown,
        Conn., to Willimantic, in August, 1873.
Length of main line from New Haven to Willi-
    mantic,   -   -   -   -   -   50.00m.
Length of road (main line) owned by the com-
    pany,   -   -   -   -   -   50.00m.
Length of sidings, or other tracks not included
    above,   -   -   -   -   -   5.05m.
Length of track of road, including sidings, in
    single track miles,   -   -   -   -   55.05m.
Length of track laid with steel rails (weight per
    yard, 56 lbs.)   -   -   -   -   41.00m.
Weight per yard of iron rails in main line, 56 lbs.
Number of new ties put in track during the year
    (cost, $7,007.65),   -   -   -   -   17,500
Aggregate length of wooden bridges, in feet,   -   8,355
Number of spans of 25 feet or over,   -   -   5
Aggregate length of iron bridges, in feet,   -   5,230
Number of spans of 25 feet or over,   -   -   18

Number of highway crossings over the track, -	12
Number of highway crossings under the track, -	6
Number of highway crossings at grade, - -	51

Number of railroads crossed at grade, and names
of each,
    Hartford & Connecticut Valley Railroad.

Name, termini, and length of each road operated
by this company under lease or contract:
    Colchester Railroad, from Turnerville,

Conn., to Colchester, Conn., - -	3.59m.
Length of all roads operated by this company, -	53.59m.
Number of stations on main line, - - -	15
Number of stations on leased lines, - -	1

EQUIPMENT.

Number of locomotives (not including switching engines), - - - - -	7
Average weight of same, including tender, water, and fuel, - - - - -	54 tons.
Number of passenger cars, -	7
Number of baggage and mail cars, -	5
Number of merchandise cars, -	118
Number of coal, gravel, and other cars, - -	22
Number of locomotives equipped with train brakes,	3
Number of cars equipped with train brakes, -	7
Name of brake, - - - Westinghouse Air Brake.	
Number of passenger train cars with patent platform, buffer, and coupler, - - -	12
Name of patent, - - - Miller.	

FARES, FREIGHT, ETC.

Average rate per mile received from passengers on roads operated by this company, excluding season-ticket passengers, - .. -	.0432
Average rate per mile for season-ticket passengers, reckoning one round trip per day to each ticket, - - - - -	.0085
Average rate of fare per mile from all passengers,	.0405
Total number of passengers carried, - -	94,378
Passenger mileage, or passengers carried one mile,	1,703,812
Miles run by passenger trains, - - -	123,635

Miles run by freight trains,	37,080
Miles run by all other trains,	9,791
Total miles run,	170,506
Total number of tons of freight carried,	66,081
Freight mileage, or tons carried one mile,	2,070,200
Average rate of freight per ton per mile,	.0358
Number of men employed in operating road, including officers,	114

ACCIDENT.

1882.

April 14. Extra engine with freight car struck a horse and wagon, slightly injuring the driver and damaging wagon. This happened on Ferry street crossing, in New Haven, Conn. All the usual signals were given, engine reversed and brakes called for. The driver persisted in driving over ahead of train, when he saw it coming. Train had nearly stopped when it struck the wagon.

OFFICERS.

President, H. B. HAMMOND, New York, N. Y.
Secretary, T. L. WATSON, Bridgeport, Conn.
Treasurer, D. B. HATCH, New York.
Superintendent, JOSEPH H. FRANKLIN, New Haven, Conn.
Auditor, A. DUPRAT, New York.

BOARD OF DIRECTORS.

H. B. HAMMOND, New York.
JAMES D. SMITH, New York.
D. B. HATCH, New York.
S. S. SANDS, New York.
A. DUPRAT, New York.
THEODORE ADAMS, Philadelphia.
T. L. WATSON, Bridgeport, Conn.
S. E. BALDWIN, New Haven, Conn.
H. G. LEWIS, New Haven, Conn.
J. N. CAMP, Middletown, Conn.
S. T. LOOMER, Willimantic, Conn.

Attest,   H. B. HAMMOND, *President.*
Attest,   D. B. HATCH, *Treasurer.*

STATE OF NEW YORK, ⎱ NEW YORK, Nov. 3, 1882.
  COUNTY OF NEW YORK. ⎰

Then personally appeared Henry B. Hammond, President, and Daniel B. Hatch, Treasurer, of the Boston & New York Air Line Railroad Company, and severally made solemn oath that they verily believed the foregoing return by them subscribed to be true and correct.   Before me,

CHARLES T. AUSTIN,
Notary Public,
Kings County, N. Y.

PROPER ADDRESS OF THE COMPANY.

BOSTON & NEW YORK AIR LINE R. R. CO.,
New Haven, Conn.

2A

COLCHESTER RAILWAY.

Return of the Colchester Railway Company, for the year ending September 30, 1882.

GENERAL BALANCE-SHEET.

Assets.

Construction account,	$50,000.00

Liabilities.

Capital stock,	$25,000.00
Bonds, first mortgage,	25,000.00
Total,	$50,000.00

GENERAL INFORMATION.

CAPITAL STOCK.

Capital stock authorized by charter,	$50,000.00
Capital stock authorized by vote of Company,	25,000.00
Capital stock issued, viz. :	
250 full shares of $100 each,	25,000.00
Stock issued for cash,	25,000.00
Amount of stock held in Connecticut,	25,000.00
Number of stockholders residing in Connecticut,	1
Whole number of stockholders,	1

BONDS AND FUNDED DEBT.

First mortgage, guaranteed by B. & N. Y. Air Line R. R. Co. at 7 per cent., accounted for in balance sheet,	25,000.00

Date when road, or different portions thereof, were
  opened for use, viz. :

    From Colchester to Turnerville, Aug., 1877.

Length of main line from Colchester to Turner-
  ville,   -   -   -   -   -   3.59m.

Length of road (main line) owned by the Company,   -   -   -   -   -   3.59m.

Length of sidings or other tracks not included
  above,   -   -   -   -   -   .50m.

Length of track of road, including sidings, in
  single track miles,   -   -   -   -   4.09m.

Weight per yard of iron rails in main line, 60 lbs.

Number of highway crossings at grade, -   -   2

Number of stations on main line,   -   2

OFFICERS.

President, ERASTUS S. DAY, Colchester, Conn.
Vice-President, GILES G. WICKWIRE, Colchester, Conn.
Secretary, IRA A. DINSMORE, Colchester, Conn.
Treasurer, GILES G. WICKWIRE, Colchester, Conn.

BOARD OF DIRECTORS.

GILES G. WICKWIRE, Colchester, Conn.
ERASTUS S. DAY, Colchester, Conn.
WILLIAM S. CURTIS, Willimantic, Conn.
GEORGE G. STANDISH, Willimantic, Conn.
LEANDER CHAPMAN, Colchester, Conn.

Attest,   ERASTUS S. DAY, *President.*
Attest,   GILES G. WICKWIRE, *Treasurer.*

STATE OF CONNECTICUT,)
COUNTY OF NEW LONDON, }   COLCHESTER, Nov. 16, 1882.

Then personally appeared Erastus S. Day, President, and Giles G. Wickwire, Treasurer, of the Colchester Railway Company, and severally made solemn oath that they verily believed the foregoing return by them subscribed to be true and correct.

Before me,·

JOSEPH N. ADAMS,

Notary Public.

PROPER ADDRESS OF THE COMPANY.

COLCHESTER RAILWAY COMPANY,

Colchester, Conn.

CONNECTICUT CENTRAL RAILROAD.

Return of the Connecticut Central Railroad Company for the year ending September 30, 1882.

[Road leased to New York & New England Railroad Co.]

GENERAL BALANCE-SHEET.

Assets.

Construction account,	$770,655.25
Materials on hand,	2,338.01
Accounts receivable,	473.53
Other assets in detail, profit and loss,	12,905.24
Cash on hand,	42.13
Total,	$786,414.16

Liabilities.

Capital stock,	$448,500.00
Bonds payable,	325,000.00
Accounts payable,	7,214.16
Stock on which are partial payments,	5,700.00
Total,	$786,414.16

PRESENT OR CONTINGENT LIABILITIES NOT INCLUDED IN BALANCE-SHEET.

Overdue interest on bonds issued by this Company,	$67,305.00

GENERAL INFORMATION.

CAPITAL STOCK.

Capital stock authorized by charter,	$800,000.00
Capital stock authorized by vote of Company,	800,000.00

Capital stock issued, viz. :

4,485 full shares of $100 each, -	$448,500.00
Am't credited on shares not issued, 5,700.00	
Stock issued for cash, - - - -	361,600.00
Stock issued to contractors as cash, - -	86,900.00
Amount of stock held in Connecticut, - . -	325,000.00
Number of stockholders residing in Connecticut,	130
Whole number of stockholders, - -	135

BONDS OR UNFUNDED DEBT.

First mortgage, due Oct. 1, 1895. Rate of interest, 7 per cent, - - - - -	$325,000.00
Interest paid to April 1, 1879.	

DESCRIPTION OF ROAD.

Date when road, or different portions thereof, were opened for use, viz. :	
From State Line, Mass., to East Hartford, Conn., January, 1876.	
Length of main line from Massachusetts State Line to East Hartford, - : -	20.25m.
Length of branches and names, from Melrose, Conn., to West Street, Conn., - - -	7.00m.
Length of all branches, - - - -	7.00m.
Length of road (main line and branches) owned by the Company, - - - -	27.28m.
Length of sidings, or other tracks not included above, - - - -	1.31m.
Length of track of road, including branches and sidings, in single track miles. - - -	28.56m.
Weight per yard of iron rails in main line, 56 lbs.; in branches, 56 lbs.	
Aggregate length of wooden bridges, in feet, -	270
Number of spans of 25 feet or over, - -	2
Aggregate length of stone arch bridges, in feet,	50
Number of highway crossings under the track, -	2
Number of highway crossings at grade, - -	33
Number of stations on main line, - -	8
Number of stations on branch, + - -	2

OFFICERS.

President, D. D. WARREN, Springfield, Mass.
Vice-President, FRANCIS GOWDY, Melrose, Conn.
Secretary, T. M. MALTBIE, Hartford, Conn.
Treasurer, D. D. WARREN, Springfield, Mass.

BOARD OF DIRECTORS.

D. D. WARREN, Springfield, Mass.
WILLIAM BIRNIE, Springfield, Mass.
FRANCIS GOWDY, Melrose, Conn.
JOHN M. STILES, Melrose, Conn.
J. A. THOMPSON, Melrose, Conn.
LEMUEL STOUGHTON, East Windsor Hill, Conn.
N. S. OSBORNE, East Windsor Hill, Conn.
H. P. STEDMAN, East Hartford, Conn.
EDWARD PRICKETT, Hazardville, Conn.
JAMES W. PERKINS, Boston, Mass.
SIMEON E. BALDWIN, New Haven, Conn.
E. S. HENRY, Rockville, Conn.

Attest,   D. D. WARREN, *President.*
Attest,   D. D. WARREN, *Treasurer.*

STATE OF MASSACHUSETTS, }
  COUNTY OF HAMPDEN,   }   SPRINGFIELD, Mass., Oct. 30, 1882.

Then personally appeared D. D. Warren, President, and D. D. Warren, Treasurer, of the Connecticut Central Railroad Company, and severally made solemn oath that they verily believed the foregoing return by them subscribed to be true and correct.

Before me,

THOMAS B. WARREN,
Justice of the Peace.

PROPER ADDRESS OF THE COMPANY.

CONNECTICUT CENTRAL RAILROAD COMPANY,
Springfield, Mass.

DANBURY & NORWALK RAILROAD.

Return of the Danbury & Norwalk Railroad Company, for the year ending September 30, 1882.

EARNINGS AND EXPENSES.

STATEMENT OF GROSS EARNINGS.

From passenger transportation,	$93,564.73
From freight transportation,	98,546.39
From United States mails,	2,897.57
From express,	3,600.00
From rents,	2,384.91
Total gross earnings,	$200,993.60

STATEMENT OF OPERATING EXPENSES.

For repairs of road-bed and track,		$33,026.93
For repairs of bridges,		3,957.17
For repairs of fences,		770.90
For repairs of buildings and fixtures,		8,070.34
For repairs of locomotives,		8,670.59
For repairs of cars,		9,714.31
For salaries and labor, not included above,		40,939.12
For fuel for locomotives and cars,—		
3,555 tons of coal,	$16,774.87	
50 cords wood,	300.00	17,074.87
For fuel, for stations and shops,—		
125 tons of coal,	$750.00	
25 cords wood,	137.50	887.50
For oil and waste, $995.37, included in locomotives and cars,		
For damages to property,		246.83
For insurance,		315.15

For expense account,	-	-			2,916.47
For dock expenses,					195.56
For car service,	-	-	-	-	205.74
For Brookside Park,	-	-	-	-	1,011.19

Total operating expenses,	-	-	-	$128,002.67
Net earnings,	-	-	-	$72,990.93

TOTAL RECEIPTS AND EXPENDITURES.

STATEMENT OF RECEIPTS FROM ALL SOURCES.

Cash on hand at date of last report,	-	-	$4,237.09
Bills and accounts receivable at date of last report,			4,159.70
From gross earnings as stated,	-	-	200,993.60
Bills payable,	-	-	147,000.00
Total,	-	-	$356,390.39

STATEMENT OF TOTAL EXPENDITURES.

For operating expenses, as stated,	-	$128,002.67
For taxes,	-	9,836.69
For interest,	-	33,632.50
For dividends (number, 3; rate per cent., 5),	-	32,491.17
Dates when paid: Dec. 1, 1881, 1¼; April 1, 1⅔, and Oct. 1882, 2½,		
For construction,—		
Wilson Point extension,	-	125,825.02
Brookside Park,	-	1,425.14
For equipment,—		
Engine and cars,	-	16,381.80
Increase of inventory,	-	4,103.13
Bills and accounts receivable this date,	-	4,337.91
Cash on hand to balance,	-	354.36
Total,	-	$356,390.39

3A

GENERAL BALANCE SHEET.

Assets.

Construction,	$1,113,239.00
Equipment,	193,345.42
Materials, "Inventory,"	18,530.98
Due from agents and others,	4,337.91
Cash on hand,	354.36
Total,	$1,329,807.67

Liabilities.

Stock,	$600,000.00
Bonds,	500,000.00
Bills payable,	147,000.00
Profit and loss,	82,807.67
Total,	$1,329,807.67

GENERAL INFORMATION.

CAPITAL STOCK.

Capital stock authorized by charter,	$1,000,000.00
Capital stock authorized by vote of company,	600,000.00
Capital stock issued, viz.:	
12,000 full shares of $50 each,	600,000.00
Stock issued for cash,	338,416.25
Stock issued for undivided earnings,	101,583.75
Stock issued for increased valuation of road, or equipment, or both,	160,000.00
Amount of stock held in Connecticut, 5,460 shares,	273,000.00
Number of stockholders residing in Connecticut,	115
Whole number of stockholders,	152

BONDS OR UNFUNDED DEBT.

First mortgage, due July 1, 1890, 7 per cent., Interest paid to July 1, 1882.	$200,000.00
Second mortgage, due July 1, 1892, 7 per cent., Interest paid to July 1, 1882.	200,000.00
Consolidated, due July 1, 1920, 6 per cent., Interest paid to July 1, 1882.	100,000.00

DESCRIPTION OF ROAD.

Date when road, or different portions thereof, were
opened for use, viz.:

> From Danbury to South Norwalk, Feb. 22,
> 1852; Branchville to Ridgefield, June,
> 1870; Bethel to Hawleyville, July, 1872;
> South Norwalk to Wilson Point, July 4,
> 1882.

Length of main line from Danbury to Wilson Point,	26.5m.
Length of branches and names,—	
From Branchville to Ridgefield, - -	4.0m.
From Bethel to Hawleyville, - -	6.0m.
Length of all branches, - - - -	10.0m.
Length of road (main line and branches) owned by the company, - - - -	36.5m.
Length of sidings, or other tracks not included above, - - - - -	5.3m.
Length of track of road, including branches and sidings, in single-track miles, - -	41.8m.
Length of track laid with steel rails (weight per yard, 56 lbs.), - - - -	41.8m.
Weight per yard of iron rails in branches, 56 lbs.	
Miles of track laid with steel rails during the year (No. of tons, 225; weight yer yard, 56 lbs; cost, $11,851.43), - - - -	2.5m.
Number of new ties put in track during the year (cost, $6,000), - - - -	13,333
Aggregate length of wooden bridges, in feet, -	1,270
Number of spans of 25 feet or over, - -	21
Number of highway crossings over the track, -	2
Number of highway crossings under the track, -	2
Number of highway crossings at grade, - -	66
Number of highway crossings at grade with flag-men, - - - - - -	2
Railroad crossed at grade, Housatonic, - -	1
Length of all roads operated by this company, -	36.5m.
Number of stations on main line, - - -	12
Number of stations on branches, - - -	2

EQUIPMENT.

Number of locomotives (not including switching engines),	7
Average weight of same, including tender, water, and fuel,	50 tons.
Number of passenger cars,	10
Number of baggage and mail cars,	3
Number of merchandise cars,	90
Number of locomotives equipped with train brakes,	6
Number of cars equipped with train brakes,	13
Name of brake,	Westinghouse Automatic.
Number of passenger train cars with patent platform, buffer, and coupler,	13
Name of patent,	Miller.

FARES, FREIGHT, ETC.

Average rate per mile received from passengers on roads operated by this company, excluding season-ticket passengers,	.035
Average rate per mile for season-ticket passengers, reckoning one round trip per day to each ticket,	.0099
Average rate of fare per mile from all passengers,	.0256
Total number of passengers carried,	346,784
Passenger mileage, or passengers carried one mile,	3,698,860
Miles run by passenger trains,	74,745
Miles run by freight trains,	33,877
Miles run by all other trains,	15,110
Total miles run,	123,732
Total number of tons of freight carried,	78,093
Freight mileage, or tons carried one mile,	1,330,145
Average rate of freight per ton per mile,	.075
Number of men employed in operating road, including officers,	132

ACCIDENT.

1882.

Sep. 23d. An Italian, name unknown, killed by passenger train between South Norwalk and Wilson Point, while walking on track.

OFFICERS.

President, JAMES W. HYATT, Norwalk, Conn.
Vice-President, F. ST. JOHN LOCKWOOD, Norwalk, Conn.
Secretary, HARVEY WILLIAMS, Danbury, Conn.
Treasurer,   "   "   "   "
Superintendent, LEWIS W. SANDIFORTH, So. Norwalk, Conn.
General Ticket Agent, HARVEY WILLIAMS, Danbury, Conn.
Acting General Freight Agent, AARON B. HULL, Danbury, Conn.

BOARD OF DIRECTORS.

ROSWELL P. FLOWER, New York.
JAMES W. HYATT, Norwalk, Conn.
W. C. STREET, South Norwalk, Conn.
F. ST. JOHN LOCKWOOD, Norwalk, Conn.
·CHAS. E. ST. JOHN, Norwalk, Conn.
EDWIN SHERWOOD, Southport, Conn.
ORRIN BENEDICT, Bethel, Conn.
EDGAR S. TWEEDY, Danbury, Conn.
LUCIUS P. HOYT, Danbury, Conn.
NATHAN M. GEORGE, Danbury, Conn.
HENRY K. McHARG, Ridgefield, Conn.

Attest,   JAMES W. HYATT, *President.*
Attest,   HARVEY WILLIAMS, *Treasurer.*

STATE OF CONNECTICUT, }
   COUNTY OF FAIRFIELD, }   NORWALK, Oct. 25, 1882.

Then personally appeared James W. Hyatt, President, and Harvey Williams, Treasurer of the Danbury and Norwalk Railroad Company, and severally made solemn oath that they verily believed the foregoing return by them subscribed to be true and correct.

Before me,

JNO. H. PERRY,
Notary Public.

PROPER ADDRESS OF THE COMPANY.

DANBURY AND NORWALK R. R. CO.

Danbury, Conn.

HARTFORD & CONN. VALLEY RAILROAD.

Return of the Hartford and Connecticut Valley Railroad Company, for the year ending September 30, 1882.

EARNINGS AND EXPENSES.

STATEMENT OF GROSS EARNINGS.

From passenger transportation,	$102,699.25
From freight transportation,	77,930.13
From United States mails,	2,761.04
From express,	2,955.84
From rents,	1,092.17
From miscellaneous,	8,435.18
Total gross earnings,	$195,873.61

STATEMENT OF OPERATING EXPENSES.

For repairs of road-bed and track,		$24,852.16
For repairs of bridges,		8,084.67
For repairs of fences,		2,925.21
For repairs of buildings and fixtures,		2,661.77
For repairs of locomotives,		7,131.11
For repairs of cars,		12,824.07
For repairs of machinery and tools,		999.58
For salaries and labor not included above,		69,568.88
For fuel for locomotives and cars,—		
3,971.82 tons of coal,	$19,980.79	
22 cords of wood,	105.48—	20,086.27
For fuel for stations and shops, 275.59 tons of coal,		1,444.93
For oil and waste,		1,709.82
For damages, losses, and gratuities,—		
To persons,	$137.85	
To property,	5,072.25—	5,210.10
For insurance,		533.73
For renewal ties,		5,271.79

For steel rails laid,	-	-	$31,304.56	
Less old rails taken up, $11,203.00			
Less amount charged			
construction,	5,428.50	16,631.50—	14,673.06
For legal and all other expenses,	-	-	17,106.67
Total operating expenses, -	-	-	$195,083.82
Net earnings,	- - -	-	-	$789.79

TOTAL RECEIPTS AND EXPENDITURES.

STATEMENT OF RECEIPTS FROM ALL SOURCES.

Cash on hand at date of last report, - -	$94,060.05
Bills and accounts receivable at date of last report,	19,177.21
From gross earnings as stated, - - -	195,873.61
From certificates of indebtedness issued, -	124,000.00
From increase in accounts payable, - -	5,462.30
Total, - - - - -	$438,573.17

STATEMENT OF TOTAL EXPENDITURES.

For operating expenses, as stated, - -	$195,083.82
For taxes, - - - - -	260.68
For interest, - - - - -	161.54
For construction, - - - - -	48,692.89
For equipment, - - - - -	11,051.29
For lands, - - - - -	162.00
For steamboat property, - - - -	111,463.54
For increase in materials on hand, - -	18,055.04
For loss on old accounts, - - -	232.28
Bills and accounts receivable this date, - -	15,143.39
Cash on hand to balance, - - -	38,266.70
Total, - - - - -	$438,573.17

GENERAL BALANCE-SHEET.

Assets.

Nominal value of property representing the railroad formerly known as the Connecticut Valley Railroad, its property and franchises acquired by this Company, - - - -	$800,000.00

Construction account (expended by this Company),	76,657.96
Equipment account (expended by this Company),	18,600.27
Steamboat property, - . - - -	111,463.54
Materials on hand, - - . - -	45,157.28
Bills and accounts receivable, - - -	15,143.39
Cash on hand, - - - - -	38,266.70
Total, - - - - -	$1,105,289.14

Liabilities.

Capital stock, - - - - -	$704,800.00
Bonds of Connecticut Valley Railroad Company outstanding and convertible into stock of this Company, representing 80 per cent. of the par value of said bonds, - - - -	95,200.00
Certificates issued for part payments on first mortgage bonds of this Company, - - -	243,200.00
Balance of cash, accounts, and material, turned over by Trustee of Conn. Valley Railroad, -	1,955.70
Accounts payable, - - - -	23,128.36
Profit and loss, - - - - -	37,005.08
Total, - - - - -	$1,105,289.14

PRESENT OR CONTINGENT LIABILITIES, NOT INCLUDED IN BALANCE-SHEET.

State taxes for three years, conditionally abated by legislative act, - - - - -	$14,334.54

GENERAL INFORMATION.

CAPITAL STOCK.

Capital stock authorized by charter, - -	$1,200,000.00
Capital stock authorized by vote of Company, -	800,000.00
Capital stock issued, viz.:	
7,048 full shares of $100 each, $704,800.00	
Stock issued for bonds of C. V. R. R. Co., -	704,800.00
Amount of stock held in Connecticut, - -	688,800.00
Number of stockholders residing in Connecticut,	16
Whole number of stockholders, - -	19

Date when road, or different portions thereof, were
   opened for use, viz :
From Hartford to Saybrook Point, June 30, 1871;
   To Fenwick, in 1872.
Length of main line from Hartford to Fenwick, -   46.20m.
Length of road (main line) owned by the Com-
   pany,   ·   ·   ·   ·   ·   ·   46.20m.
Length of sidings, or other tracks, not included
   above, -   ·   ·   ·   ·   ·   5.80m.
Length of track of road, including sidings, in
   single track miles,   ·   ·   ·   ·   52.00m.
Length of track laid with steel rails (weight per
   yard, 33.55 miles with 56 lbs., 3.84 miles with
   62 lbs.),   ·   ·   ·   ·   37.39m.
Weight per yard of iron rails in main line, 50 lbs.
Miles of track laid with steel rails during the year
   (No. of tons, 503.68; weight per yard, 56 lbs.;
   cost, $31,304.56),   ··   ·   ·   5.72m.
Number of new ties put in track during the year
   (cost $5,271.79),   ··   ·   ·   10,385
Aggregate length of wooden bridges, in feet,   ·   16,813
Number of spans of 25 feet or over,   ·   ·   12
Aggregate length of iron bridges, in feet,   ·   167
Number of spans of 25 feet or over,   ·   ·   1
Number of highway crossings over the track,   ·   1
Number of highway crossings under the track,   ·   7
Number of highway crossings at grade,   ·   58
Number of highway crossings at grade with gates,   2
Number of highway crossings at grade with flag-
   men,   ·   ·   ·   ·   ·   ·   4
Number of railroads crossed at grade: New York,
   New Haven & Hartford Railroad, Boston &
   New York Air Line Railroad, -   ·   ·   2
Length of all roads operated by this Company,   ·   46.20m.
Number of stations on main line,   ·   22 ·

EQUIPMENT.

Number of locomotives (not including switching
   engines),   ·   ·   ·   ·   ·   9

Average weight of same, including tender, water, and fuel, • · · · ·   32 tons.

Number of passenger cars,   · · ·   14

Number of baggage and mail cars,   · ·   7

Number of merchandise cars,   · · ·   69

Number of coal, gravel, and other cars, -   ·   90

Number of locomotives equipped with train brakes,   8

Number of cars equipped with train brakes,   ·   20

Name of brake: Smith's Vacuum.

Number of passenger train cars with patent platform, buffer, and coupler,   · · ·   20

Name of patent: 18 with Miller's, 2 with Cowell's.

FARES, FREIGHT, ETC.

Average rate per mile received from passengers on roads operated by this Company, excluding season ticket passengers,   · · ·   .0223

Average rate per mile for season ticket passengers, reckoning one round trip per day to each ticket,   .0093

Average rate of fare per mile from all passengers,   .0214

Total number of passengers carried,   · ·   330,984

Passenger mileage, or passengers carried one mile,   4,882,750

Miles run by passenger trains,   · · ·   111,523

Miles run by freight trains,   · · ·   63,955

Miles run by all other trains,   · · ·   52,546

Total miles run,   - · · · ·   228,024

Total number of tons of freight carried,   63,846

Freight mileage, or tons carried one mile,   ·   1,800,142

Average rate of freight per ton per mile,   ·   .0433

Number of men employed in operating road, including officers,   · · · ·   190

ACCIDENTS.

1881.

Oct. 15th. Robert Scanlan of Saybrook, Conn., brakeman on train No. 8, killed near Cromwell by falling between two freight cars, while train was in motion.

1882.

July 5th. Charles Hill of Hartford, slightly injured by being jammed in car-house at Hartford.

OFFICERS.

President, SAMUEL BABCOCK, Hartford, Conn.
Secretary, C. H. SMITH, JR., Hartford, Conn.
Treasurer, C. H. SMITH, JR., Hartford, Conn.
Superintendent, SAMUEL BABCOCK, Hartford, Conn.
Assistant Superintendent and General Passenger Agent,
             LEVI WOODHOUSE, Hartford, Conn.
General Ticket Agent, C. H. SMITH, JR., Hartford, Conn.
General Freight Agent, R. S. DOWD, Hartford, Conn.

BOARD OF DIRECTORS.

SAMUEL BABCOCK, Hartford, Conn.
D. C. SPENCER, Old Saybrook, Conn.
R. D. HUBBARD, Hartford, Conn.
H. C. ROBINSON, Hartford, Conn.
GEO. H. WATROUS, New Haven, Conn.
NATHANIEL WHEELER, Bridgeport, Conn.
E. H. TROWBRIDGE, New Haven, Conn.
W. D. BISHOP, Bridgeport, Conn.
CHARLES M. POND, West Hartford, Conn.

Attest,   SAMUEL BABCOCK, *President.*
Attest,   C. H. SMITH, JR., *Treasurer.*

STATE OF CONNECTICUT, ⎱
   COUNTY OF HARTFORD, ⎰   November 13, 1882.
  Then personally appeared Samuel Babcock, President, and C. H. Smith, Jr., Treasurer, of the Hartford and Connecticut Valley Railroad Company, and severally made solemn oath that they verily believed the foregoing return by them subscribed to be true and correct.

Before me,
  E. W. MOORE,
           Notary Public.

PROPER ADDRESS OF THE COMPANY.

HARTFORD AND CONNECTICUT VALLEY R. R. CO.,
                Hartford, Conn.

HARTFORD & CONN. WESTERN RAILROAD.

*Return of the Hartford & Connecticut Western Railroad Company,
for the year ending September 30, 1882.*

EARNINGS AND EXPENSES.

STATEMENT OF GROSS EARNINGS.

From passenger transportation,	$110,110.30
From freight transportation,	184,078.24
From United States mails,	5,441.24
From express,	4,643.34
From rents,	2,833.67
Total gross earnings,	$307,106.79

STATEMENT OF OPERATING EXPENSES.

For repairs of road-bed and track,	138,067.93
For repairs of bridges,	29,815.96
For repairs of fences,	2,277.42
For repairs of buildings and fixtures,	10,225.79
For repairs of locomotives,	9,150.96
For repairs of cars,	8,811.40
For repairs of machinery and tools,	748.81
For salaries and labor, not included above,	25,698.03
For fuel for locomotives and cars,— 4,803 tons of coal,	30,354.96
For fuel for stations and shops,— 248 tons of coal,	1,597.81
For oil and waste,	3,537.23
For damages to property,	437.79
For insurance,	631.55

For rents of other roads, viz.:

New York & New England,	$3,000.00	
New Haven & Northampton,	240.00	
Newburgh, Dutchess & Con- necticut, · · ·	1,300.00	
New York Central & Hudson River, · · ·	1,500.00	6,040.00
For rent, · · · · · ·		1,020.04
For car service, · · · · ·		1,719.79
For water works, · · · · ·		703.57
For printing and stationery, · · ·		1,559.06
For passenger expenses, · · · ·		12,613.68
For freight expenses, : · · ·		22,749.58
For general expenses, · · · ·		6,065.41
For legal expenses, · · · ·		1,345.06
For removing snow and ice, · · ·		1,188.79
For telegraph, · · · · ·		109.58
Total operating expenses, · · ·		$316,470.20
Net deficit, · · · ·		$9,363.41

TOTAL RECEIPTS AND EXPENDITURES.

STATEMENT OF RECEIPTS FROM ALL SOURCES.

Cash on hand at date of last report, · ·	$775.70
Bills and accounts receivable at date of last report,	33,168.75
From gross earnings, as stated, · · ·	307,106.79
From increase of capital stock, · · ·	1,586,000.00
From increase of first mortgage bonds, · ·	140,000.00
From increase of bills payable, · · ·	25,000.00
From increase of accounts payable, · ·	62,118.91
Total, · · · · ·	$2,154,170.15

STATEMENT OF TOTAL EXPENDITURES.

For operating expenses, as stated, · ·	$316,470.20
For taxes, · · · · · ·	9,030.30
For interest, · · · · · ·	7,321.64
For construction, · · · · ·	736,000.00

For equipment,	·	·	·	·	115,904.00
For real estate,	·	·	·	·	93,129.81
For increase of materials,		·	·	·	56,157.51
For decrease of convertible bonds,		·	·	786,000.00
Bills and accounts receivable this date,		·	·	29,589.95
Cash on hand to balance,	·	··	·	·	4,566.74
Total,	·	· ·	·	·	$2,154,170.15

GENERAL BALANCE-SHEET.

Assets.

Construction,	·	·	·	·	$2,502,400.00
Equipment,	·	·	·	·	269,504.00
Real estate,	·	·	·	·	93,129.81
Materials on hand,	·	·	·	·	82,390.23
Accounts receivable,	·	·	·	·	29,589.95
Cash on hand,	·	·	·	·	4,566.74
Total,	· ·	·	·	·	$2,981,580.73

Liabilities.

Capital stock,	·	·	·	·	$2,165,000.00
First mortgage bonds,	·	·	·	·	140,000.00
Bills payable,	·	·	·	·	25,000.00
Accounts payable, ·	·	·	·	·	76,711.98
Convertible bonds,	·	·	·	·	555,000.00
Profit and loss,	·	·	·	·	19,868.75
Total,	·	·	·	·	$2,981,580.73

GENERAL INFORMATION.

CAPITAL STOCK.

Capital stock authorized by charter,	·	$3,000,000.00
Capital stock authorized by vote of company,	·	3,000,000.00
Capital stock issued, viz.:		
21,650 full shares of $100 each,	·	$2,165,000.00
Stock issued for bonds, ·	·	1,365,000.00
Stock issued for the purchase of the Rhinebeck &		
Connecticut Railroad,	·	800,000.00

Amount of stock held in Connecticut, - - 1,084,200.00
Number of stockholders residing in Connecticut, 483
Whole number of stockholders, - - - 595

BONDS OR FUNDED DEBT.

First mortgage, due July 1, 1902; rate of interest,
5 per cent., - - - - - $140,000.00
First mortgage bonds of the Connecticut Western
Railroad Company, due July 1, 1900; rate of
interest, 7 per cent.; interest paid to January
1, 1876; convertible into the stock of this
company on the basis of 60 per cent., - 3,200,000.00
Deduct bonds exchanged for stock, - - 2,275,000.00
925,000.00

DESCRIPTION OF ROAD.

Date when road, or different portions thereof, were
opened for use, viz.:
From Hartford, Conn., to New York State
line, Dec. 21, 1871; track privilege from
New York State line to Boston Corners,
N. Y. (6.40 miles) rented from Pough-
keepsie, Hartford & Boston Railroad
Company; from Boston Corners, N. Y.,
to Rhinecliff, N. Y., July 1, 1882.
Length of main line from Hartford to Rhinecliff, 108.30m.
Length of road (main line and branches) owned
by the company, - - - - 101.90m.
Same in Connecticut, - - - 66.70m.
Length of sidings, or other tracks not included
above, - - - - - 18.12m.
Same in Connecticut, - - - 14.66m.
Length of track of road, including branches and
sidings, in single-track miles, - - 120.02m.
Same in Connecticut, - - - 81.36m.
Length of track laid with steel rails (weight per
yard, 60 lbs.), - - - - 39.28m.
Same in Connecticut, - - - 39.28m.
Weight per yard of iron rails in main line, 60 lbs.

Miles of track laid with steel rails during the year
(No. of tons, 1,622; weight per yard, 60 lbs.;
cost, $76,563.48), all in Connecticut, - 17m.

Number of new ties put in track during the year
(cost, $19,131.43),   -   ·   ·   ·   46,322

  Same in Connecticut,   -   ·   ·   28,951

Aggregate length of wooden bridges, in feet,   ·   6,812

  Same in Connecticut,   -   ·   ·   6,112

Number of spans of 25 feet or over,   ·   ·   50

  Same in Connecticut,   -   ·   ·   26

Aggregate length of iron bridges, in feet,   -   484

  Same in Connecticut,   -   ·   ·   409

Number of spans of 25 feet or over,   -   ·   9

  Same in Connecticut,   ·   ·   ·   8

Number of highway crossings over the track, all
in Connecticut,   ·   ·   ·   ·   6

Number of highway crossings under the track,   -   9

  Same in Connecticut,   -   ·   ·   6

Number of highway crossings at grade,   -   ·   98

  Same in Connecticut,   -   ·   74

Number of highway crossings at grade with flagmen, in Connecticut, -   ·   ·   ·

Number of railroads crossed at grade, and names
of each,   ·   ·   ·   ·   ·   4

  Naugatuck, Housatonic, New Haven &
  Northampton, twice.

Name, termini, and length of each road operated
by this company under lease or contract,—

  Newburgh, Dutchess & Connecticut, from
  New York State line to Millerton,   -   1.6m.

Length of all roads operated by this company,   -   103.5m.

  Same in Connecticut,   -   ·   ·   66.7m.

Number of stations on main line,   -   ·   38

  Same in Connecticut,   -   ·   ·   27

Number of stations on leased lines,   -   ·   2

EQUIPMENT.

Number of locomotives (not including switching
engines),   -   -   ·   ·   -   13

Average weight of same, including tender, water,
and fuel,   -   ·   ·   ·   ·   52 tons.

Number of switching engines, - ·· - 2
Number of passenger cars, - ·· - 16
Number of baggage and mail cars, ·· - 5
Number of merchandise cars, - ·· - 92
Number of coal, gravel, and other cars, - · 314
Number of locomotives equipped with train brakes, 6
Number of cars equipped with train brakes, - 15
Name of brake, - - - - - Westinghouse.
Number of passenger train cars with patent plat-
    form, buffer, and coupler, - - - 16
Name of patent, - - - - - Miller.

FARES, FREIGHT, ETC.

Average rate per mile received from passengers
    on roads operated by this company, excluding
    season-ticket passengers, - - - .0297
Average rate per mile for season-ticket passen-
    gers, reckoning one round trip per day to
    each ticket, - - - - - .0088
Average rate of fare per mile from all passengers, .0285
Total number of passengers carried, - - 241,707
Passenger mileage, or passengers carried one mile, 3,868,795
Miles run by passenger trains, - - - 135,710
Miles run by freight trains, - - - 142,704
Miles run by all other trains, - - - 31,075
Total miles run, - - - - - 309,489
Total number of tons of freight carried, - - 219,172
Freight mileage, or tons carried one mile, - 7,496,478
Average rate of freight per ton per mile, - .0246
Number of men employed in operating road,
    including officers, - - - - 468

ACCIDENTS.

1882.

March 18.   Dora Lake lost one finger in coupling cars at
Canaan.

July 17.   The construction train ran over a boy at Winsted,
Michael Barry, 11 years old.   He was playing about the track.
Injuries proved fatal.

5A

OFFICERS.

President, WILLIAM L. GILBERT, West Winsted, Conn.
Vice-President, CHARLES T. HILLYER, Hartford, Conn.
Secretary, EDWARD R. BEARDSLEY, Hartford, Conn.
Treasurer,   "   "   "   "   "
Superintendent, JOHN F. JONES, Hartford, Conn.
General Ticket Agent, WALTER PEARCE, Hartford, Conn.
General Freight Agent, JOHN F. JONES, Hartford, Conn.

BOARD OF DIRECTORS.

CHARLES T. HILLYER, Hartford, Conn.
LENT B. MERRIAM, Hartford, Conn.
HENRY S. BARBOUR, Hartford, Conn.
JOHN F. JONES, Hartford, Conn.
JOSEPH TOY, Simsbury, Conn.
WILLIAM L. GILBERT, West Winsted, Conn.
EGBERT T. BUTLER, Norfolk, Conn.
LYMAN DUNNING, East Canaan, Conn.
FREDERICK MILES, Chapinville, Conn.
ALEXANDER H. HOLLEY, Lakeville, Conn.
WILLIAM H. BARNUM, Lime Rock, Conn.
THOMAS CORNELL, Rondout, N. Y.

Attest,   WM. L. GILBERT, *President.*
Attest,   EDWARD R. BEARDSLEY, *Treasurer.*

STATE OF CONNECTICUT, ⎱
  COUNTY OF HARTFORD, ⎰   HARTFORD, Nov. 1, 1882.

Then personally appeared William L. Gilbert, President, and Edward R. Beardsley, Treasurer, of the Hartford & Connecticut Western Railroad Company, and severally made solemn oath that they verily believed the foregoing return by them subscribed to be true and correct.

Before me,   J. P. TAYLOR,
Notary Public.

PROPER ADDRESS OF THE COMPANY.

HARTFORD & CONNECTICUT WESTERN RAILROAD
COMPANY,
Hartford, Conn.

HOUSATONIC RAILROAD.

Return of the Housatonic Railroad Company, for the year ending September 30, 1882.

EARNINGS AND EXPENSES.

STATEMENT OF GROSS EARNINGS.

From passenger transportation,	$230,282.98
From freight transportation,	446,956.13
From United States mails,	12,356.57
From express,	15,000.00
From milk,	40,335.92
From wharfage,	1,396.16
Total gross earnings,	$746,327.76

STATEMENT OF OPERATING EXPENSES.

For repairs of road-bed and track,		$142,552.39
For repairs of bridges,		3,417.35
For repairs of fences,		3,691.72
For repairs of buildings and fixtures,		24,634.76
For repairs of locomotives,		34,011.75
For repairs of cars,		41,656.99
For repairs of machinery and tools,		6,485.31
For salaries and labor not included above,		150,981.80
For fuel for locomotives and cars:		
12,871 tons of coal,		59,969.69
For fuel for stations and shops:		
1,003 tons of coal,		4,846.69
For oil and waste,		6,312.26
For damages, losses, and gratuities:		
To persons,	$68.25	
To property,	1,029.78—	1,098.03

For insurance, - · · · · 2,440.50
For rents of other roads:
    Berkshire, - - - $42,000.00
    Stockbridge & Pittsfield, - 31,409.00
    West Stockbridge, - - 666.92— 74,075.92
Stationery and printing, - · · · 4,659.06
Outside agencies and advertising,- ' · · 5,696.44
Rents, - · · · · · 594.56
Profit and loss, · · · · · 75.36

     Total operating expenses, ' · · · $567,200.58

     Net earnings, - · ·· · $179,127.18

TOTAL RECEIPTS AND EXPENDITURES.

STATEMENT OF RECEIPTS FROM ALL SOURCES.

Cash on hand at date of last report, - · $133,390.54
Bills and accounts receivable at date of last report, 112,403.95
From gross earnings as stated, - · · 746,327.76
Rolling stock certificates, - ·- · 200,000.00
Bills and accounts payable, - · - 77,265.67
N. Y., Hous. & No. R. R., interest on purchase, - 1,652.09

     Total, - · · · · $1,271,040.01

STATEMENT OF TOTAL EXPENDITURES.

For operating expenses, as stated, · · $567,200.58
For taxes, - · · · ·· 12,447.71
For interest, - · · \ · · 69,351.97
For dividends (number 4, on preferred stock, rate
    2 per cent.), - · · · · 94,400.00
Dates when paid,—Oct. 15, 1881; Jan. 15, 1882;
    April 15, 1882; July 15, 1882.
For steel rails in excess of iron, - •- · 18,307.77
For rolling stock, - · - · - 258,793.47
For buildings, · - · · · 9,000.00
For miscellaneous, ' · · · · 22.58
For increase in materials on hand, - - 8,558.41
For real estate, ▪ · · · · 3,988.39

Bills and accounts receivable this date,	-	-	123,144.74
Cash on hand to balance, -	-	-	-	105,824.39
Total,	-	-	-	-	$ 1,271,040.01

GENERAL BALANCE-SHEET.

Assets.

Railroad and equipment, -	-	-	-	$2,981,592.02
The Ames property,	-	-	-	-	170,889.69
Real estate,	-	-	-	-	34,231.43
Materials on hand,	-	-	-	-	75,627.76
Accounts receivable,	-	-	-	-	122,418.61
Bills receivable, -	-	-	-	-	726.13
Cash on hand, -	-	-	-	105,824.39
N. Y., Hou. & No. R. R.,	-	-	-	65,000.00
Total,	-	-	-	-	$3,556,310.03

Liabilities.

Capital stock,—old,	-	8,200 shares,	
preferred,	- 11,800 shares,	$2 000,000.00
Bonds, -	-	-	-	-	1,050,000.00
Bills payable,	-	-	-	-	188,008.37
Accounts payable,	-	-	-	94,860.93
Profit and loss, -	-	-	-	-	223,440.73
Total	-	-	-	-	$3,556,310.03

GENERAL INFORMATION.

CAPITAL STOCK.

Capital stock authorized by charter,	-	-	$2,000,000.00
Capital stock authorized by vote of Company,	-	2,000,000.00
Capital stock issued, viz.:		
20,000 full shares of $100 each,	-	-	2,000,000.00
Stock issued for cash,	-	-	-	-	2,000,000.00
Amount of stock held in Connecticut,	-	-	745,800.00
Number of stockholders residing in Connecticut,	417
Whole number of stockholders, -	-	-	633

BONDS OR UNFUNDED DEBT.

First mortgage, due 1885; rate of interest, 7 per cent. Interest paid to August, 1882, - -	$100,000.00
Second mortgage, due 1889; rate of interest 6 per cent. Interest paid to July, 1882, - -	300,000.00
Equipment, due 1883; rate of interest, 7 per cent. Interest paid to August, 1882, - - -	150,000.00
Consolidated mortgage, due 1910; rate of interest, 5 per cent. Interest paid to October, 1882, -	300,000.00
Rolling stock, due 1889; rate of interest, 5 per cent. Interest paid to October, 1882, - -	200,000.00

DESCRIPTION OF ROAD.

Date when road, or different portions thereof, were opened for use, viz.:
From Bridgeport to New Milford, 1840.
From Bridgeport to State Line, Dec. 1, 1842.

Length of main line from Bridgeport to Mass. State Line, - - - - -	74.0m.
Length of branch from Brookfield Junction to Danbury, - - - - -	5.5m.
Length of all branches, - . - - -	5.5m.
Length of road (main line and branch) owned by the Company, - - - -	79.5m.
Length of sidings, or other tracks not included above, - - - - - -	12.5m.
Length of track of road, including branch and sidings, in single track miles, - - -	92.0m.
Length of track laid with steel rails (weight per yard, 60 lbs.) ; in branches, 60 lbs., - -	74.0m.
Miles of track laid with steel rails during the year (No. of tons, 1,220½; weight per yard, 60 lbs.; cost, $75,671.00), all in Massachusetts, - -	12.0m.
Number of new ties put in track during the year (cost, $22,830.02), - - - -	45,660
Aggregate length of wooden bridges, in feet, -	975
Number of spans of 25 feet or over, - -	4
Aggregate length of iron bridges, in feet, - -	94
Number of spans of 25 feet or over, - -	2
Aggregate length of stone arch bridges, in feet, -	250

Number of highway crossings over the track, -	1
Number of highway crossings under the track, -	3
Number of highway crossings at grade, - -	118
Number of highway crossings at grade, with gates,	1
Number of highway crossings at grade, with flagmen, - - - - -	2
Number of railroads crossed at grade: New York, New Haven & Hartford, Shepaug, Hartford & Conn. Western, New York & New England, -	4
Length of all roads operated by this Company, -	126.5m.
Number of stations on main line, - -	20
Number of stations on branches,	1
Number of stations on leased lines, -	16

EQUIPMENT.

Number of locomotives (not including switching engines), - - - - -	24
Average weight of same, including tender, water, and fuel, - - - -	$48\frac{1}{2}$tons.
Number of passenger cars, -	26
Number of baggage and mail cars, -	12
Number of merchandise cars, - -	546
Number of coal, gravel, and other cars, - -	339
Number of locomotives equipped with train brakes,	16
Number of cars equipped with train brakes, -	37
Name of brake, - - - - -	Vacuum.
Number of passenger train cars with patent platform, buffer, and coupler, - - -	37
Name of patent, - - - - -	Miller.

FARES, FREIGHT, ETC.

Average rate per mile received from passengers on roads operated by this Company, excluding season ticket passengers, - - -	.0269
Average rate of fare per mile for all passengers,	.0269
Total number of passengers carried, - -	340,478
Passenger mileage, or passengers carried one mile,	8,546,740
Miles run by passenger trains, - - -	222,188
Miles run by freight trains, -	292,676

Miles run by all other trains, - - -	24,606
Total miles run, - - - - -	539,470
Total number of tons of freight carried, -	353,909
Freight mileage, or tons carried one mile, -	17,510,670
Average rate of freight per ton per mile, -	.0254
Number of men employed in operating road, including officers, - - - -	525

ACCIDENTS.

1881.

November 29th.   James Burns, brakeman, finger smashed while coupling cars at Merwinsville.

December 13th.   John Doyle, brakeman, finger smashed while coupling cars at Lime Rock.

1882.

January 5th.   Harvey Adams, citizen of New Milford, while driving a team across the track above the depot at New Milford, was struck and killed by 2d passenger train from Pittsfield.

February 1st.   Andrew Miller, citizen, run over and killed at North Avenue crossing, Bridgeport, by an extra train from New Milford.

April 15th.   Wm. Thomas, water boy, fell between the cars while in motion, at Bridgeport; had one leg cut off.

May 8th.   Alfred Strickland attempted to board milk train while in motion, at New Milford, and fell under the wheels, cutting off one leg and arm; died from his injuries, May 10th.

May 21st.   John Doyle, brakeman, two fingers smashed while coupling cars at New Milford.

July 20th.   Alvah Gregory, struck and slightly injured by express freight, at Bridgeport depot.

July 28th.   Wells Root, run over and cut in two by through freight going south, near Canaan camp-ground station.

OFFICERS.

President, WM. H. BARNUM, Lime Rock, Conn.
Vice-President, DAVID S. DRAPER, Bridgeport, Conn.
Secretary, CHARLES K. AVERILL, Bridgeport, Conn.
Treasurer, CHARLES K. AVERILL, Bridgeport, Conn.
Auditor, FRED. W. HULL, Bridgeport, Conn.
Chief Clerk, H. W. WATSON, Bridgeport, Conn.
General Ticket Agent, H. D. AVERILL, Bridgeport, Conn.
General Freight Agent, H. C. COGSWELL, Bridgeport, Conn.

BOARD OF DIRECTORS.

WM. H. BARNUM, Lime Rock, Conn.
SAMUEL WILLETTS, New York.
EDWARD LEAVITT, New York.
JOHN B. PECK, New York.
DAVID S. DRAPER, Bridgeport, Conn.
WM. D. BISHOP, Bridgeport, Conn.
HORACE NICHOLS, Bridgeport, Conn.
CHARLES K. AVERILL, Bridgeport, Conn.
A. B. MYGATT, New Milford, Conn.

Attest,   W. H. BARNUM, *President.*
Attest,   C. K. AVERILL, *Treasurer.*

STATE OF CONNECTICUT, }
COUNTY OF FAIRFIELD, }   BRIDGEPORT, November 6, 1882.

Then personally appeared Wm. H. Barnum, President, and C. K. Averill, Treasurer, of the Housatonic Railroad Company, and severally made solemn oath that they verily believed the foregoing return by them subscribed to be true and correct.

Before me,

MORRIS W. SEYMOUR,
Com. of Superior Court, Fairfield County.

PROPER ADDRESS OF THE COMPANY.

HOUSATONIC RAILROAD COMPANY,
Bridgeport, Conn.

6A

NAUGATUCK RAILROAD.

EARNINGS AND EXPENSES.

STATEMENT OF GROSS EARNINGS.

From passenger transportation,	$253,884.88
From freight transportation,	435,409.41
From United States mails,	6,276.14
From express,	10,500.00
From rents,	1,512.50
From dividends,	514.90
From interest,	3,245.56
From wharfage, weighing, and switching,	3,554.62
Total gross earnings,	$714,898.01

STATEMENT OF OPERATING EXPENSES.

For repairs of road-bed and track,		$95,840.90
For repairs of bridges,		10,921.03
For repairs of fences,		242.15
For repairs of buildings and fixtures, including new depots, engine-houses, etc.,		49,311.40
For repairs of locomotives, including new engines,		37,835.34
For repairs of cars, including new cars,		43,038.61
For machinery and tools,		4,835.99
For salaries and labor, not included above,		151,059.11
For fuel for locomotives and cars,—		
8,203.11 tons of coal,	$4.98	
140.538 cords wood,	3.25	41,308.23
For fuel for stations and shops,—		
397.85 tons of coal,	$4.55	1,810.26
For oil and waste,		5,914.30

For damages, losses, and gratuities, —

	to persons,	$525.00	
	to property,	1,611.07	2,136.07

For insurance, - · · - -		2,679.60

For rents of other roads, toll paid N. Y., N. H. & H. R. R. Co., for passengers and freight, 25,902.30

For gas, $1,559.53; demurrage, $1,205.69; telephone rent, $226.35; dredging, $5,038.08; printing and stationery, $6,436.39; car service, $2,213.07; profit and loss, $253.00,   -   16,932.11

Total operating expenses, - · -	$463,865.10
Net earnings, -	$251,032.91

TOTAL RECEIPTS AND EXPENDITURES.

STATEMENT OF RECEIPTS FROM ALL SOURCES.

Cash on hand at date of last report, - -	$64,948.44
Bills and accounts receivable at date of last report,	105,626.18
From gross earnings, as stated, - · -	714,898.01
From increase in accounts payable, - ·	43.88
Total, - · - -	$885,516.51

STATEMENT OF TOTAL EXPENDITURES.

For operating expenses, as stated, - -	$463,865.10
For taxes, · · - · - -	27,247.99
For dividends (number 2; rate per cent., 5), -	200,000.00
Paid Jan. 4, 1882, July 1, 1882.	
For increase in materials on hand, · ·	306.41
Bills and accounts receivable this date, - -	69,552.21
Cash on hand to balance, - · -	124,544.80
Total, · · ·	$885,516.51

GENERAL BALANCE-SHEET.

Assets.

Construction, - ·	$1,903,483.75
Equipment, -	234,086.57

Railroad stock,	7,600.00
Railroad bonds,	5,000.00
Real estate,	30,000.00
Materials on hand,	39,964.13
Due from station agents,	65,131.59
Due from general post-office department,	1,606.53
Due from Adams Express Company,	875.00
Due from sundry accounts receivable,	339.09
Due on notes receivable,	1,600.00
Cash on hand,	124,544.80
Total,	$2,414,231.46

Liabilities.

Capital stock,	$2,000,000.00
Sundry accounts payable,	1,547.83
N. Y., N. H. & H. R. R. Co.,	30,049.39
N. Y. & N. E. R. R. Co.	903.12
Hartford & Conn. Western R. R. Co.,	701.75
Housatonic R. R. Co.,	329.30
New Haven & Derby R. R. Co.,	126.31
September expenses,	37,727.99
Profit and loss,	342,845.77
Total,	$2,414,231.46

GENERAL INFORMATION.

CAPITAL STOCK.

Capital stock authorized by charter,	$2,000,000.00
Capital stock authorized by vote of company,	2,000,000.00
Capital stock issued, viz.:	
20,000 full shares of $100 each,	2,000,000.00
Stock issued for cash,	397,696.00
Stock issued for bonds,	273,000.00
Stock issued for undivided earnings.	142,700.00
Stock issued for increased valuation of road, or equipment, or both,	448,825.00
Stock issued to contractor for work done and materials furnished,	675,879.00

Stock charged profit and loss for loss on stock
  sold, - . . . - . .30,200.00
Stock charged profit and loss for over-issue by
  New York transfer agent, - - - 31,700.00
Amount of stock held in Connecticut, - - 1,436,400.00
Number of stockholders residing in Connecticut, 451
Whole number of stockholders, - - - 590

DESCRIPTION OF ROAD.

Date when road, or different portions thereof, were
  opened for use, viz.:
  From junction N. Y., N. H. & H. R. R. to
    Waterbury, June 11, 1849; from Water-
    bury to Winsted, completed Sept. 24,
    1849.
Length of main line from junction N. Y., N. H. &
  H. R. R. to Winsted, all in Connecticut, - 56.55m.
Length of sidings, or other tracks not included
  above, - - - - - 11.54m.
Length of track of road, including branches and
  sidings, in single-track miles, - - 68.09m.
Length of track laid with steel rails (weight per
  yard, 56 and 58 lbs.), - - - 56.55m.
Number of new ties put in track during the year
  (cost, $16,130.00), - - - - 32,260
Aggregate length of wooden bridges, in feet, - 3,899
Number of spans of 25 feet or over, - - 18
Aggregate length of iron bridges, in feet, - 163
Number of spans of 25 feet or over, - . . 1
Aggregate length of stone arch bridges, in feet, 105
Number of highway crossings over the track, - 1
Number of highway crossings under the track, 1
Number of highway crossings at grade, - - 45
Number of highway crossings at grade with gates, 1
Number of highway crossings at grade with flag-
  men, - - . - - -
Number of railroads crossed at grade, and names
  of each, - - . - - 3
  New Haven & Derby, N. Y. & N. E.,
  Hartford & Conn. Western.

Name, termini, and length of each road operated
  by this company under lease or contract,—
    Watertown & Waterbury, - - - 4.61m.
Length of all roads operated by this company, 61.16m.
Number of stations on main line, - - - 19
Number of stations on leased lines, - - 2

EQUIPMENT.

Number of locomotives (not including switching
  engines) - - - - - 13
Average weight of same, including tender, water,
  and fuel, - - - - - 101,100 lbs.
Number of switching engines, - - - 2
Number of passenger cars, - - - 16
Number of baggage and mail cars, - - 9
Number of merchandise cars, - - - 115
Number of coal, gravel, and other cars, - - 297
Number of locomotives equipped with train brakes, 9
Number of cars equipped with train brakes, - 23
Name of brake, - - - Westinghouse Automatic.
Number of passenger train cars with patent plat-
  form, buffer, and coupler, - - - 23
Name of patent, - - - - - Miller.

FARES, FREIGHT, ETC.

Average rate per mile received from passengers
  on roads operated by this company, excluding
  season-ticket passengers, - - - .0368
Average rate per mile for season-ticket passengers,
  reckoning one round trip per day to each
  ticket, - - - - - .0185
Average rate of fare per mile from all passengers, .0283
Total number of passengers carried, - - 415,391
Passenger mileage, or passengers carried one mile, 8,971,196
Miles run by passenger trains, - - - 154,650
Miles run by freight trains, - - - 152,340
Miles run by all other trains, - - - 55,756
Total miles run, - - - - - 362,746
Total number of tons of freight carried, - - 301,571

Freight mileage, or tons carried one mile,   9,363,634
Average rate of freight per ton per mile,   -   .0465
Number of men employed in operating road,
    including officers,   -   -   -   -   325

ACCIDENTS.

STATEMENT OF EACH ACCIDENT IN DETAIL.

1881.

Oct. 4. James Long, a brakeman employed in the Naugatuck yard, was badly injured while coupling cars.

Nov. 2. Daniel Horan, switchman in Bridgeport yard, was run over, making it necessary to amputate his limb.

Dec. 8. Charles White badly mashed two fingers coupling cars.

Dec. 31. Charles Stevens, brakeman on extra, fell from train at Junction, was run over and instantly killed.

1882.

April 12. Edward Welsh, Ansonia, fell under the car, one leg being run over.

May 6. Lewis Reuger caught his arm between cars, breaking it and injuring his hand.

May 26. Harvey Canfield, struck by engine, instantly killed.

June 12. P. Fallon fell from top of cars. Spine injured and skull fractured.

July 1. Bennett Smith, switchman at Naugatuck, stepped between two flat cars, loaded with steel rails, to adjust couplings. His head was caught between projecting rails. It was found that he had a deep gash back of left ear, and another on side of his face.

July 6. John S. Wells, of Bridgeport, attempted to cross the track ahead of a detached car, at Derby Junction. He was struck by said car, one leg was nearly severed from the body; the other leg was mashed obliquely from the knee to the foot. He died as the train reached Bridgeport.

July 7. John Connors killed while on track at Ansonia. Intoxicated.

July 12. Samuel Paradise, of Waterbury, a boy about fourteen years of age, fell from the train and fractured his skull.

Aug. 21. William Skiff, while switching, attempted to jump

on the locomotive while in motion. His foot went under the wheel, crushing it.

· Sept. 25. Dennis Reardon, of Thomaston, while walking on track, was killed by freight train. Intoxicated.

OFFICERS.

President, E. F. BISHOP, Bridgeport, Conn.
Secretary, H. NICHOLS, Bridgeport, Conn.
Treasurer, H. NICHOLS, Bridgeport, Conn.
Superintendent, GEORGE W. BEACH, Waterbury, Conn.
Chief Clerk, W. M. STAPLES, Bridgeport, Conn.
General Ticket Agent, HENRY A. BISHOP, Bridgeport, Conn.
Freight Agent, B. SOULES, Bridgeport, Conn.

BOARD OF DIRECTORS.

W. D. BISHOP, Bridgeport, Conn.
R. TOMLINSON, Bridgeport, Conn.
E. F. BISHOP, Bridgeport, Conn.
J. G. WETMORE, Winsted, Conn. ·
A. L. DENNIS, Newark, N. J.
HENRY BRONSON, New Haven, Conn.
JNO. B. ROBERTSON, New Haven, Conn.
R. M. BASSETT, Birmingham, Conn.
F. J. KINGSBURY, Waterbury, Conn.

Attest,   E. F. BISHOP, *President.*
Attest,   H. NICHOLS, *Treasurer.*

STATE OF CONNECTICUT, }
  COUNTY OF FAIRFIELD. } BRIDGEPORT, CONN., Nov. 8, 1882.

Then personally appeared E. F. Bishop, President, and H. Nichols, Treasurer, of the Naugatuck Railroad Company, and severally made solemn oath that they verily believed the foregoing return by them subscribed to be true and correct.

Before me,
                W. M. STAPLES,
                    Notary Public.

PROPER ADDRESS OF THE COMPANY.

NAUGATUCK RAILROAD CO.
                Bridgeport, Conn.

NEW CANAAN RAILROAD.

*Return of the New Canaan Railroad Company for the year ending
September 30, 1882.*

GENERAL BALANCE-SHEET.

Assets.

Construction account,	$230,746.03
Equipment account,	27,197.90
Interest account, funded,	4,017.64
Profit and loss,	1,966.68
Total,	$263,928.25

Liabilities.

Capital stock paid in,	$164,050.00
Funded debt,	99,878 25
Total,	$263,928.25

PRESENT OR CONTINGENT LIABILITIES NOT INCLUDED IN BALANCE-SHEET.

Overdue interest on bonds issued by this Company, $18,252.99

GENERAL INFORMATION.

CAPITAL STOCK.

Capital stock authorized by charter,	$200,000.00
Capital stock authorized by vote of Company,	200,000.00
Capital stock issued, viz. :	
3,281 full shares of $50 each,	164,050.00
Stock issued for cash,	164,050.00
Amount of stock held in Connecticut,	137,000.00
Number of stockholders residing in Connecticut,	197
Whole number of stockholders,	207

7ᴀ

BONDS OR FUNDED DEBT.

First mortgage, due 1884; rate of interest, 7 per ct., $99,878.25
Interest paid to January, 1880.

OFFICERS.

President, S. Y. ST. JOHN, New Canaan, Conn.
Vice-President, J. B. HOYT, Stamford, Conn.
Secretary, A. F. JONES, New Canaan, Conn.
Treasurer, GEO. F. LOCKWOOD, New Canaan, Conn.

BOARD OF DIRECTORS.

WILLARD PARKER, New York City.
A. S. COMSTOCK, New York City.
J. B. HOYT, Stamford, Conn.
S. B. ST. JOHN, Hartford, Conn.
W. E. RAYMOND, New Canaan, Conn.
W. G. WEBB, New Canaan, Conn.
EDWIN HOYT, New Canaan, Conn.
S. Y. ST. JOHN, New Canaan, Conn.

Attest,   S. Y. ST. JOHN, *President.*
Attest,   G. F. LOCKWOOD, *Treasurer.*

STATE OF CONNECTICUT, }
COUNTY OF FAIRFIELD, }   November 28, 1882.

Then personally appeared S. Y. St. John, President, and Geo. F. Lockwood, Treasurer, of the New Canaan Railroad Company, and severally made solemn oath that they verily believed the foregoing return by them subscribed to be true and correct.

Before me,   RUSELL L. HALL,
Notary Public.

PROPER ADDRESS OF THE COMPANY.

NEW CANAAN RAILROAD COMPANY,
New Canaan, Conn.

TRUSTEES OF THE NEW CANAAN RAILROAD.

Return of the Trustees of the New Canaan Railroad, for the year ending September 30, 1882.

EARNINGS AND EXPENSES.

STATEMENT OF GROSS EARNINGS.

From passenger transportation,	$9,641.72
From freight transportation,	4,477.16
From United States mails,	689.75
From express,	200.00
From rents,	100.00
Total gross earnings,	$15,108.63

STATEMENT OF OPERATING EXPENSES.

For repairs of road-bed and track,	$2,476.62
For repairs of fences,	4.92
For repairs of buildings and fixtures,	7.50
For repairs of locomotives,	642.81
For repairs of cars,	331.04
For salaries and labor not included above,	2,981.57
For fuel for locomotives and cars, 273 tons coal,	1,242.15
For fuel for stations and shops,	60.60
For oil and waste,	325.15
For insurance,	104.54
For N. Y., N. H. & H. R. R., use of road-bed,	500.00
For Stamford Water Company,	100.00
For stationery and printing,	35.50
For miscellaneous items,	456.14
Total operating expenses,	$9,268.56
Net earnings,	$5,840.07

TOTAL RECEIPTS AND EXPENDITURES.

STATEMENT OF RECEIPTS FROM ALL SOURCES.

Cash on hand at date of last report, - -	$5,045.65
Bills and accounts receivable at date of last report,	. 1,479.03
From gross earnings as stated, - - -	15,108.63
From accounts payable, - - - -	1,221.24
Total, - - - - -	$22,854.55

STATEMENT OF TOTAL EXPENDITURES.

For operating expenses, as stated, - -	$9,268.56
For dividends (number, two; rate, 3 per cent.), -	5,992.66
Date when paid,—Oct., 1881, and May, 1882.	
Cash paid for coal on hand, - - -	825.50
Cash paid for bills payable last report, - -	1,895.75
Bills and accounts receivable this date, - -	1,994.26
Cash on hand to balance, - - -	2,877.82
Total, - - - - -	$22,854.55

GENERAL BALANCE-SHEET.

Assets.

Coal and materials on hand, - -	$1,190.00
Accounts receivable, - - - -	1,994.26
Three coal cars, - - - - -	1,224.50
Cash on hand, - - - - -	2,877.82
Total, - - - - -	$7,286.58

Liabilities.

Accounts payable, - - - -	$1,221.24
Profit and loss, - - -	6,065.34
Total, . - - -	$7,286.58

GENERAL INFORMATION.

DESCRIPTION OF ROAD.

Date when road, or different portions thereof, were
opened for use, viz. :
From New Canaan to Stamford, July 4, 1868.

Length of main line from New Canaan to Stamford,	8.30m.
Length of road owned by the Company, - -	8.30m.
Length of sidings, or other tracks not included above, . - . .	2,480ft.
Length of track of road, including branches and sidings, in single track miles, - . .	8.77m.
Track laid with new iron rails during the year (cost $300).	
Number of new ties put in track during the year (cost $325.25), ...	1,075
Aggregate length of wooden bridges, in feet, -	107
Number of spans of 25 feet or over, - -	1
Number of highway crossings under the track, -	1
Number of highway crossings at grade, - -	10
Number of railroads crossed at grade,—N. Y., N. H. & H. Railroad, at Stamford, . -	1
Length of all roads operated by this Company, -	8.30m.
Number of stations on main line, - -	5

EQUIPMENT.

Number of locomotives (not including switching engines), - - - - -	2
Average weight of same, including tender, water, and fuel, - - - - -	26 tons.
Number of passenger cars, - . .	1
Number of coal, gravel, and other cars, - ..	3

FARES, FREIGHT, ETC.

Average rate per mile received from passengers on roads operated by this Company, excluding season ticket passengers, - - -	.0463
Average rate per mile for season ticket passengers, reckoning one round trip per day to each ticket,	.0221

Average rate of fare per mile from all passengers,   .0410
Total number of passengers carried,   -   -   41,369
Passenger mileage, or passengers carried one mile,   286,265
Miles run by passenger and freight trains,   -   18,240
Total miles run,   -   -   -   -   -   18,240
Total number of tons of freight carried,   -   5,350
Freight mileage, or tons carried one mile,   -   41,391
Average rate of freight per ton per mile,   -   .1447
Number of men employed in operating road, in-
    cluding officers,   -   -   -   -   10

OFFICERS.

BOARD OF TRUSTEES.

WILLIAM E. RAYMOND, New Canaan.
ALBERT S. COMSTOCK, New York City.

Attest,   WILLIAM E. RAYMOND, *Trustee.*

STATE OF CONNECTICUT, }
    COUNTY OF FAIRFIELD, } · NEW CANAAN, November , 1882.

Then personally appeared William E. Raymond, Trustee of the New Canaan Railroad Company, and made solemn oath that he verily believes the foregoing return by him subscribed to be true and correct.

Before me,
RUSSELL L. HALL,
Notary Public.

PROPER ADDRESS OF THE COMPANY.

TRUSTEES OF THE NEW CANAAN RAILROAD CO.,
New Canaan, Conn.

NEW HAVEN & DERBY RAILROAD.

Return of the New Haven & Derby Railroad Company, for the year ending September 30, 1882.

EARNINGS AND EXPENSES.

STATEMENT OF GROSS EARNINGS.

From passenger transportation, - - -		$70,277.78
From freight transportation, - - -		90,349.65
From United States mails, - - -		704.84
From express, - - - -		1,876.96
From hoisting, - -	$2,886.12	
wharfage, - -	262.68	3,148.80
From weighing, - - - - -		44.81
Total gross earnings, - - -		$166,402.84

STATEMENT OF OPERATING EXPENSES.

For repairs of road-bed and track, - -		$13,411.52
For repairs of bridges, - - -		7,564.07
For repairs of fences, - - -		358.29
For repairs of buildings and fixtures, -		1,153.14
For repairs of locomotives, - -		5,432.50
For repairs of cars, - - -		5,069.63
For machinery and tools, - - - -		137.22
For salaries and labor, not included above, -		38,490.42
For fuel for locomotives and cars,—		
1,932 tons of coal,	$8,655.54	
— cords wood,	43.22	8,698.76
For fuel for stations and shops,—89 tons of coal,		420.97
For oil and waste, - - - - -		950.40

For damages, losses, and gratuities,—

to persons,	$275.00	
to property,	664.70	939.70

For insurance,	-	-	-	-	-	327.84

For rents of other roads,—

N. Y., N. H. & H.,	-	-	$2,800.00	
Naugatuck,	-	-	560.04	3,360.04

For car service, $848.80; repairs of dock, $202.16;
　water stations, $489.74; rents, $74.16, · 1,614.86

Total operating expenses,	-	-	-	$87,929.36
Net earnings,	-	-	-	$78,473.48

TOTAL RECEIPTS AND EXPENDITURES.

STATEMENT OF RECEIPTS FROM ALL SOURCES.

Cash on hand at date of last report,	-	-	$9,774.36
Bills and accounts receivable at date of last report,			1,763.30
From gross earnings, as stated,	-	-	166,402.84
Naugatuck R. R. Co.,	-	-	633.88
Sale old materials,	-	-	2,880.27
Total,	-	-	$181,454.65

STATEMENT OF TOTAL EXPENDITURES.

For operating expenses, as stated,	-	-	$87,929.36
For taxes,	-	-	3,989.62
For interest,	-	-	23,325.91
Land in Ansonia, $1,000; freight cars, $5,399.40; crane, $650.00; new buildings, $795.08,	-	-	7,844.48
Machinery,	-	-	6,320.72
Legal expenses,	-	-	397.20
New bridges,	-	-	310.96
Permanent improvements (filling trestles),	-	-	11,116.12
Steel rails,	-	-	11,060.60
Decrease in accounts payable,	-	-	3,574.37
Decrease in bills payable,	-	-	6,872.97
Bills and accounts receivable this date,	-	-	2,624.88
Cash on hand to balance,	-	-	16,087.46
Total,	-	-	$181,454.65

GENERAL BALANCE-SHEET.

Assets.

Construction,	$970,316.77
Equipment,	145,141.52
Accounts receivable,	2,624.88
Materials on hand,	7,326.92
Cash on hand,	16,087.46
Safe, furniture, tools, and machinery,	9,473.76
Total,	$1,150,971.31

Liabilities.

Capital stock,	$447,100.00
Bonds payable,	525,000.00
Bills payable,	9,806.00
Accounts payable,	5,954.02
City of New Haven,	72,258.33
Profit and loss,	90,852.96
Total,	$1,150,971.31

GENERAL INFORMATION.

CAPITAL STOCK.

Capital stock authorized by charter,	$700,000.00
Capital stock authorized by vote of company,	457,000.00
Capital stock issued, viz.:	
4,471 full shares of $100 each,	447,100.00
5 shares subject to $450.00 further assessment,	450.00
Amount credited on 5 shares not issued,	50.00
Stock issued for cash,	447,100.00
Amount of stock held in Connecticut,	407,500.00
Number of stockholders residing in Connecticut,	266
Whole number of stockholders,	284

BONDS OR UNFUNDED DEBT.

First mortgage, due 1888; rate of interest 7 per cent., - $300,000.00

Interest paid to May 1, 1882.

8A

Second mortgage guaranteed by City of New
    Haven; rate of interest, 7 per cent.,   -   225,000.00
        Interest paid to August 1, 1882; due 1900.

DESCRIPTION OF ROAD.

Date when road, or different portions thereof, were
    opened for use, viz.:
      From New Haven to Ansonia August 1,
    1871.

Length of main line from New Haven to Anso-
    nia, -   -   -   -   13.00m.

Length of road (main line and branches) owned
    by the company,   -   -   -   13.00m.

Length of sidings, or other tracks not included
    above,   -   -   -   1.96m.

Length of track of road, including sidings, in
    single track miles,   -   -   -   14.96m.

Length of track laid with steel rails (weight per
    yard, 56 lbs.),   -   -   -   7.68m.

Weight per yard of iron rails in main line, 48
    and 56 lbs.

Miles of track laid with steel rails during the year
    (No. of tons, 176; weight per yard, 56 lbs.;
    cost, $11,060.60),   2.00m.

Number of new ties put in track during the year
    (cost, $2,193.90),   -   -   4,255

Aggregate length of wooden bridges, in feet,   -   5,560

Number of spans of 25 feet or over,   -   7

Number of highway crossings over the track,   -   8

Number of highway crossings under the track,   -   8

Number of highway crossings at grade,   -   19

Number of highway crossings at grade with gates,   2

Number of highway crossings at grade with flag-
    men, -   -   -   -   -   2

Number of railroads crossed at grade, and names
    of each,
      Naugatuck R. R., -   -   -   1

Length of all roads operated by this company,   -   13m.

Number of stations on main line, -   -   -   7

EQUIPMENT.

Number of locomotives (not including switching engines), - - - - -	4
Average weight of same, including tender, water, and fuel, - - - -	51 tons.
Number of passenger cars, -	4
Number of baggage and mail cars,	3
Number of merchandise cars, -	16
Number of coal, gravel, and other cars, - -	48
Number of passenger train cars with patent platform, buffer, and coupler, - - -	4
Name of patent, - - - - -	Miller.

FARES, FREIGHT, ETC.

Average rate per mile received from passengers on roads operated by this company, excluding season-ticket passengers, - - -	.0303
Average rate per mile for season-ticket passengers, reckoning one round trip per day to each ticket, - - - - -	.0072
Average rate of fare per mile from all passengers,	.0371
Total number of passengers carried, - -	197,749½
Passenger mileage, or passengers carried one mile,	1,876,919
Miles run by passenger and freight trains, - -	50,493
Miles run by all other trains, - - -	4,360
Total miles run, - - - - -	54,853
Total number of tons of freight carried,	127,192
Freight mileage, or tons carried one mile,	1,422,597
Average rate of freight per ton per mile, -	.0630
Number of men employed in operating road, including officers, - - -	91

ACCIDENTS.

STATEMENT OF EACH ACCIDENT IN DETAIL.

1882.

March 4. Harry Burnham, brakeman on gravel train, fell from the train under a car, and was injured. Died about one week after the accident.

June 26. James W. Norton, walking on the track between Birmingham and Ansonia, was struck by 3.15 P. M. train from Ansonia and injured, not fatally. Said to have been intoxicated.

Aug. 5. John Foskay, brakeman on gravel train, fell from the engine and injured one foot.

OFFICERS.

President, J. H. BARTHOLOMEW, Stony Creek.
Vice-President, CHAS. L. ENGLISH, New Haven.
Secretary, FRANCIS E. HARRISON, New Haven.
Treasurer, CHAS. ATWATER, New Haven.
Superintendent, E. S. QUINTARD, New Haven.
Chief Clerk, WILLIAM A. LAW, New Haven.
General Ticket Agent, FRANCIS E. HARRISON, New Haven.
General Freight Agent, E. S. QUINTARD, New Haven.

BOARD OF DIRECTORS.

J. H. BARTHOLOMEW, New Haven.
CHARLES L. ENGLISH, New Haven.
HENRY S. DAWSON, New Haven.
ISAAC ANDERSON, New Haven.
N. D. SPERRY, New Haven.
JOEL A. SPERRY, New Haven.
M. F. TYLER, New Haven.
CHARLES ATWATER, New Haven.
JOHN B. ROBERTSON (Mayor), *ex officio*, New Haven.
R. W. ARMSTRONG (Alderman), *ex officio*, New Haven.
EDWARD N. SHELTON, Birmingham.
GEORGE W. SHELTON, Birmingham.
GEORGE P. COWLES, Ansonia.
THOMAS WALLACE, Ansonia.
FRANKLIN FARRELL, Ansonia.

Attest, J. H. BARTHOLOMEW, *President*.
Attest, CHAS. ATWATER, *Treasurer*.

STATE OF CONNECTICUT,   }   NEW HAVEN, Oct. 31, 1882.
COUNTY OF NEW HAVEN,

    Then personally appeared J. H. Bartholomew, President, and Charles Atwater, Treasurer, of the New Haven & Derby Railroad Company, and severally made solemn oath that they verily believed the foregoing return by them subscribed to be true and correct.

Before me,

CHARLES L. SWAN, JR.

Notary Public.

PROPER ADDRESS OF THE COMPANY.

THE NEW HAVEN & DERBY RAILROAD COMPANY,
New Haven, Conn.

NEW HAVEN & NORTHAMPTON COMPANY.

Return of the New Haven & Northampton Company, for the year ending September 30, 1882.

EARNINGS AND EXPENSES.

STATEMENT OF GROSS EARNINGS.

From passenger transportation,	$200,259.43
From freight transportation,	651,863.84
From United States mails,	10,258.08
From express,	14,924.52
From wharfage,	3,611.51
From hoisting,	13,074.83
From weighing,	2,278.40
Total gross earnings,	$896,270.61

STATEMENT OF OPERATING EXPENSES.

For repairs of road-bed and track,		$125,808.35
For repairs of bridges,		9,745.08
For repairs of fences,		3,075.17
For repairs of buildings and fixtures,		30,065.68
For repairs of locomotives,		38,346.52
For repairs of cars,		55,080.70
For legal expenses,	$8,330.70	
Water,	867.33	
Station and train supplies,	4,040.61—	13,238.64
For salaries and labor not included above,		181,625.74
For fuel for locomotives and cars, —		
13,369 tons of coal,		65,957.28
For fuel for stations and shops, 598 tons of coal,		3,894.40
For oil and waste,		8,814.11

For damages, losses, and gratuities,—
    To persons, - - $5,550.66
    To property, - - 1,616.46— 7,167.12
For insurance, - - - - - 2,506.70
For rent of Holyoke & Westfield R. R.,—
    Interest on bonds, - - $17,600.00
    One-half excess over $35,200, 10,815.95— 28,415.95
For stationery, $5,505.02; advertising, $1,006.98;
    contingencies, $4,338.74, - - - 10,850.74
For rent of freight cars, $5,198.77; rents, sta-
    tions, etc., $1,409.24, - - - - 6,608.01

    Total operating expenses, - - - $591,200.19

    Net earnings, - - - - $305,070.42

TOTAL RECEIPTS AND EXPENDITURES.

STATEMENT OF RECEIPTS FROM ALL SOURCES.

Cash on hand at date of last report, - - $27,834.97
Bills and accounts receivable at date of last report, 74,361.16
From gross earnings as stated, - - - 896,270.61
From interest on H. & W. bonds, $3,600.00
    Dividend on stock, 600.00— 4,200.00
From increase in bills payable, - - 269,000.00
From increase of October coupons due, - - 200.00
From vouchers and accounts, - - - 27,625.22

    Total, - - - $1,299,491.96

STATEMENT OF TOTAL EXPENDITURES.

For operating expenses, as stated, - - $591,200.19
For taxes, - - - - - 28,926.33
For interest on bonds, - - $203,695.33
    on bills payable, - 34,931.88— 238,627.21
For construction account, northern extension,
    Hamden improvement, etc., - - - 165,747.05
For equipment, two locomotives, - - - 26,168.00
For two passenger cars, - - $5,237.24
    Machinery, - - - 4,731.03— 9,968.27
For paid bonds of 1882, - - - - 190,000.00

For sinking fund, April and October payments,	15,000.00
For real estate purchased,	13,150.00
For increase materials on hand,	363.48
For accounts charged off,	476.44
Bills and accounts receivable this date,	19,864.99
Total,	$1,299,491.96

GENERAL BALANCE-SHEET.

Assets.

Construction account,	$5,560,894.06
Equipment,	901,457.03
Lands outside location,	17,372.81
Bonds of Holyoke & Westfield Railroad,	60,000.00
Stock of Holyoke & Westfield Railroad,	20,000.00
Cash and accounts due from agents and others,	19,864.99
Materials on hand,	82,879.33
Sinking fund,	52,500.00
Total,	$6,714,968.22

Liabilities.

Capital stock,	$2,460,000.00
Seven per cent. bonds, 1st mortgage,	1,300,000.00
Six per cent. bonds, 2d mortgage, conv. S. F.,	1,200,000.00
Five per cent. bonds, Northern Extension,	700,000.00
Bills payable,	585,000.00
Coupons maturing October 1st,	62,345.00
Dividends unpaid,	659.00
Vouchers and accounts,	27,625.22
Profit and loss,	379,339.00
Total,	$6,714,968.22

PRESENT OR CONTINGENT LIABILITIES, NOT INCLUDED IN BALANCE-SHEET.

Bonds guaranteed by this Company, or a lien on its road, issued by Holyoke & Westfield Railroad Company,	$260,000.00

GENERAL INFORMATION.

CAPITAL STOCK.

Capital stock authorized by charter, - -	$5,000,000.00
Capital stock authorized by vote of Company, -	2,600,000.00
Capital stock issued, viz.:	
24,600 full shares of $100 each, - -	2,460,000.00
Stock issued for cash, - - - -	1,882,000.00
Stock issued for undivided earnings, - -	578,000.00
Amount of stock held in Connecticut, - -	970,600.00
Number of stockholders residing in Connecticut,	192
Whole number of stockholders, - - -	257

BONDS OR UNFUNDED DEBT.

First mortgage, due 1899; rate of interest, 7 per ct.,	$1,300,000.00
Interest paid to date.	
Consolidated mortgage and sinking fund, 6 per cent., due 1909, - - - -	1,200,000.00
Interest paid to date.	
First mortgage Northern Extension, due 1911, 5 per cent., - - - - -	700,000,00
Interest paid to date.	
Seven per cent. Holyoke & Westfield R. R. Co., guaranteed by this Company, - - -	200,000.00
Six per cent. Holyoke & Westfield R. R. Co., guaranteed by this Company, - - -	60,000.00

DESCRIPTION OF ROAD.

Date when road, or different portions thereof, were opened for use, viz. :

From New Haven to Plainville, 1848; Plainville to Granby, 1850; Granby to Northampton, 1857; Farmington to Collinsville, 1850; Northampton to Williamsburgh, 1869; Collinsville to New Hartford, 1870; Northampton to Bardwell's Ferry, and South Deerfield to Turner's Falls, 1881.

Length of main line from New Haven to junction
  with Troy & Greenfield Railroad at Conway, -   94.64m.
      Same in Connecticut,   ·   ·   51.26m.
Length of branches and names,—
    From Farmington to New Hartford,   ·   14.09m.
    From Simsbury to Tariffville,   ·   ·   1.04m.
    From Northampton to Williamsburgh,   -   7.51m.
    From South Deerfield to Turner's Falls,   -   10.07m.
Length of all branches,   -   ·   -   ·   32.71m.
      Same in Connecticut,   -   ·   -   15.13m.
Length of road (main line and branches) owned by
  the Company,   ·   ·   ·   ·   ·   127.35m.
      Same in Connecticut,   -   ·   -   66.39m.
Length of sidings or other tracks not included
  above,   -   ·   -   ·   ·   27.50m.
      Same in Connecticut,   -   ·   -   14.52m.
Length of track of road, including branches and
  in sidings, single track miles, . -   -   -   154.85m.
      Same in Connecticut,   -   ·   ·   80.91m.
Length of track laid with steel rails (weight per
  yard, 60 lbs.),   -   ·   -   ·   ·   106.00m.
      Same in Connecticut,   -   · ·   -   51.26m.
Weight per yard of iron rails in main line, 60 lbs.;
  in branches, 60 lbs.
Miles of track laid with steel rails during the
  year, (No. of tons, $331\frac{9}{10}$ tons; weight per yard,
  60 lbs.: cost, $21,088.13),   -   -   -   3.00m
Number of new ties put in track during the year
  (cost, $23,087.60),   -   -   \ -   -   61,931
      Same in Connecticut,   -   -   -   31,739
Aggregate length of wooden bridges, in feet, . -.   881
      Same in Connecticut,   ·-   -   · ·   662
Number of spans of 25 feet or over,   ·   ·   7
      Same in Connecticut,   -   -   ·   5
Aggregate length of iron bridges, in feet,   -   3,140
      Same in Connecticut,   -·   · ·   -   897.5
Number of spans of 25 feet or over,   -   -   59
      Same in Connecticut,   -   -   -   18
Number of highway crossings over the track,   -   ·· 19
      Same in Connecticut,   -   -   -   17

Number of highway crossings under the track,   -   21
    Same in Connecticut,   -   -   -   9
Number of highway crossings at grade,   -   •   134
    Same in Connecticut,   -   •   -   86
Number of highway crossings at grade, with gates,   3
    Same in Connecticut,   -   •   -   2
Number of highway crossings at grade, with flag-
    men,   -   •   •   •   -   •   2
Number of railroads crossed at grade,— New
    York & New England, at Plainville; Hartford
    & Connecticut Western, at Pine Meadow and
    Simsbury; Boston & Albany, at Westfield,   -   4
    Same in Connecticut,   -   •   -   3
Name, termini, and length of each road operated
    by this company under lease or contract,—
      Holyoke & Westfield Railroad,   -   10.32
      Branches and side tracks to mills,   -   6.90—   17.22
Length of all roads operated by this Company,   -   144.57m.
    Same in Connecticut,   -   •   -   66.39m.
Number of stations on main line,   -   •   19
    Same in Connecticut,   -   •   -   12
Number of stations on branches,   -   •   -   10
    Same in Connecticut,   -   •   •   4
Number of stations on leased lines,   -   •   1

EQUIPMENT.

Number of locomotives (not including switching
    engines),   -   •   •   •   •   25
Average weight of same, including tender, water,
    and fuel,   -   •   •   •   -   68,000 lbs.
Number of switching engines,   -   •   -   2
Number of passenger cars,   -   •   -   22
Number of baggage and mail cars,   -   •   15
Number of merchandise cars,   -   •   -   440
Number of coal, gravel, and other cars,   -   -   99
Number of locomotives equipped with train brakes,   16
Number of cars equipped with train brakes,   -   37
Name of brake,   •   •   -   •   -   Westinghouse.
Number of passenger train cars with patent plat-
    form, buffer, and coupler,   -   -   -   37
Name of patent,   -   •   •   •   •   Miller.

FARES, FREIGHT, ETC.

Average rate per mile received from passengers on roads operated by this Company, excluding season ticket passengers,	.023
Average rate of fare per mile for all passengers,	.023
Total number of passengers carried,	483,229
Passenger mileage, or passengers carried one mile,	8,726,851
Miles run by passenger trains,	372,185
Miles run by freight trains,	231,628
Miles run in switching,	51,599
Miles run by all other trains,	27,910
Total miles run,	683,322
Total number of tons of freight carried,	498,621
Freight mileage, or tons carried one mile,	24,800,865
Average rate of freight per ton per mile,	.0263
Number of men employed in operating road, including officers,	539

ACCIDENTS.

STATEMENT OF EACH ACCIDENT.

1881.

November 11th. Godfrey Marquette of Southington, killed at that station while passing under a freight train at private crossing.

November 22d. James Beard, brakeman, fell between the cars while switching at New Haven, and died two weeks later, from injuries.

November 29th. Wm. Cooney, brakeman, fell from the cars at Simsbury, while switching, necessitating the amputation of a leg.

1882.

January 16th. Charles Johnson, (colored,) killed by passenger train at crossing near Webster street, New Haven.

May 27th. Michael Fox of New Haven, struck by passenger train while walking on track between Court and Grand streets, and killed.

September 23. John Oxley of Southington, intoxicated, was run over while attempting to board a morning train, and subsequently died from injuries.

OFFICERS.

President, CHARLES N. YEAMANS, New Haven, Conn.
Secretary, EDWARD A. RAY, New Haven, Conn.
Treasurer, EDWARD A. RAY, New Haven, Conn.
Superintendent, C. A. GOODNOW, New Haven Conn.
General Ticket Agent, EDWARD A. RAY, New Haven, Conn.
General Freight Agent, M. C. PARKER, New Haven, Conn.

BOARD OF DIRECTORS.

CHARLES N. YEAMANS, New Haven, Conn.
GEO. J. BRUSH, New Haven, Conn.
DANIEL TROWBRIDGE, New Haven, Conn.
HORATIO G. KNIGHT, Easthampton, Mass.
GEO. H. WATROUS, New Haven, Conn.
WILLIAM D. BISHOP, Bridgeport, Conn.
CHARLES M. POND, Hartford, Conn.
EZEKIEL H. TROWBRIDGE, New Haven, Conn.
EDWIN M. REED, New Haven, Conn.

Attest,   CHAS. N. YEAMANS, *President.*
Attest,   EDWARD A. RAY, *Treasurer.*

STATE OF CONNECTICUT, }
COUNTY OF NEW HAVEN, }   NEW HAVEN, Nov. 18, 1882.

Then personally appeared Chas. N. Yeamans, President, and Edward A. Ray, Treasurer, of the New Haven & Northampton Company, and severally made solemn oath that they verily believed the foregoing return by them subscribed to be true and correct, according to their best knowledge and belief.

Before me,

CLARENCE E. THOMPSON,
Commissioner of the Superior Court.

PROPER ADDRESS OF THE COMPANY.

NEW HAVEN & NORTHAMPTON COMPANY,
New Haven, Conn.

NEW LONDON NORTHERN RAILROAD.

Return of the New London Northern Railroad Company, for the year ending September 30, 1882.

[NOTE.—Items relative to operation are for 100 miles—New London to Miller's Falls. The remaining 21 miles—Miller's Falls to Brattleboro—was bought by this Company, subject to a lease to the Central Vermont Railroad Company, under which they are still operating it.]

LESSEES' STATEMENT OF

EARNINGS AND EXPENSES.

STATEMENT OF GROSS EARNINGS.

From passenger transportation, - - -	$212,274.96
From freight transportation, - - -	345,467.27
From United States mails, - - -	7,461.20
From express, - - -	8,874.47
From rents, - - - - -	10,336.56
Total gross earnings, - - -	$584,414.46
From net earnings of steamers, - - -	2,970.02
Total income, - - - -	$587,384.48

STATEMENT OF OPERATING EXPENSES.

For repairs of road-bed and track, - -		$168,499.05
For repairs of bridges, - - - -		8,380.56
For repairs of fences, - - - -		7,463.04
For repairs of buildings, fixtures, and water-works, - - - - -		14,571.36
For repairs of locomotives, - - -		24,006.96
For repairs of cars, - - - -		31,606.18
For repairs of machinery and tools, - -		2,767.94
For fuel for locomotives and cars,—		
11,483 tons of coal, -	$55,963.16	
2,770 cords of wood, -	10,036.17—	65,999.33

For fuel for stations and shops,—

440 tons of coal,	-	-	$2,483.97
450 cords of wood,		-	1,611.00—	4,094.97

For oil and waste,   -   -   -   -   7,103.24

For damages, losses, and gratuities,—

To persons,	-	-	$334.06
To property,	-	-	491.72—	825.78

For insurance,   -   -   -   -   -   2,472.00
For general and office expenses, etc.,   -   -   12,187.30
For salaries, wages, and incidentals of passenger department, - - - - - 37,839.13
For salaries, wages, and incidentals of freight department, - - - - - 87,953.88
For watchmen, switchmen, flag and signalmen, - 5,146.77
For telegraph expenses, - - - 2,016.87
For balance mileage of freight cars, - - 12,723.75
For taxes, - - - - - 23,654.07

Total operating expenses, - - - $519,312.18

Net earnings, - - - - $68,072.30

TOTAL RECEIPTS AND EXPENDITURES.
[Company's Account.]

STATEMENT OF RECEIPTS FROM ALL SOURCES.

Cash on hand at date of last report, - - $32,028.45
Bills and accounts receivable at date of last report, 98,558.32
From rent of road, and other rents, - : 216,812.50
From interest, - - - - - 38,531.11
From increase of bills payable, - - - 15,000.00
From increase of accounts payable, - - 30.59
From dividends unpaid, - - - - 1,257.00
From coupons unpaid, - - - - 676.50

Total, - - - - - $402,894.47

STATEMENT OF TOTAL EXPENDITURES.

For general expenses, - - - - $14,941.91
For new depot at Brattleboro, - - - 12,364.68
For interest, - - - - - 97,310.28

For dividends (number, 4; rate per cent., 1½),	-	90,000.00
For improvement account,	- - -	33.50
For old dividends,	- - - -	214.50
For old coupons,	- - - -	1,028.50
Bills and accounts receivable this date,	- -	155,677.72
Cash on hand to balance, -	- - -	31,323.38
Total,	- - - - -	$402,894.47

GENERAL BALANCE-SHEET.

[Company's Account.]

Assets.

Construction account,	- - -	$2,771,888.40
Equipment account,	- - -	248,420.44
Bonds of Brattleboro & Whitehall Railroad,	-	150,000.00
Steamboat property,	- - -	110,000.00
Accounts receivable,	- - -	155,677.72
Cash on hand,	- - -	31,323.38
Total,	- - -	$3,467,309.94

Liabilities.

Capital stock,	- - -	$1,500,000.00
Funded debt,	- - -	1,499,500.00
Unfunded debt,	- - -	227,000.00
Accounts payable,	- - -	133.33
Dividends unpaid,	- - -	2,218.75
Coupons unpaid,	- - -	1,271.34
Profit and loss,	- - -	237,186.52
Total,	- - -	$3,467,309.94

GENERAL INFORMATION.

CAPITAL STOCK.

Capital stock authorized by charter,	-	$2,000,000.00
Capital stock authorized by vote of Company,	-	1,500,000.00
Capital stock issued, viz.:		
15,000 full shares of $100 each,	-	1,500,000.00

Stock issued for cash, - - - -	340,673.33
Stock issued for bonds, - - - -	1,102,660.00
Stock issued for stock of Amherst, Belchertown & Palmer Railroad, - - - -	56,666.67
Amount of stock held in Connecticut, - -	1,003,900.00
Number of stockholders residing in Connecticut,	224
Whole number of stockholders, - - -	321

BONDS OR UNFUNDED DEBT.

First mortgage, due 1885; rate of interest, 6 per cent., - - - - -	300,000.00
Interest paid to April 1, 1882.	
Second mortgage, due 1892; rate of interest, 7 per cent., - - - - -	387,500.00
Interest paid to June 1, 1882.	
Consolidated mortgage due 1910; rate of interest, 5 per cent., - - - - -	812,000.00
Interest paid to July 1, 1882.	

DESCRIPTION OF ROAD.

Date when road, or different portions thereof, were opened for use, viz.:

From New London to Palmer, 1849; Palmer to Amherst, ——; Amherst to Miller's Falls, 1867; Miller's Falls to Brattleboro, ——.

Length of main line, from New London to Brattleboro, ' - . - - -	121.00m.
Same in Connecticut, - - -	56.00m.
Length of road (main line) owned by the Company,	121.00m.
Same in Connecticut, - - -	56.00m.
Length of sidings, or other tracks not included above, - - - - -	23.48m.
Same in Connecticut, - - -	13.15m.
Length of track of road, including sidings, in single track miles, - - - -	144.48m.
Same in Connecticut, - - -	69.15m.
Length of track laid with steel rails (weight per yard, 57, 58, and 60 lbs.), - - -	62.00m.
Same in Connecticut, - - -	56.00m.

10A

Weight per yard of iron rails in main line, 56 and
   60 lbs.

Miles of track laid with steel rails during the year
   (number of tons, 2,498; weight per yard,
   57 and 58 lbs.; cost, $94,368.69), -   -   29.38m.

   Same in Connecticut,   -   -   -   23.38m.

Number of new ties put in track during the year,   59,126

   Same in Connecticut,   -   -   -   33,110

Aggregate length of wooden bridges, in feet,   -   12,252

   Same in Connecticut,   -   -   -   6,176

Number of spans of 25 feet or over,   -   -   39

   Same in Connecticut,   -   -   -   21

Aggregate length of iron bridges, in feet,   -   -   629

   Same in Connecticut,   -   -   -   609

Number of spans of 25 feet or over (all in Conn.),   6

Aggregate length of stone arch bridges, in feet, -   30

Number of highway crossings over the track,   -   4

   Same in Connecticut,   -   -   -   3

Number of highway crossings under the track,   -   4

   Same in Connecticut,   -   -   -   2

Number of highway crossings at grade, -   -   106

   Same in Connecticut,   -   -   -   71

Number of highway crossings at grade, with flagmen, -   -   -   - , -   -   4

   Same in Connecticut,   -   -   -   3

Number of railroads crossed at grade,—
New York & New England, in Connecticut; Boston & Albany, and Springfield & N. Eastern,
   in Massachusetts.   -   -   -   -   3

Length of all roads operated by Lessees,   -   121.00m.

   Same in Connecticut,   -   -   -   56.00m.

Number of stations on main line,   -   -   45

   Same in Connecticut,   -   -   -   23

EQUIPMENT.

Number of locomotives (not including switching
   engines),   -   -   -   -   23

Average weight of same, including tender, water,
   and fuel,   -   -   -   -   45 tons.

Number of switching engines,   -   1

Number of passenger cars,   -   -   -   15
Number of baggage and mail cars,   -   -   10
Number of merchandise cars,   -   -   -   106
Number of coal, gravel, and other cars, -   -   254
Number of locomotives equipped with train brakes,   13
Number of cars equipped with train brakes,   -   24
Name of brake,   -   -   -   Westinghouse Automatic.
Number of passenger train cars with patent plat-
    form, buffer, and coupler,   -   -   -   24
Name of patent,   -   -   -   -   -   Miller.

FARES, FREIGHT, ETC.

Average rate per mile received from passengers on
    roads operated by this Company, excluding
    season ticket passengers,   -   -   -   .03
Average rate per mile for season ticket passengers,
    reckoning one round trip per day to each ticket,   .0072
Average rate of fare per mile from all passengers,   .029
Total number of passengers carried,   -   -   420,066
Passenger mileage, or passengers carried one mile,   7,207,081
Miles run by passenger trains,   -   -   -   276,506
Miles run by freight trains,   -   -   -   285,449
Miles run by all other trains,   -   -   -   4,013
Total miles run,   -   -   -   -   565,968
Total number of tons of freight carried,   -   458,231
Freight mileage, or tons carried one mile,   -   20,421,443
Average rate of freight per ton per mile,   -   .016
Number of men employed in operating road, in-
    cluding officers,   -   -   -   -   500

ACCIDENTS.

STATEMENT OF EACH ACCIDENT.

1881.

October 7th. At South Coventry, a man called Major Main, suffered injuries resulting in the loss of a leg.

1882.

February 21st. At Norwich, a man was slightly injured by a freight car coming in contact with one in which he was loading freight.

March 30th. At New London, an employe was slightly injured while switching.

April 20th. At Willimantic, a child was run over by a freight train, and received injuries resulting in death.

April 24th. At New London, a switchman, named James McLeary, slipped and fell under the cars, and was instantly killed.

OFFICERS.

President, ROBERT COIT, New London, Conn.
Secretary, J. A. SOUTHARD, New London, Conn.
Treasurer, ROBERT COIT, New London, Conn.
Superintendent, GEO. W. BENTLEY, New London, Conn.
Auditor, J. A. SOUTHARD, New London, Conn.
General Ticket Agent, M. R. MORAN, New London, Conn.
General Freight Agent, C. F. SPAULDING, New London, Conn.

BOARD OF DIRECTORS.

ROBERT COIT, New London, Conn.
WILLIAM W. BILLINGS, New London, Conn.
WILLIAM H. BARNS, New London, Conn.
BENJAMIN STARK, New London, Conn.
AUGUSTUS BRANDEGEE, New London, Conn.
JONATHAN N. HARRIS, New London, Conn.
THOMAS RAMSDELL, Windham, Conn.
C. H. OSGOOD, Norwich, Conn.
WILLIAM ALLEN BUTLER, New York.
WILLIAM H. HILL, Boston, Mass.
JAMES A. RUMRILL, Springfield, Mass.

Attest,   ROBERT COIT, *President.*
Attest,   ROBERT COIT, *Treasurer.*

STATE OF CONNECTICUT,   }
  COUNTY OF NEW LONDON, }   NEW LONDON,.November 3, 1882.

Then personally appeared Robert Coit, President and Treasurer of the New London Northern Railroad Company, and made solemn oath that he verily believed the foregoing return by him subscribed to be true and correct.

Before me,

JUSTUS A. SOUTHARD,

Notary Public.

PROPER ADDRESS OF THE COMPANY.

NEW LONDON NORTHERN RAILROAD COMPANY,

New London, Conn.

NEW YORK & NEW ENGLAND RAILROAD.

Return of the New York & New England Railroad Company for the year ending September 30, 1882.

EARNINGS AND EXPENSES.

STATEMENT OF GROSS EARNINGS.

From passenger transportation, - . -	$1,171,623.02
From freight transportation, - . -	1,837,890.35
From United States mails, - - -	48,898.38
From express, - - - - -	87,475.77
From miscellaneous earnings, including rents, -	156,901.96
Total gross earnings, - - -	$3,302,789.48

STATEMENT OF OPERATING EXPENSES.

For repairs of road-bed and track, -		$334,843.89
For repairs of bridges, - - - -		61,527.49
For repairs of fences, - - - -		15,802.78
For repairs of buildings and fixtures, - -		28,441.82
For repairs of locomotives, - - -		154,753.99
For repairs of cars, - - - -		173,475.83
For repairs of machinery and tools, - -		26,099.65
For salaries and labor, not included above, -		873,892.41
For fuel for locomotives and cars,—		
88,257½ tons of coal,		428,340.97
For fuel for stations and shops, - - - -		29,288.06
For oil and waste,		21,136.27
For damages, losses, and gratuities,—		
to persons,	$18,588.64	
to property,	29,381.34	47,969.98
For insurance, - - - - -		10,486.53

For rents of other roads,—

Rhode Island & Mass.,	$24,000.00	
Norwich & Worcester,	17,690.56	
Newburgh, Dutchess & Conn.,	12,975.34	
Springfield & North Eastern (Estimated),	10,000.00	
Springfield & New London,	5,500.00	
Rockville,	4,800.00	74,965.90
For stationary and printing,		29,579.55
For advertising,		15,841.95
For rent of depot grounds and buildings,		29,553.18
For rent of engines,		1,107.60
For hire of cars,		13,562.05
For expense of stations,		18,285.76
For legal expenses,		20,250.65
For expenses at general office,		6,445.31
For water station expenses,		23,739.90
Miscellaneous,		5,676.93
Total operating expenses,		$2,445,068.45
Net earnings,		$857,721.03

TOTAL RECEIPTS AND EXPENDITURES.

STATEMENT OF RECEIPTS FROM ALL SOURCES.

Cash on hand at date of last report,	$83,723.44
Bills and accounts receivable at date of last report,	508,466.06
From gross earnings as stated,	3,302,789.48
From earnings from other sources,	93,546.72
From first mortgage bonds sold,	1,032,000.00
From second mortgage bonds sold,	1,742,000.00
From premium on bonds sold,	54,895.01
Total,	$6,817,420.71

STATEMENT OF TOTAL EXPENDITURES.

For operating expenses, as stated,	$2,445,068.45
For taxes,	117,816.81
For interest,	791,211.68

For construction, equipment, or property account, -	*1,353,681.79
From decrease in accounts payable, - -	306,435.14
Bills and accounts receivable this date, including	
balance due on second mortgage bonds sold,	1,717,239.41
Cash on hand to balance, - • - -	85,967.43
Total, • • - - -	$6,817,420.71

---

* Statement of New Construction and expenditures charged to Property during the fiscal year ending September 30, 1882 :

New buildings,—

Paint shop, Norwood Central shops, -	$20,441.57	
Blacksmith shop, • • -	9,662.71	
Foundry, - • • -	6,596.14	
Transfer table, • - -	4,649.52	
Additional water supply, - -	7,633.42	
Machine and repair shops other than		
foregoing, - - • -	2,206.89	
Engine-houses, - - - -	3,109.53	
Freight-house, Waterbury, - -	8,158.18	
Freight-house, Hartford, - -	3,411.37	
Renewal and improvement of stations,	8,245.71	
Sand-house, Boston, - • -	2,354.00	
Section and watch-houses, • •	425.52	
Water and coal stations, • -	3,671.83	
		$80,566.39
New sidings, - - - -		144,663.92
New safety-gates and stop-signals, -		2,873.36
Steel rails,—difference in value and weight between steel rails of 66 lbs. weight, and steel and iron rails of 60 lbs., the former being used to replace the latter :		
Number of tons replacing steel, 1,536₇₈₈₃⁄₈₈₄₀,		
Number of tons replacing iron, 1,974₁₄₄₉⁄₈₈₄₀,		40,892.41
Bridges,—iron bridge at Readville, replacing wood, and new overhead drive bridge at Waterbury, -		6,151.12
New tools and machinery for shops,		16,960.90
New hand and push cars, -		861.87
New track scales, - • -		3,126.97
New freight-yard, Hartford, - • -		10,102.77
Riprapping East Hartford embankment,		10,289.72
Miscellaneous improvements at stations, filling, grading, etc., - -		3,264.58

Real estate.—*Deduct* the following sales :

Sale of land at Hartford to the Hfd. & C. W. Railroad, - , -		69,879.81		
Sale of land at Medway to Wm. B. Hodges, - -		150.00		
Sale of land at So. Boston to Marg. Patterson, - -		200.00		
Sale of land at Norfolk to Elvira Fisher,		50 00		
		$70,279.81		
Less real estate purchased :				
1.156 acres land at E. Hfd.,	$1,311.08			
Land at Norfolk,	125.00			
Sundry expenses in connection with land at various points,	74.44			
Right of way,	33,239.79	34,753 31	35,526.50	
				$284,227.51
Extension of double track :				
Grading, - - -			$35,583.48	
Bridging, - - -.			19,077.99	
Cross ties, - - -			9,224.67	
Steel rails, - - -			55,064.23	
Track laying and surfacing, -			15,999.75	
Miscellaneous, , - -			6,596.16	
				141,546.28
Improvement at South Boston Flats,—				
Fifty-acre lot :				
Grading, dredging, and filling, -		$17,269.18		
Paving, - - - -		7,504.16		
Buildings :				
Grain elevator,—				
Material,	$20,582.13			
Machinery,	78,575.71			
Labor,	20,950.50			
		$120,117.34		
Warehouses,—				
Material,	$2,406.49			
Labor,	233.27			
		2,639.76		
			122,757.10	
Piers :				
Material,	$97,061.03			
Dredging and filling,	18,252.45			
Labor,	32,986.61			
		148,300.09		
Miscellaneous, - - - ' -		11,831.33		
			307,661.86	
Twenty-five-acre Lot ;				
Grading, dredging and filling, -		$35.20		
Paving, - - - -		7,783.56		

Warehouses:

Material,	-	-	$101,596.46	
Labor,	-	-	32,386.24	
				133,982.70

Piers:

Material,	-	-	$5.43	
Dredging,	-	-	1,090.80	
Filling,	-	-	90.34	
				1,186.57
Miscellaneous,	-	-	-	11,660.20
					154,648.23

Twelve-acre Lot:

Grading, dredging, and filling,			$55,094.14	
Miscellaneous,	-	-	-	4,622.94	59,717.08
					522,027.17
Extension of road west of Waterbury,					206,223.09
Underlying liens bought,	-	.-			22,271.99
Highland Lake Grove, additions to improvements,				.	389.80
New transfer steamer Wm. T. Hart,	-	-			176,995.95
					$1,353,681.79

GENERAL BALANCE-SHEET.

Assets.

Cost of road, estimated,	-	$27,845,828.32
Cost of equipment, estimated,		2,280,274.36
Actual cost of road and equipment east of Waterbury,		$30,126,102.68
Extension of road west of Waterbury,	-	2,683,972.04
Stock of New Eng. Transfer Co.,		40,900.00
$325,000 Bonds of Conn. Central R. R.,		283,642.37
Total permanent investment,	- -	$33,134,617.09
Cash,	- . -	$85,967.43
Due from agents and companies,	-	754,898.72
Materials and supplies,	. -	306,552.48
Debit balances,	- -	40,410.69
Due on subscriptions to the capital stock formerly held by State of Massachusetts,	-	921,930.00
Total cash assets,	- - -	2,109,759.32
Total,	- - -	$35,244,376.41

Liabilities.

Capital Stock,		$20,000,000.00
Funded debt,—		
First mortgage bonds,	$10,000,000.00	
Second mortgage bonds,	1,742,000.00	
Funded indebtedness incurred		
for purchase of real estate		
secured by estate purchased		
(Boston Terminal lands),—		
Note to B. & A. R. R.	300,000.00	
Due Com. of Massachusetts		
(25 and 12-acre lots),	886,532.00	
Mort. note, Drake's wharf,	125,000.00	13,053,532.00
Unfunded debt, viz.,—		
Interest unpaid,	188,155.00	
*Notes payable,	422,900.06	
Vouchers and accounts,	649,246.16	1,260,301.22
Profit and loss balance,		930,543.19
Total,		$35,244,376.41

GENERAL INFORMATION.

CAPITAL STOCK.

Capital stock authorized by charter,	$20,000,000.00
Capital stock authorized by vote of company,	20,000,000.00
Capital stock issued, viz.:	
165,020 full shares of $100 each,	16,502,000.00
Berdell bonds, entitling holders of same to	
34,980 shares,	3,498,000.00
Amount of stock held in Connecticut, not including	
Berdell bonds,	62,500.00
Number of stockholders residing in Connecticut,	
not including Berdell bondholders,	14
Whole number of stockholders, not including	
Berdell bondholders,	806

*These notes have been paid off from the proceeds of the stock formerly held by the Commonwealth of Massachusetts, so that, at the time of making up this report (Nov. 27), the amount of notes payable is only $80,500.00, and these are not yet due.

BONDS OR UNFUNDED DEBT.

First mortgage, due Jan. 1, 1905; rate of interest,
    7 per cent.,   -   -   -   -   - $6,000,000.00
    First mortgage, 6 per cent.,   -   -   4,000,000.00
Second mortgage, issued Aug. 1st, 1882, 7 per cent.,   1,742,000.00
      · Due Aug. 1, 1902.
Interest paid to July 1, 1882.

DESCRIPTION OF ROAD.

Date when road, or different portions thereof, were
    opened for use, viz.:

      From Boston, Mass., to Putnam, Conn.,
      1855; from Putnam, Conn., to Willi-
      mantic, Conn., 1872; from Willimantic,
      Conn., to Hartford, Conn., 1849; from
      Hartford, Conn., to Bristol, Conn., 1850;
      from Bristol, Conn., to Waterbury,
      Conn., 1855; from Waterbury, Conn.,
      to Fishkill on Hudson, N. Y., 1881;
      from Providence, R. I., to Willimantic,
      Conn.; 1854; from East Thompson,
      Conn., to Southbridge, Mass., 1867;
      from Brookline, Mass., to Woonsocket,
      R. I., 1863.

Length of main line from Boston to Hopewell
    Junction,   -   -   -   -   -   214.90m.
    Same in Connecticut,   -   -   -   134.13m.
Length of main line from Hopewell Junction to
    Fishkill on the Hudson,   -   -   -   1.80m.
Length of main line from Providence to Willi-
    mantic,   -   ,   -   -   -   -   58.50m.
    Same in Connecticut,   -   -   -   32.18m.
Length of branches and names, from—
    Brookline to Woonsocket, -   -   -   33.75m.
    Islington to Dedham,   -   -   -   2.00m.
    Dedham Junction to Dedham,   -   -   .91m.
    Charles River to Ridge Hill,   -   -   1.64m.
    Dorrance St., Providence,   -   -   .82m.
    East Thompson to Southbridge,   -   -   17.50m.
      Same in Connecticut,   -   -   5.00m.

Hartford Freight Branch, -   .50m.
Length of all branches, -   57.12m.
    Same in Connecticut, -   5.50m.
Length of road (main line and branches) owned
    by the company, -   332.32m.
    Same in Connecticut, -   171.81m.
Length of double track road in main line, -   30.88m.
    Same in Connecticut, -   2.70m.
Length of sidings, or other tracks not included
    above, -   88.16m.
    Same in Connecticut, -   39.56m.
Length of track of road owned, including branches
    and sidings, in single-track miles, -   451.36m.
    Same in Connecticut, -   214.07m.
Length of track laid with steel rails (weight per
    yard, 60 and 66 lbs.), -   236.99m.
    Same in Connecticut, -   147.34m.
Weight per yard of iron rails in main line, 60 lbs.;
    in branches, 56 and 60 lbs.
Miles of track laid with steel rails during the year
    (No. of tons, total, $3,967\frac{440}{2240}$; in Connecti-
    cut, $2,419\frac{1018}{2240}$; weight per yard, 66 lbs.;
    cost, total, \$217,794.24; in Connecticut,
    \$133,069.74), -   38.25m.
    Same in Connecticut, -   23.79m.
Number of new ties put in track during the year,   138,365
    Same in Connecticut, -   72,399
Aggregate length of wooden bridges, in feet, -   21,719
    Same in Connecticut, -   13,046
Number of spans of 25 feet or over, -   132
    Same in Connecticut, -   66
Aggregate length of iron bridges, in feet, -   1,680
    Same in Connecticut, -   905
Number of spans of 25 feet or over, -   32
    Same in Connecticut, -   18
Aggregate length of stone arch bridges, in feet, -   1,052
    Same in Connecticut, -   440.5
Number of highway crossings over the track, -   89
    Same in Connecticut, -   29

Number of highway crossings under the track,   -   75
    Same in Connecticut,   -   -   -   39
Number of highway crossings at grade,   -   -   363
    Same in Connecticut,   -   -   -   224
Number of highway crossings at grade with gates,   21
    Same in Connecticut,   -   ,   -   8
Number of highway crossings at grade with flag-
    , men, -   -   -   -   -   -   35
    · Same in Connecticut,   -   -   -   10
Number of highway crossings at grade with elec-
    tric signals,   -   -   -   :   -   4
Number of railroads crossed at grade, and names
    of each (in Connecticut, 9),   -   -   -   12
     · Old Colony at Walpole; same at Medfield;
       New London Northern at Willimantic;
       N. Y., N. H. & H. at Hartford; N. H.
       & Northampton at Plainville; Norwich
       & Worcester at Webster; Norwich &
       & Worcester at Putnam; same at Plain-
       field; Naugatuck at Waterbury; Housa-
       tonic at Danbury; same at Hawleyville;
       Shepaug at Hawleyville.
Name, termini, and length of each road operated
    by this company under lease or contract,—
       Norwich & Worcester,   -   -   66.40m.
        Same in Connecticut,   -   49.07m.
       Rhode Island & Massachusetts,   -   13.60m.
       Rockville Branch, -   -   -   4.40m.
       Connecticut Central & Melrose Branch,   -   34.77m.
Length of all roads operated by this company, not
    including Norwich & Worcester,   -   -   385.09m.
    Same in Connecticut,   -   203.71m.
Number of stations on main line, -   -   -   121
    Same in Connecticut,   -   -   -   62
Number of stations on branches, -   -   -   23
    Same in Connecticut,   -   :   -   13
Number of stations on leased lines,   -   -   24
    Same in Connecticut,   -   -   -   11

EQUIPMENT.

Number of locomotives (not including switching engines),	101
Average weight of same, including tender, water, and fuel,	62 tons.
Number of switching engines,	16
Number of passenger cars,	136
Number of baggage and mail cars,	39
Number of merchandise cars,	1,494
Number of coal, gravel, and other cars,	1,932
Number of locomotives equipped with train brakes,	50
Number of cars equipped with train brakes,	175

Name of brake,—engine, Westinghouse, 45; Vacuum, 5; cars, Westinghouse, 127, Vacuum, 17; both, 43.

Number of passenger train cars with patent platform, buffer, and coupler,	175

Name of patent,—Miller, 173; Janney, 2.

FARES, FREIGHT, ETC.

Average rate per mile received from passengers on roads operated by this company, excluding season-ticket passengers,	.0229
Average rate per mile for season-ticket passengers, reckoning one round trip per day to each ticket,	.0085
Average rate of fare per mile from all passengers,	.0209
Total number of passengers carried,	4,536,082
Passenger mileage, or passengers carried one mile,	55,853,672
Miles run by passenger trains,	1,297,838
Miles run by freight trains,	926,074
Miles run by all other trains,	564,981
Total miles run,	2,788,893
Total number of tons of freight carried,	1,522,374
Freight mileage, or tons carried one mile,	103,668,653
Average rate of freight per ton per mile,	.01772
Number of men employed in operating road, including officers,	3,845

ACCIDENTS.

1881.

Oct. 15. Dave Cotton, trespasser, struck by engine and killed, at Putnam.

Oct. 24. Byron Stedman, trespasser, struck by train while lying on track and slightly injured about head, at East Windsor Hill.

Nov. 4. C. H. Watson, freight brakeman, fell under train and killed, at Putnam.

Nov. 6. John Sullivan, freight brakeman, fell under train and killed, at Hartford.

Nov. 23. Heber Miller, freight brakeman, struck by overhead bridge, and had back of head bruised, at Putnam.

Nov. 25. Chas. Butler, freight brakeman, hand bruised while coupling cars, at East Hartford.

Dec. 2. Thos. Purcell, freight brakeman, fell under train and killed, at Bolton.

Dec. 3. W. P. Harrington, freight conductor, killed by collision, at Thompson.

Dec. 3. Albert Clark, engineer, killed by collision, at Thompson.

Dec. 3. Ernest Wood, fireman, killed by collision, at Thompson.

Dec. 3. A. Russell, baggage-master, spine injured by collision, at Thompson.

Dec. 3. A. M. Decatur, express messenger, slightly bruised, in collision, at Thompson.

Dec. 3. James Tracey, car inspector, slightly bruised in collision, at Thompson.

Dec. 3. Mrs. A. H. Brown, passenger, wrist fractured and bruised in collision at Thompson.

Dec. 6. Horace Moore, freight brakeman, fell from train, dragged and badly bruised, at Putnam.

Dec. 30. Edwin Adams, freight brakeman, left arm fractured while coupling cars, at Hampton.

1882.

Jan. 3. J. O. Brien, trespasser, struck by engine, extent of injuries unknown, at Hartford.

Jan. 4. Mrs. F. Harrington, trespasser, attempting to cross

bridge, struck by step on mail car and head slightly cut, at Putnam.

Feb. 4. Thos. Ward, trespasser, run over while walking on
track and right leg cut off, at Danbury.

Feb. 6. A. C. Bradley, trespasser, struck by engine and right
side bruised, at New Britain.

Feb. 18. Geo. Bradley, freight brakeman, leg crushed while
coupling cars, at Hawleyville.

Feb. 22. J. A. Bailey, freight brakeman, fell from car and
slightly injured, at Hartford.

March 15. —— Ross, trespasser, fell under car and had one
finger cut off, at Forestville.

March 16. Mrs. H. Harvey, struck by train while crossing
track in a team and head slightly injured, at Willimantic.

March 19. C. E. Brooks, freight brakeman, arm bruised while
coupling cars, at Hartford.

March 27. S. Sweet, while attempting to cross track between
two cars, was caught and jammed to death, at Willimantic.

April 13. J. C. Terry, trespasser, truck by train and elbow
dislocated, at Hartford.

April 15. Wm. Yale, foot caught under pilot and run over
and jammed, at Waterbury.

April 15. Wm. Merritt, employee, fell off car, run over and
had arm cut off, at Sandy Hook.

April 19. C. A. Johnson, freight brakeman, thumb broken
while coupling cars at Hartford.

April 26. L. Olds, freight brakeman, fell from train and face
disfigured, at Hartford.

May 2. M. Donahue, freight brakeman, two fingers crushed
while coupling cars, at Hartford.

June 8. Wm. Willis, passenger, shoulder dislocated by jump-
ing from train in motion, at North Windham.

June 13. C. S. Brigham, freight conductor, arm pinched while
pulling pin, at Bristol.

June 14. M. McGurn, freight brakeman, foot caught between
draw heads and crushed, at Willimantic.

June 15. F. M. Burgess, yard brakeman, caught between engine and car and crushed to death while coupling cars, at Putnam.

June 18. John Griffin, freight brakeman, thrown from top of
train by brake rachet wheel slipping, hip fractured, at Southbury.

12A

June 21. B. Burns, freight conductor, hand split in coupling cars, at Hartford.

July 1. Thos. O'Brien, trespasser, struck by train and killed while walking on track, at New Britain.

July 4. Spencer Cushing, collided with side of freight train; injuries slight, if any, at Waterbury.

July 4. Richard S. Kelly, trespasser, struck by train while standing on track, face bruised and foot cut off, at Clayton's.

July 8. Peter. Keegan, freight brakeman, two fingers crushed while coupling cars, at Hazardville.

July 11. M. Burke, trespasser, struck by train while standing on track and killed, at Hartford.

July 11. P. Hughes, trespasser, struck by train while standing on track, arm and side bruised, at Hartford.

July 14. Geo. Cable, freight brakeman, thumb smashed in pulling pin, at New Britain.

July 18. J. Harrington, trespasser, found dead on track, at Willimantic.

July 23. W. H. Goodwin, fireman, leg sprained in collision, at Putnam.

July 25. John Cheney, fireman, fell from tender, and left shoulder and back sprained, at Danbury.

Aug. 4. T. Sullivan, trespasser, drunk, asleep on track, struck by engine, collar bone broken, at Waterbury.

Aug. 12. M. Sullivan, fireman, jumped from engine and was bruised in collision, at Putnam.

Aug. 12. H. Hobart, engineer, jumped from engine, sprained ankle and bruised elbow, at Putnam.

Aug. 29. E. E. Kelly, trespasser, drunk, walking on track, struck by engine and ribs broken, hurt internally, at Hartford.

Sept. 5. Chas. Miller, teamster, struck by engine and killed while attempting to cross track, at Hartford.

Sept. 5. W. F. Bean, engineer, badly bruised and hurt internally in collision, at Burnside.

Sept. 12. J. Slavin, conductor, fell from train while in motion, fracturing hip, at East Hartford.

Sept. 13. Samuel C. Hoffman, freight conductor, fell under train and killed, at Bristol.

Sept. 16. M. Mahoney, trespasser, struck by train and killed while sitting on track, at Waterbury.

Sept. 16. Chas. Randall, yard foreman, thrown from engine and hip hurt, at Hartford.

Sept. 16. John Sherry, yard brakeman, thrown from engine and ankle hurt, at Hartford.

Sept. 16. Owen Collins, yard brakeman, thrown from engine and ankle hurt, at Hartford.

Sept. 21. Horace Holt, passenger, fell between cars and was killed, at Hawleyville. (This passenger fell between the cars and lost his life through no fault of this compaay.)

Sept. 26. Jas. Connell, pass. brakeman, thrown against car seat by collision, scalp wound, at Towantic.

Sept. 27. Henry Gray, brakeman, right arm broken while coupling cars, at Putnam.

Sept. 27. P. Clancy, brakeman, fell under train while pulling a pin and instantly killed, at Willimantic.

Sept. 28. Chauncy P. Welton, merchant, struck by train while attempting to cross track in team, and killed, at Pratt's.

Sept. 28. Mrs. Chauncy P. Welton, struck by train while attempting to cross track in team, and fatally injured, at Pratt's.

STATEMENT OF ACCIDENTS RESULTING IN PERSONAL INJURY TO VARIOUS PERSONS IN CONNECTICUT FROM SEPT. 30, 1881, TO OCT. 1, 1882.

Date.	Name of Injured Person.		Classification.	Extent of Injury.	Cause.	Place.
1881.						
Oct. 15,	Dave Cotton,	B	Other,	Fatal,	Struck by engine,	Putnam.
24,	Byron Sith,	B	"	Slightly injured about head,	Lying on track,	E. Windsor Hill.
Nov. 4,	C. H. Van,	B	Employee,	Fatal,	Fell from train, run over,	Putnam.
6,	John Sullivan,	B	"		" " "	Hartford.
23,	Heber Mer,	B	"	Back of head bruised,	Struck by bridge,	Putnam.
Dec. 9,	Chas. Butler,	B	"	Hand slightly bruised,	Coupling cars,	E. Hartford.
25,	Thos. Bull,	B	"	Fatal,	Fell under train,	Bolton.
3,	W. P. Harrington,	B	"	"	Collision,	Thompson.
3,	Albert Gik,	A	"	"	"	"
3,	Ernest Wood,	A	"	Spine injured,	"	"
3,	A. Russell,	A	Other,	Slight bruises,	"	"
3,	A. M. Mur,	A	Employee,	"	"	"
3,	Jas. Tracy,	A	Passenger,	Wrist fractured and bruised,	Fell from train and dragged,	Putnam.
6,	Mrs. A. H. Brown,	B	Employee,	Badly bruised,	Coupling cars,	Hampton.
30,	Horace Moore,	B	"	Left arm fractured,		
	Edwin Adams,					
1882.						
Jan. 3,	J. O. Brien,	B	Other,	Unknown,	Struck by inge,	Hartford.
4,	Mrs. F. Harrington,	B	"	Slight cut on head,	Struck by mail car steps,	Putnam.
Feb. 4,	Thos. Ward,	B	"	Right leg cut off,	Walking on tak,	Danbury.
6,	A. C. Bdy,	B	Employee,	Bruise on right side,	Struck by engine,	New Britain.
18,	Gd. Bradley,	B	"	Leg crushed,	Coupling cars,	Hawleyville.
22,	J. Bailey,	B	"	Slightly injured,	Fell from car,	Hartford.
Mar. 15,	Ross,	B	Other,	One finger cut off,	Fell under car,	Forestville.
16,	Mrs. H. Harvey,	B	"	Scalp und,	Crossing track in wagon,	Willimantic.
19,	C. E. Brooks,	B	Employee,	Arm bruised,	Coupling cars,	Hartford.
27,	S. Sweet,	B	Other,	Fatal,	Jammed deon ars,	Willimantic.
Apr. 13,	J. C. Terry,	B	"	Elbow dislocated,		Hartford.
15,	Wm. Yale,	B	Employee,	Left foot crushed,	Caught in pilot,	Waterbury.
15,	Wm. Merritt,	B	"	Arm cut off,	Fell off car,	Sandy Hook.
19,	C. A. Johnson,	B	"	Thumb broken,	Coupling cars,	Hartford.

Date	Name	Class		Injury	Cause	Location
Apr. 26,	L. Olds,	Employee,	B	Side of face disfigured,	Fell from train,	Hartford.
May 2,	M. Donahue,	"	B	Two fingers ...,	Coupling cars, in,	No. Windham.
June 8,	Wm. Willis,	Passenger,	B	...	... fell from	Bristol.
13,	C. S. Brigham,	Employee,	B	Arm pinched,	Pulling pin,	Willimantic.
14,	M. McGurn,	"	B	Foot crushed,	... (brake dog slip'd),	Putnam.
15,	F. M. Burgess,	"	A	Fatal,	Fell from train,	Southbury.
18,	John Griffin,	"	B	Hip fractured,	Coupling cars,	Hartford.
21,	B. Burns,	"	B	Hand split,	Walking on track,	New Britain.
July 1,	Thos. O'Brien,	"	B	Fatal,	... with side of train,	Waterbury.
4,	Spencer Cushing,	Employee,	B	Unknown, if any,	Coupling,	Hazardville.
8,	Peter Keegan,	Other,	B	Two fingers ... hurt,	Standing on track,	Hartford.
11,	M. Burke,	"	B	Fatal,	"	"
14,	P. ...,	Employee,	B	Arm and side bruised,		
14,	Go ...,	"	B	... smashed,	Pulling pin,	New Britain.
18,	J. ...,	Empl yee,	A	Found ... on track,		Willimantic.
23,	W. H. ...,	"	B	Leg sprained,	Collision,	Putnam.
25,	...	Employee,	B	Left ... and back sprained,	Fell from tender,	Danbury.
Aug. 4,	T. ...,	"	B	Collar bone ...,	Asleep on track (drunk),	Waterbury.
12,	M. Sullivan,	Other,	B	Bruised,	Jumped from engine, collision,	Putnam.
12,	H. Hart,	"	B	... sprained, bruised,	"	"
29,	E. E. Kelly,	Employee,	A	Ribs broken, hurt internally,	Walking on track (drunk),	Hartford.
Sept. 5,	Chas. Miller,	"	B	Fatal,	Struck at crossing,	"
5,	W. F. Bean,	Employee,	B	Badly bruised, hurt internally,	Collision,	Burnside.
13,	Sam'l C. Hoffman,	"	B	Fatal,	Fell under train,	Bristol.
16,	M. ...,	Employee,	B	Hip hurt,	Sitting on track,	Waterbury.
16,	Chas. Randall,	"	B	... hurt,	Thrown from engine,	Hartford.
16,	John Sherry,	"	B	...,	"	"
16,	... Collins,	Passenger,	B	...,	"	"
21,	Horace Holt,	Employee,	A	Scalp ...,	Fell ... cars,	Hawleyville.
26,	Jas. Connell,	Other,	B	Fatal,	Struck at crossing,	Towantic.
28,	...cy P. Welton,	"	B	Foot ... off, face bruised,	"	Pratts.
July 4,	Mrs. C. P. Welton,	Employee,	B	Hip fractured,	Standing on track,	"
Sept. 12,	Richard S. Kelly,	"	B	Arm broken,	Fell from train,	Claytons.
27,	Henry Gray,	"	B	Fatal,	Coupling cars,	E. Hartford.
27,	P. ...,	B.			Fell under train,	Putnam.
						Willimantic.

Those marked "A" represent persons injured from causes beyond their own control.

Those marked "B" are persons injured from their own misconduct or carelessness.

OFFICERS.

President, JAMES H. WILSON, Boston, Mass.
Secretary, JAMES W. PERKINS, Boston, Mass.
Treasurer, GEORGE B. PHIPPEN, Boston, Mass.
General Manager, SAMUEL M. FELTON, JR., Boston, Mass.
Division Superintendents, C. C. F. BENT, Boston, Mass., T. W.
    KENNAN, Hartford, Conn., L. W. PALMER, Providence,
    R. I.
Auditor, ERASTUS YOUNG, Boston, Mass.
General Ticket Agent, A. C. KENDALL, Boston, Mass.
General Freight Agent, G. H. WILLIAMS, Boston, Mass.

BOARD OF DIRECTORS.

JAMES H. WILSON, Boston, Mass.
JESSE METCALF, Providence, R. I.
LEGRAND B. CANNON, New York.
SIDNEY DILLON, New York.
EUSTACE C. FITZ, Boston, Mass.
CYRUS W. FIELD, New York.
JONAS H. FRENCH, Boston, Mass.
JAY GOULD, New York.
R. SUYDAM GRANT, New York.
WILLIAM T. HART, Boston, Mass.
HENRY L. HIGGINSON, Boston, Mass.
HUGH J. JEWETT, New York.
FREDERICK J. KINGSBURY, Waterbury, Conn.
GEO. B. ROBERTS, Philadelphia, Pa.
RUSSEL SAGE, New York.

    Attest,   J. H. WILSON, *President.*
    Attest,   GEO. B. PHIPPEN, *Treasurer.*

STATE OF MASSACHUSETTS, }
  COUNTY OF SUFFOLK.   }   BOSTON, Nov. 29, 1882.

Then personally appeared James H. Wilson, President, and Geo. B. Phippen, Treasurer, of the New York & New England Railroad Company, and severally made solemn oath that they verily believed the foregoing return by them subscribed to be true and correct. Before me,

JAMES W. PERKINS,
Notary Public.

PROPER ADDRESS OF THIS COMPANY.

NEW YORK & NEW ENGLAND RAILROAD COMPANY,
Boston,
Mass.

NEW YORK, NEW HAVEN & HARTFORD RAIL. ROAD.

Return of the New York, New Haven & Hartford Railroad Company, for the year ending September 30, 1882.

EARNINGS AND EXPENSES.

STATEMENT OF GROSS EARNINGS.

From passenger transportation,	$3,393,513.86
From freight transportation,	2,065,855.52
From United States mails,	144,256.48
From express,	234,867.93
From rents,	69,481.60
From extra baggage,	18,135.71
From interest,	11,696.54
Total gross earnings,	$5,937,807.64

STATEMENT OF OPERATING EXPENSES.

For repairs of road-bed and track,		$529,502.01
For repairs of bridges,		47,135.44
For repairs of fences,		12,879.48
For repairs of buildings and fixtures,		229,528.18
For repairs of locomotives,		144,107.34
For repairs of cars,		392,228.50
For repairs of machinery and tools,		32,250.21
For salaries and labor, not included above,		1,088,023.65
For fuel for locomotives and cars,—		
75,267 tons of coal,	$383,251.75	
922 cords wood,	5,091.61	388,343.36
For fuel for stations and shops,—		
2,103 tons of coal,		9,083.98
For oil and waste,		52,976.63

For damages, losses, and gratuities,—

to persons,	$20,263.72	
to property,	9,001.79	29,265.51

For insurance, - - - - -	2,777.75
For rent of Shore Line Railway, - - -	100,000.00

The payments to the New York & Harlem Railroad Company for its share of receipts (which are not included in gross earnings of this company) was $291,503.67. The amount paid for interest on Harlem River & Portchester Railroad bonds, as rental, and charged in interest account, was $170,-000. The amount paid the Boston & New York Air Line Railroad, as per contract, over and above the earnings of that company, was $145,241.05. This is deducted from the gross earnings of this company, being reported by the Boston & New York Air Line Railroad Company to the Commissioners.

For freight car service, - - - -	75,810.77
For water stations, - - - -	19,472.26
For station labor and expenses, - - -	285,146.91
For office expenses, - - - -	4,821.08
For contingent expenses, - - -	22,022.65
For advertising expenses,	4,086.79
For printing and stationery, - - -	20,896.13
For rent of Grand Central depot and grounds connected therewith, - - - -	148,281.63
For rent of other depots and lands, - -	23,945.09
For legal expenses, - - - -	31,745.07
For barge expenses, -	38,303.67
For dock expenses, - - - -	30,097.10
For horse haulage,	32,022.25
For train supplies, - -	8,925.53
Total operating expenses, - - -	$3,803,678.97
Net earnings, - - -	$2,134,128.67

TOTAL RECEIPTS AND EXPENDITURES.

STATEMENT OF RECEIPTS FROM ALL SOURCES.

Cash on hand at date of last report, - -	$759,675.85
Bills and accounts receivable at date of last report,	1,531,077.43
From gross earnings, as stated, - - -	5,937,807.64
From increase in accounts payable, - -	429,681.87
From decrease in materials, - - -	25,728.51
Total, - - - - - -	$8,683,971.30

STATEMENT OF TOTAL EXPENDITURES.

For operating expenses, as stated, - -		$3,803,678.97
For taxes, - - - - -		264,440.54
For interest, - - - -		170,000.00
For dividends (number, 2; rate per cent 5 per cent. each), - - - -		1,550,000.00
Dates when paid, Jan. 2d and July 1st, 1882.		
For sinking fund, as follows:		
Note of New Canaan Railroad,	$6,045.43	
Notes of White Mountain R.R.,	6,667.00	
$160,000 bonds New Haven & Derby Railroad, - -	105,874.03	
4,994 shares Vermont Valley Railroad stock, - -	242,320.00	
375 shares New England Transfer Co. stock, - -	37,500.00	
12,298 shares New Haven & Northampton Co. stock, -	737,880.00	1,136,286.46
For 6,730 shares Hartford & Connecticut Valley R. R. stock, -	$841,250.00	
$518,000 certificates of indebtedness of H. & C. V. R. R. Co., 40 per cent. paid in, - - -	217,560.00	
$18,000 bonds of Connecticut Valley R. R. Co., - - -	18,000.00	1,076,810.00
Bills and accounts receivable this date, - -		461,758.11
Cash on hand to balance, - - - -		220,997.22
Total, - - - - -		$8,683,971.30

Spécial account of appropriations made in 1881:

Appropriated for new lands and bridges, - - - -		$200,000.00
Paid for Cazanova land, - - -	$104,894.87	
Paid for South Norwalk land, - - -	530.00	
Paid for New Haven land, - - . -	21,530.00	
Paid for Wallingford land, - - -	1,750.00	
Paid for Meriden land, - - - -	14,247.50	
Paid for Conn. River and Westbrook bridges, -	45,797.63	
Paid for Thames River bridge, - - -	11,250.00	200,000.00
Appropriated for new equipment, - - - -		$100,000.00
Paid for three new locomotives, - . -	$43,000.00	
Paid for new passenger and drawing-room cars, -	57,000.00	100,000.00

GENERAL BALANCE-SHEET.

Assets.

Construction, - - - - -	$12,889,584.40
Equipment, . . - - -	2,154,454.71
Real estate, - - - - -	560,274.67
Docks and wharves, - - , - -	128,688.31
Sinking fund, - - . - -	1,136,286.46
Materials and supplies on hand, - - -	347,802.41
Due from agents, - - - - -	187,518.20
Due from connecting roads, - - -	164,670.07
Advances to Harlem River & Portchester R. R., -	15,809.84
Stock of Harlem River & Portchester R. R., -	42,160.00
Stock of New York Transfer Company, - -	1,600.00
Stock, etc, of Hartford & Conn. Valley Railroad and Conn. Valley Railroad, - - -	1,076,810.00
Bills receivable, - - - - -	50,000.00
Cash, - - - - - -	220,997.22
Total, -. - - -	$18,976,656.29

Liabilities.

Capital stock, - - . - -	$15,500,000.00
Bills payable, - - - - -	514,762.40
Accounts payable, - - - -.	579,584.45
Interest unpaid, - - \ - .	13,333.33
Contingent account, - - - -	189,018.09
Profit and loss, - - - - -	2,179,958.02
Total, - - -	$18,976,656.29

PRESENT OR CONTINGENT LIABILITIES, NOT INCLUDED IN BALANCE-SHEET.

Bonds guaranteed by this company, issued by
    Harlem River and Portchester R. R. Co., - 3,000,000.00

GENERAL INFORMATION.

CAPITAL STOCK.

Capital stock authorized by charter,   -   - $15,500,000.00
Capital stock authorized by vote of company, - 15,500,000.00
Capital stock issued, viz.:
    155,000 full shares of $100 each, -   - 15,500,000.00
Stock issued for stock of New York & New
    Haven R. R. Co. and Hartford & New
    Haven R. R. Co,   :   -   -   - 15,500,000.00
Amount of stock held in Connecticut,   -   - 6,950,700.00
Number of stockholders residing in Connecticut,   1,938
Whole number of stockholders, -   -   -   3,464

BONDS OR FUNDED DEBT.

Bonds issued by Harlem River & Port Chester Railroad Co ,
    as follows:

First mortgage, due 1903, rate of int., 6 per cent., $1,000,000.00
First mortgage, due 1903, rate of int., 7 per cent.,   1,000,000.00
Second mortgage, due 1911, rate of int., 4 per cent.,   1,000,000.00
    Interest paid to October 1, 1882.
    Guaranteed principal and interest by this company.

DESCRIPTION OF ROAD.

Date when road, or different portions thereof, were
    opened for use, viz.:
        From New Haven to Hartford, Dec. 14,
        1839; Hartford to Springfield, Dec. 19,
        1844; New York to New Haven, Dec.
        27, 1848; Middletown R. R., March, 1850;
        New Britain R. R., January, 1865; Suf-
        field Branch, Nov., 1870; Middletown
        & New Britain railroads were merged
        with the Hartford & New Haven R. R.
        Aug, 19, 1866, and the whole road was

opened Oct. 1, 1872, as the New York,
New Haven & Hartford R. R.; Shore
Line Railway included Oct. 1, 1881.

Length of main line from Harlem Junction, N. Y., to Springfield, Mass., and from New Haven to New London, Conn.,	174.17m.
Same in Connecticut,	154.25m.
Length of branches and names,—	
From Berlin to New Britain,	3.00m.
From Berlin to Middletown,	10.00m.
From Windsor Locks to Suffield,	4.50m.
Length of all branches,—all in Conn.,	17.50m.
Length of road (main line and branches) owned by the company,	140.70m.
Same in Connecticut,	120.78m.
Length of double-track road in main line,	123.20m.
Same in Connecticut,	103.28m.
Length of sidings, or other tracks not included above,	77.87m.
Same in Connecticut,	69.38m.
Length of track of road, including branches and sidings, in single-track miles,	392.84m.
Same in Connecticut,	344.41m.
Length of track laid with steel rails (weight per yard, 60 lbs.),	308.21m.
Same in Connecticut,	268.41m.
Miles of track laid with steel rails during the year (No. of tons, 1,022.8; weight per yard, 60 lbs.; cost, $55),	9.32m.
Same in Connecticut,	5.52m.
Number of new ties put in track during the year (cost, $88,782.32),	201,778
Same in Connecticut,	179,278
Aggregate length of wooden bridges, in feet,	17,844
Same in Connecticut,	17,624
Number of spans of 25 feet or over,	59
Same in Connecticut,	54
Aggregate length of iron bridges, in feet,	4,434
Same in Connecticut,	4,378

Number of spans of 25 feet or over, - -	42
Same in Connecticut, - - -	41
Aggregate length of stone arch bridges, in feet,	2,121
Same in Connecticut, - - -	1,655
Number of highway crossings over the track, -	52
Same in Connecticut, - - -	44
Number of highway crossings under the track,	29
Same in Connecticut, - - -	22
Number of highway crossings at grade, - -	294
Same in Connecticut, - - -	267
Number of highway crossings at grade with gates,	34
Same in Connecticut, - - -	32
Number of highway crossings at grade with flag- men, - - - - - -	8
Same in Connecticut, - - -	5
Number of railroads crossed at grade, all in Conn., - - - - -	5
New Canaan R. R., Housatonic R. R., Shore Line Railway, New York & New Eng- land R. R., Hartford & Conn. Valley R. R.,	
Name, termini, and length of each road operated by this company under lease or contract,— Shore Line Railway, New Haven to New London, Conn.,—all in Conn., - -	50.97m.
Harlem River & Port Chester R. R., Har- lem River to Port Chester, N. Y., -	11.80m.
Length of all roads operated by this company,	203.47m.
Same in Connecticut, - - -	171.75m.
Number of stations on main line, - - -	49
Same in Connecticut, - - -	36
Number of stations on branches,—all in Conn., -	10
Number of stations on leased lines, - -	31
Same in Connecticut, - - -	20

EQUIPMENT.

Number of locomotives (not including switching engines) - - - - -	91
Average weight of same, including tender, water, and fuel, - - - - -	$54\frac{1}{2}$ tons.

Number of switching engines, - - -	14
Number of passenger cars, • - -	228
Number of baggage and mail cars, - -	82
Number of merchandise cars, - - -	1,818
Number of coal, gravel, and other cars, , - -	335
Number of locomotives equipped with train brakes,	64
Number of cars equipped with train brakes, -	309
Name of brake, - - - - -	Westinghouse.
Number of passenger train cars with patent platform, buffer, and coupler, - - -	309
Name of patent, - - - -	Miller—Janney, 2.

FARES, FREIGHT, ETC.

Average rate per mile received from passengers on roads operated by this company, excluding season-ticket passengers, - - -	.0231
Average rate per mile for season-ticket passengers, reckoning one round trip per day to each ticket, - - - -	.00586
Average rate of fare per mile from all passengers,	.0191
Total number of passengers carried, - -	6,397,385
Passenger mileage, or passengers carried one mile,	185,261,407
Miles run by passenger trains, - - -	2,017,635
Miles run by freight trains, - - -	1,559,368
Miles run by all other trains, - - -	120,208
Total miles run, - - - - -	3,697,211
Total number of tons of freight carried, - -	1,908,322
Freight mileage, or tons carried one mile, -	117,459,231
Average rate of freight per ton per mile, -	.0198
Number of men employed in operating road, including officers, - - - -	3014

ACCIDENTS.

STATEMENT OF EACH ACCIDENT IN DETAIL.

1881.

Oct. 10. Michael Balfe, while walking on the track at Hartford, was struck and killed by the 5.35 P. M. train from New Haven.

Oct. 11.   John Ryan, while intoxicated, attempted to board the 6 P. M. freight train, when leaving New Haven depot.   He fell under the wheels and was severely injured.

Oct. 11.   Thos. Ganey, brakeman on Middletown Branch, fell from top of car and was killed.

Oct. 12.   Wm. Arnold, brakeman, had his shoulder injured while coupling cars at Berlin.

Oct. 14.   George Kelley, laborer on gravel train, had his leg crushed at Meriden.

Oct. 15.   Mr. Huntley was struck and fatally injured while driving over the track, near East Lyme, by the 3.38 P. M. train from New London.

Oct. 19.   Howard Bussey, a water boy on New Haven & Northampton Railroad, crossed the track at New Haven in front of the 3 P. M. train from New York, and had his foot badly crushed.

Oct. 20.   An unknown man was struck, near Bridgeport, by the 4.12 P. M. train from New Haven; not seriously injured.

Oct. 20.   Walter Williams, brakeman on the 5.55 A. M. extra freight train from Harlem River, was struck by bridge at Southport, but not seriously injured.

Oct. 21.   Charles White, brakeman, was caught between cars while coupling, at New Britain, and slightly injured.

Oct. 21.   George Reardon, a boy, was struck and severely injured, near the Hartford Tunnel, by the 3.15 P. M. train from New Haven.

Oct. 22.   An unknown man was struck and killed, near Westport, by the 8 P. M. train from New York.

Oct. 24.   M. S. Perry, conductor, was struck by overhead bridge, on Berlin Grade, and was severely bruised.

Oct. 28.   N. Hoyt was slightly injured at Stamford, while attempting to save his horse, which was struck by two freight cars run off the end of turnout.

Oct. 31.   J. Hynes was injured while coupling cars of the 3.15 A. M. freight train from New Haven, at South Norwalk station.

Nov. 8.   George W. Chaffee, brakeman on switch train at Hartford, was caught between cars, bruising his head and shoulders.

Nov. 8.   Charles Post, watchman at Berlin, while assisting in switching train, fell from car, breaking two ribs.

Nov. 8.   George Weed was struck and killed at Stamford station by the 4 P. M. train from New York.

Nov. 12. Philip Sullivan, while walking on the track near South Norwalk, was struck and killed by the 8 P. M. train from New York.

Nov. 17. F. O. Meunsell, brakeman at branch, Hartford, was slightly injured coupling.

Nov. 18. George H. Hills, brakeman on branch, Hartford, fell from car, breaking his ankle.

Nov. 21. Joseph Fanning, while driving over track, Belle Dock branch, New Haven, was struck by switch engine and slightly injured.

Nov. 25. C. B. Collins, brakeman on the 8.55 A. M. freight train from New Haven, jumped from train at Berlin, spraining his ankle.

Nov. 30. Frank Dyer, brakeman on the 5 A. M. freight train from New Haven, stepped from caboose on North Haven bridge, and, falling through, was slightly bruised.

Dec. 5. Charles D. Lee, brakeman, stepped in front of switch engine, at Bridge street crossing, New Haven, and was killed.

Dec. 8. F. D. Strong, brakeman on the 8.55 A. M. freight train from New Haven, was caught between cars at Berlin, and slightly injured.

Dec. 8. M. Reed, brakeman switch gang, New Britain, severely bruised in coupling.

Dec. 9. C. B. Collins, brakeman on 5.10 P. M. freight train from Springfield, fell from train near Hayden's, and severely bruised his head.

Dec. 14. Thomas Mathews, brakeman on 4 P. M. extra freight train from Harlem River, was struck by bridge, near Stamford, and badly cut about the face.

Dec. 21. T. Nottingham, brakeman, was slightly injured in the finger while coupling, on Hartford branch.

Dec. 23. A man, supposed to be William Coleman, boarded the 1 P. M. train from New York, at Bridgeport station. Not intending to take this train, he jumped off, and, falling under train, was killed.

Dec. 24. An unknown man was struck and killed at Westport by the 9.30 P. M. train from New York.

Dec. 31. James Bracken, laborer on gravel train, while crossing the track ahead of train, near Windsor Locks, was struck and killed by the 11.35 A. M. train from Springfield.

14A

1882.

Jan. 4. —— Reilly, while driving over the track at East Bridgeport, was slightly injured by the 6.30 A. M. train from New Haven.

Jan. 5. J. R. Fulton, while driving over the track at Bridgeport, was slightly injured by the 4.12 P. M. train from New Haven.

Jan. 11. C. H. Barton, brakeman switch gang on Hartford branch, was caught between cars and slightly injured.

Jan. 11. J. H. McIntosh, brakeman on extra freight, south bound, was caught while coupling and slightly injured.

Jan. 12. John Devine, in attempting to get on the 7.45 P. M. train from New Haven, as it was leaving Stamford station, fell under the rear car, receiving fatal injuries.

Jan. 18. Richard Barry, brakeman, while coupling at brick yard, near Quinnipiac, was severely injured in the hand.

Jan. 20. Michael Zahule, while walking on the track, was struck and killed by the 1.21 P. M. train from New Haven, when near Charter Oak Park, Hartford.

Feb. 1. An unknown man, lying on the track between Stratford and Bridgeport, was struck by the 4.12 P. M. train from New Haven, receiving fatal injuries.

Feb. 3. E. W. Glover, brakeman on the 10.25 P. M. train from Hartford, was killed near Olive street bridge, New Haven. He is supposed to have fallen from the train.

Feb. 9. E. Tuttle, brakeman in Belle Dock yard, had arm broken while coupling.

Feb. 9. George Reynolds, brakeman on 6 P. M. freight train from New Haven, fell from train between Greenwich and Portchester, and was dead when found.

Feb. 16. John Buckley was found dead on the track between Stony Creek and Leete's Island, supposed to have been run over by one of the night trains.

Feb. 17. A man, thought to be Timothy O'Neil, was found lying near the track, at Housatonic River bridge, severely injured.

Feb. 17. James Coffay was caught between two cars of the 9.30 P. M. freight train from New Haven, at Bridgeport, and severely injured.

Feb. 25. G. W. Hazard, brakeman on the 9.55 A. M. freight from New Haven, had a finger crushed at Bridgeport.

Feb. 28. Thomas Benjamin Cartwright, while driving over the track at Woodmont, was slightly injured by the 11 A. M. freight train from Harlem River.

March 3. Henry McShene, one of the night switch gang at New Haven, was knocked from top of car, at Fair street bridge, and killed.

March 6. E. Flaherty, brakeman at Belle Dock, New Haven, attempted to board switch engine, was knocked down and slightly injured.

March 14. Peter Lynch, a boy, attempted to get on a car of the 11 A. M. freight train from Harlem River, when at South Norwalk station. He slipped, and his foot was severely injured.

March 15. Carl Gruttka jumped from the 3.15 P. M. train from New Haven, when near Berlin, and was severely injured.

March 17. Park Wilbur jumped from the 6 35 P. M. train from Springfield, near Hartford station, and was slightly injured.

March 21. J. F. Cassidy, switchman at Berlin, was caught between cars while coupling and killed.

March 21. Nehemiah Bouton, while driving over the track at Bridgeport, was struck by the 8 P. M. train from New York and severely injured.

March 27. F. D. Strong, brakeman on the 5.10 P. M. freight train from Springfield, when passing Berlin looked out from car, and, striking water-pipe, was knocked off and severely injured.

April 6. J. Bartley, brakeman, was slightly injured at Stamford station, while staking a car.

April 7. Garrett Dalton, brakeman on the 5 A. M. freight train from New Haven, had his arm severely injured while coupling at Meriden.

April 8. William Warner, while lying on the track near Berlin, was struck and killed by the 10.25 P. M. train from Hartford. He was thought to have been intoxicated at the time.

April 14. M. B. Fitch, conductor switch gang on branch, Hartford, lost one finger while coupling.

April 22. C. S. Coles, conductor on 12.30 P. M. train from Springfield, was knocked from train at Wallingford by whistling post and slightly injured.

April 28. Larry O'Neil, brakeman on 12.30 P. M. train from Springfield, fell from car at Meriden while switching, and was fatally injured.

April 30. L. L. Jackson, telegraph operator at Hartford, jumped from engine passing through Hartford depot, and sprained his wrist.

May 1. Peter Hammond, while driving across the track at New Haven, was struck and slightly injured by the 5.40 P. M. train from New York.

May 1. An unknown man jumped from the 8.12 P. M. train from New Haven, at North Haven, and received slight bruises.

May 3. Chris. Miller, trackman, was killed, and two others (names unknown) injured, near Glenbrook station. While standing on down track to avoid east-bound freight train, they were struck by the 8.30 A. M. train from New Haven. .

May 9. S. Elder, a tramp, while walking on the track near Kelsey's crossing, was struck by the 5.35 P. M. train from New Haven, and injured in the side and shoulder.

May 18. Patrick Mulvihill, a boy, playing about the cars near Morgan street, Hartford, was run over and fatally injured.

May 23. An unknown man was struck and killed between Fairfield and Bridgeport by the 8.30 A. M. train from New Haven.

June 4. Samuel Newberry, while sitting by side of track near branch switch, Hartford, was struck and fatally injured by the 2.07 A. M. train from Springfield.

June 7. Arthur Adams, while intoxicated, jumped from the 1.42 P. M. train from Springfield, near Thompsonville, and was slightly injured.

June 10. ——— Payne, brakeman on the 7.05 P. M. freight train from New York, had his arm crushed while coupling at at Bridgeport.

June 13. F. Parsons, brakeman on the 10.15 A. M. freight train from New Haven, lost three fingers while coupling at Milford.

June 17. Michael Doyle, a passenger on the 4.30 P. M. express from New York, had his arm out of the window. It was struck by a loose door of a car on a passing freight train and broken.

June 20. Oscar Sope, a boy, jumped or fell from the 3 P. M. train from Springfield, when near Charter Oak Park, and had one leg cut off.

June 27. G. C. Fiske, conductor switch gang at Hartford, crushed one finger unloading frogs.

June 27. Daniel Nottingham, brakeman at Belle Dock, was slightly injured coupling.

July 4. Charles Sheridan, while intoxicated, swung himself

out from a car of the 9.25 A. M. train from Springfield, when at
Windsor Locks, was struck by switch gate, and falling off, broke
one leg.

July 6.   William Ahern, a passenger on the 1.42 P. M. train
from Springfield, stepped out on platform, when three miles north
of Meriden, and, falling off, was slightly injured.

July 13.   Thomas Nodine, while driving across the track, one
mile east of Stamford, was struck and killed by the 5.45 P. M.
train from New York.

July 13.   T. Stafford was found near Laurel street bridge,
Hartford, with one foot crushed.   He was intoxicated, and is
thought to have fallen or jumped from the 9.55 P. M. freight train
from New Haven.

July 17.   Palmer Crocker, brakeman on 9.30 P. M. extra freight
train from New Haven, was killed by striking drop signal at East
Norwalk.

July 20.   John Tobin, a boy, while lying by the side of track,
near Branford station, was struck and slightly injured by delayed
night freight train.

July 22.   John McGrath, section man, while working on track
at Belle Dock, New Haven, was struck and killed by switch engine.

July 30.   F. Dwyer, a brakeman on extra freight train, south
bound, slipped from car at Berlin and was slightly injured.

Aug. 8.   An unknown man, lying on the track, near South
Norwalk, was struck and killed by the 11.50 P. M. train from
Harlem River.

Aug. 11.   James T. Maloney, brakeman on the 1.30 A. M. freight
train from New Haven, fell from train between Cos-Cob and
Greenwich, and was severely injured.

Aug. 11.   Joseph Harvey, while walking on the track intoxicated, was struck by the switch engine at New London and killed.

Aug. 21.   Michael Reynolds, a passenger on the 6.35 A. M.
train from Stamford, jumped or fell from train at New Haven,
and was fatally injured.

Aug. 22.   Mary McGourn stepped in front of engine, at New
Britain, and was fatally injured.

Aug. 29.   D. Maher, while walking on the track near Yales-
ville, was fatally injured by the 11.30 P. M. freight train from
Hartford.

Aug. 31.   Julian Smith, brakeman on the 11.16 A. M. freight train from Harlem River, was struck by a cross-piece of the Bridgeport draw and severely injured.

Sep. 1. M. Glaughlin, brakeman on the 9.30 P. M. freight train from New Haven, lost one finger coupling cars at Bridgeport.

Sep. 4. Henry O'Leary, a boy, while walking on the track near Windsor Locks, was struck and killed by the 6.10 P. M. train from Hartford.

Sep. 11. W. G. Jenner, brakeman on the 9.55 P. M. freight train from New Haven, fell from train at Hartford, and was severely injured.

Sep. 11. J. O'Hara. brakeman on switch gang at Meriden, fell from car, and was slightly injured.

Sep. 11. An unknown man was killed between Westport and South Norwalk by the 10.25 P. M. freight train from New Haven.

Sep. 11. Oscar Van Nostrand, employee on the 11.15 A. M. extra freight train from New Haven, was struck by West Haven bridge and killed.

Sep. 15. Charles Moseley stepped in front of the 11 A. M. express from New York, when between Milford and Woodmont, and was severely injured.

Sep. 15. Silas Baldwin, brakeman on the 10:44 A. M. extra freight trains from Harlem River, had foot crushed while coupling at New Haven.

Sep. 16. Thomas Doyle was found dead in the Hartford tunnel. He was seen about the station intoxicated, and was supposed to have been run over by the 9.55 P. M. train from New Haven.

Sep. 23. A. Charist, while driving over track at Meriden, was slightly injured by the 6.54 P. M. train from Springfield.

OFFICERS.

President, GEORGE H. WATROUS, New Haven, Conn.
Vice-President, E. M. REED, New Haven, Conn.
2d Vice-President, CHARLES P. CLARK, New York, N. Y.
Secretary, E. I. SANFORD, New Haven, Conn.
Treasurer, W. L. SQUIRE, New York, N. Y.
Superintendent N. Y. Div., J. T. MOODY, New York, N. Y.
Superintendent Hartford Div., C. S. DAVIDSON, Hartford, Conn.
Superintendent Shore Line Div., WM. H. STEVENSON, New Haven, Conn.

Auditor, E. C. ROBINSON, New York, N. Y.
General Ticket Agent, C. F. HEMPSTEAD, New York, N. Y.
General Freight Agent, CHAS. ROCKWELL, New Haven, Conn.

BOARD OF DIRECTORS.

GEORGE H. WATROUS, New Haven, Conn.
E. M. REED, New Haven, Conn.
W. D. BISHOP, Bridgeport, Conn.
WILSON G. HUNT, New York, N. Y.
GEORGE N. MILLER, New York, N. Y.
CHESTER W. CHAPIN, Springfield, Mass.
A. R. VAN NEST, New York, N. Y.
HENRY C. ROBINSON, Hartford, Conn.
E. H. TROWBRIDGE, New Haven, Conn.
NATHANIEL WHEELER, Bridgeport, Conn.
C. M. POND, Hartford, Conn.
AUGUSTUS SCHELL, New York, N. Y.
W. H. VANDERBILT, New York, N. Y.

Attest,   GEO. H. WATROUS, *President.*
Attest,   WM. L. SQUIRE, *Treasurer.*

STATE OF NEW YORK, } .Nov. 15, 1882.
COUNTY OF NEW YORK, }

Then personally appeared Geo. H. Watrous, President, and Wm. L. Squire, Treasurer, of the New York, New Haven & Hartford Railroad Company, and severally made solemn oath that they verily believed the foregoing return by them subscribed to be true and correct.

Before me,

WM. E. BARNETT,
Notary Public.

PROPER ADDRESS OF THE COMPANY.

NEW YORK, NEW HAVEN & HARTFORD RAILROAD COMPANY,

GRAND CENTRAL DEPOT,
4th Ave. and 42d St.,
New York, N. Y.

NEW YORK, PROVIDENCE & BOSTON RAILROAD.

Return of the New York, Providence & Boston Railroad Company, for the year ending September 30, 1882.

EARNINGS AND EXPENSES.

STATEMENT OF GROSS EARNINGS.

From passenger transportation,	$562,000.53
From freight transportation,	432,808.46
From United States mails,	19,058.13
From express,	28,053.68
From rents,	7,583.60
From ferry saloon,	600.00
From hoisting engine,	1,188.63
From harbor junction wharfage,	3,146.78
From Pawtuxet Valley Railroad,	11,210.50
Total gross earnings,	**$1,065,650.31**

STATEMENT OF OPERATING EXPENSES.

For repairs of road-bed and track,	$115,896.09
For repairs of bridges,	14,146.52
For repairs of fences,	2,937.31
For repairs of buildings and fixtures,	11,561.95
For repairs of locomotives,	13,615.36
For repairs of cars,	32,226.94
For repairs of machinery and tools,	3,219.29
For salaries and labor not included above,	216,316.39
For fuel for locomotives and cars:	
14,950 tons of coal,	70,354.21
For fuel for stations and shops:	
475 tons of coal,	2,171.40
For oil and waste,	7,742.49

For damages to property, - - -	1,845.65
For insurance, - - - - -	2,117.18
For illuminating, - - - - -	4,579.39
For stationery and printing, - - -	7,130.73
For advertising, - - - - -	12,544.55
For general expenses, - - - -	9,579.56
Legal services, - - - - -	4,322.00
For car service, - - - - -	644.25
For ferry, - - - - -	28,424.36
Total operating expenses, - - -	$561,375.62
Net earnings, - - - -	$504,274.69

TOTAL RECEIPTS AND EXPENDITURES.

STATEMENT OF RECEIPTS FROM ALL SOURCES.

Cash on hand at date of last report, - -	$158,332.36
Bills and accounts receivable at date of last report,	29,081.68
From gross earnings as stated, - - -	1,065,650.31
Total, - - - - -	$1,253,064.35

STATEMENT OF TOTAL EXPENDITURES.

For operating expenses, as stated, - -	$561,375.62
For taxes, - - - - -	28,943.96
For interest, balance of account, - - -	78,402.18
For dividends (number 4, rate per cent., 2 each), -	240,000.00
Paid Nov. 1st, Feb. 1st, May 1st, Aug. 1st.	
For harbor junction wharf, - - -	1,112.09
For Pintsch gas-works, - - - -	14,887.71
For new engines, Nos. 30, 31, 32, - -	35,004.95
For new parlor cars, - - - -	12,960.00
For new passenger cars, - - - -	15,823.71
For new baggage cars, - - - -	2,510.80
For new freight cars, - - - -	10,340.19
For new depots, - - - - -	2,836.32
For car and engine house, etc., at Auburn, -	16,392.68
For real estate at Westerly, - - -	1,000.00
For dredging, - - - - -	3,382.68

15A

Bills and accounts receivable this date, - -	62,442.64
Cash on hand to balance, - - - -	165,648.82
Total, - - - - -	$1,253,064.35

GENERAL BALANCE-SHEET.

Assets.

Cost of road and equipment, - - -	$3,065,309.21
Real estate at Groton, - - - - -	10,000.00
Extension road, New London to Stonington, -	440,686.34
Ferry-boats "Thames River" and "Groton," -	157,140.01
Warwick branch, Auburn to Buttonwood, -	67,454,38
Harbor junction wharf, - - - -	64,791.16
Pintsch gas-works, at Stonington, -	14,887.71
Stock in Providence & Stonington S. S. Co., -	804,900.00
Stock in Narragansett Pier R. R., -	15,000.00
Stock in Wood River Branch R. R., -	20,000.00
Materials and supplies on hand, - -	136,359.14
Accounts receivable, - - -	62,442.64
Cash on hand, - - - -	165,648.82
Total, - - - - -	$5,024,619.41

Liabilities.

Capital stock, - - - - -	$3,000,000.00
Bonds due 1899, secured by mortgage between Providence and Stonington, - - -	1,000,000.00
Bonds due 1901, secured by mortgage between Stonington and New London, - -	300,000.00
Profit and loss, - - - - -	724,619.41
Total, - - - - -	$5,024,619.41

PRESENT OR CONTINGENT LIABILITIES, NOT INCLUDED IN BALANCE-SHEET.

Bonds guaranteed by this Company, or a lien on its road,—Pawtuxet Valley Railroad bonds,	$60,000.00

GENERAL INFORMATION.

CAPITAL STOCK.

Capital stock authorized by charter, - -	$4,000,000.00
Capital stock authorized by vote of Company, -	4,000,000.00
Capital stock issued, viz.:	
30,000 full shares of $100 each, - -	3,000,000.00
Stock issued for cash, - - - -	3,000,000.00
Amount of stock held in Connecticut, 655 shares,	65,500.00
Number of stockholders residing in Connecticut,	18
Whole number of stockholders, - - -	607

BONDS OR UNFUNDED DEBT.

First mortgage, due 1899; rate of interest, 7 per cent.; interest paid to July 1, 1882: mortgage on road between Providence and Stonington, $1,000,000.00

First mortgage on road between Stonington and New London, due 1901: rate, 4 per cent.; interest paid to April 1, 1882,   -   -   300,000.00

Bonds issued by Pawtuxet Valley R. R. Co., guaranteed by this Company, secured by first mortgage on their road between Pontiac and River Point, and second mortgage on their road between River Point and Hope, R. I.; due 1900; rate, 6 per cent.; interest paid to April 1, 1882,   -   -   -   -   -   60,000.00

DESCRIPTION OF ROAD.

Date when road, or different portions thereof, were opened for use, viz :

From Stonington, Conn., to Providence, R. I., November 10, 1837. From Stonington, Conn., to Groton, with ferry to New London, December 30, 1858.

Length of main line from Groton to Providence,	62.500m.
Same in Connecticut, - - -	17.000m.
Length of branches from Auburn to Buttonwood (Warwick branch), - - - -	9.875m.
Length of all branches, - -	9.875m.

Length of road (main line and branch) owned
    by the Company,   -   -   -   -   72.375m.
            Same in Connecticut,   -   -   -   17.000m.
Length of double track road (in main line),   -   50.000m.
            Same in Connecticut,   -   -   -   5.500m.
Length of sidings, or other tracks, not included
    above,   -   -   -   -   -   11.000m.
            Same in Connecticut,   -   -   -   5.000m.
Length of track of road, including branch and
    sidings, in single track miles,   -   -   -   133.375m.
            Same in Connecticut,   -   -   -   27.500m.
Length of track laid with steel rails (weight per
    yard, 60 lbs.),   -   -   -   95.750m.
            Same in Connecticut,   -   -   -   18.000m.
Weight per yard of iron rails in main line, 60 lbs.;
    in branches, 60 lbs.
Miles of track laid with steel rails during the year
    (No. of tons, 500; weight per yard, 60 lbs.;
    cost, $46.25),   -   -   -   -   5.750m.
            Same in Connecticut,   -   -   -   0.750m.
Number of new ties put in track during the year
    (cost $26,747.70),   -   -   -   -   65,442
            Same in Connecticut,   -   -   -   12,738
Aggregate length of wooden bridges, in feet,   -   3,014
            Same in Connecticut,   -   -   -   1,435
Number of spans of 25 feet or over,   -   -   26
            Same in Connecticut,   -   -   -   11
Aggregate length of stone arch bridges, in feet,   -   350
Number of highway crossings over the track,   -   22
            Same in Connecticut,   -   -   -   2
Number of highway crossings under the track,   -   8
            Same in Connecticut,   -   -   -   1
Number of highway crossings at grade,   -   -   46
            Same in Connecticut,   -   -   -   17
Number of highway crossings at grade with gates,   10
            Same in Connecticut,   -   -   -   1
Number of highway crossings at grade with flag-
    men,   -   -   -   -   -   -   9
            Same in Connecticut,   -   -   -   3

Name, termini, and length of each road operated
  by this Company under lease or contract:
Pawtuxet Valley R. R., Hope, R. I., to Pontiac, -   5.670m.
Pontiac Branch R. R., Pontiac to Auburn, R. I., -   4.690m.
Length of all roads operated by this Company, •   82.735m.
      Same in Connecticut,   •   •   •   17.000m.
Number of stations on main line,   •   •   27
      Same in Connecticut,   •   •   •   8
Number of stations on branches,   •   •   9
Number of stations on leased lines,   •   •   13

EQUIPMENT.

Number of locomotives (not including switching
  engines),   •   •   •   •   •   27
Average weight of same, including tender, water,
  and fuel,   •   •   •   •   •   54 tons.
Number of switching engines,   •   •   •   2
Number of passenger cars,   •   •   •   35
Number of baggage and mail cars,   •   •   13
Number of merchandise cars,   •   •   •   285
Number of coal, gravel, and other cars, -   •   61
Number of locomotives equipped with train brakes,   23
Number of cars equipped with train brakes,   •   53
Name of brake,   -   •   •   Westinghouse Automatic.
Number of passenger train cars with patent plat-
  form, buffer, and coupler,   •   •   •   53
Name of patent,   -   •   •   •   •   Miller.
      12 Steamboat train baggage crates,
      13 Shore Line passenger cars, $\frac{64}{232}$
       7 Shore Line baggage cars, $\frac{64}{232}$
      10 Parlor cars, $\frac{12}{100}$
       2 Shore Line postal cars, $\frac{64}{232}$
       2 Shore Line baggage cars, $\frac{64}{155}$
      13 Steamboat train passenger cars, $\frac{50}{94}$
       2 Steamboat train baggage flats, $\frac{40}{94}$
       2 Ferry boats.

FARES, FREIGHT, ETC.

Average rate per mile received from passengers
  on roads operated by this Company, excluding
  season ticket passengers,   •   •   •   .025

Average rate per mile for season ticket passengers,
    reckoning one round trip per day to each ticket,   .0075
Average rate of fare per mile from all passengers,   .0235
Total number of passengers carried,   -   -   1,026,495
Passenger mileage, or passengers carried one mile,   23,836,502
Miles run by passenger trains,   -   -   -   431,731
Miles run by freight trains,   -   -   -   148,951
Miles run by all other trains,   -   -   -   60,671
Total miles run, -   -   -   -   -   641,353
Total number of tons of freight carried,   394,631
Freight mileage, or tons carried one mile,   -   14,700,005
Average rate of freight per ton per mile,   -   .029
Number of men employed in operating road, in-
    cluding officers,   -   -   -   -   700

OFFICERS.

President, SAMUEL D. BABCOCK, 50 Wall street, N. Y.
Vice-President, DAVID S. BABCOCK, 177 West street, N. Y.
Secretary, A. R. LONGLEY, JR., Stonington, Conn.
Treasurer, HENRY MORGAN, 39 William street, N. Y.
Superintendent, J. B. GARDINER, Providence, R. I.
Assistant Superintendent and Purchasing Agent,
    G. F. WARD, Stonington, Conn.
Chief Engineer, A. S. MATHEWS, Stonington, Conn.
General Ticket Agent and P. M., F. B. NOYES, Stonington, Conn.
General Freight Agent, J. L. PROUTY, Stonington, Conn.
    "   "   " (acting), A. F. KENYON, Providence, R. I.

BOARD OF DIRECTORS.

SAMUEL D. BABCOCK, 50 Wall street, New York.
HENRY MORGAN, 39 William street, New York.
J. BOORMAN JOHNSTON, Wall street, New York.
D. S. BABCOCK, 177 West street, New York.
GEO. M. MILLER, Drexel Building, New York.
EDWARD MORGAN, 39 William street, New York.
HENRY HOWARD, Coventry, R. I.
CHAS. H. SALISBURY, Providence, R. I.
NATHAN F. DIXON, Westerly, R. I.

JOHN A. BURNHAM, Boston, Mass.
A. S. MATHEWS, Stonington, Conn.

Attest,   S. D. BABCOCK, *President.*
Attest,   HENRY MORGAN, *Treasurer.*

STATE OF NEW YORK,   }
   COUNTY OF NEW YORK, }   October 31, 1882.

Then personally appeared Samuel D. Babcock, President, and Henry Morgan, Treasurer, of the New York, Providence & Boston Railroad Company, and severally made solemn oath that they verily believed the foregoing return by them subscribed to be true and correct.

Before me,

EDWIN F. COREY,
Commissioner for the State of Connecticut,
Office 54 Wall Street, N. Y.

PROPER ADDRESS OF THE COMPANY.

NEW YORK, PROVIDENCE & BOSTON R. R. CO.,
Stonington, Conn.

NORWICH & WORCESTER RAILROAD.

Return of the Norwich & Worcester Railroad Company, for the year ending September 30, 1882.

EARNINGS AND EXPENSES.

STATEMENT OF GROSS EARNINGS.

From passenger transportation, - - -	$203,798.35
From freight transportation, - - -	586,570.80
From United States mails, - - -	5,344.96
From express, - - - - -	17,112.12
From rents, - - - -	2,522.51
From excess baggage, - - -	821.89
From dividend Boat Company, - - -	21,600.00
Total gross earnings, - - -	$837,770.63

STATEMENT OF OPERATING EXPENSES.

For repairs of road-bed and track, - -		$76,228.59
For repairs of bridges, - - -		1,443.08
For repairs of fences, - - -		685.73
For repairs of buildings and fixtures, -		9,871.63
For repairs of locomotives, - -		23,583.23
For repairs of cars, - - -		46,700.74
For machinery and tools, - - -		3,745.17
For salaries and labor, not included above, -		166,391.41
For fuel for locomotives and cars,—		
About 12,200 tons of coal,	$59,781.40	
About 60 cords of wood,	400.00	60,181.40
For fuel for stations and shops, about 1,239 tons of coal, - - - - -		6,689.03
For oil and waste, - - - - -		3,449.19

For damages, losses, and gratuities,—

to persons,	$264.21	
„ to property,	1,478.58	1,742.79

For rent of N. L. N. R. R., - - -	37,210.00
For other operating expenses, - - -	35,501.67
Total operating expenses, - - -	$473,423.66
Net earnings , - - - -	$364,346.97

TOTAL RECEIPTS AND EXPENDITURES.

STATEMENT OF RECEIPTS FROM ALL SOURCES.

Cash on hand at date of last report, - -		$37,349.57
Bills and acc'ts receivable at last report,	127,515.32	
Inventory at date of last report, -	- 56,904.14	
	184,419.46	

Less bills owed by Comp'y, at date of last report,	$65,403.82		
Unpaid dividends at date of last report, - -	3,074.00		
Bills payable at date of last report, - -	11,983.93—	80,461.75	—103,957.71
From gross earnings, - - - -			837,770.63
From N. Y. & N. E. R. R., - -			18,061.83
From Putnam station, - -			3.35
From sale of land in Worcester, - -			6,843.80
Total, - - - - -			$1,003,986.89

STATEMENT OF TOTAL EXPENDITURES.

For operating expenses, - - - -		$473,423.66
For taxes, - - -		44,046.23
For interest, - - - - -		24,658.55
For dividends (number 2; rate per cent., 5), dates when paid, Jan. 10, and July 10, - -		259,780.00
For N. Y. & N. E. R. R. Co., - - - -		6,971.19 .
Bills and accounts receivable, -	$174,614.40	
Inventory, - - - -	54,823.48	
	229,437.88	

16ᴀ

Less bills owed by Co.,	$86,657.45		
Unpaid dividends, -	3,074.00		
Bills payable, - -	5,140.13—	94,871.48—	134,566.40
Cash on hand, - - - -			59,358.93
North Webster depot, - - -			1,181.93
Total, - - - -		-	$1,003,986.89--

GENERAL BALANCE-SHEET.

Assets.

Cost of road, - - - -	$3,270,95.936
Equipment, - - -	179,750.67
Lands in Massachusetts and Connecticut, -	3,107.08
Stock of Nor. & N. Y. Trans. Co., - -	270,000.00
Materials on hand, - - -	54,823.48
Accounts receivable, - - -	174,614.40
Debit balances, - - - - :	12,270.00
Cash on hand, - - - -	59,358.93
Total, - - -	$4,024,883.02

Liabilities.

Capital stock, - - - -	$2,604,400.00
Funded debt, - - - -	400,000 00
Bills payable, - - -	5,140.13
Accounts payable, - - -	86,657.35
Dividends unpaid, - - -	3,074.00
Coupons unpaid, as per books, - -	12,270.00
Profit and loss, - - -	913,342.44
Total, - ' - -	$4,024,883.92

PRESENT OR CONTINGENT LIABILITIES, NOT INCLUDED IN BALANCE-SHEET.

Bonds of the Norwich & New York Transportation Company to the amount of $200,000.00, endorsed by the Treasurer of the N. & W. R. R. Co., by vote of its board.

GENERAL INFORMATION.

CAPITAL STOCK.

Capital stock authorized by charter, - -	$3,825,000.00

Capital stock authorized by vote of company,	-	3,825,000.00
Capital stock issued,	- - - -	2,604,400.00
Stock issued for cash,	- - - -	2,604,400.00

66 shares old stock not converted into preferred stock, and on which no dividends
are paid.

Amount of stock held in Connecticut,	- -	80,600.00
Number of stockholders residing in Connecticut,		30
Whole number of stockholders,	- - -	734

BONDS OR UNFUNDED DEBT.

First mortgage, due March 1, 1897; rate of interest, 6 per cent.,   -   -   -   - $400,000.00
Interest paid to Sept. 1, 1882.

DESCRIPTION OF ROAD.

Date when road, or different portions thereof, were
opened for use, viz.:
From Norwich to Worcester, March, 1840.

Length of main line from Norwich to Worcester,	59.75m.
Same in Connecticut, - - -	41.25m.
Length of branches and names,— .	
From Allyn Point to Norwich, - -	6.30m.
N. L. N. R. R., connection in Norwich, -	.43m.
Length of all branches, - - - -	6.73m.
Length of road (main line and branches) owned	
by the company, - - - -	66.48m.
Same in Connecticut, - - -	47.98m.
Length of sidings, or other tracks not included	
above, - - - -	14.87m.
Same in Connecticut, - - -	9.97m.
Length of track of road, including branches and	
sidings, in single track miles, -	81.35m.
Same in Connecticut, - - -	57.95m.
Length of track laid with steel rails (weight per	
yard, 56 and 60 lbs.), - - - -	18.50m.
Same in Connecticut, - - -	14.20m.

Weight per yard of iron rails in main line, 56
and 60 lbs.
Miles of track laid with steel rails during the year

(No. of tons, 892; weight per yard, 60 lbs.; cost, $34,701.32), all in Connecticut,	9.70m.
Number of new ties put in track during the year (cost, $7,681.22),	25,104
Same in Connecticut,	17,574
Aggregate length of wooden bridges, in feet,	2,539
Same in Connecticut,	2,373
Number of spans of 25 feet or over,	17
Same in Connecticut,	13
Aggregate length of iron bridges, in feet,	764
Same in Connecticut,	493
Number of spans of 25 feet or over,	5
Same in Connecticut,	2
Aggregate length of stone arch bridges, in feet,	514
Same in Connecticut,	400
Number of highway crossings over the track,	6
Same in Connecticut,	4
Number of highway crossings under the track,	6
Same in Connecticut,	2
Number of highway crossings at grade,	63
Same in Connecticut,	34
Number of highway crossings at grade with gates,	1
Number of highway crossings at grade with flag-men,	10
Same in Connecticut,	2
Number of railroads crossed at grade, and names of each,—2 in Conn.,	4
N. Y. & N. E. at Plainfield; same at Putnam.	
Length of all roads operated by this company,	59.75m.
Same in Connecticut,	41.25m.
Number of stations on main line,	24
Same in Connecticut,	15
Number of stations on branches,	1
Same in Connecticut,	1

EQUIPMENT.

Number of locomotives (not including switching engines),	17
Average weight of same, including tender, water, and fuel,	40 tons.

Number of switching engines,   -   -   -   2
Number of passenger cars,   -   -   -   10
Number of smoking cars, -   -   -   -   1
Number of baggage and mail cars,   -   -   8
Number of merchandise cars,   -   -   -   256
Number of coal, gravel, and other cars,   -   -   486
Number of passenger train cars with patent plat-
    form, buffer, and coupler,   -   -   -   19
Name of patent,   -   -   -   -   -   Miller.

FARES, FREIGHT, ETC.

Average rate per mile received from passengers
    on roads operated by this company, excluding
    season-ticket passengers,   -   -   -   .03
Average rate per mile for season-ticket passengers,
    reckoning one round trip per day to each
    ticket,   -   -   -   -   -   .009
Average rate of fare per mile from all passengers,   .028
Total number of passengers carried,   -   -   423,720
Passenger mileage, or passengers carried one mile,   7,273,405
Miles run by passenger trains,   -   -   -   162,979
Miles run by freight trains,   -   -   -   223,476
Miles run by all other trains,   -   -   -   121,049
Total miles run,   -   -   -   -   -   507,504
Total number of tons of freight carried,   -   605,553
Freight mileage, or tons carried one mile,   -   21,598,654
Average rate of freight per ton per mile,   -   .027
Number of men employed in operating road, in-
    cluding officers,   -   -   -   -   437

ACCIDENTS.

STATEMENT OF EACH ACCIDENT IN DETAIL.

1881.

Oct. 1. Charles G. Oswald, brakeman, 23 years of age, was instantly killed above West Thompson, at about 2 P. M. He was running over coal cars to answer a brake call, and jumped short and fell between the cars.

1882.

Feb. 20. Harley W. Bromley, brakeman on special train at Putnam, while pulling a pin, fell from a coal car he was on, and was run over. One leg, between ankle and knee, was badly jammed, and was amputated. The other leg was some injured. Accident between 2 and 3 o'clock, P. M. Died March 19, 1882.

Feb. 20. Frank P. Johnson, brakeman, jammed his hand while coupling cars on the extension road.

Feb. 23. L. H. Vincent, brakeman, was hurt by a draw-bar falling on his foot, which he was removing from a car in Norwich yard.

April 20. On 18th inst., Samuel Troland, of Preston, attempted to get on freight train while crossing wharves, failed to do it, and jammed his foot in falling.

July 31. Train No. 6 struck carriage of Samuel Reynolds at first crossing north of Danielsonville. Killed both man and horse. Reynolds' age, 90 years. Jury exonerated company and employees from all blame.

Aug. 21. Charles H. Lester, conductor extra freight, lost three fingers of right hand coupling cars in Norwich yard.

OFFICERS.

President, F. H. DEWEY, Worcester, Mass.
Secretary, EDWARD T. CLAPP, Norwich, Conn.
Teasurer, G. L. PERKINS, Norwich, Conn.
Superintendent, P. ST. M. ANDREWS, Norwich, Conn.
Accountant, M. M. WHITTEMORE, Norwich, Conn.
Ticket Agent, EDWARD T. CLAPP, Norwich, Conn.
Freight Agent, GEO. A. HARRIS, Norwich, Conn.

BOARD OF DIRECTORS.

F. H. DEWEY, Worcester, Mass.
CHAS. W. SMITH, Worcester, Mass.
EDW. L. DAVIS, Worcester, Mass.
THOS. B. EATON, Worcester, Mass.
JOHN F. SLATER, Norwich, Conn.
WM. G. WELD, Boston, Mass.
W. BAYARD CUTTING, New York, N. Y.

Attest,   FRANCIS H. DEWEY, *President.*
Attest,   G. L. PERKINS, *Treasurer.*

State of Connecticut, }
County of New London, }   Norwich, Nov. 23, 1882.

Then personally appeared G. L. Perkins, Treasurer of the Norwich & Worcester Railroad Company, and made solemn oath that he verily believed the foregoing return by him subscribed to be true and correct.

Before me,

CHARLES W. GALE,
Notary Public.

State of Massachusetts, }
County of Worcester, }   November 27, 1882.

Then personally appeared before me, Francis H. Dewey, President of the Norwich & Worcester Railroad Company, and made solemn oath that he verily believed the foregoing return by him subscribed to be true.

GEO. E. MERRILL,
Justice of the Peace.

PROPER ADDRESS OF THE COMPANY.

NORWICH & WORCESTER RAILROAD COMPANY,
Norwich, Conn.

RIDGEFIELD & NEW YORK RAILROAD.

Return of the Ridgefield & New York Railroad Company, for the year ending September 30, 1882.

GENERAL BALANCE-SHEET.

Assets.

Cost of grading and masonry, - - -	$136,776.84
Cost of engineering expenses, - - -	15,095.09
Cost of land damages, - - - - -	15,980.50
Cost of contingent expenses, - - -	28,597.57
Total, - - - - -	$196,450.00

Liabilities.

Cash from stock subscriptions, - - -	$182,150.00
Cash received from stock of delinquent subscribers sold at auction and part-paid stock,	14,300.00
Total, - -	$196,450.00

GENERAL INFORMATION.

CAPITAL STOCK.

Capital stock authorized by charter, - -	$1,250,000.00
Capital stock authorized by vote of company, -	1,250,000.00
Capital stock issued, viz.:	
4,571 full shares of $50 each, - -	228,550.00
Stock issued for cash, - - - -	182,150.00
Stock of delinquent subscribers sold at auction, -	46,400.00
Amount of stock held in Connecticut, - -	71,500.00
Number of stockholders residing in Connecticut,	54
Whole number of stockholders, - - -	103

DESCRIPTION OF ROAD.

Length of main line from Ridgefield to Port Chester, N. Y.,   -   -   -   -   -   23.29m.
    Same in Connecticut,   -   -   -   15.94m.

OFFICERS.

President, ELLWOOD BURDSALL, Portchester, N. Y.
Vice-President, WILLIAM J. MEAD, Greenwich, Conn.
Secretary, HIRAM K. SCOTT, Ridgefield, Conn.
Treasurer,   "   "   "   "   "

BOARD OF DIRECTORS.

ELLWOOD BURDSALL, Portchester, N. Y.
WILLIAM P. ABENDROTH, Portchester, N. Y.
GEORGE W. QUINTARD, Portchester, N. Y.
HANFORD LOCKWOOD, Greenwich, Conn.
WILLIAM J. MEAD, Grenwich, Conn.
SETH S. COOK, Stamford, Conn.
DANIEL L. ADAMS, Ridgefield, Conn.
EBENEZER JONES, Ridgefield, Conn.
HIRAM K. SCOTT, Ridgefield, Conn.

Attest,   ELLWOOD BURDSALL, *President.*
Attest,   HIRAM K. SCOTT, *Treasurer.*

STATE OF CONNECTICUT, . }
COUNTY OF FAIRFIELD,   }   Nov. 6, 1882.

Personally appeared Ellwood Burdsall, President of the Ridgefield & New York Railroad Company, and affirmed that he verily
believes the foregoing return by him subscribed to be true and
correct.   Before me,

JOSEPH H. MARSHALL,
Notary Public.
Post Office, Portchester, N. Y.

GREENWICH, Conn.
17A

STATE OF CONNECTICUT,   }
    COUNTY OF FAIRFIELD,   }   Nov. 4, 1882.

Then personally appeared Hiram K. Scott, Treasurer of the Ridgefield & New York Railroad Company, and made solemn oath that he verily believes the foregoing return by him subscribed to be true and correct.

Before me,

JOHN F. GILBERT,

Justice of the Peace.

PROPER ADDRESS OF THE COMPANY.

RIDGEFIELD & NEW YORK RAILROAD COMPANY,

Ridgefield, Conn.

ROCKVILLE RAILROAD.

Return of the Rockville Railroad Company, for the year ending September 30, 1882.

[NOTE.—Reference for questions unanswered to N. Y. & N. E. R. R Co., to whom this road is leased.]

TOTAL RECEIPTS AND EXPENDITURES.

STATEMENT OF RECEIPTS FROM ALL SOURCES.

Cash on hand at date of last report,	$710.50
From rent of road,	4,800.00
From rent of lands and tenements,	654.08
From sale of locomotives,	3,000.00
Personal accounts,	123.09
Total,	$9,287.67

STATEMENT OF TOTAL EXPENDITURES.

For taxes and insurance,	$555.27
For interest,	1,236.05
For dividends (number, 2; rate per cent., 3),	2,400.00
Dates when paid, Jan. 1st and July 1st.	
For repairs of tenements, etc.,	143.03
For salary of treasurer,	400.00
Bills payable reduced,	3,000.00
Cash on hand to balance,	1,553.32
Total,	$9,287.67

GENERAL BALANCE-SHEET.

Assets.

Construction,	$144,247.66
Equipment,	25,857.99

Railroad stock,	-	-	-	-	500.00
Track repairs,	-	-	-	-	1,695.68
Cash on hand,	-	-	-	-	1,553.32
Total,	-	-	-	-	$173,854.65

Liabilities.

Capital stock,	-	-	-	-	$68,750.00
Capital stock, preferred,	-	-	-	-	40,000.00
Bonds,	-	-	-	-	6,000.00
Bills payable,	-	-	-	-	12,549.75
Personal accounts,	-	-	-	-	849.35
Real estate,	-	-	-	-	250.00
Profit and loss,	-	-	-	-	45,455.55
Total,	-	-	-	-	$173,854.65

GENERAL INFORMATION.

CAPITAL STOCK.

Capital stock authorized by charter,	$120,000.00
Capital stock authorized by vote of company,	100,000.00
Capital stock issued, viz.:	
687½ full shares of $100 each—com., $68,750	
400 full shares of $100 each—pref'd, 40,000	108,750.00
Stock issued for cash,	108,750.00
Amount of stock held in Connecticut,	108,750.00
Number of stockholders residing in Connecticut,	47
Whole number of stockholders,	47

BONDS OR UNFUNDED DEBT.

First mortgage, due July 1, 1883; rate of interest, 6 per cent.,	$6,000.00

Interest paid to July 1, 1882.

DESCRIPTION OF ROAD.

Date when road, or different portions thereof, were opened for use, viz.:

From Rockville to Vernon, Aug. 10, 1863.

Length of main line from Rockville to Vernon,—
  all in Connecticut,   .   .   .   4.80m.
Length of road (main line) owned by the company,   4.80m.
Length of sidings, or other tracks not included
  above, ...75m.
Length of track of road, including branches and
  sidings, in single-track miles,   .   .   5.55m.
Weight per yard of iron rails in main line, 50 lbs.
Aggregate length of wooden bridges, in feet,   .   66
Number of spans of 25 feet or over,   .   .   1
Number of highway crossings over the track,   2
Number of highway crossings at grade,   -   .   6
Number of stations on main line,   .   .   4

EQUIPMENT.

Number of passenger cars,   .   .   .   2
Number of baggage and mail cars,   .   .   1

OFFICERS.

President, GEORGE MAXWELL, Rockville, Conn.
Secretary, J. C. HAMMOND, Jr., Rockville, Conn.
Treasurer, J. C. HAMMOND, Jr., Rockville, Conn.

BOARD OF DIRECTORS.

Geo. Maxwell, Rockville, Conn.
C. Fitton, Rockville, Conn.
H. L. James, Rockville, Conn.
Geo. Talcott, Rockville, Conn.
J. C. Hammond, Jr., Rockville, Conn.

Attest,   GEO. MAXWELL, *President.*
Attest,   J. C. HAMMOND, Jr., *Treasurer.*

STATE OF CONNECTICUT, }   ROCKVILLE, Oct. 17, 1882.
     COUNTY OF TOLLAND, }

Then personally appeared George Maxwell, President, and J. C. Hammond, Jr., Treasurer, of the Rockville Railroad Company, and severally made solemn oath that they verily believed the foregoing return by them subscribed to be true and correct.

Before me,

E. C. CHAPMAN,
Notary Public.

PROPER ADDRESS OF THE COMPANY.

ROCKVILLE RAILROAD COMPANY,

Rockville, Conn.

SHEPAUG RAILROAD.

Return of the Shepaug Railroad Company, for the year ending September 30, 1882.

EARNINGS AND EXPENSES.

STATEMENT OF GROSS EARNINGS.

From passenger transportation,	$12,914.80
From freight transportation,	40,613.49
From United States mails,	1,456.04
From express,	766.50
From rents,	125.00
From train service on Danbury & Norwalk R. R.,	7,056.00
Total gross earnings,	$62,931.83

STATEMENT OF OPERATING EXPENSES.

For repairs of road-bed and track,		$18,628.39
For repairs of bridges,		1,153.16
For repairs of fences,		509.27
For repairs of buildings and fixtures,		293.20
For repairs of locomotives,		5,428.34
For repairs of cars,		1,903.80
For repairs of machinery and tools,		78.28
For salaries and labor not included above,		16,104.85
For fuel for locomotives and cars,—		
1,356½ tons of coal,	$7,274.38	
8 cords of wood,	14.00—	7,288.38
For fuel for stations and shops, 13 tons of coal,		90.10
For oil and waste,		585.18
For damages to property,		413.42
For insurance,		356.25
For new buildings,		1,256.62

For stationery, advertising, and printing, -	229.43
For car service, - - - - -	75.16
Total operating expenses, - - -	$54,393.83
Net earnings, - - - -	$8,538.00

TOTAL RECEIPTS AND EXPENDITURES.

STATEMENT OF RECEIPTS FROM ALL SOURCES.

Cash on hand at date of last report, - -	$16,272.57
From gross earnings as stated, - - -	62,931.83
Total, - - - - -	$79,204.40

STATEMENT OF TOTAL EXPENDITURES.

For operating expenses, as stated, - -	$54,393.83
Bills and accounts receivable this date, - -	6,385.69
Cash on hand to balance, - -	18,424.88
Total, - - - - -	$79,204.40

GENERAL BALANCE-SHEET.

Assets.

Construction account, - - -	$257,459.58
Equipment, - - - -	11,064.20
Accounts receivable, - - -	6,385.69
Profit and loss, - - - -	6,365.65
Cash on hand, - - - -	18,424.88
Total, - - - -	$299,700.00

Liabilities.

Capital stock, - - - -	$299,700.00
Total, - - - -	$299,700.00

PRESENT OR CONTINGENT LIABILITIES, NOT INCLUDED IN BALANCE-SHEET.

Shepaug Valley R. R. Co. bonds, a lien on its road,	$400,000.00
Overdue interest on the same, - -	154,000.00
Taxes due State of Conn., Oct., 1881, - -	669.68
Total, - - - -	$554,669.68

GENERAL INFORMATION.

CAPITAL STOCK.

Capital stock authorized by charter,	- -	$700,000.00
Capital stock authorized by vote of Company,	-	300,000.00
Capital stock issued, viz. :		
2,970 full shares of $100 each, $297,000		
30 shares subject to $10 further		
assessment, 2,700—		299,700.00
Stock issued for cash,	- - -	89,700.00
Stock issued for bonds,	- - -	210,000.00
Amount of stock held in Connecticut,	- -	296,700.00
Number of stockholders residing in Connecticut,		14
Whole number of stockholders,	- -	16

BONDS OR UNFUNDED DEBT.

First mortgage bonds Shepaug Valley R. R. Co., due April 1, 1891; rate of interest, 7 per ct., Interest paid to October 1, 1876.	$400,000.00

DESCRIPTION OF ROAD.

Date when road, or different portions thereof, were opened for use, viz. :	
From Litchfield to Hawleyville, January 1, 1872.	
Length of main line from Litchfield to Hawleyville,	32.28m.
Length of road owned by the Company, - -	32.28m.
Length of sidings, or other tracks not included above, - - - - -	1.52m.
Length of track of road, including sidings, in single track miles, - - - -	33.80m.
Length of track laid with steel rails (weight per yard, 50 lbs.), - - - - -	0.38m.
Weight per yard of iron rails in main line, 50 lbs.	
Miles of track laid with new iron rails during the year (No. of tons, $50\frac{108}{2240}$; weight per yard, 47 lbs.; cost, $1,957.86), - - -	0.64m.
Number of new ties put in track during the year (cost $6,305.81), - - - -	17,928
Aggregate length of wooden bridges, in feet,	2,244

18A

Number of spans of 25 feet or over,   -   -   8
Aggregate length of stone arch bridges, in feet,   59
Number of highway crossings over the track,   -   1
Number of highway crossings under the track,   -   1
Number of highway crossings at grade,   -   -   37
Number of railroads crossed at grade,—New York
    & New England Railroad, Housatonic R. R.,   2
Length of all roads operated by this Company,   -   32.28m.
Number of stations on main line,   -   -   12

EQUIPMENT.

Number of locomotives (not including switching
    engines),   -   -   -   -   3
Average weight of same, including tender, water,
    and fuel,   -   -   -   -   50 tons.
Number of passenger cars,   -   -   -   3
Number of baggage and mail cars,   -   -   2
Number of merchandise cars,   -   -   -   3
Number of coal, gravel, and other cars,   -   -   20
Number of passenger train cars with patent plat-
    form, buffer, and coupler,   -   -   -   2
Name of patent,   -   -   -   -   Miller.

FARES, FREIGHT, ETC.

Average rate per mile received from passengers
    on roads operated by this Company, excluding
    season ticket passengers,   -   -   .0403
Average rate of fare per mile from all passengers,   .0403
Total number of passengers carried,   -   16,524
Passenger mileage, or passengers carried one mile,   320,164
Miles run by passenger trains,   -   -   -   18,585
Miles run by freight trains,   -   -   -   23,460
Miles run by all other trains,   -   -   -   870
Total miles run on Shepaug R. R.,   -   -   42,915
Total miles run on D. & N. R. R.,   -   -   9,930
Total number of tons of freight carried,   -   29,787
Freight mileage, or tons carried one mile,   -   625,651
Average rate of freight per ton per mile,   -   .065
Number of men employed in operating road, in-
    cluding officers,   -   -   -   -   60

OFFICERS.

President, HENRY W. BUEL, Litchfield, Conn.
Vice-President, HENRY R. COIT, Litchfield, Conn.
Secretary, WILLIAM DEMING, Litchfield, Conn.
Treasurer, HENRY R. COIT, Litchfield, Conn.
Superintendent, EDWIN McNEILL, Litchfield, Conn.
General Ticket Agent, EDWIN McNEILL, Litchfield, Conn.
General Freight Agent, EDWIN McNEILL, Litchfield, Conn.

BOARD OF DIRECTORS.

HENRY W. BUEL, Litchfield, Conn.
HENRY R. COIT, Litchfield, Conn.
EDWARD W. SEYMOUR, Litchfield, Conn.
WILLIAM DEMING, Litchfield, Conn.
DORSEY NEVILLE, Poughkeepsie, N. Y.
HOLMES O. MORSE, Litchfield, Conn.
LEVERETT W. WESSELLS, Litchfield, Conn.
ASAHEL H. MORSE, Litchfield, Conn.
EDWIN McNEILL, Litchfield, Conn.

Attest,   HENRY W. BUEL, *President.*
Attest,   HENRY R. COIT, *Treasurer.*

STATE OF CONNECTICUT, }
COUNTY OF LITCHFIELD, }   November 4, 1882.

Then personally appeared Henry W. Buel, President, and Henry R. Coit, Treasurer, of the Shepaug Railroad Company, and severally made solemn oath that they verily believed the foregoing return by them subscribed to be true and correct.

Before me,

GEO. E. JONES,
Notary Public.

PROPER ADDRESS OF THE COMPANY.

SHEPAUG RAILROAD COMPANY,
Litchfield, Litchfield County, Conn.

SHORE LINE RAILWAY.

Return of the Shore Line Railway Company for the year ending September 30, 1882.

TOTAL RECEIPTS AND EXPENDITURES AS LESSORS.

STATEMENT OF RECEIPTS FROM ALL SOURCES.

Cash on hand at date of last report, - -	$2,690.73
From Lessees—The New York, New Haven & Hartford Railroad Co., for rent, - -	100,000.00
Total, - - - - -	$102,690.73

STATEMENT OF TOTAL EXPENDITURES.

For taxes, - - - - -	$13,973.10
For interest, - - - - -	9,118.46
For dividends (number, two; rate per cent., 3.60 and 4), - - - - -	76,000.00
Paid Jan. 5, 1882, 3.60 per cent., and July 5, 1882. 4 per cent.	
Petty expenses, - - - -	33.67
Treasurer's salary, - - -	400.00
Cash on hand to balance, - - -	3,165.50
Total, - - - -	$102,690.73

GENERAL BALANCE-SHEET AS LESSORS..

Assets.

Construction account, - - - -	$1,169,496.10
Profit and loss, - - - -	27,338.40
Cash, - - - - -	3,165.50
Total, - - - -	$1,200,000.00

Liabilities.

Capital stock,	-	-	-	-	$1,000,000.00
Funded debt,	-	-	-	-	200,000.00
Total,	-	-	-	-	$1,200,000.00

GENERAL INFORMATION.

CAPITAL STOCK.

Capital stock authorized by charter, - -	$1,000,000.00
Capital stock authorized by vote of Company, -	1,000,000.00
Capital stock issued, viz.:	
10,000 full shares of- $100 each, - -	1,000,000.00
Stock issued for cash, - - - -	62,845.20
Stock issued for bonds, - - - -	678,125.00
Stock issued for increased valuation of road, or equipment, or both, - - - -	259,029.80
Amount of stock held in Connecticut, - -	663,600.00
Number of stockholders residing in Connecticut,	184
Whole number of stockholders, - - -	224

BONDS OR UNFUNDED DEBT.

First mortgage, due March 1, 1910; rate of interest, 4½ per ct., - - - -	$200,000.00
Interest paid to Sept. 1, 1882.	

DESCRIPTION OF ROAD.

Date when road, or different portions thereof, were opened for use, viz. :

From New Haven to New London, July 22, 1852.

Length of main line from New Haven to New London, - - - - -	50.97m.
Length of road (main line) owned by the Company, - - - - -	50.97m.
Length of sidings, or other tracks not included above, - - - - -	6.97m.
Length of track of road, including sidings, in single track miles, - - - -	57.94m.
Length of track laid with steel rails (weight per yard, 60 lbs.), - - - -	50.06m.

Miles of track laid with steel rails during the year
 (No. of tons, ——; weight per yard, 60 lbs.;
 cost, $55.00),   -   -   -   -   -   .26m.
Number of new ties put in track during the year
 (cost, $11,102.96),   -   -   -   -   25,234
Aggregate length of wooden bridges, in feet,   -   12,402
Number of spans of 25 feet or over,   -   -   35
Aggregate length of iron bridges, in feet,   -   280
Number of spans of 25 feet or over,   -   -   1
Aggregate length of stone arch bridges, in feet, -   46
Number of highway crossings over the track,   -   6
Number of highway crossings under the track,   -   6
Number of highway crossings at grade, -   -   67
Number of railroads crossed at grade: New York,
 New Haven & Hartford, and Hartford & Con-
 necticut Valley,   -   -   -   -   2
Number of stations on main line,   -   -   21

[NOTE.—The statistics under "Description of Road" for the Shore
Line are included in the return of the N. Y., N. H. & H. R. R. Co.—
R. R. COMS.]

OFFICERS.

President, S. B. CHITTENDEN, New York.
Vice-President, E. H. TROWBRIDGE, New Haven.
Secretary, WILBUR F. DAY, New Haven.
Treasurer, WILBUR F. DAY, New Haven.
Superintendent, W. H. STEVENSON, New Haven.

BOARD OF DIRECTORS.

S. B. CHITTENDEN, New York.
CHAS. G. LANDON, New York.
E. H. TROWBRIDGE, New Haven.
HENRY L. HOTCHKISS, New Haven.
WILBUR F. DAY, New Haven.
WILLIAM T. BARTLETT, New HAVEN.
ARTHUR D. OSBORNE, New Haven.

STATE OF CONNECTICUT, }
 COUNTY OF NEW HAVEN, }   October 11, 1882.

Then personally appeared E. H. Trowbridge, Vice-President, and Wilbur F. Day, Treasurer, of the Shore Line Railway Company, and severally made solemn oath that they verily believed the foregoing return by them subscribed to be true and correct.

Before me,

ROBERT I. COUCH,
Notary Public.

PROPER ADDRESS OF THE COMPANY.

THE SHORE LINE RAILWAY,
WILBUR F. DAY, Treasurer,
New Haven, Conn.

SOUTH MANCHESTER RAILROAD.

Return of the South Manchester Railroad Company, for the year ending September 30, 1882

EARNINGS AND EXPENSES.

STATEMENT OF GROSS EARNINGS.

From passenger transportation, - - -	$6,609.25
From freight transportation, - - :	4,569.19
From United States mails and express, - -	50.04
Total gross earnings, - - -.	$11,228.48

STATEMENT OF OPERATING EXPENSES.

For repairs of road-bed and track, - -		$1,747.37
For repairs of buildings and fixtures, - -		187.36
For repairs of locomotives, - - -		252.46
For repairs of cars, - - - -		129.22
For repairs of machinery and tools, - -		47.89
For salaries and labor not included above, -		4,970.85
For fuel for locomotives and cars,—		
202 tons of coal, - -	$1,284.30	
5½ cords of wood, -	24.90—	1,309.20
For fuel for stations and shops, 11 tons of coal, -		74.25
For oil and waste, - - - -		302.08
For car service, N. Y. & N. E. R. R. - -		23.05
For stationery, etc., - - - -		222.43
Total operating expenses, - - ₰		$9,266.16
Net earnings, - - . . -		$1,962.32

TOTAL RECEIPTS AND EXPENDITURES.

STATEMENT OF RECEIPTS FROM ALL SOURCES.

From gross earnings as stated, - - -	$11,228.48
From sundries sold, etc., - • • •	90.27
From decrease of inventory, - • •	1,718 15
Total, - - - -	$13,036.90

STATEMENT OF TOTAL EXPENDITURES.

For operating expenses, as stated, • -	$9,266.16
For taxes, • ·· • · - -	285.85
For construction account, bank wall, - •	446.71
Paid in reduction of floating debt, • -	3,038.18
Total, · • • • -	$13,036.90

GENERAL BALANCE-SHEET.

Assets.

Cost of construction to October 1, 1882, - •	$65,376.65
Cost of equipment to October 1, 1882, · - •	17,172.46
Materials and supplies on hand, - • •	2,297.70
Total, • • • • •	$84,846.81

Liabilities.

Capital stock, • • • • •	$40,000.00
Accounts payable, • • • •	23,871.72
Profit and loss, • • • • •	20,975.09
Total, • • • • •	$84,846.81

GENERAL INFORMATION.

CAPITAL STOCK.

Capital stock authorized by charter, - •	$40,000.00
Capital stock authorized by vote of Company, -	40,000.00
Capital stock issued, viz.·	
400 full shares of $100 each, · -	40,000.00
Stock issued for cash, - · - •	40,000.00

· 19A

Amount of stock held in Connecticut,   -   -   40,000.00

Number of stockholders residing in Connecticut,   9

Whole number of stockholders, -   -   -   9

DESCRIPTION OF ROAD.

Date when road, or different portions thereof, were
opened for use, viz.:

From South Manchester to North Manchester,
June, 1869.

Length of main line from South Manchester to
North Manchester,   -   -   -   -   2.25m.

Length of road (main line) owned by the Company,   2.25m.

Length of sidings or other tracks not included
above,   -   -   -   -   -   1.36m.

Length of track of road, including sidings, in
single track miles,   -   -   -   -   3.61m.

Length of track laid with steel rails (weight per
yard, 56 lbs.),   -   -   -   -   2.25m.

Number of new ties put in track during the year
(cost, $150.00),   -   -   -   -   300

Number of highway crossings over the track,   -   1

Number of highway crossings at grade,   -   -   5

Length of all roads operated by this Company,   -   2.25m.

Number of stations on main line,   -   -   2

EQUIPMENT.

Number of locomotives (not including switching
engines),   -   -   -   -   -   1

Average weight of same, including tender, water,
and fuel,   -   -   -   -   -   23 tons.

Number of passenger cars,   -   -   -   3

Number of locomotives equipped with train brakes,   1

Number of cars equipped with train brakes,   -   3

Name of brake,   -   -   -   -   -   Westinghouse.

Number of passenger train cars with patent platform, buffer, and coupler,   -   -   -   3

Name of patent,   -   -   -   -   -   Miller.

FARES, FREIGHT, ETC.

Average rate per mile received from passengers on roads operated by this Company, excluding season ticket passengers, - - -	.04515
Average rate per mile for season ticket passengers, reckoning one round trip per day to each ticket,	.01718
Average rate of fare per mile from all passengers,	.03111
Total number of passengers carried, - -	94,445
Passenger mileage, or passengers carried one mile,	212,501
Miles run by passenger trains, - - -	13,140
Miles run by freight trains, - - -	2,808
Total miles run, - - - - -	15,948
Total number of tons of freight carried, -	$14,104\frac{560}{3240}$
Freight mileage, or tons carried one mile, -	$31,734\frac{112}{3240}$
Average rate of freight per ton per mile, -	.1432
Number of men employed in operating road, including officers, - - - -	9

OFFICERS.

President, F. W. CHENEY, South Manchester, Conn.
Secretary and Gen. Manager,
    RICHARD O. CHENEY, South Manchester, Conn.
Treasurer, C. S. CHENEY, South Manchester, Conn.

BOARD OF DIRECTORS.

RALPH CHENEY, South Manchester, Conn.
FRANK CHENEY, South Manchester, Conn.
F. W. CHENEY, South Manchester, Conn.
RICHARD O. CHENEY, South Manchester, Conn.

Attest,   F. W. CHENEY, *President.*
Attest,   C. S. CHENEY, *Treasurer.*

STATE OF CONNECTICUT,   }
    COUNTY OF HARTFORD, }   October 31, 1882.

Then personally appeared F. W. Cheney, President, and C. S. Cheney, Treasurer, of the South Manchester Railroad Company, and severally made solemn oath that they verily believed the foregoing return by them subscribed to be true and correct.

Before me,

RICHARD O. CHENEY,

Notary. Public.

PROPER ADDRESS OF THE COMPANY.

SOUTH MANCHESTER RAILROAD COMPANY,

South Manchester, Conn.

WATERTOWN & WATERBURY RAILROAD.

*Return of the Watertown & Waterbury Railroad Company, for the
year ending September 30, 1882.*

[The Watertown & Waterbury Railroad is still operated by the Naugatuck Railroad Company, as heretofore has been done; they paying all
taxes, expenses, and repairs, and receiving all income and receipts of every
nature.]

GENERAL BALANCE-SHEET.

Assets.

Construction account,	$134,248.43
Profit and loss,	2,951.57
Total,	$137,200.00

Liabilities.

Capital stock,	$118,200.00
Bonds funded,	19,000.00
Total,	$137,200.00

PRESENT OR CONTINGENT LIABILITIES, NOT INCLUDED IN BALANCE-SHEET.

Overdue interest on bonds issued by this Company,	$11,880.00

GENERAL INFORMATION.

CAPITAL STOCK.

Capital stock authorized by charter,	$150,000.00
Capital stock authorized by vote of Company,	130,000.00
Capital stock issued, viz.:	
2,364 full shares of $50 each,	118,200.00
Stock issued for cash,	118,200.00

Amount of stock held in Connecticut,   ·   ·   118,200.00
Number of stockholders residing in Connecticut,   56
Whole number of stockholders, ·   ··   ·   56

BONDS OR UNFUNDED DEBT.

First mortgage, due Nov. 17, 1885; rate of interest,
   7 per cent.; interest paid to May 15, 1873, - $19,000.00

DESCRIPTION OF ROAD.

Date when road, or different portions thereof, were
   opened for use, viz :
From Watertown to junction of Naugatuck Rail-
   road, Waterbury, November 1, 1870.
Length of main line from Watertown to Water-
   bury,   -   -   -   -   -   4.60m.
Length of road (main line) owned by the Company,   4.60m.
Length of sidings, or other tracks, not included
   above,   ·   -   -   -   -   .25m.
Length of track of road, including sidings, in
   single track miles,   -   ·   -   -   4.85m.
Weight per yard of iron rails in main line, 56 lbs.
Number of new ties put in track during the year,   2,200
Aggregate length of wooden bridges, in feet,   ·   1,531
Number of spans of 25 feet or over,   · ·   ·   5
Aggregate length of iron bridges, in feet,   -   125
Number of spans of 25 feet or over,   ·   ·   1
Number of highway crossings under the track,   ·   3
Number of highway crossings at grade, -   ·   3
Number of stations on main line, -   ·   ·   2

OFFICERS.

President, WM. D. BISHOP, Bridgeport, Conn.
Secretary, LEMAN W. CUTLER, Bridgeport, Conn.
Superintendent, GEORGE W. BEACH, Waterbury, Conn.

BOARD OF DIRECTORS.

WM. D. BISHOP, Bridgeport, Conn.
RUSSELL TOMLINSON, Bridgeport, Conn.
HORACE NICHOLS, Bridgeport, Conn.

ROYAL M. BASSETT, Derby, Conn.
F. J. KINGSBURY, Waterbury, Conn.
GEO. W. BEACH, Waterbury, Conn.
MERRIT HEMINWAY, Watertown, Conn.
HENRY MERRIMAN, Watertown, Conn.
O. B. KING, Watertown, Conn.
L. W. CUTLER, Watertown, Conn.

Attest,   WM. D. BISHOP, *President.*
Attest,   LEMAN W. CUTLER, *Treasurer.*

STATE OF CONNECTICUT,
COUNTY OF LITCHFIELD,   October 7, 1882.

Then personally appeared Wm. D. Bishop, President, and Leman W. Cutler, Treasurer, of the Watertown & Waterbury Railroad Company, and severally made solemn oath that they verily believed the foregoing return by them subscribed to be true and correct.

Before me,

CALEB T. HICKOX,
Justice of the Peace.

PROPER ADDRESS OF THE COMPANY.

WATERTOWN & WATERBURY RAILROAD COMPANY,
Watertown, Conn.

LAWS

RELATING SPECIALLY TO

RAILROADS.

STATUTES OF CONNECTICUT RESPECTING RAILROADS.

SECTION 1. The Governor shall, annually, within sixty days from the organization of the general assembly, nominate, and with the advice and consent of the senate shall appoint, one Railroad Commissioner, who shall hold his office for the term of three years from and after the next succeeding first day of July. The senate shall act on all nominations of the Governor within ten days after they are made. If the Governor shall fail to nominate, within sixty days after the organization of the general assembly, some person for Railroad Commissioner who shall be confirmed by the senate, the general assembly shall fill the vacancy which will arise during the year.

1877.
Railroad commissioners, how appointed.

SEC. 2. One of the Railroad Commissioners shall be a lawyer in good standing in his profession, and of at least ten years' practice One of said Railroad Commissioners as hereafter appointed shall be a capable and experienced civil engineer, of at least ten years' practice in his said business as civil engineer; and the other of said Railroad Commissioners as hereafter appointed shall be a good practical business man, and they shall be and constitute the Board of Railroad Commissioners.

Composition of the board.

SEC. 3. If any vacancy occurs in said Board of Railroad Commissioners at a time when the general assembly is not in session, the Governor shall appoint a Railroad Commissioner to fill such vacancy until the rising of the next session of the general assembly; and all other vacancies shall be filled for the remainder of their respective terms in the manner provided by section one of this act; and no stockholder or agent of any railroad company shall be a Commissioner.

Vacancy, how filled.

Office and clerk.   SEC. 4.   The board shall appoint a clerk and have an office in Hartford, where its records shall be preserved, which shall be kept open during the usual business hours. If the comptroller does not furnish said board a proper office, it may hire one at an annual rent not exceeding five hundred dollars.

Records.   SEC. 5.   The Railroad Commissioners shall keep a record of all communications addressed to them officially, of all their official acts and proceedings, and of all facts learned in relation to any casualty, with the names of the persons from whom they were derived, or by whom they may be proved, may employ experts or other agents when necessary, and shall have the powers and be subject to the duties specified in chapter two, part nine, of title seventeen, of the general statutes.

1878.
Salaries and contingent expenses.   SEC. 6.   The office expenses and salaries of the board shall be paid monthly from the treasury, and in July in each year the whole amount so paid during the year ending the fourth day of July shall be apportioned by the comptroller among the several railroad companies, in proportion to the length of the main track or tracks of their respective railroads in this state, and each company and the trustees, assignees, lessees, or other parties operating any such railroad, shall pay the treasurer their proportion of such amount.*

Repeal.   SEC. 7.   All acts and parts of acts inconsistent herewith are hereby repealed.

2. RAILROAD COMMISSIONERS.

To pass free on railroads.   SEC. 8.   The Railroad Commissioners shall have the right to pass free of charge, in the performance of their duties, on all the railroads in the State, and to take with them any person in their official employment.

To give notice before approval of lay-out, etc.   SEC. 9.   Before the Railroad Commissioners shall approve the laying out of any railroad, or the taking of any real estate for the purposes of said road, or any change or alteration of the same, they shall give reasonable notice to all persons having an interest in such estate to attend and be heard; and the appraisers shall cause a like notice to be given to all persons interested in the real estate taken or proposed to be taken; and if any such person resides out of this State, or is a *feme covert*, infant, or *cestui que trust*, or *non compos mentis*, any judge of the Superior Court may prescribe the notice to be given to such person.

[1856.
To certify that road is safe before it is opened.   SEC. 10.   No part of any railroad shall be opened for public travel unless the railroad company shall first obtain a certificate, signed by the Railroad Commissioners, that such road is in a suitable and safe condition.

*See sec. 1, act 1882, page 14.

SEC. 11. The Railroad Commissioners shall, at least 1850. 1856. twice in each year, examine the several railroads in this To examine State, and shall make a like examination of any railroad railroads at within the limits of any town, when thereto requested in year. writing by the selectmen, and shall see that the same are kept in suitable repair, and that the railroad companies faithfully comply with all provisions of law.

SEC. 12. Said Commissioners shall cause such portion 1874. of the laws relative to railroads, as they deem proper, to Commissioners. be posted as they shall direct; and may at any time, and on the complaint in writing of five of the stockholders or creditors of any railroad company, assigning sufficient reason, shall examine its railroad and all its appurte- nances, engines and cars, and its by-laws and rules, and in such examinations shall pass over the road at a rate not exceeding six miles an hour, and shall stop at each culvert, bridge, and piling, and examine the same, and ; hall examine the rails and ties in every mile; notifying he company in writing of the time of such examinations; and shall notify the company to make all repairs required within a time limited; shall make such rules as to plat- forms and out-buildings at stations as are for the public interest; may prescribe the time during which any ticket office shall be open for the sale of tickets, and no com- pany neglecting such order shall receive more than the regular ticket price for fare; shall make necessary orders for compelling companies to furnish comfortable seats for passengers, and for regulating the manner in which companies shall manage their engines and cars at high- way crossings; shall direct that suitable warning-boards be put up at dangerous crossings; may require companies to maintain a gait across a highway at any crossing, and to provide an agent to open and close the same; shall, when two roads meet or intersect, at the request of the directors of the company owning either, prescribe rules relative to the exchange of passengers and luggage; and shall cause printed copies of the sixty-ninth, seventieth, and seventy-first sections of this article to be kept posted up at all railroad stations.

SEC. 13. Said Commissioners, when requested in 1860. 1865. writing by the selectmen of the town to order a gate or May order electric signal to be erected, or a flagman to be stationed or signals. at any railroad crossing, shall visit such place, first giv- ing said selectmen reasonable notice thereof; and if the public safety requires it, shall order the company operat- ing said railroad to maintain a gate or electric signal, or to keep a flagman at said place, or to do any other act at said place needful for the protection of the public; and may specify when said gate shall be opened and closed, or when flagmen shall be on duty; and may change any such order when they deem it necessary, first visiting said town and there giving said selectmen an opportunity to be heard thereon. And if any railroad company shall neglect to station flagmen as ordered by said Commissioners, it shall forfeit to the State fifty dollars for each day of such neglect.

1875.
Appeals from order of Railroad Commissioners as to gates, flagmen, etc.

When the Railroad Commissioners, on the application of the selectmen of any town, shall make an order as provided herein, or refuse to make the same, their decision shall be communicated to the parties in interest within twenty days from the final hearing on the same, and either party aggrieved by such decision may appeal therefrom to the Superior Court, in the manner and with like effect as provided for appeals in section fifty-two of this article. But in all cases where a flagman, gate, or electric signal shall be ordered by the Superior Court upon an appeal taken by the selectmen of any town, such court may, at its discretion, order a portion of the expense of maintaining or erecting the same, but not exceeding one-half, to be borne by the town in which the crossing is situated; and the Superior Court may at any time, upon the application of either party, with due notice to adverse parties, annul or vary any order passed as aforesaid: *provided,* such court shall find there has been a change of circumstances surrounding such crossing.

1880.
Railroad crossings in cities and boroughs.

That all the provisions of section thirteen, article two of chapter two, part nine, title seventeen, of the general statutes, and the acts amending the same, applying to the selectmen of towns in regard to gates, signals, or flagmen at any railroad crossing be, and the same are hereby, extended to mayors and common councils of cities, and to the warden and burgesses of boroughs, in regard to streets crossing or crossed by said roads in any said city or borough.

1853.
May make recommendations.

Sec. 14. The Railroad Commissioners shall recommend in writing to the several railroad companies, or any of them, from time to time, the adoption of such measures and regulations as such commissioners deem conducive to the public safety and interest; and shall report any neglect to adopt such recommendations to the next general assembly.

ADDITIONAL PROTECTION TO BRIDGES, TRESTLES, AND PILINGS.

1878.
Guard-rails to be placed on railroad bridges.

Section 1. Whenever the Railroad Commissioners shall deem it necessary for the safety of persons traveling upon any railroad in this state, that guard-rails or any other appliances to secure safety should be placed upon any bridge belonging to such railroad, said Commissioners may order the corporation owning or operating such railroad to place such additional guards upon said bridge as they may deem necessary and proper to accomplish the object aforesaid.

SEC. 2. Any railroad company which shall neglect or refuse to comply with the orders of the Railroad Commissioners, given in pursuance of section one of this act, shall forfeit and pay to the treasurer of this state twenty-five dollars per day for each day of such neglect or refusal. *Penalty.*

SEC. 15. If, upon examination of any railroad, or the affairs of any railroad company, the Commissioners shall be of opinion that such road is in such condition, or that its affairs are so conducted as to endanger the safety of the public, or that the company has violated the law or refused to obey the directions of said Commissioners or of any judge of the Superior Court, made pursuant to the powers given in this Part, they may within one year after said examination make application to any judge of the Superior Court for an injunction to restrain any person from exercising or attempting to exercise the duties of any officer in such company; and said judge may proceed thereon as the Supreme Court may do on petitions for any injunction. *1853. May apply for injunction against corporation, when.*

SEC. 16. The Railroad Commissioners may summon and examine under oath such witnesses as they may think proper in relation to the affairs of any railroad company; and whoever shall refuse, without justifiable cause, to appear and testify, or who shall in any way obstruct any Railroad Commissioner in the discharge of his duty, shall be fined not exceeding one thousand dollars, or imprisoned not exceeding one year, or both. *1872. Power to examine witnesses. Penalty for resisting.*

The fees of witnesses summoned by the Railroad Commissioners to appear before them under the provisions of the sixteenth section of part nine, chapter two, title seventeen (page 321) of the general statutes, and the fees for summoning such witnesses, shall be taxed by the Commissioners and paid by the treasurer of the state upon the order of the comptroller. *1881. Witness fees to be paid.*

SEC. 17. The Railroad Commissioners shall make a report of the general conduct and condition of all railroads, and of any violation of law by any of them, to each general assembly in the second week of its session, with such suggestions for legislature as they deem proper. *1876. Report to General Assembly.*

Title VI.

SEC. 8. No petition for the incorporation of any railroad, horse railroad, canal, or turnpike company, or for *1844. 1865. Notice of petitions concern-*

ing railroad,
canal, or turn-
pike charters.

an alteration of the charter of any such company, shall be heard by the General Assembly, unless public notice shall have been given by advertisement in some newspaper published in the county where such railroad, horse railroad, canal, or turnpike is proposed to be, or is located, at least three weeks before the first day of the session to which such petition is brought, designating the intended route of such railroad, canal, or turnpike, the streets, highways, and other intended route of such horse railroad, or the proposed alteration of such charter; nor unless the petition for such railroad company is accompanied with, and supported by, the report of a skillful engineer, founded on examination, showing the general profile of the surface of the country through which said railroad is proposed to be made, the manner of its construction, the feasibility of the route, the character of the soil, and the probable expense of constructing the same.

1849.
Petitions to be
accompanied by
report of engi-
neer.

Title XVII, Chap. 2, Part 9.

ARTICLE I.

ORGANIZATION OF COMPANIES.

1871.
General railroad
law.

SECTION 1. Any number of persons not less than twenty-five may form a company for the purpose of constructing, maintaining, and operating a railroad for public use in the conveyance of persons and property.

Articles of as-
sociation.

SEC. 2. The persons forming such railroad company shall make and sign articles of association in which shall be stated: first, the name of the company; second, the place where its principal office or place of business is located, which shall be and continue in this State; third, the places from and to which, and the names of all the towns through or into which it is proposed to construct, maintain, and operate said road; fourth, the length of said railroad, as nearly as may be, and the amount of capital stock of the company, which shall not be less than ten thousand dollars for every mile of road proposed to be constructed; fifth, the names and residence of not less than nine directors of said company, who shall be chosen by the persons subscribing said articles of association, and a majority of whom shall always be residents of this State and who shall manage its affairs for one year; but the amount of the funded and floating debt of any such corporation shall at no time exceed the amount of cash actually paid in upon its capital stock.

Capital stock.

SEC. 3. The capital stock of said company shall be divided into shares of one hundred dollars each, and

each subscriber to such articles of association shall subscribe thereto his name, residence, and the number of
shares he agrees to take in such company; and on compliance with the provisions of the succeeding section .
such articles of association may be filed in the office of
the Secretary of this State, who shall endorse thereon
the day they are filed, and record them ; and thereupon
the persons who have subscribed such articles, together
with all persons who shall become stockholders of such
company, shall be a corporation by the name specified in Name.
such articles.

SEC. 4. Such articles of association shall not be filed Engineer's re-
and recorded unless they are accompanied by the report, pany the arti-
under oath, of a skillful engineer, founded on an actual cles of associa-
examination of the route, showing the character and tion.
structure of the proposed road-bed, with its indications
of rock or earth-cuttings; the manner in which it is proposed to construct said railroad; the general profile of
the surface of the country through which it is proposed to be made; the feasibility of the route, and an
estimate of the probable expense of constructing the
same; a copy of which report shall be kept on file in the
office of the Secretary of this State; nor shall such
articles of association be filed and recorded until at least
five thousand dollars of stock for every mile of railroad
proposed to be made is subscribed thereto, and ten *per
cent.* of such subscription paid in cash to the directors
named in said articles, nor unless there is annexed there-
to an affidavit made by at least three of said directors, Affidavit by di-
that the amount of stock required by this section has rectors.
been in good faith subscribed, and ten *per cent.* in cash
paid thereon as aforesaid, and that it is intended in good
faith to construct the road named in such articles; and
a copy of any articles of association filed and recorded
as aforesaid, or of the record thereof, certified by the
Secretary of this State, shall be *primá facie* evidence of
the due formation, existence, and capacity of said corporation.

SEC. 5. When such articles of association are re- Subscriptions
corded in the office of the Secretary, the directors may, stock.
in case the whole of the capital stock is not subscribed,
open books of subscription to the same in such places
and on such notice as they may deem expedient, and
may continue to receive subscriptions until the whole of
the capital stock is subscribed; and no subscription shall
be received or taken without such payment of ten *per
cent.;* but such company shall not commence the construction of its road until at least ten thousand dollars a
mile is subscribed to the capital stock thereof by responsible persons.

Powers of the company.

SEC. 6. Every railroad company may hold such real estate as may be convenient for accomplishing the objects of its organization; may by its agents enter upon such places as may be designated by its directors, for the purpose of making surveys and determining the line whereon to construct said railroad; and may construct, equip, and maintain a railway, with one or more tracks, over the route specified in its charter or articles of association, and transport persons and property theron by any power.

1867.
Right of way to be obtained in twelve months.

SEC. 7. No land shall be taken without the consent of its owner except within twelve months after the approval of the location of the route by the Railroad Commissioners;* and when the lands of any *feme covert*, infant, *cestui que trust*, or person *non compos mentis*, shall be necessary for the construction of any railroad, said lands may be taken on giving notice to the husband of such

Trustees may release.

feme covert, the trustee of any such *cestui que trust*, the guardian, either natural or appointed, of such infant, and the conservator of such person *non compos mentis*, who may respectively release all damages for lands so taken, as fully as if the same were holden in their own right.

1882.
Time for taking land.

SECTION 1. Every railroad company organized under the general railroad law may take land subject to the law in such case provided, at any time within two years after the approval of the location by the Railroad Commissioners.

When corporate existence ceases and Commissioners may extend time for taking land.

SEC. 2. If any railroad company formed under the provisions of article one, part nine, chapter two, title seventeen of the general statutes, shall not within two years after its articles of association are filed and recorded in the office of the secretary of this state, commence the construction of its road and expend thereon ten per cent. of the amount of its subscribed capital, or shall not finish or put in operation its railroad within five years from the time of filing and recording its articles of association as aforesaid, its corporate existence and powers shall cease; *provided*, that the Railroad Commissioners shall extend the time for the commencement of such railroad and expending ten per cent and for taking lands, for a period or periods not exceeding, in the whole, two years beyond the time of two years hereinbefore referred to, if said railroad company has been prevented by litigation, or by the opposition of any party, from complying with the provisions of this statute.

Under what conditions navigable waters may be bridged.

SEC. 3. Any railroad company organized under the provisions of the general railroad law may construct its railroad across navigable waters, when said railroad company shall have filed in the office of the secretary of

*See Secs. 1 and 6, Act 1882, pages 10 and 12.

this state a sworn statement of a competent engineer, approved by the railroad commissioners and the president
and treasurer of said railroad company, that there has
been expended in the construction of their railroad in
this state a sum equal to ten thousand dollars for each
mile of their said railroad within this state between either
terminal point in the location of said road and the proposed location of said bridge; *provided, however,* that no
bridge shall be constructed across any river or harbor
nearer the sea than some existing bridge across such
river or harbor; and further *provided,* that all such
bridges shall be constructed in such manner, and of such
materials and with draws of such width for the passage
of vessels, as the Railroad Commissioners of this state
shall authorize and direct; but nothing herein shall be
construed to authorize any railroad company to construct
or use a bridge for any but railroad purposes.

SEC. 4. Any railroad company may, subject to the The issue of
existing provisions of law, issue bonds and execute bonds.
mortgages to an amount not exceeding one-half of the
sum which its president, treasurer, and an engineer approved by the railroad commissioners shall certify under
oath to the comptroller of this state has been actually
expended upon its railroad; and any false swearing
in the matter shall be perjury. *Provided, however,* That
the whole amount of bonds outstanding at any one time
shall not exceed one-half of the actual cost of the construction of such railroad.

SEC. 5. No other railroad company shall subscribe Ownership in
for, take, or hold any stock or bonds of any railroad other railroad
company established under the general railroad law, prohibited un-
either directly or indirectly, unless specially authorized authorized.
by the general assembly.

SEC. 6. Every railroad company, after its line of How additional
railroad shall have been located, approved, and estab- land is obtained.
lished, may take land for additional tracks, turnouts, and
freight and passenger stations and depots, in the manner
provided by law for the taking of lands by railroad companies; also for the purpose of supplying water for the
use of its engines and stations.

SEC. 7. Section nine of article one, part nine, chapter Repeal.
two, title seventeen (page 317) of the general statutes,
and all acts and parts of acts inconsistent herewith, are
hereby repealed.

SEC. 8. In case the capital stock of any railroad com- Increase of cap-
pany is found to be insufficient, it may, with the concur- ital stock.
rence of two-thirds in amount of the stock represented
at a meeting of the stockholders called for that purpose,

increase its capital stock to such amount as may be required for the purposes of said road, and in such manner and on such terms as may be prescribed by said meeting; and the board of directors of any railroad company may at any time, with the consent of the stockholders, increase its capital stock to an amount sufficient to extinguish its funded and floating debt; but the amount of such increased capital stock, at its par value, shall not exceed the amount of such debts, and such increased stock shall only be issued to take up and cancel an equal amount of debts as aforesaid.

1878.
Proceedings by railroad company desiring to increase its capital stock.

SECTION 1. Whenever any railroad company shall desire to increase its capital stock, it shall make application to the Railroad Commissioners in writing, setting forth the amount to which and the purpose for which it is desired to make such increase. Whereupon the commissioners shall fix a time and place for hearing such application, and require such notice thereof to be given as they may deem reasonable.

Finding of facts, report and recommendation by R. R. Commissioners.

SEC. 2. The Commissioners shall make a finding of all the essential facts presented to them in regard to such proposed increase of capital stock, and report the same to the next session of the general assembly, with a recommendation whether such increase should be allowed or not, and if allowed, the manner in which and terms upon which such stock should be issued.

Capital stock not to be increased by R. R. Co. without special authority.

SEC. 3. No railroad company shall increase its capital stock except by special authority of the general assembly nor shall such authority be given except upon the recommendation of the railroad commissioners as herein provided.

This act operative without special acceptance.

SEC. 4. It shall not be necessary for the provisions of this act to be accepted by any railroad company before the same shall become operative as an amendment to the charter of such company.

Repeal.

SEC. 5. All acts and parts of acts inconsistent herewith are hereby repealed.

These provisions not to apply to horse railroads, nor authorize bridging navigable waters, or interfering with existing railroads.

SEC. 10. Nothing contained in this article shall be construed to authorize the construction of any horse railroad in any city or borough; or the bridging of navigable waters* or the taking or using the track, wharves, depot or depot grounds of any other company without its consent, except for the purpose of crossing or connection.

---

* See Section 3, Act 1882, page 11.

ARTICLE II.

STEAM RAILROADS.

1. OFFICERS AND MEMBERS.

SECTION 1. All railroad companies which transport passengers or freight on their roads otherwise than by animal power alone, shall have all the powers and be subject to all the provisions contained in the succeeding sections of this article respecting such companies, except otherwise specially provided in their charters.

1840.
1862. 1871.
What railroads included in the provisions of this article.

Company officers and by-laws.

SEC. 2. The direction of the affairs of every such company shall be vested in a board of not less than nine directors, annually chosen by the company, who may fill any vacancies which may occur in their number, and shall elect one of their own number president of the board, who shall also be president of the company, and may also choose a secretary, who shall also be secretary of the company, and be sworn to a faithful discharge of his duty, and a treasurer, who shall give bonds to the company in such sum as shall be required by the by-laws, for the faithful discharge of his trust, and such other officers as they may deem expedient, and may make by-laws and regulations in regard to the management of the stock, property, and affairs of said company.

1849.
Meetings, how called; stock votes.

SEC. 4. All meetings of the company shall be called in such a manner as shall be provided in the by-laws, and at such meetings each member shall be entitled to one vote for each share held by him.

1853.
Officers, when not to vote on stock of others.

SEC. 5. Every railroad company may prohibit the officers from voting in the election of directors upon any other stock than their own; and no officer of such company shall request any stockholder to execute a power of attorney to vote upon his stock; and no person shall be allowed to vote by virtue of a power so obtained;

Penalty.

and any person who shall violate the provisions of this section shall be disqualified from holding any office in said company for one year thereafter.

Title XVII., Chap. I.

Stock not to be voted on, if assessments are unpaid.

SEC. 6. No subscriber to the capital stock of any railroad company shall be allowed to vote on any of said stock, unless all assessments or installments on it, legally called in by such company, shall have been paid in full.

Who may vote on share of railroad stock subscribed for by towns.

SEC. 7. The agent appointed by the town to subscribe for stock in any railroad company may vote on the shares of stock subscribed for by him, in all meetings of such company, unless such town shall otherwise direct.

1831. 1852.
Proxies, limitation of.

SEC. 11. No person shall vote at any meeting of the stockholders of any bank or railroad company, by virtue of any power of attorney not executed within one year next preceding such meeting; and no such power shall be used at more than one annual meeting of such corporation.

1882.

SECTION 1. Every railroad corporation, before applying to the Railroad Commissioners for their approval of the location of its road, shall deposit with the state treasurer a sum equal to eleven dollars per mile of the length of its proposed road in this state. And the comptroller shall include such corporation among the several railroad companies in his next annual apportionment of the office expenses and salaries of the board, estimating the length of its main track or tracks as equal to said proposed length of road. And the state treasurer shall deduct the amount so apportioned to such corporation from said deposit, and return the remainder to the treasurer of such corporation.

SEC. 2. This act shall take effect on the first day of January, A. D. 1883.

3. LOCATION AND CONSTRUCTION.

SEC. 18. Every railroad company may lay out its road not exceeding six rods wide, and for the purpose of cuttings, embankments, and procuring stone and gravel, and for necessary turnouts, may take as much more real estate within the limits of its charter as may be necessary for the proper construction and security of the road; but no real estate without the limits of said road shall be so taken, without the permission of the parties interested therein, unless the Railroad Commissioners, on application of such company, and after notice to said parties, shall first prescribe the limits within which real estate shall be taken for said purposes; and no railroad company shall lay out and finally locate its road, without the written approbation of the location by said Commissioners, except so far as the location is definitely fixed in the charter or articles of association, provided that all damages that may be occasioned to any person by the taking of any real estate for said purposes, shall be paid for by said company, as hereinafter provided. *1849. Company may lay out road and take land on payment of appraisal. Commissioners shall prescribe limits.*

SEC. 19. Every railroad company, after its line of road shall have been located, approved, and established, may so far alter the location of such road as to change the radius of its curves, straighten and improve its lines, with, and extent of depot grounds, slopes and embankments, and extend its lines of sight, when such changes are approved by the Railroad Commissioners; * a certificate of which changes, duly signed by such Commissioners, shall be lodged for record in the town clerk's office, in the town or towns where such changes are made. *1863. Alteration of location. Certificate of alteration to be recorded.*

No railroad company shall hereafter lay out or locate its road, or any part thereof, through any cemetery or any approach in common use from the highway thereto, and within one-quarter of a mile thereof, unless the Railroad Commissioners, when called upon to approve the proposed *1881. Road not to be built through cemeteries.*

* See Sec. 6, Act 1882, page 12.

lay-out of said road, shall find that said cemetery or the approach thereto was located for the purpose of obstruct-ing such lay-out, or unless said Commissioners shall unanimously approve such lay-out or location.

1849. 1863.
1871. 1874.
Land, now taken, appraisal, damages, etc.

SEC. 20. When any railroad company shall have the right to take real estate for railroad purposes, and can-not obtain it by agreement with the parties interested therein, it may apply to any judge of the Superior Court for the appointment of appraisers to estimate all dam-ages that may arise to any person from the taking and occupation of such real estate for railroad purposes, and after reasonable notice of said application shall have been given to all parties in interest, such judges shall appoint three appraisers, who shall be sworn, and give reason-able notice to said parties in regard to the time and place of making such estimate, and shall view the premises and estimate such damage, but shall not include in such estimate the expense of erecting and maintaining fences along the line of such railroad; and shall return an ap-praisal of such damages in writing, under their hands, to the clerk of the Superior Court in the county where the estate lies, who shall record it; and when so re-turned and recorded such appraisal shall have the effect of a judgment, and execution may issue at the end of sixty days from the time of such return, in favor of the persons respectively to whom damages may be appraised;

Railroad not to be worked until damages have been paid.

and said appraisers shall be paid by said company for the time actually spent in making such appraisal and re-turn; but no railroad shall be worked upon, or opened across any real estate, until the damages, appraised to any person interested therein, shall have been paid or secured to be paid to his satisfaction, or deposited with the treasurer of the county for his use.†

[1876.
How a railroad company may be relieved of an easement re-served in a deed to them, in some cases.

SECTION 1. Whenever any grant or conveyance to any railroad company of any parcel or parcels of land or right of way, reserves any right, title, interest, easement, or privilege in such land, or subject such company to special conditions or covenants, which reservations, con-ditions, or covenants may interfere with said company furnishing reasonable and proper depot accommodations to the public, and such company cannot agree with the party or parties in interest as to the compensation or damages to be paid for the release of such reservation, condition, or covenant, then such company may, with the approval of the Railroad Commissioners first had and obtained, condemn such reservation, condition, cove-

---

† Owners of fee highway, on which a railroad is located, entitled to dam-ages. 26 Conn., 249. Incidental injury to adjacent land of same proprietor to be considered. 21 Conn., 294.

nant, or restriction in the same manner as is provided Gen. Statutes, p. 321. for taking, appraising, and paying for land in section twenty, of part nine, chapter two, of title seventeen, of the General Statutes of this State.

SEC. 2. This act shall not affect any suit now pending. Pending suits not affected.

SEC. 21. When any real estate shall have been laid out for railroad purposes, and the damages shall have been appraised, and such road, or any part thereof, shall have been abandoned or discontinued before the same shall have been opened and worked, no such execution shall issue, nor shall an action be brought against said company for the recovery of such damages by any of the owners of land over which such road or part of a road shall have been laid out and discontinued as aforesaid; but any such owner may recover of such company the actual damage which he may have suffered in consequence of the laying out of such road, or from any unreasonable delay in opening and working the same. 1858. Land owners to recover actual damages only, where road is discontinued.

SEC. 22. When any railroad company shall take any property for the purposes of its railroad, the owner of such property may at any time within three years thereafter in writing of the treasurer of the company a written description of the property so taken, and said company shall within thirty days deliver to him such description; and if it fail to do so all its rights to enter upon or use said property, except for making surveys, shall be suspended until it shall have so delivered such description. 1849. Owners may require a plan of land taken.

SEC. 23. Within ninety days after the railroad of any company shall have been laid out in any town and approved by the Railroad Commissioners, such company shall deposit with the town clerk a correct plan, signed by its president, or so much of said railroad as lies in said town, drawn upon a scale of at least five inches to the mile, upon which shall be accurately delineated the direction and length of each course, and the width of the land taken. Corporations to deposit plan of road with town clerk.

SEC. 24. Every railroad company shall, within six months after the final location of its road, file a statement of such location, defining the courses and distances, with the Secretary of this State. Location of road to be filed in Secretary's office.

SEC. 25. Every railroad company in making contracts for the building of its road shall require sufficient security from the contractors for the payment of all labor thereafter performed in constructing the road by persons in their employ; and such company shall be liable to the laborers employed, for labor actually performed on the road, if they within twenty days after the 1870. Security from contractors for paying laborers, liability of company therefor.

2

completion of such labor shall in writing notify its treasurer that they have not been paid by the contractors.

Title XVIII, Chap 7.

**1871.
Lien on railroad for services or materials furnished for its construction.**

SEC. 13.   Every railroad for the construction of which, or of any of its appurtenances, any person shall have a claim for materials furnished or services rendered under any contract with or approved by the corporation owning or managing such railroad, shall, with its real estate, right of way, material, equipment, rolling stock, and franchise, be subject to the payment of such claim ; and said claim shall be a lien on said railroad, railroad property, and franchise, and the manner of asserting and perfecting such lien, by notice, certificate, and foreclosure, shall be in all respects in accordance with the provisions of the four preceding sections of this chapter ; except that the certificates of the lien and of its discharge shall be filed in the office of the Secretary of this State, who shall record them in a book kept for that purpose.

**1882.
Intersections or connections with other roads.**

SECTION 1.   Any railroad company may in the construction of its railroad cross the railroad of any other company or connect with the same ; and if it cannot agree with such other railroad company, or the managers thereof, as to such crossing or connection, the Railroad Commissioners may determine the place and manner of such crossing or connection, after reasonable notice to the several companies in interest to appear and be heard in relation to the matters contained in such notices, and may make such orders as to bridges, abutments, piers, tunnels, arches, excavations, retaining walls, embankments, and approaches as they shall judge necessary; but no railroad shall cross any other railroad at grade without the consent and approval of the Railroad Commissioners.

SEC. 2.   This act shall not affect any existing grade crossing, or any grade crossing which has been authorized or approved by the Railroad Commissioners.

SEC. 3.   This act shall not affect the crossing of the New York & New England Railroad by the Hartford & Connecticut Valley Railroad, authorized at this session of the General Assembly.

Contracts with connecting or intersecting roads.

SEC. 27.   Any railroad company may make lawful contracts with any other railroad company with whose railway its tracks may connect or intersect, in relation to its business or property, and may take a lease of the property or franchises of, or lease its property or franchises to, any such railway company ; and may construct

Branches.

branches from the main line to any place in this State, subject to the provisions of this Part.

Sec. 1. No lease of any railroad hereafter made shall be binding on either of the contracting parties for a period of more than twelve months, unless the same shall be approved by the stockholders of the company or companies that are parties to the lease, by a vote of two-thirds of the stock represented in person or by proxy, at a meeting of the stockholders called for that purpose, and at least one month's notice shall be given of such meeting by advertising twice a week for four weeks in a daily paper published in the State, and also by mailing a copy of the call and of the lease to each stockholder; and said notice and call shall state that at the meeting the lease will be submitted for the approval of the stockholders.

1878.
Leases of railroads regulated.

Sec. 28. When it shall be necessary for the construction of a railroad to intersect or cross any water-course not navigable, or any public highway, the railroad company may construct said railroad across or upon the same if the Railroad Commissioners shall judge it necessary ; but said company shall restore said watercourse or highway, thus intersected, to its former state ; or in a sufficient manner not to impair its usefulness ; and in case any highway is so located that said railroad cannot be judiciously constructed across or upon the same without interfering therewith, said company may, with the consent of said Commissioners, cause such highway to be changed or altered, so that said railroad may be made on the best site for that purpose; but said company shall put such highway in as good situation and repair as it was previous to such alteration, under the direction of said Commissioners, whose determination thereon shall be final.*

1849.
Crossing highways or water-courses.

Sec. 29. When any railroad company shall be authorized by the Railroad Commissioners to cross any stream of water, or water-course, not navigable, or pond of water, an appeal shall be allowed to any interested person aggrieved by such permission, to any judge of the Superior Court, within twenty days after the owners of the land adjoining said stream, at the point of said crossing, shall have had actual notice of the manner in which said Commissioners have permitted said stream to be crossed ; which appeal shall be by a suitable petition, in writing, for a hearing in regard to the crossing, with a citation attached thereto, returnable within twelve days after its date, and served at least five days before the return day, upon such company. And said judge shall have, for the purpose of disposing of said appeal,

1869.
Appeals from order authorizing the crossing of non-navigable streams.

---

* Determination of Commissioners cannot be reviewed by the Superio. Court. 27 Conn., 146.

all the powers of the Superior Court, and may proceed,
by himself or by committee, to a hearing in regard to
the propriety of said manner of crossing ; and may
render a decree either establishing more and sufficient
water-way at the place of crossing, or providing such
method of crossing that the usefulness and safety of
said stream may be preserved, and that the safety of the
public may not be endangered ; or may confirm said
mode of crossing; and if said alteration is so decreed
may award costs against said company; and if said
Award of costs. mode of crossing is confirmed, may award costs against
the appellants, and may issue execution in favor of either
party for costs, to be taxed as in civil actions in court.
Appeal to be a Said appeal shall be a *supersedeas*, so far as said crossing
supersedeas. is concerned, until judgment shall be rendered thereon
by said judge.

1849.
May change lo-
cation or alter
level of roads,
intersected un-
der direction of
Commissioners.
SEC. 30. Every railroad company, which may locate
and construct a railroad across any turnpike, highway,
or public street, shall construct it so as to cross over or
under the same; and may, under the direction of Railroad Commissioners, raise or lower the same at said
crossing, or change the location thereof ; and shall make
and maintain such bridges, abutments, tunnels, arches,
excavations, embankments, and approaches, as the convenience and safety of the public travel upon said turnpike, highway, or street may require ; but the Railroad
Commissioners may, upon due notice to said company
and to the selectmen of the town or mayor of the city in
which said crossing is situated, direct such company
to construct its railroad at such crossing, upon a level
with the turnpike, highway, or street.*

1865.
Warning boards
at grade cross-
ings.
SEC. 31. Every railroad company shall keep and maintain at each crossing at grade of any highway, at which
there is no gate, warning boards of such a description as
the Railroad Commissioners may approve.

1871.
Right of way
for highways
for railroads,
how obtained.
SEC. 32. When any highway or street shall be
changed or altered by any railroad company with the
consent of the Railroad Commissioners, and it shall be
necessary to take any land for a highway to which such
company has not obtained a title, and over which neither
said company nor the town in which such change shall
be made has any right of way, and said company is
unable to agree with the owner thereof in regard to the
amount of damages to be paid therefor, the same proceedings shall be had for the purpose of procuring the
required right of way as are provided by the twentieth
section of this Article, in regard to taking land for railroad purposes.

* To what extent the company is bound to maintain approaches, &c. 39
Conn., 128.

SEC. 33. All covered bridges constructed on the line of any railroad shall not be less than eighteen feet in height from the top surface of the rail laid in the track on the bridge to the under side of the cross-beams overhead.* 1869.
Covered bridges, height of.

RAILROAD BRIDGES AND BRIDGE GUARDS.

SECTION 1. Every railroad corporation shall, within six months from the passage of this act, if required by the Railroad Commissioners, erect and thereafter maintain suitable bridge guards at every bridge over its railroad less than eighteen feet in height above the track; such bridge guards to be approved by the railroad commissioners, and to be erected and adjusted to their satisfaction. 1878.
Railroad companies to erect bridge guards.

SEC. 2. Any railroad corporation refusing or neglecting to comply with the provisions of this act, shall, for each month of continuance in such refusal or neglect, forfeit and pay to any person who shall sue therefor, the sum of fifty dollars, to be recovered in an action of debt on this statute. Penalty for neglect.

SEC. 34. When, in the opinion of the selectmen of any town, or of the Common Council of any city, a footway upon the line of any railroad bridge or causeway within the limits of such town or city would be of public convenience, and the railroad company owning such bridge or causeway shall not consent thereto, such selectmen or common council may call out the Railroad Commissioners, who, after due notice to such company, shall inquire into the facts, at the expense of such town or city. And if said Commissioners shall find that a footway along such bridge or causeway would be of public convenience or accommodation, they shall authorize such town or city to construct and maintain the same at their own expense, and to attach the same for support to such bridge or causeway: *provided*, such footway be constructed entirely outside of the bridge or causeway to which it is attached, and so constructed, used, and maintained as not to interfere with the necessary and proper use of such bridge or causeway by such company. 1866.
Footways upon Railroad bridges.

SEC. 45. Every railroad company shall construct suitable cattle-guards and fences therefrom at all crossings of passways or highways, to prevent cattle from passing upon its railroad, except when the Railroad Commissioners deem it unnecessary.† 1850. 1874.
Cattle-guards.

---

* For the height required for bridges in highways over railroads, see Title XVI, Chapter VII, Part I.
† See 37 Conn., 479.

1881.
Where Rail-
road Companies
shall erect and
maintain
fences.

SECTION 1. Every railroad company shall erect and maintain fences on the sides of the railroads operated by it at such place or places as the Railroad Commissioners shall direct; and every railroad company operating any railroad constructed under any act of incorporation passed since the first Wednesday of May, 1850, or hereafter constructed, shall cause sufficient fences to be erected and maintained on the sides of such railroads, except at such place or places as the Railroad Commissioners shall adjudge them unnecessary; such fences to be erected by all companies hereafter organized, within twelve months after they enter upon and take possession of the lands through which their railroads pass.

Commissioners
shall judge as to
necessity of
fences. Order
to be served on
secretary of
company.

SEC. 2. Said Commissioners shall make special investigation as to the necessity or condition of fences on the line of any railroad, when so requested in writing, and when judged necessary shall issue their order directing the company operating said railroad to erect or repair said fences. Said order shall specify the place or places, the manner in which, and the time within which the fence is to be erected or repaired; which order shall be served upon said company by some indifferent person by leaving with its secretary, or at his usual place of abode, a true and attested copy thereof within six days from its date.

Penalty.

SEC. 3. If any railroad company shall neglect to comply with any such order it shall forfeit to the state of Connecticut one hundred dollars per month for each and every month of such neglect. The Railroad Commissioners shall give notice of all such forfeitures to the state treasurer, who shall collect the same. And any person who, without neglect on his part, shall suffer damage by reason of the neglect of any railroad company to erect or maintain fences as required by law, may recover such damage from such company.

Lien of com-
pany on land of
owners neglect-
ing to fence.

SEC. 4. When it shall be the duty of the owner of land adjoining any railroad to erect or maintain a fence between said land and said railroad, and such owner shall have unduly neglected to erect or maintain the same, and it shall have been erected or maintained by the railroad company in conformity to the order of the Railroad Commissioners, said company may collect the cost of erecting and maintaining such fence from such owner. Such cost shall be a lien in favor of such company on said land, and it shall take precedence of every other lien or incumbrance on said land, and may be foreclosed in the same manner as a mortgage lien, but shall not continue in force unless said company shall, within sixty days after the completion of said fence, lodge a certificate with the town clerk of the town in which said land is situated, describing said land and specifying the amount claimed as a lien thereon, and the dates of the commencement and completion of said fence, which certificate shall be recorded by said town clerk on the land records of said town.

SEC. 5. When by contract neither the owner of such land, nor the railroad company, can oblige the owner to erect or maintain the fence; or such owner or his grantor has agreed not to require the railroad company to erect or maintain such fence, and the same shall have been so erected or maintained by any company by order of the Railroad Commissioners as aforesaid, said railroad company may collect one-half of the cost of erecting and maintaining the same from such owner, and the same shall be a lien on the lands of such owner as provided in the preceding chapter. *Mode of procedure when contract protects both parties.*

SEC. 6. When any railroad shall be operated by a trustee or trustees the duties and liabilities imposed and the rights conferred by the preceding sections upon companies operating railroads are hereby imposed and conferred upon such trustee or trustees. All orders of the Commissioners upon such trustees shall be served by leaving a true and attested copy of such order with or at the usual place of abode of one of such trustees by some indifferent person within six days of the date thereof. *Order for fence binding on trustees.*

SEC. 7. Sections thirty-five, thirty-seven, thirty-eight, thirty-nine, forty, forty-one, forty-two, forty-three, and forty-four, title seventeen, chapter two, part nine, article two, of the general statutes ; an act entitled "An Act concerning Railroads," approved July twenty-third, 1875; an act entitled "An Act in addition to an Act entitled 'Civil Actions,'" approved March twenty seventh, 1878; an act entitled "An Act amending an Act in relation to Railroads," approved March twenty-eighth, 1878, and all other acts inconsistent herewith, are hereby repealed, but this act shall not affect any suit now pending, nor any order of the Railroad Commissioners heretofore made. *Repeal.*

SEC. 46. When any railroad company shall neglect to construct any highway or bridge, which it is its duty to construct, or to keep in repair any bridge, embankment, filling, or abutment, which it is its duty to maintain, the State's attorney in any county wherein such neglect exists, or in which the whole or any part of said highway or bridge is situated, shall make complaint thereof to the Superior Court for such county, which shall proceed in the same manner against said railroad company as is required against towns neglecting to con- *1857. State's Attorney to complain if company neglect to repair highway.*

struct any road laid out by the Superior Court, or to keep in repair any public road within their limits, which it is their duty to construct or keep in repair.

4. DEPOTS.

1866.
When railroad trains shall stop near villages.
SEC. 47. When the business center of any village containing two hundred inhabitants is more than one and a half miles from the nearest station on a railroad, and not more than one-third of a mile from said road, the Railroad Commissioners, upon the petition of twenty of said inhabitants, after due inquiry, may make such orders in regard to the stoppage of any of the trains upon said railroad, at or near said village, for the purpose of receiving and discharging passengers and freight, as they shall deem just and reasonable; and no railroad company, whose trains may be thus required to stop, shall charge more than five cents for each mile and fraction of a mile, for transporting passengers between such stopping-place and the next station.

1865.
Stations, how established.
SEC. 48. When twenty electors shall present their petition to a judge of the Superior Court, alleging that the managers of any unfinished railroad ought to establish a station at or near a place named, and that they have reason to fear that said managers do not intend so to do, he shall, after due notice to said managers, appoint a practical engineer skilled in the construction of railroads, who, after being duly sworn, shall, with the Railroad Commissioners, hear said petition, after due notice to all parties in interest; and if on such hearing said Commissioners concur with said engineer in finding such petition true, they shall in writing designate the place within the limits embraced in said petition, where said company would establish and maintain a suitable station; and said company shall establish and maintain said station at such place; if the Commissioners shall concur

Petition to be dismissed if found untrue; engineer and Commissioners to make separate reports, if they disagree.
with said engineer in finding said petition untrue, they shall dismiss the same; and if said engineer shall not concur with said Commissioners, he and they shall each make a written report of the facts found by them, respectively, and of their respective opinions thereon, to said judge, who shall thereupon make such order as, upon an examination of said reports, he may deem reasonable; and any order so made by him against said company shall be binding upon it.

Security for compensation of engineer.
SEC. 49. Said judge may at any time require said petitioners, on penalty of dismissal of their petition, to give such security as he shall order for the payment of such fees and expenses of said engineer as shall be taxed by him after due hearing of the parties thereon, which

shall be paid by the petitioners ; but, if said judge shall
so order, the whole or a part thereof shall be refunded
by said company to the petitioners.

SEC. 50. No railroad company shall abandon any
station on its road, in this State, after the same has been
established for twelve months, except by the approval of
the Railroad Commissioners, given after a public hearing held at such station, notice of which shall be posted
conspicuously in said station for one month previous to
the hearing.

SEC. 51. Any station on any railroad in this State,
which was abandoned between the first day of January
and the fourth day of July, 1866, shall upon the petition to the Railroad Commissioners of thirty freeholders
residing in the town where said station was located, be
restored, upon the approval of said Commissioners given
after a public hearing held at the station nearest to said
abandoned station, and after notice of said hearing shall
have been conspicuously posted at the place of hearing
for one month previously to the hearing.*

SEC. 52. Any person aggrieved by any order of the
Railroad Commissioners made after the fourteenth day
of August, 1874, upon any proceeding relative to the
location, abandonment, or changing of dépôts or stations,
to which he was or ought to have been made a party,
may appeal from the same to the Superior Court of the
county in which the cause of appeal shall arise, within
twenty days after the publication of such order, by a
petition in writing, with a proper citation, signed by
competent authority, to all parties to said proceedings
having an interest adverse to him, to be served upon
them at least five days before the return day ; and said
court may hear said appeal and re-examine the question
of the propriety and expediency of the order appealed
from, either by itself or a committee, and shall proceed
thereon in the same manner as upon petitions in equity ;
and in case said order is not affirmed, may make any
other order in the premises that it may deem proper ;
and may award costs at its discretion. Such appeal
shall be a *supersedeas* of the order appealed from, until
the final action of said court thereon, and said final order
may be enforced by said court by attachment, *mandamus*
or otherwise, as it shall deem proper.

SEC. 53. When any railroad company in this State
shall refuse to stop any of its passenger trains at any
station, any ten freeholders of the town in which such
station is situated may make their application in writing
to the Superior Court, and if said court is not in session

Margin notes:
1866. Stations not to be discontinued without approval of Commissioners.
Abandoned stations, how re-established.
1874. Appeals from Railroad Commissioners.
1868. Application to Superior Court to compel companies to stop passenger trains at dépôt.

* As to what constitutes a station, see 37 Conn., 153.

to any judge thereof, praying that said company may be ordered to stop the train or trains mentioned in said application at said station ; to which application a citation shall be annexed, and the same shall be served upon such company at least six days before the return day named therein.

Hearing before committee. SEC. 54. Said court, or judge, as the case may be, shall appoint a committee of three disinterested persons, who, being first duly sworn, shall hear and decide upon said application at such time and place, and with such notice to those interested, as said court or judge shall order ; and if said committee shall be of opinion that said application ought to .be granted, they may order said company to stop its train or trains in the manner prescribed in said order, and make such other order as they shall deem just and reasonable, and shall make return of their doings to the next term of said court.

Report of committee. SEC. .55.' Upon such return, either party may object to the acceptance of the same for irregularity or improper conduct, and the court for such cause may set it aside and order a rehearing ; but if the court accept the same it shall be conclusive, and said company shall obey said order.

Order, how enforced. Costs. SEC. 56. Said order may be enforced by *mandamus*, and the costs of said proceedings may be taxed by said committee against either or both of said parties.

5. OBLIGATIONS OF AND TO COMPANIES.

1859. 1864. Companies to afford each other mutual facilities. SEC. 57. Every railroad company shall run its trains each way for passengers at such times and in such manner as to afford reasonable facilities for receiving passengers from, and delivering them to, the other railroads in this State, connected therewith ; and when the business connections of the railroad of any company with the railroad of any other company are not convenient and reasonable for the accommodation of passengers over said road, said company shall make such connections as the public travel and business may require.

1864. How compelled to make proper connections. SEC. 58. Any person who shall be aggrieved by the neglect of any railroad company to make such connections may prefer a petition against such company to any judge of the Superior Court, who is not resident of the county in which the grievance complained of exists, averring such neglect, which petition shall be served upon the respondents at least twelve days before it is made returnable ; and said judge shall, by himself or by **Hearing before a committee. Order.** a committee, inquire into the allegations of the petition, after such notice of the hearing as he shall order, and, if the allegations in the petition are found to be true, shall order such company to make such connections, on penalty of forfeiting to the petitioner not less than fifty dollars for each day that it shall fail to comply with said order ; and in such case the judge may tax costs at his discretion, and issue execution therefor. Costs.

SEC. 59. When the railroad of any company, being a trunk road, shall, at or near the same place, connect with or be intersected by two or more other railroads, which are competing lines for the business to or from such trunk railroad, equal facilities, including price and rates, shall be afforded by the company operating said trunk road to each of said competing roads, in the interchange of cars and transportation of freight, as well as in ticketing passengers and checking baggage. *1859. Trunk roads to afford equal facilities to intersecting roads.*

SEC. 60. If any such competing railroad company shall at any time deem itself aggrieved in reference to such facilities, its managers may complain to the Railroad Commissioners, who, after due notice and hearing, shall prescribe such regulations as will, in their judgment, secure reasonable facilities for the accommodation of the business of each of said connecting railroads, and fix the terms on which such facilities shall be afforded by or to each of said railroad companies ; and the Superior Court may compel the performance thereof, by attachment, *mandamus*, or otherwise, and the expenses of the proceedings shall be paid by said parties, as shall be determined on by said court. *How to compel such facilities to be furnished.*

SEC. 61. When it shall appear to the Railroad Commissioners, by the written complaint of the president, or a majority of the directors, of any railroad company in this State, or of a majority of the selectmen of any town through which any railroad passes, that the business connections of any other railroad connected with such railroad are not convenient and reasonable for the accommodation of the inhabitants on the line of such road, said Commissioners shall forthwith cause a notice to be given to all parties interested, specifying the time and place of hearing such complaint, and on such hearing, if good and sufficient cause exist, shall make such regulations in relation thereto as they shall deem proper ; and any railroad company neglecting to comply with such regulations shall forfeit to the state twenty-five dollars for each day of such neglect. *1856. 1859. Order by Railroad Commissioners as to connections to be made.*

SEC 62. Every person or corporation owning or operating any railroad, located wholly or in part within this State, which connects with any other railroad in this State, shall receive, and with reasonable dispatch draw over the same, the passengers, merchandise, and cars of the person or corporation owning or operating such con- *1874. All connecting roads to have equal facilities.*

necting railroad, and shall not in any manner discriminate as to time and price for such hauling against said
connecting railroad, in favor of other shippers at said
point of connection ; and if any such person or corporation shall fail so to do, complaint may be made thereof by
such connecting railroad to the Railroad Commissioners,
who, after reasonable notice to such person or corporation complained of, shall, if, upon a hearing, they find
the complaint true, order such person or corporation to
receive and forward, as herein provided for. such passengers, merchandise, and cars as may be delivered to
him or it by said connecting railroad.

Penalty.   SEC. 63.   Any person or corporation owning or operating any railroad, as aforesaid, refusing to conform to
any order made, as aforesaid, shall be fined twenty-five
dollars for each offense.

1882.
Couplers for   SECTION 1.   Every corporation, company, or associa-
freight cars. tion, operating any railroad located partially or wholly
in this State, shall cause every freight car that shall be
hereafter built or purchased for use on such railroad. to
be provided with couplers so arranged as to render the
presence of any person between the ends of the cars unnecessary for the purpose of coupling the same.

To be approved   SEC. 2.   No couplers shall hereafter be placed on any
by the Commis- freight cars built or purchased as before stated, nor
sioners. shall any new couplers be substituted for any that are
now in use, until the same shall have been approved by
the Railroad Commissioners, and such couplers shall be
hung at such height above the face of the railroad track
as shall be designated by such Commissioners.

Penalty.   SEC. 3.   Every corporation, company, or association
operating any railroad, who shall permit a violation of
this statute, shall forfeit for every such violation the sum
of fifty dollars to the treasury of this State, the same
to be recovered in a proper action founded on this
statute.

SEC. 4.   This act shall take effect on the first day of
July, A. D. 1882.

1866. 1867. 1872.   SEC. 64.   Every railroad company shall provide its
Connecting
aprons. passenger, baggage. mail, and express cars with suitable
platforms to secure the safety of persons passing from
car to car, or connecting aprons or bridges, to the approbation of said Commissioners, except that freight or
baggage cars need not be thus connected with the platform of a passenger car attached to a freight train; shall
1866. not allow any hand car, or other car not moved by steam,
Hand-cars. belonging to it, and used upon its railroad, when removed
from the railroad track (except when placed in a build-
ing prepared for it), to remain within fifty feet of any

road or highway crossing said track; shall from the first day of May until the first day of November, annually, carry through each passenger car, once an hour, a suitable quantity of good drinking-water for the free use of the passengers, with suitable appurtenances for carrying it, and a clean glass tumbler for using it; shall give each passenger, who shall be separated from his baggage by said company, a receipt or check for it at the time of receiving it; and shall conspicuously post on each passenger dépôt building the name of the station, and on each passenger car which leaves the *termini* of their own or any other road, a legible card, or cards, not less than three feet in length, with large letters, distinguishing way from express trains, and designating the direction in which the trains are next to move, unless such cards shall be dispensed with by the Commissioners.

1864.
Water.

1848.
Checks.

1872.
Name of station.

1866.
Designation of way and express trains.

SEC. 65. No person shall fraudulently evade, or attempt to evade, the payment of any fare lawfully established by a railroad company, and whoever does not, upon demand, first pay such fare, shall not be entitled to be transported over any railroad; but conductors or employees of railroad companies shall not put a passenger off from trains between stations.

1867.
Penalty for fraudulently evading payment of fare.

SEC. 66. No railroad company, which has had a system of commutation fares in force for more than four years, shall abolish or alter it, except for the regulation of the price charged for such commutation; and such price shall, in no case, be raised to an extent that shall alter the ratio as it existed on the first day of July, 1865, between such commutation and the rates then charged for way fare, on the railroad of such company.

1865.
Change in commutation fare.

SEC. 67. Every railroad company shall transport milk for every person by the same trains and upon the same conditions as the milk of any other person is transported by it.

1873.
Transportation of milk.

Any railroad company which shall refuse to transport over the line of its road any railroad ties, sleepers, or material to be used in the construction or repair of any other railroad, at the same rate or price as other freight of the same class, shall be deemed guilty of a misdemeanor, and liable to a fine not less than fifty dollars, nor more than three hundred dollars for each and every offense, half to him who shall sue therefor, and half to the state.

1879.
Penalty of railroad company refusing to transport material for repair of another road.

SEC. 68. All the conductors, brakemen, and baggagemen, employed upon the passenger trains of any railroad company, shall wear, when on duty, in a conspicuous place, a badge denoting their respective duties, and the name of such company.

1856.
Certain employees to wear badges.

1849.
1865. 1867.
Being on car
platform, or
grounds,or driv-
ing on track.

SEC. 69. No person shall, without the permission of the managers of the railroad, be upon, or attach himself to, any engine or car upon the track of any railroad, or occupy any part of the platform, or grounds of any railroad station, nor ride, drive, or lead any beast on said track, except for the purpose of crossing it.

Agents of com-
panies to make
complaint.

SEC. 70. Any station agent of any railroad company, who shall know or have immediate information that any person has violated any provision of the preceding section, shall forthwith inform a grand juror of the town in which said offense shall have been committed.

Punishment.

SEC. 71. Every person who shall violate any provision of the two preceding sections shall be fined not exceeding fifty dollars, or imprisoned not exceeding thirty days, or both.

1851.
Engines to have
bell and whis-
tle.

SEC. 72. Every engine used upon any railroad shall be supplied with a bell of at least thirty-five pounds weight, and a suitable steam whistle, which bell and whistle shall be so attached to such engine as to be conveniently accessible to the engineer, and in good order for use.

Engineers to
sound bell or
whistle when
crossing high-
way, etc.

SEC. 73. Every person controlling the motions of any engine upon any railroad, shall commence sounding the bell or steam whistle attached to such engine when such engine shall be approaching, and within eighty rods of the place where said railroad crosses any highway at grade, and keep such bell or whistle occasionally sounding until such engine has crossed such highway; and

Liability of cor-
poration.

the railroad company in whose employment he may be shall pay all damages which may accrue to any person in consequence of any omission to comply with the provisions of this section; and no railroad company shall knowingly employ any engineer who has been twice convicted of violating the provisions of this section.

1882.
Whistle may be
sounded for
crossing over or
under the track.

When it shall appear to the Railroad Commissioners, upon the written complaint of the selectmen of any town, that public safety requires the sounding of the engine whistle at any highway crossing where the train passes over or under such highway, they shall make such order in relation thereto as they shall deem proper.

Engineers to
have copies of
this law and be
sworn to obey
it.

SEC. 74. No railroad company shall permit any person to drive any engine upon any railroad operated by such company unless he shall have first received a printed copy of this and the two preceding sections, and shall have made oath that he will faithfully comply with the provisions thereof.

1853. 1869.
Trains to stop
before crossing
draw-bridges or
railroad cross-
ings.

SEC. 75. All railroad trains shall be brought to a full stop, at a distance not less than two hundred feet, nor more than eight hundred feet, from the draw in every draw-bridge upon the line of the railroad over which they are to be run, and from every point where such railroad is crossed by another railroad, and in plain sight of the same, before being run upon or over such draw or crossing; but the Railroad Commissioners may in writing authorize the passing of any draw or any railroad crossing, without stopping as aforesaid, when, in their opinion, it can be done consistently with public safety.

Commissioners may authorize passing without stopping.

SEC. 76. Every person running such a train, who shall violate the provisions of the preceding section, shall be fined not exceeding one hundred dollars, or imprisoned not exceeding three months; and the president and directors of any railroad company, who shall knowingly permit any violation of the same, shall be fined five hundred dollars.

Penalty for violation.

SECTION 1. Whenever the selectmen of any town, the mayor and common council of any city, or the warden and burgesses of any borough, shall bring their petition in writing to the Railroad Commissioners, representing that the interests of the public require that the blowing of the locomotive whistle upon a railroad at certain points within the limits of such town, city, or borough should be dispensed with, said Commissioners shall appoint a time and place for hearing said petition, and shall give reasonable notice thereof to the petitioners and the railroad company in question; and if after such hearing they shall be of opinion that the sounding of the whistle can be dispensed with, without danger to the public, they shall direct said railroad company to omit the same, and require that the engine bell shall be rung in lieu thereof, at such points as they may specify.

1881. When whistling may be dispensed with.

SEC. 2. Whenever any railroad company shall receive such directions from the Railroad Commissioners, it shall thereafter omit the sounding of the whistle at the points named in said order.

SEC. 77. All trains which are obliged to come to a full stop before crossing any draw-bridge, shall, when the Railroad Commissioners shall so order, stop at the regular station nearest to such draw-bridge for a sufficient length of time to accommodate passengers who may desire to enter or leave said trains, if said station is in full view of said draw-bridge, and not more than one hundred and twenty rods therefrom.

1865. Passenger trains to stop at nearest regular station to a draw-bridge.

SEC. 78. No railroad company shall permit any passenger train to be run over any switch, at any railroad junction of different roads, or any station where such train does not regularly stop, or is not then to be stopped, unless there be, at the time when such train shall arrive near such switch, a switchman standing at

1853. 1856. Switches at railroad junctions.

such junction switch, or the station switch so first approached, with a white flag by day, or a light at night, to indicate that such switches are in a proper position for the passage of such train; or unless, in the absence of such switchmen, said train shall be first brought to a full stop, at the distance of not less than two hundred feet, nor more than seven hundred feet therefrom; and every person who shall run a train over any such switch contrary to the provisions of this section, shall be fined not exceeding one hundred dollars, or imprisoned not exceeding sixty days, or both; and the president and directors of any railroad company, who shall permit such train to be run over any such switch, contrary to the provisions of this section, shall be fined five hundred dollars; but the Railroad Commissioners may dispense with such switchmen, at any places.

Penalty for violation by engine-man.

Penalty for violation by president and directors.

SEC. 79. The Commissioners may permit passenger trains to be run past any switch, station, or highway crossing without stopping, at such rate of speed as they may prescribe, upon the provision by said company of such safeguards for the protection of its passengers and the public as said Commissioners may require; and for neglecting to make such provision, such company shall pay a fine of five hundred dollars.

1873.
When trains may pass switch, &c., without stopping.

SEC. 80. Upon every train run, or intended to be run, upon any railroad in this State, at a greater average speed than thirty miles an hour, between stations, and consisting of more than two passenger cars, one brakeman shall be kept at the brake of each car; but when the double-action brake is used on any such train, but one brakeman need be kept upon and for every two cars connected with such train; and the Railroad Commissioners may grant permission to any railroad company to reduce the number of brakeman required upon passenger trains, when such company may have adopted a system of brakes to be operated by the engineer, which in the opinion of said Commissioners may render such number of brakeman unnecessary; but said Commissioners may revoke such permission when they consider the public safety requires; and on such revocation such company shall place upon its trains the number of brakemen required by law.

1853. 1854.
Number of brakeman on train.

SEC. 81. Every railroad company shall, within twenty-four hours after the occurrence of any accident attended with personal injury, give notice of the same to the Railroad Commissioners, in writing, who, upon receiving such notice, or upon public rumor of such accident, may repair, or dispatch one of their number to the scene of said accident, and inquire into the facts

1853.
Companies to give notice to Commissioners of accidents.

and circumstances thereof; and the Commissioners shall, without charge, furnish any person injured, or the friends of any person killed, any information they may have acquired in relation to any disaster, and the names of the persons from whom the same was obtained, or by whom the same may be proved.

6. BONDS AND MORTGAGES.

SEC. 82. Every railroad company may borrow money, and may secure the repayment of the same by its bonds, signed by its president, and countersigned by its treasurer; but before being issued, said bonds shall be registered in the office of the Comptroller, and a certificate thereof shall appear on the face of each bond; and the Comptroller shall cancel any bonds, so registered, which may be brought to him for that purpose, and enter said act of cancelling in his register; but no railroad company shall issue any bonds of a less denomination than one hundred dollars,* and the Comptroller shall not permit the bonds of any railroad company, registered in his office, and uncancelled, to exceed the amount limited in this section.† Such company may dispose of its bonds, as shall be authorized by its stockholders. 1842.
Corporation may borrow money, and issue bonds. 1860. 1867.
May sell bonds.

SEC. 83. The company may secure said bonds by a mortgage of its property, or any part thereof, by deed duly executed by its president, under the corporate seal, to the Treasurer of the State, and his successors in office, in trust for the holders of said bonds, and recorded in the office of the Secretary of this State. 1849.
Railroad may be mortgaged to secure bonds.

Concerning Railroad Mortgages.

SEC. 1. Whenever any railroad company has mortgaged, or shall mortgage its railroad, pursuant to law, to secure its bonds, and has included, or shall include in said mortgages all or any part of its rolling stock, locomotives, and cars, whether those owned by it at the date of said mortgage, or those thereafter to be acquired by it for use upon said railroad, or both, such mortgage shall be deemed valid and effectual, as respects all the property therein included as aforesaid; and may be foreclosed in the same manner as ordinary mortgages of real estate; and the record thereof in the office of the secretary of this state shall be a sufficient record and notice to protect the title under the mortgage, notwithstanding such com- 1877.
Mortgages of railroad property.

---

* See Sec. 4, Acts 1882, page 11.
† Various points as to liability of railroad companies upon their bonds. 26 Conn., 121.

pany may remain in possession of all or any part of the mortgaged property.

SEC. 84. When any railroad company shall have mortgaged its property, or any part thereof, to any person, in trust, for the security of its creditors, or for the security of any class of them, and shall have made default in the payment of principal or interest, due to such creditors, any such creditor may prefer his petition to the Superior Court, in any county in which such railroad, or any part thereof, is located, setting forth such fact, and praying that such trustee may be placed in the possession of such property, for the benefit of such creditors; and such petition shall be heard and determined at the first term of the court to which it is returnable, unless continued for reasonable cause; and if the allegations therein are found true, such court shall decree that the said company and its president and directors, under a suitable penalty, shall surrender such mortgaged property to the trustee, for the benefit of such creditors.

1858.
Surrender of
road to mort-
gage trustees.

SEC. 85. When any such trustee shall have taken possession of any property in pursuance of the provisions of the preceding section, or in pursuance of any authority contained in the mortgage or deed of trust, he shall take charge of, and operate, such railroad, or railroad property, for the benefit of the creditors for whom such trust was created, and shall not be personally liable for any cause or injury arising from the operation of such road, or while he may operate it; except for his willful mismanagement, or for any contracts made by him as such trustee; but all such property shall be liable for the acts and proceedings of such trustee, in the execution of his trust, to the extent of the interest of the creditors, for whose benefit he may act; and any proceeding, for the purpose of making such property liable, shall be brought against such trustee, describing him as such.

Limitation of
liability of
trustee in pos-
session.

Trust estate
liable for acts
of trustee.

SEC. 86. The trustee, upon taking possession of such property, shall make an inventory of all which may come into his possession under oath, and lodge it for record in the office of the Secretary of this State; and if any other property shall, from time to time, be discovered by him, he shall make and lodge a like inventory, under oath, as aforesaid.

Trustee to make
and return in-
ventory.

SEC. 87. The trustee shall, from time to time, while operating such road, file his account, quarterly, in the office of the Secretary of this State, of all moneys received or disbursed by him, in the course of his agency; and may proceed at his discretion, in the Superior Court, in any county in which such railroad, or any part

Trustee to ren-
der quarterly
accounts to
Secretary.

thereof, is located, to foreclose said railroad company, and all subsequent incumbrances, for the use of the bondholders, or other creditors for whom he acts; and such court may limit the time for the redemption of the mortgaged property, as in ordinary proceedings for the foreclosure of real property. *May foreclose for the bondholders.*

SEC. 88. If such trustee shall neglect or unnecessarily delay to perform his duties, any creditor, represented by such trustee, may apply to any Superior Court aforesaid, for the removal of such trustee, which application shall be heard at the first term of said court; and upon such facts being found true, such court may remove the trustee from his office, and appoint another in his stead, and may, upon the application of any such creditor, remove a trustee, and fill the vacancy. *Superior Court may remove trustee for cause, and appoint another.*

SEC. 89. Nothing in the five preceding sections shall affect any mortgage, trust, or lien upon the property foreclosed, which was created prior to the mortgage, trust or lien, under which said trustee may act; but the trustee for all such prior incumbrances may proceed, by foreclosure or otherwise, notwithstanding any act or proceeding by subsequent incumbrances, or their trustees. *Right of prior incumbrances not to be affected.*

SEC. 90. When any such railroad is in the possession of an assignee, or trustee, he shall have the same rights, powers, and privileges as are conferred upon railroad companies; and all expenses and damages incurred by such persons so in possession, in good faith, to improve the lines of the railroads so in their charge, shall be reimbursed to them from the earnings of such railroad while they have the possession thereof. *1874. Trustees to have the same powers, etc., as the corporation.*

SEC. 91. The expenses of operating such railroad, or other property, including repairs and all other reasonable expenses of the trustee, and any damages incurred for any injury sustained during the time of his execution of said trust, and all claims secured by any prior mortgages or incumbrances, which shall have become payable before or during said time, and also a reasonable compensation to be allowed to the trustee, by the Superior Court, shall be deducted from the earnings of the road, before any part of such earnings shall be paid to the creditors. *1858. Expenses of road, damages, compensation of trustees, etc. to be deducted from earnings.*

Title XVII, Article 4.

SECTION 1. Every person who shall violate any provision of this Part, for which no other penalty is prescribed or provision made, shall be fined not less than ten dollars nor more than five hundred dollars. *General Penalty.*

Title III, Chap. 4, Part 4.

1861.
Appointment of railroad and steamboat police. SEC. 2. The Governor may, from time to time, upon the application of any railroad or steamboat company, engaged in the business of transportation in this State, commission, during his pleasure, one or more persons designated by such company, who, having been duly sworn, may act at its expense as policemen upon the premises used by it in its business, or upon its cars or vessels. When any such commission is issued, or revoked, the Executive Secretary shall notify the clerk of the Superior Court of each county in which it is intended that such policemen shall act.

Badge of railroad and steamboat police. SEC. 3. Every such policeman shall, when on duty, wear in plain view a shield, bearing the words, "Railroad Police," or "Steamboat Police," as the case may be, and the name of the company for which he is commissioned.

Their power to arrest. SEC. 4. Every railroad or steamboat policeman may arrest in his precincts, for all offenses committed therein, and bring the offenders before proper authority.

Title XX, Chap. 13, Part 2.

1867.
Jurisdiction of offenses on cars or steamboats. SEC. 3. All persons arrested by railroad or steamboat policemen, for offenses committed upon cars or steamboats when in motion, may be prosecuted before any court, in the same manner as if such offenses had been committed in the town in which such court is held.

Title XII, Chap 5.

1864.   1869.
1871.   1877.
Returns by railroad companies. SEC. 5. The secretary or treasurer of every railroad company, any portion of whose road is in this State, shall, within the first ten days of October, annually, deliver to the Comptroller a sworn statement of the number of shares of its stock, and the market value of each share,—the amount and market value of its funded and floating debt, the amount of bonds issued by any town or city of the description mentioned in the twelfth section of Chapter I of this Title, when the avails of such bonds, or stock subscribed and paid for therewith, shall have been expended in such construction, the amount of cash on hand the first day of said month, the whole length of its road, and the length of those portions thereof lying without this State, and also the number, name, and length of each of its branches lying in the State.

In making the statement required in section five, chapter five, title twelve of the general statutes (page

168), by the secretary or treasurer of any railroad company, the funded and floating debt and bonds therein
included shall be returned and valued at par, unless the
market value thereof shall be below par, in which case
the market value shall be the rule of-valuation.

1889.
Basis for report-
ing bonds.

SECTION 1. The secretary or treasurer of any railroad
company, any portion of whose road is in this State,
shall, in addition to and as a part of the returns required
by the act to which this is an addition, make and deliver
to the Comptroller a sworn statement of the number,
amount, and market value of any and all unpaid bonds
which may have been secured by mortgage on the railway and railway property of said company by any of its
predecessors in the Title, and which, at the time of such
return, shall be legally entitled to conversion into the
capital stock of said company.

1882.
Unpaid bonds to
be reported to
Comptroller.

SEC. 2. Each of such railroad companies shall, in
addition to the tax now required by said act, hereafter
pay to the State one per cent. of the valuation of such
bonds so entitled to conversion as aforesaid at the times,
in the manner, and subject to the conditions and regula·
tions now provided by said act for the payment of taxes
by railroad companies. And any tax paid by any such
railroad company for and on account of any such bonds
so entitled to conversion shall constitute in behalf of said
company a lien on the right, title, and interest of the
holders of such bonds in the estate of said company.

SEC. 6. Each of such railroad companies shall, on or
before the twentieth day of October, annually, pay to the
State one per cent. of the valuation of said stock, and
funded and floating debt, and bonds, as contained in said
statement, after deducting from such valuation the
amount of cash on hand, and from said sum required to
be paid, the amount paid for taxes upon the real estate
owned by it and not used for railroad purposes ; and the
valuation so made and corrected by the Board of Equalization shall be the measure of value of such railroad,
its rights, franchises, and property in this State, for pur·
poses of taxation ; and this sum shall be in lieu of all
other taxes on its franchises, funded and floating debt,
and railroad property in this State.

1864.　1868.
1867.　1877.
Amount of tax
to be paid by
railroad com-
panies.

SEC. 7. When only part of a railroad lies in this
State, the company owning such road shall pay one per
cent. on such proportion of the above-named valuation
as the length of its road lying in this State bears to the
entire length of said road. But in fixing the aforesaid
valuation and lengths, neither the value nor length of
any branch thereof in this State, which the Board of
Equalization shall determine to be of less value per

1864.　1876.
Tax on railroad
of which only a
part lies in the
State.
Gen. Statutes,
p. 168.

mile than one-fourth of the average value per mile of
the trunk road, shall be included ; but every such branch
shall be estimated at its true and just value by the Board
of Equalization, and such railroad company shall pay to
the treasurer of this State one per cent. on such value,
at the time fixed in the next previous section for the
payment of other railroad taxes ; and when any such
sum becomes due, and such company shall not then have
the management and control of its road, or the road
bearing its name, the person or corporation then owning
or managing such railroad shall pay such sum to the
State within the time above prescribed.

1862.
Lessee of rail-
road may de-
duct taxes from
rent.

SEC. 8.   The taxes paid by the lessee of any railroad,
under any contract or lease, existing on the tenth day of
July, 1862, may be deducted from any payment due, or
to become due to the lessor, on account of such contract
or lease.

1875.
Lien on rail-
roads for taxes
due the State.
Gen. Statutes,
p. 168.

Any and all taxes which shall become due to the
State from any railroad company, under sections five,
six, and seven, of chapter five, title twelve, of the General Statutes, shall be and remain a lien on the road and
estate of said company, until such taxes are paid, and
shall take precedence and priority of any and all other
incumbrances whatsoever.

1877.
Taxation of
dwelling-
houses belong-
ing to railroad
companies.

Any dwelling-house belonging to any railroad company shall be set in the list and be liable to taxation in
the town where said dwelling-house is situated, notwithstanding the fact that the same may be rented to, or
occupied by, an employee of said railroad company ; and
the amount paid for taxes on any such dwelling-house
or houses, shall be deducted from the sum required by
law to be paid by such railroad company for taxes to
the State.

Any railroad company in this State which holds by
lease or otherwise a railroad in another State, which is
not a part of its own road, shall state, in its annual return
for purposes of taxation, how much of its funding and
floating debt was occasioned by and how much of its
capital stock was issued for any amount which has been
expended by it in the construction or permanent improvement of such railroad in another State, or in the
purchase of equipment for exclusive use thereon; and in
computing the amount of the tax to be paid by said
company to this State the amount of such funding or
floating debt and of such stock so occasioned or issued
as aforesaid shall be first deducted from the total amount
of its funded and floating debt and stock.

1875.
Trustees in
possession of

SECTION 1.   The mortgagees or trustees of any railroad
lying in whole or in part in this State, who have, or shall

hereafter come into the possession of the same, by virtue mortgaged rail- of any mortgage thereof, shall, within the first ten days road to make annual returns. of October, annually, so long as they remain in possession of said railroad, deliver to the Comptroller a sworn statement of the value of said road, its equipment, and other property, located in this State, and in their hands as such mortgagees or trustees. And the Board of Equalization shall have all the powers, in respect to such returns and values, which are conferred upon them in other cases by section eleven, chapter five, title twelve, Gen. Statutes, of the General Statutes. p. 169.

SEC. 2. Any person, whose duty it shall be to deliver Penalty. the statement required by the preceding section. who shall fail so to do within the time prescribed, shall forfeit five hundred dollars to the State.

SEC. 3. Said mortgagees or trustees shall, on or be- Tax on such roads. fore the twentieth day of October, in each year, or as soon thereafter as the earnings of said road, or other moneys in their hands, will allow, pay to the State a sum equal to one per cent. on the value of said road, equipment, and other property, less the amount of taxes paid by them on any real estate in their hands, not used for railroad purposes.

SEC. 4. In all cases in which the road and estate of When a mort- any railroad company shall have been, or shall hereafter gaged road be- comes the prop- be, foreclosed under any mortgage executed by it for the erty of another corporation. security of its creditors, and any other railroad corporation shall have, or shall hereafter become, by purchase or otherwise, the owner of said road and estate so foreclosed, said corporation shall make the returns and payments required by sections five and six, chapter five, title Gen. Statutes, twelve, of the General Statutes; and any funded or p. 168. floating indebtedness, to which said railroad and estate is liable, shall be considered for the purposes of this act as the indebtedness of said corporation, whether the same may have been contracted by it or by some predecessor in its title.

SEC. 5. Any sums which shall become due to the Lien on road for taxes. State, for taxes under this act, shall rest as a lien on the road and property on account of which said tax is imposed, until the same shall be paid, and shall take precedence of any and all other liens and incumbrances whatsoever.

SECTION 1. No highway which does not cross a rail- 1878. road track shall hereafter be laid out or opened to the Highway not to be laid out near public within one hundred yards of any railroad track railroad track. unless the layout has been approved by a judge of the Superior Court. after notice to all parties in interest, and his written approval has been lodged in the offices of the town clerk of the town in which the proposed highway is situated.

Power of judge of Superior Court as to this. SEC. 2. A judge of the Superior Court shall not approve the layout of any highway, which does not cross a railroad track, within one hundred yards of any railroad track, unless he finds that public convenience and necessities require such highway to be within such distance; and he shall have power to require any town opening a highway to the public within such distance, to erect and maintain such a fence between such highway and the railroad track as, in his opinion, the safety of the public may require.

Effect of this act. SEC. 3. This act shall take effect from its passage, but shall not affect any suit now pending.

Title XVI, Chap. 7, Part 1.

1870. Laying out highways across railroads. SEC. 6. No highway shall be laid out or constructed across and upon a level with any railroad, unless the Railroad Commissioners, upon written application of the party proposing to lay out or construct such highway, and after giving to said party, and to the company whose railroad it is so proposed to cross, reasonable notice in writing of the time and place when and where they may be heard thereon, allow said crossing; and if they, upon such hearing, shall disallow it, they shall further determine whether said highway shall cross over or under said railroad; and half of the expense of said crossing shall be borne by said railroad company, which, upon the completion of said highway and crossing, shall pay the same to the party entitled thereto.

Expenses of maintaining bridge at railroad crossing. SEC. 7. If said highway shall cross over said railroad, the structure necessary therefor shall be maintained and kept in repair by the party bound to maintain said highway; but if it shall cross under said railroad, such structure shall be maintained and kept in repair by said company.

1871. Height of railroad bridges. SEC. 8. The bottom timbers of all bridges, hereafter constructed over any railroad track, shall not be less than eighteen feet above the rails, unless the Railroad Commissioners require a less height and prescribe the same in writing.

1861. Railings to be erected on roads and bridges. SEC. 9. The party bound to maintain any bridge or road shall erect and maintain a suitable railing or fence on the side of such bridge, and of such parts of such road as are so made or raised above the adjoining ground as to be unsafe for travel; and whoever shall suffer damage in his person or property, by reason of the want of any such railing or fence, may recover damages from such party.

SEC. 10.   Any person, injured in person or property, by means of a defective road or bridge, may recover damages from the party bound to keep it in repair; but no action for any such injury, received subsequent to the seventh day of July, 1874, shall be maintained against any town, city, or borough, unless written notice of such injury, and of the time and place of its occurrence, shall, within sixty days thereafter, be given to a selectman of such town, or the clerk of such city or borough; and when the injury is caused by a structure legally placed on said road by a railroad company, it, and not the party bound to keep the road in repair, shall be liable therefor.

1862.
Liability for defective highways or bridges.

1874.

1869.

SEC. 36.   The Superior Court of the county in which is any highway, or any portion thereof, taken by any other than a horse railroad company for railroad purposes, but not in a city, nor constructed since such railroad, may, upon the petition of any party interested, served upon said company as other civil process, appoint a committee of three to inquire whether such highway or portion thereof is unsafe for travel by reason of such railroad, or whether any alteration of such highway or the construction of a new highway is thereby rendered necessary for the public safety and convenience; and such committee shall hear said parties and report their opinion thereon to said court, which may make any proper order in the premises; and if it shall order any such alteration or construction, and said company shall refuse to comply with such order, said town shall alter or construct such highway, and may recover the expense thereof from said company.

1866.
Proceeding to alter a highway taken by a railroad company.

SECTION 1.   The selectmen of any town within which a highway crosses or is crossed by a railroad, or the directors of any railroad company whose road crosses or is crossed by a highway, may bring their petition in writing to the Railroad Commissioners, therein alleging that public safety requires an alteration in such crossing, its approaches, the method of crossing, the location of the highway or railroad, or the removal of obstructions to the sight at such crossing, and praying that the same be ordered.   Whereupon the Railroad Commissioners shall appoint a time and place for hearing the petition, and shall give such notice thereof as they judge reasonable, to said selectmen, the railroad company, and to the owners of the land adjoining such crossing, and after such notice and hearing, said Commissioners shall determine what alterations or removals shall be made, by whom done, and at whose expense.

1876.
Provision for safety of highway at railroad crossing.

SEC. 2.   In case the party by whom the changes are to be made cannot agree with the owner of the land or

Assessment of damages.

other property to be removed or taken under the said decision of the Railroad Commissioners, the damages shall be assessed in the same manner as is provided in case of land taken by railroad companies. The expense of such assessment to be paid in the same manner as the expense of the alterations.

Appeal.

SEC. 3. The decision of the Commissioners shall be communicated to the selectmen, to the railroad company, and to the owners of any property directed to be removed or taken, within twenty days after final hearing, and any person aggrieved by such decision may appeal therefrom in the same manner and with like effect as is provided in the case of appeals from any order of the Railroad Commissioners upon any proceedings relative to the location, abandonment, or changing of dépôts or stations.

1877. Provision for safety of highway at railroad crossing.

That all the provisions of chapter thirty-six, entitled "An Act in regard to Railroad Crossings," of the acts of 1876, applying to selectmen of towns, in regard to highways crossing or crossed by railroads, be and the same are hereby extended to mayors and common councils of cities, and to the warden and burgesses of boroughs, in regard to streets crossing or crossed by railroads.

1878. Obstruction of highway travel by railroad cars, etc.

SECTION 1. Any person traveling upon any public street or highway which is crossed by a railroad, who shall be obstructed or prevented from crossing such railroad for a longer time than five minutes by reason of trains, cars or locomotives standing upon or across such street or highway, may recover not exceeding fifty dollars from the corporation owning or operating said railroad : *provided*, suit is brought within thirty days after the date of such obstruction.

Repeal. Gen. Statutes, p. 234.

SEC. 2. Section twenty-third, part first, chapter seven, title sixteen of the general statutes is hereby repealed.

1881. Highway crossings near bridge.

SECTION 1. Where any railroad crosses a highway in any city at grade, within two hundred feet of a covered bridge on said highway, such highway shall not be obstructed by the making up of railroad trains, nor by allowing any train, car or locomotive to stand on or across said highway, for more than three minutes at one time ; and whenever such highway has been once so used or occupied, or whenever a locomotive or train has passed entirely over it, said highway shall not again be so used or occupied, or crossed by locomotive or cars, until a sufficient time has been allowed to enable all teams which are ready, and waiting for the purpose, to cross the tracks of said railroad.

SEC. 2. Any servant, agent, or employee of any railroad corporation, willfully violating any provision of

the preceding section, shall be deemed guilty of a misdemeanor, and on conviction thereof, on complaint of any
grand juror of the town where the offense is committed,
shall be punished by a fine not exceeding seven dollars,
or by imprisonment not exceeding thirty days, or by
both.

Title XVIII, Chap. 6, Part 1.

SEC. 20. If the owner or occupant of any land, adjoining any railroad or canal has, since the tenth day of
June, one thousand eight hundred and thirty-one, taken,
or shall take, into his enclosure any part of the land belonging to said railroad or canal, as located and established, or since that time has erected, or shall erect, any
building upon any such land, no adverse possession of
the land so enclosed or built upon shall confer any title
thereto.

1846. Right to land within limits of railroad or canal, not granted by possession.

Title XVIII, Chap. 9.

SEC. 2. All goods of a nature not perishable, left
with any person, or upon any public wharf or highway,
and all goods, other than personal baggage of passengers, left at any railroad station, or in any railroad car,
or carriage, the owner of which goods is unknown, or
neglects to take them away for six months from the time
when they were left, shall be advertised one month in a
newspaper published in the county where such goods
were left ; and if the owners thereof shall not take them
away within said month, may be sold, and the proceeds
disposed of, in the manner provided in the preceding
section, except that such proceeds, not claimed by the
owner within one year, shall escheat to the State.

1854. 1858. 1865. If not perishable, how disposed of.

Title XVIII, Chap. 11, Part 2.

SEC. 20. The trustee of any railroad corporation,
whose estate is in settlement as an insolvent estate, may,
if the assets of such estate shall not otherwise be sufficient to pay the claims allowed by the Commissioners,
and the expenses of settling the estate, release, subject
to any prior existing lien or title, to any proprietors of
land any right of way or other incumbrance which said
corporation may have in or upon the same upon such
terms as shall be approved by the Court of Probate.

1858. Trustee may re- lease interest of a railroad cor- poration, when.

Title XIX, Chap. 2.

SEC. 45. In an action brought against the president
and directors of a railroad company for a forfeiture incurred under the provisions of Part IX, Chapter II of

1853. 1856. Service on non- resident rail- road directors.

Title XVII, service of the writ upon such of them as are inhabitants of this State, or as may be found therein by the officer serving the same, shall be sufficient notice to maintain the suit against all the defendants.

1877.
Limit and distribution of damages for negligence causing death. Gen. Statutes, p. 422.

SECTION 1. In all actions by an executor or administrator for injuries resulting in death from negligence, such executor or administrator may recover from the party legally in fault for such injuries, just damages not exceeding five thousand dollars, to be distributed as is provided in section nine, chapter six, title nineteen, of the general statutes, revision of 1875 ; *provided*, that no action shall be brought upon this statute but within one year after the neglect complained of ; *and provided, further*, that if suit for the injuries caused by such neglect shall be pending when the death occurs, and the executor or administrator of such deceased person shall enter and prosecute the same to final judgment, the damages recovered in such suit shall be distributed as provided in said ninth section.

Repeal Gen. Statutes, p. 448.

SEC. 2. The third section of part seventeen, title nineteen, chapter seventeen, of the general statutes, and all other acts or parts of acts inconsistent herewith, are hereby repealed.

Title XIX, Chap. 18.

1865. 1867.
Suit against railroad company for loss of life.

SEC. 14. No suit against a railroad company for damages for the loss of any life shall be brought by the executor or administrator of the deceased person, except within eighteen months from and after the death of such person.

Title XIX, Chap. 6.

1853.
1869. 1874.
Limit and distribution of damages.

SEC. 8. No action to recover damages for injury to the person, reputation, or property of the plaintiff, or to the person of his wife, child, or servant, shall abate by reason of his death ; but his executor or administrator may enter and prosecute the same in the same manner as is provided by law in other actions ; and if there be two or more plaintiffs, and one or more of them shall die before final judgment, such action shall not abate, but, such death being suggested on the record, the action shall proceed.*

Title XIX, Chap. 11.

1836. 1848.
What actions of tort survive.

SEC. 29. In all actions to recover for any injury occasioned by fire communicated by any railway locomotive engine in this State, the fact that such fire was so communicated shall be *primâ facie* evidence of negli-

---

*Death of plaintiff after verdict will not prevent rendition of judgment, though the action cannot survive. 18 Conn., 207, 208.

gence on the part of the person or corporation, who shall, at the time of such injury by fire, be in the use and occupation of such railroad, either as owner, lessee, or mortgagee, and of those who shall at such time have the care and management of such engine.

SECTION 1. Where any injury is done to a building or other property of any person or corporation, by fire communicated by a locomotive engine of any railroad corporation, without contributory negligence on the part of the person or corporation entitled to the care and possession of the property injured, the said railroad corporation shall be held responsible in damages to the extent of such injury to the person or corporation so injured ; and any railroad corporation shall have an insurable interest in the property for which it may be so held responsible in damages along its route, and may procure insurance thereon in its own behalf. *1850. Fire communicated by railway engine.*

SEC. 2. All acts and parts of acts inconsistent herewith are hereby repealed.

SEC. 3. No suit shall be brought under this act unless written notice of the claim is given to the defendant company within twenty days after the fire, specifying the day and hour of the fire, the property injured, and the amount claimed as damages. Such notices may be given by a letter signed by the claimant or his agent, and mailed to the superintendent of the railroad or delivered to its station agent at a station in the town where the fire occurred.

SEC. 4. No appraisal of damages for land taken or injured by the location or construction of a railroad shall hereafter include any compensation for the increased risk of fire to any buildings erected on or to be erected on land outside of such location, on account of sparks from locomotive engines on such railroad.

Title XIX, Chap. 16.

SEC. 25. The levy of executions on the equitable rights of interest which any railroad corporation may have in the whole, or any part of the real estate; right of way, or roadbed of any other railroad corporation, together with the income, rents, and profits which may be due or coming due thereon, shall be by leaving a true and attested copy thereof with the treasurer, secretary, or clerk of said last-named corporation, with an attested certificate by the officer making such levy, that he levies upon such right or interest to satisfy such execution; and thereupon he shall post the same upon some sign-post in the town where such last corporation has its office or principal place of business in this State, and as in cases *1856. Levy of interest of one railroad company in road of another.*

of personal property, shall, at vendue, sell the same, together with such income, rents, and profits, or so much
of them as shall be sufficient to satisfy said execution,
and shall give to the purchaser a written conveyance of
such right and interest, and shall also leave with such
treasurer, secretary, or clerk, a true and attested copy of
such execution, and of his return thereon; and the purchaser shall thereupon become entitled to said right and
interest, and to all rents, profits, and income thereon,
which such debtor was entitled to.

Title XX, Chap. 2.

1801. 1846.
.1873.
Homicide when
punished by
death.

SEC. 2. Every person who shall commit murder in
the first degree, or who shall cause the death of another
by willfully placing any obstruction upon any railroad,
or by loosening, taking up or removing any part of the
superstructure of such railroad, or by willfully burning
any building or vessel, shall suffer death.

1853.
Loss of life,
etc., by intoxi-
cation of ser-
vants of rail-
road company.

SEC. 5. Every servant of any railroad company who
shall, in consequence of his intoxication, or any gross or
willful misconduct or negligence, cause any loss of life,
or the breaking of a limb, shall be imprisoned in the
State prison not more than ten years.

Title XX, Chap. 4.

1852. 1873.
Placing obstruc-
tions on rail-
roads.

SECTION 1. Every person who shall willfully place
any obstruction upon any railroad, or who shall loosen,
tear up, or remove any part of a railroad, shall be imprisoned in the State prison not more than ten years; and
if he shall do the same with intent to throw any locomotive or car from the track of such railroad, or to obstruct
any car in motion, he shall be imprisoned in such prison
not more than thirty years.

1871.
Injury to elec-
tric signals on
railroads.

SEC. 2. Every person who shall willfully displace
any switch upon any railroad, or injure or destroy any
electric signal in use thereon, or any material or property
appertaining thereto, or who shall interrupt the use of
any wire, lever, pin, or battery, used to operate such signal, or its connection therewith, shall be fined not more
than one thousand dollars, and imprisoned in the State
prison not more than ten years.

1873.
Throwing mis-
siles at railroad
trains.

SEC. 27. Every person who shall willfully throw or
shoot any missile at any locomotive or railroad car,
whereby the safety of any person is endangered, shall be
fined not less than fifty dollars, nor more than five hundred dollars, or imprisoned not more than one year, or
both.

SEC. 28. Every person who shall willfully injure any *1852.* engine or car, used upon any railroad, shall be fined not *Injuring railroad engines,* more than one hundred and fifty dollars, or imprisoned *etc.* not more than one year, or both.

SEC. 29. Every person who shall cast, empty, or dis- *1866.* charge, or permit to be cast, emptied, or discharged, any *Nuisances on railroad tracks,* filth, rubbish, foul or offensive wash, or water, or the *or in dépôts.* contents of any privy, vault, cess-pool, or sewer, upon or into any railroad or railroad dépôt in any city, shall be fined not more than fifty dollars, half of which shall be paid, by order of court, to the person furnishing to the proper officer information that leads to a conviction.

SEC. 30. Every person who shall commit any nui- *1869.* sance in or upon any railroad bridge, shall be fined not *Committing nuisances on railroad bridges.* more than seven dollars, or imprisoned not more than thirty days, or both.

SECTION 1. Any person who shall unlawfully, mali- *1878.* ciously, and in violation of his duty or contract, unneces- *Penalty for unlawfully ob-* sarily stop, delay, or abandon any locomotive, car, or *structing railroad travel.* train of cars, or shall maliciously injure, hinder, or obstruct the use of any locomotive, car, or railroad, shall, upon conviction, be liable to a fine not exceeding one hundred dollars, or imprisonment in the county jail not exceeding six months.

SEC. 2. Every person who shall threaten, or use any *Use of threats* means to intimidate any person to compel such person, *or intimidation.* against his will, to do, or abstain from doing, any act which such person has a legal right to do, or shall persistently follow such person in a disorderly manner, or injure, or threaten to injure his property, with intent to intimidate him, shall, upon conviction, be liable to a fine not exceeding one hundred dollars, or imprisonment in the county jail six months.

SEC. 3 Chapter seventy-seven of public acts approved *Repeal, Chapter* March 22, 1877, is hereby repealed. *LXXVII, Acts 1877, p. 190.*

Title XX, Chapter 11.

SEC. 8. Every person who shall fraudulently evade, *1867. 1871.* or attempt to evade, the payment of any fare lawfully *Fraudulent evasion of payment* established by any steamboat company located in this *of fare.* State, or by any railroad company, shall be fined not less than five nor more than twenty dollars.

Title XX, Chapter 12.

SEC. 41. Every railroad company which shall will- *1873.* fully refuse to transport milk for any person according *Neglect of railroad company to* to law, shall forfeit twenty dollars. *transport milk.*

SEC. 42. The forfeitures imposed by the four preced- *To whom penalties under four* ing sections shall be paid to him who shall sue therefor. *preceding sections are payable.*

1867.
Neglect of railroad company to give receipts.

SEC. 45. Any railroad company which shall refuse to give a receipt to the owner or shipper of any commodity, delivered to it for transportation, describing such commodity, shall forfeit to such owner or shipper fifty dollars.

1882.
Railroad companies to maintain waterclosets.

SECTION 1. It is hereby made the duty of all corporations operating steam railroads in this state to maintain at each and every regular passenger dépôt on the railroad operated by them respectively, such suitable water-closets as in the judgment of the Railroad Commissioners of the State the public convenience may require; and said Commissioners are hereby empowered to make all necessary orders in the premises, and to enforce the same by mandamus, in the name of the State.

Repeal.

SEC. 2. Section seven, chapter twelve, title twenty, of the general statutes, is hereby repealed.

1875.
Effects of deeds given by railroad companies.

Whenever any railroad company shall make and properly execute a deed in fee simple of any lands which said company has derived by purchase, said deed by said railroad company shall effectually convey the title to said land, and when by said company so conveyed shall be to the absolute use of the grantee.

1876.
Penalty for neglect to secure private way opening on railroad.

Whoever enters upon or crosses a railroad at any private way, which is closed by gates or bars, and neglects to securely close them, shall forfeit for each offense a sum not less than two nor more than ten dollars, and shall be liable for any damage resulting therefrom.

1875.
Railroad companies to report balance sheet of accounts.

In addition to the returns which the railroad companies are now required to make to the Railroad Commissioners annually, the said companies shall each report a balance sheet of its accounts as they may appear on the books of the company on the thirtieth of September of each year.

1876.
Annual returns of railroad companies, when to be made.

SECTION 1. The annual returns made by the several railroad companies, and by trustees operating a railroad, shall be made to the Railroad Commissioners on or before the first day of November ; and the Railroad Commissioners shall make their report to each general assembly not later than the second week of its session.

Repeal, Gen. Stat., pp. 321, 338.

SEC. 2. So much of the seventeenth and of the ninety-third sections of article two, part nine, chapter two, title seventeen of the general statutes as are inconsistent with this act are hereby repealed.

1878.
Form of railroad returns,

SECTION 1. The Railroad Commissioners shall, on or before the first day of September, annually, furnish to the company or trustees operating each railroad, duplicate blank forms for returns, as follows :

Return of the _____ Railroad Company for the year ending September 30, 18—

EARNINGS AND EXPENSES.

Statement of Gross Earnings.

From passenger transportation.
" freight transportation.
" United States mails.
, " express.
" rents.
" other sources (specifying each).
Total gross earnings.

STATEMENT OF OPERATING EXPENSES.

For repairs of road-bed and track.
" " bridges.
" " fences.
" " buildings and fixtures.
" " locomotives.
" " cars.
" " machinery and tools.
" salaries and labor, not included above.
For fuel for locomotives and } —— tons of coal, $
    cars, . . . } —— cords of wood, $
" fuel for stations and } —— tons of coal, $
    shops, . . . } —— cords of wood, $
" oil and waste.
" damages, losses, and gratuities, { to persons, $
    { to property, $
For insurance.
" rents of other roads (naming each).
" other operating expenses (in detail).
Total operating expenses.
Net earnings (or deficit).

TOTAL RECEIPTS AND EXPENDITURES.

Statement of Receipts from all Sources.

Cash on hand at date of last report.
Bills and accounts receivable at date of last report.
Receipts from gross earnings, as stated.
" " other sources (specifying each).
Total.

Statement of Total Expenditures.

For operating expenses (as stated).
" taxes.
" interest.
" dividends—number, ——; rate per cent., ——; date
when paid.

4

For construction, equipment, or property account, giving
    each separately.
" any other purposes (in detail).
Bills and accounts receivable this date.
Cash on hand to balance.
       'Total.

GENERAL BALANCE SHEET.

Showing condition of accounts at close of business, Sep-
    tember 30, 18—.

Assets.

Construction account.
Equipment account.
Other permanent investments (in detail).
Sinking fund.
Materials on hand.
Accounts receivable.
Other assets (in detail).
Cash on hand.
       Total.

Liabilities.

Capital stock.
Bonds payable, or funded debt.
Bills payable, or unfunded debt.
Accounts payable.
Other liabilities (in detail).
Profit and loss.
       Total.

*Present or Contingent Liabilities, not included in Balance-
Sheet.*

Bonds guaranteed by this company, or a lien on its road.
Over-due interest on the same.
Over-due interest on bonds issued by this company.
Any other liabilities.

GENERAL INFORMATION.

Capital Stock.

Capital stock authorized by charter.
      "   " by vote of company.
      " issued, —— full shares of $—— each.
      "   " —— shares subject to $——
                    further assessment.
    Amount credited on —— shares not issued.
Stock issued for cash.
Stock issued for bonds.

Stock issued for stock of other corporations (naming such corporations).

Stock issued for undivided earnings.

Stock issued for increased valuation of road, or equipment, or both.

Stock issued without any payment thereon or in any manner or for any purpose not named above, stating the amount in each case separately, and including the remainder of the stock issued.

Amount of stock held in Connecticut.

Number of stockholders residing in Connecticut.

Whole number of stockholders.

Bonds or Funded Debt.

Describe all issues in the following manner (and if any bonds issued by other parties have been guaranteed by this company, or are a lien on its road, describe them in the same manner, and state also by whom issued), viz. :

First mortgage due ———. Rate of interest, ———.

Interest paid to ———.

Description of Road.

Date when road or different portions thereof were opened for public use, viz. :

From —— to ——.

In Conn. Total.

Length of main line from —— to ——
" branches and names from —— to ——
" all branches.
" road (main line and branches) owned by the company.
" double track road, $\begin{cases} \text{in main line} \text{———} \\ \text{in branches} \text{———} \end{cases}$
" sidings or other tracks not included above.
" track of road, including branches and sidings in single track miles.
" track laid with steel rails (weight per yard, ——— lbs.)

Weight per yard of iron rails in main line, ——— lbs.

Weight per yard of iron rails in branches, ——— lbs.

Miles of track laid with steel rails during the year. (No. of tons, ———; weight per yard, ——— lbs.; costs, $———).

Miles of track laid with new iron rails during the year (No. of tons, ———; weight per yard, ——— lbs.; cost, $———).

No..of new ties put in track during the year (cost,
$———).
Aggregate length of wooden bridges, in feet.
Number of spans of 25 feet or over.
Aggregate length of iron bridges, in feet.
Number of spans of 25 feet or over.
Aggregate length of stone arch bridges, in feet.
Number of highway crossings over the track.
"   "   "   under the track.
"   "   "   at grade.
"   "   "   "   with gates.
"   "   "   "   "   flagmen.
"   "   "   "   "   electric
signal.
No. of railroads crossed at grade and names of
each.
Name, termini, and length of each road operated
by this company under lease or contract.
Length of all roads operated by this company.
Number of stations on main line.
"   "   branches.
"   "   leased lines.

Equipment.

Number of locomotives (not including switching
engines).
Average weight of same, including tender, water,
and fuel.
Number of switching engines.
"   passenger cars.
"   baggage and mail cars.
"   merchandise cars.
"   coal, gravel, and other cars.
"   locomotives, equipped with train brakes.
"   cars   "   "   "   "
Name of brake.
Number of passenger train cars with patent platform, buffer, and coupler.
Name of patent.

Fares, Freight, etc.

Average rate per mile received from passengers on roads
operated by this company, excluding season ticket
passengers.
Average rate per mile for season ticket passengers, reck-
oning one round trip per day to each ticket.
Average rate of fare per mile from all passengers.
Total number of passengers carried.
Passenger mileage, or passengers carried one mile.

Miles run by passenger trains.
  "   "   freight trains.
  "   "   all other trains.
        Total miles run.
Total number of tons of freight carried.
Freight mileage, or tons carried one mile.
Average rate of freight per ton per mile.
Number of men employed in operating road, including
    officers.
Statement of each accident in detail.
Names and residences of officers.
Proper address of the company.

SEC. 2. All companies or trustees receiving such blank forms shall return one of them to the Commissioners, on or before the first day of November, in each year, with all questions fully answered, except where the answers would be "none" or "nothing," in which case the question itself may be stricken out. Said returns shall be signed and sworn to by the president and treasurer of the company, or by a majority of the trustees making the same. *(Returns, how and when made.)*

SEC. 3. Every company whose president and treasurer or trustees shall refuse or neglect to make such returns shall forfeit to the State twenty-five dollars for each day of such neglect or refusal, and said Commissioners shall report such forfeiture to the treasurer, and the books of every railroad company shall at all times be open to the inspection of any committee of the general assembly appointed for that purpose. *(Penalty for neglect. Books to be open to inspection of committee of general assembly.)*

SEC. 4. Every railroad company shall make its annual returns strictly according to the forms provided, and if the officers or trustees find it impracticable to return all the items in detail as required, they shall in their report give the reasons why they cannot be given ; but no company shall be excused for not giving such details because it does not keep its accounts in such manner as will enable it so to do. And when any such returns seem to said Commissioners defective or erroneous, they shall notify the company or trustees making the same, and require the amendments of such returns within fifteen days under the same penalty as is provided for refusing or neglecting to make returns. *(Returns to conform strictly to prescribed schedule.)*

SEC. 5. All acts and parts of acts inconsistent with this act are hereby repealed. *(Repeal.)*

SECTION 1. When the railroad of the Connecticut Central Railroad Company, or any of the branches, as now constructed, meets or lawfully crosses another railroad at the same level therewith, the corporations or persons by which either of said railroads is owned or *(1878. Connections of Connecticut Central Railroad.)*

operated may, with the written consent of the board of
Railroad Commissioners, and upon such terms as said Railroad Commissioners, shall after due hearing, prescribe,
enter its road upon or unite the same with and use the
road of the other; but no locomotive engine or other
motive power shall be allowed to run upon a railroad
except such as is owned or controlled by the corporation
owning or operating such railroad, or with the consent
of such corporation; and every such corporation or persons shall, at all reasonable times and for a reasonable
compensation, draw over its or their railroad the passengers, merchandise, and cars of the other, and each of
them shall for a reasonable compensation provide upon
its railroad convenient and suitable depot accommodations for the passengers and merchandise of the other
road passing to and over it, and shall receive and deliver
the same in the manner it receives and delivers its own
passengers and freight.

Determination of points on which the companies cannot agree. SEC. 2. If the corporations or persons cannot agree
upon the stated periods at which the cars of one shall be
drawn over the other, and the compensation to be paid
therefor, or cannot agree upon the terms and conditions
upon which accommodations shall be furnished for the
passengers and merchandise of the other, the railroad
commissioners, upon the petition of either party and
notice to the other, shall hear the parties and shall in
each case determine (having reference to the convenience
and interest of the corporations and of the public to be
accommodated thereby) the stated periods for drawing
cars and the compensation therefor, or the terms and conditions for passengers and merchandise, or the requisite
terminal accommodations as aforesaid. And upon
application of either party shall determine all questions
between the parties in relation to the transportation of
freight and passengers, and other business upon and connected with said railroads in which they are jointly
interested, and the manner in which the business shall be
done, and apportion to such corporations or persons their
respective shares of the expenses, receipts, and income
of the same. And the award of the Commissioners, or a
major part of them, shall be binding upon the respective
corporations and persons interested therein, for one year
or until the Commissioners shall revise and alter the same:

Appeal. *provided, however,* that any person or corporation aggrieved
by any order of the Railroad Commissioners, made under
the provisions of this act, may appeal from the same to
the Superior Court of the county wherein said railroads
meet within twenty days after the date of such order,
in the same manner that appeals are now allowed upon

any proceeding relative to the location, abandonment, or changing of depots or stations.

None of the provisions of this act shall apply to any railroad except the Connecticut Central and such other railroads whose tracks are now intersected or crossed by the track or tracks of said Connecticut Central railroad.

This act confined to Conn. Central and its intersecting railroads.

SECTION 1. The provisions of chapter eighty-nine of the public acts passed January session, 1878, shall apply to the Rockville railroad and to such other railroads as connect therewith or are intersected thereby, and to the several railroad companies owning or operating said respective railroads.

1879.
Chap. lxxxix. Acts of 1878, p. 313, extended to Rockville R. R.

SEC. 2. This act shall take effect from its passage.

SECTION 1. The standard of time for the meridian of the city hall in the city of New York, shall be, and is hereby, made the standard of time for this state.

1881.
Standard time.

SEC. 2. To enable this standard of time to be accurately determined and furnished each day, the comptroller of this state is hereby authorized to contract with the corporation known as "The President and Fellows of Yale College in New Haven," at a sum not exceeding two thousand dollars a year, to furnish such time at least once every day (except Sunday) to the New York, New Haven and Hartford Railroad Company, at their depot at New Haven, to be transmitted by telegraph by said railroad company, as railroad business, over its entire line, and to all other railroad companies in this state connecting with said railroad.

Furnished by Yale College.

SEC. 3. It shall be the duty of every railroad company in this state, upon receiving such standard of time, to transmit the same by telegraph, as railroad business, each day to all their depots having telegraphic communication, and to all other railroads having connection with them, and to keep at such depots a clock regulated by said time.

Duty of companies to transmit to depots.

CONSTITUTIONAL AMENDMENT.

Article XXV.

[Adopted October, 1877.]

When this act
takes effect.   No county, city, town, borough, or other municipality
shall ever subscribe to the capital stock of any railroad
corporation, or become a purchaser of the bonds, or
make donation to, or loan its credit, directly or indirectly in aid of any such corporation ; but nothing
herein contained shall affect the validity of any bonds
or debts incurred under existing laws, nor be construed
to prohibit the General Assembly from authorizing any
town or city to protect, by additional appropriations of
money or credit, any railroad debt contracted prior to
the adoption of this amendment.

INDEX TO RAILROAD LAWS.

RAILROAD COMPANIES.

INCORPORATION AND ORGANIZATION.

GENERAL INDEX.

Lightning Source UK Ltd.
Milton Keynes UK
UKHW02f0708220218
318315UK00009B/567/P

9 780266 118732